WHO'S WHO
in the law

◆

EMINENT PRACTISING LAWYERS IN THE UK

EDITED BY **JOHN PRITCHARD**

LEGALEASE

Published by Legalease, 3 Clifton Road,
London W9 1SZ

Editor: John Pritchard
Assistant Editor: Mark Stone
Editorial Staff: Noelle Ralph, Sophia Ollard,
Marty Murrihy
Designer: Jane Olswang
Printed and bound by: The KPC Group,
London and Ashford (Kent)

First published 1991

© Legalese Limited and John Pritchard 1991

ISBN: 1 870854 41 1

Further copies of *Who's Who in the Law* can be
ordered from Legalease, 3 Clifton Road,
London W9 1SZ (phone: 071 286 1890).

INTRODUCTION

Who's Who in the Law is intended to be a practitioner's book – a guide to eminent and well-known figures in the day-to-day world of practising lawyers.

To a large extent, my selection of the people to be included within this book is subjective (and, some would say, idiosyncratic). I have concentrated on practitioners – that is, solicitors and barristers whom one is likely to come across in the day-to-day business of the law. Thus there are many partners in law firms, and also eminent barristers. There are writers on the law, in-house lawyers, and also civil servants. On the other hand, there are few judges in this book; this is not because I have anything against judges, but simply that I wanted this to be a book of practising lawyers. After all, there are many other standard reference works that contain biographical information about judges.

Inevitably, there will be those who are offended because they have not been invited to appear in these pages. To them, I offer my sincere apologies and the hope that they will not be overlooked in the second edition!

JOHN PRITCHARD   January 1991

AARON Julian

partner AARON & PARTNERS
5/7 Grosvenor Court, Foregate Street,
Chester CH1 1HG.

Career: assistant law lecturer Kansas State
University (1961-1962); assistant to
Queen's Counsel in Canada (1962-1963);
articled Manches & Co (1963-1965);
admitted (1965); partner (1965-1967); legal
department Pilkington Brothers plc (1967-
1970); founded Aaron & Partners (1970);
admitted barrister and solicitor in New
Zealand (1990).

Activities: participant in solicitor exchange
scheme between Law Society and
Auckland Law Society (1987); former
officer Royal Artillery (V); former member
Council of the Vegetarian Society of the
UK; member Cheshire County Employer
Liaison Team (Reserve Army); Lloyds
Underwriter; member City of Chester
Economic Development Forum.

Biography: lives Chester and Waipu, New
Zealand; born 22.05.1939; married to
Elizabeth. Educated at Red House School,
Norton-on-Tees (1944-1953); Framlingham
College, Suffolk (1953-1958); St John's
College Oxford (1961 MA); Kansas State
University (1961-1962 NBA course).

Leisure: vegetarian; gardening; minor
historian; walking.

AARONS Elaine

partner and head of employment law
department JAQUES & LEWIS 2 South
Square, Gray's Inn, London WC1R 5HR.

Career: articled Norton Rose (1980-1982);
admitted (1982); assistant solicitor (1982-
1989); became partner Jaques & Lewis
(1989).

Activities: member City of London
Solicitors' Company Employment Law
Sub-committee; member Employment
Lawyers' Group; member Industrial Law
Society; co-ordinator London Legal
Education Committee Employment Law
Workshop at Queen Mary College;
affiliated member Association Pension
Lawyers; lecturer; member David Lloyd
Slazenger Clubs.

Biography: lives London N10; born
07.02.1958; married with 2 children.
Educated at Manchester High School for
Girls; King's College London (1979 LLB
hons); articles in Financial Times and The
Director.

Leisure: editing local magazine; co-chair
local fund raising committee.

AARONSON Graham

Queen's Counsel Queen Elizabeth
Building, Temple, London EC4.

Career: called to the Bar Middle Temple
(1966); pupillage and early practice
commercial bar; revenue bar (1968-1973);
managing director Worldwide Plastics
Development Ltd (1973-1977); revenue bar
specialising in commercial taxation (1978
to date); QC (1982).

Activities: founder Standford Grange
Rehabilitation Centre for ex-offenders
(1974); chairman Dietary Research
Foundation (1989); director Bridgend
Group PLC (1973 to date); adviser on
taxation to Treasury, State of Israel (1986 to
date).

Biography: lives London NW11; born
31.12.1944; married to Linda with 3
children. Educated at City of London
School; Trinity Hall Cambridge (1966 BA)
(1970 MA); contributor to Chitty on
Contracts (1968 23rd ed).

ABBEY Robert

conveyancing and probate partner
RUSSELL JONES & WALKER Swinton
House, 324 Gray's Inn Road, London
WC1X 8DH.

Career: articled Cecil Altman & Co;
admitted (1974); became partner (1974-
1984); became partner Russell Jones &
Walker (1984).

Activities: conveyancing forms
editor/draftsman for Oyez Services Group
PLC; former chairman Solicitors Users
Groups for Solitaire KPG Computers;
member Haringey Joggers' Club.

Biography: lives London; born 11.06.1948;
married to Alison with 1 son and 1
daughter. Educated at Woodhouse
Grammar School, North Finchley; Keele
University (1970 BA Joint hons).

Leisure: marathon and long distance
running (completed London Marathon
(1989); gardening; computer programming;
pottery.

ABRAHAMS Anthony

partner PICTONS WADE GERY FARR
30-32 Bromham Road, Bedford.

Career: articled Woodham Smith &
Greenwood (1972-1976); commissioned
4(v) Battn The Royal Green Jackets (1976);
admitted (1978); assistant solicitor (1978-
1980); partner Wade Gery & Brackenbury
(1980); became partner in Pictons Wade
Gery Farr (1989).

Activities: TA Major (1984); TD (1988);
Liveryman Glaziers; member various
committees of Bedford School; member
The Bedford Club.

Biography: lives Bedford; born 30.10.1951;
married to Kathryn with 3 children.
Educated at Bedford School; College of
Law Lancaster Gate (1970-1971); College of
Law Guildford (1976).

Leisure: rugby (County Cap for
Huntingdon and Peterborough 1976);
squash; tennis.

ABRAHAMSON Max

consultant BAKER & MACKENZIE
Aldwych House, Aldwych, London
WC2B 4JP.

Career: admitted Ireland (1953); admitted
Jamaica; admitted Victoria; lecturer in law
Trinity College Dublin (1955); lecturer in
Dublin University; special examiner to
Incorporated Law Society of Ireland;
visiting professor London University
King's College Centre of Construction Law
& Project Management (1987 to date);
founded own practice (1956); became
consultant McCann Fitzgerald in Ireland,
and Baker & MacKenzie internationally.

Activities: has advised or arbitrated on
contracts and disputes in over 60 countries;
companion Institution of Civil Engineers;
hon Fellow Institution of Engineers of
Ireland (1972); Fellow Chartered Institute
of Arbitrators (first chairman Irish branch);
member arbitration panels of Institution of
Civil Engineers; Chartered Institute of
Arbitrators & American Arbitration
Association; member Federation
Internationale des Ingenieurs - Conseil
Task Committee on Construction Law and
Insurance; member Institution of Civil
Engineers Legal Affairs Committee and
New Style Contract Working Group;
conducted solo seminars in many
countries.

Biography: lives London and Dublin; born
29.10.1932; married with 4 children.
Educated at Sandford Park School, Dublin;
Trinity College Dublin (1953); author of
'Engineering Law and the ICE Contracts'
(1979); Japanese edition (1989); articles and
notes in The Modern Law Review,
International & Comparative Law
Quarterly, New Law Journal, International
Construction Law Review; chapters in: The
Ombudsman; Yearbook of Commercial
Arbitration of the International Council for
Commercial Arbitration; The Liability of
Contractors.

Leisure: sculpture (exhibitor Royal
Hibernian Academy).

A

ACKLAND Martin

conveyancing partner STRINGER SAUL Marcol House, 293 Regent Street, London W1R 7PD.

Career: English language teacher in Italy (1975-1976); articled Bower Cotton & Bower (1977-1979); admitted (1979); assistant solicitor (1979-1983); became partner (1983).

Activities: member Magdalen Park Tennis Club.

Biography: lives London SW11; born 26.06.1954; single with 2 children. Educated at Mosley Hall Grammar School, Cheadle; Slough Grammar School; Wadham College Oxford (1975 BA).

Leisure: cooking; tennis; motorcycling.

ADAM David

senior partner VANDERPUMP & SYKES PO Box 150, 58/60 Silver Street, Enfield, Middlesex EN1 3LT.

Career: articled Roper & Whateley (1955-1958); admitted (1958); assistant solicitor Vanderpump & Sykes (1959-1962); became equity partner (1962); became senior partner (1975); consultant (1990).

Activities: Notary Public; member panel of Solicitors Complaints Bureau; former president North Middlesex Law Society; member Enfield Solicitors' Association (former secretary); member Enfield Thirty Club.

Biography: lives London N21; born 26.01.1930; married to Shirley with 3 children. Educated at Ayr Academy; Enfield Grammar School; Trinity College Cambridge.

Leisure: family; golf; DIY.

ADAMS David

senior partner COLEY & TILLEY Neville House, Waterloo Street, Birmingham B2 5UF.

Career: articled local government and private practice; admitted (1949); assistant solicitor (1949-1951); became partner AH Coley & Tilley (1951).

Activities: part-time lecturer in law University College Oxford (1948-1949); senior part-time lecturer Birmingham University (1948-1982); regional chairman West Midland Mental Health Review Tribunal; chairman West Midlands Rent Assessment Panel; councillor Birmingham City Council (1960-1963); member Law Society Panel to advise solicitors in trouble or experiencing difficulties; member

Birmingham Club.

Biography: lives Birmingham and Elmley Castle; born 19.06.1922; married to Joan with 2 children. Educated at King Edward's School, Stourbridge; Birmingham University (1942 LLB) Lady Barber Scholarship; University College Oxford (1948 BCL).

Leisure: walking; reading.

ADAMS John

director of training TITMUSS SAINER & WEBB 2 Serjeants' Inn, London EC4Y 1LT.

Career: articled Wansbroughs (1948-1956); National Service in UK and Hong Kong (1949-1951); admitted (1956); assistant solicitor in Cardiff (1956); partner Pepperell Pitt & Aylett (1956-1968); partner Adams Brown & Co (1968-1978); consultant Adams Brown & Co and Peter Browne & Co (1978-1987); director of training Titmuss Sainer & Webb (1988 to date).

Activities: member Bristol Law Society (1957-1978) (member Council 1968-1978); (president 1976-1977); member Law Society Land Law Committee (1969-1988); member Education Committee of City Council (1968-1970) and City councillor (1970-1974); councillor Avon County Council (1973-1977); lecturer Bristol University (1956-1978); professor of law Queen Mary College London (1978-1987); chairman Board of Studies in Law London University (1984-1986); various external examinerships; emeritus professor of law Queen Mary and Westfield College (1988 to date); Law Society chief examiner (1983 to date); member London Hospital Ethical Committee (1986-1988); member Ministry of Defence Underwater Personnel Research Ethics Committee (1988 to date); numerous conference and seminar activities on wide range of topics; member Nugee Committee on Blocks of Flats; member Avonmouth Old Boys' RFC.

Biography: lives Bristol and London E1; born 26.06.1931; married to Sheila with 6 children. Educated at Sea Mills Infant and Junior School, Bristol; Colston's School, Stapleton; Bristol University (1954 LLB hons); Clement's Inn Prize; Maurice Norden Prize; John Mackrell Prize (joint); Fellow Chartered Institute of Arbitrators (1979); precedents editor of 'The Conveyancer'; co-author of 'Rent Review and Variable Rents'; contributor to 'Modern Conveyancing Precedents'; chapters in 'All England Reports Review' and 'Tolleys Tax Planning'; numerous articles in legal periodicals on variety of

topics.

Leisure: rugby refereeing; grand-parenting.

ADAMS Peter

assistant general counsel ESSO PETROLEUM CO LTD GRO House, Ermyn Way, Leatherhead, Surrey KY22 8UX.

Career: articled Warmingtons & Hasties; admitted (1972); assistant solicitor Gregory Rowcliffe & Co (1972-1973); assistant legal adviser Cleveland Petroleum Ltd (1973).

Activities: Major Royal Artillery (V); member City of Westminster Law Society (secretary 1979-1985); member of: Honourable Artillery Company; Cavalry & Guards Club; Law Society.

Biography: lives London; born 11.12.1946; married to Alice with 2 sons. Educated at Wellington College, Berkshire; College of Law.

Leisure: skiing.

ADKINSON Derek

senior partner NORTON PESKETT & FORWARD 148 London Road North, Lowestoft, Suffolk.

Career: articled Bromley & Walker (1952-1957); admitted (1957); National Service 2nd Lt Royal Artillery; assistant solicitor Greene & Greene; assistant solicitor Andrew Race & Co; assistant solicitor Norton Peskett & Forward (1962-1964); became partner (1964).

Activities: member Legal Aid Committee (1974 to date); solicitor to several golf, cricket and rugby clubs; member of: Royal Norfolk & Suffolk Yacht Club; Southwold Cricket Club (chairman (1981 to date); Etc's Cricket Club; Lowestoft Rotary Club.

Biography: lives Beccles, Suffolk; born 04.06.1933; divorced with 1 child. Educated at Ashville College, Harrogate; Leeds University (1954 LLB).

Leisure: cricket; tennis; travel; owning and looking after house in Spain; organising and going on cricket tours to Yorkshire and Spain.

ADLINGTON Jonathan

partner TROWERS & HAMLINS 6 New Square, Lincoln's Inn, London WC2A 3RP.

Career: articled Trowers & Hamlins (1971-1973); admitted (1973); assistant solicitor (1973-1976); became partner (1976).

Activities: lectures frequently on housing association law and practice; lectured for

Law Society Local Government Group, Institute of Housing, Public Finance Foundation, etc; member RAC.

Biography: lives Goring; born 26.04.1949; married with 2 daughters and 1 son. Educated at Downside, Somerset; Liverpool University (LLB).

Leisure: sailing.

AIKENS Richard

Queen's Counsel Brick Court Chambers, 15/19 Devereux Court, London WC2R 3JJ.

Career: called to the Bar Middle Temple (1973); pupillage 4 Essex Court and 1 Brick Court (1973-1974); called to the Bar Gibraltar (1982); QC (1986); Junior Counsel to the Crown (1981-1986); Assistant Recorder (1989).

Activities: member Supreme Court Rules Committee (1984-1988); director Bar Mutual Insurance Fund Ltd (1987 to date); governor Sedbergh School (1988 to date); member Leander Club.

Biography: lives London W11 and Warwickshire; born 28.08.1948; married to Penny with 2 sons and 2 step-daughters. Educated at Norwich School; St John's College Cambridge (1973 MA) McMahon Law Studentship (1972); Harmsworth Scholarship Middle Temple (1974); contributing editor to 13th ed (forthcoming) of Bullen Leake and Jacobs on Precedents of Pleadings and Practice; also titles on arbitration, carriage, contact, insurance, indemnity, etc., etc.

Leisure: music; collecting pictures; walking.

AITMAN David

partner and head of EEC and competition law group DENTON HALL BURGIN & WARRENS Five Chancery Lane, Clifford's Inn, London EC4A 1BU.

Career: articled Denton Hall & Burgin (1980-1982); admitted (1982); assistant solicitor (1982-1988); became partner (1988).

Biography: lives London SE27; born 11.04.1956; married with 3 children. Educated at Northwood Preparatory School; Clifton College, Bristol; Sheffield University; College of Law; Licentiate of Royal Academy of Music.

Leisure: music; literature; theatre; cinema; fell walking; wind surfing; squash.

ALDRIDGE Arthur

consultant COCKS LLOYD & CO Riversley House, Coton Road, Nuneaton, Warwickshire CV11 5TX.

Career: junior office boy Clay & Cocks (now Cocks Lloyd & Co) (1938-1943); Royal Navy (1943-1946); managing clerk Clay & Cocks (1943-1958); articled (1958-1961); admitted (1961); partner (1961-1983); senior partner (1983-1990); became consultant (1990).

Activities: committee member Warwickshire Law Society (1960s); member Nuneaton British Legion Edyvean Walker Court, Nuneaton, House Committee (1981 to date); member Nuneaton Golf Club Committee (1979-1981) (former captain).

Biography: lives Nuneaton; born 05.10.1924; married to Vilma with 1 child. Educated at Bedworth Central Church of England Boys' School.

Leisure: golf; dancing; gardening.

ALDRIDGE Trevor

law commissioner Conquest House, 37/38 John Street, Theobald's Road, London WC1N 3BQ.

Career: admitted (1960); assistant solicitor (1960-1962); partner Bower Cotton & Bower (1962-1984); general editor Property Law Bulletin (1980-1984); became law commissioner (1984).

Activities: chairman Commonhold Working Group; chairman Conveyancing Standing Committee; member Law Society Land Law & Conveyancing Committee and Sub-committee Drafting 1980/84 Edition of Law Society's Conditions of Sale and Drafting Committee Standard Conditions of Sale, 1st ed; speaker at professional education conferences; member of: Clarity; United Oxford & Cambridge Universities Club.

Biography: lives near Hitchin; born 22.12.1933; married to Joanna with 2 children. Educated at Frensham Heights; Sorbonne, Paris; St John's College Cambridge (1955 BA MA); John Mackrell Prize; author of: 'Boundaries Walls & Fences'; 'Finding Your Facts'; 'Service Agreements'; 'Betterment Levy'; 'Letting Business Premises'; 'Rent Control & Leasehold Enfranchisement'; 'Managing Business Property' (joint); 'Leasehold Law'; 'Your Home & The Law'; 'The Law of Flats'; 'Guides to Local Authority Enquiries'; 'Enquiries Before Contract'; 'National Conditions of Sale'; 'Law Society's Conditions of Sale'; 'Criminal

Law Act 1977'; Registers & Records'; Questions of Law'; 'Powers of Attorney' (ed); 'Housing Act 1980'; 'Practical Conveyancing Precedents'; 'Practical Lease Precedents'; 'Companions to Standard Conditions of Sale'; 'Property Information Forms'; numerous articles.

ALDWINCKLE Ralph

partner LINKLATERS & PAINES Barrington House, 59/67 Gresham Street, London EC2V 7JA.

Career: articled Linklaters & Paines (1961-1964); admitted (1965); assistant solicitor (1965-1969); became partner (1969).

Activities: Chairman Law Society's Standing Committee on Company Law (1987-1990).

Biography: lives London; born 13.07.1937; married to Elizabeth. Educated at Haileybury; Clare College Cambridge (1961 BA) (1962 LLB); various articles in legal periodicals.

ALEXANDER Anthony

partner and head of banking and financial markets group and member of corporate finance and taxation groups DENTON HALL BURGIN & WARRENS Five Chancery Lane, Clifford's Inn, London EC4A 1BU.

Career: articled Oppenheimers (1969-1971); admitted (1971); assistant solicitor (1971-1973); became partner (1973); became senior partner (1988).

Biography: lives Chislehurst; born 07.10.1945; married to Ilana with 2 children. Educated at St Paul's School; Downing College Cambridge (1967 BA) (MA); College of Law (1969); chapter (Setting Out Position in England) in 'Legal Aspects of Alien Acquisition of Real Property'.

Leisure: music; classical studies.

ALEXANDER Kevin

partner BRACEWELL & PATTERSON 43 Brook Street, London W1Y 2BL.

Career: articled Lovell White & King (1977-1979); admitted (1979); assistant solicitor Boodle Hatfield (1979-1981); associate Bracewell & Patterson (1981-1983); became partner (1988); partner Boodle Hatfield (1983-1986); admitted New York (1985); attorney solicitor Sidley & Austin (1986-1988).

Activities: secretary Society of English and American Lawyers; member of: United

A

Oxford & Cambridge Universities Club; St George's Hill Tennis Club.

Biography: lives Weybridge; born 26.12.1953; married to Barbara with 1 son. Educated at Wimbledon College; St John's College Cambridge (MA); various articles.

Leisure: jogging; tennis; golf.

ALEXANDER Peter James

divorce partner PENNINGTONS 99 Aldwych, London WC2B 4LJ.

Career: articled Gamlens; admitted (1970); assistant solicitor (1970-1972); became partner (1972); Gamlens merged with Penningtons (1990).

Activities: member Solicitors Family Law Association.

Biography: lives Alton; born 16.11.1943; married with 3 sons. Educated at Summer Fields, St Leonard's; Haileybury; University of Tours (Certificat des Etudes Francaises); Manchester University (1968 LLB).

Leisure: family activities; languages; long distance running.

ALEXANDER Roger

head partner and chair of management board LEWIS SILKIN 1 Butler Place, Buckingham Gate, London SW1H 0PT.

Career: articled Lewis Silkin; admitted (1965); became partner (1965); head of marketing services group.

Activities: hon solicitor London Marriage Guidance Council.

Biography: lives London NW3; born 29.06.1942; married with 2 children. Educated at Dulwich College Preparatory School; Dulwich College; College of Law (1965 hons); 2 courses in European organisations at International Faculty of Comparative Law in Strasbourg; writes articles and gives seminars on marketing services industry.

Leisure: theatre; cinema; reading history and literature; gardening; photography.

ALEXIOU Douglas

senior partner GORDON DADDS 80 Brook Street, Mayfair, London W1Y 2DD.

Career: articled Bolton & Lowe; admitted (1970); assistant solicitor Boodle Hatfield (1970-1971); assistant solicitor Gordon Dadds (1971); partner (1971); became senior partner (1986).

Activities: member International Academy of Matrimonial Lawyers; member

Solicitors Family Law Association; member City of Westminster Law Society; vice-chairman Tottenham Hotspur Football Club; deputy Chairman Tottenham Hotspur PLC; member of: Law Society; Old Pauline Club; Richmond Golf Club; Southwold Golf Club; Coombe Wood Lawn Tennis Club.

Biography: King's College London (1965 LLB); College of Law.

Leisure: golf; tennis; watching football (Tottenham Hotspur!).

ALLAN Robert W

partner in entertainment department DENTON HALL BURGIN & WARRENS Five Chancery Lane, Clifford's Inn, London EC4A 1BU.

Career: articled FH Carpenter & Oldham; admitted (1967); assistant solicitor Roney & Co; became partner (1973); co-founded Simons Muirhead & Allan (1973); became partner Denton Hall (1986); member Conflict Committee, 1992 Committee and Articled Clerks' Committee.

Activities: UK committee member for the International Association of Entertainment Lawyers; founding chairman Music Business Lawyers' Association; member Grouchos.

Biography: lives London W9 and Hove; born 04.05.1945; married with 2 children. Educated at Xavierian College; College of Law (1967); contributor to annual publication by IAEL on its legal seminar.

Leisure: music; travel; skiing; clay pigeon shooting; food; wine.

ALLCOCK John PM

partner BRISTOWS COOKE & CARPMAEL 10 Lincoln's Inn Fields, London WC2A 3BP.

Career: technical assistant Gill Jennings & Every (1964-1969); patent agent and manager patent department Honeywell Ltd (1969-1972); patent agent Langner Parry (1972-1973); patent agent, articled clerk and assistant solicitor Coward Chance (1973-1978); assistant solicitor Bristows Cooke & Carpmael (1978-1981); became partner (1981).

Activities: member Bar/Law Society Joint Working Party on Intellectual Property.

Biography: lives Sussex; born 08.07.1941; married to Caroline with 3 children. Educated at St Edward's School, Oxford; King's College London (1963 BSC); Faculte Polytechnique de Mons, Belgium (1964 Maitrise en Science Appliquee); Chartered

Patent Agent (1968); Chartered Engineer (1972).

ALLEN Jeremy

managing partner HUNT DICKINS Leeds House, 14 Clumber Street, Nottingham NG1 3DS.

Career: articled Johnstone Sharp & Walker (1962-1968); and Raleigh Industries (1968-1970); admitted (1970); assistant solicitor (1970-1972); assistant solicitor Hunt Dickins & Willatt (1972-1973); partner (1973 to date); became managing partner (1987).

Activities: secretary Nottinghamshire Law Society (1977-1984); secretary East Midlands Association of Local Law Societies (1981-1986); founder chairman Law Society's Child Care Working Party; member Law Society Council (1986 to date); hon solicitor Nottingham CAB; hon solicitor Nottinghamshire branch British Red Cross Society; member Magistrates' Courts Rule Committee (1982 to date); member various Law Society Committees including National Advocacy Training Team; chairman Law Society's Criminal Law Committee (1987 to date); member Lord Chancellor's Efficiency Commission (1987-1989); member of Home Office Review of Procedure Committee; member of: Nottingham & Notts United Services Club; Beeston Hockey Club; Park Tennis Club.

Biography: lives Nottingham; born 05.07.1944; married to Maggie with 3 children. Educated at Bedales; College of Law; various articles.

Leisure: theatre; hockey; running; tennis.

ALLEN-JONES Charles

partner and head of corporate department LINKLATERS & PAINES Barrington House, 59/67 Gresham Street, London EC2V 7JA.

Career: articled clerk to the Justices Uxbridge Magistrates' Court (1958-1960) and Vizard Oldham Crowder & Cash (1960-1963); admitted (1963); assistant solicitor Linklaters & Paines (1964-1968); became partner (1968); Hong Kong office (1976-1981).

Activities: member City Tax Committee (1973-1975); member HK Banking Advisory Committee (1978-1981).

Biography: lives London W8 and Essex; born 07.08.1939; married with 3 children. Educated at Caldicott Prep; Clifton College; Clabon Prize (1963).

Leisure: gardening; tennis; reading; travel.

ALLERHAND Ludwik

partner commercial property department BIRD & BIRD 2 Gray's Inn Square, London WC1R 5AF.

Biography: lives London; born 04.05.1949; single. Educated at York University (BA hons).

ALLIOTT Peter Alexander

senior partner ROOTES & ALLIOTT 27 Cheriton Gardens, Folkestone, Kent CT20 2AR.

Career: admitted (1960); assistant solicitor (1960-1962); became partner Rootes & Alliott (1962).

Activities: President Kent Law Society (1976) (member Special Purposes Committee); Committee member Kent branch Country Landowners' Association; Council member and past President Romney Sheep Breeders' Society; member Folkestone Old Peoples' Welfare Committee of Age Concern; member of: Nulli Secundus Club; Kent County Cricket Club; etc.

Biography: lives Upper Hardres nr Canterbury; born 19.05.1934; married to Jennifer with 3 children. Educated at Charterhouse, Godalming; Peterhouse Cambridge (1957 MA hons).

Leisure: farming sheep, cows, pigs, ducks, chickens and canaries.

ALLISON Raymond

senior partner INGLEDEW BOTTERELL Milburn House, Dean Street, Newcastle upon Tyne NE1 1NP; a member of EVERSHEDS.

Career: National Service commissioned RN (1953-1955); management trainee James A Jobling & Co (1958); articled Ingledew Mather & Dickinson (1958-1962); admitted (1962); assistant solicitor (1962-1964); partner (1964-1982); became senior partner Ingledew Botterell (1982).

Activities: vice-president Newcastle upon Tyne Incorporated Law Society; hon consul for Chile; member North East Board of Princes Youth Business Trust; member of: British Field Sports; Atlantic Salmon Trust; Royal Naval Winter Sports Association; British Ski Club; Northern Counties Club.

Biography: lives Barrasford near Hexham; born 12.12.1934; married to Pauline with 3 children. Educated at Gilling Castle; Ampleforth College; Pembroke College Cambridge (1958 BA hons); holder of Reserve Decoration.

Leisure: fishing; shooting; stalking; skiing; golf; tennis; swimming; gardening.

ALLSOPP Ronald J

administrative partner City office and head of company/commercial department PENNINGTONS 37 Sun Street, London EC2M 2PY.

Career: articled Richard Wilson & Co (1968-1971); admitted (1972); lecturer College of Law Guildford (1971-1973); assistant solicitor Penningtons (1973-1974); became partner (1974).

Activities: member Cannons.

Biography: lives Godalming; born 12.05.1947; married to Greta with 2 children. Educated at Wallingford Grammar School; Queen's College, St Andrew's (1968 LLB); Law Society Part II (1971 hons).

Leisure: cooking; wine; shooting; walking.

ALSOP Patricia

group legal adviser and company secretary WILLIAM BAIRD PLC 79 Mount Street, London W1Y 5HJ.

Career: articled Young Jones Hair & Co (1979-1981); admitted (1981); assistant solicitor Middleton Potts (1981-1983); associate (1983-1984); group legal adviser Debenhams PLC (1984-1987); became group legal adviser and company secretary William Baird PLC (1987).

Activities: member Trading Law Committee of British Retailers Association (1984-1987); member Pension Scheme Committee of British Clothing Industry Association (1987 to date).

Biography: lives London SW11; born 20.04.1956; married to Mark with 1 child. Educated at Henrietta Barnett; Sheffield University (1978 BA hons); College of Law Lancaster Gate (1979).

Leisure: walking; skiing; opera; bridge.

AMLOT Donald

partner STEPHENSON HARWOOD One St Paul's Churchyard, London EC4M 8SH.

Career: admitted (1961); assistant solicitor (1961-1966); became partner Stephenson Harwood (1966).

Biography: born 29.09.1933; married with 2 children. Educated at Dulwich College; Cambridge (1957 BA) (1958 LLB).

AMOO-GOTTFRIED Hilda

principal AMOO-GOTTFRIED & CO 256 Lavender Hill, London SW11 1LJ.

Career: called to the Bar Inner Temple (1972); pupillage Yahuda's Chambers, 3 King's Bench Walk and Ashe Lincoln's Chambers, 12 Harcourt Buildings (1972-1973); tenant No 9 Stone Buildings (1974-1979); Unemployment Benefit Office, Department of Employment, Brixton (1982); assistant solicitor Harazi & Co (1982-1983); founded own practice (1984).

Activities: former vice-chairperson Law Society's Race Relations Committee; member Law Society's Working Party on Women's Careers; former secretary Society of Black Lawyers; former member Minority Access to the Legal Profession Project; member Law Society specialists' panel of solicitors dealing with child care law (1985); member 24-hour duty solicitor scheme (1985); member Court duty solicitor rota.

Biography: lives West Wickham; born 13.12.1945; married to Jacob with 3 sons. Educated at Mmofraturo Girls' Boarding School; Wellesley Girls' High School; Inns of Court School of Law (1972); Holborn College of Law (1967-1970); College of Law Chancery Lane (1971 LLB); article on 'Racism within the Legal Profession' in the Law Society's Gazette (1988).

Leisure: jogging; theatre.

AMOS Jack

partner and head of tax department ASHURST MORRIS CRISP Broadgate House, 7 Eldon Street, London EC2M 7HD.

Career: trainee entrant BBC (1964); Middle East Economic Digest; Financial Times; Daily Telegraph Colour Magazine; BBC Radio 3/4; freelance journalist and broadcaster; BBC TV News as writer/producer (1964-1974); articled tax department Clifford Turner (1976-1978); admitted (1978); assistant solicitor Ashurst Morris Crisp (1978-1980); became partner (1980).

Activities: member City Gym.

Biography: lives London W11; born 25.02.1941; married to Sally with 3 children. Educated at St Michael's College, Leeds; Exeter College Oxford (1964 BA) Open Scholarship; called to the Bar Middle Temple (1975); chapter on 'Investment Trust Companies' in Tolley's Tax Planning (1989); article in International Financial Law Review 'How CCF securitised its LDC debt' (1989).

Leisure: horse riding; tennis; gardening;

A

travel; swimming; reading novels; learning Spanish.

ANDERSON Anthony

Queen's Counsel 2 Mitre Court Buildings, Temple, London EC4Y 7BX.

Career: called to the Bar Inner Temple (1964); QC (1982) .

Activities: tribunal chairman of The Securities Association; member Garrick.

Biography: lives London W4; born 12.09.1938; married to Fenja. Educated at Harrow School; Magdalen College Oxford (1962 MA); joint editor 'Ryde on Rating' (12th & 13th eds).

Leisure: reading; walking; golf.

ANDERSON David

partner TODS MURRAY WS 66 Queen Street, Edinburgh EH2 4NE.

Career: articled Tods Murray WS (1970-1972); admitted (1972); assistant solicitor (1972-1975); became partner (1975).

Activities: devised and prepared documentation for first timeshare development in UK; member of: Gullane Golf Club; Bruntsfield Links Golfing Society.

Biography: lives Edinburgh; born 03.12.1948; married to Kath with 3 children. Educated at Perth Academy; Edinburgh University (1970 LLB hons); articles on timesharing.

Leisure: golf.

ANDERSON Hamish

partner and head insolvency department BOND PEARCE 1 The Crescent, Plymouth PL1 3AE.

Career: part-time lecturer in law (1969-1971) and research assistant (1970-1971) Kingston Polytechnic; articled Bond Pearce (1971-1973); admitted (1973); assistant solicitor (1973-1976); became partner (1977).

Activities: insolvency practitioner (1987); vice-president Insolvency Lawyers' Association; member Joint Working Party on Insolvency Law of the Bar and Law Society (1984 to date); assessor Law Society Insolvency Casework Committee (1986 to date); member editorial board 'Insolvency Law & Practice'; member of Insolvency Practitioners' Association; Law Society; Plymouth Law Society; Justice.

Biography: lives Maristow; born 12.07.1948; married to Linda with 2 children.

Educated at Plymouth College Preparatory School; Clifton College Preparatory School; Clifton College; Kingston Polytechnic (1969 LLB Lond); University College London (1970 LLM); College of Law (1971); author of 'Administrators: Part II of the Insolvency Act 1986'; sundry lectures, articles and reviews, etc.

Leisure: shooting; cycling; photography.

ANDERSON Lesley

training manager M5 LTD 12 The Priory Queensway, Birmingham B4 6BS.

Career: lecturer in law Manchester University (1984-1989); became training manager M5 Ltd (1989); called to the Bar Middle Temple (1989).

Activities: various internal university committees.

Biography: lives Birmingham and Manchester; born 06.04.1963; single. Educated at King Edward VI Camp Hill School, Birmingham; Manchester University (1984 LLB hons); author of 'Antiquity in Action - Ne Exeat Regno Revived' (1987); various other articles; production of research paper with Margaret Brazier commissioned by Law Commission on punitive damages.

Leisure: modern literature; wine; theatre; cinema.

ANDREAE-JONES William

Queen's Counsel 6 King's Bench Walk.

Career: called to the Bar Inner Temple (1965); Recorder of the Crown Court (1982); QC (1984).

Activities: member of: Royal Thames Yacht Club (Rear Cdre 1981-1984); Frewen; Leander Club; Royal Lymington Yacht Club; South West Shingles Yacht Club.

Biography: lives Lymington; born 21.07.1942; married to Anne with 1 son. Educated at Canford School; Corpus Christi College Cambridge (BA hons).

ANDREWS Ann

director legal education and training LEGAL RESOURCES GROUP Post & Mail House, 26 Colmore Circus, Birmingham B4 6BH.

Career: called to the Bar Gray's Inn (1971); Midland and Oxford circuit (1971-1979); director Money Advice Services, Birmingham Settlement (1983-1988); director Legal Education and Training Legal Resources Group (1988); became secretary Legal Education and Training

Group (1990).

Activities: developed first national debt counselling training programme; lectured widely on debt related issues; chair Money Advice Association (1985-1987); trustee/director Broadcasting Support Services (1987 to date).

Biography: lives Birmingham; born 14.07.1949; married to Peter with 2 daughters. Educated at Warstones Road Primary School, Wolverhampton; Wolverhampton High School for Girls; Bristol University (1970 LLB hons); co-author 'How to Cope with Credit and Deal with Debt' (1986); numerous articles and conference papers on debt management and on legal training and management skills for lawyers.

Leisure: music; literature; theatre; travel; art; architecture; horse riding.

ANDREWS Denys

senior partner commercial conveyancing SHEPHERD & WEDDERBURN WS 16 Charlotte Square, Edinburgh EG2 4YS.

Career: apprentice Shepherd & Wedderburn WS (1952-1955); admitted (1955); assistant solicitor (1955-1962); became partner (1962).

Activities: CBE (1980); Writer to the Signet; conveyancing tutor and external examiner in conveyancing Edinburgh University (1956-1963); part-time member Lands Tribunal for Scotland (1980 to date); council member Law Society of Scotland (1972-1981) (vice-president 1977-1978) (president 1978-1979); legal panel member (Scotland) Building Societies' Association (1984); Fiscal Society of Writers to the Signet (1987); member New Club.

Biography: lives Edinburgh and Ballantrae; born 03.06.1931; married to May. Educated at Girvan High School; Worksop College; Edinburgh University (1955 BL); co-compiler 'Land Registration (Scotland) Practice Book' (1981); author of section on building societies 'Stair Memorial Encyclopaedia'.

Leisure: gardening.

ANGEL Peter

partner and head of company and commercial department MANCHES & CO Aldwych House, 71/91 Aldwych, London WC2B 4RB and 3 Worcester Street, Oxford OX1 2PZ.

Career: articled Manches & Co (1968-1970); admitted (1970); assistant solicitor (1970-1972); became partner (1972).

Activities: regular speaker at seminars on corporate finance topics; chairman Shepherds Bush Housing Association Ltd (1975-1988); member Board of Management of College of Estate Management at Reading University (1989 to date); member Clarendon Club, Oxford.

Biography: lives Oxford; born 27.07.1946; married to Elizabeth with 2 daughters. Educated at Maidstone Grammar School; University College London (1967 LLB); Solicitors Finals (1968).

ANGELL Naomi

partner BINDMAN & PARTNERS 1 Euston Road, King's Cross, London NW1 2SA.

Career: articled Lawfords (1971-1973); admitted (1973); assistant solicitor Darlington & Parkinson (1973-1974); solicitor Camden Law Centre (1975-1978); assistant solicitor Wilford McBain (1978-1979); co-founder and project worker of Children's Legal Centre for International Year of the Child (1979-1981); assistant solicitor Bindman & Partners (1982); specialising in children's law; became partner.

Activities: member Law Society Child Care Panel and Family Law Committee; trustee and hon solicitor of Child Psychotherapy Trust; Council member of Central Council for Education and Training in Social Work; lecturer; member The Law Society.

Biography: lives London NW11; born 13.10.1948; married to Gerald with 2 children. Educated at Notting Hill High School; Ealing High School; King's College London (1970 LLB); various articles.

Leisure: tennis; music; dinghy sailing; her children.

ANSELL Anthony

litigation partner WOOLF SEDDON ROSCOE PHILLIPS 5 Portman Square, London W1H 9PS.

Career: called to the Bar Gray's Inn (1968); pupillage with John Hazan (1968-1969) and Israel Finestein (1969); tenant Lamb Building (1969-1979); Clifford Turner (1979-1980); admitted (1980); assistant solicitor Kleinman Klarfeld (1980-1981); partner (1981-1985); partner Ingram Ansell Levy (1985-1990); became partner Woolf Seddon Roscoe Phillips (1990).

Activities: Assistant Recorder (1987 to date); member North Middlesex Law Society; member Solicitors Family Law Association; member The London Criminal Court Solicitors' Association; member

London Solicitors' Litigation Association; representative for Area 14 Legal Aid Practitioners' Group; member Committee of The Lawyers' Group of Tel Aviv University Trust and Lawyers' Association working for Soviet Jewry; member Hendon Synagogue; committee member Caroline Lawson Children's Leukaemia Fund; member of Victoria and Albert Museum Club.

Biography: lives London NW4; born 09.09.1946; married to Karen with 1 son and 1 daughter. Educated at Dulwich College; London University (1968 LLB); article on Misuse of Drugs Law for New Law Journal.

Leisure: opera; concerts; walking.

ANSTEY Margaret

partner TOZERS 10 St Paul's Road, Newton Abbot, Devon TQ12 4PR.

Career: articled in Stratford upon Avon (1953-1958); admitted (1958); assistant solicitor (1958-1959); assistant solicitor Stanley Wasbrough & Co (1959-1963); assistant solicitor Cocks Ashford & Co (1963); assistant solicitor Ford Simey & Ford (1964-1965); assistant solicitor Tozers (1967-1975); became partner (1975).

Activities: former chairman and hon secretary Devon Young Solicitors Group; president Devon and Exeter Incorporated Law Society (1979-1980); member Council of the Law Society (1983 to date); governor College of Law; member Law Society Property and Commercial Services Committee (chairman Land Law and Conveyancing Committee (1988 to date).

Biography: lives Torquay; born 01.01.1935; widowed with 3 children. Educated at The Croft School, Stratford upon Avon; Lowther College, Abergele, North Wales; Birmingham University (1956 LLB hons); Gibson and Weldon (1957-1958).

ANSTIS Ray

senior partner GLOVERS 115 Park Street, London W1Y 4DY.

Career: National Service in North Africa and Malta; articled Glovers (1960-1963); admitted (1963); partner (1964-1982); became senior partner (1982); assistant solicitor Norton Rose (1963-1964).

Activities: assistant examiner Law Society business organisations paper (chief examiner revenue law 1970-1981); Liveryman of Horners' Company; actively involved with National Adoption Society; former chairman Middle Thames Marriage

Guidance Council; president West Surrey Family History Society (former chairman); member Law Society.

Biography: lives Maidenhead; born 12.01.1937; married to Janet with 3 children. Educated at Peter Symonds, Winchester; Keble College Oxford (1960 MA); various articles and precedents in legal press and in family history publications.

Leisure: family history; collecting smoothing irons; bird watching; bridge; watching athletics.

APPLEBY John

managing partner TRUMAN CLOSE KENDALL & APPLEBY 22 Park Row, Nottingham NG1 6GX.

Career: admitted (1970); assistant solicitor in Leicester (1970-1972); assistant solicitor RH Truman & Appleby (1972); became partner.

Activities: secretary Nottinghamshire Young Solicitors Group (1973) (National Committee representative 1976-1982); chairman (1976) National Committee of Young Solicitors (1980-1981); member Council of Law Society for Lincolnshire and Nottinghamshire (1984); chairman Law Society Family Law Committee (1987-1990); chairman Courts and Legal Services Committee (1990 to date); member Remuneration & Practice Development Committee (1986-1989); director Solicitors Indemnity Fund Ltd (1987-1990); vice-president Nottingham Hockey Club; vice-president Notts Forest Cricket Club; member of: Bacchanalians Hockey Club; Wollaton Park Golf Club.

Biography: lives Nottingham; born 04.11.1945; married to Barbara with 1 son. Educated at The Dolphin Preparatory School; Dauntseys; Nottingham University (1967 LLB) (president Law Students' Society) (captain University and UAU Hockey teams); contribution to 'Organisation and Management of a Solicitor's Practice'.

Leisure: hockey; golf; jogging; travel; wine; theatre.

APPLETON Kevin E

partner BRISTOWS COOKE & CARPMAEL 10 Lincoln's Inn Fields, London WC2A 3BP.

Career: legal clerk Bristows Cooke & Carpmael; legal executive; articled; admitted (1983); assistant solicitor (1983-1989); became partner (1989).

A

Biography: lives Gravesend; born 18.04.1956; married to Lorraine with 2 children. Educated at Springhead, Northfleet; Kingsway-Princeton College for Inst Legal Executive Course; College of Law Chancery Lane.

Leisure: building design and refurbishment; general DIY; motor racing; golf; karate; theatre and general social activities.

ARBER Will

partner in charge BOWER & BAILEY 35 High Street, Banbury, Oxon OX16 8ER.

Career: admin/personnel British Petroleum (1965-1974); articled Linnells (1974-1977); admitted (1977); assistant solicitor Bower & Bowerman (now Bower & Bailey) (1980-1982); became partner (1982).

Activities: member of: Vincents Club; Oxford University.

Biography: lives Combe; born 13.11.1942; married to Pat with 3 children. Educated at Dragon School, Oxford; Charterhouse; Oriel College Oxford (MA).

Leisure: golf; cricket; skiing.

ARCHER Bill

consultant DARBY & SON 50 New Inn Hall Street, Oxford OX1 2DN.

Career: articled Slatter Son & More; admitted (1945); assistant solicitor (1945-1946); assistant solicitor Darby & Son (1946-1953); partner (1953-1989); became consultant (1989).

Activities: president Berks Bucks and Oxon Law Society (1965-1966); chairman City of Oxford Conservative Association (1962-1965 & 1967-1971); MBE (1971); Liveryman of the Worshipful Company of Wheelwrights; member The Clarendon Club.

Biography: lives Oxford; born 21.06.1923; married to Mary with 2 sons. Educated at King Edward VI Grammar School, Stratford upon Avon; Birmingham University (1944 LLB hons); Sir Henry Barber Prize.

Leisure: politics; doing nothing! enjoying semi-retirement.

ARCHER Peter

Queen's Counsel 5 Raymond Buildings, Gray's Inn, London WC1R 5BP.

Career: called to the Bar Gray's Inn (1952); QC (1971); Recorder (1980); Bencher Gray's Inn (1974).

Activities: Solicitor General (1974); MP; Methodist (treasurer DSR); chairman Society of Labour Lawyers.

Biography: lives Wraysbury; born 20.11.1926; married to Margaret with 1 son. Educated at Wednesbury Boys' High School (1937-1943); (1946 External London LLB); London School of Economics (1950 LLM); University College London (1952 BA); Bacon Scholar Gray's Inn (1952); Fellow University College (1978); author of 'The Queen's Courts' (1956); 'Communism and the Law' (1963).

Leisure: gardening; music.

ARCHER Tim

litigation partner with RICHARDS BUTLER Beaufort House, 15 St Botolph Street, London EC3A 7EE, specialising in employment law.

Career: articled Richards Butler & Co (1965-1968); admitted (1968); assistant solicitor (1968-1972); became partner (1972).

Activities: member International Bar Association; member Law Society; member of: United Oxford & Cambridge Universities Club; Salcombe Yacht Club; Island Cruising Club.

Biography: lives Great Bardfield; born 09.02.1943; married to Gill with 2 children. Educated at Woolpit Preparatory School, Ewhurst; Sutton Valence School, Kent; Merton College Oxford (MA); College of Law Lancaster Gate (1965-1966); College of Law Guildford (1968); Alfred Syrett Prizeman; contributor to 'International Handbook on Contracts of Employment' (1989).

Leisure: family; sport; travel; art; garden.

ARDEN Andrew

barrister 11 King's Bench Walk, Temple, London EC4.

Career: called to the Bar (1974); director of law centre in Birmingham (2 years).

Activities: former part-time lecturer in law Warwick University; former housing consultant to Legal Action Group (former committee member); conducted local government inquiries; member Administrative Law Bar Association.

Biography: lives London N1; born 20.04.1948; single. Educated at Stowe; University College School, London; University College London (1972 LLB hons); Council of Legal Education (1973); editor of: 'Encyclopaedia of Housing Law & Practice'; 'Housing Law Reports'; author of: 'Manual of Housing Law'; 'Housing the Homeless'; 'Private Tenants' Handbook'; 'Public Tenants' Handbook'; 'Homeless Persons' Handbook'; joint author of: 'Housing Law'; 'Assured Tenancies'; 'Rent Acts and Regs'; 'Quiet Enjoyment'; numerous annotated statutes and articles; author of three novels.

ARKWRIGHT Tom

senior partner CYRIL MORRIS ARKWRIGHT Churchgate House, 30 Churchgate, Bolton BL1 1HS.

Career: articled Alsop Stevens & Co (1950-1955); admitted (1955); assistant solicitor (1955); assistant solicitor Cyril Morris & Co (1955-1957); became partner Cyril Morris Arkwright (1957); became senior partner (1971).

Activities: president Bolton Law Society (1972); member Joint Advisory Committee of the Law Society and HM Land Registry (1972 to date); member Remuneration Certificate Committee (1975 to date); Council member Bolton Law Society (3 times 3 years each time); president Bolton Chamber of Commerce and Industry (1971-1973) (council member 1966-1990); chairman North West Chambers of Commerce (1973); Bolton West Conservative Association: secretary (1961-1966); chairman (1966-1971); president (1972-1974) and (1989 to date) second period of office; treasurer (1981-1984); trustee (1965 to date); life deputy president (1974); deputy treasurer NW area Conservative Party (1972-1973); president Bolton Catholic Musical and Choral Society (1968 to date); North West Catholic History Society: treasurer and manager (1987-1990); hon life member (1990); publicity and membership officer (1990 to date); deputy president Bolton Coronary Care (1970 to date); member Bolton Club.

Biography: lives Chorley; born 22.03.1932; married to Muriel with 6 children. Educated at Mount St Mary's College; Liverpool University (1953 LLB hons); College of Law Guildford (1954-1955); vice-chancellor of the County Palatine of Lancaster Prize; Sheffield Prize; John Mackrell Prize; Daniel Reardon Prize; Enoch Harvey Prize; Timpron Martin Prize; Rupert Bremner Prize.

Leisure: walking; gardening; local history; family history; researching all persons bearing surname Arkwright; editing 17th-century recusant lists.

ARMSTRONG Michael

consultant with WARNERS
180 High Street, Tonbridge, Kent TN9 1BD.

Career: admitted (1956); assistant solicitor
Kent County Council (1959-1961); assistant
solicitor Warners (1961-1962); partner
(1962-1981); senior partner (1981-1989).

Activities: clerk to Commissioners of
Income Tax (1981 to date); Kent County
Councillor (1977-1985); president
Tunbridge Wells, Tonbridge & District Law
Society (1985-1986); president Kent Law
Society (1987-1988); president, chairman
and treasurer Tonbridge & Malling
Constituency Conservative Association
(1972-1985); area chairman Kent Round
Table (1968-1969); chairman Tonbridge
Round Table (1965-1966); president
Tonbridge Rotary (1987); member Council
of St John Ambulance for Kent (1974-1990).

Biography: lives Hildenborough, Kent;
born 21.05.1934; married to Sandra with 3
daughters. Educated at Hanley Castle,
Worcestershire; Newton Abbot Grammar
School, Devon; University College of South
West (1957 LLB).

Leisure: farmer.

ARMSTRONG Peter

partner and head of entertainment
department MISHCON DE REYA
125 High Holborn, London WC1V 6QP.

Career: legal assistant Morgan Finnegan
Pine Foley & Lee, New York (1977-1978);
articled Bartlett & Gluckstein Crawley &
de Reya (1980-1982); admitted (1982);
assistant solicitor; became partner.

Activities: member IBA Committee L/W
Intellectual Property, Entertainment and
Communications and Committee 16
Defamation and Media Law; member
Royal Commonwealth Society.

Biography: lives London SW10; born
04.08.1949; married to Susan. Educated at
St Andrew's College, Grahamstown, South
Africa; University of Cape Town (1970 BA);
University College London (1973 LLM);
New York University; author of "Is the
common law defence of qualified privilege
too restrictive to the media?' (1988).

Leisure: the arts; travel.

ARNOLD Christopher

director of professional development
RICHARDS BUTLER Beaufort House,
15 St Botolph Street, London EC3A 7EE.

Career: called to the Bar Gray's Inn (1973);
legal adviser Save & Prosper Group (1973-
1974); lecturer in law UCL (1964-1969);

senior lecturer in law Sydney University
(1974-1979); visiting Fellow ANU
(Canberra) Australia (1977-1978); professor
of law University of Windsor, Canada
(1979-1983); visiting professor of law
Osgoode Hall Law School, Canada (1979-
1980); visiting professor of law University
of Detroit (1982); professor of law and head
of department Leicester Polytechnic (1983-
1988); director of education and training
Rowe & Maw (1988); became director of
professional development Richards Butler
(1989).

Activities: foundation chairman British &
Irish Legal Education Technology
Association (1983-1988); chairman British
Association for Canadian Studies Law
Group (1987 to date); member Law Society
Advisory Committee on Continuing
Education; member UK Advisory
Committee on Information Technology;
member CNAA Legal Studies Board;
executive member Legal Education &
Training Group; member European
Computer & Law Group, Brussels (1987 to
date); frequent speaker to sixth formers on
careers in law; promoter of work-
shadowing in law in the City; interest in
desktop publishing in law firms.

Biography: lives London EC2; born
15.12.1942; divorced with 3 children.
Educated at Brockley County Grammar
School (1954-1961); University College
London (1964 LLB) Joseph Hume Scholar;
Bedford College London (1970 MA); Balliol
College Oxford (1972 BPhil); Inns of Court
School of Law (1973 Bar Finals);
Leverhulme Fellowship, Paris (1967-1968);
editor 'Yearbook of Law Computers &
Technology' (1984 to date); author of
'Institutional Aspects of Law' (1979).

Leisure: opera; canoeing; fishing.

ARNOLD Karl

senior partner BIRD & BIRD 2 Gray's Inn
Square, London WC1R 5AF.

Career: became partner Bird & Bird (1964).

Biography: lives London; born 17.06.1933;
married to Janet with 3 children. Educated
at Merchant Taylors' School; Bristol
University (LLB hons).

Leisure: sailing; golf.

ARNOTT Jim

partner MacROBERTS 27 Melville Street,
Edinburgh EH3 7JF.

Career: articled Brodies; admitted (1956);
National Service in RAF; assistant solicitor
MacRoberts (1962-1963); became partner

(1963).

Activities: secretary Scottish Building
Contract Committee; member Council of
Law Society of Scotland (1985) (convenor
law reform 1983-1986); lectures on
arbitration and construction law; acts as
arbitrator; member New Club, Edinburgh.

Biography: lives Edinburgh; born
22.03.1935; married to Jean with 3 children.
Educated at Merchiston Castle School,
Edinburgh; Edinburgh University (1956
LLB); writes on building law topics.

Leisure: cricket; walking.

ARNULL Anthony

legal secretary in the chambers of
Advocate-General Jacobs COURT OF
JUSTICE OF THE EUROPEAN
COMMUNITIES L-2925 Luxembourg.

Career: articled Coward Chance (1981-
1983); admitted (1983); lecturer in law
Leicester University (1983 to date); became
Legal Secretary in Chambers of Advocate
General Jacobs (1989).

Activities: member of the Committee of the
Law Society Solicitors European Group
(1986-1989) (represented the Group on the
Law Society's Entry and Training
Committee (1987-1989); correspondent for
European Law Review (1986 to date).

Biography: lives Luxembourg; born
16.08.1958; married. Educated at Finchley
Catholic High School; School of European
Studies, Sussex University (1980 BA hons);
Institut D'Etudes Europeennes Universite
Libre de Bruxelles (1978-1979); College of
Law Chancery Lane (1980-1981); Leicester
University (1988 PHD); numerous
publications.

Leisure: swimming; photography.

ARROWSMITH-BROWN
Matthew

partner MILLS & REEVE, Francis House,
3-7 Redwell Street, Norwich NR2 4TJ.

Career: articled Slaughter and May (1974-
1976); admitted (1976); assistant solicitor
(1976-1979); assistant solicitor Mills &
Reeve (1979-1981); became partner (1981);
leader of firm's family tax planning group.

Activities: churchwarden.

Biography: lives South Walsham, Norfolk;
born 25.07.1951; married to Nicola with 2
daughters. Educated at St Michael's
Preparatory School, Barnstaple, Devon and
Clifton College; York University (1972 BA
hons); College of Law Lancaster Gate
(1973-1974).

A

Leisure: advanced driving; horse racing; reading fiction.

ARSCOTT Michael

partner commercial property LOVELL WHITE DURRANT 21 Holborn Viaduct, London EC1A 2DY.

Career: articled Roche Son & Neale (1958-1961); admitted (1961); assistant solicitor Simmons & Simmons (1961-1964); assistant solicitor Piesse & Sons (1965-1968); partner (1968-1973); partner Durrant Piesse (1973-1988); became partner Lovell White Durrant (1988).

Activities: governor Hazelwood Prep School, Limpsfield.

Biography: lives Limpsfield; born 29.01.1935; married to Judy with 4 children. Educated at Norwood Prep School, Exeter; Whitgift School, Croydon; Magdalene College Cambridge (1958 BA).

Leisure: golf; sport generally.

ASH Peter

consultant WRIGHT WEBB SYRETT 10 Soho Square, London W1V 6EL.

Career: Pilot in Fleet Air Arm RNVR (1943-1946); articled Manset Phillips & Co (1946-1949); admitted (1949); assistant solicitor Wright & Webb (1949-1950); assistant solicitor JR Spencer Young (1950-1952); assistant solicitor Syrett & Sons (1952-1956); partner (1956-1982); became senior partner Wright Webb Syrett (1982); consultant (1989).

Activities: legal adviser to Music Publishers' Association and Personal Managers' Association.

Biography: lives Banstead; born 26.12.1924; married to Audrey (nee Betts) with 2 children. Educated at Henry Thornton School; College of Law (1948-1949).

Leisure: reading; gardening; watching cricket.

ASH Robert

senior trust and tax partner THOMAS EGGAR VERRALL BOWLES 5 East Pallant, Chichester, West Sussex PO19 1TS.

Career: articled Rooper & Whately; admitted (1967); assistant solicitor Baileys Shaw & Gillett (1968-1971); assistant solicitor Thomas Eggar & Son (1971-1972); became partner (1972).

Activities: director Thesis (formerly Thomas Eggar & Son Investment Services); trustee very large number private and charitable trusts.

Biography: lives Chichester; born 05.03.1942; married to Carolyn with 2 children. Educated at Whitgift School, Croydon; Clare College Cambridge (1963 BA) (1964 LLB) (1968 MA).

Leisure: travel; literature; theatre; music; ornithology; walking.

ASHBY Michael James

senior Crown Prosecutor with CROWN PROSECUTION SERVICE Exeter.

Career: articled Arthur Blackman Hailey & Co (1968-1973); admitted (1973); assistant solicitor Turberville Smith & Co (1973-1975); partner (1975-1983); senior criminal litigation partner Turberville Woodbridge (1983-1990); became senior Crown Prosecutor with Crown Prosecution Service at Exeter (1990).

Activities: member Law Society.

Biography: lives High Wycombe; born 15.11.1946; married to Micheline with 3 children. Educated at Tiffin School, Kingston upon Thames; College of Law Lancaster Gate and Guildford.

Leisure: sailing; yoga; golf.

ASHCROFT Charles

partner specialising in corporate finance and financial services ROWE & MAW 20 Black Friars Lane, London EC4V 6HD.

Career: articled Rowe & Maw; admitted (1977); assistant solicitor (1977-1980); became partner (1980).

Biography: lives London; born 21.10.1951; married to Josanne. Educated at Rossall Junior School; Uppingham School; Christ Church Oxford (hons); Open Exhibition; Clifford's Inn Prize; John Marshall Prize; City of London Solicitors Company Prize.

Leisure: bridge; opera; walking; reading.

ASHWORTH Philip

partner CASTLE SANDERSON Edward Baines House, 7 King Street, Leeds LS1 2HH.

Career: articled Sanderson Kaye & Martin; admitted; assistant solicitor Halliwell Landau (2 years); director property finance company in York (2 years); became partner Sandersons (now Castle Sanderson) (1987).

Activities: member Round Table.

Biography: lives York; born 11.06.1958; married to Sally with 1 child. Educated at Hulme Grammar School, Oldham; Hull University (1980 LLB); College of Law Chester.

Leisure: squash; skiing; golf.

ASPINALL Michael

senior partner THOMSON SNELL & PASSMORE 3 Lonsdale Gardens, Tunbridge Wells, Kent TN1 1NX.

Career: articled Fladgate & Co; admitted (1948); assistant solicitor (1948-1951); assistant solicitor Snell & Co (1951-1954); became partner (1954); amalgamated to form Thomson Snell & Passmore (1968).

Activities: member of: MCC; Royal Ocean Racing Club; Ski Club of Great Britain.

Biography: lives Wadhurst; born 22.11.1926; married to Avril with 2 children. Educated at Sutton Valence School; College of Law (1948).

Leisure: sailing; travel; appreciation of the countryside; Bordeaux wines.

ASTON Howard

commercial property partner FEW & KESTER Montagu House, Sussex Street, Cambridge CB1 1PB.

Career: articled Few & Kester; admitted (1968); assistant solicitor (1968-1972 & 1973-1974); became partner (1974); assistant solicitor Hatch & Hatch (1972-1974); Notary Public.

Activities: director Cambridge Building Society (1984) (former principal legal adviser to Board of Directors); treasurer Cambridgeshire & District Law Society.

Biography: lives Cambridge; born 23.10.1943; married to Julie. Educated at Balsham Village Primary School; St Faith's Preparatory School, Cambridge; The Leys School, Cambridge; St Catharine's College Cambridge (1965 BA) (1969 MA).

Leisure: folk singing and associated musical activity; running; cycling (Cambridge University half-blue (1965); various sports pursuits; keep fit; general interest in old buildings and conservation.

AUCOTT John

senior partner EDGE & ELLISON Rutland House, Edmund Street, Birmingham B3 2JR.

Career: articled EH Kenshole (1963-1969); admitted (1969); assistant solicitor; became partner Edge & Ellison (1974).

Activities: former deputy High Court Registrar; member Council of Law Society (1984 to date) (member Strategy Committee 1988 to date) (chairman Remuneration & Practice Development Committee (1988 to date); member Council of Birmingham Law Society (1978 to date) and deputy vice-president (1990-1991); advisor to sporting bodies; member Wig & Pen Club.

Biography: lives London WC2 and near Coleshill; born 02.01.1946; married to Angela with 2 daughters. Educated at Coleshill Grammar School; College of Law Guildford; articles on practice management and remuneration issues.

Leisure: country sports; golf; family; gastronomy; visiting house in France.

AUDEN Derek

commercial office partner GOODGER AUDEN Walpole House, 50 Lichfield Street, Burton on Trent DE14 3TL.

Career: Major in 2nd Gurkha Rifles (Indian Army) (1946); articled to father Auden & Son (1947-1949); admitted (1949); assistant solicitor (1949-1950); partner (1950-1984); became senior partner Goodger Auden (1984).

Activities: president Derby Law Society (1985-1986); HM Coroner for East District of Staffordshire & Burton-upon-Trent (1959-1974); member Burton Club.

Biography: lives Repton near Derby; born 23.01.1924; married to Joan with 3 children. Educated at Repton School; Travers Smith Scholarship (1949).

Leisure: gardening; fishing.

AUGHTERSON William

sole practitioner 53 Victoria Road, Colchester, Essex CO3 3NU formerly senior partner AUGHTERSON KEEBLE & PASSMORE.

Career: articled in Melbourne, Australia; admitted Victoria (1964); founded Aughterson & Lamb (1964); admitted England & Wales (1978); founded Aughterson Keeble & Passmore (1981).

Activities: part-time tutor in law Melbourne University (1964-1966); part-time tutor in law Royal Melbourne Institute (1965-1971); chairman Articled Clerks' Monitoring Committee (1988-1989); chairman Frating Parish Council (1977-1978); clerk to Stanway Parish Council (1978-1980); governor Colchester Royal Grammar School (1985 to date); member of: Surrey County Cricket Club; Birch Grove Golf Club; North Countryman's Club.

Biography: lives Colchester; born 21.12.1937; married to Patricia with 5 children. Educated at Xavier College, Melbourne; Melbourne University (1963);

Essex University (1975 MA); Law Institute of Victoria Solicitors Prize (1966).

Leisure: watching cricket; golf; bee-keeping; London theatre.

AUSTIN Ian

practice development and training consultant with various firms. SLT CONSULTANTS South Bar, Todley Hall, Todley Hall Road, Laycock, Keighley, West Yorkshire.

Career: lecturer in law Southwest Polytechnic, Oxford College and Oxford Polytechnic (1977-1985); consultant in employment law and agreement planning; director of training and information Pennington Ward Bowie (1988); training director Hammond Suddards (1989).

Activities: member Legal and Education Training Group; member of Association of Law Teachers; member of: Round Table; Napoleon's, Bradford; Bradford City Supporters' Club.

Biography: lives Keighley; born 05.02.1952; married to Susan with 1 son. Educated at Greenford County Grammar School; London University; Polytechnic of Central London; Bristol University; (1975 LLB hons); (1979 MBIM); (1987 LLM); various articles in journals.

Leisure: writing fiction; travel; gardening; horticulture; winter sports; people; the law; Bradford City FC.

AVERY JONES John

senior partner SPEECHLY BIRCHAM 154 Fleet Street, London EC4A 2HX.

Career: admitted (1966); assistant solicitor; partner Bircham & Co; became senior partner Speechly Bircham (1985).

Activities: visiting professor LSE; president Institute of Taxation (1980-1982); CBE; member Meade Committee; member Keith Committee; member Council of The Law Society (1986-1990); member Council of Institute for Fiscal Studies; member Executive Committee and chairman of the British Branch of International Fiscal Association; member Athenaeum.

Biography: lives London W2; born 05.04.1940; single. Educated at Rugby School; Trinity College Cambridge (1962 MA) (1965 LLM); FTII; editor 'British Tax Review'; numerous articles; consulting editor 'Encyclopaedia of VAT'.

Leisure: opera.

AWFORD Ian

senior aviation partner BARLOW LYDE & GILBERT Beaufort House, 15 St Botolph Street, London EC3A 7NJ.

Career: admitted (1967); assistant solicitor Barlow Lyde & Gilbert (1969-1973); became partner (1973); admitted Hong Kong (1988).

Activities: chairman Outer Space Committee of the International Bar Association Section on Business Law; chairman Aerospace Committee of the Asia Pacific Aerospace Law Association; co-chairman Aerospace Law Committee of the Inter-Pacific Bar Association; member International Institute of Space Law of the International Astronautics Federation; member British Space Society; member International Forum of Travel and Tourism Advocates; member International Society of Air Safety Investigators; member Shipping and Aviation Sub-committee of the City of London Law Society; international associate of American Bar Association; member Air Law Group of the Royal Aeronautical Society.

Biography: lives London E14; born 15.04.1941; divorced; married to Leonora with 3 sons by first wife. Educated at Stagenhoe Park Prep School, Hitchin; Wellingborough School; Sheffield University (1963 LLB hons); FRAeS (1987); numerous publications and articles.

Leisure: art; theatre; golf; computers.

AYLWIN John M

executive partner RICHARDS BUTLER Beaufort House, 15 St Botolph Street, London EC3A 7EE.

Career: articled Richards Butler (1965-1967); admitted (1967); assistant solicitor (1967-1972); partner (1972); became executive partner (1984).

Activities: member City of London Solicitors' Company Problems of Practice Sub-committee; member City of London Law Society Practice Rules Working Party; member of: Richmond Football Club; Dorking Rugby Football Club.

Biography: lives Dorking; born 23.07.1942; married to Angela with 2 sons. Educated at Uppingham; Emmanuel College Cambridge (1964 BA MA); College of Law Guildford (1965 Solicitors Finals).

Leisure: tennis; golf; gardening; theatre.

B B

BACH John

partner STEPHENSON HARWOOD One St Paul's Churchyard, London EC4M 8SH.

Career: became partner Stephenson Harwood (1966).

Activities: governor Moorfields Eye Hospital.

Biography: lives London NW3; born 18.02.1936; married to Hilary with 2 daughters and 1 son. Educated at Rugby School (1949-1954); New College Oxford (1959 MA).

BADCOCK Ashley

partner SHARPE PRITCHARD Elizabeth House, Fulwood Place, London WC1V 6HG.

Career: articled Sharpe Pritchard (1970-1973); admitted (1973); became partner (1973).

Activities: London Deputy for Sheriffs of Kent, Warwickshire, Northants, Tyne and Wear and Dyfed; member Legal Aid Area Committee (1986); member General Committee Legal Aid Scheme (1981) (chairman's panel 1985); member Interview Panel for Law Society Monitoring of Articles Scheme (1987); member Committee of London Solicitors Litigation Association; Freeman of City of London (1986); Freeman of Company of Watermen and Lighterman (1986); member UK Environmental Law Association; member of: Hurlingham; Old Pauline.

Biography: lives London SW6; born 03.05.1948; married to Fabienne with 2 children. Educated at St Paul's School; King's College London (1969 LLB); contributor to Longman's Litigation Practice (chapter on Official Referee).

Leisure: shooting; tennis; fishing.

BAGNER Hans

senior partner VINGE 44/45 Chancery Lane, London WC2A 1JB.

Career: associate Squire Sanders & Dempsey, Cleveland (1963-1964); called to the Swedish Bar (1965); associate Vinge (1964-1968); became partner (1968); Stockholm office (1964-1979); opened London office (1979).

Activities: visiting professor Louisianna State University Law School (1966); lecturer trade law Stockholm University Law School (1964-1968); lecturer trade law

Stockholm School of Economics (1967-1979); ad hoc lecturer in various seminars and conferences in trade law (M & A joint ventures) and international commercial arbitration; Associate Fellow London Court of Arbitration; panellist American Arbitration Association; arbitrator and/or counsel in international commercial arbitration proceedings in UK, US and Sweden; member of: Annabel's; Roehampton (golf) Country Club; Lidingo Golf Club, Stockholm.

Biography: lives London W14 and Stockholm; born 22.08.1937; married to Susanne with 3 children. Educated at Sodra Latin High School (1956); Stockholm University Law School (1959 LLB jur kand); Michigan University Law School (1963 Master Comparative Law); several articles in legal publications in UK, US, China and Sweden.

Leisure: political history; theatre; golf.

BAGWELL PUREFOY Peter

partner THOMSON SNELL & PASSMORE 3 Lonsdale Gardens, Tunbridge Wells, Kent TN1 1NX.

Career: regular officer in the Royal Artillery (1953-1969); articled Haines Bonniface & Franks (1969-1971); articled Thomson Snell & Passmore (1971-1973); admitted (1973); assistant solicitor (1973-1976); salaried partner (1976-1983); became partner (1983).

Activities: solicitor to the Royal Artillery Museum Project (1988 to date); hon solicitor to the British Art Medal Society (1982 to date); member Law Society Financial Services Act Working Party (1989); hon legal adviser to the Royal Numismatic Society; member Army & Navy Club.

Biography: lives Crowborough; born 01.10.1932; married to Leslie with 1 son. Educated at St Neot's School, Eversley; Wellington College; Royal Military Academy Sandhurst (1953 regular commission); Staff College, Camberley (1964); College of Law Lancaster Gate (1971 & 1973); articles in Law Society's Gazette; author of: 'The Fee Earner's Compliance Manual'; 'The Practice Manager's Guide' together forming the Law Society's Guide to the Solicitors Investment Business Rules (1988).

Leisure: painting; studying ancient Spanish coins; collecting coins and medallions; reading history.

BAHL Kamlesh

company secretary and manager DATA LOGIC LIMITED Queen's House, Greenhill Way, Harrow, Middlesex HA1 1YR.

Career: articled GLC (1978-1980); admitted (1980); assistant solicitor (1980-1981); legal adviser British Steel Corporation (1981-1984); solicitor Texaco Limited (1984-1987); legal and commercial manager Data Logic Limited (1987-1989); became company secretary and manager legal services (1989).

Activities: member Law Society Commerce and Industry Group (chairman 1988-1989) (chairman Public Relations Sub-committee Group 1987-1988) (member Activities Sub-committee Group 1984); member Law Society Race Relations Committee (1986 to date); member Law Society's Young Solicitors Group Main Committee (1984-1986); member Law Society's Council (1990 to date).

Biography: lives London N14; born 28.05.1956; married to Nitin. Educated at Minchenden School, Southgate; Birmingham University (1977 LLB hons); Pettit Bursary; College of Law Lancaster Gate; OU Certificate (1987); Texaco Limited Spirit of the Star Award; written articles on the in-house lawyer in the Ivanhoe Guide to Commerce and Industry and Ivanhoe Guide to the Legal Profession; appeared on BBC2 Open Space and BBC Radio 4 Open Mind; general editor 'Managing Legal Practice in Business: (published 1989 as Gazette Practice Handbook).

Leisure: swimming; squash; tennis; walking.

BAILLIE Iain

resident European partner LADAS & PARRY 52-54 High Holborn, London WC1V 6RR.

Career: plant manager Scottish Gas Board (1953-1955); technical assistant Monsanto Chemicals Ltd (1955-1959); technical assistant Eric Potter & Clarkson (1959-1960); international patent law advisor American Cyanamid Patent Law Department (1960-1961); associate Langner Parry Card & Langner (now Ladas & Parry) (1961-1969); became partner (1969-1976); resident London partner and resident European partner (1976 to date); opened Munich office (1978).

Activities: member American Bar Association; member International Bar Association; member European

Communities Trade Mark Practitioners Association; member Canadian Patent and Trade Mark Association; member Licensing Executives Society; on panel of Arbitrators, American Film Marketing Association; lecturer to students on intellectual property in Queen Mary College and Chartered Institute of Patent Agents; member of: Institute of Directors; Caledonian Club.

Biography: lives London SW1; born 14.07.1931; married to Joan with 1 son. Educated at High School of Glasgow; Glasgow University (1953 BSc hons); Fordham University School of Law, New York (1965 JD); member New York Bar (1966); member US Federal Bars including Supreme Court of USA; registered US Patent Attorney (1967); Fellow of the Institute of Chartered Patent Agents (UK) (1961); European Patent Attorney (1978); Fellow of the Institute of Trade Mark Agents (1986); Fellow of the International Institute of Licensing Practitioners (1985); Jospeh Rossman Memorial Award (1976); admitted Canadian Patent Office (1967); AIPPI; FICPI; UNION; member Institute of Patent Attorneys of Australia; Fellow of the Royal Society of Arts and other professional bodies; author of: 'Practical Guide to Intellectual Property Management: (1986); 'Licensing A Practical Guide' (1987); contributor to: International Franchising - An Overview' (1984); 'Joint Ventures in the United States' (1988); numerous other contributions to professional and commercial journals on intellectual property, technology transfer, image licensing, competition law EEC and USA, character merchandising, franchising; lectured in UK, USA, Sweden, Germany and Japan and been published in German, Spanish and Japanese.

Leisure: ballroom dancing; walking; model and clock making.

BAILY Mark

partner STEPHENSON HARWOOD One St Paul's Churchyard, London EC4M 8SH.

Career: admitted (1966); assistant solicitor (1966-1970); became partner Stephenson Harwood (1970).

Biography: born 13.09.1940; married to Penelope with 3 children. Educated at Eton College; Christ Church Oxford (1962).

Leisure: most sports; dinghy sailing; tennis; countryside pursuits (particularly Norfolk); theatre; concerts in London.

BAKER Alan

partner and head residential property department WALKER MORRIS SCOTT TURNBULL St Andrew House, 119-121 The Headrow, Leeds LS1 5NP.

Career: articled Walker Morris & Coles (1972-1974); admitted (1974); assistant solicitor (1974-1976); became partner (1976); firm merged to become Walker Morris Scott Turnbull (1988).

Activities: chairman Non-Contentious Business Committee Leeds Law Society (1982-1988); member General Committee Leeds Law Society; board member and former vice-chairman Harrogate Theatre; treasurer two local welfare charities; former member Law Society Computer Sub-committee; local chorister; trustee of West Yorkshire Drama Trust.

Biography: lives Leeds; born 04.06.1950; married with 2 children. Educated at Roundhay School, Leeds; Leeds University (1971); articles in local press on property related matters.

Leisure: senior grade rugby union referee; club cricket; member Yorkshire CCC; all ball sports; theatre; classical music.

BAKER Anthony James Morton

senior partner FLADGATE FIELDER Heron Place, 3 George Street, London W1H 6AD.

Career: articled to Sir Dingwall Bateson at Walters Hart (1955-1958); admitted (1958); assistant solicitor (1958-1961); partner (1961-1964); managing partner (1964-1987); became senior partner Fladgate Fielder (1988).

Activities: Captain in the Territorial Army; assistant examiner Law Society Finals (1965-1974); member Council of the Rainer Foundation; trustee Pennycress Trust; former president Bucks County Hockey Association; former chairman Truman South Hockey League; former member Hockey Association Council; former secretary and president Old Greshamian Society; chairman family companies; member of: The Law Society; Beaconsfield Golf Club; Sheringham Golf Club; Royal Norwich Golf Club.

Biography: lives London NW1 and West Runton, Norfolk; born 30.01.1932; married to Vivienne with 1 son and 1 daughter. Educated at Gresham's School, Holt; Emmanuel College Cambridge (1955 BA) (1956 LLB) (1988 LLM); John Mackrell Prize (1958); contributor to Michael Simmon's 'Successful Mergers - Planning Strategy and Execution'.

BAKER Jeremy

partner specialising in town & country planning and local government law RADCLIFFES & CO 10 Little College Street, Westminster, London SW1P 3SJ.

Career: articled Wilkinson Kimbers & Staddon; admitted (1968); local government: Croydon LBC; Southwark LBC; Oxford City; secretary and returning officer Cherwell District (Oxfordshire) and secretary Sevenoaks District; assistant solicitor Radcliffes (1987-1988); became partner (1988).

Activities: founder member and area chairman Association of District Secretaries; member Camping Liaison Committee; director and camp leader Forest School Camps.

Biography: lives London SE21; born 19.01.1942; married to Malgorzata with 1 son. Educated at Dulwich College; Pembroke College Oxford (1965 MA); College of Law.

Leisure: sailing (sailed to South Pacific); children's camps; travel; DIY.

BAKER Nicholas

partner FRERE CHOLMELEY 28 Lincoln's Inn Fields, London WC2A 3HH.

Career: National Service in King's African Rifles (1957-1959); admitted (1967); assistant solicitor Frere Cholmeley (1968-1973); became partner (1973).

Activities: Conservative Parliamentary candidate for Peckham (1974); GLC candidate (1973); MP for North Dorset (1979 to date); Parliamentary Private Secretary to Rt Hon Michael Heseltine (1984-1986) and to Rt Hon Lord Young of Graffham (1987-1989); Government Whip (1989 to date); member Lloyd's; member Blandford Constitutional Club and Wimborne Conservative Club.

Biography: lives Wimborne Minster and London SW1; born 23.11.1938; married to Carol with 2 children. Educated at St Neot's School, Eversley; Clifton College (scholar); Exeter College Oxford (1963 MA); author of 'Better Company, Proposals for Company Law Reform' (1973); 'This Pleasant Land', a new strategy for planning (1987); 'Low-Cost Housing in Rural Areas' (1989).

Leisure: environmental matters including planning, agriculture, trade and industry; music; shooting; countryside; keeping fit.

B

BAKER Simon

partner and chairman VEALE
WASBROUGH 17 Berkeley Square, Bristol
BS8 1HD.

Career: admitted (1971); assistant solicitor
Bircham & Co (1971-1972); assistant
solicitor Stanley Wasbrough (1972-1973);
became partner (1973); member
Management Committee on Formation of
Veale Wasbrough (1988); elected chairman
(1990).

Activities: Council member The Law
Society of England and Wales; chairman
Bristol Young Solicitors Group (1975-1977);
member Law Society Young Solicitors
Group National Committee (1977-1981);
chairman National Young Solicitors Law in
Schools Working Party (1979-1981);
member Council of Bristol Law Society
(1980) (chairman Conveyancing and Non-
Contentious Committee 1987-1987); vice-
president Bristol Law Society (1990);
member International Bar Association
(1984); chairman Solicitors Conveyancing
Group, Bristol (1985-1987); member Society
for Computers and Law; supervising
computerisation of Bristol Law Society
(1989); member Rotary International.

Biography: lives Bristol; born 15.04.1945;
married to Ruth. Educated at Clifton
College, Bristol; Clare College Cambridge
(1967 BA) (1968 LLB); author (for Bristol
Law Society) of: 'Guidelines for Residential
Conveyancing Practice' (1985);
'Conveyancing and Competition' (1984);
'The Independence of the Legal Profession'
(1987); occasional contributor to Law
Society's Gazette on conveyancing, future
of the profession and law in schools.

Leisure: fine wine; travel; political history.

BALEN Paul

partner FREETH CARTWRIGHT
Willoughby House, 20 Low Pavement,
Nottingham NG1 7DL.

Career: articled Freeth Cartwright (1975-
1977); admitted (1977); assistant solicitor
(1977-1980); became partner (1980).

Activities: founder and Steering Committee
member Benzodiazipine Solicitors Group;
'legal eagle' Radio Nottingham; joint hon
secretary and press officer
Nottinghamshire Law Society (1984-1989);
member Notts Medico-Legal Society;
member American Trial Lawyers'
Association; member of: Old
Nottinghamians Cricket Club; Wollaton
Park Rotary Club.

Biography: lives Melbourne, Derbyshire;
born 25.02.1952; married to Helen with 2

children. Educated at Nottingham High
School; Peterhouse Cambridge (MA hons);
Roosevelt Scholar (1977).

Leisure: playing and watching most sports
(particularly cricket; squash and golf).

BALL Peter

staff partner ABSON HALL 30 Greek
Street, Stockport, Cheshire SK3 8AD.

Career: articled Neville Holt (1973-1975);
admitted (1975); assistant solicitor Abson
Hall & Co (1975-1977); became partner
(1977).

Activities: member Child Care Panel; part-
time chairman Social Security Appeal
Tribunal; secretary Stockport Law Society
(1985-1987); deputy president Stockport
Law Society (1990); lectures; member of:
Stockport Harriers; Bramhall Park Golf
Club; Bramhall Park Tennis Club;
Wilmslow Rotary Club.

Biography: lives Stockport; born 20.07.1951;
married to Claire with 1 child. Educated at
Great Moor Primary School; Stockport
Grammar School; Manchester Grammar
School; Leicester University (1972 LLB
hons); College of Law Guildford (1973 Law
Society Finals).

Leisure: running; golf; tennis; squash.

BALLARD Andrew

head of litigation RIGBEYS 42-44 Waterloo
Street, Birmingham B2 5QN.

Career: admitted (1981); assistant solicitor
in Swindon (1981-1983); became head of
litigation Rigbeys (1983).

Biography: lives Birmingham; born
01.12.1955; married with 1 child. Educated
at St Joseph's, Swindon; Bristol Polytechnic
(BA hons).

Leisure: all sports.

BALLARD Richard

partner in corporate tax department
FRESHFIELDS Whitefriars, 65 Fleet Street,
London EC4Y 1HS.

Career: admitted (1978); assistant solicitor
(1978-1984); became partner Freshfields
(1984).

Biography: lives Pakenham; born
03.08.1953; married to Penny with 3
children. Educated at St Edmund's
College, Ware; Queen's College Cambridge
(1975 MA); contributions to various books
and journals.

BALLINGALL Patrick

consultant BARWELL BLAKISTON &
BALLINGALL 10 Sutton Park Road,
Seaford, East Sussex BN25 1RB.

Career: 1st Lt Royal Artillery serving in
Greece, Palestine and Egypt (1944-1948);
articled Reynolds Gorst & Porter (1950-
1953); admitted (1953); assistant solicitor
(1954-1955); assistant solicitor RV Stokes &
Metcalfe (1955-1958); assistant solicitor
Barwell & Blakiston (1958-1959); partner
(1959-1980); senior partner (1980-1989);
became consultant (1990).

Activities: MBE (1984); chairman Lewes
Constituency Conservative Association
(1978-1981); chairman East Sussex
Conservative European constituency
Council (1984 to date).

Biography: lives Seaford; born 05.12.1926;
married with 2 children. Educated at
Loretto School, Musselburgh; Edinburgh
University; Emmanuel College Cambridge
(1950 MA).

BAMFORD Carmel

legal director WICKES PROPERTIES
LIMITED 19/21 Mortimer Street, London
W1N 7RJ.

Career: articled Tweedie & Prideaux (1983-
1985); admitted (1985); assistant solicitor
Rowe & Maw (1985-1987); assistant
solicitor Lovell White Durrant (1987-1988);
became legal director Wickes Properties
Limited (1988).

Activities: member Riverside Racquets
Club.

Biography: lives London SW14; born
04.11.1959; married. Educated at
Maricourt Convent School; Sheffield
University (1982 BA); College of Law
Guildford (1983).

Leisure: tennis; skiing; literature.

BAMFORD Richard

senior partner ARCHER & ARCHER
Market Place, Ely, Cambs CB7 4QN.

Career: articled Taylor & Humbert (1961-
1964); admitted (1964); assistant solicitor
(1964-1966); assistant solicitor Archer &
Archer (1966-1967); partner (1967-1987);
became senior partner (1987).

Activities: clerk to General Commissioners
for Income Tax Ely and South Witchfield;
clerk to Association of Drainage
Authorities Great Ouse branch; member
Cambridgeshire & District Law Society;
member Solicitors Disciplinary Tribunal
(1984 to date); local councillor; Mayor of
Ely (1988-1989); Deputy Lt,

Cambridgeshire (1987); secretary PCC St Mary's, Ely (1986 to date); member of: Royal West Norfolk; Royal Worlington; City of Ely.

Biography: lives Ely; born 1938; married with 2 children. Educated at Winchester House; Wellington; Selwyn College Cambridge (1961 BA MA).

Leisure: family; golf; shooting.

BANKES U William

partner FIELD FISHER WATERHOUSE 41 Vine Street, London EC3N 2AA.

Career: admitted (1954); assistant solicitor (1954-1961); became partner Field Fisher Waterhouse (1961).

Activities: secretary Bow Group (1952); secretary Holborn Law Society (1979-1984) (president 1987-1988) (chairman Conveyancing Section); secretary Radcliffe Medical Foundation; member Middleton Stoney PCC; member United Oxford & Cambridge Universities Club.

Biography: lives London SW1 and Middleton Stoney; born 15.10.1927; married to Mary with 2 children. Educated at Eltham College; New College Oxford (1950 BA) (1951 BCL) (MA); Solicitors Finals (hons).

Leisure: opera; bridge; watching village cricket and tennis; travel.

BANNAR-MARTIN David

partner REDFERN & STIGANT 167 High Street, Strood, Kent ME2 4TH.

Career: articled Kenneth Redfern & Co; admitted (1971); assistant solicitor (1971-1972); became partner (1972).

Activities: immediate past chairman Medway Towns Victims' Support Scheme; member St Mark's Gillingham Parochial Church Council; trustee and hon legal advisor to Gillingham Kent branch of the CAB; president Rochester, Chatham & Gillingham Law Society (1989-1990); member Lawyers' Christian Fellowship; member Durham University Society.

Biography: lives Gillingham; born 11.11.1943; married to Jane with 3 children. Educated at King's School, Rochester; Newcastle University (1966 LLB).

Leisure: Church; sport; music.

BARCLAY Jonathan

partner MILLS & REEVE 3-7 Redwell Street, Norwich NR2 4TJ.

Career: articled Withers (1969-1971);

admitted (1971); assistant solicitor (1971-1973); assistant solicitor Mills & Reeve (1974-1976); became partner (1976).

Activities: chairman Norton Rose M5 Group; member Norfolk Country Landowners' Association Committee; member CLA National Taxation Committee.

Biography: lives Norfolk; born 09.03.1947; married with 2 children. Educated at Eton College; East Anglia University (1968 BA).

Leisure: opera; golf; skiing; wine.

BARLOW Roy

senior partner ASHTONS Yorkshire Bank Chambers, Fargate, Sheffield S1 1LN.

Career: assistant solicitor local government (Doncaster CB, Leeds City, Derbyshire CC, Sheffield City (1952-1962); became partner Ashtons (1962).

Activities: Recorder.

Biography: lives Barlow nr Sheffield; born 13.02.1927; married to Kathleen with 3 children. Educated at King Edward VII School, Sheffield, Queen's College Oxford; Sheffield University (1948 LLB).

BARNES Judith

partner company/commercial department JAQUES & LEWIS 2 South Square, Gray's Inn, London WC1R 5HR.

Career: teacher with Voluntary Service Overseas in Egypt (1972-1974); articled Bischoff & Co (1975-1977); admitted (1978); assistant solicitor (1977-1979); assistant solicitor Jaques & Lewis (1979-1984); became partner (1984).

Activities: member management Committee of Camden Community Law Centre; member Camden Council.

Biography: lives London NW5; born 17.01.1950; single. Educated at Mary Erskine School, Edinburgh; Huyton College, Liverpool; Somerville College Oxford (1968-1972); Gilbert Murray Scholarship; College of Law Chester (1974-1975); College of Law Lancaster Gate (1977-1978).

Leisure: mountain walking; cinema; opera.

BARNES Nigel

senior partner BARNES AND PARTNERS 4 Little Park Gardens, Enfield, Middlesex EN2 6PQ.

Career: commerce (2 years); property development; founded own practice.

Activities: member Executive Committee

local NSPCC; member Bush Hill Park Golf Club.

Biography: lives Essex; born 18.03.1945; married to Nicola with 3 children. Educated at The Manchester Grammar School; College of Law.

Leisure: golf; tennis; skiing; bridge.

BARNES Rachel

partner BEALE AND COMPANY Garrick House, 27-32 King Street, Covent Garden, London WC2E 8JD.

Career: partner Beale and Company.

Activities: member Law Society Interviewing Panel for the Monitoring of Articles; member International Bar Association; member Solicitors European Group; member City of Westminster Law Society; member The Law Society; member French Chamber of Commerce.

Biography: lives Twickenham; born 07.03.1951; married to David with 2 children. Educated at North Foreland Lodge, Basingstoke; Bristol University (1972 LLB).

Leisure: reading; film; theatre; QPR Football Club.

BARNES Simon

partner HEMPSONS 33 Henrietta Street, London WC2E 8NH.

Career: articled Withers Nicholl Manisty (1962-1966); admitted (1966); assistant solicitor Jacobs and Greenwood (1967-1971); became partner (1971); merged with Woodham Smith Borrowdaile and Martin (1972); became senior partner (1988) firm dissolved (1990); partner Hempsons (1990).

Activities: governor Combe Bank School, Sundridge near Sevenoaks Kent; member East London Legal Aid Area Committee (1980-1988); member Athenaeum.

Biography: lives near Tonbridge; born 13.12.1939; married to Helen Gresford-Jones with 3 children. Educated at Bradfield College, Berkshire; Corpus Christi College Cambridge (1962 BA) (1965 MA).

Leisure: fishing; cricket; reading; skiing.

BARNETT William Evans

Queen's Counsel 12 King's Bench Walk, Temple, London EC4Y 7EL Tel 071-583 0811 Fax No. 071-583 7228 LDE 1037.

Career: called to the Bar Inner Temple (1962); Recorder (1981); QC (1984); member Personal Injuries Litigation Procedure

B

Working Party (1976-1979); one of the Arbitrators with the Motor Insurers' Bureau (Compensation of Untraced Drivers) Agreement (1987 to date).

Activities: member of: The Royal Automobile Club; Surrey Tennis and Country Club; Croydon Medico Legal Society.

Biography: lives Croydon; born 10.03.1937; married to Lucinda with 2 sons. Educated at Brightlands Preparatory School, Newnham on Severn; Repton; Keble College Oxford (1961 BA) (1965 MA); Major Scholarship Inner Temple (1962).

Leisure: photography; gardening; DIY.

BARNSLEY Graham

professor of law UNIVERSITY OF LEICESTER Faculty of Law, Leicester LE1 7RH.

Career: articled Fentons Stansfield & Co (1956-1960); admitted (1960); assistant lecturer Manchester University (1960-1963); lecturer (1963-1966); senior lecturer Leicester University (1966-1973); professor of law (1973 to date); dean Faculty of Law (1976-1982); head of department of law (1987-1988); part-time solicitor (1963-1975).

Activities: chief examiner in tort for Solicitors Qualifying Examinations part I (1967-1973); moderator in land law for the College of Law's Common Professional Examinations (1985 to date); Church worker and lay preacher; member The Gideons International.

Biography: lives Oadby, Leicestershire; born 16.01.1936; married to Blanche with 2 children. Educated at Stand Grammar School, Whitefield; Manchester University (1956 LLB) (1960 LLM); Dauntsey Senior Legal Scholarship (1956); author of: 'Barnsley's Conveyancing Law and Practice' (3rd ed) (1988); 'Land Options' (1978).

Leisure: philatelist; gardening and plant propagation; walking; lapsed jogger.

BARR Outram David Guy

former senior partner DAWBARNS 1 & 2 York Row, Wisbech, Cambridgeshire PE13 1EA, now consultant.

Career: admitted (1939); Army; assistant solicitor Dawbarns (1946); became partner.

Activities: former deputy chairman Agricultural Land Tribunal; former president Cambridgeshire Law Society; member Royal West Norfolk Golf Club.

Biography: lives Elm; born 26.03.1917; married to Marjorie with 2 children.

Educated at King's School, Canterbury; regular contributor to legal and other publications; author of 'A Family Way' and 'Twice Hooked' (to be published Autumn 1990); editor of: 'The Haig Guide to Salmon Fishing in Scotland'; 'The Haig Guide to Trout Fishing in Britain'; Country Life's fishing correspondent.

BARR William

partner MILLS & REEVE 112 Hills Road, Cambridge CB2 1PH.

Career: articled Mills & Reeve (1971-1973); admitted (1973); assistant solicitor (1973-1975); became partner (1975).

Activities: member Agricultural Law Association; frequent lectures on agricultural law topics; member Norwich Rowing Club.

Biography: lives Norwich; born 10.05.1949; married to Erica with 2 children. Educated at Nowton Court; Wisbech Grammar School; Sheffield University (1970 LLB) Edgar Allen Scholar; joint author of 'Farm Tenancies'.

Leisure: rowing; (4 wins Boston Marathon); marathon running; fishing.

BARR-SMITH Adrian

partner DENTON HALL BURGIN & WARRENS 5 Chancery Lane, Clifford's Inn, London EC4A 1BU.

Career: articled Rubinstein Callingham (1975-1977); admitted (1977); assistant solicitor (1977-1978); director Artlaw Services Ltd (1979-1981); assistant solicitor Denton Hall Burgin & Warrens (1982-1986); became partner (1986).

Activities: hon secretary Design and Artists' Copyright Society Ltd; chairman Interlink Trust; member of: MCC; Groucho.

Biography: lives London SW3; born 23.01.1952; married to Annie. Educated at Rossall School; Emmanuel College Cambridge (1973 BA) (1979 MA); College of Law (1974-1975); contributor to 'International Media Law Newsletter' and 'Broadcast'; co-author 'Denton Hall Encyclopaedia of Entertainment Law'.

Leisure: cricket; travel; theatre; cinema; contemporary art.

BARRETT David

consultant in charge of telecommunications and information technology matters THEODORE GODDARD 150 Aldersgate, London EC1A 4EJ.

Career: called to the Bar (1979); legal adviser IBM United Kingdom Limited (1979); divisional legal adviser; senior legal adviser; counsel (1988-1989); special assistant to the vice-president and general counsel and senior legal adviser IBM Europe SA (1985-1988); became consultant Theodore Goddard (1989).

Activities: member Telecommunications and Computer Law Committees of IBA; member Computer Law Association; Computer Law Group; IT Lawyers' Group; former member Legal Committee of Business Equipment and Technology Association; participant in numerous computer law and telecommunications law conferences as delegate and speaker; member Royal Over-Seas League.

Biography: lives Hertfordshire; born 30.04.1953; married to Anne with 1 child. Educated at Ryley's Preparatory School, Alderley Edge; King's School, Tynemouth; Gonville and Caius College Cambridge (1972-1976); University of Michigan Law School (postgraduate scholarship 1976-1977) (MA LLB LLM hons); Full Right Award; State Scholarship in Private International Law; participant in Hague Academy of International Law.

Leisure: theatre; music; sailing; travel; politics.

BARRINGTON John

senior partner MOORE & BLATCH 11 The Avenue, Southampton SO1 2SQ.

Career: admitted (1957); National Service in Army Pay Corps (1957-1959); assistant solicitor Moore & Blatch (1959-1966); became partner (1966).

Activities: consultant on development land/capital gains taxes and land options to various public companies, landowners and solicitors.

Biography: lives Hythe; born 26.07.1935; married to Daphne with 2 children. Educated at Hugh Sexey's, Bruton.

Leisure: all sport.

BARRY Quintin

managing partner DONNE MILEHAM & HADDOCK 42/46 Frederick Place, Brighton, East Sussex BN1 1AT.

Career: articled Mileham Scatliff & Allen (1953-1958); admitted (1958); assistant solicitor Cronin & Son (1958-1960); (1960-1961); assistant solicitor Mileham Scatcliff & Allen (1960-1961); partner (1961-1970); became partner Donne Mileham & Haddock (1970).

Activities: Labour Parliamentary candidate for Lewes (1970), Shoreham (1974) and Brighton Kemp Town (1979); chairman Legal Aid Practitioners' Group (1982-1985); director Southern Sound PLC (chairman 1982-1985); director Southern Radio Holdings PLC; former member Law Society Remuneration Committee; chairman Law South; solicitor to Sussex County Cricket Club; hon solicitor British Red Cross (Sussex).

Biography: lives Shoreham by Sea; born 07.03.1936; married with 6 children. Educated at Tyttenhanger Lodge School; Eastbourne College; OU (1983 BA).

Leisure: history; horse racing.

BARTLETT Bernard

partner and head corporate department BERWIN LEIGHTON Adelaide House, London Bridge, London EC4R 9HA.

Career: articled Bower Cotton & Bower (1963-1968); admitted (1968); assistant solicitor Berwin & Co (1968-1972); partner Berwin Leighton (1972); became head corporate department (1988); member Board of Management.

Activities: member Wentworth.

Biography: lives Chobham; born 10.06.1941; married to Jenny with 2 children. Educated at Leighton Park School .

Leisure: tennis; golf; bridge; old sports cars.

BARTLETT Pierre

partner BARTLETT & SON 16 Nicholas Street, Chester CH1 2NX.

Career: became partner Bartlett & Son (1968) (fourth generation).

Biography: lives Mold; born 05.05.1942; married with 3 children. Educated at Eton; Christ Church Oxford (MA).

Leisure: farming; conservation of historic buildings.

BATES John

partner and commercial property group head FLADGATE FIELDER Walgate House, 25 Church Street, Basingstoke, Hants RG21 1QQ.

Career: articled Courts & Co (1961-1966); admitted (1966); assistant solicitor Walters & Hart; salaried partner; partner; became partner Fladgate Fielder (1988).

Biography: lives Winchester; born 01.09.1944; married to Gillian with 3 children. Educated at Highgate School; London University (LLB external).

Leisure: sailing; family.

BATESON Fergus

consultant THOMAS COOPER & STIBBARD 52 Leadenhall Street, London EC3A 2DJ.

Career: articled Thomas Cooper & Stibbard (1952-1955); admitted (1956); assistant solicitor (1956-1959); partner (1959); senior partner (1986-1990); became consultant (1990).

Activities: trustee Nautical Museums Trust (1982 to date); member Law Society working party on civil evidence (1964-1965); member Advisory Committee on Historic Wreck Sites (Runciman Committee) (1974 to date); member of 'Company of Ten', St Albans (set designer and painter - designed sets for company's tour to Detroit, USA (1985); member Mitre Club.

Biography: lives St Albans; born 26.04.1930; married to Ann with 4 children. Educated at Lockers Park (1937-1943); Westminster School (1943-1948); Hertford College Oxford (1952 BA); College of Law Lancaster Gate (1953 & 1954-1955); fluent written and spoken French; some Italian and little Romanian; author of 'Notes on International Maritime Law as applied by the Law of England' (1966).

BATESON George

senior partner SMEATHMANS PO Box 1, 10 Queensway, Hemel Hempstead, Herts HP1 1LU.

Career: articled Smeathmans (1954-1957); admitted (1957); assistant solicitor (1957-1963); became partner (1963) .

Activities: deputy Coroner Hemel Hempstead District (1974); Coroner (1984); president Hertfordshire Law Society (1985); solicitor to governors of Berkhampsted Schools; member of: Little Gaddesden Art Club; Berkhamsted Strathspey and Reel Club.

Biography: lives near Berkhamsted; born 20.04.1932; married to Alison with 3 children. Educated at Leighton Park School; Magdalene College Cambridge (1954 BA).

Leisure: Scottish country dancing; photography; playing bagpipes; white water rafting; keeping hens and sheep.

BAXTER David HW

a senior partner in the Corporate Services Department of FOSTER BAXTER COOKSEY now based at 7/10 George Street, Snow Hill, Wolverhampton, West Midlands WV2 4DN.

Career: articled in family firm JH Baxter & Son; admitted (1958); 34 years as partner in the Willenhall office now based since December (1989) at the Head Office of the Group Practice in Wolverhampton.

Activities: a member of the Governing Council of the Law Society representing Constituency 24 now including Wolverhampton, Walsall and Staffordshire; non-executive director in a number of substantial private limited companies; a member of the International Committee of the Law Society; Chairman of the International Promotions Working Party of the Law Society; a member of the Child Care Appeal Casework Committee of the Law Society; a member of the Specialisation Committee of the Law Society; a Council member of the Local Law Societies of Birmingham, Wolverhampton and Walsall; member of the Solicitors European Group.

Biography: lives in Pattingham; born 16.05.1935; married to Jennifer with 2 sons, Nicholas and Steven; Nicholas practising law in Omaha, Nebraska; Steven in computers. Educated at Malvern College.

Leisure: golf; gardening; horse riding; motor racing.

BEALE Diana

member LEGAL AID BOARD Newspaper House, 8-16 Great New Street, London EC4A 3BN.

Career: housing welfare assistant GLC (1966-1969); housing welfare officer London Borough of Camden (1969-1970); estate manager LBC (1971-1972); research & information officer Housing Aid Centre LBC (1971-1972); lecturer in housing management South Gwent College (part-time) (1973-1975); advice worker Abergavenny CAB (part-time) (1974 to date); member Legal Aid Board (1988).

Activities: member NACAB legal services group (1978-1988) (member Council (1984-1988); Lord Chancellor's nominee Legal Aid (Duty Solicitor) Committee (1985-1989); chair South Wales Legal Services Steering Group (1986-1988); member Legal Action Group Management Committee (1987-1988).

Biography: lives Powys; born 28.12.1944; married with 2 children. Diploma in Sociology (1971); co-author with B Stow: 'CAB & Access to Legal Services In South Wales' (1986); with G Maddocks: 'A Legal Services Committee for South Wales' for Law Society's Gazette (1988).

B

BEARE Stuart N

senior partner RICHARDS BUTLER
Beaufort House, 15 St Botolph Street,
London EC3A 7EE.

Career: assistant plebiscite supervisory
officer Northern Cameroons Trust Territory
(1960-1961); articled Simmons & Simmons
(1961-1964); admitted (1964); assistant
solicitor (1964-1966); assistant solicitor
Richards Butler & Co (1966-1969); partner
(1969-1988); became senior partner (1988).

Activities: member Court of Assistants of
The City of London Solicitors' Company;
member Shipping and Aerospace Sub-
committee of The City of London Law
Society; member The Baltic Exchange;
supporting member The London Maritime
Arbitrators' Association; titulary member
of the Comite Maritime International;
member of: Alpine Club; City of London
Club; Oriental Club; MCC; Aldgate Ward
Club.

Biography: lives London N1; born
06.10.1936; married to Cheryl. Educated at
Clifton College; Clare College Cambridge
(1960 BA MA LLB).

Leisure: mountaineering; skiing; travel.

BEAUMONT Rupert

partner SLAUGHTER AND MAY
35 Basinghall Street, London EC2V 5DB.

Career: articled Beaumont & Son (1962-
1968); admitted (1968); assistant solicitor
Appleton Rice & Perrin, New York City
(1968-1969); assistant solicitor Slaughter
and May (1969-1974); became partner
(1974); Hong Kong office (1976-1981).

Activities: member Technical Committee of
Association of Corporate Treasurers;
numerous speaking engagements at
seminars, conferences, universities and
client training/education sessions on
several subjects; member Cavalry &
Guards.

Biography: lives West Green; born
27.02.1944; married to Susie with 2
children. Educated at Wellington College,
Crowthorne; Grenoble Foreign Faculty;
several articles in legal journals and books
especially on debt financing and
securitisation.

Leisure: reading; theatre; opera; tennis;
fishing.

BECK Anthony

head of training HOLMAN FENWICK &
WILLAN Marlow House, Lloyd's Avenue,
London EC3N 3AL.

Career: articled Titmuss Sainer & Webb;

admitted (1961); pupillage S Stammler QC
and RAK Wright QC; called to the Bar
(1968); principal lecturer Essex Institute of
Higher Education (1979-1984); head of
department Ealing College of Higher
Education (1984-1989).

Activities: contributor to conferences of
critical legal studies and semiotics.

Biography: lives London SW6; born
25.04.1936; married to Rosemary Ann with
2 children. Educated at Haberdashers'
Aske's, Hampstead; Tapp Scholar, Gonville
and Caius College Cambridge (1957 BA)
(1958 MA); Harvard Law School (1958
LLB) (1966 LLM); Visiting Research Fellow
Sussex University (1967-1968); author of
articles on Contract, Criminal Law, Legal
Semiotics.

Leisure: piano.

BECKWITH Peter

deputy chairman LONDON &
EDINBURGH TRUST PLC
243 Knightsbridge, London SW7 1DH.

Career: articled Herbert Smith & Co (1967-
1970); admitted (1970); assistant solicitor
Norton Rose (1970-1972); founded London
& Edinburgh Trust Ltd (1972).

Activities: vice-president Old Harrovian
Association Football Club; chairman
Riverside Racquets Club.

Biography: lives London SW19; born
20.01.1945; married with 2 daughters.
Educated at Merchant Taylors' (1956-1958);
Harrow School (1958-1963); Emmanuel
College Cambridge (1966 MA hons).

Leisure: tennis; skiing; dogs; music; travel;
reading.

BEER Andrew

senior commercial property partner
WILDE SAPTE Queensbridge House, 60
Upper Thames Street, London EC4V 3BD.

Career: articled Theodore Goddard (1958-
1963); admitted (1964); assistant solicitor
Wilde Sapte (1968-1969); became partner
(1969).

Activities: regular lecturer upon property,
landlord and tenant and insolvency
subjects; Blundell Memorial lecturer (1985);
chairman Law Society Rugby Football
Club.

Biography: lives North Bucks; born
26.08.1939; married with 2 children.
Educated at Dragon School, Oxford (1948-
1953); Shrewsbury School (1953-1957);
contributor to: Encyclopaedia of Forms
and Precedents (fifth edition); Landlord
and Tenant (Butterworths).

Leisure: old cars; bee keeper.

BEESLEY Peter

partner LEE BOLTON AND LEE 1 The
Sanctuary, Westminster, London SW1P 3JT.

Career: articled Windeatt and Windeatt
(1965-1967); admitted (1967); assistant
solicitor (1967-1968); assistant solicitor Lee
Bolton and Lee (1968-1969); became
partner (1969).

Activities: joint registrar Diocese of St
Alban's (1969-1978) and Archdeaconries of
St Alban's and Bedford (1969-1978);
chapter clerk St Alban's Cathedral (1973 to
date); joint registrar Diocese of Ely (1978 to
date); registrar Diocese of Guildford (1981
to date); joint registrar Diocese of Hereford
(1983 to date); registrar Faculty Office of
the Archbishop of Canterbury (1981 to
date); solicitor to the National Society (C of
E) for Promoting Religious Education and
the General Synod Board of Education
(1975 to date); registrar Woodard
Corporation (1987 to date); hon auditor of
The Law Society (1984 & 1985); treasurer
City of Westminster Law Society; secretary
Ecclesiastical Law Association; secretary
Ecclesiastical Law Society; solicitor and
secretary to various private companies,
charitable companies, trusts both
charitable and non-charitable and various
Diocesan Boards of Finance and Education
of the Church of England; member
working party of the National Society
which published report on employment in
Sector Ministries (1983); Livery man of the
Worshipful Company of Glaziers and
Painters of Glass (Master's Steward 1988-
1989); chairman governors Hampstead
Parochial School; member of: Athenaeum;
St Stephen's Constitutional Club.

Biography: lives London NW11; born
30.04.1943; married to Elizabeth with 1 son
and 2 daughters. Educated at Montpelier
School, Paignton; The King's School,
Worcester; Exeter University (1964 LLB);
College of Law Guildford (1964-1965); joint
contributor to volume 13 Encyclopaedia of
Forms and Precedents 'Ecclesiastical Law'.

BEHARRELL Steven

founding partner BEHARRELL
THOMPSON & CO 4 Dean's Court,
London EC4V 5AA in association with
COUDERT BROTHERS.

Career: articled Denton Hall Burgin &
Warrens; admitted (1969); assistant
solicitor (1969-1973); became partner
(1973); founded Beharrell Thompson & Co
(1990).

Activities: JP (1976-1986); member IBA Committee on Oil Law.

Biography: lives London SW3 and Hatfield Broad Oak; born 22.12.1944; married to Julia with 2 children. Educated at St Ronan's School, Hawkhurst; Uppingham School; British Institute and Sorbonne University, Paris; College of Law London; various articles in professional journals and publications of lectures and papers.

Leisure: fishing; shooting; performing arts; reading; travel.

BELCHAMBER Peter

partner STEPHENSON HARWOOD One St Paul's Churchyard, London EC4M 8SH.

Career: admitted (1964); assistant solicitor (1964-1968); became partner Stephenson Harwood (1968).

Biography: born 27.03.1932. Educated at Wellington Avenue Secondary Modern, Chingford.

Leisure: reading; walking; photography; bird watching.

BELL Cedric

director of training and research RAWSTHORN EDELSTONS St George's Chambers, 4 Fishergate Walk, Preston PR1 2LH.

Career: called to the Bar Middle Temple (1976); pupillage in Chambers in Nottingham; lecturer in law Trent Polytechnic (1976-1980); senior lecturer in law Huddersfield Polytechnic (1980-1984); principal lecturer in law Lancashire Polytechnic (1984 to date); became director of training and research Rawsthorn Edelstons (1988).

Activities: member editorial board of Trust Law and Practice; member Legal Education and Training Group.

Biography: lives Preston; born 20.06.1952; single. Educated at Royal Belfast Academical Institution (1963-1970); Birmingham University (1974 LLB) (1975 LLM) (1985 PHD); contributes regularly to national legal periodicals.

Leisure: committed Christian and active Church member; swimming; walking; Border Collie dogs; association football (supporter Northern Ireland international team).

BELL Malcolm

partner ADDLESHAW SONS & LATHAM Dennis House, Marsden Street, Manchester M2 1JD.

Career: articled in London; admitted (1959); assistant solicitor (1959-1960); assistant solicitor Addleshaw Sons & Latham (1960-1963); became partner (1964).

Activities: member Law Society and Bar Council Joint Working Party on Insolvency Law; chairman North East Cheshire Lawn Tennis League; member of: Alderley Edge Cricket Club; Wilmslow Golf Club; Sheringham Golf Club.

Biography: lives Alderley Edge; born 29.05.1936; married to Beryl with 3 daughters. Educated at Manchester Grammar School; University College London (1956 LLB hons).

Leisure: tennis; golf.

BELL Martin

senior partner ASHURST MORRIS CRISP Broadwalk, 5 Appold Street, London EC2A 2HA.

Career: admitted (1961); assistant solicitor Ashurst Morris Crisp (1961-1963); partner (1963-1986); became senior partner (1986).

Biography: lives Loughton; born 16.01.1935; married to Shirley with 2 children. Educated at Charterhouse; College of Law; Alfred Syrett Prize.

BELL Mike

senior partner FOYEN & BELL Norway House, 21-24 Cockspur Street, London SW1Y 5BN; consultant ADVOKATFIRMAET FOYEN & CO Ans Oscars Gate 52 Oslo, Norway.

Career: articled Pritchard Englefield Leader Henderson (1962-1967); admitted (1969); assistant Cripps Harries Hall & Co (1968-1969); legal adviser Trust House Forte Group (1969-1971); assistant solicitor JM Rix & Kay (1971-1973); partner (1973-1982); senior partner (1982-1985); consultant Advocatfirmaet Foyen & Co, Oslo (1984); became partner Foyen & Bell (1987).

Activities: member of the board of: Norbrit Invest A/S, Norway; Tria Aktiv A/S, Norway; member Foyen International Committee; adviser to board of 5 substantial Norwegian Corporations; adviser to various companies in Norway and Finland on trading matters with USSR and Poland and on African affairs; member of: East India Club; National Liberal Club; Buxted Park Cricket Club (vice-president); Cryptics CC; Hamar Seil Klubb; Anglo Norse Society; British Business Forum; International Bar Association. Present directorships: Aluminium H Windows Ltd;

Anebyhus (UK)Ltd; EM Tatton Ltd; Expograph Ltd; Fringehill Developments Ltd; The H Window UK Ltd; Mayfair Fine Art Ltd; New Barn Farm Ltd; Qualitex Building Co Ltd; Qualitex (Conversions) Ltd; Rjukan Metall UK Ltd; Scantrade International Ltd; Solofair Developments Ltd; Ticon UK Ltd; Timber H Windows Ltd; Tria-Aktiv (UK) Ltd; UPVC H Windows Ltd; Watchlight Properties Ltd; Westad UK Limited. Past directorships: Aidaprop Ltd; Churchdown Country Homes Ltd; Creative Marketing Consultants (UK) Ltd; Crowson Fabrics Ltd; Derek Crowson Ltd; Derek Crowson (Design) Ltd; Derek Crowson (Fabrics) Ltd; Finnav Companies Ltd; Nordic Light Ltd; Sagahus Ltd; Sagahus (London) Ltd; Sagahus (Sussex) Ltd; Sharlaine Ltd.

Biography: lives London and Hamar, Norway; born 02.10.1943; married to Aud with 2 children. Educated at Brightlands Preparatory School, Newnham, Glos; Oundle School; a number of articles on Norwegian/UK trading and commercial laws; article on Norwegian exchange control regulations.

Leisure: sailing; cricket; skiing .

BELL Murray

senior partner COFFIN MEW & CLOVER 29 Middle Road, Park Gate, Southampton SO3 7AL.

Career: articled in London (1957-1960); admitted (1960); assistant solicitor in Eastcote (1960-1962); assistant solicitor in Wedmore (1963-1964); assistant solicitor Coffin Mew & Clover (1964-1965); became partner (1965).

Activities: Notary Public.

Biography: lives Alverstoke; born 16.06.1934; divorced with 3 children. Educated at Bristol Grammar School; Bristol University (1955 LLB).

Leisure: sailing; theatre; cinema; cooking; kite flying.

BELL Robin

senior partner TODS MURRAY WS 66 Queen Street, Edinburgh EH2 4NE.

Career: National Service commissioned in The Royal Scots serving in British Troops, Berlin (1951-1953); apprentice Morton Smart MacDonald & Prosser WS (1956-1960); admitted (1960); assistant solicitor Coward Chance (1961-1962); became partner Tods Murray WS (1963).

Activities: non-executive director Upton & Southern Holdings plc; member The Law

B

Society of Scotland Company Law Committee (member Council 1975-1978); member Company Law Committee of the Council of the Bars & Law Societies of The European Community; member New Club, Edinburgh.

Biography: lives Edinburgh; born 28.02.1933; married to Patricia with 4 sons (1 deceased). Educated at The Edinburgh Academy; Loretto School; Worcester College Oxford (1956 BA); Edinburgh University (1959 LLB).

Leisure: salmon fishing; gardening.

BELL Rodger

Queen's Counsel and head of chambers 1 Crown Office Row, Temple, London EC4Y 7HH.

Career: called to the Bar Middle Temple (1963); Recorder (1980); QC (1982).

Activities: legal member Mental Health Review Tribunals (1983 to date); member of: Thames Hare and Hounds; Dacre Boat Club; Vincent's Club; Achilles Club.

Biography: lives London SW15; born 13.09.1939; married to Claire with 1 son and 3 daughters. Educated at Moulsham Primary School for Boys (1948-1951); Brentwood School (1951-1958); Brasenose College Oxford (1962 BA).

Leisure: running; rowing.

BELL Tony

partner responsible for staff training and head of commercial property department KNIGHT & SONS 31 Ironmarket, Newcastle under Lyme, Staffordshire ST5 1RL.

Career: articled Knight & Sons (1963-1966); admitted (1966); assistant solicitor (1966-1967); became partner (1967).

Activities: part-time lecturer in law Keele University (1966-1981); taught trainee legal executives and students doing external degrees for London University; chairman West Midland Rent Assessment Committee; former governor Ellesmere College; hon legal adviser Newcastle under Lyme School; member of the North Staffs District Health Authority; member of: Newcastle under Lyme Rotary Club; Basford Lawn Tennis Club; Stone Master Marathoners.

Biography: lives Newcastle under Lyme; born 24.02.1942; married to Wendy with 2 children. Educated at Ellison Street School, Wolstanton; Ellesmere College, Shropshire; Emmanuel College Cambridge (1963 BA) (1965 LLB) (MA).

Leisure: marathon runner (completed 22 marathons including 6 London marathons); skiing.

BELOFF Michael

Queen's Counsel 4-5 Gray's Inn Square, Gray's Inn, London WC1R 5AY.

Career: called to the Bar Gray's Inn (1967); lecturer in law Trinity College Oxford (1965-1966); legal correspondent New Society (1969-1979); The Observer (1979-1981); QC (1981); Recorder (1985); Bencher Gray's Inn (1988); Deputy High Court Judge in Queen's Bench Division (1989 to date).

Activities: chairman Administrative Law Bar Association (1986 to date); member Bingham Law Reform Committee on Discovery of Documents and Disclosure (1982 to date); hon member International Athletes' Club; member of: Reform; Vincent's (Oxford).

Biography: lives London W8 and Oxford; born 19.04.1942; married to Judith with 2 children. Educated at Dragon School, Oxford; Eton College (King's School, Captain of School 1960); Magdalen College Oxford (1962 BA) (1963 Law) (1965 MA) HWC Davis Prizeman; president Oxford Union Society (1962); Oxford Union tour of USA (1964); Gerald Moody Scholar (1963); Atkin Scholar (1967); author of: 'A Short Walk on the Campus' with J Aitken (1966); 'The Plateglass Universities' (1968); 'The Sex Discrimination Act' (1976); 'Judicial Safeguards in Administration Proceedings' (1989); Halsbury's Laws of England (Time) (1983); contributor to: Encounter, Minerva, Irish Jurist Political Quarterly, Current Legal Problems, Public Law, etc.

Leisure: marathon running.

BENHAM David Hamilton

senior litigation partner BISCHOFF & CO PO Box 613, Epworth House, 25 City Road, London EC1Y 1BY.

Career: articled John Mowlem & Co Ltd and Finnis Downey Linnel & Price; admitted (1970); assistant legal adviser British Oxygen Co Ltd; contracts solicitor British Petroleum Co Ltd; assistant solicitor Bischoff & Co (1974-1975); became partner (1975).

Activities: member Solicitors Family Law Association; member London Litigation Solicitors' Association; Freeman of the City of London; Liveryman City Company; member of: Lambs Squash Club; Colets Club (Old Paulines); Royal Southampton Yacht Club.

Biography: lives Thames Ditton and Southampton; born 1942; married to Ann with 1 son and 1 daughter. Educated at public school; Southampton University (1963 BA).

Leisure: former county rugby and national standard sprinter; squash; photography; collecting antiques; boating.

BENJAMIN Victor

partner BERWIN LEIGHTON Adelaide House, London Bridge, London EC4R 9HA.

Career: became partner Berwin Leighton (1963).

Activities: deputy chairman Tesco PLC; non-executive deputy chairman LEX Service PLC; director Blackheath Concert Halls; chairman Central Council of Jewish Social Services; member of: City of London Club; Savile Club.

Biography: lives East Sussex; born 02.03.1935; married with 5 children. Educated at Malvern.

Leisure: sailing; skiing; opera.

BENNETT David

partner AC BENNETT & ROBERTSONS WS 16 Walker Street, Edinburgh EH3 7NN.

Career: became partner AC Bennett & Robertsons WS (1964).

Activities: chairman Oswalds of Edinburgh Ltd (director 1964 to date); director Jordan Group Ltd (1986 to date); council member Law Society of Scotland (1984-1990) (convener Company Law Committee 1985 to date).

Biography: lives Edinburgh; born 27.03.1938; married to Marion with 2 daughters. Educated at Fettes College, Edinburgh; Edinburgh University (1959 MA) (1961 LLB); Scottish editor 'Palmer's Company Law' (1967 to date); 'Gore-Browne on Companies' (1972 to date).

BENNETT G Colin

partner LAMB & HOLMES West Street, Kettering, Northants NN15 0AZ.

Career: articled Alsop Stevens & Co (1949-1952); admitted (1952); assistant solicitor (1952-1954); assistant solicitor Lamb & Holmes (1954-1956); became partner (1956).

Activities: Clerk to Corby Justices (1959-1974); president Rotary Club (1987-1988); member MCC; President Kettering Town Cricket Club (1982-1985).

Biography: lives Corby; born 10.05.1924; married with 3 children. Educated at Rydal School, Colwyn Bay; Trinity Hall Cambridge (1949 MA LLB).

Leisure: sport (now including gardening); photography.

BENNETT Henry

consultant DONNE MILEHAM & HADDOCK with WHITLEY HUGHES & LUSCOMBE 36 High Street, Steyning, West Sussex.

Career: articled Mr HE Major (1929-1934); admitted (1934); assistant solicitor Bulmer Lawson & Roberts (1935-1939); 7th Battalion West Yorkshire Regiment (Leeds Rifles) converted into 45th Royal Tank Regiment in TA (1936-1939); 45th Royal Tank Regiment in UK and Middle East and deputy legal adviser to British Administration of Eritrea and legal adviser to British Military Administration of the Dodecanese (1939-1945); assistant solicitor Nye & Donne and (1946-1948); partner (1948-1990); became consultant (1990); firm amalgamated to become Donne Mileham & Haddock (1970) .

Activities: MBE New Year's Honours List (1990); holder of Territorial Decoration; chairman West Sussex War Pensions Committee; Officers' Association representative for Shoreham and Worthing; examiner for the Diocese of Chichester under Ecclesiastical Jurisdiction Measure (1963); serving brother of Most Venerable Order of the Hospital of St John of Jerusalem; member of: Naval & Military; West Sussex Golf Club.

Biography: lives Steyning; born 01.03.1912; married to Phyllis (deceased) with 4 children. Educated at Greyfriars School; Beechlawn, Leamington Spa; Brighton College.

Leisure: golf; gardening.

BENNETT Hugh

barrister Queen Elizabeth Building, Temple, London EC4Y 9BS (Tel: 071-583-7837).

Career: called to the Bar Inner Temple (1966); pupil to Mr Justice Johnson and Lord Justice Staughton; common law practice; assistant Recorder (1987); QC (1988); Recorder (1990).

Activities: member Supreme Court Rules Committee (1988); part-time chairman Horse Race Betting Levy Appeal Tribunal (1989); member London Common Law and Commercial Bar Association; Bar European

Group; Union International des Avocats; International Bar Association; Family Law Bar Association: Fellow of Woodard Corporation (SE Division); governor of Lancing College; member MCC.

Biography: born 08.09.1943; married to Elizabeth with 4 children. Educated at Marlborough House School, Hawkhurst; Haileybury and ISC, Hertford; Churchill College, Cambridge (1965 MA hons); Duke of Edinburgh Entrance Scholarship to Inner Temple.

Leisure: cricket; tennis; fishing; shooting.

BENNETT Laurence

managing partner, head of non-contentious department and marketing partner YAFFE JACKSON & OSTRIN 81 Dale Street, Liverpool L2 2HZ.

Career: articled David Carr & Roe (1967-1972); admitted (1972); assistant solicitor Yaffe Jackson & Ostrin (1972-1973); became partner (1973).

Activities: committee member National Association of Solicitors Property Centres (1985-1987); founded Prescot Solicitors Property Centre (1988); member Legal Aid Practitioners' Group (1988 to date); member Liverpool Law Society (assistant hon secretary); secretary North End Wirral Workshop and chairman Southern Training (YOP schemes); secretary Priority Area Development; chairman Articled Clerk Monitoring Committee; chairman of governors primary school; research with management consultancies on various developments on marketing, information technology and on group marketing of practices; lobbying Law Society over rule changes and lobbying consumers' association and building societies.

Biography: lives Liverpool; born 15.11.1948; married to Myrna with 2 daughters. Educated at Northway County Primary School, Liverpool; Liverpool Institute; Liverpool Polytechnic Law School (1970); Margaret Bryce Scholarship (1960).

Leisure: motorsport; swimming; traveller touring in USA/Canada.

BENNETT Margaret

a senior partner and head of matrimonial department MALKIN JANNERS 29 Bedford Street, Covent Garden, London WC2E 9RT.

Career: admitted (1972); assistant solicitor (1972-1973); became partner Malkin Cullis & Sumption (1973); merged to become Malkin Janners .

Activities: member Legal Aid Board West London Appeal Committee (1977) (vice-chairman (1988-1990); member Solicitors Family Law Association; member International Bar Association Family Law Committee (1986) (vice chairman (1988) (founder chairman working party on intercountry adoption); founding fellow International Academy of Matrimonial Lawyers (treasurer 1986) (vice-president 1989 to date); lectured and participated in various educational programmes for IAML IBA Commonwealth Lawyers Asssociation New Jersey State Bar Association (1989); spoken and broadcast on various family law and other topics at Oxford University and the Confederation of British Industry; member Panel in Educational Programmes for Foreign Law Associations; vice-president British Association of Women Entrepreneurs; member of: the Law Society; RAC; IOD.

Biography: lives London; born 01.03.1946; married with 2 children. Educated at Corona Academy; City of Westminster College; London School of Economics (1968 LLB); College of Law London; various papers and newspaper articles.

Leisure: travel; photography.

BENNETT Peter

managing partner HOWES PERCIVAL Oxford House, Cliftonville, Northampton NN1 5PN.

Career: articled in Liverpool (1968-1969); articled Howes Percival & Budge (1969-1971); admitted (1971); assistant solicitor (1971-1972); partner (1972); part-time managing partner (1983-1986); became full-time managing partner (1986).

Activities: member East Midlands branch of the Institute of Directors; governor Nene College Northampton; lecturer on the management of law firms; non-executive director Forman Hardy Holdings Ltd; member Jesters Club.

Biography: lives Northamptonshire; born 21.11.1945; married to Sarah with 1 son and 1 daughter. Educated at Waterloo Grammar School; Aston University, Birmingham (1968 LLB hons); various articles in Law Society's Gazette and Independent.

Leisure: golf; reading; listening to music; family.

BENNETT Philip

branch partner and head of family law department HART BROWN & CO Victoria Road, Farnham, Surrey GU9 7RG.

B

Career: articled Hart Brown & Co (1977-1979); admitted (1979); assistant solicitor (1979-1983); became partner (1983).

Activities: treasurer Surrey branch of Solicitors Family Law Association; original member Law Society Child Care Panel.

Biography: lives Godalming; born 25.03.1955; single. Educated at King Charles 1st Grammar School, Kidderminster; Wolverhampton Polytechnic (1976 BA hons); College of Law Guildford (1976-1977).

Leisure: sport (particularly cricket).

BENNION Charles

managing partner HOWES PERCIVAL Oxford House, Cliftonville, Northampton NN1 5PN.

Career: articled Bristows Cooke & Carpmael (1972-1974); admitted (1974); US multinational in Leicester (1974-1979); assistant solicitor Howes Percival (1979-1980); became partner (1980); member Strategic Board.

Activities: member Northamptonshire Chamber of Commerce and Industry; member of: Institute of Directors; North Norfolk Sailing club.

Biography: lives South Leicestershire; born 22.10.1948; married to Judy with 3 daughters. Educated at Winchester House School, Brackley; Radley College; Fitzwilliam College Cambridge (1971 MA hons) Fellowship in Management of Training (1977).

Leisure: sheep farming; sailing.

BENZIE Alasdair

partner STEVENS BOLTON 1 The Billings, Walnut Tree Close, Guildford, Surrey GU1 4YD.

Career: articled Clifford Turner (1974-1976); admitted (1976); Tax Department (1977-1978); lecturer College of Law Guildford (1978-1984); senior lecturer (1982-1985); assistant solicitor Stevens & Bolton (1985-1986); became partner (1986).

Activities: director Blackwater Valley Enterprise Trust Ltd; Thames Valley Branch of The Institute of Taxation; lectures and writes for College of Law; member of: Sunningdale Golf Club; The Bourne Club.

Biography: lives Farnham; born 25.09.1950; married to Dena with 1 child. Educated at Earleywood School (1958-1962); Stubbington House School (1962-1963); Merchiston Castle School, Edinburgh (1963-1968) Scholarship; Bristol University (1973 BA hons); College of Law Guildford

(1973-1974 & 1976-1977 2nd Class Honours in Law Society Finals); ATII (1981); author of: chapter on Retirement Relief in Longman's Practical Tax Planning; articles in Law Notes and Law Society's Gazette; 'Taxation of Companies and Their Shareholders'; various chapters for booklets produced by College of Law; contributor to Tax Case Analysis.

Leisure: golf; football; squash; badminton; tennis; skiing; playing piano; bridge; chess; amateur dramatics; gardening; family.

BERKOWITZ Leonard Terry

partner LINKLATERS & PAINES Barrington House, 59/67 Gresham Street, London EC2V 7JA.

Career: advocate attorney South Africa (1959-1964); executive/director Anglo-African Shipping Co Ltd (1965-1967); became partner Linklaters & Paines (1972).

Biography: lives London W11; born 11.10.1936; married to Ruth with 3 children. Educated at Parktown Boys' High School, Johannesburg (1952); University of Witwatersrand (BCom LLB).

Leisure: golf; tennis.

BERLINS Marcel

presenter BBC RADIO 4 LAW IN ACTION and freelance writer and journalist 7 Leighton Crescent, London NW5.

Career: legal assistant Lord Chancellor's department (1969-1971); legal correspondent and leader writer The Times (1971-1982); freelance writer and journalist (including broadcaster and TV presenter) (1982-1987); conceived and presented The Law Machine, a 10-part television series on the legal system LWT (1982) and Once a Thief, an 8-part television series on the criminal justice system LWT (1985); editor Law Magazine (1987-1988); presenter BBC Radio 4 Law in Action and freelance writer and journalist (1988 to date).

Activities: member Lady Marre's Committee into the Future of the Legal Profession; member Justice Committee on Sentencing Policy.

Biography: lives London NW5; born 30.10.1941; single. Educated at schools in France and South Africa; University of Witwatersrand (1964 BCom LLB); London School of Economics (1968 LLM); co-author: 'Caught in the Act' (1974); 'Living Together' (1982); 'The Law Machine' (1982); author of: 'Barrister Behind Bars' (1976); general editor of 'The Which Guide to your Rights' (1980) and 'The Law and

You' (1986).

Leisure: cinema; jazz.

BERNHARD Richard

director of legal services ROYAL COLLEGE OF NURSING 20 Cavendish Square, London W1M 0AB.

Career: teacher (1973-1975); articled Joynson-Hicks (1975-1980); management experience at indoor tennis club (1979-1981); admitted (1980); assistant solicitor (1980-1985); partner (1985-1987); claims solicitor London Insurance Brokers Ltd (1987-1988); became director of legal services RCN (1988).

Activities: chief officer of the RCN; chairman of the Board RCN Membership Services Ltd; chairman Management Side Joint Consultation & Negotiating Committee; Liveryman of the Worshipful Company of Gardeners; associate member of the Society of Young Freemen; member Institute of Advanced Motorists; acting member Torch Players; member of: Uppingham Rovers Cricket Club; Law Society Cricket Club; Surrey Tennis and County Club.

Biography: lives London SE24; born 28.11.1950; married to Martine with 1 son. Educated at Nevill Holt Preparatory School, Leicestershire; Uppingham School; Mid-Essex Technical College and School of Art; London (1973 LLB external); prepared papers on the Court system of England for a London seminar (1985).

Leisure: refurbishment of Edwardian property; DIY; amateur drama; summer sports (particularly cricket and tennis).

BERNS Richard

joint senior partner PIPER SMITH & BASHAM 31 Warwick Square, London SW1V 2AF.

Career: articled Francis Basham & Co; admitted (1971); became partner (1971); acquired practice (1973); merged with Piper Smith & Piper (1975); became joint senior partner.

Activities: director of number of property companies.

Biography: lives London SW1 and Cobham; born 16.08.1947; married to Bobbi with 2 children. Educated at Dulwich College; College of Law Guildford (1971).

Leisure: skiing; tennis; sailing; reading.

BERRY Christopher

senior litigation partner EDWIN COE 11 Stone Buildings, Lincoln's Inn, London WC2.

Career: articled Edwin Coe; admitted (1969); assistant solicitor (1969-1973); became partner (1973).

Activities: nominated by Lord Chancellor as non-Law Society council member solicitor on Supreme Court Rules Committee; member panel of solicitor assessors to sit on hearings of costs reviews in High Court; Law Society representative on Insolvency Users' Committee; Committee member (formerly secretary) London Solicitors Litigation Association; member Law Society and Bar Joint Working Party on Company Law and Insolvency; chairman Warman Sports Trust; member of: Bromley Rugby Football Club; Hayes (Kent) Cricket Club; Hayes (Kent) Tennis Club; RAC.

Biography: lives Shortlands; born 16.03.1946; married with 2 sons and 1 daughter. Educated at Sevenoaks; FCIArb; joint author: 'Bankruptcy Law & Practice'; Vols 7 & 10 Atkins Court Forms.

Leisure: early morning squash.

BERRY Tim

senior partner HARRIS & HARRIS Diocesan Registry; 14 Market Place, Wells, Somerset BA5 2RE.

Career: articled Harris & Harris; admitted; became partner (1970).

Activities: member Agricultural Land Association; hon solicitor Shepton Mallet CAB; member Lawyers'Christian Fellowship; certain company directorships; member Wells Conservative Club.

Biography: lives Shepton Mallet; born 01.01.1945; married with 2 sons. Educated at Bruton Primary School; Sexey's Grammar School, Bruton; Liverpool University (LLB); Bristol Polytechnic.

Leisure: Christianity (member PCC); music; walking.

BERTRAM John

partner THOMSON SNELL & PASSMORE Lyons, East Street, Tonbridge, Kent TN9 1HL.

Career: articled Ellis & Fairbairn (1952-1957); admitted (1957); 2nd Lt in the Army (1957-1959); assistant solicitor Thomson Snell & Passmore (1959-1963); became partner (1963); chairman firm's Conveyancing Committee.

Activities: president Tunbridge Wells Tonbridge & District Law Society (1983-1984); member Army & Navy Club.

Biography: lives Tunbridge Wells; born 02.03.1934; divorced with 2 children. Educated at Forest School; Dover College; London University (1957 LLB).

BESANT David

partner KEENE MARSLAND 6 Clanricarde Gardens, Tunbridge Wells, Kent TN1 1PH.

Career: became partner Keene Marsland (1961).

Activities: director Mid-Sussex Building Society; director Fellowship of St Nicholas; member General Synod of Church of England (1969-1972); Liveryman City of London Solicitors' Company.

Biography: lives Mayfield; born 11.06.1931; married with 3 children. Educated at Uppingham School; Trinity College Cambridge (MA).

Leisure: music; tennis; walking.

BETHEL Martin

Queen's Counsel Pearl Chambers, 22 East Parade, Leeds LS1 5BU.

Career: called to the Bar Inner Temple (1965); North-Eastern circuit (1966); Recorder (1979); QC (1983).

Biography: born 12.03.1943; married to Kathryn with 3 children. Educated at Kingswood School; Fitzwilliam College Cambridge (MA LLM).

Leisure: sailing; music; skiing.

BETHELL-JONES Richard

partner WILDE SAPTE Queensbridge House, 60 Upper Thames Street, London EC4V 3BD.

Career: admitted (1970); assistant solicitor (1970-1975); became partner Wilde Sapte (1975).

Activities: member City of London Solicitors' Company Insolvency Law Sub-Committee.

Biography: lives London SW18; born 16.09.1945; married to Sarah with 2 children. Educated at St John's School, Leatherhead; Churchill College Cambridge (1967 MA).

BETTELHEIM Eric

resident partner ROGERS & WELLS 58 Coleman Street, London EC2R 5BE.

Career: admitted California Bar (1976); associate Lillick McHose & Charles, San Francisco (1976-1978) & (1980-1983); called to the Bar England and Wales (1979); pupillage in commercial and maritime chambers 4 Essex Court, Middle Temple (1979-1980); associate Sidley & Austin (1983-1986); admitted New York Bar (1984); partner Finley Kumble Wagner (1986-1987); became partner Rogers & Wells (1987).

Activities: member American Bar Association; member New York Bar Association; member California Bar Association; member Inner Temple, member Options and Futures Society; member Futures Industry Association; member Maritime Law Association of the US.

Biography: born 27.01.1952; single. Educated at University of Chicago Laboratory High School (1964-1968); Rochester University(1972 AB); Oxford University (1975 BA) (1980 MA); Chicago University (1976 JD); Inns of Court School of Law (1979); author of: 'An Investor's Guide to the Commodity Futures Markets' (1986); 'Reconstruction and Regulation since October 19, 1987' Financial Futures and Options (1989); various articles.

BETTERIDGE Tony

partner TALBOT & CO 148 High Street, Burton upon Trent; DE14 1JY.

Career: articled Talbot & Co; admitted (1983); assistant solicitor (1983-1986); became partner (1986).

Activities: member of: Derbyshire County Cricket Club; The Burton Club.

Biography: lives Midway; born 16.10.1958; married with 1 son. Educated at The Granville School, Woodville; The Pingle School, Swadlincote; Warwick University (1977-1980 LLB hons); Trent Polytechnic (1981 Law Society Finals).

Leisure: cricket.

BETTINSON John

partner SHAKESPEARES 10 Bennetts Hill, Birmingham B2 5RS.

Career: admitted (1955); Lt 3rd Carabiniers (1955-1957); partner Bettinsons (1957-1990).

Activities: founder/chairman Mercian Housing Society Ltd (1964-1973); chairman Birmingham Area Health Authority (1973-1982); chairman National Association of Health Authorities (1976-1979); chairman Concentric PLC (1981-1986) (vice-chairman 1986 to date); chairman Victoria Carpet

B

Holdings PLC (1986 to date); chairman Birmingham Assay Office (1988 to date); chairman Birmingham Research Park Ltd (1988 to date); Deputy Clerk of the Peace Birmingham (1959-1969); General Commissioner of Income Tax (1970 to date); president West Midlands Rent Assessment Panel (1985 to date); member Birmingham Law Society Council (1962-1973 & 1983-1989) (president 1987-1988); member Legal Aid No 6 Area (1972-1988) (chairman 1985-1987); chairman of governors Birmingham Blue Coat School (1974-1987); member Hallmarking Council (1989 to date); chairman Birmingham Repertory Theatre (1986 to date); deputy treasurer Birmingham University (1989 to date); chairman Age Concern England (1989 to date); member of: Birmingham Club; Cavalry & Guards Club; Worshipful Company of Glaziers.

Biography: lives Birmingham; born 27.06.1932; married to Angela with 2 children. Educated at West House School, Birmingham; Haileybury; Birmingham University (1953 LLB).

Leisure: woodworking; bricklaying; reading.

BEUSELINCK Oscar Albert

media consultant MIRROR GROUP NEWSPAPERS Holborn Circus, London EC1P 1DQ.

Career: office boy Wright & Webb; articled (1948-1950); admitted (1950); became senior partner (1963); War service in Artillery and Intelligence Corps (1940-1946); founded own practice (1951-1963); became media consultant Mirror Group Newspapers (1989).

Activities: founder member and incorporating solicitor Multiple Sclerosis Society; first president Copinger Society; chairman Executive Committee of the British Film & Television Producers' Association; lectured on libel copyright, film and theatre law and practice; broadcast on Capital Radio and BBC; numerous directorships; member of: Garrick Club; MCC.

Biography: lives London WC1; Folkestone and Bruges; born 10.10.1919; married and divorced (3 times) with 2 sons. Educated at Rosebery Avenue LCC Elementary School; letters to the press.

Leisure: business of entertainment and the media; getting married; sport; country walking; serious music.

BEVAN Hugh

professor of law THE UNIVERSITY OF HULL Law School, Hull HU6 7RX.

Career: called to Bar Middle Temple (1959); part-time practice at the Bar (1960 to date); assistant lecturer Hull University (1950-1951); lecturer (1951-1961); senior lecturer (1961-1969); professor (1969-1989); Professor Emeritus (1989 to date); Honorary Doctor of Laws, Hull University (1990).

Activities: pro vice-chancellor Hull University (1981-1985); Justice of the Peace (1972 to date); chairman Bench of Kingston-upon-Hull Justices (1984-1989); chairman Humberside Magistrates' Committee; chairman Rent Assessment Committee; past president of the Society of Public Teachers of Law (1988); member of the Policy and Resources Group of the National Children's Bureau; chairman Hull and North Humberside Conciliation Service (1986-1990); Director of Training and Education for Taylor Vinters, Solicitors, Cambridge.

Biography: lives Hull; born 08.10.1922; married to Mary with 2 children. Educated at Neath Grammar School; The University College of Wales (1949 LLB) (1966 LLM); visiting Fellowship Emmanuel College Cambridge (1974); visiting Fellowship Wolfson College Cambridge (1986 & 1989-1990); Fellow of Wolfson College, Cambridge (1990 to date); author of: 'Casebook on Family Law' (1964) with PRH Webb; 'The Children Act 1975' (1979) with ML Parry; sole editor: 'Child Law' (1989); 'Law Relating to Children' (1973); joint editor 'Butterworths Family Law Service' (1983 to date).

Leisure: golf; classical music.

BEVAN Peter

deputy group general counsel and head of corporate legal services THE BRITISH PETROLEUM COMPANY plc Britannic House, Moor Lane, London EC2Y 9BU.

Career: articled Kennedys; admitted (1969); assistant solicitor BP Chemicals; manager Lands and Concessions, BP Exploration; assistant secretary British Petroleum Company plc; became deputy group legal adviser (1982).

Activities: co-founder member and committee member UK Oil Lawyers' Group; trustee The Petroleum and Mineral Law Education Trust .

Biography: lives East Horsley; born 12.04.1944; married to Susan with 2 children. Educated at Ealing College;

University College of Wales (LLB hons); various articles and speeches primarily on oil and gas law.

Leisure: music (choral and orchestral); wine; walking; sailing; gardening.

BEVERIDGE John

Queen's Counsel 4 Pump Court, Temple, London EC4.

Career: called to the Bar (1963); NSW, Australian Bar (1975); QC NSW (1975); QC (1979); member Western Circuit; Bencher Inner Temple (1986).

Activities: director Avery's of Bristol; member of: Beefsteak; Brooks's; Pratts; The Turf.

Biography: lives London SW1; born 26.09.1937; married to Moira. Educated at Jesus College Cambridge (MA LLB).

Leisure: private investment; hunting (former MFH Westmeath); shooting.

BEVINGTON Christian

barrister and head of chambers 1 Pump Court, Temple, London EC4Y 7AA.

Career: called to the Bar Inner Temple (1961); Lincoln's Inn (1971); tax consultant City firm (1976); became head of Chambers (1981); Assistant Recorder in the Crown Court.

Activities: founded Charitable Housing Trust (1971); member of: The Reform; Pall Mall.

Biography: lives London NW3; divorced with 3 children. Educated at St James's School, West Malvern; London School of Economics (LLB) .

Leisure: music (plays organ and harpsichord).

BICKERTON Patricia

senior solicitor in London Regional Counsel Office of THE FIRST NATIONAL BANK OF CHICAGO First Chicago House, 90 Long Acre, London WC2E 9RB.

Career: articled Clifford-Turner; admitted (1978); assistant solicitor (1978-1979 & 1982-1985); legal adviser European Investment Bank, Luxembourg (1979-1982); became senior solicitor at The First National Bank of Chicago (1985).

Biography: lives London N6; born 30.01.1952; married to Jon with 1 daughter. Educated at Marple Hall County Grammar School for Girls; New Hall Cambridge (1973 MA); articles in Law Society's Gazette and The International Contract

Law and Finance Review.

Leisure: bridge; tennis; skiing; aerobics; gardening.

BIDDLE Michael

senior non-contentious partner WOODFORD & ACKROYD 20 Havelock Road, Southampton SO9 5TT.

Career: articled Biddle & Co (1961-1964); admitted (1965); assistant solicitor Hill & Perks (1965-1967); assistant solicitor Woodford & Ackroyd (1967-1970); became partner (1970).

Activities: member Law Society Revenue Law Committee (1980-1989) and Bye-Laws Revision Committee (1984-1989); member Hampshire Incorporated Law Society (1973 to date) (secretary 1974-1977) (president 1987-1988); member South Coast Chapter VAT Practitioners' Group; committee worker for Southampton & District Relate; member Royal Southampton Yacht Club.

Biography: lives Winchester; born 23.06.1937; married to Gillian (deceased 1967); Elaine with 2 daughters. Educated at Radley College; Trinity Hall Cambridge (1961 BA) (1962 LLB) (1965 MA); anonymous author Hampshire Incorporated Law Society's responses re Benson Committee and Lord Chancellor's Green Paper on work and organisation of the profession.

Leisure: gardening; theatre; sailing; family life; committee work on home village organisations.

BIGGART Thomas Norman

partner BIGGART BAILLIE & GIFFORD WS 105 West George Street, Glasgow G2 1QP.

Career: apprentice Maclay Murray & Spens (1951-1954); admitted (1954); National Service Sub Lt (RNVR) (1954-1955); assistant solicitor Biggart Lumsden & Co (1955-1957); partner (1958-1974); amalgamated to become Biggart Baillie & Gifford WS (1974); partner (1974); became senior partner (1988).

Activities: CBE; WS; member Council of Law Society of Scotland (1977-1986) (vice-president (1981-1982) (president (1982-1983); chairman Business Archives Council, Scotland (1977-1986); member Executive Committee of Scottish Council (Development and Industry) (1984 to date); member Scottish Tertiary Education Advisory Council (1984-1987); member Scottish Records Advisory Council; director Clydesdale Bank (1985 to date);

New Scotland Insurance Group (1986 to date); hon member American Bar Association (1982); Order St John (1968); member Council on Tribunals (chairman of its Scottish Committee (1990); trustee Scottish Civic Trust (1989).

Biography: lives Kilmacolm; born 24.01.1930; married to Eileen with 2 children. Educated at Morrisons Academy, Crieff; Glasgow University (1951 MA) (1954 LLB).

Leisure: golf; hill walking.

BIGGS John

partner DOLMANS 17 Windsor Place, Cardiff CF1 4PA.

Career: called to the Bar Gray's Inn (1959); senior lecturer in law Australian National University, Canberra (1959-1962); articled Dolman & Sons (1962-1965); admitted (1965); assistant solicitor (1965-1966); became senior partner (1966).

Activities: member Society for Computers and Law; member Silver Society of London; member Royal Fowey Yacht Club.

Biography: lives London SW1 and Bristol; born 04.06.1933; married to Paula with 2 children by previous marriage. Educated at Eltham College; King's College London (1954 LLB) (1956 PHD) Jelf Medallist and post graduate Fellowship; Harvard Law School (1956-1957) (1959 SJD); Yale Law School (1957-1958); University of California at Berkeley (1958); Commonwealth Fund Fellowship to Harvard, Yale and Berkeley; Law Society Herbert Ruse Prize (1965); author of 'The Concept of Matrimonial Cruelty' (1962); various articles .

Leisure: computers; boats; antique silver and porcelain; wine; food.

BIGNELL Geoffrey

assistant secretary-general THE LAW SOCIETY 113 Chancery Lane, London WC2A 1PL.

Career: social work Essex and Nottinghamshire (1971-1974); articled Nottinghamshire County Council (1975-1977); admitted (1977); assistant prosecuting solicitor Nottinghamshire Police (1977-1978); assistant and senior assistant solicitor Leicestershire County Council (1980-1983); principal solicitor Warwickshire County Council (1983-1987); became assistant secretary-general The Law Society (1987).

Activities: secretary The Law Society Services Ltd; secretary The Law Society Trustees Ltd; director Law Society Pension

Scheme Ltd.

Biography: lives Guildford; born 07.03.1949; married to Susie with 2 children. Educated at Isleworth Grammar School; Trinity Hall Cambridge (1971 BA) (1975 MA); articles in Community Care (1986-1987).

Leisure: Roman Catholic; yoga; photography; shares; railways.

BILLINGS David Michael

senior partner responsible for the corporate and corporate finance department RIGBEYS 42-44 Waterloo Street, Birmingham B2 5QN.

Career: articled Pepper Tangye & Winterton; admitted; lectured on company law at Ronald Ind Accountancy School; became partner Rigbey Loose & Mills (1970-1971); became senior partner Rigbeys (1988).

Activities: member Edgbaston Priory Club.

Biography: lives Stratford-upon-Avon; born 20.03.1943; married to Ann with 2 children. Educated at Chad's Prep School, Prestatyn; Wrekin College, Wellington.

Leisure: soccer (founder Tankards football team); tennis; National Hunt Racing (amateur rider 1976-1982); wine and general ambrosia.

BILLINGTON Guy

partner and head of corporate finance department MCKENNA & CO Mitre House, 160 Aldersgate Street, London EC1A 4DD.

Career: articled Lovell White & King (1969-1972); admitted (1972); assistant solicitor McKenna & Co (1972-1977); became partner (1977).

Activities: member Law Society; member City of London Solicitors' Company; member of: The Gresham; Rosslyn Park Football Club; British Sub-Aqua Club.

Biography: lives London SW19; born. 12.11.1946; married to Christine with 2 children. Educated at King's College School, Wimbledon; St John's College Cambridge (MA); author of Practical Commercial Precedents Longmans 'Organisation of a Business'.

Leisure: rugby; music; scuba diving.

BINDMAN Geoffrey

senior partner BINDMAN & PARTNERS 1 Euston Road, London NW1 2SA.

Career: articled Rowley Ashworth & Co

B

(1956-1959); admitted (1959); partner Lawford & Co (1965-1974); founded present practice (1974).

Activities: tutor Workers' Educational Association (1956-1959); teaching Fellow Northwestern University School of Law (1959-1960); visiting professor University of California at Los Angeles (1982); hon senior lecturer in law University College London (1988 to date); legal adviser Race Relations Board (1966-1977); legal adviser Commission for Racial Equality (1977-1983).

Biography: lives London; born 03.01.1933; married to Lynn with 3 children. Educated at Newcastle Royal Grammar School; Oriel College Oxford (BCL MA); numerous publications, books, pamphlets and articles and reviews on anti-discrimination law, citizenship, immigration, human rights, legal services, legal profession, etc.

Leisure: jogging; book collecting.

BIRD Brian

senior partner WANNOP & FALCONER South Pallant House, 8 South Pallant, Chichester, West Sussex PO19 1TH.

Career: articled Kenwright & Cox (1951-1957); admitted (1957); National Service as subaltern with Royal Artillery (1957-1959); became partner Kenwright & Cox (1959-1970); became partner Wannop & Falconer (1971); senior partner (1977).

Activities: legal adviser to West Sussex Institute of Higher Education; member Chichester and District Law Society (former committee member) (president (1981-1982); marking examiner and assistant examiner for the Family Law Paper (1960-1971); member Rotary Club of Chichester (president (1978-1979).

Biography: lives Eastergate; born 03.07.1934; married to Lyn with 2 children. Educated at Brentwood School; College of Law.

Leisure: sailing; walking; gardening; DIY; railways and railway modelling.

BIRD Stephan

partner WILDE SAPTE Queens Bridge House, 60 Upper Thames Street, London EC4V 3BD.

Career: admitted (1960); became partner Wilde Sapte (1972); partner in charge New York office (1978-1981); Singapore office (1981-1983).

Biography: lives London EC2; born 03.01.1934; married to Tan Aw Yee (1983). Educated at King Edward VII School,

Sheffield; Brasenose College Oxford (1957 BA); author of: 'How to prune those Loan Agreements' (1979); 'The State Immunity Act 1978' (1980).

Leisure: Tai Chi.

BIRNBERG Benedict

senior partner BM BIRNBERG & CO 103 Borough High Street, London SE1 1NN.

Career: admitted (1958); assistant solicitor Philcox Sons & Edwards and Coward Chance (1958-1962); founded own practice (1962).

Activities: executive National Council for Civil Liberties (1960s) (chairman (1974); former governor Greenwich Theatre; former company secretary War on Want; former chairman Lewisham CAB; member Labour party; member Law Society.

Biography: lives London SE3; born 08.09.1930; married to Felitsa with 1 daughter. Educated at Minehead Grammar School; The Kings School, Canterbury; Corpus Christi College Cambridge (1954 BA hons); occasional contributions to the press and TV.

Leisure: theatre; music.

BIRRELL David

senior partner DUNDAS & WILSON CS 25 Charlotte Square, Edinburgh.

Career: apprentice legal office in Edinburgh, Kilmarnock and Lochgiephael; admitted; assistant solicitor Davidson & Syme; merged with Dundas & Wilson CS (1952); became senior partner.

Activities: director of: Martin & Co (Edinburgh) Ltd; Clydesdale Bank PLC; Securities Trust of Scotland; Saltire Insurance Investment; Lawrie & Symington Ltd; Prestonfield House Hotel; Open Arms Hotel; Wm Nimmo & Co Ltd; Morgan Grenfell (Scotland) PLC; member Advisory Committee of RSPCC; trustee Scottish Business Achievement Award Trust; trustee Holyrood Brewery Foundation; hon member Haddington Rugby Football Club; member of: The Honourable Company of Edinburgh Golfers; Haddington Rugby Club; Bruntsfield Golf Club; The Clubhouse, Elie.

Biography: lives Edinburgh; born 06.11.1926; widower with 3 children. Educated at Knox Academy, Haddington; Edinburgh University (1950 LLB); advised IBA on interpretation of law of contempt in Scotland and England and advised Scottish Television; The Scotsman Publications; Radio Forth and other members of the

media.

Leisure: golf.

BISHOP Archie

senior partner HOLMAN FENWICK & WILLAN Marlow House, Lloyds Avenue, London EC3N 3AL.

Career: Deck officer with P & O Line (7 years); joined Holman Fenwick & Willan (1960); articled (1965-1970); admitted (1970); became partner (1970); became senior partner (1989).

Activities: legal adviser to International Salvage Union; Freeman of the City of London; member of: The Company of Watermen and Lightermen; member City of London Solicitors' Company.

Biography: lives London SW6; born 21.07.1937; separated with 2 children. Educated at Dr Morgan's, Bridgwater; HMS Worcester, Greenhythe; Thames Nautical Training College (1952 First Class Extra Nautical Studies); Sir John Cass College (1959 1st Mate's Foreign Going Certificate); College of Law (1970 Solicitors' Finals).

Leisure: hunting; fishing; golf; swimming; reading; music; painting.

BISHOP David Henry Barnardo

senior partner GILL AKASTER Scott Lodge, Milehouse, Plymouth PL2 3DD.

Career: articled Gill Akaster; National Service in the Army; admitted (1951); assistant solicitor (1951-1956); became partner (1956-1975); became senior partner (1975).

Activities: HM Coroner for Plymouth and SW Devon (1979); president Plymouth Law Society (1984); president South Western Coroners Society (1987); member SW Electricity Consultative Council (1980-1990); member The Lord Chancellor's Advisory Committee for the Exeter Group of Courts; member No 4 (South Western) Legal Aid Area Committee; attended Comonwealth and Empire Law Conference in Ottawa and American Bar Association meeting in Washington (1960); member of: Royal Western Yacht Club of England; Royal Ocean Racing Club; Plymouth Lions Club (former president).

Biography: lives Plymouth; born 03.04.1927; married to Patricia with 2 children. Educated at St Olaves Preparatory School, Ripon; Manchester Grammar School; College of Law Guildford.

Leisure: sailing (mainly cruising in own 30 ft sloop) (one-time competitor in Round

Britain and Ireland Race, Fastnet Race and other offshore and local races); theatre (president The Tamaritans Amateur Dramatic Society); DIY; silversmithing.

BJORNSTAD Finn

resident partner WIKBORG REIN & CO 1 Knightrider Court, London EC4V 5JP.

Career: Wikborg, Rein & Co (1985); admitted; assistant solicitor; became partner.

Activities: shipping, financing, security markets and business law in general.

Biography: lives London; born 05.05.1958. Educated Bergen University.

BLACK Alastair

senior partner BURCHELL & RUSTON 2 Serjeants' Inn, Fleet Street, London EC4Y 1LL.

Career: National Service as Lt Intelligence Corps (1953-1955); admitted (1953); became partner William T Burchell (1953); became senior partner (1974).

Activities: Under Sheriff of Greater London; president Under Sheriff's Association; clerk to the Bowyers Company; clerk to the General Commissioners of Income Tax for Divisions of Holborn, Finsbury and Covent Garden; member Committee of the London Solicitors' Litigation Association; member Ecclesiastical Fees Advisory Commission; CBE (1989); Deputy Lt of Greater London (1976 to date); member General Synod of Church of England (1982 to date) and member Bishop's Council (Guildford Diocese) lay reader (1983 to date); vice-chairman Guildford Diocese Council for Social Responsibility.

Biography: lives Effingham; born 14.12.1929; married with 3 children. Educated at Sherborne School; College of Law Lancaster Gate; contributed to vols 25 and 42 Halsbury's Laws of England (4th ed); Atkins Court Forms: 3rd ed vol 19 Execution (1972 & 1985); vol 22 Interpleader (1968); vol 36 Sheriffs & Bailiffs (1977 & 1988); author of 'Enforcement of a Judgement' (7th ed) (1986).

Leisure: gardening; horse racing.

BLACKBURN Bill

consultant THEODORE GODDARD 167 St Martins-le-Grand, London EC1A 4EJ.

Career: partner Theodore Goddard (1957-1962); staff attorney IBM Europe SA, Paris

(1962-1966); counsel (1980-1982); company secretary IBM UK Ltd (1966-1972); member Management Committee (1982-1985); managing director IBM European office, Brussels (1972-1980) .

Activities: Law Society Council member; chairman Law Society International Committee; member Law Society Strategy Committee; member British Council Legal Advisory Committee; member UK delegation to Council of European Bars and Law Societies; former chairman Law Society Law Office Management and Technology Committee; member of: RAC; Royal Mid-Surrey Golf Club; Cercle de L'Union Interallie, Paris.

Biography: lives London NW8; born 23.12.1932; married to Chloe with 2 sons. Educated at Holt School; Liverpool University (1953 LLB hons).

Leisure: opera; golf; property in France.

BLACKMORE Anthony

senior partner SIMPSON CURTIS 41 Park Square, Leeds LS1 2NS.

Career: articled Simpson Curtis (1954-1957); admitted (1957); assistant solicitor (1959-1962); partner (1962-1988); became senior partner (1988); Slaughter and May (1957-1959).

Activities: non-executive director Liberty PLC; Visiting Professor in Commercial Practice at Leeds Polytechnic; member City of London Solicitors' Company; President Leeds Law Society; member Society for Computers and Law; member British Computer Society; member Leeds Club.

Biography: lives North Yorkshire; born 13.04.1933; married with 3 children. Educated at Winchester College; Emmanuel College Cambridge (1954 BA); Solicitors Finals (1957 hons).

Leisure: skiing; computers; tennis; swimming.

BLAIR Alan

senior partner BLAIR & BRYDEN 34 Union Street, Greenock PA16 8DJ.

Career: apprentice Black Cameron Campbell (1960-1963); admitted (1963); assistant solicitor Maclay Murray & Spens (1963-1965); assistant solicitor Wright Johnston MacKenzie (1965-1967); founded Blair Bryden Greenock (1967).

Activities: Magistrate in Greenock (1968-1975); JP (1975); leader Inverclyde District Council (1977-1980); Liberal Councillor for: Greenock Town Council (1965-1975); Invercylde District Council (1975-1984);

Democrat Councillor Inverclyde District Council (1989 to date); joint treasurer Scottish Liberal Party (1974); Elder St Andrew's Church of Scotland, Greenock; member Council of Law Society of Scotland; member Legal Education Committee; Professional Remuneration Committee and Complaints Committee of Law Society of Scotland; member of: Greenock Golf Club (former captain); Kilmacolm Golf Club; Son Servera Golf Club, Majorca; Scottish Liberal Club; Greenock Imperial Club; Greenock Wanderers RFC.

Biography: lives Greenock; born 24.02.1939; married to Mhairi. Educated at Greenock Academy; Glasgow University (1960 MA hons) (1963 LLB).

Leisure: golf; watching football; local politics; reading; travel.

BLAIR Michael

general counsel and director legal division SECURITIES AND INVESTMENTS BOARD 3 Royal Exchange Buildings, London EC3V 3NL.

Career: called to the Bar Middle Temple (1965); pupillage Eric Stockdale (1965); pupillage Ian Edwards-Jones (1966); Lord Chancellor's department (1966-1987); became general counsel and director legal division Securities and Investments Board (1987).

Activities: intern in United Nations Human Rights Commission (1963); stagiaire at European Commission of Human Rights (1965); private secretary to Lord Chancellor Gardiner (1968-1970); private secretary to Lord Chancellor Hailsham of St Marylebone (1970-1971); Deputy Serjeant at Arms House of Lords (1968-1971); Green Staff Officer Investiture at Caernarvon (1969); UK delegation to Council of Europe Committee of Experts on: State Immunity (1967-1968); Custody of Children (1973-1979); secretary of Law Reform Committee (1977-1979); Under Secretary (1982-1987); circuit administrator Midland and Oxford circuit (1982-1986); received Red Bag from Desmond Fennell QC (1985); head Policy and Legal Services Group (1986-1987); member General Council of the Bar (1989 to date); member Bar Committee (1989 to date); member General Management Committee concerned with the Government's Green Papers on the legal profession (1989); member General Committee of Bar Association for Commerce Finance and Industry (1988 to date) (vice-chairman 1989-1990); door tenant, 3 Gray's Inn Place, London WC1R

B

5EA; member Athenaeum.

Biography: lives London SE24; born 26.08.1941; married to Halldora with 1 son. Educated at Edinburgh Academy; Cargilfield School, Edinburgh; Rugby School (top scholar); Clare College Cambridge (1962 MA) (1965 LLM) (Open Minor Scholar); Yale University (Mellon Fellowship); Harmsworth Scholar Middle Temple (1965-1966); Cabinet Office top management programme (1986); articles in: legal periodicals (1964-1966); Civil Justice Quarterly (1981-1983); author of book on the Sale of Goods Act (1980).

Leisure: family life; skiing; music; theatre; languages.

BLAIR Robin

managing partner responsible for administration and finance DUNDAS & WILSON 25 Charlotte Square, Edinburgh EH2 4EZ.

Career: apprentice Fraser Stodart & Ballingall WS (1963-1965); admitted (1965); assistant solicitor Maclay Murray & Spens (1965-1966); assistant solicitor Slaughter and May (1966-1967); partner Davidson & Syme WS (1967); merged with Dundas & Wilson CS (1972); managing partner (1976-1983); became current managing partner (1988).

Activities: chairman Scottish Solicitors Staff Pension Fund; member Law Society of Scotland Organisation and Methods Committee (convenor 1979-1982 & 1985-1986) and Future of the Profession Committee; director Technology & Law Ltd; Purse Bearer to the Lord High Commissioner to the General Assembly of The Church of Scotland; member of: New Club, Edinburgh; Honourable Company of Edinburgh Golfers; Royal Company of Archers; The Queen's Bodyguard for Scotland.

Biography: lives Edinburgh; born 01.01.1940; married to Caroline with 3 children. Educated at Rugby; St Andrew's (1961 MA); Edinburgh (1963 LLB); co-author of Report on Law Offices and Technology (1983); Report on a Legal Electronic Network (1985).

BLAKE Allan

associate dean Leeds Business School, LEEDS POLYTECHNIC Queen Square House, Woodhouse Lane, Leeds LS2 8AB.

Career: CAB volunteer, Twickenham (1976-1977), Chorley (1977-1979); lecturer in law Lancashire Polytechnic (1977-1979) (senior lecturer 1979-1988); chairman Preston Free

Legal Information Service (1978-1987); became head department of law Leeds Polytechnic (1988) and Associate Dean, Leeds Business School (1990).

Activities: member Legal Aid Board (1988 to date); member Area (9A) Regional Duty Solicitor Committee; former chairman Lancashire Committee of North-Western Legal Services Committee; former chairman Area 7B Regional Duty Solicitor Committee; member Legal Action Group Executive Committee (1984-1988); member Lord Chancellor's Legal Services Conference (from 1986); member Management Committee and researcher HMP Strangeways Duty Solicitor Scheme (1986); co-ordinator Enquire Within Project (1986-1988); chairman Preston Free Legal Information Service (1978-1984 & 1985-1987); member Chorley Police Liaison Committee (1982-1983); chairman Management Committee Chorley Rights Centre (1982-1984); member University of Lancaster Court (1986-1988).

Biography: lives Stockport; born 05.02.1955; married with 1 child. Educated at Isleworth Grammar School; Ealing College of Higher Education (1976 BA hons); University College London (1977 LLM); numerous articles, books, videos, conference/research papers and casenotes/book reviews.

BLAKE-DYKE Jimmy

partner BURT BRILL & CARDENS Rochester House, Rochester Gardens, Hove, East Sussex BN3 3BD.

Career: articled Wilson & Wilson (1950-1955); admitted (1955); assistant solicitor (1955-1957); assistant solicitor Burt Brill & Edwards (1957-1959); became partner (1960).

Activities: first chairman Sussex Society of Young Solicitors (1960); chairman National Committee of Young Solicitors (1961-1963); member Committee of Sussex Law Society (librarian 1965-1977) (president 1977-1978); member Eastbourne Law Society Committee (1984-1987); clerk to Brighton and Hove Almshouse Charity (1973 to date).

Biography: lives Eastbourne; born 07.07.1929; married to Diana with 3 children. Educated at Hampton House Preparatory School, Chester; St Bees School, Cumbria.

Leisure: travel; interesting railways; music; cinema; theatre.

BLANCO WHITE Thomas

Queen's Counsel Francis Taylor Building, Temple, London EC4Y 7BY.

Career: called to the Bar Lincoln's Inn (1937); RAFVR (1940-1946); QC (1969); Bencher (1977); retired (1990).

Biography: lives London; born 19.01.1915; married to Anne with 3 children. Educated at Gresham's; author of 'Patents for Inventions' (1950 etc); joint editor of 'Kerly on Trademarks' and 'Encyclopaedia of Patent Law'.

Leisure: gardening.

BLATHERWICK Peter

partner TALLENTS GODFREY & CO 3 Middlegate, Newark, Notts NG24 1AQ.

Career: articled Hodgkinson & Beevor and Andrew & Co; admitted (1958); assistant solicitor (1958-1960); became partner (1960).

Activities: Notary Public; chairman Newark Advertiser Co Ltd.

Biography: lives Newark; born 12.03.1935; married to Dorothy with 3 children. Educated at Rydal School, Colwyn Bay.

Leisure: Methodist local preacher and Church activities generally especially in the Healing Ministry of the Church.

BLOCK Simon

partner WITHERS CROSSMAN BLOCK 199 Strand, London WC2.

Career: articled Linklaters & Paines (1958-1960); admitted (1960); assistant solicitor (1960-1962); became partner Crossman Block & Keith (1962); became senior partner Crossman Block (1989).

Activities: gave UK paper on doctrine of 'Piercing Corporate Veil' at IBA meeting, Atlanta; Sheriff of City of London (1988-1989); member Life Assurance Legal Society Committee (1981-1984); member Court of Common Council of City of London; former Master The Broderers' Company; president The Embroiderers' Guild; member of: City Livery Club; Leander; The Grannies.

Biography: lives North Molton; born 19.07.1935; married to Tishy with 3 sons. Educated at Marlborough College; Pembroke College Cambridge (1958 MA hons); Harvard Summer Law School (1977).

Leisure: fine wine; field sports; marathon runner.

BLOOM Charles

Queen's Counsel and head of Chambers 28 St John Street, Manchester M2 4DJ.

Career: called to the Bar (1963); deputy circuit Judge (1979); Crown Court Recorder (1983); QC (1987).

Activities: chairman Medical Appeal Tribunals (1979); committee member Family Law Bar Association; member of: Dunham Golf Club; Friedland Postmusaf Tennis Club.

Biography: lives Cheadle; born 06.11.1940; married to Janice with 2 children. Educated at Manchester Central Grammar School; Manchester University (1962 LLB hons); College of Law London (1962-1963).

Leisure: tennis; theatre.

BLOOR Richard

senior partner OWSTON & CO 23 Friar Lane, Leicester LE1 5QQ.

Career: articled Billson & Sharp; admitted (1960); assistant solicitor Owston & Co (1960-1966); became partner (1966); occasional lecturer in company law Leicester Polytechnic (1960-1970).

Activities: secretary College Law Society; hon solicitor to: Building Employers' Federation, Leicestershire; St John Ambulance, Leicestershire; Leicestershire & Rutland County Football Association and numerous local charitable organisations; Commander of the Order of St John Ambulance (1983); county chairman Leicestershire; member St John Council for Leicestershire (17 years); Church warden; member several Diocesan Committees; President Leicestershire Law Society; member Leicestershire Club.

Biography: lives Burton Overy; born 20.11.1936; married to Anne with 3 children. Educated at Lutterworth Grammar School, Leicestershire; University College London (1957 LLB hons).

Leisure: walking; tennis; sailing.

BLUNDELL David

partner JEROME & CO 98 High Street, Newport, Isle of Wight PO30 1BD.

Career: articled Jerome & Co (1958-1963); admitted (1963); assistant solicitor (1963-1964); became partner (1964).

Activities: hon solicitor to Isle of Wight Chamber of Commerce; former marking examiner Law Society Finals.

Biography: lives Newport; born 20.01.1939; married to Gillian (deceased 16.02.1990) with 3 children. Educated at King James I Grammar School, Newport.

Leisure: reading.

BOARDMAN John

marketing partner; training partner; information technology partner and head of corporate department ALEXANDER TATHAM 30 St Ann Street, Manchester M2 3DB.

Career: articled Alexander Tatham (1977-1979); admitted (1979); assistant solicitor (1979-1984); associate (1984-1986); became partner (1986).

Activities: board member - Eversheds; National Product Group Coordinator - Eversheds.

Biography: lives Hayfield, Derbyshire; born 26.07.1955; married to Julie with 2 children. Educated at Manchester Grammar School; Downing College Cambridge (1976 MA); National Handwriting Prize (1962).

Leisure: pottery; walking; countryside; computers; reading; eating; drinking; music; frogs; quantum mechanics; prehistory; space; meaning of life.

BODDEN John

senior partner PLATT BODDEN & CO in association with BUTCHER & BARLOW Old Colony House, South King Street, Manchester M2 6DQ.

Career: Royal Navy Anti-submarine Electrical Branch in home waters, Indian Ocean and Pacific Ocean (1943-1946); HMS Adamant and 4th Submarine flotilla Eastern Fleet and British Pacific Fleet (1944-1946) (demobbed Lt); articled Wrigley Claydon & Co, Oldham and Manchester (1946-1949); admitted (1949); assistant solicitor (1949-1951); became partner (1951-1962); acquired practice of Platt & Co in association with Butcher & Barlow (1964).

Activities: trustee Oldham Foundation; chairman Ernest Broadbelt Investments Ltd; president Bury & District Law Society (1989-1990).

Biography: lives Hale, Cheshire; born 15.05.1923; married to Patricia. Educated at Felsted School (1937-1940); Manchester University (1943 BSC hons); Wadham College Oxford (1950-1951 PPE); Manchester University (1974 BA); articles in Law Society's Gazette on the Gillies Report, the Euro-currency market and historical sketch of the Solicitors branch of the profession.

BODDINGTON Christopher

partner NABARRO NATHANSON 50 Stratton Street, London W1.

Career: articled Western Sons & Neave (1963-1966); admitted (1966); assistant solicitor (1966-1969); assistant solicitor McKenna & Co (1969-1972); partner Ziman & Co (1972-1977); became partner Nabarro Nathanson (1977).

Activities: former Committee member City of Westminster Law Society; member Brooks's.

Biography: lives London W11; born 04.05.1941; divorced with 2 daughters. Educated at Rugby School (1954-1959); The Queen's College Oxford (1963 MA hons); College of Law Lancaster Gate (1966).

Leisure: food; opera; cinema; travel.

BODLEY Kevin F

commercial partner EDWARDS & BODLEY Bargates House, 33a Bargates, Christchurch, Dorset BH23 1QD.

Career: articled Arthur Goldberg; admitted (1979); assistant solicitor (1979-1981); partner Johnsons (1980-1981); became partner Edwards & Bodley (1982).

Activities: member Law Society Panel of Solicitors in Child Care Cases; currently engaged in establishing international network of associated offices; specialist in air law and aviation matters; promoter and director in newly formed regional airline based at Bournemouth International Airport; member of: Royal Lymington Yacht Club; Bournemouth Flying Club; Aircraft Owners' & Pilots' Association; Institute of Air Transport.

Biography: lives Frogham nr Fordingbridge; born 06.11.1953. Educated at Lancaster Royal Grammar School; Lancashire, Bristol and Preston Polytechnics; College of Law Chester (1973-1974 and 1977); Fellow of the Institute of Legal Executives (1978); articles on office computerisation and lexis in Computers and Law and The Lawyer, Hong Kong; articles on air law in Pilot International and other publications.

Leisure: flying (holder of private pilot's licence and training/studying for commercial pilot's licence); motoring; classic cars; music; (former professional); collecting guitars; literature; travel; dogs.

BOLGER Chris

partner with responsibility for professional standards and member litigation department KNIGHT & SONS

B

31 Ironmarket, Newcastle under Lyme, Staffordshire ST5 1RL.

Career: articled Corner & Co (1964-1966); admitted (1966); assistant solicitor (1966-1967); assistant solicitor and senior assistant solicitor Plymouth City Council (1967-1971); deputy town clerk Burton on Trent CBC (1971-1974); assistant solicitor Knight & Sons (1980-1982); became partner (1982); edits firm's newsletters.

Activities: sometime governor Thistley Hough School; former chairman Stoke on Trent Legal Advice Centre; member editorial board 'Midlands Medicine'; member Medical Ethics Committee of North Staffordshire Hospital Centre; organises annual sponsorship by Knight & Sons of Keele University law students' Mooting Competition; part-time tutor Keele University (1987-1988) (supervised dissertation (1988-1989); hon life member Keele University Law Society; country friend Royal Academy; member KCLA (Laws Branch); member of: Amnesty International; NCCL.

Biography: lives Stoke on Trent; born 18.05.1942; married to Elizabeth with 3 children. Educated at St Francis Xavier's, Liverpool; King's College London (1963 LLB); article in Midlands Medicine; occasional letters to press on legal topics.

Leisure: cinema (used to run film society); music; literature; the arts generally; languages; occasional political involvement; travel; watching cricket and football.

BOLTON James

former partner LONGMORES PO Box 17, 24 Castle Street, Hertford SG14 1HP.

Career: articled Longmores; admitted (1950); assistant solicitor (1950-1959); became partner (1959); retired (1989).

Activities: assistant deputy Coroner E Herts District (1956); deputy Coroner (1964); Coroner (1966-1990); chairman Lee Valley Water Company (1986 to date) (director 1976); deputy Lt Hertfordshire (1968); council member of the Law Society (1975-1990); chairman non-contentious business (1984-1986); chairman remuneration casework (1987-1989).

Biography: lives Harpenden; born 04.02.1921; married to Margaret with 1 son and 1 daughter. Educated at Oundle School; Cambridge (1947 BA hons).

BOND Christopher

partner FIELD FISHER WATERHOUSE 41 Vine Street, London EC3N 2AA.

Career: articled Herbert Smith (1966-1968); admitted (1969); assistant solicitor Frere Cholmeley (1968-1972) London and Paris; assistant company secretary and legal adviser Reuters Ltd (1972-1976); UK Law Briger & Associates (1976-1978); became partner Field Fisher and Martineau (1979).

Activities: lectured at international legal conferences on financial and EC law in America, Japan, Korea, Taiwan and the UK; member BIEC missions to Korea (1987) and Taiwan (1988).

Biography: lives Richmond and Somerset; born 28.06.1943; married to Lindsay with 2 children. Educated at Hurst Court, Hastings; Wellington College, Berkshire; Trinity Hall Cambridge (BA hons); author of: 'Investing in the United Kingdom' (1990); 'Investing in the United Kingdom - The Basic Issues' (1987); '1992 and Telecommunications' (1989); articles in International Law Journal on EC distribution law (1986-1988); articles for Japan Securities Research Institute on the Financial Services Act and the EC Banking and Investment Services Directives (1987 & 1989).

Leisure: music; hill walking; reading; sailing.

BOND Julie

partner MANCHES & CO Aldwych House, 71-91 Aldwych, London WC2B 4RP and 3 Worcester Street, Oxford OX1 2PZ.

Career: articled Speechly Bircham (1977-1979); admitted (1979); assistant solicitor Boodle Hatfield & Co (1980-1981); assistant solicitor Bruce Lance & Co (1981-1983); assistant solicitor Manches & Co (1983-1986); became partner (1986).

Biography: lives Oxford; born 31.08.1954; married to Christopher. Educated at Burlington School for Girls (1966-1972); University College of Wales (1976 LLB hons).

Leisure: reading; walking; theatre; history of art.

BONEHILL Roger Charles

associate partner and head of private client department EDGE & ELLISON Rutland House, 148 Edmund Street, Birmingham B3 2JR.

Career: admitted (1963); sole practitioner Roger Bonehill & Co (1969-1979); partner Bonehill & Jones (1979-1986); associate partner Wragge & Co (1987-1988); became associate partner Edge & Ellison (1988).

Activities: senior lecturer in law Birmingham Polytechnic (1979-1984); examiner in conveyancing Law Society Finals; member Law Society Final Advisory Board; hon secretary to King Edward VI High School for Girls Parents' Association, Birmingham; member Royal St David's Golf Club, Harlech.

Biography: lives Sutton Coldfield; born 16.01.1942; married to Jill with 3 children. Educated at King Edward's School, Birmingham; London University (1981 LLB hons) (1983 LLM); Brigid Cotter Prize for Law of Landlord & Tenant; co-author of 'Law and Practice of Intestate Succession'.

BONHAM-CARTER Norman A

consultant RADCLIFFES & CO 5 Great College Street, London SW1Y 3SJ.

Career: junior clerk National Provincial Bank (1947-1950); articled family firm Thorold Brodie Bonham-Carter & Mason (1950-1956); admitted (1956); became partner (1959); merged with Radcliffes & Co (1974); assistant solicitor Trower Still & Keeling (1956-1959).

Activities: vice-president Solicitors Wine Society (former chairman); vice-president and hon solicitor to Anglo-Belgian Society (former chairman) (Council member 1969-1990); Council member Law Society (1980-1989) (former secretary and president City of Westminster); former chairman Young Solicitors Group; chairman The Old Gownboys Committee Charterhouse; director Anglo-Belgian Club (1987-1990); former member Editorial Board of the Law Guardian; member number of wine orders and an Officer of The Ordre des Coteaux de Champagne; former member London Athletic Club; trialist Wembley Lions Ice Hockey team; life member Wig & Pen Club.

Biography: lives London W6 and Old Windsor, Berks; born 28.05.1928; married with 3 children and 4 step-children. Educated at St John's College, Winnipeg; Gordon Bell High School, Winnipeg; Charterhouse; AIB; Solicitors Finals (hons).

Leisure: a member of the Cave de Cocumont (Cotes du Marmandais A.O.C.) with a small vineyard attached to cottage in France.

BONNAR Brian

deputy senior partner ROSS HARPER & MURPHY 38 Strathmore House, Princes Square, East Kilbride.

Career: National Service; industry; became partner Ross Harper & Murphy (1971).

Activities: secretary East Kilbride Centre Ltd; secretary Platthorn Business Project Ltd; member local school board; member heritage group; member East Kilbride Kittoch Rotary Club.

Biography: lives Hamilton; born 08.03.1936; married with 8 children. Educated at Our Lady's High School, Motherwell; Glasgow University (1962 MA); (1969 LLB).

BONNETT Ralph

partner LINKLATERS & PAINES Barrington House, 59/67 Gresham Street, London EC2V 7JA.

Career: partner Linklaters & Paines.

Biography: lives London SW15; born 06.01.1928; married to Pearn with 1 child. Educated at Bedford School; Pembroke College Cambridge (1952 BA).

BOOTH Roger

barrister and head of chambers 3 Peter Street, Manchester M2 5QR.

Career: called to the Bar Gray's Inn (1966); practice (1966-1976); philatelic publishing and investment portfolio company (1976-1983); private practice at Bar (1984).

Activities: county councillor for Tyne & Wear (1978-1982); deputy leader of opposition (1976-1978); Parliamentary candidate (1979); member Royal Philatelic Society of London; international medallist for philatelic literature (1978-1984); Major in TA; member RAC Club.

Biography: lives Stockport; born 11.08.1942; married to Joan with 2 children. Educated at King Edward VI Grammar School, Stourbridge; Sheffield University (1964 LLB hons); Holker Senior Scholar Gray's Inn (1966-1969).

BOOTHMAN Chris

senior assistant solicitor LONDON BOROUGH OF HACKNEY Legal Directorate, 298 Mare Street, London E8 1HE.

Career: articled Gordon & James Morton (1980-1981); articled Jeffrey Gordon & Co (1981-1982); admitted (1982); assistant solicitor Gordon & James Morton (1982-1983); research assistant London Borough of Camden (1983-1984); legal assistant GLC (1984-1985); joint deputy head police committee support unit (1985-1986); legal officer The London Strategic Policy Unit (1986); assistant legal adviser (1986-1987);

acting legal adviser (1987-1988).

Activities: part-time housing and employment advice worker Forest Hill Youth Project (1979-1986); member Law Society's Criminal Law Committee (former member Race Relations Committee); Council member of the Law Society (July 1990); chair The Society of Black Lawyers (1987-1990); former Martial Arts instructor; member Black Music Association; member National Black Caucus; member Harringay Youth Steel Orchestra; member London Brotherhood of Steel; member of Dougie's.

Biography: lives London SE4; born 11.12.1955; married to Andrea with 1 son and 1 daughter. Educated at Brockley County School; City of London Polytechnic (BA) Business Law.

Leisure: all aspects of carnival and music.

BOREHAM Michael

consultant FRERE CHOLMELEY 28 Lincoln's Inn Fields, London WC2A 3HH.

Career: commissioned with 16th/5th Lancers; articled Allen & Overy; admitted; assistant solicitor in Ghana (1958-1959); assistant solicitor Frere Cholmeley (1959-1960); partner (1960-1979); became senior partner (1979); retired as senior partner (1990); appointed consultant (1990).

Activities: number of company directorships.

Biography: lives London SW3 and West Sussex; born 07.06.1928; married to Alison with 2 children. Educated at Highgate School; University College London (LLB hons); City of London Solicitors' Company Prize; Grotius Prize.

BORRIE Sir Gordon

Director General of Fair Trading Field House, 15-25 Bream's Buildings, London EC4A 1PR.

Career: called to the Bar Middle Temple (1952); National Service Army Legal Services HQ Brit Commonwealth Forces in Korea (1952-1954); barrister London (1954-1957); lecturer and senior lecturer College of Law (1957-1964); senior lecturer in law Birmingham University (1965-1968); professor of English law and director Institute of Judicial Administration (1969-1976); dean of Faculty of Law (1974-1976); Bencher (1980); QC (1986); became Director General of Fair Trading (1976).

Activities: member Law Commission Advisory Panel on Contract Law (1966 to date); member Parole Board of England and Wales (1971-1974); member CNAA

Legal Studies Board (1971-1976); member Circuit Advisory Committee Birmingham Group of Courts (1972-1974); member Council of Consumers' Association (1972-1975); member Consumer Protection Advisory Committee (1973-1976); member Equal Opportunities Commission (1975-1976); vice-president Institute of Trading Standards Admin (1985 to date); sen treasurer National Union of Students (1955-1958); contested Labour Croydon NE (1955) and Ilford S (1959); governor Birminghamm College of Commerce (1966-1970); Kt (1982); member Reform Club.

Biography: lives Abbots Morton; born 13.03.1931; married to Dorene. Educated at John Bright Grammar School, Llandudno; Manchester University (LLB LLM); Harmsworth Scholar; author of 'Commercial Law' (1962) (6th ed 1988); co-author: 'The Consumer Society and the Law' (1963) (4th ed 1981); 'Law of Contempt' (1973) (2nd ed 1983) .

Leisure: gastronomy; piano playing; travel.

BOSWOOD Anthony

Queen's Counsel Fountain Court, Temple, London EC4.

Career: called to the Bar (1970); pupillage with WAB Forbes QC; QC (1986).

Activities: member Hurlingham.

Biography: lives London SW18 and Siena, Italy; born 01.10.1947; married to Sarah with 3 daughters. Educated at St Paul's School; New College Oxford (1968 BA) (1969 BCL).

Leisure: opera; concert going; riding; tennis; Church activities; walking dogs; driving children around.

BOTT Rosemary

partner FRERE CHOLMELEY 28 Lincoln's Inn Fields, London WC2A 3HH.

Career: articled Frere Cholmeley (1978-1980); admitted (1980); assistant solicitor (1980-1986); became partner (1986).

Activities: member Editorial Advisory Board of MCB University Press's new publication 'Professional Practice Development'.

Biography: lives London SW20; born 27.11.1956; divorced with 1 son. Educated at Convent of Our Lady of Sion, Worthing; Southampton University (1977 LLB hons); College of Law Guildford (1977-1978); Maxwell Law Prize (1976).

B

BOTTOMLEY Alan

joint senior partner and head company and commercial department HAMMOND SUDDARDS Empire House, 10 Piccadilly, Bradford BD1 3LR and Joseph's Well, Hanover Walk, Leeds LS3 1AB.

Career: National Service as 2nd Lt Royal Artillery; Major RATA TD; articled Gaunt Fosters and Bottomley; admitted (1957); assistant solicitor (1957-1959); became partner (1959); amalgamated with AV Hammond & Co (1971); became joint senior partner (1983); firm name changed to Hammond Suddards on amalgamation (1988).

Activities: president Bradford Law Society (1973); chairman Harrogate Festival of Arts & Sciences (1965-1972); director of companies; member of: Army & Navy Club; Bradford Club; Cruising Association.

Biography: lives Harrogate; born 14.11.1931; married with 2 children. Educated at Shrewsbury School.

Leisure: opera; theatre; travel; sailing.

BOUNDY Charles

partner FLADGATE FIELDER and partner-in-charge of office at Walgate House, 25 Church Street, Basingstoke, Hants RG21 1QQ.

Career: articled London; admitted (1970); became partner Malkin Cullis & Sumption (1970-1973); partner Martin Clore & Co (1974-1977); founded own practice (1977); merged with Walters Fladgate (1985); became finance partner (1988); member management board (1985-1990).

Activities: non-executive director Pourshins PLC (1988-1989); co sec numerous companies; member Basingstoke Hospice Project Committee (1989); member Chamber of Commerce Legal & Taxation Committee (1989); gave seminars at Henley Management College (1980); temporary part-time lecturing post at local technical college (1987).

Biography: lives North Hampshire; born 21.11.1945; married to Hazel with 3 sons. Educated at Liverpool College; Emmanuel College Cambridge (1967 BA) (1970 MA); articles in Journal of General Management and local Business Gazette; numerous internal booklets and practice notes.

Leisure: folk music (founder and active member ceilidh band 1980-1987); walking; music; eating/dining out; reading; theatre; golf; tennis; badminton; keep fit; holidays.

BOURNE Teddy

partner property department CLIFFORD CHANCE Blackfriars House, 19 New Bridge Street, London EC4V 6BY.

Career: articled Linklaters & Paines; admitted (1972); assistant solicitor Clifford Chance (1972-1981); became partner (1981).

Activities: hon legal adviser to Amateur Fencing Association; member City of London Solicitors' Company Education & Training Sub-Committee.

Biography: lives London NW3; born 30.09.1948; married to Marcy with 1 stepson. Educated at Brentwood School, Essex; King's College London (1969 LLB hons); College of Law Lancaster Gate; author of 'Handbook of Conveyancing Searches' (1984 & 1986).

Leisure: cross country skiing; Punch & Judy; chess; cooking.

BOWCOCK Philip

consultant and recently senior partner BOWCOCK & PURSAILL 54 St Edward Street, Leek, Staffordshire ST13 5DJ.

Career: National Service commissioned 15/19 the King's Royal Hussars (1947-1949); Sudan political service District Commissioner Central Nuer (1949-1955); HM Overseas Civil Service provincial administration Northern Rhodesia (Zambia); district commissioner Judiciary Magistrate first class (1955-1965); Principal Home Civil Service Ministry of Technology (1965-1968); joined family practice (1968).

Activities: chairman of Board Leek United and Midlands Building Society; chairman Medical Appeal Tribunal Stoke on Trent and West Midlands; deputy chairman Agricultural Land Tribunal South Eastern England; chairman Lichfield Diocesan Pastoral Committee; vice-chairman governors Newcastle under Lyme School; member Royal Commonwealth Society.

Biography: lives Endon; born 28.04.1927; married to Brenda with 3 children. Educated at The High School, Newcastle under Lyme; St John's College Oxford School of Modern History (1947 MA); Middle East Centre of Arab Studies, Lebanon (1950 Higher Arabic).

Leisure: Church; gardening; reading; walking; visiting buildings and beautiful places.

BOWEN John

partner in company and commercial department MORGAN BRUCE Bradley Court, Park Place, Cardiff CF1 3DP.

Career: articled Marchant Harries & Co (1957-1960); admitted (1960); assistant solicitor G Houghton & Son (1960-1961); assistant solicitor Gamlens (1961-1964); assistant solicitor Morgan Bruce & Nicholas (1964-1966); became partner (1966); chairman Management Committee.

Activities: deputy chairman Institute of Welsh Affairs; vice-chairman Area No 5 (South Wales) Legal Aid Board; member of executive of Tenovus Cancer Appeal.

Biography: lives Cardiff; born 07.06.1937; married to Helen with 1 child. Educated at Aberdare County Grammar School; University College of Wales (1957 LLB).

BOWER David

senior partner BOWER & BAILEY 41 Cornmarket Street, Oxford OX1 3HA.

Career: articled Linnell & Murphy (1965-1970); admitted (January 1971); regional legal adviser Midland Bank PLC (1972-1973); founded own practice (1973).

Activities: member of: MCC; Frilford Heath Golf Club; sporting clubs.

Biography: born Birmingham; lives Oxford; born 29.03.1947; married to Jane with 4 children. Educated at Stamford School, Lincolnshire.

Leisure: sport; gardening.

BOWLER Michael Harold Denton

managing partner HARBOTTLE & LEWIS 14 Hanover Square, London W1R 0BE.

Career: National Service commission XX The Lancashire Fusiliers; active service in Cyprus; admitted (1965); assistant solicitor in the country and the City (1965-1974); partner Harbottle & Lewis (1974); became managing partner (1987).

Activities: member Oriental Club.

Biography: lives London SW14 and East Sussex; born 23.05.1939; married to Ann with 2 children. Educated at Wellington School, Somerset; Mellersh Prize; Eastbourne Law Society Prize.

BOWLES Anthony

partner in construction department MCKENNA & CO Mitre House, 160 Aldersgate Street, London EC1A 4DD.

Career: voluntary service overseas Serdang College of Agriculture, Malaya (1968-1969); articled McKenna & Co (1970-1972); admitted (1973); assistant solicitor (1973-1979); became partner (1979).

Activities: Fellow of the Royal
Meteorological Society; member Lawyers'
Flying Association.

Biography: lives London W14; born
07.05.1946; married to Miranda with 3
children. Educated at Eton College; Sussex
University (1968 BA hons); College of Law
Lancaster Gate.

Leisure: meteorology; aviation; music;
opera; walking.

BOWMAN Brian

partner BOYCE HATTON 12 Tor Hill
Road, Torquay, Devon TQ2 5RB.

Career: articled Wansbroughs & Co (1959-
1964); admitted (1965); assistant solicitor
Bath Corporation (1965-1967); deputy town
clerk Torquay Borough Council (1967-
1969); social science research council
fellowship Kent University (1969-1970);
assistant town clerk London Borough of
Greenwich (1970-1972); assistant solicitor
Boyce Hatton (1972-1973); became partner
(1973).

Activities: Deputy District Registrar;
chairman Rent Assessment Committee;
chairman Education and Training Sub-
committee of Devon & Exeter Law Society
(1986-1989); member Devon & Exeter Law
Society (1982-1989); lectures in law at
South Devon College; to legal profession;
surveyors; etc; occasional chats on local
radio re legal matters.

Biography: lives Torquay; born 04.07.1941;
married with 2 children. Educated at
Clifton College, Bristol; Kent University at
Canterbury (1970 MA).

Leisure: long distance and mountain
walking; wind surfing; gardening;
archaeology.

BOWN Philip

barrister and head of chambers,
24 Millstone Lane, Leicester LE1 5JN.

Career: British Horse Society Instructor
(1967); called to the Bar Middle Temple
(1974); established Millstone Lane
Chambers with John Borneo (1976).

Activities: co-founder Highfields
Community Law Centre; member Leicester
Legal Aid Appeals Committee; member of:
Leicestershire Club; Leicestershire Golf
Club; Rushcliffe Golf Club.

Biography: lives Melton Mowbray; born
02.05.1949; divorced with 1 child.
Educated at Gateway School, Leicester;
Leicester Polytechnic (LLB).

Leisure: ornithology; golf; squash; current
affairs; good books.

BOWYER David

partner CLIFFORD CHANCE Blackfriars
House, 19 New Bridge Street, London
EC4V 6BY.

Career: articled Clifford Turner (1963);
admitted (1965); assistant solicitor (1965-
1968); became partner (1968); firm merged
with Coward Chance (1987).

Activities: member International Academy
of Estate and Trust Law; member of:
Boodles Club; Huntercombe GC.

Biography: lives Overton; born 27.08.1940;
married to Ann with 3 children. Educated
at Highfield School; Tonbridge School;
Trinity Hall Cambridge (1962 BA).

Leisure: golf; tennis; skiing.

BOYCE Tony

senior partner BOYCE HATTON 12 Tor
Hill Road, Castle Circus, Torquay TQ2 5RB;
offices also at Bristol and Brixham.

Career: articled Hutchings & Hutchings
and HW & S Patey; admitted (1953);
founded own practice (1954).

Activities: chairman Torbay Health
Authority; president Torquay United
Association Football Club PLC (chairman
1965-1985); member Torbay Hospital
Management Committee (1965-1974);
member South Western Regional Health
Authority (1974-1982); director numerous
companies; former chairman Torquay
Round Table; president Devon County
Football Association; council member
South West Industrial Council; board
member Prince's Youth Business Trust;
honorary legal adviser to a number of
Devon-based voluntary organisations.

Biography: lives Torquay; born 19.02.1930;
married with 3 children. Educated at
Repton School.

Leisure: music; professional football;
restoration of vintage cars.

BOYD Stewart

Queen's Counsel 4 Essex Court, Temple,
London EC4Y 9AJ.

Career: called to the Bar Middle Temple
(1967); QC (1981); Bencher of the Middle
Temple (1989).

Activities: Department of Trade Inquiry
Minet Holdings PLC (1982); chairman
Lloyd's Disciplinary Committee (1986);
Falkland Islands Government Inquiry
Seamount Ltd (1988); member
Departmental Advisory Committee on
Arbitration law; appointed arbitrator in
numerous disputes in England and
overseas under ad hoc and institutional

arbitration agreements concerning
international commercial disputes.

Biography: lives London NW3 and West
Dorset; born 25.10.1943; married to
Catherine with 4 children. Educated at
Winchester College; Trinity College
Cambridge (1965 BA) (1971 MA);
Trevelyan Scholar; Harmsworth Scholar;
Colombos Prize in International Law; joint
editor of Scrutton on Charter Parties and
Bills of Lading; joint author of Mustill and
Boyd on Commercial Arbitration; many
lectures and articles on international
commercial law and arbitration.

Leisure: sailing; gardening; playing the
piano.

BOYD-CARPENTER M Henry

partner FARRER & CO 66 Lincoln's Inn
Fields, London WC2A 3LH.

Career: articled Farrer & Co (1962-1965);
admitted (1965); assistant solicitor (1965-
1968); became partner (1968).

Activities: solicitor to the Duchy of
Cornwall (1976 to date); hon auditor of the
Law Society (1979-1981); member
governing body of Charterhouse School
(1981 to date); member Brooks's.

Biography: lives Ascot; born 11.10.1939;
married to Lesley with 2 children.
Educated at Charterhouse (1953-1958);
Balliol College Oxford (1962 BA) (1967
MA).

Leisure: reading; listening to music; motor
boating; hill walking; gardening.

BOYDELL Peter

The Worshipful Chancellor 2 Harcourt
Buildings, Temple, London EC4.

Career: War service (1939-1945); Adjt 17th
Field Regt RA (1943); Bde Major RA 1st
Armoured Div (1944); Bde Major RA 10th
Indian Div (1945); admitted (1947); called
to the Bar Middle Temple (1948); QC
(1965); Bencher (1970).

Activities: chairman Local Government
and Planning Association of the Bar (1986
to date); leader Parliamentary Bar (1975 to
date); chancellor of Dioceses of Truro (1957
to date); Oxford (1958 to date); Worcester
(1959 to date); chairman Planning and
Local Government Committee of the Bar
(1973-1986); member Legal Board of
Church Assembly (1958-1971); contested
Conservative Carlisle (1964); associate
RICS (1982); member of: Garrick; RAC;
Climbers.

Biography: lives London SW1; born
20.09.1920; single. Educated at Arnold
School, Blackpool; Manchester University

(1940 LLB).

Leisure: mountaineering; music; travel.

BOYLE Anthony

professor of law QUEEN MARY AND WESTFIELD COLLEGE Law Faculty, Mile End Road, London E7.

Career: called to the Bar Gray's Inn (1958); lecturer Durham University (1961-1963); lecturer Birmingham University (1963-1965); lecturer King's College London (1965-1971); reader Queen Mary College (1971-1974); professor of law at Queen Mary and Westfield College, London University (1974 to date).

Activities: general editor Gore Browne on Companies (1972-1989); member Jorans & Sons Editorial Committee; member Bearings; member of: MCC Squash Club at Finchley.

Biography: lives London N6; born 11.12.1934; married to Joan with 1 son. Educated at Salesian College, Farnborough; St Peter's School, Guildford; University College London (1956 LLB) (1958 LLM); Harvard Law School (1967 SJD); joint author of 'Boyle and Birds on Company Law'; various articles in MLR, JBL, JCLQ and The Company Lawyer; contributions to various monographs on company and commercial law.

Leisure: squash; gardening.

BRADLEY David

partner in charge of probate and trust department HEWITSON BECKE & SHAW Shakespeare House, 42 Newmarket Road, Cambridge CB5 8EP.

Career: articled Payne Hicks Beach & Co (1970-1972); admitted (1972); assistant solicitor (1972-1975); assistant solicitor Wild Hewitson & Shaw (1975-1976); became partner (1977).

Activities: clerk to sundry village charitable trusts.

Biography: lives Cottenham; born 15.12.1946; married to Margaret with 3 children. Educated at King's School, Ely; Christ's College Cambridge (1969 BA (MA); University of Lyon (1966 Diplome de Langue et de Civilisation Francaise).

Leisure: natural history; photography; France; Church; family.

BRADSHAW John

partner and head of litigation department and recruitment SIMMONS & SIMMONS 14 Dominion Street, London EC2M 2RJ.

Career: National Service subaltern 4RHA

(1957-1959); articled Simmons & Simmons (1962-1965); admitted (1965); assistant solicitor (1965-1971); became partner (1971).

Activities: member Bosham Sailing Club.

Biography: lives West Clandon; born 22.10.1938; married to Alison with 3 children. Educated at Corpus Christi College Cambridge (MA).

Leisure: sailing; skiing; walking.

BRAFMAN Guilherme

partner CAMERON MARKBY HEWITT Sceptre Court, 40 Tower Hill, London EC3N 4BB.

Career: articled Slaughter and May (1977-1979); admitted (1979); assistant solicitor Herbert Oppenheimer Nathan & Vandyk (1979-1983); founded own practice (1983); merged to form Brafman Morris (1984); merged to form Cameron Markby Hewitt (1989).

Activities: member Panel of Arbitrators of American Arbitration Association (1988); member International Marketing Committee of the ICC (UK); involved in seminars on company law and mergers and acquisitions of business which exploit intellectual property; deals extensively with North and South America; involved in marketing aspects of legal profession; member RAC.

Biography: lives London NW11; born 09.10.1953; married to Jane with 2 children. Educated at Kingston Grammar School; Lycee Francais de Londres; Downing College Cambridge (1976 BA hons) (1979 MA); Associate of Chartered Institute of Arbitrators (1986); fluent in Portuguese, French and Spanish; often quoted in legal/advertising press.

Leisure: tennis; cycling; eating out; reading; spending time with wife and kids and travelling with them.

BRAHAMS Diana

barrister 15 Old Square, Lincoln's Inn, London WC2A 3UH.

Career: called to the Bar Middle Temple (1972); pupillage with TRF Jennings (1974-1975); pupillage with GB Parker (1975-1976); tenancy E Scamell's Chambers (1976).

Activities: legal correspondent to The Lancet (1981 to date); editor Medico-Legal Journal (1983 to date); editor Estates Times Law Reports (1985-1986); council member Medico-Legal Society of London; member Health Watch; member International Society for the Prevention of Iatrogenic

Complications; member Concern; member working party convened by Spastics Society on compensation (1986); participation in workshops, round table discussions and seminars on variety of subjects with bias on anaesthesia and product liability and compensation; lectures widely on medico-legal matters; member Royal College of Physicians Working Party on Compensation for Adverse Consequences of Medical Intervention; member of Royal College of General Practitioners Ethics Committee; addressed Bar Conference on attractions of no fault compensation and reform of computation and awarding of damages for personal injury (1988); Fellow of Royal Society of Medicine; member of Apil (Association of Personal Injury Lawyers); member of : National Trust; Hampstead Theatre Club; King's Head Threatre Club.

Biography: lives London NW11; born 18.02.1944; married to Malcolm with 2 sons and 1 daughter. Educated at Roedean, Johannesburg (1955-1959); Queen's College London (1959-1961); Sir John Cass College of Art, London (1964-1965); College of Law Chancery Lane (1968-1970 & 1971-1972); author of: 'A Casebook on Rent Review and Lease Renewal' (with Mark Pawlowski) Collins Professional Books (1986) (now belongs to Blackwells); (since 1986) responsible for up-dating a section of loose-leaf work on 'Premises Management' Croner Publications; (from 1977-1986) regular publications in both legal and property journals including Estates Gazette, Estates Times, Chartered Surveyors Weekly, New Law Journal and in particular a regular series called Property Law Round-up (with Malcolm Brahams) published in the Law Society's Gazette and a series of articles on Adverse Possession published in the Estates Gazette (1978); chapters contributed to: The Law and You 'Family and Personal/Health'– 'Which? Books' (1987) edited by Marcel Berlins, Hodder and Stoughton; Encyclopaedia Britannica's Medical and Health Annual (1985) 'The Rights of Mental Patients: The Case in the UK' (1986); 'Under-age sex' (1987); 'No Fault Compensation in Scandinavia' (1989) and in press 'Computers as Decision Aids in the Law' (with Dr Jeremy Wyatt); No Fault Compensation in Medicine: 'No Fault Compensation in Finland with an overview of the Scandinavian approach to compensation of medical and drug injuries' edited by Ronald Mann and John Havard, Royal Society of Medicine (1989); Medical Malpractice Solutions: 'The Swedish and Finnish Patient

Insurance Scheme' edited by Halley, Fowks et al (1989); Charles C Thomas USA; Human Genetic Information: Science, Law and Ethics 'The Legal implications of Human Genetic Information: edited by J Whelan published by the Ciba Foundation (1990); Journals: (since 1981) legal correspondent to The Lancet; regular contributions to The New Law Journal and The Law Society's Gazette and The Medico-Legal Journal, Anaesthesia and Dispensing Doctors' Journal on a wide varietymedico-legal issues; topics include: Medical Negligence; the case of R v Arthur (1981); Premenstrual Syndrome and the Law; Clinical trials; Informed Consent; Assisted Reproduction and the Law; AIDS; No Fault Compensation for Medical and Drug Injuries; an Analysis of Swedish and Finnish Insurance Schemes; Product Liability; Computers as Decision Aids; Medical Frauds; Heat-illness in the Armed Forces; Military Law and the Defence of Obeying Orders; Sterilisation of Incapable Women; Under-age Girls and Contraception; Monitoring and Awareness in Anaethesia; Benzodiazepins; Ownership of Patient data; Enthuanasia; International Legal Perspectives; Comparative Overviews of Foreign Decisions on Medico-Legal issues; Human Genetic Information; Inquests; Adverse effects of drugs; Automatism; Iatrogenic crime; NHS reforms; Suspended Doctors in the NHS; The General Medical Council; other publications include:' The AIDS Letter; Independent Health News; Criminal Law Review; the Hastings Center Report; Self Health; Journal of Medical Ethics; the Physician; The Practitioner; British Medical Bulletin; Psychiatry in Practice; the New England Journal of Medicine; in preparation: Preimplantation Diagnosis, Legal Implications, edited by Professor Robert Edwards, Cambridge; in press: Pharmaceutical Medicine (2nd edition) Legal Implications and Product Liability, edited by Burley et al, Edward Arnold (1990).

Leisure: walking; reading; theatre; travel; music; 3 cats; Victorian paintings and furniture; historical houses .

BRAHAMS Malcolm

joint senior partner BRAHAMS KILLEN MARK EISENTHAL Savoy Hill House, Savoy Hill, Strand, London WC2R 0BU.

Career: articled Bartlett & Gluckstein (1963-

1965); admitted (1966); assistant solicitor (1966-1969); partner Malcolm Slowe & Co (1969-1972); partner Kaufman Kramer Shebson (1972-1982); founded own practice (1982); merged to become Brahams Killen Mark Eisenthal (1985).

Activities: hon treasurer Concern; council member Medico-Legal Society; council member Campaign against Health Fraud; addressed various conferences on the subject of no-fault compensation and product liability.

Biography: lives London NW11; born 28.08.1941; married to Diana with 3 children. Educated at Leighton Park School, Reading; Balliol College Oxford (1962 BA hons); College of Law (1963 & 1965); author of 'Commercial Leases' (1985); articles in New Law Journal (1988); occasional contributions to Law Society's Gazette and Estates Gazette.

Leisure: travel; reading; theatre; photography; movie-making.

BRAMSON David

senior partner property department NABARRO NATHANSON 50 Stratton Street, London W1X 5FL.

Career: articled Kaufman & Segal (1963-1966); admitted (1966); commercial lawyer Mobil Oil Co Ltd (1967-1969); assistant solicitor Nabarro Nathanson (1969-1970); became partner (1970).

Activities: adviser RICS Committee on Property Unitisation; lectures on property development and funding; voluntary adviser on inner city regeneration; member RAC.

Biography: lives London NW3; born 08.02.1942; married to Lilian with 2 children. Educated at Willesden County Grammar School; University College London (1963 LLB); Law Society Finals (hons); various articles on property development and property funding in professional journals.

Leisure: visual arts; opera; literature.

BRANDES Antonia

partner CANNONS 11-15 Arlington Street, St James's, London SW1A 1RD.

Career: articled Malkin Cullis and Sumption; admitted; assistant solicitor Collyer-Poinstow; became partner Cannons.

Biography: lives London NW3; born 10.12.1952; married to Stephen with 1 son. Educated at Stoke Park School; University College London (1975 LLB).

Leisure: opera; wine.

BRENNAN Daniel

Queen's Counsel 2 Garden Court, Temple, London EC4Y 9BL and 18 St John Street, Manchester M3 4EA.

Career: Recorder of the Crown Court (1982); QC (1985).

Activities: legal assessor to UK Central Council for Nursing; member of Criminal Injuries Compensation Board.

Biography: lives London and Cheshire; born 19.03.1942; married to Pilar with 4 sons. Educated at St Bede's Grammar School, Bradford; Manchester University (1964 LLB); author of 'Provisional Damages' (1986); contributor to Bullen & Leake (1990 ed).

BRENT Michael

Queen's Counsel and head of chambers 2 Dr Johnson's Buildings, Temple, London EC4Y 7AY.

Career: called to the Bar Gray's Inn (1961); Northern circuit (1961-1967); Circuit Junior (1964); Midland & Oxford circuit (1967 to date); QC (1983); Assistant Recorder (1985-1990); Recorder (1990).

Activities: Deputy Chairman Agricultural Land Tribunal (1979 to date).

Biography: lives London NW8; born 08.06.1936; married to Rosalind with 2 children. Educated at Manchester Grammar School; Manchester University (1957 LLB hons).

BRETHERTON Jeremy

senior partner BRETHERTON & CO 6 Romeland Hill, St Albans, Herts AL3 4ET.

Career: admitted (1957); assistant solicitor Ottaways (1957-1959); solicitor share and loan department Stock Exchange (1959-1963); assistant solicitor legal department Industrial and Commercial Finance Corporation Ltd (1963-1964); became partner AG Tooth (1964-1965); founded own practice (1965).

Activities: part-time chairman Social Security Appeal Tribunal; member Legal Aid Area Committee No 11 Legal Aid Area; member of: Professional and Business Club; Constitutional Club.

Biography: lives King's Walden; born 10.10.1929; married to Vera with 3 children. Educated at Packwood Haugh Preparatory School; Shrewsbury School; Queen's College Cambridge (1954 MA); Chartered Institute of Secretaries (1960).

Leisure: sailing (boat in Porto Colom, Majorca); gardening; farming; tennis.

B

BRETT Alan

partner and head of commercial property department (Cambridge office) HEWITSON BECKE & SHAW Shakespeare House, 42 Newmarket Road, Cambridge CB5 8EP.

Career: admitted (1972); assistant solicitor Wild Hewitson & Shaw (1973-1977); became partner (1977); merged to become Hewitson Becke & Shaw (1989); member Management Committee Wild Hewitson & Shaw (1984-1989) and Hewitson Becke & Shaw (1989 to date); member Merger Committee (1989); part-time supervisor in company law Sidney Sussex (1974-1975) and Magdalene College Cambridge (1975-1976); member Management Committee Wild Hewitson & Shaw (1984-1989) and Hewitson Becke & Shaw (1989 to date); member Merger Committee (1989).

Biography: lives nr Royston; born 02.08.1947; married to Jane with 2 daughters. Educated at Chatham House Grammar School, Ramsgate (1959-1963); Andover Grammar School (1963-1966); Birmingham University (1969 LLB hons) (1970 LLM distinction) Lady Barber Faculty Scholarship; AE Hills University Scholarship; Sidney Sussex College Cambridge (1974 LLB) (LLM); Diploma in International Law; Evan Lewis-Thomas Law Studentship.

BRETT Alastair

company solicitor to TIMES NEWSPAPERS LIMITED Legal Department, 1 Pennington Street, London E1 9XN.

Career: articled Stephenson Harwood & Tatham (1973-1975); admitted (1975); assistant solicitor Macfarlanes (1975-1977); senior legal assistant Times Newspapers Ltd (1977-1984); became company solicitor (1984).

Activities: specialist in media law lecturing to all Times journalists (1989); member Law Society Sub-committee on Privacy and Related matters (1989); member Professional Development Sub-committee of Commerce and Industry Group; pioneered rights of audience for solicitors in the High Court; member Hurlingham Club.

Biography: lives London SW6; born 16.05.1950; married to Patricia. Educated at Bow School, Durham; Sedbergh School, Yorkshire; Exeter College Oxford (1972 BA hons); contributed regularly to The Times and The Sunday Times; numerous articles on the need to reform the profession or an area of law.

Leisure: tennis; squash; skiing; running; writing; theatre; opera.

BRETT Hugh

partner DALLAS BRETT Pembroke House, Pembroke Street, Oxford OX1 1BL.

Career: articled Linklaters & Paines (1967); head of legal department Allied Breweries Ltd (1974-1981); founded Dallas Brett (1981).

Activities: appointed by the Secretary of State to the UK Copyright Tribunal (1990); member Intellectual Property Committee of Law Society; founder member British Literary and Copyright Association; founder member The Common Law Institute of Intellectual Property; member of the copyright section of the British Computer Society; member of: Aldeburgh Golf Club; Oxford & Cambridge Universities Club.

Biography: lives Oxford; born 14.06.1941; married to Margaret with 3 children. Educated at Sedbergh School; Keble College Oxford (1963 MA); editor of The European Intellectual Property Review; author of: 'The Patents Act' (1977); 'The Protection of Computer Software'; numerous articles on intellectual property law.

Leisure: fishing; golf.

BRETTEN (George) Rex

Queen's Counsel 24 Old Buildings, Lincoln's Inn, London WC2A 3UJ.

Career: assistant lecturer Nottingham University (1964-1967); visiting lecturer Faculty of Law, University of Auckland (1967); assistant director Institute of Law Research & Reform, Edmonton, Canada (1968-1970); commenced practice as barrister (1970); QC (1980); Bencher Lincoln's Inn (1989).

Biography: lives Cambridge; born 21.02.1942; married to Gillian with 1 daughter. Educated at King Edward School, King's Lynn; Sidney Sussex College Cambridge (1964 MA LLB).

Leisure: hobby farming; tennis.

BRIANT Gill

partner DENTON HALL BURGIN & WARRENS 5 Chancery Lane, Clifford's Inn, London EC4A 1BU.

Career: articled Denton Hall Burgin (1977-1979); admitted (1979); assistant solicitor (1979-1984); became partner (1984).

Activities: legal training partner and

chairman in-house committee on 'Women in the Law'; member IBA; member Law Society; member of: Hurlingham; Wimbledon Squash and Badminton.

Biography: lives London SW20; born 12.11.1953; married to Nicholas with 2 children. Educated at Cheltenham Ladies' College; Bristol University (1975 BA hons); Oxford University (1976 PGCE); College of Law.

Leisure: squash; cooking.

BRICE Nuala

assistant secretary-general THE LAW SOCIETY 113 Chancery Lane, London WC2A 1PL.

Career: articled March Pearson & Green; admitted (1963); assistant solicitor the Law Society (1963-1964); assistant secretary (1964-1973); senior assistant secretary (1973-1982); departmental secretary (1982-1987); became assistant secretary-general (1987).

Activities: secretary Revenue Law Committee (1972-1982); member University Women's Club.

Biography: lives London SW1 and Lane End, Bucks; born 22.12.1937; married to Geoffrey with 1 son. Educated at Loreto Convent, Manchester; University College London (1959 LLB hons) (1976 LLM) (1982 PHD); Stephen Heelis Gold Medal and John Peacock Conveyancing Prize (1963).

Leisure: music; reading; gardening.

BRIDGE Richard

partner in entertainment division of the commercial department MISCHON DE REYA 125 High Holborn, London WC1V 6QP.

Career: patents clerk GEC; articled to Edward F George; admitted (1977); assistant solicitor Bird & Bird (1977-1978); assistant solicitor Crawley & De Reya (1978); became partner (1978); firm became Mishcon de Reya (1988).

Activities: member of: Copinger Society; BLACA; CLIP; Law Society; SEG; CLA .

Biography: lives Higham nr Gravesend; born 07.09.1948; married to Jacqueline with 1 stepdaughter, 1 stepson and 1 daughter. Educated at Wahroonga Preparatory School, Australia; Alcuin House School; Orley Farm School; Aldenham School (Bursary; member Duodecim Society); College of Law Chester and Lancaster Gate; Nottingham University (1970 BSC) (1973 BA) (Hallward Debating Cup; president Wortley Hall); co-author of

'Video Law'; various articles and papers.

Leisure: walking 3 pointers; cutting the grass; trying to lose weight and keep fit; folk, blues and rock music; trying to maintain and restore a Fiat 124 Sport Coupe.

BRIDGES-ADAMS Nicholas

barrister and head of chambers 4 Verulam Buildings, Gray's Inn, London WC1R 5LU.

Career: called to the Bar Lincoln's Inn (1958); Recorder of the Crown Court (1972); head of chambers (1979).

Activities: chairman Criminal Justice and Sentencing Committee; member Society of Conservative Lawyers; chairman Representation Committee under the Food and Environmental Protection Act; member of: Savile Club; Garrick Club; Bar Yacht Club.

Biography: lives London WC1 and Bury St Edmunds; born 16.09.1930; married to Jenifer. Educated at Orwell Park; Stowe; Oriel College Oxford (MA Dip Ed) Scholar; contribution on collisions at sea to 3rd ed Halsbury.

Leisure: shooting; sailing; skiing; cooking.

BRIDGEWATER Martin

partner and head of construction department NABARRO NATHANSON 50 Stratton Street, London W1X 5FL.

Career: articled Evershed & Tomkinson (1974-1976); admitted (1976); assistant solicitor (1976-1977); admitted Hong Kong (1978); assistant solicitor Johnson Stokes & Master, Hong Kong (1978-1979); assistant solicitor Nabarro Nathanson (1980-1984); became partner (1984).

Activities: member: International Bar Association; American Bar Association; West India Committee; Middle East Association; British-Florida Chamber of Commerce.

Biography: lives Teddington; born 27.06.1952; married to Hattie with 1 son. Educated at King Edward's School, Birmingham; Oriel College (1973 BA) (1977 MA).

Leisure: travel; science fiction; watching sport; wicket-keeping.

BRIGGS Richard M

partner TUCKER TURNER KINGSLEY WOOD & CO 5 Stone Buildings, Lincoln's Inn, London WC2A 3YD.

Career: articled Tucker Turner & Co (1966-1972); admitted (1972); assistant solicitor (1972); became partner (1972).

Activities: lectured on various legal aspects of communications particularly mobile communications.

Biography: lives Essex; born 07.08.1948; married with 1 child. Educated at Highgate School; College of Law; part-author of: 'The Telecomms User's Guide to Regulations' and 'The Telecomms User's Handbook'.

Leisure: gardening.

BRINDLEY Peter

member of Board of Management and Director of Continuing Education THE COLLEGE OF LAW 33-35 Lancaster Gate, London W2 3LU.

Career: articled Heald Johnson Garton (1961-1964); John Mackrell Prize; admitted (1964); lecturer The College of Law (1964).

Activities: general editor Law Notes (1972-1980); member Law Society Revenue Law Committee and Advocacy Training Sub-Committee.

Biography: lives St Albans; born 30.10.1938; married to Sybil with 2 children. Educated at Beaumont College; Oriel College Oxford (1961 BA).

Leisure: photography; gardening.

BRINLEY-CODD Patti

partner BARLOW LYDE & GILBERT Beaufort House, 15 St Botolph Street, London EC3A 7NJ.

Career: called to the Bar (1976); pupillage at 1 Essex Court and 2 Temple Gardens (1976-1977); legal advisor ICI Ltd (1977-1985); admitted (1983); assistant solicitor Barlow Lyde & Gilbert (1985-1987); became partner (1987).

Biography: lives London SW19; born 27.06.1954; married to Peter. Educated at St Margaret's School For Girls, Exeter; University College London (1975 LLB); College of Law.

Leisure: fly fishing; gardening.

BRISLEY Christopher

senior partner LLOYD BRAGG St Nicholas House, High Street, Bristol BS1 2AW.

Career: articled Lloyd Burch Inskip & Co (1955-1958); admitted (1958); assistant solicitor (1958-1961); partner (1961-1981); senior partner (1981); merged to become Lloyd Bragg (1988).

Activities: hon secretary to Bristol Commercial Rooms; local director Sun Alliance & London Insurance Group;

secretary Paragon Concert Society .

Biography: lives Bristol; born 03.08.1931; married with 3 children. Educated at Rendcomb College; Cirencester; Bristol University (1955 LLB).

BRITTON Andrew

partner and head of corporate/commercial department DAVIES ARNOLD COOPER 12 Bridewell Place, London EC4V 6AD.

Career: articled Baker & McKenzie; admitted (1975); assistant solicitor (1975-1980); assistant solicitor Davies Arnold Cooper (1980-1981); became partner (1981).

Activities: gives seminars and participates in conferences on legal topics.

Biography: lives Barnet; born 18.01.1951; married to Valerie with 2 children. Educated at Nailsea Grammar School; King's College London (1972 LLB AKC); College of Law Lancaster Gate.

Leisure: music (sings in London Choral Society); theatre; classic sports cars; tennis.

BROADIE Charles

partner CRIPPS HARRIES HALL 84 Calverley Road, Tunbridge Wells, Kent TN1 2UP.

Career: articled Field Roscoe & Co (1967-1969); admitted (1969); assistant solicitor Hedleys (1970-1972); Secretariat of the European Commission of Human Rights, Strasbourg (1972-1974); assistant solicitor Cripps Harries Hall & Co (1974-1976); became partner (1976).

Activities: assistant deputy coroner for West Kent (1988); member No 2 (South Eastern) Legal Aid Area Committee (1984 to date); governor Wadhurst College; governor Rose Hill School, Tunbridge Wells .

Biography: lives Tunbridge Wells; born 15.03.1945; married to Eun-Ja with 4 children. Educated at Wellington House, Westgate on Sea (1953-1958); Bradfield College, Berks (1958-1963); Sidney Sussex College Cambridge (1963-1966 MA LLM); Universite de Nancy, France (1969-1970); .

Leisure: relaxing with family; reading; walking.

BROCK Duncan

partner and head commercial property department COBBETT LEAK ALMOND Ship Canal House, King Street, Manchester M2 4WB.

Career: assistant solicitor Cobbett Whitaker & Cobbett (1963-1967); became partner

B

(1968); head of legal department Lyon Group (Northern) Ltd (1971-1974).

Activities: chapter clerk Manchester Cathedral; member St James's Club, Manchester.

Biography: lives Henbury; born 30.04.1937; married to Judy with 3 children. Educated at Terra Nova; Trinity College, Glenalmond; Clare College Cambridge (1960 MA).

Leisure: gardening; sheep; occasional golf.

BRODIE Bruce

chairman FRERE CHOLMELEY 28 Lincoln's Inn Fields, London WC2A 3HH.

Career: became partner Frere Cholmeley (1971).

Biography: lives London NW1; born 19.03.1937; married to Louise with 2 daughters. Educated at Union High School, South Africa; Natal University (BA); Fitzwilliam College Cambridge (MA).

Leisure: cricket; fishing.

BRODIE Colin Queen's Counsel 24 Old Buildings, Lincoln's Inn, London WC2.

Career: called to the Bar Middle Temple (1954); QC (1980); Bencher Lincoln's Inn (1988).

Activities: member Guards Polo Club.

Biography: lives Dorking; born 19.04.1929; married to Julia with 2 children. Educated at Eton College; Magdalen College Oxford.

Leisure: polo.

BRODIE Stanley

Queen's Counsel 2 Hare Court, Temple, London EC4Y 7BH.

Career: called to the Bar Inner Temple (1954); lecturer in law Southampton University (1954); QC (1975); Bencher Inner Temple (1983); Recorder of the Crown Court (1975-1989).

Activities: member Bar Committee (1987) and member Finance and General Purposes Committee of the Bar Council (1988); member working party in Ethical Aspects of Aids Vaccine Trials (Medical Research Council); member Flyfishers' Club.

Biography: lives London SW1 and Dalrymple, Ayrshire; born 02.07.1930; married to Elizabeth Gloster QC with 2 children. Educated at Bradford Grammar School; Balliol College Oxford (1952 MA); president Oxford University Law Society (1952).

Leisure: country pursuits; opera.

BROMAGE Peter

partner EVERSHED WELLS & HIND 10 Newhall Street, Birmingham B3 3LX.

Career: articled Eversheds & Tomkinson (1955-1958); admitted (1958); assistant solicitor (1958-1960); became partner (1960); senior partner (1984-1989); chairman of Eversheds (1988-1990).

Activities: hon treasurer Rugby Football Union; chairman Discipline Committee of the Test and County Cricket Board; chairman General Purposes and Finance Committee of Warwickshire CCC; member of: MCC; Oriental; East India; Walsall RFC; Little Aston Golf Club; XL Club; British Sportsman's Club.

Biography: lives Walsall; born 08.07.1933; married to Barbara with 3 children. Educated at Queen Mary's Grammar School, Walsall; St John's College Cambridge (1954 BA) (MA); John Mackrell Prizeman; Birmingham Law Society Bronze Medallist.

Leisure: golf; music; bridge; gardening.

BROOKE Lynne

senior partner BROOKE BLAIN RUSSELL The Smokery, Greenhill's Rents, Cowcross Street, London EC1M 6BN; main professional interests Corporate Law & Finance, natural resources law and making deals.

Career: articled Benson Mazure & Co; admitted; assistant solicitor Wildman Millington & Wallace; assistant solicitor Douglas Wiseman Karsberg & Collyer; founded Yudolph & Brooke; merged to become Brooke Kirschel & Redstone (1978); sole practitioner (1979); merged to become Brooke Blain Russell (1985); editor firm's newsletter.

Activities: secretary and founder member Law Society's Group for the Welfare of People with a Mental Handicap; vice-chairman Westminster Society for Mentally Handicapped Children and Adults; Kith & Kids parent support group; Network for the Handicapped (legal advisory centre for people suffering from a disability); Park Lodge Project (provides temporary accommodation for homeless people with a disability); chairman of the Newham Riding School & Association providing riding for the disabled and people who could not normally afford to ride; presently in negotiations with LDDC to build an equestrian centre.

Biography: lives City of London; born

12.04.1943; married to Lesley with 3 daughters and 1 son. Educated at Godwin Road Primary School; Plaistow Grammar School; Holborn College of Law; London University (LLB external).

Leisure: running; squash.

BROOKE Michael

barrister 2 Crown Office Row, Temple, London EC4 and 250 Bis, Boulevard St Germain, 75007 Paris, France.

Career: called to the English Bar Gray's Inn (1968); tenant in Chambers 2 Crown Office Row (1969 to date); admitted to the Paris Bar (1987).

Biography: lives London W1; born 08.05.1942; divorced with 3 sons. Educated at Lycee Francais de Londres; Edinburgh University (1965 LLB).

Leisure: boating; cycling; wild mushrooms; comparing England with France.

BROWN Bradley

senior partner SPEECHLY BIRCHAM Bouverie House, 154 Fleet Street, London EC4A 2HX.

Activities: member Society for Computers and Law Information Technology and the Courts.

Biography: lives London NW6; born 10.11.1934; married with 2 children. Educated at Westminster School; London University (LCB).

BROWN David

senior partner BUDD MARTIN BURRETT Anglia House, Culver Street West, Colchester, Essex CO1 1JG.

Career: articled Landons; admitted (1972); assistant solicitor; partner; assistant solicitor Budd Martin Burrett (1976-1977); became partner (1977).

Activities: member Council of Suffolk and North Essex Law Society; former treasurer Colchester Solicitors Group; member of: Law Society; Law Society Motor Club; Solicitors Benevolent Association; British Association for Shooting & Conservation; Classic Corvette Club; Colchester and District Fencing Club.

Biography: lives Hadleigh; born 16.05.1947; married to Tessa with 3 children. Educated at Brentwood Grammar School; London School of Economics (1968 LLB hons).

Leisure: clay/rough shooting; collecting antique prints; motorsport; reading (particularly history); American cars; fencing (foil).

BROWN David

partner BRISTOWS COOKE & CARPMAEL 10 Lincoln's Inn Fields, London WC2A 3BP.

Career: Royal Corps of Naval Constructors naval architect warship design and construction (1960-1966); technical assistant Bristows Cooke & Carpmael (1966); admitted (1972); assistant solicitor (1972-1974); became partner (1974).

Biography: lives London SW10 and Oxfordshire; born 08.05.1942; married with 4 children. Educated at Royal High School, Edinburgh; The High School of Glasgow; Royal Naval Engineering College, Plymouth; Royal Naval College, Greenwich (1965 naval architecture).

Leisure: family; the turf.

BROWN Douglas

assistant solicitor building and engineering group JAQUES & LEWIS 2 South Square, Gray's Inn, London WC1R 5HR.

Career: admitted (1973); assistant solicitor Jaques & Lewis.

Activities: Greater London Council senior planning advocate; specialising in offshore and onshore construction British Gas PLC; social secretary Society of Construction Law; former full committee member Law Society's Commerce and Industry Group; member Beckenham Cricket Club.

Biography: lives London SE21; born 01.04.1948; married to Lani. Educated at The Marr College, Troon; Sir William Borlases School, Marlow; King's College London (1970 LLB hons).

Leisure: tennis; golf; riding.

BROWN Gordon

consultant BRACHERS Somerfield House, 59 London Road, Maidstone, Kent ME16 8JH.

Career: articled Frank Miskin (1934-1937); admitted (1937); became partner Bracher Son & Miskin (now Brachers) (1939).

Activities: vice-president Branch Prayer Book Society; former chairman Parish Council; voluntary Church organist.

Biography: lives Chart Sutton; born 25.06.1912; married to Joan with 3 children. Educated at Palmer's Grays; St John's College Cambridge (1934 BA hons) (1937 MA); McMahon Studentship; Scholar St John's College.

Leisure: music; travel; gardening.

BROWN Graham Stephen

partner and head of tax and trust department PAYNE HICKS BEACH 10 New Square, Lincoln's Inn, London WC2A 3QG.

Career: admitted (1969); assistant solicitor (1969-1972); became partner Payne Hicks Beach (1972).

Activities: member Revenue Law Committee; Capital Taxes Sub-committee of the Law Society; member Law Society Financial Services Act Working Party; member Committee and Professional Purposes Sub-committee of Holborn Law Society; member Agricultural Law Association; member International Fiscal Association; member Farmers' Club.

Biography: born 28.11.1944; married to Jacqueline. Educated at Farnborough; Bristol University (1966 LLB); King's College (1975 LLM); Catholic University of Louvain (1969-1970); Associate of the Institute of Taxation in Ireland; papers on tax, trusts, probate, international succession and charities to various major international legal conferences in London, Amsterdam and Munich; published translations on legal/fiscal subjects from French.

Leisure: wide interest and involvement in arts and heritage.

BROWN Ken

solicitor and company secretary THE GEORGE PHILIP PROPERTIES GROUP OF COMPANIES AND DANBURY GROUP PLC 12/14 Long Acre, London WC2E 9LP.

Career: articled Norton Rose; admitted (1982); assistant solicitor; assistant solicitor Alsop Wilkinson; became solicitor and company secretary George Philip Publishing and George Philip Properties (1984).

Activities: former member Publishers' Association Law Panel; formerly on secondment to Tower Hamlets Law Centre; provided advice at free local law surgeries.

Biography: lives London SE6; born 13.01.1957; married to Rosie with 1 son and 1 daughter. Educated at Christ's Hospital, Horsham (1967-1975); Downing College Cambridge (1979 BA hons); (1983 MA); College of Law Guildford (1980).

Leisure: reading; involvement with local Church.

BROWN Michael

senior partner BROWN COOPER 7 Southampton Place, London WC1A 2DR.

Career: articled Denton Hall & Burgin (1954-1957); admitted (1957); assistant solicitor (1957-1958); partner (1959-1980); founded Brown Cooper (1981).

Activities: chairman Urwick Orr & Partners Ltd (1983) (director 1981-1983); chairman Pooh Properties Trust (1982-1990); director Channel Television (1979-1982); secretary Society of English & American Lawyers (1983-1986) (chairman 1989) (president 1989 to date); assistant secretary Holborn Law Society (1960s); hon legal adviser to the Variety Club of Great Britain (23 years); member Garrick.

Biography: lives Chorleywood; born 23.09.1932; widowed with 3 sons. Educated at Berkhamsted School; New College Oxford (1954 BA) (1957 MA); pamphlets, articles and letters on the law of libel.

Leisure: conversation and the company of friends; reading history; all kinds of music; home and family activities.

BROWN Peter Stewart

resident partner WINTHROP STIMSON PUTNAM & ROBERTS 2 Throgmorton Avenue, London EC2N 2AP.

Career: associate attorney Winthrop Stimson Putnam & Roberts (1977-1984); became partner (1 January 1985).

Activities: member International Bar Association.

Biography: lives London SW3; born 08.01.1951; married to Charlotte with 1 son and 2 daughters. Educated at Regis High School, New York (1969); Drew University (1974 BA); Harvard University (1977 JD).

BROWN Philip

managing partner WILDE SAPTE 60 Upper Thames Street, London EC4V 3BD.

Career: Peace Corps volunteer, Botswana (1966-1969); attorney Newark-Essex Law Reform Project (1969-1971); articled Ormerod Morris & Dumont (1972-1974); admitted (1975); became partner Wilde Sapte (1975); became managing partner (1988).

Biography: lives London SW12; born 24.06.1942; married to Geraldine with 2 children. Educated at Cheshunt Grammar School; Albion High School, New York; Hobart College (1963 BA); Columbia

B

B

University (1966 LLB); New York Bar (1966); New Jersey Bar (1969).

Leisure: pottery.

BROWN Roy

litigation partner HAMLIN SLOWE PO Box 4SQ. Roxburghe House, 273-287 Regent Street, London W1A 4SQ.

Career: admitted (1964); assistant solicitor father's practice Hamlin Brown Veale & Twyford (1964-1967); became partner (1967); firm became Hamlin Slowe (1984).

Activities: member of: MCC; Wentworth Golf Club; Aldworth Cricket Club (treasurer).

Biography: lives Streatley; born 06.12.1937; married to Wendy with 2 children. Educated at the Hall School, Hampstead; Westminster School; Trinity College Oxford (MA).

Leisure: golf; cricket; reading.

BROWN Tony

senior partner PATTERSON GLENTON & STRACEY Law Court Chambers, Waterloo Square, South Shields, Tyne and Wear NE33 1AW.

Career: Indian Army (1944-1948); articled to town clerk of South Shields; admitted (1949); became partner Patterson Glenton & Stracey (1953).

Activities: legal member Royal Town Planning Institute; member Newcastle-upon-Tyne Incorporated Law Society Standing Committee; member No 8 (Northern) Legal Aid Area Appeals Committee; member Lord Chancellor's Judicial Appointments Committee (Tyneside); former member and chairman South Shields Hospital Management Committee; member Northern Regional Health Authority; chairman South Tyneside Family Practitioner Committee and its Service Committees.

Biography: lives Cleadon Village; born 09.07.1925; married to Bunny with 1 daughter and 3 sons. Educated at Corby Hall, Sunderland.

Leisure: skiing; fell walking; gardening; bridge.

BROWNE Michael

managing partner RICHMONDS 35 Potter Street, Worksop, Notts S80 2AG.

Career: articled Rotheras; admitted (1965); assistant solicitor Mee and Co (1965); partner (1967-1989); upon merger became managing partner Richmonds (1989).

Activities: Colonel in Territorial Army; former chairman Bassetaw Conservative Association; Deputy Coroner for Retford (1970s); Deputy County Court Registrar; panel member Solicitors Complaints Bureau; organiser Chamber Park Horse Trials; founder member Retford Squash Club; member of: Retford Golf Club; Army & Navy Club.

Biography: lives Retford; born 06.12.1942; married to Sue with 2 daughters. Educated at Uppingham; Law Society Finals (hons).

BRUCE-SMITH Keith

partner WITHERS 20 Essex Street, London WC2R 3AL.

Career: articled Withers (1976-1978); admitted (1978); assistant solicitor (1978-1983); became partner (1983).

Activities: Territorial Army Officer.

Biography: lives Purley; born 11.06.1953; married to Susan with 2 children. Educated at Oundle School; Christ Church Oxford (1985 MA hons); joint author of: 'Practical Trust Precedents' (1986); 'Practical Will Precedents' (1987); joint editor 'International Trust Precedents' (1989).

BRUMMER Malcolm

partner and chairman of Board of Management BERWIN LEIGHTON Adelaide House, London Bridge, London EC4R 9HA.

Career: articled Leighton & Co (later Berwin Leighton) (1970-1972); admitted (1972); assistant solicitor (1972-1975); became partner Berwin Leighton (1975); chairman Finance Committee; chairman of Board of Management (May 1990).

Activities: lectured widely (particularly on property banking issues).

Biography: lives London; born 21.03.1948; married to Yvonne with 1 son and 1 daughter. Educated at Haberdashers' Aske's School, Elstree; Downing College Cambridge (1969 BA hons) (MA hons).

Leisure: family; opera.

BRYAN Howard

head of litigation and employment law and member management committee HEPWORTH & CHADWICK Cloth Hall Court, Infirmary Street, Leeds LS1 2JB.

Career: admitted (1968); assistant solicitor Hepworth & Chadwick (1968-1971); became partner (1971).

Activities: governor and clerk to the Board

of Governors Silcoates School; Liveryman of the Wheelwrights' Company; chairman Leeds Law Graduates' Association; member Leeds Law Society Committee (1978 to date); member Industrial Law Society; member British Germany Jurists' Association; frequent lecturer on employment and trades union issues; member of: Leeds Club; Royal Yachting Association; Clyde Cruising club.

Biography: lives York; born 24.04.1944; married to Jacqui with 2 children. Educated at Silcoates School (1953-1962); Leeds University (LLB).

Leisure: sailing; tennis; skiing.

BUCHANAN David

senior partner STEEDMAN RAMAGE & CO WS 6 Alva Street, Edinburgh EH2 4QQ.

Career: apprentice Fraser Stoddart & Ballingall WS and J & RA Robertson WS; admitted (1955); National Service with Royal Scots (1956-1958) (commissioned); assistant solicitor Maclay Murray & Spens (1958-1959); assistant solicitor Steedman Ramage & Co WS (1959-1960); became partner (1960).

Activities: former president Auchinleck Boswell Society; non-executive director Macdonald Martin Distilleries PLC; governor St Margaret's School, Edinburgh; chairman Book Selection Committee, Signet Library; member of: New Club, Edinburgh; Gullane Golf Club; Edinburgh Photographic Society.

Biography: lives Edinburgh; born 02.07.1933; single. Educated at Merchiston Castle School, Edinburgh; Edinburgh University (1953 MA) (1955 LLB distinction); winner of the Medal in the class of Scots law; Thow Scholarship; Writer to the Signet (1956); various contributions to the Journal of the Law Society of Scotland on rent review in commercial leases; various lectures to professional bodies on commercial leasing and rent review clauses, the text of which are in specialist libraries.

Leisure: classical music (both as concert and opera goer and as performer on piano and cello); photography; wines; foreign travel; golf; skiing; bridge; literature; authorship.

BUCHANAN Nigel

partner J & F ANDERSON WS 48 Castle Street, Edinburgh EG2 3LX.

Career: articled Maclay Murray & Spens (1957-1959) and Shepherd & Wedderburn (1959-1961); admitted (1961); became partner J & F Anderson (1961).

Activities: member Council of Society for Computers and Law; member Executive Committee and convener of Countryside Advisory Panel of National Trust for Scotland; member of: New Club; Puffins.

Biography: lives Edinburgh and Stirlingshire; born 22.07.1933; married to Caroline. Educated at Cargilfied School; Rugby School; Trinity College Oxford (1957 BA); Glasgow University (1959 LLB).

Leisure: shooting; skiing; curling.

BUCKINGHAM John

senior litigation partner SHAKESPEARES 10 Bennetts Hill, Birmingham B2 5RS.

Career: articled Dennis Fenton Cave (1962-1967); admitted (1967); assistant solicitor Harold Roberts and Lea (now Shakespeares) (1968-1969); became partner (1969).

Activities: Commissioner for Oaths (1974); member Area Legal Aid Committee; Deputy Registrar Midland and Oxford Circuit (1983 to date); council member and joint hon secretary Birmingham Law Society; member Birmingham Medico-Legal Society; vice-chairman Birmingham District CAB; member British Insurance Law Association.

Biography: lives Birmingham; born 27.07.1944. Educated at Splott Mixed Infants' School, Cardiff; Stacey Road Junior School, Cardiff; Holly Lodge Grammar School for Boys, Smethwick; College of Law Guildford (1963); College of Commerce Birmingham (1966).

Leisure: good company; food; wine; running family property company; broadcasting; pursuit of excellent beer; gardening; sailing; appreciation of music; literature; the arts; watching the sea.

BUCKLE Jennifer

partner WRIGHT HASSALL & CO 9 Clarendon Place, Leamington Spa CV32 5QP.

Career: articled Zelin & Zelin; admitted (1971); legal department Forward Trust; legal department Automotive Products PLC (1972); became partner Duggan Lea & Co (1982); became partner Wright Hassall & Co (1990).

Activities: lectured extensively on legal topics; member Warwickshire Family Practitioner Committee (1985 & 1989); chairman Medical Services Committee and Opthalmic Services Committee for Warwickshire.

Biography: lives Kenilworth; married to Allan. Educated at Preston Manor County Grammar School; College of Law; numerous articles in popular press and professional journals on employment law and intellectual property.

Leisure: hot air ballooning (own balloon).

BUCKLEY James

partner MACFARLANES 10 Norwich Street, London EC4.

Career: became partner Macfarlanes (1964).

Activities: member Garrick.

Biography: lives London W11; born 25.05.1936; married with 2 children. Educated at Eton College; Magdalen College Oxford (1959 BA).

Leisure: sailing; hill farming.

BUCKLEY Michael

partner and head of Shipping Group WALTONS & MORSE Plantation House, 31/35 Fenchurch Street, London EC3M 3NN.

Career: clerk Sun Life Assurance Society (1959-1960); conveyancing assistant Waltons & Co (1960-1962); articled (1962-1967); admitted (1967); assistant solicitor (1967-1971); became partner (1971); became managing partner Waltons & Morse (1982).

Activities: member Admiralty Sub-committee of Society of Conservative Lawyers; member Institute of Maritime Law; associate member Association of Average Adjusters; subscribing member London Maritime Arbitrators' Association; member Australian British Chamber of Commerce; member Maritime Law Association of Australia and New Zealand; member Wig & Pen Club.

Biography: lives Rayleigh and Hickling; born 20.11.1942; married to Marie with 4 children. Educated at Buckhurst Hill County High School; College of Law Lancaster Gate.

Leisure: sailing; gardening; theatre; cinema; jazz music.

BUCKLEY Thomas

partner SLAUGHTER AND MAY 35 Basinghall Street, London EC2V 5DB.

Career: articled Slaughter and May (1955); admitted; assistant solicitor; became partner (1966).

Biography: lives Newnham; born 14.01.1932; married to Valerie with 3 sons. Educated at Horris Hill, Newbury; Eton

College; Magdalen College Oxford (1955 MA); Solicitors Finals (hons); Citizen of London Solicitors Company Prize.

Leisure: yachting.

BUCKWELL Jeremy

senior partner FITZHUGH GATES 3 Pavilion Parade, Brighton, East Sussex BN2 1RY.

Career: articled Gates & Co; admitted; assistant solicitor; became partner (1961); became senior partner (1986); became senior partner Fitzhugh Gates (1988).

Activities: legal member Royal Town Planning Institute (1971) (council member 1978 to date); member Sussex Law Society Committee (former dinner secretary); former secretary National Young Solicitors; former member AIJA; former president Brighton and Hove Chamber of Commerce & Trade; member of: Dyke and West Sussex Golf Club; Itchener Sailing Club.

Biography: lives Brighton; born 12.04.1934; married to Gilda with 3 children and 4 stepchildren. Educated at Bedford; Trinity Hall Cambridge (1957 MA); LMRTPI (1971).

Leisure: golf; sailing; skiing.

BUENO Antonio

Queen's Counsel 5 Paper Buildings, Temple, London EC4Y 7HB.

Career: called to Bar (1964); pupillage with Sir Anthony Barrowclough and Sir James Miskin; present chambers (1965 to date); Assistant Recorder (1984); Recorder (1989); QC (1989).

Activities: member of: Flyfishers; East India.

Biography: lives London W8; born 28.06.1942; married to Christine with 3 daughters. Educated at Worth Preparatory School; Downside School; Salamanca University; Council of Legal Education; Blackstone Pupillage Award (1964); assistant editor 'Byles on Bills of Exchange' 24th ed (1979) and 25th ed (1983); joint editor 26th ed (1988); assistant editor 9th ed (1982) 'Paget's Law of Banking'; joint editor/banking 'Atkins Court Forms' 2nd ed (1976 issue).

Leisure: fishing.

BUIST David

senior partner WALTERS & WELCH 9 Station Road, Stone, Staffordshire ST15 8JS.

Career: articled Rowe & Maw (1961-1966); admitted (1966); assistant solicitor Brown

B

Turner Compton Carr & Co (1966); assistant solicitor Eric Whitehead & Co (1966-1968); became partner Walters and Welch (1968).

Activities: member Leek Golf Club.

Biography: lives Stafford; born 28.04.1942; married to Barbara. Educated at Repton.

Leisure: golf; music.

BULLWORTHY Roger William

head of planning and rating unit TITMUSS SAINER & WEBB 2 Serjeants' Inn, London EC4Y 1LT.

Career: planning departments in various county and district councils in the South East (10 years); land department in the South East with national house builder (2 years); Titmuss Sainer & Webb (1974).

Biography: lives Purley; born 01.06.1943; married to Anne with 2 daughters. Educated at Sutton County Grammar School; London University (cert in transport studies).

Leisure: family; railway history; local history.

BUNKER Anthony

senior associate specialising in tax litigation BERWIN LEIGHTON Adelaide House, London Bridge, London EC4R 9HA.

Career: HM Inspector of Taxes (1967-1980); became tax consultant Berwin Leighton (1980).

Activities: pensions trustee; member Policy Committee (1986-1987); member Entertainment Committee (1985-1988); member National Liberal Club.

Biography: lives Letchworth; born 03.10.1944; married to Elizabeth with 2 children. Educated at Hitchin Boys' Grammar School; King's College London (BA); author of: 'Inland Revenue Clearance'; 'Tax Case Analysis'.

Leisure: reading; walking; wine.

BUNKER David

partner BUNKER & CO 32 Keymer Road, Hassocks, West Sussex BN6 8AL.

Career: admitted (1962); became partner Bunker & Co (1962) .

Activities: member University Committee University of Sussex and chairman Careers Advisory Board; vice-president Sussex Association of Youth Clubs (former chairman Executive Committee; former member Council of National Association of Youth Clubs.

Biography: lives Hove, East Sussex; born 22.06.1934; married to Connie with 3 children. Educated Brighton Hove & Sussex Grammar School; Gonville andCaius College Cambridge (1957 MA) (1960 LLM); University of Michigan Law School (1958 Diploma in Comparative Law).

Leisure: family; camping; concerts; theatre; opera; swimming; skiing; convivial meals with friends.

BUNKER Peter

senior partner BUNKER & CO 9 The Drive, Hove, Sussex BN3 6JS.

Career: admitted (1954); assistant solicitor; became partner; became senior partner Bunker & Co.

Activities: president Sussex Law Society (1979-1980); chairman Frederick Soddy Trust; OBE (1988); founder chairman People and Churches Together; first chairman Martlet Housing Association; first chairman East Sussex Council on Alcoholism; former chairman of governors of Blatchington Mill (Comprehensive) School and of Goldstone Junior School; member National Executive United Reformed Church.

Biography: lives Hove; born 26.02.1928; married to Angela with 4 children. Educated at Brighton Hove and Sussex Grammar School; Gonville and Caius College Cambridge (1951 MA LLM); Law Society Broderip and Mellersh Prizes.

Leisure: gardening; skiing; listening to music.

BUNTING Chris

marketing and public relations manager RUSSELL JONES & WALKER Swinton House, 324 Gray's Inn Road, London WC1X 8DH.

Career: family's arable farm North Essex; administrator National Federation of Young Farmers' Clubs (1984-1986); development officer United Nations Children's Fund (1986-1988); Russell Jones & Walker (1989).

Activities: chairman National Federation of Young Farmers' Clubs Agricultural Policy Committee (1979-1982); first ever NFYFC delegate to Council of national Farmers' Union (1982-1984); co-chairman Organising Committee World Food Conference (1987-1989); UK delegate to European Council of Young Farmers (1980-1985); responsible for creation of starter tenancies for new entrants to farming contained in (1984) Agricultural Holdings Act; spokesman East Anglian Inter-City Commuters' Association; member Essex County Cricket Club.

Biography: lives Diss; born 14.02.1956; single. Educated at Bradfield College, Berkshire; Writtle Agricultural College (1978 Higher National Diploma in Agriculture).

Leisure: sport; cinema; music; literature.

BUNTING Gerald Leeson

partner GILBERT BUNTING CO Exchange Building, 66 Church Street, Hartlepool, Cleveland.

Career: commissioned in Army (1947); served in MELF, Egypt; Territorial Army (1952-1960) Captain 508 Field Sgn Re TA; admitted (1952); became partner with father Gilbert Bunting Co.

Activities: Deputy Coroner Cleveland North (1968 to date); president Hartlepool Law Society (1972); Deputy Lt for the County of Cleveland (1988); president Durham & North Yorkshire Law Society (1988-1989); Hartlepool Hospital Management Committee (1969-1974); member Hartlepool Community Health Council (1974-1982); vice-chairman Hartlepool District Health Authority (1982 to date); member Cleveland Family Practitioner Committee (1982 to date); member the Hospitals Trust for the Hartlepools; member Legal Aid Local and Area Committees (20 years); member of: Seaton Carew Golf Club; Bamburgh Castle Golf Club; Bedale Golf Club.

Biography: lives Northallerton; born 01.03.1928; married to Diana with 3 children. Educated at Uppingham School; Gibson & Weldon (1952).

Leisure: golf; shooting; gardening.

BURDER Robert

senior partnr BATCHELORS The Outer Temple, 222-225 Strand, London WC2R 1BG.

Career: articled Tamplin Joseph & Flux (1947-1954); National Service with 4th RTR in Egypt and Jordan (1948-1949); admitted (1955); assistant solicitor Ross & Son (1955-1957); assistant solicitor Batchelor Fry Coulson & Burder (1957-1960); became partner (1960); became senior partner (1986); firm became Batchelors (1987).

Activities: member West End local Board Commercial Union Assurance Company PLC; governor St Christopher's School,

Farnham; director private companies; Liveryman City of London Solicitors Company; Churchwarden Seale & Sands Parish; member of: Frensham Pond Sailing Club; Bourne Club.

Biography: lives Farnham; born 27.12.1929; married to Diana with 1 son and 1 daughter. Educated at Ashbury College, Ottawa; Tonbridge School.

Leisure: raising money for Church Urban Fund; gardening; walking; dinghy sailing.

BURDETT David

partner and member partnership management committee BROWNE JACOBSON 44 Castle Gate, Nottingham NG1 6EA.

Career: admitted (1972); assistant solicitor (1972-1973); assistant solicitor Browne Jacobson (1973-1976); became partner (1976).

Activities: member MHRT Panel; member local duty solicitor schemes; SFLA.

Biography: lives West Bridgford; born 03.09.1946; married to Gillian with 4 children. Educated at West Bridgford Grammar School; Manchester University (LLB hons).

Leisure: cricket; football; walking holidays.

BURGESS David

partner and head of company department GOULDENS 22 Tudor Street, London EC4Y 0JJ.

Career: articled Gouldens; admitted (1972); assistant solicitor (1972-1974); became partner (1974).

Activities: member of: Naval & Military; Leander; Bosham SC.

Biography: lives London; born 31.10.1944; 3 children. Educated at Beaumont College; Gonville and Caius College, Cambridge.

Leisure: rowing; shooting; sailing; reading; music; painting.

BURKE John

Queen's Council 18 St John Street, Manchester M3 4EA and 14 Gray's Inn Square, London.

Career: called to the Bar (1965); QC (1985); Recorder (1980).

Biography: lives Mobberley; born 04.08.1939; married to Margaret with 3 children. Educated at Stockport Grammar School.

Leisure: painting; drawing; skiing.

BURKE Michael

partner banking department CAMERON MARKBY HEWITT Sceptre Court, 40 Tower Hill, London EC3N 4BB.

Career: articled Carter & Bell; admitted (1958); Major Army Legal Corps (1959-1962); became partner Layton & Co (1964-1967); became partner Markbys (1967).

Activities: licensed insolvency practitioner; Dowgate Ward Clerk; deputy clerk Worshipful Company of Carmen; member of City of London Law Society Problems of Practice Committee; member City of London Corporation Livery Consultative Committee; member Insol; member AEPPC; committee member East Coast Mutual; member of: Essex Yacht Club (hon solicitor); City Livery (council member).

Biography: lives London and Leigh on Sea; born 22.06.1934; married to Margaret with 4 children. Educated at Westcliff High School; Nottingham University (1955 LLB); various articles in Business Law Review and New Law Journal.

Leisure: sailing; golf; travel; Livery Company affairs.

BURN John

senior partner BURN TURNBULL BUCHANAN 37 Frederick Street, Sunderland, Tyne & Wear SR1 1LN.

Career: articled Crutes; admitted (1962); assistant solicitor Robinsons Todd Hope & Wood (1962-1966); became partner (1966-1977); founded own practice (1977).

Activities: postal tutor Gibson & Weldon (1962-1964); part-time lecturer in law Monkwearmouth College of Further Education, Sunderland and Newcastle upon Tyne College (1963-1965); president Sunderland Law Society (1988-1989); member No 8 (Northern) Legal Aid Area Committee; member Legal Aid Board.

Biography: lives Cleadon; born 05.02.1939; married with 1 son. Educated at Redby School, Sunderland; Monkwearmouth Grammar School, Sunderland; Durham University (1957-1960 Law hons).

Leisure: cricket (Durham Senior League and Durham University); chess (represented Sunderland); family; ardent follower of Sunderland Football Club and Yorkshire County Cricket Club; travel abroad (especially USA and West Indies).

BURNELL Roger

partner and head commercial property department HOWES PERCIVAL Oxford House, Cliftonville, Northampton NN1 5PN.

Career: articled Mulready & Co (1969-1971); admitted (1971); assistant solicitor Clifford Turner (1971-1976); assistant solicitor Ray & Vials (1976-1977); partner (1977-1986); became partner Howes Percival (1986).

Biography: lives between Banbury and Stratford on Avon; born 26.02.1947. Educated at Highgate School; Bristol University (1968 LLB hons).

Leisure: farming.

BURNET George

senior partner MURRAY BEITH & MURRAY WS 39 Castle Street, Edinburgh EH2 3BH.

Activities: secretary Scottish Building Contracts Committee (1964-1987); member Joint Contracts Tribunal for the Standard Form of Building Contract (1966-1987); legal adviser to Royal Incorporation of Architects in Scotland; convener Church of Scotland General Finance Committee (1980-1983); chairman Life Association of Scotland Ltd; deputy chairman Hibernian Life Association Ltd; director number of companies; Brigadier Royal Company of Archers Queen's Bodyguard for Scotland; hon Fellow Royal Incorporation of Architects in Scotland; member New Club, Edinburgh.

Biography: lives Inveresk; born 26.12.1927; married with 3 children. Educated at Edinburgh Academy; Lincoln College Oxford (BA); Edinburgh University (LLB); numerous articles on variety of different subjects relating to the architectural profession and the building industry.

BURNETT-HALL Richard

partner and head environmental law group MCKENNA & CO Mitre House, 160 Aldersgate Street, London EC1A 4DD.

Career: Carpmaels & Ransford (1961-1968); manager patents and licensing The International Synthetic Rubber Co Ltd (1968-1917); articled McKenna & Co (1971-1974); assistant solicitor (1974); became partner (1974); also a Chartered Patent Agent and European Patent Attorney.

Activities: council member The UK Environmental Law Association; member Laws Committee The Licensing Executives' Society (Britain and Ireland); member United Oxford and Cambridge University Club.

Biography: lives London W11; born 05.08.1935; married to Judith with 3 children. Educated at Marlborough

B

College; Trinity Hall Cambridge (1959 BA) (MA); Fellow Chartered Institute of Patent Agents; numerous articles and conference papers on UK and EEC environmental issues, their impact on commercial organisations, and legal and management responses; co-author of European section of 'Global Environmental Issues and International Business' (BNA Inc); numerous articles on intellectual property licensing, freedom of movement of goods and intellectual property rights, competition law (UK and EEC) and intellectual property, patent litigation; contributor to intellectual property section of 'Practical Commercial Precedents'; author of Industrial Property section of Kluwer's 'Business Law Handbook'.

BURNLEY John

partner SIMPSON CURTIS 41 Park Square, Leeds LS1 2NS.

Career: articled Booth & Co; admitted (1949); assistant solicitor (1949-1955); became partner Simpson Curtis (1955); became senior partner (1984-1988).

Activities: General Commissioner of Income Tax; member Leeds Law Society (president 1983-1984); member Law Society's Standing Committee on Company Law (1973-1989); member Finance Committee and Development Committee of Opera North; treasurer Service to the Arts in Leeds; governor Leeds Festival; chairman Leeds branch Friends of BLESMA; member Leeds Club.

Biography: lives Leeds; born 20.11.1924; married to Yvonne with 2 sons. Educated at Worksop College; Leeds University (1947 LLB).

BURNTON Stanley

Queen's Counsel 1 Essex Court, Temple, London EC4Y 9AR.

Career: called to the Bar (1965); QC (1982).

Biography: lives London NW3; born 25.10.1942; married to Gwenyth with 3 children. Educated at Hackney Downs Grammar School; St Edmund Hall Oxford (1964 BA).

Leisure: music; theatre.

BURR Michael

senior partner PETER WILLIAMS & COMPANY 93 Walter Road, Swansea SA1 5QA.

Career: articled Hilliard & Ward (1959-1964); admitted (1964); assistant solicitor

(1964-1969); family picture framing business (1969-1972); acquired Peter Williams & Co (1972).

Activities: committee member Swansea and District Law Society (secretary 1980-1983); Assistant Recorder Wales and Chester Circuit (1983); Recorder (1988); non-Council member Law Society's Adjudication Committee (1986-1989); member Lawyers' Flying Association.

Biography: lives Swansea; born 31.08.1941; married with 5 children. Educated at Brecon County Grammar School; King Edward VI School, Chelmsford; College of Law Lancaster Gate.

Leisure: aircraft owner and pilot interested in navigation and touring by air.

BURROUGHS Philip

commercial property partner LAWRENCE GRAHAM 190 Strand, London WC2R 1JN.

Career: articled Sedgwick Turner Sworder & Wilson (1978-1980); admitted (1980); assistant solicitor Freshfields (1980-1983); assistant solicitor Lawrence Graham (1983-1985); became partner (1985).

Activities: member British Council of Shopping Centres; member City of London Solicitors' Company; member City of London Law Society; member Westminster Law Society; member Round Table.

Biography: lives Berkhamsted; born 02.10.1955; married to Katharine with 2 children. Educated at Hemel Hempstead Grammar School; Bristol University (LLB hons); College of Law Lancaster Gate; articles relating to shopping centres.

Leisure: sport; wine; gardening.

BURROW Robert

partner and head of corporate finance SJ BERWIN & CO 236 Gray's Inn Road, London WC1X 8HB.

Career: articled Clifford-Turner (1973-1975); admitted (1975); assistant solicitor (1975-1976); assistant solicitor Linklaters & Paines (1976-1977); J Rothschild & Co Ltd (1978-1982); became a managing director (1982-1985); became partner SJ Berwin & Co (1985).

Biography: lives London SW19; born 24.03.1951; married with 2 children. Educated at Woburn Hill Preparatory School, Weybridge; St George's College, Weybridge; Fitzwilliam College Cambridge (1972 MA); College of Law Lancaster Gate (1972).

BURSTOW Don

head of commercial services BURSTOWS 8 Ifield Road, Crawley, West Sussex RH11 7YY.

Career: articled Donne Mileham & Haddock; admitted; assistant solicitor Tarran Jones & Co (1972-1975); founded Burstow & Burstow with brother (1975).

Activities: company secretary Radio Mercury PLC; involvement in community affairs including local youth organisation, charitable trust for the disabled and local independent radio; member Royal Ocean Racing Club.

Biography: lives Horsham; born 18.09.1947; married with 2 children. Educated at Hove County Grammar School; Southampton University (1969 LLB); College of Law Guildford (1969-1970). ·

Leisure: sailing; golf; skiing.

BURTON Carl

partner RAWLISON AND BUTLER Griffin House, 135 High Street, Crawley, West Sussex RH10 1DQ.

Career: articled Horsham District Council (1977-1979); admitted (1979); planning solicitor (1979-1981); principal solicitor (1981); assistant secretary (legal) Dartford Borough Council; assistant solcitior Rawlison & Butler (1985-1986); became partner (1986).

Biography: lives Horsham; born 29.07.1955; married to Carol with 2 sons. Educated at Derby Grammar School; Birmingham Polytechnic (BA); Diploma in Local Government Law & Practice (Local Government Trust Fund Prize).

Leisure: cricket; football; squash; family.

BURTON Ian

senior partner BURTON COPELAND Royal London House, 196 Deansgate, Manchester M3 3NF.

Career: articled Nigel Copeland Glickman & Co; admitted; founded own practice (1975); became senior partner Burton Copeland (1982).

Activities: special interest in extending the service of experienced lawyers to those facing criminal prosecution particularly in the field of commercial fraud; the extension of Legal Aid availability; member of the International Bar Association; member of: Confrererie de la Chaine de Rotisseurs; Aston Martin Drivers' Club.

Biography: lives Hale Barns, Cheshire; born

25.03.1947; married to Sarah with 1 daughter and 1 son. Educated at Whittingeham College, Brighton.

Leisure: squash; shooting; horticulture; food; wine.

BURTON Michael

Queen's Counsel 2 Crown Office Row, Temple, London EC4.

Career: lecturer in law Balliol College Oxford (1970-1973); called to the Bar Gray's Inn (1970); QC (1984); Recorder (1989).

Activities: Labour Party candidate for Kensington Borough Council (1971); Labour Party Parliamentary candidate Stratford upon Avon (1974); Social Democrat candidate for Putney GLC election (1981).

Biography: lives London SW19; born 12.11.1946; married to Corinne with 4 daughters. Educated at Bilton Grange School; Eton College; King's Scholar; captain of the school; Balliol College Oxford (MA) Scholar; president Balliol College JCR; first president Oxford University Students' Union.

Leisure: spending time with children; amateur dramatics; singing and lyric writing; bridge; watching Wimbledon Football Club.

BUSHELL Standley

consultant EMMETT & TACON 4 Cathedral Street, Norwich NR1 1NB.

Career: articled Hatch & Hatch (1952-1955) and Emmett & Tacon (1955); admitted (1956); assistant solicitor (1956-1960); became partner (1960); became senior partner (1979); became consultant (1989).

Activities: president Norfolk & Norwich Law Society (1989-1990) (publicity and press officer 1972-1989) (committee member; founder member Norwich CAB chairman (1977-1984) (secretary) (hon solicitor 21 years); member Broads Authority; chairman Norfolk & Suffolk Yachting Association; founder member and trustee Norwich Samaritans; member of: Norfolk Broads Yacht Club; Norwich Frostbite Sailing Club; Norwich Exiles Hockey Club; East Anglia Squash Club; Aula Club.

Biography: lives Norwich; born 28.08.1925; married to Vivien with 2 sons. Educated at City of Norwich; Trinity Hall Cambridge (1946 BA) (1950 MA); Diploma of Education (1947).

Leisure: yachting (Cambridge half Blue

1947) (winner Norfolk Broads Gold Cup 1983); hockey (umpire 1953 to date) (president Norfolk Eastern Counties Grade I (1965).

BUTLER Peter

partner GWILYM HUGHES & PARTNERS 30 Grosvenor Road, Wrexham, Clwyd LL11 1BU.

Career: articled Gwilym Hughes & Partners (1976-1978); admitted (1978); assistant solicitor (1978-1980); became partner (1980).

Activities: assistant secretary and treasurer of the Law Society's Associate Members' Group (1977-1978) (chairman 1978-1979); member Law Society's Young Solicitors Group (1979-1988) (treasurer 1982-1984) (vice-chairman 1984-1985); (chairman 1985-1986); served on miscellaneous Law Society Committees including Standing Committee on Education and Training (6 years); former Parliamentary & Public Relations Officer Chester & North Wales Incorporated Law Society; member joint SCDC/Law Society Law in Education Committee; member Law Society; governor College of Law (1989 to date).

Biography: lives Wrexham; born 22.10.1952; married to Lynne with 2 children. Educated at March Grammar School; Grove Park Grammar School; University College of Wales (1974 LLB); Emmanuel College Cambridge (1976 LLB).

Leisure: reading; listening to music; spending weekends with wife and children in Anglesey.

BUTT Geoffrey

principal assistant solicitor, currently in charge of litigation, VAT appeals, EEC, legislative and advisory work for HM CUSTOMS AND EXCISE New King's Beam House, 22 Upper Ground, London SE1 9PJ.

Career: articled Pepperell Pitt & Aylett and Durrant Cooper & Hambling; admitted (1970); joined Office of the Solicitor for the Customs and Excise (1971); assistant solicitor (1982-1986); became principal assistant solicitor (1986).

Biography: lives Tunbridge Wells; born 05.05.1943; married to Lee with 3 children. Educated at Royal Masonic School, Bushey; Reading University (1965 BA).

Leisure: classical music; art; literature; family life.

BUTTERFIELD Chris

partner THOMAS MALLAM 126 High Street, Oxford OX1 4DG.

Career: career in road transport; teacher in further education; law teacher; became partner Thomas Mallam.

Activities: chairman Rent Assessment Committees and Rent Tribunals; local Law Society public relations officer; press spokesperson .

Biography: lives Thame; born 14.04.1943; married to Madeleine with 1 daughter. Educated at Undercliffe Primary School, Bradford; Bradford Grammar School; Jesus College Oxford (1965 MA); Leeds University (1969 Cert Ed); London University (1974 LLB external); various articles in Law Society's Gazette on road haulage licensing and liquor licensing; numerous contributions to road haulage technical press on legal subjects.

Leisure: DIY; swimming; driving buses for coach-operating clients.

BUTTERS Paul

senior partner PRETTYS Elm House, 25 Elm Street, Ipswich, Suffolk IP1 2AD.

Career: articled Bankes Ashton & Co (1957-1962); admitted (1962); assistant solicitor (1962-1965); became partner Prettys (1965); became senior partner (1984).

Activities: deputy coroner for South Eastern District of Suffolk (1967-1972); governor of the School of Jesus and Mary Educational Trust; member of: Ipswich Sports Club; Ipswich Golf Club.

Biography: lives Ipswich; born 01.02.1939; married to Penelope with 3 children. Educated at Radley College, Abingdon.

BUXTON James

partner BURGES SALMON Narrow Quay House, Prince Street, Bristol BS1 4AH.

Career: called to the Bar (1971); pupillage to Gilbert Rodway QC (Hong Kong) and Peter Scott QC (1971-1972); tenant of Chambers late Joseph Jackson QC (1972-1978); tenant of Chambers David Calcutt QC (1978-1982); admitted (1984); became partner Burges Salmon (1984).

Activities: lectures on the law relating to agricultural holdings at public seminars and seminars/conferences organised by professional organisations; member of: Brooks's Club.

Biography: lives Galhampton near Castle Cary; born 14.03.1948; married with 4 children. Educated at Harrow School;

C

Trinity College Cambridge (MA); contributor to: Halsbury's 'Agriculture'; Scammell & Densham's 'Law of Agricultural Holdings' (7th ed); various articles in farming periodicals.

Leisure: fishing; shooting; tennis; bicycling.

BYAM-COOK David

partner corporate services department BIRD & BIRD 2 Gray's Inn Square, London WC1R 5AF.

Career: admitted (1976); assistant solicitor (1976-1984); became partner Bird & Bird (1984).

Activities: member Hurlingham Club.

Biography: lives London SW15; born 28.07.1951; married with 2 children. Educated at Kent University (1973 BA hons).

CAIRD Richard

partner litigation department WILDE SAPTE Queensbridge House, 60 Upper Thames Street, London EC4V 3BD.

Career: articled Radcliffes & Co (1980-1982); admitted (1982); assistant solicitor Wilde Sapte (1983-1987); became partner (1987).

Biography: lives London SW12; born 20.01.1958; married with 1 daughter. Educated at Glasgow Academy; New College Oxford (1979 MA); College of Law Guildford (1979-1980).

Leisure: sport; reading; theatre.

CAIRNS Elizabeth

solicitor specialising in charity law at Knowle Hill Farm, Ulcombe, Maidstone, Kent ME17 1ES.

Career: called to the Bar (1968); charity commission (1972-1978); admitted (1977); assistant solicitor (1977-1979); assistant solicitor Jaques & Lewis (1979-1984); partner (1984-1990).

Activities: member Law Society Wills and Equity Committee; spoken occasionally at seminars and conferences on charity law and practice.

Biography: lives London SW10 and Ulcombe; born 14.09.1943; married to Andrew with 2 children. Educated at Priors Field School, Godalming; Trinity College Dublin (1966 BA hons LLB); author of 'Charities: Law and Practice' (1988).

Leisure: gardening; fishing; browsing in art galleries and antique shops.

CALDERAN John

senior litigation partner THEODORE GODDARD 150 Aldersgate Street, London EC1A 4EJ.

Career: assistant solicitor Theodore Goddard (1955-1957); became partner (1957).

Activities: immediate past president British-Italian Law Association; immediate past president London Solicitors Litigation Association; member The Law Society.

Biography: lives Aldbury nr Tring; born 27.09.1927; married to Barbara with 3 children. Educated at Ealing College; College of Law Lancaster Gate (1950); King's College London University (1952 LLB).

Leisure: riding; walking; gardening.

CALVERT Colin

company and commercial partner THOMPSON QUARRELL 35 Essex Street, London WC2R 3BE.

Career: articled Worcestershire County Council (1960-1963); admitted (1963); assistant solicitor Sharpe Pritchard & Co (1964-1966); assistant solicitor Thompson Quarrell & Megaw (1966-1968); became partner (1968); firm merged and changed name (1975).

Activities: member of: MCC; United Oxford & Cambridge University Club.

Biography: lives Kew, Surrey and Bricqueville, Normandy; born 04.10.1936; married with 2 daughters. Educated at Manchester Grammar School; Glasgow Academy; Corpus Christi College Cambridge (1960 MA LLM); Diploma of Comparative Law Luxembourg; languages: French; German; miscellaneous articles in legal and commercial journals mainly on topics relating to Europe.

Leisure: books; travel; cricket; cycling.

CALVERT John

partner SIMMONS & SIMMONS 14 Dominion Street, London EC2M 2RJ.

Career: articled Simmons & Simmons (1954-1959); admitted (1960); National Service (1960-1962); assistant solicitor Simmons & Simmons (1962-1965); became partner (1966).

Activities: member Cavalry & Guards Club.

Biography: lives Frensham; born 17.02.1936; married to Carolyn with 3 children. Educated at Epsom College.

Leisure: golf; skiing; shooting.

CALVERT Roger

partner CUFF ROBERTS NORTH KIRK 25 Castle Street, Liverpool L2 4TD.

Career: National Service Commission with King's Own Royal Regiment in Aden and Kenya (1957-1959); articled Maxwell Batley & Co (1963-1966); admitted (1966); assistant solicitor Slaughter and May (1966-1969); assistant solicitor North Kirk & Co (1969-1971); became partner (1971); merged to become Cuff Roberts North Kirk (1982).

Activities: secretary The Pool Promoters' Association; member of: The Liverpool Racquet Club; Waterloo Rugby Club; The Northern Cricket/Hockey/Squash Club (former president); Formby Golf Club; Liverpool Rotary Club.

Biography: lives Crosby; born 18.05.1938; married to Moira with 2 children. Educated at Liverpool College; Rossall School; Selwyn College Cambridge (1962 BA MA) (1963 LLB LLM).

Leisure: music; gardening; rugby; golf.

CAMERON Henry

senior partner and head of commercial department PETERKINS Burgh House, 7-9 King Street, Aberdeen AB2 3AA.

Career: office/accounts manager and finance director motor and agricultural dealership; articled C & PH Chalmers (1968); admitted; partner (1971-1978); founded Cameron Thom & Co (1978); took over Peterkin & Duncans (1979).

Activities: chairman Pentex Oil Ltd.

Biography: lives Aberdeen; born 09.12.1939; married with 2 children. Educated at Aberdeen Grammar School; Aberdeen University (BL).

Leisure: skiing; golfing.

CAMP Peter

director and principal EDUCATIONAL & PROFESSIONAL SERVICES LTD 1 The Close, Wonersh, Guildford, Surrey GU5 0PA.

Career: admitted (1974); lecturer College of Law Guildford (1974-1976 & 1977-1979); senior lecturer (1979-1985); principal lecturer (1985); assistant solicitor Crossman Block & Keith (1976-1977); head of education and ethics Clifford

Turner/Clifford Chance (1985-1987); became director and principle Educational & Professional Services Ltd (1988).

Activities: member Accounts Rules Sub-committee of the Law Society; member Law Society's Working Party on Financial Services; president West Surrey Law Society (1990-1991); regular lecturer for The Law Society; College of Law; Lowe & Gordon seminars; etc.

Biography: lives Guildford; born 13.05.1950; married to Susan with 2 children. Educated at Bexley Grammar School; Leeds University (1971 LLB); College of Law (1974); John Mackrell Prizeman; author/editor of 'The Professional Conduct of Solicitors'; author of: 'Solicitors and Financial Services - a Practitioners' Handbook'; co-author of 'Practical Partnership'; 'Individual Employment Law'; author of 'The Financial Services Act in Practice - A Solicitors Guide'.

Leisure: narrow boating; clay pigeon shooting.

CAMPBELL Alistair

partner corporate department BRODIES WS 15 Atholl Crescent, Edinburgh EH3 8HA.

Career: partner Brodies WS.

Biography: lives Edinburgh; born 14.02.1954; married to Cara with 2 children. Educated at Cargilfield School; Fettes College; University of Edinburgh (LLB hons).

CAMPBELL Andrew

partner specialising in construction and property litigation SIMMONS & SIMMONS 14 Dominion Street, London EC2M 2RJ.

Career: admitted (1975); assistant solicitor Stilgoes (1975-1976); assistant solicitor Simmons & Simmons (1976-1980); became partner (1981).

Activities: member of: The Coningsby Club; Worcester Lawn Tennis Club.

Biography: lives London; born 03.06.1950; single. Educated at Clifton College Preparatory School; Rugby School; St John's College Oxford (1972 BA hons).

Leisure: tennis; cricket; golf; skiing; fishing; travel; theatre; film; classical music (particularly opera); history (particularly military); natural history.

CAMPBELL Andrew

commercial property partner WILDE SAPTE Queensbridge House, 60 Upper Thames Street, London EC4V 3BD.

Career: articled Farrer & Co (1972-1976); admitted (1976); assistant solicitor Christopher Frere-Smith (1976-1977); assistant solicitor Wilde Sapte (1977-1982); became partner (1982).

Activities: public lectures on landlord and tenant subjects; member of: Flora and Fauna Preservation Society; Ocean Cruising Club.

Biography: lives London SW6; born 09.11.1950; married to Ann with 2 sons. Educated at Cheltenham College; College of Law Lancaster Gate; co-contributor to Butterworths Encyclopaedia of Forms and Precedents 'Business Tenancies' (5th ed Vol 22).

Leisure: sailing; skiing; Southern African wildlife; history.

CAMPBELL James H

senior partner BIRD SEMPLE FYFE IRELAND WS 249 West George Street, Glasgow G2 4RB.

Career: RAF British Commonwealth Occupation Force, Japan (1945-1948); apprentice Bird Son & Semple; admitted (1950); assistant solicitor (1950-1952); became partner (1952).

Activities: vice-president of the Law Society of Scotland member of: Royal Scottish Automobile Club; East Renfrewshire Golf Club.

Biography: lives Giffnock; born 13.11.1926; married to Iris with 3 children. Educated at Bearsden Academy; Glasgow University (1950 BL).

Leisure: music; golf; charitable activities.

CAMPBELL Russell

solicitor NATIONAL HOUSING LAW SERVICE Woolwich House, 43 George Street, Croydon CR9 1EY.

Career: articled Bindman & Partners (1980-1982); admitted (1982); solicitor Camden Law Centre (1984-1990).

Activities: member Law Society's Housing Working Party (1987 to date); member Law Society Legal Services Committee (1987-1988) and Courts & Legal Services Committee (1988 to date); member Association of London Authorities Legal Advisory Panel (1988-1989); member Law Centres Federation's Housing Policy Working Group (1984-1990); vice-chair

Threshold Advice Centre (1987-1988); freelance teaching in housing law.

Biography: lives Brighton; born 13.07.1957; married to Rosemary with 1 daughter. Educated at Cheltenham Grammar School; Balliol College Oxford (1979 BA); College of Law Chester (1978-1980); co-author: Law Centres Federation's submissions on public law and housing law to the Civil Justice Review; 'The Courts and the Housing Crisis' (1985); 'A Law Fit to Live In?' (1987); many articles and reviews on legal services, law centres and housing law in the Law Society' Gazette, The New Law Journal, Legal Action; The Guardian, Roof Magazine and the Adviser (1985-1989).

Leisure: chess; bridge; running; cycling; family.

CAMPS Graham

partner and head private client department BIRD & BIRD 2 Gray's Inn Square, London WC1R 5AF.

Career: articled in Godalming; admitted (1970); assistant solicitor (1970-1975); became partner Bird & Bird (1975).

Biography: lives Guildford; born 18.11.1945; single. Educated at The Leys School, Cambridge.

Leisure: gardening; walking; lawn tennis.

CANNINGS Colin

partner commercial property department SAUNDERS SOBELL LEIGH & DOBIN 20 Red Lion Street, Holborn, London WC1R 4AE.

Career: articled local government; admitted (1973); Royal London Insurance (1976-1989); head legal department (1981-1989); director (1986-1989); became partner Saunders Sobell Leigh & Dobin (1989).

Biography: lives London N1; born 18.08.1948; separated. Educated at Dunstable Grammar School; University Hall, Buckland (BA hons); Fellow of the Chartered Insurance Institute.

Leisure: theatre.

CAPPER Phillip

special adviser MASONS 30 Aylesbury Street, London EC1R 0ER.

Career: worked on major programming project IBM UK (1969-1970); lecturer in law Durham University (1973-1976); fellow and tutor in law Keble College Oxford (1976-1988); academic adviser in law to Hong Kong government; chairman Faculty of Law Oxford University (1984-1988); joined

C

C

Masons and became Masons Professor of Construction Law at King's College London (1988 to date).

Activities: served on committees advising government and construction industry on professional liability; member British Computer Society Committee on Individual Rights; lecturer at conferences for professions and industry.

Biography: lives Oxford; born 25.01.1952; married to Helen with 3 children. Educated at Peter Symonds School, Winchester; Durham University (1973 BA hons); Oxford University (1977 MA); Special Contribution Award for work at IBM's UK Laboratories (1969-1970); editor Construction Industry Law Letter (1983 to date); author of 'Latent Damage Act - Impact on the Professions and the Construction Industry'; co-author 'Latent Damage Law - The Expert System'; contributor of numerous articles.

Leisure: horses; equestrian competitions; computers.

CARL Michael

partner and head of Anglo-German Group FRERE CHOLMELEY 28 Lincoln's Inn Fields, London WC2A 3HH.

Career: articled Herbert Smith; admitted (1979); admitted to the Courts at Dusseldorf; assistant solicitor (1979-1981); partner Herbert Smith (1981-1987); became partner Frere Cholmeley (1987).

Biography: Educated at Universities of Freiburg; Lausanne and Berlin (1974 DR IUR (Freiburg), European Community Prize (1976); several publications on English and German banking and commercial law.

CARLILE Alexander

Queen's Counsel 1 Dr Johnson's Buildings, Temple, London EC4 and Sedan House, Stanley Place, Chester.

Career: called to the Bar Gray's Inn (1970); QC (1984); Recorder (1986).

Activities: SLD MP for Montgomery; Liberal Democrat spokesman on Trade and Industry; lay member General Medical Council; member Advisory Council on Public Records; vice-chairman Great Britain East Europe Centre; member of Council of Howard League; secretary of all party barristers' group in Parliament; member of: Reform Club; National Liberal Club.

Biography: lives Mid-Wales and London; born 12.02.1948; married to Frances Soley with 3 daughters. Educated at Epsom

College; King's College London (LLB AKC).

CARNWATH Robert

Queen's Counsel 2 Paper Buildings, Temple, London EC4.

Career: called to the Bar (1968); practice in planning and local government law (1970 to date); Junior Crown Counsel (1978-1980); Junior Counsel to Inland Revenue (1980-1985); QC (1985); Attorney General to Prince of Wales (1988); Assistant Recorder (1990).

Activities: Governing body of Royal Academy of Music; member Executive Committee of Interights; chairman of Shepherds Bush Housing Association; member Garrick.

Biography: lives London W2; born 15.03.1945; married. Educated at Pinewood School; Eton; Trinity College Cambridge (1967 MA) (1968 LLB); author of: 'Compulsory Purchase & Compensation'; DOE Report 'Enforcement of Planning Control' (1989).

Leisure: music (singing; violin); tennis; golf; squash; cinema.

CARRELL John

partner and head of tax department STEPHENSON HARWOOD One St Paul's Churchyard, London EC4M 8SH.

Career: called to the Bar (1972); tax consultancy (1972-1981); joined Stephenson Harwood and admitted (1981); became partner (1983).

Biography: lives Marlow; born 18.11.1945; married to Jean with 1 child. Educated at Leys School, Cambridge; Pembroke College Oxford (1967 hons).

CARROLL Stuart

senior litigation partner and head of litigation NABARRO NATHANSON 50 Stratton Street, London W1X 5FL.

Career: senior litigation partner Nabarro Nathanson.

Biography: lives London; born 24.07.1951. Educated at London University (LLB hons).

CARRON Buron

senior litigation partner TOWNSENDS 42 Cricklade Street, Swindon, Wilts SN1 3HD.

Career: admitted (1965); assistant solicitor Townsends; became partner .

Activities: former member, chairman and

secretary Glos & Wilts Young Members' Group (national representative); member Glos & Wilts Law Society; former vice-chairman Wiltshire County Council (former chairman Finance Committee); member of Action for Victims of Medical Negligence; founder member Headway Group, Swindon; member Swindon Rotary Club.

Biography: lives nr Swindon; born 18.03.1942; married with 5 children. Educated at The Gables, Swindon; The College, Swindon.

Leisure: gardening; walking; music.

CARRUTHERS Andrew

partner insurance and commercial litigation ROWE & MAW 20 Black Friars Lane, London EC4V 6HD.

Career: articled Milners Curry & Gaskell (1973-1975); admitted (1975); assistant solicitor Lovell White & King (1975-1977); assistant solicitor Bond Pearce (1977-1980); assistant solicitor Linklaters & Paines (1980-1983); assistant solicitor Rowe & Maw (1983-1985); became partner (1985).

Activities: former committee member London Solicitors Litigation Association; member UIA; member International Litigation Practitioners' Forum.

Biography: lives Winchester; born 29.11.1949; married to Patricia with 2 children. Educated at Harrow County Boys' School (1961-1968); Pembroke College Oxford (1972 MA); College of Law (1972-1973).

Leisure: singing; learning to play piano (at 40!); swimming; gardening; reading.

CARTER Jane Barham

director of studies PENNINGTONS Clement House, 99 Aldwych, London WC2B 4LJ.

Career: journalist including fashion editor The Ambassador; senior beauty writer Woman and freelance for BBC Radio (1966-1972); articled Penningtons (1972-1975); admitted (1975); assistant solicitor (1975-1976); associate (1976-1978 & 1982-1984); became director of studies (1989); taught law in the VIth form Charterhouse.

Activities: Freeman by gift of The Worshipful Company of Clockmakers (1987); Freeman of The City of London (1990); trustee various public and private trusts; member Royal Over-Seas League.

Biography: lives Godalming; born 15.07.1944; married to Clive. Educated at Bishop's Strachan School, Toronto; Queenswood; Herts & Essex High School;

Girton College Cambridge (1969 MA).

Leisure: theatre; classical music; piano; tennis; Airedales and Rolls Royces.

CARTER Roger

senior litigation partner HILL BAILEY 20 Red Lion Street, London WC1R 4AE and in Bromley, Reading and West Wickham.

Career: articled Herbert & Gowers (1963-1968); admitted (1968); became partner (1968-1971); assistant solicitor Watts Vallance & Vallance (1971-1973); became partner (1973-1984); became partner Hill Bailey (1985); consultant to Saunders Sobell Leigh and Dobin (1989).

Biography: lives Sevenoaks; born 08.12.1943; married to Cherrilyn with 2 sons. Educated at East Grinstead County Grammar School (1955-1962); College of Law; frequently asked to comment for newspapers and periodicals upon matters relating to matrimonial disputes, legislation, etc.

Leisure: travelling; reading; walking; photography; tennis; motoring.

CARTER-RUCK Peter F

senior partner PETER CARTER-RUCK AND PARTNERS Essex House, Essex Street, Strand, London WC2R 3AH.

Career: admitted (1937); Captain Instructor in Gunnery Royal Artillery (1939-1944); senior partner Oswald Hickson Collier & Co (1944-1981); founded Peter Carter-Ruck and Partners (1981).

Activities: specialist member of the Council of the Law Society (1971-1984); member Council of Justice (English section of the International Commission of Jurists); former president City of Westminster Law Society; former president the Media Society; governor St Edward's School, Oxford (1950-1978); former chairman and founder governor Shiplake College, Henley; member Livery City of London Solicitors' Co; underwriting member of Lloyd's; chairman Law Society's Law Reform Committee (1980-1983); chairman Media Committee International Bar Association (1983-1985); former commodore Law Society Yacht Club; member of: Carlton; Garrick; Press; Royal Yacht Squadron; Lloyd's Yacht Club; Royal Ocean Racing; Ocean Cruising (former commodore).

Biography: lives London and Bishop's Stortford; born 26.02.1914; married to Pamela Ann with 2 children (1 deceased).

Educated at St Edward's School, Oxford; author of: 'Libel and Slander' (1953) (3rd ed 1985); 'The Cyclist and the Law' with Ian Mackrill (1953); 'Copyright: Modern Law and Practice' with Edmund Skone James (1965); writes and lectures on the law of defamation, the media.

Leisure: sailing; wood-turning; filming.

CARUTH David

group legal adviser SCHRODERS PLC and director J HENRY SCHRODER WAGG & CO LTD.

Career: articled in Dorset; admitted (1956); admitted Kenya (1958); assistant solicitor Linklaters & Paines (1960-1966); became partner (1966); member Management Committee (1977-1983); partner in charge Commercial Group (1979-1983); admitted legal consultant New York Bar (1983); in charge New York office (1983-1986); retired (1990).

Activities: member Lowtonian Society (1973 to date); DTI investigator (1988-1989); non-executive director of Matthew Hall & Co Ltd (1979-1983) and Bradbury Wilkinson & Co Ltd (1972-1983); member National Appeal Committee of Cancer Research Campaign (1987 to date); member British Sporting Art Trust; governor of Wallingford School (1977-1981) and St Mary's School, Calne (1978-1983); member Boodles.

Biography: lives London SW7; born 31.07.1931; married to Ann with 3 children by first marriage. Educated at Wellington College; Southampton University Law School.

Leisure: swimming; racing; shooting.

CARVER Robin

managing partner MILLS & REEVE Francis House, 112 Hills Road, Cambridge CB2 1PH.

Career: called to the Bar (1956); articled Clifford Turner & Co; admitted (1960); assistant solicitor (1960-1964); partner (1964-1970); became partner Mills & Reeve (1970).

Biography: lives Cambridge; born 17.01.1932; married to Rose with 3 children. Educated at Eton; Trinity College Cambridge (MA).

Leisure: farming; shooting.

CASTLE Andrew

senior partner CASTLE SANDERSON Russell House, St Paul's Street, Leeds LS1 2JG.

Career: articled City of Bradford Metropolitan Council (1974-1977); admitted (1977); company secretary and managerial positions Transport Development Group PLC (1977-1981); managing director group subsidiary of Atlas Express Ltd (1981-1983); founded own practice (1983).

Biography: lives Batley; born 02.01.1952; married to Julie with 1 daughter and 1 son. Educated at Batley Grammar School; King's College London (LLB hons).

Leisure: sport; participating in or watching the activities undertaken by his children.

CASTLE Leslie

senior partner GOTELEE & GOLDSMITH 35 & 37 Elm Street, Ipswich IP1 2AY.

Career: articled Roberts Son & Hinchliffe (1952); National Service with the army (1958); commissioned as 2nd Lt Royal Army Service Corps (1959); served in Singapore (1959-1960); admitted (1961); assistant solicitor Gotelee & Goldsmith (1963); became partner (1965); became senior partner (1987).

Activities: chairman Town ward branch Ipswich Conservative Association; active Conservative.

Biography: lives Ipswich; born 25.08.1933; married to Belinda with 5 children. Educated at St Andrew's Infants and Junior Schools; Rastrick Grammar School; Leeds University (1955 LLB hons); College of Law Guildford (1961).

Leisure: enjoys cricket and most sport; reading; music (Mozart); opera; gardening; being with family.

CATES Armel

partner CLIFFORD CHANCE Royex House, Aldermanbury Square, London EC2V 7LD.

Career: articled Coopers & Lybrand (6 months); articled Theodore Goddard and Vinters; admitted; assistant solicitor Coward Chance (1969-1972); assistant solicitor Clifford Turner (1972-1975); became partner (1975).

Activities: trustee Charterhouse-in-Southwark; editorial adviser International Financial Law Review.

Biography: lives Saffron Walden; born 03.05.1943; married to Sue with 3 children. Educated at Charterhouse; Southampton University (1965 LLB); Travers Smith Scholarship; various articles in Euromoney publications on matters relating to

C

international finance; contributed part of chapter in Shea & Shea's Banking Law on Swaps; chapter on Sovereign immunity in Euromoney book.

Leisure: golf; tennis; photography; grasscutting.

CATTRALL Peter

assistant general counsel ESSO EXPLORATION AND PRODUCTION UK LIMITED Esso House, Victoria Street, London SW1E 5JW.

Career: schoolmaster Holmewood House (1969-1972); articled Baileys Shaw & Gillett (1972-1974); admitted (1974); assistant solicitor Knocker and Foskett (1974-1977); assistant legal adviser Esso Petroleum Co Ltd (1977-1980 & 1982-1984); counsel Esso Europe Inc (1980-1982); senior assistant legal adviser Esso Exploration and Production UK Ltd (1984); became assistant general counsel (1988).

Activities: member UK Offshore Operators' Association (UKOOA) Legal Committee; member Exploration and Production Forum (E & P Forum) Legal and Insurance Committee; member International Bar Association; member Law Society; member UK Offshore Lawyers' Group; member of: United Oxford and Cambridge University Club; MCC; Rye Golf Club; Vincents; Jesters Club; I Zingari; Free Foresters; Band of Brothers.

Biography: lives Beckenham; born 08.01.1947; married to Amanda with 2 children. Educated at Cliftonville Preparatory School; The King's School, Canterbury; Trinity College Oxford (1968 jurisprudence hons); petroleum law seminar Churchill College Cambridge (1978); Oxford University Business Summer School (1980); Windsor management seminar (1983).

Leisure: cricket; squash (Kent County Squash Player (1970-1979); golf; occasionally tennis; walking; swimming; cinema; theatre; music; current affairs.

CHADWICK Julian

private client partner PENNINGTONS INCORPORATING GAMLENS Clement House, 99 Aldwych, London WC2B 4LJ.

Career: articled Gamlens (1980-1982); admitted (1982); assistant solicitor (1982-1983); associate (1983-1985); partner (1985-1989); became partner Penningtons (1990).

Activities: communicant member of the Church of England; member Oxford and Cambridge Club.

Biography: lives Beaconsfield; born 03.01.1957; single. Educated at Royal Grammar School, High Wycombe; Christ Church Oxford (1978 MA); open exhibitioner.

Leisure: part-time farmer; master of hounds.

CHALFEN Stuart P

the solicitor and head of legal and secretarial departments BAT INDUSTRIES PLC Windsor House, 50 Victoria Street, London SW1H 0NL.

Career: articled Bristows Cooke & Carpmael; admitted (1967); assistant solicitor Smiths Industries Ltd (1967-1969); assistant solicitor Rank Xerox Ltd (1970-1973); legal manager (1976-1977); general counsel and director (1983-1987); staff counsel Xerox Corp, USA (1974-1975); senior counsel (1981-1982); admitted New York Bar (1982); associate general counsel (1987); vice-president secretary and general counsel Xerox of Canada Inc, Canada (1977-1980); became The Solicitor BAT Industries PLC (1988).

Activities: member American Corporate Counsel Association; associate member Canadian Bar Association; member Law Society Commerce & Industry Group; council member University College London; chairman UCLi Ltd.

Biography: lives London NW3; born 14.07.1940; married to Frances with 3 children. Educated at Haberdashers' Aske's School, Hampstead; University College London (BSC hons); DSIR Research Scholar (LLB hons); several articles on law department management.

Leisure: walking; music; photography; tennis.

CHALTON Simon

partner DIBB LUPTON BROOMHEAD & PRIOR Beech House, High Kilburn, York YO6 4AJ.

Career: National Service with Royal Artillery; articled Dibb Lupton & Co (1953-1958); admitted (1958); became partner (1963).

Activities: former secretary Leeds Law Students' Society; former secretary and president Leeds Law Society; founder member National Young Solicitors Group; former member Law Society's Revenue Law Committee (chairman Income Tax Sub-committee); former member Law Society's Law Office Management and Technology Committee; former member

Council of the Society for Computers and Law; member British Computer Society's Intellectual Property Committee; former committee vice-chair within computer division of American Bar Association's Economics of Law Practice Section; former officer Section on General Practice International Bar Association; director Northern Europe International Bar Association's Section on Business Law Committee on International Computer and Technology Law; chairman Section on General Practice Committee on Professional Development and Technology; UK member CELIM; co-founder Law Data Systems Limited (former chairman); member working party established by Society for Computers and Law to make recommendations in connection with the development of computer-assisted legal information retrieval systems in the UK (1979); member Appeal Committee of the Disciplinary Committee of the Institute of Chartered Accountants in England and Wales; associate of the Institute of Arbitrators; director of: Intellectual Property International Limited; Jordan Group Limited; Yorkshire Post Newspapers Limited; several other UK and overseas directorships; gives papers and presentations at number of international conferences and seminars in overseas countries; life member National Trust; member Leeds Club.

Biography: lives North Yorkshire; born 07.06.1932; married to Linda with 1 son and 2 daughters. Educated at Stowe School; primary draftsman of 'A National Law Library - The Way Ahead' (1979); author of: 'Computers and Word Processors in a Solicitor's Office' (4th ed 1988); 'Encyclopaedia of Data Protection' with Shelagh Gaskill (1988); numerous articles on information technology, the use of technology in law offices, data protection, intellectual property and related topics.

Leisure: music; literature; walking; gardening; countryside.

CHAMBERLAIN Kevin John

deputy legal adviser FOREIGN AND COMMONWEALTH OFFICE London SW1A 2AH.

Career: called to the Bar Inner Temple (1965); assistant legal adviser Foreign Office (1965-1979); Legal counsellor (1979-1990); appointed Deputy Legal Adviser (1990).

Activities: member UK delegation to many bilateral and multilateral intergovernmental negotiations including ICAO Legal Committee and Diplomatic conferences on air law at the Hague, Montreal and Rome (1970-1972); member Preparatory Committee on Law of the Sea (1971-1973); member Legal Sub-committee of UN Outer Space Committee (1979-1982 and 1988-1990); legal adviser British Military Government, Berlin (1974-1976); legal adviser British Embassy, Bonn (1976-1977); counsellor (Legal Adviser) Office of the United Kingdom Permanent Representative to the European Communities, Brussels (1983-1987).

Biography: lives Kingswood; born 31.01.1942; married to Pia with 1 daughter. Educated at Wimbledon College; King's College London (1963 LLB hons); author of 'Collective Suspension of Air Services with States which Harbour Hijackers' (1983).

Leisure: opera; tennis; riding; skiing.

CHAMBERS Nicholas

Queen's Counsel 1 Brick Court, Temple, London EC4Y 9BY.

Career: called to the Bar (1966); QC (1985); Recorder (1987).

Activities: member of: Garrick; Lansdowne.

Biography: born 25.02.1944; married to Sarah with 3 children. Educated at King's School, Worcester; Hertford College Oxford (1965 BA MA).

Leisure: sketching.

CHANDLER Christopher

partner CAPSTICK-DALE & PARTNERS 8 Holgate Court, Western Road, Romford, Essex RM1 3JS.

Career: articled Raggett Wakefield & Co (1963-1968); admitted (1968); assistant solicitor (1968-1970); became partner Capstick-Dale (1971).

Activities: occasionally sits as Deputy Registrar in County Courts and District Registries; member Council of The Law Society; member Law Society Courts and Legal Services Committee and Civil Litigation Committee; former chairman Young Solicitors Group; former president Mid-Essex Law Society; member of: Royal Ocean Racing Club; Royal Burnham Yacht Club; Little Ship Club; Wig & Pen Club.

Biography: lives Brentwood; born 06.02.1944; married with 2 children. Educated at St Bonaventure's School, London; College of Law.

Leisure: coastal and offshore cruising.

CHAPMAN Colin

partner RALPH C YABLON TEMPLE-MILNES & CARR 13 Henry Street, Keighley, West Yorkshire BD21 3DT.

Career: articled at Ilkeston (1957-1960); admitted (1960); assistant solicitor (1960-1964); became partner (1964-1972); sole practitioner (1972); senior partner Wright Atkinson & Pearson (1972-1990).

Activities: president Keighley & Craven Law Society (1985-1986); member Committee (1977 to date); hon solicitor to Keighley Amateur Operatic and Dramatic Society; ex-member and former chairman Haworth & District Round Table (area treasurer 2 years); former committee member Bingley Cricket Club; member of: Haworth & District 40 Club and 41 Club; Bradford & Bingley Sports Club Ltd (member House Committee); Bingley Harriers.

Biography: lives Bingley; born 07.12.1936; married to Carolyn with 2 children. Educated at Skegness Grammar School; Nottingham University (1957 LLB).

Leisure: jogging (completed London marathon 1988); squash; walking; watching cricket and soccer; theatre.

CHAPMAN Frank

barrister 6 Fountain Court, Steelhouse Lane, Birmingham 4.

Career: Recorder; 6 Fountain Court (1969).

Activities: deputy chairman Agricultural Tribunal; member Bar Council.

Biography: lives Worcestershire; born 28.05.1946; married with 1 son and 1 daughter. Educated at Newton-le-Willows Grammar School; University College London (LLB).

Leisure: travel; mountaineering; angling; practising Anglican.

CHAPMAN Norman

partner litigation department FRERE CHOLMELEY 28 Lincoln's Inn Fields, London WC2A 3HH.

Career: admitted (1980); assistant solicitor (1980-1986); became partner Frere Cholmeley (1986).

Biography: born 11.01.1956. Educated at Leeds University (LLB hons).

CHAPMAN Tim

partner ELLIOTT & COMPANY Centurion House, Deansgate, Manchester M3 3WT.

Career: articled Fentons Stansfield & Elliott

(1967-1968) and Elliott & Buckley (1968-1972); admitted (1972); became partner (1972).

Activities: member St James's Club, Manchester.

Biography: lives Lymm; born 21.05.1949; married to Lynda with 2 children. Educated at Heronwater, North Wales (1957-1962); Rugby School (1962-1966); Liverpool College of Commerce.

CHARITY David

partner HOLMAN FENWICK & WILLAN Marlow House, Lloyds Avenue, London EC3.

Career: articled Holman Fenwick & Willan (1964-1966); admitted (1966); assistant solicitor (1966-1971); became partner (1971).

Activities: member Alpine Club.

Biography: lives London E1 and East Sussex; born 06.04.1941; divorced with 4 children. Educated at William Hume Grammar School; Kingswood School, Bath; London School of Economics (1964 LLB).

Leisure: mountaineering; chess; opera.

CHARMAN Michael

consultant, former senior partner FREER BOUSKELL 10 New Street, Leicester LE1 5ND.

Career: articled Owston & Co (1938); admitted (1945); Leicestershire Regt TA (1939-1945); assistant solicitor Freer Bouskell (1945-1948); became partner (1948), retired 1990 and became consultant.

Activities: HM Coroner for City of Leicester and S Leics (1969 to 1990); appointed assistant deputy coroner; hon Lay Canon Leicester Cathedral (1969 to date); hon solicitor to the Samaritans (1975-1988) (ex-director Samaritans of Leicester); hon solicitor to Boys' Clubs of Leicestershire (1946 to date); chairman Glebe Committee Diocese of Leicester; chairman Royal Leicestershire Society for the Blind (committee member 1948 to date); chairman Leicestershire Rutland & Wychief Society for the Blind; member of: Leicestershire Golf Club; The Leicestershire Book Society; The Leicestershire; the Far & Near.

Biography: lives Leicester; born 28.05.1920; married to Joy with 1 son and 1 daughter. Educated at St Paul's School; author of 'Confidentiality' for the Samaritans.

Leisure: golf; books; bridge.

C

CHATE Ian

group legal adviser OCEAN GROUP PLC, 47 Russell Square, London WC1B 4JP.

Career: admitted (1970); assistant solicitor Stephen Jaques & Stephen, Sydney, Australia (1970-1972); assistant solicitor Linklaters & Paines (1972-1975); head of law department Gulf Oil (Great Britain) Ltd (1975-1977); legal adviser Gulf Oil Company - Eastern Hemisphere (1977-1984); vice-president and general counsel Texas Eastern North Sea Inc (1984-1989); became group legal adviser Ocean Group plc (1989).

Activities: member of: The Law Society; International Bar Association; American Corporate Counsel Association; Institute of Petroleum; United Kingdom Environmental Law Association; member RAC.

Biography: lives Richmond; born 12.05.1945; married to Anne with 2 children. Educated at Walton Lodge Prep School, Clevedon (1956-1959); Reed's School, Cobham (1959-1962); The English School, The Hague (1962-1964); Bristol University (1967 LLB hons); College of Law Guildford (1968); Sydney University (1971).

Leisure: collecting signed first editions; theatre; swimming.

CHATFIELD John

consultant HART READE & CO 104 South Street, Eastbourne, East Sussex BN21 4LW.

Career: admitted (1951); assistant solicitor Shrewsbury Corporation (1952-1954); assistant solicitor and prosecuting solicitor Reading County Borough (1954-1956); partner Hart Reade & Co (1956-1976); senior partner (1976-1989); became consultant (1989).

Activities: CC Deputy Registrar (1965-1978); president Eastbourne Law Society (1972-1973); chairman Sussex Police Authority (1982-1985); chairman Official Side Police Negotiating Board for UK (1982-1985); vice-chairman Association of County Councils (1986-1989) (chairman Police Committee 1982-1985); CBE (1982); Deputy Lt for East Sussex (1986); chairman Association of County Councils (1989 to date); chairman UK Local Authority International Bureau (1989 to date); chairman Consultative Council of Regional and Local Authorities in Europe (1990 to date).

Biography: lives London SW3 and Eastbourne; born 28.10.1929; married. Educated at Southdown College,

Eastbourne; Roborough School, Eastbourne; Lawrence Sheriff School, Rugby; Lewes Grammar School; College of Law Lancaster Gate.

Leisure: music; theatre.

CHAVASSE Patrick

senior partner commercial property department WANSBROUGHS WILLEY HARGRAVE 103/104 Temple Street, Bristol.

Career: National Service with Royal Artillery (1954-1956); articled Slaughter and May (1959-1962); admitted (1962); assistant solicitor (1962-1964); assistant solicitor Wansbroughs (1964-1967); became partner (1967).

Activities: hon legal adviser to Bristol Chamber of Commerce Industry and Shipping (1980 to date); member of: Lions Club of Portishead; Clevedon Golf Club; Progressive Businesses Club.

Biography: lives Portishead; born 06.08.1935; married to Ann with 3 children. Educated at Winchester House School, Brackley (1944-1949); Bedford School (1949-1954); Clare College Cambridge (1959 BA MA).

Leisure: jogging; golf; bridge; motoring; foreign travel.

CHEAL Jonathan

agricultural partner THRINGS & LONG Midland Bridge Road, Bath BA1 2HQ.

Career: articled in London, Brighton and Chichester; admitted (1976); Chinese practice and international trust company in Hong Kong (1976-1982); legal adviser to the Country Landowners' Association (1982-1987); assistant solicitor Thrings & Long (1987-1989); became partner (1989).

Activities: member Wig & Pen Club.

Biography: lives Beckington; born 30.06.1950; married to Miriam with 1 daughter. Educated at Great Walstead School, Lindfield; St Lawrence College, Ramsgate; College of Law Guildford and Chester; regular contributor to Country Life and Country Landowner.

Leisure: amateur theatre; cricket (some live BBC commentary); writing (two best-selling books); music; architecture; politics.

CHEESEMAN Guy

secretary P & O CONTAINERS LTD Beagle House, Braham Street, London E1 8EP.

Career: articled Linklaters & Paines; admitted (1974); assistant solicitor Richards

Butler (1974-1975); assistant legal adviser Overseas Containers Ltd (1975-1980); legal adviser (1980-1986); became company secretary/legal adviser P & O Containers Ltd (1986).

Biography: lives London SE3; born 22.03.1947; married with 2 children. Educated at St Edward's School, Oxford (1960-1965); Keble College Oxford (1969 BA).

Leisure: photography; architecture; history.

CHEETHAM John

senior partner KNIGHT & SONS 31 Ironmarket, Newcastle-under-Lyme, Staffordshire ST5 1RL.

Career: commissioned RAF (1956-1958); articled Knight & Sons (1961-1964); admitted (1964); assistant solicitor (1964-1965); became partner (1965); became senior partner (1987).

Activities: member Law Society Area Committee; chairman North Staffordshire Articled Clerks Monitoring Committee; member Newcastle-under-Lyme School Appeals Committee; governor Betley C of E (C) School; founder chairman Stoke-on-Trent Wedgwood Round Table; founder member Newcastle-under-Lyme Blackfriars Rotary.

Biography: lives Newcastle-under-Lyme; born 01.02.1938; married to Susan with 2 children. Educated at Newcastle-under-Lyme School; St John's College Cambridge; North Staffs Law Society F Livingstone Dickson Prize.

Leisure: sport; walking; gardening; amateur dramatics.

CHILD Graham

partner SLAUGHTER AND MAY 35 Basinghall Street, London EC2V 5DB.

Career: tutorial assistant University of East Africa Law Faculty (1964-1966); articled Slaughter and May (1966-1968); admitted (1968); assistant solicitor (1969-1974); became partner (1975); Stagiaire Legal Service, Commission of the European Communities (1968-1969).

Activities: member joint Bar and Law Society working party on competition law; member of: Hurlingham Club; Highgate Golf Club.

Biography: lives London W11; born 24.06.1943; single. Educated at Bedford School; Worcester College Oxford (1964 BA MA); co-author of 'Common Market Law of Competition' (3rd ed 1987).

Leisure: golf; outdoor pursuits.

CHRISTIE Penelope

partner BIRD & BIRD 2 Gray's Inn Square, London WC1R 5AF.

Career: admitted (1977); assistant solicitor Payne Hicks Beach & Co (1977-1980); assistant solicitor Bird & Bird (1980-1983); became partner (1983).

Biography: lives London; born 23.09.1951; married. Educated at Brighton and Hove High School; Girton College Cambridge (1973).

CHRISTIE Stuart

partner ALSOP WILKINSON 701 India Buildings, Water Street, Liverpool L2 0NH.

Career: articled Alsop Stevens & Co (1954); admitted; assistant solicitor; became partner (1963).

Activities: member Legal Advice Centre Toynbee Hall (1963-1965); Notary Public; Commissioner for Oaths; hon treasurer Liverpool Philharmonic Choir; senior trustee Patronage of St Matthew and St James, Mossley Hill, Liverpool; Sidesman St Mary The Virgin, Grassendale; clerk to the managers of Bishop Martin CE School, Liverpool (1965-1988); member of: Athenaeum, Liverpool (hon secretary 1988-1989); Artists' Club, Liverpool.

Biography: lives Liverpool; born 26.11.1934; married to Elizabeth with 2 children. Educated at Liverpool Institute High School; Liverpool University.

CHRISTIE William

barrister and head of Chambers 13 Old Square, Lincoln's Inn, London WC2A 3UA.

Career: Lt Coldstream Guards (1941-1943); FO South American Dept (1944-1946); 3rd secretary British Embassy Buenos Aires (1946-1948); called to the Bar Lincoln's Inn (1952); Bencher (1989); member Falkland Islands Bar; Northern Ireland Bar.

Activities: member Council Inland Waterways Association (1950-1952) (hon life member 1968); member Chelsea Metropolitan Borough Council (1956-1965); (chairman of Committees of Council); hon sec UK Falkland Islands Committee (1968-1976); chairman Falkland Islands Research and Development Association Ltd (The Falkland Islands Office) (1976-1983); chairman South Atlantic Fisheries Committee (1977-1982); member Court of Worshipful Company of Clockmakers (1968) (Master 1979); president British Horological Institute (1979); president National Clock and Watchmakers' Benevolent Society (1979); FBHI; member

Flyfishers Club.

Biography: lives London SW1 and NW Sussex; born 18.08.1922; married with 2 sons and 2 daughters. Educated at St Peter's School, Seaford; Marlborough College; RMC Sandhurst (1941); Scott Polar Research Institute Cambridge (1948-1950); FBHI; author of: 'The Antartic Problem: An Historical and Political Study' (1950); 'Portrait of Trent' in Collection 'Portraits of Rivers' (1953); contributor to legal and specialist publications.

Leisure: forestry; country life.

CHRYSTIE Kenneth

senior corporate partner MCCLURE NAISMITH ANDERSON & GARDINER 292 St Vincent Street, Glasgow G2 5TQ.

Career: articled McClure Naismith Anderson & Gardiner; admitted; assistant solicitor; became partner (1971).

Activities: member Mustill Committee (DTI); member Law Society of Scotland's working party on damages; member joint working party on intellectual property law; member of the Scottish Advisory Committee on Arbitration; chairman Fraser Foundation and Emily Fraser Trust; member of: Glasgow Golf Club; Carrbridge Golf Club; Western Lawn Tennis & Squash Club; Western Baths.

Biography: lives Glasgow and Boat of Garten; born 24.11.1946; married with 3 children. Educated at Eastwood Senior Secondary; Duncamrig Senior Secondary; Glasgow University (1968 LLB hons) Phd Faulds Fellowship and Rotary Fellowship Virginia University (1971); McCormick Prize; contributor to International Handbook on Contracts of Employment and Encylcopaedia of Scots Law.

Leisure: golf; tennis; squash; curling.

CHUBB Joseph

partner DAVIS POLK & WARDWELL 1 Frederick's Place, London EC2R 8AB

Career: admitted New York (1966); second circuit Court of Appeals (1974); southern district New York (1976); associate Professor Mississippi University School of Law (1966-1967); minority counsel to Committee on the Standing Rules of US Senate (1967); assistant solicitor Davis Polk & Wardwell (1968-1974); became partner (1974); London office (1978-1979 & 1984 to date); Paris office (1979-1981).

Activities: member American Bar Association; member New York State Bar Association; member Association of the

Bar the City of New York (member Committee on Banking 1976-1978); member International Bar Association; member of Knickerbocker Club; Yale Club of NYC; Automobile Club de France.

Biography: born 23.10. 1940; Yale (1962 BA) (1966 LLB).

CHURCH David

partner WOLLASTONS 35-37 Moulsham Street, Chelmsford, Essex CM2 0HY and Rue du Taciturne 44, Brussels 1040.

Career: volunteer work in Cyprus; articled Gotelee & Goldsmith (1972-1974); admitted (1974); assistant solicitor Bawtree & Sons (1974-1977); became partner (1977-1984); became partner Ellison & Co (1984); developed Brussels office (1986-1988); became partner Wollastons (1988).

Activities: member Royal Rasante Hockey Club, Brussels.

Biography: lives Colchester and Brussels; born 20.03.1950; divorced with 3 children. Educated at Felsted; University College London (1971 LLB); College of Law Lancaster Gate.

Leisure: children; hockey.

CHURCH Eric

senior partner COLE & COLE St George's Mansions, George Street, Oxford.

Career: admitted (1955); assistant solicitor (1955-1959); became partner Cole & Cole (1959); became senior partner (1987).

Activities: member of: Clarendon Club; Frewen Club; Chipping Norton Golf Club.

Biography: lives near Burford; born 02.10.1929; married with 3 children. Educated at Magdalen College School Oxford.

Leisure: walking; shooting; fishing.

CHURCHOUSE Michael

senior partner DAYNES HILL & PERKS 3 Princes Street, Norwich NR3 1BD.

Career: articled Hill & Perks (1952-1955); admitted (1955); assistant solicitor (1955-1959); partner (1959-1981); senior partner (1981-1987); became senior partner Daynes Hill & Perks (1987).

Activities: part-time chairman SSAT; Deputy Registrar; member Council of Law Society (1983 to date) (chairman Legal Aid Committee 1987-1989); member of: Army & Navy Club.

Biography: lives Norwich; born 26.01.1929; married to Marion with 2 children.

C

Educated at Oakham School, Rutland; Keble College Oxford (1952 BA) (1956 MA).

CLAPHAM John

senior partner BISCHOFF & CO PO Box 613, Epworth House, 25 City Road, London EC1Y 1BY.

Career: articled Bischoff & Co (1956-1959); admitted (1959); assistant solicitor (1959-1962); became partner (1962).

Activities: treasurer Lowtonian Society; member Oriental Club.

Biography: lives Great Bromley; born 18.04.1935; married to Anne with 3 daughters. Educated at Epsom College; Trinity College Oxford (1956 BA MA).

CLARK James

partner BRODIES WS 15 Atholl Crescent, Edinburgh EH3 8HA.

Career: articled Brodies WS; admitted; became partner (1972).

Activities: director of Tenement Investments Ltd and Heritable Investors Trust; secretary Edinburgh Sheltered Housing Charitable Society; past council member Law Society of Scotland (1981-1984) (member Guarantee Fund, Professional Practice, Post Qualifying Legal Education, Insurance and Revenue Committees); member Society of Writers to Her Majesty's Signet; member of: Bruntsfield Links Golfing Society; Crail Golfing Society; Scottish Ski Club.

Biography: lives Edinburgh; born 14.07.1946; married to Tessa with 3 children. Educated at the Edinburgh Academy; Edinburgh University (1968 LLB); occasional articles for business magazines.

Leisure: hill walking; fishing; skiing; golf; squash; bridge.

CLARK John

senior tax partner NORTON ROSE Kempson House, PO Box 570, Camomile Street, London EC3A 7AN.

Career: articled Norton Rose Botterell & Roche (1968-1971); admitted (1971); assistant solicitor trust department (1971-1973); assistant solicitor tax department (1973-1978); became partner tax department (1978); senior tax partner (1987).

Activities: assistant clerk to the St Pancras General Commissioners (1974-1979); co-opted member Technical Committee of the Institute of Taxation (1980); (full member 1981); council member the Institute of Taxation (1981); member of Confederation Fiscale Europeene (CFE) Committee the Institute of Taxation (1983); member of administrative board CFE (1983); member of fiscal committee CFE (1983-1985); vice-chairman technical committee the Institute of Taxation (1984-1986) (chairman 1986-1988); lectures on various taxation subjects.

Biography: lives Woking; born 13.01.1947; married to Marion with 3 children. Educated at St Helen's College; Surbiton County Grammar School; St Catherine's College Oxford (1968 BA); (1971 MA); Associateship Final Examination the Institute of Taxation (1974); awarded the Spofforth Prize; Fellowship Thesis the Institute of Taxation (1980) joint winner 1980 Thesis Prize; written articles in British Tax Review; New Law Journal; Leasing Digest; co-author Ring and Clark on 'Tax Warranties and Indemnities'.

Leisure: photography; listening to and playing music (classical guitar and other instruments); fell walking; foreign languages; 'dabbling' in all kinds of other interests.

CLARK Peter

partner and head of matrimonial department EDWIN COE 2 Stone Buildings, Lincoln's Inn, London WC2A 3TH.

Career: articled Booth & Co (1972-1974); admitted (1974); assistant solicitor Withers (1974-1980); became partner Edwin Coe (1980).

Activities: member Solicitors Family Law Association Conciliation Sub-committee and Pensions Ad hoc Sub-committee.

Biography: lives London; born 19.12.1947; married to Therese with 2 children. Educated at Bradford Grammar School; Sheffield University (1970 LLB); secretary of Students' Union (1970-1971); College of Law Guildford (1971-1972); co-author of 'Practical Matrimonial Precedents' (1988); 'The Lawyer's Factbook - Family Law Section' (1985).

Leisure: cricket.

CLARK Tim

partner SLAUGHTER AND MAY 35 Basinghall Street, London EC2V 5DB.

Career: admitted (1976); assistant solicitor (1976-1983); became partner Slaughter and May (1983).

Activities: member of: Euston Club; Malaprops Club.

Biography: lives London SW18; born 09.01.1951; married to Caroline with 2 children. Educated at Sherborne School; Cambridge (1972 BA) (MA).

Leisure: sport; music; history.

CLARKE Anthony

Queen's Counsel 2 Essex Court, Temple London EC4Y 9AP.

Career: called to the Bar (1965); QC (1979); Recorder.

Activities: Wreck Commissioner; Lloyd's arbitrator; ICC arbitrator; member des Chambre Arbitrator Maritime de Paris; member Gibraltar Bar; called (on occasion) to Hong Kong and Singapore Bars.

Biography: lives Horsmonden; born 13.05.1943; married to Rosemary with 3 children. Educated at Oakham School; King's College Cambridge (1961-1964).

Leisure: tennis; golf; skiing; travel.

CLARKE Charles

senior partner OSBORNE CLARKE 30 Queen Charlotte Street, Bristol BS99 7QQ.

Career: Welsh Guards (1944-1948); admitted (1951); partner Clarke Gwynn & Press (1952-1970); became partner Osborne Clarke (1970).

Activities: Notary Public (1953); member and chairman various NHS Boards and Authorities (1952-1986); chairman various small local companies; Master Society of Merchant Venturers (1967); chairman Bristol Municipal Charities (1977-1988); CBE (1987); member of: Army & Navy Club; Clifton Club, Bristol.

Biography: lives Flax Bourton; born 03.08.1926; married to Stella with 5 children. Educated at Radley; member of the Council of Bristol University (1969-1986) (hon DLitt).

CLARKE Christopher

Queen's Counsel 1 Brick Court, Temple, London EC4.

Career: QC (1984); Recorder.

Activities: chairman Committee of Inquiry of States of Guernsey re Barnet Christie Finance Ltd; member International Practice Committee; councillor International Bar Association; attorney of the Turks and Caicos Islands; member of: Brooks's; Hurlingham.

Biography: lives London SW4; born 14.03.1947; married to Caroline with 3

C

children. Educated at Marlborough College; Gonville and Caius College Cambridge (1968 MA); Harmsworth Law Scholar; JJ Powell and Lloyd Stott Prizeman.

CLARKE Christopher

partner DENTON HALL BURGIN & WARRENS Five Chancery Lane, Clifford's Inn, London EC4A 1BU.

Career: admitted (1974); admitted Hong Kong (1975); assistant solicitor Denton Hall Burgin & Warrens Hong Kong (1978); became partner (1978); became joint managing partner Hong Kong (1978-1984); London office (1984); member firm's Business Development Committee (1985-1986) (chairman 1986-1988); member firm's Policy and Finance Committee (1986-1990).

Activities: member Oriental Club.

Biography: lives London SW3; born 21.03.1950; divorced. Educated at Fettes College.

Leisure: travel; restaurants.

CLARKE David

Queen's Counsel 5 Essex Court, Temple, London EC4Y 9AH.

Career: in practice (Northern Circuit) (1965 to date); QC (1983); Recorder (1981).

Activities: hon treasurer Northern Circuit.

Biography: lives Birkenhead; born 16.07.1942; married to Alison with 3 children. Educated at Winchester College; Magdalene College Cambridge (1964 BA) (1968 MA).

Leisure: sailing; canal boating; swimming.

CLARKE John

senior partner CLARKE & SON Manor House, Winchester Road, Basingstoke, Hants RG21 1UG.

Career: became senior partner Clarke & Son (1957).

Activities: Coroner for Basingstoke, Andover, Whitchurch and Hampshire (1962-1989); president The Coroners' Society of England & Wales (1985); president Hampshire Incorporated Law Society (1976); Captain (rtd) RNR; member of: Naval Club; Island Sailing Club, Cowes.

Biography: lives Whitchurch; born 20.08.1923; married to Joan with 4 children. Educated at Harcourt School, Weyhill; St Edward's School, Oxford (1937-1941); St Edmund Hall Oxford (1948-1951).

CLARKE Robert

senior partner WOOD NASH KIMBER 6 Raymond Buildings, Gray's Inn. London WC1R 5DA.

Career: RNR Midshipman (1953); Sub Lt (1954) Lt (1955); admitted Herbert Smith (1961); Cabinet Goddard, Paris (1962-1963); assistant solicitor Theodore Goddard (1964-1965); became partner Wood Nash (now Wood Nash Kimber) (1966).

Activities: chairman Fieldsports Associations of the EEC (UK) (1980-1985); chairman International Council for Hunting and Conservation of Game (UK) (1985-1990); vice-president, Fellow and hon solicitor to Game Conservancy Trust; trustee Conservation Trusts; member of: Turf Club; Oxford & Cambridge Universities Club.

Biography: lives Abinger Manor, Surrey and Cheyne Mews, Chelsea SW3; born 09.05.1934; married to Cherry nee Waudby of Molo, Kenya with 3 children. Educated at Westminster; Ecole des Roches, France; Christ Church Oxford (1958 MA hons); former editor Droit et Affaires (UK); articles on English law for EEC publications.

Leisure: offshore cruising; hunting; shooting; conservation; tennis; fencing; skiing; travel.

CLAY Malcolm

partner and head of commercial and conveyancing RAMSBOTTOM & CO 25-29 Victoria Street, Blackburn, Lancs BB1 6DN.

Career: admitted; partner Horne Graham & Clay; partner Rushton Ibbotson & Clay; partner Ramsbottom & Co.

Activities: secretary Association of Circus Proprietors; member Blackburn Enterprise Trust Ltd; member Blackburn Rotary Club.

Biography: lives Blackburn; born 03.11.1945; married to Nora with 3 sons. Educated at Heath Grammar School, Halifax.

Leisure: circus historian.

CLAYDEN Paul

deputy secretary NATIONAL ASSOCIATION OF LOCAL COUNCILS 108 Great Russell Street, London WC1B 3LD.

Career: admitted (1969); assistant solicitor (1969-1970); National Association of Parish Councils (1970-1973); Building Societies Association (1973-1976); secretary Open Spaces Society (1976-1984); became deputy secretary National Association of Local Councils (1984).

Activities: hon sec Henley Society.

Biography: lives Henley-on-Thames; born 05.11.1941; married to Lyn with 3 sons. Educated at Ampleforth College; Jesus College Oxford (1963 BA); co-author of 'Rights of Way: A Guide to Law & Practice' (1983); author of 'Our Common Land: The Law & History of Commons and Village Greens' (1985).

Leisure: walking; bell ringing.

CLAYTON Graham

senior solicitor NATIONAL UNION OF TEACHERS Hamilton House, Mabledon Place, London WC1H 9BD.

Career: articled Richards Butler & Co (1972-1974); admitted (1974); assistant solicitor (1974-1976); solicitor National Union of Teachers (1976-1988); became senior solicitor (1988).

Activities: frequent lecturer to practising teachers on the law of education and to student prospective teachers and others involved in education; regular annual programme of student lectures.

Biography: lives Denham; born 01.01.1949; married to Penelope with 2 sons. Educated at Dudley Grammar School; Jesus College Cambridge (BA); College of Law; regular contributor to journals within education service in England and Wales; author of chapters in number of publications on education law and education management including 'Headteachers' Legal Guide' and 'Education and the Law'.

Leisure: politics; skiing.

CLEARY Alan

solicitor and chief executive HINCKLEY AND BOSWORTH BOROUGH COUNCIL, Argents Mead, Hinckley, Leicestershire LE10 1BZ.

Career: management trainee Beecham Group; articled in private practice; admitted (1965); Deputy Town Clerk Carlisle City Council; head of legal division Leeds City Council; director legal department Building Employers' Confederation; became Solicitor and Chief Executive Hinckley and Bosworth Borough Council.

Activities: former hon legal adviser Leeds Polytechnic; former hon legal adviser Yorkshire Microsystems Centre; member National Schedule of Rates Management Board; secretary to Cavendish Conference Centre Companies and Insurance Brokers; secretary Technical Education Trust; former

C

Employers' Permanent Representative National Joint Consultative Committee for Building; former Board member Quality Assurance Board, British Constructional Steelwork Association; expert witness and adviser; expert in field of UK public authority practice and protocol (MBAE); member Council of the British Academy of Experts; member of: The British Butterfly Conservation Society; Budokwai Judo Club; various luncheon clubs; Catenian Association.

Biography: lives London W1 and Milton Keynes; born 13.05.1939; married to Dinah with 1 child. Educated at St Piran's School, Maidenhead; The John Ruskin School; Bristol University (1960 LLB); Birmingham University (1975 Advanced Management Program); Leeds University (1985-1986 Computer Program for mature students); New College Oxford (1964-1965 Theft Act research team); (1966 ATII); member Operational Research Society (1978); Fellow of the Land Institute (1985); EEC Certificate (OU); Rixham Prizeman; various privately published advisory papers; contributions to many committees concerned with reform of the law and public finance; Parliamentary draftsmanship and expert evidence.

Leisure: cycling; swimming; general exercise program; microscopy; British wildflowers and insects.

CLEGG J Lawrence

consultant INGLEDEW BROWN BENNISON & GARRETT International House, 26 Creechurch Lane, London EC3A 5AL.

Career: articled Bracewell & Leaver ; admitted (1971); assistant solicitor Wilde Sapte (1971-1973); partner (1973-1990); resident in Singapore (1981-1985); became consultant Ingledew Brown Bennison & Garrett (1990).

Activities: former member Management Committee of The Singapore Town Club; former secretary Keel Boat Squadron, Singapore; former member Singapore's 1985 Admiral's Cup Team on Highland Fling; former chairman Wimbledon Squash and Badminton Club; member of: Walton Heath Golf Club; St Enodoc Golf Club; Royal Ocean Racing Club; Little Ship Club.

Biography: lives Cobham; born 05.07.1943; married to Rosamund with 2 daughters. Educated at King's College School, Wimbledon; College of Law (1971); solicitor and barrister of the Supreme Court of Victoria.

Leisure: golf; sailing.

CLEMENTS Paul

managing partner WITHERS CROSSMAN BLOCK 199 Strand, London WC2R 1DR.

Career: articled Bird & Bird (1975-1977); admitted (1977); assistant solicitor (1977-1979); assistant solicitor Crossman Block & Keith (1979-1980); became salaried partner (1981-1984); became equity partner (1985); equity partner and head of litigation Withers Crossman Block (1988-1989).

Activities: member City of Westminster Law Society; member London Solicitors Litigation Association; lectures on the rules of discovery and the law of nuisance as concerns neighbours; member Medico-Legal Society; member British Insurance Law Association; member RAC.

Biography: lives New Malden; born 29.04.1953; married to Pamela with 1 son. Educated at Haberdashers' Aske's School, Elstree (1962-1971); Birmingham University (1974 LLB hons); College of Law (1975).

Leisure: amateur drama; opera; classical music; sport (former player member Wasps Rugby Club); especially golf.

CLIFTON John

senior partner GODWIN BREMRIDGE & CLIFTON 12 St Thomas Street, Winchester SO23 9HF.

Career: National Service with Royal Signals (1948-1949); TA (1949-1960) (Captain and Major); articled in Winchester (1950-1955); admitted (1955); assistant solicitor (1955-1957); became partner Godwin Bremridge & Clifton (1957); became senior partner (1974).

Activities: chairman Southern Area Legal Aid Committee (1971); president Hampshire Law Society (1987) (member main committee); clerk of trustees of Hospital of St Cross & Almshouse of Noble Poverty; member Ski Club of Great Britain.

Biography: lives Upham; born 21.09.1930; married to Buffy with 3 children. Educated at Charterhouse.

Leisure: sailing; skiing; mountain walking; ornithology.

CLITHEROE John

partner KINGSLEY NAPLEY 107-115 Long Acre, London WC2E 9PT.

Career: articled in local government; admitted (1959); assistant solicitor in Portsmouth, Kingston and Bromley; assistant solicitor Kingsley Napley (1962-1965); became partner (1965).

Activities: solicitor to Council for Professions Supplementary to Medicine; past member Law Society Standing Committee on Criminal Law; chairman editorial board of Journal of Criminal Law; lectures on case preparation and consultation for Diploma of Medical Jurisprudence, on science and the law and on development of fraud; member Law Society Advocacy Training Team; member London Criminal Courts (Solicitors) Association; member British Academy of Forensic Sciences (former council member); member Exchange Team of Russian and UK Lawyers (Moscow 1989); member of RAC; St James.

Biography: lives Kingston upon Thames; born 03.06.1935; married to Irene with 4 children. Educated at Royal Grammar School, Guildford; London (LLB hons); author of 'Guide to Conducting a Criminal Defence'.

Leisure: reading; opera; theatre; sport (spectator); travel.

CLOGG Christopher

partner THEODORE GODDARD 16 St Martin's le Grand, London EC1A 4EJ.

Career: articled Theodore Goddard; admitted (1964); assistant solicitor (1964-1969); became partner (1969).

Activities: member of: Whites; The City University Club; Royal St George's Golf Club; Berkshire Golf Club.

Biography: lives London; born 26.03.1936; married to Clodagh with 3 children. Educated at Aysgarth Preparatory School; Eton; Christ Church Oxford (1961 MA); contributor to Tolley's Company Law.

Leisure: theatre; reading ancient history and literature; golf; wine.

CLOSE David

senior partner TRUMAN CLOSE KENDALL & APPLEBY 30 Avenue Road, Grantham, Lincs NG31 6TH.

Career: articled Langleys (1955-1960); (served RNVR during articles); admitted (1960); assistant solicitor Kenneth FM Bush & Co (1960-1963); assistant solicitor Peake Snow & Jeudwine (1963-1966); became partner (1966-1986); founded Close Kendall & Co (1986); merged with Truman & Appleby (1988).

Activities: president Lincolnshire Law Society (1987-1988); chairman Lincolnshire Young Solicitors Group (1965); member No 10 (East Midlands) Legal Aid Area Committee; member Council of

Lincolnshire Law Society; founder member Grantham Victim Support scheme; member Rotary Club of Grantham.

Biography: lives Welbourn; born 17.07.1938; married to Stephanie with 2 children. Educated at Christ's Hospital, nr Horsham.

Leisure: squash; golf; tennis; gardening; music; food; wine; rugby (spectator now!).

CLOSE John

partner CLARKE WILLMOTT & CLARKE 6 Hammet Street, Taunton, Somerset TA1 1RG.

Career: National Service in Italy; articled Christopher Rowe; admitted (1952); assistant solicitor Clarke Willmott & Clarke (1952); partner (1956); joint senior partner (1987); became senior partner (1989).

Activities: joint founder Abbeyfield movement in Taunton (1960s) (chairman 1966-1988); legal chairman for Somerset Rent Tribunal (1960s to date); first president Taunton Junior Chamber of Commerce (1960s); president Somerset Law Society (1989-1990); hon solicitor to St Margaret's Somerset Hospice.

Biography: lives Taunton; born 06.03.1927; married to Margaret with 2 sons and 1 daughter. Educated at Colstons, Bristol; Bristol University (1948 LLB).

COATES Ross

partner BIRKETT WESTHORP & LONG 5 Bridge Street, Framlingham, Woodbridge, Suffolk IP13 9DR.

Career: articled Woodham Smith and Birketts (1977-1979); admitted (1979); assistant solicitor RJ Hughes & Co (1979-1982); assistant solicitor Birketts (1982-1984); became partner (1984).

Activities: awarded MBE in Queen's Birthday Honours List (1989) for political and public services; part-time law lecturer Suffolk College of Further and Higher Education (1977-1990); member Examining Board for the Institute of Legal Executives (1986 to date); member Conservative Party (1972 to date); chairman Ipswich Conservative Association (1984-1988); chairman Eastern Area Political Committee (1986-1989); youth leader and formed Ipswich Youth Advice Centre (1977-1986); member Ipswich Junior Chamber; National Debating Champion (1987) (member national winning team 1988); member of Suffolk Family Health Services Authority (1990); selected as prospective Parliamentary candidate for Blackburn (1990).

Biography: lives Martlesham; born 28.03.1954; married with 1 daughter. Educated at Woodbridge School; Chelmer Institute of Further and Higher Education, Chelmsford; London University (1975 external LLB hons); author of 'Conveyancing' Longman Practice Notes Series (1988) and 'Real Property and Conveyancing' (Blackstone Press 1990) .

Leisure: cruiser sailing; gardening.

COATON John

senior partner commercial property DAVIES ARNOLD COOPER 12 Bridewell Place, London EC4V 6AD.

Career: Wright & Webb; assistant solicitor Davies Arnold Cooper (1978-1980); became partner (1980).

Biography: lives Harpenden; born 15.12.1951; married to Catherine with 3 children. Educated at Spalding Grammar School; Nottingham University (LLB hons); College of Law.

Leisure: theatre; hockey; tennis; golf.

COCKBURN David

partner PATTINSON & BREWER 30 Great James Street, London WC1N 3HA.

Career: articled Pattinson & Brewer (1972-1975); admitted (1975); assistant solicitor; (1975-1977); became partner (1977).

Activities: treasurer Institute of Employment Rights; former chairman Industrial Law Society; member Employment Law Committee of the Law Society; member Editorial Committee of the Industrial Law Journal; editorial adviser to Encyclopaedia of Labour Relations Law; member Legal Aid Area Committee; member Board of Management, Centre for Legal Studies, Hatfield Polytechnic; frequent speaker at conferences on employment law.

Biography: lives Harpenden; born 30.11.1948; married with 3 children. Educated at The King's School, Pontefract; London School of Economics (1970 LLB) (1972 MScEcon); contributor to 'Labour Law in Britain'.

Leisure: family life; tennis; sailing; theatre; cinema; talking politics.

COCKSEDGE Christopher

senior partner BIRKETT WESTHORP & LONG 20-32 Museum Street, Ipswich IP1 1HZ.

Career: National Service with RAF; Barclays Bank; articled Birketts; admitted

(1968); became partner (1968).

Activities: member Suffolk and N Essex Law Societies (1968 to date) (president 1986-1987); director Christchurch Park Hospital (1987 to date); governor School of Jesus and Mary, Ipswich (chairman 1980 to date); treasurer Suffolk Golf Union (1988 to date); member of: Ipswich, Woodbridge & Aldeburgh Golf Clubs (captain Ipswich 1976); Ipswich & Suffolk Club (chairman (1980, 1984 & 1990); Ipswich Sports Club (life member); Haven Ports Yacht Club (1986 to date).

Biography: lives Playford; born 06.08.1934; married to Rosemary with 2 daughters. Educated at Felixstowe Grammar School; College of Law.

Leisure: golf; private pilot's licence; sailing.

COCKSEDGE Simon

partner SHARMAN & TRETHEWY 1 Harpur Street, Bedford MK40 1PF.

Career: articled Markbys; admitted (1974); assistant solicitor Sharman & Trethewy (1974-1977); became partner (1977).

Activities: member North Bedfordshire Borough Council (1973 to date); Conservative group leader (1977-1988); chairman Finance & General Purposes Committee (10 years); chairman Policy Committee (3 years); member Child Care Panel; member MCC.

Biography: lives Bedford; born 06.01.1950; married to Rosaria with 2 children. Educated at Headford School, Kells, Co Meath; Bedford School; University College of Wales, Aberystwyth (1971 LLB hons).

Leisure: motor sport; gardening; politics.

CODRINGTON Eddie

partner in pensions and employment department SLAUGHTER AND MAY 35 Basinghall Street, London EC2V 5DB.

Career: articled Slaughter and May (1974-1976); admitted (1976); assistant solicitor Slaughter and May (1976-1985); became partner (1985).

Biography: lives London W5; born 12.04.1951; married to Philomena with 6 children. Educated at St Benedict's School, Ealing; Birmingham University (LLB).

Leisure: family.

CODRINGTON Ian

senior partner SHARMAN & TRETHEWY 1 Harpur Street, Bedford MK40 1PF.

Career: articled Sharman & Trethewy

C

C

(1956-1959); admitted (1962); assistant solicitor (1962-1967); became partner (1967).

Activities: secretary/clerk Abbeyfield Bedford Society Ltd; solicitor Bedford School Boarding House Trust and Bedford School Trust; chairman Neighbourhood Revitalisation Services, Bedford; secretary Bedford Regatta; Bedford Head of River; rowing umpire; member of: Leander Club (committee member); Bedford Rowing Club (deputy president and committee member); Old Bedfordian Club; Rotary Club of Bedford Castle (former president).

Biography: lives Bedford; born 11.02.1938; divorced with 3 children. Educated at Bedford School; Fitzwilliam College Cambridge (1959 MA).

COHEN David

corporate and employee tax partner PAISNER & CO Bouverie House, 154 Fleet Street, London EC4A 2DQ.

Career: articled Titmuss Sainer & Webb (1978-1980); admitted (1980); assistant solicitor (1980-1986); became partner Paisner & Co (1986).

Activities: frequent lecturer at legal and tax seminars; trustee Aleh Charitable Foundation; Fellow of the Institute of Taxation.

Biography: lives London NW3; born 15.12.1955; married to Barbara with 2 children. Educated at Howardian High School, Cardiff; Jesus College Oxford (1977 first class hons); won the Institute of Taxation's prize for the best fellowship thesis (1987); contributor of section on Schemes and Benefits for Employees in the Encyclopaedia of Forms and Precedents; contributor to 'Practical Tax Planning with Precedents'; co-author of 'Tax Aspects of Going Public'; author of 'Employee Participation in Flotations'; frequent contributor on legal topics to Financial Times and professional press.

COHEN Harvey

director of training STEPHENSON HARWOOD One St Paul's Churchyard, London EC4M 8SH.

Career: articled Emanual Round & Nathan (1959-1961); admitted (1962); founded own practice (1962-1969); lecturer Holborn College of Law (1962-1964); called to the Bar Lincoln's Inn (1969); pupil to RJS Thompson (1969-1970); barrister 5 and 3 New Square, Lincoln's Inn (1970-1988); lecturer in equity and trusts the Inns of Court School of Law (1971-1974); visiting

professor of law University of Western Ontario (1975-1976); lecturer in laws University College London (1964-1988); became director of training Stephenson Harwood.

Activities: member Joint Staff/Student Committee UCL (1970-1972); member Standing Sub-committee for External Students' Board of Studies in Law University of London (1984-1988); member London Legal Education Committee (1985-1987); chairman Refectory Management Committee University College London (1981-1988).

Biography: lives London N3; born 06.06.1936; married to Kathleen with 1 son and 1 daughter. Educated at Quintin Grammar School, London (1947-1953); Faculty of Laws University College London (1956 hons) (1968 PHD); Joseph Hume Scholarship in Jurisprudence (1956-1958); articles in: Current Legal Problems; The Conveyancer and Property Lawyer; New Journal Annual Charities Review; New Law Journal; The Journal of International Banking Law.

Leisure: reading; theatre; gardening; walking.

COHEN Laurence

partner specialising in intellectual property rights and litigation BRISTOWS COOKE & CARPMAEL 10 Lincoln's Inn Fields, London WC2A 3BP.

Career: articled Bristows Cooke & Carpmael (1974-1976); admitted (1976); assistant solicitor (1976-1981); became partner (1981).

Biography: lives Radlett; born 12.09.1951; married to Madelaine with 3 children. Educated at Highgate School; Emmanuel College Cambridge (1973 BA) (1977 MA) Entrance Exhibitioner; College of Law Chester (1974); author of 'World Litigation Law & Practice, England' (1986).

Leisure: squash; tennis.

COHEN Philip

partner and head of commercial litigation JEFFREY GREEN RUSSELL Apollo House, 56 New Bond Street, London W1Y 9DG.

Career: articled Bennetts & Partners; admitted (1979); assistant solicitor (1979-1981); became partner (1981-1982); became partner Jeffrey Green Russell (1982).

Activities: member of: Royal Automobile Club; Wig & Pen Club; Mosimann's Club.

Biography: lives London NW1; born 27.09.1952; married to Libby with 1

daughter. Educated at Latymer Upper School; Peterhouse Cambridge (1975); Senior Scholarship; writes and lectures on litigation tactics, copyright and employment law .

Leisure: creative writing (Bayliss Award for Drama; Orme Film Award for a screenplay; Westminster Arts Council Poetry Award); preparation and consumption of gastronomic delights; body building.

COHN Michael L

partner and head of litigation department PRITCHARD ENGLEFIELD & TOBIN 23 Great Castle Street, London W1N 8NQ.

Career: articled Menasse & Tobin (1961-1967); admitted (1967); assistant solicitor (1967-1968); salaried partner (1968-1970); became equity partner (1971).

Biography: lives London N22; born 15.12.1943; married to Susan with 4 sons. Educated at the Hall School, London; William Ellis Grammar School, London.

Leisure: reading; spending as much time as possible with family.

COLBEY Richard

barrister 1 Gray's Inn Square, Gray's Inn, London WC1R 5AA; tel: 071-405 8946.

Career: called to the Bar Inner Temple (1984); pupillage 1 Garden Court; tenant at 1 Gray's Inn Square (1989).

Biography: lives London N10; born 03.05.1960. Educated at Rickmansworth School; Exeter University (1982 LLB); Paul Methuen Scholarship Inner Temple (1984); editor 'Litigation'; author of: 'Resident Landlords & Owner Occupiers' (1987); 'Residential Tenancies' (1988, 1990); articles for The Guardian; Solicitors Journal; Legal Action; Litigation; Road Law, The Economist.

Leisure: travel; art galleries; cricket; tennis.

COLE Peter

managing partner ALEXANDER TATHAM 30 St Ann Street, Manchester M2 3DB.

Career: articled Alexander Tatham (1965-1967); admitted (1967); assistant solicitor (1967-1969); became partner (1969).

Activities: board member Eversheds.

Biography: lives Millington; born 13.08.1942; divorced with 2 children. Educated at Colyton Grammar School; University College London (1963 LLB); Tulane University, New Orleans (1964 LLM).

COLE Richard

co-partner in charge London office MAYER BROWN & PLATT 162 Queen Victoria Street, London EC4V 4BS.

Career: associate Mayer Brown & Platt, Chicago (1976-1981); associate London office (1981-1983); became partner (1983).

Biography: lives London SW13; born 21.02.1951; married to Lois. Educated at Brown University (1973 AB Magna Cum Laude); Cornell Law School (1976 JD Magna Cum Laude); Phi Beta Kappa; Order of the Coif; co-author: 'International Banking Centres' (1982); 'Commercial Paper - The Bankers Trust Case' (1986); 'The College Retirement Equities Fund No-Action Letter' (1987); 'Securities Exchange Act Arbitration' (1987); 'Multi-Currency Global Medium Term Notes' (1987); 'Preliminary Merger Talks may Require Disclosure' (1988).

Leisure: travel; food; wine.

COLEMAN Sylvia

company secretary and legal manager CBS (UNITED KINGDOM) LTD 17-19 Soho Square, London W1V 6HE.

Career: articled Stephenson Harwood (1980-1982); admitted (1982); assistant solicitor (1982-1985); commercial lawyer Gallaher Ltd (1985-1986); legal manager CBS (United Kingdom) Ltd (1986-1989); became company secretary (1989).

Activities: member The Kensington Close.

Biography: lives London SW5; born 10.12.1957; single. Educated at Harrow County Grammar School for Girls; Birmingham University (1979 LLB hons); College of Law Lancaster Gate (1979-1980).

Leisure: promotion of Ceroc dance (co-organiser of annual Ceroc charity ball).

COLES Richard

partner SHAW AND CROFT 30 St Mary Axe, London EC3A 8DE.

Career: articled Derrick Bridges & Co (1969-1971); admitted (1972); assistant solicitor (1972-1973); assistant solicitor Holman Fenwick & Willan (1973-1977); assistant solicitor Carter & Co (now Carter Faber) (1977-1978); partner (1978-1990); became partner Shaw and Croft (1990).

Activities: supporting member London Maritime Arbitrators' Association; Liveryman City of London Solicitors Company; Liveryman Carmen's Company; honorary treasurer British Motor Ship Owners' Association; officer Territorial Army; member of: Honourable Artillery Company; Aldgate Ward Club.

Biography: lives Felden; born 27.03.1947; married to Jane with 2 children. Educated at Queen Elizabeth's Grammar School, Barnet; Hull University (1968 LLB); College of Law Guildford (1971-1972); part-time research student in maritime law University College London (1974-1975); member Chartered Institute of Transport (MCIT) (1985); articles on ship registration, Merchant Shipping Acts.

COLLCUTT Michael

senior partner TOLLER HALES & COLLCUTT 55 Headlands, Kettering, Northamptonshire NN15 7EY.

Career: articled to the clerk Kent County Council (1952-1955); admitted (1955); senior assistant solicitor Northants County Council (1955-1959); became partner Toller Son and Hales (1959-1969); became senior partner Toller Hales & Collcutt (1969).

Activities: HM Coroner for East Northamptonshire (1969); HM Coroner for the County and Borough of Northampton (1974); former council member Northants Law Society; member of: Institute of Directors; Hawks Club; The Luffenham Heath Golf Club; president Kettering Golf Club (former captain).

Biography: lives Finedon; born 28.07.1928; married to Iris with 2 children. Educated at Cathedral School, Truro; Pembroke College Cambridge (1952 BA hons); Kent Law Society Prize.

Leisure: reading; golf; fishing; shooting.

COLLIER Richard

managing partner DAYNES HILL & PERKS Holland Court, The Close, Norwich NR1 4DX.

Career: articled Becke Greene & Stopps; admitted; assistant solicitor Goodger Auden; assistant solicitor Daynes Chittock & Back (now Daynes Hill & Perks) (1971-1972); became partner (1972).

Activities: convener of the Norwich Duty Solicitors Scheme; founder and first chairman Norfolk Family Conciliation Service; hon assistant curate St Peter Mancroft, Norwich; director Northampton Machinery Co Ltd (1966-1979); director Bonds (Norwich) Ltd (1979-1981); director and chairman Norwich Arts Centre Ltd (1986-1989); member of: Royal West Norfolk Golf Club; Norfolk Punt Club.

Biography: lives Norwich; born 18.04.1945; married to Sally with 2 children. Educated at Winchester House, Brackley; The King's

School Canterbury; ordained priest in the Church of England (1981).

Leisure: sailing; listening to music; conversation.

COLLINS Anthony Ralph

senior partner ANTHONY COLLINS & CO Pearl Assurance House, 4 Temple Row, Birmingham B2 5HG.

Career: articled Wragge & Co; admitted (1970); articled and admitted in Toronto, Canada (1970-1972); assistant solicitor in Birmingham (1972-1973); founded Anthony Collins & Co (1973).

Activities: clerk to the Commissioners of Income Tax.

Biography: lives Birmingham; born 23.06.1942; married to Fiona with 3 children. Educated at Bradfield College, Berkshire .

Leisure: family; friends; fly fishing.

COLLINS Brian

senior partner BP COLLINS & CO Collins House, 32-38 Station Road, Gerrards Cross, Bucks SL9 8EL.

Career: articled Taylor Willcocks & Co (1958-1963); admitted (1963); assistant solicitor Hollands & Co (1963-1965); founded own practice (1966).

Activities: managing director Staines Metal Products (Group) Ltd; trustee Wexham Gastrointestinal Trust and other charities; member of: Gerrards Cross Sports Club (president); Gerrards Cross Golf Club.

Biography: lives Gerrards Cross; born 29.04.1939; married with 3 children. Educated at John Lyon School, Harrow; College of Law Lancaster Gate.

Leisure: cricket; golf; gardening.

COLLINS David

senior conveyancing and property partner BLAKE LAPTHORN 8 Landport Terrace, Portsmouth PO1 2QW.

Career: articled Kimber Bull & Co (1957-1962); admitted (1962); assistant solicitor (1962-1964); assistant solicitor Blake Lapthorn (1964-1966); became partner (1966).

Activities: Notary Public (1976); member Council of the Notaries Society; member of: Royal Naval Club; Royal Albert Yacht club; Stewards' Enclosure Henley Royal Regatta; Molesey Boat Club; Portsmouth & Southsea Rotary Club.

Biography: lives Adsdean nr Chichester;

C

C

born 20.04.1939; married to Ann with 1 daughter and 2 sons. Educated at Kingston Grammar School; London University (1961 LLB).

Leisure: rowing; theatre; travel; gardening.

COLLINS Ivor

senior property partner FORSYTE KERMAN 79 New Cavendish Street, London W1M 8AQ.

Career: articled Forsyte Kerman (1947-1952); admitted (1952); assistant solicitor (1952-1955); became partner (1956); first chairman partnership board (1985-1988).

Activities: member RAC.

Biography: lives London W1 and nr Cirencester; born 28.10.1929; married to Bobby with 1 daughter and 1 son. Educated at Bradfield College, Berkshire; College of Law Lancaster Gate.

Leisure: bridge; theatre; travelling to Europe, USA, Far East, and Australia; swimming; walking.

COLLINS John

barrister Pearl Chambers, 22 East Parade, Leeds LS1 5BZ and 11 King's Bench Walk, Temple, London EC4.

Career: called to the Bar (1956); pupillage to Jonathan Sofer, Basil Wigoder and Stanley Snowden; Chambers of Eric Greenwood (1957); became head of Chambers (1966 to date); Deputy County Court Judge (1970-1971); Assistant Recorder (1971); Deputy Circuit Judge (1972-1979); Recorder (1980 to date).

Activities: member Legal Aid Committees (1960 to date); member NE Circuit Committee; president Leeds Jewish Representative Council (1986-1989) (hon life vice-president); member various committees.

Biography: lives Leeds; born 25.06.1931; married to Sheila with 1 child. Educated at Leeds Grammar School; Queen's College Oxford (1953 BA) (1956 MA); author of 'Summary Justice' (1963); several legal articles; representative of the Law Reports and All England Law Reports on NE Circuit (1968 to date).

COLLINS John

Queen's Counsel 10 Essex Street, Outer Temple, London WC2R 3AA.

Career: called to the Bar (1952); Queen's Counsel (1972); Recorder of the Crown Court (1972-1988); Bencher Gray's Inn (1981).

Activities: deputy chairman Cumberland Quarter Sessions (1969-1972); Judge of the Courts of Appeal, Jersey and Guernsey (1984 to date); Deputy High Court Judge; member Bar Council (1981-1984) (member Professional Standards Committee 1986 to date); chairman Management Committee Gray's Inn (1990); member of: Athenaeum; Carlton Club.

Biography: lives London SW1; born 24.01.1929; married to Daphne with 3 children. Educated at Uppingham School; Manchester University (LLB).

Leisure: oriental art; theatre; keeping fit.

COLLINS John

head of chambers Westgate Chambers, 144 High Street, Lewes, East Sussex BN7 1XT.

Career: auditor of King's Inns (1966); practising member Irish Bar (1968-1974); practising member English Bar (1975 to date).

Activities: member Bar in the Republic of Ireland and New South Wales, Australia; member St Luke's Social club, Pinner.

Biography: lives Pinner; born 23.05.1944; married to Eline Mary with 2 sons and 1 daughter. Educated at Redemptorist College, Limerick; Presentation College, Dun Laoghaire; King's Inns Dublin (1961-1966).

Leisure: family; walking the dog; swimming; travel.

COLLINS Julian

legal adviser and solicitor BRITISH COAL CORPORATION Hobart House, Grosvenor Place, London SW1X 7AE.

Career: articled National Coal Board (1965-1967); admitted (1967); assistant solicitor (1967-1973); head of industrial branch legal department (1973-1984); deputy legal adviser (1984-1988); became legal adviser British Coal Corporation (1988).

Activities: member Law Society Standards and Guidance Committee (1989).

Biography: lives London SW14; born 15.11.1942; single. Educated at Nottingham High School; Gonville and Caius College Cambridge (MA LLM).

Leisure: theatre; travel.

COLMAN Anthony

Queen's Counsel 4 Essex Court, Temple, London EC4Y 9AJ.

Career: called to the Bar Gray's Inn (1962); pupil to CS Staughton, 3 Essex Court,

Temple (1962-1963); practice at the Commercial Bar (1963); QC (1977); Recorder of the Crown Court (1985).

Activities: member Committee of Enquiry into Fidentia Lloyd's (1982); chairman Lloyd's Disciplinary Committee in respect of PCW and Minet (1984); Master of the Bench Gray's Inn (1987); deputy High Court Judge Queen's Bench Division (1987); chairman Trust Funds Committee of Bar Council (1988 to date); Treasurer and member Executive of COMBAR (1989 to date); author of The Practice and Procedure of the Commercial Court, 3rd edn (1990); substantial number of lectures on commercial litigation procedure, insurance and re-insurance laws, Lloyds and self-regulation in London, San Francisco, San Diego, New York, Singapore (1977 to date); governor British American Drama Academy.

Biography: lives Sarratt; born 27.05.1938; married to Angela with 2 daughters. Educated at Harrogate Grammar School; Trinity Hall Cambridge; Aldis Scholar; (1962 BA double first Law) (1965 MA); Fellow of Chartered Institute of Arbitrators (1977).

Leisure: tennis; cricket; gardening; collecting antiquarian books; the island of Siphnos; the River Chess.

COLSON Daniel

partner STIKEMAN ELLIOTT Cottons Centre, Cottons Lane, London SE1 2QL.

Career: assistant solicitor Stikeman Elliott (1971-1977); became partner (1977); lecturer in commercial law Concordia University and Loyola (1972-1974).

Activities: member Hong Kong Law Reform Commission (1982-1983); non-executive director various companies incl: Daily Telegraph PLC; Hollinger Inc; The Spectator (1828) Ltd; Fednav Europe Ltd.

Biography: lives London SW3; born 05.05.1947; married to Suzanne with 2 children. Educated at Loyola (1968 BA); Laval University (1971 LLL); various articles on commercial law.

COLTHORPE David

senior commercial litigation partner BIRKETT WESTHORP & LONG Essex House, 42 Crouch Street, Colchester, Essex CO3 3HH.

Career: National Service commissioned into the 5th Royal Inniskilling Dragoon Guards (1954-1956); articled Smith Morton & Long (1956-1961); admitted (1961);

assistant solicitor (1961-1963); became partner (1963).

Activities: deputy registrar South Eastern Circuit (1980); president Halstead Combined Division St John Ambulance; former chairman Halstead Round Table; former president Halstead Rotary Club; member of: Oriental Club; Gentlemen of Essex Cricket Club.

Biography: lives Sible Hedingham; born 18.10.1935; married to Elizabeth with 2 daughters. Educated at Selwyn House Preparatory School, Broadstairs; Marlborough College.

Leisure: sailing; shooting; gardening.

COLVIN Andrew

comptroller and city solicitor
THE CORPORATION OF LONDON
PO Box 270, Guildhall, London EC2P 2EJ.

Career: articled London Borough of Ealing; admitted (1975); assistant town clerk; deputy town clerk and borough solicitor Royal Borough of Kensington & Chelsea (1982-1989); became comptroller and city solicitor The Corporation of London (1989).

Biography: lives London W13; born 28.04.1947; married to Helen with 4 children.

Leisure: cycling; sailing; music.

COLYER John

Queen's Counsel 11 King's Bench Walk, Temple, London EC4.

Career: National Service (2nd Lt RA) (1953-1955); called to the Bar Middle Temple (1959); instructor (1959-1960) and assistant professor (1960-1961) University of Pennsylvania Law School, Philadelphia, USA; English Bar (1961 to date); QC (1976); Bencher Middle Temple (1983); Recorder (1985); lecturer (1970-1989) and Hon Reader (1985 to date) Inns of Court School of Law.

Activities: member Council of Legal Education (1985 to date); chairman Lawyers' Christian Fellowship (1981-1989); member of: Wig & Pen Club; Anglo-American Real Property Institute (past treasurer).

Biography: lives Kent; born 25.04.1935; married with 2 daughters. Educated at Dudley Grammar School (1943-1948); Shrewsbury (1948-1953); Worcester College Oxford (BA) (Open History Scholarship); editor vols 11 & 12 Encyclopaedia of Forms & Precedents (1966); author of 'A Modern View of the Law of Torts' (1966); editor Halsbury's Laws of England 'Landlord & Tenant'; general editor 4th ed 'Rent Acts' (1988); various articles.

Leisure: gardening (keen collector of Lithops and cacti); opera; travel.

CONDON Peter

chief executive LEGAL RESOURCES GROUP Post & Mail House, 26 Colmore Circus, Birmingham B4 6BH.

Career: articled Coopers & Lybrand (1962-1965); admitted chartered accountant (1965); audit supervisor (1965-1967); accountant Pilkington Group (1967-1969); finance director Hawker Marris Ltd (1969-1977); finance director Tricentrol Trading Ltd (1977-1983); finance director Amalgamated Foods Ltd (1983-1989); became chief executive Legal Resources Group (1989).

Activities: member of: Worcestershire County Cricket Club; St Paul's Club, Birmingham.

Biography: lives Leamington Spa; born 03.01.1941; married to Barbara with 3 children. Educated at St Philip's Grammar School, Birmingham; Jesus College Oxford (1959-1962).

Leisure: music; theatre; local historical research.

CONI Peter

Queen's Counsel 1 Gray's Inn Square, Gray's Inn, London WC1R 5AG.

Career: called to the Bar Inner Temple (1960); QC (1980); Master of the Bench Inner Temple (1986); Recorder (1985).

Activities: chairman BAAB Enquiry into Drug Abuse in British Athletics (1988); chairman Henley Royal Regatta (1978 to date); member Amateur Rowing Council (1962 to date) (member Executive Committee 1968 to date); president London Rowing Club; member of: Athenaeum; Garrick Club; Leander Club.

Biography: lives London SW1 and Henley on Thames; born 20.11.1935; single. Educated at Uppingham; St Catharine's College Cambridge (MA).

Leisure: good food; modern art; Bosnian stamps!.

CONINGSBY Thomas

Queen's Counsel and head of Chambers 3 Dr Johnson's Buildings, Temple, London EC4.

Career: called to the Bar Gray's Inn (1957); head of Chambers (1982); Recorder (1986); QC (1986).

Activities: chancellor of the dioceses of York (1977) and Peterborough (1989); vicar-general of the Province of York (1980); member Family Law Bar Association Committee (1979 to date) (secretary 1986-1988) (chairman 1988-1990); member Lord Chancellor's Matrimonial Causes Rule Committee (1985-1989); member Supreme Court Procedure Committee (1988 to date); member Bar Council (1988-1990); member General Synod of Church of England (1970 to date) (member Legal Advisory Commission 1973 to date) (member Legal Officers Fees Advisory Commission (1979 to date) (member Lichfield Commission on Divorce and Marriage (1975-1978).

Biography: lives Chipstead; born 21.04.1933; married to Elaine with 5 children. Educated at Epsom College (1945-1951); Queen's College Cambridge (1956 BA) (1959 MA).

CONLON Thomas Francis

director HENDERSON ADMINISTRATION LTD
3 Finsbury Avenue, London EC2M 2PA.

Career: called to the Bar (1970); legal adviser Manufacturers Hanover Trust Co; associate Graham & James; partner Tigert & Roberts, Washington DC; general counsel Philadelphia National (1984-1986); became director Henderson Administration Ltd (1986).

Activities: member British Bankers' Association Committee on EEC law; general counsel Democrats Abroad (1980-1984); delegate Democratic Party National Convention (1980 & 1984); member National Platform Committee of Democratic Party (USA) (1983-1984); member Broadgate Club.

Biography: lives Richmond; born 04.03.1943; single. Educated at St Johnsbury Academy; University of Denver (1966 & 1969 BA Juris Dr); London School of Economics (1973 LLM); University of London (1973 Dipl in law); AAA Hague Academy of International Law (1975 Grand Prize for International Law); author of: Insider Dealing (series of articles on the law in the US, UK and EEC) 'Financial Times' (1989-1990); 'EEC Law Fifth Company Law Directive' 24 ICLQ 348; 'Unlawful Seizure of Aircraft' Annuire de AAA vol 45/46; 'The Aircraft Mortgages Convention' in Journal of Air Law and Commerce.

Leisure: tennis; running; writing.

C

CONN Philip

senior partner PHILIP CONN & CO
Lincoln House, 1 Brazennose Street,
Manchester M2 5JF.

Career: articled to conveyancing probate
practice (1950-1956); admitted (1956);
assistant solicitor Peter Goldstone (1956-
1957); founded own practice (1957);
became Conn Goldberg & Co (now
Pannone Blackburn) (1959); founded Philip
Conn & Co (1975).

Activities: visited Republic of China with
First English Lawyers' Group (1979).

Biography: lives Manchester; born
30.03.1933; divorced with 3 sons. Educated
at Bolton School; Manchester University
(1951).

Leisure: sport (particularly rugby union);
bridge; theatre; cinema; music; opera;
visual arts; antiques; food; wine; travel.

CONNELL Michael

Queen's Counsel Queen Elizabeth
Buildings, Temple, London EC4.

Career: called to the Bar Inner Temple
(1962); Recorder of the Crown Court
(1980); QC (1981); Bencher Inner Temple
(1988) .

Activities: member Bucks Club.

Biography: lives Northamptonshire; born
06.08.1939; married to Anne with 4
children. Educated at Harrow School
(1953-1958); Brasenose College Oxford
(1961 BA).

Leisure: racing; foxhunting.

CONNICK H Ivor

senior partner THORNTON LYNNE &
LAWSON 56 Portland Place, London
W1N 4BD.

Career: RAF (1946-1948); (attached War
Crimes, Singapore (1947); articled
Thornton Lynne & Lawson (1950-1952);
admitted (1952); assistant solicitor (1952-
1953); became partner (1953).

Activities: director UDS Group PLC (1975-
1983) (latterly deputy chairman); director
Land Securities PLC (1987 to date); vice-
president British ORT; vice-chairman
Administrative Committee World ORT
Union; member of: MCC; Roehampton
Club.

Biography: lives London SW15; born
25.01.1927; married to Claire with 3
children. Educated at Ealing Grammar
School; London School of Economics &
Political Science (1950 LLB).

Leisure: cricket; golf; music.

CONSTANT Richard Michael

general counsel POLYGRAM GROUP
30 Berkeley Square, London W1X 5HA

Career: articled Jaques & Co (1976-1978);
admitted (1978); assistant solicitor (1978-
1980); Polygram Group (1980).

Activities: member United Oxford and
Cambridge University Club.

Biography: lives London SW1; born
15.04.1954; single. Educated at Sherborne;
St John's College Cambridge (1975 BA)
(1978 MA).

Leisure: private pilot.

COODE Colin

barrister and head of chambers St Ive's
Chambers, Fountain Court, Steelhouse
Lane, Birmingham B4 6DR.

Career: war service RA (1942-1947); called
to the Bar Middle Temple (1950); London
practice (1950-1956); founded St Ive's
Chambers (1965).

Activities: member Birmingham Legal Aid
Committees.

Biography: lives Fairoak, Staffs; born
05.12.1923; widower with 9 children, now
remarried. Educated at George Watson's
College, Edinburgh; Edinburgh University
(1947 MA); author of 'The Law of the
Individual' (1968).

Leisure: writing; teaching; bee-keeping;
reading; classical music; country walking.

COOK Michael

partner RICE-JONES & SMITHS 17
Southampton Place, London WC1A 2EH.

Career: partner Adam Burn & Metson;
became partner Rice-Jones & Smiths.

Activities: clerk to the Worshipful
Company of Needlemakers; Livery and
City companies and charities.

Biography: lives London, Barnet and
Bosham; born 17.03.1949; married to Jill
with 2 children. Educated at Highgate
School; College of Law.

Leisure: playing violin; sailing; walking.

COOK Richard

senior property partner BOOTH &
BLACKWELL 3 and 4 Berners Street,
London W1P 4AT.

Career: admitted (1972); became salaried
partner Booth & Blackwell (1972-1978);
became equity partner (1978).

Activities: hon solicitor Royal Tunbridge
Wells Civic Society (1977-1987) (chairman

1981 & 1982).

Biography: lives Wadhurst; born 17.04.1946;
married. Educated at Emmanuel School;
College of Law Lancaster Gate (1972).

Leisure: fell walking; trekking;
photography; music.

COOK Trevor Martin

partner BIRD & BIRD 2 Gray's Inn Square,
London WC1R 5AF.

Career: admitted (1977); assistant solicitor
(1977-1981); became partner Bird & Bird
(1981).

Activities: member Law Society; member
International Bar Association Section on
Business Law, Committee R (International
Technology and Computer Law); member
Licensing Executives' Society; member
Parliamentary Information Technology
Committee; associate member British
Computer Society; associate member
Chartered Institute of Patent Agents.

Biography: lives Woking; born 21.08.1951;
married to Janet with 2 children. Educated
at Southampton University (1973 BSc hons
chemistry); contributor to: 'Information
Technology and the Law' (1986); 'CIPA
Guide to the Patents Acts' (1990).

COOKE David

senior partner PINSENT & CO
Post & Mail House, 26 Colmore Circus,
Birmingham B4 6BH.

Career: admitted (1961); assistant solicitor
Hall Brydon & Co (1961-1964); assistant
solicitor Orr Dignam, Calcutta and King
and Partridge, Madras (1964-1967);
assistant solicitor Pinsent & Co (1967-1969);
became partner (1969); became senior
partner (1987).

Activities: director Legal Resources
Limited; secretary West Midlands
Development Agency Ltd (1989); member
Law Society Standing Committee on
Company Law (1987-1989); member
Birmingham Law Society Committee on
Company Law (1988-1990).

Biography: lives Birmingham; born
22.03.1938; 2 daughters. Educated at
Bolton School; Accrington Grammar
School; Manchester University (1958 LLB).

Leisure: classical music; fell walking.

COOKE Howard

partner FRERE CHOLMELEY 28 Lincoln's
Inn Fields, London WC2A 3HH.

Career: articled Frere Cholmeley (1973);
admitted; assistant solicitor; became

partner (1980).

Biography: lives London SE24 and N Devon; born 07.01.1952; married to Liz with 2 children. Educated at Exeter School; Queen Mary College, London (1972 LLB).

Leisure: country pursuits.

COOKE Paul

partner and head of company law unit and chairman of the marketing committee BRISTOWS COOKE & CARPMAEL 10 Lincoln's Inn Fields, London WC2A 3BP.

Career: articled Bristows Cooke & Carpmael; admitted (1972); assistant solicitor (1972-1976); became partner (1976).

Activities: director various companies.

Biography: lives London; born 18.04.1948; married to Maureen with 4 children. Educated at Winchester College; Swiss School, Lausanne; College of Law Lancaster Gate (hons); City of London Solicitors Company Prize for commercial law.

Leisure: sailing; historic racing cars.

COOKE Peter

partner responsible for employment/pensions practice THEODORE GODDARD 150 Aldersgate Street, London EC1.

Career: articled with Greater London Council; admitted (1974); assistant solicitor (1974-1978); legal adviser to Engineering Employers' Federation (1978-1983); assistant solicitor Theodore Goddard (1984-1986); became partner (1986).

Activities: member Employment Sub-committee of City of London Solicitors Company.

Biography: lives London EC2; born 13.04.1948; married to Elizabeth with 2 children. Educated at Royal Grammar School, Guildford; Southampton University (1970 BSC); College of Law Guildford and Lancaster Gate; author of 'Croners Employment Law' (1980); contributor to Croners Industrial Relations Law (1989).

Leisure: sailing; cycling; music.

COOKE Simon Henry

partner BRISTOWS COOKE & CARPMAEL 10 Lincoln's Inn Fields, London WC2A 3BP.

Career: articled Bristows Cooke & Carpmael (1954-1957); assistant solicitor

(1957-1960); became partner (1960).

Activities: chairman Critchley Ltd; chairman of governors Newport Free Grammar School, Essex; director Bausch & Lomb Limited, Trico-Folberth Ltd; Associate member Chartered Institute of Patent Agents (1960 to date); former member Patents Procedure Committee; former council member International Association for Protection of Industrial Property British Group; clerk to Clavering Parish Council (1966 to date); Fellow RSPB.

Biography: lives Clavering; born 16.04.1932; married to Gillian with 3 sons. Educated at Dragon School, Oxford; Marlborough College; Gonville and Caius College Cambridge (1954 Natural Sciences and Law) (1987 MA).

Leisure: conservation; gardening; bird watching; skiing.

COOKE Stephen

partner WITHERS 20 Essex Street, London WC2R 3AL.

Career: articled Clay Allison & Clark (1966-1971); admitted (1971); assistant solicitor Withers (1971-1973); became partner (1973).

Activities: member General Committee of the Ockenden Venture; former member Council of City of Westminster Law Society; frequent lecturer at seminars on trust law, probate, administration of estates and all associated taxation; and on business planning for estate owners.

Biography: lives Farnham; born 30.07.1946; married to Jane with 2 sons. Educated at Stamford School; Leicester College of Art and Technology; College of Law; Sidney Herbert Clay Prize; co-author of 'Inheritance Tax and Lifetime Gifts' (1987); consultant editor Trusts and Estates; contributor to Tax Cases Analysis; various articles in magazines on taxation.

Leisure: gardening; tennis.

COOPER Beryl

Queen's Counsel 2 Dr Johnson's Buildings, Temple, London EC4.

Career: called to the Bar Gray's Inn (1960); Bencher (1988); Recorder (1977 to date).

Activities: Deputy High Court Judge Family Division (1980 to date); member Criminal Injuries Compensation Board (1978 to date); (Departmental Committee on Criminal Statistics 1964-1968); member Housing Corporation (1975-1978); member review body for nursing staff, midwives, health visitors and professions allied to

medicine (1983 to date); member Council of Justice (1985 to date); member of: English Speaking Union; Royal Eastbourne Golf Club; Dulwich & Sydenham Golf Club; Caledonian Club, Edinburgh.

Biography: lives London SE21 and Eastbourne; single. Educated at Wimbledon High School; Surbiton High School; Birmingham University (1950 BCM); author of 'Fraud Trials for Justice' (1984).

Leisure: travel; reading; golf; gardening.

COOPER Edward

partner and head of trade union and employment department RUSSELL JONES & WALKER Swinton House, 324 Gray's Inn Road, London WC1X 8DH.

Career: articled Simmons & Simmons (1982-1984); admitted (1984); assistant solicitor (1984-1985); assistant solicitor Russell Jones & Walker (1985-1988); became partner (1988).

Activities: volunteer legal adviser to National Council of Civil Liberties (1982-1985); fundraiser for National Jazz Centre Project (1982-1986); member Society of Labour Lawyers; member Industrial Law Society; founder member and fixture secretary Crocodiles Cricket Club; member of: MCC; Lord's Taverners; Labour Party.

Biography: lives London SW12; born 12.06.1959; single. Educated at Winchester House, Sevenoaks; Tonbridge School; Bristol University (1980 LLB); author of section on trade unions in Encyclopaedia of Forms and Precedents (5th ed) (1988).

Leisure: jazz and improvised music (jazz critic for London magazine); tennis; films; theatre.

COOPER Robert

partner SHOOSMITH & HARRISON 8 Clarendon Street, Nottingham NG1 6HG.

Career: National Service commissioned in the Royal Corps of Signals (1954-1956); trainee and junior manager Boots Pure Drug Co (1959-1961); articled Hunt Dickins & Willatt and Linklaters & Paines (1961-1964); admitted (1964); assistant solicitor Perry Parr and Ford (1964-1967); became partner (1967-1974); merged with Rotheras; became partner Shoosmith & Harrison (1984).

Activities: chairman Placketts Holdings Ltd; member Services Club, Nottingham.

Biography: lives Nottingham; born 13.05.1936; married with 3 children. Educated at Repton; Pembroke College

C

Oxford (1959 Jurisprudence); Solicitors Finals (hons); articles for Taxation Practitioner.

Leisure: fishing; squash; tennis; gardening.

COOPER STEVENS Marie

group solicitor LADBROKE GROUP PLC Chancel House, Neasden Lane, London NW10.

Career: articled Slaughter and May (1971-1973); admitted (1973); assistant solicitor (1973-1977); consultant legal advisor to TIL (Medical) Ltd; United Biscuits PLC; Colgate-Palmolive Ltd; Radio 4; sole practitioner; became Group Solicitor Ladbroke Group plc.

Biography: lives London SW1; born 05.07.1950; married to David with 3 children. Educated at Wadhurst College; London School of Economics (1971 LLB hons); College of Law.

Leisure: opera; theatre.

CORBETT Helen

partner ROBBINS OLIVEY BURLEY & GEACH 62 Woodbridge Road, Guildford, Surrey GU1 4DX.

Career: articled Robbins Olivey Lake (1978-1980); admitted (1980); became partner (1981).

Activities: treasurer National Committee of the Law Society's Young Solicitors Group; member Law Society's Entry and Training Committee; member of: The West Surrey Society; Godalming and Haslemere Rambling Group (former secretary).

Biography: lives Guildford; single. Educated at Turmead School for Girls, Guildford; Guildford County School for Girls; Surrey University (1976 BSC); College of Law Guildford (1977-1978).

Leisure: country rambling; swimming; cinema; theatre; tennis; travel.

CORMAN Charles

partner corporate finance TITMUSS SAINER & WEBB 2 Serjeants' Inn, London EC4Y 1LT.

Career: articled Titmuss Sainer & Webb (1955-1958); admitted (1959); assistant solicitor (1960-1961); became partner (1963); associate Goldstein Judge & Gurfein, New York (1960).

Activities: governor Carmel College; treasurer Friends of Israel Cancer Association; council member Jews College, London.

Biography: lives London; born 23.10.1934; married to Ruth with 5 children. Educated at The Hall School, Hampstead; St Paul's School, Kensington; University College London (1955 LLB hons); Fullbright Scholar; University of California at Berkeley (1960 LLM) Walter Perry Johnson Fellowship.

CORNES David

senior partner WINWARD FEARON & CO 35 Bow Street, London WC2E 7AU.

Career: design and construction John Laing Construction Ltd; articled Masons; admitted (1979); assistant solicitor (1979-1982); partner Fenwick Elliott & Co (1982-1986); founding partner Winward Fearon & Co (1986).

Activities: supporter and occasional speaker for The Centre of Construction Law and Management King's College London; member Society of Construction Law; member British Insurance Law Association; regular public speaker at construction law conferences; member National Liberal Club.

Biography: lives Little Gaddesden; born 31.08.1944; married with 3 children. Educated at Rydal School; King's College London (1966 BSC AKC); MICE (1970); CEng (1970); Concrete Society Prize (1969); author of 'Design Liability in the Construction Industry'; contributor to 'Construction Contract Policy'; occasional articles on construction law for publications; monthly articles for New Builder magazine; joint author of 'Collateral Warranties - A Practical Guide for the Construction Industry'.

Leisure: walking; gardens; reading; opera.

CORNWELL Nigel R

partner specialising in construction law and litigation BRISTOWS COOKE & CARPMAEL 10 Lincoln's Inn Fields, London WC2A 3BP.

Career: articled Hedleys (1980-1982); admitted (1982); assistant solicitor (1982-1983); assistant solicitor Bristows Cooke & Carpmael (1983-1987); became partner (1987).

Activities: member Construction Law Society; Freeman City of London Solicitors' Company; member Lansdowne.

Biography: lives Henley-on-Thames; born 07.11.1954; married to Alison with 2 children. Educated at Dover College; Sir Roger Manwood's; Bristol University (1977 BA); College of Law Guildford (1979).

Leisure: listening to and performing choral works and oratorio; playing piano; squash; tennis.

CORSER David

partner and head of conveyancing and probate department CHALLINOR & ROBERTS COOKSEY 16/18 South Road, Smethwick, Warley, West Midlands B67 7BW.

Career: articled Pinsent & Co (1963-1967) and Tyndall Mirams (1967-1970); admitted (1970); assistant solicitor (1970-1971); assistant solicitor Challinor & Roberts (1971-1972); became partner (1972).

Activities: Notary Public; member International Property Lawyers' Association; member of: Smethwick Rotary Club; Birmingham Philatelic Society; Welsh Philatelic Society; Montgomery Midlands Society (chairman); Smethwick Twenty Investment Club.

Biography: lives Halesowen; born 03.04.1944; married to Luned with 1 son and 1 daughter. Educated at Repton Preparatory School; Malvern College; College of Law Guildford.

Leisure: philately; antiques; stockmarket; watercolour painting (landscapes); foreign travel; inland waterways.

COSTIN Martin Christopher

senior partner WYNNE BAXTER GODFREE Dial House, 221 High Street, Lewes, East Sussex BN7 2AE.

Career: legal training Dawe & Co; Royal Army Pay Corps in Holland and Germany (2 years); articled in Kingston on Thames (1957-1962); admitted (1962); assistant solicitor (1962-1964); assistant solicitor Wynne E Baxter & Son (1964); became partner.

Activities: trustee Lewes Old Grammar School.

Biography: lives Ringmer; born 10.01.1937; married to Jane with 2 children. Educated at Epsom College.

Leisure: family; all sports including: sailing; swimming; rugby; cricket; association football.

COTTON Diana

Queen's Counsel Devereux Chambers, Devereux Court, Temple, London WC2R 3JJ.

Career: called to the Bar (1964); Midland and Oxford circuit; part-time lecturer in law Holborn College of Law, Languages and Commerce (1963-1967); pupillage with Peter Weitzman QC and Leslie Joseph QC (1964-1965); tenant (1965); Assistant Recorder (1978); Recorder (1982); QC (1983).

Activities: member Thalidomide Panel (1973-1976); member Criminal Injuries Compensation Board; arbitrator for Motor Insurers' Bureau; member Western Club.

Biography: lives London; born 30.11.1941; married to Richard Allan with 3 children. Educated at Berkhamsted School for Girls; Lady Margaret Hall Oxford (1963 BA) (1967 MA); Exhibitioner; Council of Legal Education Bar Finals.

Leisure: family; gardening; sport; music; opera; theatre; reading; foreign travel.

COULSTON Leo

senior partner LEO COULSTON & CO 29 Billing Road, Northampton.

Career: articled late Eric Green; admitted (1957); founded own practice (1976).

Activities: group director and legal adviser to Gerald White (Northampton) Ltd and Kislingbury Hire Ltd Group of Companies; secretary and member council Northants Law Society.

Biography: lives Northampton and Cheltenham; born 27.03.1935; married with 3 children. Educated at Lydney Grammar School; Cheltenham Grammar School.

Leisure: sailing; golf; walking.

COUPER Dudley

head of property department ROWE & MAW 20 Black Friars Lane, London EC4V 6HD.

Career: articled in Farnham; admitted; assistant solicitor in Kent (1961-1964); assistant solicitor Rowe & Maw (1964-1965); became partner (1965); formerly finance partner (for 20 years).

Activities: governor Cranleigh School; member MCC.

Biography: lives Haslemere; born 09.04.1935; married to Jill with 2 daughters and 1 son plus 2 grandchildren. Educated at Cranleigh School; Keble College Oxford (hons); College of Law Guildford.

Leisure: family; gardening; golf; sport generally; swimming; walking.

COVER Michael

partner and head of intellectual property unit DAVIES ARNOLD COOPER 6/8 Bouverie Street, London EC4Y 8DD

tel: 071 936 2222 Fax 071 936 2020.

Career: called to the Bar (1973); Allied Lyons PLC (latterly deputy head of legal services) (1974-1987); admitted (1988); assistant solicitor (1988-1989); became partner Davies Arnold Cooper (1989).

Activities: member of: Royal Ocean Racing Club; Bosham Sailing Club.

Biography: lives London; born 29.11.1950. Educated at Portsmouth Grammar School; Southampton University (1972 LLB); joint author of articles in Financial Times and Trademark World (1989); papers given include British Institute of Regulatory affairs (1989) and Crisis Management and Product Tamper (1990).

Leisure: ocean racing; skiing.

COVERLEY Chris

partner HAWLEY & RODGERS 23 New Walk, Leicester LE1 6TA.

Career: articled Cuthbert Barker (1952-1957); admitted (1957); assistant solicitor Hawley & Rodgers (1957-1960); became partner (1960).

Activities: member Kirby Fields Road Fund Committee; member of: Old Humberstone Constitutional Club (president); Kirby Muxloe Golf Club; Kirby Muxloe Sports and Social Club.

Biography: lives Kirby Muxloe; born 13.02.1930; married to Joan with 3 children. Educated at Market Drayton Grammar School; Woodlands School, Matlock; Manchester University.

Leisure: gardening; walking; DIY.

COWARD Stephen

Queen's Counsel 2 Crown Office Row, Temple, London EC4Y 7HJ.

Career: National Service with RAF (1957-1959); lecturer in law and constitutional history University College London and Police College Bramshill (1962-1964); called to the Bar (1964); Recorder of the Crown Court (1980); QC (1984).

Activities: member Northampton and County Club.

Biography: lives Northampton; born 15.11.1937; married to Pye with 4 children. Educated at King James I Grammar School, Almondbury; University College London (1962 LLB).

Leisure: wine; gardening.

COWEN Maurice

partner and head of company law BOOTH & CO Sovereign House, South

Parade, Leeds LS1 1HQ.

Career: articled Slaughter and May (1968-1970); admitted (1970); assistant solicitor (1970-1973); became partner Booth & Co (1974).

Biography: lives Ilkley; born 29.01.1946; married to Anne with 2 sons. Educated at Haverstock School; Sheffield University (1967 LLB hons).

Leisure: music; theatre; hill walking; squash; fishing; reading good books.

COWLES Ronald

consultant NORTON ROSE Kempson House, PO Box 570, Camomile Street, London EC3A 7AN.

Career: articled Monro Saw & Co (1950-1955); admitted (1955); National Service (1955-1957); head of commercial branch British Coal Corporation legal department (1957-1988); legal adviser and solicitor British Coal Corporation (1973-1988); Norton Rose (1988).

Activities: chairman Law Society's Commerce and Industry Group (1983-1984); member International Bar Association Competition Law Committee; Environmental Law Committee (former deputy chairman); Coal Law Committee (chairman and council member 1982-1986); member Surrey Magistrates' Courts Committee; member Lord Chancellor's Advisory Committee for Surrey; JP for Surrey (1969 to date); chairman Dorking Bench (1986 to date); former chairman Probation Liaison Committee; former Chairman Juvenile Panel; member RAC.

Biography: lives Enton in Surrey; born 05.03.1932; married to Susan with 4 children. Educated at Bancroft's School; College of Law Lancaster Gate (1954 solicitor's finals hons); editor World Coalmining Law (1984); author of articles on mining law, environmental law, administrative law, in-house legal departments.

Leisure: family; reading; listening to music; collecting 18th-Century books and prints; riding.

COX Brian Robert Escott

Queen's Counsel 1 King's Bench Walk, Temple, London EC4Y 7DB.

Career: called to the Bar Lincoln's Inn (1954); Junior Counsel on Midland and Oxford circuit (1954-1974); Recorder of the Crown Court (1972); QC (1974); Master of the Bench Lincoln's Inn (1985); Lord Chancellor's List of Deputy High Court Judges (1978 to date).

C

C

Activities: member Nottingham United Services Club.

Biography: born 30.09.1932; married to Noelle with 2 children. Educated at Rugby School; Oriel College Oxford (BA).

Leisure: music.

COX Christopher

partner NABARRO NATHANSON 50 Stratton Street, London W1X 5FL.

Career: articled Coward Chance (1968-1970); admitted (1970); assistant solicitor (1970-1977); tax consultant Financial Techniques (Planning Services) Ltd (1977-1980); tax research and consultancy dept Spicer and Pegler (1981-1984); assistant solicitor Nabarro Nathanson (1984-1986); became partner (1986).

Activities: member Taxation Committee of International Chamber of Commerce.

Biography: lives London N1; born 21.07.1944; married to Kate with 2 children. Educated at St Edward's School, Oxford; Hertford College Oxford (1966 BA) (MA); (1967 BCL); College of Law (1968); co-author of: 'Partnership Taxation'; 'Capital Gains Tax on Businesses'.

Leisure: mountain walking; music; theatre.

COX George

senior partner BOOTH & CO Sovereign House, South Parade, Leeds LS1 1HQ.

Career: articled to town clerk of Leeds (1950-1952); admitted (1952); solicitor Leeds City Council (1952-1962); became partner Armitage Speight and Ashworth (1962-1972); merged with Booth & Co (1972); became senior partner (1978).

Biography: lives Harrogate; born 17.07.1927; married to Yvonne with 2 children. Educated at Leeds Grammar School; St Peter's College Oxford (1950 BA).

COX Norman

senior partner KENWRIGHT & COX Elizabeth House, 4/7 Fulwood Place, Gray's Inn, London WC1V 6GH.

Career: admitted (1950); assistant solicitor (1950-1951); became partner Kenwright & Cox (1951); became senior partner (1971).

Activities: Law Society's examiner in family law (1961-1964); president West Essex Law Society (1974-1975); committee member London Solicitors Litigation Association (treasurer 1987 to date).

Biography: lives Loughton; born 19.10.1927;

married to Pamela with 3 children. Educated at County High School, Ilford; College of Law London; John Mackrell Prize (1950); City of London Solicitors Company Prize.

COXALL David

senior partner 5 Sheep Street, Bicester, Oxon OX6 7JB.

Career: articled in London; admitted (1968); assistant solicitor (1968-1972); became partner (1972); now tending towards EEC work.

Biography: lives Oxfordshire; born 19.07.1943; divorced with 2 children from first marriage and 2 from second. Educated at Clarkes College, Ealing; Bursary from Law Society Trust.

Leisure: all ball sports; fishing; skiing; motorcycling; reading; eating; drinking; amusing his children.

CRADICK Roger

senior litigation partner MORGAN BRUCE Bradley Court, Park Place, Cardiff CF1 3DP.

Career: articled Thomas John & Co; admitted (1954); assistant solicitor Myer Cohen & Co (1954); prosecuting solicitor County Borough of Cardiff (1954-1956); assistant solicitor Garelick & Co (1956-1959); assistant solicitor Hardwickes (1959-1963); became partner (1963); firm merged to form Morgan Bruce & Hardwickes (1987).

Activities: deputy District Registrar High Court of Justice; deputy County Court Registrar; part-time chairman Medical Appeals Tribunal; member Area Committee No 5 (South Wales) Area Law Society Legal Aid Committee; former member Law Society Bye Laws Revision Sub-committee; vice-president Old Penarthians RFC (former chairman); member Cardiff & District Rugby Referees' Society.

Biography: lives Dinas Powis; born 06.11.1932; married to Jill with 4 children. Educated at Penarth County Grammar; Llandovery College; College of Law Guildford (1953-1954).

Leisure: rugby football; rugby referee; cricket; gardening; visiting family in Crete.

CRAWFORD Andrew

partner and head of residential conveyancing THOMAS EGGAR VERALL BOWLES East Pallant, Chichester, West Sussex PO19 1TS.

Career: admitted (1980); assistant solicitor (1980-1984); became partner Thomas Eggar & Son (1984); became head of conveyancing (1989).

Activities: Notary Public; member East India Devonshire and Public Schools Club.

Biography: lives Chichester; born 22.05.1956; married to Penelope. Educated at Hurstpierpoint College (1964-1974); Birmingham Polytechnic (1977).

Leisure: cricket; skiing; tennis; squash; infrequent sailing.

CRAWLEY Thomas

partner TURNER KENNETH BROWN 100 Fetter Lane, London EC4A 1DD.

Career: Martin's Bank (1959-1961); articled Turner Kenneth Brown (1961-1964); admitted (1965); assistant solicitor (1965-1967); became partner (1967); admitted Hong Kong (1986); senior resident partner TKB Hong Kong (1988-1990).

Activities: Liveryman of City of London Solicitors' Company; member International Bar Association; member International Fiscal Association; member Asia Pacific Lawyers' Association; member Justice and International Commission of Jurists; member of: Travellers Club; Hong Kong Club; Monmouthshire Hunt Club.

Biography: lives London and Gwent; born 17.05.1936; married to Felicity with 3 children. Educated at St Faith's School, Cambridge (1944-1949); Rugby School (1949-1954); Trinity College Cambridge (1959 BA) (1964 MA); College of Law (1964); City of London Solicitors Company Prize; Charles Steele Prize; author of 'Using Tax Havens Successfully' (English edition of 'Guide des Paradis Fiscaux' (1978).

Leisure: hill walking; swimming; theatre; gardening; wine.

CREAGH Giles PV

senior partner GREENE & GREENE 80 Guildhall Street, Bury St Edmunds, Suffolk IP33 1QB.

Career: articled RM Beckwith (1948-1951); admitted (1951); assistant solicitor (1951-1956); became partner Greene & Greene (1956).

Activities: Notary Public (1958); clerk to St Edmundsbury Cathedral Council (1956-1979); registrar of Diocese of St Edmundsbury and Ipswich (1956-1975); registrar of Archdeaconry of Sudbury (1956-1975); member General Assembly of Church of England; president Suffolk and

North Essex Law Society (1984-1985); officer in TA (1955-1967) (retired Major) TD (1967); served with Suffolk Regiment, Reserve Reconnaissance Unit, SAS and Intelligence Corps; member of: United Oxford & Cambridge University; Special Forces.

Biography: lives Market Weston; born 21.11.1927; married with 2 sons. Educated at Marlborough; Clare College Cambridge (1948 BA) (1951 MA).

Leisure: travelling in Far East; history (particularly military and Chinese); Chinese culture.

CRERAR Lorne

senior partner commercial conveyancing and banking departments HARPERS the commercial division of ROSS HARPER & MURPHY Ca'd'Oro Building, Gordon Street, Glasgow G1 3PE.

Career: articled Mackenzie Roberton & Co; admitted (1978); assistant solicitor (1978-1979); became partner (1979-1984); assistant solicitor Ross Harper & Murphy (1984-1985); became partner (1985); chairman firm's client development committee; elected member firm's management committee.

Activities: lecturer in Scottish private law at Glasgow University (1982 to date); clerk of Incorporation of Cardiners in Glasgow; member of: Royal Scottish Automobile Club; Glasgow High/Kelvinside RFC; numerous climbing and fishing clubs.

Biography: lives Glasgow; born 29.07.1954; single. Educated at Kelvinside Academy, Glasgow; Glasgow University (1976 LLB hons); Bennett Miller and Shaw Stewart Jubilee Memorial Prizes.

Leisure: rugby referee; hill climbing; fishing; devoted to Western Highlands of Scotland and its history.

CRESSWELL Peter

Queen's Counsel 3 Gray's Inn Place, London WC1R 5EA; Tel: 071-831 8441.

Career: called to the Bar Gray's Inn (1966); QC (1983); Recorder (1986).

Activities: chairman General Council of the Bar (1990); chairman Common Law and Commercial Bar Association (1985-1987); member Senate of Inns of Court and Bar (1981-1984 & 1985-1986); member General Council of the Bar (1987 to date) (vice-chairman 1989); member Supreme Court Procedure Committee (1982-1988); member Executive Committee of Cystic Fibrosis Research Trust (1983 to date); member of:

Athenaeum; Flyfishers' Club.

Biography: lives London SW1; born 24.04.1944; married to Caroline with 1 son (1 son deceased). Educated at St John's School, Leatherhead; Queen's College Cambridge (MA LLM); Malcolm Hilbery Award Gray's Inn; editor of 'Encyclopaedia of Banking Law' (1982) (and subsequent service issues); contributions to various domestic and international journals on banking law.

Leisure: fly fishing; fishery management.

CROLY Colin

partner BARLOW LYDE & GILBERT Beaufort House, 15 St Botolph Street, London EC3A 7NJ.

Career: articled Webber Wentzel & Co, Johannesburg; admitted (1974); assistant solicitor Barlow Lyde & Gilbert (1976-1981); became partner (1981).

Activities: participates in many reinsurance conferences and seminars delivering talks and acting as chairman; member International Bar Association Committee H (Insurance); Secretary General of the Association Internationale de Droit des Assurances (AIDA); member British Insurance Law Association (former committee member); chairman all day session on Asbestos Related Claims - The Insurance and Reinsurance Implications thereof, Buenos Aires (1988); member of: RAC; North London Bowling Club (hon solicitor).

Biography: lives London N8 and Beer, Devon; born 09.10.1949; married to Clare. Educated at St Andrew's College, Grahamstown, RSA; University of Cape Town (1971 BCom LLB); University College London (1975 LLM); numerous articles on reinsurance and articles in the Review, Reinsurance and other magazines.

Leisure: politics/current affairs; gardening; tennis; bowls; history; theatre.

CROMBIE John

partner GUILLAUME & SONS 20 Queen's Road, Weybridge, Surrey KT13 9UZ.

Career: Guillaume & Sons (1959).

Biography: lives Weybridge; born 28.09.1938; single. Educated at Gorsecliffe School, Bournemouth; Shrewsbury School.

Leisure: golf.

CROSSBY Michael

partner MOORE & BLATCH 48 High Street, Lymington, Hants SO41 9ZQ.

Career: articled Janson Cobb Pearson & Co (1963-1966); admitted (1966); assistant solicitor (1966-1970); assistant solicitor Moore & Blatch (1970-1972); became partner (1972); Notary Public (1985).

Activities: hon secretary Southern Area Association of Law Societies; solicitor to Lymington & Pennington Town Council; secretary to Abbeyfield Lymington Society; committee member (secretary 1984-1987) Hampshire Incorporated Law Society; member of: Lymington Rotary Club; Lymington 41 Club.

Biography: lives Milford-on-Sea; born 03.04.1941; married to Margaret with 2 children. Educated at County Grammar School, Wallington; Bristol University (1963 LLB hons).

Leisure: travel; family; commercial tomato growing.

CROWE David

partner GOULDENS 22 Tudor Street, London EC4Y 0JJ.

Career: articled Gouldens (1961-1964); admitted (1964); became partner HA Crowe & Co (1964-1968); became partner Gouldens (1968).

Activities: member of: Oxford & Cambridge University Club; National Liberal Club.

Biography: lives Beckenham; born 31.08.1939; married to Helen with 2 daughters. Educated at Cranleigh School; Christ Church Oxford (1961 MA); Law Society Finals (hons).

CRUSH Harvey

senior partner commercial and marine litigation department NORTON ROSE Kempson House, PO Box 570, Camomile Street, London EC3A 7AN.

Career: articled to Thomas Boyd Whyte (1957-1962); admitted (1963); assistant solicitor Norton Rose (1963-1968); became partner (1968).

Activities: director The TOSG Trust Fund Ltd·(1970 to date); vice-president City of London Law Society (chairman of Committee 1989 to date); member Supreme Court Rule Committee (1984-1988); member No 13 (London East) Legal Aid Area Local and General Committees (1970-1983) (Area Committee 1983 to date) (panel chairman); Liveryman Worshipful Company of Solicitors of the City of London (senior steward); member Royal Aeronautical Society (1980); member and hon solicitor to Association of British

C

Aviation Consultants; member International Rally Drivers Club.

Biography: lives Swanley Village; born 12.04.1939; married to Maggie with 3 children. Educated at Chigwell School; Law Society's School of Law (1959); College of Law (1962); numerous papers on air transport regulation and liabilities presented to International Bar Association and various international conferences.

Leisure: flying (private pilot); travel; motor sport.

CRUTE Alan

senior partner CRUTES 7 Osborne Terrace, Newcastle upon Tyne NE2 1RQ.

Career: articled Sinton & Co (1950-1954) and Crute & Sons (1954-1955); admitted (1955); assistant solicitor (1955-1957); became partner (1957-1979); became senior partner (1979).

Activities: chairman Social Services Appeal Tribunal; member Newcastle Family Practitioner Committee (chairman Dental, Medical, Opthalmic and Pharmaceutical Services Sub-committee); president North of England Medico-Legal Society; former chairman Newcastle & District Beagles; member of: Border Club; Northumberland Golf Club.

Biography: lives Newcastle upon Tyne; born 30.08.1932; married to Joy with 1 child. Educated at Appleby Grammar School; Durham School; King's College Durham University (1953 LLB); William Hutton Prize (1955).

Leisure: beagling; fell fox hunting; watching Sunderland AFC; golf.

CRUTWELL Christopher

partner and head of trust department GOULDENS 22 Tudor Street, London EC4Y 0JJ.

Career: articled Wood Nash & Co (1955-1958); admitted (1958); assistant solicitor Gregory Rowcliffe & Co (1958-1961); assistant solicitor Gouldens (1961-1963); became partner (1963).

Activities: hon solicitor to the National Philatelic Society.

Biography: lives Purley; born 25.07.1932; married to Patricia with 2 children. Educated at King's School, Bruton; St John's College Oxford (1955 BA); Law Society Finals (hons).

Leisure: philately (exhibitor at national and international exhibitions).

CRYSTAL Michael

Queen's Counsel specialising in commercial and financial law 3/4 South Square, Gray's Inn, London WC1R 5HP.

Career: called to Bar Middle Temple (1970); lecturer in law Pembroke College Oxford (1971-1976); QC (1984).

Activities: secretary Justice Committee on Bankruptcy (1973-1975); member Joint Working Party of Law Reform Committees of the Senate and the Law Society on the Draft EEC Bankruptcy Convention (1975-1976) and on the Reform on Insolvency Law and Practice (1977-1981); associate member Association Europeene Des Practiciens Des Procedures Collectives (1982 to date); hon senior visiting fellow of the Centre for Commercial Law Studies Queen Mary and Westfield College London (1987 to date); chairman Lloyd's Disciplinary Committee (1984); DTI Inspector into County Nat West Limited and County Nat West Securities Limited (1988-1989); appearances in the Courts of Hong Kong, Bahamas, Cayman Islands, Bermuda and Gibraltar; expert witness on commercial law in the Courts of the USA and Sweden; governor Royal Shakespeare Company; member of: RAC; MCC.

Biography: lives London NW3; born 05.03.1948; married to Felicia with 2 children. Educated at Leeds Grammar School; Queen Mary College London (1969 LLB hons); Magdalen College Oxford (1969-1971 BCL); Blackstone Major Entrance Exhibition Middle Temple (1967); Drapers Company Prize (1969); Lloyd Stott Memorial Prize (1970); Harmsworth Law Scholarship (1971); Blackstone Pupillage Prize (1971); assistant editor Halsbury's Laws of England (4th ed) vol 3 'Bankruptcy' (1974); joint editor 'Handbook on the Law of Bankruptcy' (3rd ed) (1978); assistant editor Williams and Muir Hunter on Bankruptcy (19th ed) (1979); joint editor 'Loose on Liquidators' (2nd ed) (1981); joint editor 'Totty and Crystal on Corporate Insolvency' (1982); joint contributor title 'Arrangements with Creditors' vol 3 The Encyclopaedia of Forms and Precedents (5th ed) (1985); editor Butterworths Insolvency Law Handbook (1987 second edition 1990); joint editor Halsbury's Laws of England (4th ed reissue) vol 7 (2) 'Companies' (1988).

Leisure: travel; music; theatre.

CRYSTAL Peter

senior partner MEMERY CRYSTAL 31 Southampton Row, London WC1B 5HT.

Career: articled Simpson Curtis (1970-1972); admitted (1973); assistant solicitor Clifford Turner (1973-1978); founded own practice (1978).

Activities: part-time Law Society examiner company law (1973-1978); Parliamentary Candidate SDP Leeds NE (1983 & 1987); member Liberal Democratic Lawyers' Association; captain Otley RUFC (1970-1972); member Reform Club; Vincents Club; Athenaeum; Hurlingham.

Biography: lives London SW13; born 07.01.1948; married to Lena with 2 daughters. Educated at Leeds Grammar School (1956-1966); St Edmund Hall Oxford (1969 BA hons) (1974 MA) Oxford Blue boxing (1968); College of Law Lancaster Gate (1969-1970); McGill University Institute of Comparative Law, Montreal (1973 LLM); Rotary Foundation Graduate Fellowship (1972-1973); Max Binz Research Scholarship (1973); author of 'Legal Aspects of Control on Entry of Multinational Companies by EEC' (1973).

Leisure: politics; sport; tennis; travel.

CULLEN Christopher

partner BEALE AND COMPANY Garrick House, 27/32 King Street, Covent Garden, London WC2E 8JD.

Career: factory floor JS Robertson & Sons; taught comprehensive school, South London (1971-1972); articled Beale and Company (1975-1977); assistant solicitor (1977-1978); became partner (1978).

Activities: part-time legal advice centre, Hackney (1975-1980); public speaking.

Biography: lives East Horsley; born 04.10.1947; married to Carol with 2 children. Educated at St George's School, Windsor Castle; Rugby School, Warwickshire; Exeter University (1969 BA hons); London University (1971-1972); London School of Economics (1982 LLM); articles in Law Society's Gazette and Construction News.

Leisure: golf; tennis; squash; plays; films; books.

CULLEN Joyce

partner BRODIES WS 15 Atholl Crescent, Edinburgh EH3 8HA.

Career: admitted (1981); assistant solicitor (1981-1986); became partner Brodies WS (1986).

Biography: lives Edinburgh; born 07.01.1958; married to Paul with 1 son. Educated at Leith Academy; Dundee University (1979 LLB).

Leisure: travel.

CULLEN Terence

Queen's Counsel 13 Old Square, Lincoln's Inn, London WC2 3UA.

Career: Royal Navy (1948-1955); Prestige Group Ltd (1955-1961); called to the Bar Lincoln's Inn (1961); QC (1978); Singapore Bar (1978); Malaysia Bar (1980); Hong Kong Bar (1986); Bermuda Bar (1990); Bencher Lincoln's Inn (1986).

Biography: lives London N1 and Newnham; born 29.10.1930; married to Muriel with 3 children. Educated at Royal Naval College Dartmouth (1944-1948); Royal Naval College Greenwich (1950).

Leisure: racing; opera; painting.

CULLIMORE William

consultant BIRCH CULLIMORE & CO Friars, Whitefriars, Chester CH1 1XS.

Career: land commissioners and legal department of Ministry of Agriculture; Birch Cullimore & Co.

Activities: clerk to Dean and Chapter Chester Cathedral; clerk to Chester Municipal Chambers; former president Chester and North Wales Law Society; former chairman Cheshire CLA; trustee Water Companies Pension Fund; former chairman Wrexham & East Denbighshire Water Co; director Chester Water Co (former chairman); local director Sun Alliance Insurance Co; chairman family property and trading companies; member Farmers' Club.

Biography: lives Chester; born 28.11.1918; married to Russell with 2 children. Educated at Shrewsbury; Gonville and Caius College Cambridge (MA); professional Associate of Royal Institute of Chartered Surveyors.

Leisure: farming (dairy Friesian herd).

CUNLIFFE John

partner in charge of Employee Benefits Group MCKENNA & CO Mitre House, 160 Aldersgate Street, London EC1A 4DD.

Career: law lecturer Liverpool University; became partner McKenna & Co.

Activities: member of the Association of Pension Lawyers Main Committee (chairman International Sub-committee); co-chair International Foundation of Benefit Plans European Committee; member of the Law Society Sub-committee on pensions; member of the Council & Management Committee of the Occupational Pensions Advisory Service; editor International Pension Lawyer; adviser to insurance companies and employers and trustees of occupational pension schemes; regular speaker at pension conferences and courses organised by: the National Association of Pension Funds; the Pensions Management Institute; the Association of Pension Lawyers; commercial conferences; international pensions conferences in London, Holland, Budapest and Berlin; gave paper at 7th World Congress of Insurance Law in Budapest.

Biography: lives in a village 10 miles south of Sevenoaks, Kent; born 06.03.1935; married. Educated at Liverpool University; Oxford University; author of 'The Role of the Pension Fund Trustee'; regular contributor to Pensions World, Pensions Intelligence, Pensions Management.

CUNNINGHAM David

partner CUNNINGHAM JOHN & CO Fairstead House, 7 Bury Road, Thetford, Norfolk IP24 3PL.

Career: articled Cozens-Hardy & Jewson; admitted; became partner TE Rudling & Co (1960-1972); founded own practice (1973).

Activities: chairman Eastern Regional Rent Assessment Committee; new 'Purchasers Charter' legal audit; member of: Thetford Rotary; Thetford Rugby; Thetford Golf.

Biography: lives Rushford College; born 30.12.1933; married to Jacqueline with 4 children. Educated at King Edward VI, Norwich; John Mackrell Prize.

CURNOW Ann

Queen's Counsel 6 King's Bench Walk, Temple, London EC4Y 7DR.

Career: Prosecuting Counsel to the Crown Middlesex Crown Court (1972); Junior Prosecuting Counsel Central Criminal Court (1977); Senior Prosecuting Counsel to the Crown (1981); QC (1985); Bencher Gray's Inn (1985); Recorder of the Crown Court.

Activities: member Criminal Bar Association Committee (1969-1980).

Biography: lives London SW8; born 05.06.1935; married to Neil Denison. Educated at St Hilda's School, Whitby; King's College London (1955 LLB AKC).

Leisure: reading; tapestry; walking; listening to music; opera; cats.

CURRAN Gerard

solicitor to the council for LONDON BOROUGH OF NEWHAM Town Hall, East Ham, London E6 2RP.

Career: articled Greater Manchester Council (1983-1985); admitted (1985); assistant solicitor London Borough of Newham (1985-1986); senior solicitor (1986); principal solicitor (1987); became solicitor to the Council (1987).

Activities: hon legal adviser North East London Polytechnic (1987-1989); member Haldane Society.

Biography: lives London E17; born 09.12.1959; married. Educated at De La Salle College, Salford; Bristol University (1981 LLB hons); Manchester Polytechnic (1983 Law Society Finals).

Leisure: eating out; football; reading; the pub.

CURTIS Nigel

a senior conveyancing partner with HAMLIN SLOWE Roxburghe House, 273-287 Regent Street, London W1A 4SQ.

Career: articled Malcolm Slowe & Co (1953-1959); admitted (1959); assistant solicitor (1959-1960); became partner (1960).

Activities: member Worshipful Company of Glaziers and Painters of Glass; member of: Arts Club; Dyrham Park Golf Club; The Magic Circle.

Biography: lives Stanmore; born 05.07.1935; married to Carol with 3 children. Educated at Midhurst Grammar School, Sussex; College of Law Lancaster Gate.

Leisure: golf; magic; the arts (particularly theatre).

CURTIS Penelope

director compliance department NM ROTHSCHILD & SONS LIMITED New Court, St Swithin's Lane, London EC4P 4DU.

Career: articled Freshfields (1979-1981); admitted (1981); assistant solicitor (1981-1987); compliance department NM Rothschild & Sons Ltd (1987).

Biography: lives London; born 20.02.1957; married to Christopher Crouch. Educated at St Michael's School, Limpsfield; Exeter University (1978 LLB hons); Law Society Finals (1979 hons).

D

CUTHBERTSON Evan

partner BRODIES WS 15 Atholl Crescent, Edinburgh EH3 8HA.

Career: apprentice Lindsay Howe WS (1960-1963); admitted (1963); assistant solicitor (1963-1964); became partner Brodie Cuthbertson & Watson WS (1964).

Activities: Notary Public; member of: New Club; Farmers' Club; Gullane Golf Club; Hon Company of Edinburgh Golfers.

Biography: lives Gullane; born 15.09.1938; married to Judy with 3 daughters. Educated at Edinburgh Academy; Sedbergh; Edinburgh University (1960 MA) (1963 LLB).

Leisure: gardening; golf; shooting.

D

D'SA Rose

international relations and information consultant EDWARDS GELDARD, SOLICITORS 16 St Andrew's Crescent, Cardiff CF1 3RD; a newly created role to develop the firm's domestic and international strategy in the context of the single European market in 1992.

Career: called to the Bar Middle Temple (1981); practised at the Bar in Newport, South Wales; became international relations and information consultant Edwards Geldard (1989).

Activities: visiting lecturer Kenya School of Law (1982); lecturer Department of Law, University College Cardiff (1983-1984); lecturer in law, Faculty of Law, Bristol University (1984-1985); research officer, Human Rights Unit, Commonwealth Secretariat, London (1985-1988); Legal Consultant, Commonwealth Law Ministers' Meeting, New Zealand (1990).

Biography: lives Cardiff; born 07.10.1957 Nairobi, Kenya; married to Dr John A Matthews. Educated at Loreto Convent, Nairobi; Millfield School, Somerset; Birmingham University (1979 LLB First Class Honours) (1982 PHD in public international law on the relationship between the United Nations and the organisation of African unity in the fields of international peace and security and of economic and social development); Lady Barber Postgraduate Scholarship (1981-1982); British Government Overseas Research Students' Award (1981-1982); Middle Temple Major Award: Jules Thorn Law Scholarship (1988-1989); numerous law papers in academic journals on public international law, human rights, European Community law; member of the Board of Editors of the Journal of Third World Legal Studies, New York (1988 to date).

Leisure: tennis; scholarship to Millfield School; captained ladies' team (1976); school winners of the Aberdare Cup; Kenya National Tennis Ranking No 3 (1975); selected for South Wales County (1984); hockey: played for Somerset County (1975); member Kenya National Squad (1980).

DALGLEISH Andrew

partner BRODIES WS 15 Atholl Crescent, Edinburgh EH3 8HA.

Career: apprentice MacKenzie & Black WS; admitted (1975); assistant solicitor Brodies WS (1975-1977); became partner (1978).

Activities: lectured at Law Society of Scotland courses; Notary Public; Writer to the Signet.

Biography: lives Edinburgh; born 09.06.1951; married to Sheila with 1 child. Educated at George Watson's College, Edinburgh; Edinburgh University (1973 LLB hons); contributor to Lawrence, International Personal Tax Planning Encyclopaedia; Withers, International Trust Precedents.

Leisure: wine.

DALKIN Eric

company secretary and legal adviser BLUE CIRCLE INDUSTRIES PLC 84 Eccleston Square, London SW1V 1PX.

Career: articled Goundry & McCallum (1951-1956); admitted (1956); National Service with RAF (1956-1958); assistant solicitor National Coal Board (1958-1959); solicitor Norfolk CC (1959-1960); solicitor BBC (1960-1965); solicitor APCM (1965-1968); solicitor Laporte Industries PLC (1968-1970); chief solicitor Blue Circle Industries PLC (1970-1984); became company secretary and legal adviser (1984).

Activities: member Law Society; member of: Yorks CCC; Surrey CCC.

Biography: lives London SW11 and Marlborough; born 09.04.1934; married to Sheila with 1 child. Educated at Homewood School, Middlesbrough; Acklam Hall Grammar School; Sir William Hutton Prizeman (1956); N Yorks and S Durham Law Society Prizeman (1956).

Leisure: horse racing; cricket; running.

DALLY Brian

partner specialising in commercial and international work TAYLOR JOYNSON GARRETT 180 Fleet Street, London EC4A 2NT.

Career: RNR Lt Commander 1952-1975 (retired) (RD); admitted (1954); assistant solicitor and partner Donaldson & Burkinshaw, Singapore (1956-1966); partner Bircham & Co (1966-1968); partner Wilde Sapte & Co (1968-1970); became partner Parker Garrett & Co (1971); merged to become Taylor Joynson Garrett.

Activities: responsibility for Interlex; ward clerk Lime Street Ward (1972-1982); member of: Royal Lymington Yacht Club; Tanglin Club, Singapore.

Biography: lives London SW19; born 11.10.1930; married to Philida with 2 children. Educated at Silcoates School, Wakefield; University College School, Hampstead; College of Law.

Leisure: sailing; skiing; squash; opera; travel.

DALRYMPLE Hew

partner private client department BRODIES WS 15 Atholl Crescent, Edinburgh EH3 8HA.

Career: apprentice Brodies WS; admitted; assistant solicitor; became partner (1980).

Activities: Writer to the Signet; member of: New Club; Drumsheugh Baths Club; The Edinburgh Academical Club; The Dalmahoy Golf and Country Club.

Biography: lives Edinburgh; born 12.11.1952; married to Deirdre with 1 son. Educated at The Edinburgh Academy; Edinburgh University (LLB hons).

Leisure: swimming; golf; fishing; shooting; skiing; music.

DARLINGTON Alured

crown prosecutor CROWN PROSECTUTION SERVICE, Acton W3..

Career: articled to Town Clerk Chingford; admitted; founded own practice (now) Darlington & Parkinson (1966)..

Activities: local secretary Central & South Middlesex Law Society (1965-1971); former member National Committee and chairman Fundraising and Publicity Committee of International Voluntary Service.

Biography: lives Ealing; born 03.01.1935; divorced with 3 children. Educated at Kent College, Truro; Colet Court, Hammersmith; St John's, Leatherhead;

College of Law; letters to the press and article in Justice of the Peace Review.

Leisure: music; hill walking; chess; motorcycling.

DAVID Irving

senior partner DAVID WINEMAN Craven House, 121 Kingsway, London WC2B 6NX.

Career: articled Wright & Webb (1968-1972); admitted (1982); head of legal affairs WEA Records Ltd (1972-1973); head of legal and business affairs GTO Records Ltd (1974-1975); became partner Rubinstein Callingham (1976-1978); became partner Clintons (1978-1981); founded David Elton & Wineman (1981); became David Wineman (1988).

Activities: member RAC.

Biography: lives London N3; born 21.03.1947; single. Educated at Hasmonean Grammar School; London School of Economics (1965-1968 LLB); College of Law Lancaster Gate (1971-1972).

Leisure: private flying; travel; photography.

DAVIDSON David

partner matrimonial department PENNINGTONS INCORPORATING GAMLENS Clement House, 99 Aldwych, London WC2B 4LJ.

Career: geologist's assistant Widgiemooltha, W Australia (1968); teacher Parramatra High School, NSW, Australia (1969); articled Theodore Goddard & Co (1970-1972); admitted (1972); assistant solicitor (1972-1975); assistant solicitor Kenwright & Cox (1975-1976); associate (1976-1977); partner (1977-1985); became partner Gamlens (1986); firm merged to become Penningtons incorporating Gamlens (1990).

Activities: member Solicitors Family Association Sub-Committee; member MCC.

Biography: lives Surrey; born 30.01.1947; married with 3 children. Educated at Winchester College; Edinburgh University (1968 LLB); author of: Kenwright & Cox 'A Simple Guide to Divorce'; 'Tax and Divorce - A Guide to the Taxation Consequences of Separation and Divorce'; Gamlens Divorce Guides; contributor to Encyclopaedia of Forms and Precedents - Jointly Owned and Matrimonial Property (5th ed).

Leisure: cricket; ornithology.

DAVIDSON Keith

senior partner HEWITSON BECKE & SHAW 7 Spencer Parade, Northampton NN1 5AB.

Career: articled South East London (1950-1955); admitted (1955); National Service at Army School of Education, Beaconsfield; assistant solicitor Herbert Smith & Co; assistant solicitor De La Rue Co Ltd; assistant solicitor Frere Cholmeley; assistant solicitor Phipps & Troup (1962-1963); became partner (1963); firm became Becke Phipps, then Hewitson Becke & Shaw.

Activities: strong interest in corporate and financial affairs particularly corporate structure and taxation; clerk to the General Commissioners of Taxes Northampton County Division (1970 to date); member General Synod Legal Aid Committee; Church Assembly member (1965-1970); General Synod member (1965 to date); chairman Peterborough Diocesan House of Laity (1982-1988); councillor Northampton County Borough Council (1965-1972) (deputy chairman Housing Committee (1970-1972); member Northampton Red Cross Finance Committee (1980 to date); member Northampton and County Club.

Biography: lives Northampton; born 12.09.1932. Educated at Whitgift School, South Croydon; London (1955 LLB).

Leisure: walking; travelling.

DAVIDSON Richard

partner and member International Policy Committee BAKER & MCKENZIE Aldwych House, Aldwych, London WC2B 4JP.

Career: articled Baker & McKenzie (1968-1970); admitted (1970); assistant solicitor (1970-1972 & 1973-1975); associate Chicago office (1972-1973); became partner (1975).

Biography: lives Twickenham; born 02.09.1946; married to Alison with 2 children. Educated at Newcastle on Tyne Preparatory School; Fettes College, Edinburgh; Worcester College Oxford (1967 BA MA); Worcester College Law Prize (1966).

Leisure: oil painting; sculpture; art collection.

DAVIES Andrew

senior partner LEE BOLTON & LEE 1 The Sanctuary, Westminster, London SW1P 3JT.

Career: National Service with the Royal Fusiliers; articled family firm Evan Davies & Co; admitted (1962); assistant solicitor and partner Lee Ockerby & Co (1962-1964); became partner Evan Davies & Co (1964); merged with Lee Bolton & Lee (1981); became deputy senior partner (1983); became senior partner (1987).

Activities: Registrar and legal adviser Diocese of Canterbury (1982); legal adviser Dean and Chapter Canterbury Cathedral; director Snowdon Mountain Railway PLC; director Faversham Oyster Fishery Company; member Canterbury Industrial Consultative Committee; member Boodle's Club.

Biography: lives London SW11 and Faversham; born 12.01.1936; married to Margaret with 1 son and 2 daughters. Educated at Highfield; Shrewsbury; College of Law London.

Leisure: family; country activities; theatre; ballet.

DAVIES Aubrey

consultant HAMBLY SMITH HURLEY & VIZARD 6 Priory Street, Monmouth, Gwent NP5 3DZ.

Career: articled to Mr Reginald Edwards of Aberystwyth (1954-1957); admitted (1957); National Service with Directorate of Army Legal Services; short service commission in DALS (1957-1961); legal advisor to Financings Group of Companies; assistant solicitor Prentice Kirkwood & Co; assistant solicitor Vizard & Co (1966-1968); partner (1968-1990); became consultant with Hambly Smith Hurley & Vizard (1990).

Activities: president Monmouthshire Incorporated Law Society (1983-1984); member Council of the Law Society (1983 to date); clerk to the General Commissioners of Income Tax Monmouth Division; part-time chairman Social Security Appeal Tribunals; member Law Society Law Reform Committee (1984-1987); Courts and Legal Services Committee (1987-1988); Property and Commercial Services Committee (1988 to date); Race Relations Committee; Law Society/Institute of Legal Executives Joint Committee; member of Army and Navy Club.

Biography: lives Monmouth; born 22.01.1934; married to Eirlys with 3 children. Educated at Ardwyn Grammar School, Aberystwyth; University College Wales, Aberystwyth (LLB hons).

Leisure: choral singing; gardening.

D

D

DAVIES David

senior partner PENNINGTONS
99 Aldwych, London WC2B 4LJ.

Career: Royal Navy (1944-1947); articled
Penningtons (1947-1950); admitted (1950);
assistant solicitor (1950-1953); became
partner (1953); became senior partner
(1974).

Activities: Lt-Commander RNR (retired);
member of: Travellers' Club; HMS
President Wardroom Mess.

Biography: lives Newport, Essex; born
21.05.1926; married to Pauline with 3
children. Educated at Sherborne School;
College of Law; Fellow of Institute of
Taxation; author of: 'Will Draftsman's Aid'
(1970); 'Will Precedents and Capital
Transfer Tax' (1978 & 1983); 'Will
Precedents and Inheritance Tax' (1988);
general editor Butterworths Wills, Probate
and Administration Service (1990); various
articles in Law Society's Gazette.

DAVIES Geoffrey

partner and head of one of the corporate
finance teams TITMUSS SAINER & WEBB
2 Serjeants' Inn, London EC4Y 1LT.

Career: articled Reynolds Porter
Chamberlain (1971-1972); admitted (1972);
assistant solicitor Titmuss Sainer & Webb
(1973-1976); became partner (1976).

Activities: director Starlight Foundation
Ltd.

Biography: lives London WC2; born
28.09.1947; married. Educated at Clifton,
Bristol; King's College London.

DAVIES Jennet

partner GOULDENS 22 Tudor Street,
London EC4Y 0JJ.

Career: articled Herbert Smith & Co;
admitted; assistant solicitor (2 years);
assistant solicitor Gouldens (1981-1985);
became partner (1985).

Activities: member Anglo-Italian
Association.

Biography: lives London; born 28.09.1951;
single. Educated at The Grammar School,
Lymm; Wellingborough High School for
Girls, Northants; Godalming Grammar
School; Reading University (1974 BA
hons); Naples University (1972-1973); Liege
University (1978).

Leisure: theatre; painting; canalling.

DAVIES John Verdin

head of legal department BRITISH
MEDICAL ASSOCIATION Tavistock
Square, London WC1H 9JP.

Career: called to the Bar Gray's Inn (1955);
pupillage and practice in provincial
Chambers; legal secretary to the National
Farmers' Union (1957-1965); steel industry
(1965-1968); construction plant (1968-1973);
food manufacturing industry (1973-1975);
London Chambers.

Activities: secretary BMA Services Ltd;
legal adviser British Steel Corporation;
director/chief executive of Contractors'
Association and Federation of Bakers;
member Bar Association for Commerce
Finance and Industry General Committee
(1965-1968 & 1977-1987) (treasurer 1983-
1987); member Athenaeum.

Biography: lives London SW1; born
23.04.1932; married to Judith with 3
children. Educated at Manchester
Grammar School; Manchester University
(1953 LLB hons); Associate of Institute of
Taxation (1963); Fellow Chartered Institute
of Arbitrators (1976); author of: 'The
Farmers' Guide to the Law' (1963);
'Encyclopaedia of Health Services and
Medical Law' (1987).

Leisure: music; languages; literature;
walking in the Yorkshire Dales.

DAVIES Leslie

senior partner IVESONS PO Box 119, 19
Bowlalley Lane, Hull HU1 1YL.

Career: articled JA Iveson (1953-1956);
admitted (1956); National Service in Air
Ministry Legal Department RAF (1956-
1958); assistant solicitor JA Iveson & Co
(1958-1960); became partner (1960).

Activities: Under Sheriff City of Kingston
upon Hull (1965); president Hull
Incorporated Law Society (1975-1976);
member Council of the Law Society (1976
to date); chairman Education & Training
Committee (1983-1986); member Land Law
& Conveyancing Committee; member
Remuneration & Practice Development
Committee; governor College of Law (1984
to date); member of: Brough Golf Club;
Royal Overseas Club; St James's.

Biography: lives North Ferriby; born
23.12.1931; single. Educated at Ruthin
School, North Wales (1942-1950); Jesus
College Oxford (1953 BA).

Leisure: golf; holidays in warm, sunny
Spain; gardening.

DAVIES Martin

senior partner TA MATTHEWS & CO
6 & 7 King Street, Hereford HR4 9BS.

Career: articled in Newport (1953-1958);
admitted (1958); became senior partner TA

Matthews & Co.

Activities: part-time chairman Social
Security Appeal Tribunal.

Biography: lives Hereford; born 04.06.1935;
married with 2 children. Educated at
Newport High School.

DAVIES Patrick P

management partner PETERKINS
Burgh House, 7-9 King Street, Aberdeen,
AB2 3AA.

Career: apprentice J Downie Campbell and
Milne (1965-1967); admitted (1967);
assistant solicitor Clapperton and Brands
(1967-1971); firm amalgamated with J
Downie Campbell and Milne (1968);
became partner (1971); amalgamated with
Peterkins (1987).

Activities: member Council of the Law
Society of Scotland; secretary Rotary Club
of Aberdeen; convenor Law Society Legal
Education Committee; member President's
International Relations and Practice
Committees; chairman Chinook Disaster
Legal Group; chairman Piper Disaster
Group; member Royal Northern &
University Club.

Biography: lives Aberdeen; born 05.10.1944;
married with 1 child. Educated at Bristol
Grammar School; Ellon Academy,
Aberdeenshire; Aberdeen University (1965
LLB).

Leisure: hill walking; motoring in pre-war
vehicles.

DAVIES Richard

partner WILSON COWIE & DILLON
13 The Cross, Neston, South Wirral,
Cheshire L64 9UB.

Career: articled Wilson Cowie & Dillon
(1972-1979); admitted (1979); assistant
solicitor (1979-1982); became partner
(1982).

Activities: member of: Hightown Hockey
Club; Liverpool Cricket Club; West Derby
Golf Club; Merseyside Ski Club.

Biography: lives Liverpool; born 16.07.1952;
married to Pamela with 2 children.
Educated at Liverpool College; co-author
with Marilyn Mornington 'Matrimonial
Proceedings' (1988).

Leisure: skiing; hockey (Wales, Lancashire);
cricket; golf.

DAVIES Rowland

partner and head of commercial property
department EDWARDS GELDARD
16 St Andrew's Crescent, Cardiff CF1 3RD.

D

Career: articled Edwards Geldard (1976-1978); admitted (1978); assistant solicitor (1978-1981); became partner (1981); became head of department (1986).

Activities: immediate past president Rotary Club of Cardiff St David's; secretary of Wine Imbibers' Club.

Biography: lives Cardiff; born 27.08.1953; married to Sian with 1 son. Educated at Cardiff High School; Downing College Cambridge (1975 BA hons) (MA); Squire Scholarship; Senior Harris Scholarship.

Leisure: Rotary International; rugby football; wine; art; reading; travel; DIY.

DAVIES Timothy John

partner company department FIELD FISHER WATERHOUSE 41 Vine Street, London EC3N 2AA.

Career: admitted (1979); assistant solicitor (1979-1985); became partner Field Fisher Martineau (1985-1989); became partner Field Fisher Waterhouse (1989).

Biography: lives Sutton; born 14.05.1955; single. Educated at Wallington High School; Southampton University (1976 LLB); author of corporate reorganisations section of Butterworths 'UK Corporate Finance Handbook'.

DAVIS Grahame

consultant HEXTALL ERSKINE & CO 28 Leman Street, London E1 8ER and solicitor WINCH AND WINCH 20 Manor Road, Chatham, Kent ME4 6AG.

Career: National Service in Royal Army Service Corps (1953-1955); articled Booth Hearn & Stratton (1955-1961); admitted (1961); assistant solicitor (1961-1962); became partner Hextall Erskine & Co (1962); became senior partner (1985); became consultant (1990); appointed Chairman Industrial Tribunals (part-time) (1990).

Activities: member Law Society; member Institute of Directors; formed trade association for clients; lectured on contract, tort and employment law; area chairman and member National Council of the Round Table (former Table chairman); member of: Wig & Pen Club; Castle Club, Rochester; Medway 41 Club; Maidstone Rugby Football Club (vice-president); Bobbing Court Cricket Club; Roffen Club, Rochester.

Biography: lives Shorne; born 09.09.1934; married to Wendy with 2 children. Educated at King's School, Rochester; College of Law Lancaster Gate; paper for

British Security Industry Association on effect of employment legislation on small businesses.

Leisure: golf; cricket; cine and video photography.

DAVIS James

partner FRESHFIELDS Whitefriars, 65 Fleet Street, London EC4Y 1HT.

Career: admitted (1971); assistant solicitor (1971-1976); became partner Freshfields (1976); partner in charge of Singapore office (1980-1984).

Activities: member of: Singapore Cricket Club; MCC; Berkshire Golf Club; Hurlingham Club.

Biography: lives London SW19; born 23.09.1946; married to Sally with 4 children. Educated at Charterhouse; Balliol College Oxford (1968 BA).

Leisure: cricket; golf; family.

DAVIS Michael

solicitor in the professional indemnity department PINSENT & CO, Post & Mail House, 26 Colmore Circus, Birmingham B4 6BH.

Career: articled Fitzhugh Gates; admitted (1982); assistant solicitor (1982-1985); became partner (1985-89); solicitor Pinsent & Co (1989).

Activities: press and public relations officer Young Solicitors Group National Committee.

Biography: lives Birmingham; born 13.09.1956; single. Educated at Holy Trinity School, Crawley; Brunel University (1979 LLB); College of Law Guildford (1980 SFE); articles in various legal and other periodicals.

Leisure: sailing; golf; squash; skiing; theatre; industrial archaeology.

DAWS Andrew

partner DENTON HALL BURGIN & WARRENS 5 Chancery Lane, Clifford's Inn, London EC4 1BU.

Career: articled Wilkinson Howlett & Moorhouse; admitted; assistant solicitor Markbys (2 years); Bank of London & South America; assistant solicitor Denton Hall & Burgin (1971-1975); became partner (1975).

Activities: member of: Royal Mid-Surrey Golf Club; Roehampton Club; Richmond Squash Rackets Club.

Biography: lives Kew; born 11.03.1943;

married to Phoebe with 1 son and 1 daughter. Educated at King's School, Grantham; Exeter University (1964 LLB hons); College of Law (hons).

Leisure: squash; golf; family.

DAWSON Colin Frederic

senior partner WOODCOCK & SONS West View, Princess Street, Haslingden, Rossendale, Lancs.

Career: articled Woodcock & Sons; admitted (1966); assistant solicitor and partner (1966-1984); became senior partner (1984).

Activities: Commissioner for Oaths (1973); Notary Public (1982); member (1970 to date) and Chairman Area Legal Aid (No 7) District Committee (1988); Clerk to the Commissioners of Taxes for Rochdale Division (1988) (deputy clerk 1970-1988); former Secretary and Treasurer Bury and District Law Society (Parliamentary Relations Officer 1978 to date); former member Bury CAB Management Committee; member Association of Clerks to the Commissioners of Taxes for GB (Executive Committee member 1988 to date); member BMA Panel Medical Partnerships (1988 to date); member MOD Liaison Committee re: Holcombe Moor Camp, Bury; member local residents' groups and committees; Hon Solicitor re: Bridleways Association (Rochdale and Bury Group).

Biography: lives Bury, Lancashire; born 01.09.1942; married to Joyce with 4 sons. Educated at Bury Grammar School; Leeds University (1963 LLB hons).

Leisure: gardening; tennis; crown green bowling; snooker.

DAY Michael

chairman COMMISSION FOR RACIAL EQUALITY Elliot House, 10/12 Allington Street, London SW1E 5EH.

Career: senior officer West Sussex (1964-1967); chief probation officer Surrey (1968-1976); chief probation officer West Midlands (1976-1988); became chairman of Commission for Racial Equality (1988).

Activities: OBE (1980); chairman Chief Probation Officers' Conference (1974-1977); first chairman Association of Chief Officers of Probation (1981-1983); member of Council of Grubb Institute; member Advisory Council of Prince's Youth Business Trust.

D

Biography: lives Bridgnorth, Shropshire; born 04.09.1933; married to June with 1 daughter and 1 son. Educated at University College School, Hampstead; Selwyn College Cambridge (MA); London School of Economics (Cert in Social Work and Social Admin).

Leisure: gardening; friends and family life; the countryside; church; reading.

DE CHAZAL Paul

partner SIMMONS & SIMMONS
14 Dominion Street, London EC2M 2RJ.

Career: articled Crossman Block & Keith (1964-1967); admitted (1967); assistant solicitor Simmons & Simmons (1967-1969); admitted Hong Kong (1981); partner Brussels office (1969-1971); became partner (1971).

Activities: member of Law Society; International Bar Association; British Institute of International & Comparative Law; International Law Association; City of London Solicitors' Company; AIPPI; (The Competition Law Association); American Bar Association; Law Society Working Group on EEC & Insurance Law; Belgo-Luxembourg Chamber of Commerce (hon general secretary); French Chamber of Commerce; Portuguese Chamber of Commerce; US Chamber of Commerce; Sino-British Trade Council; L'Association des Juristes Franco-Britanniques; Japan Association; Union Internationale des Avocats; The European Centre of Space Law; director British-American Insurance Co Ltd (1972-1988); director Windsor Group Ltd (1987-1988); director Windsor Life Assurance Co Ltd (1978-1988); director Hamilton Life Assurance Co Ltd (1983 to date); director Hamilton Insurance Co Ltd (1983 to date).

Biography: lives London SW15; born 25.09.1942; married to Donatienne with 2 children. Educated at Downside School (1956-1960); Madrid University, Spain (1960-1961); Cambridge (1961-1964); (1964 BA); College of Law London (1966).

DE HAAS Margaret Ruth

barrister 5th Floor, The Corn Exchange, Liverpool, L2 7QS .

Career: called to the Bar Middle Temple (1977).

Activities: member Family Law Bar Association; British Insurance Law Association; International Union of Lawyers; author Domestic Injunctions (Sweet & Maxwell); co-author (with Iain S. Goldrein) Personal Injury Litigation,

Practice & Precedents; The Butterworths Personal Injury Litigation Service; co-author (with KHP Wilkinson) Property Distribution on Divorce (Longmans); lectures regularly on matrimonial finance and personal injury litigation for European Conference Studies

Biography: lives Liverpool; born 21.05.1954; married to Iain S Goldrein with 2 children. Educated at Townsend Girls' School, Bulawayo, Zimbabwe, Bristol University (LLB Hons)

Leisure: family, swimming, law, theatre.

DE LA GUARDIA Rogelio

senior resident lawyer ARIAS FABREGA & FABREGA 6th Floor, 17 Cockspur Street, London SW1Y 5BS.

Career: legal assistant Icaza Gonzalez Ruiz & Aleman (1974-1979); special associate Haight Gardner Poor & Havens, New York (1981); became associate Arias Fabrega & Fabrega (1981).

Activities: secretary Panama Maritime Law Association; member of: Panama Bar Association, International Bar Association, International Tax Planning Association, Union Club, Panama India House.

Biography: lives London SW1Y; born 26.01.1957; married with 1 child. Educated at Colegio Javier; Panama University (1979 licenciate in law and political science); New York University (1981 LLM in Corporation Law); member Sigma Lambda Honour Chapter; author of 'Regulation of Professional Ethics'; 'Arrest of Vessels in Panama'.

Leisure: swimming; photography; cooking.

DE MAIN John

partner HAMMOND SUDDARDS
Josephs Well, Hanover Walk, Leeds LS3 1AB.

Career: articled Hammond Suddards.

Activities: member Law Society Planning Law Committee; member of the Bradford Club.

Biography: lives Bingley; born 19.11.1945; married to Caroline with 2 daughters. Educated at Hymers College; Manchester University (1967); author of a booklet on the Community Land Act and Development Land Tax for the National Association of Estate Agents; article on Retail Warehousing for URPI.

Leisure: family; cinema; theatre; golf.

DE SILVA Desmond

Queen's Counsel and head of Chambers 2 Paper Buildings, Temple, London EC4.

Career: called to the Bar Middle Temple (1964); Sierra Leone Bar (1968); Gambia Bar (1981); QC (1984).

Activities: deputy circuit Judge (1976-1980); Councilman of the City of London (1980 to date); Freeman of the City of London; Liveryman of Worshipful Company of Fletchers; member of: Carlton; City Livery.

Biography: lives London; born 13.12.1939; married to HRH Princess Katarina of Yugoslavia. Educated at Dulwich College PS; Trinity College, Kandy, Ceylon; consulting editor 'English Law and Ethnic Minority Customs' (1986).

DE STE CROIX Richard

partner and head of commercial litigation department BRISTOWS COOKE & CARPMAEL 10 Lincoln's Inn Fields, London WC2A 3BP.

Career: Morgan Guaranty, London and New York (1969-1970); Rubinstein Nash (1972-1975); assistant solicitor Bristows Cooke & Carpmael (1975-1978); became partner (1978).

Activities: contested Chertsey & Walton (1983); General Election & Westminster North (1987); General Election for the Alliance.

Biography: lives London NW8; born 15.07.1947; married to Hillary with 2 daughters. Educated at Victoria College, Jersey; Pembroke College Oxford (1969 BA); King Charles I Exhibition.

Leisure: theatre; reading; politics.

DE VOIL Paul

principal PAUL DE VOIL & CO
Water Lane Barn, Denston, Newmarket, Suffolk CB8 8PP.

Career: flying officer Royal Air Force (instructor at OCTU) (1950-1953); HM Inspector of Taxes (1953-1960); taxation manager Ford Motor Company (1960-1963); taxation specialist Herbert Smith & Co (1964-1969); admitted (1967); head of company tax department Baker Sutton & Co (1969-1978); head office taxation controller Lonhro PLC (1978-1987); principal Arthur Young (now Ernst & Young) (1987-1989); founded own practice (1989).

Activities: examiner/senior examiner to the Institute of Taxation (1967-1978) (council member 1979-1989); member Law Society Revenue Law Committee (1986 to date); member VAT sub-committee (1982 to date) (chairman 1986-1989); member Royal Air Force Club.

Biography: lives Denston; born 29.09.1929; married to Sheila with 1 son and 1 daughter. Educated at Fettes College, Edinburgh; Hertford College Oxford (1950 BA) (1987 MA); Fellow of the Institute of Taxation; author of: 'de Voil on Tax Appeals' (1989); 'de Voil on VAT' (1972); contributor to Simon's Taxes 3rd edn; UK paper on VAT 1982 Venice Congress of the International Fiscal Association.

Leisure: wine; music; statues; bright-eyed love; theology; church warden and reader.

DEACON David

senior and managing partner DEACON GOLDREIN GREEN Peel House, 5/7 Harrington Street, Liverpool L2 9XP.

Career: articled Goldrein & Co (1965-1967); admitted (1967); assistant solicitor; partner Sydney Levy & Co; merged with Goldrein & Co (1985).

Activities: committee member Liverpool Law Society (1989 to date); vice-chairman Legal Aid Practitioners' Group; frequent speaker and commentator on legal subjects; member Athenaeum, Liverpool.

Biography: lives Liverpool; born 09.10.1942; married to Jennifer with 2 children. Educated at The Alsop, Liverpool; Liverpool University (1964 LLB hons).

Leisure: films; music; gymnastics.

DEAN Barry

director of training and know-how LINKLATERS & PAINES Barrington House, 59/67 Gresham Street, London EC2V 7JA.

Career: admitted as advocate South Africa and solicitor in England and Wales; professor of public law and Dean of the Faculty of Law, Cape Town University, South Africa; visiting scholar Michigan University Law School (1981); Alexander von Humbolt Fellow Max Planck Institute for Public and International Law, Heidelberg (1985); became director of training and know-how Linklaters & Paines (1986).

Biography: lives Great Missenden; born 25.08.1943; married to Becky with 2 children. Educated at Cape Town University (BCom LLB); London University (PhD); variety of booklets and articles on legal education and public law.

Leisure: walking; reading.

DEAR Stuart

partner MARSHALLS 102 High Street, Godalming, Surrey GU7 1DS.

Career: trainee chartered accountant Price Waterhouse (1976-1978); articled Barlows (1979-1981); admitted (1981); assistant solicitor Marshalls (1981-1983); became partner (1983).

Activities: member of: Rolls Royce Enthusiasts' Club; Caravan Club.

Biography: lives Ash Vale; born 08.03.1953; divorced with 2 children. Educated at Emmanuel School; University College Buckland (1975 LLB); College of Law Guildford (1979).

Leisure: motorcycling; foreign touring; skiing; windsurfing; cycling; tennis; canoeing; old cars.

DEARING Geoffrey

partner BRACHERS Somerfield House, 59 London Road, Maidstone, Kent ME16 8JH.

Career: admitted (1972); assistant solicitor (1972-1974); became partner Bracher Son & Miskin (1974).

Activities: Deputy Registrar (1983-1987); member Child Care Panel; secretary Kent Law Society (1988 to date); vice-chairman Kent Family Conciliation Service; served on two small working parties of the Law Society; member of: The Maidstone Club; various cricket and golf clubs.

Biography: lives Maidstone; born 26.04.1948; married to Elisabeth with 2 children. Educated at Sutton Valence School; College of Law Lancaster Gate and Guildford.

Leisure: cricket; golf; motor sport; travel.

DEBENHAM Richard

partner TURNER & DEBENHAMS 6 St Peter's Street, St Albans, Hertfordshire AL1 3LG.

Career: articled Sedgwick Turner Sworder and Wilson (1965-1970); admitted (1970); assistant solicitor family firm Thompson & Debenhams (1970-1973); became partner (1973); amalgamated to form Turner & Debenhams (1978).

Activities: president Hertfordshire Law Society (1988-1989); director Solicitors Benevolent Association (vice-chairman 1990).

Biography: lives St Albans; born 09.09.1946; married to Frances with 3 children. Educated at Berkhamsted.

DEHN Conrad

Queen's Counsel, Fountain Court, Temple, London EC4Y 9DH.

Career: Army (1945-1948); 2nd Lt Royal Artillery (1947); called to the Bar Gray's Inn (1952); pupillage with Leslie Scarman (1952-1953); Chambers of Melford Stevenson QC (1953); Recorder of the Crown Court (1974); Bencher Gray's Inn (1977); head of Fountain Court (1984-1989).

Activities: president of Inns of Court Students' Union (1951-1952); director of Bar Mutual Indemnity Fund (1988 to date); member Planning Committee of Senate of Inns of Court & Bar (1978-1983) (chairman 1980-1983); member Foster Committee of Inquiry into Operators' Licensing Dept of Transport (1978); member Management Committee of Gray's Inn (1985-1987) chairman (1987); chairman Bar Council Working Party on Liability for Defective Products (1975-1977); member Council of Legal Education (1981-1986; appeared in the ECJ and in High Court in Hong Kong and Bermuda; member Reform Club.

Biography: lives London; born 24.11.1926; married to Marilyn with 3 children by first wife. Educated at Gibbs (1935-1940); Charterhouse (1940-1945), Senior Exhibitioner; Christ Church Oxford (1950 BA) 1st class hons Philosophy, Politics and Economics; (1952 MA) Holford Scholar; Best Cadet Mons OCTU (1946); Holker Junior Scholar; Holt Scholar; WEA tutor (1951-1955); member Governing Body United Westminster Schools (1953-1957); chairman London University Appellate (Disciplinary) Committee (1986 to date).

Leisure: theatre; travel; walking.

DEIGHTON Richard

barrister 4 Verulam Buildings, Gray's Inn, London WC1R 5LW.

Career: articled in Cheltenham; admitted as a solicitor(1970); former managing partner Rapers, solicitors of Chichester; called to the Bar Middle Temple (1990).

Activities: former president Chichester & District Law Society; former vice- chairman Regional Duty Solicitor Committee for Surrey, Kent and Sussex; former chairman Local Duty Solicitor Scheme; former member Crown Court Liaison Committee for the South Eastern Circuit; lecturer in advocacy training for West Sussex Magistrates' Courts Association and Sussex Advocacy Training Course; chairman Selsey Illuminations Committee; member of: West Sussex County Club; Regnum Club.

D

Biography: lives Church Norton; born 06.02.1946; married to Chrissie with 1 son and 1 daughter. Educated at Cheltenham College; College of Law Guildford.

Leisure: active in local community; swimming; walking.

DELEMORE Ceri Lynn

associate EDWARDS GELDARD 16 St Andrews Crescent, Cardiff CF1 3RD.

Career: articled Slaughter and May (1984-1986); admitted (1986); assistant solicitor Slaughter and May (1986-1988); assistant solicitor Edwards Geldard (1988-1989); became associate (1989); member firm's articled clerks group.

Biography: lives Porthcawl; born 19.08.1961. Educated at Cynffig Comprehensive School; University of Kent at Canterbury (1983 BA hons first class); University of Paris, Sud a Sceaux - Diplome de droit francais.

DENISON Edward

senior partner DENISON TILL Chancery House, 143 Holgate Road, York YO2 4DF.

Career: articled Hepworth Chadwick (1951-1954); admitted (1954); assistant solicitor Simpson Curtis (1955-1956); assistant solicitor and then partner Hepworth & Chadwick (1957-1960); head of legal department Shepherd Building Group (1960-1967); became partner Last Suddards (1967); became Denison Till Group.

Activities: first chairman legal group to NFBTE (now Builders' Employers' Confederation); founder and deputy chairman Pennine Property Unit Trust; professional board appointee to companies in textiles, computers, optics; chairman pension fund management company; speaker on legal aspects of inland revenue tax investigations; former leader North Yorkshire County Council and many local government interests; member Yorkshire, Humberside and East Midlands Development Board; Lt Col (retired) TA; member YH TAVR Association; vice-chairman governors St Peter's School, York; director University of Leeds Foundation; member of: Army & Navy; Vincents; Yorkshire.

Biography: lives York; born 13.09.1928; married with 1 son and 1 daughter. Educated at St Peter's School, York; Brasenose College Oxford (1950 BA hons) (MA); (1951 BCL).

Leisure: shooting; tennis; swimming;

skiing; theatre; reading; good food.

DENKER James

partner ROWE & MAW 20 Black Friars Lane, London EC4V 6HD.

Career: admitted (1976); assistant solicitor (1976-1980); became partner Rowe & Maw (1980).

Activities: academician International Academy of Estate and Trust Law; member International Bar Association; member Association Internationale des Jeunes Avocats; Phi Beta Kappa.

Biography: lives London W2 and Brighton; born 07.03.1947; single. Educated at University of Pennsylvania (1969 BA hons); University of Cape Town (1967); Caius College Cambridge (1971 BA hons) (1976 MA); author of 'International Estate Planning' in Accountancy (1989).

Leisure: reading; travel.

DENOON DUNCAN Russell

consultant CAMERON MARKBY HEWITT Sceptre Court, 40 Tower Hill, London EC3N 4BB.

Career: South African Artillery, Egypt and Italy (1943-1945); admitted South Africa (1949); assistant solicitor Webber Wentzel (1951-1952); partner (1952-1961); admitted England (1962); assistant solicitor Cameron Markby Hewitt (1962-1963); partner (1963); senior partner (1987-1990); became consultant (1990).

Activities: non-executive chairman National Australia Finance (UK) Ltd, the UK holding company of Clydesdale Bank plc, Yorkshire Bank plc; Northern Bank Ltd and National Irish Bank Ltd; vice-chairman British Polish Legal Association; member of: City of London Club; The Royal Tennis Court; City Law Club; Rand Club; City Solicitors' Company.

Biography: lives Thames Ditton; born 11.03.1926; married to Caroline with 2 children. Educated at Michaelhouse, Natal, South Africa.

Leisure: mountain walking; painting; tennis.

DENSHAM Andrew

partner BURGES SALMON Narrow Quay House, Prince Street, Bristol BS1 4AH.

Career: articled Stanley Wasbrough & Co (1962-1965); admitted (1965); assistant solicitor (1965-1968); assistant solicitor Burges Salmon & Co (1968-1969); became partner (1970).

Activities: member Bristol Law Society Committee (1976-1977) (member Land Law and Conveyancing Committee 1978-1982); member Council of the Bristol University (1981-1983); Crown Court Assistant Recorder (1990 to date).

Biography: lives Bristol; born 30.11.1940; married to Fiona with 3 children. Educated at Tonbridge School; Bristol University (1962 LLB); College of Law Guildford (1965); author of Scammell & Densham's Law of Agricultural Holdings 6th ed (1978) and 7th ed (1989); principal contributor to 5th ed Halsbury's Encyclopaedia of Forms and Precedents Title 'Agriculture' (1986) and a contributor to Halsbury's Laws of England (edition in preparation) (1990).

Leisure: golf; long distance walking; skiing.

DENSLOW Simon

partner in charge of conveyancing and housing association department RIGBEYS 42-44 Waterloo Street, Birmingham B2 5QN.

Career: articled Rigbey Loose & Mills (1982-1984); admitted (1984); assistant solicitor (1984-1988); became partner (1989).

Activities: member of: Rover Sports Register; Cambridge Oxford Owners' Club.

Biography: lives Bromsgrove; born 02.03.1958; married. Educated at Boldmere Infant & Juniors' School, Sutton Coldfield; Bishop Vesey's Grammar School, Sutton Coldfield; Trent Polytechnic (1980 BA hons).

Leisure: shooting; motor racing; swimming.

DERBYSHIRE Paul

partner in charge of civil litigation FORD SIMEY DAW ROBERTS 8 Cathedral Close, Exeter, Devon EX1 1EZ.

Career: articled Cartwrights; admitted (1973); assistant solicitor Cartwrights and Sansbury Hill (1973-1977); assistant solicitor Ford Simey Daw Roberts (1977-1979); became partner (1979).

Activities: Deputy High Court/County Court Registrar (1986); legal adviser to Joint Agencies Child Abuse Team; legal adviser to Adoption Panel; member of the Committee of the Devon & Exeter Law Society (1984-1990); member Ide Cricket Club.

Biography: lives Exeter; born 1949; married with 3 children. Educated at St Brendan's College; Exeter University (1970 LLB hons).

Leisure: family; fly fishing; cricket; moorland walking.

DESCH Stephen

Queen's Counsel 2 Crown Office Row, Temple, London EC4Y 7HJ.

Career: Called to the Bar (1962); Deputy Circuit Judge/Recorder (1979); QC (1980).

Activities: junior lecturer in law Magdalen College Oxford (1963-1965) .

Biography: lives Sussex; born 17.11.1939; married to Julia with 2 children. Educated at Dauntsey's School; Magdalen College Oxford (MA BCL); Northwestern University, Chicago .

Leisure: mountain walking; farming; country pursuits.

DETHRIDGE David

barrister and head of Chambers 12 Old Square, Lincoln's Inn, London WC2P 3TX.

Career: called to the Bar Lincoln's Inn (1975); pupillage 3 New Square and 1 King's Bench Walk; 12 Old Square (1977); became head of Chambers (1986).

Biography: lives London N1; born 25.06.1952; married to Alexandra with 1 son, Christopher. Educated at Kingston Grammar School (1963-1967); King Edward VI School, Bath (1967-1970); Queen's College Oxford (1974 BA hons) (1978 MA) Open Scholar; College of Law (1974-1975).

DEVEREUX Mark

partner and head of entertainment department SIMON OLSWANG & CO 1 Great Cumberland Place, London W1H 7AL.

Career: articled Brecher & Co; admitted (1981); assistant solicitor Simon Olswang & Co (1981-1982); became partner (1982); admitted as US attorney in California (1983).

Activities: chaired debate on new Copyright Bill at Edinburgh Television Festival (1988); contributed to international media law; regularly lectures on all aspects of film and television production, financing and distribution and on music in films and television.

Biography: lives London W2; born 02.08.1956; single. Educated at Lycee Francais de Londres; University College London (1978 LLB hons); College of Law (1979); member of the State Bar of California (1983).

Leisure: tennis; film; music.

DEWAR Donald

partner ROSS HARPER & MURPHY 163 Ingram Street, Glasgow .

Career: Labour MP for Aberdeen South and Parliamentary Private Secretary to Tony Crosland (1966-1970); reporter to Children's Panel in Lanark County (1970-1975); assistant solicitor Ross Harper & Murphy (1975); became partner.

Activities: Labour MP for Glasgow Garscadden (1978 to date); chairman Select Committee on Scottish Affairs (1979-1981); Labour party's Scottish front bench team (1981 to date) (principal spokesman on Scottish Affairs 1983); elected to Shadow Cabinet (1984 to date).

Biography: lives London and Glasgow; born 21.08.1937; divorced with 1 son and 1 daughter. Educated at Glasgow Academy; Glasgow University (MA LLB).

Leisure: politics; broadcasting; journalism.

DEWAR John

fellow in law HERTFORD COLLEGE Oxford OX1 3BW .

Career: lecturer in law Lancaster University (1981-1983); lecturer School of Law Warwick University (1983-1988); became head of education and training Allen & Overy (1988-1990); appointed to Fellowship of Hertford College, Oxford .

Activities: hon senior lecturer in law University College London (1989-1990); member Legal Education and Training Group.

Biography: lives London SW4; born 11.09.1959; married to Rosie. Educated at Dragon School, Oxford (1968-1972); Abingdon School (1972-1975); Brockenhurst 6th Form College (1972-1975); Hertford College Oxford (1980 BA); Martin Wronker Prize in Law; (1981 BCL); articles in academic journals; contributor to number of books; author of 'Law and the Family' (1989).

Leisure: reading; cinema; theatre; occasional creative writing; gardening.

DI BIASE Paul

chairman partnership board and senior partner corporate and commercial department FORSYTE KERMAN 79 New Cavendish Street, London W1M 8AQ.

Career: articled Forsyte Kerman (1957-1960); admitted (1961); assistant solicitor (1961-1964); became partner (1965); became finance partner (1977-1988); chairman of the partnership board (1988).

Activities: director of family controlled ladies' hairdressing businesses (1957 to date); founder member East Molesey residents' association (1964-1967); director property development companies; partner with wife in her design consultancy; member of Richmond Golf Club, Petersham; (lessee and captain-elect (1991) (centenary year).

Biography: lives London W1 and Weston Green, Surrey; born 21.07.1934; married to Susan with 2 sons and 1 daughter. Educated at Rutlish School, Merton; University College Oxford (1957 LLB hons) .

Leisure: golf; good food; fine wine; watching sports; art; architecture; design; classical music; cinema; theatre; travel (particularly Italy).

DIAMOND Anthony

Circuit Judge 1 Cannon Place, London NW3 1EH.

Career: called to the Bar Gray's Inn (1953); Bencher (1985 to date); Silk (1974); head of Chambers (1984 to date); Recorder of the Crown Court; sits regularly as arbitrator; Circuit Judge (1990).

Activities: Fellow of the Chartered Institute of Arbitrators; member number of tribunals.

Biography: lives London; born 04.09.1929; married with 2 children. Educated at Rugby School; Corpus Christi College Cambridge; numerous articles on aspects of transport and shipping law.

Leisure: visual arts.

DIAMOND Aubrey L

professor of law and co-director UNIVERSITY OF NOTRE DAME London Law Centre, 7 Albemarle Street, London W1X 3HF.

Career: admitted (1951); assistant solicitor (1951-1959); became partner Lawford & Co (1959-1971); became consultant (1987 to date); law teacher LSE (1957-1966); professor of law Queen Mary College London (1966-1971); Law Commissioner (1971-1976); director Institute of Advanced Legal Studies (1976-1986); professor of law and co-director University of Notre Dame (1987).

Activities: former part-time chairman Industrial Tribunals; deputy chairman Data Protection Tribunal; visiting professor LSE; hon Fellow LSE; Fellow QMC; member Law Society Council (1976 to date); member Council of Justice (1976 to

D

date); Senate of the University of London; member Court of Governors LSE; former chairman of the Social Science Research Council Committee on Social Sciences and the Law; former chairman IBA Advertising Advisory Committee; former member Latey Committee on the Age of Majority; former member UNIDROIT Governing Council, Rome; vice-president Institute of Trading Standards Administration; member Reform.

Biography: lives London; born 28.12.1923; married to Eva with 2 children. Educated at Central Foundation School, London; LSE (1950) (1956 LLM); author of: 'A Review of Security Interests in Property' (1989); 'Commercial and Consumer Credit' (1982); 'The Consumer, Society and the Law' (1981) (with Sir Gordon Borrie QC) .

DIBBLE Robert

banking and finance partner and head of transport and trade finance group WILDE SAPTE Queensbridge House, 60 Upper Thames Street, London EC4V 3BD.

Career: Royal Naval Officer (retired Commander) (1958-1977); articled Linklaters & Paines (1978-1980); admitted (1980); assistant solicitor (1980-1981); assistant solicitor Wilde Sapte (1981-1982); became partner (1982).

Activities: member IBA; member Worshipful Company of Shipwrights.

Biography: lives London SE; born 28.12.1938; married to Teresa with 4 children. Educated at Westcliff High School for Boys; Royal Naval College, Dartmouth (1955-1958); Queen's Gold Medal and Telescope; communications and electronic warfare specialist cruise (1966-1967); Russian interpreter (first class); Defence Fellow King's College London.

Leisure: tennis; music; family.

DICKINSON Donald

partner PAPE DICKINSON & CO 7 Starkie Street, Preston PR1 3LU.

Career: articled in Preston; admitted (1958); assistant solicitor in Windsor and Tonbridge; founded own practice (1964).

Activities: chairman British Legal Association (1987-1989) (member Executive Committee); member Law Society president's working party on sole practitioners; member of: Lancaster Golf Club; Preston Grasshoppers.

Biography: lives near Lancaster; born 01.11.1930; married with 3 children. Educated at Ulverston & Hutton Grammar

Schools; Manchester University (1955 LLB hons).

Leisure: swimming; golf; reading; walking; gardening; studying Spanish, Italian and Russian.

DICKINSON Robert

senior partner DICKINSON DEES Cross House, Westgate Road, Newcastle upon Tyne NE99 1SB.

Career: admitted (1960); assistant solicitor (1960-1963); became partner Dickinson Dees (1963); became senior partner (1987).

Activities: deputy chairman Northern Rock Building Society; deputy chairman Tyne Tees Television PLC; High Gosforth Park PLC; Grainger Trust PLC; Northern Investors Co PLC; Reg Vardy PLC; local director Barclays Bank PLC; trustee University of Newcastle upon Tyne Development Trust; member of: Boodles; Northern Counties Club.

Biography: lives Stocksfield; born 12.05.1934; married to Kyra with 3 children. Educated at Harrow School; Christ Church Oxford (1957 Hons).

DIGBY-BELL Christopher

partner property department FRERE CHOLMELEY 28 Lincoln's Inn Fields, London WC2A 3HH.

Career: articled Taylor & Humbert (1966-1971); admitted (1972); assistant solicitor (1972-1975); became salaried partner (1975-1977); became equity partner (1977-1984); became partner Taylor Garrett following merger (1984-1987); managing partner (1987-1989); became partner Frere Cholmeley (1989).

Activities: active interest in the legal rights of the mentally handicapped particularly in relation to education; member Downs Syndrome Association; member Law Society Group for the Welfare of People with a Mental Handicap; member Home Farm Trust; member of: MCC; Berkshire Golf Club; Stewards Henley on Thames; Leander Rowing Club.

Biography: lives London SW15; born 21.06.1948; married to Claire with 3 children. Educated at Marlborough College; College of Law London; Distinction in conveyancing paper.

Leisure: cricket (founder The Briefs XI); golf; tennis; swimming; American football (spectator); rugby (spectator); current affairs; reading; pop music; refurbishing period houses; cinema; photography.

DIGGLE Catherine

commercial property and training partner FORSYTE KERMAN 79 New Cavendish Street, London W1M 8AQ.

Career: articled John Laing & Son Ltd; admitted (1980); assistant solicitor Forsyte Kerman (1980-1984); partner (1984 to date); became training partner (1988).

Biography: lives London N1; born 05.07.1955; single. Educated at Lanchester Polytechnic, Coventry (1976 BA hons).

Leisure: Egyptology; Manchester United.

DILGER John

partner and head of tax and financial planning department MACFARLANES 10 Norwich Street, London EC4A 1BD.

Career: national service (1953-1955); articled Macfarlanes (then Neish Howell & Haldane) (1958); admitted (1961); assistant solicitor (1961-1964); partner (1964).

Activities: chairman Law Society Revenue Law Committee (member since 1974); member Athenaeum.

Biography: lives Banstead; born 30.09.1935; married to Kay with 2 children. Educated at Wimbledon College; Brasenose College Oxford (BA 1958 MA); Solicitors Finals (1961 Hons Clifford's Inn Prize).

DILLON Jerome

partner MARSLAND & BARBER 51 Hawley Square, Margate, Kent CT9 1NY.

Career: articled Rashleigh & Co; admitted (1968); assistant solicitor Malcolm Borg & Borg (1968); firm became known as Marsland & Barber; became partner.

Activities: president of the Isle of Thanet Law Society (1986-1987); member South East Regional Duty Solicitor Committee; hon solicitor to Broadstairs & St Peter's Town Council (1987 to date); member of team of solicitors conducting advocacy training courses at Kent police headquarters training school; member of: Royal Cinque Ports Yacht Club; Broadstairs Sailing Club; The Margate Club.

Biography: lives London NW3 and Broadstairs; born 06.05.1944; married to Susan with 3 children. Educated at Worth Preparatory School; Downside School; College of Law.

Leisure: sailing; boating; stage lighting.

DIXON Christopher

deputy senior partner NORTON ROSE Kempson House, Camomile Street, London EC3A 7AN.

Career: National Service as Lt RA (1947-1950); Major RATA in Territorial Army (1951-1960); articled Norton Rose (1955); assistant solicitor (1955-1959); became partner (1959).

Activities: member of: City University Club; Royal Artillery Yacht Club.

Biography: lives Oxted; born 17.08.1928; married to Ethelwyn with 4 children. Educated at King's College Junior School; Rugby School; College of Law Lancaster Gate (1955).

Leisure: sailing; gardening.

DIXON David

partner WITHERS 20 Essex Street, London WC2R 3AL.

Career: articled Allen & Overy (1950-1952); admitted (1953); assistant solicitor (1954-1957); became partner Withers (1957); senior partner (1982-1986).

Activities: chairman Elf UK PLC; hon legal adviser The British Olympic Association (1978 to date); solicitor to Ascot Authority (1980 to date); various directorships; hon secretary The Commonwealth Games Federation (1982 to date); member of: Brooks's; RAC; Vincent's; Achilles; Hurlingham; Royal Wimbledon Golf Club.

Biography: lives London SW19 and Blackford; born 01.05.1926; married to Alison with 3 children. Educated at Whitgift School; Oxford University (1950 BA MA); Harvard University Law School (1954 LLM) (Commonwealth Fund Fellowship); papers and lectures on aspects of sport and law.

Leisure: sport (Oxford Athletics Blue; president OUAC 1950); travel.

DIXON Peter

consultant RADCLIFFES & CO 10 Little College Street, Westminster, London SW1P 3SJ.

Career: articled Milles Day & Co (1955-1958); admitted (1958); assistant solicitor Radcliffes & Co (1959-1960); became partner (1961-1980); senior partner (1981-1990); became consultant (1990).

Activities: TA hon Col 81 Signal Squadron (V) (1980-1986); member of: East India Club; Leander.

Biography: lives London W8 and Shrewsbury; born 03.10.1931; married to Christine with 1 son. Educated at Shrewsbury School; Christ's College Cambridge (MA LLB); Clabon Prize.

DIXON Roger

partner HAGUE & DIXON Bank House, 1 The Square, Stamford Bridge, York.

Career: articled to father at Hague & Dixon (1970-1972); admitted (1972); became partner (1972).

Activities: hon secretary Yorkshire Law Society (1981 to date); chairman and vice-president MacMillan Cancer Relief Fund York Committee; trustee York Boys' Club; vice-chairman of the Board of Governors of Welburn Hall School; member of the Committee of the York and District Friends of the Home Farm Trust; solicitor to St Leonard's Hospice; presented occasional legal talks particularly on the topic of testamentary provision and associated matters for the mentally handicapped.

Biography: lives Holtby; born 13.03.1948; married to Wendy with 1 son and 1 daughter. Educated at St Olave's Preparatory School, York; St Peter's School, York; Durham University (1969 BA hons); College of Law Guildford (1969-1970).

Leisure: messing about in boats; gardening; running (completed half marathon); classic cars; playing the guitar.

DIXON Roger

partner TRAVERS SMITH BRAITHWAITE 10 Snow Hill, London EC1A 2AL.

Career: articled Travers Smith Braithwaite (1953-1956); admitted (1957); assistant solicitor (1957-1961); became partner (1962).

Activities: Senior Warden of City of London Solicitors' Company; governor Christ's Hospital; member of: City of London Club; MCC.

Biography: lives London; born 19.06.1929; married to Kathleen with 1 son and 2 daughters. Educated at Christ's Hospital (1939-1948); St Catharine's College Cambridge (1953 BA) (MA).

Leisure: travel; books; music; theatre; stamps.

DOBBS Oliver Louis

consultant to FAIRCHILD DOBBS & CO 1 Bulstrode Way, Gerrards Cross, Bucks SL9 7QT and Walter C Hetherington & Co, Gerrards Cross.

Career: articled Howard Davidson & Co; admitted (1953); National Service; assistant solicitor Freshfields (1955-1960); Mobil Oil Co (1960-1963); partner Fairchild Greig & Co (1963-1974); senior partner (1974-1989); became consultant (1989).

Activities: elder of Goldhill Baptist Church (1970-1990).

Biography: lives Gerrards Cross; born 20.04.1931; married to Ruth with 3 children. Educated at Queen Elizabeth's School, Barnet; College of Law Lancaster Gate.

Leisure: sailing; windsurfing; tennis; skiing; promoting Christian faith.

DOBIAS Michael

senior litigation partner, practising in the insurance/reinsurance section of DAVIES ARNOLD COOPER 12 Bridewell Place, London EC4V 6AD.

Career: articled Davies Arnold Cooper (1973-1975); admitted (1975); assistant solicitor (1975-1980); became partner (1980).

Activities: committee member London Solicitors Litigation Association; member International Bar Association; member International Association of Defense Council.

Biography: lives Ilford; born 28.09.1950; married to Alison with 3 children. Educated at Hackney Downs Grammar School; Birmingham University (1972 LLB hons); articles published and papers delivered at seminars on insurance/reinsurance matters and UK civil procedures; contributor to Longman Litigation Practice Trial and Judgment Section.

Leisure: cinema; sports.

DOBRIN Michael

senior conveyancing partner HOWARD KENNEDY 23 Harcourt House, 19 Cavendish Square, London W1A 2AW.

Career: articled Franks Charlesly & Co; admitted (1962); assistant solicitor Winston & Co (1962-1964); assistant solicitor Howard Kennedy (1965-1966); became partner (1966); hotel and catering speciality.

Biography: lives London NW11; born 24.07.1937; married to Barbara with 3 daughters. Educated at Caterham; University College London (1958 LLB hons).

Leisure: skiing; tennis.

DOBSON Andrew

commercial litigation partner LAWRENCE GRAHAM 190 Strand, London WC2R 1JN.

Career: articled Macfarlanes (1978-1980); admitted (1980); assistant solicitor (1980-

D

1986); partner Knapp Fishers (1986-1987); became partner Lawrence Graham (1987).

Biography: lives London; born 20.02.1956; married to Janet with 2 children. Educated at Oundle School (1969-1973); St Catharine's College Cambridge (1977 MA); College of Law Guildford (1978).

Leisure: reading (particularly modern European history); social rugby; sport; travel.

DODD Graham

senior partner JAMES & CHARLES DODD 18 Tranquil Vale, Blackheath, London SE3 0AZ.

Career: articled James & Charles Dodd; admitted (1963); became partner; became senior partner.

Biography: lives Westerham; born 03.03.1940; married to Theresa with 4 children. Educated at King's School, Canterbury .

DODD Ian

senior partner GRIFFITH SMITH 47 Old Steyne, Brighton, East Sussex BN1 1NW.

Career: articled Griffith Smith Dodd & Riley (1961-1965); admitted (1965); became partner (1967); prosecuting solicitor to Eastbourne Borough Council (1966-1967).

Activities: solicitor to Shoreham Port Authority; hon solicitor to Brighton & Hove District Samaritans; solicitor to Brighton & Hove District MENCAP; solicitor and governor of Brighton College and other schools; director of number of companies; trustee various charities; hon secretary International Committee re Polio Plus; member of: Dyke Golf Club; Shoreham Yacht Club.

Biography: lives Hove; born 16.07.1942; married to Pat with 7 children. Educated at Brighton College; Britannia Royal Naval College (1960-1961); College of Law; Royal Naval Scholarship.

Leisure: Rotary; theatre; travel.

DODDS-SMITH Ian

partner MCKENNA & CO Mitre House, 160 Aldersgate Street, London EC1A 4DD.

Career: articled McKenna & Co; admitted (1976); assistant solicitor (1976-1984); seconded to pharmaceutical company (1979-1982);·became partner (1984).

Activities: temporary advisor to WHO on the law relating to clinical trials (1987); legal adviser to the Clinical Sciences Ethics Committee of University of London and University College Hospital; member of the Royal College of Physicians Working Party on Research at Phase 1 in Healthy Volunteers (1985-1986); member of the Medical Research Council Working Party on legal and ethical issues raised by research in the mentally incapacitated (1988); frequent speaker at symposia on regulatory and product liability issues relevant to the pharmaceutical and medical product and device sectors; member American Bar Association.

Biography: lives London SW6 and Cuckfield; born 31.07.1951; married to Caroline with 1 daughter and 1 son. Educated at Solihull School; Downing College Cambridge (1972 BA) (1973 MA); author of: The Implications of Strict Liability under the Consumer Protection Act for the Pharmaceutical Sector - book chapter in 'Risk and Consent to Risk' (1989); Legal Liabilities in Clinical Trials - book chapter in 'Early Phase Human Drug Evaluation' (1990); Chapter 21 on Product Liability for Medicinal Products in 'Medical Negligence' (1990); The European Product Liability Directive - The Personal & Medical Injuries Law Letter (1985): The Legal Implications of Studies in Healthy Volunteers - The Journal of the British Institute of Regulatory Affairs (1985); Product Liability: US Smoking and Health Litigation - The Personal & Medical Injuries Law Letter (1986); Patient Information and the Supply of Oral Contraceptives in the UK - The Contraceptive Foundation (1986).

Leisure: walking; gardening; all aspects of natural history; keen interest in national hunt racing.

DODSON Eric

consultant ADDLESHAW SONS & LATHAM Dennis House, Marsden Street, Manchester M2 1JD.

Career: Lt Inns of Court Regt RAC (1943-1947); Civil Affairs branch British Military Administration, East Africa; assistant custodian Enemy property, Mogadishu; articled Addleshaw Sons & Latham (1949-1951); admitted (1951); assistant solicitor (1951-1953); became partner (1953-1978); became senior partner (1978-1987); became consultant (1987).

Activities: director Halifax Building Society (1984 to date); member Commercial Law Committee of Association of British Chambers of Commerce (1969-1981) (later chairman); member Committee of Solicitors European Group (1973 to date) (chairman 1988); member of: St James's Club, Manchester; National Liberal Club.

Biography: lives Stockport; born 18.01.1924; married to Mary with 3 children. Educated at Manchester Grammar School; Rugby School; Trinity Hall Cambridge (1948 BA) (1949 LLB) (LLM) (1952 MA). ,

Leisure: travel (particularly to Italy and France - good working knowledge of Italian); rowing (Amateur Rowing Association umpire).

DOHMANN Barbara

barrister 2 Hare Court, Temple, London EC4Y 7BH.

Career: called to the Bar Gray's Inn (1971); Recorder (1990); QC (1987).

Activities: Committee member Commercial Bar Association; member CWIL.

Biography: lives London NW3. Educated in schools in Germany and USA; Universities of Erlangen, Mainz and Paris.

DOLMAN James

senior partner BIRCHAM & CO 1 Dean Farrar Street, Westminster, London SW1H 0DY.

Career: articled Jaques & Co; admitted; became partner Bircham & Co (1970); became senior partner (1985).

Activities: chairman Samuel Gardner Memorial Trust; hon solicitor and member Executive Committee King Edward VII's Hospital for Officers; Hon Fellow Purcell School of Music.

Biography: lives London SW15; born 26.04.1934; married to Jean with 4 children. Educated at Ilminster Grammar School; St John's College Cambridge (1957 MA LLM); McMahon Law Studentship.

Leisure: arts; all rough sports.

DONALDSON David

Queen's Counsel 2 Hare Court, Temple, London EC4Y 7BH.

Career: called to the Bar (1968); QC (1984).

Biography: lives London; born 30.09.1943; married to Therese. Educated at Glasgow Academy; Gonville and Caius College Cambridge (1964 BA) (1967 MA); University of Freiburg, West Germany (1967 Dr Jur).

DONN Raymond

senior partner DONN & CO 26 Cross Street, Manchester M2 7AN.

Career: articled Betesh Singer & Co; admitted (1969); founded own practice (1969).

D

Activities: developing legal advisory services within NHS hospitals; former director and vice-chairman Altrincham Association Football Club.

Biography: lives Manchester; born 17.03.1944; married with 4 children. Educated at Stand Grammar School, Whitefield; College of Law Guildford (1969).

DOOLAN Kevin

head of banking department PHILLIPS & BUCK Fitzalan House, Fitzalan Road, Cardiff CF2 1XZ.

Career: admitted (1977); assistant solicitor Phillips & Buck (1977-1980); became partner (1980); member executive committee.

Activities: national chairman Eversheds Banking Group; regular provider of seminars on developments in the law and upon negotiating skills for those in the finance industry; appointed member Urban Investment Grants Panel by Secretary of State for Water (1989).

Biography: lives Cardiff; born 14.11.1953; married to Deborah with 1 child. Educated at De La Salle Prep School; St Illtyd's College, Cardiff; University of Wales (1976 LLB hons).

Leisure: badminton; swimming; golf; skiing; computer programming.

DOUGLAS-JONES Peter

partner DOUGLAS-JONES & MERCER 147 St Helen's Road, Swansea SA1 4DB.

Career: admitted (1970); assistant solicitor Dennis Berry & Co (1970-1971); became partner Douglas Jones & Mercer (1971).

Activities: member Area Committee of Legal Aid Board; Notary Public; member of Clarity.

Biography: lives Swansea; born 30.04.1947; married to Christine with 2 children. Educated at Mill Hill School.

DOULTON Roger

partner WINWARD FEARON & CO 35 Bow Street, London WC2 7AU.

Career: articled Herbert Smith; admitted; assistant solicitor; assistant solicitor Davies Arnold & Cooper (1978-1980); partner Fenwick Elliott & Co (1980-1985); founder partner Winward Fearon & Co (1986).

Activities: member British Academy of Experts; liability correspondent and committee member British Insurance Law Association; member of: Wig & Pen Club; Salcombe Yacht Club.

Biography: lives London N1; born 28.03.1949; divorced with 2 children. Educated at Rugby; Oxford MA (Oxon) PPE; articles for BILA.

Leisure: French horn playing; opera; the arts generally; sport; politics; eating and drinking.

DOWLER Bryan

partner and head commercial property department FLADGATE FIELDER Heron Place, 3 George Street, London W1H 6AD.

Career: articled Copley Singleton & Billson; admitted; assistant solicitor Walters & Hart (1965-1971); legal adviser Glade Group of Companies (1972-1976); partner Walters Fladgate (1980-1989); became head commercial property department Fladgate Fielder (1989).

Activities: chairman and/or vice-chairman governing body of karate in England & Wales (professional karate instructor (1978-1989).

Biography: lives Croydon; born 01.12.1938; divorced. Educated at Winton House Preparatory; Whitgift School.

Leisure: study of things oriental; speaking Thai.

DOYLE Julian

partner GOULDENS 22 Tudor Street, London EC4Y 0JJ.

Career: law clerk Arthur Robinson & Co, Melbourne; founded own practice; Australian Trade Commissioner, London; Commercial Counsellor Australian Mission to EC, Brussels; became partner Ellison Hewison & Whitehead; founding chief executive Victorian Economic Development Corporation; Managing Director Sirotech Limited.

Activities: city councillor, Prahran; member Victorian Parliament; member International Trade Law Committee, Law Council of Australia; member of Australian Club, Melbourne.

Biography: lives Saffron Walden; married to Sally Anne with 4 children. Educated at Xavier College, Melbourne; Melbourne University (LLB); University of California (Berkeley).

Leisure: music; surfing.

DOYLE Michael

partner OXLEY & COWARD 275 Glossop Road, Sheffield S10 2HB.

Career: articled Knight & Sons (1968-1973); admitted (1973); assistant solicitor Arthur F Clark & Son (1973-1975); solicitor and

senior assistant regional solicitor with Trent Regional Health Authority (1975-1989); became partner Oxley & Coward (1989).

Activities: lectures to health authorities on the law and the health service; member South Yorkshire Medico-Legal Society.

Biography: lives Sheffield; born 12.07.1947; married to Gillian with 2 children. Educated at Douai School; Liverpool Polytechnic.

Leisure: travel; photography; mountaineering; cycling.

DRABBLE Timothy

senior partner GREGORY ROWCLIFFE & MILNERS 1 Bedford Row, London WC1R 4BZ.

Career: articled Mr Hugh Rowcliffe; admitted (1960); assistant solicitor (1960-1962); became partner Gregory Rowcliffe & Co (1962); became equity partner (1965); senior partner (1987); became senior partner Gregory Rowcliffe & Milners (1988).

Activities: committee member Holborn Law Society (1977 to date) (president (1988-1989); member Cavalry & Guards Club.

Biography: lives London W11 and Billingshurst; born 06.01.1935; married to Daphne with 1 child. Educated at St Peter's School, Seaford; Winchester College; Law Society School of Law.

Leisure: shooting; gardening; tidying up indoors and outdoors.

DRAKE John

managing partner STEVENS DRAKE & POPE Midland House, 117/119 High Street, Crawley, West Sussex RH10 1YN.

Career: articled Stevens Son & Pope (1963-1965); admitted (1965); assistant solicitor (1965-1966); became partner (1966).

Activities: co-founder first Solicitors Property Centre in Crawley (1985); speaker at seminars on solicitors selling property; member executive Committee of NASPYC; secretary Mid-Sussex MENCAP; member Haywards Heath Rugby Club .

Biography: lives Staplefield; born 29.08.1940; married to Janet with 5 children. Educated at Churchers College, Petersfield; Chichester High School; Lewes Grammar School; Gonville and Caius College Cambridge (1962 MA).

Leisure: travel; golf; rugby; reading; theatre; gardening.

D

DREW Jeff

partner and head of insolvency department EDGE & ELLISON Rutland House, 148 Edmund Street, Birmingham B3 2JR.

Career: articled (1978-1980); admitted (1980); assistant solicitor (1980-1984); became partner (1984).

Activities: member Oxford and Cambridge Club.

Biography: lives Birmingham; born 12.10.1954; married to Ann. Educated at Ruckleigh School; Solihull School; St Edmund Hall Oxford (1977 BA).

Leisure: squash; badminton; tennis; reading.

DRIFFIELD John

head of property department McKENNA & CO Mitre House, 160 Aldersgate Street, London EC1A 4DD.

Career: articled Morrish & Co (1955-1960); Army (1960-1965) (latterly as major Army Legal Services Staff List (BAOR and Aden); became partner Lomer & Co (1965-1974); assistant solicitor McKenna & Co (1974-1976); became partner (1976).

Biography: lives Kelvedon; born 19.08.1937; married to Yvonne with 3 sons. Educated at Leeds Grammar School; Leeds University (1958 LLB); co- author with other members of department of the Business Property section of Kluwer's 'Business Law Handbook'.

Leisure: music (organ, choral singing); ecclesiastical duties; dabbles in classic cars.

DROOP Peter

partner TAYLOR JOYNSON GARRETT 180 Fleet Street, London EC4A 2NT.

Career: articled Taylor & Humbert (1966-1968); admitted (1968); assistant solicitor (1968-1972); became partner (1972-1982); became finance partner Taylor Garrett (1982-1989); became partner Taylor Joynson Garrett (1989) .

Activities: member of: Roehampton Club; Jesters Club.

Biography: lives London SW13; born 28.03.1944; married to Pauline with 3 children. Educated at Marlborough College; Trinity College Cambridge (1965 MA).

Leisure: lawn tennis; golf; travel; photography.

DRUMMOND William (Bill)

partner commercial property department BRODIES WS 15 Atholl Crescent, Edinburgh EH3 8HA.

Career: apprentice Brodies WS (1980-1982); admitted (1982); assistant solicitor (1983-1986); became partner (1986); assistant solicitor Shepherd & Wedderburn WS (1982-1983).

Activities: Writer to Her Majesty's Signet (1986); member of: The North Berwick Golf Club; The Highland Club.

Biography: lives Edinburgh; born 26.01.1959; married to Caroline. Educated at North Berwick High School; Aberdeen University (1979 LLB).

Leisure: Scottish countryside; skiing; hill walking; fishing; golf.

DRYSDALE Tom

managing partner SHEPHERD & WEDDERBURN WS 16 Charlotte Square, Edinburgh EH2 4YS.

Career: admitted (1966); assistant solicitor (1966-1967); partner Shepherd & Wedderburn WS (1967); became managing partner (1988).

Activities: chairman Edinburgh Solicitors Property Centre (1981-1988); member New Club, Edinburgh.

Biography: lives Edinburgh; born 23.11.1942; married to Caroline with 2 daughters and 1 son. Educated at Glenalmond; Edinburgh University (1964 LLB).

Leisure: skiing; walking.

DU-FEU Viv

partner and head of employment and contentious department PHILLIPS & BUCK Fitzalan House, Fitzalan Road, Cardiff CF2 1XZ.

Career: admitted (1979); assistant solicitor (1979-1983); became partner Phillips & Buck (1983).

Activities: part-time lecturer in labour law at University College Cardiff (1983-1987); member Institute of Personnel Management.

Biography: lives Cardiff; born 17.04.1954; married to Lynn. Educated at Priory Boys' School; Guildford Technical College (1973); University College Cardiff (1976 LLB); author of 'Conduct of Proceedings before Industrial Tribunals' (1988).

Leisure: musician; squash.

DUBOW Leslie

general secretary SOLICITORS PROPERTY GROUP 30 Station Road, Cuffley, Herts EN6 4HE.

Career: articled Jacklyn Dawson & Meyricke Williams (1956-1959); admitted (1960); assistant solicitor HW Pegden & Co (1960-1963); became junior partner (1963-1967); became senior partner (1967-1980); senior partner Pegden & Dubow (1980-1984); sold practice (1984); sabbatical (1984-1985); partner Norman Cecil and Martin (1978-1982); became principal Solicitors Property Centres (1986).

Activities: member Law Society Ad hoc Committee on relations with French Notaries; lectures on practice rules affecting the solicitor property seller; runs seminars on buying and selling property in France, Spain and Portugal; estate agency for solicitors; past chairman Enfield Community Relations Council; chairman North London branch English Speaking Union; member of Law Society.

Biography: lives Cuffley; born 30.08.1933; married to Leila with 2 children. Educated at Cardiff High School (1944-1951); Jesus College Oxford (1954 MA Oxon) University College Cardiff Law School (1956-1957).

DUCKWORTH John

partner TURNER KENNETH BROWN 100 Fetter Lane, London EC4A 1DD.

Career: articled White Brooks & Gilman (1955-1958); admitted (1958); assistant solicitor Culross & Co (1959); assistant solicitor Kenneth Brown Baker Baker (1960-1965); became partner (1965).

Biography: lives London and Nether Wallop; born 27.10.1931; single. Educated at Sedbergh (1945-1950); Downing College Cambridge (1952-1955).

Leisure: sailing; skiing; DIY.

DUFFIELD Peter

partner TRAVERS SMITH BRAITHWAITE 6 Snow Hill, London EC1A 2AL.

Career: articled Travers Smith Braithwaite (1958-1961); admitted (1961); assistant solicitor (1961-1966); became partner (1966).

Activities: non-executive director CE Heath PLC; member City Solicitors Company Revenue Law Committee; member of: City of London Club; City Livery Club; Flyfishers' Club.

Biography: lives Sussex; born 1935; married to Diana with 2 children. Educated at Bancroft's; St John's College Oxford (MA).

Leisure: fishing.

D

DUFFY John

senior partner BRETHERTON TURPIN & PELL 16 Church Street, Rugby.

Career: articled Bretherton Turpin & Pell (1950); National Service; admitted; assistant solicitor; became partner (1958).

Activities: sometime chairman Social Security Appeal Tribunal; chairman governors Lawrence Sheriff School, Rugby; member of: The Rugby Club; The Northamptonshire County Golf Club.

Biography: lives Rugby; born 16.08.1932; married to Muriel. Educated at Lawrence Sheriff School, Rugby; Rugby School.

Leisure: golf; fishing.

DUNCAN Ken

partner STEPHENSON HARWOOD One St Paul's Churchyard, London EC4M 8SH.

Career: admitted (1971); assistant solicitor (1971-1977); became partner Stephenson Harwood (1977).

Biography: born 30.12.1946. Educated at King William's College, Isle of Man; Downing College Cambridge (1968).

DUNSMORE Ian

partner BISHOP AND ROBERTSON CHALMERS 2 Blythswood Square, Glasgow G2 4AD.

Career: National Service in Royal Navy (1956-1958); apprentice McGrigor Donald (1959-1962); admitted (1962); became partner Bishop Milne Boyd & Co (now Bishop and Robertson Chalmers).

Activities: member Glasgow Junior Chamber of Commerce (1963-1976); president Pollok Curling Club (1986-1987); Elder in Church of Scotland (1968 to date); session clerk Merrylea Parish Church (1985 to date); secretary Glasgow Leukaemia Trust; secretary Institute of Neurological Sciences Research Trust; clerk Incorporation of Weavers of Glasgow; member of: RNVR Club (Scotland); Royal Scottish Automobile Club.

Biography: lives Glasgow; born 24.12.1936; married to Eileen with 2 daughters. Educated at Giffnock School (1941-1946); Glasgow Academy (1946-1956); Glasgow University (1962 BL).

Leisure: sailing; hill walking; philately; naval affairs; curling.

DURBIN Peter

partner FOOT & BOWDEN 70/76 North Hill, Plymouth PL4 8HH.

Career: articled GD Cann & Hallett (1958-1963); admitted (1964); assistant solicitor Farrer & Co (1964-1968); assistant solicitor Whitford Bennett & Co (1968-1970); assistant solicitor Shelly & Johns (1970-1971); became partner (1971); amalgamated with Foot & Bowden (1981).

Activities: formerly retained by police as prosecutor Plymouth Magistrates' Court; occasionally represents defendants in Courts Martial; Colonel TA (Deputy Commander 43 Infantry Brigade (1964 to date); TD (1976); OBE (1987); Freeman of the City of London; member Worshipful Company of Carmen; member of: Royal Western Yacht Club of England; Saltash Rotary Club; MBIM.

Biography: lives Saltash; born 29.04.1941; married to Linda with 2 children. Educated at Marlborough College; College of Law Guildford.

Leisure: keen sailor.

DURIE Robyn

partner Intellectual Property Department LINKLATERS & PAINES Barrington House, 59-67 Gresham Street, London EC2V 7JA.

Career: articled Allen Allen & Hemsley, Sydney (1975-1977); admitted NSW (1977); assistant solicitor (1978-1981); legal assistant International Federation of Record Companies, UK (1977-1978); called to the Bar (1981); entertainment division News Limited (1982); Freehill Hillingdale & Page, Sydney; solicitor Linklaters & Paines (1987-1990); became partner (1990).

Activities: member Australian Copyright Law Review committee (1986-1987); member Queen's Club, Sydney.

Biography: lives London; born 11.12.1952; married. Educated PLC Pymble; Sydney University (1974 BA) (1977 LLB hons); London University (1978 LLM); author of 'Broadcasting Law & Practice'; articles on intellectual property in: European Intellectual Property Review; IIC the Australian Law Journal and Entertainment Law Review.

Leisure: theatre; writing; cooking; gardening.

DURRANT Anthony

senior partner HORWOOD AND JAMES 7 Temple Square, Aylesbury, Bucks HP20 2QB.

Career: articled Kingsfords; admitted (1956); assistant solicitor in London (1956-1958); assistant solicitor Horwood and James (1958-1960); partner (1960-1974); became senior partner (1974).

Activities: Recorder of the Crown Court (1987); deputy chairman Agricultural Land Tribunal (South Western Area) (1987); president Berks Bucks & Oxon Incorporated Law Society (1977-1978); first chairman Berks Bucks & Oxon Professional Council; joint chairman Joint Consultative Committee of Barristers and Solicitors in Berks Bucks and Oxfordshire; hon solicitor to: British Paraplegic Sports Society; Stoke Mandeville (member Executive Council) and Stoke Mandeville Hospital Post Graduate Society (member Executive Council).

Biography: lives Little Kimble; born 03.01.1931; married to Jacqueline with 3 children. Educated at Rose Hill Preparatory School, Tunbridge Wells; Rochester Grammar School.

Leisure: reading; boating.

DYKSTRA Ronnie

senior partner ADDLESHAW SONS & LATHAM Dennis House, Marsden Street, Manchester M2 1JD.

Career: articled Addleshaw Sons & Latham (1951-1956); admitted (1957); assistant solicitor (1957-1961); became partner (1961); became senior partner (1987).

Activities: president Society of Construction Arbitrators; Fellow of Chartered Institute of Arbitrators; member of Wilmslow Green Room Society; member Wilmslow Amateur Swimming Club.

Biography: lives Wilmslow; born 04.03.1934; married to Sonia with 3 sons. Educated at The Edinburgh Academy.

Leisure: swimming; amateur drama; walking; cycling (cycled Land's End to John O'Groats 1986).

DYMOND Geraldine

senior partner JUDGE SYKES & HARRISON 9 Kingsway, London WC2B 6YF.

Career: shorthand typist; articled (3 years); admitted (1965); assistant solicitor and salaried partnerships in two firms; founded own practice (1984); became senior partner (1988).

Activities: member of: RAC; Wig & Pen Club.

Biography: lives London W1; born 21.05.1933; married to Geoffrey with 2 children. Educated at East Ham Grammar School for Girls; writes occasional articles for the journal of the German Chamber of Commerce.

E

Leisure: theatre; cinema; reading; listening to music; walking; cooking.

DYSON George

employment law partner BURGES SALMON Narrow Quay House, Prince Street, Bristol BS1 4AH.

Career: teaching fellow Osgoode Hall Law School, Toronto (1967-1968); articled; admitted; assistant solicitor Coward Chance (1969-1973); assistant solicitor Burges Salmon (1973-1977); became partner (1977).

Biography: lives Bristol; born 25.08.1945; married to Gill with 2 sons and 2 daughters (2 of the children from first marriage). Educated at Wallington County Grammar School for Boys; Balliol College Oxford (1967 BA); Balliol Open Scholarship.

Leisure: family; gardening; reading (especially history); travelling in France; wine.

EADY David

Queen's Counsel 1 Brick Court, Temple, London EC4Y 9BY.

Career: called to the Bar Middle Temple (1966); QC (1983); Recorder (1986).

Activities: member The Calcutt Committee on Privacy and Related Matters (1989-1990); working party on Pleadings in Defamation Cases (1990).

Biography: lives Tenterden; born 24.03.1943; married to Catherine with 2 children. Educated at Brentwood School; Trinity College Cambridge (1964 BA) (1965 LLB) (1968 MA); co-author 'The Law of Contempt' (1982).

Leisure: music; watching cricket.

EAGLES Brian

partner SJ BERWIN & CO 236 Gray's Inn Road, London WC1X 8HB.

Career: articled Bulcraig & Davis; admitted (1960); assistant solicitor J Sanson & Co (1960-1961); became partner (1961); firm merged with Herbert Oppenheimer Nathan & Vandyk (1967); partner (1967); finance partner (1974-1984); head of entertainment media and leisure group (1980-1988); became partner SJ Berwin & Co (1988).

Activities: arbitrator American Film

Marketing Association; hon solicitor Celebrities Guild of Great Britain; member of: Copenhagen Club; Variety Club of Great Britain.

Biography: lives London NW3; born 04.02.1937; married to Marje with 3 children. Educated at Kilburn Grammar School; London University (1959 LLB); writes for various journals.

Leisure: music; film; theatre; walking; skiing.

EALAND David

senior admiralty partner SINCLAIR ROCHE & TEMPERLEY Stone House, 128-140 Bishopsgate, London EC2M 4JP.

Career: holiday/work experience Wood & Audrey (1960-1963); articled Wellington & Clifford (1963-1968); admitted (1968); assistant solicitor Holman Fenwick & Willan (1968-1972); assistant solicitor Sinclair Roche & Temperley (1972-1974); became partner (1974); admitted Hong Kong; in part responsible for creation of firm's Hong Kong office; member firm's management committee; chairman committee responsible for office space and accommodation.

Activities: proprietor of one of England's most successful vineyards and wineries Chiltern Valley Wines.

Biography: lives nr Henley-on-Thames; born 15.09.1945; married to Fiona with 4 children. Educated at Cokethorpe Park.

Leisure: skiing; sailing.

EASBY Dennis

senior partner BRAIN & BRAIN 73 London Street, Reading RG1 4DB.

Career: RAF (1943-1947); articled Brain & Brain (1942-1950); admitted (1950); assistant solicitor (1950-1957); partner (1957-1985); became senior partner (1985).

Activities: President Reading & District Solicitors Association; Representative on Rugby Football Union for Berkshire (1971 to date); representative Rugby Football Union on International Rugby Football Board; chairman Rugby Football Union Laws Committee; former president and secretary Berkshire County Rugby Football Union; former chairman Reading Golf Club (captain 1975); former captain Old Redingensians Rugby Union Football Club and Cricket Club; former first class rugby referee with London Society of Rugby Referees; member of: RAF Club; East India Club.

Biography: lives Reading; born 15.02.1925;

married to Helen with 3 children and 2 stepchildren. Educated at Reading School (1934-1942); Gonville and Caius College Cambridge (1943 RAF short course); Air Efficiency Medal.

Leisure: gardening; golf; rugby administration.

EATON Andy

solicitor SHEFFIELD CITY COUNCIL Town Hall, Sheffield S1 2HH.

Career: articled Sheffield City Council (1986-1988); admitted (1988); assistant solicitor (1988-1990); became solicitor (1990).

Activities: president Sheffield Trainee Solicitors Group (1988-1989); regular volunteer in the Free Legal Information Service.

Biography: lives Sheffield; single. Educated at Doncaster Grammar School; Liverpool University (1985 LLB hons); College of Law Chester (1986).

Leisure: tennis; golf; ballroom dancing; indoor cricket; five-a-side football; camping/hiking; travelling.

EATON John

financial services & practice development partner LUPTON FAWCETT Yorkshire House, Greek Street, Leeds LS1 5SX.

Career: became partner in family firm Eaton & Co (1967-1985); became senior partner (1985); became consultant; became financial services & practice development partner Lupton Fawcett (1988).

Activities: member Bradford Law Society Council (1968); PR and press officer (1985); president Bradford Junior Chamber of Commerce (1973-1974) (hon life member 1984); Iceland award for most outstanding member in British Junior Chamber (1979); runner-up in national public speaking competition (1980-1982); president Bradford Law Society (1987); Fellow Institute of Directors; director Jarvis Porter Group PLC; Holiday Property Bond Limited and other private companies; member Law Society SBA British Legal Association; member Society for Computers and Law; member National Federation of Self Employed; senator Jaycees International; trustee Bingley Little Theatre; deputy chairman West Yorkshire County Scouts Council; chairman Bradford Businessmen's Association; hon solicitor Bradford & District Wool Federation; hon solicitor and 'legal eagle' on local radio (Radio Pennine); lecturer on marketing, financial services and computerisation for solicitors; contributer and panel speaker at Law Society national conferences (1987 & 1988).

Biography: lives Bingley; born 24.06.1943; married to Margaret with 1 daughter and 1 son. Educated at Charney Hall; Charterhouse (1956-1961); Cambridge (1964 MA); author of over 100 taped topics for 'Lawline'; contributer to several financial and investment journals.

Leisure: music; cabaret work (runs barbershop quartet); theatre; skiing; squash; tennis; walking; swimming; travel; naturopathy; organic lifestyle; environmental matters (member Soil Association; Conservation Society; Green Party; World Wildlife Fund; Friends of the Earth; Greenpeace; etc); campaigning for minority causes (anti-fluoridation; diet reform; etc).

EATON Paul

tax partner PENNINGTONS Clement House, 99 Aldwych, London WC2B 4LJ.

Career: articled Gamlens (1968-1970); admitted (1970); assistant solicitor (1970-1972); partner (1972); managing partner (1987-1990); became partner Penningtons on merger (1990).

Activities: member Holborn Law Society Revenue Law Committee; member Institute for Fiscal Studies/Society for Computers and Law; treasurer Law Society Rugby Football Club.

Biography: lives West Horsley; born 17.01.1945; married to Pauline with 2 sons and 1 daughter. Educated at St Wilfrid's Roman Catholic Primary School, Northwich; Sir John Dean's Grammar School, Northwich; Trinity Hall Cambridge (1967) (MA).

Leisure: music particularly opera; literature; languages particularly French, German, Russian; mountain walking; skiing.

EATON Tom

senior partner OVERBURY STEWARD & EATON 3 Upper King Street, Norwich, Norfolk NR3 1RL.

Career: 4 Bn Royal Norfolk Regt (TA) (1936-1950); served WWII (wounded despatches POW Singapore 1942-1945); admitted and Notary Public (1947); assistant solicitor (1947-1948); became partner Overbury Steward (1948).

Activities: president Norfolk & Norwich Incorporated Law Society (1960s); member Norwich City Council (1949-1974) (leader

1969-1970); Lord Mayor of Norwich (1957-1958); Conservative party candidate Norwich North (1951 & 1955); trustee East Anglian Trustee Savings Bank (1957-1980); governor Theatre Royal (Norwich) Trust Ltd (1972-1985); chairman Memorial Trust 2 Air Division USAAF (1975 to date); member Norfolk Club (president 1990-1991).

Biography: lives Norwich; born 13.10.1918; married to Robin with 3 children. Educated at Stowe.

Leisure: theatre; travel.

EDDIS Richard

former senior partner and head private client department STEPHENSON HARWOOD One St Paul's Churchyard, London EC4M 8SH.

Career: Army (1946-1949) commissioned The Rifle Brigade; ADC to Deputy Military Governor, Berlin (1948-1949); articled Stephenson Harwood (1950-1955); admitted (1955); assistant solicitor (1955-1957); partner (1957); chairman Executive Committee (1974-1981); senior partner (1981-1987).

Activities: member panel of Tribunal Chairman - TSA (1987-1990); member RHS Ridley Review Committee (1984-1985); magistrate (Essex) Halstead and Hedingham Bench (1969) (deputy chairman 1973-1989) (chairman 1990); member of: The City Club; Cavalry & Guards Club; Boodles; Lansdowne Club; The Lowtonian Society.

Biography: lives North Essex; born 10.06.1928; married with 5 children. Educated at Eton College.

Leisure: gardening (garden open for National Gardens Scheme 1985-1989); shooting; tennis.

EDELEANU Claire

partner in company department and responsible for training GOULDENS 22 Tudor Street, London EC4Y 0JJ.

Career: admitted (1975); assistant solicitor (1975-1979); became partner Gouldens (1979).

Biography: lives London W2; born 27.08.1949; single. Educated at Queen Victoria High School, Stockton on Tees; Leeds University (1972 LLB); College of Law Guildford (1972-1973).

EDELL Stephen

BUILDING SOCIETIES' OMBUDSMAN Grosvenor Gardens House, 35/37

Grosvenor Gardens, London SW1X 7AW.

Career: articled to father Edell & Co (1953-1958); admitted (1958); assistant solicitor (1958-1959); became partner Knapp-Fishers (1959-1975); Law Commissioner (1975-1983); became partner Crossman Block & Keith (1984-1987); Building Societies' Ombudsman (1987).

Activities: president City of Westminster Law Society (1982-1983); former member Law Society's Planning Law and Development Committee and By-Laws Revision Committee; member council and executive of Oxfam; Chairman Retailing and Property Committee; member City Livery Club.

Biography: lives Haywards Heath; born 01.12.1932; married with 3 children. Educated at Uppingham; London University (external) (LLB); author of: 'Inside Information on the Family and the Law' (1969); 'The Family's Guide to the Law' (1974); numerous magazine and newspaper articles.

Leisure: music; opera; theatre; early astronomical instruments.

EDEN John

consultant BEVAN ASHFORD Curzon House, Southernhay West, Exeter EX4 3LY.

Career: articled Wansbroughs (1952-1955); admitted (1956); assistant solicitor (1956-1958); assistant solicitor FE Metcalfe & Co (1958-1960); assistant solicitor Sparkes & Co (1961); became partner (1962-1976); became partner Ashford Sparkes & Harward (1976-1986); became senior partner (1985-1986); became senior partner Bevan Ashford (1987-1989).

Activities: Deputy Registrar High Court and County Court (1977 to date); Deputy Coroner East Devon (1980-1983); clerk to the Dean and Chapter of Exeter (1966-1989); company inspector Department of Trade and Industry (1987-1989); member Devon and Exeter Incorporated Law Society (1963-1969 & 1986 to date) (assistant secretary 1963-1968) (president 1988-1989); member Association of South Western Law Societies (1964-1969 & 1988-1989) (president 1968-1969); member Lord Chancellor's Judicial Review Committee (Devon) (1988 to date); hon secretary and librarian Exeter Law Library Society (1963-1976); founding hon secretary Exeter Weekend Course (1964); member of Court Exeter University (Law Society representative) (1968 to date); director Solicitor's Benevolent Association (1985-1987); member Territorial Army (1952-1961) (Major 1959-1961); trustee Exeter

E

Cathedral Preservation Trust; member Exeter Archaeological Advisory Committee; elder United Reformed Church.

Biography: lives Exeter; born 09.03.1929; married to Mary with 4 children. Educated at Forres School, Swanage; St Peter's College, Adelaide, South Australia; St John's College Cambridge (1950 BA) (1967 MA); author of articles in Law Society Gazette; The Conveyancer and Bracton Law Journal.

Leisure: music; roses.

EDGE Stephen

corporate tax partner SLAUGHTER AND MAY 35 Basinghall Street, London EC2V 5DB.

Career: articled Slaughter and May (1973-1975); admitted (1975); assistant solicitor (1975-1982); became partner (1982).

Biography: lives London SW8; born 29.11.1950; married to Melanie with 2 daughters. Educated at Canon Slade Grammar School, Bolton; Exeter University (1972 LLB hons); contributions to many publications.

Leisure: cricket; golf; fell walking; reading biographies; listening to early music.

EDMUND John

senior partner BEOR WILSON & LLOYD Calvert House, Calvert Terrace, Swansea SA1 6AP.

Career: articled Beor Wilson & Lloyd (1958-1961); admitted (1961); assistant solicitor (1961-1963); became partner (1963).

Activities: Under Sheriff West Glamorgan (1983 to date); clerk to General Commissioners of Taxes (Swansea Division) (1986 to date); member Law Society Land Law and Conveyancing Committee (1985 to date); member of: Vincents Club, Oxford; Bristol Channel Yacht Club, Swansea.

Biography: lives Swansea; born 06.03.1935; married to Myfanwy. Educated at Swansea Grammar School; Jesus College Oxford (1958 MA); Associated Law Societies of Wales Prize (1961).

EDNEY Robert

licensing partner KINGSFORD STACEY 14 Old Square, Lincoln's Inn, London WC2.

Career: articled Routh Stacey Pengelly & Co; admitted (1970); assistant solicitor (1970-1972); became partner Routh Stacey Pengelly & Boulton (1972).

Activities: chairman Legal Aid Area (No 13) Committee; chairman Aston Tennis Club; treasurer Aston Cricket Club.

Biography: lives near Stevenage; born 08.09.1946; married to Susan with 5 children. Educated at King Edward VI Grammar School, Nuneaton; Christ's College Cambridge (1968 BA).

Leisure: sport (particularly tennis).

EDWARD David

Judge of the Court of First Instance of the European Communities; Rue du Fort Niedergrunewald, L-2925 Luxembourg.

Career: National Service RNVR (1956-1957) (Sub Lt); advocate (Scotland) (1962); QC (1974); clerk and treasurer Faculty of Advocates (1967-1977); president Consultative Committee of Bars & Law Societies of the EC (1978-1980); Salvesen Professor of European Institutions Edinburgh University (1985-1989).

Activities: trustee National Library of Scotland; president Scottish Council for Arbitration (former chairman); former member Panel of Arbitrators ICSID; former member Law Advisory Committee of British Council; former chairman Continental Assets Trust PLC; former director Adam & Company PLC; former director Harris Tweed Association Ltd; former specialist adviser to House of Lords Select Committee on the European Communities; chairman Hopetoun House Preservation Trust; Fellow Royal Society of Edinburgh; member of: Athenaeum; New (Edinburgh).

Biography: lives Edinburgh and Luxembourg; born 14.11.1934; married to Elizabeth with 4 children. Educated at Sedbergh School; University College Oxford (1960 MA); Edinburgh University (1962 LLB); numerous articles.

EDWARDES JONES John

partner and head of company/commercial department DRUCES AND ATTLEE Salisbury House, London Wall, London EC2M 5PS.

Career: articled Trower Still & Keeling (1959-1962); admitted (1963); assistant solicitor (1963-1967); became partner (1967-1970); became partner Druces & Attlee (1971).

Activities: clerk of the Worshipful Company of Innholders; member Council of Distressed Gentlefolks Aid Association; Liveryman of the City of London Solicitors' Company; member of: Royal

and Ancient Golf Club; Brancaster Staithe Sailing Club; Royal West Norfolk Golf Club.

Biography: lives London EC2 and Buntingford; born 11.11.1936; married to Caroline with 1 son and 1 daughter. Educated at Marlborough College; Pembroke College Cambridge (1959 MA).

Leisure: golf; tennis; sailing; sport generally; food; drink; reading; theatre; cinema; music; travel abroad.

EDWARDS Alan

partner McKENNA & CO Mitre House, 160 Aldersgate Street, London EC1A 4DD.

Career: articled Coward Chance (1977-1979); admitted (1979); assistant solicitor (1979-1985); assistant solicitor McKenna & Co (1986); became partner.

Biography: lives London NW1; born 05.08.1955; single. Educated at Alun Grammar School, Mold, Clwyd; University College of Wales.

EDWARDS Anthony

senior partner WILSONS Steynings House, Chapel Place, Fisherton Street, Salisbury, Wilts SP2 7RJ.

Career: articled Ryland Martineau & Co (1963-1969); admitted (1969); assistant solicitor Farrer & Co (1969-1973); became partner (1973-1976).

Activities: chairman Salisbury Festival; chairman Cassidy Davis Members Agency Ltd; local director Coutts & Co (Winchester Branch); governor Sherborne School for Girls; governor Hawtreys School; member Court of Assistants Worshipful Company of Distillers; Liveryman Vintners' Company; member of: Brooks's Club; Flyfishers' Club; Zingari Cricket Club; Butterflies CC; MCC.

Biography: lives near Salisbury; born 13.03.1946; married to Celia with 4 children. Educated at Hillstone School, Malvern; Rugby School.

Leisure: music of all kinds; fishing; shooting; reading; gardening; wine; cricket.

EDWARDS Anthony

senior partner JOHN HODGE & CO 27-31 Boulevard, Weston-super-Mare, Avon BS23 1NY.

Career: articled (1950 for 4 months); National Service commissioned (NS) (1951); regular commission Royal Artillery (1953); articled John Hodge & Co and Waterhouse & Co (1953-1957); admitted

(1957); assistant solicitor John Hodge & Co (1957-1959); became partner (1959); senior partner (1980).

Activities: president Mental Health Review Tribunal (1980 to date); member of: Clifton Club; Royal Western YC of England; Royal Thames Yacht Club; Royal Fowey YC.

Biography: lives Banwell and Polruan-by-Fowey; born 26.04.1932; married to Patricia Mary with 1 son and 1 daughter. Educated at Cheltenham College.

Leisure: sailing; skiing; walking; reading.

EDWARDS John

partner COOK FOWLER AND OUTHET Albemarle Chambers, Albemarle Crescent, Scarborough, North Yorkshire YO11 1LA.

Career: articled to father with Cook Fowler and Outhet; admitted (1971).

Activities: past president Scarborough Law Society; president Scarborough Round Table; chairman and hon solicitor Derwent Anglers' Club; RYA dinghy instructor; member and hon solicitor of: Scarborough Yacht Club; Scalby Beck Anglers' Club; Filey Sailing Club; Scarborough Rugby Union FC; member of: Ski Club of Great Britain; Scarboro Cricket Club; the Naval Club.

Biography: lives Scalby nr Scarborough; born 22.10.1946; married to Jennifer with 2 children. Educated at Greshams School; College of Law.

Leisure: sailing; skiing; squash.

EDWARDS John

partner LINKLATERS & PAINES Barrington House, 59-67 Gresham Street, London EC2V 7JA.

Career: articled Linklaters & Paines (1967-1969); admitted (1969); assistant solicitor (1969-1973); became partner (1974); head of international finance (1986); head of European transactions unit (1989); merchant banking Hill Samuel (1973-1974)

Activities: hon senior visiting Fellow Queen Mary College London University; co-chairman Euromarket Securities Committee Q3 (IBA); member working party No 1 of International Organisation of Securities Commissions; regular speaker at Euromoney; IFLR Conferences; IBA; ABA; member of: Cresta Club; RAC; Marks'; Annabel's; City Club Hurlingham.

Biography: lives London SW3; born 06.11.1941; married to Annemarie with 2 children. Educated at Kantonsschule (Realgymnasium), Zurich; Trinity College Cambridge (1965 BA hons) (1968 MA).

Leisure: collecting 18/19th Century European paintings; music (classical, jazz, pop); playing clarinet/guitar; literature; skiing; psychology; philosophy; people.

EDWARDS Keith

senior partner EDWARDS GELDARD 16 St Andrew's Crescent, Cardiff CF1 3RD.

Career: articled C & M Edwards Shepherd & Co with time at Speechly Mumford and Soames & Jacques & Co; admitted (1967); assistant solicitor C & M Edwards Shepherd & Co (1967-1969); partner (1969); administration partner Edwards Geldard & Shepherd (1973); managing partner Edwards Geldard (1983-1990); became senior partner (1985).

Activities: member of: Cardiff and County Club; Cardiff Athletic Club; Glamorgan Wanderers Rugby Football Club.

Biography: lives South Glamorgan; born 17.10.1940; married to Susan with 3 children. Educated at Downs School, Colwall and Uppingham School.

Leisure: gardening; walking; photography.

EDWARDS Kenneth

senior managing partner BURT BRILL & CARDENS 30 Old Steyne, Brighton BN1 1FL.

Career: articled Blandy & Blandy; admitted (1961); 1 year in Richmond; assistant solicitor Cardens (1963); sole principal (1965); firm merged with Burt Brill & Edwards (1986).

Activities: head office solicitor to major national building society (1965-1985); member Law Society Land Law and Conveyancing Committee; member Law Commission Conveyancing Standing Committee; chairman working party on deposits in residential conveyancing; president Sussex Law Society.

Biography: lives Arlington; born 29.05.1930; married to Evelyn with 2 sons and 1 daughter. Educated at Reading Blue Coat School; part-author Law Society's booklet on home buying; member editorial board Law Society's Conveyancing Manual.

Leisure: home; family.

EDWARDS Martin

partner MACE AND JONES Drury House, 19 Water Street, Liverpool L2 0RP.

Career: articled in Leeds; admitted (1980); assistant solicitor Mace and Jones (1980-1984); became partner (1984).

Activities: member Law Society's

Employment Law Committee; Liverpool Law Society Admin Committee; Business Law Review - Editorial Committee; member Editorial Advisory Board of European Business Law Review; member of: Athenaeum Club, Liverpool; Crime Writers' Association; Society of Authors.

Biography: lives Lymm; born 07.07.1955; married to Helena. Educated at Sir John Deane's Grammar School (1966-1974); Balliol College Oxford (1977 hons); College of Law Chester; author 'Understanding Computer Contracts'; 'Understanding Dismissal Law'; 'Managing Redundancies'; 'Executive Survival'; co-author 'Careers in the Law'; written articles for various magazines.

Leisure: writing crime fiction; music; films; travel; cricket; soccer.

EDWARDS Michael

litigation partner LAWRENCE GRAHAM 190 Strand, London WC2R 1JN.

Career: articled Lawrence Graham (1969-1971); admitted (1971); assistant solicitor (1971-1973); became partner (1973-1976 & 1980); assistant solicitor Russell Jones & Walker (1978-1980).

Biography: lives New Malden; born 13.05.1947; married to Alison with 2 children. Educated at Tiffin Grammar School; Newcastle upon Tyne University (1968 LLB hons); article in Law Society's Guardian Gazette (1989).

Leisure: travel; supporting Chelsea Football Club.

EGERTON-SMITH David

partner LINKLATERS & PAINES Barrington House, 59/67 Gresham Street, London EC2V 7JA.

Career: became partner Linklaters & Paines (1974).

Activities: council member and former chairman section on energy and natural resources law of the International Bar Association; chairman Executive of Journal of Energy and Natural Resources Law; member MCC.

Biography: lives London W11; born 20.06.1942; married to Susan. Educated at Shrewsbury School; Cambridge.

EGERTON-VERNON Paul

partner NIGEL HARRIS & PARTNERS Oak Walk, St Peter, Jersey, Channel Islands JE3 7EF.

Career: articled Slaughter and May (1969);

E

seconded to Cleary Gottlieb Steen and Hamilton, Brussels; assistant solicitor Slaughter and May; founded London office associated with Nigel Harris & partners in Jersey (1978); moved to Jersey (1984).

Activities: international editor Law Society's Gazette (1973 to date); British representative on the Legal Committee of the Permanent Conference of European Chambers of Commerce (1973-1976); member Law Society's Competition Law Committee; member Law Society's Intellectual Property Law Committee (1975-1984); regular speaker at conferences on Common Market International Law; member of Oriental Club.

Biography: lives Grouville, Jersey; born 22.03.1945; married to Tricia with 2 sons. Educated at The Knoll School; Aldenham School; Durham University (1967 BA hons); College of Law (1968 & 1970); written numerous articles for the Law Society's Gazette; Competition Law contributor to Kluwar's 'Handbook on Business Law'; United Kingdom contributor on Kluwar's 'Competition Law in Western Europe and the USA'.

Leisure: riding; sailing; running.

EISDELL Anton HM

group legal adviser ALEXANDER & ALEXANDER EUROPE PLC 6 Devonshire Square, London EC2M 4YE; Assistant General Counsel Alexander & Alexander Services Inc, New York, NY, USA.

Career: articled Bartier Perry & Purcell, Sydney (1968-1970); Clifford Turner (1973-1975); Alireza & Colombolts, Bahrain (1978-1980); Appleby Spurling & Kempe, Bermuda (1981-1984); became group legal adviser Alexander & Alexander Europe PLC (1984); appointed Assistant General Counsel Alexander & Alexander Services Inc (1988).

Activities: member of: MCC; Saffron Walden Golf Club.

Biography: lives Arkesden nr Saffron Walden; born 23.12.1945; married to Juliet with 3 children. Educated at The Scots' College, Sydney; Sydney University (1970 LLB); London School of Economics (1976 LLM).

Leisure: shooting; tennis; skiing; fishing; golf; gardening.

ELDRIDGE David

partner and head of property department LEE & PEMBERTONS 45 Pont Street, London SW1X 0BX.

Career: articled Lee & Pembertons; admitted (1963); assistant solicitor (1963-1966); became partner (1966).

Activities: Fellow Institution of Analysts and Programmers; member British Sporting Art Trust; member Sloane Club.

Biography: lives Amersham; born 21.06.1939; married to Sheila with 2 children. Educated at University College School; College of Law Lancaster Gate.

Leisure: local Church work; community activities; country and mountain walking; keen photographer; computers; international friendship.

ELDRIDGE David John

partner AMHURST BROWN COLOMBOTTI 2 Duke Street, St James's, London SW1Y 6BJ and in AMHURST BROWN SP.20.0 of Warsaw, Poland.

Career: articled Stanley Attenborough & Co (1951-1956); admitted (1956); assistant solicitor (1956-1958); became partner (1958-1973); became partner Martin & Nicholson (1975-1977); became partner Amhurst Brown Martin & Nicholson (1977-1988); became partner Amhurst Brown Colombotti (1988); partner Amhurst Brown SP.20.0 which opened in Warsaw, Poland (1990).

Activities: past Master Guild of Freemen of City of London and past Master Worshipful Company of Fletchers (currently on Court of both); member of: City Livery Club; RAC.

Biography: lives London SW15; born 12.01.1935; married to Anna and has 3 children by first wife (deceased). Educated at KCS, Wimbledon.

ELDRIDGE James

senior partner JAMES ELDRIDGE & SONS 17 Lind Street, Ryde, Isle of Wight PO33 2NS.

Career: became partner James Eldridge & Sons (1947); (firm established by grandfather 1832); now senior partner.

Activities: Commissioner for Oaths; past president Isle of Wight Law Society; member Brading Haven Yacht Club.

Biography: born 25.04.1924; married to Elizabeth with 3 children. Educated at Sherborne.

Leisure: sailing.

ELDRIDGE Rob

assistant solicitor BERWIN LEIGHTON Adelaide House, London Bridge, London EC4R 9HA.

Career: articled Burton & Rind; admitted (1982); assistant solicitor Dibb Lupton & Co (1982-1986); assistant solicitor Hempsons (1986-1987); assistant solicitor Titmuss Sainer & Webb (1987-1989); assistant solicitor Berwin Leighton (1989).

Activities: great interest in employment law; member Industrial Law Society; ex-chairman Ashford Lawn Tennis Club; member Putney Lawn Tennis Club.

Biography: lives London SW12; born 19.06.1957; single. Educated at Ashford Grammar School; Birmingham University (1978 LLB hons).

Leisure: tennis; reading anything historical.

ELFER David

Queen's Counsel 1 Paper Buildings, Temple, London EC4Y 7EP and Guildhall Chambers, Broad Street, Bristol.

Career: called to the Bar Inner Temple (1964); pupillage with LKE Boreham; common law junior Western circuit; taught criminal law and evidence at Southampton University (1965-1968); Recorder (1978); QC (1981); Bencher of Inner Temple (1989).

Activities: Master of Bench of Inner Temple; member Wine Committee of Western Circuit (1979-1981); elected Western circuit representative on the General Council of the Bar Committee of Law Reform and Clerks' Liaison (1986-1988); member Henley Royal Regatta.

Biography: lives Virginia Water; born 15.07.1941; married to Alexandra with 3 sons. Educated at St Bede's College, Manchester; Emmanuel College Cambridge (1963 BA) (1968 MA).

Leisure: music (especially opera); theatre; skiing; jogging; dining in good company.

ELIA Giancarlo

partner STUDIO LEGALE BISCONTI 1 College Hill, London EC4R 4RA.

Career: National Service with Italian Navy (1966-1968); Mobil Oil, Rome (1968); called to the Bar (1969); Mobil Oil International, New York (1970); legal department IBM, Milan (1971-1973); Studio Legale Ardito (1974-1977); London office (1977-1980); consultant (1980-1984); became London resident partner Studio Legale Bisconti (1985).

Activities: lecturer on Italian law and speaker at various legal conferences and seminars in England and abroad; member IBA Banking and Business Organisation Committees; chairman Christian Mediation and Arbitration Service; member Full

Gospel Businessmen's Fellowship International; trustee several Christian charities.

Biography: lives London SW3; born 28.02.1943; married to Catherine. Educated at Liceo Dante, Rome (1958-1959); Liceo Umberto I, Naples (1959-1961); Rome University Faculty of Law (1966); Academy of American and International Law, Dallas (1970).

Leisure: mountaineering; sailing.

ELKS Laurence

partner NABARRO NATHANSON 50 Stratton Street, London W1X 5FL.

Career: voluntary service overseas (1970-1971); community worker (1971-1973); welfare rights worker Child Poverty Action Group (1973-1976); articled Withers (1978-1980); admitted (1980); assistant solicitor (1980-1981); assistant solicitor Nabarro Nathanson (1981-1984); became partner (1984).

Activities: co-ordinator of Nabarro Nathanson's activities for the Lawyers for Enterprise Scheme for Hackney Business Venture; hon legal adviser to business in the community; chairman local school governors.

Biography: lives London; born 25.03.1949; married with 3 children. Educated at Haberdashers' Aske's, Elstree; Trinity College Cambridge (1970 hons) Open Scholar; former regular contributor to Legal Action Group bulletin; regular contributor on behalf of Nabarro Nathanson to Corporate Briefing.

Leisure: active in various local environmental groups.

ELKS Michael

litigation partner RADCLIFFES & CO 5 Great College Street, Westminster, London SW1P 3SJ.

Career: articled Wilson & Berry (1972-1973); articled Radcliffes & Co (1973-1974); admitted (1974); assistant solicitor (1974-1976); became litigation partner (1977).

Activities: deputy registrar of Courts of Appeal of Falklands, British Antarctic Territories and St Helena; registrar of Court of Appeal of British Indian Ocean Territories; member sub-committee of the Law Society's Land Law and Conveyancing Committee; member International Bar Association; member of Royal Automobile Club.

Biography: lives London SW20; born 02.03.1949; married to Barbara with 3

children. Educated at Ipswich School; Clare College Cambridge (1971 BA); College of Law Lancaster Gate (1971-1972).

Leisure: theatre; cinema; squash.

ELLINGTON Paul

senior partner in Company Group and head of insolvency MCKENNA & CO 71 Queen Victoria Street, London EC4V 4EB.

Career: articled T Weldon Thomson & Co (1958-1961); articled Marcan & Dean (1961-1963); admitted (1963); assistant solicitor Clifford Turner & Co (1963) (Paris office 1963-1965); assistant solicitor Allen & Overy (1965-1968); assistant solicitor McKenna & Co (1968-1970); became partner (1970).

Activities: licensed insolvency practitioner; member Law Society Insolvency Law Panel; member CBI Companies Bill Working Group and CBI Company Law Working Group; arbitrator of the Westminster Court of Arbitration; member Editorial Committee of the Revue de Droit des Affaires Internationales.

Biography: lives London SE26, Tewkesbury and Aix-en-Provence; born 02.08.1937; married to Mireille with 3 children. Educated at Ipswich School; Dauntsey's School, Devizes; College of Law; recent articles and papers: 'Initiating liquidations'; 'Responsibilities of Officers of Insolvent Companies'; 'Insolvency Law in the UK: Current Developments' (1988); 'Securities and their Enforcement'; Confidentiality Obligations under English Law'; 'Best and Reasonable Endeavours'.

Leisure: reading; singing; theatre; concerts; walking.

ELLIOT Gordon

partner in charge of recruitment CLYDE & CO 51 Eastcheap; London EC3M 1JP.

Career: articled Clyde & Co (1970-1972); admitted (1972); assistant solicitor (1972-1975); became partner (1975).

Biography: lives London SW7; born 28.06.1948; divorced with 3 children. Educated at Nottingham High School; Bristol University (1969 LLB); Law Society Finals (1970).

Leisure: classical music; opera; theatre; cinema; literature; travel; sport.

ELLIOTT Brian

senior partner SEWELL RAWLINS & LOGIE 7 Dollar Street, Cirencester, Gloucestershire GS7 2AS.

Career: articled Slaughter & May; admitted

(1949); assistant solicitor (1949-1952); became partner Sewell Rawlins & Logie (1952).

Activities: High Steward of Cirencester; member of: Cirencester Bull Club; Cirencester Society in London; Old Coxwell Club.

Biography: lives Cirencester; born 02.06.1921; married with 2 children. Educated at Rugby School; Edinburgh University (1942 MA LLB); School of Oriental and African Studies London (Japanese translation).

Leisure: taking it easy.

ELLIOTT John

senior partner ELLIOTT & COMPANY Centurion House, Deansgate, Manchester M3 3WT.

Activities: chairman Young SolicitorsW Group - National; president Manchester Law Society; chairman Manchester & Salford branch of the NSPCC; member St James's Club, Manchester.

Biography: lives Sandbach; born 13.03.1937; married to Angela with 4 children. Educated at Mill Hill School; Manchester University.

ELLIOTT Robert

partner and head of banking and finance WILDE SAPTE Queensbridge House, 60 Upper Thames Street, London EC4V 3BD.

Career: articled Malkin Cullis & Sumption (1974-1976); admitted (1976); assistant solicitor Wilde Sapte (1976-1979); became partner (1979).

Activities: member Commercial Panel of American Arbitration Association; member of: Royal Ocean Racing Club; New York Yacht Club.

Biography: lives London; born 03.07.1952; married to Sara with 3 children. Educated at Leeds Grammar School; London University (1973 LLB); College of Law (1974); articles in IFLR and Solicitors Journal.

Leisure: reading; sailing.

ELLIS Brian

partner and head of probate and trust department WOOLLEY BEVIS & DIPLOCK 79 Church Road, Hove, East Sussex BN3 2BB.

Career: admitted (1968); assistant solicitor Verrall & Son (1969-1970); partner (1970-1990); amalgamated to become Thomas

E

Eggar Verrall Bowles (1989); became partner Woolley Bevis & Diplock (1990).

Activities: council member St Barnabas Hospice; committee member Petworth House Real Tennis Court; member of: the Jesters; Sussex Martlets; Worthing Golf Club; Brighton & Hove Golf Club; Brighton Squash Rackets Club (life vice-president).

Biography: lives East Preston; born 05.12.1943; married with 2 children. Educated at Brighton College; Emmanuel College Cambridge (1965 BA) (1968 MA); College of Law Guildford (1968).

Leisure: real tennis; golf; travelling; gardening; the arts.

ELLIS Carol

editor THE LAW REPORTS AND WEEKLY LAW REPORTS 11 Old Square, Lincoln's Inn, London WC2A 3TS.

Career: called to the Bar Gray's Inn (1951); silk (1980); law reporter The Times (1952-1969); law reporter The Law Reports and Weekly Law Reports (1954-1969) (managing editor 1970-1976) (became editor 1976); case editor Solicitors' Journal (1970); consultant editor Mason's Road Traffic Reports (1970).

Activities: JP West Central Division Inner London (1972 to date); member Inner London Probation Committee (1989 to date).

Biography: lives London NW8; born 06.05.1929; married to Ralph Gilmore with 2 sons. Educated at The Abbey School, Reading; Pensionnat La Ramee, Lausanne; Lausanne University; University College London (LLB hons).

Leisure: travel; music; theatre.

ELLISON Hugh

joint senior partner CARTMELL SHEPHERD Bishop Yards, Penrith, Cumbria CA11 7XS.

Career: articled QLW Little; admitted (1960); became partner Little & Shepherd (1960-1978); became senior partner (1978-1989); became joint senior partner Cartmell Shepherd (1989).

Activities: part-time Clerk to the Penrith Justices (1968-1989); member committee Carlisle & District Law Society (president 1986-1987); member General Synod of the Church of England (1970-1987); chairman Carlisle Diocesan Board of Finance (1982 to date).

Biography: lives Penrith; born 03.07.1932; married to Susan with 2 children. Educated

at Elstree School, Berkshire; Sedbergh School; Queen's College Oxford (1956 BA) (1967 MA).

Leisure: fell walking.

ELLISON Robin

senior partner ELLISON WESTHORP Glade House, 52 Carter Lane, London EC4.

Career: partner Cecil Ellison & Co (1973-1975); Fellow European Law Wolfson College Cambridge (1975-1980); managing director Finance for Housing (1981-1987); senior partner Ellison Westhorp (1982).

Activities: founder Association of Pensions Lawyers (1984); member Occupational Pensions Board; council member National Association of Pension Funds; chairman Law Society Pensions Committee; member RAC.

Biography: lives London NW3; born 03.02.1949; married to Micheline with 2 children. Educated at Manchester Grammar School; author of: 'Pensions Law and Practice' (1988); 'Pensions Law Reform' (1986); 'Pensions for Partners' (1989); 'Pension Schemes for Controlling Directors' (1987); legal correspondent Pensions World; Law Society's Gazette; articles in The Times; Daily Telegraph.

Leisure: social housing; housing associations; sailing; fell-walking; antiquarian books.

ELLMAN Michael Peter David

partner responsible for international work (company, commercial and general litigation) including Paris & Milan offices and international relations VIZARDS 42/3 Bedford Row, London WC1R 4LL.

Career: articled Denton Hall and Burgin; admitted (1962); assistant solicitor Theodore Goddard & Co (1965-1970); became partner Herbert and Gowers (1971-1981); merged with Vizards (1981).

Activities: hon vice-president Association Internationale des Jeunes Avocats; member International Committee of Haldane Society; member of Council of Justice; member 'Defence de la Defense' Committee of Union International des Avocats and responsible for UIA-IBA-AIJA Coordinating Committee; member Human Rights Missions for International Commission of Jurists to Greece; for Federation International des Droits de L'Homme to South Africa, Fiji and Sicily; Parliamentary candidate (Liberal) Greenwich (1964); member Labour Party (1980 to date); member of: Law Society; Wig & Pen Club.

Biography: lives London; born 25.11.1937; separated with 2 children. Educated at Epsom College; Merton College Oxford; University for Foreigners, Perugia, Italy; Nancy University, France; author of: 'Motor Accidents in France'; 'The Financial Consequences of Divorce in France' and other articles for the Law Gazette; 'China and the Law' and other articles in Commerce International.

Leisure: political activities; travel; theatre; swimming; cycling.

ELLY Charles

partner REYNOLDS PARRY-JONES & CRAWFORD 10 Easton Street, High Wycombe, Bucks HP11 1NP.

Career: articled Reynolds Parry-Jones & Crawford (1963); admitted (1966); became partner (1968).

Activities: part-time lecturer in law High Wycombe College of Technology (1970s); (deputy registrar until 1987); president Berks Bucks & Oxon Incorporated Law Society (1988-1989); (secretary 1975-1982); secretary Southern Area Association of Law Societies (1975-1982); secretary Joint Consultation Committee with Barristers (1975 to date); secretary Berks Bucks & Oxon Professional Council (1978-1982); (chairman 1983-1984); member of Council of Law Society (1981 to date); chairman Legal Aid Committee (1984-1987); chairman Standards & Guidance Committee (1987-1990); chairman Advocacy Training Sub-committee (1987 to date); Training Committee; Criminal Law Committee; Specialisation Committee; Joint Committee Legal Executives; chairman Advocacy Training Team and course leader; governor College of Law; chairman High Wycombe Citizens' Advice Bureau (1983-1988); trustee/on management committees of various charities; former Church warden; former chairman Maidenhead Deanery's Synod; member Oxford Diocesan Synod; member of Berkshire County Council (1979-1981); member of: Oxford & Cambridge Club; Sloane Club.

Biography: lives Cookham; born 20.03.1942; married to Marion with 2 children. Educated at Crown House Preparatory School; Sir William Borlase's School; Hertford College Oxford (1963 BA); (1967 MA); College of Law Lancaster Gate (1965-1966); Stephen Nicholls Prize; co-author advocacy training material for local Law Societies.

Leisure: gardening; ornithology; walking; theatre.

ELY Philip

senior partner PARIS SMITH & RANDALL Lansdowne House, Castle Lane, Southampton SO9 4FD.

Career: articled Southampton (1953-1958); admitted (1958); National Service with Royal Navy (1958-1960); assistant solicitor Paris Smith & Randall (1960-1961); became partner (1961); senior partner (1982).

Activities: assistant hon secretary Hampshire Law Society (1961-1966); hon secretary (1966-1974); treasurer (1974-1979); president (1979); council member Law Society (1979-1990); chairman Committee of Enquiry (Glanville Davies) (1982); chairman Adjudication Committee (1986-1989); deputy vice-president (1989); member Reform Club.

Biography: lives Compton; born 22.03.1936; married with 5 children. Educated at Douai School; LLB London - external.

Leisure: dry fly fishing; gardening; music.

EMERSON Tim

partner in charge of probate/trusts/wills and tax department FOOT & BOWDEN 70/76 North Hill, Plymouth PL4 8HH.

Career: articled Bond Pearce & Co; admitted (1965); assistant solicitor Stafford Clark & Co, London EC4 and Heppenstalls Lyndhurst (1965-1973); became partner Foot & Bowden (1973).

Activities: Notary Public (1978); clerk to governors of two independent schools; Church warden; member Yelverton Parochial Church Council; trustee Lady Modiford's Trust; hon sec Plymouth Proprietary Library; member Royal Western Yacht Club of England.

Biography: lives Yelverton; born 14.02.1942; married to Susanna with 2 children. Educated at Mount House School, Tavistock; Kelly College, Tavistock; College of Law.

Leisure: skiing; shooting; sailing; tennis.

EMMERSON John

head of private client department McKENNA & CO Mitre House, 160 Aldersgate Street, London EC1A 4DD.

Career: administrative class of Home Civil Service (Air Ministry) (1961-1963); became partner Warmingtons & Hasties (1967-1983); became partner McKenna & Co (1983); admitted as a solicitor in Hong Kong.

Activities: Fellow of the Woodard Corporation; governor of Ardingly College, Sussex; Committee Member of the London Chamber of Commerce; member Brooks's Club.

Biography: lives London W11; born 10.09.1937; married to Anne with 2 children. Educated at Merchant Taylors' School; Magdalen College Oxford (1961 MA); Richards Essay Prize (Gray's Inn) (1961); written articles in British Tax Review and other publications.

Leisure: fly fishing.

ENGLEHART Robert

Queen's Counsel 2 Hare Court, Temple, London EC4Y 7BH.

Career: called to the Bar (1969); QC (1986); Recorder of the Crown Court.

Activities: Chairman London Common Law and Commercial Bar Association; member MCC.

Biography: lives London; born 01.10.1943; married to Rosalind with 3 children. Educated at St Edward's School, Oxford; Trinity College Oxford (1966 MA); Harvard Law School (1969 LLM); Diploma in International Relations, Bologna, Italy (1967); contributed to 'Il Controllo Giudiziario: a comparative study of civil procedure' (1968).

Leisure: shooting; cricket; windsurfing.

ENSOR George Anthony (Tony)

partner WEIGHTMAN RUTHERFORDS Richmond House, 1 Rumford Place, Liverpool L3 9QW.

Career: articled Rutherfords (1956-1960); Gibson & Weldon law tutor (1960-1961); admitted (1961); assistant solicitor Rutherfords (1961-1962); became partner (1963); firm merged with Weightmans (1988).

Activities: deputy coroner (Liverpool) (1966 to date); part-time chairman Industrial Tribunals (1975 to date); deputy Circuit Judge/assistant Recorder (1979-1983); Recorder (1983 to date); member Judicial Studies Board (1987-1989); member Liverpool Law Society (1969 to date); assistant hon secretary (1970-1980); vice-president (1981); president (1982); member Law Society Legal Aid Committee (local area) (1964-1988); trustee Empire Theatre (Merseyside) Ltd (1987 to date); director Liverpool FC (1985 to date); member of: Artists' Club (Liverpool); Formby Golf Club; Pwllheli Golf Club; Waterloo Rugby Union FC.

Biography: lives Liverpool; born 04.11.1936; married to Jennifer with 2 children.

Educated at Malvern College; Liverpool University (1958 LLB); Atkinson Conveyancing Prize; Rupert Bremner Medal.

Leisure: association football; theatre; golf.

EREIRA David

senior manager FRESHFIELDS Whitefriars, 63-67 Fleet Street, London EC4Y 1HP.

Career: National Westminster Bank Ltd (1977-1978); Herbert Oppenheimer Nathan & Vandyk (1979-1981); assistant solicitor Wilde Sapte (1981-1984); partner (1989); became senior manager Freshfields (1989).

Activities: member International Bar Association (Section on Business Law) (Sub-Committee B Aeronautical Law) (Sub-Committee E Banking Law); member Justice Committee reviewing the legal protection for the small investor.

Biography: lives London NW11; born 11.08.1956; married to Vivien with 2 daughters and 1 son. Educated at Kingsbury High School; Manchester University (LLB hons); Hulme Major Entrance Scholarship .

Leisure: cosmology (occasional student at Birkbeck College).

ERVING Chris

senior litigation partner STEGGLES PALMER 2 Bedford Row, London WC1R 4BU.

Career: police cadet Hull City Police; Sergeant (1969); articled Blatchfords (1973-1977); articled Rowleys & Blewitts (1977); admitted (1980); assistant solicitor (1980-1981); became partner (1981); became head of Litigation Steggles Palmer (1983).

Activities: chairman Lockerbie Air Disaster Steering Committee; member Association of Personal Injury Lawyers; member Royal Mid-Surrey Golf Club.

Biography: lives London W5; born 15.01.1946; married with 2 children. Educated at Withernsea High School; College of Law Guildford.

Leisure: golf; bridge.

EVANS Brian

senior consultant BRUTTON & CO West End House, Fareham, Hants PO16 0AJ.

Career: articled in St Albans (1949-1954); admitted (1954); assistant solicitor Brutton & Birkett (1960-1961); became partner (1961); senior partner (1979-1988).

E

Activities: member of Lord Chancellor's Independent Panel of Inspectors; chairman Southern Rent Assessment Panel; treasurer and main committee member Hampshire Incorporated Law Society; chairman of governors Wykeham House School; active council member of the Sail Training Association involved in organisation of tall ships racing throughout world; senator Junior Chamber International; member of: Royal Southern Yacht Club; Rotary Club of Fareham (past president).

Biography: lives Titchfield; born 10.05.1931; married with 3 children. Educated at St Albans; College of Law.

Leisure: playing piano; travelling; sailing/ocean racing.

EVANS David

managing partner SIMPSON CURTIS 41 Park Square, Leeds LS1 2NS.

Career: articled Crombie Wilkinson & Robinson (1956-1959); lectured in law York College of Further Education (1956-1957); admitted (1959); assistant solicitor Crombies (1959-1961); assistant solicitor Simpson Curtis (1961-1963); became partner (1963); became managing partner (1982).

Activities: director Legal Resources Limited; former president St Catharine's College Cambridge Law Society; former hon treasurer Cambridge Society of York; former president Durham Cathedral Old Choristers' Association; warden Leeds Parish Church; trustee (1984) Appeal Fund; committee member St Catharine's College Cambridge; chairman Yorkshire Branch; governor Leeds Grammar School; member Leeds Club.

Biography: lives Leeds; born 08.03.1935; married to Sonia with 3 children. Educated at Durham Cathedral Chorister School; Durham School; St Catharine's College Cambridge (1956 BA hons) (1958 LLB hons); Yorkshire Law Society Prize (1959).

Leisure: music; bee-keeping.

EVANS David

litigation partner specialising in landlord and tenant and charity law WILDE SAPTE Queensbridge House, 60 Upper Thames Street, London EC4V 3BD.

Career: National Service as 2nd Lieutenant Green Howards; articled Trowers & Hamlins; admitted (1962); assistant solicitor; became partner Pritchard Englefield .

Activities: sponsor ENO; member of: MCC; HAC; Royal Horticultural Society.

Biography: lives Sevenoaks; born 31.01.1935; married to Sue with 2 daughters. Educated at Bromsgrove; Trinity College Oxford (BA); author of article on JP Monnet Father of Europe.

Leisure: bee keeping; cricket.

EVANS Michael

partner and head of company and commercial department GREENWOODS 30 Priestgate, Peterborough PE1 1JE.

Career: articled and assistant McKenna & Co (1955-1961); admitted (1961); assistant solicitor Clifford Turner & Co (1961-1963); assistant solicitor Greenwoods (1963-1966); became partner (1966).

Activities: local Parish council; chairman local approved school; member of board of governors local village school; chairman local youth club; member International Bar Association; member Institute of Directors; Director Peterborough Evening Telegraph Ltd; Director/Secretary Peterborough Enterprise Programme; member Solicitors' European Group and Eurolink; member Peterborough Port Club.

Biography: lives Peterborough; born 24.07.1937; married to Margaret with 3 children. Educated at Welbury, Ampleforth.

Leisure: fishing; shooting; collecting ceramics, glass, books and prints; food and drink (port and wine).

EVANS Michael

senior partner DAVIES BLUNDEN AND EVANS 43/45 Victoria Road, Farnborough, Hampshire GU14 7PD.

Career: articled Denis H Blunden (1952-1957); admitted (1957); National Service commissioned Second Lt; Platoon Commander with ambulance company Germany; Assistant Adjutant to 1 Corp Troop Column Bielefeld (1957-1959); became senior partner (1981).

Activities: chairman Social Security Appeals Tribunal; member Area Legal Aid Committee; member management committee old people's home Knellwood; hon solicitor Farnborough Chamber of Commerce (past president); founder member Farnborough Round Table (chairman 1964); governor three local schools; former church warden; presently completing 30 years member Parochial Church Council; member of: Rotary Club of Farnborough (past president); 41 Club;

Farnborough & RAE Operatic Society; Somerset County Cricket Club; Hampshire County Cricket Club.

Biography: lives Farnborough; born 27.08.1932; married to Susan. Educated at Ilminster Grammar School, Somerset; Farnborough Grammar School; College of Law (1957 hons); West Surrey Law Society prize; Hampshire Incorporated Law Society prize.

Leisure: cricket (including firm's team); golf; swimming; antiquarian horology.

EVANS Rachel Anne

senior partner MORGAN BRUCE Bradleys Court, Park Place/Boulevard de Nantes, Cardiff.

Career: articled Morgan Bruce & Nicholas (now Morgan Bruce); admitted (1967); assistant solicitor (1967-1970); became partner (1970).

Activities: part-time Deputy County Court and High Court Registrar; part-time MAT chairman; executive Cardiff Family Conciliation Service; legal adviser Relate; legal adviser Girl Guides' Association of Wales; accredited member of the Law Society's Child Care Panel.

Biography: lives Cardiff; born 14.01.1943; married to Robert Chegwin with 1 daughter. Educated at Alderman Davies' Church in Wales School, Neath; Neath Girls' Grammar School; Cardiff High School; Westfield College London University (1964 hons); College of Law Guildford (1967 hons); Robert Innes Prize (1965); Travers-Smith Scholarship (1967); Geoffrey Howard-Watson Prize (1965); Associated Law Societies of Wales Prize (1967).

Leisure: enjoying family and their activities; making and listening to music.

EVANS Sir Vincent

Judge of the European Court of Human Rights 2 Hare Court, Temple, London EC4Y 7BH.

Career: called to the Bar Lincoln's Inn (1939); HM Forces (RA) (1939-1946); N Africa (1941-1946); legal officer Occupied Enemy Territories Administration (1942); legal appointments in Eritrea, Cairo and Cyrenaica; legal adviser (Lt Col) to British Military Administration, Cyrenaica (1945-1946); legal branch HM Diplomatic Service (1947-1975); assistant legal adviser Foreign Office (1947-1954); legal counsellor UK Mission to United Nations, New York (1954-1959); deputy legal adviser FO (1960-

1968); legal adviser FCO (1968-1975); QC (1973); retired (1975).

Activities: UK representative on European Committee on Legal Cooperation Council of Europe (1965-1975) (chairman 1969-1971); member Diplomatic Service Appeals Board (1976-1986); UK representative on Council of Europe Steering Committee on Human Rights (1976-1980); (chairman 1979-1980); member Human Rights Committee set up under International Covenant on Civil and Political Rights (1977-1984); Judge of the European Court of Human Rights (1980 to date); member Permanent Court of Arbitration (1987 to date); director (chairman) Bryant Symons & Co Ltd (1964-1985); president Old Merchant Taylors' Society (1984-1985); member Council of Management of British Institute of International and Comparative Law; member Advisory Board Centre for International Human Rights Law Essex University (1983 to date); member School Committee of Merchant Taylors' Company (1985 to date); governor British Institute of Human Rights (1988 to date); lectures on human rights and international law; member Athenaeum.

Biography: lives Moor Park; born 20.10.1915; married to Joan with 1 son and 2 daughters. Educated at Merchant Taylors' School, Northwood (1925-1934); Wadham College Oxford (1938 BA BCL) (1941 MA); Honorary Fellow (1981); Cassel Scholar Lincoln's Inn (1937); Honorary Bencher (1983); Honorary Doctor Essex University (1986); MBE (Military) (1945); CMG (1959); KCMG (1970); GCMG (1976).

Leisure: gardening.

EVANS Tony

partner MANBY & STEWARD 1st Floor, Mander House, Wolverhampton, West Midlands WV1 3NE.

Career: articled Stirk & Co (1956-1959); admitted (1959); commissioned National Service assistant adjutant; assistant solicitor Stirk Adams & Co (1961-1964); assistant solicitor Manby & Steward (1964-1966); became partner (1966).

Activities: member Wolverhampton Law Society; member Legal Aid Area Committee.

Biography: lives Brewood; born 20.07.1935; married to Marie with 2 children. Educated at St Chad's College, Wolverhampton; Birmingham University (1956 LLB).

Leisure: music (plays oboe).

EVANS-LOMBE Edward

silk practising mainly at the Chancery Bar 4 Stone Buildings, Lincoln's Inn, London WC2.

Career: called to the Bar Inner Temple (1963); standing Counsel Department of Trade in Bankruptcy matters (1971-1978); Bencher Inner Temple (1985); QC (1978); Recorder of the Crown Court (1983); chairman SE Area Agricultural Land Tribunal (1983); Bencher Inner Temple (1985) .

Activities: member Bar/Law Society Committee on the Reform of Insolvency Law (1977); member Norfolk Club.

Biography: lives London W14 and Norfolk; born 10.04.1937; married to Frances with 4 children. Educated at Abberley Hall, Worcestershire; Eton College; Trinity College Cambridge (MA); contributor to Atkins Bankruptcy Court Forms.

Leisure: farming; forestry; country pursuits (particularly fishing); amateur archaeology (in particular Rome).

EVERATT Henry

partner OXLEY & COWARD 71/79 St Sepulchre Gate, Doncaster DN1 1RX.

Career: articled Oxley & Coward (1962-1971); admitted (1971); assistant solicitor (1971-1972); became partner (1972).

Activities: member Doncaster & District Law Society; legal advisor to Doctors' Accident Rescue Team (DART), Doncaster and Rotherham.

Biography: lives Doncaster; born 04.06.1944; married to Audrey with 2 children. Educated at Wath Grammar School.

Leisure: reading; music; sport.

EVERETT PR

retired partner LOVELL WHITE & KING (now LOVELL WHITE DURRANT) Randolph House, Hillcrest Waye, Gerrards Cross, Bucks SL9 8DN.

Career: served in Royal Navy (1940-1946); Lt RNVR; Captain MTBs and MGBs; articled Lovell White & King (1946-1949); admitted (1949); assistant solicitor (1949-1955); became partner (1955-1982).

Activities: awarded DSC (1944); member Council of Tribunals (1977-1985); member Justice Administrative Law Committee (1970 to date); member Law Society Planning Law Committee (1977-1988); member Sir Patrick Neill's All Souls Justice Committee on Administrative Law in the

UK (1978-1988); member of: United Oxford and Cambridge University Club; Old Merchant Taylors' Football Club.

Biography: lives Gerrards Cross; born 11.03.1921; married to Pamela Needham (1956). Educated at Merchant Taylors' School (1934-1939); Wadham College Oxford (MA).

Leisure: swimming (open air only); watching rugby football; cricket; reading; visiting cathedrals.

F

FABER Peter

head of corporate department CARTER FABER 10 Arthur Street, London EC4R 9AY.

Career: articled Simmons & Simmons (1971-1973); admitted (1974); assistant solicitor (1974-1978); became partner (1978-1980); founded own practice (1980); merged to form Carter Faber (1986).

Activities: panel member City of London Law Society for Monitoring of Articles; member Riverside Racquet and Tennis Centre.

Biography: lives London SW14; born 12.06.1948; married to Ann with 4 children. Educated at Shrewsbury School; Brasenose College Oxford (1969 hons).

Leisure: family; theatre; travel; squash; tennis; photography.

FAGAN Neil

partner in financial services and commercial litigation LOVELL WHITE DURRANT 21 Holborn Viaduct, London EC1A 2DY.

Career: articled Durrant Cooper & Hambling; admitted (1971); assistant solicitor (1971-1975); became partner (1975).

Biography: lives Crondall nr Farnham; born 05.06.1947; married to Catherine with 3 daughters. Educated at Cheam; Charterhouse; Southampton University (LLB hons); contributor to New York Law School Review and elsewhere on UK casino gaming law.

Leisure: reading; walking; eating and drinking; sailing; talking.

FAGELSON Ian

head of commercial and finance law department WARNER CRANSTON Pickfords Wharf, Clink Street, London SE1 9DG.

F

Career: lecturer in law Reading University (1975-1977); articled Lovell White & King (1977-1979); admitted (1980); co-founder Warner Cranston (1979).

Activities: member United Oxford & Cambridge Universities Club.

Biography: lives London N1; born 22.04.1952; married with 1 son. Educated at Southend on Sea High School for Boys; Southampton University (1973 LLB); Keble College Oxford (1975 BCL); various publications in Modern Law Review; Law Quarterly Review; International Financial Law Review; Business Law Journal; Financial Times.

Leisure: theatre; music; loafing.

FAIR Stuart

partner THORNTONS WS Whitehall Chambers, 11 Whitehall Street, Dundee DD1 4AE.

Career: apprentice Edinburgh; admitted and WS (1956); assistant solicitor (1956-1960); became partner (1960); became senior partner (1984); resigned as senior partner (1990).

Activities: examiner in Revenue Law for Law Society of Scotland (1970-1978); member Scottish Solicitors Discipline Tribunal (1978-1988); lecturer in revenue law (1972-1990) and lecturer in professional ethics (1988-1990) at Dundee University; member Tayside Health Board (1984-1990); former dean of Faculty of Procurators and Solicitors in Dundee; former member of the Council of WS Society; clerk to the Commissioners of Inland Revenue Dundee Districts; director of two private investment companies; trustee Caird's Travelling Scholarships Trust; honorary Sheriff; temporary sheriff; member Dundee Port Authority; chairman University of Dundee Court; president Dundee Choral Union; member of: New Club; Royal Scottish Automobile Club.

Biography: lives Dundee and pied a terre, Kensington, London W8; born 30.09.1930; married to Lesley with 3 children. Educated at Perth Academy; St Andrew's University (1952 MA); Edinburgh (1956 LLB).

Leisure: bridge; opera; travel; community service.

FALLOWS Peter

senior partner FALLOWS & CO 83 Great Bridge, Tipton, West Midlands DY4 7HD.

Career: National Service (1949-1951); firm of international printers; office

communications company; articled; admitted (1966); assistant solicitor with firm in the Black Country; founded own practice.

Activities: past president Sandwell Solicitors Club; past president Dudley and District Law Society; member Solicitor's Complaints Bureau; member Hereford & Worcester County Council (1958 to date) chairman Appeals Panel; chairman GP Committee; chairman Planning Committee and Personnel Committee; vice-chairman West Mercia Police Authority; member West Midlands TAVRA (Incidental Committees to the above); member of: Teifi Boat Club (Cardigan); RYA; Worcester County Cricket Club; Camping Club of Great Britain; president West Hagley Cricket Club.

Biography: lives Hagley; born 26.09.1930; married to Jessica with 2 children. Educated at Sacred Heart College; Sebright School; King Charles I Grammar School; Birmingham University.

Leisure: sailing; cricket (spectator); travel.

FARLEY Alastair Hugh

senior partner WATSON FARLEY AND WILLIAMS Minories House, 2-5 Minories, London EC3N 1BJ.

Career: articled Norton Rose (1968-1970); admitted (1971); assistant solicitor (1971-1974); partner (1974-1982); founded own practice (1982).

Activities: court assistant Worshipful Company of Shipwrights; member of: RAC; Roehampton Club.

Biography: lives London W8; born 02.01.1946; married to Hilary with 3 children. Educated at Felsted, Essex (1955-1964); Jesus College Cambridge (MA).

Leisure: sport; 'Norfolk'; shooting.

FARMER David

executive director CHARTERED WESTLB LIMITED 33-36 Gracechurch Street, London EC3V 0AX (formerly Standard Chartered Merchant Bank Ltd).

Career: articled Slaughter and May (1959-1962); admitted (1962); assistant solicitor (1962-1966); legal adviser Roan Selection Trust Ltd and associated companies (1967-1976); group secretary Lonrho Ltd (1976-1979); assistant director project finance Standard Chartered Merchant Bank Ltd (1979); director overseas administration (1984).

Biography: lives London SW1; born 19.10.1935; married to Johanna with 3

stepchildren. Educated at Tonbridge School; St John's College Cambridge (1959 BA) (MA).

Leisure: travel.

FARMER Derek

solicitor AMALGAMATED METAL CORPORATION PLC 7th Floor, Adelaide House, London Bridge, London EC4R 9DT.

Career: articled Roney & Co (1972-1974); admitted; assistant solicitor (1974-1979); became solicitor Amalgamated Metal Corporation (1980).

Biography: lives Harpenden; born 03.12.1949; married to Susan. Educated at St Martin's Preparatory School, Northwood; Aldenham School, Elstree; Queen Mary College London (LLB hons).

Leisure: literature; theatre; exploring Greek Islands; food and wine; collecting books.

FARRAND Julian

insurance ombudsman INSURANCE OMBUDSMAN BUREAU 31 Southampton Row, London WC1B 5HJ.

Career: articled Herbert Oppenheimer Nathan & Vandyk (1957-1960); admitted (1960); assistant lecturer and lecturer King's College London (1960-1963); lecturer Sheffield University (1963-1965); reader in law University of London Queen Mary College London (1965-1968); professor of law Victoria Manchester University (1968-1988); Law Commissioner (1984-1988); became insurance ombudsman Insurance Ombudsman Bureau (1989).

Activities: Dean of Faculty of Law Manchester University (1970-1972 & 1976-1978); chairman Government Conveyancing Committee (1984-1985); chairman Greater Manchester Rent Assessment Panel (1973); chairman London Rent Assessment Panel (1984).

Biography: lives London WC1 and Stockport; born 13.08.1935; married with 3 children. Educated at Portsmouth Grammar School; Haberdashers' Aske's; London University (1957 LLB hons) Joseph Hume Scholar; (1966 LLD); Manchester (1972 hon LLM); Sheffield (1990 hon LLD); editor 'Emmet on Title' (1986 19th ed); author 'Contract & Conveyancing' (1983 4th ed).

FARREN Peter

partner property department and PR partner LINKLATERS & PAINES Barrington House, 59-67 Gresham Street, London EC2V 7JA.

Career: assistant solicitor Linklaters & Paines (1967-1973 & 1976-1979); became partner (1979); lending officer in banking department Wm Brandt Son & Co Ltd (1973-1976).

Activities: member Hadley Wood Golf Club.

Biography: lives Hadley Wood; born 16.10.1944; married to Victoria with 3 children. Educated at Mill Hill School; University de Grenoble (1961-1962); King's College London (1965 LLB hons).

Leisure: flying; golf; squash.

FARRER Mark

partner FARRER & CO 66 Lincoln's Inn Fields, London WC2A 3LH.

Career: partner Farrer & Co (1968 to date).

Activities: elected member Council of Lloyd's; director Lyonnaise UK plc; deputy chairman Essex Water Co; deputy chairman East Anglian Water Co; director Association of Lloyd's members; member Brooks's Club.

Biography: lives London; born 25.03.1941; married to Zara with 1 daughter. Educated at Stone House, Broadstairs; Eton College.

Leisure: gardening; the steam railway; salmon fishing.

FARRER William

senior partner FARRER & CO 66 Lincoln's Inn Fields, London WC2A 3LH.

Career: Coldstream Guards (1945-1948); admitted (1953); assistant solicitor (1953-1956); became partner Farrer & Co (1956); senior partner (1976).

Activities: solicitor to the Duchy of Lancaster; member Solicitors Disciplinary Tribunal; member Holborn Law Society; member of Brooks's Club; MCC; R & A Club.

Biography: lives Haslemere; born 23.06.1926; married with 3 children. Educated at Eton College; Balliol College Oxford (1949 MA).

Leisure: golf; music.

FARRINGTON David

head of chambers 2 Garden Court, Temple, London EC4Y 9BL.

Career: called to the Bar (1972); tenant Louis Blom-Cooper's Chambers (1974-1976); deputy head of Richard Slowe's chambers (1976-1985); head of Chambers 2 Garden Court (1985); part-time lecturer in law Polytechnic of Central London (1972-

1988); part-time lecturer in law Morley College (1972-1976); guest lecturer 'Temple lectures'.

Activities: member sub-committee of the Bar Council.

Biography: lives London W14; born 02.12.1948; single. Educated at Balshaw's Grammar School, Leyland; University College London (1971 LLB hons); Council of Legal Education (1971-1972); editor and proof reader of: 'Know Your Rights' (1976); 'Law For The Consumer' (1978); co-author and editor accompanying manuals for 'Temple lectures' (1988 Xmas tour).

Leisure: theatre; films; ballet; travel.

FARTHING Peter

partner CLYDE & CO
51 Eastcheap, London EC3.

Career: articled Rowberry Morris (1971-1973); admitted (1974); assistant solicitor Clyde & Co (1974-1977); became partner (1977).

Biography: lives London; born 01.1949; single. Educated at Crypt School Gloucester; Pembroke College Oxford (MA).

Leisure: farming; gardening; birdwatching; skiing.

FAULL David

senior partner WINCKWORTH & PEMBERTON 35 Great Peter Street, Westminster, London SW1P 3LR.

Career: articled Leanings Carr; admitted (1955); assistant solicitor Allen & Overy (1955-1959); became partner Milles Day & Co (1960-1964); (amalgamated with Lee Bolton & Lee); became partner (1964-1978); became partner Winckworth & Pemberton (1978); became senior partner (1985).

Activities: involved with housing associations; assisted in formation of Paddington Churches Housing Association; involved with nursing profession; Registrar of the Diocese of London, Southwark; legal secretary to the Bishop of Rochester; Registrar of Diocese of Chelmsford (1964-1989); Chapter Clerk to St Paul's Cathedral; member committee of Sutton and Hastoe Housing Association; member committee of Abbey National Housing Association; trustee Wimbledon YMCA; chairman Ecclesiastical Law Association; treasurer Ecclesiastical Law Society; member Athenaeum Club; Nobody's Friends.

Biography: lives Wimbledon; born 25.02.1929; single. Educated at Taunton

School; Law Society School of Law.

Leisure: theatre; walking; gardening; housing; amateur theatricals; Cornish history.

FAWSSETT Robert

senior partner BIDDLE & CO 1 Gresham Street, London EC2V 7BU.

Career: articled Biddle & Co (1954-1957); admitted (1957); assistant solicitor (1957-1958); became partner (1958); became senior partner (1976).

Activities: member Lowtonian Society; member of: Naval Club; City University Club.

Biography: lives West Malling; born 04.05.1931; married to Philippa with 3 children. Educated at Westbourne House Prep School; Bradfield College; Pembroke College Cambridge (1954 BA).

Leisure: gardening; tennis; opera.

FEARON Guy

partner WINWARD FEARON & CO 35 Bow Street, London WC2E 7AU.

Career: partner Fenwick Elliott & Co (1981-1985); founding partner Winward Fearon & Co (1986).

Activities: member Bucks.

Biography: lives London SW3; born 16.05.1955; married with 1 child..

FELL John

partner WILDE SAPTE Queensbridge House, 60 Upper Thames Street, London EC4V 3BD.

Career: articled Kimbers (1952-1955); admitted (1955); assistant solicitor (1955-1956); assistant solicitor Conquest Clare & Binns (1956-1958); assistant solicitor Hatchett Jones & Co (1958-1963); became partner Wilde Sapte (1964).

Activities: common councilman for Queenhithe Ward on the Corporation of London; director of: Portman Family Settled Estates Ltd; Portman Burtley Estate Co; Moor Park (1958) Ltd; Seymour Street Nominees Ltd; chairman Trustees of Truro Fund; trustee Royal Academy of Arts Trust; trustee Housing Associations Charitable Trust; trustee of Lord Mayor's 800th Anniversary Awards Trust; governor of City of London School; donation governor Christ's Hospital; past chairman Broad Street Ward Club; past chairman Queenhithe Ward Club; member of: Old Merchant Taylors' Society; Guildhall Club; City Livery Club.

F

Biography: lives Northwood; born 31.08.1928; married with 2 daughters. Educated at Merchant Taylors' School; Pembroke College Oxford (1951 MA).

FELLINGHAM Michael

partner and head of private client department PENNINGTONS Highfield, Brighton Road, Godalming, Surrey GU7 1NS.

Career: articled (1963-1966); admitted (1966); lecturer College of Law (1966-1972); became partner Penningtons (1973).

Activities: member West Surrey Golf Club.

Biography: lives Chiddingfold; born 21.04.1941; married to Jan with 2 children. Educated at Stowmarket Grammar School; St Catharine's College Cambridge (1960-1963).

Leisure: tennis; golf; bridge; shooting.

FENNER John

BERWIN LEIGHTON Adelaide House, London Bridge, London EC4R 9HA.

Career: articled Zeffertt Heard & Morley Lawson (1956-1959); admitted (1959); assistant solicitor Lionel Leighton & Company (1959-1962); became partner (1962); merged to form Berwin Leighton (1970); became managing partner Berwin Leighton (1980); became chairman (1984-1990).

Activities: member of: City of London Club; Royal Automobile Club; Carlton Club.

Biography: lives London N6; born 07.12.1935; married to Simmons with 2 sons. Educated at Tonbridge School; University College London (1956 LLB); City of London Solicitors Company Grotius Prize.

Leisure: political fund-raising; charity work; actively involved with human rights; opera; theatre; skiing; tennis; bridge.

FENWICK ELLIOTT Robert James

senior partner FENWICK ELLIOTT & BURNS 353 Strand, London WC2R 0HS.

Career: articled in Norwich; admitted (1977); assistant solicitor Masons (1977-1980); founded own practice (1980).

Activities: member Committee of City of Westminster Law Society; member Steering Committee of Official Referees' Solicitors Association; member Euston Club.

Biography: lives Chiswick; born 17.03.1952;

married to Sue with 2 children. Educated at Eastbourne College; Kent University (1972 BA); president university students' union; author of 'Building Contract Litigation'; numerous articles in magazines on construction law topics and papers delivered at construction law conferences; contributions to the Architect as Arbitrator.

Leisure: ocean racing; scuba diving; gardening; old pianos and new motor bikes.

FERGUSON Richard

Queen's Counsel and head of Chambers 1 Crown Office Row, Temple, London EC4.

Career: called to the Bar Northern Ireland (1956); QC (NI) (1973); Senior Counsel (Ireland) (1983); QC (England and Wales) (1986).

Activities: chairman Mental Health Review Tribunal (NI); Crown Counsel (NI); member Kilbrandon Commission on Devolution; member Criminal Bar Association; member Kildare Street Club, Dublin.

Biography: lives London and Derrygonnelly, Northern Ireland; born 22.08.1935; married first to Janet with 4 children; second to Roma with 1 child. Educated at Rainey School, Magherafelt; Methodist College, Belfast; Queen's Belfast (1955 LLB hons); Trinity College Dublin (1956 BA).

Leisure: Irish politics; swimming; hill walking.

FERMAN Gary

founder GARY M FERMAN 19/20 Grosvenor Street, London W1X 9FD.

Career: admitted New York Bar (1973); associate attorney, Kronish Lieb Shainswit Weiner & Hellman, New York City (1973-1978); associate attorney Crane & Hawkins (1978-1979); senior associate attorney Graham & James (1979-1981); founded own practice (1981).

Activities: adjunct associate professor of law Notre Dame University Law School (1982); adjunct lecturer in law United States International University - Europe (1988); member Amcham Tax Committee; member Executive Committee of Society of English and American Lawyers; member American Bar Association; American Immigration Lawyers' Association; member of: Chess Valley Bridleways Association; Lansdowne Club.

Biography: lives Chorleywood; born 09.02.1947; married to Jacqueline with 3

children. Educated at Riverdale Country School; University of California, Berkeley (1968 AB with Great Distinction); Sussex University (1970 MA); Harvard University Law School (1972 JD); New York University Law School (1975-1977) (LLM Taxation Programme); author of 'Acquisition Strategy: Legal Aspects' in Corporate Investments and Acquisitions by Foreign Companies in the USA (1979).

FERMOR Andrew

partner in commercial division CRIPPS HARRIES HALL 84 Calverley Road, Tunbridge Wells, Kent TN1 2UP.

Career: articled Slaughter and May; admitted; assistant solicitor; seconded to Boden Oppenhoff u Schneider, Germany; assistant solicitor Cripps Harries Hall (1976-1980); became partner (1980).

Activities: member Rural Development Commission County Committee for Sussex (1986-1989).

Biography: lives Tunbridge Wells; born 30.07.1949; married to Margo with 2 children. Educated at Felsted School; King's College London (1971 LLB); Associate of King's College (1970).

Leisure: amateur dramatics; horticulture.

FERNYHOUGH Richard

Queen's Counsel 10 Essex Street, Outer Temple, London WC2R 3AA.

Career: called to the Bar Middle Temple (1970); tenant 11 King's Bench Walk (1972); Recorder of the Crown Court (1986); QC (1986).

Activities: member Official Referees Users Committee (1983 to date); member Council and Executive Committee of Justice; chairman Fellowship Committee of British Academy of Experts; frequently lectures on legal topics to conferences in UK and abroad; member Champneys Club.

Biography: lives London and Belstone; born 27.11.1943; married to Diane with 3 children. Educated at Merchant Taylors' School, Northwood (1957-1962); University College London (1966 LLB hons) .

Leisure: opera; tennis; shooting; arboriculture.

FIELD Richard

Queen's Counsel 11 King's Bench Walk; Temple, London EC4Y 7EQ; practices in commercial law.

Career: Assistant Professor Faculty of Law British Columbia University (1969-1971);

Lecturer in law Hong Kong University (1971-1973); Associate Professor, McGill University, Montreal (1973-1977); called to the Bar Inner Temple (1977); QC (1987).

Activities: member of: Reform Club; Roehampton Club.

Biography: lives London SW13; born 17.04.1947; married to Lynne with 4 children. Educated at Ottershaw School, Chertsey; Bristol University (1968 LLB hons); London University (1969 LLM); Mark of Distinction; numerous articles and book reviews in UBC Law Review; The Hong Kong Law Journal; McGill Law Journal.

Leisure: theatre; opera; dog walking; cricket and rugby football (spectator); reading.

FIELD Sally

partner intellectual property department BRISTOWS COOKE & CARPMAEL 10 Lincoln's Inn Fields, London WC2A 3BP.

Career: articled Clifford Turner (1979-1981); admitted (1981); assistant solicitor (1981-1983); assistant solicitor Bristows Cooke & Carpmael (1983-1987); became partner (1987).

Biography: lives London W11; born 16.05.1957; single. Educated at Oakwood School (1968-1973); Thomas Rotherham Sixth Form College (1973-1975); Durham University (1978 BA hons); Law Society Finals (1977 hons).

Leisure: skiing; tennis.

FIELD-FISHER Thomas

Queen's Counsel 2 Kings Bench Walk, Temple, London EC4Y 7DE.

Career: Queen's Counsel.

Biography: lives London SW6; born 16.05.1915; married.

FIELDEN Anthony

senior partner COBBETT LEAK ALMOND Ship Canal House, King Street, Manchester M2 4WB.

Career: articled Emerson & Fielden (1958-1961); admitted (1961); became partner (1962-1968); became partner Whitworths (incorporating Emerson & Fielden) (1968-1970); became partner Leak Almond & Parkinson (incorporating Emerson & Fielden) (1970-1987); became senior partner (1985); became senior partner Cobbett Leak Almond (1987).

Activities: member of: MCC; Manchester

Tennis & Racquet Club; XL Club; Cryptics .

Biography: lives Knutsford and Chipping Campden; born 18.03.1937; married with 2 children. Educated at Heronwater (1945-1950); Rossall (1950-1955); Keble College Oxford (1955-1958).

Leisure: cricket (playing and watching); old houses; antiques; squash rackets; real tennis; good food and wine.

FIELDING Michael

partner and head of banking and asset finance BRECHER & CO 78 Brook Street, London W1Y 2AD.

Career: financial management trainee Ford Motor Company (1967-1968); articled Arthur Andersen & Co (1968-1969); articled London Borough of Hackney (1969-1971); admitted (1971); assistant solicitor Simmons & Simmons (1972-1973); became partner Grangewood Allen (1973-1974); founding partner Grangewoods (1974-1988); became partner and head of banking and asset finance Brecher & Co (1989).

Activities: vice-chairman Palmerston Holding PLC; member of: Annabels; Harry's Bar.

Biography: lives London NW1; born 27.03.1946; married to Sandra with 2 children. Educated at Hackney Downs Grammar School (1957-1964); Sheffield University (1967 LLB); Scott Scholar, Clement's Inn; Edmund Thomas Child, Sheffield; Cecil Karuth and John Marshall Prizes.

Leisure: tennis; travel; reading.

FIFE Jon

partner FIELD FISHER WATERHOUSE 41 Vine Street, London EC3N 2AA.

Career: articled Waterhouse & Co (1971-1973); admitted (1973); assistant solicitor (1973-1978); became partner (1978).

Biography: lives Godalming; born 18.09.1948; married to Jean with 1 son and 2 daughters. Educated at Leeds Modern School; Lincoln College Oxford (1970 MA).

Leisure: football; opera.

FIFIELD Guy

partner WILDE SAPTE Queensbridge House, 60 Upper Thames Street, London EC4V 3BD.

Career: articled Winterbothams; admitted (1982); assistant solicitor Robins & Co (1982-1984); assistant solicitor Wilde Sapte (1984-1989); became partner (1989).

Activities: member Whittington Committee of CLSC.

Biography: lives London; born 07.03.1957; single. Educated at Cheltenham College (LLB hons).

Leisure: current affairs.

FILLEUL Richard

partner BRODIES WS 15 Atholl Crescent, Edinburgh EH3 8HA.

Career: articled Peacock Fisher & Finch; admitted (1970); partner Field Fisher & Martineau (1971-1979); assistant solicitor Bond Pearce & Co (1979-1982); admitted Scotland (1983); assistant solicitor Brodies WS (1983-1986); became partner (1986).

Activities: member Society for Computers and the Law.

Biography: lives Dunfermline; born 28.05.1945; married to Kate. Educated at Sandle Manor, Fordingbridge; Kelly College, Tavistock; Keble College Oxford (1967 MA hons); author of 'Estate Planner' an in-house program for IBM PLC.

Leisure: computing; gardening .

FILLINGHAM Graham

justices' clerk Haringey Magistrates' Court, Bishops Road, Archway Road, Highgate, London N6 4HS.

Career: administration in magisterial service; trainee Court clerk (1972); principal assistant Ormskirk magistrates Court (1976-1983); deputy clerk to the Highgate Justices (1983-1986); became clerk to the Haringey Justices (1986).

Activities: member Brookmans Park Tennis Club.

Biography: lives Hertfordshire; born 09.09.1949; married to Suzanne with 3 children. Educated at Aspull High School; Bristol Polytechnic (1973-1976 Diploma in Magisterial Law); Manchester Polytechnic (1980 Common Professional Examination); Law Society Finals (1981).

Leisure: golf; tennis; music.

FINCH Robert

partner commercial property department LINKLATERS & PAINES Barrington House, 59-67 Gresham Street, London EC2V 7JA.

Career: partner Linklaters & Paines.

Activities: member Law Society; member City of London Solicitors Company; member of: Alpine Ski Club; Ski Club of Great Britain.

F

Biography: lives London SW19; born 20.08.1944; married to Patricia with 2 daughters. Educated at Felsted .

Leisure: sailing; skiing; mountaineering.

FINCH Stephen

partner HARRIS ROSENBLATT & KRAMER 26-28 Bedford Row, London WC1R 4HE.

Career: articled Withers; admitted (1975); assistant solicitor Sydney, Australia (1 year); assistant solicitor Lloyds Bowmaker (4 years); company solicitor Citibank (3 years); became partner Hill Bailey; became partner Harris Rosenblatt and Kramer.

Activities: former member Finance Houses Legislation Committee; examiner for the Finance Houses Diploma Examination; lectured extensively on the Consumer Credit Act; delivered lecture on Data Protection Act; member of: David Lloyd Tennis Club; London/Australia Society.

Biography: lives Worcester Park; born 28.11.1950; married to Leonie with 3 children. Educated at Raynes Park Grammar School; London University (1973 LLB hons).

Leisure: tennis; golf; cricket; eating out.

FINDLEY Christopher

partner and head of agricultural and commercial property department THOMAS MALLAM 18 High Street, Woodstock, Oxford OX7 1TF.

Career: articled Boyce Evans & Sheppard (1976-1978); admitted (1979); assistant solicitor (1979-1980); assistant solicitor Kenwright & Cox (1980-1981); assistant solicitor Preston & Redman (1981-1983); senior assistant solicitor Thomas Mallam (1983-1985); became partner (1986).

Activities: member of: Agricultural Law Association (elected member Committee 1988 and Parliamentary sub-committee 1989); National Farmers' Union; Tenant Farmers' Association; Country Landowners' Association; Barton & District Farming Club.

Biography: lives Oxford; born 14.03.1953; married to Julie. Educated at The Downs School, Colwell (1962-1966); Surbiton Grammar School (1966-1971); Polytechnic of Central London School of Law (1975 LLB hons); languages: French.

Leisure: travelling; wine; fishing; gardening; cooking; reading.

FINNEMORE Paul

senior partner in commercial property department COLE & COLE Sterling House, 19/23 High Street, Kidlington, Oxford OX5 2DH.

Career: admitted attorney, notary and conveyancer in South Africa (1956); assistant solicitor Cole & Cole (1964-1968); became partner (1968).

Activities: member Committee of Oxford & District Society for Mentally Handicapped (former treasurer); local director Solicitors Benevolent Association; member Board of Directors of City of Oxford Orchestra; member Oxford Theatre Club.

Biography: lives Oxford; born 26.07.1930; married to Bridget with 4 children. Educated at Grey High School, Port Elizabeth; University of Cape Town (1950 BA) (1952 LLB).

Leisure: music (especially opera); scrambling about old ruins; foreign travel; tennis; theatre; swimming.

FISHER Kenneth

senior partner KENDALL & FISHER 68 Market Street, Dalton in Furness, Cumbria LA15 8AD.

Career: Royal Navy (1945-1948) (discharged Sub Lt RNVR); articled to father Stanley J Fisher of WC Kendall & Fisher; Boxall & Boxall; Gibson & Weldon; admitted (1953); became partner Kendall & Fisher (1954).

Activities: chairman Agricultural Land Tribunal (Northern Area); chairman Social Security Appeal Tribunals; chairman Medical Services Committee and Opthalmic Services Committee for Cumbria; member Cumbria Family Practitioners' Committee; member No 7 Area Legal Aid Committee; chairman Governors Chetwynde Preparatory School; president Barrow in Furness branch of the Royal Society of St George; chairman Dalton & District Recreational Trust; past president North Lonsdale Law Association; past president Cartmel North Lonsdale and Lowick Agricultural Societies; member of: Hawks Club; Uppingham Rovers; LX Club; Lancashire RFC; Furness RUFC.

Biography: lives Ulverston; born 26.06.1927; married to Mary Florence with 2 children. Educated at Craig Preparatory School; Uppingham School; St John's College Cambridge (1951 BA MA): (LLB LLM).

Leisure: spectator rugby and cricket; skiing; gardening.

FISHER Tony

employment partner FIELD FISHER WATERHOUSE Lincoln House, 296-302 High Holborn, London WC1V 7JL.

Career: Regular Army Officer with Royal Engineers (1957-1963); ACIS (1963); admitted (1976); became partner (1979).

Activities: lectures to students at London School of Economics on practical employment law.

Biography: lives Maidstone; born 19.01.1939; married to Sylvia. Educated at St Paul's; Royal Military Academy Sandhurst (1957-1959); writes occasional articles on employment matters in various journals.

FISHWICK Tom

senior partner FRANK PLATT & FISHWICK Victoria Buildings, King Street, Wigan WN1 1DB.

Career: articled Edwin Berry & Co; pilot training with RAF; admitted (1950); assistant solicitor (1950-1958); became partner (1958).

Activities: member Wigan Law Society (1950 to date) (president 1975) (treasurer 1976-1989); solicitor to Wigan Rugby League Club.

Biography: lives Wigan; born 13.01.1925; married to Avril with 2 daughters. Educated at Rossall School; Exeter College Oxford; one or two publications on precedents in The Conveyancer and Property Lawyer.

Leisure: incurable skier; curable gardener.

FITZGERALD Christopher

partner SLAUGHTER AND MAY 35 Basinghall Street, London EC2V 5DB.

Career: admitted (1971); assistant solicitor (1971-1976); became partner Slaughter and May (1976); executive partner (finance) (1986-1990); head of banking (1990).

Activities: member of: MCC; RAC.

Biography: lives London; born 17.11.1945; married to Jill (1986); has 3 children and 2 stepchildren. Educated at Downside School; Lincoln College Oxford (1967 MA).

Leisure: reading; music; travel.

FITZGERALD David

partner and head of the commercial property department PAYNE HICKS BEACH 10 New Square, Lincoln's Inn, London WC2A 3QG.

Career: articled Ivens Thompson & Green

(1963-1968); admitted (1968); assistant solicitor Payne Hicks Beach (1968-1970); became partner (1970).

Activities: member of: RAC; Roehampton; St James's.

Biography: lives London SW13; born 05.10.1944; married to Elisabeth with 2 children. Educated at Kingswood School, Bath; College of Law.

Leisure: skiing; golf; tennis; windsurfing; running.

FITZGERALD Michael

Queen's Counsel 2 Mitre Court Buildings, Temple, London EC4 7BX.

Career: called to the Bar (1961) Middle Temple Astbury Scholar; QC (1980); Master of the Bench Middle Temple .

Activities: committee member Parliamentary Bar; committee member local government and planning Bar; committee member Annual Joint Planning Conference of Bar, Law Society and Royal Institution of Chartered Surveyors; member of: Athenaeum; Special Forces Club.

Biography: lives London SW7; born 09.06.1936; married with 4 children. Educated at Downside; Christ's College Cambridge (MA hons).

Leisure: opera; music; the arts; shooting; fishing; horse racing.

FITZGERALD Peter

partner and head private client department FLADGATE FIELDER 9 Queen Anne Street, London W1M 0BQ.

Career: articled Walters & Hart; admitted; assistant solicitor; became partner; firm merged to become Fladgate Fielder; specialist in agricultural and urban estates.

Activities: member Travellers Club.

Biography: lives London SW7 and Somerset; born 23.07.1943; married to Sarah with 3 children. Educated at Canford School; Trinity College Oxford (MA).

Leisure: farming; foxhunting; forestry.

FLANAGAN Terry

partner CHAFFE STREET Brook House, 70 Spring Gardens, Manchester M2 2BQ.

Career: articled Alexander Tatham & Co (1975-1977); admitted (1978); assistant solicitor Harold Chaffe & Co (1982-1984); became partner Chaffe Street (1984).

Activities: lecturer in law Manchester University (1970-1975 & 1978-1982) (part-time 1975-1978) .

Biography: lives Hebden Bridge; born 27.03.1948; married to Margaret with 3 children. Educated at St Bede's Grammar School, Bradford; Manchester University (1970 LLB) (1978 LLM); co-author 'Milman and Flanagan - the Modern Law of Partnership' (1983); various articles and contributions to legal works.

Leisure: game fishing; music.

FLATHER Gary

Queen's Counsel Lamb Building, Temple, London EC4Y 7AS.

Career: National Service as 2nd Lt serving in the Aden Protectorate; WT Flather (family steel business); called to the Bar (1962); pupillage Elwyn Jones QC's Chambers (1963); became tenant (1965); QC (1984); Recorder (1986).

Activities: TA commission (1958-1962); member panel of chairman for Teachers' Disciplinary Tribunal ILEA (1974); chairman of the William Tyndale Teachers' Tribunal (1976); assistant Parliamentary Boundary Commissioner (1982); member panel of chairman for ILEA Polytechnics Disciplinary Tribunal (1982); a chairman of the Police Disciplinary Appeal Tribunal (1987); a legal member of the Mental Health Review Tribunal (1987); a legal assessor to the General Medical Council (1987); a legal assessor to the General Dental Council (1987); inspector appointed by the DTI to conduct an enquiry into insider dealing under the Financial Services Act 1986 (1987-1988); chairman of the Statutory Committee of the Royal Pharmaceutical Society (1990); vice-president of the Community Council for Berkshire; president of the Maidenhead Rotary Club (1990); member of Oriental Club.

Biography: lives Maidenhead; born 04.10.1937; married to Shreela (Baroness Flather) with 2 children. Educated at Oundle School; Pembroke College Oxford (1961 BA) (1967 MA).

Leisure: played fives and rowed for Oundle; rowed for Pembroke Oxford; South Yorkshire junior squash champion; travelled extensively in India and Africa; climbed Mt Kilimanjaro and Mt Sinai; music; gardening; reading history; being sociable.

FLEGG Michael

partner CRIPPS HARRIES HALL Seymour House, 11-13 Mount Ephraim Road, TN1 1EN and 84 Calverley Road, Tunbridge Wells, Kent TN1 2UP.

Career: articled West London practice; admitted (1960); assistant solicitor Aylesbury (1960); assistant solicitor George Wimpey & Co Ltd (1966); solicitor private practice West End London (1973); Port of London Authority (1975); private practice (1979).

Activities: secretary to: local Chamber of Trade; Rugby Club and Round Table (1961-1966); chairman local Round Table; National Conference Registration Officer; secretary 41 Club; treasurer 41 International (1988-1989); chairman of trustees of Kidney Research Aid Fund; governor St James CE Infant School; interested in computing especially for lawyers and membership of Society for Computers and Law; Commissioner for Oaths; former Church warden and member St James' Church Tunbridge Wells; member Wang Legal User Group.

Biography: lives Tunbridge Wells; born 10.03.1938; married to Wendy (deceased 09.05.1990). Educated at Preston Manor County Grammar School; College of Law; Institute of Administrative Management Certificate and Diploma; Open University (BA); legal associate member Royal Town Planning Institute.

Leisure: film and video making; photography; computing; town and country planning; historic development of towns.

FLEMING John

partner STEPHENSON HARWOOD One, St Paul's Churchyard, London EC4M 8SH.

Career: admitted (1953); assistant solicitor (1953-1955); partner Evill & Coleman (1955-1959); became partner Stephenson Harwood (1960).

Activities: chairman Beaconsfield Cricket Club; chairman The Gresham Club; craftsman Incorporation of Gardeners of Glasgow; freeman of The Worshipful Company of Gardeners; Freeman of the City of London Solicitors' Company; member of: Beaconsfield Golf Club; MCC; Western Club; Royal Overseas League.

Biography: born 02.02.1926; married to Margaret with 3 children. Educated at Lincoln School; Trinity College Cambridge (1950 BA); (1954 LLB); Scott Scholar; Clement's Inn; City of London Solicitors' Company's Grotius, Maurice Nordon Prize; John Mackrell Prize.

Leisure: gardening; music; reading; collecting early English watercolours.

F

FLESCH Michael

barrister practising at Revenue Bar Gray's Inn Chambers, Grays' Inn, London WC1.

Career: Bigelow Teaching Fellow University of Chicago Law (1963-1964); variety of pupillages; part-time lecturer in revenue law University College London; Revenue Bar (1966 to date); QC (1983).

Activities: chairman Taxation and Retirement Benefits Committee of Bar Council (1985 to date); member of: MCC; Middlesex CCC; Arsenal FC; Brondesbury Lawn Tennis & Cricket Club.

Biography: lives London NW2; born 11.03.1940; married with 1 daughter and 1 son. Educated at Gordonstoun (1953-1958); University College London (1962 LLB); University of London Scholarship; Lord Justice Holker Senior Scholarship (1963); frequent contributor of articles, notes, reviews, etc to legal periodicals on tax subjects.

Leisure: all forms of sport (watching); playing tennis; watching Arsenal FC & Middlesex CCC; backgammon.

FLETCHER John

senior partner COZENS-HARDY & JEWSON Castle Chambers, Opie Street, Norwich NR1 3DP.

Career: articled Solly Marshall & Co; admitted (1953); National Service with Army Intelligence Corps (1953-1955); assistant solicitor Garerd Hill & Curl (1955-1959); partner (1959-1970); amalgamated with Cozens-Hardy & Jewson (1970); partner (1970-1988); became senior partner (1988).

Activities: trustee Anorexia Family Aid; member of: Norwich Rugby FC; Norwich CEYMS; Norfolk Dog Training Society.

Biography: lives Norwich; born 01.04.1930; married to Janet with 2 daughters. Educated at Birkenhead School (1940-1947); Liverpool University (1950 LLB hons); Cambridge (1954 Russian language short course).

Leisure: formerly rugby; cricket; gardening; obedience dog training; antiques (particularly clocks).

FLETCHER Kevin

partner JACKSONS 7/15 Queen's Square, Middlesbrough, Cleveland TS2 1AL.

Career: articled Andrew M Jackson & Co (1969-1971); admitted (1971); assistant solicitor Jacksons Monk & Rowe (1971-1972); became salaried partner (1972-1973); became equity partner (1973); became partner Jacksons on merger with Cohen Jackson (1989).

Activities: frequent contributor to employment law seminars and advised local polytechnic on employment law course; member Industrial Law Society; member of: The Cleveland Club; Middlesbrough Cricket Club.

Biography: lives Nunthorpe; born 06.03.1947; married to Susan with 1 son and 1 daughter. Educated at Hull Grammar School (1958-1964); St Catharine's College Cambridge (1968 BA MA); College of Law Guildford (1968-1969); articles on employment law in local newspaper.

Leisure: interested in all forms of sport; jogging; cricket; avid reader; collecting Art; music enthusiast.

FLETCHER Rod

partner and head of criminal law department RUSSELL JONES & WALKER Swinton House 324 Gray's Inn Road, London WC1X 8DH.

Career: articled Kingsley Napley & Co; admitted (1981); assistant solicitor (1981-1983); assistant solicitor Russell Jones & Walker (1983-1985); became partner (1985).

Activities: member Clerkenwell Magistrates' Court Duty Solicitor Committee; administrator Clerkenwell & Hampstead 24-Hour Duty Solicitor Scheme; member International Bar Association.

Biography: lives Twickenham; born 21.04.1957; single. Educated at Berkhamsted School; Birmingham University (1978 LLB); College of Law Lancaster Gate (1979).

Leisure: sailing (RYA/DOT Practical Certificate Coastal Skipper); rugby; golf; cricket.

FLETT Andrew

company secretary and head of legal division Shell UK Limited Shell-Mex House, Strand, London WC2R 0DX.

Career: articled Ashurst Morris Crisp & Co; admitted (1970); assistant solicitor (1970-1971); legal adviser Shell International Petroleum Co Ltd (1971-1976); advocate of Brunei (1976-1979); managerial jobs in Shell organisation (1979-1980 & 1981-1985); legal adviser Brunei Shell Petroleum Co Ltd (1980-1981 & 1985-1987); legal adviser Shell UK Limited (1976-1979 & 1987-1988); company secretary and head of legal Shell UK Ltd (1988).

Biography: lives London W8; born 05.10.1943; married to Carol with 3 daughters. Educated at St Paul's School, London; St John's College Oxford (1965 BA).

FLINT Charles JB

partner SHAKESPEARES 10 Bennetts Hill, Birmingham B2 5RS.

Career: articled Harold Roberts & Lea (1963-1966); admitted (1966); became partner (1966); amalgamated to become Shakespeares; Theodore Goddard (1966).

Activities: chairman Young Solicitors Group England & Wales (1973-1974); chairman Solicitors European Group (1990) (founder Birmingham branch 1968); member Council of Birmingham Law Society (1974-1989); member Public and Professional Relations and Gazette Committees of the Law Society; member West Midlands Area Legal Aid Committee (1975-1989); Institute of European Law University of Birmingham Advisory Board (1990 to date).

Biography: lives near Stratford upon Avon and Quercy, France; born 21.04.1942; married to Marie with 2 children. Educated at Uppingham School; Birmingham University (LLB); author of 'Directors' Rights and Responsibilities'; various articles for press and journals.

Leisure: family; sport; shooting; fishing; consumption and study of wine; France; charitable activities (especially NSPCC).

FLINT David

partner MACROBERTS 152 Bath Street, Glasgow G2 4TB.

Career: assistant solicitor MacRoberts (1979-1984); became partner (1984).

Activities: licensed insolvency practitioner under the Insolvency Act (1986); Notary Public (1980); member joint working party of Scottish, English and Northern Irish Law Societies and Bars on competition law (1981 to date); member joint working party of Scottish and English Law Societies and Bars on intellectual property law (1984 to date); member Law Society of Scotland EEC Company Law sub-committees; working party on EEC Competition Procedures; working party on banking law; 1992 Committee; member Computer Law Association Inc; lecturer on company law at Scottish Police College; chairman Scottish Lawyers' European Group (1985 to date); member Insolvency Practitioners'

Association; member of: Western Club; Royal Scottish Automobile Club.

Biography: lives Glasgow; born 07.07.1955; married to Marie with 2 children. Educated at High School of Glasgow (1964-1973); Glasgow University (1976 LLB) (1982 LLM); Europa Instituut Universiteit van Amsterdam (1978 Diploma in European Integration with distinction); various articles in LIEI; EIPR; Journal of the Glasgow Chamber of Commerce; The Accountant's Magazine; author of 'A Guide to Liquidation in Scotland' (2nd edition 1989); editor of 'Insolvency Law in Scotland Guide and Practice Series'; Scottish insolvency editor of 'Gore-Browne on Company Law'; author of 'Trade Regulation - EEC Aspects' in Stair Memorial Encyclopaedia of Scots Law.

Leisure: computers; reading.

FLINT Michael

chairman DENTON HALL BURGIN & WARRENS Five Chancery Lane, London EC4A 1BU.

Career: articled Denton Hall & Burgin (1951-1956); admitted (1956); assistant solicitor (1956-1966); managing director Paramount British Pictures Ltd (1967); became vice-president (1968-1970); chairman London Screen Enterprises Ltd (1970-1972); became partner Denton Hall & Burgin (1973); firm became Denton Hall Burgin & Warrens (1985).

Activities: Director General of Association of Independent Radio Contractors (1975); chief executive Capital Radio Limited (1974); vice-chairman Limehouse Productions Limited (1982-1986); member of British Association of Film & Television Arts (BAFTA); Fellow of the Society of Antiquaries (1960 to date); treasurer of British Archaeological Association (1959-1989) (currently vice-president); editorial board of International Media Law; council member of the Common Law Institute of Intellectual Property; chairman committee L Intellectual Property Entertainment & Communications; International Bar Association Council member; member of standing committee on communications and database International Bar Association; member of the planning committee of the Assise Europeenes de l'Audiovisuel; lectured at University of Oxford, University of Southern California, Stamford University, University of California, Los Angeles, Paris Bar, Anglo-German Jurists' Association; CLIP conferences; IBA conferences, MIDEM, MIPCOM, Cannes Film Festival,

Australian Television School, National Broadcasting School, BAFTA; executive producer: 'Glastonbury Fayre' (feature film 1972); 'Can I Help You' (short film 1980); member of: Savile Club; Variety Club of Great Britain; Lord's Taverners' Club; Wig & Pen Club; Hurlingham Club.

Biography: lives London SW7 and Boulouris, Var, France; born 07.05.1932; married to Phyllida Margaret Medwyn with 2 sons and 1 daughter. Educated at St Peter's York; Kingswood School; Law Society's School of Law Lancaster Gate; author of: 'A User's Guide to Copyright'; 'Intellectual Property - The New Law' (with Alan Williams and Clive Thorne); contributor to 'Television by Satellite - Legal Aspects'; numerous articles on copyright related topics and space law for: European Intellectual Property Review; International Media Law; Cable & Satellite Europe; New Law Journal; Business Law Review; Law Society's Gazette.

Leisure: painting (winner of Law Society Art Group Annual Prize 1977); photography; tennis; opera .

FLOUNDERS Andrew

partner and manager of commercial and corporate department READ HIND STEWART 29 Park Place, Leeds LS1 2RU.

Career: articled Reads (1981); admitted; assistant solicitor; partner Read Hind & Co (1984); became manager commercial department (1989).

Activities: governor Bradford Centre for Deaf People; member of: the Bradford Club; Round Table.

Biography: lives Calverley nr Leeds; born 24.11.1958; married to Susan with 2 sons. Educated at Benton Park Grammar School, Rawdon; Manchester University (1977-1980); Leeds Polytechnic (1981).

Leisure: most sports (captain firm's five-a-side football team).

FOCKE Paul

Queen's Counsel and head of chambers 1 Mitre Court Buildings, Temple, London EC4.

Career: called to the Bar Gray's Inn (1964); QC (1982); called to the Bar New Zealand (1982); QC New South Wales (1984); Recorder.

Activities: director Bar Mutual Indemnity Fund Ltd; member of: Turf Club; Cavalry & Guards Club; Beefsteak Club; Pratts Club.

Biography: lives London SW3; born

14.05.1937; married to Lady Tana with 2 children. Educated at Worth Preparatory School; Downside School; Exeter College Oxford; Trinity College, Dublin.

Leisure: aeroplanes; travelling.

FOGEL Steven

head of property department TITMUSS SAINER & WEBB 2 Serjeants' Inn, London EC4Y 1LT.

Career: Cohen & Meyohas, Paris (1974); articled Titmuss Sainer & Webb (1974-1976); assistant solicitor (1976-1980); partner (1980); became trainee solicitor recruitment partner (1982); head of development division (1986-1990); became head of property department (1990).

Activities: member Law Commission working party on landlord and tenant (Privity of Contract) - LCWP 95 HMSO (1985-1986); member joint working party of Law Society and RICS on commercial leases (1987); member of Old Carmeli Association; Blundell Law Lecturer (1985); member British Council of Shopping Centres (1989); member British Council for Offices (1990); member of Anglo American Property Institute (1990).

Biography: lives London NW11; born 16.10.1951; married to Joan with 2 sons and 1 daughter. Educated at Carmel College (1963-1969); King's College, London (1972 LLB); Hickling prize winner; (1973 LLM); co-author 'Rent Reviews' (1987); consulting editor Vol 22 Butterworth Encyclopaedia of Forms and Precedents; member of board of Journal of Property Finance (1989) and writes and lectures frequently for Law Society; RICS; commercial publishers.

Leisure: cycling; jazz; photography; gardening; creative writing; family.

FORBES David

senior partner PICKWORTHS 6 Victoria Street, St Albans, Herts AL1 3JB.

Career: articled West Sussex County Council (1971-1973); admitted (1973); assistant solicitor (1973-1974); assistant solicitor Pickworths (1974-1976); became partner (1976-1989); senior partner specialising in town and country planning (1986).

Activities: secretary Dacorum Enterprise Agency; vice-chairman Dacorum Relate; secretary Friends of Dacorum College; part member Herts Law Society Committee (member of panel for monitoring articled clerks); talks to local schools on how the law affects sixth formers; takes part in

F

firm's seminars run twice-yearly for clients; secretary junior school PTA.

Biography: lives St Albans; born 07.12.1947; married to Helen with 3 children. Educated at KEGS Grammar School; Birmingham University (1969 LLB); (1970 LLM); Distinction in Mercantile Law; Aitchison Memorial Prize for Leadership; Henry Menton Scholarship and Scholarship from DES for LLM course; Guildford College of Law (1970) (Distinction in revenue and conveyancing).

Leisure: reading; eating; drinking; meeting people.

FORMBY Roger

managing partner MACFARLANES 10 Norwich Street, London EC4A 1BD.

Career: articled Macfarlanes (1961-1964); admitted (1965); assistant solicitor (1965-1967); became partner (1967); head of property department (1970-1986); became managing partner (1987).

Activities: member City of London Club.

Biography: lives Thames Ditton; born 15.03.1938; married to Jane with 2 children. Educated at Winchester College; Magdalen College Oxford (1961 BA); Law Society Finals (1964 hons).

Leisure: golf; swimming; skiing; travel; ballet; theatre.

FORSTER David

partner CHURCH ADAMS TATHAM & CO 23/25 Bell Street, Reigate, Surrey RH2 7AD.

Career: articled Griffinhoofe & Brewster and Malkin Cullis & Sumption (1954-1959); admitted (1959); National Service 2nd Lt RASC (1959-1961); became partner Malkin Cullis & Sumption (1961-1964); became partner Mole Metters & Forster (1965-1975); became senior partner (1975-1986); became partner Church Adams Tatham & Co upon merger (1986).

Activities: committee member South East Surrey Law Society (1980 to date) (president 1986-1988); member Surrey Legal Aid Local Committee (1969-1974); director property company; member of Lloyds; member of: Worshipful Company of Loriners (Liveryman); Lloyds Yacht Club.

Biography: lives Tonbridge; born 15.11.1936; married to Belinda with 3 children. Educated at Bradfield College, Berkshire (1950-1954); College of Law Lancaster Gate (1955-1956 & 1959 hons).

Leisure: sailing; riding; tennis.

FOSTER James

partner and head of litigation department MANCHES & CO Aldwych House, 71/91 Aldwych, London WC2B 4RP.

Career: articled Slaughter and May (1979-1981); admitted (1981); assistant solicitor (1981-1983); assistant solicitor Withers (1983-1985); assistant solicitor Manches & Co (1985-1986); became partner (1986).

Activities: member International Litigation Practitioners' Forum; member London Litigation Solicitors Association; member British Academy of Experts; member British-German Jurists' Association.

Biography: lives London N12; born 24.02.1957; married to Susan with 2 children. Educated at Clifton College, Bristol (1969-1974); Magdalen College Oxford (1978 MA) Herbert Warren Exhibitioner.

Leisure: photography; chess; walking.

FOWELL David

partner JAQUES & LEWIS 2 South Square, Gray's Inn, London WC1R 5HR.

Career: articled Jaques & Lewis (1967-1969); admitted (1969); assistant solicitor (1969-1976); established Jaques & Co in Jersey (1972-1976); became partner (1976); head of litigation department (1980-1990); member Management Committee (1982-1990); director of marketing (1987-1990).

Activities: member London Solicitors Litigation Association; member Justice; member Old Boys Club.

Biography: lives London E8; born 07.10.1944; married to Jane with 2 stepchildren. Educated at Mill Hill School (Scholar); Pembroke College Oxford (1966 BA hons).

Leisure: antique silver; restoring antique furniture; garden; cinema; theatre; some tennis.

FOWLE Ivo

joint senior partner WILLIAM DAWES & CO Watchbell Chambers, Rye, E Sussex TN31 7HB.

Career: articled Hudgell Yeates & Co (1962-1967); admitted (1967); assistant solicitor William Dawes & Co (1967-1969); became partner (1969).

Activities: past president Hastings & District Law Society; immediate past chairman Rye Festival Council; member SFLA; president local Round Table; immediate past chairman Rye & Romney Marsh 41 Club; member of: Tenterden Golf Club; Senlac Golfing Society.

Biography: lives Rye; born 27.11.1944; married with 2 children. Educated at Bexleyheath Boys' School; College of Law Lancaster Gate.

Leisure: squash; tennis; golf; helping to organise local arts festival.

FOWLE Richard

senior partner HATCH & HATCH 4 Theatre Street, Norwich, Norfolk NR2 1QY.

Career: articled Turberville Smith & Co; admitted (1970); assistant solicitor (1970-1972); assistant solicitor Hatch & Hatch (1972); became partner; became senior partner (1988).

Activities: chairman Non-Contentious Business Committee; member Committee Norfolk & Norwich Inc Law Society; former chairman Wymondham Heritage Museum; vice-chairman Wymondham Heritage Society; vice-chairman Mid-Norfolk Railway Project.

Biography: lives Wymondham; born 12.06.1946; married to Valerie with 3 children. Educated at Slough Grammar School; College of Law; member of team which produced 'Norfolk Conveyancing Protocol'.

Leisure: local history research.

FOX Ronnie

senior partner FOX WILLIAMS City Gate House, 39-45 Finsbury Square, London EC2A 1UU.

Career: articled Oppenheimers (1969-1972); admitted (1972); assistant solicitor (1972-1974); became partner (1974-1988); became partner Denton Hall Burgin & Warrens (1988-1989) founded Fox Williams (1989).

Activities: member Law Society Completion Cheque Scheme working party (1981-1982); member Law Society Standing Committee on Company Law (1985-1989); Law Society representative on the Registrar of Companies Users' Group (1985-1989); member City of London Law Society Problems of Practice Sub-committee (1985 to date); chairman working party preparing the evidence of the CLLS to Lady Marre's Committee on the Future of the Legal Profession (1986); coordinator of the CLLS Survey on City Solicitors' attitudes to multi-disciplinary practices (1987); member CLLS Committee (1988); elected Deputy Chairman of CLLS Committee (1989); member Executive Committee of the British-Israel Chamber of

Commerce; member of the Council Membership Committee of the Law Society of England and Wales; chairman CLLS working party preparing the response of City solicitors to the Government Green Paper on the work and organisation of the legal profession (1989); hon solicitor to the British-Israel Chamber of Commerce; member of the British-German Jurists' Association; member International Bar Association; frequently attends IBA and Law Society national conferences; addressed Committee G of the IBA Conference on Due Diligence Disclosures and Warranties in Corporate Acquisition Practice (1987); member of: Royal Automobile Club; Law Society Motor Club.

Biography: lives London NW11; born 27.09.1946; married to Sonya with 2 children. Educated at Mercers School (1957-1958 Exhibitioner); City of London School (1958-1964); Lincoln College Oxford (1968 MA); City of London Solicitors Company Distinguished Service Award (1989); author of 'Payments on Termination of Employment' (1981, 1984 & 1990); 'Legal Aspects of Doing Business in the United Kingdom' (1984); 'Due Diligence, Disclosures and Warranties in Corporate Acquisition Practice - the United Kingdom' (1988); 'International Business Transactions - Service Agreements for Multinational Corporate Executives in the United Kingdom' (1988); 'Legal Aspects of Doing Business in England and Wales' (1990); articles in the Law Society's Gazette; City of London Law Society Newsletter; International Business Lawyer; British-Israel Trade Journal; Office and Information Management International; Financial Times; Legal Business.

Leisure: opera; theatre; cinema; swimming; skin diving; scuba diving; motoring and other forms of transport; management studies.

FOX Stephen

senior partner BETESH FOX & CO 17 Ralli Courts, West Riverside, Manchester M3 5FT.

Career: specialist commercial fraud lawyer.

Activities: managing director Van-Dade Chocolatier Ltd.

Biography: lives Manchester; born 08.10.1948; single. Educated at Manchester Grammar School; College of Law.

Leisure: raconteur.

FRANKEL William

finance partner BIRKBECK MONTAGU 7 St Bride Street, London EC4A 4AT.

Career: articled Birkbeck Montagu (1966-1969); admitted (June 1970); assistant solicitor (1970); became partner (September 1970).

Activities: Governor University College School (1980 to date); trustee various school trusts and pension funds and member governing council's general purposes committee; UK solicitor representing government of Jamaica and director of companies owned by that government; trustee of Inter-Action Trust and director Inter-Action Social Enterprise Trust Limited (1968 to date); director of a number of companies and trustee of various charitable trusts; member Solicitors European Group; involved in all aspects of human rights activities particularly pertaining to South Africa; member Morton's.

Biography: lives London NW3; born 14.12.1944; married to Bridget with 2 children. Educated South African schools; Universities of Cape Town and Sydney.

Leisure: skiing; swimming; cross country walking; classical music; theatre; bridge.

FRANKS John

senior partner CHETHAMS 84 Baker Street, London W1M 1DL.

Career: articled Smiles & Co (1949-1952); admitted (1952); assistant solicitor Chethams (1952-1956); became partner (1956).

Activities: Law Society Council member (1974); chairman Sunlight Service Group PLC (1975-1989); deputy chairman Godfrey Davis (Holdings) PLC (1987 to date); chairman Franks Committee (1979-1980); report on profits allowed for dispensing by retail pharmacists under the National Health Service; chairman Disciplinary Committee of the Architects' Registration Council (1982-1988); chairman Appeals Committee of the National House Builders' Registration Council (1988 to date); member various committees of Council of the Law Society; member Export Advisory Council of the Sir Percival David Foundation; Liveryman of the Worshipful Company of Arbitrators; member of RAC; Institute of Directors.

Biography: lives London W9; born 10.12.1928; married with 3 children and 1 stepdaughter. Educated at Acton County Grammar School; The Grammar School, Shaftesbury; University College London

(1949 LLB); Institute of Advanced Legal Studies London (1951 LLM); Fellow of the Chartered Institute of Arbitrators; numerous articles particularly in the Solicitors Journal; author of: 'Companies Act (1967)'; 'Company Director and the Law'.

Leisure: archaeology; collecting antiques; specialist collection of Vanity Fair caricatures.

FRASE Anthony

partner DENTON HALL BURGIN & WARRENS Banking and Financial Markets group; currently on secondment to THE ASSOCIATION OF FUTURES BROKERS AND DEALERS LIMITED B Section, 5th Floor, Plantation House, 5-8 Mincing Lane, London EC3M 3DX.

Career: 2nd Lt TAVR (1976-1978); 9th Bn Royal Green Jackets (1977-1978); articled Allen & Overy (1978-1980); admitted (1981); assistant solicitor (1981-1983); assistant solicitor Denton Hall Burgin & Warrens (1983-1988); became partner (1988); compliance officer and editor Denton Hall Banking and Financial Services Newsletter (1988-1989); seconded to The Association of Futures Brokers and Dealers Limited (1989).

Activities: member International Bar Association; member City of London Solicitors' Company; member Law Society; member of: United Oxford and Cambridge University Club; Wig & Pen Club; Cavalry & Guards Club.

Biography: lives London SW11; born 08.07.1954; married to Sarah. Educated at Repton School; Exhibitioner Trinity College Cambridge (1976 BA) (1980 MA); publications: various articles on banking and financial markets.

Leisure: art; theatre; travel.

FRASER Alan

county secretary and solicitor CUMBRIA COUNTY COUNCIL The Courts, Carlisle CA3 8LZ.

Career: articled West Sussex CC (1958-1960); assistant solicitor East Suffolk CC (1960-1962); assistant solicitor and assistant clerk Derbyshire CC (1962-1971); deputy clerk Cumberland CC (1971-1974); director of legal and administrative services (later redesignated county secretary and solicitor) (1973).

Activities: secretary: Cumbria Probation Committee; Cumbria Tourist Board; Cumbria Sea Fisheries Committee;

F

president Carlisle and District Law Society (1988-1989); member Law Society Planning Law Committee (1983-1989); member Society of County Secretaries (1973 to date); hon secretary (1989 to date); chairman Joint Liaison Group on Child Care Law; member of: United Oxford & Cambridge Universities Club; Border Club.

Biography: lives Carlisle; born 11.02.1936; single. Educated Bramcote Hall; Trent College; Hertford College Oxford (1961 MA); LMRTPI; author of: miscellaneous articles on constitutional law, child care law, professional issues; 'National Parks Policy and the Law' (Oxford Planning Law Conference 1982).

Leisure: hockey (chairman & secretary Cumbria County Hockey Association); cricket; golf; music particularly opera.

FRASER Colin

partner TAYLOR JOYNSON GARRETT 10 Maltravers Street, London WC2R 3BS and 180 Fleet Street, London EC4A 2NT.

Career: National Service in the Army; Rifle Brigade (1952-1953); commissioned into Queen's Own Royal West Kent Regiment (1953); served with the 1st Bn as a platoon commander in Malaya (1953-1954) Baor (1954); articled Joynson-Hicks (1957-1960); admitted (1960); assistant solicitor (1960-1964); became partner (1964).

Activities: former Deputy to the Under Sheriff of Surrey; member British Literary and Artistic Copyright Association; Associate, Centre for Commercial Law Studies, Queen Mary College; one of the legal advisers to the Music Copyright Reform Group; gave the (1987) Otto Blau Memorial lecture on copyright and music; followed the copyright part of the Copyright, Designs and Patents Act (1988) through Parliament; served in the Territorial Army (1954-1968) (rose to rank of Major); awarded the TD; chairman of two committees in Dorking; member United Oxford & Cambridge Universities Club.

Biography: lives Dorking; born 18.02.1934; married to Gay with 2 adult children. Educated at Cottesmore School (1940-1947); Aldenham School (1947-1952); Trinity Hall Cambridge (1954-1957) (1960 MA); writes articles and speaks at seminars on copyright matters.

FRASER John

senior partner LEWIS SILKIN 1 Butler Place, London SW1H 0PT.

Career: worked in banking; army

education instructor; articled; admitted (1960); became senior partner Lewis Silkin.

Activities: Opposition spokesman on legal affairs; MP (1966); Minister of Employment (1974-1976); Minister for Consumer Affairs (1976-1979); dealt as Minister with competition policy and spearheaded many legal reforms eg Unfair Contract Terms Act and Estate Agents Act; campaigning for leasehold reform and for housing rights for 25 years.

Biography: lives London; born 30.06.1934; married to Ann with 3 children. Educated at Sloane Grammar School; Law Society School of Law; John Mackrell Prizeman.

Leisure: walking; football; athletics; music; travel.

FRAZER Christopher

barrister 2 Harcourt Buildings, Temple, London EC4Y 9DB; also Harcourt Chambers, St Aldate's Courtyard, St Aldates, Oxford.

Career: called to the Bar Middle Temple (1983) (Astbury Scholar); Inner Temple ad eundem; Midland and Oxford Circuit; Family Law and Criminal Bar Associations.

Activities: chairman Cambridge University Conservative Association (1980); chairman and founder Conservative Young Lawyers (1984); Freeman of the City of London (1986); member Court of Common Council, Corporation of London (1986 to date); vice-chairman and treasurer Twickenham Conservative Association (1986-1989); patron Richmond Music Festival (1986 to date); member Corporation of London Police Committee (1987 to date); editor 'Thoughts for a Third Term' (1987); secretary Society of Conservative Lawyers (1988-1989); member General Council of the Bar (1989 to date); chairman Bar Council Parliamentary Group (1989-1990); vice-chairman Young Barristers' Committee (1990); vice-chairman Bar Conference (1990); Director of 'Law Aid '90'; prospective Conservative Parliamentary Candidate, Peckham; member of Guildhall Club.

Biography: lives London W6; born 17.06.1960; married to Victoria (younger daughter of Mr and Mrs JP Hess, Chorlton Hall, Chester) 20.05.1989. Educated at King's College School, Wimbledon; St John's College Cambridge (MA LLM); Entrance Exhibition; College Prizeman; McMahon Law Student; Macauley Scholar.

Leisure: dinghy sailing; music; architecture and heritage.

FREEDMAN Lionel

senior partner ALEXANDER TATHAM & CO 30 St Ann Street, Manchester M2 3DB.

Career: articled Alexander Tatham; admitted; assistant solicitor; became senior partner (1983).

Activities: hon lecturer in company law Manchester University; member Advisory Board of the University of Manchester Centre for Law and Business; hon secretary Manchester Financial and Professional Forum; chairman of the Institute for Fiscal Studies North West (1989); president Jewish Representative Council of Greater Manchester & Region (1977-1980); chairman Provincial Committee of Board of Deputies of British Jews (1980-1985); hon officer Trades Advisory Council Manchester (1980 to date); member of: St James's Club; Dunham Forest Golf Club.

Biography: lives Bowdon; married to Freda with 2 children. Educated at Foyle College, Londonderry; Manchester University (LLB hons).

Leisure: communal activities; walking.

FREEDMAN Philip

partner in charge of managing the conveyancing department MISHCON DE REYA 125 High Holborn, London WC1V 6QP.

Career: articled Victor Mishcon & Co (1969-1971); admitted (1972) .

Activities: member editorial board of Journal of Rent Review and Lease Renewal; member Law Society's Land Law and Conveyancing Committee; frequent speaker at legal conferences and seminars on property related matters; delivered a Blundell Memorial lecture (1987).

Biography: lives London NW11; born 29.11.1947; married to Rhona with 1 child. Educated at Christ's College Grammar School, Finchley; London School of Economics University of London (1968 LLB hons); College of Law Lancaster Gate (1968-1969); numerous property related articles in the Law Society's Gazette; The Solicitors Journal; The Estates Gazette; Journal of Rent Review & Lease Renewal; author of: 'Checklist for Commercial Lettings'; 'Service Charges - Law and Practice'; legal chapters in 'Valuation & Investment Appraisal'.

Leisure: photography; music (listening); reading; cycling; travel.

FREEMAN David

senior partner DJ FREEMAN & CO 43 Fetter Lane, London EC4A 1NA.

Career: Army Lt (1946-1948); admitted (1952); founder and senior partner DJ Freeman & Co (1952).

Activities: Department of Trade Inspector into the affairs of AEG Telefunken (UK) Ltd and Credit Collections Ltd (1977); governor Royal Shakespeare Theatre (1979 to date); member of the Law Society; member: Huntercombe Golf Club; Reform Club.

Biography: lives London W2; born 25.02.1928; married to Iris with 2 sons and 1 daughter. Educated at Christ's College Finchley.

Leisure: golf; reading; theatre.

FREEMAN Mark

senior resident partner FRESHFIELDS 24th Floor, One Exchange Square, Hong Kong.

Career: articled Crossman Block and Keith (1967-1969); admitted (1969); assistant solicitor Freshfields (1969-1974); partner (1974); head of finance team (1974-1985); became resident senior partner Hong Kong (1985).

Activities: member City of London Solicitors' Company Banking Law Sub-committee; member Hong Kong Law Society Banking and Company Law Committee; member Hong Kong Club.

Biography: lives Hong Kong; born 29.09.1943; 2 daughters. Educated at Eton College (1956-1961); Emmanuel College Cambridge (1967 MA LLB); articles in Air Finance Journal and Air Finance Yearbook.

Leisure: skiing; scuba diving; motor racing.

FREEMAN Michael

senior partner MICHAEL FREEMAN & CO One Great Cumberland Place, London W1H 7AL.

Career: articled Middleton Lewis & Co; admitted (1961); assistant solicitor (1961-1967); founded own practice (1967).

Biography: lives Stanmore; born 12.01.1939; married to Ruth with 2 children. Educated at Epsom College; College of Law Lancaster Gate (1958 & 1960).

Leisure: cricket; Mozart.

FREEMAN Richard

senior partner BANKES ASHTON 81A Guildhall Street, Bury St Edmunds, Suffolk IP33 1PZ.

Career: articled Jackaman Smith & Mulley; admitted (1957); assistant solicitor (1957-1960); assistant solicitor Bankes Ashton &

Co (1960-1963); became partner (1963); became senior partner (1987).

Activities: member Royal Harwich Yacht Club.

Biography: lives Bury St Edmunds; born 05.11.1931; married to Jean with 3 children. Educated at Culford School; Christ's College Cambridge (1954 BA) (1955 LLB) (1957 MA).

Leisure: Scouts (former Suffolk county commissioner); sailing; fell walking.

FREEMAN Roger

group legal adviser COSTAIN GROUP PLC 111 Westminster Bridge Road, London SE1 7UE.

Career: articled to the town clerk Epsom and Ewell BC (1962-1965); admitted (1965); assistant solicitor and senior assistant solicitor (1965-1969); senior solicitor Costain (1969-1971); became group legal adviser (1971); chairman of Lysander Insurance Brokers Ltd (wholly-owned subsidiary of Costain) (1988).

Activities: committee member Law Society Commerce and Industry Group and its Recruitment and Training Sub-committee; lectures on construction and business law.

Biography: lives Epsom; born 04.02.1939; married with 2 children. Educated at Enfield Grammar School; Jesus College Cambridge (1962 BA) (MA); contributor to 'Managing Legal Practice in Business' in Law Society's Gazette.

Leisure: golf; walking; poetry.

FREER Gillian

commercial property partner NABARRO NATHANSON 50 Stratton Street, London W1X 5FL.

Career: articled Nabarro Nathanson (1966-1968); admitted (1968); assistant solicitor (1968-1972); became first female partner (1972).

Activities: member various committees supporting music; member of: Dulwich & Sydenham Hill Golf Club; West Cornwall Golf Club.

Biography: lives Bickley and St Ives; born 15.06.1944; married to Michael. Educated at Bromley High School for Girls; University College London (1965 LLB); College of Law Lancaster Gate (1966).

Leisure: enthusiastic supporter of music; trying to learn to play piano; keen golfer; horse riding.

FREER Penny

partner FRESHFIELDS Whitefriars, 65 Fleet Street, London EC4Y 1HS.

Career: articled Lee & Pemberton (1971-1973); admitted (1973); assistant solicitor Nabarro Nathanson (1973-1975); assistant solicitor Freshfields (1975-1979); became partner (1979).

Activities: member Reform Club.

Biography: lives London SE26; born 06.02.1950; married to Terry Fuller with 2 children. Educated at Bromley High School for Girls; Lady Margaret Hall Oxford (1967-1970) Exhibitioner; College of Law (1970-1971).

FRESHWATER Tim

partner SLAUGHTER AND MAY 35 Basinghall Street, London EC2V 5DB.

Career: articled Slaughter and May (1967-1969); admitted (1969); assistant solicitor (1969-1975); became partner (1975); Hong Kong office (1979-1985).

Activities: president Law Society of Hong Kong (1984-1985); joint chairman Joint Working Party on China of the Law Society and the Bar; member Japan Committee of the British Invisible Exports Council.

Biography: lives London SW7; born 21.10.1944; married to Judy. Educated at Eastbourne College (1958-1963); Emmanuel College Cambridge (1966 BA) (MA) (1967 LLB); contributor to 'A Practitioner's Guide to the City Code on Take-overs and Mergers'.

FRETTEN Ian

senior partner IAN FRETTEN & PARTNERS The Saxon Centre, 11 Bargates, Christchurch, Dorset BH23 1PZ.

Career: articled Lickfolds Wiley and Powles (1968-1970); admitted (1971); assistant solicitor Christopher Frere-Smith (1972); assistant solicitor Jeffrey Gordon and Co (1972-1973); assistant solicitor Aldridge Myers (1973-1975); assistant solicitor Cousins Burbidge and Connor (1975-1977); founded own practice (1978).

Activities: secretary and committee member Bournemouth District Housing Society; secretary and committee member Society of Self Build Consultants; hon solicitor Christchurch Hospital League of Friends; chairman Christchurch CAB.

Biography: lives Christchurch; born 27.06.1947; divorced with 3 children. Educated at Sir Roger Manwood's School, Sandwich; University College London (1968 LLB hons); Solicitors Finals (1971).

Leisure: squash; bridge; chess; foreign travel; food and wine.

FRIMOND Nicholas

senior partner FRIMONDS Chronicle House, 72/78 Fleet Street, London EC4A 2BU and Haslemere and Guildford, Surrey.

Career: articled Borm-Reid & Co; admitted (1971); founded own practice (1971).

Activities: director of various companies; member of: Royal Thames Yacht Club; Little Ship Club.

Biography: lives Roundhurst, West Sussex; born 18.07.1945; married with 2 sons. Educated at Lycee d'Anvers, Antwerp, Belgium; Lycee Francais, London; College of Law Lancaster Gate.

Leisure: sailing; skiing; painting; walking the dog.

FROSTICK Raymond

partner and chairman of partnership board DAYNES HILL & PERKS Holland Court, The Close, Norwich, Norfolk NR1 4DX.

Career: articled (1954-1957); admitted (1957); assistant solicitor Sydney Morse & Co (1957-1961); became partner Hill & Perks (now Daynes Hill & Perks) (1962).

Activities: board member Eversheds; Lord Mayor of Norwich (1976); (councillor 1966-1979); chairman Norfolk County Council (1983) (councillor 1973-1985); chairman Norfolk Area Health Authority (1978-1982); chairman Norwich Health Authority (1982-1985); president Norwich and Norfolk Chamber of Commerce and Industry (1985-1988); council member East Anglia University (1972) (Pro-Chancellor and Chairman of the Council 1990 to date); deputy lieutenant for Norfolk (1979); chairman Radio Broadland Limited; chairman Relate national executive (1986-1990); member Royal Commonwealth Society.

Biography: lives Norwich; born 18.05.1931; married to Claire with 4 children. Educated at Norwich School; Corpus Christi College Cambridge (1954 BA) (1955 LLB) (MA) (LLM); Fellow Royal Society of Arts (1985).

Leisure: local history; cartography; travel.

FRYER Anthony

criminal partner CARTWRIGHT & LEWIS VERNON & SHAKESPEARE 179 Corporation Street, Birmingham.

Career: articled Cartwright & Lewis Vernon & Shakespeare (1969-1971);

admitted (1971); assistant solicitor (1971-1975); became partner (1975).

Biography: lives Worcester; born 26.12.1940; single. Educated at Sebright School, Wolverley; King Edward VI School, Stourbridge; Manchester University (1964 LLB); Diploma in Education TD.

Leisure: soccer (former captain Manchester University Football Club full maroon (colours); cricket; tennis.

FYNN Lionel

partner and head of licensing in the leisure industries department PENNINGTONS 70 Richmond Hill, Bournemouth, Dorset BH2 6JA.

Career: articled Philip Evans & Co (1958-1963); admitted (1963); assistant solicitor (1963-1965); became partner (1965); founded McInerney & Fynn (1970); merged with Penningtons.

Activities: produced Plato's Law series of audio cassettes on legal subjects; produces and appears in audio cassettes and video tapes on licensing subjects; member of: West Hants Lawn Tennis Club; Bournemouth Flying Club and Sea Vixen Society.

Biography: lives Bournemouth; born 14.04.1940; married to Katherine with 2 children. Educated at Gorsecliff School, Bournemouth; Oratory School, Reading; contributes legal articles on licensing topics and lectures on licensing subjects.

Leisure: aviation; all modes of travel and transport; general photography; films; reading; classical music; travel; playing squash; cricket.

GABBITASS David

senior partner WOLFERSTANS Deptford Chambers, 62/64 North Hill, Plymouth PL4 8EP.

Career: police officer Plymouth City Police (1956-1959); articled Wolferstan Snell & Turner (1959-1964); admitted (1964); assistant solicitor (1964-1965); became partner Wolferstans (1965-1980); became senior partner (1980).

Activities: former agent for Director of Public Prosecutions; prosecuting agent for treasury solicitor and Department of Transport; president Plymouth Law Society (1987-1988); chairman Social Security Appeal Tribunal; member Legal Aid Area Committee; Regional Duty

Solicitor; member Justice Committee on Fraud Trials; president Plymouth Albion RFC; past president Drake Rotary Club of Plymouth; member Lord's Taverners.

Biography: lives Plymouth; born 19.07.1935; married to Pam with 2 sons. Educated at Huish's Grammar School, Taunton; Sir George Fowler Prize; FCI ARB.

Leisure: all sports; watching Somerset CC.

GAISFORD Robert

partner SINCLAIR ROCHE & TEMPERLEY Stone House, 128-140 Bishopsgate, London EC2M 4JP.

Career: articled Corner & Co; admitted (1971); assistant solicitor (1971-1974); assistant solicitor Sinclair Roche & Temperley (1974-1976); became partner (1976).

Activities: occasional lectures on legal aspects of the maritime industry; member of Baltic Exchange and International Bar Association.

Biography: lives Stonegate; born 04.12.1946; married to Susan with 5 children. Educated at Chigwell School; Southampton University (1968 LLB).

Leisure: swimming; tennis.

GAMMIE Malcolm

partner LINKLATERS & PAINES Barrington House, 59/67 Gresham Street, London EC2V 7JA.

Career: articled Linklaters & Paines (1973-1975); admitted (1975); assistant solicitor tax department (1975-1978); deputy head of taxation department Confederation of British Industry (1978-1979); director National Tax Office Thomson McLintock & Co (1979-1984); director National Tax Services KMG Thomson McLintock (1984-1985); taxation department Linklaters & Paines (1985-1987); became partner (1987).

Activities: member Council of the Institute of Taxation (1983 to date) (chairman Administration Committee 1987-1988) (chairman Technical Committee (1990 to date); secretary and member Executive Committee and Council of the Institute for Fiscal Studies (1985 to date) (chairman Capital Taxes Working Party); member Taxation Committee Institute of Directors; member London Chamber of Commerce and Industry's Taxation Committee (1976 to date) (chairman 1989) (member of the Council 1989); member Law Society's Revenue Law Committee (1990 to date) (member of the Corporation Tax sub-committee); member British Branch

Committee of the International Fiscal Association; member Special Committee of Tax Law Consultative Bodies (1987 to date); Senior Visiting Fellow Queen Mary and Westfield College University of London (1989 to date).

Biography: lives Carshalton; born 18.02.1951; married to Rosalind with 3 daughters and 1 son. Educated at Edge Grove School, Aldenham (1957-1964); Merchant Taylors' School, Northwood (1964-1968); Sidney Sussex College Cambridge (1969-1972); College of Law Lancaster Gate (1972-1973); Institute of Tax (Associate 1976) (Fellow 1981); author of: 'Land Taxation" (1985); 'Tax on Company Reorganisations' with Susan Ball (2nd edition 1982); 'Tax Strategy for Companies' (4th edition 1986); 'Tax Strategy for Directors, Executives and Employees' (2nd edition 1985); 'Stock Relief' with David Williams (1981); 'Tax Focus on Interest and Discounts' with David Williams (1983); 'Whiteman on Capital Gains Tax' with Peter Whiteman and Mark Herbert (4th edition 1988); 'The Enactment of Tax Legislation 1979 to 1987' (1988); 'The Process of Tax Reform in The United Kingdom' (1990); contributor to: Simon's Taxes; Butterworths Income Tax Service; Strategic Tax Planning; Financial Times on tax matters (1983-1987); editor of Law & Tax Review (1982-1988) (member editorial board); regular lecturer and writer of articles on taxation subjects.

Leisure: English mediaeval church architecture; playing recorder; jogging.

GARDINER Ronald

partner BRODIES WS 15 Atholl Crescent, Edinburgh EH3 8HA.

Career: National Service as 2nd Lt with The Cameronians (Scottish Rifles) (1957-1959); admitted (1963); assistant solicitor (1963); became partner John C Brodie Cuthbertson & Watson WS (1964).

Activities: chairman Rent Assessment Committee (1973 to date); governor Fettes College (1986 to date); member Revenue Committee Law Society of Scotland (1966-1978); council member Society of Writers to HM Signet (1978-1981); member New Club.

Biography: lives Edinburgh; born 25.10.1938; married to Aileen with 3 children. Educated at St Mary's School, Melrose; Fettes College; Edinburgh University (1962 BL).

Leisure: fishing; shooting; golf.

GARDNER Michael

senior litigation partner BINKS STERN AND PARTNERS Queen's House, 55/56 Lincoln's Inn Fields, London WC2A 3LT.

Career: articled Harold Stern & Co (now Binks Stern & Partners); admitted (1970); assistant solicitor (1970-1971); partner (1971); became senior partner.

Activities: member Lincoln's Inn Fields Association; member Holborn Law Society; member London Litigation Solicitors Association; member of: David Lloyd Slazenger Club; the Alibi Club; Zanzibar.

Biography: lives London; born 16.06.1946; married to Frances with 2 daughters. Educated at Hendon County Grammar School; College of Law Lancaster Gate; written articles for the Guardian newspaper.

Leisure: interested in civil and human rights; current affairs; a general interest in the Arts; socialising; travel.

GARLAND Michael

senior partner in the securities and general division of the property department TITMUSS SAINER & WEBB 2 Serjeants' Inn, London EC4Y 1LT.

Career: articled Alfred Neale & Co (1955-1961); admitted (1961); assistant solicitor Titmuss Sainer & Webb (1961-1967); became partner (1967).

Activities: member Law Society.

Biography: lives Purley; born 16.11.1937; married with 3 children. Educated at Queen Elizabeth Grammar School, Barnet; College of Law.

Leisure: classical music; good food and wine; a 'Spanophile' with second home in Andalucia.

GARNER Graham

barrister and head of Chambers Southsea Chambers, PO Box 148, Southsea, Hants PO5 2TU.

Career: founder Southsea Chambers (1988).

Activities: member of: Royal Naval & Royal Albert Yacht Club; Thames Rowing Club.

Biography: lives Southsea; born 12.03.1943; married to Ynskje with 3 children. Educated at Westminster.

Leisure: sailing; clay shooting.

GARNETT Patrick

senior partner and head of commercial property department CUMBERLAND

ELLIS PEIRS Columbia House, 69 Aldwych, London WC2.

Career: articled Darley Cumberland; admitted (1956); National Service in the RAF; assistant solicitor; became partner (1960); became senior partner when firm merged to become Cumberland Ellis Peirs (1989).

Activities: former chairman Surrey & Hampshire Gliding Club and Lasham Gliding Society; chairman North Downs Gliding Trust Ltd.

Biography: lives Effingham; born 27.03.1933; married to Sarah with 4 children. Educated at St Michael's School; Bootham School.

Leisure: glider pilot; skiing; equestrian events.

GARNHAM Caroline

partner TAYLOR JOYNSON GARRETT 10 Maltravers Street, London WC2R 3BS.

Career: admitted (1981); assistant solicitor Allen & Overy, DJ Freeman & Wilde Sapte (1981-1987); became partner Joynson-Hicks (1987); merged with Taylor Garrett (1989).

Activities: in-house and external talks on personal tax and international tax planning.

Biography: lives London E1 and Gloucestershire; born 10.10.1955; divorced. Educated at George Abbott School for Girls, Guildford; Exeter University (1974-1977 BSC); articles for Financial Times Saturday Family & Finance page on Personal Tax (1987 to date); International Magazine monthly article (1988 to date).

Leisure: reading; hunting; skiing.

GARRETT Colin

group solicitor and compliance officer 3i GROUP PLC 91 Waterloo Road, London SE1 8XP.

Career: articled Waterhouse & Co (1965-1967); admitted (1969); assistant solicitor Few & Kester (1968-1969); company solicitor and secretary Amoco (UK) Ltd (1969-1973); legal adviser Shell International Petroleum Co Ltd (1973-1977); counsel Asiatic Petroleum Corp New York (1977-1979); admitted to New York Bar (1978); senior legal adviser Shell International Petroleum Co Ltd (1979-1981); group solicitor 3i Group plc (1981).

Activities: chairman Law Society Commerce & Industry Group (1989-1990); member Law Society Council Standards & Guidance Committee (1987-1989); FBIM (1988).

G

Biography: lives Berkhamsted; born 03.06.1942; married to Sarah with 2 daughters. Educated at the Downs School Colwall; Leighton Park School; King's College Cambridge (1964 BA) (1968 MA); College of Law London (1964-1965); Universite de Nancy, France (1968 Diplome d'Etudes Superieures) .

Leisure: music (violin & clarinet player); violin making and restoration.

GARRY Brendan

senior partner WITHAM WELD 70 St George's Square, London SW1V 3RD.

Career: admitted (1959); assistant solicitor Witham Weld (1959-1960); became partner (1960); became senior partner (1987).

Activities: foundation trustee with Sir Dingle Foot QC and others to increase graduates from Kenya (1961); Kenya Government guest at Independence celebrations (1963); personal and professional concern with the law relating to charities (in particular education); member MCC.

Biography: lives London NW3; born 22.09.1934; single. Educated at Stonyhurst College; Liverpool University (1957 LLB); Rupert Bremner Medal (1959).

Leisure: history; fine art; literature; music; watching cricket.

GARSTON Clive Richard

senior partner HALLIWELL LANDAU St James's Court, Brown Street, Manchester M2 2JF.

Career: articled clerk Hall Brydon; admitted (1968); assistant solicitor (1968-1971); partner (1971-1978); became partner Halliwell Landau (1978).

Activities: sat on boards of private and public companies; director of: The Intercare Group plc; First Manchester Properties plc; member of: Lancashire County Cricket Club; St James's Club.

Biography: lives Hale; born 25.04.1945; married to Racheline with 1 son and 1 daughter. Educated at Manchester Grammar School; Leeds University (1965 LLB hons).

Leisure: interested in most sports as a spectator; skiing; swimming; keen supporter Lancashire County Cricket Club and Manchester United.

GARVIN Michael

partner LASS SALT GARVIN 16 Bell Yard, London WC2A 2JR.

Career: articled Malcolm Slowe & Co; admitted; assistant solicitor Oswald Hickson Collier; assistant solicitor Pickering Kenyon; partner (1973-1990); became partner Lass Salt Garvin (1990).

Activities: director family group companies; director Waterglade International Holdings PLC; member of: RAC; Tramp; Zanzibar.

Biography: lives London NW3 and Harpenden; born 08.02.1944; married to Helga with 3 children. Educated at The Hall; Charterhouse; University College London.

Leisure: walking; travelling; speedboats; reading.

GARWOOD Christopher

partner in charge of commercial department and managing partner CARRICK CARR & GARWOOD Norwich House, Savile Street, Hull HU1 3ES.

Career: articled in Hull (1971-1973); admitted (1973); assistant solicitor (1973-1976); founded own practice (1976).

Activities: immediate past president Hull Incorporated Law Society; (member Council); member Law Society's Insolvency Casework Committee; authorised Insolvency Practitioner; founder member and initial council member Insolvency Lawyers' Association; member of Insolvency Practitioners' Association; speaker at Law Society Conference (1989); member and treasurer Driffield Town Council; member Hessle Golf Club; former member and chairman Driffield Round Table.

Biography: lives Wansford nr Driffield; born 15.06.1949; married to Susan with 1 son and 1 daughter. Educated at Gembling County Primary School; Pocklington School; Worcester College Oxford (1967-1970); College of Law Guildford; occasional articles on legal subjects in local newspapers and journals.

GASKELL Sir Richard Kennedy Harvey

senior partner LAWRENCE TUCKETTS Shannon Court, Corn Street, Bristol BS99 7JZ.

Career: articled Burges Salmon (1955-1960); admitted (1960); assistant solicitor Tucketts Williams & Kew (1960-1963); became partner Tucketts (1963-1985); became partner Lawrence Tucketts (1985).

Activities: national chairman Young Solicitors Group of the Law Society (1964-

1965); president Bristol Law Society (1978-1979); president Association of South Western Law Societies (1980-1981); president Law Society of England and Wales (1988-1989); council member and solicitor to the Wildfowl Trust (Wildfowl & Wetlands Trust) (1978 to date) (chairman 1983-1987); legal adviser to the Laura Ashley Foundation (1988 to date) (trustee 1990 to date); chairman Contentious Business Committee of the Law Society (1979-1982); chairman The Law Society's Advocacy Training Committee and Team (1974-1987); chairman The Law Society Trustees Ltd (1982 to date); member the Court of Bristol University (1973 to date); member Lord Justice Watkins working party on criminal trials (1986-1988); member Crown Court Rules Committee (1977-1983); member the Lord Chancellor's Efficiency Commission (1986-1988 & 1989 to date); member the Marre Committee on the future of the legal profession (1986-1988); heavily involved in the LS response to the LC Green Papers; member Farmers' Club.

Biography: lives Wiltshire; born 17.09.1936; married to Judy with 2 children. Educated at St Ronan's Preparatory School, Hawkhurst; Marlborough College; Bristol University Law School (1955-1956), (1989 hon LLD); Bristol Polytechnic (1989 hon LLM); Knight Bachelor (1989); member Security Service Tribunal (1989 to date).

GASSON John

head of policy and legal services group LORD CHANCELLOR'S DEPARTMENT Trevelyan House, 30 Great Peter Street, London SW1.

Career: called to Bar Gray's Inn (1957); advocate at High Court of S Rhodesia (1959-1964); Lord Chancellor's Department (1964); CB (1980).

Activities: secretary of Law Commission (1982-1987); member of: Bulawayo Club; Cycle Touring Club.

Biography: lives London; born 20.08.1931; married to Lesley with 3 children. Educated at Diocesan College Cape Town (1946-1949); University of Cape Town (1952 BA); Oxford (1956 MA BCL).

Leisure: gardening; cycling.

GATENBY Ian

partner & head of planning group MCKENNA & CO Mitre House, 160 Aldersgate Street, London EC1A 4DD.

Career: assistant company secretary to a group of engineering companies; articled

G

Lovell White & King (1966-1968); admitted (1968); assistant solicitor; associate in planning department; assistant solicitor McKenna (1975-1977); became partner (1977).

Activities: member of: Ski Club of Great Britain; Ranelagh Sailing Club.

Biography: lives London SW14; born 30.06.1942; divorced with 2 children. Educated at Royal Grammar School Newcastle upon Tyne; Exeter College Oxford (MA); various scholarships; numerous articles on planning, rating and landlord and tenant; former co-editor of commercial property section of Business & Financial issue of Law Society's Gazette; editor Foreshores section of Encyclopaedia of Forms & Precedents; editor of property section of Croner Handbook of Business Law; author of McKenna & Co guide to rating; treatise on local plans.

Leisure: skiing; sailing; English National Opera; gardening.

GATENBY John Keirl

commercial litigation partner; member international committee and responsible for language training programme ADDLESHAW SONS & LATHAM Dennis House, Marsden Street, Manchester M2 1JD.

Career: articled Linklaters & Paines (1973-1975); admitted (1975); assistant solicitor (1975-1983); became head of litigation department Withers (1983-1984); became associate Addleshaw Sons & Latham (1984); became partner (1985).

Activities: conference speaker on civil procedure topics; member IBA; member Solicitors European Group; member Commonwealth Law Association; member London Solicitors Litigation Association; member Poynton Baptist Church; member Halle Concerts Society; member National Trust; member RSPB.

Biography: lives Prestbury; born 26.04.1950; married to Eunice with 2 daughters. Educated at Hartlepool Grammar School; Trinity Hall Cambridge (1971 BA) (1972 LLB now LLM) (1975 MA); ACI Arb; barrister and solicitor New Zealand; author of: casenote 'More Bother in Bognor' (1973); 'Notes on Discovery and Inspection of Documents' 2nd edn (1975); 'Recovery of Money' 7th edn (1989); 'Discovery - is it really necessary?' (1985).

Leisure: music (listening and playing organ, piano, clarinet); gardening; photography; computers; reading; walking the dog.

GAYMER Janet

partner and head of employment law department SIMMONS & SIMMONS 14 Dominion Street, London EC2M 2RJ.

Career: articled Simmons & Simmons (1971-1973); admitted (1973); assistant solicitor (1973-1976); became partner (1977).

Activities: chairman Employment Law Sub-committee of City of London Law Society; member Editorial Advisory Board of Sweet & Maxwells's Encyclopaedia of Labour Relations; member Law Society's Committee on Employment Law; member Justice Committee on Industrial Tribunals; affiliate member Institute of Personnel Management; member IBA; member Union Internationale des Avocats.

Biography: lives Effingham; born 11.07.1947; married with 2 children. Educated at Nuneaton High School for Girls; St Hilda's College Oxford (MA); London School of Economics (LLM); author of article 'Aids in the Workplace' in The Independent; chapter on transfers and acquisitions as they affect employees in 'The Acquisition of Private Companies' by W Knight.

Leisure: learning to play the flute; theatre; riding; swimming; tennis.

GAYNOR-SMITH Adrian

senior partner GAYNOR-SMITH OWEN & CO 133/135 Barnards Green Road, Malvern, Worcs WR14 3LT.

Career: articled Markby Stewart & Wadesons (1960-1963); admitted (1963); assistant solicitor (1963-1966); assistant solicitor and partner Russell & Co (1966-1972); assistant solicitor and partner Gordon Bancks & Co (1972-1975); founded Gaynor-Smith & Owen with wife (1975) (Owen wife's maiden name).

Activities: chairman Hereford & Worcs Supplementary Benefit Appeal Tribunal (later Social Security Appeal Tribunal) (1978-1988); member Solicitors Disciplinary Tribunal (1984); deputy Registrar High Court and County Court & Oxford Circuit (1985); assistant deputy Coroner (1987); past president Worcester & Worcestershire Incorporated Law Society; lectures to local clubs and organisations on legal topics; attended careers conventions in schools.

Biography: lives Malvern; born 23.09.1937; married to Sue with 2 sons. Educated at The John Lyon School, Harrow; London School of Economics (1960 LLB); occasional articles on family law.

Leisure: trying to keep abreast of sons;

trying to find social time with wife; photography; reading; composing poetry; theatre.

GAYTHWAITE Miles

partner intellectual property department BIRD & BIRD 2 Gray's Inn Square, London WC1R 5AF.

Career: admitted (1978); became partner Bird & Bird (1978).

Biography: lives London; born 28.05.1943; single. Educated Glasgow (1964 BSC); Cambridge (1967 PHD); Chartered Patent Agent (1972).

GELDARD Robin

partner EDWARDS GELDARD 16 St Andrew's Crescent, Cardiff CF1 3RD.

Career: articled Allen Pratt & Geldard (1952-1958); admitted (1958); commissioned Royal Marines (1958-1960); assistant solicitor (1960-1963); became partner (1963); founded new corporate department (1970).

Activities: deputy High Court Registrar (1978-1984); president Cardiff Law Society (1988-1989); president Cardiff Chamber of Commerce (1987-1989); president Federated Welsh Chambers of Commerce (1989-1991); member Solicitors European Group; member Council of University of Wales; member Cardiff Incorporated Law Society; member Associated British Chambers of Commerce Council Economic & Industrial Committee; frequently travels for clients to Hong Kong, China, Australia, America; director several companies; member of: IOD and CBI; Naval Club; Royal Porthcawl Golf Club; Cardiff & County Club.

Biography: lives Cowbridge; born 09.08.1935; married to Susan with 3 children. Educated at Aldenham School, Elstree; Gibson & Weldon Guildford and London.

Leisure: fly fishing; ocean sailing; walking; music; good food and wine; photography.

GEORGE Peter

partner CHARLES RUSSELL WILLIAMS & JAMES Hale Court, Lincoln's Inn, London WC2A 3UL.

Career: admitted (1962); assistant solicitor (1962-1964); became partner Charles Russell & Co (1964).

Biography: lives Winchester; born 12.01.1935; married to Denise with 7 children. Educated at Ampleforth College,

G

York.

Leisure: mainly with family; chess; bridge; music; reading.

GEORGE Tony

partner in charge of recruitment INCE & CO Knollys House, 11 Byward Street, London EC3R 5EN.

Career: articled Ince & Co (1969-1971); admitted (1971); assistant solicitor (1971-1974); became partner (1975).

Activities: panel member of Monitoring of Articles at the City of London Law Society; supporting member London Maritime Arbitrators Association; annual subscriber to Association of Average Adjusters; frequent lecturer at home and abroad on political risk insurance, cargo insurance, oil cargo claims, general average, multimodal transport; member Law Society; member City of London Solicitors' Company; member of: Alleyn Club; Old Alleynian Rugby Club; Mosimann's; Friends of Dulwich; National Trust; Sierra Park Club; Aloha Golf Club.

Biography: lives London SE23; born 15.04.1946; married to Monica with 3 children. Educated at Dulwich College; Pembroke College Oxford (1968 BA hons); co-editor of Admiralty section of latest edition of Halsbury's Laws of England; occasional contributor on marine and insurance law subjects to Lloyd's List, Lloyd's Log, Reaction, Fairplay, Lloyd's Maritime & Commercial Law Quarterly, Reinsurance Market Report.

Leisure: collecting Oriental porcelain; collecting antiques; jazz, rock & classical music; rugby (spectating); tennis; travel; wining & dining; reading modern novels.

GEORGE William

head of chambers 20 North John Street, Liverpool L2 9RL.

Career: called to the Bar Lincoln's Inn (1968); part-time lecturer Liverpool University (1968-1976) and Manchester University (1968-1973); pupillage (1968-1969).

Activities: Junior Counsel to the Treasury in charity matters in Liverpool; treasurer Northern Chancery Bar Association; member Athenaeum (Liverpool).

Biography: lives Liverpool; born 28.09.1944; married to Susan with 2 daughters. Educated at Herbert Strutt Grammar School, Belper; Manchester University (1966 LLB) (1967 LLM); Mansfield Scholar Lincoln's Inn (1968).

Leisure: gardening; reading (English and European history); travel; repose.

GIBBON Lawrence

senior partner BEETENSON & GIBBON Lauriston House, Town Hall Square, Grimsby, Humberside DN31 1JB.

Career: articled Skipton Yorkshire; commission Royal Army Service Corp (1949-1950); admitted (1952); assistant solicitor (1952-1953); sole practitioner (1953).

Activities: past president and past secretary Grimsby & Cleethorpes Law Society; assistant deputy Coroner; member local Law Society; regularly attends College of Law courses to keep up to date; past president Grimsby Rotary Club; former member Grimsby Round Table; member of: Grimsby 41 Club; Jaguar Drivers' Club; Grimsby Golf Club.

Biography: lives Grimsby; born 29.03.1928; married to Patricia with 3 sons. Educated at Ermysteds Grammar School; Leeds University (1948 LLB hons).

GIBBONS Christopher

partner STEPHENSON HARWOOD One St Paul's Churchyard, London EC4M 8SH.

Career: Bar Middle Temple (1954-1960); admitted (1962); assistant solicitor (1962-1966); became partner Stephenson Harwood (1966).

Activities: member Company Law Committee of Law Society (1978 to date); leader Accounting Matters Group (1987 to date); City of London Solicitors Company member (Liveryman) (member Professional Business Committee (1976-1984) (deputy chairman (1982-1984); chairman Banking Law Sub-committee (1980-1984); member Company Law Sub-committee (1968-1986).

Biography: born 14.05.1930; married to Charlotte with 3 daughters. Educated at Charterhouse; Trinity College Cambridge .

Leisure: racing; walking.

GIBSON Andrew

partner FOOT & BOWDEN 70/76 North Hill, Plymouth PL4 8HH.

Career: articled Foot & Bowden (1974-1976); admitted (1979); assistant solicitor (1979-1984); became partner (1984).

Activities: chairman Plymouth Civil Litigation Solicitors' Association (1987-1990); member SW Area Legal Aid Area Committee (1988 to date); member of: St

Mellion Golf & Country Club; Saunton Golf Club; Delverton Golf Club; Saints Cricket Club.

Biography: lives Plymouth; born 27.07.1951; single. Educated at Plymouth College; Monkton Combe School, Bath; The Queen's College Oxford (MA).

Leisure: golf; cricket; music (bassoon).

GIBSON Kenneth

senior partner WANSBROUGHS WILLEY HARGRAVE 103 Temple Street, Bristol BS1 6EN.

Career: articled Wansbroughs Robinson Taylor and Taylor (1959); admitted (1962); assistant solicitor (1962-1965); became partner (1965).

Activities: past president Bristol Law Society; member Common Law Committee of the Law Society; occasional lecturer on civil procedure and on contentious costs.

Biography: lives Bitton; born 16.09.1935; married to Jill with 4 children. Educated at Monkton Combe School; Clare College Cambridge (1959 MA LLM).

Leisure: St Mary's Church Bitton; golf.

GIDNEY David

partner commercial property department ROWE & MAW 20 Black Friars Lane, London EC4V 6HD.

Career: articled Rowe & Maw (1975-1977); admitted (1977); assistant solicitor (1977-1981); became partner (1981); ran firm's articled clerk recruitment and training (1985-1988).

Biography: lives Farnham; born 21.02.1952; married with 3 children. Educated at Eagle House Preparatory School, Crowthorne; Sherborne School; Christ Church Oxford (1974 hons).

Leisure: sport; theatre; relaxing with family.

GIFFORD Lord Anthony

barrister 8 King's Bench Walk, London EC4Y 7DU (071 353 7851).

Career: called to the Bar Middle Temple (1962); Queen's Counsel (1982); called to the Northern Ireland Bar (1984); called to the Jamaican Bar (1990).

Activities: co-founder first law centre (North Kensington) (1970); founder and head of Wellington Street Chambers (1974-1990); visiting lecturer in Human Rights Latrobe University, Melbourne (1984-1986); chair Legal Action Group (1980-1983); vice-president Haldane Society of Socialist

Lawyers (1986 to date); vice-chairman British Defence and Aid Fund (1983 to date); member Labour Party in the House of Lords (1965 to date); human rights missions in Northern Ireland; Southern Africa; Hungary; Portugal; Spain; Greece; West Germany; Morocco; Ghana; Grenada; Chile; Turkey; Puerto Rico.

Biography: lives London; born 01.05.1940; married to Elean Thomas; 2 children from first marriage. Educated at Winchester College (1953-1958); King's College Cambridge (1961 BA); College of Law London (1962-1963); author of 'South Africa's Record of International Terrorism' (1981); 'Death on the Streets of Derry' (1981); 'Political Policing in Wales' (1984); 'Supergrasses - the Use of Accomplice Evidence in Northern Ireland' (1984); 'Where's the Justice - A Manifesto for Law Reform' (1986); 'Broadwater Farm Inquiry' (1986); 'Broadwater Farm Revisited' (1988); 'Loosen the Shackles' (1989); numerous newspaper articles.

Leisure: political and community work.

GILBERT Stephen

partner BIRKBECK MONTAGU'S
7 St Bride Street, London EC4A 4AT.

Career: articled Birkbeck Montagu's (1975-1977); admitted (1977); assistant solicitor (1977-1980); became partner (1980).

Activities: member of Worshipful Company of Plaisterers; member The Law Society; member of: RAC; City Livery Club; Farringdon Ward Club.

Biography: lives Woodford Green; born 24.11.1953; married to Caroline with 2 children. Educated at King's School, Rochester (1964-1966); Harrow County School for Boys (1966-1971); Southampton University (1974 LLB hons).

Leisure: theatre; golf; swimming.

GILES A Patrick

partner LANE & MITTENDORF
22 Grosvenor Square, London W1X 0DY.

Career: vice-president Intermar Inc (1968-1970); managing director Meridian Corporation SA (1970-1972); partner Montgomery McCracken Walker & Rhoads (1972-1983); became partner Lane & Mittendorf (1983).

Activities: member of: Brooks's Club; Queen's Club; Annabel's; Foxhills.

Biography: lives London; born 18.03.1940; married to Nancy with 2 children. Educated at Dartmouth College, Hanover (BA) (MBA); Michigan University (JD).

GILLESPIE Robert Munro

partner THOMPSON SMITH & PUXON
41 Station Road, Clacton on Sea, Essex CO15 1RN.

Career: articled Thompson Smith & Puxon (1962-1967); admitted (1967); assistant solicitor AH Page (1967-1968); assistant solicitor RA Roberts (1968-1969); became partner Thompson Smith & Puxon (1.01.1970).

Activities: former member Legal Aid Committee; former member Committee of local branch of Law Society; legal adviser to many local sporting clubs and local hotel association; chairman town cricket club; former chairman Round Table; Rotarian (1977 to date).

Biography: lives Clacton on Sea; born 18.05.1944; married to Susan with 2 children. Educated at St Felix Preparatory School; Charterhouse; College of Law.

Leisure: golf; veteran hockey and veteran cricket; local community.

GILLOTT Roland

partner RADCLIFFES & CO
10 Little College Street, Westminster, London SW1P 3SJ.

Career: articled Linklaters & Paines (1967-1972); admitted (1972); assistant solicitor (1972-1977); assistant solicitor Radcliffes & Co (1977-1978); became partner (1979).

Activities: member International Bar Association; member Parochial Church Council of St Michael's, Amersham; member Amersham & Chesham Bois Churches Committee; member of: MCC; RAC; City Livery Club.

Biography: lives Amersham; born 22.08.1947; married to Rae with 3 children. Educated at St Martin's School, Northwood and Haileybury.

GILTHORPE Ian

managing and commercial partner ROBERT MUCKLE Norham House, 12 New Bridge Street West, Newcastle upon Tyne NE1 8AS.

Career: articled Robert Muckle (1976-1978); admitted (1978); assistant solicitor (1978-1979); became partner (1979).

Activities: licensed insolvency practitioner (1986); member Newcastle upon Tyne Incorporated Law Society Standing Committee (1988); member of: Northumberland Golf Club; South Northumberland Cricket Club.

Biography: lives Gosforth; born 09.05.1953; married to Gillian with 3 children. Educated at Ascham House School, Gosforth; Oundle School; Leeds University (LLB); College of Law Chester.

Leisure: golf; cricket; bringing up 3 children.

GIRLING Tony

chairman and managing partner GIRLINGS 158 High Street, Herne Bay, Kent CT6 5NP.

Career: admitted (1966); became partner Girlings (1966).

Activities: hon secretary Kent Law Society (1974-1980); member Council of Law Society for Kent (1980 to date) (twice re-elected); president Kent Law Society (1982); president Isle of Thanet Law Society (1985); chairman Law Society's Remuneration Committee (1984-1987); member Law Society's Strategy Committee; chairman Law Society's Property and Commercial Services Committee; director Solicitors Financial and Property Services Limited; member Lord Chancellor's County Court Rules Committee (1983-1987); campaigner for rights of audience for solicitors; member Law Society's Rights of Audience working party (1985-1988); participated in Radio 4 'You the Jury' debate on the topic (1987); member Law Society's Advocacy Training Team (1981-1990); chairman of the Law Society's Transaction Working Party; High Court Costs Assessor; Board member of Law South.

Biography: lives Canterbury; born 21.08.1943; married to Lynne with 1 son and 1 daughter. Educated at Tonbridge School; College of Law Lancaster Gate (1965-1966); various articles in the Law Society's Gazette and regular lecturer on subject of legal costs.

Leisure: golf; skiing; tennis; reading; music; theatre.

GISBY Stephen

litigation partner JW WARD AND SON
52 Broad Street, Bristol BS1 2EP.

Career: articled Sansbury Hill and Co; admitted (1979); assistant solicitor JW Ward and Son (1980-1983); became partner (1983).

Activities: member Bristol Law Society Council (1987 to date); chairman Bristol Law Society Education and Training Committee; member Bristol Chancery Users' Group.

Biography: lives Bristol; born 23.04.1954;

G

married to Sarah. Educated at Bishop Wordsworth's School, Salisbury; Magdalen College Oxford (1975 BA) (1982 MA); contributed to Longman Litigation Practice (1988).

Leisure: singing; sailing; cricket; travel.

GITELSON Bruce

senior resident partner (London office) GIBSON DUNN & CRUTCHER 30/35 Pall Mall, London SW1Y 5LP.

Career: assistant solicitor Gibson Dunn & Crutcher (1964-1971); became partner (1971).

Activities: teaching assistant (1964-1965); visiting instructor (1971 & 1972); acting professor of law (1979-1980); instructor (1981-1985) Stanford Law School; visiting instructor Southwestern University School of Law (1967); visiting instructor University of Southern California Law Center (1968, 1969 & 1970); adjunct professor Loyola Law School (1973-1978); periodic guest lecturer Stanford Law School (1980 to date); various lectures and presentations; member Kara Funding Advisory Committee (1985-1987) (Board of Directors 1987-1989) (chair Funding Development Committee 1986-1989); member Board of Visitors of Stanford Law School (1978-1980 & 1987-1989); member American Bar Association Committee on Accreditation of Law Schools and Section of Legal Education and Admissions to the Bar; Section of Banking and Business Law; Section of Real Property and Probate Law (1977-1980); member State Bar of California Committee on Continuing Education of the Bar and the CEB Joint Advisory Committee (1976-1978); member Committee on Corporations of the Business Law Section (1978-1979); member Citizens' Advisory Panel to the California Secretary of State (1978); president The Constitutional Rights Foundations (Los Angeles) (1977-1979); director and vice-president Education and member Executive Committee; member Lawyers' Advisory Board Education Council; member Board of Managers Westside YMCA, Los Angeles (1978-1980); member Mosimann's.

Biography: lives London SW7 and Carmel, California; born 04.06.1941; married to Margaret with 1 son and 1 daughter. Educated at University High School, Los Angeles; Stanford University (1963 BA); Stanford Law School (1964 JD).

Leisure: travel (particularly English countryside and Wales); sea travel.

GLASS Anthony

Queen's Counsel Queen Elizabeth Building, Temple, London EC4.

Career: called to the Bar Inner Temple (1965); Recorder of the Crown Court (1985); QC (1986).

Biography: lives London; born 06.06.1940; married to Deborah with 2 children. Educated at Royal Masonic School (1948-1958); Lincoln College Oxford (1963 BA hons).

GLASS David

senior UK company/commercial partner PRITCHARD ENGLEFIELD & TOBIN 23 Great Castle Street, London W1N 8NQ.

Career: articled Macfarlanes (1972-1974); admitted (1974); assistant solicitor (1974-1976); assistant solicitor Coward Chance (1976-1980); assistant solicitor Courts & Co (1980-1982); became partner (1982-1984); became partner Pritchard Englefield & Tobin (1984).

Activities: part-time volunteer at Camden Community Law Centre (1973-1977); speaker in seminars arranged by current firm with firm of accountants and spoken on the Budget; spoken on 'management buy-outs' to Anglo-Belgian Jurists' Association; speaker at seminar in Hong Kong; member Holborn Law Society.

Biography: lives Barnet; born 23.08.1950; married to Yvonne with 1 son and 2 daughters. Educated at Kerem Preparatory School; Christ's College; Gonville and Caius College Cambridge (1971 BA); (1972 LLB); College of Law (1971-1972); Tapp postgraduate scholarship at Cambridge (1974 MA); written articles for the Law Society's Gazette on franchising and investment advertising and for various other legal periodicals on company and commercial matters.

Leisure: theatre; local politics; cinema; classical music.

GLASSER Cyril

managing partner and head of litigation department SHERIDANS 14 Red Lion Square, London WC1R 4QL.

Career: articled Bernard Sheridan & Co (now Sheridans); admitted (1967); assistant solicitor (1965-1974); became partner and head of litigation department (1977); became managing partner (1989).

Activities: research assistant Legal Research Division LSE (1966-1968); special consultant Legal Aid Advisory Committee (attached to Lord Chancellor's

Department) (1974-1977); consultant National Board for Prices and Incomes (1967); assessor Race Relations Board (1973); member Social Sciences and the Law Committee (SSRC) (1977-1983); member Council of Management Institute of Judicial Administration (Birmingham University) (1984 to date); visiting professor of law University College London (1987 to date); member Justice Committee on Civil Procedure (1974); member working party to review Legal Aid legislation (Lord Chancellor's Department) (1974-1977); chairman Legal Aid Financial Provisions working party (Lord Chancellor's Advisory Committee on Legal Aid) (1975-1977); co-founder and a director Legal Action Group (1972-1974); trustee Legal Assistance Trust (1985 to date).

Biography: lives London NW5; born 31.01.1942. Educated at Raine's Foundation GS; London School of Economics (1963 LLB) (1966 LLM); articles in legal periodicals including Modern Law Review, New Law Journal, Law Society's Gazette and Legal Action.

GLASSON John

partner and head trust department JAQUES & LEWIS 2 South Square, Gray's Inn, London WC1R 5HR.

Career: articled Jaques & Lewis (1959-1962); admitted (1962); assistant solicitor (1962-1966); became partner (1966).

Activities: registered legal practitioner Isle of Man (1988); chairman New Philharmonic Society; member RAC.

Biography: lives London N2; born 07.02.1936; married to Sheena with 2 children. Educated at Belmont College, nr Barnstable (1944-1949); Wellington School, Somerset; Fitzwilliam House Cambridge (1959 MA LLM); Precedents for 'Charities: Law and Practice' by Elizabeth Cairns; co-author 'Trusts, Tax and Estate Planning through the Isle of Man' (1989); contributor to 'International Money Marketing'; 'Taxation'.

Leisure: 'English' concertina player; gardening.

GLAZEBROOK Bill

senior partner LACE MAWER Castle Chambers, 43 Castle Street, Liverpool L2 9SU.

Career: 2nd Lt South Wales Borderers (1948-1949); captain Cheshire Yeomanry (TA) (1953-1959); articled Laces & Co (1952-1955); admitted (1956); assistant solicitor (1956-1959); became partner (1960).

Activities: chairman Liverpool Merchants' Guild (1974-1989); legal adviser British Association for Shooting and Conservation (BASC) (1984-1989); member Taxation Committee of Country Landowners' Association (1978-1983); member of: Liverpool Racquet Club; Delamere Forest Golf Club.

Biography: lives Denbigh; born 18.06.1929; married to Sara with 2 sons. Educated at Leas School (1939-1942); Eton (1942-1947); Pembroke College Cambridge (1952 MA).

Leisure: golf; tennis; fishing; shooting; gardening; farming 400 acre stock and arable farm in Vale of Clwyd.

GLAZEBROOK Peter

partner and head of licensing department FIELD FISHER WATERHOUSE 41 Vine Street, London EC3N 2AA.

Career: articled Russell Steward Stevens & Hipwell (1965-1970); admitted (1970); assistant solicitor Stilgoes (1971-1974); assistant solicitor Field Fisher Waterhouse (1974-1978); became salaried partner (1978); became equity partner (1980); took over licensing department (1985).

Activities: Bromley Round Table (1978-1987) (chairman 1985-1986); member Bromley 41 Club.

Biography: lives Bickley; born 14.02.1947; married to Sue with 2 children. Educated at Guildford Grammar School; Guildford Technical College; writes occasional articles and letters on licensing in the legal journals.

Leisure: cricket; tennis; golf; sailing; travel; music; reading.

GLAZIER Barry

partner (Head of Strategy) LESTER ALDRIDGE Russell House, 31 Oxford Road, Bournemouth, Dorset BH8 8EX.

Career: articled Pennington & Son (1963-1966); admitted (1966); assistant solicitor Clifford Turners (1966-1971); assistant solicitor Mooring Aldridge & Haydon (1971-1972); became partner (1972); became senior partner Mooring Aldridge (1984-1988); became senior partner Lester Aldridge following merger (1988); member of Management Committee and Chairman of Strategy and Development Committee.

Activities: Notary Public; vice-president of the Dorset Chamber of Commerce and Industry; director of and solicitor to the Dorset Training and Enterprise Council;

senior vice-president Bournemouth & District Law Society; governor of The Bournemouth and Poole College of Further Education; member Dorset War Pensions Committee; lectures nationally and locally on inheritance tax and other related taxes and on trusts.

Biography: lives Wimborne Minster; born 01.07.1941; married to Patsy with 4 daughters. Educated at Hurstpierpoint College, Sussex (1950-1960); St Peter's College Oxford (1963 BA) (1967 MA); College of Law London (1965-1966).

Leisure: playing piano; concerts; theatre; gardening; bird watching.

GLEDHILL Mike

senior partner FINN GLEDHILL & CO 1/4 Harrison Road, Halifax HX1 2AG.

Career: articled Wilkinson Woodward and Godfrey Rhodes & Evans; admitted (1962); became partner Godfrey Rhodes & Evans (1962-1965); purchased Frederick Walker Son & Dickie with Hugh Finn (1965); firm became Finn Gledhill & Co (1966); became senior partner (1979).

Activities: clerk to Waterhouse Charities (1965); clerk to Abbotts Ladies Homes (1966); Notary Public (1980); clerk to Rishworth School (Wheelwright Charity 1984); hon solicitor Calderdale Chamber of Commerce & Industry (1979); president Halifax & District Incorporated Law Society (1989); Fellow of the Institute of Directors (1984); director nine local companies; member of: West End Golf Club; Old Rishworthians RUFC; Old Rishworthians Club (vice-president 1990).

Biography: lives Halifax; born 28.10.1937; married to Margaret with 3 sons. Educated at Rishworth School; Leeds University.

Leisure: rugby; golf; gardening; music.

GLICK Ian

Queen's Counsel 1 Essex Court, Temple, London EC4.

Career: called to the Bar (1970); Junior Counsel to the Crown (1985-1987); Standing Counsel to the Department of Trade and Industry in Export Credit Cases (1985-1987); QC (1987).

Biography: lives London NW8; born 18.07.1948; married to Roxane. Educated at Bradford Grammar School; Balliol College Oxford (1970 MA BCL).

GLOIN David B

director litigation and advisory department The Solicitor's Office, BRITISH TELECOMMUNICATIONS PLC 81 Newgate Street, London EC1A 7AJ.

Career: articled Gaunt Foster & Hill; admitted (1969); became salaried partner (1969); conveyancing department Post Offices Solicitor's Office (1970-1982); divisional solicitor commercial department British Telecommunications Solicitor's Office (1982-1987); director property law department (1987-1989); became director litigation and advisory department (1989).

Biography: lives Orpington; born 28.02.1946; married to Francis with 2 children. Educated at Alleyn's School, Dulwich; College of Law; articles in Law Society's Gazette.

Leisure: swimming; singing; Church activities.

GLOVER Malcolm

deputy senior partner WILDE SAPTE Queensbridge House, 60 Upper Thames Street, London EC4V 3BD.

Career: articled Bridge Sanderson (1966-1968); admitted (1968); assistant solicitor (1968-1970); assistant solicitor Wilde Sapte (1970-1971); became partner (1971); became deputy senior partner (1988).

Biography: lives London N2; born 03.11.1943; married to Diane with 3 children. Educated at Doncaster Grammar School; Bristol University.

Leisure: tennis; theatre.

GODFREY David

partner MIDDLETON POTTS 3 Cloth Street, Long Lane, London EC1A 7LD.

Career: articled Herbert Oppenheimer Nathan & Vandyk (1966-1968); admitted (1968); assistant solicitor (1968-1970); assistant solicitor Crawley & de Reya (1970-1971); partner (1971-1976); founding partner Middleton Potts (1976); member firm's management committee.

Activities: uses Italian, French and German in international practice.

Biography: lives London NW11; born 16.11.1943; married to Sharon with 2 children. Educated at Grosvenor House School, Harrogate; Uppingham School, Rutland; British Institute in Paris; Bristol University (1965 LLB hons); College of Law Guildford.

Leisure: antique collecting; the arts; photography.

G

GOLD Anthony

senior partner ANTHONY GOLD
LERMAN & MUIRHEAD The Hop
Exchange, 24 Southward Street, London
SE1 1TY.

Career: articled in the City of London;
admitted (1957); National Service
commissioned in RASC; assistant solicitor
Stephenson Harwood; founded own
practice (1963) .

Biography: lives London NW11; born
13.01.1934; married to Joan with 2 children.
Educated at City of London School; King's
College London (LLB); Solicitors Finals
(hons).

Leisure: sailing; walking; reading history.

GOLD Antony

commercial litigation partner
ALEXANDER TATHAM & CO 30 St Ann
Street, Manchester M2 3DB.

Career: articled (1980-1983); admitted
(1983); assistant solicitor Alexander
Tatham & Co (1984-1988); became partner
(1988).

Activities: represented investors in Barlow
Clowes in their successful claim for
compensation from the Government; acts
for investors in other similar collapses; co-
presented talks on commercial litigation
for Greater Manchester Economic
Development Council; advises local
bridleways group on rights of way.

Biography: lives Wilmslow; born
26.08.1958; married to Sally with 1 child.
Educated at Birkenhead School (1969-
1976); Manchester University (1979 LLB);
Chester College of Law; wrote article on
trade secrets for North West Business
Monthly; contributed to seminar on
environmental legislation .

Leisure: horse riding; squash; music;
gardening; reading.

GOLD David

partner HERBERT SMITH Watling House,
35 Cannon Street, London EC4M 5SD.

Career: articled Herbert Smith; admitted
(1975); assistant solicitor (1975-1983);
became partner (1983).

Activities: member Advisory Committee of
International Litigation Practitioners'
Forum; Freeman of City of London
Solicitors Company.

Biography: lives Thorpe Bay and
Hampstead; born 01.03.1951; married to
Sharon with 1 daughter and 2 sons.
Educated at Westcliff High School; London

School of Economics (1972 LLB).

Leisure: travel; theatre; family; friends.

GOLDBERG David

barrister practising at the Revenue Bar
Gray's Inn Chambers, Gray's Inn, London
WC1.

Career: called to the Bar Lincoln's Inn
(1971); QC (1987); practice at Revenue Bar
(1971 to date).

Activities: casenote editor British Tax
Review (1975-1981).

Biography: lives London; born 12.08.1947;
married to Alison with 2 children.
Educated at Plymouth College; London
School of Economics (1969 LLB) (1970
LLM); joint author of: 'An Introduction to
Company Law' (4th ed 1987); 'The Law of
Partnership Taxation' (2nd ed 1979);
numerous articles on tax and company
law.

Leisure: reading; letter writing; thinking.

GOLDBERG Melvin

senior partner DOUGLAS GOLDBERG
HENDELES & CO 1 Holly Hill,
Hampstead, London NW3 6UB.

Career: articled Sylvester Amiel & Co;
admitted (1963); assistant solicitor; junior
partner Parker Thomas & Co; founded
own practice (1968); worked in lawyers'
offices in America and has associate legal
practice in Tampa, Florida where is also the
president of an American sports agency.

Activities: Commissioner for Oaths;
member Law Society; vice-chairman
British Olympic Games Travel Committee
for the Russian Olympics (1980); director
and legal advisor to the International
Squash Players' Association; founder
member Olympic Gold Financial Services
Limited; London Rotary Tennis Champion
(1988); president elect Hampstead Rotary
Club; member of: Cumberland Lawn
Tennis Club; Chandos Lawn Tennis Club;
RAC Club Pall Mall; David Lloyd Club.

Biography: lives London NW3; born
05.06.1937; married to Isabel with 3
children. Educated at Westminster City; St
John's College Cambridge (1963 MA);
College of Law.

Leisure: keen sportsman; swimming;
tennis; squash.

GOLDENBERG Philip

partner SJ BERWIN & CO 236 Gray's Inn
Road, London WC1X 8HB.

Career: articled Linklaters & Paines (1969-

1972); admitted (1972); assistant solicitor
(1972-1982); assistant solicitor SJ Berwin &
Co (1982-1983); became partner (1983).

Activities: former member Executive
Committee Wider Share Ownership
Council; member London Regional
Council Confederation of British Industry;
Liberal/SDP Alliance Parliamentary
Candidate Woking (1983 and 1987); Eton &
Slough (1974 & 1979); elected Woking
Borough Council (1984) (re-elected 1988);
chair Highways Committee (1988-1990);
legal adviser to the Liberal Party in relation
to its merger with SDP; adviser to Liberal
Democrat Parliamentarians in both Houses
in particular on corporate and taxation
matters; member Federal Conference
Committee of the Liberal Democrats;
member Liberal Party Council (1975-1988);
National Executive Committee (1977-1984);
successor National Executive (1984-1985 &
1986-1987); Candidates Committee (1976-
1985); Assembly Committee (1985-1987);
vice-chairman Electoral Reform Society
(1980-1982); governor Slough College of
Higher Education (1980-1986); responsible
for conception and enactment of Liberal
proposals for employee profit sharing in
1978 Finance Act; member National Liberal
Club.

Biography: lives Woking; born 26.04.1946;
married to Lynda with 3 children.
Educated at St Paul's School; Pembroke
College Oxford (1968); joint author,
Constitution of the Social and Liberal
Democrats; joint editor New Outlook
(1974-1977); author Fair Welfare (1968);
editor and part author: 'The Businessman's
Guide to Directors' Responsibilities' (1988);
'Sharing Profits' (1986); editor Guide to
Company Law (CCH, 1990); contributing
author 'Gore Brown on Companies'
(Jordans, 1990).

Leisure: family.

GOLDINGHAM Christopher

partner commercial property department
TOWNSENDS 42 Cricklade Street,
Swindon, Wilts SN1 3HD.

Career: admitted (1978); assistant solicitor
Townsends (1978-1980); became partner
(1980).

Activities: member Colston LTC.

Biography: lives Broadwell; born
09.08.1952; married with 2 sons. Educated
at West Downs, Winchester; Stowe School,
Buckingham; Oxford Polytechnic (1974
BSC); College of Law Chester (1975);
College of Law Lancaster Gate (1977-1978).

Leisure: tennis; playing harmonica in blues
band.

G

GOLDMAN Alfred

consultant ISADORE GOLDMAN
125 High Holborn, London WC1V 6QF.

Career: articled Isadore Goldman (1937-
1939); Territorial Army (1939); served
overseas in Middlesex Regiment (1943-
1946) (Captain 1942); solicitor to Middlesex
Regimental Association; articled (1946-
1947); admitted (1947); assistant solicitor
(1947-1950); became partner (1950); senior
partner (1961-1988); consultant (1988).

Activities: assistant Recorder (1979-1985);
member Insolvency Law Review
Committee (1976-1982); member
Insolvency Rules Committee (1976-1983);
member panel appointed under the
Banking Acts (1981 to date); general
commissioner for taxes City of London
(1988 to date); president Holborn Law
Society (1972-1973); member interview
panel Solicitors Complaints' Bureau (1988);
president Old Millhillians; member MCC.

Biography: lives Arkley; born 24.07.1920;
married with 3 children. Educated at Mill
Hill School; Open University (BA Arts
1990); contributor to: 'Insolvency' (1980);
'The Book of Humorous Legal Anecdotes'
(1988).

Leisure: gardening; cricket.

GOLDMAN Ian

senior partner GODLOVE SAFFMAN
15 St Paul's Street, Leeds LS1 2LZ.

Career: articled Brecher & Co; admitted
(1971); took over and became senior
partner Louis Godlove & Co and successor
firms (1971).

Activities: director Commercial & Financial
Investments Ltd (1972-1987); member
Committee Leeds Law Society and
chairman Non Contentious Business
Committee; lay member Leeds Family
Practitioner Committee (1985 to date); lay
member Leeds East District Health
Authority (1988 to date).

Biography: lives Leeds; born 28.01.1948;
married to Diane with 3 daughters.
Educated at Liverpool College; London
University (1968 LLB).

GOLDMEIER Michael

partner and head construction litigation
department BERWIN LEIGHTON
Adelaide House, London Bridge, London
EC4R 9HA.

Career: partner Berwin Leighton.

Biography: lives London; born 27.11.1946;
married to Philippa with 3 children.
Educated at London School of Economics
(LLB).

GOLDREIN Iain S

barrister and joint head of chambers 5th
Floor, Corn Exchange Building, Fenwick
Street, Liverpool L2 7QS and 1 Harcourt
Buildings, Temple, London EC4Y 9DA.

Career: called to the Bar Inner Temple
(1975); specialisations are: personal injury
litigation with particular reference to
medical negligence actions and disaster
claims; product liability with particular
reference to pharmaceutical products;
general commercial law.

Activities: member of Middle Temple;
member The UIA - the International Union
of Lawyers (Union Internationale des
Avocats); member International Litigation
Practitioners' Forum Advisory Committee;
Associate of the Chartered Institute of
Arbitrators; member The British Academy
of Experts; member The British Insurance
Law Association; regular lecturer for the
major professional conference
organisations on pharmaceutical product
liability, medical negligence, disaster
claims and commercial litigation (with
particular reference to litigation technique
and pre-emptive injunctions); in-house
training for solicitors with particular
reference to litigation technique; member
Athenaeum, Liverpool.

Biography: lives Liverpool and London;
born 10.08.1952; married to Margaret with
2 children. Educated at Merchant Taylors'
School, Crosby; Pembroke College
Cambridge (1974 BA) (1978 MA) Squire
Scholarship for Law; Exhibitioner; Ziegler
Prize for Law; Duke of Edinburgh
Entrance Scholarship Inner Temple; co-
author of: 'Personal Injury Litigation -
Practice and Precedents' (1985);
'Commercial Litigation - Pre-emptive
Remedies' (1987); Butterworths 'Personal
Injury Litigation Service' (1988); 'Pleadings
- Principles and Practice'; general editor
'Bullen & Leake and Jacob's Precedents of
Pleadings' 13th edition; author of 'Ship
Sale and Purchase - Law and Technique'
(1985).

Leisure: law; new ideas; the family; riding.

GOLDRING John

Queen's Counsel 2 Crown Office Row,
Temple, London EC4Y 7HJ.

Career: called to the Bar (1969); pupillage 2
Crown Office Row; QC (1987); Recorder;
specialisations: commercial, international
and tax fraud, disciplinary tribunals of
professional bodies, licensing, negligence
crime.

Activities: former standing prosecuting

counsel to the Inland Revenue Midland
and Oxford Circuit (1985-1987); faculty
member National Institute for Trial
Advocacy programmes, United States.

Biography: lives London WC1 and country;
born 09.11.1944; married to Wendy with 2
children. Educated at Wyggeston
Grammar School, Leicester; Exeter
University (LLB).

Leisure: gardening; skiing.

GOLDSMITH Peter

Queen's Counsel Fountain Court, Temple,
London EC4.

Career: called to the Bar Gray's Inn (1972);
member Chambers (1973); Junior Counsel
to the Crown Common Law (1985-1987);
QC (1987).

Biography: lives London NW3; born
05.01.1950; married to Joy with 4 children.
Educated at Quarry Bank High School,
Liverpool; Gonville and Caius College
Cambridge (1971 BA hons MA); University
College London (1972 LLM); Entrance
Exhibitioner; Senior Scholar; Schuldham
Plate Winner; McNair Prize Winner; Tapp
Postgraduate Scholar Caius College; Lord
Justice Holker Junior Exhibitioner;
Birkenhead Scholar Gray's Inn; Stuart
Cunningham MacCaskie KC Prizewinner.

GOLDSPINK Robert

partner and head of litigation DENTON
HALL BURGIN & WARRENS
Five Chancery Lane, Clifford's Inn,
London EC4A 1BU.

Career: supervisor in legal studies
Fitzwilliam and Sidney Sussex College
Cambridge (1973-1975); articled Wild
Hewitson & Shaw (1973-1975); admitted
(1975); solicitor Freshfields (1975-1980);
solicitor Denton Hall Burgin & Warrens
(1980-1981); became partner (1981).

Activities: lectures widely on subject of
international litigation and arbitration .

Biography: lives London; born 08.08.1949;
married to Margo with 1 son. Educated at
Eltham College; Fitzwilliam College
Cambridge (1968-1972 MA LLM); Squire
Scholar; Rebecca Flower Scholar.

Leisure: restoring Victorian waterside
chapel in Docklands in which he now lives;
tennis; water sports; gardening.

GOLDSTEIN John Arthur

general commercial litigation partner
TITMUSS SAINER & WEBB
2 Serjeants' Inn, London EC4Y 1LT.

Career: articled Sidney L Samson & Nyman (1954-1959); admitted (1959); assistant solicitor (1959-1960); assistant solicitor Titmuss Sainer & Webb (1960); became partner and served as head of Litigation.

Activities: Commissioner for Oaths; member of City of London Solicitors' Company; personal concern in children's leukaemia research; member Wig and Pen Club.

Biography: lives London NW6; born 14.07.1937; married to Daniele d.o. Colonel & Madame G Wry of Paris with 18 year old daughter (young son lost from leukemia at 5 years). Educated at Kilburn Grammar School; College of Law (hons).

Leisure: keen sportsman; Law Society cricket; Francophile also with affection for Tuscany; opera; gardening; cooking.

GOLDSTRAW Stephen

partner MANCHES & CO
Aldwych House, 71-91 Aldwych, London WC2B 4RP.

Career: articled Slaughter and May (1981-1983); admitted (1983); assistant solicitor (1983-1985); tax consultant Thomson McLintock/Peat Marwick McLintock (1985-1988); assistant solicitor Manches & Co (1989); became partner (1990).

Biography: lives London SW15; born 28.07.1959; single. Educated at Crewe County Grammar School for Boys; St Catherine's College Oxford (1980 BA hons); regular contributor to: Tolleys Company Secretary Review; Certified Accountant.

Leisure: music; squash; computers.

GOODACRE Michael

partner COFFIN MEW & CLOVER
17 Hampshire Terrace, Portsmouth, Hants PO1 2PU.

Career: articled Beale & Co; temporary legal assistant/solicitor Lambeth Town Hall (1968-1969); admitted (1969); assistant solicitor Coffin Mew & Clover (1969-1971); became partner (1971).

Activities: committee member Hampshire Incorporated Law Society (1988 to date) (chairman European sub-committee (1989 to date) (hon treasurer Portsmouth area); vice-chairman (1985 1986 & 1989); chairman (1987 & 1988) of Board of Visitors and member Local Review Committee of the Parole Board of HM Prison Kingston (Portsmouth); member and former chairman Promotion of International

Gastronomy Society; member of: Royal Naval Club and Royal Albert Yacht Club.

Biography: lives Titchfield; born 10.08.1941; married to Yvonne with 2 sons. Educated at Shrewsbury School; Keble College, Oxford (1964 BA MA).

GOODE Roy

Norton Rose Professor of English Law UNIVERSITY OF OXFORD, Fellow, St John's College, Oxford OX1 3JP.

Career: assistant solicitor (1955-1963); partner Victor Mishcon & Co (1963-1971); consultant (1971-1988); transferred to the Bar (1988); QC (1990); tenant of Chambers of Mr Colin Ross-Munro QC, 2 Hare Court, Temple; appointed Professor of Law University of London (Queen Mary College) (1971); acting Dean of the Faculty of Law (1971-1972); Crowther Professor of Credit and Commercial Law in the Department of Law (1976-1980); founder and director of the Centre for Commercial Law Studies Queen Mary College (1979-1989); elected Norton Rose Professor of English Law in the University of Oxford (1990) and Fellow of St John's College (1989).

Activities: visiting professor, Melbourne University (1976); Monash University (1984); Falconbridge visiting professor, York University (1981); Commonwealth Banking Corp; visiting professor Monash (1988); member of the Civil and Family Committee of the Judicial Studies Board (1988 to date); member of Council of the Banking Ombudsman (1989 to date); member of Council and vice-chairman of Executive Committee of Justice; member Crowther Committee on Consumer Credit (1968-1971); chairman Advertising Advisory Committee of the Independent Broadcasting Authority (1976-1980); member of the Monopolies and Mergers Commission (1981-1986); member Department of Trade and Industry Advisory Committee on Arbitration (1985 to date); elected Fellow of the British Academy (1988) and Fellow of the Royal Society of Arts (1990); member Governing Council of Unidroit (1988 to date); president-elect of the International Academy of Commercial and Consumer Law; joint honorary president British-Czech Legal Association; Freeman of the City of London; member Wig & Pen Club.

Biography: lives Oxford; born 06.04.1933; married to Catherine Anne Rueff with 1 daughter. Educated at Highgate School (1946-1949); Gladstone Scholar; (1954 LLB) (1976 LLD); OBE (1972); author of: 'Hire

Purchase Law and Practice' (1962, 1970 & Supplement 1975); 'Hire Purchase and Conditional Sale: A Comparative Survey of Commonwealth and American Law' with Jacob S Ziegel (1965); 'Consumer Credit Legislation'; 'Commercial Law' (1982); 'Legal Problems of Credit and Security' (1982 & 1988); 'Payment Obligations in Commercial and Financial Transactions' (1983); 'Proprietary Rights and Insolvency in Sales Transactions' (1985 & 1989); 'Principles of Corporate Insolvency Law' (1990); numerous articles in legal periodicals and contributions to encyclopaedic works.

Leisure: walking; chess; browsing in bookshops.

GOODHART Sir William

Queen's Council 3 New Square, Lincoln's Inn, London WC2A 3RS.

Career: called to the Bar (1957); Chambers of Peter Foster QC (1960); head of Chambers (1975); QC (1979); Bencher Lincoln's Inn (1986).

Activities: member Council of Legal Education; member Professional Standards Committee; member Direct Professional Access Committee; director Bar Mutual Indemnity Fund Ltd; member Conveyancing Standing Committee of the Law Commission; chairman Executive of Justice (vice-chairman 1978-1988); chair Social & Liberal Democratic Lawyers' Association; Knighted (1989); leading member Social and Liberal Democrats; chair Party's Conference Committee and member Policy Committee; contested Parliamentary elections in Kensington (1983 & 1987 general elections and 1988 by-election); member Brooks's.

Biography: lives London W8 and Oxford; born 18.01.1933; married to Celia with 2 daughters and 1 son. Educated at Eton College; Trinity College Cambridge (1956 MA); Harvard Law School (1958 LLM); Harkness Fellow; co-author of 'Specific Performance' (1986); sections in Halsbury's Laws of England on Corporations and Specific Performance; articles in legal periodicals.

GOODIER Roger

senior partner ROWLEY ASHWORTH
247 The Broadway, Wimbledon, London SW19 1SE.

Career: admitted (1970); assistant solicitor (1970-1974); became partner Rowley Ashworth (1974).

Activities: part-time chairman Social

Security Appeals Tribunal (1982-1985); hon legal adviser to Walthamstow Dogs; member Wig & Pen Club.

Biography: lives Twickenham; born 07.09.1944; married with 2 children. Educated at Gatley Primary School, Moseley Hall Grammar School, Cheadle; Sheffield University (1967 LLB hons).

Leisure: family; Morris dancing.

GORDON Charles

head of litigation and insolvency group CARTER FABER 10 Arthur Street, London EC4R 9AY.

Career: barrister commercial practice (1976-1989); assistant Clifford-Turner (1980-1984); admitted (1981); assistant solicitor (1981-1984); became partner Carter & Co (1984); merged to form Carter Faber (1986); became head of litigation (1987); became managing partner (1987-1989).

Activities: president Younger Society (Balliol College Oxford) (1974); clerk of the Candlewick Ward City of London; frequent speaker at seminars on insolvency litigation and employment law; organiser of network of European lawyers - Eurolex Groupe EEIG; licenced insolvency practitioner.

Biography: lives Sevenoaks; born 21.04.1953; married to Ann (legal conference organiser); with 3 children. Educated at St George's College, Weybridge; Balliol College Oxford (1974 hons); Coolidge Atlantic Crossing Trust (1974); Inns of Court School of Law (1975 Bar Finals); Solicitors Finals (1981).

Leisure: family; tennis; all things French and Italian; chairman Special Care Baby Fund (registered charity).

GORDON Grahame

joint managing director LOWE & GORDON SEMINARS and partner MCCOMBIE GORDON & LOWE 34 Queen Anne Street, London W1M 9LB.

Career: articled Norton Rose Botterell & Roche (1969-1971); admitted (1972); lecturer at College of Law Guildford (1972-1974); assistant solicitor Slowes (1974-1976); became partner (1976-1980); founded McCombie Gordon & Lowe and Lowe & Gordon Seminars (1981).

Activities: associate of Ashridge Management College.

Biography: lives London N3; born 12.03.1948; married to Claire with 2 children. Educated at Leeds Grammar School; University College Oxford (1969

BA) (1971 MA); College of Law Guildford (1971-1972); contributed to booklets published by College of Law (pre-1980).

Leisure: fundraising; bridge; cinema; theatre; good food; trying (unsuccessfully) to control two young children!.

GORDON-SAKER Paul

senior litigation partner and head of litigation ALSOP WILKINSON 6 Dowgate Hill, London EC4R 2SS.

Career: articled Alsop Stevens; admitted (1970); assistant solicitor (1970-1972); became partner (1972); became head of litigation on merger with Wilkinson Kimbers (1988); licensed insolvency practitioner.

Activities: Notary Public; member INSOL project on cross-border insolvencies; lectures at various seminars on insolvency; member Law Society; member Insolvency Lawyers' Association; member Insolvency Practitioners' Association.

Biography: lives Sanderstead; born 06.08.1944; married to Vickie with 2 children. Educated at Stonyhurst College; author of 'Insolvency Procedure Notes' with Michael Stubbs; various magazine articles.

Leisure: theatre; travel; reading; photography.

GORE Robert Michael

senior partner and head of company commercial department ROBERT GORE AND COMPANY 17 Grosvenor Street, London W1X 9FD.

Career: articled Nicholson Graham & Jones (1967-1969); admitted (1969); assistant solicitor (1969-1971); executive merchant bank/finance house (6 months); founded own practice (1972).

Activities: member Solicitors European Group; former trustee and treasurer Apex Charitable Trust; founder member and promoter of Association of Business and Property Lawyers in the EEC; member of: English Stage Society; Heath & Old Hampstead Society; Jaguar Drivers' Club; Law Society Motor Club; Fitness Club; RPO Club; South End Green Association.

Biography: lives London NW3; born 10.03.1945; widowed; remarried to Diana with 4 children. Educated at The Hall School (1953-1958); University College School (1958-1963); King's College, London (1966 LLB hons); College of Law Lancaster Gate (1967).

Leisure: family leisure; music; theatre; motor sport; classic cars; private flying.

GORMAN John

Queen's Counsel 2 Dr Johnson's Buildings, Temple, London EC4Y 7AY.

Career: Royal Artillery (1945-1948); called to Bar Inner Temple (1953); Birmingham Chambers (1953-1974); Midland & Oxford Circuit; QC (1974); Bencher Inner Temple (1983); Recorder of Crown Court.

Activities: deputy chairman Northamptonshire Quarter Sessions (1970-1971); sat as Deputy High Court Judge (QBD) (1982 to date); Fellow RSPB; life member National Trust; member Reform Club.

Biography: lives Ilminster; born 29.06.1927; married; 4 children. Educated at Stonyhurst College; Balliol College Oxford (1951 MA).

Leisure: fresh air; music; painting.

GORTY Peter

partner corporate finance, banking and energy NABARRO NATHANSON 50 Stratton Street, London W1X 5FL.

Career: articled Gilbert Samuel & Co (1966-1968); admitted (1969); assistant solicitor Withers (1969-1970); assistant solicitor Nabarro Nathanson (1970-1972); became partner (1972).

Biography: lives Weybridge; born 03.11.1944; married with 2 children. Educated at Owens School Islington; LSE (1965 LLB).

Leisure: sport; opera; architecture.

GOTHERIDGE Martin

senior partner EKING MANNING 44 The Ropewalk, Nottingham NG1 5EL.

Career: articled in Mansfield (1965-1967); admitted (1967); assistant solicitor Eking Manning (1967-1969); became partner (1969); became senior partner (1988).

Activities: assistant Deputy Coroner for Nottinghamshire; vice-president designate Nottinghamshire Law Society; member Area Legal Aid Committee; chairman Hockey Association Competitions Committee; president Midlands Counties Hockey Association; member European Hockey Federation; member Nottingham Squash Racquets Club; member Notts United Services Club.

Biography: lives Nottingham; born 23.02.1943; married to Margaret. Educated at West Bridgford Grammar School; University College London (1964 LLB hons).

GOUDIE James

Queen's Counsel 11 King's Bench Walk, Temple, London EC4Y 7EQ.

Career: articled (1964-1966); admitted (1966); assistant solicitor (1966-1970); called to the Bar Inner Temple (1970); Assistant Recorder (1982); QC (1984); Recorder (1985).

Activities: member Executives of Administrative Law Bar Association Society of Labour Lawyers; councillor London Borough of Brent (1967-1978) (chairman Housing and Planning Committees; deputy leader; leader); Parliamentary candidate (Labour) Brent North (1974).

Biography: lives London NW3; born 02.06.1942; married with 2 sons. Educated at Dean Close School, Cheltenham; London School of Economics (1963 LLB hons); Distinction in Commercial Law; various articles.

GOUGH James Benjamin (Ben)

commercial partner FRERE CHOLMELEY 28 Lincoln's Inn Fields, London WC2A 3HH.

Career: articled Frere Cholmeley (1961); admitted; assistant solicitor; became partner (1969).

Activities: senior vice-president Holborn Law Society; Committee member British-Italian Legal Association.

Biography: lives 26.04.1938; divorced with 1 child. Educated at Eton College; Christ Church Oxford (1961 LLB); Boulter Exhibitioner in Law.

GOULD Nicholas

resident partner LOVELL WHITE DURRANT 11th Floor, West Tower, Bond Centre, Queensway, Hong Kong.

Career: articled Lovell White & King; admitted (1967); assistant solicitor (1967-1971); partner (1971); admitted Hong Kong (1982); became resident partner Hong Kong (1987).

Activities: vice-chairman Committee T (International Construction Contracts) of the International Bar Association; member The Hong Kong Club.

Biography: lives Hong Kong; born 02.08.1942; married to Britta with 1 son. Educated at Oundle School; Magdalene College Cambridge (1964 BA); number of articles in journals on aspects of construction and arbitration law.

Leisure: classical music; antique furniture and pictures; tennis; scuba diving.

GOWAR Martyn

partner and head of tax department LAWRENCE GRAHAM 190 Strand, London WC2R 1JN.

Career: articled Lawrence Graham (1967-1970); admitted (1970); assistant solicitor (1970-1973); became partner (1973).

Activities: member Law Society Revenue Law Committee (1979 to date); editor taxation section Law Society's Gazette (1980 to date); clerk to the trustees of the Hamlyn Trust; member of: MCC; Gresham Club; Lord's Taverners; Elstead CC (chairman).

Biography: lives Elstead; born 11.07.1946; married to Sue with 3 sons. Educated at King's College School, Wimbledon (1957-1964); Magdalen College Oxford (1967 MA); FTII (1981); Institute of Taxation Thesis Prize (1981).

Leisure: golf; cricket; gardening; birdwatching; keeping fit.

GRABINER Anthony

Queen's Counsel 1 Essex Court, Temple, London EC4 Tel: 071 583 2000; Fax: 071 583 0118.

Career: called to the Bar (1968); pupillage SA Stamler QC (1968-1969); commercial lawyer; QC (1981); Bencher of Lincoln's Inn (1989); Recorder of the Crown Court (1990).

Activities: Standing Junior Counsel to the DTI Export Credits Guarantee Department (1976-1981); a Junior Counsel to the Crown (1978-1981); sometime lecturer in law London University; member of: Garrick; MCC; RAC.

Biography: lives London NW8; born 21.03.1945; married to Jane with 2 children. Educated at Central Foundation Boys' Grammar School, London; London School of Economics (1966 LLB) (1967 LLM); author of: 'Sutton & Shannon on Contracts' (7th ed) (1970); 'Banking Documents' in the Encyclopaedia of Forms and Precedents (1986).

Leisure: swimming; theatre.

GRACIE Diana

partner LEWIS SILKIN 1 Butler Place, Buckingham Gate, London SW1H 0PT.

Career: admitted (1972); assistant solicitor (1972-1973); became partner Lewis Silkin (1973).

Biography: lives London. Educated at London University (LLB).

GRAFTON-GREEN Paddy

partner, management committee member and head of the Media Group THEODORE GODDARD 150 Aldersgate Street, London EC1A 4EJ.

Career: articled Theodore Goddard; admitted (1969); assistant solicitor (1969-1982); became associate (1982); became partner (1983).

Activities: lectured extensively on the taxation of income arising from the exploitation of copyright and other 'media rights' both within and outside UK; lectured on general law of copyright; member MCC.

Biography: lives London SW13; born 30.03.1943; married to Deborah with 4 children. Educated at St Richards, Little Malvern; Ampleforth College; Wadham College Oxford (1965 MA); College of Law Lancaster Gate.

Leisure: cricket (player and spectator); travel; medieval European history; arts generally (especially opera and theatre).

GRAHAM Dan

partner responsible for in-house training BRISTOWS COOKE & CARPMAEL 10 Lincoln's Inn Fields, London WC2A 3BP.

Career: articled Bristows Cooke & Carpmael (1965-1967); admitted (1967); assistant solicitor (1967-1971); became partner (1971).

Activities: regular speaker in UK and overseas on aspects of electrical and mechanical engineering contracts; chairman Business Law Section Holborn Law Society (1989-1990); European rapporteur of the Committee on General Contract Conditions of the industrialisation working group of the Euro-Arab dialogue (1974-1977); IEE/I Mech E Model Forms Drafting Panel; member FIDIC E & M task force; member of: Porters Park Golf Club; Radlett Cricket Club; Tabard Rugby Club; Old Salopian Club.

Biography: lives Little Gaddesden; born 06.05.1942; married to Jenny with 3 children. Educated at Ashfold School, Dorton (1949-1956); Shrewsbury School (1956-1961); Gonville and Caius College Cambridge (1961-1964); College of Law Lancaster Gate (1964-1965); Ralph Yablon Bursary (1967); occasional articles on electrical and mechanical engineering contracts in construction law journals.

Leisure: golf; performing in amateur dramatics, light opera and old-time music halls; planting rhododendrons and azaleas; collecting prints and lithographs by modern artists.

GRAHAM Peter

partner NORTON ROSE Kempson House, Camomile Street, London EC3A 7AN.

Career: articled Norton Rose Botterell & Roche (1969-1971); admitted (1971); assistant solicitor (1971-1977); (seconded to Cleary Gottlieb Steen & Hamilton Paris office (1973-1974); became partner Norton Rose (1977).

Activities: member Law Society's Standing Committee on Company Law (1980 to date); member City of London Solicitors' Company.

Biography: lives London NW11; born 15.06.1946; married to Susan with 1 son. Educated at Colet Court (1955-1960); St Paul's School (1960-1963); Magdalene College Cambridge (1967 BA) (1968 LLB); Exhibitioner (1966); Scholar (1968); (Associate of the Institute of Taxation (1971).

Leisure: theatre; opera.

GRAHAM MAW Nigel

senior partner ROWE & MAW 20 Black Friars Lane, London EC4V 6HD.

Career: articled Rowe & Maw (1958-1961); admitted and became partner (1961); became senior partner (1976).

Activities: hon solicitor to the Barristers' Clerks' Association; lectures generally on company and commercial matters with particular reference to the City Code and takeover tactics; numerous company directorships including Decca Limited (chairman 1980) and Telephone Rentals plc (1982-1989); member of: Oxford & Cambridge United Universities Club; Royal Southern Yacht Club.

Biography: lives Avington, Hampshire; born 04.07.1933; married to Gill with 4 children. Educated at Westminster School; Pembroke College Cambridge (1958 MA LLM); publications: 'Rowe & Maw on Public Takeovers and Mergers in the United Kingdom' (1990).

Leisure: gardening; music; sailing.

GRAMATIDIS Yanos

managing partner BAHAS GRAMATIDIS & ASSOCIATES 141 Harley Street, London W1N 7DJ.

Career: admitted Athens (1977); became managing partner Bahas Gramatidis &

Associates (1988).

Activities: member Special Representation in Greece of the International Franchise Association; member Athens Bar; member International Bar Association; member Business Law Section and General Practice Section of International Bar Association; member American and Inter-American Bar Associations; member Law Society of London; member Hellenic-American Chamber of Commerce; member British-Hellenic Chamber of Commerce; member Anglo-Hellenic Law Association, London (chairman 1988 to date); member of: Champneys; IOD.

Biography: lives London W1; born 12.05.1952; married to Mariella. Educated at Larissa A High School (1967); Athens B High School (1969); Athens University Law School (LLB); The Hague Academy of International Law; Institut International des Droits de l'Homme, Strasbourg; author of: 'The Protection of Human Rights in Europe' (1982); 'La Nouvelle Loi qui concerne les Relations entre les Hommes et les Femmes' (1983); 'Acquisition of Real Property in Greece by Aliens' (1985); 'The New Law on Leasing in Greece' (1987); 'Hotel Contracts in Greece' (1987); 'Time-sharing in Greece' (1987); 'The Establishment of the Lawyers in the EEC' (1983); 'Franchising: The Greek Legislation' (1988); 'Investment Incentives in Greece' (1988); 'Mergers and Acquisitions in the EEC' (1988); 'Acquisitions of Greek Securities' (1988); 'Bank Confidentiality in Greece' (1989).

Leisure: tennis; antiques collection.

GRANT Donald

chairman SCOTTISH LEGAL AID BOARD 44 Drumsheugh Gardens, Edinburgh EH3 7SW.

Career: war service in Royal Artillery (1939-1946) (retired Major); admitted chartered accountant (1948); partner Moody Stuart & Robertson CA (1950) partner Thomson & McLintock & Co CA on merger (1975); retired as senior partner in Dundee (1986).

Activities: chairman Tayside Health Board; chairman Dundee & London Investment Trust PLC; chairman Mathew Trust; trustee other charitable trusts; formerly director of Hat Group PLC and Don Brothers Buist PLC; vice-president Institute of Chartered Accountants of Scotland (1977-1979) (president 1979-1980); member of: New Club; Royal & Ancient Golf Club; Panmure Golf Club; Blairgowrie Golf Club.

Biography: lives Dundee; born 08.10.1921;

married to Lavinia with 3 daughters. Educated at Dundee High School; Dundee University (hon LLD).

Leisure: golf; shooting; fishing; bridge.

GRANT Gregor

senior partner NEEDHAM & GRANT 14 Lincoln's Inn Fields, London WC2A 3BP.

Career: articled Hempsons (1962-1967); admitted (1967); assistant solicitor Bird & Bird (1968-1971); founded Needham & Grant (1971).

Activities: member Patent Solicitors Association.

Biography: lives London; born 10.02.1944; married to Jeanie with 4 children. Educated at University College School.

Leisure: cycling; motorcycling; cooking; boogie-woogie.

GRAY David

partner LOVELL WHITE DURRANT 65 Holborn Viaduct, London EC1A 2DY.

Career: articled Coward Chance (1957-1960); admitted (1960); assistant solicitor (1960-1962); assistant solicitor Bischoff & Co (1962-1963); assistant solicitor Lovell White & King (1963-1965); became partner (1966-1988); became partner Lovell White Durrant (1988).

Activities: Master City of London Solicitors' Company (1984-1985) (Almoner 1988 to date); vice-president and chairman of the Committee the City of London Law Society (1985-1988); hon auditor of the Law Society (1988-1990); assistant treasurer of the International Bar Association (1988 to date); trustee of the International Bar Association Educational Trust (1987 to date); member of the Court of the City of London Solicitor's Company (1974 to date); member various committees and sub-committees; member International Bar Association section on Business Law and Committees G and Q; member Solicitors European Group; former member and hon treasurer Law Society Hockey Club; member London Solicitors Golf Society; member Solicitors Wine Society; Liveryman of the Glaziers' Company; member of: Ski Club of Great Britain; Liphook Golf Club.

Biography: lives London and Haslemere; born 18.05.1936; married to Rosemary with 3 children. Educated at Bilton Grange; Rugby; Trinity College Oxford (1957 BA) (1961 MA); management course at Ashridge College (1976).

G

Leisure: skiing; golf; tennis; swimming; music; theatre; wine; travel.

GRAY Roger

Queen's Counsel Queen Elizabeth Building, Temple, London EC4Y 9BS.

Career: commissioned RA (1942); Ayrshire Yeomanry (1942-1945); campaign Normandy and NW Europe (1944-1945); GSO III 8 Corps (War Criminals) (1945); GSO III (Mi/Ops) GHO Delhi (1946); called to the Bar SE Circuit (1947); QC (1967); Deputy Recorder of Andover (1967-1971); a Recorder of the Crown Court (1971); a Deputy High Court Judge Family Division (1975 to date).

Activities: president Oxford Union (1947); Conservative candidate Dagenham General Election (1955); member of: Carlton Club; Pratts Club; MCC.

Biography: lives London W11; born 16.06.1921; married to Lynne; 1 son by former marriage. Educated at Wycliffe College; Queen's College Oxford (1941 jurisprudence 1st class hons).

Leisure: cricket (OU Authentics); reading; talk.

GRAYSON Edward

barrister 4 Paper Buildings, Temple, London EC4Y 7EX.

Career: called to the Bar Middle Temple (1948); pupillage and practising barrister Chancery Bar Lincoln's Inn (1949-1953); practising barrister Temple (1953 to date).

Activities: hon legal adviser to: Kensington Citizens Advice Bureau (1950-1960); Mary Ward Settlement Legal Advice Centre (1950-1970); Freedom in Sport International (1981 to date); counsel to Professional Footballers' and Trainers' Union (1953-1957); consultant and contributor to Central Council of Physical Recreation and Sports Council (1978 to date); member of: MCC; Middlesex Surrey and Sussex County Cricket Clubs; Corinthian-Casuals, Harlequins and Littlehampton Town Football Clubs; British Association of Sports and Medicine.

Biography: lives The Temple, London EC4 and Rustington, West Sussex; born 01.03.1925; married to Wendy (nee Shockett) with 1 son, Harry. Educated at Taunton's School, Southampton; Exeter College Oxford (1947 BA hons) (1951 MA); author of: 'Sport and the Law' (1978 and 1988); 'Corinthian-Casuals and Cricketers (1955 and 1983); The Way Forward: Gleneagles Agreement (1982); co-author of:

'Sponsorship of Sport, Arts and Leisure: Law Tax and Business Relationships' (1984); 'Royal Baccarat Scandal' (1977 and 1988); 'Medicine, Sport and the Law' (1990); contributions to national, legal and sporting media (1953 to date).

Leisure: working; writing; creative thinking for the Rule of Law to expunge cheating by violence, administrative malpractices and government gaps from all sports, games, pastimes and leisure activities, including monitoring 'The Royal Baccarat Scandal' on stage, screen, radio and in book form.

GREEN Alan Laurence

barrister practising from chambers of Robin Stewart QC at 2 Harcourt Buildings, Temple, London EC4Y 9DB.

Career: investment analyst Grieveson Grant & Co (1969-1970); pupillage Chambers of M Finer QC (1972); called to the Bar Gray's Inn (1973); pupillage A Logan Petch (1973); tenant Ship Canal House (1973-1980); head of chambers 1 Verulam Buildings (1985-1990); door tenant 2 Old Bank Street, Manchester.

Activities: voluntary civil rights work .

Biography: lives Beaconsfield; born 02.02.1946; married to Charlotte with 2 sons. Educated at Carmel College; Altrincham Grammar School; Sussex University (BA hons).

Leisure: fell walking; skiing; sailing; tennis; classical Greek.

GREEN Allan

Director of Public Prosecutions and head of the Crown Prosecution Service 4-12 Queen Anne's Gate, London SW1H 9AZ.

Career: Royal Navy (1953-1955); called to the Bar Inner Temple; Bencher (1985); junior prosecuting counsel to the Crown Central Criminal Court (1977); senior prosecuting counsel (1979); first senior prosecuting counsel (1985); Recorder (1979-1987); became Director of Public Prosecutions (1987).

Activities: member of: Athenaeum; Brooks's.

Biography: born 01.03.35; married to Eva with 1 son and 1 daughter. Educated at Charterhouse; St Catharine's College Cambridge (1958 BA) (1963 MA) Open Exhibitioner.

Leisure: listening to music.

GREEN Christopher

senior partner CHRISTOPHER GREEN & PARTNERS 35 Carlton Crescent, Southampton, Hampshire SO9 2RF.

Career: articled Taylor Simpson & Mosley (1959-1964); admitted (1964); assistant solicitor and partner Farnfield & Nicholls (1964-1969); became partner Jasper & Vincent (1969-1981); founded Christopher Green & Partners (1981).

Activities: chairman Southampton Glyndebourne Association.

Biography: lives Winchester; born 24.07.1936; married with 4 children. Educated at Uppingham.

Leisure: opera; motorcycles.

GREEN David

consultant VJG JOHNS & SONS 19 West Street, Fishguard, Dyfed.

Career: articled George Davies & Co (1955-1959); admitted (1959); assistant solicitor (1959-1962); became partner (1963-1970); legal adviser Nuclear Power Group Ltd (1970-1973) (part-time 1973-1980); adviser 'This is Your Right' Granada TV Ltd (1971-1988); became consultant VJG Johns & Sons (1973); partner in charge litigation (1977-1982).

Activities: member Law Society Family Law Committee (1966-1988); member Law Society Revenue/Family Law Sub-committee (1980-1981); member Abortion Law Reform Association National Executive (1965-1968); member International Editorial Board Land Use Policy (1983-1989); contributions to: First International Colloquium on the Law of Sport Louvain University (1965); First International Symposium on Gender Identity (1969); Institute of Biology Symposium on the role of vegetables in feeding people and livestock Royal Geographical Society (1979); Institute of Fiscal Studies Conference 'The Taxation of the Family' Royal Institution (1981); Second Conference on the Family Court Bristol University (1984); evidence to Commons Select Committee on the Divorce Reform Act and Lords Select Committee on taxation of husband and wife (1985); Liberal candidate Nantwich Division (1964 & 1966) General Election; Oldham West by-election (1968); occasional contributor to GTV programmes; Credo (LWT); TV Eye (Thames); contributor to Radio Wales 'Fair Play' and 'Money Box' and 'Small Country Living' (BBC Radio 4); winner Welsh Region Times National Microcomputer Challenge (1984); author:

'Maintenance & Capital Provision on Divorce' (Law Society 1987); 'Splitting Up' (Kogan Page 1988); 'Moving to the Country' (Kogan Page 1990); 'Green Living' (Kogan Page 1990-1991).

Biography: lives Castle Morris nr Haverfordwest; born 13.02.1935; widowed with 2 daughters and 1 son. Educated at The Manchester Grammar School (1946-1952); Manchester University (1955 LLB).

Leisure: horticulture; music; building; writing; computers; chess; bridge.

GREEN Guy

partner and joint head company/commercial department PAYNE HICKS BEACH 10 New Square, Lincoln's Inn, London WC2A 3QG.

Career: articled Payne Hicks Beach (1970-1972); admitted (1972); assistant solicitor (1972-1974); became partner (1974).

Activities: joint recruitment partner.

Biography: lives Winchester; born 24.07.1947; married to Janet with 2 sons and 1 daughter. Educated at Eagle House, Sandhurst (1956-1960); Wellington College, Crowthorne (1960-1965); Exeter University (1966-1969); College of Law (1969-1970).

Leisure: all sports; gardening; the arts.

GREEN Jeffrey

senior partner JEFFREY GREEN RUSSELL Apollo House, 56 New Bond Street, London W1Y 9DG.

Career: admitted (1958); founded own practice (1972).

Activities: frequent lecturer on tax and commercial matters and for various organisations; member RAF Club.

Biography: lives London; born 24.12.1933; married to Susan with 3 children. Educated at London School of Economics (1955 LLB); general editor of Practical Commercial Precedents; articles on international and domestic tax and acquisitions and mergers in legal and other periodicals.

GREEN Michael Ian

partner FINERS 179/185 Great Portland Street, London W1.

Career: articled Mr Arnold A Finer (1951-1956); admitted (1956); National Service in Royal Air Force (1956-1957); assistant solicitor (1957-1960); became partner as Arnold Finer & Green (1960); firm became Gershon Young Finer & Green (1981) and then Finers (1989).

Activities: member of: Finchley Golf Club; RAC.

Biography: lives London N3; born 12.10.1934; married to Stefanie with 2 sons (one of whom is a partner in Finers). Educated at Malvern College (1948-1950); Law Society Finals (hons).

Leisure: golf; social bridge; listening to music; opera.

GREEN Nicholas

barrister Brick Court Chambers, Devereux Court, Temple, London EC4.

Career: lecturer in European and commercial law Southampton University (1981-1985); visiting Fellow Queen Mary College London (1986-1989); called to the Bar Inner Temple (1986); specialises in EEC law, competition law, restraint of trade, intellectual property licensing.

Activities: member correspondents' panel 'Computer Law and Security Journal'; given papers at international conferences on European law topics; Editorial Board member, Competition Journal.

Biography: lives London N1; born 15.10.1958. Educated at King Edward's, Birmingham (1970-1977); Leicester University (1980 LLB); Toronto University (1981 LLM); Southampton University (1985 PHD); author of 'Commercial Agreement and Competition Law: Practice and Procedure in the UK and EEC' (1986); co-author of 'The Legal Foundations of the Single European Market' (1991).

Leisure: swimming (former international); music; Victorian watercolours.

GREEN Stephen

senior partner MARCH PEARSON & SKELTON 41 Spring Gardens, Manchester M2 2BB.

Career: articled March Pearson & Green; admitted (1962); assistant solicitor Simmons & Simmons (1962-1965); assistant solicitor March Pearson & Green (1965-1966); became partner (1966).

Activities: Consul for the Netherlands for Greater Manchester, East Lancashire and East Cheshire; director Manchester & District Housing Association; member of: St James's Club Manchester; Royal Overseas League.

Biography: lives Buxton; born 02.01.1937; married to Margaret with 3 children. Educated at Terra Nova School, Cheshire; Kingswood School, Bath; Manchester University (1955 LLB).

Leisure: walking; reading; music; gardening.

GREENBURY Toby

company and commercial partner DJ FREEMAN & CO 43 Fetter Lane, London EC4A 1NA.

Career: articled Stephenson Harwood (1974-1976); admitted (1976); assistant solicitor (1976-1979); associate (on secondment) Lord Day & Lord (1976-1977); assistant solicitor DJ Freeman & Co (1979-1980); became partner (1980).

Activities: New York Bar (1978); member the Law Society of England & Wales, City of London; the City of London Law Society; chairman of the Whittington Committee of the City of London Solicitors' Company; editor of the newsletter of the City of London Solicitors Company; member of RAC .

Biography: lives London SE11; born 18.09.1951; single. Educated at Clifton College; University College London.

Leisure: gardening; music; polo.

GREENE John

partner MACROBERTS 152 Bath Street, Glasgow G2 4TB.

Career: assistant solicitor Joseph Kirkland & Son (1958-1960); assistant solicitor MacRoberts (1960-1961); became partner (1961).

Activities: former vice-convenor Company Law Committee of Law Society of Scotland; former member Bankruptcy and Liquidation Committee; member Insolvency Practitioners' Adjudication Panel; former tutor Glasgow University in Diploma of Legal Education; frequent contributor at seminars run by Law Society of Scotland and Institute of Chartered Accountants; member of: Royal Troon Golf Club; Prestwick Golf Club; Caledonian Club; Royal Scottish Automobile Club.

Biography: lives Troon; born 02.06.1932; married to Catriona with 1 child. Educated at Merchiston Castle School, Edinburgh; Edinburgh University (1955 MA) (1957 LLB); joint author of 'The Law and Practice of Receivership in Scotland'.

Leisure: golf.

GREENHALGH David

tax partner LINKLATERS & PAINES Barrington House, 59-67 Gresham Street, London EC2V 7JA.

Career: articled March Pearson & Skelton; admitted (1968); assistant solicitor Linklaters & Paines (1969-1974); became partner (1974).

G

Activities: member City of London Law Society's Revenue Law sub-committee; member St George's Hill and West Sussex Golf Clubs.

Biography: lives Weybridge; born 04.12.1943; married to Jill. Educated at Sedbergh School.

Leisure: gardening; golf.

GREENHOUS Guy

recruitment partner RADCLIFFES & CO 10 Little College Street, Westminster, London SW1P 3SJ.

Career: articled Radcliffes & CO (1967-1972); admitted (1972); assistant solicitor (1972-1976); became partner (1976).

Activities: chairman Law Society Monitoring of Articles Panel; hon legal adviser to: Marlow Society; Forty Green Preservation Society; Marlow Rowing Club; lay member Berkshire Family Practitioner Committee (chairman Dental Service, Pharmaceutical Service; Pharmaceutical Practice and Hours of Service Committees) (1985 to date); member Radleian Society Committee (1988 to date); member East India Club.

Biography: lives Marlow; born 06.09.1947; married to Sarah with 2 children. Educated at Radley College; CIPFA lecture paper on 'Legal aspects of NHS trust funds' (1984).

Leisure: rowing; cycling; gardening; Hellenic studies; ancient and military history; archaeology; conservation generally.

GREENLEAVES Michael

senior partner HUMPHRIES KIRK 4 Rempstone Road, Swanage, Dorset BH19 1DP (also at Wareham, Dorchester, Upton and Boscombe).

Career: articled Dorchester (1964-1970); admitted (1970); assistant solicitor Brecon (1970-1971); assistant solicitor Humphries Kirk (1971-1973); became partner (1973); became senior partner (1985).

Activities: member committees of 5 local charitable organisations.

Biography: lives Nr Swanage; born 04.11.1945; married to Valentine with 3 children. Educated at Bryanston School, Blandford.

Leisure: walking; climbing; photography; cycling; running.

GREENSTONE Nicolas

head of corporate finance SIMON OLSWANG & CO 1 Great Cumberland Place, London W1H 7AL.

Career: articled Herbert Smith (1968-1970); admitted (1970); assistant solicitor Donne Mileham & Haddock (1971-1972); assistant solicitor Berwin Leighton Paris office (1973-1976); assistant solicitor London (1976-1978); became partner (1978-1985); partner Simon Olswang (1985).

Biography: lives London NW3; married with 4 stepchildren. Educated at St Paul's School (1958-1962); University College Oxford (1966 BA hons); College of Europe Bruges, Belgium (1967 Masters in EEC competition law); co-author of 'Management Buy-outs (published Butterworths 1990); articles in Investment Management; Butterworths Journal of International Banking and Financial Law.

Leisure: opera; music; theatre; films; food; wine; travel; current affairs.

GREENWOOD Anthony

partner and managing partner ELLIOTT AND COMPANY 8 Breams Buildings, London EC4A 1EA.

Career: articled Elliott and Company (1980-1982); admitted (1982); assistant solicitor (1982-1984); became partner (1984); became managing partner (1985); active participant in firm's overseas legal association.

Activities: vice-president Manchester Trainee Solicitors Group (1981); member National Committee of Trainee Solicitors (1981); member Manchester and Holborn Law Societies; member The Euro-American Lawyers' Group; member of: St James's Club, Manchester; Reciprocal Clubs.

Biography: lives London; born 31.07.1958. Educated at Giggleswick School; Liverpool Polytechnic (1979 BA hons); College of Law Chester (1979-1980).

Leisure: sport of all varieties; cinema; theatre; food; drink.

GREENWOOD Brian

partner in commercial property and planning department NORTON ROSE Kempson House, PO Box 570, Camomile Street, London EC3A 7RN.

Career: articled Westminster City Council (1972-1975); admitted (1976); assistant solicitor South Yorkshire County Council (1976-1978); senior assistant solicitor Kent County Council (1978-1980); assistant County solicitor (1980-1982); chief solicitor Bedfordshire County Council (1982-1985);

assistant solicitor Norton Rose (1985-1988); became partner (1988).

Activities: past member Executive Committee Law Society Local Government Group; member Law Society Planning Law Committee; chairman City of London Law Society Planning and Environmental Law sub-committee; lecturer for the College of Law on Planning Law and Practice.

Biography: lives Bedford; born 15.04.1950; married to Julia with 3 children. Educated at Forest School; Southampton University; College of Law Guildford (1975-1976); author of: articles for various legal journals including Law Society's Gazette; local government Chronicle and Journal of Planning Law; quarterly law review for the 'Planner' (the journal of the Royal Town Planning Institute); general editor of Butterworth's Planning Law Service.

Leisure: family; classical music (violinist); golf; tennis; soccer.

GREENWOOD Jeffrey

senior partner NABARRO NATHANSON 50 Stratton Street, London W1X 5FL.

Career: articled Bartlett & Gluckstein (1957-1960); admitted (1960); assistant solicitor (1960-1961); assistant solicitor Nabarro Nathanson (1961-1963); partner (1963); head property department (1971-1987); became senior partner (1987); chairman Managing Committee.

Activities: director Bank Leumi (UK) PLC; Chairman Jewish Care; Law Society appointee to Hampstead Garden Suburb Trust Council (1984-1987); member RAC.

Biography: lives London N6; born 21.04.1935; married to Naomi with 4 children. Educated at Raines Foundation Grammar School (1944-1953); London School of Economics (1953-1954); Downing College Cambridge (1957 MA LLB); articles on property law and other legal topics in variety of magazines and newspapers.

Leisure: daily jogging on Hampstead Heath; competitive running events; swimming; skiing; voluntary social welfare work; the arts; literature; opera; theatre; modern painting.

GREENWOOD William

senior partner STEELE & SON Castlegate, Clitheroe, Lancs BB7 1AZ.

Career: taught chemistry Churchill School, Salisbury, S Rhodesia (1952-1954); articled (1954-1959); admitted (1959); assistant solicitor (1959-1962); became partner Steele & Son (1962).

Activities: president Agricultural Land Tribunal Western Region; president Mental Health Review Tribunal North Western Area; chairman SSAT; chairman Milk and Dairies Tribunal Midlands and Western Region; member of: Clitheroe Golf Club; Earby Cricket Club.

Biography: lives Kelbrook; born 23.02.1928; married to Jean with 5 children. Educated at Sedbergh School (1940-1946); Leeds University (1952 BSC) Teaching Certificate.

Leisure: farming; gardening.

GREGG Andrew DMcCallum

litigation partner OSBORNE CLARKE 30 Queen Charlotte Street, Bristol BS99 7QQ.

Career: articled Raper Fovargue (1965-1970); admitted (1970); assistant solicitor Heringtons (1970-1972); became partner Geoffrey Borg Wotton & Young (1972-1974); assistant solicitor Osborne Clarke (1974-1975); became partner (1975).

Activities: chairman Avon & Bristol Federation of Boys' Club's Fund-Raising Committee; past chairman Bristol Young Solicitors Group; past president Bristol Law Students' Society; past and current member Council Bristol Law Society; chairman Law Society Monitoring of Articles Panel; past panel member Central & Kingswood CAB; member of: the Lagonda Club; The Teign Corinthian Yacht Club.

Biography: lives Bristol; born 12.09.1943; married with 2 children. Educated at The Dragon School, Oxford; The King's School, Canterbury; The University of Aix-en-Provence.

Leisure: restoration and driving of vintage cars; sailing; skiing; rugby.

GREGORY Tony

senior partner KEEBLE HAWSON Old Cathedral Vicarage, St James Row, Sheffield S1 1XA.

Career: articled Bury & Walkers (1964-1967); admitted (1967); assistant solicitor Keeble Hawson Steele Carr & Co (1967-1970); became partner (1970).

Biography: lives Worksop; born 11.01.1943; 2 children; married to Doreen. Educated at Becket School, Nottingham; Leeds University (1964 LLB hons).

Leisure: public speaking; golf; reading.

GREGORY ROBSON Lancelot William

training and library partner FLADGATE FIELDER Heron Place, 3 George Street, London W1H 6AD.

Career: voluntary service overseas teaching English in Thailand (1969-1970); articled Marcan & Dean (1976-1978); admitted (1978); assistant solicitor Denton Hall & Burgin (1978-1982); associate Walters Fladgate (1982-1986); became partner Walters Fladgate (1986); merged to become Fladgate Fielder (1988).

Activities: research into EEC law (1973-1974); school governor (1985-1987); articles editor for Lawtel Database (1989 to date); Associate of Chartered Institute of Arbitrators; member Immigration Law Practitioners' Association; Legal Education and Training Group.

Biography: lives Epsom; born 16.08.1951; married to Vanapa with 2 children. Educated at King Edward VI Grammar School, Morpeth; Newcastle University (1973 LLB hons); Cert D'Etudes Superieures du Federalisme (AOSTA) (1973); French and Thai languages.

Leisure: contact karate; hill walking; playing Northumbrian small pipes.

GREIG Lindsey

editor THE LAWYER 103-109 Wardour Street, London W1.

Biography: lives London; born 17.11.1951; married to Hannah with 2 daughters. Educated at Ottershaw School; Warwick University (1973 BA).

GRIESBACH Alan Keith

senior partner CARTWRIGHT & LEWIS 53-55 High Street, Harborne, Birmingham, West Midlands B17 9NU.

Career: articled Wallace Robinson & Morgan (1950-1955); admitted (1956); RAF Legal Services London and Middle East (Cyprus) (1956-1958); assistant solicitor Cartwright & Lewis (1958); became partner (1958); became senior partner (1983).

Activities: Commissioner for Oaths; Deputy Registrar (1978 to date); member County Court Rules Committee (1982-1986); former member Law Society's working parties on practice and procedure and small claims; former member Law Society's Standing Committee on Remuneration in Contentious Costs; former member Birmingham Law Council; former chairman No 6 Area Legal Aid Committee; former captain Robin Hood

Golf Club; member Kings Norton RFC (former captain, chairman and president).

Biography: lives Solihull; born 26.05.1931; married to Joyce with 2 sons. Educated at Bablake School, Coventry (1941-1948).

Leisure: sport (in particular rugby and golf).

GRIEVE Alan

consultant, company director and former senior partner TAYLOR JOYNSON GARRETT 180 Fleet Street, London EC4A 2NT.

Career: assistant solicitor Slaughter and May (1953-1955); personal assistant to the chairman of the Prestige Group Ltd and legal officer (1955-1958); became partner Taylor & Humbert (1958); became senior partner (1979); became senior partner Taylor Garrett (1982-1988); consultant Taylor Joynson Garrett (1989).

Activities: principal directorships: Baggeridge Brick plc; Medical Insurance Agency Limited; Reliance Resources Limited; Stenham plc; trustee the Jerwood Foundation; trustee Oakham School; trustee the British Racing School (Newmarket); board member Educational Assets Board; chairman Awards Panel for the Courage Award to Racehorse Owners; member Finance Committee Royal College of Physicians; member Boodles; Aula; Asparagus.

Biography: lives Berkshire and London NW1; born 22.01.1928; married to Karen with 3 sons and 2 daughters. Educated at Northcliffe House; Aldenham; Trinity Hall Cambridge (1948 MA hons) (1951 LLM).

Leisure: skiing; boating; shooting; theatre; books.

GRIEVES John K

senior partner FRESHFIELDS Whitefriars, 65 Fleet Street, London EC4Y 1HS.

Career: admitted (1961); assistant solicitor Freshfields (1963-1964); became partner (1964-1979); became managing partner (1979-1985).

Activities: member of: Athenaeum; Roehampton Club.

Biography: lives London SW15; born 07.11.1935; married to Ann with 2 children. Educated at King's School, Worcester; Oxford University (1958 MA); Harvard Business School (1979 Advanced Management Program).

Leisure: the Arts; running.

G

GRIFFITHS Griffin

senior partner JEFFREYS & POWELL
4 Lion Street, Brecon, Powys LD3 7AU.

Career: admitted (1965); assistant solicitor
Jeffreys & Powell (1965-1967); became
partner (1967).

Biography: lives Erwood; born 10.11.1940;
single. Educated at Builth Wells Grammar
School; University College of Wales,
Aberystwyth (1962-1965) LLB.

Leisure: farming.

GRIFFITHS John

Queen's Counsel 1 Brick Court, Temple,
London EC4.

Career: called to the Bar Middle Temple
(1956); QC (1972); Attorney General of
Hong Kong (1979-1983); Recorder of
Crown Court (1972).

Activities: chairman Hong Kong Law
Reform Commission (1979-1983) (member
Legislature and Executive Council);
treasurer of Bar Council (1988); council
member Council of Legal Education (1983-
1988); member of Court Hong Kong
University (1983-1988); member Executive
Committee of Commercial Bar Association
(1970s & 1989); member Hong Kong Bar;
member of: Flyfishers Club; Hong Kong
Club.

Biography: lives London; born 16.01.1931;
married to Jessamy with 3 daughters.
Educated at St Peter's School, York;
Foundation Scholar; Emmanuel College
Cambridge (1955 BA) (1959 MA); Senior
Exhibitioner; Harmsworth Scholar.

Leisure: fishing; gardening; collecting first
editions.

GRIFFITHS Mark

senior partner HENRIQUES GRIFFITHS &
CO The Old Vicarage, 18 Portland Square,
Bristol BS2 8SJ.

Career: articled PRQ Henriques (1972-
1974); admitted (1977); became partner
Henriques Griffiths & Co (1977); became
senior partner (1980).

Activities: former secretary and committee
member of Rolls Royce Enthusiasts' Club
in the South West.

Biography: lives Bristol; born 31.10.1950;
single. Educated St Chad's Cathedral
School (1960-1964); Worksop College (1964-
1969); Bristol Polytechnic (1972 LLB).

GRIFFITHS Richard

managing partner FARRER & CO
66 Lincoln's Inn Fields, London
WC2A 3LH.

Career: articled Farrer & Co; admitted
(1963); partner (1966); became managing
partner (1986).

Activities: founder member General
Committee of the Solicitors Family Law
Association; member Oxford & Cambridge
Universities Club.

Biography: lives London and Orford; born
30.10.1936; married to Sheila with 2
daughters. Educated at Denstone College;
Trinity College Cambridge.

Leisure: golf; walking; theatre.

GRIFFITHS Richard

head of Chambers 30 Spilman Street,
Carmarthen, Dyfed SA31 1LQ.

Career: pupillage 1 Dr Johnston's
Buildings; 30 Park Place, Cardiff (1984-
1985); opened new Chambers in
Carmarthen (1985).

Activities: Master Pembrokeshire &
Carmarthenshire Minkhounds; chairman
Carmarthenshire Foxhounds.

Biography: lives Carmarthen and Whitland;
born 11.05.1958; single. Educated at
Monkton Combe School; Fishguard
County Secondary; Bristol Polytechnic
(1982); Inns of Court School of Law (1982-
1983).

Leisure: field sports.

GRIGGS Patrick

senior partner INCE & CO Knollys House,
11 Byward Street, London EC3R 5EW.

Career: articled Ince & Co (1958-1963);
admitted (1963); assistant solicitor (1963-
1966); partner (1966); became senior
partner (1989).

Activities: member Executive Committee
and CMI Sub-committee - Damages in
Collision Cases of British Maritime Law
Association; supporting member London
Maritime Arbitration Association;
subscribing member of Average Adjusters'
Association; solicitor member of
Commercial Court Committee; solicitor
member of Lloyds Insurance Brokers'
Committee; member of: Gresham Club;
City Law Club.

Biography: lives Ongar; born 09.08.1939;
married with 3 sons. Educated at The Old
Ride Preparatory School; Stowe School;
Tours University, France; College of Law
Lancaster Gate; joint author 'Limitation of

Liability for Maritime Claims' (1987).

Leisure: tennis; hockey; shooting; walking;
gardening.

GROARKE Roger Joseph

senior partner SLATER HEELIS
1 Tatton Road, Sale, Greater Manchester
M33 1XR and 71 Princess Street,
Manchester 2.

Career: articled Slater Heelis (1955-1958);
admitted (1958); National Service as
captain in RAOC Adjutant 17 Bn (1958-
1960); assistant solicitor Slater Heelis (1961-
1962); became partner (1962).

Activities: Commissioner for Oaths;
member Trafford Family Practitioner
Committee; member Manchester Law
Society; member Trafford Solicitors
Association and Law Society; vice-
chairman governors Mount St Mary's
College; member of: Wilmslow Golf Club;
Wilmslow Rugby FC .

Biography: lives Bramhall; born 22.03.1933;
married to Bernadette with 5 children.
Educated at Mount St Mary's College,
Sprinkhill; Manchester University (1955
LLB hons); College of Law Lancaster Gate
(1958 hons).

Leisure: squash; walking; opera; theatre.

GROSE-HODGE Peter

partner specialising matrimonial law
DRUCES & ATTLEE Salisbury House,
London Wall, London EC2M 5PS.

Career: articled in London (1947-1952);
admitted (1952); National Service pilot
officer RAF; partner Speechly Bircham
(1962-1990); became partner Druces &
Attlee (1990).

Activities: former member Committee
Holborn Law Society (7 years); former
secretary Solicitors Family Law
Association (5 years); President
International Academy of Matrimonial
Lawyers; member Law Society Standing
Committee on Family Law; several radio
and television broadcasts on law and
associated topics; member of: Lasham
Gliding Club; Ferrari Owners' Club.

Biography: lives Bramley; born 18.12.1929;
married to Jane with 2 children. Educated
at Bedford School; The Diocesan College,
Rondebosch, Cape Town; numerous items
in The Solicitors Gazette; Family Law; etc.

Leisure: motor racing; motoring; gliding.

GROSSE Lorna

consultant LEE BOLTON & LEE
1 The Sanctuary, Westminster, London
SW1P 3JT.

Career: articled Evan Davies & Co (1978-
1980); admitted (1980); assistant solicitor in
merger with Lee Bolton & Lee (1980-1985);
became first female partner in 129 years
(1985); became first female consultant in
practice (1990).

Activities: member Westminster Law
Society; member Solicitors Family Law
Association; member St Stephen's
Constitutional Club.

Biography: lives London SE10; born
24.08.1955; married to Paul with 1 child.
Educated at Prendergast Grammar School;
University College Buckland (LLB hons).

Leisure: music; singing in local choir;
learning flute; fencing; jogging; squash;
sailing; gardening.

GROSZ Stephen

partner BINDMAN & PARTNERS 1 Euston
Road, King's Cross, London NW1 2SA.

Career: Stagiaire European Commission of
Human Rights, Strasbourg (1975); articled
Bindman & Partners (1976-1978); admitted
(1978); assistant solicitor (1978-1981);
became partner (1981).

Activities: member Executive Committee of
Interights; sometime member Justice
Committee on administration of the
Courts; sometime member Management
Committee of Victims' Helpline.

Biography: lives London N1; born
14.04.1953; married to Judith. Educated at
William Ellis School; Clare College
Cambridge (1974 BA) (1975 MA); Institut
d'Etudes Europeennes (Universite Libre de
Bruxelles) (1976); contributor to 'Public
Interest Law' (1987); joint author of
revision of Atkin's Court Forms title on
Personal Rights.

Leisure: cycling; sailing; swimming; wine-
tasting and collecting; eating.

GROUND Alan

partner LINKLATERS & PAINES
Barrington House, 59-67 Gresham Street,
London EC2V 7JA.

Career: articled Pollard & Co (1958-1962);
admitted (1962); assistant solicitor
Linklaters & Paines (1962-1969); became
partner (1969); group leader Linklaters &
Paines anti-trust practice.

Activities: member Law Society
International Committee and International
Human Rights Working Party; chairman

Dunsfold branch south west Surrey
Conservation Association; member of:
RAC; Royal Overseas League.

Biography: lives Dunsfold; born 05.04.1935;
married to Sarah with 3 sons and 1
daughter. Educated at Beckenham
Grammar School (1946-1954); Jesus College
Cambridge (1958 MA LLB) Exhibitioner.

Leisure: tennis; music; reading.

GROVES Peter

partner and head of intellectual property
EEC MANCHES AND CO
Aldwych House, 71-91 Aldwych, London
WC2B 4RP.

Career: articled Cohen Jackson Scott &
Simon (now Jacksons) (1978-1980);
admitted (1980); assistant legal adviser to
Society of Motor Manufacturers and
Traders (1980-1984 & 1985-1986); head of
commercial law CBI (1984-1985); formed
information technology team Speechly
Bircham (1986-1987); head of intellectual
property and EEC Manches and Co (1987);
became partner (1990).

Activities: member Solicitors European
Group Committee (1985 to date); member
Law Society International Promotion WP
on Central and Eastern Europe; member
Competition Law Association Committee;
Conservative Parliamentary candidate
South Shields (1983); member North Beds
Borough Council (1986-1990); Robert
Shumann Silver Medal for work for
European unity (1984).

Biography: lives Harwell, Oxon; born
26.08.1956; married to Hilary with 2
daughters. Educated at Barnard Castle
School; Warwick University (1977 LLB);
College of Law Guildford; City of London
Polytechnic (part-time 1982 MA); part-time
research student writing MPhil/Phd thesis
on law and competition in the motor
industry (1982 to date); numerous articles
in Business Law Review (reviews editor
and member editorial board); member
editorial advisory board European
Business Law Review; associate editor of
Intellectual Property in Business; co-
founder of 'Motor Law' bi-monthly legal
newsletter for motor industry managers;
articles also published in European
Competition Law Review; NLJ; Road Law;
The Lawyer; joint author of Institute of the
Motor Industry's student guide to motor
industry law; book on Copyright, Designs
and Patents Act 1988 (due out late 1990);
external lecturer, College of Law.

Leisure: politics; motor cars; travelling;
collecting Biggles books and Bob Dylan
records.

GRUNDY Milton

barrister and head of revenue chambers
Gray's Inn Chambers, Gray's Inn, London
WC1R 5JA.

Career: called to the Bar Inner Temple
(1954); practised in Chambers of Sir John
Foster (1955-1962); established own
Chambers with Francis Brennan (1962).

Activities: draftsman Trust Law of the
Cayman Islands (1967); president
International Tax Planning Association
(1975 to date); chairman International
Management Trust; founder and chairman
Gemini Trust for the Arts (1959-1966);
charter member Peggy Guggenheim
Collection (1980-1989); founder and
chairman The Warwick Arts Trust (1979 to
date); trustee National Museums and
Galleries of Merseyside (1986 to date).

Biography: lives London SW1 and
Oxfordshire; born 13.06.1926; single.
Educated at Cowley School, St Helens;
Sedbergh School; Caius College Cambridge
(1951 BA) (1956 MA); author of 'Venice'
(1971); 'Tax and the Family Company'
(1956); 'Tax Havens' (1968); 'The World of
International Tax Planning' (1984).

GUEST Professor Anthony Gordon

Queen's Counsel 4 Raymond Buildings,
Gray's Inn, London WC1.

Career: army and TA (Lt RA) (1948-1950);
lecturer University College (1954-1955);
Fellow and Praelector in Jurisprudence
(1955-1965); Dean (1963-1964); called to the
Bar Gray's Inn (1956); Bencher (1978);
Reader in common law to Council of Legal
Education Inns of Court (1967-1980);
professor of English law London
University (1966 to date); QC (1987).

Activities: Fellow King's College (1982);
UK delegate to UN Commission on
International Trade Law New York,
Geneva and Vienna (1964-1988); to UN
Conference on Limitation of Actions
(1974); CBE (1988); member Lord
Chancellor's Law Reform Committee
(1963-1984); member governing body of
Rugby School (1968-1988); member
Advisory Committee on Establishment of
Law Faculty in Hong Kong University
(1965); member Garrick Club.

Biography: lives London SW7; born
08.02.1930; single. Educated at Colston's
School, Bristol; St John's College Oxford
(1954 MA hons); FCIArb; book review
editor Law Quarterly Review (1980-1984);
editor Arbitration International (1985 to
date); editor Anson's Principles of the Law
of Contract (21st-26th eds 1959-1984);

G

general editor Chitty on Contracts (23rd-26th eds 1968-1989); general editor Benjamin's Sale of Goods (1st-3rd eds 1974-1986); The Law of Hire Purchase (1966); joint editor Encyclopaedia of Consumer Credit (1975); joint editor Introduction to the Law of Credit and Security (1978).

GUILD Ivor

senior partner SHEPHERD & WEDDERBURN WS 16 Charlotte Square, Edinburgh EH2 4YS.

Career: admitted Writer to the Signet; became partner Shepherd & Wedderburn WS (1950).

Activities: member of the Council on Tribunals; Immigration Appeal Adjudicator; member of the Interception of Communications Tribunal; clerk to the Episcopal Synod of the Scottish Episcopal Church; Bailie of Holyrood House; director of 5 investment trust companies; governor Donaldson's Hospital for the Deaf; trustee Edinburgh University; convenor Investment Committee National Trust for Scotland; former chairman National Museum of Antiquities of Scotland; member of: New Club; Honourable Company of Edinburgh Golfers.

Biography: lives Edinburgh; born 02.04.1924; single. Educated at Cargilfield; Rugby; New College Oxford (1946 MA); Edinburgh University (1948 LLB).

Leisure: golf; genealogy.

GULBENKIAN Paul

senior partner ISADORE GOLDMAN 125 High Holborn, London WC1V 6QF and GULBENKIAN MARSHALL & CAMPBELL 181 Kensington High Street, London W8 6SH.

Career: articled Lewis & Lewis (1961-1964); admitted (1964); assistant solicitor Penningtons & Lewis & Lewis (1964-1966); assistant solicitor Isadore Goldman & Son (1966-1970); became partner (1970-1989); became senior partner Isadore Goldman and Gulbenkian Marshall & Campbell (1989 to date).

Activities: chairman Camden Citizens Advice Bureau Service Management Committee (1978-1983); president Holborn Law Society (1984-1985); chairman Monitoring of Articles Panel of the Law Society (1986-1989); hon auditor of the Law Society (1987-1989); hon auditor of the Holborn Law Society (1988 to date); part-time immigration adjudicator (1989 to date); former member of: the Family Law Committee; the Immigration Law

Committee and the Duty Solicitor Committee; founder member of the Principal Registry Committee that set up the Conciliation Service at the Principal Registry also of the Solicitors Family Law Association, the Immigration Law Practitioners' Association and the European Immigration Law Group; trustee of a number of charitable trusts including associate trust of the Calouste Gulbenkian Foundation (The St Sarkis Charity Trust) and a number of trusts for the benefit of the Armenian community; hon treasurer of Aid Armenia; administrator of two Armenian educational charities; hon treasurer of the Church of St Sarkis and of the Apcar Trust.

Biography: lives Weybridge; born 23.03.1940; separated with 2 daughters. Educated at King's College School, Wimbledon (1953-1958); The London School of Economics (1961 LLB); articles in the Law Society's Gazette on US immigration; conciliation in divorce; specialised referral lists.

Leisure: music (one of the organisers of Music Armenia 1978); playing tennis and squash; walking.

GUMERSALL Arthur Geoffrey Stewart

senior partner (1960-1990) COTTON GUMERSALL & PALMER then senior consultant to GUMERSALL & PALMER 16 Waterloo Road, Epsom, Surrey KT19 8AZ.

Career: RAF Volunteer Reserve (1937-1939); articled Theodore Bell Cotton & Co (1938-1943); admitted (1944); assistant clerk to the Justices at Epsom; assistant clerk to the Income Tax Commissioners Copthorne Division; has now completed over 52 years continuous service with the firm and its predecessors.

Activities: Commissioner for Oaths (1950); Notary Public (1959); member Law Society London; member (past committee member and bulletin editor) mid Surrey Law Society; member Society of Provincial Notaries Public; life governor Imperial Cancer Research Fund; life member Stewart Society of Edinburgh; Liveryman of the Worshipful Company of Arbitrators; Freeman of the City of London; Horton Hospital Epsom (serving Paddington General Hospital): member Management Committee (1963); chairman Establishment Committee (1963); vice-chairman hospital (1972); chairman Finance and General Purposes Committee (1972); founder member Surrey Area Health Authority

(resigned 1975); Fellow of the Chartered Institute of Arbitrators 1973); nominee and chairman of tribunals Whitely Council; legal adviser and member of committee of League of Friends of Horton Hospital; hon auditor League of Friends of Epsom and Ewell Cottage Hospital; member Epsom and Ewell Ratepayers' Association; past chairman of College Ward; past secretary of the parent body for the whole of Epsom; past member Surrey Archives Committee; member and past president Rotary Club of Epsom; founder chairman and secretary Rotary Club of Epsom charity fund trustees; past trustee Epsom Parochial Charities; governor and solicitor to Epsom College (1950 to date); hon legal adviser Epsom and Ewell Cruse Club; past president Hakiro Judo Club; chairman Helen Gordon Crook Trust (Eastbourne Lifeboat Christmas dinner); capital gains tax and capital transfer tax consultant; property development and management; court of protection practice and management; history of development of land law including lecturing thereon; hon tutor to the Forces for Solicitors professional examinations; direct descendant of Stewart of Appin.

Biography: lives Epsom; born 01.07.1920; widowed. Educated at Shrewsbury House School, Surbiton; Epsom College (First Violin School Orchestra); College of Law; Prizeman Trust Accounts and Bookkeeping (99 percent).

Leisure: stamp collecting; voluntary service to the aged; music; opera.

GURLAND Robert

senior partner ROBERT GURLAND & ASSOCIATES 5 Deanery Street, London W1Y 5LH.

Career: admitted New York; the Southern and Eastern Federal District Courts of New York, US Tax Court and US Supreme Court; partner Nierenberg Zeif & Weinstein (1967-1970); partner Crotti and Gurland (1974-1982); co-founded Satterlee Burke & Gurland (1987); founded own practice (1990).

Activities: chairman Tax Equity for Americans Abroad; participant in organisation of seminars on tax, arbitration and contracts in developing countries in US, England and Belgium; member New York State and American Bar Associations (member International Tax and other committees); member Solicitors Law Society; member American Chamber of Commerce in London; member Institute of Directors; member American Tax Institute;

member Woolnoth Society; member of: Hurlingham Club; Itchenor Sailing Club.

Biography: lives London. Educated New York University School of Law (1956 JD); author of: 'Taxation Without Representation' (1972); 'The Common Market: A Common Sense Guide for Americans' (1974); 'Banking in Britain' (1976); 'Banking in Germany' (1976); 'Britain Banking Capital of the World' (1981); contributing editor 'International Tax Report' (1973-1976); various articles on tax and other subjects.

Leisure: tennis.

GUTHRIE Robin

Chief Charity Commissioner for England and Wales THE CHARITY COMMISSION St Albans House, 57-60 Haymarket, London SW1Y 4QX.

Career: Head of Cambridge House (1962-1969); teacher ILEA (1964-1966); social development officer Peterborough Development Corporation (1969-1976); Office of the Chief Scientist and Social Work Service Department of Health & Social Security (1976-1979); director Joseph Rowntree Memorial Trust (1979-1988).

Activities: member Arts Council of Great Britain (1979-1981 and 1986-1988); chairman Yorkshire Arts Association (1984-1988); chairman Council of Regional Arts Associations (1985-1988); member of United Oxford & Cambridge University Club.

Biography: lives London WC1 and York; born 27.06.1937; married to Sally with 2 sons and 1 daughter. Educated at Clifton College; Trinity College Cambridge (1961 BA); (1966 MA); Liverpool University (1962); London School of Economics (1968 MSC).

Leisure: music; mountaineering.

GUY Diana

partner (corporate department), head of EEC Group and responsible for firm's Brussels office THEODORE GODDARD 150 Aldersgate Street, London EC1A 4EJ.

Career: articled Theodore Goddard (1966-1968); admitted (1968); assistant solicitor property department (1968-1971); assistant solicitor commercial department (1971); became partner (1973).

Activities: chairman Solicitors European Group (1985); chairman Law Society's 1992 Working Party (1988 to date); member Solicitors European Group, Union Des Avocats Europeens.

Biography: lives Richmond; born 27.03.1943; married to Robert with 2 children. Educated at Queen Anne's School, Caversham; Lady Margaret Hall Oxford (1965 BA hons); author of 'The EEC and Intellectual Property' (1981); articles in European Law Review; European Intellectual Property Review; International & Comparative Law Quarterly.

Leisure: reading; opera; family.

GUY John

former consultant VEALE WASBROUGH 17 Berkeley Square, Bristol BS8 1HD.

Career: Captain R Signals (India, Sumatra, Malaya) (1943-1947); ADC to HM Governor Malayan Union (1945-1946); articled Bayliss Rowe & Co (1950); admitted (1953); assistant solicitor Stanley Wasbrough (1953); became senior partner (1980-1985); consultant Stanley Wasbrough (later Veale Wasbrough) (1986); retired (May 1990).

Activities: member Solicitors Disciplinary Tribunal (1974 to date); president Bristol Rent Assessment Panel (1982 to date); chairman SW Region Mental Health Review Tribunal (1984 to date); president Association of SW Law Societies (1988-1989) (hon secretary 1960-1976); member Area Committee of Law Society (1960-1975); hon secretary Board of Legal Studies (Bristol University) (1960-1963); member Council Bristol Law Society (1969-1978); governor & council member Clifton College Bristol (1965 to date) (chairman finance committee 1979 to date); member of: Royal Western Yacht Club of England; Bristol & Clifton Golf Club; Thurlestone Golf Club.

Biography: lives Bristol; born 30.08.1925; married to Anne. Educated at King's College Choir School; Clifton College; King's College Cambridge (MA LLM) Choral Scholar.

Leisure: music; sailing; golf.

HACKING Chris

senior partner HACKING ASHTON JERVIS & CO Berkeley Court, Borough Road, Newcastle under Lyme, Staffordshire ST5 1TT.

Career: articled John Ekserdjian; admitted (1968); assistant legal adviser Geigy UK Ltd (1969); company secretary and solicitor to Ernest Scragg & Sons Ltd (1971); director

joint venture company with Oceaneering International Inc, Houston; founded practice with Bob Ashton (1978).

Activities: non executive director of: Reiter Scragg Ltd; Unikeller Great Britain Ltd; Fluka Chemicals Ltd; Baumann Springs & Pressings Ltd; solicitor to British Textile Machinery Association; former secretary to the North West Section of the Law Society Commerce & Industry Group; particular interest in developing close working arrangements with European lawyers.

Biography: lives Macclesfield and Tetbury; born 05.05.1945; married to Jo with 4 daughters. Educated at Bury Grammar School; College of Law Guildford; Manchester Polytechnic.

Leisure: motor cycling; aviation history.

HACKMAN Michael

senior partner LARCOMES 168 London Road, North End, Portsmouth, Hants PO2 9DN.

Career: articled Portsmouth (1958-1963); admitted (1963); became partner Larcomes (1963).

Activities: solicitor/advisor to: several sporting interests; local fishing industry; member of: Chichester Lawn Tennis and Squash Club; Law Society Yacht Club; Emsworth Slipper Sailing Club; Royal Navy and Royal Albert Yacht Club; Petersfield Rugby Club; Hampshire RFU.

Biography: lives Westbourne nr Emsworth; born 15.02.1936; married to Marilyn with 2 children. Educated at Lancing.

Leisure: sailing; squash; skiing; rugby; restoration of old buildings; gardening; keen interest in farming and the countryside.

HAGGER David

partner and head commercial department BRAY & BRAY 1 3 & 5 Welford Road, Leicester, LE2 7AN.

Career: partner Bray & Bray.

Activities: committee member Nuffield Hospital, Leicester; supporter and member Leicestershire County Cricket Club; supporter and member Leicester Football Club.

Biography: lives Leicester; born 31.01.1942; married to Patricia with 2 children. Educated at Humphrey Perkins Grammar School; University College London (LLB hons); College of Law Lancaster Gate.

H

HAGGER Robert

sole principal ROBERT HAGGER & CO
32 Church Road, Tunbridge Wells, Kent
TN1 1JP.

Career: articled Brandon & Nicholson
(1960-1966); admitted (1966); assistant
solicitor Wilde Sapte & Co (1966-1967);
became partner Hamlins Grammer &
Hamlin (1967-1969); became partner Buss
Stone & Co (1969-1979); managing partner
(1979-1988); founded own practice (1988).

Activities: councillor Chigwell Urban
District (1967-1969); designed and
marketed the 'Priory Software'
computerised conveyancing package to
run on IBM compatible equipment (1985);
president Tunbridge Wells and District
Law Society (1988).

Biography: lives Tunbridge Wells; born
27.03.1942; married to Margaret with 2
children. Educated at Chigwell School;
author of articles of a political nature as to
reform of employment, criminal and
housing law.

Leisure: music; politics; cricket; football;
theatre; opera.

HAGGETT David

senior partner EVERSHED WELLS &
HIND 10 Newhall Street, Birmingham
B3 3LX.

Career: assistant solicitor Wragge & Co
(1962-1966); assistant solicitor Roythorne &
Co (1966-1967); assistant solicitor Evershed
& Tomkinson (1967-1969); became partner
(1969-1984); deputy senior partner (1984-
1989); senior partner Evershed Wells &
Hind (1989).

Activities: referred to as 'the King of the
Management Buyout' in July 1989 issue of
the USM Review; member Warwickshire
County Cricket Club; played hockey for
Staffordshire (1958); County schoolboys'
hockey coach .

Biography: lives Four Oaks, Sutton
Coldfield; born 28.03.1938; married to Janet
with 2 sons and 2 daughters. Educated at
Bromsgrove School (1951-1956); Trinity
Hall Cambridge (1962 MA LLM); Dr
Cooper's Law Studentship Trinity Hall
(1961); author of various articles mainly on
taxation matters and management
buyouts.

HALES Christopher

partner HOLMAN FENWICK & WILLAN
Marlow House, Lloyds Avenue, London
EC3N 3AL.

Career: served at sea with Alfred Halt &

Co (the Blue Funnel Line) as apprentice
(1949) to second officer (1958); master
mariner (1957); barrister Gray's Inn (1960);
articled Alsop Stevens & Co (1961-1964);
admitted solicitor (1964); assistant solicitor
Holman Fenwick & Willan (1965-1968);
became partner (1968).

Activities: Deputy District Registrar of
High Court and Deputy Registrar County
Court (1989); Liveryman of Hon Company
of Master Mariners; Freeman of City of
London Solicitors' Company; Freeman of
City of London.

Biography: lives London SW1 and Elmdon,
Essex; born 26.08.1931; married to Barbara
with 2 sons and 4 daughters. Educated at
Wellingborough School (1945-1947); HMS
Worcester (1947-1949).

Leisure: concerts; theatre; following cricket;
history; reading; swimming; gardening.

HALL Christopher

partner CRIPPS HARRIES HALL
84 Calverley Road, Tunbridge Wells, Kent
TN1 2UP.

Career: articled Clifford Turner; admitted;
assistant solicitor; became partner Cripps
Harries Hall (1964).

Activities: served with Territorial Army
(TAVR) (1956-1968); president Tunbridge
Wells Tonbridge & District Law Society
(1987); Deputy Lt East Sussex (1986 to
date); chairman of boards of British
Equestrian Promotions Ltd and A Burslem
& Son Ltd; former chairman of Council
South of England Agricultural Society; past
master City Livery Company Worshipful
Company of Broderers; council member
British Horse Society; steward National
Hunt Ascot, Folkestone, Plumpton;
member Cavalry & Guards Club.

Biography: lives Tunbridge Wells; born
09.03.1936; married with 3 sons. Educated
at Temple Grove School (1944-1949); Rugby
School (1949-1954); Trinity College
Cambridge (1959 MA); contributions to
various equestrian publications.

Leisure: running farm (300 acres); field
sports; national hunt racing.

HALL David

partner CLYDE & CO
51 Eastcheap, London EC3M 1JP.

Career: articled Loxley Sanderson &
Morgan (1965-1968); admitted (1968);
assistant solicitor (1968-1970); assistant
solicitor Joelson & Co (1970-1971); assistant
solicitor Clyde & Co (1971-1974); became
partner (1974).

Biography: lives nr Guildford; born
10.12.1941; married. Educated at
Cheltenham College; Trinity College
Dublin (BA).

HALL Norman

consultant HALLS 8/16 Earl Street,
London EC2A 2AL.

Career: articled Lance E Hall (1935-1939);
admitted (1946); became partner (1946);
became senior partner (1958-1985); became
consultant (1985).

Activities: CBE (1976); Master City of
London Solicitors' company (1979); one of
Her Majesty's Commission of Lieutenancy
for the City of London; Common
Councilman Corporation of London (1952-
1981); Chief Commoner (1973); hon
Freeman Worshipful Society of
Apothecaries; Butchers' Company Clerk
(1948-1960) (Master 1977); Master
Innholders' Company (1965); Barbers'
Company Clerk (1970-1975); member
Guildhall Club.

Biography: lives Harrow; born 06.04.1917;
married to Maureen with 2 children.
Educated at Malvern College; London
University (1939 LLB).

HALLAM Ted

senior partner THATCHER & HALLAM
Island House, Midsomer Norton, near
Bath, Avon BA3 2HJ.

Career: articled FE Greathead & Co (1941-
1943 & 1947-1948); active service in bomber
command as pilot Royal Air Force (1943-
1946); Distinguished Flying Cross (1945);
admitted (1948); assistant solicitor AFB
Thatcher (1949-1953); became partner
Thatcher & Hallam (1953).

Activities: member and former president
Somerset Law Society; member RAF Club.

Biography: lives Kilmersdon near Bath;
born 28.07.1923; married to Barbara with 3
children. Educated at Bryntirion School,
Bridgend; Denstone College, Uttoxeter.

Leisure: numerous charities; gardening;
flying; travel.

HALLATT Diane

partner and manager of Sheffield branch
office OXLEY & COWARD 275 Glossop
Road, Sheffield S10 2HB.

Career: articled in local government (1975-
1980); admitted (1980); assistant solicitor
(1980-1986); assistant regional solicitor
Trent Regional Health Authority (1986-
1989); became partner Oxley & Coward
(1989).

Activities: lectures to Health Authorities on the law and the health service; Church treasurer; Sunday School teacher.

Biography: lives Sheffield; born 25.02.1956; single. Educated at Abbeydale Grammar School for Girls; Sheffield University (1977 LLB); College of Law Chester; article in Therapy Weekly on professional negligence (1989).

Leisure: choral singing; cooking; gardening; swimming.

HALLGARTEN Anthony

Queen's Counsel and head of chambers 3 Essex Court, Temple, London EC4Y 9AL.

Career: called to the Bar Middle Temple (1961); pupillage with A Lloyd; tenant 3 Essex Court (1962); QC (1978); Bencher Middle Temple (1987); Recorder (1990).

Activities: chairman Committee on Sea Waybills of British Maritime Law Association; chairman of Bar's Joint Regulations Committee; member of executive of Commercial Bar Association; chairman Management Committee of Camden Victim Support; patron of LAWS (Lawyers Working for Soviet Jewry); speaker on London Arbitration at International Bar Association, Moscow (1988); member of: Garrick Club; MCC.

Biography: lives London NW3; born 16.06.1937; married to Katherine with 3 daughters and 1 son. Educated at Merchant Taylors' School, Northwood; Downing College Cambridge (BA) Harris Law Scholar; Barstow Law Scholar; chapter on Shipping Agents in 'Shipowners', vol 13 of British Shipping Laws; articles on arbitration, insurance, etc.

Leisure: cycling; reading historical novels; cricket; learning French.

HALPERN Ann

director education & training ROWE & MAW 20 Black Friars Lane, London EC4V 6HD.

Career: called to the Bar Gray's Inn (1972); lecturer Ealing Technical College (1972-1977); senior lecturer Ealing College of HE (1977-1987); principal lecturer Council of Legal Education (1987-1989); Reader (1989-1990).

Activities: Legal Skills Research Group - IALS; coordinated development of the vocational course for Bar students; member Executive Committee Legal Education and Training Group.

Biography: lives London SW19; born 15.04.1950. Educated at Copthall County

Grammar School; Barnet College of FE; Queen Mary College London (1971 LLB) (1973 LLM); Inns of Court School of Law; Barrister of Gray's Inn (1972); various articles in Family Law Journal; Journal of Social Welfare Law and skills books.

HALSTED Nick

head of legal department REED INTERNATIONAL PLC 6 Chesterfield Gardens, London W1A 1EJ.

Career: articled Slaughter and May (1965-1968); admitted (1968); assistant solicitor (1968-1971); assistant attorney CPC Europe Ltd, Brussels (1971-1973); co secretary and legal adviser CPC (UK) Ltd (1973-1976); Reed International (1976); became head of legal dept (1983).

Biography: lives London NW5; born 24.10.1942; married to Clare with 3 children. Educated at Westminster School (1956-1961); Wadham College Oxford (1964 MA).

Leisure: fencing (president Amateur Fencing Association); tennis; theatre.

HALTON Nicholas

general counsel ESSO EUROPE-AFRICA SERVICES INC Esso House, Victoria Street, London SW1.

Career: articled Church Adams Tatham & Co; admitted (1966); assistant solicitor (1966-1968); Esso Group of Cos (1968); legal advisor Esso Chemical Ltd (1977-1979); legal advisor and company secretary Esso Petroleum Co Ltd (1979-1982); senior counsel Esso Europe Inc (1983-1986); general counsel Esso Europe-Africa Services Inc (1986).

Activities: executive trustee Petroleum & Mineral Law Education Trust; chairman Insolvency Practitioner Tribunal; treasurer and vice-president of section on energy and natural resources law of International Bar Association (former council member); member Roehampton Club.

Biography: lives London; born 26.08.1940; divorced with 1 child. Educated at Marlborough College; Emmanuel College Cambridge.

Leisure: music; literature; walking/climbing.

HALTON Nicholas Roger

partner HILL DICKINSON DAVIS CAMPBELL Pearl Assurance House, Derby Square, Liverpool L2 9XL.

Career: articled Roger Hill; admitted

(1967); assistant solicitor (1967-1971); became partner (1971).

Activities: member of: Aughton Lawn Tennis Club; Altcar Rifle Club; Ormskirk Golf Club; Ormskirk Cricket Club; Salcombe Yacht Club.

Biography: lives Aughton nr Ormskirk; born 30.09.1944; married to Kathleen with 1 child. Educated at Downside School, Somerset.

Leisure: tennis; walking; golf; classical music; sailing; theatre.

HAMILTON Adrian

Queen's Counsel and head of chambers 7 King's Bench Walk, Temple, London EC4Y 7DS.

Career: Lt RNVR (Atlantic; Mediterranean; English Channel) (1942-1946); called to the Bar Lincoln's Inn (1949); member Oxford Circuit; ad eundem member Middle Temple and Inner Temple; QC (1973); Recorder of the Crown Court (1974); Bencher Lincoln's Inn (1979).

Activities: deputy High Court Judge; chairman Mental Health Review Tribunals (1986); inspector Peek Foods Ltd (1977); member Senate of Inns of Court and the Bar (1976-1982) (treasurer 1979-1982); member Council of Legal Education (1977-1987); commercial arbitrator; supporting member of the London Maritime Arbitrators' Association; member of: Garrick Club; Roehampton Club; Piltdown Golf Club; Bar Yacht Club.

Biography: lives London; born 11.03.1923; married to Jill with 2 daughters. Educated at Highgate School; Balliol College Oxford (1948 MA hons); Jenkyns Law Prize; Paton Memorial Student; Cassel Scholar Lincoln's Inn.

Leisure: golf; sailing; walking; family.

HAMILTON David

partner CARTWRIGHTS Marsh House, Marsh Street, Bristol BS99 7BB.

Career: Instructor officer in Gunnery School, Royal Navy, Devonport (1956-1959); production and General Manager aluminium and corrugated board industry (1959-1973); articled Tuckett Williams & Kew; admitted (1976); assistant solicitor Cartwrights (1976-1981); became salaried partner (1981); became equity partner (1985); specialist subjects: betting, gaming and liquor licensing; club registration; public entertainment licensing; food safety; trade descriptions and weights and measures legislation and particularly advocacy relating to these subjects in the Magistrates' Court.

Activities: member Royal Naval Sailing Association.

Biography: lives Dartmouth and Bristol; born 13.03.1934; married to Josephine with 3 children. Educated at St Albans County Grammar School; Fitzwilliam House Cambridge (1953-1956) Qualification MA (Natural Sciences).

HAMILTON Douglas

senior partner NORTON ROSE Kempson House, Camomile Street, London EC3N 7AN.

Career: articled Edridges & Drummonds (1948-1953); admitted (1953); National Service (1953-1955); assistant solicitor Botterell & Roche (1955-1959); amalgamated with Norton Rose (1960); became executive partner Norton Rose (1976-1982); became senior partner (1982).

Activities: hon treasurer British Maritime Charitable Foundation; treasurer British Polish Legal Association; member City Law Club.

Biography: lives East Sussex; born 20.04.1931; married to Judith with 3 sons. Educated at John Fisher School, Purley; London (1955 LLB).

Leisure: tennis; golf; travelling.

HAMILTON Eben

Queen's Counsel 1 New Square, Lincoln's Inn, London WC2.

Career: called to the Bar Inner Temple (1962); QC (1981); Bencher Inner Temple (1985); FRSA (1988); specialises corporate and insolvency law.

Activities: member Garrick Club.

Biography: lives London W8; born 12.06.1937; married to Themy. Educated at Winchester College; Trinity College Cambridge (MA).

Leisure: travel.

HAMILTON Graeme

Queen's Counsel 2 Crown Office Row, Temple, London EC4Y 7HJ.

Career: called to the Bar Gray's Inn (1959); Recorder of the Crown Court (1974); QC (1978); Bencher Gray's Inn (1987).

Activities: member Criminal Injuries Compensation Board (1987 to date); member of: Cavalry & Guards Club; Royal Thames Yacht Club; RAC.

Biography: born 01.06.1934. Educated at

Eton; Magdalene College Cambridge (MA).

Leisure: sailing; shooting; gardening.

HAMILTON Nigel

Queen's Counsel 1 Essex Court, Temple, London EC4
071-936-3030 (FAX 071-583-1606).

Career: National Service 2nd Lt Royal Engineers; called to the Bar (1965); QC (1981); schoolmaster.

Activities: member Bar Council; member Avon County Council; member Flyfishers' Club.

Biography: lives London WC1 and Bristol; born 13.01.1938; married to Leone with 2 children. Educated at St Edward's School, Oxford; Queen's College Cambridge (1961 MA).

Leisure: fishing.

HAMILTON Sophie

partner property department FRERE CHOLMELEY 28 Lincoln's Inn Fields, London WC2A 3HH.

Career: articled Frere Cholmeley; admitted (1979); assistant solicitor (1979-1985); partner (1985); recruitment partner (1985-1990); became training partner (1990).

Biography: educated at St Mary's School, Calne; Marlborough College; Clare College Cambridge.

HAMLETT Peter

partner FINN GLEDHILL & CO
1-4 Harrison Road, Halifax, West Yorkshire HX1 2AG.

Career: articled Godfrey Rhodes & Evans (now Finn Gledhill & Co); admitted (1967); became partner (1967).

Activities: Evangelical Christian; member Salvation Army; president Halifax chapter of Full Gospel Businessmen's Fellowship International; partner Christian bookshop business in Halifax.

Biography: lives Halifax; born 12.05.1943; married to Beryl with 1 daughter. Educated at Bradford Grammar School; Leeds University (1964 LLB hons).

Leisure: music (especially brass bands); art; sport (spectator).

HAMLYN Peter

partner ROOKS RIDER 8 New Square, Lincoln's Inn, London WC2A 3QJ.

Career: articled Jaques & Co (1958-1961);

admitted (1961); assistant solicitor (1961-1963); assistant solicitor Rooks & Co (now Rooks Rider) (1963-1965); became partner (1965).

Activities: member of: Royal Overseas League; MCC; Hurlingham Club.

Biography: lives London; born 06.01.1935; married to Philippa with 1 son and 3 daughters. Educated at St Edward's School Oxford; Trinity College Cambridge (MA LLB).

HAMMETT Stephen

partner PRINCE EVANS
77 Uxbridge Road, Ealing, London W5 5ST.

Career: admitted (1971); assistant solicitor; became partner J Hostettler & Co (now Hostettler & Hammett) (1972-1987); became partner Prince Evans (1987).

Activities: member Central & South Middlesex Law Society Committee (1974 to date); president (1982-1983); secretary (1983-1986); council member Law Society (1986 to date); member Courts & Legal Services Commitee (1988-1989); chairman Standards & Guidance Committee (1990-1991) (vice-chairman (1989-1990).

Biography: lives London W4; born 06.04.1947; married to Sarah with 2 children. Educated at Ealing Grammar School; author of 'Law Society's Office Manual' (1989).

Leisure: opera; sailing; reading; theatre; family activities; amateur dramatics.

HANCOCK Roger

partner CLARKE WILLMOTT & CLARKE 6 Hammet Street, Taunton, Somerset TA1 1RG.

Career: articled Clarke Willmott & Clarke (1967-1969); admitted (1969); assistant solicitor (1969-1972); became partner (1972).

Activities: member Somerset Law Society (former Committee member); member National Committee of Aim Charter Users' Association; member Society for Computers and Law; member of: Taunton Rotary Club; Taunton Deane Deaf Association.

Biography: lives Taunton; born 10.02.1945; married to Denise with 2 daughters. Educated at Clifton College, Bristol; Exeter University (1966 LLB).

Leisure: inland waterways; swimming; walking; computers; gardening; travel; book collecting; hearing impairment.

HAND John

Queen's Counsel and head of Crown Square Chambers, 1 Dean's Court, Manchester M3 3HA and 15 Old Square, Lincoln's Inn, London.

Career: called to the Bar (1972); pupillage with JA Price QC; QC (1988); Assistant Recorder.

Biography: lives Manchester and London NW8; born 16.06.1947. Educated at Huddersfield New College; Nottingham University.

Leisure: sailing.

HAND Sean

head of pensions department EDGE & ELLISON Rutland House, 148 Edmund Street, Birmingham B3 2JR.

Career: called to the Bar Middle Temple (1981); inhouse legal adviser/company secretary: life industry Transamerica Corporation; Lloyd's broking (reinsurance) Sedgwick Group plc; merchant banking (Morgan Grenfell Group plc; became head of pensions department Edge & Ellison (1989).

Activities: member Association of Pension Lawyers (assisted in setting up regional branch of APL, West Midlands); member Guild of Pastoral Psychology; occasional lecturer to Royal College of Nursing.

Biography: lives Kings Norton; born 03.09.1955; single. Educated at Salvatorian College, Harrow; Sussex University; Leicester University (1980 LLB).

Leisure: opera; theatre; sub-aqua; marine archaeology.

HANDLER Tom

partner commercial litigation, environmental law, Hungarian affairs BAKER & MCKENZIE Aldwych House, Aldwych, London WC2B 4JP.

Career: admitted NSW, Australia (1962); admitted England (1966); assistant solicitor Baker & McKenzie (1967-1973); became partner (1973).

Activities: member Editorial Board Environmental Brief; member International Litigators' Forum; member London Solicitors Litigation Association; member UK Environmental Law Association; member British Hungarian Society; lectured on legal topics in England, France, Hungary, USA; Neighbourhood Watch Co-ordinator.

Biography: lives London N6; born 25.05.1938; married to Adrienne with 2

children. Educated at Fort Street Boys' High School, Sydney; Sydney University (1958 BA) (1962 LIB).

Leisure: languages (Hungarian, French, German); music; reading; writing; collecting; gardening; nature; travel, photography; tennis; rambling; sailing; cross-country skiing.

HANSON Brian

registrar and legal adviser to the General Synod of the Church of England Church House, Great Smith Street, London SW1V 2AR.

Career: articled Wilson Houlder & Co (1957-1962); admitted (1963); assistant solicitor (1963-1965); solicitor with the Church Commissioners for England (1965-1970); assistant legal adviser General Synod (1970-1975); solicitor to the General Synod (1975-1977); became legal adviser (1977); became registrar (1980).

Activities: admitted ecclesiastical notary (1980); joint principal registrar Province of Canterbury and Province of York (1980 to date); registrar Convocation of Canterbury (1982 to date); member General Synod's Legal Advisory Commission (1980 to date) (secretary 1970-1986); member Council Ecclesiastical Law Society (1987 to date); member Council St Luke's Hospital for the Clergy; Fellow of the Woodard Corporation; governor St Michael's School, Burton Park; Guardian of the Shrine of Our Lady of Walsingham; member House of Laity, Chichester Diocesan Synod; member Royal Commonwealth.

Biography: lives Bolney; born 23.01.1939; married with 2 sons and 3 daughters. Educated at Hounslow College; College of Law; editor of: 'The Canons of the Church of England' (2nd ed 1975) (4th ed 1986); 'The Opinions of the Legal Advisory Commission' (6th ed 1985).

Leisure: family; gardening; genealogy.

HANSON George Walker

consultant CLARKSONS & STEELE 25 Harrison Road, Halifax, W Yorks HX1 2AS.

Career: articled Clarkson & Thomas (1933-1938); admitted (1938); War Service (1939); commissioned in Royal Artillery (1940); served with Field Regiment in Western Desert, Sicily and NW Europe; Major.

Activities: TA (6 years); former chairman Yorkshire & Lancashire Milk & Dairies Tribunal; formerly deputy chairman Agricultural Land Tribunal; former

chairman DHSS Appeals Tribunal; member Freemasons' Lodge of Probity No 61.

Biography: lives Halifax; born 10.06.1916; married to Ruth Ashley with 2 children. Educated at Heath Grammar School, Halifax; part-time Leeds University (LLB).

Leisure: hill walking; model railways; eventing (spectator).

HARBOTTLE G Laurence

senior partner HARBOTTLE AND LEWIS Hanover House, 14 Hanover Square, London W1R 0BE.

Career: commissioned in the Royal Artillery (1942) later serving in Burma and India; captain and adjutant of the 9th Field Regiment Royal Artillery (1945-1947); articled Newcastle upon Tyne; admitted (1952); assistant solicitor (1952-1955); founded Harbottle and Lewis (1955).

Activities: first chairman various theatre companies including Prospect Productions Ltd; Royal Exchange Manchester; Cambridge Theatre Company; Theatre Centre; member Arts Council (1976-1978); chairman of a number of Arts Council Committees; president Theatrical Management Association (1979-1985); deputy chairman Theatres Trust and Theatres national Committee; chairman Institute of Contemporary Arts; chairman governors of the Central School of Speech and Drama; director City Literary Institute; member Justice Committee on Privacy (1970); member The Savile Club.

Biography: lives London SW10; born 11.04.1924; single. Educated at the Leys School, Cambridge; Emmanuel College Cambridge (MA).

Leisure: works of art; gardening.

HARDCASTLE Michael

senior partner WHITEHEAD MONCKTON 72 King Street, Maidstone, Kent ME14 1BL.

Career: articled Longmores (1956-1961); admitted (1961); assistant solicitor Monckton Son & Collis (1961-1965); became partner (1965); firm amalgamated to become Whitehead Monckton (1968).

Activities: Under Sheriff of Kent (1989 to date); Deputy Coroner for Maidstone (1981 to date); clerk to Maidstone Division of Commissioners of Taxes (1985 to date).

Biography: lives Cranbrook; born 04.05.1938; married with 2 children. Educated at Haileybury.

Leisure: fly fishing.

H

HARDING Geoffrey

partner WILDE SAPTE Queensbridge House, 60 Upper Thames Street, London EC4V 3BD.

Career: National Service with Royal Air Force; assistant secretary (legal) Federation of Civil Engineering Contractors (1958-1960); legal adviser British Insurance (Atomic Energy) Committee (1960-1963); exchange lawyer through Harvard Law School program Isham Lincoln and Beale, Chicago (1963-1964); assistant solicitor Joynson Hicks (1965-1967); assistant solicitor Wilde Sapte (1967); became partner (1967).

Activities: member joint working party on banking law of the Law Society and Bar; occasional lecturer/conference speaker; member Kent Autistic Community Trust; member Guild of Freemen of The City of London; member National Autistic Society.

Biography: lives Kent; married to Margaret with 1 son (Peter) and 1 daughter (Kate). Educated at Preston Grammar School; Gravesend County Grammar School; King's College London (1956 LLB hons AKC); Northwestern University School of Law, Chicago (1965 LLM) General Electric Foundation Fellow; Queen Mary College London (1982 Phd); Gray's Inn, Barrister, (1957-1963); author of: 'Refusal to sell as a means of enforcing retail price maintenance - UK legislation and US experience' Northwestern University Law Review; 'Banking Act 1987 - Current Law Statutes Annotated'; joint consulting editor 'Encyclopaedia of Competition Law' (1987).

Leisure: mountain biking; disco dancing; piano playing; avoiding domestic DIY.

HARGREAVES Don

managing partner ALEXANDER TATHAM St James Court, 107 Wilderspool Causeway, Warrington WA4 6PS.

Career: National Service at HQ military records, Nairobi; admitted (1957); assistant solicitor and senior partner general practice in Warrington (1957-1988); became partner Alexander Tatham (1988).

Activities: former president Warrington Law Society.

Biography: lives Mouldsworth; born 05.03.1930; married to Anne with 3 children. Educated at Queen Elizabeth's Grammar School, Blackburn.

Leisure: fishing; walking; golf.

HARMAN Robert

Queen's Counsel 2 Harcourt Buildings, Temple, London EC4.

Career: called to the Bar Gray's Inn (1954); SE circuit; junior prosecuting counsel to the Crown at Central Criminal Court (1967-1972); senior treasury Counsel (1972-1974); Recorder of the Crown Court (1972); QC (1974); a Judge of the Courts of Appeal, Jersey & Guernsey (1986); Bencher (1984).

Activities: member Senate of the Inns of Court and the Bar (1985-1987); jt hon sec Barristers' Benevolent Association; appeal steward BBB of C; Liveryman Goldsmiths' Company; member of: Garrick Club; Beefsteak Club; Pratt's Club; Swinley Forest Golf Club.

Biography: lives London SW7; born 26.09.1928; married to Sarah (deceased 1965) with 2 sons; married to Rosamond (1968) with 2 daughters. Educated at St Paul's School; Magdalen College Oxford.

HARMAN Robert

managing partner TRAVERS SMITH BRAITHWAITE 10 Snow Hill, London EC1A 2AL.

Career: articled Travers Smith Braithwaite (1970-1972); admitted (1972); assistant solicitor (1972-1976); became partner (1977); became managing partner (1986).

Biography: lives Woking; born 30.07.1947; married to Wendy with 2 children. Educated at Caldicott School (1956-1961); Wellington College (1961-1965); St Catharine's College Cambridge (1969 BA) (1972 MA).

HARMER Caroline

reader THE COLLEGE OF LAW Braboeuf Manor, Guildford GU3 1HA.

Career: worked as secretary BBC and others (1964-1968); called to the Bar Middle Temple (1968); lecturer College of Law (1969); senior lecturer (1974); principal lecturer (1979); reader (1984).

Activities: member Law Society's Family Law Committee (1976-1989); member editorial board of Lawline; Executive Committee member Asssociation of Personal Injury Lawyers; member Law Society's Civil Litigation Committee; council member Society of Public Teachers of Law; SPTL Family Law Committee; director FW Harmer (Holdings) Ltd; parent governor Kingsclere Primary School.

Biography: lives between Newbury and Basingstoke; born 10.07.1944; divorced with 1 daughter. Educated at West Heath, Sevenoaks; Universite de Caen, Normandy (1962 Diploma); Council of Legal Education; author of: 'Law and Practice in Matrimonial Causes'; 'Practical Partnership'; editor of Butterworths Family Law Service; 'Personal Injury Litigation', 'Commercial Litigation' and various lecture transcripts for the College of Law.

Leisure: music (piano and singing); gardening; riding; 'housewife'.

HARPER Jack

corporate tax partner TITMUSS SAINER & WEBB 2 Serjeants' Inn, London EC4Y 1LT.

Career: chartered accountant (1972); articled (1972-1976); admitted (1976).

Biography: lives London; born 02.08.1947; married with 2 children. Educated at St Joseph's Academy, Blackheath; Queen's College, Cambridge (1969 BA) (1972 MA); Fellow of Institute of Taxation (1979); author of book on Stamp Duty and Capital Duty (1979).

HARPER Ross

senior partner ROSS HARPER & MURPHY 163 Ingram Street, Glasgow G1 1DW.

Career: admitted (1959); founded Ross Harper & Murphy with James P Murphy (1961).

Activities: pioneered TV commercials in Scotland; president of the Law Society of Scotland (1988-1989); part-time Professor of Law Strathclyde University; President Glasgow Bar Association (1975-1988); secretary of section on general practice International Bar Association; former Conservative candidate Parliamentary elections; former president Scottish Conservative & Unionist Association; member of: Western Club; RSAC; has 28 partners and 20 branch offices, largest branch network in Europe.

Biography: lives Glasgow; born 20.03.1935; married to Ursula with 3 children. Educated at Hutcheson's Boys' Grammar School; Glasgow University (1956 MA) (1958 LLB); author of 'My Client, My Lord' (1983); 'Practitioners' Guide to Criminal Procedure' (1985); 'The Glasgow Rape Case' (1984); 'Fingertip Guide to Criminal Law' (1987); various management pamphlets.

Leisure: angling; bridge; shooting.

HARPUR Oonagh

principal executive BERWIN LEIGHTON Adelaide House, London Bridge, London EC4R 2HA.

Career: operations research scientist (1976-1980); assistant to Board Member for Science and the Executive Secretary (1980-1981); section leader Operational Research Executive (1981-1983); senior member of central policy group British Coal (London) (1983-1985); consultant and senior consultant Spicer & Oppenheim (1985-1986); managing consultant (1986-1987); associate Strategic Planning Associates, Washington DC (1987-1988); principal executive Berwin Leighton (1989).

Activities: leading personal growth workshops; member of Network.

Biography: lives London; born 26.09.1953; divorced with 1 child. Educated at Altringham County Grammar School for Girls; Keele University (1976 BA hons); Brunel University, Certificate of Advanced Study Operational Research (1978).

Leisure: clarinet; opera; white water rafting and canoeing.

HARREL David

partner and head of commercial litigation SJ BERWIN & CO 236 Gray's Inn Road, London WC1X 8HB.

Career: articled William Charles Crocker; admitted (1974); assistant solicitor and partner (1974-1978); partner Burton & Ramsden (1979-1982); founding partner SJ Berwin & Co (1982).

Activities: member Royal St George's Golf Club.

Biography: lives nr Maidstone; born 23.06.1948; married to Julia with 3 children. Educated at Marlborough College; Bristol University (1971 LLB); College of Law (1972).

Leisure: golf; gardening; sailing; tennis; skiing.

HARRIS Brian

director professional conduct department INSTITUTE OF CHARTERED ACCOUNTANTS IN ENGLAND AND WALES Gloucester House, Silbury Boulevard, Central Milton Keynes, Bucks MK9 2HL.

Career: deputy chief clerk London Magistrates' Courts (1963-1967); clerk to the Justices Poole (1967-1985); director professional conduct department Institute of Chartered Accountants in England and Wales (1985).

Activities: OBE (1983); secretary Executive Committee Joint Disciplinary Scheme; member Juvenile Courts Committee; Magistrates' Association (1973-1985); NACRO Juvenile Crime Adv Committee (1982-1985); former member CCETSW working party on legal training of social workers (report 1974); NACRO committee on diversion (Zander report 1975); HO/DHSS working party on operation of Children and Young Persons' Act 1969 (report 1978); ABAFA working party on care proceedings (report 1979); president Justices' Clerks' Society (1981-1982).

Biography: lives Northamptonshire; born 14.08.1932; married to Jan with 2 children. Educated at Henry Thornton Grammar School; King's College London (LLB hons); editor Justice of the Peace Review (1982-1985); author of:'Criminal Jurisdiction of Magistrates' 10th edn (1986); 'Warrants of Search and Entry' (1973); 'The Courts, the Press and the Public' (1976); 'The Rehabilitation of Offenders Act 1974' (2nd ed 1989); 'New Law of Family Proceedings in Magistrates' Courts' (1979); joint ed 'Clarke Hall and Morrison on Children' (1985); entry on Magistrates in Halsbury's Laws of England 4th edn (1979).

HARRIS Bryan

senior partner EVERY PHILLIPS AND DUNNINGS The Laurels, 46 New Street, Honiton, Devon EX14 8BZ.

Career: articled Herbert W Milnes; National Service with Intelligence Corps; admitted (1952); assistant solicitor Milnes & Milnes (1952-1954); became partner (1954-1957); acquired practice Every & Phillips (1957); sole practitioner (1957-1968); now senior partner; acquired firm Dunning & Bicknell (now Dunnings) (1968).

Activities: chairman Devon & Cornwall Rent Tribunal; past president Devon & Exeter Incorporated Law Society; member of: Reform Club; Sidmouth Club; Rotary Club of Honiton.

Biography: lives Sidmouth; born 28.11.1927; married to Hazel with 2 children. Educated at Finchley Catholic Grammar School (1939-1946); Law Society's School of Law (1946); Gibson and Weldon (1951).

Leisure: gardening; golf; music; travel; photography.

HARRIS David

senior partner RICHMONDS 35 Potter Street, Worksop, Nottinghamshire S80 2AG (other offices at Gainsborough, Retford, Doncaster and Maltby).

Career: articled Hayes Son & Richmond (1967-1969); admitted (1969); assistant solicitor (1969-1971); became partner (1971); senior partner (1987).

Activities: OBE; TD; ADC; Commissioner for Oaths (1973); Deputy Registrar (1978-1984); Parliamentary candidate (1974 & 1979); Colonel in Territorial Army; Deputy Commander 49 Infantry Brigade; (to be TA Colonel RMA Sandhurst 1991); member East India Club.

Biography: lives Haxey nr Doncaster; married to Veronica. Educated at Ranby House; Worksop College; King's College London (1966 LLB).

Leisure: gardening; good food and wine; shooting.

HARRIS Philip

senior partner CLARKE WILLMOTT & CLARKE Flower's House, 15 Hendford, Yeovil, Somerset BA20 1TB.

Career: articled Mr SDF Campbell (1951-1956); admitted (1956); assistant solicitor WJ Fraser & Son (1956-1961); assistant solicitor Clarke Willmott & Clarke (1962-1964); became partner (1965).

Biography: lives Tintinhull; born 12.04.1934; married to Jillian with 2 children. Educated at East Barnet School; College of Law.

Leisure: reading; gardening.

HARRIS Richard

partner FRESHFIELDS Whitefriars, 65 Fleet Street, London EC4Y 1HT.

Career: admitted (1966); assistant solicitor (1966-1970); became partner Freshfields (1970); partner in company department (1970 to date).

Activities: member of City of London Club.

Biography: lives London N1; born 14.10.1941; single. Educated at Stamford School; Peterhouse Cambridge.

HARRIS Rosina M

consultant TAYLOR JOYNSON GARRETT 180 Fleet Street, London EC4A 2NT.

Career: served with American Ambulance of Great Britain (1941); called to the Bar at Lincoln's Inn (1944); admitted (1953); assistant solicitor (1953-1954); partner Joynson-Hicks (1954-1989); became senior partner (1977-1986); became consultant on merger of Joynson-Hicks and Taylor Garrett to form Taylor Joynson Garrett (1989).

H

Activities: Queen's Jubilee Medal (1977); non-executive director Blundell-Permoglaze Holdings PLC (1979-1986) (deputy chairman 1981-1986); non-executive director London Brick PLC (1983-1984); member Committee chaired by The Hon Mr Justice Whitford appointed to consider and report on the changes desirable in the law of copyright including the protection of registered designs under the Registered Designs Act 1949; member Goodwood Country Club.

Biography: lives London W1 and West Wittering; born 30.05.1921; single. Educated at St Swithin's School, Winchester; St Hilda's College, Oxford (MA BCL).

Leisure: theatre; opera.

HARRISON David

senior partner POOLE ALCOCK & CO and TIMPERELY & CO 'The Hollies', Wesley Avenue, Sandbach, Cheshire CW11 9DQ.

Career: admitted (1963); assistant solicitor Poole Alcock & Co; became partner; Notary Public (1975).

Activities: former part-time adjudicator with Immigration Tribunals in Birmingham; former part-time chairman Industrial Tribunals in Liverpool; present part-time chairman Social Security and Supplementary Benefit Tribunals at Hanley; keen and active interest in the horse field; member Race-owners Association; a racehorse owner; in partnership with wife and daughters in an equestrian centre at Alsager, Cheshire holding shows 52 weeks in the year.

Biography: lives Alsager; born 13.04.1939; married to Gillian with 4 children. Educated at Newcastle under Lyme High School; Manchester University.

HARRISS David

partner BIRD & BIRD 2 Gray's Inn Square, London WC1R 5AF.

Career: trainee patent agent AA Thornton & Co (1965-1969); chartered patent agent (1969); patent agent with Langner Parry (1970-1973); articled Bird & Bird (1973-1977); admitted (1977); became partner (1977).

Activities: member joint working party of the Bar and Law Society on intellectual property.

Biography: lives Chobham; born 15.03.1943; married to Penny with 1 son and 1 daughter. Educated at Epsom College; Christ's College Cambridge (MA).

Leisure: tennis; golf.

HARROP Stuart

legal director THE STOCK EXCHANGE London EC2N 1HP.

Career: articled Yorkshire Water Authority; admitted (1980); solicitor The Costain Group; company solicitor Albright & Wilson Ltd; manager ICI; became legal director The Stock Exchange (1988).

Activities: former member CBI Competition Law Panel; various Stock Exchange-related committees; member Association des Juristes Franco-Britanniques.

Biography: lives Tunbridge Wells; born 11.01.1956; married to Tracy with 2 children. Educated at Beverley Grammar School; Leeds University (LLB hons); College of Law Chester.

Leisure: freelance photography (business and natural history); natural history generally.

HART J Neil

partner THOMAS EGGAR VERRALL BOWLES Sussex House, North Street, Horsham, West Sussex RH12 1BN.

Career: articled Norton Rose Botterell & Roche; admitted (1978); assistant solicitor (1978-1980); admitted Hong Kong (1980); assistant solicitor Johnson Stokes & Master, Hong Kong (1980-1984); associate solicitor Thomas Eggar & Son (1984-1986); became partner (1986).

Activities: vice-chairman Federation Sussex Industries; FSI Council member; member of: Royal Hong Kong Yacht Club; Itchener Sailing Club; Law Society Institute of Directors.

Biography: lives Bepton nr Midhurst; born 27.02.1953; married to Rosalind with 2 children. Educated at Oundle School; Exeter University (1975 LLB).

Leisure: sailing; squash.

HART Michael

Queen's Counsel 2 New Square, Lincoln's Inn, London WC2A 3RU.

Career: called to the Bar (1970); QC (1987).

Activities: member Committee of Chancery Bar Association (1986-1988).

Biography: lives London; born 07.05.1948; married to Melanie with 2 children. Educated at Winchester College; Magdalen College Oxford (1969 BA) (1970 BCL); Vinerian Law Scholar (1970); Eldon Law Scholar (1970); Fellow All Souls College Oxford (1970-1977 & 1979-1986).

HARTLEY Elizabeth

litigation partner DJ FREEMAN & CO 43 Fetter Lane, London EC4A 1NA.

Career: articled DJ Freeman & Co (1980-1982); admitted (1982); assistant solicitor (1982-1986); became partner (1987).

Activities: member Law Society (1982); member London Young Solicitors Group Committee (1986-1990) (chairman 1988-1989); hon Fellow American Bar Association; member City of London Solicitors' Company; member Association Internationale des Jeunes Avocats; representative of London Young Solicitors Group on National Committee of Young Solicitors (1988-1990).

Biography: lives London; born 15.05.1957; married to Dr Peter Dzwig. Educated at The Royal Masonic School for Girls, Rickmansworth; Sheffield University (LLB hons); Law Society Finals (1980).

Leisure: music; riding; skiing; theatre; opera.

HARTLEY Michael

partner commercial property services SPEECHLY BIRCHAM Bouverie House, 154 Fleet Street, London EC4A 2HX.

Activities: member Reform Club.

Biography: lives Kent; born 18.03.1944; married to Jenice with 4 sons.

Leisure: photography; books; family.

HARTWIG Hans Joseph

partner HARTWIG 15 William Mews, London SW1X 9HF and Croydon.

Career: licensed in New York (1976) and West Germany (1978); Notary Public.

Activities: chairman Commercial Law Committee of British Chamber of Commerce; Council Notaries Society with special interest in European notarial practice.

Biography: lives London SW1; born 1936; married to Patricia with 1 daughter and 1 son. Educated in India and Pakistan (1939-1949); London School of Economics (1954 LLB hons); Cornell University (1968); joint author of 'Administrative Receivership' (1989); consulting editor International Credit Securities; various legal articles including International and Comparative Law Quarterly, Conveyancer, Versicherungsrecht, Insolvenzrecht; joint editor Journal of Society of English and American Lawyers.

Leisure: family; friends; involvement with manufacturing industry.

HARVEY Adam

senior partner MORRISON & MASTERS 17/20 Commercial Road, Swindon, Wilts SN1 5NR.

Career: articled Bournemouth; admitted; assistant solicitor Morrison & Masters (1961); became partner .

Activities: former member Wilts Squash Committee; member of: Wessex Squash Club; Swindon Golf Club; Swindon Rugby Club (former secretary).

Biography: lives Swindon; born 12.08.1937; married with 1 child. Educated at Cranleigh; Southampton University.

Leisure: sport particularly rugby; squash; golf.

HARVEY Guy

partner and head of litigation and insolvency department SIMPSON CURTIS 41 Park Square, Leeds LS1 2NS.

Career: articled Simpson Curtis (1974-1976); admitted (1976); assistant solicitor (1976-1978); became partner (1978).

Activities: former national vice-chairman and Yorkshire representative Law Society Trainee Solicitors Group; former committee member Leeds Law Students' Society; former chairman Yorkshire Young Solicitors Group; former public relations officer Leeds Law Society Committee; taken part in radio phone-ins and appeared on various television programmes being interviewed about legal developments; member North Yorkshire Board Prince's Youth Business Trust; member Board of Management Education 2000 Leeds Project; active in Friends of Opera North.

Biography: lives Ripon; born 26.02.1951; married to Henrietta with 1 son and 1 daughter. Educated at Stowe School (1964-1969); Trinity College Cambridge (1983 BA hons); College of Law Lancaster Gate (1983).

Leisure: arts (especially music and opera); gardening.

HARVEY Michael

Queen's Counsel 2 Crown Office Row, Temple, London EC4Y 7HJ.

Career: called to the Bar Gray's Inn (1966); pupillage with Raymond Kidwell QC (1966-1967); 2 Crown Office Row (1967); QC (1982); Recorder of the Crown Court (1986).

Activities: tutor in advocacy at Council of Legal Education (1972-1977); member Bar

Council sub-committee on codification of the criminal law (1970); member Surrey Legal Aid Local Committee (1970-1980); member Legal Aid Area Committee (West London) (1980 to date); chairman of Bar working party on Civil Justice Review (1989 to date); attorney in the Cayman Islands (1986); admitted to the Bar in Hong Kong (1987); arbitrator; member of: Athenaeum; Hawks (Cambridge).

Biography: lives Central London and Surrey; born 22.05.1943; married to Denise with 2 children. Educated at St John's School, Leatherhead; Christ's College Cambridge (1964 BA hons) (1965 LLB) (1967 MA); Uthwatt Scholarship (1965); Mould Scholarship (1966); joint contributor of 'Damages' in Halsbury's Laws of England 4th Ed (1975).

Leisure: shooting; golf.

HARVEY Terence

senior partner LEES LLOYD WHITLEY Castle Chambers, Castle Street, Liverpool L2 9TJ.

Career: articled Edward Russell Lloyd (1948-1952); admitted (1952); assistant solicitor Edward Lloyd & Co (1952-1956); became partner (1956-1988); became senior partner Lees Lloyd Whitley (1988).

Activities: former member Lord Chancellor's Chancery Practice sub-committee; joint master Royal Rock Beagle Hunt (1959-1984); chairman Shrewsbury House Community Centre (1978 to date).

Biography: lives Neston; born 16.01.1927; married to Liz with 5 children. Educated at The Old Hall, Wellington; Shrewsbury School.

HARWOOD-SMART Philip

pensions partner ASHURST MORRIS CRISP Broadwalk House, 5 Appold Street, London EC2A 2HA.

Career: articled Herbert Smith & Co (1968-1970); admitted (1971); assistant solicitor (1971-1973); associate partner (1973-1975); assistant solicitor Farrer & Co (1977-1980); assistant solicitor Ashurst Morris Crisp (1980-1983); became associate partner (1983-1984); became partner (1984).

Activities: commissioned King's Own Royal Regiment Territorial Army (1965); former member Constitutional Committee Society of Pension Consultants (1981-1982) and Activities Committee Association of Pension Lawyers (1984-1989); member Honourable Artillery Company (1986); member of: Carlton Club; City Livery

Club; Henley Regatta Club; Coleman Street Ward Club.

Biography: lives Winchester; born 01.10.1944; married to Juliet with 2 daughters. Educated at Eastbourne College (1958-1963); Lancaster University (1967 BA hons); author of 'The History of Jevington' (1961, 1972).

Leisure: heraldry and genealogy.

HATCHER William

senior partner HATCHER ROGERSON 25 Castle Street, Shrewsbury, Shropshire SY1 2DA.

Career: marketing trainee Gillette Industries; articled Denton Hall & Burgin; admitted; founded own practice (1973).

Activities: member Vincent's Club; Leander Club; Upper Tanat Fishing Club.

Biography: lives nr Wem, N. Shropshire; born 20.09.1942; married to Karen with 1 son and 2 daughters. Educated at Adams' Grammar School, Wem; St Edmund Hall Oxford (1965 BA); College of Law Lancaster Gate.

Leisure: fishing; agricultural/equestrian pottering; Welsh coast; occasional rowing.

HATTRICK Ian

consultant WALTONS & MORSE Plantation House, 31/35 Fenchurch Street, London EC3M 3NN.

Career: articled Skelton & Co (1955-1958); commissioned Lancashire Regiment (1958-1960); assistant solicitor Waltons & Co (1960); became partner (1964).

Activities: member Admiralty Court Committee; chairman City of London Admiralty Solicitors Group; council member Regimental Council; member of: Naval & Military Club; City Club; City Law Club; Little Ship Club; Law Society Yacht Club; Colne Yacht Club.

Biography: lives Kersey; born 20.01.1933; married to Chatterton with 3 daughters. Educated at William Hulmes School; Victoria University (1955 LLB).

Leisure: Regimental charity work; RNLI fund raising; sailing; walking; tennis; music.

HAVERY Richard O

barrister 4 Raymond Buildings, Gray's Inn, London WC1R 5BP.

Career: called to the Bar Middle Temple (1962); QC (1980); Recorder of the Crown Court (1986) (sits on Official Referees'

H

Business); Bencher Middle Temple (1989).

Activities: member of: Garrick; Hurlingham.

Biography: lives London SW1; born 07.02.1934. Educated at St Paul's; Magdalen College Oxford (1957 BA) (1961 MA); Harmsworth Entrance Exhibitioner; Astbury Law Scholarship; Eldon Law Scholarship; Barstow Scholarship; joint editor Kemp & Kemp 'The Quantum of Damages' (1967 3rd ed).

Leisure: music; croquet; steam locomotives.

HAWES Robert

partner THOMAS MALLAM 126 High Street, Oxford OX1 4DG.

Career: articled Thomas Mallam (1965); admitted; assistant solicitor; became partner (1970).

Activities: member Committee of Berks Bucks & Oxon Law Society (1979 to date) (vice-president (1988-1989); president (1989-1990); part-time chairman Social Security Appeal Tribunals (1985); Rotarian; Sidesman at the City Church; member of: Lawyers' Fishing Club; Clarendon Club; Vincent's Club.

Biography: lives Oxford; born 17.07.1939; married to Ann with 2 children. Educated at Dragon School, Oxford (1945-1953); Marlborough (1953-1957); Brasenose College Oxford (1962 MA).

Leisure: trout fishing; season ticket holder Oxford United; tennis; formerly hockey (Final England Trial; reserve for Olympic side at Tokyo 1964).

HAWLEY Peter

managing partner WALKER MARTINEAU 64 Queen Street, London EC4R 1AD.

Career: National Service in Johore, Malaya (1957-1959); articled Walker Martineau (1964-1967); assistant solicitor (1967-1969); became partner (1970); principal partner banking department (1972); managing partner (1983); chairman firm's executive committee.

Activities: member of: Gresham Club; Institute of Directors.

Biography: lives London SW7 and Oxfordshire; born 20.07.1938; married to Tanya with 1 child. Educated at Wyggeston School; Magdalene College Cambridge (1962 BA) (1963 LLB) (1965 MA).

Leisure: college association; village twinning; foreign travel; local history.

HAYDEN Julian

partner and head of tax and trust department MANCHES & CO Aldwych House, 71-91 Aldwych, London WC2B 4RP.

Career: articled Withers (1978-1981); admitted (1981); assistant solicitor (1981-1984); partner Alexanders (1985-1988); became partner Manches & Co (1988).

Activities: seminar presentations.

Biography: lives Epsom; born 12.12.1955; married to Gillian. Educated at Dorking Grammar School; St John's College Cambridge (1978 BA (MA).

Leisure: fishing; sailing.

HAYES David

senior partner HAYES & STORR 18 Market Place, Fakenham, Norfolk NR21 9BH.

Career: articled Mills & Reeve; admitted; assistant solicitor; assistant solicitor Hayes & Storr (1969-1981); became partner (1981).

Activities: legal member Mental Health Review Tribunal (1987 to date); president King's Lynn and West Norfolk Law Society (1987-1988).

Biography: lives Little Snoring; born 11.02.1943; married to Sue with 5 children. Educated at St Faith's Prep School, Cambridge; The Leys School, Cambridge; Sidney Sussex College Cambridge (1964 BA) (1969 MA).

Leisure: sports; gardening.

HAYES Michael

partner MACFARLANES 10 Norwich Street, London EC4A 1BD.

Career: articled Macfarlanes (1966-1968); admitted (1968); assistant solicitor (1968-1973); became partner (1974).

Activities: member Law Society Wills and Equity Committee; member Law Society Standing Committee on Entry and Training (1987-1989); member Committee of the City of London Law Society (1978 to date); vice-chairman City of London CAB Advisory Committee; member London Legal Education Committee; actively involved in fund-raising for Tower Hamlets Law Centre from City solicitors; member Roehampton Club.

Biography: lives Wimbledon; born 10.01.1943; married to Jackie with 3 children. Educated at Wimbledon College; University College Oxford (1965 BA) (1968 MA); article in Law Society's Gazette 'Putting One's House in Order' (1984); contributor to 'International Handbook on

Pensions Law' (Graham & Trotman 1989).

Leisure: old cars; windsurfing; theatre; reading.

HAYES Stephen

partner HAYES DIXON 146 Strand, London WC2R 1JH.

Career: articled Denis Hayes & Co (1968-1970); admitted (1970); law lecturer (2 years); assistant solicitor (1970-1973); became partner Denis Hayes & Co (1973); firm merged with Dixon & Co (1980).

Activities: member Westminster and Holborn Law Societies.

Biography: lives Walton-on-Thames; born 31.05.1946; married to Penelope with 3 children. Educated at Milbourne Lodge School; Leighton Park School; London School of Economics (1967 LLB hons).

Leisure: opera; travel in France.

HEAL Jeremy

tax partner, head of group tax department and head of information technology HOWES PERCIVAL 52 Colegate, Norwich, Norfolk.

Career: admitted (1967); assistant solicitor E Edwards Son & Noice; partner (1970); assistant solicitor Turner Martin & Symes (1971-1972); partner (1972-1988); became tax partner Howes Percival (1988).

Activities: hon treasurer Cambridge Footlights (1962-1964); lectures on tax and property law and related subjects; member of: Norfolk Gliding Club; Ipswich & Suffolk Club.

Biography: lives nr Norwich; born 18.09.1942; married to Joanna with 4 children. Educated at Edge Grove Preparatory School, Aldenham; Marlborough College; Queen's College Cambridge (1964 BA) (1965 LLB) (1968 MA) (1985 LLM).

Leisure: gliding; private flying (motor gliders); sailing; photography; playing flute and saxophone.

HEALEY Arthur John

senior partner HARTLEY & WORSTENHOLME 20 Bank Street, Castleford, West Yorkshire WF10 1JD.

Career: articled large general practice in Hull (1954-1959); admitted (1959); assistant solicitor Hartley & Worstenholme (1961-1964); became partner (1964); became senior partner (1983).

Activities: assistant Recorder (1985).

Biography: lives Pontefract; born 19.07.1935; married to Jan with 2 children. Educated at Barnsley Grammar School; Hull Grammar School.

Leisure: game fishing; golf; walking.

HEAP Sir Desmond

consultant HAMMOND SUDDARDS 10 Piccadilly, Bradford BD1 3LR; SUGDEN AND SPENCER Avondale House, Charles Street, Bradford BD1 1ER.

Career: articled Thos Thornton (1930-1933); admitted solicitor of the Supreme Court (1933); deputy Town Clerk of Leeds (1947); comptroller and City solicitor to Lord Mayor and Corporation of City of London (1947-1973); consultant Coward Chance, London (1974-1984); consultant in local government and town and country planning law to Hammond Suddards and Sugden and Spencer (1974 to date).

Activities: member Council of Law Society (1955-1978) (member several Council Committees); president of the Law Society (1972-1973); president Royal Town Planning Institute (1955-1956); senior past Master Worshipful Company of Solicitors of the City of London (Master 1965-1966); Honorary Associate (1987); visiting Professor in Law of urban renewal at University of Hawaii (1980); associate member Royal Institution of Chartered Surveyors; hon assistant Worshipful Company of Chartered Surveyors; hon member Incorporated Society of Valuers and Auctioneers; hon member American Bar Foundation; Gold Medallist Royal Town Planning Institute (1983); hon life member Council International Bar Association; hon life president International Bar Association Section on General Practice; member Editorial Board of Journal of Planning and Environmental law; hon member City (of London) Law Club; member of: Athenaeum; Guildhall Club.

Biography: lives Sevenoaks; born 17.09.1907; married to Adelene Mai with 2 daughters and 1 son. Educated at the Grammar School, Burnley; Victoria University of Manchester (1929 LLB hons) (1937 LLM) (1973 Hon LLD); author of: 'Planning Law for Town & Country' (1938); 'The Town & Country Planning Act 1944' (1944); 'The New Towns Act 1946' (1946); 'An Outline of Planning Law' (1949 - 10th edition 1991); Halsbury's Laws of England 'Housing' (1979) and 'Town & Country Planning' (1986); 'The Land and the Development; or The Turmoil and the Torment' (1975); numerous lectures and articles on legal topics; general editor, Encyclopaedia of Planning Law and Practice.

Leisure: swimming; the London Opera; the theatre; music; biking (until 1988); reading; writing.

HEAPS Christopher

partner JAQUES & LEWIS 2 South Square, Gray's Inn, London WC1R 5HR.

Career: admitted (1967); assistant solicitor Jaques & Lewis (1967-1971); became partner (1971).

Activities: elected to Law Society Council (1985); deputy chairman London Regional Passengers' Committee; member Holborn Law Society (1973 to date) (president 1983-1984); chairman Law Society Planning Committee (1988 to date); panel chairman Law Society Adjudication Committee (1988 to date); member Railway Heritage Trust Advisory Panel (1985 to date).

Biography: lives Dorking; born 15.11.1942; married to Ann with 2 children. Educated at Ashtead Preparatory School; Dorking Grammar School; Exeter University (1964 LLB); member Chartered Institute of Transport; author of: 'London Transport Railways Album' (1977); 'Western Region in the 1960s' (1981); 'This is Southern Region Central Division' (1982); 'BR Diary 1968-1977' (1988).

HEASELGRAVE Bill

managing partner THURSFIELD ADAMS & WESTONS 14 Church Street, Kidderminster, Worcs DY10 2AJ.

Career: articled Lee Crowder & Co (1965-1967); admitted (1967); assistant solicitor Thursfield & Adams (1967-1970); became partner (1970).

Activities: member of the Council of the Birmingham Law Society; secretary non-contentious business committee (1985 to date); member Edgbaston Priory Club.

Biography: lives Harborne; born 25.07.1943; married to Vivien with 2 daughters. Educated at King Edwards; Birmingham University (1964 LLB hons); College of Law Guildford (1965).

Leisure: reading especially history; running (marathons); golf; theatre; all ball sports; chauffeur to 2 teenage daughters!.

HEATH Brian

senior partner CHALLENOR & GARDINER 38-40 Westgate, Oxford OX1 1LN.

Career: articled Huntbatch & Co (1956-1959); admitted (1959); assistant solicitor Halliley & Morrison (1959-1962); assistant solicitor Challenor & Gardiner (1962-1964); became partner (1964).

Activities: director Solicitors Benevolent Association; member Frewen Club.

Biography: lives Oxford; born 02.01.1935; married to Maureen with 2 sons. Educated at Newcastle under Lyme High School; Fitzwilliam College Cambridge (1956 BA hons).

Leisure: veterans' squash; golf; camping; walking.

HEATH Jane

partner ROWE & MAW 20 Black Friars Lane, London EC4V 6HD.

Career: articled Highwood & Smith (1954-1959); admitted (1959); assistant solicitor Richards Butler (1959-1971); assistant solicitor and partner Warren Murton & Co (1972-1977); became partner Rowe & Maw (1978).

Biography: lives London SW18; born 13.11.1935; single. Educated at Upper Tooting High School.

Leisure: ballet; theatre; music.

HEATH William

senior partner WILLIAM HEATH & CO 16 Sale Place, London W2 1PX.

Career: articled Charles Caplin & Co (1960-1963); admitted (1963); assistant solicitor (1963-1965); partner (1965-1969); founded own practice (1969).

Activities: president West London Law Society (1979 & 1988-1989) (treasurer 1981 to date); member Council of Law Society (1979-1986 & 1990 to date); participation in board meetings of variety of private companies; advises solicitors in partnership disputes or professional problems; governor of old school and trustee of school and youth charities; supports former TA Regiment at home and abroad; member of: Wimbledon Squash & Badminton Club; Artists' Rifles Association; Cricketers' Club of London.

Biography: lives Wimbledon; born 20.05.1939; married with 3 children. Educated at Westminster City School (1950-1957); Durham University (1960 LLB hons); College of Law (1963 2nd class hons); articles on private investment in New Law Journal (1983); Cayman Islands Year Book (1986-1987); promotion of 'Solicitors Building Society' (1984-1985).

Leisure: squash; supporting Wimbledon Football Club; walking; travel.

H

H

HEDLEY Mark

barrister and head of chambers 5th Floor, Corn Exchange, Fenwick Street, Liverpool L2 7QS.

Career: pupillage with Derek Hill Smith; head of Chambers (1983); Recorder (1988).

Activities: Reader Church of England (1975).

Biography: lives Liverpool; born 23.08.1946; married to Erica with 4 children. Educated at Framlingham College; Liverpool University (1968 LLB); Inns of Court School of Law.

Leisure: cricket; railways.

HEESOM Karen Barbara

training manager HAMMOND SUDDARDS Bradford and Leeds.

Career: Administrator for English language schools for foreigners; articled; admitted (1987); Assistant Solicitor Few & Kester (1987-1990); taught trainee legal executives at Anglia Regional College in evening classes (1988-1989); became Training Manager Hammond Suddards (1990).

Activities: member Legal Education & Training Group.

Biography: lives Leeds; born 19.07.1949. Educated at Rosebery Grammar School, Epsom; Newcastle University (1976-1979); College of Law Chancery Lane (1982-1984).

Leisure: cycling; listening to music (especially rock); concerts; old railways; pre-Raphaelite paintings.

HEFFRON Niall

senior partner HEFFRONS Ternion Court, 258-262 Upper Fourth Street, Central Milton Keynes, Bucks MK9 1DP.

Career: articled Hawkins & Co (1958-1961); admitted (1961); assistant solicitor (1961-1966); became partner (1966); senior partner (1983-1990) merged with Russell Jones & Co (1987); founded own practice (1990).

Activities: co-founder National Association of Solicitors Property Centres (1984) (chairman 1986-1989); governor of Kingshott Preparatory School.

Biography: lives Hitchin; born 13.09.1935; married to Hilary with 3 children. Educated at St Bede's Preparatory School, nr Stafford; Ampleforth College, York; St Catherine's College Cambridge (1958 BA) (1959 LLB) (1961 MA); occasional articles in Law Society Gazette; joint author of Response to the Lord Chancellor's recent Green Papers; Response to the Law

Commission's Green Paper on part II of the Landlord and Tenant Act 1954.

Leisure: learning languages and embarrassing family on holiday by 'having a go' in French, German and Greek; gathering material for that book which will be written in retirement.

HEGARTY Richard

senior partner and head of commercial department HEGARTY & CO 16 Lincoln Road, Peterborough PE1 2RG.

Career: articled Harding & Barnett and Gardner & Millhouse; admitted (1974); founded own practice (1974).

Activities: secretary Peterborough & District Law Society (1983-1989); member of the Council of the Law Society (1989); member Law Society Employment Committee and Practice and Remuneration Committee.

Biography: lives Peterborough; born 15.08.1949; married to Sheelah with 3 children. Educated at Stamford School; Leicester University (1971 LLB hons).

Leisure: drinking wine; cycling; swimming; travelling; skiing.

HEILBRON Hilary

Queen's Counsel 1 Brick Court, Temple, London EC4Y 9BY.

Career: called to the Bar Gray's Inn (1971); QC (1987).

Activities: member Commercial Court Committee; vice-chairman London Common Law and Commercial Bar Association.

Biography: lives London; born 02.01.1949; single. Educated at Huyton College; Lady Margaret Hall Oxford (1970 MA).

HELLER John

managing partner NABARRO NATHANSON 50 Stratton Street, London W1X 5FL.

Career: articled Nabarro Nathanson (1976-1978); admitted (1978); assistant solicitor (1978-1982); partner (1982-1987); articled clerk recruitment partner (1987-1989); became managing partner (1989).

Activities: member of: Oriental Club; Ski Club of Great Britain; Wine Society.

Biography: lives Henley on Thames; born 29.12.1952; married to Amanda with 3 children. Educated at St Edward's School, Oxford (Exhibitioner); Clare College Cambridge (BA hons) (MA).

Leisure: skiing; tennis; sailing; family; garden; old cars; wine.

HELLER Lawrence

managing partner BERWIN LEIGHTON Adelaide House, London Bridge, London EC4R 9HA.

Career: articled Silkin & Silkin (1956-1959); admitted (1959); assistant solicitor Titmuss Sainer & Webb (1959-1962); became partner (1962-1963); equity partner Lionel Leighton & Co (1963); firm merged to become Berwin Leighton (1970); (founding partner); became managing partner (1986-1990).

Activities: trustee Westminster Association for Youth; occasionally lectures on legal topics upon which specialises.

Biography: lives London W1; born 14.04.1934; married to Patricia with 1 daughter. Educated at Battersea Grammar School; Sidney Sussex College Cambridge (1956 BA) Scholar; (MA first class hons); author of the section 'Commercial Property Development' in Practical Commercial Precedents; contributor of the chapter on 'Property Warranties' in 'Warranties and Indemnities on Share Sales'.

Leisure: skiing; gardening; theatre; reading.

HENCHLEY Richard

general counsel and secretary ROLLS ROYCE PLC 65 Buckingham Gate, London SW1E 6AT.

Career: admitted (1965); assistant solicitor Simmons & Simmons (1965-1966); assistant solicitor Richards Butler & Co (1966-1967); assistant solicitor British-American Tobacco Co Ltd (1967-1972); deputy head of department (1972-1977); solicitor and secretary British American Cosmetics Ltd (1977-1984); senior solicitor BAT Industries (1984-1989); became general counsel and secretary Rolls Royce PLC (1989).

Activities: voluntary advice worker Lambeth Law Centre (1975-1976); council member Trade Marks Patents & Designs Federation (1977-1982); director Brixton Enterprise Centre Ltd (1984-1989); chairman Law Society Commerce & Industry Group (1984-1985); elected to Law Society Council (1987); director Solicitors Financial and Property Services Ltd (1988); CBI Committees and sub-committees on Equal Opportunities; Product Liability; Competition Law; City Working Party; originator of Lawyers for Enterprise concept.

Biography: lives London SE21; born

23.03.1943; married to Gillian with 2 children. Educated at Clifton College Bristol.

Leisure: squash; swimming; art; architecture; design (1875-1925).

HENDERSON Giles

partner specialising in corporate finance SLAUGHTER AND MAY 35 Basinghall Street, London EC2V 5DB.

Career: articled Slaughter and May (1968-1970); admitted (1970); assistant solicitor (1970-1975); became partner (1975).

Activities: part-time tutor in law Magdalen and St Catherine's Colleges Oxford (1968-1970).

Biography: lives London W2 and Sevenoaks; born 20.04.1942; married to Lynne with 3 children. Educated at Michaelhouse, South Africa; Witwatersand University, South Africa (1962 BA); Magdalen College Oxford (1965 BA hons) (1966 BCL); Associate in Faculty of Law University of California at Berkeley (1967); article in International Financial Law Review (1985); speaker at International Bar Association and other seminars.

Leisure: music; sport.

HENDERSON Hugh

senior partner in commercial department and managing partner MORTON FRASER MILLIGAN WS 19 York Place, Edinburgh EH1 3EL.

Career: apprenticed Morton Smart MacDonald & Milligan WS; admitted (1966); assistant solicitor (1966-1970); became partner Morton Fraser & Milligan WS (1970); set up firm's commercial department (1972).

Activities: Writer to the Signet (1972); external examiner Diploma in Legal Practice Edinburgh University; Law Society of Scotland lecturer (1988); PQLE courses convenor (1990); trustee Music is Pleasure Trust; chairman Musselburgh Sea Cadet unit; council member Musselburgh Conservation Society; member Royal Forth Yacht Club.

Biography: lives Musselburgh; born 24.02.1941; married to Sheila with 4 children. Educated at Galashiels Academy; George Heriot's School; Edinburgh University; author of Law Society of Scotland PQLE course paper 'Practical Elements in Commercial Missives'.

Leisure: sailing; mountaineering; skiing.

HENDERSON Roger

Queen's Counsel and head of chambers 2 Harcourt Buildings, Temple, London EC4Y 9DB.

Career: called to the Bar Inner Temple; QC (1980); Recorder (1983).

Activities: president British Academy of Forensic Sciences (1986-1987); ordinary governor London Hospital Medical College; member Council of Legal Education (1983-1990); chairman Public Affairs Committee of the Bar (1989 to date); chairman Bar Conference Committee (1988-1989); counsel to King's Cross Inquiry.

Biography: lives London; born 21.04.1943; married to Catherine with 3 children. Educated at Radley College (1956-1961); St Catharine's College Cambridge (1964 MA hons); Adderley Prize for Law (1964); Inner Temple Duke of Edinburgh and major scholarships; various papers in Medicine Science and the Law.

Leisure: fly fishing; gardening; shooting.

HENDERSON Schuyler

international partner BAKER & MCKENZIE Aldwych House, Aldwych, London WC2B 4JP.

Career: admitted New York (1972); admitted Illinois (1973); associate Mayer Brown & Platt (1973-1976); became partner (1977-1985); became partner Sidley & Austin (1985-1989); became partner Baker & McKenzie (1989).

Activities: member editorial advisory boards of: International Banking and Financial Law Bulletin; Journal of International Banking Law; Butterworths Journal of International Banking and Financial law; member Special Committee on Relations with European Bars of the Bar Association of the City of New York (1984-1989); member Legislative Committee of the American Chamber of Commerce (UK) (1986-1988); regular speaker on international finance at conferences in London, New York and Tokyo; member of: Annabels; Hurlingham Club; Cannons.

Biography: lives London W8; born 02.02.1945; married to Paula with 2 children. Educated at Princeton University (1967 BA); University of Chicago Law School (1971 JD); University of Chicago Business School (1971 MBA); numerous publications.

HENDERSON William James Carlaw

partner residential conveyancing department BRODIES WS 15 Atholl Crescent, Edinburgh EH3 8HA.

Career: admitted (1973); assistant solicitor (1973-1976); partner Allan McDougall & Co SSC (1976-1983); became partner Brodies WS (1983).

Activities: Notary Public (1978); Writer to the Signet (1981); secretary Society of Scottish Artists (1980-1983); member Edinburgh CAB; Tenovus - Scotland for Medical Research - Edinburgh Area Committee member.

Biography: Educated at George Heriot's School, Edinburgh; University of Edinburgh, Faculty of Law (1971 LLB).

HENDRY John

partner BRODIES WS 15 Atholl Crescent, Edinburgh EH3 8HA.

Career: became partner Brodies WS (1977).

Activities: member of: New Club; Honourable Company of Edinburgh Golfers; Luffness New Golf Club; Panmure Golf Club; Grange Club.

Biography: lives North Berwick; born 28.09.1949; married to Gillian with 3 children. Educated at Lathallan School, Montrose; Rugby School, Warwickshire; Edinburgh University (1968-1971 LLB).

Leisure: hockey; golf; shooting.

HENDY John

Queen's Counsel 15 Old Square, Lincoln's Inn, London WC2A 3UH.

Career: called to the Bar Gray's Inn (1972); QC (1987).

Activities: chairman Institute of Employment Rights (1989 to date).

Biography: lives London; born 11.04.1948; married. Educated (1969 London external LLB); Queen's University Belfast (1971 LLM).

HENEKER Michael

partner HYDE MAHON BRIDGES 52 Bedford Row, London WC1R 4UH.

Career: articled clerk Hyde Mahon & Pascall (1965); admitted (1967); assistant solicitor (1967-1969); became partner (1969).

Activities: founder and chairman National Independent Solicitors Group (NIS Group); governor local primary school; previously held various positions with local

H

H

Conservative association; treasurer local CPRE branch; member Glyndebourne Festival Society; member RAC.

Biography: lives Reigate; born 13.10.1942; married to Julia with 2 sons. Educated Cheltenham College (1956-1960); Bristol University (1964 LLB hons).

Leisure: tennis; music; opera; philately.

HENMAN Anthony

senior partner HENMANS 116 St Aldates, Oxford OX1 1HA.

Career: articled Henman Ballard (now Henmans) and Birkbeck Montagues; admitted (1964); assistant solicitor Hextall Erskine (1964-1968); assistant solicitor Henmans (1968-1969); became partner (1969); became senior partner (1980).

Activities: Deputy Registrar of High Court and County Court Oxford and Midland Circuit (1984 to date); represented Oxfordshire at hockey; tennis; squash; football and cricket; chairman Oxfordshire Squash RA; member of: Travellers' Club; Tramps; Jesters; Cumberland LTC; Vanderbilt LTC.

Biography: lives Weston on the Green, Oxfordshire; born 12.04.1940; married to Jane with 3 children. Educated at New College Preparatory School; Oxford and Malvern College; College of Law.

HENNIKER Chris

managing partner STEGGLES PALMER 2 Bedford Row, London WC1R 4BU.

Career: articled Tyrrell Lewis & Co; admitted (1978); assistant solicitor Steggles Palmer (1978-1981); became partner (1981); became managing partner (1983).

Activities: member Hurlingham Club.

Biography: lives London W4 and East Sussex; born 20.10.1952; married with 3 children. Educated at Bedford School; Manchester University (1974 LLB).

Leisure: tennis; squash; skiing.

HENNIKER SMITH Ian

head of legal department and company secretary BROWN & ROOT (UK) LTD Brown & Root House, 150 The Broadway, Wimbledon, London SW19 1RX.

Career: articled Balmer Son & Ritchie (1971-1973); admitted (1973); assistant solicitor (1973-1975); assistant solicitor Three Rivers District Council (1975-1978); assistant solicitor Brown & Root (UK) Ltd (1978-1980); deputy head of legal dept (1980-1982); became head of legal dept

(1982).

Activities: member of: Rudgwick Lawn Tennis Club; Pennthorpe Badminton Club; The Caravan Club; The Camping & Caravanning Club.

Biography: lives Cranleigh; born 20.04.1949; married to Jillian with 3 children. Educated at Douai School, Berkshire (1962-1967); Bristol University (1970 LLB).

Leisure: family life; badminton; tennis; shooting; swimming; gardening; walking; caravanning.

HENSHAW Hugh

partner LOVELL WHITE DURRANT 65 Holborn Viaduct, London EC1A 2DY.

Career: articled Clifford Turner & Co (1956-1961); admitted (1961); assistant solicitor Freshfields (1961-1964); assistant solicitor Lovell White & King (1964-1968); became partner (1968).

HERBERT Anthony James

partner ALLEN & OVERY 9 Cheapside, London EC2V 6AD.

Career: admitted (1965); assistant solicitor Allen & Overy (1965-1970); became partner (1970); became managing partner (1989).

Activities: member of the Law Society; City of London Law Society; International Bar Association; member of Roehampton Club.

Biography: lives London SW15; born 28.03.1940; married to Lowell with 3 children. Educated at Eton (1952-1958); King's College Cambridge (1962 BA); Alfred Syrett Prize (1964).

Leisure: painting pictures; tennis; skiing; listening to music.

HERBERT Bryan

partner and head of private client department BOOTH & CO Sovereign House, South Parade, Leeds LS1 1HQ.

Career: Royal Artillery (2 years); articled Booth & Co (1954-1957); admitted (1957); assistant solicitor (1957-1960); became partner (1960).

Activities: occasional lecturer on tax matters at Leeds Polytechnic; member of: The Leeds Club; Rotary Club of Leeds; Junior Chamber International.

Biography: lives Leeds; born 23.07.1930; married to Mary with 2 sons and 1 daughter. Educated at Bingley Grammar School; The Leys School, Cambridge; Christ's College Cambridge (1954 MA LLB); pamphlets on settlements and

inheritance tax.

Leisure: charity work; touring in Europe especially Germany.

HERBERT Max

company secretary and solicitor NATIONAL POWER PLC Sudbury House, 15 Newgate Street, London EC1A 7AU.

Career: articled in local government; admitted; solicitor to London Borough of Merton (1973-1976); Surrey County Council (1976-1979); solicitor CEGB (1979-1985); founded own practice (1985-1989); National Power (1989).

Activities: Planning Litigation Administrator.

Biography: lives Wimbledon; born 03.10.1946; married to Jane with 1 son. Educated at Strodes School, Egham; Chelsea College London (1968 BSC).

Leisure: golf; racing.

HERMAN Tony

senior partner BERRY & BERRY 11 Church Road, Tunbridge Wells, Kent.

Career: articled in Central London; admitted (1965); assistant solicitor Berry & Berry (1965-1970); became partner (1970); became senior partner (1984).

Activities: member Kent & Sussex Club.

Biography: lives Tunbridge Wells; born 21.01.1938; married to Dorita with 4 children. Educated at Hitchin Grammar School (1949-1957); London School of Economics (1961 BSC hons).

Leisure: association football; basketball; tennis; athletics; Spanish language and culture.

HEWETSON Sir Christopher

partner LACE MAWER 43 Castle Street, Liverpool L2 9SU.

Career: National Service as 2nd Lt in 4 RHA (1951-1953); articled Abercromby & Wood (1953-1956); admitted (1956); assistant solicitor (1956-1959); became partner (1959-1961); firm merged with Laces & Co (1961); became partner Laces & Co (1961); firm became Lace Mawer (1988).

Activities: Territorial Army with 359 Medium Regiment in Liverpool (1953-1968); commanded as Lt Colonel (1965); awarded TD (1966); president Liverpool Law Society (1975-1976); chairman governors of the College of Law (1977-1982) (governor 1969 to date); president The Law Society (1983-1984); Knighted

(1984); appointed Deputy Lt for Merseyside (DL) (1986); member Liverpool Law Society Committee (1964-1987); council member of The Law Society (1966-1987); member of: Athenaeum, Liverpool; Army & Navy Club; The Royal Birkdale Golf Club.

Biography: lives Southport; born 26.12.1929; married to Alison with 3 children. Educated at Terra Nova Preparatory School, Cheshire (1939-1943); Sedbergh, Cumbria (1943-1948); Peterhouse Cambridge (1951 BA) (1955 MA); Major Open Scholarship in Classics to Peterhouse; Timpron Martin Prize in Solicitors Finals; member editorial boards for a Guide to the Professional Conduct of Solicitors (1974) and the Professional Conduct of Solicitors (1986).

HEWITSON Charles

partner HEWITSON BECKE & SHAW Shakespeare House, 42 Newmarket Road, Cambridge CB5 8EP.

Career: articled Mills & Reeve; admitted (1977); assistant solicitor (1977-1979); assistant solicitor Wild Hewitson & Shaw (1979-1980); became partner (1980).

Activities: committee member The Evelyn Hospital, Cambridge; member of: CVC Squash Club; Cambridge Windsurfing; Ski Club of Great Britain.

Biography: lives Cambridge; born 09.11.1952; married to Julie with 2 children. Educated at Uppingham School; Leicester University (1975 LLB).

Leisure: squash; skiing; windsurfing; tennis.

HIBBARD Michael

partner CLYDE & CO Beaufort House, Chertsey Street, Guildford GU1 4HA.

Career: admitted (1966); assistant solicitor (1966-1972); became partner Clyde & Co (1972).

Biography: lives Guildford; born 28.03.1942. Educated at Nottingham High School; Bedford School; Corpus Christi College Cambridge (1963 MA); College of Law.

Leisure: squash; languages; music.

HIBBERT Randal

senior partner BIRCH CULLIMORE & CO Friars White Friars, Chester CH1 1XS.

Career: articled Lowndes & Co (1959-1962); admitted (1963); assistant solicitor Campbell & Co (1963-1964); assistant

solicitor Birch Cullimore (1964-1966); became partner (1966).

Activities: president Chester and North Wales Incorporated Law Society (1988-1989) (hon treasurer 1968-1986 & 1989 to date); under-sheriff for County of Cheshire (1981 to date); deputy Chapter clerk Chester Cathedral; treasurer Under-Sheriffs Association (1986 to date); life member National Trust (first vice-chairman Chester centre); life member Friends of Lake District; life member Cheshire branch CPRE; Fellow Royal Society of Arts; vice-chairman Cheshire Community Council; member of: Chester City Club; Henley Royal Regatta; Royal Chester Rowing Club.

Biography: lives Christleton; born 12.04.1936; married to Gill with 3 children. Educated at Kingsmead School (1945-1949); Shrewsbury School (1949-1954); Magdalene College Cambridge (1959 MA).

Leisure: tennis; golf; fell-walking; music; cathedrals.

HICKSON Paul

partner commercial property department BIRD & BIRD 2 Gray's Inn Square, London WC1R 5AF.

Career: admitted (1983); assistant solicitor (1983-1987); became partner Bird & Bird (1987).

Biography: lives Essex; born 10.10.1958; married with 1 child. Educated at Felsted School, Dunmow; St Catharine's College Cambridge (1980 MA).

Leisure: cricket; bridge.

HIGGINS Rosalyn

professor of international law UNIVERSITY OF LONDON 4 Essex Court, Temple, London EC4Y 9AJ.

Career: Research Fellow Royal Institute of International Affairs (1962-1973); Research Fellow Centre for International Studies LSE (1974-1976); called to the Bar (1975); door tenant 4 Essex Court (1975); QC (1986); professor of international law University of Kent (1977); professor of international law University of London at LSE (1980); Bencher of Inner Temple (1989).

Activities: legal adviser Foreign Affairs Select Committee on Abuse of Diplomatic Privileges; UK member UN Committee on Human Rights under Article 40 of the Covenant on Civil and Political Rights (1984 to date); member Editorial Board of Journal of Energy and Natural Resources Law; Energy Committee of International

Bar Association; former member Editorial Board American Journal International Law; Advisory Council, Interights; Council of Management British Institute of International Law; Associe of Institut de Droit International (1988); lectures given at Hague Academy of International Law; member Crockfords.

Biography: lives London SE3; born 02.06.1937; married to Terence with 2 children. Educated at Burlington Grammar School; Girton College Cambridge (1958 LLB) (1955 LLM); Yale Law School (1961 JSD).

Leisure: watching and playing golf; cooking and eating.

HIGGS David

senior partner HIGGS & SONS Blythe House, 134 High Street, Brierley Hill, West Midlands DY5 3BG.

Career: articled to uncle RGH Higgs (1957-1962); admitted (1963); became partner Higgs & Son (1963).

Activities: General Commissioner for Income Tax; member Birmingham Law Society Council (1974-1990); member Education and Lectures Committee and Social Committee; president Dudley & District Law Society (1984-1985); president Birmingham Law Society (1988-1989); feoffee and governor of Oldswinford Hospital; member of: Stourbridge Golf Club; Brierley Hill Rotary Club.

Biography: lives Stourbridge; born 21.03.1940; married to Vaari with 2 children. Educated at The Old Ride Preparatory School, Little Horwood; Bromsgrove School; Birmingham University (1957-1958); College of Law Lancaster Gate (1962-1963).

Leisure: bridge; swimming; golf; gardening.

HIGHAM Nicholas

partner SJ BERWIN & CO 236 Gray's Inn Road, London WC1X 8HB.

Career: articled Bristol; film and music law Richards Butler & Co (1968); intellectual property Linklaters & Paines; co-founder S J Berwin & Co (1982).

Activities: member CBI Intellectual Property Forum; participant in CBI Initiative on 1992.

Biography: lives London; born 02.03.1947; married to Ursula with 2 sons. Educated at Sherborne School; Bristol Polytechnic; Law Society exams (hons); Associate of Chartered Institute of Patent Agents;

H

author of 'The Businessman's Guide to Intellectual Property'; articles on data protection, service marks and exhaustion of rights under community law.

Leisure: sailing; bridge; marine art.

HILDITCH Brian

partner commercial property department MANCHES & CO Aldwych House, 71/91 Aldwych, London WC2B 4RP.

Career: articled Frank Platt & Fishwick (1971-1973); admitted (1973); assistant solicitor Linklaters & Paines (1973-1979); became partner Harold Benjamin & Collins (1979-1983); assistant solicitor Manches & Co (1983-1986); became partner (1986).

Activities: treasurer centre and grounds and council member Hadley Wood Association.

Biography: lives Hadley Wood; born 19.01.1949; married with 2 children. Educated at Holmwood School, Formby; Shrewsbury School; Liverpool University (LLB hons).

HILL Robert

member of the board of management THE COLLEGE OF LAW Bishopthorpe Road, York YO2 1QA.

Career: junior clerk Hall Brydon & Co (1964-1967); articled MPG Bowman (1968-1973); admitted (1974); lecturer College of Law Chester (1974-1978); senior lecturer (1978-1983); principal lecturer (1983-1988); appointed to board of management (1988); co-principal.

Activities: Deputy Registrar of the High Court of Justice and the County Court (1985 to date); special interests include advocacy training (studied this aspect in the USA); Territorial Army (1968); commissioned 33 Signal Regiment (1980).

Biography: lives York; born 19.10.1947; married to Ann with 2 children. Educated at Salford Grammar School; Manchester College of Commerce (1964-1967); College of Law Lancaster Gate (1969-1970 & 1972); Associate Institute of Legal Executives (1967) (Fellow 1972); author of 'Civil Litigation' with John O'Hare; author of 'How to survive your articles'; numerous articles and lectures published.

HILL Roy

partner and chairman HILL DICKINSON DAVIS CAMPBELL Equity & Law House, 47 Castle Street, Liverpool L2 9UB.

Career: admitted (1947); Royal Air Force

Second World War; assistant solicitor Hill Dickinson & Co; became partner (4th generation) (1951); became senior partner (1984); chairman (1987); chairman Hill Dickinson Davis Campbell (1989).

Activities: engaged in commercial practice with a width of experience covering shipping, insurance, pension property and its development; Manager the Liverpool and London War Risks Insurance Association Ltd; Chairman of trustees the National Union of Marine Aviation and Shipping Transport and its welfare activities; served on various committees relating to British Shipping including various advisory committees set up by HMG (1955-1965); legal adviser to various pension funds including relating to the shipping industry; examiner Solicitors Qualifying Examination Commercial Paper (1950s-1970s); member of: The Sloane Club; Alvis Owners' Club; RAC; the Royal Horticultural Society.

Biography: lives Caldy, Wirral; born 05.01.1922; married to Norah with 2 children. Educated at Wallop Preparatory School, Weybridge; Chigwell School.

Leisure: swimming; walking; gardening; writing; music and opera.

HILLYER John

senior partner PHILIP JONES HILLYER AND JACKSON 9 Hunter Street, Chester CH1 2AQ.

Career: admitted (1965); taught students taking solicitor finals at Liverpool Polytechnic for 6 months; articled Philip Jones; assistant solicitor; became partner; became senior partner (1984).

Activities: assistant recorder (1984); recorder (1988); chairman of Regional Duty Solicitor Panel; member of: Rotary Chester; 41 Club Chester.

Biography: lives Chester; born 22.10.1940; 2 children. Educated at Chester City Grammar School; LSE (LLB hons).

Leisure: very active sportsman in the past; golf; bridge.

HINDE Keith

partner POTHECARY & BARRATT Talbot House, Talbot Court, Gracechurch Street, London EC3V 0BS.

Career: articled Stibbard Gibson & Co (1958-1961); admitted (1961); assistant solicitor (1961-1965); became partner Thomas Cooper & Stibbard (1965-1976); became partner Pothecary & Barratt (1976).

Activities: clerk to the City of London

Solicitors' Company (1969-1976); Master to the City of London Solicitors' Company (1988-1989); clerk to the Worshipful Company of Cutlers (1975 to date); director Scaffolding Construction Limited; member General Council King George's Fund for Sailors (1970 to date); chairman City Solicitors Professional Business Committee (1978-1981); president City of London Law Society (1988-1989); trustee Stretham Old Engine; trustee Suffolk & Norfolk Yeomanry Trust; member of United Oxford & Cambridge Club.

Biography: lives Waterbeach; born 1934; married with 1 son. Educated at Colchester Royal Grammar School (1942-1953); Corpus Christi College Cambridge (1958 MA); author of sundry articles on the history of Fenland drainage.

HINE Alan

partner FORD SIMEY DAW ROBERTS Hereford House, Southernhay Gardens, Exeter EX1 1NP.

Career: articled to the town clerk of Torquay; seconded to the formation of new County Borough of Torbay; admitted (1966); tutor College of Law (1966-1970); assistant solicitor London (1970-1971); assistant solicitor/partner Woodfine and Company (1971-1972); litigation partner Ford Simey and Ford (1972-1979); became commercial partner (1979).

Activities: formerly part of the Law Society's examining team in the Law of Contract; Deputy County Court Registrar and Deputy District Registrar (1983 to date); assisted various local voluntary organisations.

Biography: lives Exeter; born 01.09.1940; married with 2 children and 2 stepchildren. Educated at Hele School, Exeter; King's College London (1962 LLB); written articles during years as tutor.

Leisure: obsessive interest in one acre of land in the Haldon Hills, Devon; old motor cars; music especially medieval music; literature; eating; drinking.

HODGE Henry

senior partner HODGE JONES & ALLEN 148/150 Camden High Street, London NW1 0NG.

Career: articled Durrant Cooper Hambling; admitted (1970); legal secretary Justice (1971); solicitor and deputy director Child Poverty Action Group (1972-1977); founded Hodge Jones & Allen (1977).

Activities: member Islington Council (1974-

1978); chairman National Council for Civil Liberties (1974-1975); member Lord Chancellor's Legal Aid Advisory Committee (1977-1983); member Council of Law Society (Legal Aid specialist) (1984 to date); chairman Camden Citizens Advice Bureau (1983-1988); chairman national Citizens Advice Bureau Training Committee (1982-1984); chairman Courts and Legal Services Committee Law Society (1987-1990); member Supplementary Benefits Commission (1978-1980); member Social Security Advisory Committee (1980 to date); interested in discrimination/family law/poverty issues/Labour Party (active member); Arsenal supporter.

Biography: lives London N1; born 12.01.1944; married to Margaret with 4 children. Educated at Chigwell School; Balliol College Oxford (1965); author of 'Legal Rights' (1974); various articles on law and legal practice; writing on and promoter of the need for solicitors to provide an effective Legal Aid service.

HODGE John Bater

consultant to GREGORY ROWCLIFFE & MILNERS 1 Bedford Row, London WC1R 4BZ.

Career: articled to brother Harold R Hodge; admitted; assistant solicitor Mills Curry & Gaskell; assistant solicitor JH Milner & Son; litigation partner; amalgamated to become Milners Curry & Gaskell and then amalgamated to become Gregory Rowcliffe & Milners; became consultant.

Biography: lives Chislehurst; born 04.07.1925; married with 4 daughters. Educated at Chigwell School; Haileybury College; Queen's College Cambridge (1949 MA LLM); author of small book 'Vicarious Liability' or 'Liability for the Acts of Others'; various articles in Law Society's Gazette; Solicitors Journal; New Law Journal.

Leisure: wildlife; walking.

HODGETTS Clifford

senior partner THOMAS EGGAR VERRALL BOWLES 5 East Pallant, Chichester PO19 1TS.

Career: articled Rickerbys; National Service commission Royal Artillery; assistant solicitor Thomas Eggar & Son (1960); became partner (1962); senior partner (1986).

Activities: Diocesan Registrar (1971 to date); Bishop's legal secretary (Chichester);

clerk to Dean & Chapter of Chichester; legal secretary to Dean & Chapter of Westminster; member of MCC.

Biography: lives Graffham nr Petworth; born 12.05.1934; married with 3 children. Educated at Dean Close School; Bristol University (LLB).

Leisure: fishing; golf; tennis; walking.

HODGKINSON George

partner SINCLAIR ROCHE & TEMPERLEY Stone House, 128-140 Bishopsgate, London EC2M 4JP and SINCLAIR ROCHE 42nd Floor, Bank of China, Tower No. 1 Ganden Road, Central, Hong Kong.

Career: voluntary service overseas (India) (1963); articled Coward Chance; admitted (1970); assistant solicitor BP Tanker Company Limited (1971-1973); assistant solicitor Sinclair Roche & Temperley (1973-1975); became partner (1975).

Activities: speaker on ship loans in default; class captain Aldeburgh Yacht Club Wayfarers.

Biography: lives Aldham, Colchester; born 04.03.1945; married to Sarah with 3 children. Educated at Rugby School; Oxford (1966 BA Jurisprudence).

Leisure: sailing; tennis; golf.

HODGSON Anthony

senior partner HODGSON & SONS 7 Ribblesdale Place, Preston .

Career: articled to father (1947-1952); admitted (1953); RAF (1953-1955); assistant solicitor (1955-1958); became partner (1958).

Activities: deputy chairman Agricultural Land Tribunal (West Midlands Region) (1983); Notary Public; commissioner for Oaths; president Preston Incorporated Law Society (1988); member Law Society Legal Aid Appeals Committee; member Preston Rotary Club.

Biography: lives Preston; born 25.10.1929; married to Jean with 2 sons. Educated at Rossall; Manchester University.

Leisure: music; steam railways.

HODSON Philip

partner and head of litigation department COBBETT LEAK ALMOND Ship Canal House, King Street, Manchester M2 4WB.

Career: articled Manchester City Council (1966-1969); admitted (1969); assistant solicitor (1969-1973); assistant solicitor Leak Almond & Parkinson (1973-1974);

became partner (1974-1987); became partner Cobbett Leak Almond (1987).

Activities: chairman Manchester Young Solicitors Association (1980); president Manchester Law Society (1988-1989); treasurer South Manchester Law Centre (1982-1987) (chairman 1987-1989); former secretary Manchester Lawyers' Golfing Society; member Legal Aid Area Committee; former member local Duty Solicitor Committee; member South Manchester Law Centre Management Committee; member Salford Players Theatre; member Salford Playhouse Management Committee; member St James's Club.

Biography: lives Eccles; born 02.10.1944; married to Diane. Educated at Oundle School; St Edmund Hall Oxford (1966 BA) (1969 MA); Francis Bennion Prize (1964).

Leisure: squash (playing and refereeing); golf; theatre.

HOFFMAN Anthony Edward

senior partner HAMLIN SLOWE PO Box 4SQ, Roxburghe House, 273/287 Regent Street, London W1A 4SQ.

Career: articled Thornton Lynne & Lawson (1954-1959); admitted (1959); assistant solicitor (1959-1960); became junior partner Joelson & Co (1960-1962); founded own practice (1962); acquired to form Hamlin Slowe (1984 to date).

Activities: member of The Law Society.

Biography: lives London NW1 and Peterborough; born 21.02.1937; divorced with 3 daughters. Educated at City of London School; various articles on intellectual property law.

Leisure: shooting; fishing; walking; gardening.

HOFFMAN Paul

head of chambers 25 Park Square, Leeds LS1 2PW.

Career: called to Bar (1964); head of chambers (1981 to date); Recorder on NE Circuit (1985).

Activities: standing prosecuting Counsel to Inland Revenue on NE Circuit (1985).

Biography: lives Leeds; born 29.07.1942; married to Elaine with 3 sons. Educated at Roundhay Boys, Leeds; Sheffield University (1962 LLB) Edgar Allen Scholar; Law Society junior prize (1960); Law Society senior prize (1962).

Leisure: gardening; walking; rambling; theatre; concerts.

HOGG Graham Edwyn Trevor

partner HOLMAN FENWICK & WILLAN Marlow House, Lloyds Avenue, London EC3N 3AL.

Career: clerk Ince & Co (1956-1957); articled (1960-1964); admitted (1964); assistant solicitor Roney & Co (1964-1966); assistant solicitor Richards Butler & Co (1966-1969); assistant solicitor Waltons Bright & Co (1969-1971); assistant solicitor Holman Fenwick & Willan (1971); became partner (1973); member Staff & Salaries Sub-committee (1975-1983); member Management Committee (1989 to date); practice development partner (1989).

Activities: member RAC.

Biography: lives Amersham; born 22.12.1936; married to Margaret with 2 children. Educated at Gresham's School, Holt (1947-1955); Fitzwilliam College Cambridge (1964 MA) College of Law (1963-1964).

Leisure: squash; swimming; tennis; fell walking; golf; music; wine; food; travel.

HOLBROOK Richard

chairman board of management THE COLLEGE OF LAW Braboeuf Manor, St Catherine's, Guildford, Surrey GU3 1HA.

Career: articled in Holborn (1957-1960); admitted (1960); Gibson & Weldon (1960-1962); The College of Law (1962).

Activities: member the Lord Chancellor's Advisory Committee on Legal Education; member The Law Society's Training Committee; member the Common Professional Examination Board; member the Law Society's Finals Advisory Board; member West Surrey Law Society; member Surrey Law Club.

Biography: lives Guildford; born 05.12.1934; married with 2 children. Educated at Sir William Borlases, Marlow; Rutherford Grammar School, Newcastle-upon-Tyne; King's College Durham (LLB hons); author of joint edition Gibson's Conveyancing Twenty-First Edition.

HOLDEN Lawrence

managing partner BRABNER HOLDEN 1 Dale Street, Liverpool L2 2ET.

Career: articled Banks Kendall Taylor & Gorst and Duncan Oakshott & Co; admitted (1965); assistant solicitor Duncan Oakshott & Co (1965-1966); became partner (1966); merged with Toulmin Hodgson & Brabner (1968); became managing partner Brabner Holden & Co (1988).

Activities: vice-president of Council of

Liverpool University (1987 to date); treasurer Liverpool Council of Social Services (1982 to date); member Law Society (1983-1988); member Law Office Management and Technology Committee (1988); member Business Improvement Committee (1988-1989); member Society for Computers in Law Council (1982-1987); vice-president Liverpool Law Society; former chairman Legal Education Committee; former chairman Legal Advice Services Committee and Professional and Public Relations Committee; member Athenaeum.

Biography: lives Prenton; born 19.09.1940; married to Rosemary with 3 children. Educated at Liverpool University (1962 LLB); articles in the Law Society Gazette and the Journal of the Society for Computers and Law.

Leisure: mountain walking; sculpting in wood.

HOLLAND Christopher

Queen's Counsel Pearl Chambers, 22 East Parade, Leeds LS1 5BU.

Career: practice in Leeds (1963); junior North Eastern Circuit (1966); QC (1978); Bencher Inner Temple (1985) .

Activities: vice-chairman Committee of Inquiry into Outbreak of Legionnaire's Disease at Stafford (1986); Deputy High Court Judge (1988); member United Oxford & Cambridge Universities Club.

Biography: born 01.06.1937; married to Jill with 2 children. Educated at Leeds Grammar School; Emmanuel College Cambridge (MA LLB).

HOLLAND Paul

partner STAMP JACKSON & PROCTER 5 Parliament Street, Kingston-upon-Hull, Humberside HU1 2AZ.

Career: articled Philip Hamer & Co (1978-1980); admitted (1980); assistant solicitor Philip Hamer & Co and Payne & Payne (1980-1982); assistant solicitor Stamp Jackson & Procter (1982-1983); became partner (1983).

Activities: member Law Society Child Care Panel; Regional Duty Solicitor Committee; local Court users' group .

Biography: lives Kingston-upon-Hull; born 11.09.1956; married to Lin. Educated at Chipping Sodbury Grammar School; North Staffordshire Polytechnic.

Leisure: sport; cuisine; foreign travel; literature; fashion & design.

HOLLAND Peter

partner ALLEN & OVERY 9 Cheapside, London EC2V 6AD.

Career: assistant solicitor Allen & Overy (1968-1971); became partner (1972).

Activities: member Law Society's Company Law Committee (1978-1988) (chairman 1983-1987); member City EEC Committee (1983-1987); member City of London Law Society's Company Law Sub-committee (1983-1987).

Biography: lives Basingstoke; born 31.07.1944; married to Susan Okeby with 1 son and 1 daughter. Educated at St Edmund's School, Canterbury; Oxford (1965 BA); contributor to: 'Mergers & Acquisitions' (1986); 'The City Code on Take-Overs & Mergers: A Practitioner's Guide' (1988).

Leisure: travel; skiing; outdoor activities.

HOLLAND Tony

partner FOOT & BOWDEN 70-76 North Hill, Plymouth PL4 8HH.

Career: admitted (1962); assistant solicitor Foot & Bowden (1962-1964); became partner (1964).

Activities: chairman National Committee of Young Solicitors Group of the Law Society (1972-1973); elected to the Council of the Law Society (1976); chairman Non-Contentious Business Committee of the Council of the Law Society (1982-1985); Governor Plymouth College; chairman Social Security Appeal Tribunal; former chairman BBC South Western Regional Advisory Council (1984); member Marre Committee on the future of the legal profession (1986); President of the Law Society (1990); member Royal Western Yacht Club of England.

Biography: lives London EC2 and Plymouth; born 09.11.1938; married to Kay with 3 children. Educated Gracedieu Manor Preparatory School; Ratcliffe College; Nottingham University (1959 LLB); co-author of 'Principles of Registered Land Conveyancing' and 'Landlord and Tenant'; joint advisory editor on Mining Precedents in Encyclopaedia of Forms and Precedents.

Leisure: opera; journalism; broadcasting; sailing.

HOLLINGSWORTH Bernard

partner and head of property department JAQUES & LEWIS 2 South Square, Gray's Inn, London WC1R 5HR.

Career: articled Jaques & Lewis (1957-

1960); admitted (1960); assistant solicitor (1960-1963); became partner (1963).

Biography: lives Cuckfield; born 08.06.1936; married to Barbara with 2 children. Educated at George Watson's College, Edinburgh; Whitgift School, South Croydon; King's College London (1957 LLB) (1957 AKC) (1959 LLM).

Leisure: sailing; gardening.

HOLLIS Dan

Queen's Counsel and head of chambers Queen Elizabeth Building, Temple, London EC4Y 9BS.

Career: first prosecuting Counsel to Inland Revenue CCC (1965); QC (1968); Recorder (1972); Bencher (1975); Deputy High Court Judge (1982).

Activities: member Home Secretary's Advisory Board on Restricted Patients (1986).

Biography: born 30.04.1925; married to Stella with 3 children; 2 stepchildren. Educated at Geelong Grammar School; Brasenose College Oxford.

HOLMAN Richard

partner DAVIES WALLIS FOYSTER 37 Peter Street, Manchester M32 5GB.

Career: articled Foysters (1969-1971); admitted (1971); assistant solicitor (1971-1973); became partner (1973); became head litigation department (1979); became managing partner (1988-1989); firm merged with Davies Wallis (1989).

Activities: Deputy District Registrar of the High Court and Deputy Registrar of the County Court (1982-1988); Assistant Recorder (1988); council member Manchester Law Society (1983-1990); member North West Legal Aid Area Committee; Notary Public; governor Pownall Hall School, Wilmslow (1990 to date); member of: the Wilmslow Golf Club; Valley Lodge Country Club.

Biography: lives Wilmslow; born 16.06.1946; married to Susan with 2 sons. Educated at Eton College (1959-1964); Gonville and Caius College Cambridge (1968 BA) (1972 MA); College of Law Guildford (1969 hons).

Leisure: golf; gardening; theatre; listening to music.

HOLMES Murray

senior partner DENNIS FAULKNER & ALSOP Beethoven House, 32 Market Square, Northampton NN1 2DQ.

Career: articled Rance & Co (1962); admitted (1966); assistant solicitor Lucien Fior (1966-1967); assistant solicitor Dennis Faulkner and Alsop (1967-1969); became partner (1969); became senior partner (1989).

Activities: ex-president Northamptonshire Law Society (1988-1989); ex-chairman Northamptonshire Duty Solicitor Committee; member Northamptonshire Family Health Services Authority; trustee and general committee member Northampton Rugby Football Club; chairman of two local trusts and local Conservation Area Committee; member of: Old Millhillians Club; Northampton and County Club; Dallington Country Club; Black Bottom Jazz Club.

Biography: lives Northampton; born 26.05.1940; married to Jill with 3 children. Educated at Eaglehurst College, Northampton; Mill Hill School; University of Wales (1962 LLB).

Leisure: reading; sailing; rugby football; exercise; jazz.

HOLT Jonathan

co-founding and joint senior partner HOLT PHILLIPS 11/12 Queen Square, Bristol BS1 4NT.

Career: articled Husband Tillyard Rees & Peterson; admitted (1980); assistant solicitor (1980-1982); assistant solicitor Cartwrights (1982-1984); co-founded Holt Phillips (1984).

Activities: member of: Bridgwater & Albion RFC; Welshback Squash Club.

Biography: lives Chew Magna nr Bristol; born 08.09.1955; married to Jennifer with 2 children. Educated at Windsor Grammar School; Penarth Grammar School; University of Wales (1977 LLB hons).

Leisure: motorsports; squash; running; keeping-fit; eating out; wine; spending as much time as possible with 2 daughters.

HOLT Neville

senior partner ABSON HALL 30 Greek Street, Stockport SK3 8AD.

Career: admitted (1956); National Service with Army Lt Intelligence Corps, Berlin (1956-1958); became senior partner Abson Hall (1986).

Activities: former Liberal Councillor Stockport Town Council; former president Stockport Law Society; former chairman Association of Manchester Area Law Societies; chairman Social Security Appeal Tribunal; life member National Trust;

member of: RSPB; CHA; Intelligence Corps Association; Social & Liberal Democrat Party; Camping & Caravanning Club; Caravan Club; Forum Music Society.

Biography: lives Stockport; born 27.07.1931; married to Patricia with 1 son. Educated at Our Lady's Primary, Stockport Convent High School; Stockport Grammar School; Manchester University (1953 LLB hons).

Leisure: environmental issues; rambling; caravanning; bird watching; gardening; beer brewing; swimming; men's lacrosse; music; theatre.

HOLT Nick

legal and compliance director SMITH NEW COURT PLC Chetwynd House, 24-30 St Swithin's Lane, London EC4N 8AE.

Career: articled Coward Chance (1980-1982); admitted (1982); assistant solicitor (1983-1984); admitted Hong Kong (1984); assistant solicitor corporate legal department Jardine Matheson & Co Ltd, Hong Kong (1984-1986); manager (1986-1987); legal adviser Smith New Court PLC (1987-1989); became legal and compliance director (1989).

Activities: member The Reform Club.

Biography: lives London SE21; born 02.04.1958; married to Georgina with 1 son and 1 daughter. Educated at the Manchester Grammar School; Fitzwilliam College Cambridge (1979 BA hons) (1983 MA).

Leisure: sport; football; squash; wine.

HOMAN Hugh

head of asset finance group and staff partner BERWIN LEIGHTON Adelaide House, London Bridge, London EC4R 9HA.

Career: articled clerk and assistant Allen & Overy (1967-1973); assistant solicitor Berwin Leighton (1973-1975); partner (1975).

Activities: frequent lecturer on leasing, lectures both in UK and abroad.

Biography: lives London and Suffolk; born 26.06.1945; married to Lyn with 2 children. Educated at Sherborne School, Dorset; Worcester College, Oxford (MA 1967).

Leisure: indian affairs; local (Suffolk village) politics; sailing; golf.

HONNYWILL Godfrey C

senior partner THE BUSS MURTON PARTNERSHIP The Priory, Tunbridge Wells, Kent TN1 1JJ.

H

Career: admitted (1957); assistant solicitor (1957-1959); became partner (1959).

Activities: president Kent Law Society (1974-1975); member Kent Law Society Special Purposes Committee; member Commonwealth Lawyers' Association; member Tonbridge Rugby Club.

Biography: born 14.03.1934; married with 4 children. Educated at Temple Grove Prep School, Sherborne; College of Law Lancaster Gate.

Leisure: holiday house in South of France; gardening.

HOOBERMAN Ronald

partner in commercial property department and business development partner SAUNDERS SOBELL LEIGH & DOBIN 20 Red Lion Street, London WC1R 4AE.

Career: articled Nabarro Nathanson; admitted (1970); assistant solicitor; became partner David Alterman & Sewell (1973-1985); became partner Saunders Sobell Leigh & Dobin (1985).

Activities: Freeman of the City of London; Liveryman of the Worshipful Company of Basketmakers; member Savile Club.

Biography: lives London NW1; born 11.06.1943; single. Educated at City of London School; Cours de Civilisation Francaise at the Sorbonne, Paris (1962); University College (1966 LLB hons).

Leisure: photography; modern art; music; wine; food; cookery; pottering in the garden; languages (French and Russian).

HOOD Brian (Buzz)

partner WINCKWORTH & PEMBERTON Guy Harlings, 53 New Street, Chelmsford CM1 1NG.

Career: articled Anthony Polson & Robertson, New Zealand (1965-1966); admitted NZ (1966); supply teacher in London (1967-1968); English language teacher to various oil companies in Libya (1969-1972); articled Kershaw Gassman & Matthews (1973-1974); articled Lee Bolton & Lee (1974-1976); admitted UK (1976); assistant solicitor (1976-1977); partner (1977-1978); became partner Winckworth & Pemberton (1978).

Activities: Deputy Diocesan Registrar Chelmsford (1978-1989); Registrar & Bishop's legal secretary (1989); Ecclesiastical Notary Public (1976); member Law Society Golf Society.

Biography: lives Fairstead; born 08.02.1943; married with 2 children. Educated at

Marlborough College; University of Canterbury, New Zealand (1966 LLB) (1967 LLM hons).

Leisure: golf; tennis; sailing.

HOOD Stephen

partner and head of capital markets CLIFFORD CHANCE Royex House, Aldermanbury Square, London EC2V 7LD.

Career: articled Morris Fletcher & Cross, Brisbane, Queensland; admitted Queensland (1969); admitted England (1974); assistant solicitor Coward Chance (1974-1978); became partner (1978); admitted Hong Kong (1980); became senior resident partner Hong Kong (1981-1986).

Activities: chairman London Young Solicitors Law Society (1979-1980); chairman Financial Law Sub-committee Hong Kong Law Society (1984-1986); chairman Royal Commonwealth Society Hong Kong (1983-1986); chairman Executive Committee Sir Robert Menzies Memorial Trust (1988 to date); council member Royal Commonwealth Society (1987 to date); council member Britain Australia Society (1980 to date); British board member European Association for Chinese Law; member Boards of Management - Institute for Commonwealth Studies and Centre for Australian Studies, University of London; member Oriental Club, London; Hong Kong Club, Hong Kong.

Biography: lives London SW3 and Haslemere; born 12.02.1947; married to Maya nee Togonal with 4 sons and 1 daughter. Educated at Brisbane Boys' College; Queensland University (1974-1978); London University (1973 LLM); co-author of: UK chapter 'Doing Business in Europe'; 'Equity Joint Ventures in the People's Republic of China'; 'Technology Transfer to the People's Republic of China'.

HOOLE Sir Arthur

consultant TUCK & MANN King's Shade Walk, 123 High Street, Epsom, Surrey KT19 8AU.

Career: RAF Navigator and flying officer (1943-1946); articled Tuck & Mann (1948-1950); admitted (1951); became partner (1951-1988); became consultant (1989).

Activities: member Law Society Council (1969-1987) (chairman Education and Training Committee (1979-1982); president Law Society (1984-1985); president Mid-Surrey Law Society (1971-1972); chairman governors of College of Law (1983-1990); member Criminal Injuries Compensation

Board (1985 to date); member Mental Health Tribunal; member Lord Chancellor's Advisory Committee on Legal Education; governor St John's School, Leatherhead; governor Sutton Manor High School; chairman Epsom Sports Club; member RAC.

Biography: lives Leatherhead; born 14.01.1924; married to Eleanor with 4 children. Educated at Sutton County School; Emmanuel College Cambridge (1947 MA LLM); Solicitors Finals (1951 hons).

Leisure: music; books; wine; cricket.

HOOPER John

partner SELWOOD LEATHES HOOPER 6/7 St George's Road, Kemp Town, Brighton, East Sussex BN2 1EB.

Career: articled Selwood Leathes Hooper (1957-1962); admitted (1962); assistant solicitor (1962-1963); became partner (1963).

Activities: member Sussex Law Society; President Sussex Law Society (1988-1989) (advocacy training officer 1981 to date) (chairman Continuing Education Committee) (member General Committee and various sub-committees); former chairman Sussex Society of Young Solicitors; Deputy County Court and District Registrar; member No 2 (South Eastern) Legal Aid Area Committee; member Brighton Hove & Lewes Duty Solicitor Committee; member Law Society Child Care Panel; member of: Old Azurians Association; Worthing Rowing Club.

Biography: lives West Sussex; born 04.12.1938; married to Celia with 2 daughters and 1 son. Educated at Worthing High School for Boys; Gibson & Weldon Chancery Lane; London University (external LLB).

Leisure: family; theatre; gardening; going to France.

HOOSON Lord Emlyn

Queen's Counsel 1 Dr Johnson's Buildings, Temple, London EC4.

Career: called to the Bar (1949); QC (1960); Bencher Gray's Inn (1968); leader Wales & Chester circuit (1971-1974); Recorder of Merthyr Tydfil (1971); Recorder of Swansea (1971); Recorder of the Crown Court (1972 to date).

Activities: deputy chairman Merioneth QS (1960-1967) (chairman 1967-1971); deputy chairman Flint QS (1960-1971); Liberal MP for Montgomery (1962-1979); leader Welsh Liberal party (1966-1979) (president 1983-1986); Life Peer (1979); vice-treasurer Gray's Inn (1985) (treasurer 1986); non-executive director Laura Ashley PLC (1985 to date); hon professional Fellow University College of Wales (1971 to date); vice-chairman Political Committee North Atlantic Assembly (1975-1979); president Llangollen International Musical Eisteddfod (1987 to date); chairman governors of the London Welsh School; member Surrey County Cricket Club.

Biography: lives London and Llanidloes; born 26.03.1925; married to Shirley with 2 daughters. Educated at Denbigh Grammar School; University College of Wales (LLB).

Leisure: farming.

HOPKINS Carl

partner NABARRO NATHANSON 50 Stratton Street, London W1X 5FL.

Career: admitted (1971); assistant and senior assistant solicitor Kent County Council (1971-1976); assistant county secretary Kent (1976-1981); secondment principal DOE New Towns Directorate (1979-1980); solicitor and secretary London Docklands Development Corporation (1981-1987); became partner Nabarro Nathanson (1987).

Activities: member CBI London Region Council (member task force on urban regeneration); member Reform Club.

Biography: lives nr Rochester; born 18.08.1945; married to Jennifer with 1 child. Educated at Haverfordwest Grammar School; Milford Haven Grammar School; College of Law.

Leisure: fishing; sailing..

HOPKINS Roger

senior partner HOPKINS & WOOD 2-3 Cursitor Street, London EC4A 1NE.

Career: called to Bar Inner Temple (1969); pupillage with John Griffiths QC (1969-1970); tenant 2 Crown Office Row (1970-1974); articled Clifford Turner (1974-1976); admitted (1976); assistant solicitor (1976-1980); founded Hopkins Fuller (1980); became Hopkins & Wood (1982).

Activities: member of: Flyfishers' Club; Lansdowne Club.

Biography: lives London and Steventon; born 21.04.1947; married with 2 children. Educated at Uppingham School; Worcester College Oxford (1968 BA hons 1st Class) (1972 MA); Duke of Edinburgh Entrance Scholar Inner Temple (1967); Major Scholar

Inner Temple (1969).

HOPKINS Rowland

barrister and head of chambers Victoria Chambers, 177 Corporation Street, Birmingham B4 6RG.

Career: pupillage with JR Hopkin (1970-1971); Court clerk Northampton Magistrates' Court (1972-1974); Court clerk Birmingham Magistrates' Court (1974-1984); Birmingham Bar (1984 to date); became head of Chambers (1986).

Activities: volunteer United Evangelical Project Legal Advice Service, Aston; member General Synod of Church of England (until 1990); chairman House of Laity of Birmingham Diocesan Synod.

Biography: lives Birmingham; born 19.12.1948; married to Ann with 1 daughter Sarah (born 24.10.1989). Educated at Lawrence Sheriff School, Rugby; University College London (1970 LLB); articles in Justice of the Peace; New Law Journal and other journals (1975-1978).

Leisure: skiing; hill walking.

HORNER Nigel

partner WHATLEY WESTON & FOX 15 & 16 The Tything, Worcester WR1 1HD.

Career: articled Pinsent & Co (1971-1973); admitted (1973); assistant solicitor (1973-1976); became partner Whatley Weston & Fox (1976).

Activities: Insolvency Practitioner (1987); member Law Society's Insolvency Practitioners' Association.

Biography: lives Worcestershire; born 15.07.1948; married to Helen with 2 daughters. Educated at Solihull School; Nottingham University; on the editorial board of 'Insolvency Law & Practice'.

Leisure: skiing; sailing .

HORROCKS Peter

partner LOVELL WHITE DURRANT 21 Holborn Viaduct, London EC1A 2DY.

Career: articled Cameron Kemm Nordon & Co; admitted (1968); assistant solicitor (1968-1970); assistant solicitor Lovell White & King (1970-1975); became partner (1975); New York office (1980-1983); admitted as licensed consultant in New York (1982).

Activities: licensed insolvency practitioner; member Law Society; member Insolvency Sub-committee of the City of London Law Society; member Law League of America; member Joint Committee of the law Society and the Bar on Insolvency Matters;

council member Insolvency Lawyers' Association Limited; Liveryman of the City of London Solicitors' Company; member of: Brickendon Grange Golf & Country Club; The Wig & Pen Club; the Williams Club, New York.

Biography: lives Roydon; born 25.06.1944; married to Nerys with 2 children. Educated at High Storrs, Sheffield; Rutherford College, Newcastle; King's School, Macclesfield.

Leisure: sport (particularly cricket and golf).

HORSEY John

senior partner and joint chairman PENNINGTONS Phoenix House, 9 London Road, Newbury, Berks RG13 1JL.

Career: articled London and Weston super Mare (1961-1966); admitted (1966); assistant solicitor (1966-1967); became partner Penningtons (1967); became joint chairman (1986); chairman strategy/planning committee and marketing committee.

Activities: member of the board of West Berkshire Housing Association; director several private companies.

Biography: lives Marlborough; married with 7 children. Educated at Streete Court Preparatory School; St John's Leatherhead Public School; City of London University (1961); College of Law Lancaster Gate; Bristol University (Law Society finals).

Leisure: shooting; music (part-time organist); travel; tennis; gardening; study of horology.

HORSEY Paul

senior partner BEVAN ASHFORD Gotham House, Tiverton, Devon EX16 6LT.

Career: articled in London; admitted (1962); assistant solicitor (1962-1969); became partner Bevan Ashford (1969).

Activities: Notary Public; former president Devon and Exeter Incorporated Law Society; deputy chairman Area 4 Legal Aid Committee; governor FE College; member Rotary.

Biography: lives Tiverton; born 23.05.1937; married to Els with 4 children. Educated at St John's School, Leatherhead .

Leisure: choral singing; tennis; sailing.

HORSFALL TURNER Richard

senior resident partner Middle East Regional Office located in Dubai of ALLEN & OVERY 9 Cheapside, London EC2V 6AD.

H

Career: articled Allen & Overy (1963-1966); admitted (1966); assistant solicitor (1966-1970); became partner (1970); opened firm's Middle East regional office Dubai (1978).

Activities: member Law Society (1967); member City of London Solicitors' Company; licenced as legal consultant Dubai (1977); admitted solicitor Supreme Court for Hong Kong (1988); member Law Society of Hong Kong; Associate of the Chartered Institute of Arbitrators; member European and Asia-Pacific Users' Councils of the London Court of International Arbitration; member International Bar Association Committee on International Construction Contracts (1989); member of: Dubai Hilton Beach Club; World Trade Club, Dubai; Dubai Polo Club; Emirates Golf Club, Dubai; Amstel Club, Amsterdam.

Biography: lives London N1 and Jumeirah, Dubai; born 04.02.1942. Educated at Dragon School, Oxford (1950-1955); King's School, Canterbury (1955-1960); Jesus College Oxford (1963 BA hons).

Leisure: restoration and refurbishment of period properties.

HORSFIELD Peter

Queen's Counsel 8 Stone Buildings, Lincoln's Inn, London WC2A 3TA.

Career: National Service RNR; called to the Bar Lincoln's Inn (1959); practices at the Chancery Bar; QC (1978); Bencher Middle Temple.

Activities: member Garrick Club.

Biography: lives Kingston upon Thames; born 15.02.1932; married to Anne with 3 sons. Educated at Beaumont; Trinity College Oxford (hons); RNR Russian interpreter.

Leisure: painting; observational astronomy.

HOUGHTON Deryck

partner and head of criminal/magistrates' court department OXLEY & COWARD 34 Moorgate Street, Rotherham, South Yorkshire S60 2HB.

Career: articled in Chesterfield (1979-1981); admitted (1981); assistant solicitor (1981-1986); assistant solicitor Oxley & Coward (1986-1988); became partner (1988).

Activities: inaugural member National Child Care Panel.

Biography: lives Chesterfield; born 08.07.1957; single. Educated at The Wallace High School, Lisburn; Newton le Willows Grammar School; Sheffield University (1978 LLB hons).

HOULDSWORTH David

partner private client - land and rural estates department BRODIES WS 15 Atholl Crescent, Edinburgh EH3 8HA.

Career: apprentice Brodies WS (1975-1977); admitted (1977); assistant solicitor (1978-1981); became partner (1981); assistant solicitor Cameron Markby Hewitt (1977-1978).

Activities: director Cairngorm Chairlift Company; member of: New Club; Honourable Company of Edinburgh Golfers; Royal Company of Archers; MCC.

Biography: lives Edinburgh; born 19.02.1953; married to Jane. Educated at Belhaven Hill, Dunbar (1961-1966); Eton College (1966-1971); Edinburgh University (1974 LLB).

Leisure: Scottish art; skiing; shooting; fishing; golf.

HOULTON David

partnership secretary BRISTOWS COOKE & CARPMAEL 10 Lincoln's Inn Fields, London WC2A 3BP.

Career: commission in the Army (1956) Royal Regiment of Fusiliers; commanded 1st Battalian (1977-1980); Colonel in Ministry of Defence; retired (1988); became partnership secretary Bristows Cooke and Carpmael (1988).

Activities: Deputy Colonel of the Regiment for Northumberland; member Army & Navy Club.

Biography: lives Greenwich; born 21.06.1937; married to Veronica with 2 children. Educated at Nautical College, Pangbourne; Army Staff College (1970 PSC).

Leisure: keen sailor (own yacht).

HOUSLEY Keith

partner and head of commercial property department BRABNER HOLDEN 1 Dale Street, Liverpool L2 2ET.

Career: articled Toulmin Hodgson & Brabner (1968-1970); admitted (1970); assistant solicitor Brabner Holden (1970-1972); became partner (1972).

Activities: secretary Turner Memorial Home, Dingle; former chairman, president and secretary Liverpool Round Table; member of: Royal Aeronautical Society (Chester branch); Liverpool Rotary Club (secretary); Liverpool 41 Club.

Biography: lives Parkgate; born 04.11.1945; married with 2 children. Educated at Lower Bebington Church of England Primary School; Birkenhead School; Nottingham University (1967 LLB).

Leisure: reading; vehicle and aeronautical technology; walking; computers.

HOWARD Michael

Queen's Counsel, 2 Essex Court, Temple, London EC4Y 9AP.

Career: lecturer in law LSE (1970-1974); called to the Bar (1971); QC (1986); visiting professor in law Essex University (1987 to date); Assistant Recorder.

Activities: member of: United Oxford & Cambridge Universities Club; RAC.

Biography: lives London EC4 and Oxfordshire; born 10.06.1947; single. Educated at Clifton College; Magdalen College Oxford (1968 BA) (1970 MA BCL); joint editor Phipson on Evidence (12th, 13th & 14th ed); articles in learned journals.

Leisure: reading; squash; music.

HOWELL WILLIAMS Peter

senior partner BELL LAMB & JOYNSON 6 Castle Street, Liverpool L2 0NB.

Career: articled GH Morgan & Sons (1950-1952); admitted (1952); assistant solicitor (1952-1953); became partner Bell Lamb & Joynson (1953-1990); consultant solicitor (1990).

Activities: president Liverpool Law Society (1980-1981); Chairman Mental Health Tribunal; member Keith Lucas report on local Government finance; active in town planning specialising in conservation; Borough Councillor (1955-1964); leader of party group; North-West chairman Liberal Party (1964); Parliamentary candidate (1964 & 1966); founder and chairman Maritime Housing Association (1963); chairman Merseyside Civic Society (1966-1971); chairman Friends Cleft Palate Association; director Liverpool Everyman Theatre (chairman 1983 to date); member Council North Wales Arts Festival; national chairman The Abbeyfield Society (1985 to date); member of: Athenaeum Liverpool (president 1980); Athenaeum London.

Biography: lives Rhuthun; born 22.06.1926; married to Fiona with 3 children. Educated at Rydal School, N Wales; Downing College Cambridge (1950 MA LLB); author of: 'A Gentleman's Calling - Liverpool Attorney-at-Law' (1981); 'Liverpolitana' (1971).

Leisure: antiquarian books; golf.

HOWELL-JONES Keith

senior partner HOWELL-JONES &
PARTNERS 75 Surbiton Road; Kingston
upon Thames, Surrey KT1 2AF.

Career: articled London (1964-1969);
admitted (1969); assistant solicitor
Kingston upon Thames (1969-1970);
became partner Spencer Young & Partners
(1970-1972); became partner Murray
MacLean & Co (1972-1977); founded
Howell-Jones & Partners (1977).

Activities: secretary to mid-Surrey Law
Society; member Association of Surrey
Law Societies (member Clarity
Committee); promotion of modern
management methods in running a
solicitor's firm; assistant organist Esher
Parish Church.

Biography: lives Surbiton; born 23.01.1946;
married to Peggy with 2 sons. Educated at
St Paul's School, London; College of Law
Lancaster Gate; Associate Royal College of
Organists.

Leisure: music; gardening; travel; food and
wine.

HOWELLS Ian

partner DOOTSONS 23 Jackson Avenue,
Culcheth, Warrington WA3 4EJ.

Career: admitted (1976); assistant solicitor
(1976-1977); became salaried partner
Dootsons (1977); became equity partner
(1979).

Activities: president Leigh Law Society
(1988-1989); chairman Leigh Round Table
(1989-1990) .

Biography: lives Leigh; born 28.05.1951;
married to Elaine with 3 children.
Educated at Leigh Grammar School;
Newcastle upon Tyne Polytechnic (1973
hons).

Leisure: swimming; squash.

HOWELLS Mike

senior partner PRICE & KELWAY
17 Hamilton Terrace, Milford Haven,
Pembs SA73 3JA.

Career: articled Price & Kelway; admitted
(1966); assistant solicitor (1966-1972);
became partner (1972).

Activities: clerk to the Haverfordwest
General Commissioners of Income Tax
(1978); HM Coroner for Pembrokeshire
(1980); member Council of the Law Society
(1983) (chairman Civil Litigation
Committee); vice-chairman board of
management of local professional theatre;
president Milford Haven Civic Society;

member of: RAC; Neyland Yacht Club;
Waterloo Club.

Biography: lives Milford Haven; born
29.05.1939; married to Pam with 2 sons.
Educated at Dean Close School,
Cheltenham; University College London;
articles and reviews in the Law Society's
Gazette.

Leisure: reading; collecting books; keeping
bees; messing about in boats; theatre.

HOWELLS Roger

senior partner GOMER WILLIAMS AND
CO 19/21 John Street, Llanelli, Dyfed.

Career: articled Gomer Williams and
Company; (Helder Roberts & Co 1 year);
admitted (1966); assistant solicitor (1966-
1968); became partner (1968); became
senior partner (1987).

Activities: chairman Social Security
Appeals Tribunal; town clerk Kidwelly
Town Council; hon cases secretary Llanelli
NSPCC; member Law Society Child Care
Panel; trustee Llanelli Citizens Advice
Bureau; president Kidwelly Rugby Social
Club; member of: Llanelli Conservative
Club; Bury Port Reading Room and Club.

Biography: lives Kidwelly; born 08.09.1942;
married to Mary with 2 children. Educated
at Llandovery College; Swansea
University.

Leisure: cricket; rugby.

HOWS Tony

senior partner LAWFORD & CO
Watchmaker Court, 65 St John Street,
London EC1M 4HQ.

Career: articled Lawford & Co (1970-1972);
admitted (1972).

Activities: chairman Legal Aid Committee
Area 13; chairman of Industrial Tribunals;
qualified flying instructor; member Royal
Southampton Yacht Club.

Biography: lives Richmond, Surrey and
Lymington; born 23.12.1947; divorced.
Educated at King Edward VI School,
Southampton; Queen Mary College
London (LLB hons).

Leisure: sailing; flying; skiing.

HUCKER Michael

barrister and head of common law
chambers 3 New Square, Lincoln's Inn,
London WC2 3RS.

Career: commissioned Royal Engineers
(1957); served BAOR; West Africa;
Malaysia; Northern Ireland; MOD; Captain

(1961); Major (1967); retired Pay (1976);
called to the Bar Lincoln's Inn (1974); army
legal service (1974-1976); head of
Chambers (1978); Counsel to Army Board
(1979); Judge Advocate (part-time) (1983);
Assistant Recorder (1988); called to
Gibraltar Bar (1988).

Activities: member SE Circuit; member
Central Criminal Court Bar Mess; Freedom
of City of London (1978); member Pegasus
Club.

Biography: lives Winchester; born
25.10.1937; married to Hazel Zoe (JP) with
2 sons and 1 daughter. Educated at St
Dunstan's College; London School of
Economics.

Leisure: music; study of English history;
historical biography; gardening.

HUDD David GT

head of structured finance department
PARIBAS LIMITED 33 Wigmore Street,
London W1H 0BN.

Career: articled Linklaters & Paines (1981-
1983); admitted (1983); assistant solicitor
(1983-1985); corporate finance officer
Paribas Limited (1985-1986); head of new
issues execution team (1986-1988); head of
international finance and legal department
(1988-1990); became head of structured
finance department (1990).

Biography: lives London W8; born
21.06.1958; single. Educated at Gravesend
Grammar School; Christ Church Oxford
(1980 MA hons).

Leisure: literature; cinema; theatre.

HUDSON James

partner BRISTOWS COOKE & CARPMAEL
10 Lincoln's Inn Fields, London WC2A
3BP.

Career: called to the Bar (1972); admitted
(1977); assistant solicitor (1977-1979);
assistant solicitor Bristows Cooke &
Carpmael (1979-1984); became partner
(1984).

Activities: member of: Garrick; Rye GC;
New Zealand GC.

Biography: lives London SW18 and
Wittersham; born 13.05.1949; married with
4 children. Educated at Highfield School,
Liphook; Winchester College; King's
College London (1971 LLB).

Leisure: golf; tennis; cricket.

HUDSON Michael

partner OSWALD HICKSON COLLIER &
CO Essex House, Essex Street, Strand,
London WC2R 3AQ.

H

Career: articled Gardner Leader; admitted (1971); assistant solicitor Oswald Hickson Collier & Co (1971-1972); became partner (1972).

Biography: lives Epping; married to Susan with 1 child. Educated at St Bartholomew's Grammar School, Newbury,

Leisure: bridge; gardening; golf; Scouting.

HUDSON William

Queen's Counsel 5 King's Bench Walk, Temple, London EC4Y 7ND.

Career: called to the Bar Middle Temple (1943); QC (1967); Bencher (1972).

Activities: chairman Blackfriars Settlement; member Hawks.

Biography: lives London W6; born 17.11.1916; married to Pamela with 4 children. Educated at Haileybury Imperial Service College; Trinity Hall Cambridge (1943 MA); Harmsworth Law Scholar.

Leisure: athletics (Cambridge Blue); golf; theatre.

HUGHES Allan

senior partner PAYNE HICKS BEACH 10 New Square, Lincoln's Inn, London WC2A 3QG.

Career: 7th (Queen's Own) Hussars (1951-1953); articled Payne Hicks Beach & Co (1953-1959); admitted (1959); assistant solicitor (1959-1960); became partner (1960).

Activities: member London Rent Assessment Panel (1965-1970); director Colonial Mutual Life American Society Limited; chairman Iris Fund for Prevention of Blindness; chairman governors Heathfield School; director Solicitors Benevolent Association; hon secretary The Justinians; member of: Buck's; MCC.

Biography: lives London and nr Cirencester; born 27.02.1933; married to Ann with 2 sons. Educated at Wellington College, Berkshire.

Leisure: gardening; watching cricket; shooting.

HUGHES Brian

senior partner HUGHES DOWDALL 216 Bath Street, Glasgow G2 4HS.

Career: assistant solicitor Hughes Dowdall (1961-1967); became partner Hughes Dowdall (1967); became senior partner (1986).

Activities: founder member Glasgow Bar

Association (1965-1972) (president 1969-1970); commissioned temporary Sheriff (1984); former member Law Society of Scotland Contempt of Court Committee; former member Royal Faculty of Procurators Court House Commission; conducted number of district and general courts martial.

Biography: lives Glasgow; born 22.01.1938; married with 2 children. Educated at St Aloysius College, Glasgow; Mount St Mary's College, nr Sheffield; Glasgow University (1960 BL); author of 'Stair Memorial Encyclopaedia of the Laws of Scotland' for Law Society of Scotland; contributor 'Betting Gaming & Lotteries'.

Leisure: sailing; computing; travel.

HUGHES Gwilym Caesar

senior partner GWILYM HUGHES & PARTNERS Ashgrove, 30 Grosvenor Road, Wrexham LL11 1BU and Midland Bank Chambers, Llangollen, Clwyd.

Career: articled Cyril Jones & Co (1951-1954); National Service (1954-1956); assistant solicitor Cyril Jones & Co (1956-1960); became partner (1960); founded Gwilym Hughes & Partners (1970).

Activities: past chairman 12A Regional Duty Solicitor Committee; restaurateur at Caesar's Restaurant, Llangollen; member of: Royal St David's Golf Club; Rotary Club; Wrexham Business Club; Wrexham Golf Club; Wrexham 41 Club; Gresford Sailing Club.

Biography: lives Wrexham and Harlech; born 06.05.1930; married to Pat; 3 children. Educated at Llangollen Grammar School; Liverpool University (1951 LLB hons); Gibson and Weldon London (1954).

Leisure: dining in Good Food Guide restaurants; golf; walking; country/village life; gardening.

HUGHES Rupert

partner and head of commercial department WRAGGE & CO Bank House, 8 Cherry Street, Birmingham B2 5JY.

Career: National Service commissioned in the Loyal Regiment in Malaya (1956-1958); district officer in the Colonial Service in Fiji (1962-1966); director and company secretary Maxim Investments Ltd Property & Construction Company (1967-1972); articled Wragge & Co (1972-1975); admitted (1975); assistant solicitor (1975-1978); became partner (1978).

Activities: member Lord Chancellor's Committee on Patent Litigation (Oulton

Committee); member Patent Solicitors Association; specialist in intellectual property law and competition law; hon sec SOS International; member of: Birmingham Club; Birmingham Book Club.

Biography: lives Worcestershire; born 16.09.1937; married with 3 daughters. Educated at Queen Mary's Grammar School, Walsall; St John's College Cambridge (MA hons).

Leisure: walking; fly fishing; collecting books; opera; classical music.

HUGILL John

Queen's Counsel and head of chambers 2 Old Bank Street, Manchester M2 7PF.

Career: 2nd Lt Royal Artillery (1949-1950); called to the Bar (1954); Northern circuit (1954); Recorder (1972): QC (1976); Bencher Middle Temple (1984).

Activities: former member General Council of the Bar and Northern circuit Executive Committee; member Bar Yacht Club.

Biography: lives London SW5 and Cheshire; born 11.08.1930; married to Patricia with 2 children. Educated at Sydney C of E Grammar School, Australia; Fettes College; Trinity Hall Cambridge (1953 MA).

Leisure: sailing.

HULME Leonard

managing partner WANSBROUGHS WILLEY HARGREAVE Park Lane House, Westgate, Leeds LS1 2RD.

Career: Eagle Star Insurance Co Ltd (1948); head motor claims dept (1955); area claims inspector Northern Insurance Group (1955-1965); branch manager Lloyds syndicate, Lloyds (1965-1969); articled Willey Hargreave (1969-1974); admitted (1974); became partner (1974); head of Leeds and London offices (1975-1979); managing partner (1979-1989).

Activities: panel solicitor member of Law Society's various schemes for professional indemnity cover for solicitors since inception and of other similar schemes for other professions (1976); became associate of Chartered Insurance Institute (1953) (membership lapsed).

Biography: lives Harrogate; born 18.11.1931; married to June Anne with 1 child. Educated at Sutton High School for Boys, Plymouth; submission of papers to Lord Chancellor re Civil Justice Review on the Work and Organisation of the Legal Profession.

Leisure: literature; music; gardening.

HUME David William

senior partner KENNETH BUSH & CO
11 New Conduit Street, King's Lynn,
Norfolk PE30 1DG.

Career: articled Kenneth Bush & Co (1960-
1966); admitted (1966); assistant solicitor
(1966-1968); became equity partner (1968).

Activities: hon consul of the Federal
Republic of Germany for King's Lynn and
Norfolk (1988); hon vice-consul of the
Netherlands at King's Lynn, Norfolk,
Lincolnshire, Cambridgeshire,
Northamptonshire & Leicestershire (1987);
past president King's Lynn Junior
Chamber of Commerce; past president
King's Lynn & West Norfolk Law Society;
director West Norfolk Enterprise Agency
Trust; representative of King's Lynn
Chamber of Trade & Commerce; member
of: Institute of Advanced Motorists; West
Norfolk RUFC (past president); King's
Lynn Priory Rotary Club (chairman of
youth exchange); King's Lynn Golf Club;
Leziate Park Sailing Club.

Biography: lives King's Lynn; born
05.05.1942; married to Carla with 2
children. Educated at King's School, Ely;
College of Law (1961-1962 & 1965).

Leisure: walking; cycling; swimming;
tennis; clay pigeon shooting.

HUME John

litigation partner TITMUSS SAINER &
WEBB 2 Serjeants' Inn, London EC4Y 1LT.

Career: articled Titmuss Sainer & Webb;
admitted (1970); assistant solicitor (1970-
1973); became partner (1973).

Activities: Liveryman City of London
Solicitors' Company; member Law Society;
member of: RAC; Jaguar Drivers' Club;
Roehampton Club; Old Cranleighan
Society; Old Cranleighan Rugby Club.

Biography: lives London SW13; born
22.09.1945; married with 2 sons. Educated
at Cranleigh School; College of Law
Lancaster Gate.

Leisure: shooting; motor racing; holidays;
travel; collecting cars; enjoying company of
family and friends.

HUMPHREY Tony

partner ALLEN & OVERY 9 Cheapside,
London EC2V 6AD.

Career: articled Allen & Overy (1973);
admitted; assistant solicitor; became
partner (1981).

Activities: member Law Society; member
International Bar Association; member City

of London Solicitors' Company; member
RAC.

Biography: lives London SE5 and Caston,
Norfolk; born 12.01.1951; married to Ann.
Educated at Douai School, Berkshire;
Durham University (1972 BA hons).

Leisure: horse riding; skiing; tennis; golf.

HUMPHRIES John

senior partner TRAVERS SMITH
BRAITHWAITE 6 Snow Hill, London EC1.

Career: served RNVR (1943-1946) .

Activities: OBE (1980); member Thames
Water Authority (1983 to date); chairman
Water Space Amenity Commission (1973-
1983); vice- president Inland Waterways
Association (1973 to date) (chairman 1970-
1973); member Inland Waterways Amenity
Advisory Council (1971 to date); adviser to
HM Government on amenity use of water
space (1972); member National Water
Council (1973-1983); chairman Evans of
Leeds PLC (1982 to date); member London
Board Halifax Building Society (1985 to
date); deputy chairman CoEnCo (1985 to
date); Chairman Southern Council for
Sport and Recreation (1987 to date);
member Sports Council (1987 to date);
member of: RNVR; City Club.

Biography: lives London SW19; born
15.06.1925; married to Olga with 4
daughters. Educated at Fettes; Peterhouse
Cambridge (1946-1948); (Solicitors finals
hons).

Leisure: inland waters; gardening.

HUNT Anthony

senior partner HUNT & HUNT
157 High Street, Colchester, Essex
CO1 1PG.

Career: articled Hunt & Hunt (1938); HM
Forces; articled (1945-1946); admitted
(1946); assistant solicitor (1946-1954);
became partner (1954).

Biography: lives Stoke by Nayland; born
16.03.1915; married to Joan. Educated at
The Oratory School, Caversham; Queen's
College Oxford (BCL MA).

Leisure: fishing; shooting.

HUNT James

Queen's Counsel 1 King's Bench Walk,
Temple, London EC4.

Career: Midland and Oxford Circuit (1968
to date); Circuit Junior (1976); Recorder of
the Crown Court (1982); QC (1987).

Activities: member General Council of the

Bar (1989) .

Biography: lives Stamford; born 26.01.1943;
married to Susan with 4 children.
Educated at Ashby de la Zouch Boys'
Grammar School; Keble College Oxford
(MA); Gray's Inn.

Leisure: singing; stonework; tennis; circuit
life.

HUNT Jonathan

senior partner WAKE SMITH & CO
Telegraph House, High Street, Sheffield
S1 1SF.

Career: articled Wake Smith & Co (1961-
1966); admitted (1966); assistant solicitor
(1966-1967); became partner (1967); became
senior partner (1988).

Activities: OBE; TD; DL; chairman
Sheffield Enterprise Agency Limited;
member Planning Committee for Sheffield
Training and Enterprise Council; Territorial
Army; member of: The Sheffield Club;
Cavalry & Guards Club; Aldeburgh Yacht
Club; Linderick Golf Club.

Biography: lives Sheffield; born 06.03.1943;
married to Susan with 2 sons. Educated at
Stowe.

HUNT Ken

senior partner KIDD & SPOOR Norfolk
House, 90 Grey Street, Newcastle upon
Tyne NE1 6AG.

Career: admitted (1970); assistant solicitor
(1970-1973); partner provincial law firm
(1973-1975); North London (1975-1976);
partner Kidd & Spoor (1976); became
senior partner (1983).

Activities: developed first Property Centres
in the North of England (1985); member
Institute of Directors; commercial
developer of Newcastle's premier four star
hotel The Newcastle Copthorne; director of
a number of other local companies in a
wide range of market sectors.

Biography: lives Whitley Bay; born
10.06.1946; married to Geraldine with 4
daughters. Educated at King's School,
Tynemouth; College of Law Guildford;
regular articles on commercial law to
prestigious local magazine.

Leisure: running; cricket; tennis; golf;
music; reading; travel.

HUNT Matthew

partner FOOT & BOWDEN 70/76 North
Hill, Plymouth PL4 8HH.

Career: articled Foot & Bowden (1977-
1979); admitted (1979); assistant solicitor

H

Wansbroughs (1979-1985); assistant solicitor Moore & Blatch (1985-1987); assistant solicitor Foot & Bowden (1987-1988); became partner (1988).

Activities: secretary Mount Cricket Club.

Biography: lives Plymouth; born 14.09.1952; married to Alison with 1 child. Educated at Clifton College, Bristol; Nottingham University (1974 LLB); Bristol Polytechnic (1974-1975).

Leisure: cricket.

HUNT Tim

company secretary/legal co-ordinator ULTRAMAR PLC 141 Moorgate, London EC2M 6TX.

Career: law clerk Lawrence Messer (1964-1966); part-time lecturer City of London College (1965-1972); corporate lawyer Freshfields (1966-1969); legal coordinator Ultramar PLC (1970-1982); became company secretary/legal coordinator (1982).

Activities: member of: City of London Club; Royal Lymington Yacht Club; Ganton Golf Club.

Biography: lives Hartley Mauditt; born 24.06.1941; married to Sylvia with 2 sons. Educated at Giggleswick School; Bristol University (LLB hons); College of Law Guildford; Oxford University (business course).

Leisure: sailing; golf.

HUNTER Ian

Queen's Counsel 4 Essex Court, Temple, London EC4.

Career: called to the Bar Inner Temple (1967); pupillage 4 Essex Court; QC (1980); Arent Fox, Washington DC (3 months); Bencher Inner Temple (1986).

Activities: member and rapporteur Anti-Trust Committee of the International Law Association (1968-1972); member Bar Council Consolidated Regulations and Transfer Committee (1982-1985) (chairman 1986-1987); member Executive Committee (1985-1986); member International Relations Committee (1982 to date); UK vice-president Union Internationale des Avocats (1982-1986) (first vice-president 1986-1987) (president elect 1988-1989) (president 1989-1990) (Director of Studies 1990 to date); director Lioncourt PLC (1986-1989) (chairman 1988-1989).

Biography: lives London W8; Abbotts Ann nr Andover and Cannes, France; born 03.10.1944; married to Maggie with 2 sons. Educated at Reading School; Pembroke

College Cambridge (1966 BA) (MA) (1967 LLB) Open Scholar; State Scholar; Squire University Law Scholar; Trevelyan Scholar; Harvard Law School (1968 LLM) Kennedy Memorial Scholar; Inner Temple Duke of Edinburgh Entrance Scholar; Major Scholar articles on international law.

Leisure: bebop; French eating and lifestyle; speaking French; property investment.

HUNTER Martin

partner FRESHFIELDS Whitefriars, 65 Fleet Street, London EC4Y 1HT.

Career: articled Freshfields (1961-1963); admitted (1963); assistant solicitor (1963-1967); became partner (1967).

Activities: senior visiting Fellow Queen Mary College London; chairman ICC Commission's Working Group on Dissenting Opinions and Interim and Partial Awards (1985-1990); member International Council for Commercial Arbitration (1988 to date); member ICC's Court of Arbitration (1988 to date); member ICC's Commission on International Commercial Arbitration (1985 to date); member Arbitration Court of the London Court of International Arbitration (1987 to date); Deputy Chairman United Kingdom Dept of Trade Committee on Arbitration Law Reform (1989); member International Law Association's International Arbitration Committee (1982-1989); member Chartered Institute of Arbitrators' Arbitration Committee (1979-1990); member Law Society's Working Group on Arbitration Law Reform (1985-1988); member World Arbitration Institute International Advisory Committee (1986 to date); member International Bar Association delegation to the United Nations Commission on International Trade Law in relation to arbitration matters (1983-1986); member editorial board of 'Arbitration International'; numerous lectures and conference speeches on practice and procedure in international arbitration; visiting lecturer at the Asser Institute, the Hague; member of: Royal Cruising Club; Royal Lymington Yacht Club; Sunningdale Golf Club; Roehampton Club.

Biography: lives Weybridge; born 23.03.1937; married to Linda. Educated at Shrewsbury School; Pembroke College Cambridge (1960 BA) (1986 MA); joint author 'Law and Practice of International Commercial Arbitration' (1986); editor 'Encyclopaedia of Forms and Precedents' arbitration title (1985); numerous articles in ICCA Yearbook Commercial Arbitration;

Arbitration International; Journal of International Arbitration; International Business Lawyer; Journal of the Chartered Institute of Arbitrators; Lloyd's Maritime and Commercial Law Quarterly; etc; contributor to: ICCA Congress Series No 3 (1986); 'Contemporary Problems in International Arbitration' (1986).

Leisure: cruising under sail; golf.

HUNTER Muir

Queen's Counsel 3/4 South Square, Gray's Inn, London WC1R 5HP.

Career: called to the Bar Gray's Inn (1938); Armed Forces (1940-1946); 2 Royal Glos Hussars; 149 Regt RAC; Gen Staff Intelligence GHQ India; Judge of Special Criminal (Anti-Corruption) Tribunal Govt of India (1943-1945); retd Hon Lt Col GSOI; head of Chambers (1960-1989); QC (1965); Bencher Gray's Inn (1975).

Activities: deputy chairman Armed Forces Candidates' Tribunal, Home Office; member Departmental Advisory Committee of DTI on the Draft European Bankruptcy Convention (1973-1976); member Insolvency Law Review Committee of DTI (1977-1982); seminar and conference speaker on Insolvency Act 1986; vice-chairman Insolvency Committee J of International Bar Association (1975-1985); founder chairman North Kensington Neighbourhood Law Centre (1970-1971); council member Justice (1962-1988); Amnesty International observer (1963, 1969 & 1972); life member Commercial Law League of America; member Hurlingham Club.

Biography: lives Donhead St Andrew; born 19.08.1913; married to Gillian with 1 child and 4 stepchildren. Educated at Westminster; Christ Church Oxford (1936 BA hons MA) Scholar; Holke Senior Scholar Gray's Inn (1938); MRI; editor 'Williams on Bankruptcy' later 'Williams & Muir Hunter on Bankruptcy' (1949-1985); author 'Muir Hunter on Personal Insolvency' (1987); contributing editor: (Bankruptcy & Insolvency) Butterworths 'County Court Precedents and Pleadings'; Butterworths 'Financial Law Review' (1988); joint editor: 'Kerr on Receivers and Administrators' (1989); 'Insolvency Law and Practice'.

Leisure: helping to found hospices for the dying overseas (Gdansk, Nairobi) with wife Gillian; theatre; travel.

HUTCHINGS Graham

partner LOVELL WHITE DURRANT 21 Holborn Viaduct, London EC1A 2DY.

Career: articled Lovell White Durrant (1952-1957); admitted (1957); assistant solicitor (1957-1961); became partner (1961); seconded to Hughes Hubbard & Reed, New York (1958-1959).

Activities: member of: Royal Ashdown Forest Golf Club; Hurlingham Club; Seaford Golf Club.

Biography: lives London and Hartfield; born 04.10.1934; married to Susan with 3 children. Educated at Rugby School; Law Society's Finals (1957 hons).

Leisure: tennis; golf; photography; travel.

HUTCHINGS Michael

partner in EEC group LOVELL WHITE DURRANT 65 Holborn Viaduct, London EC1A 2DY.

Career: articled McKenna & Co; admitted (1973); assistant solicitor Lovell White & King (1974-1981); became partner (1981); resident partner Brussels office (1982-1986).

Activities: chairman London Young Solicitors' Group (1981); chairman Solicitors' European Group (1989); member Solicitors' European Group; member of: St Enodoc Golf Club; Woking Golf Club; Hurlingham Tennis Club.

Biography: lives London W14; born 08.11.1948; divorced with 2 children. Educated at Marlborough College, Wiltshire; College of William & Mary, Virginia, USA (1969 BA); College of Law Guildford (1969-1970 & 1972-1973); UK contributor European Competition Law Review; articles on EEC law published in various law journals.

Leisure: golf; tennis; windsurfing; carpentry; buying secondhand books.

HUWS Hywel

senior partner RL EDWARDS & PARTNERS 20 Nolton Street, Bridgend, Mid Glam CF31 1DU.

Career: articled Brinley Richards & Huws; admitted (1962); assistant solicitor (1962-1965); became partner (1965); amalgamated with RL Edwards & Evans; Williams Simons & Thomas (1970).

Biography: lives Bridgend; born 16.01.1932; married with 3 children. Educated at Pontardawe Grammar School; University College of Swansea (1953 BA hons); University College of Wales (1955 LLB hons); Travers Smith Scholarship.

Leisure: charity work; church activities; golf; music; photography; travel.

HYTNER Benet Alan

Queen's Counsel 5 Essex Court, Temple, London EC4Y 9AH and 25 Byrom Street, Manchester M3 4PF.

Career: called to the Bar (1952); QC (1970); Recorder of the Crown Court (1972); Bencher Middle Temple (1977).

Activities: Judge of Appeal Isle of Man (1980 to date); leader Northern Circuit (1984-1988); member General Council of Bar (1969-1973 & 1984-1989); member Senate of Inns of Court & Bar (1977-1981) .

Biography: born 29.12.1927. Educated at Manchester Grammar School; Trinity Hall Cambridge (MA).

I

IBBOTSON Roger

senior litigation partner BOOTH & CO Sovereign House, South Parade, Leeds LS1 1HQ.

Career: articled Burton & Burton; admitted (1966); assistant solicitor Booth & Co (1966-1970); became partner (1970).

Activities: member Leeds Law Society Contentious Business Sub-committee (Civil); member Law Society Area Committee; advocacy training officer Leeds Law Society; chairman Leeds Girls' High School Parents' and Friends' Association; trustee WW Spooner Charitable Trust.

Biography: lives Leeds; born 02.01.1943; married to Susan with 3 children. Educated at Cockburn High School, Leeds; Manchester University (1963 LLB hons); College of Law Guildford (1966 hons).

ILLER Martin Stuart

principal lecturer COLLEGE OF LAW 33/35 Lancaster Gate, London W2.

Career: articled Freeman & Son; admitted (1970); lectured College of Law (1970-1973); became partner Wright Webb Syrett (1974-1980); lecturer College of Law (1980); became senior lecturer (1981-1987); principal lecturer (1987).

Activities: member Law Society's Criminal Law Committee (1986 to date); member West London Law Society (1982 to date); member Law Society's Academic Consultative Committee (1989 to date);

member British Academy of Forensic Science (1980 to date) and member of BAFS Executive Council (1990 to date); given number of public recitals on the piano; taking part in a series of chamber music concerts during lunchtimes in various churches in the City; broadcast on television as Max's accompanist in 'Max Headroom Show'.

Biography: lives London W5; born 09.06.1944; married to Helen (1969-1981) with 2 children; married to Diana (1983 to date). Educated at Queen Elizabeth's Grammar School, Barnet (1955-1963); Nottingham University (1966 LLB hons); Honours in Law Society's Final Examination (August 1969); awarded John Mackrell Prize and John Marshall Prize; author of: 'Criminal Litigation' (1985); written numerous articles in the Law Society Gazette, Law Notes and Legal Action Bulletin; supplied the text for two Consumer's Association publications one on 'Divorce' and one on 'Children, Parents & the Law'; writes humorous works under the pseudonym of Stewart Miller.

Leisure: music both classical and 'other'; enjoying good food and wine; supporting Tottenham Hotspur FC.

ING David Newson

senior partner DOWNS 156 High Street, Dorking, Surrey RH4 1BQ.

Career: articled to Mr ED Gosschalk; admitted (1957); National Service in RAF (commission and Sword of Honour); assistant solicitor Down Scott & Down (1961-1963); partner (1963); became senior partner (1985).

Activities: director Surrey Building Society (1969 to date) (chairman 1981); Notary Public (1976); Law Society's Remuneration Certificate Panel (1974 to date) with status of Council member; hon solicitor to Fire Services National Benevolent Fund; hon solicitor to Lutyens Trust; past Master Worshipful Company of Woolmen of the City of London; member of: MCC; The Law Society; Surrey Law Club.

Biography: lives Abinger Hammer; born 30.05.1934; married to Ann with 2 sons. Educated at Pocklington School, York; Solicitors' Finals (1956).

Leisure: walking; cricket; reading; gardening; opera; theatre .

I

INGLIS Alistair

senior partner MCCLURE NAISMITH ANDERSON & GARDINER 292 St Vincent Street, Glasgow G2 5TQ.

Career: apprentice McClure Naismith Brodie & Co (1949-1952); admitted (1952); Royal Corps of Signals (1952-1954); assistant solicitor (1954-1956); became partner (1956).

Activities: professor of conveyancing (1979) and professor of professional legal practice (1984) of Glasgow University (part-time chairs); dean of the Royal Faculty of Procurators in Glasgow (1989); chairman Scottish Universities Joint Rating and Revaluation Committee (1980 to date); member Law Society of Scotland Conveyancing Committee; member Joint Liaison Committee with the Registers of Scotland; member Rent Assessment Panel for Scotland (1966 to date) (president 1976-1987); CBE (1984); member Greater Glasgow Health Board (1975-1983); convenor Ad Hoc Committee of the General Assembly of the Church of Scotland into Legal Services of the Church (1978-1979); session clerk Caldwell Parish Church; member of: Western Club; Royal Scottish Automobile Club; College Club Glasgow University.

Biography: lives Glasgow; born 24.12.1928; married to Elizabeth with 2 sons and 3 daughters. Educated at Kilmarnock Academy; Fettes College; St Andrew's University (1949 MA); Glasgow University (1952 LLB); numerous opinions and articles in journals; chapters in certain books.

Leisure: golf; gardening.

INGLIS George

senior partner SLAUGHTER AND MAY 35 Basinghall Street, London EC2V 5DB.

Career: articled Slaughter and May (1956-1959); admitted (1959); assistant solicitor (1959-1966); partner (1966-1986); became senior partner (1986).

Biography: lives NW Essex; born 19.04.1933; married with 3 children. Educated at Winchester College; Pembroke College Oxford (1953 jurisprudence hons).

Leisure: gardening.

INGLIS Ian

senior corporate partner SHEPHERD & WEDDERBURN WS 16 Charlotte Square, Edinburgh EH2 4YS.

Career: apprentice clerk; clerk; apprentice solicitor The Royal Bank of Scotland (1957-1966); apprentice Shepherd & Wedderburn

WS (1966-1967); admitted (1967); assistant solicitor (1967-1968); became partner (1968).

Activities: member Scottish panel of experts assisting the Department of Trade & Industry in reviewing the law and practice relating to insolvency; member panel Scottish experts assisting Prof AL Diamond in connection with his report 'A Review of Security Interests in Property'; member Law Society of Scotland Bankruptcy & Liquidation Committee (1979-1987); member of: New Club, Edinburgh; Polmont Rotary Club.

Biography: lives Polmont; born 06.02.1941; married with 2 daughters. Educated at Lanark; University of Edinburgh (1965 LLB); Institute of Bankers in Scotland (AIB Scot).

Leisure: golf; reading.

INGLIS-JONES Nigel John

Queen's Counsel Lamb Building (Ground Floor), Temple, London EC4Y 7AS.

Career: National Service with Grenadier Guards; called to the Bar Inner Temple (1959); Recorder of the Crown Court (1976); Bencher (1981); QC (1982).

Activities: member Association of Pension Lawyers; member MCC.

Biography: lives Richmond; born 07.05.1935; married to (1) Lenette (deceased 09.01.1986) with 2 sons and 2 daughters and (2) Ursula Jane Drury. Educated at Eton; Trinity College Oxford (BA); author of 'The Law of Occupational Pension Schemes' (1989).

Leisure: gardening; fishing.

ISAACS Anthony

senior partner STEPHENSON HARWOOD One St Paul's Churchyard, London EC4M 8SH.

Career: Sub-Lt RNVR; admitted (1960); assistant solicitor (1960-1964); became partner Stephenson Harwood (1964-1987); became senior partner (1987).

Activities: member Solicitors' Disciplinary Tribunal (1988); co-opted member Company Law Committee of Law Society; DTI inspector (1988); member of Garrick Club.

Biography: born 09.08.1934; married to Jennifer with 5 children. Educated at Cheltenham College; Pembroke College Cambridge (1957 BA).

Leisure: charities; music; gardening.

ISAACS Lewis

senior partner of the company and commercial department WILD HEWISTON & SHAW Shakespeare House, 42 Newmarket Road, Cambridge CB5 8EP.

Career: assistant to company secretary Hall & Ham River Limited (subsequently part of RMC Group); articled Eland Hore Patisons (1964-1966); admitted (1967); assistant solicitor (1967-1971); became partner Wild Hewitson & Shaw (1971).

Biography: lives Cambridge; born 20.03.1942; married to Mary with 2 children. Educated at Merchant Taylors' School; Brasenose College Oxford (1963 MA).

Leisure: reading; theatre; cinema; tennis; sail boarding; cross country skiing.

ISAACS Sydney

senior partner MERRILS EDE Principality Buildings, Queen Street, Cardiff CF1 4LR.

Career: war service with Welsh Regiment; admitted (1956); founded own practice (1956); following various amalgamations became senior partner Merrils Ede (1989).

Activities: member the Finer Committee (1969-1974); subsequently lectured on work of the committee; member Board of Management of St Donat's Arts Centre and Music Theatre; member of: Llanishen Golf Club; Cardiff Solicitors' Golf Society.

Biography: lives Cardiff; born 13.01.1923; married to Della with 2 children. Educated at Howard Gardens High School; Cardiff College of Technology; external student London University (1949 BCom).

Leisure: music; golf.

ISRAEL Jennifer

sole practitioner JENNIFER ISRAEL & CO 1346 High Road, Whetstone N20 9HJ.

Career: articled AL Philips & Co; admitted (1969); managed Barnet branch office (1969-1988); founded own practice (1988).

Activities: president North Middlesex Law Society (1982-1983); Council member of Law Society (1986); member Adjudication Committee of Solicitors' Complaints Bureau; member Law Society Land Law and Conveyancing Committee; chairman Race Relations Committee; member RICS inter-professional working party on land transfer; member of working party on women solicitors' careers; member Solicitors' Benevolent Association; member of: Totteridge Tennis Club; Laings Sports Club.

Biography: lives Barnet; born 03.03.1946; married to Victor with 2 children. Educated at Finchley County Grammar School; College of Law; Law Society paper 'management and sale of flats' (1983); articles on conveyancing in Law Society's Gazette; Blundell Memorial Lecture (1988); various commercial lectures on Landlord and Tenant Act 1987.

Leisure: tennis; gardening; reading; natural history.

IVES Matthew

City solicitor and secretary CITY OF WESTMINSTER City Hall, Victoria Street, London SW1E 6QZ.

Career: articled London Borough of Waltham Forest (1973-1975); admitted (1975); senior property lawyer (1976-1980); deputy chief solicitor London Borough of Haringey (1980-1982); deputy City solicitor City of Westminster (1982-1985); became City solicitor and secretary (1985).

Activities: hon Parliamentary officer of London Boroughs Association.

Biography: lives Woodford Green; born 05.03.1948; married to Julia with 1 son and 1 daughter. Educated at St Ignatius College, London; London University (1971 BA hons); College of Law Lancaster Gate (1972-1973); Legal Associate of the Royal Town Planning Institute (1980).

Leisure: history; historic buildings; gardening.

JACK Raymond

Queen's Counsel 1 Hare Court, Temple, London EC4Y 7BE.

Career: called to the Bar Inner Temple (1966); QC (1982); Recorder of the Crown Court (1989).

Activities: commercial practice at the Bar.

Biography: lives London N1 and Wiltshire; born 13.11.1942; married to Elizabeth with 2 daughters and 1 son. Educated at Hawtreys; Rugby School; Trinity College Cambridge (1965 MA).

Leisure: trees and wood; music; reading; poetry; horses; educating his children; gardening; landscape.

JACKS Peter

senior partner FRASER BROWN 84 Friar Lane, Nottingham NG1 6ED.

Career: articled Nottingham; admitted (1966); assistant solicitor Fraser Brown (1966); became partner (1969).

Activities: vice-president Nottinghamshire Law Society; member Nottingham Appeals Committee of Cancer Research Campaign; director Nottingham & Notts United Services Club; member of: Beeston Hockey Club; Notts Casuals Hockey Club; Nottingham Squash Racquets Club; Notts Amateurs Cricket Club; Wollaton Park Golf Club; Notts Golf Club; Societe de Golf des Deux Magots.

Biography: lives Nottingham; born 13.04.1944; married to Philippa with 2 children.

Leisure: travelling; squash; golf; hockey; cricket; rugby union; football; skiing.

JACKSON Christopher

partner MILLS & REEVE Francis House, 112 Hills Road, Cambridge CB2 1PH.

Career: articled Rawlison & Butler; admitted (1959); National Service in Army (1959-1961); assistant solicitor Farrer & Co (1961-1968); partner Francis & Co (1969); senior partner (1981-1987); senior Cambridge partner Mills & Reeve Francis (1987-1989); became partner Mills & Reeve (1989).

Activities: Commissioner for Oaths; committee member Cambridgeshire and District Law Society (1976-1984); member Law Society Bye-laws Revision Committee (1984-1989); member Cambridgeshire Advisory Panel on Archives since (1981).

Biography: lives Cambridge; born 29.11.1934; married to Sheila with 3 children. Educated at Collyers School, Horsham (1945-1952); University College London (1956 LLB); article in Law Society Gazette 'Residential Conveyancing Guidelines: The Cambridge Experience' (1986); author of 'A Cambridge Bicentenary - the History of a Legal Practice 1789-1989'.

Leisure: books; art; architecture; drawing; painting.

JACKSON Rodney

partner in charge of litigation department ANDREW M JACKSON & CO PO Box 47, Victoria Chambers, Bowlalley Lane, Hull HU1 1XY.

Career: articled Andrew M Jackson & Co (1959-1962); admitted (1962); assistant solicitor (1962-1964); became partner (1964); head of litigation department (1971).

Activities: Territorial Army (1955-1967); member Humberside County Council (1972-1975); Notary Public (1967); Recorder (1985 to date); hon solicitor Hull Boys' Club; Hull Medical Society; member Royal Commonwealth Society.

Biography: lives Swanland nr Kingston upon Hull; born 16.04.1935; married to Anne with 2 sons. Educated at King Edward VII School, Sheffield (1943-1945); Queen Elizabeth's Grammar School, Wakefield (1946-1953); Queen's College Cambridge (1958 BA) (1959 LLB) (1962 MA) (1985 LLM).

Leisure: fell walking; photographing preserved steam railways.

JACKSON Roger

partner property department RADCLIFFES & CO 10 Little College Street, Westminster, London SW1P 3SJ.

Career: articled Gordon Dadds & Co (1974-1976); admitted (1976); assistant solicitor (1976-1978); assistant solicitor Slaughter and May (1978-1985); assistant solicitor Radcliffes & Co (1985); became partner (1985).

Biography: lives Haywards Heath; born 26.07.1952; married with 3 children. Educated at Hymers College, Hull; Mansfield College Oxford (1973 BA).

JACKSON Rupert

Queen's Counsel 2 Crown Office Row, Temple, London EC4Y 7HJ.

Career: called to the Bar (1972); QC (1987).

Biography: lives Surrey; born 07.03.1948; married to Claire with 3 daughters. Educated at Christ's Hospital; Jesus College Cambridge (MA LLB) president Cambridge Union (1971); co-author with John Powell QC 'Professional Negligence' (1982 & 1987).

JACKSON Tom

senior partner trust department SLAUGHTER AND MAY 35 Basinghall Street, London EC2V 5DB.

Career: admitted (1955); assistant solicitor Slaughter and May (1958-1970); became partner (1970).

Activities: member editorial board of Trust Law and Practice; member Court of Common Council in the City of London; member of: The Court of the Honourable Irish Society; The Livery of The Solicitors' Company; The Wheelwrights' Company.

Biography: lives London N1; born

J

01.02.1929; married to Paula with 4 children. Educated at Queen Mary's School, Basingstoke; King's College London (1954 LLB); ATII.

Leisure: avid old car enthusiast.

JACOB Robin

Queen's Counsel Francis Taylor Building, Temple, London EC4Y 7BY.

Career: called to the Bar Gray's Inn (1965); pupillage with Nigel Bridge (1966-1967) and AM Walton (1967-1968); Chambers of TA Blanco (1968); Junior Counsel to the Treasury in Patent Matters (1976-1981); QC (1981); Bencher Gray's Inn (1989); called to Bar of New South Wales (1990).

Activities: QC for Secretary of State in Trade Mark Appeals (1989); Deputy Chairman Copyright Tribunal (1989); member Council of Common Law Institute of Intellectual Property; member of: Garrick Club; RAC.

Biography: lives London and Oxfordshire; born 26.04.1941; married to Wendy with 3 children. Educated at King Alfred School, London; Montgrase Secondary Comprehensive School, Potters Bar; St Paul's; Trinity College Cambridge (1963 BA) (MA); LSE (1967 LLB); Atkin Scholar Gray's Inn (1966); author of 'Kerly's Law of Trade Marks and Trade Names' (1972 and sub eds); co-author of: 'Passing off Trade Marks, Registered Designs'; 'Encyclopaedia of European and UK Patent Law'; 'Patents, Trade Marks Copyright & Designs'; miscellaneous articles.

Leisure: photography; gardening; music; theatre.

JACOBS Francis

advocate-general COURT OF JUSTICE OF THE EUROPEAN COMMUNITIES Luxembourg.

Career: barrister Middle Temple (1964); lecturer in jurisprudence Glasgow University (1963-1965); lecturer in law London School of Economics (1965-1969); secretariat European Commission of Human Rights and legal directorate, Council of Europe, Strasbourg (1969-1972); legal secretary Court of Justice of the European Communities (1972-1974); barrister specialising in European Community law (1974-1988); professor of European law University of London (King's College 1974-1988); QC (1984); advocate-general Court of Justice of the European Communities (1988).

Biography: lives Luxembourg and

Teddington; born 08.06.1939; married to Susan with 5 children. Educated at City of London School; Christ Church Oxford; Nuffield College Oxford (1964 MA) (1967 D Phil); several books and numerous articles especially on European law.

JACOBS Norman

former partner SLAUGHTER AND MAY 35 Basinghall Street, London EC2V 5DB.

Career: articled Kennedy Genese & Syson (1954-1957); admitted (1958); assistant solicitor (1958-1959); partner (1959-1966); assistant solicitor Slaughter and May (1967-1972); partner (1973-1990).

Activities: member Land Law Committee City of London Solicitors' Company (1980-1990); Sports Law Committee (1982-1986) and Property Law Committee (1974-1984) of International Bar Association; Chairman of Football Licensing Committee; holder of the Emergency Reserve Decoration (ERD); Freeman of City of London; member Sports Council; Steward British Boxing Board of Control; Governor of Christ's Hospital; member of MCC; FRSA (1989).

Biography: lives Pinner; born 08.08.1930; married to Elizabeth with 4 children. Educated at Christ's Hospital; Exeter College Oxford (1958 MA); written various papers for IBA on sports and property law.

Leisure: hill walking; trekking; music; theatre.

JAFFA Tony

partner FOOT & BOWDEN 70/76 North Hill, Plymouth PL4 8HH.

Career: articled Boyce Hatton & Co (1978-1980); admitted (1980); assistant solicitor Wilde Sapte (1980-1983); assistant solicitor Foot & Bowden (1983-1987); became partner (1987).

Activities: chairman Devon Young Solicitors' Group (1989-1990) (Devon rep National Committee 1988-1989); chairman SW region of UK Boardsailing Association (1983-1987).

Biography: lives Ivybridge; born 06.08.1956; married with 1 child. Educated at St Boniface's College, Plymouth; Oxford (1977 BA) (1983 MA).

Leisure: windsurfing.

JAMES Christopher John

senior partner MARTINEAU JOHNSON St Philips House, St Philips Place, Birmingham B3 2PP.

Career: articled Johnson & Co (1955-1958);

admitted (1958); assistant solicitor (1958-1959); became partner (1960-1987); became senior partner (1985-1987); became deputy senior partner of Martineau Johnson upon amalgamation (1987); became senior partner (1989).

Activities: president Birmingham Law Society (1983); member Birmingham Law Society Council (1974-1987); member Company Law Committee of the Law Society (1980-1982); member Management Consultants' Steering Committee of the Law Society (1984-1987); deputy chairman Birmingham Midshires Building Society (1988-1990) (chairman 1990 to date); joined Board of Birmingham Building Society (1980); chairman of the governing body Edgbaston High School for Girls (1987-1990); member of: the Birmingham Law Club; Little Aston Golf Club.

Biography: lives Sutton Coldfield; born 20.03.1932; married to Elizabeth with 1 son and 1 daughter. Educated at Clifton College; Magdalene College Cambridge (1955 BA): (1963 MA); writes occasional articles for the local press.

Leisure: golf; photography.

JAMES Glen William

partner SLAUGHTER AND MAY 35 Basinghall Street, London EC2V 5DB.

Career: articled Slaughter and May (1974-1976); admitted (1976); assistant solicitor (1976-1983); became partner (1983).

Biography: lives London SW15; born 22.08.1952; married to Amanda. Educated at Wimbledon Park Primary School; King's College School, Wimbledon; New College Oxford (BA MA); College of Law; author of chapters in: 'The Mergers and Acquisitions Handbook'; 'A Practitioner's Guide to the Stock Exchange Yellow Book'.

Leisure: golf; squash; swimming; music; theatre; gardening.

JAMES Keith

chairman PHILLIPS & BUCK Fitzalan House, Fitzalan Road, Cardiff CF2 1XZ.

Career: articled Phillips & Buck (1967-1969); admitted (1969); became partner (1969); chairman (1987).

Activities: vice-chairman Eversheds Group (1989); director of various companies in the Hamard Group (1977-1986); director of the Bank in Wales PLC (1988); chairman Welsh Executive of United Nations Association (1977-1980); chairman Welsh Centre for International Affairs (1979-1984); member UK management committee Freedom from

Hunger Campaign (1978-1987); member Welsh management committee of Institute of Directors (1985 to date); member of the Court of UWIST (University of Wales Institute of Science & Technology); (1985-1988); member of the Council of UWIST (1985-1988); member advisory panel to the Cardiff Business School (1986 to date); vice-president Cardiff Business Club (1987 to date); founder member and deputy chairman of Institute of Welsh Affairs (1987 to date); member of the Council of University of Wales College of Cardiff (1988 to date); member of: Cardiff & County Club; Royal Porthcawl Golf Club.

Biography: lives Peterson super Ely; born 16.08.1944; married to Linda with 2 daughters and 1 son. Educated at Cowbridge Grammar School; Cardiff High School; West Monmouth School; Queen's College Cambridge (1966 BA); (1970 MA).

Leisure: skiing; squash; golf.

JAMES Keith

senior partner NEEDHAM & JAMES Windsor House, Temple Row, Birmingham B2 5LF.

Career: admitted (1954); assistant solicitor (1954-1956); became partner Needham & James (1956); became senior partner (1980).

Activities: chairman Society for Computers & Law (1988-1990); member ITAC (Information Technology & Courts); member Birmingham Law Society Information Technology Committee; managing director Technology & Law Ltd; member of: Birmingham Club; The Athenaeum.

Biography: lives Warwickshire; born 22.08.1930; married to Venice with 4 children. Educated at King Edward VI School, Camp Hill; articles on information technology and law; joint author: 'A Guide to the Electronic Office'.

Leisure: shooting; walking; tennis; cooking.

JAMES Laurence

partner company commercial department PHILLIPS & BUCK and national quality assurance partner EVERSHEDS Fitzalan House, Fitzalan Place, Cardiff CF2 1XZ.

Career: articled in Manchester (1973-1975); admitted (1975); assistant solicitor Evershed & Tomkinson (1977-1979); assistant solicitor Phillips & Buck (1979-1980); became partner (1980).

Activities: company secretary Valentec International Limited; director and company secretary Ogwr Partnership Trust

(Enterprise Agency); director Cardiff & Vale Enterprise Agency; council member Cardiff Chamber of Commerce & Industry; member local residents' association; member National Trust; director and secretary South Glamorgan Training & Enterprise Council Ltd; director Attwood & Sawyer Ltd; company secretary Mid-Glamorgan Training & Enterprise Council; governor of the Welsh Sports Aid Foundation.

Biography: lives Cardiff; born 02.03.1951; married to Jennifer with 2 sons and 1 daughter. Educated at Moseley Grammar School, Birmingham; Manchester University (1972); author of: article on Management Buy-Outs in Management Today and article on Insider Dealing in Western Mail & Echo.

Leisure: skiing; fell walking; road running; photography; harrassed father!.

JAMES Michael

senior partner MORTON FISHER Carlton House, Worcester Street, Kidderminster, Worcs DY10 1BA.

Career: articled Ivens Morton & Greville-Smith (predecessor of present firm); admitted (1956); commissioned RAF during National Service (1957); qualified as Navigator; assistant solicitor Morton Fisher (1958-1959); became partner (1959).

Activities: acting Stipendiary Magistrate for West Midlands (1985 to date); long time member Legal Aid Local and subsequently Area Committees; chairman Management Committee Wyre Forest Citizens Advice Bureau; Clerk to local parish council; member local Youth Trust and various local committees and groups.

Biography: lives Droitwich; born 30.10.1933; married to Lois. Educated at King Charles I Grammar School.

Leisure: music; literature; appreciation of wine; unstrenuous walking.

JAMES Michael

partner in litigation department and head of international trade and transport unit SIMPSON CURTIS 41 Park Square, Leeds LS1 2NS.

Career: called to the Bar (1976); pupillage with David Grace at 3 Essex Court and Andrew Pugh at 2 Hare Court (1976); A Bilbrough & Co Ltd (1977); assistant director Hong Kong office (1980-1983); admitted (1983); assistant solicitor Ingledew Brown Bennison & Garrett (1983-1985); partner (1985-1988); assistant

solicitor Simpson Curtis (1988-1989); became partner (1989).

Activities: member City of London Solicitors' Company.

Biography: lives Ilkley; born 17.05.1953; married to Valerie with 2 children. Educated at Hertford Grammar School; Christ Church Oxford (1973 BA) (1977 MA); Inns of Court School of Law (1975).

Leisure: hill walking; sailing; cycling; model railways; history; literature; general family life; travel; speaking German.

JAMES Robert

senior partner HEMPSONS 33 Henrietta Street, Covent Garden, London WC2E 8NH.

Career: articled Lester Dixon & Jeffcoate (1951-1956); admitted (1956); National Service commissioned Oxfordshire & Buckinghamshire Light Infantry; served in Cyprus (1956-1958); London Rifle Brigade (TA) (1959-1967); assistant solicitor Trower Still & Keeling (1959-1961); assistant solicitor Hempsons (1961-1962); became partner (1962).

Biography: lives London NW1; born 02.12.1932; married to Elisabeth with 3 daughters. Educated at Cheltenham College (1946-1951).

Leisure: military history; tennis.

JAMES Robin

senior partner JAMES TRUMAN MOORE Hinton House, Station Road, New Milton, Hants BH25 6HZ.

Career: admitted (1970); assistant solicitor (1970-1971); became partner Trestrail & James (1971-1980); became senior partner James Truman Moore (1980-1989).

Activities: member of: RORC; RTYC: R Lym YC.

Biography: lives Lymington; born 24.05.1945; single. Educated at Lancing College; Southampton University (1966 LLB).

Leisure: offshore yacht racing; skiing; travel.

JAMES Stephen

senior partner SIMMONS & SIMMONS 14 Dominion Street, London EC2M 4RJ.

Career: admitted (1959); assistant solicitor Simmons & Simmons (1959-1961); became partner (1961); became senior partner (1980).

Activities: director of: Horace Clarkson

157

J

PLC (1975 to date); SOFIPAC (London) Ltd (1975 to date); Shipping Industrial Holdings Ltd (1972-1982); Tradinvest Bank & Trust Co of Nassau Ltd (1975-1985); Nodiv Ltd (1975-1978); Silver Line Ltd (1978-1982); Thompson Moore Associates Ltd (1984-1988); member of the Worshipful Company of Glaziers (1964); member of: Royal Yacht Squadron; Royal Ocean Racing Club; Royal Thames Yacht Club; Royal Lymington Yacht Club.

Biography: lives London SW7 and Lymington; born 19.10.1930; divorced with 4 children. Educated at Clifton College; St Catharine's College Cambridge (BA).

Leisure: yachting (yacht 'Jacobite'); gardening.

JAMES Stuart

partner ROWE & MAW 20 Black Friars Lane, London EC4V 6HD.

Career: articled Rowe & Maw; became partner Warren Murton & Co (1967); became partner Rowe & Maw (1977).

Activities: director Reliance Mutual Group; director Pulford Winstone and Tennant; member Council of the Society of Pension Consultants; Fellow of the Pension Managers' Institute.

Biography: lives Reigate; born 03.03.1944; separated with 1 son. Educated at Reed's School; written various articles.

Leisure: flying.

JAMES Wyndham

senior partner CURWENS Old Vestry Offices, 22 the Town, Enfield, Middx EN2 6LT.

Career: articled Curwen Carter & Evans (1959-1962); admitted (1962); joined father (1962); firm amalgamated with Curwen Carter & Evans; amalgamated with Jessopp & Gough.

Activities: member of: London Welsh Rugby Football Club (hon solicitor); MCC; Glamorgan County Cricket Club; Enfield Cricket Club (president 1986-1989).

Biography: lives Ware and Ogmore by Sea; born 31.03.1936; married to Jane with 2 children. Educated at Enfield Grammar School; Mill Hill School; University College London (1959 LLB).

Leisure: watching and assisting the administration of rugby football and cricket.

JAMESON Arthur Roy

sole practitioner COTMAN & JAMESON 8 Lune Street, Preston, Lancashire PR1 2LD.

Career: articled T Clifford Tipping (1948-1953); admitted (1953); assistant solicitor Cotman & Son (1954-1966); assistant solicitor Fulwood UDC (1955-1968); clerk and solicitor (1968-1974).

Activities: Notary Public (1955); hon secretary Preston Incorporated Law Society (1976-1980); president Preston ILS (1986-1987); president Association of NW Law Societies (1988-1989); local rep Solicitors' Benevolent Association; member Council of the Notaries Society (1987 to date); clerk to the governors of the Royal Cross School for the Deaf (1968-1990); clerk to Withnell Parish Council (1974-1976); governor Hutton Grammar School; chairman of Greater Manchester & Lancashire Rent Assessment Committee (1989 to date); hon sec Preston Fencing Club; member Preston Drama Club; fencing coach (Amateur Fencing Association coaching awards).

Biography: lives Preston; born 27.12.1930; married to Pauline with 1 son and 2 daughters. Educated at Hutton Grammar School (1940-1948); London University (LLB); legal member Royal Town Planning Institute.

Leisure: amateur dramatics; fencing; conjuring.

JAMIESON Colin

tax manager COOPERS & LYBRAND DELOITTE PO Box 207, 128 Queen Victoria Street, London EC4P 4JX.

Career: articled Church Adams Tatham & Co; admitted (1987); tax senior in corporate tax department Coopers & Lybrand Deloitte (1987-1988); became tax manager (1988).

Activities: member Caledonian Club.

Biography: lives London SW19; born 29.08.1962; married. Educated at Edinburgh Academy; University of Kent at Canterbury (BA hons); College of Law Guildford.

JARMAN Nicholas

Queen's Counsel and head of chambers 4 King's Bench Walk, Temple, London EC4.

Career: National Service with Royal Artillery; commissioned (1957); troop commander Cyprus (1957-1959); called to the Bar Inner Temple (1965); Recorder of the Crown Court (1982); QC (1985); head of Chambers (1988).

Activities: joint chairman Joint Committee of Barristers and Solicitors in Berkshire, Bucks and Oxfordshire.

Biography: born 19.06.1938; married to Julia with 1 daughter. Educated at Harrow School (1952-1956); Christ Church Oxford (1962 MA); Sword of Honour, Mons (1957).

Leisure: France; fly fishing.

JARVIS Alan

partner in charge private clients' department WILDE SAPTE Queensbridge House, 60 Upper Thames Street, London EC4V 3BD.

Career: articled Wilkinson Kimbers & Staddon (1974-1976); admitted (1976); assistant solicitor (1976-1980); partner (1980-1983); assistant solicitor Herbert Oppenheimer Nathan & Vandyk (1983-1985); partner (1985-1987); became partner Wilde Sapte (1988).

Biography: lives London SW20; born 04.04.1951; married with 3 children. Educated at Westminster City School; London School of Economics London University (1973 LLB).

JARVIS Brian

senior partner RUSSELL STEWARD & CO 5 Tombland, Norwich NR3 1HH.

Career: articled Russell Steward & Co (1960-1964); admitted (1964); assistant solicitor (1964-1967); became partner (1967); became senior partner (1984).

Activities: assistant Deputy Coroner; member Law Society Area Committee; member of: Church of England Young Men's Society; Yorkshire Dales Society; Long Distance Walkers' Association; Friends of Settle & Carlisle Railway; Three Peaks of Yorkshire Club.

Biography: lives Norwich; born 21.09.1938; married to Freda with 2 children. Educated at Gedling C of E School, Nottingham; Henry Mellish Grammar School, Nottingham; London School of Economics (1960 LLB).

Leisure: all sports (particularly squash and swimming); fell and long distance walking; German and German history; natural history.

JEFFCOATE Tony

senior partner LESTER DIXON & JEFFCOATE 29 Dugdale Street, Nuneaton CV11 5QN.

Career: Royal Navy; articled father's practice; admitted (1954); became partner

(1954); became senior partner (1983).

Activities: chairman Nuneaton Round Table (1967); president Warwickshire Law Society (1987).

Biography: lives Market Bosworth; born 14.12.1928; married to Mitchell with 4 children. Educated at Cheltenham College.

Leisure: farming; sailing; skiing; mountain walking in Switzerland in the summer.

JEFFERSON David

senior partner MAXWELL BATLEY 27 Chancery Lane, London WC2A 1PA.

Career: articled Simmons & Simmons; admitted (1957); National Service commission in Intelligence Corps; became partner Maxwell Batley (1963); became senior partner (1985).

Activities: member Council of the Law Society (1968 to date); chairman Incorporated Council of Law reporting for England and Wales (1987 to date); chairman the Church Adoption Society (1977-1988); member Datchet Parish Council (1965-1983) (chairman 1971-1973); member Eton Rural District Council (1967-1974); member Royal Borough of Windsor & Maidenhead Council (1974-1983); chairman joint working party of the Law Society and the Bar on banking Law; member of: Special Forces Club; Royal Thames Yacht Club; The City of London Club; Leander.

Biography: lives Datchet; born 14.06.1932; married to Barbara with 3 children. Educated at Windsor Grammar School; College of Law.

Leisure: conversation; music; ballet; opera; theatre; swimming; skiing; collecting books, drawings and water colours.

JEFFREY John

consultant STEPHENSON HARWOOD One St Paul's Churchyard, London EC4M 8SH.

Career: admitted (1961); assistant solicitor (1961-1967); partner Ashton Hill & Co (1967-1973); became Stephenson Harwood (1973).

Activities: member of: Oriental Club; Hong Kong Club.

Biography: born 30.05.1934; married to Oonagh with 2 children. Educated at Rugby; Clare College Cambridge (1957).

Leisure: theatre; piano; tennis; squash.

JEFFREYS David

Queen's Counsel in criminal practice Queen Elizabeth Building, Temple, London EC4Y 9BS.

Career: called to the Bar (1958); Recorder (1979); QC (1981).

Activities: member Magistrates Court Rules Committee; member Crown Court Rules Committee.

Biography: lives London; born 01.07.1934; married with 2 children. Educated at Harrow School; Cambridge (1957 BA hons).

JEFFRIES Jonathan David

partner in litigation and insolvency department SIMPSON CURTIS 41 Park Square, Leeds LS1 2NS.

Career: articled Simpson Curtis (1981-1983); admitted (1983); assistant solicitor (1983-1985); associate (1985-1987); became partner (1987).

Activities: licensed insolvency practitioner (1988); member Insolvency Practitioners' Association; member Institute of Directors; member Institute of Credit Managers; member Insolvency Lawyers' Association; former member Trainee Solicitors' Group, Yorkshire; former member Yorkshire Young Solicitors' Committee; member Liversedge Lawn Tennis Club.

Biography: lives Leeds; born 08.07.1959; married to Tracy with 1 son and 1 daughter. Educated at Froebel House Preparatory School, Hull; Hymers College, Hull; Newcastle Upon Tyne University (1980 LLB hons); College of Law Chester (1981); speaker at seminars and articles on: corporate recovery including retention of title; directors duties; wrongful trading; all aspects of insolvency law.

Leisure: active sportsman; running half marathons; weight training; keep fit; tennis; squash; cricket.

JEFFS Julian

Queen's Counsel Francis Taylor Building, Temple, London EC4.

Career: called to the Bar Gray's Inn (1958); Recorder (1975); Bencher Gray's Inn (1981).

Activities: chairman Patent Bar Association (1981-1989); General Commissioner of Income Tax (1985 to date); member Senate of Inns of Court & Bar (1984-1986); member Bar Council (1988-1989); member of: Beefsteak; Garrick; Reform; Saintsbury.

Biography: lives East Ilsley; born 05.04.1931; married to Deborah with 3

sons. Educated at Mostyn House School (1940-1944); Wrekin College (1944-1949); Downing College Cambridge (1953 MA); author of intellectual property chapters in Clerk & Lindsell on Torts (13th-16th eds 1969-1989); part author 'Encyclopaedia of UK & European Patent Law' (1977).

Leisure: writing; wine; walking; old cars; Iberian things.

JENKINS Ian

senior partner BARLOW LYDE & GILBERT Beaufort House, 15 St Botolph Street, London EC3A 7NJ.

Career: articled Barlow Lyde & Gilbert (1969); admitted; assistant solicitor; became partner (1974); became senior partner (1989).

Activities: member of: Royal Thames Yacht Club; Royal Southern Yacht Club; Ocean Cruising Club.

Biography: lives Richmond; born 24.08.1946; married to Judy with 2 sons. Educated at Betteshanger School; Denstone College; King's College London (LLB).

Leisure: sailing.

JERRARD Don

partner and head of intellectual property and technology law department BAKER & MCKENZIE Aldwych House, Aldwych, London WC2B 4JP.

Career: articled Lovell White & King (1974-1976); admitted (1976); assistant solicitor (1976-1977); assistant solicitor Baker & McKenzie (1977-1983); became head of intellectual property and technology law department (1983).

Activities: member of Board of Federation against Software Theft (FAST); chairman FAST Legal Advisory Group; member editorial panels of Computer Law and Practice and Computer Law and Security Report; founder member London Computer Law Group.

Biography: lives Greatham nr Liss; born 21.03.1950; married to Susan with 2 children. Educated at Oakmount School, Southampton; Winchester College; Emmanuel College Cambridge (1973 BA College Law Prize) (1976 MA); College of Law Lancaster Gate (1974); many articles in publications such as: Computer Law and Practice; The Computer Law and Security Report; The European Intellectual Property Review and others; European editor 'Protecting Computer Technology' (1986); worldwide lecturer on intellectual property, competition and computer laws.

J

Leisure: travel (mainly on business!); watching Southampton FC; swimming; croquet; tennis; landscape gardening.

JOANES Andrew

senior partner BAKER & MCKENZIE Aldwych House, Aldwych, London WC2B 4JP.

Career: National Service 2nd Lt Royal Signals (1950-1952); Bigelow teaching fellow University of Chicago Law School (1955-1956); articled Linklaters & Paines (1956-1957); lecturer in law University of British Columbia (1957-1959); articled Baker & McKenzie (1960-1962); admitted (1962); became partner (1962).

Activities: speaker on tax issues at seminars organised by European Study Conferences, Institute of Chartered Accountants, Institute of Taxation, Ernst & Whinney, Crown Eagle Communications; member of: Reform Club; Lansdowne Club; Crockfords.

Biography: lives Dulwich; born 12.04.1932; married to Ann with 3 children. Educated at Christ's Hospital; The Queen's College Oxford (1955 BA); University of Chicago (1960 LLM); Winter Williams Prize Oxford; author of 'Stare Decisis in the Supreme Court of Canada' Canadian Bar Review; 'Conditional Sales in Canada' UBC Law Review.

Leisure: golf; gardening.

JOHNSON Alan

senior partner LONGUEVILLE GITTINS 39/41 Church Street, Oswestry, Shropshire SY11 2SZ.

Career: Executor & Trustee Department of Lloyds Bank; (1958-1960); articled John C Gittins & Co (1960-1964); admitted (1964); assistant solicitor (1964-1977); became partner (1977); became senior partner (1984); amalgamated with Longueville & Co (1988).

Activities: hon solicitor to Oswestry & District Citizens Advice Bureau; member management Committee Oswestry & District Citizens Advice Bureau; former Law Society examiner in equity and succession under the old syllabus; chairman Oswestry & District Bowling League; former churchwarden local church; vice-chairman Parochial Church Council; treasurer Shamrock Gardening Club; member of: Oxford Union Society; Oswestry & District Conservative Club.

Biography: lives Oswestry; born 10.06.1933; married to Betty with 3 children. Educated

at Oswestry Boys' High School; St Edmund Hall Oxford (1956 BA) (1988 MA).

Leisure: crown green bowling; gardening; philately (Great Britain and Shropshire postal history); photography; preservation of vintage aircraft.

JOHNSON Brian

senior partner FREEMAN JOHNSON 11 Victoria Road, Darlington, Co Durham DL1 5SP.

Career: articled Latimer & Hinks; admitted (1955); assistant solicitor; assistant solicitor Freeman Johnson & Jacks (1966); became senior partner (1985).

Activities: secretary of the Durham and North Yorkshire Law Society (1971-1980); member of the National Council of the Law Society (1980-1988); chairman No 8 Northern Legal Aid Area; member Council of Durham & North Yorkshire Law Society; member of Royal Air Force Club.

Biography: lives Darlington; born 06.08.1933; married to Julie with 3 children. Educated at Darlington Queen Elizabeth Grammar School.

Leisure: cricket and other kindred sports; gardening; music.

JOHNSON Geoffrey Nicholson

assistant chief legal adviser LLOYDS BANK PLC 71 Lombard Street, London EC3P 3BS.

Career: articled Clifford Turner (1973-1975); admitted (1975); Lloyds Bank PLC (1977).

Activities: member Law Society Standing Committee on Company Law; member CBI Commercial Law Panel.

Biography: lives Colchester; born 18.05.1951; married to Patricia with 2 children. Educated at Clifton College, Bristol; Durham University (1972 BA hons).

Leisure: bridge; golf; tennis; badminton.

JOHNSON Peter

partner J & WH SALE AND SON 6 Iron Gate, Derby DE1 3PN.

Career: articled to father; admitted .

Activities: governor of the College of Law; secretary of Derby Law Society (1977-1983); member Law Society Council (1983 to date); chairman of Entry & Training Committee (1987-1989); chairman Training Committee (1989); involved in scheme for funding local private school to save it from extinction (1970s/1980s) .

Biography: lives Belper; born 13.09.1939; married to Janet with 2 children. Educated at Herbert Strutt Grammar School, Belper; Manchester University (1961 LLB hons); Bigelow Teaching Fellow University of Chicago Law School (1961-1962).

Leisure: music; hill walking.

JOHNSON Richard Trevor

senior partner BURGES SALMON Narrow Quay House, Prince Street, Bristol BS1 4AH.

Career: National Service as an officer in the Royal Signals in Egypt (1949-1950); articled Burges Salmon (1953-1956); admitted (1956); became partner (1960); senior partner (1986).

Activities: past president Bristol Law Society (1974-1975); member Bristol Benevolent Institution; past president Dolphin Society; legal member Mental Health Review Tribunal; founder M5 group of legal practices; member Farmers' Club.

Biography: lives Bristol; born 21.06.1930; married to Kate with 3 children. Educated at Clifton College; Cambridge (BA LLM).

Leisure: hill walking; theatre; opera; music.

JOHNSON Tom

partner FAEGRE & BENSON 10 Eastcheap, London EC3M 1ET.

Career: admitted Minnesota (1964) and New York (1966); associate Milbank Tweed Hadley & McCloy, New York (1965-1971); associate Gottesman & Partners (1971); opened branch offices in London for Atlanta and Chicago law firms; became partner and opened branch office in London for Faegre & Benson (1985).

Activities: member American Bar Association; member NY Bar Association; member Association of the Bar of the City of NY; member International Bar Association; member International Fiscal Association.

Biography: lives Gerrards Cross; born 18.05.1936; divorced with 5 sons. Educated at Watertown High School, South Dakota (1954); Macalester College, St Paul, Minnesota (1958 BA Phd); Harvard Law School (1964 JD); author of 'A Practical Guide to US Taxation of Overseas Americans' (1977); author, editor and publisher monthly newsletter 'US Expatriates Taxation' (1977-1987); contributing editor BNA 'Tax Planning International Review' (1977 to date); various articles in Law Society's Gazette and other publications.

Leisure: skiing; saltwater swimming; tennis; rearing children; writing for publication; stamp accumulation; gardening; participating in Democratic Party politics.

JOLLES Alicia

litigation partner CLIFFORD CHANCE Blackfriars House, 19 New Bridge Street, London EC4V 6BY.

Career: publishing (1972-1974); articled Coward Chance (1974-1977); admitted (1977); assistant solicitor (1977-1981); became partner (1981); firm became Clifford Chance (1987).

Activities: chairman City of London Law Society sub-committee on recruitment.

Biography: lives London N1; born 24.12.1947; married to Martin Herbert with 3 children. Educated at Northampton High School for Girls; Westfield College London University (1969 BA); Scholarship (1967-1969); (1974 PHD); Exhibition (1966).

Leisure: family; friends; gardening; sailing.

JONES Bryan

partner TRAPNELL & FORBES 16 Orchard Street, Bristol and JW WARD & SON 52 Broad Street, Bristol.

Career: articled George Fisher (1954-1957); admitted (1957); assistant solicitor Blake Lapthorn (1957-1962); became partner JW Ward & Son (1963); became partner Trapnell & Forbes (1990).

Activities: president Bath Law Society (1978-1980); former vice-chairman Avon County Council; chairman Wick Committee Social & Liberal Democrats; former liaison officer for Lions Clubs International District 105W with 103 NO; member Bath Lions Club.

Biography: lives Marshfield; born 20.02.1932; married to Jennifer with 3 children. Educated at Watford Boys' Grammar School; Cambridge (1954 BA); (1955 LLM).

JONES Donald W

head of corporate and commercial department TROWERS & HAMLINS 6 New Square, Lincoln's Inn, London WC2A 3RP.

Career: articled small City firm (5 years); admitted (1961); assistant solicitor Trowers & Hamlins (1961-1969); seconded to foreign government client of firm (1964-1967); became partner (1969).

Activities: chairman firm's Management Committee.

Biography: lives North Hertfordshire; born 26.05.1938; married with 3 children. Educated at Queen Elizabeth's Grammar School, Barnet; College of Law (1960).

Leisure: theatre; cinema; art.

JONES Francis

barrister 55-59 Temple Chambers, Temple Avenue, London EC4Y 0HP.

Career: called to the Bar (1980).

Activities: Labour councillor Wandsworth (1978 to date); member Battersea Labour Club.

Biography: lives London SW11; born 29.12.1951; married to Jane. Educated at King Edward VI, Norwich; Exeter College Oxford (1971-1974 PPE); Polytechnic Central London (1979 Law Diploma); Council Legal Education (1979-1980 Bar exams).

Leisure: cricket.

JONES George Anthony (Tony)

partner PITMANS 47 Castle Street, Reading RG1 7SR.

Career: articled Kent Thomas & Jones and Dudley Clarke & Son; admitted (1964); became partner Kent Thomas & Jones (1964-1974); became partner Pitmans (1974).

Activities: secretary (3 years) treasurer (2 years) Reading and District Solicitors Association (1965-1972); member Reading Local Legal Aid Committee (1965-1980) .

Biography: lives Ashford Hill; born 09.04.1939; married to Harriet with 2 children. Educated at Crossfields, Reading; Oundle, Northants; Clare College Cambridge (1961 BA); College of Law Guildford (1963-1964 hons); Berks Bucks & Oxon Law Society Prize.

Leisure: gardening and plant propagation; music; skiing; overseas travel; swimming; food and wine.

JONES Glanville

barrister Angel Chambers, 94 Walter Road, Swansea, West Glamorgan SA1 5QA.

Career: Recorder of the Crown Court (1972).

Activities: member Swansea Law Library Association; chairman The Guild for the Promotion of Welsh Music.

Biography: lives Swansea; born 01.05.1931; married to Valma with 3 sons. Educated at St Clement Danes; University College

London (LLB hons); Inns of Court School of Law.

JONES Glyn

partner HALLIWELL LANDAU St James's Court, Brown Street, Manchester M2 2JF.

Career: articled March Pearson & Skelton; admitted (1979); assistant solicitor Harold Chaffe & Co (1979-1980); assistant solicitor Halliwell Landau (1980-1981); became partner (1981).

Activities: director Gaynor Group PLC; Director Claremont Business Equipment Europe Ltd; director Mynshul Bank PLC; group corporate development director Swinton (Holdings) Limited; member of: St James's Club; Lancashire County Cricket Club.

Biography: lives Goostrey; born 26.10.1955; married to Nicola. Educated at Burnage Grammar School; Burnage High School; London School of Economics (1975 LLB hons).

Leisure: reading; theatre; spectator and participant: cricket; soccer; golf; swimming.

JONES Gordon R

senior partner CHURCH ADAMS TATHAM & CO Fulwood House, Fulwood Place, London WC1V 6HR.

Career: articled Wellington & Clifford (1954-1957); admitted (1957); assistant solicitor Church Adams (1958-1960); became partner (1960); responsible for litigation until (1976); and then established company commercial department (1973); became senior partner (1982).

Activities: Committee member London Solicitors Litigation Association (1960-1973) (secretary 7 years) (president 2 years); member Life Assurance Legal Society Committee (2 years); lectured on enforcement of mortgages in the Chancery Division (1960s); annual lecture South Bank Polytechnic on legal and commercial aspects of setting up a business (1986-1988); occasional lectures on establishing shared workspace (1970s); governor prep school (1979 to date) (chairman 1984 to date); vice-chairman Putney Conservation Association (1970s); governor two local state schools; member of: Oxford & Cambridge Universities Club; Hurlingham Club.

Biography: lives London SW15; born 14.08.1931; married to Jane with 3 children. Educated at Crypt School, Gloucester (1942-1950); Selwyn College Cambridge

J

(1954 MA LLM); College of Law Lancaster Gate (1956-1957); occasional articles on litigation topics (1960s); in (1986) article in Architects Journal on pros and cons of incorporating an architect's practice following up a previous article in (1982).

Leisure: freemasonry; sailing; skiing; squash; played for Gloucester RFC and Rosslyn Park (1950s-1960s).

JONES Harry

company solicitor and company secretary TOYOTA (GB) LTD The Quadrangle, Redhill, Surrey RH1 1PX.

Career: admitted (1980); assistant solicitor RAC Motoring Services Ltd (1980-1983); assistant solicitor Streeter Marshall & Wilberforce Jackson (1983-1985); legal adviser Society of Motor Manufacturers & Traders Ltd (1985-1989); became company solicitor and company secretary Toyota (GB) Ltd (1989).

Activities: JP Kingston upon Thames Petty Sessional Division; member Society of Motor Manufacturers & Traders Consumer Affairs Committee; Freemason.

Biography: lives Chessington; born 20.10.1954; married with 2 children. Educated at Surbiton County Grammar School; Ealing Technical College; College of Law Guildford; Associate of the Chartered Institute of Arbitrators; some articles in Road Law.

Leisure: scouting; rugby .

JONES Michael

senior partner HUGH JAMES JONES & JENKINS Arlbee House, Greyfriars Road, Cardiff CF1 4QB.

Career: articled C Hugh James (1963-1966); admitted (1966); became partner (1966); became senior partner (1970).

Activities: member Circuit Advisory Committee (Wales & Chester) (1970-1977); member Incorporated Law Society of Cardiff Council (1969 to date); member Wales & Chester Chancery Court Users Committee (1989); member Curriculum Council for Wales (1988 to date); Law Society spokesman for Wales; governor of 2 schools; member of: Cardiff & County Club; Oxford Union.

Biography: lives Cardiff; born 14.01.1943; married to Ethni with 4 children. Educated at Neath Boys' Grammar School; Jesus College Oxford (1963 BA) (1967 MA); College of Law Lancaster Gate (1965-1966); ACI Arts; Associated Law Societies of Wales Prizeman (1966).

Leisure: gardening; walking; parents' association.

JONES Norman

Queen's Counsel Park Court Chambers, 40 Park Cross Street, Leeds LS1 2QH.

Career: called to Bar (1968); QC (1985); Recorder (1986).

Biography: lives Leeds; born 12.12.1941; married with 3 children. Educated at Grammar School, Bideford; N Devon Technical College; Leeds University (1965 LLB) (1967 LLM).

Leisure: boating; walking.

JONES Peter Henry Francis

partner JOHN HOWELL & CO 427/431 London Road, Sheffield S2 4HJ.

Career: articled Coward Chance (1974-1976); admitted (1977); assistant solicitor (1977-1978); assistant solicitor Darlington & Parkinson (1978-1979); became partner (1979-1987); became partner John Howell & Co (1987).

Activities: chairman Legal Services Conference; member Lord Chancellor's Legal Aid Advisory Committee; member Family Law Committee of Law Society; Chairman Child Care sub group of Family Law Committee; member of Children Act Procedure Advisory Group chaired by Mrs Justice Booth (1990); member Domestic Procedure Sub-committee of Home Office Review of Magistrates' Courts; member of Management Committee of Family Studies Centre, Sheffield; presented paper at Child Sexual Abuse Conference organised by NCB (1988); member BASPCAN; member of: Dethreau BC; Scorpions CC.

Biography: lives Sheffield; born 25.02.1952; married to Libby with 2 daughters. Educated at Bishop Gore Grammar School, Swansea; Newport High School, Gwent; Balliol College Oxford (1973 MA hons); articles on child care law in Justice of the Peace; book reviews for legal action and family law; lecturer on child care law on College of Law course 'Acting in Children's Cases'; at police staff college Bramhill; on courses on child care law and welfare law practice for Nottingham Polytechnic and North West Law Conferences; sometime for FRG/BAA7/London Borough of Ealing.

Leisure: family; rugby; cricket; tennis.

JONES Roger

partner MERRILS EDE Dominions House South, 3rd Floor, Dominions Arcade, Queen Street, Cardiff CF1 4AR.

Career: articled Merrils Ede (1968-1970); admitted (1970); assistant solicitor (1970-1972); became partner (1972).

Activities: part-time Polytechnic law lecturer; hon secretary Cardiff Law Society (1971-1981); deputy treasurer The Law Society (1986-1988 & 1989 to date); chairman Gazette Editorial Advisory Board (1989 to date); chairman Civil Litigation Committee (1990 to date); member The Law Society's: Training Committee (1985 to date); Finance Committee (1987 to date); Employment Law Committee (1985-1990); Council member Law Society (1978 to date); president Associated Law Societies of Wales (1988-1990); chairman CAB Management Committee; former Parliamentary candidate (1974 & 1979); chairman Cardiff North Conservative Association; Rotarian; member Cardiff & County Club.

Biography: lives Cardiff; born 14.09.1945; married. Educated at Newport High School; Bridgend Grammar School; Wadham College Oxford.

Leisure: long distance running.

JONES Rupert

partner ALLEN & OVERY 9 Cheapside, London EC2V 6AD.

Career: articled Allen & Overy (1976-1978); admitted (1978); assistant solicitor (1978-1985); became partner (1985).

Activities: member London Young Solicitors Group Committee (1984-1989) (secretary 1985-1986) (treasurer 1986-1987) (chairman 1987-1988); member National Committee of Young Solicitors (1986-1989); member Law Society Special Committee on Law Office Management and Technology (1985-1987); member Law Society Business Improvement Committee (1987-1989); member Society for Computers and Law (1988 to date); member Whittington Committee of the City of London Solicitors' Company (1988 to date).

Biography: lives Dunsfold nr Godalming; born 02.09.1953; married to Sheila with 2 sons and 1 daughter. Educated at King's College School, Wimbledon (1967-1971); Birmingham University (1975 LLB hons); Sir John Barber Scholarship; The Solicitor's Law Stationery Society Ltd's Prize.

Leisure: cinema; cars; computers; enjoying living in the country.

JONES William

partner and head of commercial and planning department FOOT & BOWDEN 70/76 North Hill, Plymouth PL4 8HH.

Career: articled to the clerk of Carmarthenshire County Council (1962-1965); admitted (1965); assistant solicitor Plymouth City Council (1965-1966); senior assistant solicitor (1966-1970); assistant town clerk Birkenhead Borough Council (1970-1972); became partner Foot & Bowden (1972).

Activities: Notary Public; clerk to the General Commissioners of Income Tax; company secretary to Abbeyfield Tamar Extra Care Society; member Planning Law Committee of the Law Society (Mineral Specialist); member The Friary House Trust; member St Mellion Club.

Biography: born 11.04.1939; married with 2 children. Educated at Llandovery College; Llanelli Grammar School; University College of Wales (1962 BA); paper on 'Mineral Development' at Cambridge Seminar on Planning for Industry organised by IBA; powers of local planning authorities to impose financial obligations - 'A Case History'; Rights of the Public in Environmental Decision Making in England and Wales - IBA Conference in Vancouver.

Leisure: golf; theatre; books.

JORDAN Anthony

litigation partner MILLS & REEVE Francis House, 3-7 Redwell Street, Norwich NR2 4TJ.

Career: articled Mills & Reeve (1954-1960); admitted (1960); assistant solicitor (1960-1965); became partner (1965).

Activities: member Circuit Liaison Committee; hon solicitor Norfolk Baptist Association; Church secretary Chapelfield Road Methodist Church, Norwich; member Old Norvicensian Club.

Biography: lives Cringleford; born 21.07.1938; married to Diane with 1 son. Educated at Norwich School; College of Law Lancaster Gate (1959).

Leisure: active in Methodist Church and other non-conformist Church groups; theatre; cinema; philately.

JORDAN Kevin

chief executive AARON & PARTNERS Grosvenor Court, Foregate Street, Chester CH1 1HG.

Career: Brown & Root, UK and Bahrain (1977-1982); project manager/general

manager SBM, Monaco and Manila (1982-1987); business support manager BP Ventures (1988-1990); became chief executive Aaron & Partners (1990).

Activities: national coach Welsh Hang Gliding Club; club instructor Philippines Sub-Aqua Club; member RAC.

Biography: lives Chester; born 01.07.1956; married to Carolyn with 3 daughters. Educated at Bishop Wordsworth's School, Salisbury; University College Swansea (1977 BSc); IMI Geneva (1988 MBA); Sainsbury Management Fellowship (1987); broke British and European Hang Gliding endurance record (1976).

Leisure: squash; golf.

JOSEPH Colin

head of litigation DJ FREEMAN & CO 43 Fetter Lane, London EC4A 1NA.

Career: articled DJ Freeman (1969-1971); admitted (1971); assistant solicitor (1971-1973); became partner (1973); joint head litigation department (1978-1987); chief executive (1987-1990); head of litigation (1990).

Activities: licensed insolvency practitioner; member Insolvency Law Committee City of London Solicitors' Company; lectured in England and USA on insolvency and insurance; member of MCC.

Biography: lives London N6; born 23.12.1946; married to Anne with 1 son and 1 daughter. Educated at Bancroft's; Exeter College Oxford (1968 BA); Law Society Finals (1969); written articles on: Multi-Disciplinary Practices; the Government Green Papers; Insolvency; Insurance for: 'The Independent'; 'Estate Times'; 'Lloyd's List'.

Leisure: cricket; theatre; reading.

JOSEPH Leslie

Queen's Counsel Devereux Chambers, Devereux Court, London WC2R 3JJ.

Career: called to the Bar (1953); QC (1978); Bencher Middle Temple (1986) .

Activities: member Council of Legal Education.

Biography: lives London NW3; born 13.08.1925; widowed with 3 children. Educated at Haberdashers' Aske's, Hampstead; University College London (1950 LLB hons).

JOWETT Chris

group solicitor HALIFAX BUILDING SOCIETY Trinity Road, Halifax, West Yorkshire HX1 2RG.

Career: regular Army (1963-1970); articled (1970-1973); admitted (1973); assistant solicitor private practice (1973-1978); assistant solicitor Halifax Building Society (1978-1982); became solicitor (1982) and group solicitor (1989).

Activities: member Land Law and Conveyancing Committee of the Law Society; former member Standing Committee on Conveyancing of Law Commission (Committee wound up 1989); chairman Legal Advisory Panel (BSA); member Legal Advisory Panel (Council of Mortgage Lenders).

Biography: lives Leeds; born 01.01.1945; married to Ann with 1 son and 1 daughter. Educated at St Peter's York; Royal Military Academy, Sandhurst.

Leisure: golf; jogging.

JOWITT James

commercial and tax partner BISCHOFF & CO 25 City Road, London EC1Y 1BY.

Career: articled Bischoff & Co; admitted (1968); assistant solicitor (1968-1970); became partner (1970).

Activities: member City University Club.

Biography: lives Essex; born 11.07.1941; married to Ann with 2 children. Educated at Eton; Trinity College Cambridge (1963 MA).

JOY Robert

deputy chief executive/solicitor to the council LONDON BOROUGH OF LEWISHAM Lewisham Town Hall, Catford, London SE6 4RU.

Career: admitted (1966); borough solicitor Sunderland MDC (1974-1976); borough solicitor Lewisham LBC (1976-1982); borough secretary (1982-1990); became deputy chief executive (1990).

Biography: lives Sevenoaks; born 01.03.1942; married to Margaret. Educated at Highgate School (1951-1960); London School of Economics (1963 LLB).

Leisure: collecting antiques, books and plants.

JOYCE Thomas

managing partner London office SHEARMAN & STERLING St Helen's, 1 Undershaft, London EC3A 8HX.

Career: partner Shearman & Sterling, New York (1972); partner London office (1978-1981); managing partner Hong Kong office

K

(1985); became managing partner London office (1989 to date).

Activities: member American Bar Association; Association of the Bar of the City of New York; International Bar Association; member University Club, New York.

Biography: lives London SW3; born 05.10.1939; married to Patricia with 2 children. Educated at St John's University, Minnesota (1960 BA); Notre Dame University (1963 LLB).

Leisure: reading history; travel; walking; the arts.

JUDGE Victor

senior partner JUDGE AND PRIESTLEY 6 West Street, Bromley, Kent BR1 1JN.

Career: articled JH Milner & Son (1948-1954); admitted (1954); became senior partner Judge and Priestley upon father's death (1954); National Service (2 years).

Activities: president Bromley District Law Society; member of: Royal Cinque Port Golf Club; RAF Yacht Club; West Kent Bridge Club; Institute of Directors; Harlequins RFC; Westcombe Park RFC; Society RFU Referees.

Biography: lives Tunbridge Wells; born 05.12.1930; widowed with 3 children. Educated at Tonbridge School; College of Law.

Leisure: former rugby referee and player; bred and exhibited Shetland ponies; yachting (own yacht at Portsmouth); golf; bridge.

JULIUS Anthony

partner and head of litigation MISHCON DE REYA 125 High Holborn, London WC1V 6QP.

Career: articled Mishcon de Reya (1979-1981); admitted (1981); assistant solicitor (1981-1983); became partner (1983); became equity partner (1985); head of litigation department (1987); member of firm's management committee (1987 to date).

Activities: lectures in litigation topics.

Biography: lives London NW11; born 16.07.1956; married with 3 children. Educated at City of London School; Jesus College Cambridge (BA); (First Class; English) Coleridge Prize; Scholar; author of two chapters in 'Tribunals: Practise and Procedure'.

Leisure: researching for PHD in TS Eliot.

K

KADRI Sibghatulla

Queen's Counsel and head of chambers 11 King's Bench Walk, Temple, London EC4Y 7EQ.

Career: producer and broadcaster BBC External Urdu Service (1965-1968); presenter BBC Home Service Asian programmes (1968-1970); visiting lecturer in Urdu Holborn College London (1967-1970); called to the Bar Inner Temple (1969); head of Chambers (1973 to date); QC (1989) .

Activities: president Inner Temple Students' Association (1968-1969); chairman Society of Afro-Asian and Carribean Lawyers' (1978-1983); chairman Asian Lawyers Conference in UK; secretary of Lawyers' Committee for Justice & Human Rights in Pakistan (1985 to date); president Standing Conference of Pakistani Organisations (SCOPO) (1978-1985) (general secretary 1975-1978); convenor Asian Action Committee (1976); vice-chairman All Party Joint Committee Against Racism (1978-1980); actively involved in race-relations and immigration issues and British Pakistani's struggle for the restoration of democracy in Pakistan; member of the working party established by the Senate of the Inns of Court and the Bar to investigate race relations in the profession; established race-relations committee; member National Liberal Club.

Biography: born 23.04.1937; married to Carita with 2 children. Educated at Christian High School, Budaun UP; SM College, Karachi; Karachi University.

KAIN Bernard

senior partner WITHY KING & LEE 5 & 6 Northumberland Buildings, Queen Square, Bath BA1 2JE.

Career: articled Withy King & Lee (1954); admitted (1960); assistant solicitor (1960-1963); became partner (1963).

Activities: president Bath Law Society; past chairman (Bristol & Bath branch) National Delegate Committee of Young Solicitors Group (1969-1970); past chairman Historic Vehicle Joint Consultative Committee; past president Vintage Sports Car Club; trustee of The Bugatti Trust; member Bath and County Club.

Biography: lives Atworth and Rock; born 19.12.1937; married to Jean. Educated at Clifton College.

Leisure: driving vintage Bugatti racing

cars; sailing; golf; shooting.

KALBFLEISCH Peter

managing partner London office BLAKE CASSELS & GRAYDON Northumbrian House, 14 Devonshire Square, London EC2M 4TE.

Career: called to the Bar Ontario (1978); solicitor Blake Cassels & Graydon (1978-1984); partner (1984-1989); became managing partner London office (1989).

Activities: member Membership Committee of the Canada/UK Chamber of Commerce; member of: Canada Club; Canada Bar Association; Canada/UK Chamber of Commerce; International Bar Association.

Biography: lives Walton on Thames; born 11.07.1951; married to Barbara with 3 children. Educated at Goderich District Collegiate Institute; Waterloo University (1973 BA); Osgoode Hall Law School, Toronto (1976 LLB); Silver Medal; numerous articles on corporate and securities law matters.

Leisure: travel; duplicate bridge; history; antiques.

KALISHER Michael

Queen's Counsel 1 Hare Court, Temple, London EC4Y 7BE.

Career: admitted (1965); assistant solicitor (1965-1966); partner Avery Midgen & Co (1966-1969); called to the Bar (1970); practice at 9 King's Bench Walk (1970-1976); practice 1 Hare Court (1976 to date); QC (1984); Recorder (1985); Bencher Inner Temple (1989).

Activities: vice-chairman Criminal Bar Association (1990 to date); member Crown Courts Rules Committee (1988 to date); member Efficiency Commission (1989 to date); member Home Secretary's Working Party on Rights of Silence (1988-1989); member Roehampton Club.

Biography: lives London; born 24.02.1941; married with 3 children. Educated at Hove County Grammar School; Bristol University (LLB hons).

Leisure: reading; squash; tennis; walking.

KATZMAN Jerrold

partner and head of London office PROSKAUER ROSE GOETZ & MENDELSOHN 4 St James's Place, London SW1A 1NP.

Career: Skadden Arps Meagher & Flom, New York (1972); Cravath Swaine &

Moore, New York and London (1973-1980); became partner Proskauer Rose Goetz & Mendelsohn (1981-present).

Activities: member of: RAC; Beaconsfield Golf Club; Royal Mid-Surrey Golf Club.

Biography: lives Buckinghamshire; born 06.09.1948; married to Dr Silvia Casale with 1 child. Educated at London School of Economics and Political Science (1968-1969); Wharton School of Finance and Commerce, Pennsylvania University BS (1970 Summa Cum Laude); independent research on multinational corporations at the International Institute of Economic Studies, Stockholm, Sweden (1971); Yale Law School (1973 JD).

Leisure: golf; theatre; swimming; reading.

KAUFMAN Alan

managing partner FORSYTE KERMAN 79 New Cavendish Street, London W1M 8AQ.

Career: articled Forsyte Kerman; admitted; assistant solicitor; partner (1974); became managing partner (1988).

Activities: lectured to surveyors and estate agents on legal matters; past president and educational vice-president of Knightsbridge Speakers' Club (former winner ASC Area Speech Competition and runner-up ASC District Speech Competition); member of: Highgate Lawn Tennis Club; Rugby Club of London.

Biography: lives London NW11; born 15.04.1947; married to Vivienne with 5 daughters. Educated at Hackney Downs Grammar School; King's College Cambridge (1968 MA) Exhibitioner.

Leisure: cinema; theatre; tennis; squash; cricket; five-a-side football.

KAY John

Queen's Counsel 1 Exchange Flags, Liverpool L2 3XN.

Career: called to the Bar Gray's Inn (1968); tutor Liverpool University (1968-1969); Northern circuit (1968 to date); Recorder (1982); QC (1984).

Activities: member General Council of the Bar; member Executive Committee of Northern circuit; member of: Athenaeum, Liverpool; Racquet, Liverpool.

Biography: lives Liverpool; born 13.09.1943; married to Jeffa with 3 children. Educated at Denstone College; Christ's College Cambridge (1965 MA) Bachelor Scholar; Gray's Inn Arden Senior Scholar.

Leisure: racing; rugby football; gardening; genealogy.

KAY John Frederick

senior partner MOLESWORTHS 3/11 Drake Street, Rochdale, Lancs OL16 1RH.

Career: articled with father Frederick William Kay (1965-1966) and William Barlow Tomlinson (1966-1971); admitted (1971); became partner (1971); now senior partner.

Activities: President Rochdale Law Association; Chairman Northern Branch of the Society for Computers and Law; Director Solicitors Own Software Limited; Director Rochdale Enterprise Agency; Director Rochdale Training Enterprise Council Ltd.

Biography: lives Littleborough; born 14.11.1946; married to Elisabeth with 2 daughters. Educated at Mostin House School; Wrekin College; College of Law Guildford.

KAYE Laurence

partner in charge of the company/commercial department SAUNDERS SOBELL LEIGH & DOBIN 20 Red Lion Street, London WC1R 4AE.

Career: articled Brecher & Co (1972-1975); admitted (1975); assistant solicitor (1975-1977); became partner (1977); partner Saunders Sobell Leigh & Dobin (1980); co-founded company/commercial department.

Activities: member Law Society; member business law section International Bar Association; initiator of 'Network 92' an association of independent law firms in Europe; past chairman Mount Vernon Cleft Lip Palate Association; hon solicitor Radlett & Bushey Reform Synagogue; member Radlett Lawn Tennis Club.

Biography: lives Radlett; born 01.09.1949; married to Lauren with 2 children. Educated at Haberdashers' Aske's (1960-1967); Sidney Sussex College Cambridge (1971 BA); (1975 MA); College of Law (1972 & 1975); written in-house articles & seminars on EEC law including EC competition law and 1992; gives seminars to accountants on above; in-house seminars on communication skills; talk to Holborn Law Society: 'Intellectual Property Rights in the Electronic Age'.

Leisure: yoga; theatre; cycling; tennis.

KEANE Georgina

partner and head of employment unit TITMUSS SAINER & WEBB 2 Serjeants' Inn, London EC4Y 1LT.

Career: called to the Bar (Middle Temple) (1975); pupillage in London Chambers; general practice at the Bar in London and East Anglia (1975-1984); employment law adviser Employment Affairs Department of the Confederation of British Industry (1984-1986); consultant barrister Titmuss Sainer & Webb (1986-1988); admitted (1988); became partner (1988).

Activities: member Executive Committee of the Industrial Law Society; member Employment Committee of the Fawcett Society; lectures at various organisations eg Institute of Personnel Management; Law Society Young Solicitors in-house training.

Biography: lives London NW10; born 03.02.1954; married with 2 sons. Educated at Convent of the Sacred Heart; Inns of Court Law School; writes various booklets for clients eg equal pay; cashless pay; trade union law.

Leisure: opera; theatre; horseriding; walking; avoiding housework.

KEAT Alan

partner TRAVERS SMITH BRAITHWAITE 10 Snow Hill, London EC1A 2AL.

Career: articled Travers Smith Braithwaite (1964-1966); admitted (1966); assistant solicitor (1966-1970); became partner (1970).

Activities: non-executive director Beazer PLC (1986-1989); member Law Society Standing Committee on Company Law.

Biography: lives Guildford; born 12.05.1942; married with 3 daughters. Educated at Charterhouse; Merton College (1963 MA).

KEATING Donald

Queen's Counsel and head of chambers 10 Essex Street, Outer Temple, London WC2R 3AA.

Career: Flt Lt RAFVR (1943-1946); called to the Bar Lincoln's Inn (1950); QC (1972); Recorder of the Crown Court (1972-1987); Bencher Lincoln's Inn (1979) .

Activities: member Professional Liability Review Construction Industry Study Team (DOE (1988-1989); lectured and delivered reports on many aspects of construction law; arbitrator sole and joint home and overseas; member of the Society of Construction Arbitrators; member Garrick.

Biography: lives London; born 24.06.1924; married to Rosamond with 4 children and 1 stepdaughter. Educated at Roan; King's College London (1948 BA); Fellow

K

K

Chartered Institute of Arbitration (1982); author of: 'Building Contracts' (eds 1955, 1963, 1969, 1978 & supps 1982 & 1984); 'Guide to RIBA Form 1959'; many articles in variety of journals on construction law.

Leisure: theatre; music; travel; walking.

KEATS Terence

senior partner MARSHALL HARVEYS Argyle Chambers, Fir Vale Road, Bournemouth BH1 2JG.

Career: meteorological office Heathrow (1959-1961); Westminster Bank Ltd (1961-1962); articled Marshall Harveys (1963-1968); admitted (1968); assistant solicitor (1968-1972); partner (1972-1984); became senior partner (1984).

Activities: secretary Bournemouth & District Law Society (1982-1984) (president 1988-1989); past chairman Courts sub-committee; chairman Parliamentary liaison sub-committee; member Bournemouth Symphony Chorus; past vice-chairman Bournemouth and Boscombe Light Opera Company; chairman Canford School Society.

Biography: lives Ferndown; born 25.03.1941; married to Jenny with 1 son and 1 daughter. Educated at Bournemouth Grammar School; College of Law Guildford (1963-1967).

Leisure: cricket; tennis; skiing; sailing; music; travelling in France.

KEELY Stephen

senior partner KEELY SMITH & JOBSON 16 Bore Street, Lichfield, Staffs WS13 6LL.

Career: articled Durham Brindley & Linn; admitted; assistant solicitor Silverman & Livermore; assistant solicitor Durham Brindley & Linn (1967-1971); became partner (1971-1982); jointly founded Keely Smith & Jobson (1982).

Biography: lives Lichfield; born 05.04.1940; married to Dorothy with 3 children and 3 stepchildren.

Leisure: bridge; jogging; tennis.

KEEN Howard

managing partner FLADGATE FIELDER Heron Place, 3 George Street, London W1H 6AD.

Career: articled Philip Taylor & Co; admitted (1957); assistant solicitor (1957-1960); partner (1960-1963); partner Fielder Le Riche (1963-1975); senior partner (1975-1988); became managing partner merged firm Walters Fladgate (1988).

Activities: member of: Hartsbourne Golf Club; Dyrham Park Country Club.

Biography: lives London NW8; born 07.06.1933; married to Frances with 3 children. Educated at City of London School; University College London (1954 LLB hons); London University Scholarship in Law (1954-1956).

Leisure: relaxing at holiday home in France; bridge.

KEENE David

Queen's Counsel 4 & 5 Gray's Inn Square, Gray's Inn, London WC1.

Career: called to the Bar (1964); QC (1980); Bencher Inner Temple (1987); Recorder of the Crown Court (1989).

Activities: Chairman Examination-in-Public into Cumbria and Lake District Structure Plan (1980); inspector County Hall (London) Public Inquiry (1987); vice-chairman of Local Government and Planning Bar Association; occasional member Final Selection Board for DOE Planning Inspectorate; member Athenaeum.

Biography: lives London; born 15.04.1941; married to Gillian with 2 children. Educated at Hampton Grammar School; Balliol College Oxford (1962 BA hons) (1963 BCL); Winter Williams Prizewinner; Eldon Scholar.

Leisure: walking; opera; jazz.

KEHOE Laurence

legal adviser and head of national legal department GRANT THORNTON Grant Thornton House, Melton Street, London NW1 2EP.

Career: junior clerk Wedlake Bell (1967-1970); litigation manager Pickering Kenyon (1970-1974); articled (1974-1978); admitted (1978); assistant solicitor Lawrance Messer (1978-1982); associate partner (1982-1984); partner (1984-1987); became legal adviser Grant Thornton (1987).

Activities: member Law Society Commerce & Industry Group; former Round Tabler; former team member Wedlake Bell football team (Cup & League Double); member sports and social clubs.

Biography: lives London E12 and Great Clacton; born 08.08.1951; married to Karen with 2 sons. Educated at State primary and secondary schools; City of London Polytechnic; Tottenham Polytechnic; East Ham Polytechnic; College of Law (Distinction in criminal law and the law of tort).

Leisure: karate; weight training;

swimming; movies; photography; DIY; reading.

KEIGHLEY Richard

civil litigation and employment partner HORWOOD & JAMES 7 Temple Square, Aylesbury, Bucks HP20 2QB.

Career: articled Burges Salmon (1966-1968); admitted (1969); assistant solicitor (1970-1973); became partner (1973).

Activities: founder member Berks Bucks & Oxon Young Solicitors Group (chairman (1976); member Berks Bucks & Oxon Law Society Committee (1979-1989) (president 1987-1988); assistant Recorder (1988 to date).

Biography: lives Wingrave; born 19.02.1943; married to Jean with 1 son and 1 daughter. Educated at Chichester High School for Boys (1954-1962); Bristol University (1965 LLB).

Leisure: amateur dramatics (founder Wingrave Players); playing cricket, squash and croquet; walking in the Alps.

KELLER-HOBSON Kathleen

partner in charge European office TORY DUCHARME LAWSON LUNDELL, Canadian Barristers and Solicitors, 44/45 Chancery Lane, London WC2A 1JB.

Career: law student Tory Tory Deslauriers & Binnington (1979-1981); called to the Bar Ontario (1981); associate (1981-1987); became partner (1987).

Activities: council member Canada/United Kingdom Chamber of Commerce (member Financial Services Committee); speaker at conferences on doing business in Canada and Eurobonds; member Canada Club.

Biography: lives London W8; born 08.08.1956; married to Douglas. Educated at Ottawa University (1974-1976 Arts) (1979 LLB); frequent contributor to International Financial Law Review on capital markets, corporate finance and aircraft finance topics.

Leisure: travel; cooking; gardening.

KELLY Clive Raisman

corporate counsel PENTLAND GROUP PLC Pentland Centre, Lakeside, Squires Lane, Finchley, London N3 2QL.

Career: articled Champion & Co (1952-1957); admitted (1957); assistant solicitor Mobil Oil Co (1959-1960); Thorn EMI PLC (1960-1986); became corporate counsel Pentland Group PLC (1987).

Activities: member Law Society;

Liveryman of the City of London Solicitors' Company; member of: Oriental Club; Rand Club, Johannesburg; Greek Yachting Club; Royal Cape YC.

Biography: lives London NW6; born 07.01.1935; married to Aliki, Educated at Hampton School (1946-1952); College of Law; Administrative Staff College, Henley (1973); Fellow British Institute of Management; Fellow The Institute of Directors.

Leisure: travel; music; reading; curling.

KEMP Douglas

senior partner MILLS KEMP & BROWN 1/5 Huddersfield Road, Barnsley, South Yorkshire S70 2LP.

Career: admitted (1956); armed services (1956-1958); assistant solicitor W Winter; became partner; firm amalgamated to form Mills Kemp & Brown (1967).

Activities: member Barnsley Law Society (past president); chairman sub-committee for contentious matters; chairman Barnsley Duty Solicitor Committee; chairman 9B Regional Duty Solicitor Committee; member of local golf and tennis clubs.

Biography: lives Barnsley; born 26.6.1933; married to Barbara Julia with 2 daughters. Educated at Queen Elizabeth Grammar School; Leeds University; College of Law Guildford.

Leisure: golf; tennis; military history; fine wines and cigars.

KEMP David

Queen's Counsel and head of chambers 4 Raymond Buildings, Gray's Inn, London WC1R 5BP.

Career: called to the Bar (1948); QC (1973); Recorder (1976); Bencher Inner Temple; FCI Arb.

Activities: arbitrator in domestic and international construction arbitrations; counsel in construction disputes in UK and abroad; also in judicial review and personal injury litigation; member Council of Law Reporting; member of: Hurlingham Club; Kandahar Ski Club; Ski Club of Great Britain.

Biography: lives London; born 14.10.1921; married to Sylvia (deceased 1971); Maureen. Educated at Winchester College; Corpus Christi College Cambridge (hons); Scholarship Inner Temple; author of 'Kemp & Kemp Quantum of Damages vols I & II' (1954).

Leisure: tennis; skiing; gardening.

KENDALL John

partner and head of crime and commercial department TRUMAN CLOSE KENDALL & APPLEBY 30 Avenue Road, Grantham, Lincolnshire NG31 6TH.

Career: articled Waldy Chater & Jacks and Campbell Hooper; admitted; became partner Peake Snow & Jeudwine; demerged to become Close Kendall & Co; merged to become Trumans.

Activities: member Law Society Child Care Panel; secretary Teeside Law Students' Group (1969); trustee Aveling Barford Pension Funds; member Grantham Civic Trust; Church warden; governor Sandon School (for mentally handicapped children); member choral society; member Red Cross.

Biography: lives Grantham; born 16.08.1947; married to Liz with 2 children. Educated at Chesterfield School; University College London.

Leisure: swimming; badminton; tennis.

KENNEDY John

senior partner ALLEN & OVERY 9 Cheapside, London EC2V 6AD.

Career: admitted (1957); assistant solicitor Allen & Overy (1957-1961); became partner (1961).

Activities: member of: City of London Club; City Law Club; Hurlingham Club.

Biography: lives London W11; born 09.07.1934; married to Margaret with 4 sons. Educated at London University (1954 LLB).

Leisure: music; reading; sport.

KENNETT Richard

chief executive partner LAYTONS 16 Lincoln's Inn Fields, London WC2A 3ED.

Career: articled Laytons (1968-1970); admitted (1970); assistant solicitor (1970-1972); became partner (1972).

Activities: former chairman Harpenden Round Table.

Biography: lives Harpenden; born 01.08.1945; married to Christine with 3 children. Educated at Shirley House School; Cranleigh School; St John's College Cambridge (1967 BA) (1968 LLB) (1970 MA) (1986 LLM).

Leisure: family.

KENNY Phillip

head of law department NEWCASTLE POLYTECHNIC Ellison Place, Newcastle

upon Tyne; consultant on property law to DICKINSON DEES, Newcastle upon Tyne.

Career: lecturer Nottingham University (1971-1973); private practice (1973-1976); head of department Newcastle Polytechnic (1980); became professor (1987); legal director Education Assets Board (1989).

Activities: Law Society moderator; ILEX examiner; member Law Society Training Committee; member CPE Board; consultant on landlord & tenant, conveyancing, mobile homes law and development; member Tynemouth Sailing Club.

Biography: lives Gosforth; born 09.08.1948; married to Ann with 4 children. Educated at Lurgan College; Bristol University (1969 LLB); Cambridge (1970 Dip Crim); Columbia University, New York (1971 LLM); author of: 'Conveyancing Law' (1985); 'Studying Law' (1984); Sweet & Maxwell's 'Law Files'; Sweet & Maxwell's 'Conveyancing Practice' (1989); articles in Criminal Law Review, Housing Encyclopaedia, Current Law, Conveyancer, New Law Journal, Journal of Planning & Environment Law, Solicitor's Journal, Law Society's Gazette, Guardian Gazette, Modern Law Review, Journal of Criminal Law, Estates Gazette.

Leisure: legal journalism; sailing; walking.

KENROY James

senior partner GLANVILLES 16 Landport Terrace, Portsmouth PO1 2QT.

Career: articled Allen Sons Ward and Blake (1951-1956); admitted (1956); assistant solicitor (1956-1959); assistant solicitor Hobson Thomas Sherwell and Wells (1959-1960); became partner (1960); firm became Glanvilles Wells and Way (1970); became senior partner Glanvilles (1983).

Activities: HM Coroner for Portsmouth and South East Hampshire (1989 to date); part-time chairman Social Security Appeal Tribunals (1987 to date); hon treasurer Hampshire Incorporated Law Society (1978-1985) president (1985-1986); founder chairman Hampshire Solicitors Conveyancing Protocol (Portsmouth & SE Hampshire area) (1986-1990); chairman Portsmouth Area Solicitors (1987-1989); member Coroners' Society; Southern Coroners' Society; member of: Royal Naval Club and Royal Albert Yacht Club.

Biography: lives Prinsted; born 10.01.1932; married to Deirdre with 2 daughters. Educated at Tonbridge (1945-1950); Solicitors Finals (1956 hons).

Leisure: family life; travel.

K

KENYON David

senior partner PHILIP EVANS & CO
30 Christchurch Road, Bournemouth,
Dorset BH1 3PB.

Career: admitted (1959); National Service
(1959-1961); assistant solicitor
Poole/Bournemouth firm of solicitors
(1964-1968); became partner (1964-1968);
assistant solicitor Philip Evans & Co (1968-
1969); became partner (1969); became
senior partner (1975).

Activities: director Wessex Building Society
(1972 to date); member of: Army & Navy
Club; Royal Motor Yacht Club; Cowes
Corinthian Yacht Club; Institute of
Directors.

Biography: lives Bournemouth; born
06.10.1935; married to Shirley with 3
daughters; 2 sons; 1 stepson. Educated at
Sandle Manor Preparatory School,
Fordingbridge (1945-1949); Sherborne
School, Dorset (1949-1953).

Leisure: sailing; boat renovation; theatre;
cinema; literature.

KEOGH Malcolm

partner PANNONE BLACKBURN
123 Deansgate, Manchester M3 2BU.

Career: articled George Davies & Co (1964-
1969); admitted (1969); partner with father
Ronald Keogh & Co (1969-1974); senior
partner (1974-1987); became partner
Pannone Blackburn (1987).

Activities: deputy registrar of High Court
and County Court; Consular Agent for
France in Manchester; member Law
Society Working Party on International
Promotion; responsible for negotiation and
formation of First European Economic
Interest Grouping of Lawyers from
England, Belgium, France, Italy and Spain;
lectures for IBC, ESC, etc; lectures in
French and English in Belgium and France
on English business law and investment;
member Franco British Jurists' Association;
chairman Northern Chamber Orchestra
Ltd; chairman Franco British Business
Club; member St James's Club,
Manchester.

Biography: lives Knutsford; born
13.04.1944; married to Catherine. Educated
at Stonyhurst College, Whalley; College of
Law, London; Liverpool Polytechnic;
numerous articles on French property law
and on European Economic Interest
Groupings for Lawyers.

Leisure: flying (PPL/IR); languages (fluent
French; Spanish); overseas cultures.

KERLE Bridget

partner corporate department HEWITSON
BECKE & SHAW Shakespeare House, 42
Newmarket Road, Cambridge CB5 8EP.

Career: articled Slater Heelis & Co (1975-
1977); admitted (1977); assistant solicitor
Wild Hewitson & Shaw (1977-1980);
became partner (1980).

Activities: former secretary Cambridge
Young Solicitors; member local Law
Society Committee; member Association of
Women Solicitors.

Biography: lives Longmeadow; born
12.05.1953; married to Brian with 1 child.
Educated at Glossop School; St Hilda's
College Oxford (1974 MA); College of Law
Lancaster Gate; local newspaper articles.

Leisure: gardening; reading; opera.

KERMAN Isidore

senior partner FORSYTE KERMAN
79 New Cavendish Street, London
W1M 8AQ.

Career: admitted (1927); founded own
practice (1927).

Activities: Freeman of the City of London;
Grande Officer of the Southern Cross of
Brazil; former member Council of the Soho
Hospital for Women; former member
Council of the Shorthorn Society; director
of: BS Group Plc; Data Tote England Ltd;
Drones Restaurant Ltd; Fontwell Park
Steeplechase Co Plc; J Sheekey Ltd; Kybo
Inns Ltd; Plumpton Racecourse Plc; Scott's
Restaurant Plc; Scott's Restaurant
Investments Ltd; Wembley Plc; member of:
Naval & Military Club; Portland Club.

Biography: lives London W1 and Kent;
born 13.03.1905; married to Blanche with 2
children. Educated at Cheltenham; author
of 'Problems of the Law of Defamation in
relation to the Press, Literary Work and
Broadcasting'; 'Married Women and
Tortfeasors'.

Leisure: farmer (livestock breeder); owns
and breeds greyhounds and racehorses;
bridge.

KERR David

partner BIRD & BIRD 2 Gray's Inn Square,
London WC1R 5AF.

Career: admitted (1985); assistant solicitor
(1985-1987); became partner Bird & Bird
(1987).

Activities: spoken at many conferences on
telecommunications and information
technology.

Biography: lives London SW8; born

28.04.1960; married to Rebecca. Educated
at Sevenoaks School; Jesus College
Cambridge (1982 MA hons); many articles
in specialist telecommunications journals;
contributor to 'User's Guide to
Telecommunications'.

Leisure: golf.

KILBURN Barry

partner and head of property department
MARSHALLS 102 High Street, Godalming,
Surrey GU7 1DS.

Career: articled Ingledew Brown Bennison
& Garrett; admitted (1979); assistant
solicitor (1979-1980); became partner
Marshalls (1980).

Activities: director SOS Ltd; member West
Surrey Golf Club.

Biography: lives Headley Down; born
20.03.1955; married with 3 children.
Educated at Royal Grammar School,
Guildford; Southampton University (1976
LLB); College of Law Guildford (1977
hons).

Leisure: golf; squash; football; tennis;
cricket; DIY; travel.

KING Bob

senior partner MANBY & STEWARD
Mander House, Mander Centre,
Wolverhampton, West Midlands
WV1 3NE.

Career: commissioned into the
Worcestershire Regiment (1942); prisoner
of war in Germany (1943-1945); articled
Manby & Steward (1947-1949); admitted
(1949); assistant solicitor (1949-1953);
became partner (1953-1985); became senior
partner (1985).

Activities: president Wolverhampton Law
Society (1969-1970); chairman Solicitors
Benevolent Association (1977); member of
Council of the Law Society (1969-1988);
Council for Licensed Conveyancers (1986-
1988); chairman Wolverhampton Division
of General Commissioners for Income Tax;
very much involved in Church of England
Diocese of Lichfield (former chairman
Diocesan board of finance).

Biography: lives Wolverhampton; born
30.03.1922; married to Pauline with 2
children. Educated at Tettenhall College;
Queen's College Cambridge (LLB);
Foundation Scholar Queen's College .

KING Bryan

senior partner WAYMAN-HALES
12 White Friars, Chester CH1 1PT.

Career: articled Alsop Stevens; admitted (1955); assistant solicitor (1955-1957); assistant Solicitor Wayman-Hales (1957-1960); became partner (1960); became senior partner (1986).

Activities: member council of the Law Society (1982 to date); solicitor to the Cheshire Regiment; member Law Society's Gazette editorial advisory board; chairman Law Society Wills & Equity Committee; panel member Law Society Adjudication Committee; vice-chairman North West England and IOM territorial association; member regimental council the Cheshire Regiment; member of: Army & Navy Club; Chester City Club.

Biography: lives Chester; born 29.04.1930; married to Elizabeth with 2 children. Educated at Birkenhead School.

Leisure: president and playing member Deeside Ramblers Hockey Club; travel; gardening.

KING Henry

partner DENTON HALL BURGIN & WARRENS Five Chancery Lane, Clifford's Inn, London EC4A 1BU.

Career: admitted (1964); assistant solicitor (1964-1967); became partner Denton Hall & Burgin (1967).

Activities: member Pilgrims.

Biography: lives London; born 11.10.1936; married with 1 child. Educated at Whitgift Middle; Fitzwilliam College Cambridge (MA LLB); Harry Strouts Prize; Law Society Finals (1964).

Leisure: travel; theatre; music.

KING Lesley

principal lecturer COLLEGE OF LAW 30/32 Lancaster Gate, London W2.

Career: assistant solicitor Durrant Piesse and Pritchard Englefield & Tobin (1972-1976); College of Law (1976).

Activities: member Law Society Wills & Equity Committee.

Biography: lives London; born 06.12.1949; married to Anthony. Educated at St Joseph's Convent, Monks Kirby; Nuneaton High School for Girls; Bristol University (1971 LLB); Cambridge (1972 Dip Crim); author of 'Wills Administration & Taxation: A Practical Guide'; articles for various periodicals; Encyclopaedia of Forms and Precedents: Wills and Administration.

Leisure: theatre; eating; doing nothing.

KING-FARLOW Charles Roderick

partner PINSENT & CO
26 Colmore Circus, Birmingham B4 6BH.

Career: articled Slaughter and May; admitted (1965); assistant solicitor Pinsent & Co (1967-1969); became partner (1969).

Activities: council member and treasurer Birmingham Law Society (1976 to date) vice-president (1990); member Tax Committee Birmingham Chamber of Commerce and Industry (1974-1981); member Tax Committee Historic Houses Association (1980 to date); director ISS Europe Limited and other companies (1969 to date); trustee of: City of Birmingham Orchestral Endowment Fund; John Feeney Charitable Trust; member of City of Birmingham Symphony Orchestra Council of Management (1972-1980); member of Friends of Birmingham Art Gallery Committee (1972-1978 & 1983-1989); trustee of Birmingham Art Gallery Bellini and Canaletto Appeals (1974 & 1976); chairman Cannon Hill Trust Limited (1985-1989); board member of City of Birmingham Touring Opera (1987 to date) and Public Art Commissions Agency (1990); general commissioner for taxes (1973-1984); member Oriental Club.

Biography: lives Edgbaston; born 16.02.1940; married to Tessa (nee Raikes) with 2 children. Educated at Eton; Trinity College Oxford (1962 MA); author of: articles on taxation and heritage reliefs in International Journal of Museum Management and Curatorship; Trusts and Estates; Taxation.

Leisure: music; gardening; fishing; skiing.

KINSMAN Jeanne

senior partner BEVAN ASHFORD
6 High Street, Swindon, Wiltshire SN1 3ES.

Career: articled Kinneir & Co; admitted; assistant solicitor; became partner (1963); assistant solicitor Wallasey Borough Council (1959).

Activities: chairman Wiltshire Family Health Services Authority; member Wessex Regional Health Authority; past chairman North Wilts Legal Association; former non-council member Property and Commercial Services Committee of the Council of the Law Society; member Gloucestershire and Wiltshire Incorporated Law Society; member Association of Women Solicitors (former secretary and vice-chairman); member Soroptimist Club of Great Britain & Ireland.

Biography: lives Swindon; born 08.03.1934;

married to John with 3 children. Educated at Howells School, Llandaff; Talbot Heath School, Bournemouth; College of Law.

Leisure: riding; walking; gardening; reading; theatre.

KIRBY Michael

senior partner KIRBY SIMCOX
36 High Street, Thornbury, Bristol BS12 2AJ.

Career: articled Wilmot Thompson; admitted; partner predecessor firm of Kirby Simcox (1966); became senior partner Kirby Simcox (1972).

Activities: member Hertford College Boat Club Society; member of: Rotary Club; Parish Church Council.

Biography: lives Thornbury; born 20.07.1935; married with 2 children. Educated at Bristol Grammar School; Hertford College Oxford (1958 BA hons) (1966 MA).

Leisure: gardening; travel; tennis.

KIRK John David

senior partner FIELD SEYMOUR PARKES
1 London Street, Reading, Berks RG1 4QW.

Career: National Service commission in the Intelligence Corps; 1 year's service in Germany; articled Clarks; admitted (1956); assistant solicitor CG & GS Field (1956-1959); became partner (1959); firm merged to become Field Seymour Parkes (1987).

Activities: won Berks County Rugby Cap (1964); co founder Reading Lawyers' Golfing Society (1977); hon secretary Reading Hockey Club and founder/captain Veterans XI; former District & Parish Councillor; ex sec local VSO Committee; member of: Reading Hockey Club; Huntercombe Golf Club; Royal North Devon Golf Club; Caversham Rotary Club (immediate past president); Berkshire Athenaeum Club.

Biography: lives Pangbourne; born 11.03.1930; married to Bente with 3 daughters. Educated at Dragon School, Oxford; Oundle School; Pembroke College Cambridge (1950-1953); Gibson and Weldon Law School Chancery Lane (1955-1956); contributor of numerous articles to Law Society's Gazette and Solicitors Journal (some under pseudonym 'David Marryat').

KIRKBY John

partner in charge of criminal department FOOT & BOWDEN 70/76 North Hill, Plymouth PL4 8HH.

K

Career: National Service Royal Air Force; Northern Rhodesia Colonial Police Force (Chief Inspector); articled Foot & Bowden; admitted (1974); assistant solicitor (1974-1976); became partner (1976).

Activities: secretary Plymouth Law Society (member Committee); member Royal Western Yacht Club.

Biography: lives Downderry; born 04.10.1935; married to Jane with 1 child. Educated at Tormore Preparatory School, Deal; Westminster School.

Leisure: golf; cricket; walking.

KIRKHAM David

staff partner and head of matrimonial department OXLEY & COWARD 34 Moorgate Street, Rotherham, South Yorkshire S60 2HB.

Career: articled Oxley & Coward (1973-1977); admitted (1977); assistant solicitor (1977); became partner.

Activities: vice-chairman Round Table.

Biography: lives Rotherham; born 01.03.1952; married to Lynne with 1 child. Educated at Maltby Grammar School, Rotherham; University College London (1973).

Leisure: sports (especially squash); literature; France.

KITCHING John

partner and head of venture capital team LOVELL WHITE DURRANT 21 Holborn Viaduct, London EC1A 2DY.

Career: articled Lovell White & King (1969-1971); admitted (1971); assistant solicitor (1971-1976); became partner (1976).

Activities: member of: Mid Herts Golf Club; Hale Golf Club.

Biography: lives Harpenden; born 30.07.1946; married to Toril with 2 children. Educated at Rugby School; Caius College Cambridge (1968 BA) (1973 MA); various articles principally on venture capital and MBOs.

Leisure: golf; singing.

KLING Edward

managing partner (London office) DECHERT PRICE & RHOADS 52 Bedford Square, London WC1B 3EX.

Career: Buchalter Nemer Fields & Younger, Los Angeles; vice-president and general manager Itel International Corp; became European Counsel, partner and managing partner Dechert Price & Rhoads.

Activities: member California, American and International Bar Associations; member United Oxford & Cambridge Universities Club.

Biography: lives London SW3; born 05.11.1947; married to Trudy with 1 son. Educated at Babson College, USA (BS); Oxford (2 BA's, MA).

Leisure: skiing.

KNAPP David

partner in charge of conveyancing department HART BROWN & CO based at 1 South Street, Godalming, Surrey GU7 1DA.

Career: articled Hart Brown & Co (1982-1984); admitted (1984); assistant solicitor (1984-1986); became partner (1986).

Activities: member Steering Committee of Self-Start Workshops; member of: West Byfleet Golf Club; Guildford Hockey Club; Shackleford Cricket Club.

Biography: lives Puttenham, nr Guildford; born 18.06.1959; single. Educated at St Andrew's Preparatory School (1966-1972); Cranleigh School (1972-1977); Birmingham Polytechnic (1980 BA hons).

Leisure: hockey (plays for Wales at international level); golf.

KNIGHT Bill

partner SIMMONS & SIMMONS 14 Dominion Street, London EC2M 2RJ.

Career: admitted (1969); assistant solicitor (1969-1973); became partner Simmons & Simmons (1973); admitted Hong Kong; in charge of Hong Kong office (1979-1982).

Activities: vice-chairman Law Society Standing Committee on Company Law; trustee SCAR (Sickle Cell Anaemia Relief); trustee Haydn-Mozart Players; member Hong Kong Club.

Biography: lives London N1; born 11.09.1945; married to Stephanie with 2 children. Educated at Sir Roger Manwood's School, Sandwich; Bristol University (1966 LLB); Fellow Royal Society of Arts.

Leisure: riding; skiing; music.

KNIGHT John Walton

partner MILLS & REEVE 3 Redwell Street, Norwich NR2 4TJ.

Career: articled Ashby Rogers & Co (1953-1957); admitted (1957); assistant solicitor Victor Cooper & Lingard (1957-1958); assistant solicitor Mills & Reeve (1958-

1963); became partner (1963).

Activities: under-sheriff for Norfolk (1978-1990); member Norfolk Club.

Biography: lives Norwich and Cambridge; born 20.03.1933; married to Ann with 3 children. Educated at Reading (1941-1950).

Leisure: archaeology; local history; hockey; skiing; travel.

KNIGHT Robert

consultant and sole practitioner ROBERT J KNIGHT 1 Tolmers Gardens, Cuffley, Herts EN6 4JE.

Career: assistant Trower Still & Keeling (1956-1962); assistant Theodore Goddard & Co (1962-1964); articled Theodore Goddard & Co (1964-1969); admitted (1969); founded Faull Best & Knight (1969-1975); partner Southall & Knight (1976-1981); partner Hamlin Slowe (1981-1990); retired; became consultant and founded own practice (1990).

Biography: lives Cuffley; born 14.04.1939; married to Pamela with 2 children from previous marriage. Educated at Sheen Grammar School; John Mackrell Prize; Charles Steele City of London Solicitors Company Prize.

Leisure: reading; walking.

KRAFFT James

head of probate equity tax planning and trust department THOMSON SNELL & PASSMORE 3 Lonsdale Gardens, Tunbridge Wells, Kent TN1 1NX.

Career: management trainee ICI (1966-1967); articled Francis & Crookenden (1968-1970); admitted (1971); assistant solicitor Herbert Smith (1971-1972); assistant solicitor Stephenson Harwood & Tatham (1972-1976); assistant solicitor Thomson Snell & Passmore (1976-1980); salaried partner (1980-1982); became equity partner (1982).

Biography: lives Langton Green, Tunbridge Wells; born 01.05.1944; married to Jane with 1 son and 3 daughters. Educated at Ladycross Preparatory School, Seaford; Downside School; St Catherine's College Oxford (1966 PPP MA); College of Law Guildford (1971 hons); article on testamentary tax planning for married couples in Law Society's Gazette.

Leisure: tennis; golf; bridge; chess; reading.

KUPER Jenny

solicitor CHILDREN'S LEGAL CENTRE 20 Compton Terrace, London N2 2UN.

Career: secretary/assistant editor Penguin Books (1972-1975); articled BH Birnberg & Co (1975-1977); admitted (1978); assistant solicitor Bowling & Co (1978); solicitor Camden Law Centre (1978-1983); solicitor Children's Legal Centre (1983).

Activities: advisor Centre for War and the Child (USA); member Family Law Committee of the Law Society; member Executive Committee of Defence for Children International UK branch.

Biography: lives London N16; born 02.08.1948; 1 child. Educated at University High School, Los Angeles (1963-1966); School of Oriental and African Studies, London (1968-1969); University of California, Los Angeles (1972 BA); regular articles in Children's Legal Centre magazine Childright; articles in Legal Action Group Bulletin; Justice of the Peace; contributed research on position in UK to 'Children In Prison' by K Tomaseuski; paper published in book 'Ombudswork for Children'.

Leisure: writing (poetry, fiction); dance (modern ballet); reading; cinema; travel.

KUSTOW David

partner BRECHER & CO 78 Brook Street, London W1Y 2AD.

Career: articled Brecher & Co; admitted (1973); assistant solicitor (1973-1975); became partner (1975).

Activities: member RAC.

Biography: lives London N20; born 04.05.1949; married to Joyce with 1 son and 1 daughter. Educated at Christ's College.

Leisure: reading; tennis; swimming; walking; theatre; cinema; good food.

L

LACE John

partner company and commercial department BRISTOWS COOKE & CARPMAEL 10 Lincoln's Inn Fields, London WC2A 3BP.

Career: articled Meade-King & Co (1968-1973); admitted (1973); assistant solicitor (1973-1974); assistant solicitor Bristows Cooke & Carpmael (1974-1978); became partner (1978).

Biography: lives London W4; born 11.09.1947; married to Stephanie with 4 children. Educated at the Dragon School, Oxford; Malvern College; College of Law.

Leisure: gardening; sailing; photography.

LADBURY Rick

senior resident partner MALLESONS STEPHEN JAQUES 2nd Floor, 36-38 Leadenhall Street, London EC3A 1AP.

Career: admitted Victoria (1969); associate High Court of Australia; assistant solicitor Mallesons (1971-1974); partner (1974); became senior resident partner in London (1987); admitted Western Australia, NSW, the Australian Capital Territory, England and Wales (1990).

Activities: former director Melbourne University Law School Foundation; former secretary and treasurer and director of Australian Mining and Petroleum Law Association Ltd (former president Victorian branch); former tutor in law Monash University & Trinity College, Melbourne University; former visiting Fellow and lecturer Melbourne University Law School; member Banking Law Association; member American Bar Association (member Resources and Energy Committee); member International Bar Association (member Publications Committee of Committee E of SBL) (member Section on Business Law) (member Section on Energy and Resources Law); councillor of SERL (former chairman Committee B); Chairman of SERL; member Committee of Australian Business in Europe; IBA Councillor; member IBA Management Committee; member of: Australia Club; Melbourne Cricket Club; RACV; Royal South Yarra; Peninsula Country Golf Club; Savage Club.

Biography: lives Richmond; born 30.07.1945; married to Pam with 3 daughters. Educated at Melbourne Grammar School; Melbourne University (1968 LLB hons); contributing editor for

Australia for numerous publications; numerous papers in Australia and overseas.

LADDIE Hugh

Queen's Counsel Francis Taylor Building, Temple, London EC4Y 7BY.

Career: called to the Bar Middle Temple (1969); QC (1986).

Activities: Junior Counsel to HM Treasury in Patent Matters (1981-1986).

Biography: lives London; born 15.04.1946; married to Stecia with 3 children. Educated at Aldenham School; St Catharine's College Cambridge (MA); assistant editor in chief Annual of Intellectual Property Law (1975-1979); UK correspondent European Law Review (1978-1983); joint author of: 'Patent Law of Europe and the United Kingdom' (1978); 'The Modern Law of Copyright' (1980).

Leisure: music; gardening; fishing.

LAIRG Lord Irvine of

Queen's Counsel and head of chambers 11 King's Bench Walk, Temple, London EC4Y 7EQ.

Career: lecturer London School of Economics (1965-1969); called to the Bar (1967); QC (1978); Recorder (1985-1988).

Activities: life peer (1987); Labour front bench spokesman on legal and home affairs; member Garrick.

Biography: lives London; born 23.06.1940; married to Alison with 2 sons. Educated at Inverness Academy; Hutchesons' Boys' Grammar School, Glasgow; Glasgow University (MA LLB); Christ's College Cambridge (BA LLB).

Leisure: cinema; theatre; collecting paintings; travel.

LALLAH Ravin

senior member BERLIOZ & CO 44/46 Kingsway, London WC2B 6EN.

Career: teaching English, French and history St Andrew's School, Mauritius (1971-1972); called to the Bar Lincoln's Inn (1976); called to Mauritius Bar (1977); private practice (1977-1978); lecturer summer school City of London Polytechnic (1980 & 1981); European law internship programme University of the Pacific McGeorge School of Law, Salzburg University and Unido, Vienna (1980); twelfth study session International Institute of Human Rights, Strasbourg (1981); in charge De Chambrun & Partners

L

(1982-1985); founded London office Berlioz & Co (1985).

Activities: member Board of Directors of Franco-British Chamber of Commerce in London.

Biography: lives London N6; born 04.12.1950; married to Regine. Educated at Royal College Curepipe, Mauritius; Council of Legal Education; City of London Polytechnic (1979 MA).

Leisure: travel; theatre; bridge.

LANCELEY Ian

joint senior partner in charge of litigation FREEBOROUGHS 14/15 Vernon Street, West Kensington, London W14 0RJ.

Career: articled large provincial firm in Leicester; admitted; assistant solicitor; legal department merchant bank in the City; prosecuting solicitor New Scotland Yard; became partner Freeborough Slack & Co (1977); amalgamated with Blok Bull & Co (1988); became joint senior partner Freeboroughs (1988).

Activities: Acting Stipendiary Magistrate in the Metropolitan Courts; member Roehampton Club.

Biography: lives London SW15; born 12.02.1946; married to Valerie with 2 children. Educated at Blundell's School, Devon; College of Law Guildford (hons).

Leisure: golf; squash.

LAND Brook

partner NABARRO NATHANSON 50 Stratton Street, London W1X 5FL.

Career: articled Nabarro Nathanson (1967-1972); admitted (1972); assistant solicitor (1972-1974); became partner (1974).

Activities: non-executive director: JCI Group PLC; Theatre Royal Brighton Ltd.

Biography: lives London NW3; born 12.03.1949; married to Anita with 1 daughter and 1 son. Educated at St Paul's School; writes various periodical articles.

Leisure: racing; sport.

LANDEN Dalby

senior partner BLANDY & BLANDY 1 Friar Street, Reading, Berkshire RG1 1DA.

Career: articled in Brighton; admitted (1955); National Service in the Army; commissioned in the Royal Corps of Transport; assistant solicitor Brighton (1957); London firm (2 years); assistant solicitor Blandy & Blandy (1962-1964);

became partner (1964); became senior partner (1980).

Activities: Deputy Registrar and ecclesiastical examiner (1978); local director Sun Alliance Insurance Company (1980); treasurer Berkshire Family Conciliation Service (1982-1988); former governor local comprehensive school; has taken part in radio phone-ins on local radio.

Biography: lives Whitchurch; born 04.09.1932; married to Lesley with 3 children. Educated at Borden Grammar School, Sittingbourne; Hove County Grammar School; College of Law London.

Leisure: sings in church choir occasionally officiating at Evensong; playing piano; walking; swimming; writing history of Reading.

LANE Martin Stuart

residential property partner FLADGATE FIELDER Heron Place, 3 George Street, London W1H 6AD.

Career: partner Coleman Allebone; partner Fladgate & Co; merged to become Walters Fladgate and subsequently Fladgate Fielder.

Biography: lives London; born 21.05.1941; widowed. Educated at Stowe.

LANE Terence

senior partner LANE & PARTNERS 46/47 Bloomsbury Square, London WC1A 2RU.

Career: Major RA HM Forces (1940-1946); HM Colonial Service (Administrative) District Commissioner (Tanzania) and subordinate Judge (1947-1949); admitted (1953); assistant solicitor Linklaters & Paines (1953-1957); became partner Bracewell & Leaver (1957-1961); founded Baker & McKenzie, London (1961-1974); became senior partner Lane & Partners (1974).

Activities: arbitration particularly in Middle East, Kuwait, Saudi Arabia, Oman, Abu Dhabi, Dubai, Libya, etc; Fellow Chartered Institute of Arbitrators; ICC Panel of Arbitrators; member of: Savage Club; Hampshire Hunt.

Biography: lives London WC1 and Rake, Hampshire; born 05.10.1918; married to Jacqueline (nee Dunlop) with 7 children. Educated at King Edward's, Farnborough; London University (1940 BA); Indiana University (1939 AB); College of Law (1953); author of 'English Law of International Licensing'; 'English Law of

Trade Secrets'; 'Constitutional Aspects of British Entry to the Common Market'; 'A Businessman's Guide to the Anti-Trust Rules of the Common Market'.

Leisure: riding; hunting.

LANE-SMITH Roger

managing partner ALSOP WILKINSON 6 Dowgate Hill, London EC4R 2SS.

Career: admitted (1969); assistant solicitor John Gorna & Co (1971-1973); became partner David Blank & Co (1973-1977); founded own practice (1977); merged with Alsop Stevens (1984); merged with Wilkinson Kimbers (1988); member Executive Committee.

Activities: member of: St James's Club; Mark's Club.

Biography: born 19.10.1945; married to Pamela with 2 children. Educated at Stockport Grammar School; Robert Ellis Memorial Prize; various articles published in the Law Society's Gazette and Solicitors Journal on company commercial topics.

Leisure: golf; tennis; shooting; deep sea fishing.

LANGLEY Peter

partner SLAUGHTER AND MAY 35 Basinghall Street, London EC2V 5DB.

Career: articled Johnson Mileham & Scatliff (1960-1965); admitted (1965); assistant solicitor CF Snow & Co (1965-1966); became partner (1966-1970); assistant solicitor Slaughter and May (1970-1975); became partner (1975).

Activities: member MCC.

Biography: born 18.02.1942. Educated at Brighton Hove & Sussex Grammar School.

Leisure: collecting fine bindings specifically; bibliomania generally.

LANHAM Rex

director of legal services LONDON RESIDUARY BODY Globe House, 4 Temple Place, London WC2R 3HP.

Career: articled in LCC (1959-1962); admitted (1962); assistant solicitor (1962-1973); principal solicitor (conveyancing) GLC (1973-1976); director of legal services (1976-1981); head of legal branch (1981-1986); became director of legal services London Residuary Body (1986).

Biography: lives Hampshire; born 24.02.1935; married to Daphne with 2 children. Educated at Perse School, Cambridge; Jesus College Cambridge (1959

BA) (1962 MA) (1960 LLB) (1985 LLM).

Leisure: walking; railways; stamp collecting; snooker; Dumasiana; canals.

LARKHAM Michael

senior partner VERNON & SHAKESPEARE 15 Church Street, Oldbury, Warley, West Midlands B69 3AA.

Career: articled to father (1953-1958); admitted (1958); became partner (1958); became senior partner (1986).

Activities: General Commissioner of Income Tax (1971 to date); member of: Moseley Football Club; Barnt Green Sailing Club.

Biography: born 16.11.1934; married to Diana with 3 children. Educated at Cheltenham College.

Leisure: sailing (dinghy and offshore); golf; walking; fresh air; reading.

LATHAM David

Queen's Counsel 1 Crown Office Row, London EC4.

Career: called to the Bar Middle Temple (1964); one of the Junior Counsel to the Crown common law (1979-1985); Junior Counsel to the Department of Trade in Export Credit Guarantee matters (1983-1985); QC (1985); Bencher Middle Temple (1989); Recorder.

Activities: member Judicial Studies board; member General Council of the Bar; vice-chairman of the Professional Standards Committee; member Council of Legal Education; member Leander.

Biography: lives Sunningdale; born 18.09.1942; married to Margaret with 3 daughters. Educated at Bryanston; Queen's College Cambridge (1963 MA); Astbury Scholar; Colombos International Law Prizewinner.

Leisure: music; reading; food; wine; sailing.

LATHAM Peter

managing partner GLANVILLES 151 West Street, Fareham, Hampshire PO16 0DZ.

Career: admitted (1970); assistant solicitor (1970-1971); became partner Glanvilles (1971); became managing partner (1985).

Activities: councillor and leader Fareham Borough Council (1987-1990).

Biography: lives Fareham; born 31.12.1944; married to Barbara with 3 children. Educated at Crypt Grammar School, Gloucester; Bristol University (1964-1967).

LATHAM Robert

head of chambers 2 Plowden Buildings, Middle Temple, London EC4.

Career: called to the Bar (1976); established Chambers 2 Plowden Buildings (1978).

Activities: councillor LB of Camden (1982-1990); member Bloomsbury District Health Authority (1986-1990); governor National Hospital of Nervous Diseases (1986-1990).

Biography: lives London NW1; born 15.09.1953; married to Janet. Educated at Winchester College (1966-1971); Selwyn College Cambridge (1975 MA); College of Law (1975-1976).

Leisure: music; photography; travel.

LATTER Chris

partner corporate department BERWIN LEIGHTON Adelaide House, London Bridge, London EC4R 9HA.

Career: articled Rowe & Maw; admitted (1976); assistant solicitor Clifford Turner (1976-1981); group legal director and company secretary Brown & Jackson PLC (1981-1986); assistant solicitor Berwin Leighton (1986-1987); salaried partner (1987-1989); became equity partner (1989).

Activities: committee member local Conservative Association; conference speaker.

Biography: lives Lamberhurst; born 23.08.1951; married to Julia with 3 sons. Educated at St Dunston's College, Catford (1958-1969); Clare College Cambridge (1973 BA hons) (1977 MA); articles in Law Society's Gazette; Acquisitions Monthly; FT Mergers and Acquisitions.

Leisure: music; theatre; cricket; golf.

LAUTERPACHT Elihu

Queen's Counsel 3 Essex Court, Temple, London EC4Y 9AL.

Career: called to the Bar Gray's Inn (1950); QC (1970); Bencher Gray's Inn (1983).

Activities: practising international lawyer; director Research Centre for International Law University of Cambridge; member World Bank Administrative Tribunal (1980 to date); member Arbitration Panel World Bank Centre for the Settlement of Investment Disputes (1974 to date); member Panel of Arbitrators International Energy Agency Disputes Settlement Centre (1980 to date); member Institut du Droit International; fellow Royal Geographical Society; member Athenaeum.

Biography: lives Cambridge; born 13.07.1928; married with 4 children.

Educated at Phillips Academy, Massachusetts; Harrow School; Trinity College Cambridge (1949 BA) (1950 LLB) (LLM) (1955 MA); Whewell Scholar in International Law (1950); Holt Scholar (1948); Birkenhead Scholar (1950); fellow Trinity College Cambridge (1953 to date); University lecturer in law Cambridge (1951-1981); reader in international law Cambridge (1981-1988); visiting professor University of Delhi (1960); director of research Hague Academy of International Law (1959 & 1960); chairman East African Common Market Tribunal (1972-1985); legal adviser Department of Foreign Affairs, Australia (1975-1977); consultant on international law Central Policy Review Staff (1972-1974); author of: 'Jerusalem and the Holy Places' (1968); 'The Development of the law of International Organisation by the Decisions of International Tribunals' (1980); various articles; editor of International Law Reports (1960 to date); consulting editor of Iran-United States Claims Tribunal Reports (1982 to date); editor of British Practice in International Law (1956-1970); editor of International Law: the collected papers of Sir Hersch Lauterpacht vols i-iv (1960 to date).

LAW David

senior/managing partner DAVID LAW & CO Telegraph House, High Street, Sheffield S1 1PT.

Career: articled Taylor & Emmett; admitted; assistant solicitor Allen & Overy; assistant solicitor Farrer & Co; assistant solicitor Pye Smith & Son; founded own practice.

Activities: Hon consul for Belgium; member Sheffield Chamber of Commerce; Fellow British Institute of Management; member of: Sheffield Club; Abbeydale Golf Club; South Caernarvonshire Yacht Club.

Biography: lives Sheffield; born 09.09.1930; married to Mary with 2 children. Educated at King Edward VII School, Sheffield; Brasenose College Oxford (1949-1953).

Leisure: golf; sailing; skiing; various social/charitable organisations; full blues for athletics and cross country Oxford; one time holder the Canadian all comers mile record plus a share in 4 x 1500m world record; 4 x 1 mile Commonwealth record; ran for England 1954 Commonwealth Games.

L

LAWRENCE Ivan

Queen's Counsel 1 Essex Court, Temple, London EC4.

Career: called to the Bar Inner Temple (1962); practising barrister commercial Bar (1962 to date); QC (1981); assistant Recorder (1983); Recorder of the Crown Court (1987) .

Activities: MP for Burton (1974 to date); chairman Conservative Parliamentary Legal Committee (1987 to date) (vice-chairman 1979-1987); chairman Conservative Parliamentary Home Affairs Committee (1988 to date) (vice-chairman (1982-1988) chairman All Party Parliamentary Barristers' Group (1987 to date); member Council of Justice (1980 to date); member Executive Society of Conservative Lawyers (1989 to date): member Joint Parliamentary Committee on Commendation of Statutes (1974-1987); member Executives' State Law Society (1985 to date); broadcaster on legal matters; member All Party Parliamentary Select Committee on Foreign Affairs (1983 to date); executive member British Board of Commonwealth Parliamentary Association; member Board of Deputies of British Jews; vice-chairman European Inter-Parliamentary Conference for Soviet Jewry; chairman Burton Breweries Charitable Trust; member Burton Club.

Biography: lives Shepperton and Burton-upon-Trent; born 24.12.1936; married to Gloria with 1 daughter. Educated at Brighton Hove & Sussex Grammar School; Christ Church Oxford (1960 MA hons); Yarborough-Anderson Scholarship Inner Temple (1962); State Scholarship (1956); pamphlets and articles for The Times; Daily Telegraph; Guardian on legal and political subjects.

LAWSON Peter

partner MCKENNA & CO Mitre House, 160 Aldersgate Street, London EC1A 4DD.

Career: articled Freshfields (1954-1957); assistant solicitor (1957-1959); assistant solicitor McKenna & Co (1959-1964); became partner (1964).

Activities: member of: United Oxford and Cambridge Club; City Livery Club.

Biography: lives Oxted; born 07.01.1933; married to Susan with 4 children. Educated at Lancing College; Trinity College Cambridge (1954 BA).

Leisure: opera; gardening; mountain walking.

LAWTON Keith

partner WILLMETT & CO 13 Castle Street, Reading, Berkshire RG1 7TB.

Career: articled Knight & Maudsley; (1964-1967); assistant solicitor (1967-1971); assistant solicitor Willmett & Co (1971-1974); became partner (1974).

Activities: chairman Maidenhead Rugby Union Football Club.

Biography: lives Maidenhead; born 24.08.1942; married to Janet with 2 children. Educated at Sir William Borlase's School (1953-1961); London University (1964 LLB hons).

LE BAS Malcolm

partner PARIS SMITH & RANDALL Lansdowne House, Castle Lane, Southampton SO9 4FD.

Career: articled Paris Smith & Randall (1959-1964); admitted (1964); assistant solicitor (1964-1969); became partner (1969).

Activities: hon solicitor and member Executive Committee of Hampshire County Cricket Club; director Solent Business Fund; president Trojans Sports Club; governor Southampton Institute of Higher Education; trustee Wessex Cancer Trust; secretary Mayflower Theatre Trust; member MCC.

Biography: lives Southampton; born 28.10.1941; married to Sue with 3 sons. Educated at Oakmount Preparatory School, Southampton; Worksop College.

Leisure: playing social cricket; coaching junior rugby; great supporter of sons' sport.

LE FLEMING Peer

partner GARDNER & CROFT 2 Castle Street, Canterbury, Kent CT1 2QH.

Career: admitted (1977); assistant solicitor (1977-1978); became partner Gardner & Croft (1978).

Activities: inaugural member Law Society Mental Health Panel and Child Care Panel; member Law Society Family Law Committee; member Canterbury Area Duty Solicitor Committee (1985-1987); chairman Canterbury District Mind (1982-1985); lecturer on mental health law and childcare/child protection law; legal group member BAAF; member Family Rights Group; member Kent and Canterbury Club.

Biography: lives Canterbury; born 28.03.1952; married to Marilyn. Educated

at Tonbridge; Kent University (1974 BA hons).

Leisure: hillwalking; climbing.

LEACH John

barrister and head of chambers First National Chambers, 4th Floor, 24 Fenwick Street, Liverpool L2 7NE.

Career: Royal Navy (1944-1946); detective inspector Merseyside Police (1946-1975); called to the Bar Gray's Inn (1974); pupillage (1975).

Biography: lives Liverpool; born 15.04.1926; married to Jean (deceased 18.02.1990) with 2 children. Educated at Ellergreen and Walton Technical Institute, Liverpool; Liverpool Polytechnic (1969-1973); London University (1973 LLB external); School of Law Gray's Inn (1973-1974).

LECKY-THOMPSON Roy

personnel director CAMERON MARKBY HEWITT Sceptre Court, 40 Tower Hill, London EC3N 4BB.

Career: personnel and training British Petroleum Group (1969-1985); business analyst (1981-1984); senior policy adviser remuneration and benefits (1984-1985); director of personnel Arthur Young (1986-1987); became personnel director Cameron Markby Hewitt (1987).

Activities: chair/speaker on human resource planning conferences; seminars on beyond the recruitment crisis in the profession and on women in the law.

Biography: lives Saffron Walden; born 08.04.1948; married to Pat with 4 children. Educated at Douai; Keble College Oxford (1969 BA hons); MIPM (1971); articles on personnel issues in Lawyer; Law Society's Gazette; The Times.

Leisure: reading historical and political biographies; cinephotography; family maintenance; gardening.

LEDBROOKE Simon

senior partner KIRK JACKSON 97 Chorley Road, Swinton, Manchester M27 2AB.

Career: articled Kirk Jackson (1955-1958); admitted (1958); assistant solicitor (1958-1960); partner (1960); became senior partner; involved in commercial and construction work and developed interest in foreign jurisdictions including being involved in matters in various countries such as Mexico, Hong Kong, USA, Spain and Portugal; would like the practice to develop futher foreign connections with

1992 in mind.

Activities: formerly involved with the Royal Manchester Children's Hospital (former chairman League of Friends); secretary Whitefield Golf Club; governor Moorside Primary School.

Biography: lives Whitefield; born 24.05.1933; married to Pamela with 2 children. Educated at North Manchester Grammar School; Nottingham University (1955 LLB hons); Law Society Finals (hons).

Leisure: golf; bridge; travel.

LEE Bob

director of education WILDE SAPTE Queensbridge House, 60 Upper Thames Street, London EC4V 3BD.

Career: lecturer in law Lancashire Polytechnic; senior lecturer; lecturer Lancaster University; senior tutor; became director of education Wilde Sapte (1988).

Activities: former chair of the Board of Business and Finance, Lancaster University; former visiting Research Fellow Department of Law, Essex University; visiting senior lecturer in Law, Kent University; hon Fellow Centre for Science Policy Lancaster University of Lancaster; chairman Rent Assessment Committees and Rent Tribunals of Greater Manchester and Lancashire; former moderator Business Education Council; industrial relations editor Journal of Business Law; former member Lord Chancellor's Advisory Committee on Legal Education; former member Executive and Council of Society of Public Teachers of Law; visiting lecturer Limburg University, Maastrict, The Netherlands; campaigner on issues relating to the provision of housing and health; member of: Springfields HC; Lancashire CC; East London Runners.

Biography: lives Saffron Walden; born 27.11.1952; married to Anne with 1 son. Educated at Preston Catholic College; Brunel University (1976 LLB); Manchester University (1977); DES Major State Scholarship (1976); Social Science Faculty Prize, Brunel University (1974); various books including: 'Birthrights: Law and Ethics at the Beginnings of Life' (1989); 'Housing Act 1988: A Practical Guide to Residential Lettings' (1989); 'Public Law Statutes' (1988); 'Constitutional and Administrative Law' (1989); articles in law journals, medical and other professional journals and newspapers.

Leisure: hockey; cricket; running; theatre.

LEE Michael

managing partner commercial and marine litigation department NORTON ROSE Kempson House, Camomile Street, London EC3A 7AN.

Career: articled Lovell White & King (1963-1966); admitted (1966); assistant solicitor (1966-1967); legal assistant Solicitors department Metropolitan Police (1967-1969); assistant solicitor Norton Rose (1971-1973); became partner (1973).

Activities: secretary London International Arbitration Trust; UK member International Chamber of Commerce Commission on International Arbitration; member Arbitration Panel of ICC UK; associate Chartered Institute of Arbitrators; member of: RAC; Little Ship Club.

Biography: lives London SW10; born 22.06.1942; divorced with 3 children. Educated at Blundell's School; Durham University (LLB hons).

Leisure: skiing; sailing.

LEE Peter

managing partner OXLEY & COWARD 34 Moorgate Street, Rotherham, South Yorkshire S60 2HB.

Career: managing partner Oxley & Coward.

Activities: past president Rotherham Chamber of Commerce; chairman Association of Yorkshire & Humberside Chamber of Commerce; director and member National Council of Association of British Chambers of Commerce; lectures on legal subjects particularly capital taxation and trusts.

Biography: lives Doncaster; born 18.03.1951; married to Susan with 2 children. Fellow of the Institute of Legal Executives.

Leisure: family; cycling; motor cycling.

LEEMING Charles

senior partner WILDE SAPTE Queensbridge House, 60 Upper Thames Street, London EC4V 3BD.

Career: admitted (1959); assistant solicitor (1959-1963); became partner Wilde Sapte (1963).

Activities: chairman Banking Law Sub-committee of City of London Law Society; member Little Ship Club.

Biography: lives London W4; born 04.05.1936; single. Educated at Ampleforth College, York.

Leisure: sailing.

LEES David

partner BOYCE HATTON 12 Tor Hill Road, Castle Circus, Torquay TQ2 5RB.

Career: articled Almy & Thomas (1958-1961); admitted (1961); assistant solicitor Clifford Turner (1961-1963); assistant solicitor Nabarro Nathanson & Co (1963-1964); assistant solicitor Keene Marsland & Co (1964); assistant solicitor Boyce Hatton (1964-1968); became partner (1968).

Activities: chairman Torbay Arthritis Project.

Biography: born 19.09.1937; married to Nancy with 2 children. Educated at Rugby School; King's College London (LLB hons).

Leisure: sailing; scuba diving in warm water; stamp collecting.

LEES John

consultant to WRIGHT & WRIGHT 6/14 Devonshire Street, Keighley, West Yorkshire BD21 2AY.

Career: demobilised Royal Navy (1946); RNR (1947-1961); Lt Commander V.R.D.; articled Allan McNeil & Son WS; admitted Scotland (1950); articled JH Winstanley (1954-1957); admitted England (1957); assistant solicitor (1957-1958); became partner (1958); firm amalgamated with Wright & Wright (1981).

Activities: councillor and alderman Keighley Borough Council (1960-1974); member of: Keighley Conservative Club; Keighley Golf Club.

Biography: lives Keighley; born 23.10.1924; married to Patricia with 3 children. Educated at St Mary's, Melrose; Edinburgh Academy; Edinburgh University (1949 MA LLB); Gibson & Weldon (1956).

LEESE Paul

senior litigation partner FLADGATE FIELDER Heron Place, 3 George Street, London W1H 6AD.

Career: articled David Edwards; admitted (1973); assistant solicitor (1973-1978); became partner Walters Fladgate (1978).

Activities: member of: RAC; Hurlingham Club.

Biography: lives Wimbledon; born 23.05.1947; married with 2 children. Educated at Fulneck School, Yorkshire; Sheffield University (1970 LLB); College of Law London (1970-1971).

Leisure: family; yachting; shooting; skiing.

L

L

LEGH-JONES Nicholas

Queen's Counsel practising at the Commercial Bar 3 Essex Court, Temple, London EC4Y 9AL.

Career: legal instructor University of Pennsylvania (1966-1967); called to the English Bar (1968); lecturer in law New College Oxford (1967-1971); tenant 3 Essex Court (1969 to date); Assistant Recorder (1984); QC (1987).

Activities: member joint working party of the Law Commission to report on liability for defective products (1972-1974); arbitrator in maritime law disputes; member Travellers' Club.

Biography: lives Tonbridge; born 02.02.1943; single. Educated at Pinewood School, Bourton; Winchester College; New College Oxford (1964 BA Hist) (1966 BA Jur); Eldon Scholar (1968); Kennedy Scholar (1968); joint editor of 'MacGillivray & Parkington on Insurance Law' (6th, 7th & 8th ed); articles in Law Quarterly Review; Cambridge Law Journal and Modern Law Review (1968-1975).

Leisure: vintage cars; motor sports; historical reading; cycling; walking.

LEIFER N Anthony

partner DJ FREEMAN & CO 43 Fetter Lane, London EC4A 1NA.

Career: articled DJ Freeman & Co; admitted (1972); assistant solicitor (1972-1974); became partner (1974).

Activities: member of a committee chaired by Sir Derek Hodgson on the profits of crime and their recovery (1984).

Biography: lives London NW3; born 17.09.1945; married to Susan with 2 children. Educated at Hackney Downs Grammar School; London School of Economics (1968 LLB); University of California (Berkeley) (1969 LLM).

LEIGH John

joint senior partner LEIGH WILLIAMS Kings House, 32-40 Widmore Road, Bromley, Kent BR1 1RY.

Career: articled Middle Temple (1955-1960); admitted (1960); assistant solicitor Lincoln's Inn and Catford; founded Gunson & Leigh (1964); amalgamated to form Leigh Williams (1986).

Activities: president Bromley & District Law Society (1974-1975); president Kent Law Society (1985-1986); hon solicitor Bromley Enterprise Agency Trust; hon solicitor Bromley Chamber of Commerce.

Biography: lives Chiddingstone nr Edenbridge; born 09.08.1937; married to Lynn with 4 children. Educated at Dulwich College; Outward Bound Mountain School (hons); College of Law Lancaster Gate.

Leisure: mountaineering all over the world; squash; collecting books and stamps.

LEMAN Richard

senior partner ACTONS 2 King Street, Nottingham NG1 2AX.

Career: admitted (1965); assistant solicitor Actons (1965-1966); became partner (1966); became senior partner (1980); licensed insolvency practitioner.

Activities: deputy County Court Registrar (1982-1988); director Melton Mowbray Building Society.

Biography: lives Nottingham; born 10.03.1940; married to Judith with 2 children. Educated at Royal Masonic School, Bushey; Pembroke College Oxford (1963 BA hons) (1965 MA).

Leisure: sport; tennis; hockey (Notts county player 1964-1965); cycling; sailing.

LEMKIN James

consultant FIELD FISHER WATERHOUSE 41 Vine Street, London EC3N 2AA.

Career: articled Sharpe Pritchard (1950-1953); admitted (1953); assistant solicitor (1953-1954); assistant solicitor McKenna & Co (1954-1956); assistant solicitor Wild Collins (1956-1957); assistant solicitor Joynson Hicks (1957-1959); became partner Field Fisher Waterhouse (1959); became consultant (1990).

Activities: member Holborn Law Society (1971-1974); member Council of Justice (1970s); elected member GLC (1973-1986); GLC Opposition Chief Whip (1982-1986); member of: Athenaeum; Carlton Club.

Biography: lives London NW3; born 21.12.1926; married to Casserley with 4 children. Educated at The Hall Preparatory School (1935-1940); Charterhouse (1940-1945); Merton College Oxford (1950 MA); Solicitors Finals (1953).

LENNON Allan

senior partner METSON CROSS & CO Quality Court, Chancery Lane, London WC2A 1HP.

Career: National Service (1950-1952); commissioned (1951); Intelligence Corps; called to the Bar Inner Temple (1953); Major Army Legal Service (1954-1961);

mentioned in Despatches (Cyprus) (1956); admitted (1961); assistant solicitor Allen & Overy (1961-1964); became partner Metson Cross & Co (1964).

Activities: vice-president Agricultural Law Association; UK delegate Comite Europeen de Droit Rural; chairman Whitefriars Club; member of: Oxford & Cambridge Club; Farmers Club; Tower Ward Club; The Younger Society; Chevalier Ordre des Coteaux de Champagne; numerous wine societies.

Biography: lives Wootton-by-Woodstock; born 17.09.1929; widowed and remarried to Julia with 1 son and 1 daughter by first marriage. Educated at Bradford Grammar School; Balliol College Oxford (1950 BA MA); ACI Arb (1959); (fencing Half-Blue 1949 & 1950) (captain OUFC 1949-1950).

Leisure: wine tasting; good food and conversation; foreign travel; theatre; swimming.

LEONARD Simon

partner and head of commercial unit TITMUSS SAINER & WEBB 2 Serjeants' Inn, London EC4Y 1LT.

Career: articled Wragge & Co (1966-1969); admitted (1969); assistant solicitor (1969-1971); private practice Jaques & Partners, Lusaka, Zambia (1971-1976); assistant solicitor Titmuss Sainer & Webb (1976-1983); became partner (1983); head of commercial unit (1986).

Activities: member CBI Computer Forum.

Biography: lives London; born 11.03.1944; married to Ann with 2 sons. Educated at King Edward's School, Birmingham; Durham University (1965 BA hons); College of Law Lancaster Gate (1966).

Leisure: sailing; singing.

LERNER Perry

managing partner London office O'MELVENY & MYERS 10 Finsbury Square, London EC2A 1LA.

Career: law clerk United States Tax Court (1968-1970); attorney advisor Office of International Tax Counsel US Treasury Department (1973-1976); became managing partner O'Melveny & Myers (1987).

Activities: adjunct professor of taxation University of San Diego Law School (1984-1987); member Sections on Taxation and International Law of American Bar Association; member State Bar of California; member of: Jonathan Club, Los Angeles; Reform Club.

Biography: lives London SW3; born 20.04.1943; married to Susan with 4 children. Educated at Claremont McKenna College (1965 BA); Harvard Law School (1968 JD); editor 'International Tax Report'; various publications.

LESTER Anthony

Queen's Counsel 2 Hare Court, Temple, London EC4Y 7BH.

Career: QC (1975); Bencher Lincoln's Inn (1985); QC Northern Ireland; Irish Bar; Recorder South Eastern Circuit.

Activities: hon visiting professor of public law University College London; chairman Board of Governors James Allen's Girls' School; governor London School of Economics; chairman Interights; member Council and Executive Committee of Justice; chairman Runnymede Trust; member Council of Policy Studies Institute; special adviser to the Home Secretary (1974-1976); special adviser to Standing Advisory Committee on Human Rights in Northern Ireland (1975-1977); member of: Garrick Club; RAC.

Biography: lives London SE24; born 03.07.1936; married to Katya with 1 son and 1 daughter. Educated at City of London School; Trinity College Cambridge (1960 BA); Harvard Law School (1962 LLM); Harkness Commonwealth Fellow (1960-1962); Mansfield Scholar Lincoln's Inn; Hague Academy of International Law Research Scholar (1962).

Leisure: walking; sailing; golf; water colours; theatre.

LEVER Jeremy Frederick

Queen's Counsel, 4 Raymond Buildings, Gray's Inn, London WC1R 5BP.

Career: called to the Bar Gray's Inn (1957); QC (1972); Bencher (1985).

Activities: Fellow All Souls College Oxford (1957) (Sub-Warden 1982-1984) (Senior Dean 1988 to date); non-executive director of: Dunlop Holdings Ltd (1973-1980); The Wellcome Foundation Ltd (1983 to date); arbitrator US/UK arbitration concerning Heathrow Airport User Charges; member Council of the British Institute of International and Comparative Law; governor Berkhamsted Schools; Trustee Oxford Union Society; member Garrick Club.

Biography: lives London WC1 and Oxford; born 23.06.1933; single. Educated at Bradfield College, Berkshire; University College Oxford (1957 jurisprudence hons);

Nuffield College Oxford (1956-1957); Gray's Inn Entrance Scholar; Stuart Cunningham McCaskey Scholar; Arden Scholar; author of 'The Law of Restrictive Practices'; co-editor 'Chitty on Contracts' (22nd-25th ed); consulting editor 'Common Market Law of Competition'.

Leisure: walking; music.

LEVERTON David

managing partner and head of family law section PAYNE HICKS BEACH 10 New Square, Lincoln's Inn, London WC2A 3QG.

Career: articled Ridsdale & Son (1953-1958); admitted (1958); assistant solicitor Payne Hicks Beach (1959-1961); became partner (1961); became managing partner (1983).

Activities: former member Joint Standing Committee of Law Society and Court of Protection; member International Academy of Matrimonial Lawyers; member of: RAC; Bucks Club.

Biography: lives London NW11; born 08.09.1935; married to Corinne with 2 children. Educated at The Haberdashers' Aske's School, Hampstead.

Leisure: rugby football; theatre; cinema; family.

LEVESON Brian

Queen's Counsel 5 Essex Court, Temple, London EC4Y 9AH and 25 Byrom Street, Manchester M3 4PF.

Career: called to the Bar Middle Temple (1970); practised primarily on the Northern Circuit (1971 to date); QC (1986); Recorder of the Crown Court (1988).

Activities: lecturer in law Liverpool University (1971-1981) (member of Council 1983 to date).

Biography: born 22.06.1949; married to Lynne with 2 sons and 1 daughter. Educated at Liverpool College; Merton College Oxford (1970 BA) (1974 MA); Harmsworth Scholarship.

LEVINE Sydney

barrister and head of chambers Broadway House, 9 Bank Street, Bradford BD1 1TW.

Career: War service (1942-1947); called to the Bar (1952); prosecuting department, Bradford; pupillage Bradford Chambers; head of Chambers (1975); Recorder (1975).

Activities: deputy circuit judge (1975).

Biography: lives Leeds; born 04.09.1923; married to Cecile with 4 children.

Educated at Bradford Grammar School; Leeds University (1951 LLB).

Leisure: amateur theatre (acting and directing); gardening; running - 3 marathons (including London 1987).

LEVINSON Stephen

partner and head of employment department PAISNER & CO 154 Fleet Street, London EC4A 2DQ.

Career: articled Paisner & Co; admitted (1976); assistant solicitor in litigation dept (1976-1978); became partner (1978); founded and became head of employment department (1988).

Activities: director Solicitors Benevolent Association (1984-1988); member Law Society Reform Committee (1985-1987); Law Society Employment Law Committee (1987 to date); Executive Committee Industrial Law Society (1985 to date); National Committee of Young Solicitors (1983-1987); London Solicitors Litigation Association Committee (1986-1988); London Young Solicitors Group (1981-1987) chairman (1984-1985); member of MCC.

Biography: lives London NW8; born 12.02.1949; married to Penny with 1 daughter. Educated at Northwood Preparatory School; Clayesmore School; Leicester University (1971 LLB); College of Law; Fellow of Chartered Institute of Arbitrators (1988 FCI Arb); editor on Employment Cases for Current Law (1986-1987); articles in Law Society's Gazette; Solicitors Journal; New Law Journal and other specialist publications.

Leisure: enthusiastic village cricketer; squash; tennis; local politics; opera; collects modern first editions and illustrated books.

LEVISON Jeremy Ian

partner and head of the matrimonial department COLLYER-BRISTOW 4 Bedford Row, London WC1R 4DF.

Career: articled Theodore Goddard (1974-1976); admitted (1976); assistant solicitor (1976-1980); became partner Collyer-Bristow (1980); became head of matrimonial department (1984).

Activities: member Solicitors Family Law Association; founder member International Academy of Matrimonial Lawyers; instrumental in the setting up of the Collyer-Bristow Art Exhibition and Art Awards; responsible for Collyer-Bristow's sponsorship of the RSC; lectures and broadcasts from time to time particularly

L

L

on the subject of cohabitation law.

Biography: lives London W4 and Bordeaux, France; born 03.02.1952; single. Educated at Durlston Court Preparatory School, Barton on ea; Charterhouse School; Kent University (BA hons); College of Law Guildford; scholarship at Charterhouse.

Leisure: music; playing violin; arts; substantial collection of modern art; keen sportsman (cricket; skiing; squash); claret.

LEVISON Nicholas

partner TURNER KENNETH BROWN 100 Fetter Lane, London EC4A 1DD.

Career: articled Lovell White & King (1962); admitted; assistant solicitor Lawrance Messer & Co (1962); became senior partner (1986); became partner Turner Kenneth Brown upon amalgamation with Lawrance Messer & Co (1989).

Activities: acts on behalf Unit Trust Association, numerous unit trust managers, unit trust trustees and companies in financial services industry; member City of London Club.

Biography: lives Great Missenden; born 01.08.1935; married with 1 child. Educated at Malvern College.

Leisure: golf; skiing; reading.

LEVY Benjamin

barrister and head of chambers 9 Old Square, Lincoln's Inn, London WC2A 3SR.

Career: National Service with Army Legal Aid Unit, Cyprus; called to the Bar Lincoln's Inn (1956); Bencher Lincoln's Inn (1989).

Activities: part-time supervisor in law King's College and Pembroke College Cambridge (1960-1963).

Biography: lives London; born 02.01.1934; married to Ruth with 2 daughters. Educated at Clifton College (1947-1952); King's College Cambridge (1955 BA) (1956 LLB) (1959 MA); Scholar; Cholmeley Scholar and Sir T More Bursary Lincoln's Inn (1956); assistant editor Vols 11 & 12 'Landlord & Tenant' 4th ed Encyclopaedia of Forms & Precedents.

Leisure: books; reading; walking; people.

LEVY Brian

commercial property partner FLADGATE FIELDER Heron Place, 3 George Street, London W1H 6AD.

Career: articled SR Freed & Co; admitted; assistant solicitor; partner; senior property

partner Davies Arnold & Cooper (1968-1973); shareholder/director English & Continental Property Co Ltd (1973-1976); became partner Fielder Le Riche (1976); merged to become Fladgate Fielder (1988).

Activities: treasurer housing association; treasurer charitable trust running day nurseries.

Biography: lives London NW3; born 08.11.1938; married to Gillian with 3 children. Educated at Grocers School, London; University College London (1958 LLB hons).

Leisure: tennis; skiing; backgammon; theatre.

LEWER Michael

Queen's Counsel Farrars Building, Temple, London EC4Y 7BD.

Career: 2nd Lt Royal Artillery (1953-1954); Captain RA & Intelligence Corps (1954-1967) (TA); called to the Bar Gray's Inn (1958); Junior (1961); Recorder of SE circuit (1978); QC (1983); Recorder (1983) .

Activities: member Bar Council (1979-1982); member Criminal Injuries Compensation Board; assistant commissioner Parliamentary Boundary Commission for England; trustee local charity; member management committee of a housing association; member Western Club, Glasgow.

Biography: lives London N4; born 01.12.1933; married to Bridget with 4 children. Educated at Tonbridge School; Oriel College Oxford (1957 BA MA).

Leisure: involved with local amenity groups; holidaying in France.

LEWIS Anthony

joint senior partner TAYLOR JOYNSON GARRETT 10 Maltravers Street, London WC2R 3BS.

Career: articled Freshfields (1964-1967); admitted (1967); assistant solicitor (1967-1970); assistant solicitor Joynson-Hicks (1970-1971); became partner (1971); became senior partner (1986-1989); became joint senior partner Joynson Taylor Garrett (1989).

Activities: director Finlan Group PLC; director various property companies; member of: Bucks Club; Annabels.

Biography: lives London SW3 and Cotswolds; born 15.11.1940; married to Ewa-Maria with 2 children. Educated at Rugby School; St Edmund Hall Oxford (1963 MA); author of articles on 'Shooting and the Law'.

LEWIS Barry I

partner PENNINGTONS Highfield, Brighton Road, Godalming, Surrey GU7 1NS.

Career: admitted (1965); became partner RI Lewis & Co (1965-1973); founded own practice (1980-1988); became partner Penningtons (1988).

Activities: member of: Hankley Common Golf Club.

Biography: lives nr Farnham; born 14.08.1940; married with 4 children. Educated at Rugby School; Trinity Hall Cambridge (1962 BA hons) (1963 LLB); Rugby School Leavers' Scholarship; Cambridge University Open Scholarship.

Leisure: golf; skiing; photography; gardening.

LEWIS Charles

barrister specialising in medical negligence and personal injuries 2 Paper Buildings, Temple, London EC4.

Career: called to Bar (1963).

Activities: member Roehampton Club.

Biography: lives London SW15; born 23.10.1938; divorced with 2 children. Educated at Charterhouse (1952-1956); Oriel College Oxford (1958-1962); Open Classical Scholar; numerous articles; author of: 'Medical Negligence, a Plaintiff's Guide' (1988); 'State and Diplomatic Immunity' (3rd ed) (1990).

Leisure: opera; singing; piano; languages; walks in the countryside.

LEWIS David

partner corporate finance NORTON ROSE Kempson House, Camomile Street, London EC3A 7AN.

Career: articled Norton Rose (1969-1972); admitted (1972); assistant solicitor (1972-1977); became partner (1977); admitted Hong Kong (1977); Hong Kong office (1979-1982).

Activities: member Hong Kong Law Society Company Law and Securities Law Committees (1980-1982); member of London Law Society Company Law Committee (1983 to date); governor Dragon School, Oxford; Business magazine 40 under 40 Young Businessman of the Year (1986); member Hong Kong Club.

Biography: lives Oxford; born 01.11.1947; married with 2 children. Educated at Dragon School, Oxford (1956-1961); St Edward's School, Oxford (1961-1966); Jesus College Oxford (1969 Jurisprudence hons).

Leisure: keeping fit; collecting maps; travel.

LEWIS Eric

senior partner KENNEDYS
Longbow House, 14-20 Chiswell Street,
London EC1 4TY.

Career: RAF (1947-1949); articled Hyman
Isaacs Lewis & Mills (1949-1954); admitted
(1954); assistant solicitor Kennedys (1954-
1955); became partner (1955).

Activities: founder member and former
president Solicitors Articled Clerk Society;
member Hartsbourne Country Club.

Biography: lives London; born 09.07.1927;
married to Margaret with 2 children.
Educated at Haberdashers' Aske's; High
Wycombe Royal Grammar School; College
of Law.

Leisure: golf; society; travel; reading.

LEWIS George

senior partner KIDD RAPINET
35 Windsor Road, Slough, Berkshire
SL1 2EB.

Career: junior in legal department Slough
Borough Council (1955-1957); articled to
town clerk Slough Borough Council (1958-
1963); admitted (1963); assistant solicitor
(1963-1964); assistant solicitor Kidd
Rapinet Badge & Co (1964-1969); became
partner (1969); became senior partner Kidd
Rapinet (1985).

Activities: Notary Public (1976); member
Stoke Poges Golf Club.

Biography: lives Farnham Common; born
25.11.1939; married with 7 children.
Educated at Eton Porney Primary School;
Slough Grammar School; College of Law
(1962 hons).

Leisure: family; golf.

LEWIS Geoffrey

partner HERBERT SMITH
35 Cannon Street, London EC4M 5SD.

Career: articled Herbert Smith (1952);
became partner (1960); senior partner
Hong Kong office (1983-1986).

Activities: adviser on securities legislation
to Hong Kong Government (1988-1989);
member of Garrick Club.

Biography: lives Saffron Walden; born
11.07.1929; married to Christine with 4
children. Educated at Taunton School;
Trinity Hall Cambridge (1952 MA); author
of 'Lord Atkins' (1983); various articles on
professional topics.

Leisure: music; walking; watching football.

LEWIS Harold

partner JAQUES & LEWIS 2 South Square,
Gray's Inn, London WC1R 5HR.

Career: assistant to architectural
photographer (1976); articled Jaques &
Lewis (1977-1979); admitted (1980);
assistant solicitor (1980-1985); became
partner (1985).

Biography: lives London N7; born
12.05.1952; married to Elaine with 3
daughters. Educated at King Edward VII
Preparatory School, Johannesburg; North
Sydney Boys' High School; Sydney
University (1972 BA); Sussex University
(1975 BA); College of Law (1979).

Leisure: music; family outings; DIY.

LEWIS Jonathan

partner in property department
DJ FREEMAN & CO 1 Fetter Lane, London
EC4A 1BR.

Career: articled DJ Freeman & Co (1978-
1980); admitted (1980); assistant solicitor
(1980-1982); became partner (1982).

Biography: lives London N2; born
02.11.1955; married to Veronique with 1
son and 2 daughters. Educated at St Paul's
School (1968-1973); Manchester University
(1977 BA Econ).

Leisure: sabre fencing; charity fund raising.

LEWIS Jonathan Malcolm

senior partner within the company/
commercial department and chairman of
the Finance Committee of DJ FREEMAN &
CO 43 Fetter Lane, London EC4A 1NA.

Career: articled DJ Freeman & Co (1969-
1971); admitted (1971); assistant solicitor
(1971-1974); became partner (1974).

Activities: authorised insolvency
practitioner under the Insolvency Act 1986;
member City of London Solicitors'
Company; member International Bar
Association.

Biography: lives Pinner; born 27.03.1946;
married to Rosemary with 2 sons.
Educated at Harrow County School for
Boys; Downing College Cambridge (MA);
author of 'City Comment' in the Law
Society's Gazette (1983-1990); writes and
lectures on various business law topics.

Leisure: tennis; walking; theatre; family.

LEWIS Peter

partner LEWIS & TOMPKINS
11 King Street, Hereford HR4 9BW.

Career: articled Edwards Geldard (1970);

admitted; partner; founded own practice
(1990); joint partnership with Paul
Tompkins (1990).

Activities: member of: Hereford Motor
Club; Whitecross Squash Club.

Biography: lives Hereford; born 11.11.1946;
married with 2 daughters. Educated at
Llandovery College; University College of
Wales Aberystwyth (1969).

Leisure: keen interest in motor sport as
rally driver and co-driver.

LEWIS Rhiannon

partner in family law department
EDWIN COE 2 Stone Buildings, Lincoln's
Inn, London WC2A 3TH.

Career: articled Edwin Coe; admitted
(1981); assistant solicitor (1981-1985);
became partner (1985).

Activities: member Solicitors' Family Law
Association Ad Hoc Committee on the
recommendations of the Warnock
Committee (1987); member Solicitors
Family Law Association.

Biography: Educated at Alice Smith School
Kuala Lumpur; St Paul's Girls' School;
Bristol University (1976 BA hons); College
of Law Chancery Lane (1978); College of
Law Lancaster Gate (1980); co- author with
Peter Clark 'The Lawyer's Factbook -
Family Law Section' (1985).

Leisure: travel; cottage in Dyfed; Malaysia .

LEWIS Trevor

joint senior partner HAMMOND
SUDDARDS Britannia Chambers,
4/5 Oxford Place, Leeds LS1 3AX.

Career: assistant solicitor AV Hammond &
Co (1960-1963); became partner (1964-
1988); became joint senior partner
Hammond Suddards (1988).

Activities: president Bradford Law Society
(1982-1983); former deputy coroner for the
County of West Yorkshire (Western
District); director Bradford & Bingley
Building Society.

Biography: lives Leeds; born 21.10.1936;
married to Pam with 2 children. Educated
at Bradford Grammar School; Leeds
University (1958 LLB).

LINCOLN Ashe

head of Chambers 9 King's Bench Walk,
Temple, London EC4Y 7DX.

Career: called to the Bar Inner Temple
(1929); Royal Navy Supplementary
Reserve (1936); Sub Lt Royal Navy (1939);
Lt (1939); Lt Cmdr (1940) (King's

L

Commendation for Bravery); Commander (1945); Captain RNVR (1952); KC (1947); mentioned in Despatches (1944).

Activities: member Executive Committee of Bar Council (1957-1961); chairman Courts Committee Bar Council; Recorder of Gravesend (1967-1971); Recorder and Deputy Crown Court Judge (1972-1979); Master of the Bench Inner Temple (1955 to date); Master of the Moots Inner Temple (1955-1964 & 1968-1970); deputy president International Association of Jewish Lawyers & Jurists; Justice of the World Zionist Court; member of the Bars of Gibraltar, Nigeria, Northern Ireland, West Indies; Freeman and Liveryman of the City of London; past master Worshipful Company of Plaisterers; president London Devonian Association; president Royal Naval Reserve Officers' Club; member of: Athenaeum; Royal Automobile Club; MCC; Royal Corinthian Yacht Club; Bar Yacht Club; City Livery Club; Island Sailing Club; Naval Club.

Biography: lives London EC4; born 30.10.1907; married to Sybil with 2 children. Educated at Hoe Grammar School, Plymouth; Paterson High School, USA; Haberdashers' Aske's School; Exeter College Oxford (1929 BA hons MA BCL); author of 'The Starra' (1939) a Secret Naval Investigator (1954).

LINDSAY Gordon

sole practitioner GORDON LINDSAY & PARTNERS 7 Queen Avenue, Liverpool L2 4SL.

Career: articled family firm (1951-1956); admitted (1956); National Service 2nd Lt Queen's Own Cameron Highlanders (1956-1958); became partner Gair Roberts Fields & Co (1959-1967); became senior partner (1967); partnership dissolved (1988); founded own practice (1988).

Activities: member Liverpool Law Society (president 1979-1980); member Legal Education Committee; articled clerks' liaison officer; minor lecturing on administration of estates; local councillor:Birkenhead (1970-1974); Merseyside County (1973-1977); Wirral Metropolitan Borough (1973 to date) (Mayor 1985-1986); Parliamentary candidate (1978 & 1983); URC Elder; member National Liberal Club.

Biography: lives Birkenhead; born 28.06.1933; married to Rosemary with 3 children. Educated at Loretto (1946-1951); Liverpool University (1954 hons); Metropolitan College (Solicitors finals hons); Atkinson Prize (1956).

Leisure: music.

LING Timothy

partner and head of corporate tax department FRESHFIELDS Whitefriars, 65 Fleet Street, London EC4Y 1HT.

Career: articled Freshfields (1971-1973); admitted (1973); assistant solicitor (1973-1977); became partner (1977); became head of corporate tax department (1986).

Activities: member Law Society Revenue Law Committee; member Royal Harwich Yacht Club.

Biography: lives Stowmarket; born 17.09.1948; married to Sarah with 4 children. Educated at Dulwich College Preparatory School; The King's School, Canterbury; Queen's College Oxford (1970 MA); various articles for professional journals and contributions to tax books.

Leisure: music; sailing.

LINGARD Gordon Young

civil litigation partner STAMP JACKSON & PROCTER 5 Parliament Street, Hull, North Humberside HU1 2AZ.

Career: admitted (1973); assistant solicitor (1973-1975); became partner Dixon & Trout (1975); amalgamated with Stamp Jackson & Procter.

Activities: Deputy Registrar County Court/Deputy District Registrar (1988 to date); member local parish church; former treasurer of 250,000 pounds restoration appeal committee; Borough Councillor (1979-1987).

Biography: lives Ottringham; born 23.12.1948; married to Sue with 2 children. Educated at Hymers College, Hull; Bristol Polytechnic; external London (1970 LLB hons); College of Law Guildford; First Class Honours Law Society Final Part II (1971); New Inn Prize; James Willis Mills Memorial Prize (Hull Incorporated Law Society).

Leisure: gardening; caravanning.

LINGENS Michael

partner commercial services group SPEECHLY BIRCHAM Bouverie House, 154 Fleet Street, London EC4A 2HX.

Career: articled Simmons & Simmons; admitted (1982); assistant solicitor (1982-1983); assistant solicitor Payne Hicks Beach (1983-1985); partner and head of company/commercial department Woodham Smith (1985-1990); became partner Speechly Bircham (1990).

Activities: Conservative Parliamentary

candidate; chairman Bow Group (1984); member of: Carlton Club; Queens Club.

Biography: lives London W6; born 15.05.1957; single. Educated at St Edmund's School, Canterbury; Trinity College Oxford.

Leisure: real tennis; rackets; skiing.

LINSELL Richard

partner ROWE & MAW 20 Black Friars Lane, London EC4V 6HD.

Career: articled Rowe & Maw (1969-1971); admitted (1972); became partner (1976).

Activities: non-executive director DHL International (UK) Ltd; International Bar Association - Business Law Group .

Biography: lives London N1; born 21.06.1947; married to Briony with 1 child. Educated at Bishop's Stortford College (1956-1959); Mill Hill School (1960-1965); Jesus College Cambridge (1969 MA).

Leisure: music; walking; golf; family.

LISHMAN John

senior partner DUNHAM BRINDLEY & LINN Denning House, George Street, Wolverhampton WV2 4DP.

Career: admitted (1952); National Service with Army Legal Aid in London and Egypt (1952-1954); assistant solicitor Little & Co, Bombay (1954-1957); assistant solicitor Lilley Wills & Co Nyasaland (now Malawi) (1957-1962); assistant solicitor Dunham Brindley & Linn (1962-1963); became partner (1963); senior partner (1987).

Activities: president Wolverhampton Law Society (1984-1985); public relations officer Wolverhampton Law Society; chairman 6B Regional Duty Solicitor Committee and Wolverhampton Local Duty Solicitor Committee; member British Academy of Forensic Sciences; director Solicitors Benevolent Association; chairman Bridgnorth Theatre-on-the-Steps; church warden and treasurer local Parish Church; member of: Holdworth Club of Birmingham University.

Biography: lives Bridgnorth; born 28.01.1928; married to Beth with 3 children. Educated at Royal Grammar School, Newcastle on Tyne; King Edward's School, Birmingham; Birmingham University (1949 LLB).

Leisure: fly fisherman.

LISTER Bill (William Brian Collins)

senior partner HILL DICKINSON DAVIS CAMPBELL Pearl Assurance House, 3 Derby Square, Liverpool L2 9XL.

Career: articled in Blackpool; admitted (1953); served in Far East Air Force during emergency in Malaya during National Service; became assistant solicitor James Chapman & Co, Manchester (1957); became partner (1959); became partner Campbell & Co, Liverpool (1968); firm amalgamated to become Davis Campbell (1970); senior partner (1988-1989); senior partner newly amalgamated practice Hill Dickinson Davis Campbell (1989).

Activities: Officer Liverpool Law Society; President Union Club Southport; Fellow Royal Geographical Society.

Biography: lives Southport; born 18.12.1929; married to Joan with 2 children. Educated at Quarry Bank High School; Baines's Grammar School; Manchester University (1951 LLB hons); author of the 'Bibliography of Murray's Handbooks for Travellers'.

Leisure: cricket; book collecting; travel; wine.

LISTER Jane

managing partner FOOT & BOWDEN 70/76 North Hill, Plymouth PL4 8HH.

Career: articled Foot & Bowden; admitted (1976); became partner (1976); became managing partner (1980).

Activities: Notary Public (1977); former chairman Devon Young Solicitors Group; former member National Committee of the Young Solicitors Group; member Association of Women Solicitors; former member Professional & Public Relations Committee of the Law Society; member British Institute of Management; committee member Plymouth Law Society; former employer representative Plymouth Committee for the Employment of Disabled People; member South Western Regional Health Authority (1986-1990); member Royal Western Yacht Club of England.

Biography: lives Plymouth; born 14.06.1951; married to Paul with 2 daughters. Educated at Bath High School; Plymouth High School; College of Law Guildford.

Leisure: husband and children.

LITTLEWOOD Paul

partner BOODLE HATFIELD 43 Brook Street, London W1Y 2BL.

Career: articled Bond Pearce Eliott & Knape (1959-1962); admitted (1962); assistant solicitor Freshfields (1962-1966); assistant solicitor Boodle Hatfield (1967); became partner (1967).

Biography: lives Amersham; born 27.02.1936; married to Anne with 1 son and 1 daughter. Educated at Winchester College; Trinity Hall Cambridge (BA).

LITTMAN Mark

Queen's Counsel 12 Gray's Inn Square, London WC1R 5JP.

Career: called to the Bar (1947); QC (1961); chief legal adviser British Steel Corporation (1967) (deputy chairman 1970-1979); Bencher Middle Temple (1970); treasurer Middle Temple (1988).

Activities: president Bar Association for Commerce Finance & Industry (1974-1980); member Royal Commission on Legal Services; member General Council of the Bar (1968-1974); member Senate of the Inns of Court and the Bar (1974-1975); member advisory panel to Law Commission on Codification of Law of Contract; director of: RTZ Corporation PLC; Burton Group PLC; Granada Group PLC; member of: Reform; Garrick; RAC; United Oxford & Cambridge; Century and Harmonie, New York.

Biography: lives London SW1; born 04.09.1920. Educated at Owen's School; London School of Economics (1939 BSC hons); Queen's College Oxford (MA).

LLEWELYN David

partner MCKENNA & CO Mitre House, 160 Aldersgate Street, London EC1A 4DD.

Career: lecturer in law Reading University (1977-1978); NATO Fellow (1980); Research Fellow Max Planck Institute for Intellectual Property Law, Munich (1980-1981); assistant solicitor Linklaters & Paines (1982-1987); became partner McKenna & Co (1987).

Activities: visiting lecturer in industrial and intellectual property law London School of Economics (1984 to date); member editorial advisory panel 'Intellectual Property in Business' (1987 to date); visiting lecturer in intellectual property law at Queen Mary College, London (1983-1985); adjunct professor in EEC law at Pepperdine University, California (1984-1987); member World Intellectual Property Organisation Committee of Experts on International Registration of Marks (1985).

Biography: lives London NW6; born 15.07.1956; single. Educated at Wallingford Grammar School; Southampton University (1977 LLB); Worcester College Oxford (1979 BCL); author of: 'The International Registration of Trade Marks: Present and Future' (1985); numerous articles and papers on trade mark, copyright, computer, design, EEC and public international law; UK editor of 'Intellectual Property Reports' (1987 to date).

LLOYD Malcolm

partner commercial property department SIMPSON CURTIS 41 Park Square, Leeds LS1 2NS.

Career: articled in Liverpool (1979-1981); admitted (1981); assistant solicitor Simpson Curtis (1981-1984); associate (1984-1986); became partner (1986).

Activities: former hon legal advisor to Leeds Junior Chamber of Commerce; member Leeds Club.

Biography: lives Leeds; born 31.10.1956; married to Helen with 1 son. Educated at Sedbergh School; St Catharine's College Cambridge (1978 MA).

Leisure: family; fishing; walking; gardening.

LLOYD Roger Hall

partner HAYTHE & CURLEY 23 Albemarle Street, London W1X 3HA.

Career: associate Casey Lane & Mittendorf, New York (1958-1964); associate and partner London (1964-1980); became partner Haythe & Curley (1980).

Activities: director American Chamber of Commerce (UK) (president 1982-1984); chairman British American Arts Association; director Royal Oak Foundation (USA); trustee Glyndebourne Association America Inc (USA); member of: Knickerbocker Club, New York; Brooks's Club.

Biography: lives London W8 and West Suffolk; born 18.09.1934; married to Svetlana with 2 children. Educated at Stowe School (1948-1951); Princeton University (1955 BA); Harvard University (1958 LLB).

LLOYD Stephen

senior partner DALE & NEWBERY Clarence House, Clarence Street, Staines, Middlesex TW18 4SY.

Career: articled Dale & Newbery; admitted; assistant solicitor; became

L

partner (1968); became senior partner (1984).

Activities: Assistant Recorder (1989); committee member Legal Aid Area 14 Legal Aid Board; vice-president National Council for One parent Families; chairman Committee of Management of Mediation in Divorce; chairman Board of Governors Manor House School; broadcasting on family law and related subjects (1974-1976); Committee member Ashvillian Society; member Effingham Golf Club.

Biography: lives Dorking; born 16.09.1938; married to Joyce with 2 daughters. Educated at Ashville College; Leeds University (LLB hons).

Leisure: charity work; walking the dogs; relaxing at cottage in Yorkshire Dales; running and enjoying 1936 Morris 8 Tourer; music; golf; tennis; entertaining at home.

LLOYD-EDWARDS Norman

senior partner CARTWRIGHTS ADAMS & BLACK 36 West Bute Street, Cardiff CF1 5UA.

Career: articled Bayliss Rowe & Co (1955-1958); National Service with Royal Navy (1958-1960); assistant solicitor Cartwright Taylor & Cooper (1960-1961); became partner (1962-1989); became consultant and senior partner in Cardiff (1989).

Activities: Notary Public; member Cardiff City Council (1963-1987); deputy Lord Mayor of Cardiff (1973-1974); (Lord Mayor 1985-1986); South Wales Division Royal Navy Reserve (1960); (Reserve Decoration 1971); (Bar 1980); Commanding Officer for HMS Cambria (1981); (Captain 1982); appointed Naval ADC to HM The Queen (1984); Chapter Clerk, Parish Treasurer and Dean's Registrar Llandaff Cathedral (1975 to date); Deputy Lt for South Glamorgan (1978); (Vice-Lord Lt 1986); Lord Lt (1990); Officer of the Order of St John (1983) (Knight 1988); Prior for Wales (1989); chairman of Wales Committee Duke of Edinburgh's Award Scheme; former chairman Glamorgan TAVRA and Cardiff Festival of Music; chairman National Rescue Training Council; president Cardiff Branch of Sail Training Association Schooners; president South Glamorgan Scouts Council and president United Services Mess Cardiff; vice-president Cardiff RNLI; member Board of Outward Bound Aberdovey; member Welsh Arts Council; member BBC Wales Council; member of: Army and Navy Club; Cardiff and County Club.

Biography: lives Cardiff; born 13.06.1933;

single. Educated at Monmouth School for Boys; Quakers Yard Grammar School; Bristol University (1955 LLB).

Leisure: music; gardening; table talk.

LOCHNER Ludi

partner and head of intellectual property group STEPHENSON HARWOOD One St Paul's Churchyard, London EC4M 8SH.

Career: registered as patent agent and admitted as attorney South Africa; admitted (1981); assistant solicitor (1981-1983); became partner Stephenson Harwood (1983).

Activities: member of: Little Ship Club; The Cruising Association.

Biography: born 05.01.1938; married to Eleanor. Educated at Langchoven High School, South Africa; Rhodes University (1959 BSC); University of the Witwatersrand (1969 LLB); Higher Diploma Tax (1974).

Leisure: offshore yachting; woodwork; music; wine; photography; supervising washing-up!.

LOCKHART Alastair H

partner and head of litigation BISHOP AND ROBERTSON CHALMERS 2 Blythswood Square, Glasgow G2 4AD.

Career: apprentice McGrigor Donald & Co (1967-1969); admitted (1969); assistant solicitor Robertson Chalmers and Auld (1969-1970); became partner (1970); firm amalgamated with Bishop & Co (1986).

Activities: Notary Public; member of: the Merchants House of Glasgow; the Royal Faculty of Procurators in Glasgow; the Incorporation of Barbers; Glasgow Academical Club; Clydesdale Cricket Club; Royal Scottish Automobile Club; Balloch Fishing Club.

Biography: lives Glasgow; born 21.09.1946; married to Susan with 2 sons. Educated at Ayr Academy; Glasgow Academy; Glasgow University (1967 LLB).

Leisure: refereeing junior rugby union; organising and coaching mini-rugby; trout fishing; family; watching class sport of any kind.

LOCKHART-MIRAMS Andrew

senior partner in commercial litigation department and NHS law department HEMPSONS 33 Henrietta Street, Covent Garden, London WC2E 8NH.

Career: articled Tyndallwoods (1959-1963) and Hempsons (1963-1964); admitted

(1965); assistant solicitor (1965-1966); became partner Tyndallwoods (1966-1972); became partner Hempsons (1972); became senior commercial litigation partner (1986).

Activities: secretary Horse Race Betting Levy Board Appeal Tribunal for England and Wales; Commissioner for Oaths.

Biography: lives London SW1 and Hampshire; born 01.04.1941; married to Juliet with 2 children. Educated at Westbourne House Preparatory School; Monkton Combe School; Associate of Institute of Arbitrators.

Leisure: ocean racing; shooting; garden design.

LOCKHART-MUMMERY Christopher John

Queen's Counsel 2 Paper Buildings, Temple, London EC4Y 7ET.

Career: called to the Bar (1971); QC (1986); Assistant Recorder.

Biography: lives London W8 and Hampshire; born 07.08.1947; married to Rosamund with 3 children. Educated at St Peter's, Seaford; Trinity College Cambridge (1969 BA); editor of Hill and Redman's 'Law of Landlord and Tenant'.

Leisure: fishing; opera.

LOCKLEY Andrew

director legal practice THE LAW SOCIETY 113 Chancery Lane, London WC2A 1PL.

Career: articled Kingsley Napley; admitted (1979); legal assistant/assistant solicitor Young & Solon (1978-1980); assistant solicitor Meaby & Co (1980-1982); assistant secretary Law Society (1982-1985); secretary contentious business (1985-1987); director legal practice (1987).

Activities: member Efficiency Commission of the Criminal Courts (1986 to date); member Advisory Committee Citcom (1988 to date); director Solicitors Financial & Property Services Ltd (1988 to date).

Biography: lives Luton; born 10.05.1951; married to Ruth with 3 children. Educated at Marlborough College (1964-1968); Oriel College Oxford (1973); College of Law (1975 & 1978); research scholar for World Council of Churches in Geneva (1973-1975); occasional contributor to legal journals and national press.

Leisure: children; organic kitchen garden/orchard; travel; walking; reading; swimming.

LOFTHOUSE Janet

solicitor to the BRITISH UNITED PROVIDENT ASSOCIATION GROUP LEGAL DEPARTMENT Provident House, Essex Street, London WC2R 3AX.

Career: legal secretary Courtaulds PLC (1977-1979); legal secretary Hempsons (1983-1984); articled Le Brasseur & Bury (1984-1986); admitted (1986); appointed solicitor BUPA Legal Department (1986).

Activities: member Law Society.

Biography: lives Surrey Quays London SE16; and Guildford; born 14.05.1958; single. Educated at St Peter's and Merrow Grange, Guildford; Guildford College of Technology (1976); City of London Polytechnic (1982 BA hons); College of Law Guildford (1983).

Leisure: tennis; skiing; swimming; theatre; cinema; ballet; travel; photography; shopping.

LOMBARDI Enrico

senior partner PEGDEN & DUBOW 64A Church Street, Enfield, Middlesex EN2 6EQ.

Career: articled JR Bernstein & Co (1977-1980); admitted (1980); assistant solicitor (1980-1982); assistant solicitor Fletcher Dervish (1982); became partner; acquired own practice with Tony Johnson (Pegden & Dubow) (1984).

Activities: president North Middlesex Law Society (1987-1988) (secretary 1989-1990); member Area 14 Legal Aid Committee and Criminal Legal Aid Committee; former member Enfield Magistrates' Court Duty Solicitor Committee; member North Middlesex Law Society Committee; hon legal advisor (1982-1990) and treasurer (1987-1990) Edmonton Citizen's Advice Bureau (member management committee); disciple Charlton Athletic FC & Italian National Team.

Biography: lives London N14; born 07.12.1952; married to Conchita with 2 sons. Educated at South East London Secondary School; South East London College of Further Education (1968-1970); Walbrook College (1970-1971); Polytechnic of Central London (1976 LLB); College of Law Lancaster Gate; post qualification courses run by Law Society or College of Law (mainly advocacy and office management).

Leisure: reading; photography; snooker; squash; ten-pin bowling; driving.

LONG Colin

partner BEHARRELL THOMPSON & CO (in association with Coudert Brothers) 4 Dean's Court, London EC4V 5AA.

Career: articled Clifford Turner; admitted (1970); assistant solicitor (1970-1972); legal department ICI head office (1972-1974); assistant solicitor Clifford Turner (1974-1978); partner Bird & Bird (1979-1990); became partner Beharrell Thompson & Co (1990).

Activities: founding committee member Holborn Law Society Business Law Section; vice-chairman Communications sub-committee of the International Bar Association; member RAC.

Biography: lives Bedford Park; born 04.06.1946; married to Sheila with 2 children. Educated at Downside School, Purley; Epsom College; Bristol University (1967 LLB hons); joint author of 'Information Technology and the Law' (1986); author 'Telecommunications Law and Practice' (1988); member editorial panel of 'Computer Law and Security Report' and 'Telecomms Regulation Review'.

Leisure: swimming; relaxing in Normandy; photography; books; cinema; theatre; squash; tennis.

LONG Michael

partner and head of local government services and training partner DONNE MILEHAM & HADDOCK Frederick Place, Brighton BN1 1AT.

Career: articled Stephenson Harwood (1969-1971); admitted (1971); assistant solicitor (1971-1973); assistant solicitor Donne Mileham & Haddock (1973-1974); became partner (1975).

Activities: council member Law Society; Law Society final examiner in business law; councillor Hove Borough Council; senator Junior Chamber International; member Law Society Investigation Committee and various others; ex-chairman Law Society Constitution and Continuing Education Committees; former member Training Committee, Company Law Committee, Revenue Law Committee, etc; Liveryman of the City of London Solicitors' Company; member Sussex Law Society; member United Oxford & Cambridge Club.

Biography: lives Hove; born 15.03.1947; married to Christl. Educated at King Edward VI Grammar School, East Retford; St John's College Cambridge (1968 BA) (MA); author of 'Some Aspects of the

Family Business' (1979) with DT Sparrow.

Leisure: opera; theatre; Scotland; local politics.

LONG Robert

senior partner BELL POPE & BRIDGWATER 6 High Street, Southampton SO9 1LR.

Career: articled Kirk Jackson & Co (1961-1964); admitted (1964); assistant solicitor (1964-1967); became partner Bell Pope & Bridgwater (1967); became senior partner (1977).

Activities: secretary Hampshire Inc Law Society (1977-1981) (president 1988-1989); secretary Southern Area Association of Law Societies (1982-1988); president Southern Rent Assessment Panel (1987 to date); chairman Southampton Enterprise Agency Ltd; member Stoneham Golf Club.

Biography: lives Eastleigh; born 13.07.1939; married with 3 children. Educated at Bristol Grammar School (1947-1958); Manchester University (1961 LLB hons).

Leisure: golf; gardening; music; computers; skiing.

LONGLEY Adrian

legal adviser to NATIONAL COUNCIL FOR VOLUNTARY ORGANISATIONS 26 Bedford Square, London WC1B 3HU.

Career: Army service (1944-1947); Rifle Brigade (acting Captain 1947); Middle East (1946-1947); schoolmaster (1950-1954); articled Guscotte Fowler & Cox (1955-1958); admitted (1959); assistant solicitor Freshfields (1959-1969); associate White Brooks & Gilman (1970-1972); became legal adviser National Council for Voluntary Organisations (1972).

Activities: hon legal adviser Institute of Charity Fund-Raising Managers and Group 300 Educational Trust; member various committees of NCVO (1972 to date); member Goodman Committee on the effect of charity law & practice on voluntary organisations (1974-1976); member NCVO working party on malpractice in fundraising for charity (1985-1986); trustee St Mildred's House; trustee Cyril Wood Memorial Trust; addresses/lectures at various conferences/seminars on charity law; member of: MCC; Royal Commonwealth Society; Cavalry & Guards Club.

Biography: lives London SW11; born 27.09.1925; married to Sylvia with 3 children. Educated at Aysgarth School, Bedale; Winchester College; Trinity College Cambridge (1949 BA) (MA); co-author of

L

'Charity Trustees Guide'; articles on charity law in various publications including Law Society's Gazette, Charity, Peace and Security, Les Associations et Foundations en Europe (1990); Sunday Times; letters to Press.

Leisure: cricket; music; foreign travel; reading history, biographies and detective fiction.

LONGMORE Andrew

Queen's Counsel 7 King's Bench Walk, Temple, London EC4.

Career: teaching associate Northwestern University School of Law, Chicago (1965); member Chambers (1966); QC (1983); Assistant Recorder (1988).

Activities: member Bar Council (1982-1985) (chairman Law Reform Committee 1988); member Phillips Committee on Commercial Court Working Practices (1985-1987) .

Biography: lives London W11; born 25.08.1944; married to Meimei with 1 son. Educated at Winchester College; Lincoln College Oxford (jurisprudence hons MA); Astbury Scholar Middle Temple; co-editor 'McGillivray and Parkington on the Law of Insurance' (1975, 1981 & 1988).

Leisure: fell walking.

LONGMORE Charles John Nigel

senior partner LONGMORES 24 Castle Street, Hertford, Herts SG14 1HP.

Career: articled Radcliffes & Co; admitted; marshall to the Hon Mr Justice Haveas (1954); became senior partner Longmores (1969).

Activities: High Sheriff for the County of Hertfordshire (1969); clerk to the Commissioners of Taxes Hertford & Stevenage Divisions (1965 to date); Deputy Coroner (1986 to date); member Executive Committee and hon legal advisor to the Hertfordshire Society (1961 to date); life governor Haileybury College (1966) (member of Council and Finance & General Purposes Committee); hon legal advisor and Member of Council Ada Cole Memorial Stables (1965); county president St John Ambulance for Hertfordshire; hon legal advisor Herts Playing Fields Association; member of: The Arts; The Chelsea Arts Club; Marylebone Cricket Club.

Biography: lives Hertford Heath nr Hertford; born 02.04.1933; divorced with 1 daughter. Educated at Harrow (1946-1951).

Leisure: painting; shooting; fishing.

LOOSEMORE John

management consultant to the legal profession, LAWYERS' PLANNING SERVICES 18-19 High Street, Cardiff CF1 2BZ; senior partner LOOSEMORES 70 Bridge Street, Newport NP9 4AQ and consultant LOOSEMORES 18-19 High Street, Cardiff CF1 2BZ.

Career: National Service (2 years); supply teaching (1 year); articled Rees Currie-Jones & Simons; admitted (1965); founded own practice (1965).

Activities: founding partner Lawyers' Planning Services; speaker at numerous international and UK legal seminars and conferences; former senior lecturer in law University College Cardiff; chairman Social Security Appeals Tribunal (1977 to date); former local Law Society Council member; trustee Christians in Sport; member of: St Fagan's Cricket Club; Cardiff Lawn Tennis Club.

Biography: lives Dinas Powys, South Glamorgan; born 20.10.1937; married to Pam with 4 children. Educated at Cathays High School, Cardiff; University College Cardiff (1958 BA hons Economics); frequent contributor to various journals including Law Society's Gazette; New Law Journal; Legal Action.

Leisure: squash; tennis; Welsh league soccer referee; supporting daughter Sarah, who is full-time professional tennis player.

LOOSLEY Roger

joint head company and commercial department FLADGATE FIELDER Waldgate House, 25 Church Street, Basingstoke, Hants RG21 1QQ.

Career: outdoor clerk and clerk in HP recovery department Kennedys (1963-1964); clerk in litigation department W Bradly Trimmer & Son (1964-1966); articled (1966-1971); admitted (1971); assistant solicitor (1971-1974); became partner (1974-1987); Provincial Notary (1982); merged with Walters Fladgate (1987).

Activities: member Lawyers' Christian Fellowship; director Bagster Video Ltd; non-playing member WASPS Football Club.

Biography: lives Winchester; born 20.10.1946; married to Judith with 2 daughters. Educated at Roxeth Manor County Secondary School, South Harrow; College of Law Guildford.

Leisure: practising Evangelical Christian; travel; walking (particularly in the Lake District); watching rugby; listening to most forms of music (particularly string quartets and orchestral music); computers; reading; food (particularly Thai); wine; general family life.

LORD Geoffrey

partner ELLIOTT & COMPANY Centurion House, Deansgate, Manchester M3 3WT and 8 Breams Buildings, London EC4A 1HP.

Career: articles Alexander Tatham & Co (1970-1972); admitted (1972); assistant solicitor (1972-1973); assistant solicitor Elliott & Company (1973-1974); became partner (1974).

Activities: deputy District Registrar High Court of Justice North Western Circuit (1982-1987); company secretary and director of privately owned group of companies; member Legal Aid Appeals Committee North Western Legal Aid Area; member International Bar Association; international associate member American Bar Association; member British Insurance Law Association; member St James's Club, Manchester.

Biography: lives Wilmslow; born 08.05.1947; married to Adele with 3 children. Educated at Stockport School; Queen Mary College London (1969 LLB hons) (president students' union 1969); College of Law Lancaster Gate (1969-1970).

Leisure: playing classical guitar; model making.

LOUGHRAN James

senior partner KEVORKIAN & PARTNERS 49 Conduit Street, London W1R 9FB.

Career: 1st Lt US Marine Corps (1953-1955); admitted New York and Connecticut (1959); practice in New York and Buenos Aires (1959-1964); general counsel McKee Corp, USA (1964-1972); chief financial officer McKee, Rome (1972-1975); chief financial & admin officer McKee, USA (1976-1978); London practice (1979-1984); became partner Kevorkian & Rawlings (1985).

Activities: vice-chairman National Contractors' Association (1977); member of: Hurlingham Club; RAC.

Biography: lives London SW3; married to Margareta with 4 children. Educated at Fordham University (1953 BA); Pennsylvania University (1958 LLB); Columbia University (1959 MIA); Fulbright Scholar Argentina (1963).

LOUP Michael

senior partner BOODLE HATFIELD
43 Brook Street, London W1Y 2BL.

Career: articled Clowes Hickley & Heaver;
(amalgamated Boodle Hatfield 1951);
became partner (1958).

Activities: president City of Westminster
Law Society (1973); member Council of the
Law Society (1975-1983); former chairman
Law Society Revenue Law Committee;
former chairman Solicitors European
Group; former chairman London Small
Claims Court; former chairman Society of
English & American Lawyers; former
member Remuneration Certifying
Casework Committee; member of
Committee of MCC; member Boodle's,
Bucks.

Biography: lives London SW1; born
19.05.1929; married with 4 children.
Educated at Stowe; written and delivered
occasional papers on taxation, exchange
control, comparative law and the future of
the profession.

Leisure: walking in English and French
countryside; golf; cinema; theatre; reading.

LOWE Veronica

director Solicitors Complaints Bureau
Portland House, Stag Place, London
SW1E 5BL.

Career: articled Ryland Martineau (1976-
1978); admitted (1979); lectured in labour
law at Aston University (1979); assistant
solicitor (1979-1986); assistant area director
(legal) Legal Aid Area No. 8 Newcastle-
upon-Tyne (1986-1988); Area director (W
Midlands) Legal Aid Area No 6 (1988-
1989); Group Manager (Midlands) (1989-
1990); became Director of SCB (1990).

Activities: former member Birmingham
Law Society Litigation & Legal Aid
Committee; member of: Association of
Women Solicitors; Solicitors Family Law
Association; Romantic Novelists'
Association; St Hugh's College Senior
Members' Association.

Biography: lives Dunchurch; born
29.06.1951; married to Ian with 1 daughter.
Educated at King Edward VI Grammar
School for Girls; St Hugh's College Oxford
(1972 BA hons); Oxford Polytechnic (1972-
1973); City of Birmingham Polytechnic
(1974-1976); contributions on
employment/financial contracts/property
law to encyclopaedia of business contracts
and on commercial law for accounting
manual.

Leisure: interest in all historical subjects;
writing historical fiction; reading; food &

wine; travel; theatre; listening to music;
dancing; swimming.

LUBAR Charles

senior partner MORGAN LEWIS &
BOCKIUS 4 Carlton Gardens, Pall Mall,
London SW1Y 5AA.

Career: called to the Bar Maryland (1966);
called to the Bar Washington, DC (1967);
attorney advisor Chief Counsel's office
Internal Revenue Service, Washington
(1967-1969); Chairman of Board Haraka
Housing Ltd, Nairobi (1969-1971); legal
advisor East African Development Bank,
Kampala (1970); law school teacher
University College, Nairobi (1970); lawyer
Margulies & Sterling (1971-1974); senior
partner Lubar & Youngstein (1974-1981);
became senior partner Morgan Lewis &
Bockius (1981).

Activities: tax editor Overseas American
(1974-1978); tax editor European & Middle
East Tax Report (1974-1978); contributing
editor International Tax Report (1974-1990);
member Foreign Tax Committees of
American Bar Association; member Tax
Committee of American Chamber of
Commerce in London; frequent speaker in
UK, US and Continent on various topics of
international taxation; member Fulbright
Commission UK (1987 to date); member
American Sector Appeal Committee Prince
of Wales Youth Business Trust (1989-1990);
chairman Yale Club Alumnae Schools
Committee in London (1974 to date);
member of: RAC; Queens Club; Annabels;
Vanderbilt Tennis Club; Harvard Club,
New York; Yale Club of London.

Biography: lives London SW7; born
20.05.1941; married to Dominique with 1
son and 1 daughter. Educated at Woodrow
Wilson High School, Washington DC; Yale
University (1963 BA); Magna Cum Laude;
Harvard Law School (1966 JD);
Georgetown University (1967 LLM
Taxation); author of: Foreign Investment in
East Africa in East African Law Journal
(1971); Tax Thriller in Tax Planning
International (1987).

Leisure: tennis; golf; running; guitar
playing; reading; theatre; cinema; travel.

LUDLOW Michael

senior partner BEALE AND COMPANY
Garrick House, 27-32 King Street, Covent
Garden, London WC2E 8JD.

Career: articled Beale and Company (1956-
1959); admitted (1959); assistant solicitor
Wellington & Clifford (1960-1961); assistant
solicitor Beale and Company (1961-1965);

became partner (1965).

Activities: Fellow of Chartered Institute of
Arbitrators (1983); on panel of arbitrators
available for hearing disputes concerning
building, civil, structural and mechanical
engineering works (1983); member of CI
Arb working party on taxation of costs by
arbitrators (1988); member of CBI working
party on the GATT concerning intellectual
property rights (1989); conference speaker
at seminars/conferences on construction
law dispute issues of the Association of
Consulting Engineers (1985); Geological
Survey Annual Conference (1985); Annual
Conference of South African Association of
Consulting Engineers (1988); SE Branch of
Chartered Institute of Arbitrators (1988);
member of: Reform Club; Vincent's
(Oxford); Grannies CC.

Biography: lives London SW14; Paignton,
Devon; Malta; born 30.03.1933; married to
Diane with 4 children. Educated at Fyling
Hall School (1938-1946); Rugby School
(1946-1951); Trinity College Oxford (1956
BA hons); (1969 MA); articles in the New
Civil Engineer and Arbitration Journal on
construction law issues; author (under the
alias 'Outlaw') of 'Fair Charges? A review
of controls over Solicitors costs' (1982).

LYELL Nicholas

HM Solicitor General House of Commons,
London SW1A 0AA.

Career: Walter Runciman & Co (1962-1964);
called to the Bar Inner Temple (1965);
Queen's Counsel (1980); Bencher (1986);
private practice (1965-1986); Recorder
(1985 to date); MP (1979 to date); PPS to
Attorney General (1979-1986);
Parliamentary Under Secretary of State
DHSS (1986-1987); became Solicitor
General (1987); Privy Counsellor (1990).

Activities: joint secretary Constitutional
Committee (1979); chairman Society of
Conservative Lawyers (1982-1985); vice-
chairman BFSS (1983-1986); member
Brooks's Club.

Biography: born 06.12.1938; married to
Susanna with 4 children. Educated at
Stowe; Christ Church Oxford (MA hons).

Leisure: gardening; shooting; drawing.

LYON Thomas

partner BERWIN LEIGHTON
Adelaide House, London Bridge, London
EC4R 9HA.

Career: articled Woodham Smith
Borradaile & Martin (1962-1965); admitted
(1965); assistant solicitor (1965-1968);

L

assistant solicitor Berwin & Co (1968-1969); became partner (1969); became partner Berwin Leighton (1970).

Biography: lives London; born 26.11.1941; married to Judith with 3 children. Educated at University College School, Hampstead; Wadham College Oxford (1962 BA); London School of Economics (1967 LLM); contributions to various periodicals.

LYONS Edward

Queen's Counsel Fourth Floor, 4 Brick Court, Temple, London EC4Y 9AD and 6 Park Square, Leeds LS1 2LW.

Career: Recorder of Crown Court (1971); Bencher Lincoln's Inn (1983); QC.

Activities: former Member of Parliament; International Commission of Jurista Missives to South Africa and SW Africa (1969 & 1972); formerly executive of Justice; hon member of the Council of Justice.

Biography: lives London SW1 and Leeds; born 17.05.1926; married to Barbara with 2 children. Educated at Roundhay School, Leeds; Leeds University (1951 LLB hons); Combined Services Course Cantonese School Oriental & African Studies London (1946); Combined Services Russian Course University of Cambridge (1946).

LYONS Fergus

senior partner LYONS DAVIDSON Bridge House, 48-52 Baldwin Street, Bristol BS1 1QD.

Career: articled Bush & Bush (1949-1954); admitted (1955); National Service with Intelligence Corp in Cyprus (1956); founded Taylor Lyons with brother (1957); amalgamated to form Lyons Davison (1972).

Activities: president Bristol Law Society (1976) (former secretary); member Public Relations and Law Society's Gazette Committees of the National Law Society; deputy chairman Radio West; chairman Radio Bristol Advisory Council; governor Bristol Polytechnic; member Frenchay Hospital Management Committee; chairman Constitution Club; president Bristol Circle of the Catenian Association; chairman Governors Prior Park College; secretary and trustee of Van Neste Foundation; member Council of Bristol Law Society; chairman Mental Health Tribunal; member Council of Bristol Chamber of Commerce; interest in making law accessible to the public; involvement in establishment of free legal advice centres

throughout Bristol; starting up of Courts Conciliation Centre in Bristol and the Magistrates' Court Duty Solicitors Scheme; involved for 15 years via Amazon Trust with third world project in remote jungle of Peru where hospital and 10 clinics set up; leader of 'Booters' local walking group; member of: Clifton Club; Commercial Rooms; Institute of Directors; Lansdown Club.

Biography: lives Bristol; born 20.04.1931; married to Mary with 2 sons and 3 daughters. Educated at Prior Park College, Bath; numerous articles published in the local press on state of the practice of the law and current topics, the last being criticism of remand prisons.

Leisure: tennis; golf; hill walking; obsession for bow ties and walking sticks.

LYONS TCH (Toby)

deputy chairman and managing director MINSTER TRUST LTD Minster House, Arthur Street, London EC4R 9BH.

Career: commissioned Royal Welch Fusiliers (1956-1958) and TA to (1967); articled Gustavus Thompson Saxton & Morgan (1962-1964); articled Linklaters & Paines (1964-1965); admitted (1965); assistant solicitor (1965-1966); assistant solicitor Allen & Overy (1966-1969); Minster Trust Ltd (1969).

Activities: director of: Minster Assets PLC; Monument Oil & Gas PLC; chairman R & J Hadlee Fine Art PLC; member Law Society.

Biography: lives Stansted; born 08.03.1937; married to Heather (nee Forbes); dissolved (1971); married to Frances (nee Gosling); 4 children. Educated at Harrow School; Oriel College, Oxford (1961 MA).

Leisure: shooting; skiing; waterskiing.

M

MABERLY Elizabeth

deputy head legal department NATIONAL WESTMINSTER BANK PLC 20 Old Broad Street, London EC2N 1EJ.

Career: articled Theodore Goddard (1965-1967); admitted (1968); Esher Urban District Council (1968-1969); Caporte Industries PLC (1969-1972); National Westminster Bank PLC (1972); became deputy head of department (1982).

Activities: member Recruitment and Training Sub-committee of Commerce and Industry Group of the Law Society.

Biography: lives London SW19; born 26.03.1943; married to Adam. Educated at Bournemouth School for Girls; King's College London (1964 LLB).

Leisure: badminton; swimming; reading; cooking; gardening; travelling; unusual holidays.

MACARTNEY David

commercial property partner BRODIES WS 15 Atholl Crescent, Edinburgh EH3 8HA.

Career: apprentice Biggart Baillie & Gifford WS (1975-1977); admitted (1977); assistant solicitor Biggart Baillie & Gifford WS (1977-1978); assistant solicitor Archibald Sharp & Son (1978-1979); assistant solicitor Bird Semple Fyfe Ireland WS (1979-1983); assistant solicitor Brodies WS (1983-1985); assistant solicitor Wright Johnston & MacKenzie (1985); became partner Brodies WS (1986).

Biography: lives Edinburgh; born 01.06.1953; married to Mairi with 2 children. Educated at Hutchesons' Boys' Grammar School, Glasgow; Glasgow University (1975 LLB hons).

Leisure: running; football; golf.

MACCABE Michael

partner FRESHFIELDS Whitefriars, 65 Fleet Street, London EC4Y 1HT.

Career: articled Charles Russell & Co; admitted (1969); assistant solicitor Freshfields (1970-1974); became partner (1974); became managing partner Paris office (1981-1984); managing partner (1985-1990).

Activities: director Solicitors Indemnity Mutual Insurance Association Limited; Committee member of The City of London Law Society.

Biography: lives London SW7; born 20.11.1944; widowed with 2 children. Educated at Downside School; Lincoln College Oxford (1963-1964); London Business School (senior executive programme).

Leisure: painting; fishing.

MACDONALD Ian

Queen's Counsel and joint head of chambers 2 Garden Court, Temple, London EC4Y 9BL.

Career: called to the Bar (1963); Chambers of Sir Derek Walker-Smith (1963-1974); 2 Garden Court (1974).

Activities: British representative on Commission Speciale pour l'etude des lois anti-trust (1963-1965); member committee of inquiry into student sit-ins at Manchester University (1971); chair of inquiry into racial violence in Manchester schools (The Burnage Report) (1987-1988); president Immigration Law Practitioners' Association; member Cumberland LTC.

Biography: lives London N5; born 12.01.1939; divorced with 3 children. Educated at Glasgow Academy; Cargilfield School, Edinburgh; Rugby School; Clare College Cambridge (1960 BA) (MA) (1961 LLB); Astbury Scholar Middle Temple (1962-1965); author of: 'Resale Price Maintenance' (1964); 'The Land Commission' with DP Kerrigan QC (1967); 'Race Relations and Immigration Law' (1969); 'Race Relations: The New Law' (1977); 'The New Nationality Law' with NJ Blake (1982); 'Immigration Law and Practice' (1st ed 1983; 2nd ed 1987; 3rd ed 1991); Murder in the Playground; Inquiry into racial violence in Manchester Schools (1990); consultant editor Butterworths Encyclopaedia of Forms and Precedents - Nationality; member editorial board of Immigration and Nationality Law and Practice.

Leisure: squash; tennis; swimming; following Arsenal AFC; reading; travel.

MACDONALD Morag

partner intellectual property department BIRD & BIRD 2 Gray's Inn Square, London WC1R 5AF.

Career: called to the Bar Gray's Inn (1984); pupillage in leading intellectual property Chambers; assistant Bird & Bird (1985-1988); admitted (1988); became partner (1989).

Activities: particular interest in computers and electronics and computer law; Chairman of Brands & Trade Marks group at Bird & Bird.

Biography: lives London SW18; single. Educated at Croydon High School for Girls; Newnham College Cambridge (1983 BA hons) (1987 MA hons); College of Legal Education.

MACDONALD-BROWN Charters

partner in charge of litigation GOULDENS 22 Tudor Street, London EC4Y 0JJ.

Career: called to the Bar Middle Temple (1969); articled Gouldens (1972-1974); admitted (1974); assistant solicitor (1974-1977); became partner (1977).

Activities: clerk to General Commissioners of Taxes (East Brixton Division); hon legal

adviser to the Law and Parliamentary Committee of the Royal Society of Chemistry; delivered talks at seminars; member of: Wig & Pen Club; RAC; Annabels.

Biography: lives London SW15; born 20.08.1946; married to Patricia with 4 children. Educated at Loretto School (1959-1964); Geneva University (1966 Diploma); Inns of Court Law School (1969).

Leisure: swimming; sailing; tennis; the arts in general; collecting pictures; theatre; opera; music.

MACFADYEN Michael Robert

partner NORTON ROSE Kempson House, PO Box 570, Camomile Street, London EC3A 7AN.

Career: articled Norton Rose (1961-1966); admitted (1966); assistant solicitor (1966-1970); became partner (1970).

Activities: governor Rupert House School; member of: Berkshire GC; St Endoc golf club; MCC; City of London Solicitors' Company.

Biography: lives East Berkshire; born 21.05.1943; married to Judy with 3 children. Educated at Marlborough College.

MACFARLANE Andrew

managing partner MACFARLANE GUY 3 Kingsmead Square, Bath BA1 2AB.

Career: admitted (1968); founded MacFarlane Guy.

Activities: former chairman Local Review Committee of Parole Board, Bristol; former president Bath Law Society; member Remuneration and Practice Development Committee of the Law Society; member Bath Area Drug Advisory Service; member Bath Child in Need; member Legal Aid Board Duty Solicitor Committee; lectures on computers and practice management for Law Society and Society for Computers and Law.

Biography: lives Bath; born 03.03.1943; married to Christine with 3 sons and 1 daughter. Educated at St Christopher's Preparatory School; City of Bath Boys' School; MBIM; author of 'A Guide to Parole'; co-author loose-leaved guide to Conduct and Good Practice of Board of Visitors members.

Leisure: sailing; watercolour painting; gardening; watching his pond.

MACFARLANE Jonathan

partner MACFARLANES 10 Norwich Street, London EC4A 1BD.

Career: articled Macfarlanes (1978-1980); admitted (1980); assistant solicitor (1980-1985); became partner (1985).

Activities: member Leander Club.

Biography: lives London W6; born 28.03.1956; married to Johanna with 1 son and 1 daughter. Educated at Charterhouse; Oriel College Oxford (1977 MA); Law Society Finals (1978).

MACFARLANE Nicholas Russel

partner and coordinator for one of the intellectual property groups LOVELL WHITE DURRANT 65 Holborn Viaduct, London EC1A 2DY.

Career: articled Richards Butler; admitted (1977); assistant solicitor Faithfull Owen and Fraser (1978-1980); became partner (1980); merged with Durrant Piesse (1985); merged with Lovell White & King (1988).

Activities: member Committee of the Patent Solicitors Association; member City of London Club.

Biography: lives London SW11; born 21.02.1952; married to Lissie. Educated at Cheam School; Radley College; Lancaster University (1974 BA).

Leisure: shooting; fishing; tennis; painting.

MACGREGOR Robert

assistant solicitor CLIFFORD CHANCE Blackfriars House, 19 New Bridge Street, London EC4V 6BY.

Career: articled Titmuss Sainer & Webb (1983-1985); admitted (1985); assistant solicitor (1985-1989); partner (1989-1990); became assistant solicitor Clifford Chance (1990).

Activities: lectures extensively on property development and financing documentation; Freeman of the City of London; member of the Worshipful Company of Glovers.

Biography: lives London SW10; born 14.01.1960; married to Alison. Educated at Berkhamsted Boys' School (1967-1978) head of school; Nottingham University (1982 LLB hons).

Leisure: squash (Scottish Masters Champion 1981); sailing; cricket; vintage car restoration.

MACHIN Anthony

Queen's Counsel 1 Paper Buildings, Temple, London EC4Y 7EP.

M

Career: called to the Bar Lincoln's Inn (1951); QC (1973); Recorder (1976) .

Activities: Judge of the Courts of Appeal of Jersey and Guernsey (1989); member Bar Yacht.

Biography: lives Topsham; born 28.06.1925; married to Jean with 3 children. Educated at Christ's College Finchley; New College Oxford (1950 BCL MA); part author 'Health and Safety'; contributor to: Halsbury's Laws on Health and Safety at Work; 'Medical Negligence'.

Leisure: sailing; music; languages.

MACKARNESS Simon

senior partner MACKARNESS AND LUNT 16 High Street, Petersfield, Hants GU32 3JJ.

Career: articled Raper & Co (1966-1968); articled Mackarness and Lunt (1968-1970); admitted (1970); assistant solicitor Tuckett Williams and Kew (1971-1972); assistant solicitor Mackarness and Lunt (1972-1976); became partner (1976); became senior partner (1984).

Activities: on advisory council of Petersfield Counselling Service; retired Territorial Army (1980) (holder of Territorial Decoration TD); Captain Regular Army Reserve of Officers (RARO); member of: Lion and Unicorn Players; AJS and Matchless Owners' Club.

Biography: lives Petersfield; born 10.09.1945; married to Diana with 2 children. Educated at Marsh Court (1955-1958); Portsmouth Grammar School (1958-1963); Bristol University (1966 BA hons).

Leisure: amateur dramatics; motorcycle touring .

MACKAY Alan

senior litigation partner LINDSAYS WS 11 Atholl Crescent, Edinburgh EH3 8HE.

Career: apprentice in Edinburgh (1965-1968); admitted (1968); became partner Patrick & James WS (1968-1987); became partner Lindsays WS (1987).

Activities: Writer to the Signet; Notary Public; lectures at courses for the Law Society of Scotland, Royal Institution of Chartered Surveyors, the Chartered Institute of Arbitrators (Arbiters in Scotland) and various university and college courses on subjects relating to building and civil engineering disputes and arbitration; arbiter on the panel of the Law Society of Scotland's arbitration appointment scheme; member Scottish Council for Arbitration and of the Law

Society of Scotland Working Party on Arbitration; member of Bruntsfield Links Golfing Society.

Biography: lives Edinburgh; born 19.01.1944; married to Elizabeth with 4 children. Educated at George Watson's College, Edinburgh; Edinburgh University (1965 LLB).

Leisure: golf; tennis; fishing; reading (historical and literary); family pursuits.

MACKENZIE Andrew

senior Brighton partner JE DELL & LOADER 22/23 Regency Square, Brighton, East Sussex BN1 2FS.

Career: admitted (1976); assistant solicitor (1976-1979); became partner JE Dell & Loader (1979); became senior Brighton partner (1985).

Activities: various property and commercial interests.

Biography: lives Hove; born 01.09.1952; single. Educated at Brighton College; College of Law Guildford.

Leisure: motor racing; tennis; squash; classic cars.

MACKIE David

senior litigation partner London office ALLEN & OVERY 9 Cheapside, London EC2V 6AD.

Career: articled Allen & Overy (1968-1971); admitted (1971); assistant solicitor (1971-1975); became partner (1975).

Activities: assistant Recorder of the Crown Court (1988 to date); chairman International Bar Association Committee on Consumer Affairs, Advertising, Unfair Competition and Products Liability; member Roehampton.

Biography: lives London SW6; born 15.02.1946; married with 3 children. Educated at RAF School Changi, Singapore; Ardingly College, Sussex; St Edmund Hall Oxford (1967 BA) (1971 MA); College of Law London (1967-1968); author of 'Products Liability'; various articles.

Leisure: climbing.

MACLEOD D Iain

senior litigation partner SHEPHERD & WEDDERBURN WS 16 Charlotte Square, Edinburgh EH2 4YS.

Career: apprenticed Macpherson & Mackay WS (1957-1959) and Shepherd & Wedderburn WS (1959-1960); admitted (1960); assistant solicitor Shepherd &

Wedderburn WS (1960-1964); became partner (1964); became senior litigation partner (1970).

Activities: solicitor in Scotland to HM Customs & Excise and Department of Employment (1970 to date); solicitor in Scotland to Health & Safety Executive and Commission (1974 to date); Writer to the Signet; Notary Public; member Court of Session Rules Council and Rules Review Group; occasional lecturer and tutor for post-qualifying legal education programme of the Law Society of Scotland; Lt Cdr (retd) Royal Naval Reserve; Elder Church of Scotland; FIH Class 1 International Hockey Umpire; member of: Bruntsfield Links Golfing Society; RNVR Club (Scotland).

Biography: lives Edinburgh; born 19.04.1937; married to Mary with 1 son and 2 daughters. Educated at Dumfries Academy; Aberdeen Grammar School; Aberdeen University; Edinburgh University (1957 MA); (1959 LLB).

Leisure: hockey; golf.

MACROBERT David

partner MACROBERTS 152 Bath Street, Glasgow G2 4TB.

Career: apprentice Brechin Robb (1975-1977); admitted (1977); assistant solicitor family firm MacRoberts (1977-1980); became partner (1980).

Activities: senior tutor in finance and investment Glasgow University; member Revenue Committee of Law Society of Scotland; governor of Glenalmond; treasurer Old Glenmond Club; member of: Royal Gourock Yacht Club; Western Club; Royal Western Yacht Club; Royal Scottish Automobile Club.

Biography: lives Glasgow; born 27.09.1953; single. Educated at Dardene; Craigflower; Glenalmond; Dundee University (1975 LLB).

Leisure: shooting; sailing; skiing.

MACWILKINSON Jeffrey

litigation partner DOLMANS 17/19 Windsor Place, Cardiff CF1 4PA.

Career: articled Derek Hugh-Jones (1960-1965); admitted (1966); assistant solicitor (1966-1968); assistant solicitor Francis Ryan & Co (1968-1970); became partner (1970-1972); became litigation partner Dolmans (1972).

Activities: chairman Social Security Appeals Tribunal (1986 to date); Associate of Institute of Arbitrators; member of:

Radyr Golf Club; Radyr Tennis Club.

Biography: lives Cardiff; born 10.09.1942; married to Josephine. Educated at Penarth Grammar School.

Leisure: golf; tennis; Rotary.

MADDOX Simon

Chief Executive LAWNET GROUP Centre City Tower, 7 Hill Street, Birmingham B5 4UU.

Career: articled Rawlins Davy & Wells (1960-1965); admitted (1965); assistant solicitor and partner Tompkins & Co (1965-1967); founded own practice (1967); merged with Restall Round & Gloster to become Rees Edwards Maddox & Co (1969); became senior partner (1981); became consultant (1989).

Activities: non-executive director Labinah Management Training Limited (Time Manager International) (1978); established Solicitors Central Services Limited (1985); director Corbrook Court PLC (1986); director Business Training for Education Limited (1988); director Central Law Training Limited (1988).

Biography: lives Warwick; born 18.09.1942; married to Jane with 7 children. Educated at Forres School, Swanage; Canford School, Wimborne; author of 'The College Company' (1987).

Leisure: gardening; golf; family activities.

MADGE Nic

partner BINDMAN AND PARTNERS 1 Euston Road, London NW1 2SA.

Career: admitted (1978); solicitor Camden Community Law Centre (1978-1983); assistant solicitor Nash & Dowell (1984-1985); assistant solicitor Bindman and Partners (1985-1986); became partner (1986).

Activities: helped set up duty solicitor scheme for private tenants at Bloomsbury County Court; Deputy County Court and District Registrar; member Law Society Housing Working Party; founder member Housing Law Practitioners' Association Area 1 Legal Aid Committee; frequent lecturer on housing law.

Biography: lives London; born 14.05.1953; married with 2 children. Educated at Cannock Grammar School; St Catharine's College Cambridge (1974 MA); co-author of Legal Action Group's 'Defending Possession Proceedings'; contributed chapters on rent regulation in 2 books entitled 'Tribunals Practice and Procedure'; regular writer on housing law in Law

Society's Gazette, New Law Journal and Legal Action including quarterly 'Recent Developments in Housing Law' in Legal Action.

Leisure: walking; cycling; travel; family history.

MAHER Frank

partner WEIGHTMAN RUTHERFORDS Richmond House, 1 Rumford Place, Liverpool L3 9QW.

Career: articled Weightmans (1981-1983); admitted (1983); assistant solicitor (1983-1985); became partner (1985).

Activities: clerk to Great Altcar Parish Council (1983-1988); former member Professional & Public Relations Committee of the Law Society; former secretary Liverpool Law Society Professional & Public Relations Committee; member National Committee Young Solicitors Group (1985 to date) (former sub-committee chairman) (vice-chairman 1990-1991); committee member Liverpool Young Solicitors Group (1984 to date) (former secretary) (chairman 1990-1991); member Law Society Civil Litigation Committee (1987 to date) and Council Membership Committee (1990 to date); member Liverpool Law Society Contentious Business Committee and Future Planning Committee; member Liverpool Racquet Club.

Biography: lives Chester; born 01.01.1959; married to Marion. Educated at Liverpool University (1980 LLB); College of Law Christleton (1980-1981); Liverpool Law Society Prizewinner; articles in Law Society's Gazette & Solicitors Journal.

Leisure: fell walking; music; swimming.

MAHONEY Tony

partner, deputy managing partner and head of commercial and industrial department WINTER-TAYLORS Park House, London Road, High Wycombe, Bucks HP11 1BZ.

Career: articled Winter-Taylors; admitted; became partner .

Biography: lives High Wycombe; born 29.05.1942; married with 2 children. Educated at High Wycombe Royal Grammar School; Bristol University (LLB hons).

Leisure: general interest in youth activities including governorship of schools.

MAITLAND-WALKER Julian

partner with responsibility for EEC & competition law CHARLES RUSSELL Hale Court, Lincoln's Inn, London WC2A 3UL and at Killowen House, Bayshill Road, Cheltenham GL50 3AW.

Career: articled Clifford Turner; admitted (1974); assistant solicitor London and Brussels (1974-1978); became partner Brussels (1978-1980); became partner Risdons (1980-1989); became partner Charles Russell (1990).

Activities: county councillor for Somerset (1985 to date); chairman South Western Milk & Dairies Tribunal (1985 to date); chairman Performance Review & Special Purposes Committee Somerset County Council (1989); vice-chairman Environment Sub-committee Somerset County Council (1989); member Management Committee Centre for European Legal Studies Faculty of Law Exeter University (1980 to date); Policy and Resources Somerset County Council (1989); Finance Somerset County Council (1989).

Biography: lives Minehead; born 07.08.1949; married with 2 children. Educated at West Somerset School (1960-1967); Atlantic College (1966-1967); College of Law Guildford (1969-1971); author of: 'EEC Competition Law' (1978); 'International Anti Trust Law' (1984); 'Towards 1992 - The development of International Anti Trust' (1990); editor European Competition Law Review (1980 to date); editor 'European Business Lawyer' (1990).

Leisure: reading; opera; tennis; squash; cricket.

MALLOWS Richard

partner MCKENNA & CO Mitre House, 160 Aldersgate Street, London EC1A 4DD.

Career: articled Lovell White & King (1961-1964); admitted (1965); assistant solicitor McKenna & Co (1964-1971); became partner (1971).

Activities: member London Legal Education Committee.

Biography: born 11.12.1939. Educated at KCS Wimbledon; Magdalen College Oxford (1961 BA); contributor to the Intellectual Property section of 'Longman Commercial Precedents'; articles in 'Business Law Review' and other journals; editor of McKenna Law Letters.

MALONEY Tim

partner JAQUES & LEWIS 2 South Square, Gray's Inn, London WC1R 5HR.

M

M

Career: articled Lawford & Co (1973-1975); admitted (1975); assistant solicitor Lewis & Lewis (1975-1979); became partner (1979); firm merged with Jaques & Co (1982).

Activities: member of: St James's Club; Wig & Pen Club.

Biography: lives Surrey; born 02.01.1951; married with 2 children. Educated at Colfes Grammar School; Exeter University (1972 LLB hons).

Leisure: golf; squash; windsurfing.

MALSTER Simon

partner in charge of overseas property OSBORNES 93 Parkway, London NW1 7PP.

Career: became partner Osbornes (1981); started properties abroad department (1985).

Biography: lives London; born 15.10.1954; married to Joanne. Educated at St Alban's School; Kent University.

MALTHOUSE RH (Dick)

senior partner MCKENNA & CO Mitre House, 160 Aldersgate Street, London EC1A 4DD.

Career: articled McKenna & Co (1954-1957); admitted (1957); assistant solicitor (1957-1961); became partner (1961).

Activities: member of: Brooks's Club; City of London Club; Rosslyn Park RFC; Effingham GC.

Biography: lives East Horsley; born 21.09.1931; married to Jean with 4 children. Educated at Uppingham School; Pembroke College Cambridge (1954 BA hons); John Mackrell Prize.

Leisure: rugby football; golf; gardening; sailing; travel.

MANCHES Louis

partner and head of commercial property department MANCHES & CO Aldwych House, Aldwych, London WC2B 4RP.

Career: articled Manches & Co (1976-1978); admitted (1979); assistant solicitor (1979-1981); became partner (1981); chairman Computer Committee.

Activities: director Baillie Longstaff Ltd; trustee Peper Harrow Therapeutic Community; lectures to professional bodies; member of: MCC; Queen's Club; Roehampton Club; RAC.

Biography: lives Pyrford; born 15.04.1954; married to Corinne with 3 children. Educated at Highgate School; St John's

College Oxford (1975 BA) (1978 MA); College of Law Chester (hons).

Leisure: tennis; skiing; watching cricket and football; reading; cinema; bridge; travel.

MANNING Lawrence

partner in charge London office JONES DAY REAVIS & POGUE 1 Mount Street, London W1Y 5AA.

Career: law clerk US Court of Appeals, Fourth Circuit; Jones Day Reavis & Pogue (1969).

Activities: member of: Chevy Chase Club, Maryland; Cumberland Lawn Tennis Club.

Biography: lives London W9; born 27.04.1943; married to Diane with 1 child. Educated at Washington & Lee University; Virginia University School of Law (1968 JD).

Leisure: travel; tennis.

MANNO Christopher E

senior resident partner WILLKIE FARR & GALLAGHER Dauntsey House, 4B Frederick's Place, London EC2R 8AB.

Career: admitted New York (1979); assistant solicitor Willkie Farr & Gallagher, New York (1979-1983); Paris office (1983-1986); partner (1988); became resident partner London office (1988).

Activities: speaker/panellist at Mergers & Acquisitions magazine annual conferences England (1988) and Switzerland (1990); member Ward of Cheap Club.

Biography: lives London; born 22.11.1954; married. Educated at Colgate University, New York (1976 BA); St John's University School of Law, New York (1979 JD hons); St Thomas More Academic Scholarship; various articles in St John's Law Review; author of 'Doing Business in Europe' (1990, NY State Bar Association); contributing editor to 'Guide to Acquisitions in the US' (1989 Butterworths).

Leisure: guitar; skiing; literature; world travel; language.

MANSFIELD Michael

Queen's Counsel and head of chambers 14 Tooks Court, Cursitor Street, London EC4.

Career: called to the Bar (1967); founded Chambers (1984); QC (1989).

Activities: member Executive Committee of Criminal Bar Association; vice-chair Labour Campaign for Criminal Justice;

founder member Tottenham Neighbourhood Law Centre and Interights; chair Jacksons Lane Community Centre and ARC 73 (1970s); projects for : Haldane Society; NCCL and LAG; hon member NUM; governor Highgate Wood School (1980s); contributor and presenter to: BBC Open Space Series 'Advocacy' (1985); LWT 'The Hollis Trial' (1988); appearances in Panorama; Newsnight; Channel 4 film 'Battle for Orgreave' (1986); member Amnesty.

Biography: lives London; born 12.10.1941; lives with Yvette Vanson; 6 children. Educated at Holmewood Prep School; Highgate School; Keele University (1964 BA hons); Holken Exhibitioner Gray's Inn (1968); former columnist on drugs law for periodical; former legal consultant for historian/author.

Leisure: children; sport; jazz drumming and listening.

MARCO Alan

head of matrimonial department BAILEYS SHAW & GILLETT 17 Queen Square, London WC1N 3RH.

Career: articled in Holborn; admitted (1965); assistant solicitor (1965-1967); became salaried partner small West End firm (1967-1972); became litigation partner Baileys Shaw & Gillett (1972).

Activities: former hon legal advisor to North Kensington Citizens Advice Bureau.

Biography: lives Edgware; born 09.11.1939; married to Gail with 3 children. Educated at Christ's College, Finchley; London School of Economics (1961 LLB hons).

Leisure: watching old westerns on TV; jogging; sunbathing; non-league football; Al Bowley and 30s swing music.

MARCUS Hans Herbert

partner PRITCHARD ENGLEFIELD & TOBIN 23 Great Castle Street, London W1N 8NQ.

Career: articled Markby Steward & Wadeson; admitted; assistant solicitor William James Fullerton (1948); became partner Cardew-Smith & Ross; firm amalgamated with Pritchard Englefield Leader Henderson (1970).

Activities: Commissioner for Oaths; hon treasurer to the Grosvenor Belgravia Residents' Association; vice-president Associazione Giuristi di Lingua Italiana of Milan, Italy which represents Anglo-Italian legal interests; member of: Garrick Club; RAC.

Biography: lives London SW7; born 18.07.1921; married to Josephine. 2 sons. Educated at Hansa Schule, Humanistisches Gymnasium, Hamburg; Rugby School; Manchester University (hons); Grotius Prize for International law; various articles on the law; contribution to German property law in Germany relating to English law.

Leisure: reading; theatre; swimming.

MARGERISON J Peter

senior partner property department HEPWORTH & CHADWICK Cloth Hall Court, Infirmary Street, Leeds LS1 2JB.

Career: articled in Leeds; admitted (1960); assistant solicitor (1960-1963); assistant solicitor Hepworth & Chadwick (1963-1967); became partner (1967).

Biography: lives Harrogate; born 05.04.1938; married with 2 children. Educated at Woodhouse Grove School, Bradford; Leeds University (1958 LLB).

Leisure: various forms of relaxation.

MARKHAM Francis

partner ROWE & MAW 20 Black Friars Lane, London EC4V 6HD.

Career: articled Rowe & Maw; admitted (1965); assistant solicitor (1965-1967); became partner (1967); specialises in property law.

Activities: member of: Athenaeum Club; Holland Park Tennis Club; Horatian Society; secretary of Amicable Society of St Clement Danes.

Biography: lives London W4; born 24.05.1937; married to Diana. Educated at Eton; King's College Cambridge (1961 hons); (MA).

MARKS Nathan

managing partner KUIT STEINART LEVY & CO 3 St Mary's Parsonage, Manchester M3 2RD.

Career: articled David Blank; admitted (1956); assistant solicitor (1956-1958); assistant solicitor JM Levy & Co (1958-1959); became partner (1959); amalgamated with Kuit Steinart & Ashby (1959).

Activities: serves on Court of Manchester University; member British Airways Consumer Council; representative of Manchester Law Society on joint committee with Institute of Chartered Accountants and Manchester Institute of Taxation; founder member and former chairman Manchester Young Solicitors

Group; Council member on the Manchester Law Society Council (president 1983-1984) convener 1992 Committee.

Biography: lives Manchester; born 11.08.1932; married to Vivian with 4 children. Educated at North Manchester Grammar School; Manchester Grammar School; Manchester University (1953 LLB hons); extra-mural courses at Exeter University and Manchester University in EEC law.

Leisure: spectator and participant in sport; keen squash and tennis player; lifelong supporter Manchester City FC; bridge; communal and charitable work.

MARLOW Ed

partner corporate finance DENTON HALL BURGIN & WARRENS Five Chancery Lane, Clifford's Inn, London EC4A 1BU.

Career: articled Herbert Oppenheimer Nathan & Vandyk; admitted (1980); assistant solicitor (1980-1985); partner (1985-1987); in-house counsel Heron Corporation PLC (1987-1988); became partner Denton Hall Burgin & Warrens (1988).

Activities: member RAC Club.

Biography: lives London; born 18.12.1954; single. Educated at Haberdashers' Aske's School, Elstree; Christ's College Cambridge (1977 MA); article for Corporate Money (1989).

Leisure: tennis; snooker; swimming; cinema; theatre.

MARRIOTT David

partner and head of property department MICHAEL FREEMAN & CO One Great Cumberland Place, London W1H 7AL.

Career: articled major City firm; admitted (1972); assistant solicitor and associate; became partner Michael Freeman & Co (1978).

Biography: lives North Hertfordshire; born 05.08.1947; married to Michelle. Educated at Brentwood School, Essex; Brasenose College Oxford (1968 BA hons); minor contribution to a precedent book.

Leisure: attempting to keep a country garden tidy; various sports; music; theatre; cinema; literature.

MARRON Peter

senior partner MARRON DODDS & WAITE 31-33 Friar Lane, Leicester LE1 5RB.

Career: articled Isle of Wight County

Council (1967-1970); admitted (1970); third assistant solicitor Leicester City Council (1970-1971); second assistant solicitor (1971-1972); principal assistant solicitor (1972); assistant solicitor Gardiner & Millhouse (1972-1973); partner (1973-1978); founded own practice (1978).

Activities: executive and non-executive directorships.

Biography: lives Uppingham; born 03.06.1944; married with 3 children. Educated at St Cuthbert's Grammar School, Newcastle upon Tyne; Liverpool University (1966 LLB hons); Law Society Finals (1970 distinction).

Leisure: sailing; skiing.

MARSH Barrie

senior partner MACE & JONES 19 Water Street, Liverpool L2 0RP.

Career: articled Mace & Jones (1953); 2 years' National Service.

Activities: president Solicitors Disciplinary Tribunal; chairman Medical Appeals Tribunal; chairman Radio City PLC; chairman Chamber of Commerce (1984-1986); Belgium Consul in Liverpool; member of: Anglo-Belgian Club; Heswall Golf Club.

Biography: lives Wirral; born 18.07.1935; married with 3 children. Educated at Bury Grammar School; Loughborough Grammar School; Liverpool University (1955 LLB hons); author of 'Employer and Employee - a complete and practical guide to the Law of Employment' (1976, 1981, 1989 & 1990); numerous articles on various aspects of Employment Law.

Leisure: hill walking (trying to climb all the Munros); golf; bird watching; music.

MARSH David

partner WRAGGE & CO Bank House, 8 Cherry Street, Birmingham B2 5JY.

Career: articled Wragge & Co (1958-1961); admitted (1961); assistant solicitor (1961-1963); became partner (1963).

Activities: director Fownes Hotels PLC; director Marla Tube Fittings Ltd; member Midland Sporting Club.

Biography: lives Evesham; born 02.11.1936; married to Hilary with 3 children. Educated at Leeds Grammar School; Merton College Oxford (MA).

Leisure: watching sport; foreign travel.

M

MARSH David

partner BURGES SALMON Narrow Quay House, Bristol BS1 4AH.

Career: articled Richards Butler (1966-1968); admitted (1968); assistant solicitor (1968-1971); assistant solicitor Burges Salmon (1971-1972); partner (1972); became managing partner (1990).

Activities: member Law Society Company Law Committee (1984-1990); council member Bristol Incorporated Law Society (1979-1984); chairman Education and Courses Committee Bristol Incorporated Law Society (1982-1984); member Clifton Club.

Biography: lives Bristol; born 12.01.1944; married to Pippa with 2 children. Educated at Bristol Grammar School (1951-1955); Queen Elizabeth Grammar School, Wakefield (1955-1962); University College Oxford (1965 MA).

Leisure: music; skiing; sailing.

MARSH Paul

senior partner BELLS Eagle Chambers, 16-18 Eden Street, Kingston upon Thames, Surrey KT1 1RD.

Career: articled Bells (1970-1972); admitted (1972); assistant solicitor (1972-1973) became partner (1973).

Activities: chairman Medical Services Committee Kingston & Richmond Family Practitioner Committee; member Council of the Law Society for County of Surrey (1987 to date); member Adjudication Committee and Company Law Committee; president Mid-Surrey Law Society (1984-1985); chairman Kingston Round Table (1980-1981); member of: Vintage Sports Car Club; MG Car Club; Brooklands Society; Bentley Drivers' Club.

Biography: lives Guildford; born 06.09.1947; married to Sheila with 3 children. Educated at Raynes Park County Grammar School; Lanchester Polytechnic; College of Law Guildford.

Leisure: family; gardening; vintage cars.

MARSHALL Lawrence

partner J & F ANDERSON WS 48 Castle Street, Edinburgh EH2 3LX.

Career: apprenticed Maclay Murray & Spens WS; National Service as pilot officer RAF (1956-1958); graduate trainee ICI Paints Division; admitted (1962); assistant solicitor (1962-1966); became partner W & J Cook WS (1966-1983); became partner J & F Anderson WS (1983); specialises in trust executry and investment work and capital transfer tax planning.

Activities: clerk and treasurer Iona Cathedral Trustees; clerk and treasurer Donaldsons School for the Deaf; curator Writer to the Signet's Library; chairman Royal Victoria Hospital Tuberculosis Trust; member Edinburgh Grand Opera Co; member of: Bruntsfield Links Golfing Society; Scottish Ski Club.

Biography: lives Colinton; born 16.02.1935; married with 2 children. Educated at Strathallan School, Forgandenny; Glasgow University (1956 BL).

Leisure: golf; tennis; gardening; travelling; reading.

MARSHALL Rob

senior partner SIMPSON MILLAR 101 Borough High Street, London Bridge, London SE1 1NL.

Career: articled Stafford Clark & Co; admitted (1948); assistant solicitor (1948-1951); became partner WR Millar & Sons (now Simpson Millar) (1951).

Activities: member Council of the Law Society (1969 to date); member Land Law & Conveyancing Committee of the Law Society (chairman 5 years); member of: Savage Club; City Livery Club.

Biography: lives Godalming; born 05.10.1924; married to Jean with 2 children. Educated at Dulwich College.

Leisure: sailing; travel; classical music; reading.

MARSHALL Sir Denis

consultant BARLOW LYDE & GILBERT Beaufort House, 15 St Botolph Street, London EC3A 7NJ.

Career: articled Barlow Lyde & Gilbert (1932-1937); admitted (1937); assistant solicitor (1937-1949); (War service 1939-1946); became partner (1949-1968); became senior partner (1968-1983).

Activities: council member of the Law Society of England & Wales (1966-1986); president (1981-1982); member Royal Commission on Civil Liability (The Pearson Commission) (1973-1977); member Criminal Injuries Compensation Board; Government nominee council member Insurance Brokers' Registration Council (1979 to date); invited member Council of Fimbra (1987 to date); member Naval & Military Club.

Biography: lives Dartmouth; born 01.06.1916; married to Jane with 1 son. Educated at Dulwich College; Law Society School of Law Gibson & Weldon (1937 hons).

Leisure: sailing.

MARTELL Robert

partner BORNEO MARTELL & PARTNERS 9 Notre Dame Mews, Northampton NN1 2BG.

Career: articled Herbert & Gowers; admitted (1971); assistant solicitor (1971-1972); became partner Borneo Martell & Partners (1972).

Activities: member of: Northampton Becket Rotary; Overstone Squash Club.

Biography: lives Northampton; born 29.08.1945; married to Julie with 2 children. Educated at Bedford School.

Leisure: squash; skiing.

MARTIN Barrie

senior partner JM RIX AND KAY 84 High Street, Heathfield, East Sussex TN21 8JG.

Career: articled Sir Charles Russell Bart (1965-1968); admitted (1968); assistant solicitor (1968-1970); became partner (1971-1973); assistant solicitor Sprott & Sons (1973-1976); became partner JM Rix and Kay (1976); became senior partner (1985).

Activities: member The Sloane Club.

Biography: lives Rotherfield; born 18.08.1941; single. Educated at St John's Beaumont Preparatory School; Beaumont; Trinity College Dublin (1965 BA LLB).

Leisure: tennis; travel.

MARTIN Christopher

senior partner CHAMBERLAIN MARTIN & SPURGEON 42 Sudley Road, Bognor Regis, West Sussex PO21 1ES.

Career: articled to father Reginald Martin (1960-1964); admitted (1964); became senior partner (1982).

Activities: president Chichester and District Law Society (1985); (committee member) (former chairman Press and Publicity Committee); clerk Middleton-on-Sea Parish Council (1982 to date); member Lord's Taverners; chairman West Sussex Region; former chairman Middleton Sports Club; committee member Bognor Regis Golf Club (captain 1971); member Bognor Regis Rotary Club.

Biography: lives Middleton-on-Sea; born 21.12.1940; married with 1 son and 1 daughter. Educated at Etonhurst Prep School, Bognor Regis (1947-1954); Lancing College (1954-1959).

Leisure: golf.

MARTIN Peter

partner and head of aviation department FRERE CHOLMELEY 28 Lincoln's Inn Fields, London WC2A 3HH.

Career: admitted (1959); assistant solicitor (1959-1962); became partner Beaumont and Son (1962-1981); became partner Frere Cholmeley (1981).

Activities: Fellow Royal Aeronautical Society; clerk to HM Commission of Lieutenancy for the City of London; visiting professor of Aerospace at University College London.

Biography: lives London; born 09.05.1934; editor Shawcross & Beaumont Air Law; Halsbury's Laws of England 'Aviation'.

MARTIN Tony

senior partner MARTIN TOLHURST PARTNERSHIP 7 Wrotham Road, Gravesend, Kent DA11 0PD.

Career: demobilised from Royal Air Force (1947); articled family firm (1947-1950); admitted (1950); assistant solicitor (1950-1956); became partner (1956).

Activities: past president Kent Law Society; member Rotary Club of Gravesend.

Biography: lives Shorne; born 15.05.1925; married to Valerie with 2 children. Educated at King's School, Rochester; Gravesend Grammar School for Boys.

Leisure: gardening.

MARTIN ALEGI Lynda

partner and head of EEC group in London BAKER & MCKENZIE Aldwych House, Aldwych, London WC2B 4JP.

Career: articled Baker & McKenzie (1975-1977); admitted (1977); assistant solicitor (1977-1981); Brussels office (1979); became partner (1981); member firm's 1992 Task Force.

Activities: member competition panel Confederation of British Industry; member Advisory Committee - MCE 1990 International Company Lawyers' Conference.

Biography: lives London EC2; born 07.03.1952; married to Peter. Educated at Woodford County High School; Newnham College Cambridge (1973 BA) (1975 MA); Institute of European Studies of the Free University of Brussels (1975 MA); various articles on EEC competition law.

Leisure: food; wine.

MARTIN-KAYE Neil

senior partner MARTIN-KAYE & PARTNERS Hazledine House, Town Centre, Telford, Shropshire.

Career: National Service in Malaya during emergency with 1st Royal West Kent Regt (1952-1954); articled Pickard & Co and Royds Rawstorne & Co (1955-1960); admitted (1960); assistant solicitor Markbys (1961-1962); assistant legal adviser Esso Petroleum Co Ltd (1963-1966); assistant secretary and legal adviser BTR Industries Ltd (1966-1969); assistant legal adviser and secretary Conoco Europe Ltd (1969-1971); international patent and legal dept AMP Incorporated (1971-1974); director Participation Consultants Ltd (1974); company lawyer Amersham International Ltd (1975-1981); chief legal adviser to Michelin Tyre Co PLC (1982); founded own practice (1983).

Activities: convenor and founder member Ealing Civic Society; founder member and on steering committee of Ealing Arts Council; Liberal Parliamentary Candidate Acton (1964); Ealing S (1966); various activities and roles with Liberal Party (now ceased membership); chairman Action Committee at Amersham to save nursery school; director of Chalfont Nurses Ltd (1973-1982); involved with IAG International (international association of independent professional advisers); active on computer software; member Licensing Executive Society and International Bar Association .

Biography: lives Market Drayton; born 20.06.1934; married with 2 daughters. Educated at Highgate School; author of article 'The Theoretical Basis of Modern Company Law' in the Journal of Business Law (1976).

Leisure: opera; music; politics.

MARTYN Philip

joint general manager and chief legal adviser THE SUMITOMO BANK LIMITED Temple Court, 11 Queen Victoria Street, London EC4N 4TA.

Career: articled Coward Chance (1970-1972); admitted; assistant solicitor (1972-1977); assistant solicitor Clifford Turner (1977-1979); Sumitomo Bank Limited (1979).

Activities: trustee North and South London Waldorf Schools; director Mercury Provident PLC (green bank) .

Biography: lives London SW19; born 17.07.1948; single. Educated at St Dunstan's College, London; Exeter University (1969 LLB).

Leisure: miscellaneous green and new-age involvements based on philosophy of Rudolf Steiner; gardening; pre-history; psychology.

MASKELL John

partner NORTON ROSE Kempson House, PO Box 570, Camomile Street, London EC3A 7AN.

Career: articled Norton Rose Botterell-Roche (1964-1966); admitted (1966); assistant solicitor (1966-1971); became partner (1971).

Activities: chairman London Maritime Arbitrators' Association Supporting Members' Committee (1980-1984); associate member MCC; president Aldgate Ward Club (1986-1987); member British Maritime Law Association.

Biography: lives Witham; born 26.03.1942; widowed and divorced with 2 children. Educated at Winchester (1955-1960); Peterhouse Cambridge (1963 BA); (1964 LLB); (1967 MA); author of: 'Interest & Costs in Arbitration' in The Arbitrator; 'Disaster Litigation' in International Financial Law Review.

Leisure: travel; music; bridge; good wine.

MASON Donald

partner ALSOP WILKINSON 290 India Buildings, Liverpool L2 0NH.

Career: articled Batesons & Co (1960-1963); admitted (1963); assistant solicitor (1963-1967); became partner (1967); merged with Alsop Stevens (1967); merged with Wilkinson Kimber (1988).

Activities: chairman Liverpool School of Tropical Medicine; member Lyceum Club.

Biography: lives Wirral; born 25.06.1938; married to Joyce with 2 children. Educated at Ruthin School, North Wales; Fitzwilliam College Cambridge (1960 MA LLM).

MATHER Christopher

partner WARNER GOODMAN & STREAT 14-16 Portland Terrace, Southampton SO9 4ZQ.

Career: articled in Leeds; admitted (1973); assistant solicitor in Wareham and Bournemouth; became partner Warner Goodman & Streat (1978).

Activities: deputy district registrar/registrar (1989); member South Hampshire & Isle of Wight Valuation Panel; chairman Solicitors group acting for the victims of the Clapham rail disaster;

M

chairman Hursley Pony Club.

Biography: lives Romsey; born 20.06.1947; married to Pauline with 2 children. Educated at Ellesmere College, Shropshire.

Leisure: general rural pursuits.

MATHEW John

Queen's Counsel 5 Paper Buildings, Temple, London EC4.

Career: Royal Navy; called to the Bar Lincoln's Inn (1949); Junior Prosecuting Counsel to the Crown Central Criminal Court (1949); Senior Prosecuting Counsel (1964 & 1974); Bencher Lincoln's Inn (1970); QC (1977).

Activities: former member Bar Council; former Committee member Criminal Bar Association; appeal steward British Boxing Board of Control; non-executive director Wilton Group; member Garrick.

Biography: lives London; born 03.05.1927; married to Jane with 2 children. Educated at Beaumont College.

Leisure: golf; tennis; bridge; backgammon.

MATHEWS Michael

partner CLIFFORD CHANCE Royex House, Aldermanbury Square, London EC2V 7LD.

Career: articled Coward Chance (1963-1966); admitted (1966); assistant solicitor (1966-1971); became partner (1971); became partner Clifford Chance on merger of Coward Chance and Clifford-Turner (1987).

Activities: member committee of the City of London Law Society.

Biography: lives London SW14; born 03.11.1941; married to Ann with 2 sons and 1 daughter. Educated at Uppingham School; King's College Cambridge (1963 BA) (MA).

Leisure: walking; watching good cricket.

MAULEVERER Bruce

Queen's Counsel 4 Pump Court, Temple, London EC4Y 7AN.

Career: called to the Bar (1969); QC (1985); Recorder Crown Court (1985).

Activities: hon sec general International Law Association (1986).

Biography: lives London SE3; born 22.11.1946; married to Sara with 4 children. Educated at Sherborne; Durham University (BA).

Leisure: sailing; skiing.

MAUNDER Ben

partner and head local residential conveyancing team FLADGATE FIELDER Walgate House, 25 Church Street, Basingstoke RG21 1QQ.

Career: articled Bradly Trimmer (1961-1966); admitted (1966); assistant solicitor (1966-1970); became partner (1970); firm became part of Fladgate Fielder (1988).

Biography: lives near Basingstoke; married to Shirley. Educated at Queen Mary's Grammar School, Basingstoke.

Leisure: gardening; opera; cinema; theatre; interest in agriculture.

MAUNSELL Michael

partner LOVELL WHITE DURRANT 65 Holborn Viaduct, London EC1A 2DY.

Career: articled Lovell White & King (1965-1967); admitted (1967); assistant solicitor (1967-1971); became partner (1971); administration partner (1978-1983).

Activities: chairman Education & Training Sub-committee of City of London Law Society.

Biography: lives London N1; born 29.01.1942; married to Harriet. Educated at Monkton Combe School (1955-1960); Gonville and Caius College Cambridge (1963 BA MA) (1964 LLB LLM).

Leisure: photography; travel; exercise!.

MAX Michael Geoffrey

partner property development TITMUSS SAINER & WEBB 2 Serjeants' Inn, London EC4Y 1LT.

Career: articled SA Bailey & Co (1950-1955); admitted (1955); assistant solicitor (1957-1959); partner (1959-1963); National Service (1955-1957); assistant solicitor Titmuss Sainer & Webb (1963-1965); became partner (1965).

Activities: councillor London Borough of Barnet (1978-1986); chairman Hampstead Garden Suburb Institute; governor Henrietta Barnett School; member variety of model railway clubs.

Biography: lives London; born 04.03.1933; married to Wendy with 4 children. Educated at Haberdashers' Aske's (1943-1950); University College London (LLB).

Leisure: music; railways; model railways; gardening; walking; skiing.

MAXLOW-TOMLINSON Paul Christian

managing partner STONES Northernhay Place, Exeter EX4 3QQ.

Career: National Service commissioned with Queen's Royal West Surrey Regiment; Army PT course; Army boxing judge; Army basketball referee (1950-1952); graduate trainee Turner & Newall Salisbury, Rhodesia (1956-1958); branch manager Mercantile Credit Corporation, Bulawayo (1958-1962); Mercantile Credit Co, London (1962); branch manager Belfast, Portadown and Coleraine (1963); represented Ski Club of Great Britain in Lenzerheide and Cortina (1964); American Grand Circle Travel Co (1965-1967); articled Veitch & Co (1968-1971); admitted (1971); assistant solicitor Ford Simey and Ford (1971-1972); assistant solicitor Stones (1972); partner (1974); became managing partner (1985).

Activities: served with British South African Police as Special Reserve especially during riots of (1958-1962); Rhodesian National Basketball Selector; chairman Referees' Association in Basketball of Bulawayo; founder member and chairman The Oakfields Project (a NACRO hostel complex for ex-prisoners in Exeter (1976-1983); council member Ski Club of Great Britain (1978-1982) (chairman 1982-1987); director of British Ski Federation (1982-1987); coopted member Devon Probation Committee (1983-1986); executive council of British Academy of Forensic Sciences (1987-1990); British representative Legal Committee of Federation Internationale de Ski (FIS) (1988 to date); member of Judges Commission FIS (1989 to date); leading authority on skiing law.

Biography: lives Exeter; born 24.10.1931; 1 son and 1 daughter. Educated at Cranleigh School; Barclays Bank Scholar; Trinity College Dublin (1952); Wadham College Oxford (1953-1956); President University Judo Team (1955 and 1956); University Ski Team; various articles in the Law Society's Gazette on skiing and the law and comparative skiing law; articles on skiing law in national newspapers.

Leisure: skiing; fishing; shooting; tennis.

MAY Anthony

barrister 10 Essex Street, London WC2R 3AA.

Career: called to the Bar Inner Temple (1967); QC (1979); Recorder of the Crown Court (1985); master of the Bench of Inner Temple (1985); mixed general litigation (1967-1972); specialising as Counsel in Court and Arbitration in British and international construction contract and commercial cases in Britain, Middle East and Far East (1972 to date).

Activities: vice-chairman Official Referees'
Bar Association; chairman Guildford
Choral Society.

Biography: lives Guildford; born
09.09.1940; married to Stella with 3
children. Educated at Bradfield College
(1954-1959) Senior Scholar; Worcester
College Oxford (1960-1964); Trevelyan
Scholar (1960); First Class in Classical
Honour Moderations (1962); hon College
Scholar (1962); Second Class in Literae
Humaniores (1964); Inner Temple Major
Scholar (1965).

Leisure: music; books; gardening; bonfires.

MAY Stuart

senior partner THEODORE GODDARD
150 Aldersgate Street, London EC1A 4EJ.

Career: articled Theodore Goddard (1961);
admitted (1964); assistant solicitor (1964-
1970); became partner (1970); became
senior partner (1989).

Biography: lives near Cambridge; born
05.04.1937; married to Sarah with 4
children. Educated at Taunton School;
Wadham College Oxford (1961 MA).

Leisure: gardening; walking; reading.

MAY Trevor

partner and head of commercial litigation
department THOMSON SNELL &
PASSMORE Lyons, East Street, Tonbridge,
Kent TN9 1HL.

Career: articled in the City of London
(1963-1968); admitted (1968); assistant
solicitor Thomson Snell & Passmore (1968-
1971); became partner (1971).

Activities: Notary Public (1988); president
Tunbridge Wells, Tonbridge & District Law
Society (1990).

Biography: lives Tunbridge Wells; born
08.11.1945; married to Armoral with 1
child. Educated at Ilford County High
School for Boys; Alfred Syrett Prize.

Leisure: sailing; photography; reading.

MAYCOCK John

head of intellectual property department
CROSSMAN BLOCK 199 Strand, London
WC2R 1DR.

Career: articled Crossman Block & Keith
(1966-1969); admitted (1970); Paris office of
Hughes Hubbard & Reed, New York and
Societe d'Avocats P Chardenon & de
Mourzitch, Paris (1970-1972); became
partner Crossman Block & Keith (1971);
became managing partner (1986-1987).

Activities: member City of Westminster
Law Society Committee (1975-1981 & 1982
to date) (chairman Ethics & Guidance sub-
committee 1986-1987); member
International Young Lawyers' Association
Executive Committee (1973-1977 & 1978-
1987); (UK vice-president 1977-1980); (hon
auditor 1975-1990); president Law Courses
Commission (1981-1987); governor local
pre-prep school; member Hurlingham
Club.

Biography: lives Surrey; born 17.02.1945;
married with 3 sons. Educated at The
King's School, Canterbury; Gonville and
Caius College Cambridge (MA LLM);
Rebecca Flower Squire Scholarship (1963);
miscellaneous articles in legal journals;
editor 'Lectures on English Commercial
Law' (1983).

Leisure: cellist with local orchestra; veteran
sculling.

MAYER Stephen David

partner and head of the commercial
litigation department REYNOLDS
PORTER CHAMBERLAIN 278/282 High
Holborn, London WC1V 7HA.

Career: articled Reynolds Porter & Co;
admitted (1974); assistant solicitor (1974-
1977); became partner Reynolds Porter
Chamberlain (1977); work specialisation:
intellectual property; employment law;
competition law and general commercial
litigation.

Biography: lives Chalfont St Giles; born
12.03.1949; married to Elaine with 3
children. Educated at St Paul's School,
London; Oriel College Oxford (1971 MA
hons).

Leisure: sport (particularly tennis and
watching association football); music;
theatre; current affairs.

MAYOR Hugh

Queen's Counsel 2 Dr Johnson's Buildings,
Temple, London EC4Y 7AY.

Career: lecturer in economics Leicester
University (1964-1968); called to the Bar
Gray's Inn (1968); Recorder of the Crown
Court (1982); QC (1986); member Midland
and Oxford Circuit common law practice.

Activities: Assistant Commissioner to the
Parliamentary and European Assembly
Boundary Commission (1979-1984).

Biography: lives East Leicestershire; born
12.10.1941; married to Carolyn with 2
children. Educated at Kirkham Grammar
School; St John's College Oxford (1964 BA
Cert of Statistics) (1968 MA); Leicester

University (1967 MA).

Leisure: sailing; gardening; history.

McARDLE Brian Thomas

Chief Crown Prosecutor for Inner London
24th Floor, Portland House, Stag Place,
London SW1E 5BH.

Career: articled Shacklocks & Aston Hill
(1971-1973); part-time lecturer at
Clarendon College of FE (1971-1972);
admitted (1973); assistant solicitor
Molineux McKeag & Cooper (1973-1974);
prosecuting solicitor Northumbria Police
Authority (1974-1977); prosecuting solicitor
West Midlands County Council (1977-
1986); Branch Crown Prosecutor Inner
London (1986-1987); became Chief Crown
Prosecutor (1987).

Biography: lives Hertfordshire; born
31.01.1948; married to Alison. Educated at
St Mary's, Darlington; Newcastle
University (1970 LLB hons).

Leisure: skiing; photography; classical
music; watching cricket.

McCALL Christopher

Queen's Counsel 7 New Square, Lincoln's
Inn, London WC2A 3QS.

Career: called to the Bar Lincoln's Inn
(1966); pupillage with John Bradburn and
JE Vinelott; practice at Chancery Bar (1967);
QC (1987).

Activities: junior counsel to Attorney
General in Charity Matters (1981-1987);
second junior counsel to Inland Revenue in
Chancery Matters (1977-1987); member Bar
Council (1973-1976); chairman Young
Barristers' Committee (1976); member
Committee of Management Barristers'
Benevolent Association (1977-1986) (joint
hon treasurer 1981-1986); member of: RAC;
Leander Club; Climbers Club.

Biography: lives London N1; born
03.03.1944; married to Henrietta. Educated
at Winchester College (Scholar); Magdalen
College Oxford (1964 BA hons); Eldon Law
Scholar (1966); has contributed to
periodicals.

Leisure: mountain walking; music;
photography.

McCALL John

partner FRESHFIELDS Whitefriars,
65 Fleet Street, London EC4Y 1HT.

Career: articled local government
(Southampton) (1957-1961); admitted
(1962); assistant solicitor Freshfields (1962-
1969); became partner (1969); seconded to

M

run legal department British National Oil Corporation (1976-1979); senior resident partner New York (1983-1987).

Activities: worked extensively for Eurotunnel project and its financing (1987-1988); council member International Bar Association (chairman section on energy and natural resources law 1988-1990); member organising committee of IBA energy seminars (1978 to date); member Racquet and Tennis Club, New York.

Biography: lives London and Surrey; born 28.07.1938; married to Anne with 3 children. Educated at Winchester College; delivered papers at IBA energy law seminars (1981 & 1982); numerous chairings of topics at IBA conferences.

Leisure: real tennis; road running; sea birds.

McCARTHY David

partner company department and capital markets CLIFFORD CHANCE Royex House, Aldermanbury Square, London EC2V 7LD.

Career: articled Wragge & Co; admitted (1968); assistant solicitor Coward Chance (1976-1978); became partner (1978); became partner Clifford Chance (1986).

Activities: member City of London Company Law sub-committee; director St George's Hill Residents' Association Limited; member of: Richmond Cricket Club; St George's Hill Tennis Club; Loch Achonachie Angling Club.

Biography: lives Weybridge; born 27.01.1942; 2 sons. Educated at Ratcliffe College, Leicestershire; Birmingham University (LLB hons).

Leisure: cricket; tennis; fly fishing; reading; anything Italian.

McCAW Robert

partner WILDE SAPTE Queensbridge House, 60 Upper Thames Street, London EC4V 3BD.

Career: articled Guscotte Fowler & Cox (1962-1965); admitted (1966); assistant solicitor Linklaters & Paines (1965-1969); group secretary and legal adviser and director of subsidiary of the Brocks Group of Companies Ltd (1969-1971); assistant solicitor Wilde Sapte (1971); became partner (1971); opened firm's New York office (1976-1978).

Activities: licensed as legal consultant by the appellate division of the Supreme Court of New York; member of: Cannons Sports Club; Woodford Wells Club squash

and tennis sections.

Biography: lives London E4; born 21.12.1941; divorced with 2 sons. Educated at Solihull School; Collyers School, Horsham; University of Exeter (1962 LLB) .

Leisure: squash; tennis; golf; jogging.

McCORMICK Peter

senior and managing partner MCCORMICKS Oxford House, Oxford Row, Leeds LS1 3BE.

Career: articled J Levi & Co (1974-1976); admitted (1976); assistant solicitor (1976-1978); became partner (1978-1983); founded own practice (1983).

Activities: president of the Law Society at King's College (1971-1972); resident legal expert BBC Radio Leeds (1988 to date); chairman Chequerway Ltd; member of the Judicial Studies Board, Leeds University; member Wig & Pen Club.

Biography: lives Kirkby; born 27.06.1952; married to Kathryn with 1 son and 1 daughter. Educated at Clifton House Preparatory School, Harrogate (1958-1963); Ashville College, Harrogate (1963-1969); King's College London (1973 LLB); College of Law Chester (1976 hons).

Leisure: football; travel; theatre; music.

McDONNELL John

Queen's Counsel 1 New Square, Lincoln's Inn, London WC2A 3SA.

Career: Conservative research department (1966-1969); HM Diplomatic Service (1969-1971); 1st Secretary Assistant Private Secretary to Secretary of State; called to the Bar Inner Temple (1968); pupillage with Sir Peter Gibson and Mr Justice Waite (1971-1972); Assistant Recorder; QC.

Biography: lives London SW3; born 26.12.1940; married to Susan with 3 children. Educated at City of London School; Balliol College Oxford (1962 BA) (1964 MA); Harvard Law School (1965 LLM); Harkness Fellowship (1964-1966); American Political Science Association Congressional Fellowship (1965-1966).

Leisure: sculling.

McEVOY David

Queen's Counsel 2 Fountain Court, Steelhouse Lane, Birmingham.

Career: National Service with Black Watch in Cyprus; pupillage with Hon Mr Justice Drake DFC; Birmingham Chambers (1965); Recorder (1979); QC (1983).

Activities: member of: Caledonian Club; Blackwell Golf Club.

Biography: lives Longdon nr Tewkesbury; born 25.06.1938; married with 3 daughters. Educated at Mount St Mary's College; Lincoln College Oxford (1962 hons); College of Law (1962-1963).

Leisure: family; fishing; golf; tennis.

McFADDEN John H

partner PEPPER HAMILTON & SCHEETZ City Tower, 40 Basinghall Street, London EC2V 5DE (head office, Philadelphia, PA, USA).

Career: New York City Department of Correction (1973-1978); admitted New York (1979); associate Sidley & Austin, London (1978-1984); became partner Pepper Hamilton & Scheetz (1984).

Activities: director various companies in US and UK; member of: RAC; Piping Rock Club, Philadelphia Club.

Biography: lives London NW1; born 22.03.1947; married to Deirdre with 3 children. Educated at St Paul's School, Concord, New Hampshire; Harvard College (1970 BA); Columbia University (1973 MBA); Fordham University (1978 JD).

Leisure: family; travel.

McFARLANE Gavin

member taxation unit TITMUSS SAINER & WEBB 2 Serjeants' Inn, London EC4Y 1LT.

Career: National Service with 2nd Royal Tank Regiment (trooper) (1955-1957) (BAOR hockey XI (1956); called to the Bar Middle Temple (1962); pupillage with Sir James Miskin QC and HH Judge Bruce Campbell QC (1962-1963); practised at Bar (1962-1966); legal adviser International Computers Ltd (1966-1968); legal adviser IFPI (1968-1970); legal adviser Performing Right Society (1970-1972); senior legal assistant HM Customs and Excise (1975-1981); Assistant Solicitor HM Customs and Excise (1981-1989); Titmuss Sainer & Webb (1989).

Activities: British nominee to L'Ecole Nationale d'Administration, Paris (1976); member VAT Practitioners' Group (City of London Chapter); member Customs Practitioners' Group; member Institute of Export; member of: Wimbledon Hockey Club; Epsom Hockey Club; Haverfordwest Hockey Club; Surbiton Tennis Club; Haverfordwest Tennis Club; Morgan Sports Car Club; Pegasus Club; British Masters Cross-Country Ski Club.

Biography: lives London and Haverfordwest; born 18.07.1936; married to Stella with 2 sons. Educated at King's College School, Wimbledon; Sheffield University (1961 LLB hons) (1970 LLM) (secretary of the Union; chairman of debates; member University boxing team); London School of Economics (1976 PHD); Trieste University (1962 Diploma in International and Comparative Law); Brussels University (1966 Diploma in EEC law); Harmsworth Law Scholar (1962); author of: 'Copyright: The Development and Exercise of the Performing Right'; 'Metcalfe's General Principles of English Law'; 'A Practical Introduction to Copyright'; 'The Layman's Dictionary of English Law'; 'Copyright Through The Cases'; 'McFarlane on Customs and Excise Cases'; 'McFarlane's Customs Law Handbook'; 'The ABC of VAT'; 'VAT and Customs Law Update'; 'McFarlane's Customs and Excise Law and Practice'; contributing author to 'Grove's Dictionary of Music and Musicians' and 'The Writers' and Artists' Yearbook'; numerous articles in general and legal press; sometime general editor of The Criminal Law Library.

Leisure: islands.

McGHIE Brian

partner in charge MORLAND & SON 33 Bath Street, Abingdon, Oxon OX14 3RL.

Career: assistant solicitor Stockport, Matlock and Abingdon; became partner Morland & Son/Cole & Cole (1966).

Activities: clerk to Christ's Hospital; chairman Breast Cancer Campaign.

Biography: lives Abingdon; born 05.03.1931; married to Sybil with 2 children. Educated at Denstone College, Staffs; Manchester University (1959 LLB).

McGOLDRICK Patrick

senior partner TILSTON MACLAURIN 100 West Regent Street, Glasgow G2 2QB.

Career: admitted (1959); assistant solicitor Joseph Mellick (1959-1961); became partner Tilston & MacLaurin (1961); became senior partner.

Activities: Notary Public (1960); Temporary Sheriff throughout Scotland (1982 to date); founder member Glasgow Bar Association; former convener of Court House Committee with the Faculty of Procurators at Glasgow; member Glasgow Standing Advisory Committee during period with Court House Committee; member of: Royal Scottish Automobile Club; Old

Ranfurly Golf Club.

Biography: lives Houston; born 17.01.1934; married to Anne with 3 children. Educated at St Charles' Primary School, Paisley; St Mirin's Senior School, Paisley; (1954 MA) (1958 LLB).

Leisure: golf; boating; snooker.

MCGONIGAL Christopher

joint senior litigation partner CLIFFORD CHANCE Blackfriars House, 19 New Bridge Street, London EC4V 6BY.

Career: admitted (1965); assistant solicitor Coward Chance (1965-1968); became partner (1969-1987); senior litigation partner (1973-1979 and 1983-1987); senior resident Middle East partner (1979-1983); joint senior litigation partner Clifford Chance (1987).

Biography: lives Lamberhurst; born 10.11.1937; married to Sally with 4 children. Educated at Ampleforth College; Corpus Christi College Oxford.

McGREGOR Harvey

head of chambers 4 Paper Buildings, Temple, London EC4Y 7EX.

Career: RAF; Professor Chicago University (1950-1951); pupillage and tenancy at Bar (1955-1958); executive J Walter Thompson (advertising) (1959-1963); Visiting Professor USA (1963-1965); Bar (1965); QC (1978).

Activities: teaching law at Oxford (1955 to date); Fellow of New College (1972); Warden (1985); trustee Oxford Union; deputy chairman London and Provincial Theatre Councils; member editorial board Modern Law Review; member Garrick.

Biography: lives London WC1 and Oxford; born 25.02.1926; single. Educated at Scarborough Boys' High School; Inverurie Academy; Queen's College Oxford (1955 MA BCL) (1983 DCL); Harvard University (1962 SJD); author of 'McGregor on Damages'; variety of articles in legal journals.

Leisure: playing piano in amateur chamber music concerts; acting in amateur plays; swimming; tennis; bridge; refurbishing houses.

McINTOSH David Angus

senior partner DAVIES ARNOLD COOPER 12 Bridewell Place, London EC4V 6AD.

Career: junior clerk Ames Kent & Rathwell (1960-1962); articled Davies Arnold Cooper

(1962-1969); admitted (1969); assistant solicitor (1969); became partner (1969); became senior partner (1976).

Activities: secretary International Bar Association's Committees on: Consumer Affairs Advertising Unfair Competition and Products Liability; member International Association of Defense Counsel's Committees on: Excess and Reinsurance; Product Liability; Hazardous Substances Litigation; member joint working committee of the Senate of the Bar and Law Society on US/UK Reciprocal Enforcement of Judgements; member Law Society's working party on personal injury litigation; associate member Chartered Institute of Arbitration and of American Bar Association; active in the tort and legal profession reform debate as a speaker and panellist at, inter alia, the Times Forum at the National Theatre (1989); invited speaker at: the Oxford Union Debate on the Government's Green Papers (1989); the 33rd congress of the Union International Des Advocats in Switzerland (1989); the Law Society's National Conference in Harrogate (1989): member of: Blacksmith's Livery Company; Chigwell Golf Club; Duquesa Golf & Country Club, Spain.

Biography: lives London and Loughton; born 10.03.1944; married to Jennifer with 2 daughters. Educated at St John's Primary School, Frome; Selwood Secondary School, Frome; College of Law London (1969); prolific author and lecturer worldwide on legal, insurance and pharmaceutical affairs and recognised as having communication and media skills within high profile litigations.

Leisure: travelling; playing golf; trying to keep fit and being with family.

McINTYRE Bruce

barrister and head of chambers 1 Plowden Buildings, Middle Temple Lane, Temple, London EC4Y 9BU.

Career: called to the Bar Middle Temple (1968); pupillage with H Summerfield at Pump Court; pupillage with RAR Stroyan at 11 King's Bench Walk; tenancy at 11 King's Bench Walk (1972); practising from own Chambers (1980); assistant Recorder.

Activities: chairman Abbeyfield (Chelsea & Fulham) Society Ltd; member of: Lansdowne Club; South Kensington Squash Club.

Biography: lives London SW10 and Pembrokeshire; born 01.02.1946; single. Educated at Glasgow High School; Whitgift; Glenalmond; Manchester University (1968 LLB); Trinity Hall

M

Cambridge (1970 LLM); Inns of Court School of Law; Diploma in International Law - The Plea of Illegality in the Law of the European Communities.

Leisure: squash; golf; swimming; skiing; walking the Pembrokeshire Coastal Path; travelling to France, Italy, Spain and Portugal; languages; concerned about environmental issues; arts generally.

McIVOR Ian

barrister and head of chambers, Barristers Chambers, 38 King Street West, Manchester M3 2WZ.

Career: called to the Bar (1973); Northern Circuit; part-time lecturer in law Manchester Polytechnic, St John's College, The College of Building in Manchester, Bolton Institute and Worsley Technical College (3 years).

Activities: member Honourable Society of Inner Temple; member of: Heald Green Private Members' Club; Catenian Association; Didsbury Golf Club.

Biography: lives Sale; born 19.01.1944; married to Patricia with 5 children. Educated at Worsley High School; Bolton Institute; London (1973 LLB hons); Pupillage Scholarship; Marshall-Hall Trust Award.

Leisure: golf; fishing; windsurfing; swimming.

McKAY Graham

senior partner BROCKBANK TYSON & CO PO Box 1, 44 Duke Street, Whitehaven, Cumbria CA28 7NR.

Career: articled Brockbank Helder & Ormrod (1955-1958); admitted (1958); assistant solicitor (1959); became partner (1959); firm amalgamated with John G Tyson & Todd.

Activities: chairman Social Security Tribunals (1971); member West Cumberland Law Society (chairman 1985); member United Club.

Biography: lives St Bees; born 11.07.1935; married to Christine with 1 daughter and 1 son. Educated at Whitehaven Grammar School; King's College London (1955 LLB).

Leisure: music.

McKAY Peter

consultant ROSS HARPER & MURPHY 6A Academy Street, Coatbridge, Lanarkshire ML5 3AU.

Career: apprentice Ramsay Menzies & Wilson (1961-1964); admitted (1964);

assistant solicitor Borland King & Stewart (1964-1966); assistant solicitor Ross Harper & Murphy (1966-1969); became partner (1969); became consultant (1990).

Activities: temporary Sheriff for all Scottish Sheriffdoms; Notary Public; former lecturer in business law; director Loretto Housing Association Ltd; chairman and secretary East Stirlingshire FC Ltd; member Management Committee Scottish Football League; council member Scottish Football Association Ltd; member of: Glasgow University Union; Bothwell Castle Golf Club; Turnberry Castle Golf Club; East Stirlingshire FC; Turnberry Hotel Country Club.

Biography: lives Uddingston; born 18.05.1941; married to Mary with 3 children. Educated at St Joseph's RC Primary School, Blantyre; Our Lady's High School, Motherwell; Glasgow University (1961 MA) (1964 LLB).

Leisure: golf; association football administration.

McKENZIE Andrew N

finance partner FLADGATE FIELDER Heron Place, 3 George Street, London W1H 6AD.

Career: admitted (1971); assistant solicitor; partner Joynson-Hicks & Co; partner Gustavus Thompson & Co; became partner Fladgate Fielder.

Activities: tax planning and property.

Biography: lives London W11; born 25.12.1945; single. Educated at Wimbledon College; Trinity College Cambridge (MA).

Leisure: countryside; opera; drama.

McKERRELL Douglas

partner MACLAY MURRAY & SPENS 151 St Vincent Street, Glasgow G2 5NJ.

Career: articled McGrigor Donald; assistant solicitor Denton Hall Burgin & Warrens (1969-1970); posts in Glasgow and Linlithgow; assistant solicitor Maclay Murray & Spens (1975); became partner (1976).

Activities: senior tutor Glasgow University (1980-1989); lawyer member Rent Assessment Committee (1978 to date); chairman Glasgow & West of Scotland SPCA (1983-1987); chairman Scottish SPCA (1988 to date); director Scottish Music Information Centre, Scottish Electro Acoustic Music Association and Committee of Scottish International Piano Competition; member of Royal Scottish Automobile Club.

Biography: lives Glasgow; born 18.08.1944; married to Lizanne with 3 sons and 1 daughter. Educated at Royal High School (1949-1958); High School of Glasgow (1958-1961); Glasgow University (1964 LLB); author 'The Rent Acts - A Practitioner's Guide' (1985).

Leisure: the arts; collecting records; watching tennis.

McKICHAN Duncan James

senior partner MACLAY MURRAY & SPENS 151 St Vincent Street, Glasgow G2 5NJ.

Career: apprenticeship with Maclay Murray & Spens (1947-1950); admitted (1950); assistant solicitor (1950-1952); became partner (1952).

Activities: OBE (1990); Dean, Royal Faculty of Procurators in Glasgow (1983-1986); member Conveyancing Committee and International Relations Committee of Law Society of Scotland; honorary Consul for Canada in Scotland, Northern Ireland and North of England; member of: Western Club; Royal Northern and Clyde Yacht Club.

Biography: lives Helensburgh; born 28.07.1924; married to Leila with 2 daughters. Educated at George Watson's College, Edinburgh; Solihull School; Downing College Cambridge; Glasgow University (1950 BL); co-author of 'Drafting and Negotiating Commercial Leases in Scotland'.

Leisure: sailing; hill walking; skiing; gardening; reading.

McLEOD Wilson

partner BRYAN CAVE MCPHEETERS & MCROBERTS 29 Queen Anne's Gate, London SW1H 9BU.

Career: trust officer Shawmut Bank of Boston NA (1963-1967); consultant Crane & Hawkins (1967-1982); admitted to Massachusetts Bar (1969); admitted (1975); became partner Bryan Cave McPheeters & McRoberts (1982); admitted United States Tax Court (1987).

Biography: lives Ingatestone, Essex; born 25.08.1938; married with 2 children. Educated at Delta Secondary School; Westdale Secondary School, Hamilton, Ontario; McMaster University (1960 BA); Harvard University (1963 LLB Cum Laude).

McMULLEN John

partner ROTHERAS 24 Friar Lane, Nottingham NG1 6DW.

Career: part-time supervisor Emmanuel College Cambridge (1975); articled (1976-1978); admitted (1978); assistant solicitor (1978-1980); Fellow and lecturer in law Girton College Cambridge (1980-1986); director of studies in law (1981-1986); tutor (1981-1986); praelector (1982-1985); lecturer in law (1986-to date); Bye-Fellow in law (1988 to date); became partner Rotheras (1986).

Activities: consultant editor The Company Lawyer (1981 to date); member Law Society's Standing Committee on Employment Law; lectures widely to conferences and other talks to lawyers, personnel managers, accountants, etc; legal practice in the field of Employment and Labour Relations Law.

Biography: lives Nottingham; born 29.03.1954; married. Educated at Magnus Grammar School; Emmanuel College Cambridge (1975 BA); (1979 MA); senior scholar (1974-1975); squire Scholar University of Cambridge (1975-1976); various college prizes (1974 and 1975); author of 'Business Transfers and Employee Rights' (1987); co-author 'Allied Dunbar Business Tax and Law Guide' (1988 2nd ed 1989); contributor 'Butterworths Employment Law Guide' (1989); contributor 'Acquired Rights of Employees' (1989); contributor 'Aspects of Employment Law' (1990); numerous articles in CLJ; MLR; ILJ; NLJ; Company Lawyer; LS Gazette; CJQ and elsewhere.

Leisure: reading; travel; archaeology; Greek, Roman and Egyptian history; cinema; theatre; sport for enjoyment.

McNEIL D John

deputy chairman MORTON FRASER MILLIGAN WS 15 & 19 York Place, Edinburgh EH1 3EL.

Career: apprentice Davidson & Syme WS (1959-1962); admitted (1962); assistant solicitor (1962-1964); became partner Fraser Stodart & Ballingall (1964).

Activities: tutor in conveyancing Edinburgh University (1968-1978); president Law Society of Scotland (1986-1987) (chairman and member numerous committees of Council 1972 to date); chairman Board of Examiners LSS (1982-1985); CBE (1988); member Warnock Inquiry into Aspects of Human Fertilisation and Embryology (1982-1984); member of: New Club; Royal Scots Club;

Bruntsfield Golf Club.

Biography: lives Linlithgow; born 24.03.1937; married to Avril with 3 children. Educated at Glasgow Academy; Daniel Stewart's College, Edinburgh; Edinburgh University (1959 MA hons) (1962 LLB); various articles for Journal of The Law Society of Scotland and Scots Law Times.

Leisure: amateur theatre (acting and direction); golf; snooker; opera; concerts; theatre; cinema; good fiction; eating out.

McNEISH Maureen

personnel officer STAMP JACKSON & PROCTER 5 Parliament Street, Hull HU1 2AZ.

Career: lecturer in law (1975-1987); assistant examiner for 'A' level law; wrote correspondence course for BTEC business law option and tutored law on open learning course; involved in staff development (1985 to date); training officer Stamp Jackson & Procter (1988-1989); became personnel officer (1989); founder member Association of Legal Personnel.

Biography: lives Market Weighton; born 08.05.1952; married to Wyn. Educated at Bourne Grammar School; Caistor Grammar School; City of Westminster College (1972 HND); University College, Cardiff (1975 LLB hons).

Leisure: reading; films; crosswords; gardening; travel.

McQUAY Elizabeth

partner and head family law department WINWARD FEARON 35 Bow Street, London WC2E 7AU.

Career: articled Forsyte Kerman (1976-1978); admitted (1978); Magistrate and Deputy Registrar Attorney General's Office, Nairobi (1979-1980); assistant solicitor Gordon Dadds (1980-1983); associate partner (1983-1985); partner (1985-1988); became partner Winward Fearon (1988).

Activities: chairman Conciliation Sub-committee and member Main Committee of Solicitors Family Law Association; member of: RAC; Pall Mall.

Biography: lives London N1; born 29.08.1953; married. Educated at Harrogate Ladies' College; College of Law Chester; articles in Solicitors Family Law Association Newsletter.

Leisure: swimming; golf.

MEAD Malcolm

joint managing partner BEVAN ASHFORD Gotham House, Tiverton, Devon EX16 6LT.

Career: articled Ashford Sparkes & Harward; admitted; assistant solicitor; partner (1975); became joint managing partner (1989).

Activities: part-time industrial tribunal chairman (1989 to date); company secretary Mid-Devon Enterprise Agency; member Rotary Club of Tiverton.

Biography: lives Tiverton; born 19.11.1948; married to Helen with 2 children. Educated at Tiverton Grammar School; London University (1969 LLB); College of Law Guildford (1973); Exeter University (1980); author of 'The Reference Book on Employment Law, Unfair Dismissal Handbook' (1981); published articles based on research thesis Industrial Tribunal Procedure.

Leisure: cricket; gardening; music; art.

MEGGESON Michael

senior partner WARNER GOODMAN & STREAT Portland Chambers, 66 West Street, Fareham PO16 0JR.

Career: articled Lamports (1954-1957); admitted (1957); assistant solicitor (1957-1959); became partner Warner & Son (now Warner Goodman & Streat) (1959).

Activities: Deputy Circuit Judge (1978); Recorder of the Crown Court (1981); member Hampshire Incorporated Law Society Committee (president 1981); member Solicitors Staff Pension Fund (chairman 1988); member Committee Legal Aid Area No 3 (chairman 1986-1988); member of: Royal Southern Yacht Club; Royal Ocean Racing Club; Hayling Golf Club.

Biography: lives Petersfield; born 06.08.1930; married to Alison. Educated at Sherborne; Gonville and Caius College Cambridge (1953 BA) (1956 MA).

Leisure: sailing; golf; music; gardening.

MEHIGAN Simon

barrister 5 Paper Buildings, Temple, London EC4Y 7HB and Rue du Taciturne 42, B-1040 Brussels, Belgium practising in restraint of trade, breach of confidence, EEC competition law, defamation and media, commercial fraud.

Career: corporate finance section of a merchant bank; called to the Bar Lincoln's Inn (1980).

Biography: lives London SW1 and West

M

M

Milton; born 16.08.1956; married to Amanda. Educated at Colchester Royal Grammar School; University College London (1977 LLB); joint author 'Restraint of Trade and Business Secrets: Law and Practice' (1986); editor 'Underhill's Licensing Guide' (10th ed 1988).

Leisure: gardening; creative writing.

MEISEL Frank

director of training and research EVERSHEDS 10 Newhall Street, Birmingham B3 3LX.

Career: Johnson Jecks & Landons (later Stones Porter & Co) (1965-1970); called to the Bar Middle Temple (1974); pupillage 4 Essex Court and 7 King's Bench Walk (1974-1975); 7 King's Bench Walk (1975-1976); part-time lecturer in law University College Buckingham (1976); lecturer in law Birmingham University (1976-1989); door tenant 4 Fountain Court (1985-1989); became director of training and research Eversheds.

Biography: lives Birmingham; born 30.08.1946; married to Sian Mari with 2 children. Educated at St Marylebone Grammar School, London; Leeds University (1973 LLB); Inns of Court School of Law (1973-1974); co-author of Auctions 'Law & Practice' (1985); assistant editor 'Civil Justice Quarterly'; numerous articles.

Leisure: watching sport on television.

MELLING Peter Kenneth

assistant chief solicitor NATIONWIDE ANGLIA BUILDING SOCIETY Chesterfield House, Bloomsbury Way, London WC1V 6PW.

Career: admitted (1982); assistant solicitor (1982-1988); partner Wilson Cowie & Dillon (1988-1989); solicitor (company/commercial) Nationwide Anglia Building Society (1989); became assistant chief solicitor (1989).

Activities: member General Committee of Liverpool Law Society (1987-1988).

Biography: lives London E2; born 03.08.1958; single. Educated at St Brendan's College, Bristol; Liverpool University (1979 LLB hons); College of Law Lancaster Gate (1979-1980).

Leisure: semi-professional pianist; keen swimmer.

MELLOR Tony

senior partner and chairman of partners TOZERS 8-10 St Paul's Road, Newton Abbot, Devon TQ12 4PR and at Teignmouth, Dawlish and Exeter.

Career: articled Holt, Beever & Kinsey (1951-1956); admitted (1956); assistant solicitor Bretherton Turpin & Pell (1956-1957); legal assistant Civil Service (1957-1960); assistant solicitor Tozers (1960-1962); became partner (1962).

Activities: Deputy District Registrar; member Management Committee Teignbridge Citizens Advice Bureau; member Management Committee Newton Abbot Volunteer Bureau; member of the Committee of Friends of Dartington; member Family Law Association; member Exeter & County Club.

Biography: lives Broadhampton; born 23.04.1930; married to Moira with 2 children. Educated at Shanghai Cathedral School; St Mark's DSB, George, South Africa; Epsom College, Surrey; College of Law Lancaster Gate.

Leisure: family; friends; literature; cinema; skiing; tennis; beagling.

MENDELSOHN Martin

senior partner ADLERS 22-26 Paul Street, London EC2A 4JH.

Career: admitted (1959); assistant solicitor (1959-1961); became partner Adlers (1961).

Activities: visiting Professor of Franchising at City University Business School (1989); special consultant Belmont European Community Law Office; legal consultant British Franchise Association; UK representative International Franchise Association; frequently lectures on business and legal aspects of franchising to businessmen, lawyers and students; course director College of Marketing; first chairman International Franchising Committee of the Section on Business Law of the International Bar Association; member American Bar Association Forum Committee on Franchising; member MCC.

Biography: lives Kenton; born 06.11.1935; married to Phyllis with 2 children. Educated at Upton House School, Hackney; Hackney Downs School; College of Law; author of: 'The Guide to Franchising'; 'How to Evaluate a Franchise'; 'How to Franchise Internationally'; 'The Ethics of Franchising'; 'The BFA Franchisor Manual'; co-author of: 'How to Franchise your Business'; 'Comment Negocier une Franchise'; contributed to the UK and EC Sections of the American Bar Association publication 'Survey of Foreign Laws and Regulations affecting International Franchising' and the UK and EEC section

of the 'Canadian Franchise Guide'; editor of 'International Franchising - An Overview'; articles on the business as well as legal aspects of franchising in UK Europe, North America, South America, Africa and Australasia; general editor of The Journal of International Franchising and Distribution Law and of 'International Franchising - An Overview'.

Leisure: keen cricketer; collector of cricket books and cricketania; philately.

MEREDITH Alan

partner, member of board and head of commercial property department PHILLIPS & BUCK Fitzalan House, Fitzalan Road, Cardiff CF2 1XZ.

Career: articled Gordon Williams WN Davies & Co (1974-1976); admitted (1976); assistant solicitor (1976-1978); became partner JR Evans WN Davies & Co (1978-1985); became partner Phillips & Buck (1985).

Activities: member management Committee Swansea Cricket & Football Club (1982 to date); member Welsh Rugby Union Re-Drafting Committee - constitution and bye-laws (1989); member of: Cardiff & County Club; Royal Porthcawl Golf Club; Barbarian Rugby Football Club.

Biography: lives Cowbridge; born 08.01.1952; married to Morfudd with 1 daughter. Educated at Cathays High School, Cardiff (1961-1962); Neath Grammar School (1962-1969); University of Wales (1970-1973).

Leisure: rugby union football; golf; reading.

MEREDITH George

head of chambers 25 Southernhay East, Exeter EX1 1NW.

Career: called to the Bar (1969); practised common law Bar in London (1970-1972); practised in Exeter and South West general common law work in the civil courts (1972 to date); became head of Chambers 25 Southernhay East (1975).

Activities: hon secretary and librarian Exeter Law Library Society; member Devon & Exeter Institution.

Biography: lives Exeter; born 16.01.1943; married with 2 children. Educated at Marlborough College.

Leisure: family life; reading; photography; hill walking.

MERRICKS Walter

assistant secretary-general (communications) THE LAW SOCIETY 50 Chancery Lane, London WC2A 1SX.

Career: articled John Batt (1968-1970); admitted (1970); Hubbard travelling scholar (1971); director Camden Community Law Centre (1972-1976); lecturer in law Brunel University (1976-1981); writer on legal affairs New Law Journal (1982-1985); secretary Professional and Public Relations The Law Society (1985-1987).

Activities: member Royal Commission on Criminal Procedure (1978-1981); Fraud Trials Committee (1984-1986).

Biography: lives London N6; born 04.06.1945; married to Olivia with 2 children. Educated at Bradfield College; Trinity College Oxford (1967) (BA hons MA).

MESSER Laurence

partner DAVIES ARNOLD COOPER 12 Bridewell Place, London EC4V 6AD.

Career: articled Norton Rose Botterell & Roche (1972-1974); admitted (1974); assistant solicitor (1974-1982); assistant solicitor Nicholson Graham & Jones (1982-1983); partner (1983-1989); partner Davies Arnold Cooper (1989 to date).

Activities: member London Young Solicitors Group (1977-1983) chairman (1981-1982); member Council of the Royal Town Planning Institute (1987 to date); representative of the Royal Town Planning Institute on the Joint RTPI/Law Society Examination Board for the Law Society Proposed Planning Law Panel; member Law Society Planning and Land Development Committee (1982 to date).

Biography: lives London W5; born 27.05.1949; married with 2 daughters. Educated at Bradford Grammar School; Durham University (1971 BA hons); College of Law Guildford; Legal Associate of the Royal Town Planning Institute.

Leisure: playing and watching sport; cinema; theatre.

METCALFE Stephen

commercial litigation and partner responsible for banking and insolvency work WANSBROUGHS WILLEY HARGRAVE 103 Temple Street, Bristol BS99 7UD.

Career: articled Durrant Piese (1981-1983); admitted (1983); assistant solicitor (1983-1985); assistant solicitor Wansbroughs (1985-1988); became partner (1988).

Activities: member Bristol Law Society Chancery Users' Committee.

Biography: lives Bristol; born 10.02.1956; married to Lucy with 3 children. Educated at Bicester School; New College Oxford (1978 BA hons); College of Law Guildford (1980).

Leisure: musician (singer); theatre; cinema; reading; gardening.

METLISS Jonathan Alexander

deputy head of corporate finance SJ BERWIN & CO 236 Gray's Inn Road, London W1X 8HB.

Career: articled LM Doffman & Co (1971-1973); admitted (1973); assistant solicitor Nabarro Nathanson (1973-1976); merchant banker in corporate finance department Capel Court Corporation, Sydney, Australia (1977-1978); assistant solicitor Berwin Leighton (1978-1982); became partner SJ Berwin & Co (1982).

Activities: director Atapco (UK) Ltd; deputy chairman The Friends of the Weizmann Institute UK; lecturer for 'Euroconferences' of Sjaelsmarkvej IB, Denmark and Westminster Management Consultants Ltd; member British Israel Chamber of Commerce; member Law Society; member Holborn Law Society; member of: Marylebone Cricket Club; Middlesex and Surrey County Cricket Clubs.

Biography: lives London; born 12.06.1949; married with 3 children. Educated at Haberdashers' Aske's, Elstree; Southampton University (LLB hons).

Leisure: cricket; squash; soccer; travel; work.

MEYRICK Grant

managing partner HOWES PERCIVAL 4 Dean's Court, St Paul's Churchyard, London EC4V 5AA.

Career: articled Lawford & Co; admitted (1966); assistant solicitor (1966-1967); partner (1967-1988); became partner Howes Percival (1988).

Activities: former chairman The Queen's Club.

Biography: lives London; born 22.02.1944; divorced with 2 children. Educated at Latymer Upper.

Leisure: lawn tennis.

MIDDLETON Grant

senior partner STONEHAM LANGTON & PASSMORE 8 Bolton Street, London W1Y 8AU.

Career: admitted (1955); Army (1955-1959); assistant solicitor (1959-1961); became partner Stoneham Langton & Passmore (1961).

Activities: president City of Westminster Law Society (1989-1990); Citizens Advice Bureau; member Naval & Military Club.

Biography: lives London SW13; born 08.03.1934; married to Pamela with 3 children. Educated at Ushaw College, Durham; King's College Durham (1954 LLB); Greek interpreter (1957).

Leisure: Bach choir; motorcycling.

MIDDLETON William

senior partner MIDDLETON POTTS 3 Cloth Street, Long Lane, London EC1A 7LD.

Career: admitted (1954); became partner Crawley & de Reya (1954-1976); co-founder Middleton Potts (1976).

Activities: chairman and director numerous companies; member of: City of London Club; Hurlingham Club.

Biography: lives London SW7; born 26.02.1923; single. Educated at Rome and London Universities.

MIDGLEY Robin

partner and head of planning and environmental department BOND PEARCE 1 The Crescent, Plymouth PL1 3AE.

Career: articled to the Town Clerk of Plymouth (1954); admitted; assistant solicitor City of Plymouth; became partner Bond Pearce; specialises in town and country planning.

Activities: Notary Public; president Plymouth Law Society (1989); member Law Society's standing committee on planning law (1964-1984); chairman Abbeyfield (Plymouth) Society Ltd; director Plymouth Theatre Royal Co Ltd; chairman Stoke Damerel Plymouth Conservation Society.

Biography: lives Plymouth; born 15.07.1931; married to Beth with 4 children. Educated at The Downs School, Colwall; Bootham School, York; Worcester College Oxford (1954 BA hons) (MA); occasionally writes articles for the Journal of Planning Law.

Leisure: walking; music.

MILDRED Mark

London partner PANNONE BLACKBURN and PANNONE NAPIER 20/22 Bedford Row, London WC1R 4EB.

Career: Law Centre volunteer (1972); articled BM Birnberg & Co (1975); founded own practice (1975-1976); became partner Gasters (1976-1978); founding partner Mildred and Beaumont (1978-1986); became partner Pannone Napier (1986).

Activities: member NCC Legal Advisory Panel; member Law Society Consumer Law Working Party; member: Battersea Labour Club; Scorpions Club.

Biography: lives London SW11; born 16.09.1948; married to Sarah with 2 sons. Educated at Lancing College; Clare College Cambridge (1970 BA); author of 'Group Actions After Opren' NCC (1989); chapter in Powers ed Butterworth Medical Negligence (1990); articles in NLJ, LSG, etc on tort and multi-plaintiff litigation.

Leisure: politics; childcare; bridge; racket games; cooking; walking; choral singing.

MILES Adrian

head of Special Finance Group specialising in aviation, marine and project finance WILDE SAPTE Queensbridge House, 60 Upper Thames Street, London EC4V 3BD.

Career: assistant solicitor Boodle Hatfield (1972-1974); assistant solicitor Norton Rose (1974-1976); became partner Wilde Sapte (1976).

Biography: lives Chislehurst; born 16.11.1947; married to Hilary with 3 children. Educated at Rutlish School; Queen Mary College London (LLB hons) .

Leisure: music; chess; sport.

MILES John

partner LIGHTFOOTS The Old Red Lion, 1 & 2 High Street, Thame, Oxon OX9 2BX.

Career: articled Cole & Cole (1969-1971); admitted (1971); assistant solicitor Lightfoots (1971-1973); became partner (1973).

Activities: county manager Bucks RFU U17; member Chinnor RUFC.

Biography: lives Thame; born 04.04.1947; married to Cheryl with 3 children. Educated at Brackenwood County Primary School; Birkenhead School; St Peter's College Oxford (1968 BA) (1972 MA).

Leisure: spoken French; teacher of Tai Chi Chuan; playing piano; darts.

MILFORD John Tillman

Queens's Counsel and head of chambers 9-12 Trinity Chare, Quayside, Newcastle upon Tyne.

Career: called to the Bar Inner Temple (1969); in practice Newcastle upon Tyne (1970); Recorder (1985); QC (1989).

Activities: member Northern Counties Club, Newcastle upon Tyne.

Biography: lives Hexham; born 04.02.1946; married to Mary nee Spriggs with 3 daughters. Educated at The Cathedral School, Salisbury; Hurstpierpoint; Exeter University (LLB).

Leisure: fishing; shooting; gardening; the writings of Henry Williamson.

MILLAR Richard

partner BISCHOFF & CO Epworth House, 25 City Road, London EC1Y 1AA.

Career: admitted (1963); assistant solicitor Bischoff & Co (1965); became partner (1969).

Activities: member of Law Society Company Law Committee; chairman of the Law Society Collective Investment Scheme Working Party; hon solicitor to the British Uruguayan Society and to the West London Committee for the Protection of Children; member of: City of London Club; Little Ship Club; Offshore Yachts Class Owners' Association.

Biography: lives London W4; born 16.02.1940; married to Rosemary. Educated at Wellington College.

Leisure: sailing; gardening.

MILLAR William McIntosh

consultant MCCLURE NAISMITH ANDERSON & GARDINER 292 St Vincent Street, Glasgow G2 5TQ.

Career: captain with Royal Signals World War II; apprenticed Maclay Murray & Spens (1948-1951); admitted (1951); assistant solicitor McClure Naismith Brodie & Co (1951-1955); became partner (1955); became senior partner (1987-1989).

Activities: chairman Strathclyde Housing Society Ltd; member Scottish Housing Advisory Committee (1970-1975); director Citizens Theatre Ltd (1969-1972); governor Royal Scottish Academy of Music & Drama (1969 to date); chairman Scottish Early Music Association and Glasgow Early Music (1990); member The Scottish Arts Club.

Biography: lives Glasgow G12 and St Ann's; born 10.09.1925. Educated at

Glasgow Academy; Fettes College; Glasgow University (1950 BL); editor Journal of the Law Society of Scotland (1983-1989); editor and joint author of the Law Society's Response to the Secretary of State's Consultation Paper on the future of the legal profession in Scotland (1989); many articles (some serious) to Journal of Law Society of Scotland; monthly editorials (1983-1989).

Leisure: writing; listening to music; playing fiddle, bagpipes, harpsichord.

MILLER Anthony Russell (Tony)

senior admiralty partner CONSTANT & CONSTANT Sea Containers House, 20 Upper Ground, Blackfriars Bridge, London SE1 9PD.

Career: articled Rider Heaton Meredith & Mills (1960-1965); admitted (1965); assistant solicitor (1965-1966); assistant solicitor Constant & Constant (1966-1968 & 1969-1972); assistant solicitor Whitehouse-Vaux & Elborne (1968-1969); became partner Constant & Constant (1972).

Activities: officer in the Royal Naval Reserve; member Court of Assistants of the Haberdashers' Company; member of: Royal Ocean Racing Club; City of London Club.

Biography: lives Sandhills; born 11.01.1942; married to Sarah with 2 sons and 1 daughter. Educated at Ladycross; Wellington College, Berks; Tabor Academy, Mass, USA; College of Law; Mine Counter Measures Vessel Command (Ocean): Ship's Diving Officer; holder of the Reserve Decoration; written and lectured on law of maritime salvage and marine claims.

Leisure: sailing; gardening.

MILLER Michael

barrister and joint head of chambers 8 Stone Buildings, Lincoln's Inn, London WC2.

Career: called to the Bar (1958); QC (1974).

Activities: Bencher Lincoln's Inn (1984 to date); member Bar Council (chairman sub-committee on Computers and Information Technology); founder Clarendon Software; author of computer programs and expert systems.

Biography: lives London; born 28.06.1933; married with 2 sons and 2 daughters. Educated at the Dragon School Oxford (1941-1946); Westminster School (1946-1951) King's Scholar; Christ Church Oxford (1955 BA Litt Hum) (1958 MA); Westminster Scholar; Carey Scholar; Slade

Prizeman; Cholmeley Scholar Lincoln's Inn (1958).

Leisure: sailing; walking; travel; gardening.

MILLS Barbara

director of the SERIOUS FRAUD OFFICE, Elm House, 10-16 Elm Street, London WC1X OBJ.

Career: called to the Bar Middle Temple (1963); Junior Prosecuting Counsel to the Inland Revenue (1977); Senior Prosecuting Counsel (1979); Recorder of the Crown Court (1982); Junior Treasury Counsel Central Criminal Court (1982); QC (1986); Bencher Middle Temple (1990); Director of the Serious Fraud Office (1990).

Activities: legal assessor to the General Medical Council and General Dental Council (1988); member Criminal Injuries Compensation Board (1988); trustee King's Cross Disaster Fund (1987); member SE Circuit Bar Mess; former member Middle Temple Hall Committee; former joint honorary secretary Barristers' Benevolent Association.

Biography: lives London; born 10.08.1940; married with 4 children. Educated at St Helen's School, Northwood; Lady Margaret Hall Oxford (1962 MA) Scholar; Gibbs Open University Scholar (1961); Entrance Exhibitioner Middle Temple.

MILLS David

senior resident partner CARNELUTTI and senior partner MACKENZIE MILLS 76 Shoe Lane, London EC4A 3BQ.

Career: assistant principal Ministry of Defence (1965-1966); called to the Bar Middle Temple (1968); founded Carnelutti London office (1978); admitted (1978); senior partner Mackenzie Mills (founded 1982).

Activities: councillor Camden Council (1974-1978); member Garrick Club.

Biography: lives London and Warwickshire; born 31.05.1944; married to Tessa Jowell; 5 children. Educated at Glenalmond; University College Oxford (1965 MA); Scholar; Harmsworth Scholar Middle Temple (1967); author of: 'Doing Business in Italy' (1982 & 1990); 'Leveraged Buyouts in Italy' (1990) (IFLR).

Leisure: music - clarinet (Royal Orch Society); gardening; golf.

MILNE David

Queen's Counsel 4 Pump Court, Temple, London EC4Y 7AN.

Career: articled Whinney Murray (1966-1969); admitted chartered accountant (1969); called to the Bar (1970); QC (1987); Assistant Recorder (1989).

Activities: member Taxation Committee of Bar Council; member of: Garrick; Hurlingham; Gnomes; Walton Heath Golf Club.

Biography: lives London SW13; born 22.09.1945; married to Rosemary with 1 daughter. Educated at Harrow; Oxford (1966); FCA (1974).

Leisure: natural history and conservation; music; golf.

MILNER Patrick

senior partner JH MILNER & SON 46 Park Place, Leeds LS1 2LD.

Career: articled JH Milner & Son (1961-1966); admitted (1966); assistant solicitor (1966-1968); became partner (1968).

Activities: secretary North Leeds Cricket Club; member Leeds Lions Club.

Biography: lives Leeds; born 14.10.1941; married to Gill with 2 children. Educated at Aysgarth School, North Yorkshire (1949-1955); Rugby School (1955-1960); Leeds University (1964 LLB hons).

Leisure: cricket; wine; opera.

MIMPRISS Peter

partner ALLEN & OVERY 9 Cheapside, London EC2V 6AD.

Career: articled in Sherborne; admitted (1967); assistant solicitor Allen & Overy (1968-1972); became partner (1972).

Activities: director of: Leeds Castle Foundation; Weston Park Foundation; Chatham Historic Dockyard Trust; member of: Athenaeum; Garrick.

Biography: lives London SW7; born 22.08.1943; married to Hilary with 2 children. Educated at Sherborne School.

Leisure: heritage matters; maritime history; collecting books and pictures.

MISHCON Lord

senior partner MISHCON DE REYA 125 High Holborn, London WC1V 6QP.

Career: admitted (1937); founded own practice (1937); merged with de Reya (1988).

Activities: official spokesman for the Opposition in the House of Lords on home and legal affairs; former vice-chairman Solicitors All-Party Parliamentary Committee; former member Law sub-

committee House of Lords European Communities Committee.

Biography: lives London; born 14.08.1915; married to Joan with 3 children by former marriage.

MITSON John

partner BIRKETT WESTHORP & LONG 20-32 Museum Street, Ipswich, Suffolk IP1 1HZ.

Career: articled Town Clerk of Lincoln and Sharpe Pritchard & Co; admitted (1956); assistant solicitor Plymouth City Council (1956-1959); assistant solicitor Birketts (1959-1961); became partner (1961) .

Activities: Diocesan Registrar and Bishop's legal secretary of the Diocese of St Edmundsbury and Ipswich (1975 to date); Church warden; member MCC.

Biography: lives Dedham; born 28.02.1929; widower with 4 children. Educated at Oakham School; Sidney Sussex College Cambridge (1953 BA) (1954 LLB).

MITTING John

Queen's Counsel 4 Fountain Court, Steelhouse Lane, Birmingham 4 and 2 Harcourt Buildings, Temple, London EC4.

Career: called to the Bar (1970); QC (1987); Recorder (1988).

Activities: member Birmingham.

Biography: lives Gorosall; born 08.10.1947; married to Judith with 3 sons. Educated at Downside; Trinity Hall Cambridge; (1969 BA) (1970 LLB).

Leisure: wine; food; bridge.

MOCTON Sam

senior partner ROWLANDS 35 Fountain Street, Manchester M2 2AF.

Career: articled Maurice S Myers (1952-1955); admitted (1955); assistant solicitor (1955-1956); became partner (1956); negotiated merger of Myers Mocton & Levy with Tom Dixon to form Rowlands (1968).

Activities: senior governor Jewish High School for Girls Manchester; voluntary social/educational worker for patients at Heathlands residential home for the aged Manchester.

Biography: lives Salford; born 14.09.1931; married to Nina with 6 children. Educated at Salford Grammar School (1942-1949) Lancashire County Council Scholarship; Manchester University (1952 LLB hons); Stephen Heelis Gold Medal awarded by

M

Manchester Law Society (1955); writes occasional newspaper articles.

MOFFAT Andrew

partner MARTIN TOLHURST PARTNERSHIP 7 Wrotham Road, Gravesend, Kent DA11 0PD.

Career: admitted (1968); assistant solicitor Martin Tolhurst Partnership (1968-1970); became partner (1970).

Activities: clerk to General Tax Commissioners (Gravesend and Chatham Division) (1986 to date); Notary Public (District Notary) (1972 to date); secretary Gravesend & District Law Society (1971-1986) (president 1989-1990); chairman Gravesend Citizens Advice Bureau (1987-1990); member of: Rotary Club of Gravesend; Kent Archaeological Society.

Biography: lives Shorme nr Gravesend; born 12.02.1944; married. Educated at King's School, Rochester; College of Law.

Leisure: local history.

MOFFAT Douglas

partner in charge of commercial property department TODS MURRAY WS 66 Queen Street, Edinburgh EH2 4NE.

Career: apprentice solicitor Shepherd & Wedderburn WS; admitted (1968); assistant solicitor (1968-1973); assistant solicitor Tods Murray WS (1973-1974); became partner (1974).

Activities: tutor in conveyancing Edinburgh University (1970-1974); director (governor) Edinburgh Academy; member of Edinburgh Academical Club and Sports Club.

Biography: lives Thornton; born 03.10.1947; married to Kareen with 1 son and 1 daughter. Educated at Edinburgh Academy; Edinburgh University (1968 LLB).

Leisure: hill walking; gardening.

MOISER Cliff

magistrates' clerk PLYMOUTH MAGISTRATES' COURT St Andrew Street, Plymouth PL1 2DP.

Career: Royal Marines (1942-1946) (Murmansk 1943-1944); magistrates' courts Dewsbury; Buxton; Coventry (1947-1958); admitted (1957); assistant solicitor (1958-1959); magistrates' clerk Dudley (1960-1971); magistrates' clerk Plymouth (1971).

Activities: president Justices' Clerks' Society (1979-1980); Committees (1970-1980) (hon treasurer 1976-1979); president

Devon Justices' Clerks' Society (1987 to date); lectured in America on English Courts; attended International Juvenile Courts Meeting, Paris (1978); viewed courts and lawyer activity in Moscow and Leningrad (1989) (hosting reciprocal visit 1990); chairman 'Plymouth Self Rule' to recreate 'County Borough' or metropolitan district status for Plymouth and divorce from county council; vice-president Plymouth Albion Rugby Club; member of: Yorkshire CCC; Somerset CCC; Joint Services Officers' Mess, Plymouth; Royal Marines Commando Officers' Mess, Plymouth; Royal Marines Historical Society.

Biography: lives Plymouth; born 15.01.1925; married to Colleen with 3 children. Educated at Wheelwright School, Dewsbury; Leeds University; writes regularly for 'Justice of the Peace' and other law journals; author of: 'Practice and Procedure in Magistrates' Courts'; 'Disqualifications & Endorsements'.

Leisure: chess; swimming.

MOLE David

partner HAWKINS RUSSELL JONES 7/8 Portmill Lane, Hitchin, Herts SG5 1AS.

Career: articled Lovell White & King (1960-1965); admitted (1965); assistant solicitor (1965-1968); assistant solicitor Hawkins Russell Jones (1968-1971); became partner (1971).

Activities: member of: Wig & Pen Club; IOD; The Law Society.

Biography: lives Hitchin; born 05.10.1941; married to Rosemary. Educated at Winchester College.

Leisure: sailing; golf; gardening.

MOLYNEUX Anne

partner responsible for problem property of all types MASONS 116/118 Chancery Lane, London WC2A 1PP.

Career: articled small firm in West End of London; admitted (1983); assistant solicitor and associate partner City firm (1986); assistant solicitor Masons (1987-1989); became partner (1989).

Biography: lives Ealing; born 12.01.1959; married to Jeremy with 2 children. Educated at Southport High School for Girls; Sheffield University (1979 LLB hons); College of Law Chester (1979-1980).

Leisure: mother (no more need be said).

MONTGOMERY Nigel

partner in charge of insolvency unit DAVIES ARNOLD COOPER 12 Bridewell Place, London EC4V 6AD.

Career: commission in the Army; solicitor in the City; receiver; liquidator and administrator of wide variety of companies; became head of insolvency unit Davies Arnold Cooper (1989).

Activities: member of: National Rifle Association; London & Middlesex Rifle Association; Bentley Drivers' Club; Cavalry & Guards Club.

Biography: lives Kent; born 1956; married with 1 son and 1 daughter. Educated at Cambridge; lectured and written articles widely on various aspects of banking and insolvency law and practice.

Leisure: collecting and restoring cars; target and clay pigeon shooting.

MOODY Robert

partner TRUMP & PARTNERS 34 St Nicholas Street, Bristol BS1 1TS.

Career: articled Leo Lush; admitted (1961); assistant solicitor Reynolds Porter (1961-1963); partner (1963); became first partner Trump & Partners (1965).

Activities: former council member Bristol Law Society.

Biography: lives East Harptree; born 19.01.1939; married to Elisabeth with 3 children. Educated at Chafyn Grove School, Salisbury; Kelly College, Tavistock; Wiltshire and Glos Law Society Prize.

Leisure: gardening; choral singing; playing the violin in village orchestra; running; bell ringing.

MOON Patrick

tax partner NABARRO NATHANSON 50 Stratton Street, London W1X 5FL.

Career: articled Tarlo Lyons & Aukin; admitted (1980) assistant solicitor Nabarro Nathanson (1980-1986); became partner (1986).

Activities: frequent lecturer in UK and abroad including lecturing in French.

Biography: lives London W11 and Oxfordshire; born 08.05.1953; single. Educated at Truro School; Lincoln College Oxford (MA); College of Law Chester and Guildford; author of 'Employee Share Schemes' and occasional articles.

Leisure: opera; theatre; wine; European travel; walking; buying and occasionally painting pictures.

MOONEY Kevin

senior partner in the intellectual property department SIMMONS & SIMMONS 14 Dominion Stteet, London EC2M 2RJ.

Career: articled Simmons & Simmons (1969-1971); admitted (1971); assistant solicitor (1971-1974); became partner (1974).

Activities: member International Advisory Committee USTA; member Intellectual Property sub-committee City of London Solicitors' Company; member specialist committees of ABA; AIPLA; AIPPI and IBA; regular lecturer at conferences on intellectual law matters.

Biography: lives London; born 14.11.1945; married to Maureen with 3 children. Educated at Cardinal Vaughan School; Bristol University (LLB).

Leisure: gardening; lifelong passion for QPR.

MOORE Matthew

consultant JOHN HAMILTON ASSOCIATES and legal training consultant CENTRAL LAW TRAINING King Edward House, New Street, Birmingham B2 4QJ.

Career: teacher in Essex and Devon; articled Varley Hibbs & Co; admitted; assistant solicitor; co-ordinator M5 Group (1985-1988); director of publicity and recruitment (1988-1989); became consultant John Hamilton Associates (1989); became legal training consultant Central Law Training.

Activities: chairman and secretary Warwickshire Trainee Solicitors Group (1983-1984).

Biography: lives Sutton Coldfield; born 25.06.1954; married to Angela with 1 daughter. Educated at Bishop Vesey's Grammar School, Sutton Coldfield; Mid-Essex Technical College, Chelmsford (1972-1975); Sydney C Taylor Memorial Medal; author of 'The Law and Procedure of Meetings' (1979); frequent contributor to professional journals on practice management subjects.

Leisure: most sport especially soccer and running.

MOORE Michael

partner HENRY FALLOWS & CO Larkhill House, 160 St George's Road, Bolton BL1 2PJ and consultant MACE & JONES 4 Oxford Court, Manchester M2 3WQ.

Career: articled Henry Fallows & Co; admitted (1967); assistant solicitor (1967-1968); became partner (1968); also

consultant to Mace & Jones since November (1987).

Activities: member Bolton Law Society (1968) (president 1988); member IBA Committees; runs numerous continuing education courses on employment law in general and discrimination law in particular.

Biography: lives Bolton; born 28.08.1943; married to Kate with 2 children. Educated at Hulme Grammar School; Brasenose College Oxford (1964 BA) (MA); author of 'A Practical Guide to Discrimination Law' (1980); three books on discrimination law; two books on renting business premises; articles in Law Society's Gazette (1987 & 1988).

Leisure: tennis; walking; bridge; spectator cricket; opera; theatre; politics.

MOORE Nicholas

head of employment and industrial relations unit HILL TAYLOR DICKINSON Irongate House, Duke's Place, London EC3A 7LP.

Career: articled Hill Dickinson & Co (1970-1972); admitted (1972); assistant solicitor (1972-1974); associate partner (1974); partner (1976).

Activities: runs regular seminars in-house; delivers papers at external seminars; Freeman of the City of London; Liveryman in the Worshipful Company of Patternmakers.

Biography: lives nr Tunbridge Wells; born 22.12.1947; married to Sally with 4 children. Educated at Oundle School; Trinity College Cambridge (MA hons); contributes newspaper articles on topical industrial relations law issues.

Leisure: riding; skiing; gardening.

MOORE-BICK Martin

Queen's Counsel 3 Essex Court, Temple, London EC4Y 9AL.

Career: called to the Bar Inner Temple (1969); QC (1986); Recorder (1990).

Biography: lives Burwash; born 06.12.1946; married to Tessa with 2 sons and 2 daughters. Educated at The Skinners' School, Tunbridge Wells; Christ's College Cambridge (1972 MA).

MOORHEAD Robert

senior partner HALLETT & CO 11 Bank Street, Ashford, Kent TN23 1DA.

Career: Lt 1st Bn The Manchester Regiment (served mainly in BAOR) (1946-1948);

articled Hallett & Co (1950-1953); admitted (1953); assistant solicitor (1953-1955); became partner (1955).

Activities: Notary Public (1960); former member SE Regional War Pensions Board; former chairman Clover Trust; former district chairman Forces Help Society and Lord Roberts Workshops; former auditor of Smeeth Parish Church; chairman Smeeth Parish Council; governor Hawtreys; council member of the Paddocks Children's Trust; trustee of: the Mountbatten Charity; the Brabourne Charity; the Diana Edgson Wright Charity; director of six companies; member Farmers' Club.

Biography: lives Smeeth; born 07.01.1928; married to Shirley with 4 sons. Educated at Marlborough; Corpus Christi College Cambridge (hons).

Leisure: farming; reading; walking.

MORAN Peter

senior partner CHATTERTONS 5 South Street, Horncastle, Lincolnshire LN9 6DS.

Career: articled Kendall & Rigby; admitted (1959); assistant solicitor Chattertons (1961-1964); became partner (1964).

Activities: clerk to Horncastle Justices (1965-1970); president Lincolnshire Justices Clerks' Society (1965); Conservative candidate Lincoln (twice); part-time chairman Lincolnshire Social Security Appeal Tribunal; treasurer Society of Conservative Lawyers (co-chairman working party on the Green Papers); chairman East Lindsey Conservative Association; president Lincolnshire European Conservative Constituency Association; member Carlton Club.

Biography: lives London NW6 and Horncastle ; born 03.08.1936; married to Miriam with 2 daughters. Educated at St Edward's College, Liverpool; Liverpool University (1957 LLB); Atkinson Conveyancing Prize.

Leisure: tennis; political activities.

MORDSLEY Barry

partner HARRIS ROSENBLATT AND KRAMER 26/28 Bedford Row, London WC1R 4HE.

Career: admitted as solicitor (1972); lecturer at the City of London Polytechnic (1972); senior lecturer (1974); principal lecturer (1977); visiting lecturer City University (1974); visiting scholar and Professor Cornell Law School, Cornell

M

University, Ithaca, USA (1981-1982); visiting lecturer Queen Mary College (1986-1987); own practice (1972-1989); became partner Harris Rosenblatt & Kramer; chairman of Industrial Tribunals (England & Wales) (1984) (part-time); visiting Professor Cornell University School of Industrial and Labour Relations (1989).

Activities: member Law Society's Committee on Employment Law; chairman Mansfield Law Club (1976-1979); while at City Polytechnic Course Organiser for Law Society Part II and Finals course; a Law Society Examination Moderator; chairman External Relations Committee for the Law Faculty and also for Short Courses; consultant to Hill Bailey and Co (1980-1988); member Industrial Law Society; member of: Oakleigh Park Lawn Tennis & Squash Club; MCC and Middlesex County Cricket Club.

Biography: lives London N20; born 19.01.1947; married to Helen (BA, MSc) social worker with 3 daughters. Educated at William Ellis School, Highgate; London School of Economics (1969 LLB hons) (1972 LLM hons); co-author Butterworths Employment Law Guide (1990); authored numerous publications and presented numerous papers at home and abroad.

Leisure: squash; cricket (playing and spectator); running; theatre; music; reading.

MORE George

senior partner MORE & CO
19 Dublin Street, Edinburgh.

Career: apprenticed to Edinburgh firm of lawyers (1965-1967); admitted (1967); assistant solicitor (1967-1969); became partner Ogilvie More & Co (1969-1975); founded More & Co (1976).

Activities: tutored in criminal advocacy at Edinburgh University; president of the Society of Procurators of Midlothian (1984-1985); member George Heriot's former pupils' cricket and rugby clubs.

Biography: lives Edinburgh; born 05.06.1944; married to Barbara with 2 sons and 1 daughter. Educated at George Heriot's School; Edinburgh University (1965 LLB).

Leisure: sport particularly cricket; holiday home in Ardnamurchan in the West Highlands; enjoys the flora and fauna of the Scottish Highlands.

MORGAN David Llewellyn

partner company department RICHARDS BUTLER Beaufort House, 15 St Botolph Street, London EC3A 7EE.

Career: articled James Morgan & Co, Cardiff (1956-1959); admitted (1959); assistant solicitor Richards Butler (1959-1964); assistant solicitor Herbert Smith (1964-1965); became partner Richards Butler (1965).

Activities: non-executive director Deymel Investments Limited (1966 to date) (chairman 1977 to date); member City of London Law Society Company Law sub-committee; Liveryman Worshipful Company of Clockmakers; member of: Travellers' Club; United Oxford and Cambridge Universities Club; City University Club; Cardiff and Country Club.

Biography: lives London SW1; born 05.10.1932; single. Educated at Charterhouse; Trinity College Cambridge (MA); articles in the Journal of Business Law.

Leisure: DIY in house and garden.

MORGAN-HARRIS James

partner THOMAS EGGAR VERRALL BOWLES East Pallant, Chichester, Sussex.

Career: articled Thomas Eggar & Son; admitted (1970); assistant solicitor (1970-1975); became partner (1975).

Activities: chairman Chichester & District Law Society Litigation Sub-committee; former Crown Court Liaison Officer; member of: Wig & Pen Club; West Sussex County Club; Regnum Club.

Biography: lives Chichester; born 01.02.1946; married to Elaine with 4 children. Educated at Wellington School; Southampton University (1967 LLB hons); College of Law Guildford.

Leisure: golf; fishing.

MORGENSTERN Philip

senior partner NICHOLSON GRAHAM & JONES 19/21 Moorgate, London EC2R 6AU.

Career: articled Nicholson Graham & Jones (1954-1957); admitted (1958); assistant solicitor (1958-1961); became partner (1962).

Activities: director of bank, insurance company and other companies; trustee and patron of learned institutions.

Biography: lives London; born 15.01.1932; married to Estelle with 4 children.

Educated at St Paul's School; London University (1954 BA hons).

Leisure: Hermeneutic and rhetorical exegesis of ancient texts; music; art history.

MORRIS David

senior partner TRETHOWANS College Chambers, New Street, Salisbury, Wilts SP1 2LY.

Career: Yardley & Co Ltd; became advertising manager; articled Trethowans (1966-1970); admitted (1970); became senior partner (1979).

Activities: clerk to the General Commissioners of Income Tax South Wiltshire Division; past president Salisbury Solicitors Association; past president Gloucestershire and Wiltshire Incorporated Law Society.

Biography: lives near Salisbury; born 18.01.1935; divorced with 2 children. Educated at Charterhouse; Christ Church Oxford (1957 hons); Holford Exhibitioner and hon scholar.

Leisure: gardening; shooting.

MORRIS David

barrister and head of chambers 30 Park Place, Cardiff CF1 3BA.

Career: called to the Bar Lincoln's Inn (1965); pupillage 4 Paper Buildings and 9 Old Square (1965-1967); tenant 2 Dr Johnson's Buildings (1967-1972); member Chambers 30 Park Place (1972).

Activities: Deputy Circuit Judge (1978); Recorder (1984); Wales & Chester circuit rep for Barristers' Benevolent Association and Lincoln's Inn; local junior for Cardiff (1984-1988); founder member Round Table, 41 and Rotary Clubs of Llantwit Major and Llanmaes Community Council; member Cardiff and County Club.

Biography: lives Castleton; born 10.03.1940; married to Carolyn with 2 children. Educated at Abingdon School, Oxon; King's College London (1963 LLB hons); City of London College (1985 Diploma in Comparative Law).

Leisure: watching rugby union football; swimming; theatre; gardening; reading; enjoying family.

MORRIS John

Queen's Counsel 3 Hare Court, Temple, London EC4.

Career: called to the Bar Gray's Inn; QC (1973); Recorder of the Crown Court.

M

Activities: MP Aberavon (1959 to date); Privy Counsellor (1970); Parliamentary Secretary Ministry of Power and Ministry of Transport; Minister for Defence Equipment; Secretary of State for Wales; Shadow Attorney General.

Biography: born 05.11.1931; married to Margaret with 3 daughters. Educated at Ardwyn Grammar School, Aberystwyth University College Wales (LLB) LLD (hon CAUSA); Gonville and Caius College Cambridge (LLM); Academy of International Law, The Hague; Holker Senior Exhibitioner Gray's Inn.

MORRIS Leslie

senior partner WALKER MORRIS SCOTT TURNBULL Holbeck House, 105 Albion Street, Leeds LS1 5AY.

Career: assistant examiner/examiner Estate Duty Office Inland Revenue (1956-1961); Inspector of Taxes (1961-1963); Fellow of Institute of Taxation (1964); admitted (1966); became partner Walker Morris & Coles (1966); senior partner when Walker Morris Scott Turnbull formed (1988).

Activities: member Revenue Law Committee (1990 to date); member Law Society Revenue Law Tax Appeals Sub-committee and Capital Taxes Sub-committee; some minor directorships.

Biography: lives Leeds; born 28.02.1933; married to Pat with 3 children. Educated at High Storrs Grammar School; Sheffield University (1954 BA hons); King's College London (1959 LLB hons).

Leisure: sport; countryside; travel; reading.

MORRISH Peter

head of chambers Goldsmith Building, Temple, London EC4Y 7BL.

Career: Metropolitan Police (1948-1949); Northern Rhodesia Police (1950-1961); called to the Bar Gray's Inn (1962); Flying Officer RAF (1961-1963); deputy clerk Inner London Magistrates' Courts Service (1963-1964); clerk Courts of the County of London Quarter Sessions (1964-1965); assistant clerk Peace of the County Palatine of Lancaster Quarter Sessions (1965-1966); deputy clerk Middlesex Quarter Sessions area of Greater London (1966-1970); deputy clerk Central Criminal Court, Old Bailey (1970-1974); assistant solicitor Criminal Appeals Office RCJ (1974-1978); South Eastern circuit (1978 to date).

Activities: deputy stipendiary magistrate Bow Street Magistrates' Court (1968-1972);

member Chief Taxing Master's Committee on Legal Taxation (1974-1978; lectured on criminal law; associate member Magistrates' Association of England & Wales; member The Wig & Pen Club.

Biography: lives London E17 and Whitchurch-on-Thames; born 16.04.1927; married to Norah with 3 children. Educated at The Lion School, Winchester; Peter Symond's School, Winchester; Edinburgh University (1945); Metropolitan Police Senior Detectives Training School, Hendon (1954); various articles on criminal law and road traffic in Justice of the Peace Journal (1966-1983); co-editor Justice of the Peace Journal (1978-1982); contributor to: Archbold Criminal Pleading Evidence & Practice; Vol II Halsbury's Laws of England on Criminal Law (4th ed); co-author: 'Appeals in the Criminal Courts'; 'The Magistrates' Courts - An Index' (8 eds); 'The Crown Court - An Index' (12 eds); 'The Trial of Breathalyser Offences' (2 eds); 'Practice and Procedure in the Court of Appeal Criminal Division'.

Leisure: writing mainly legal books; reading; gardening; walking.

MORRISON Michael

senior partner TAYLOR JOYNSON GARRETT 180 Fleet Street, London EC4A 2NT.

Career: articled Allen & Overy; admitted; assistant solicitor (2 years); assistant solicitor Parker Garrett (1968-1969); became partner (1969); merged with Taylor & Humbert (1982); merged with Joynson-Hicks (1989).

Activities: director of: Ambia Marine (UK) Limited; Bessemer Group UK Limited; Futuremill Limited; Gainhalf Limited; Huntsmoor Nominees Limited; Huntsmoor Nominees (Fleet Street) Limited; Bride Developments Limited; Uxbridge Springwaters Developments Limited; Beaumont House Properties Limited; Leif Hoegh (UK) Limited; Merchant Viking Limited; Phil ot Trading Co Limited; Yuills Limited; Law 109 Limited; Law 117 Limited; former director of: Norwegian American Cruises (UK) Limited; Pomeroys Restaurants Limited; The Oxford & Cambridge Fine Wine Co Limited; secretary Autoliners (UK) Limited; former member of the Council of the Policy Signing and Accountancy Centre; member of: RAC; Moor Park Golf Club; Den Norske Klub; Danish Club.

Biography: lives Moor Park and Whitby; born 31.03.1939; married to June with 2 children. Educated at Dragon School,

Oxford; Fettes College, Edinburgh; St Catharine's College Cambridge (1962 MA LLB).

Leisure: theatre; golf; swimming; squash.

MORTIMER John

Queen's Counsel c/o 10 Buckingham Street, London WC2; Fellow of the Royal Society of Literature; CBE (1986).

Career: called to the Bar (1948); QC (1966); master of the Bench Inner Temple (1975).

Activities: member National Theatre Board (1968-1988); president Berks Bucks and Oxon Naturalists' Trust (1984 to date); chairman of the Royal Society of Literature (1989 to date); chairman of The Royal Court Theatre (1990 to date).

Biography: lives Henley on Thames; born 21.04.1923; married to Penelope (divorced) with 1 son and 1 daughter; married to Penelope with 2 daughters. Educated at Harrow; Brasenose College Oxford; hon D Litt Susquehanna University (1985); St Andrew's (1987); hon LLD Exeter (1986); Italia Prize for short play (1958); British Academy Writers Award (1979); BAFTA Writer of the Year Award (1980); Book of the Year Award Yorkshire Post (1982); Nottingham University (DLitt); Doctor of Brunel University (1990); author of: many plays, novels, film and television scripts; contributes to periodicals.

Leisure: working; gardening; opera.

MORTON Andrew

partner ALLEN & OVERY 9 Cheapside, London EC2V 6AD.

Career: assistant solicitor Allen & Overy (1968-1973); became partner (1973).

Activities: member of: Royal Harwich Yacht Club; Royal Wimbledon Golf Club.

Biography: lives Surrey; born 05.07.1943; married to Angela with 2 children. Educated at Charterhouse; Merton College Oxford (1965 BA).

Leisure: sailing; golf; skiing.

MOSS Gary

partner TAYLOR JOYNSON GARRETT 10 Maltravers Street, London WC2R 3BS.

Career: articled Wilkinson Kimbers (1975-1977); admitted (1977); assistant solicitor Clifford Turner (1977-1979); assistant solicitor Woodham Smith (1979-1980); partner (1980); became partner Taylor Joynson Garrett (1990).

Activities: member Law Society joint

M

working party on intellectual property.

Biography: lives London; born 07.04.1953; married to Nina with 3 children. Educated at Hampton Grammar School; Enfield Grammar School; Leicester University (1974 hons); College of Law (1975 hons); John Mackrell Prize.

Leisure: squash; golf; watching football; theatre; opera; reading.

MOSS Gerald

senior partner SHENTONS Star Lane House, Staple Gardens, Winchester, Hants SO23 9AD.

Career: articled Shentons (1950-1954); admitted (1954); assistant solicitor (1954-1955); became partner (1955).

Activities: president Hampshire Law Society; president Mental Health Review Tribunal; hon solicitor Winchester Chamber of Commerce; hon solicitor Hampshire Playing Fields Association; trustee Royal Winchester Golf Club.

Biography: lives Winchester; born 16.02.1927; married to Jean with 2 children. Educated at Peter Symonds School; St Edmund Hall Oxford (1950 MA); Association Football Blue; Charles Ford Trust Prize (Hampshire Law Society, 1953).

Leisure: golf.

MOSTYN Paul

family law partner HORWOOD & JAMES 7 Temple Square, Aylesbury, Bucks.

Career: articled in the Midlands; admitted (1970); assistant solicitor in the City and West End (1970-1977); assistant solicitor Bucks (1977-1980); assistant solicitor Horwood & James (1980-1982); became partner (1982).

Activities: Deputy County Court and District Registrar Midland and Oxford Circuit; part-time and/or occasional law lecturer Aylesbury College; member various motoring clubs.

Biography: lives Granborough; born 08.10.1945; married to Elizabeth with 3 children. Educated at Ampleforth College; College of Law.

Leisure: vintage cars; gardening.

MOSTYN-WILLIAMS Stephen

partner BARLOW LYDE & GILBERT Beaufort House, 15 St Botolph Street, London EC3A 7NJ.

Career: articled Travers Smith Braithwaite; admitted (1981); assistant solicitor (1981-

1985); assistant solicitor Barlow Lyde & Gilbert (1985-1986); became partner (1986).

Biography: lives London N5; born 25.02.1956; married with 4 children. Educated at St Peter's School, Bournemouth; Bristol University (1979 LLB).

Leisure: theatre; opera; riding; wind-surfing; rugby; squash.

MOUGHTON Barry

partner TURNER KENNETH BROWN 100 Fetter Lane, London EC4A 1DD.

Career: articled Robins Olivey & Lake; admitted (1958); assistant solicitor (1958-1961); assistant solicitor Turner Kenneth Brown (1961); became partner (1963).

Activities: chairman Dorking Urban District Council (1967-1968); magistrate (1967-1971); past president Rotary Club of London; member Law Society European Group; chairman Churches of Dorking Housing Association.

Biography: lives Dorking; born 28.05.1932; married to Elizabeth with 3 children. Educated at Merchant Taylors' (Scholar); Oxford (1954 MA); McGill University, Canada (1960 MCL).

Leisure: choral singing.

MOYSE Richard

partner and head of tax and financial planning department BOODLE HATFIELD 43 Brook Street, London W1Y 2BL.

Career: articled Peacock Fisher (1966-1969); admitted (1970); assistant solicitor Lawrence Graham (1970-1973); assistant solicitor Boodle Hatfield (1973-1974); became partner (1974).

Activities: member Revenue Law Committee of Law Society of England and Wales; member Westminster Law Society Revenue Law Committee; member Executive Committee of the International Academy of Estate and Trust Law; member International Bar Association Revenue Law and Estate Planning Law Section.

Biography: lives London SW18 and Shipdham; born 29.09.1943; married to Elizabeth with 4 children. Educated at Plymouth College Preparatory School; Plymouth College; Oxford (1965 BA); various legal periodicals, articles and contribution to Business Law Encyclopaedia.

Leisure: choral singing; fishing; walking; genealogy; watching cricket.

MULLIGAN Richard

senior partner DODSON HARDING King William House, 16/17 King Square, Bridgwater, Somerset TA6 3AN.

Career: left army (1948); articled Mooring Aldridge & Haydon (1948-1953); admitted (1953); assistant solicitor Dodson & Pulman (now Dodson Harding) (1954-1958); became partner (1958).

Activities: vice-president Somerset Law Society (1989-1990); prospective president Somerset Law Society (1990-1991); member and hon legal adviser for Somerset Archaeological & Natural History Society; clerk Clatworthy Parish Council; ex church warden and member Huish Champflower Parochial Church Council; hon legal adviser Taunton Deane Research & Excavation Committee; trustee Westonzoyland Engine Trust; trustee Carew & James Charity; member Society of Nautical Research; member Naval Record Society; member of Ferrari Owners' Club.

Biography: lives Wiveliscombe; born 05.02.1927; single. Educated at Bloxham; Gibsons of Chancery Lane.

Leisure: following hounds (stag); railway preservation (part owner of one steam locomotive and owner of one GWR syphon G and toad guards van); motoring; naval history.

MUNDAY Peter

senior partner MUNDAYS The Bellbourne, 103 High Street, Esher, Surrey.

Career: National Service RCS (1957-1959); admitted (1968); partner Mundays (1968); senior partner (1976).

Activities: Notary Public (1975); chairman and trustee Princess Alice Hospice Esher; trustee Esher War Memorial Property Fund; Friend of St George's Church; Freeman City of London; Liveryman Worshipful Company of Bakers; member Law Society (1968); Notaries' Society (1975); member of MCC.

Biography: lives Oxshott; born 31.10.1938; married to Lin with 2 children.

Leisure: hockey; squash; cricket.

MURPHY Brian Gordon

partner FARRER & CO 66 Lincoln's Inn Fields, London WC2A 3LH.

Career: articled Smiles & Co; admitted (1966); assistant solicitor Roythorne & Co; assistant solicitor Russell & Dumoulin, Vancouver, Canada; became partner Knapp-Fishers (1968-1987); became partner Farrer & Co (1987).

Activities: president City of Westminster Law Society (1983-1984); council member of the Law Society (1982 to date); chairman Law Society's Employment Law Committee; council member Incorporated Council of Law reporting for England and Wales; member Law Society's Courts and Legal Services Committee.

Biography: lives London SW3 and Bourne End; born 18.10.1940; married to Judy. Educated at Mill Hill School.

MURPHY Francis

consultant HAROLD G WALKER & COMPANY Lansdowne House, Bournemouth BH1 3JT.

Career: Royal Navy (1942-1951) (Lt); articled late Col AW Malim (1951-1953); admitted (1954); assistant solicitor Luff Raymond & Williams (1954-1958); assistant solicitor Harold G Walker & Company (1958-1959); became partner (1959); became consultant (1988).

Activities: member of: Royal Naval Sailing Association; Law Society Yacht Club.

Biography: lives Blandford; born 04.03.1923; married to Pauline with 2 children. Educated at Panton College .

Leisure: sailing.

MURPHY John

corporate partner THEODORE GODDARD 150 Aldersgate Street, London EC1A 4EJ.

Career: articled Coward Chance (1969-1971); admitted (1971); assistant solicitor (1971-1974); assistant solicitor Crawley & De Reya (1974-1976); partner (1976-1978); partner Bartletts De Reya (1978-1988); became partner Theodore Goddard (1988).

Activities: member DTI/Soviet Working Party on Consortia; member Law Society Working Party on USSR and East Europe; vice-chairman of The Anglo-Polish Legal Association; member International Chamber of Commerce East/West Committee; numerous talks at seminars on East/West trade legal matters throughout Europe; secretary of British-Hungarian Law Association; member of the Advisory Board to HM Government Know-How Funds; founder member East Europe Business Club; member of: RNVR Yacht Club; Law Society Yacht Club.

Biography: lives London; born 16.01.1948; married to Jocelyn with 1 daughter. Educated at St Peter's School, Downside (Major Scholarship); Magdalen College Oxford (1968 MA hons) (Major

Scholarship); author of: 'Joint Ventures in Poland'(1989); 'Joint Ventures in The Soviet Union'(1988); 'Joint Ventures in Poland: The New Legislation'(1989); 'Joint Ventures in Hungary'(1989).

Leisure: sailing; music; eating; drinking; reading; swimming; talking; sleeping.

MURRAY Iain

partner LINKLATERS & PAINES Barrington House, 59-67 Gresham Street, London EC2V 7JA.

Career: articled Freshfields (1956-1959); admitted (1959); assistant solicitor Robert Fleming & Co (including 9 months on secondment to GH Walker (Investment Bankers) Wall Street 1960-1962); assistant solicitor Linklaters & Paines (1963-1967); became partner (1967).

Activities: member Law Society Company Law Committee (1970s); member City of London SolicitorsCompany (1970s); member inflation accounting and property bonds working parties (1970s); member CBI Companies Committee; various lectures at home and abroad; member of: City of London Club; Travellers' Club; New Club.

Biography: lives London; born 12.11.1932; married to Ursula with 3 children. Educated at Rugby School; Corpus Christi College Cambridge (1956 BA MA); writes papers relating to legal matters.

Leisure: walking.

MYERS Ronnie

senior partner MYERS LISTER PRICE 376 Palatine Road, Northenden, Manchester M22 4FZ.

Career: articled Smith Fort & Symonds (1960-1963); admitted (1963); assistant solicitor (1963-1965); partner Linder Myers (1965-1975); senior partner (1975-1988); became senior partner Myers Lister Price (1988).

Activities: Commissioner for Oaths; member Manchester Law Society Conveyancing Committee; interview panelist SolicitorsComplaints Bureau; hon life president South Manchester FC; company director.

Biography: lives Manchester; born 29.08.1939; married to Denise with 1 son and 1 daughter. Educated at Bootham School, York (1953-1957); Manchester University (1960 LLB hons).

Leisure: Bel Canto Opera; Pavarotti; Manchester City FC.

NAPIER Michael

senior partner IRWIN MITCHELL and partner PANNONE NAPIER St Peter's House, Hartshead, Sheffield S1 2EL.

Career: articled Moss Toone & Deane, Loughborough; admitted (1970); assistant solicitor WH Thompson (1970-1972); partner Irwin Mitchell (1973); joint founding partner Pannone Napier (1985).

Activities: appointed to Mental Health Act Commission (1983) (vice-chairman 1985-1988) chairman North East Region (1985-1990); joint founder and past president South Yorkshire Medico-Legal Society; member Governing Board Association of Trial Lawyers of America; member JUSTICE/World Federation for Mental Health; MIND/American Society of Law & Medicine; British Academy of Experts; Trial Lawyers for Public Justice; Law Society Negligence Panel; Law Society Mental Health Panel; first UK solicitor to appear as advocate before European Court of Human Rights Strasbourg; joint founder and trustee Pitsmoor Citizens Advice Bureau; regular chairman of seminars on all aspects of personal injury claims; frequent lecturer and broadcaster on compensation and medico-legal matters; joint founder and secretary Association of Personal Injury Lawyers (1990); member Abbeydale Sports Club.

Biography: lives Derbyshire and Norfolk; born 11.06.1946; married to Denise with 3 children. Educated at Loughborough Grammar School; open exhibition to Hulme Hall Manchester University (1967 LLB) (president of Hall 1967); member editorial board Personal & Medical Injuries Law Letter and The Journal of Forensic Psychiatry; author of: 'Psychiatrist & Lawyer - total incompatibility?'(1986); 'Compensation for traumatically induced psychiatric injury'(1989); 'Adverse Drug Reactions: The legal implications of signal generation'(1989); 'The Battle for Compensation'(1990).

Leisure: sport generally; occasional cricket; relaxing on North Norfolk coast and messing about in small boat with family.

NAPLEY Sir David

senior partner KINGSLEY NAPLEY 107-115 Long Acre, London WC2E 9PT.

Career: admitted (1937); served with Queen's Royal (W Surrey) Regt (1940); command (1942); Indian Army (1942);

N

Captain (1942); invalided (1945); senior partner Kingsley Napley.

Activities: president of the Law Society (1976-1977) (vice-president 1975-1976); contested (C) Rowley Regis and Tipton (1951); Gloucester (1955); president Criminal Courts SolicitorsAssociation (1960-1963): chairman Executive Council British Academy of Forensic Sciences (1960-1974) (president 1967) director (1974 to date); member Council Law Society (1962 to date); member Judicial Exchange with USA (1963-1964); chairman Law Society's Standing Committee on Criminal Law (1963-1976); president City of Westminster Law Society (1967-1968); member Editorial Board Criminal Law Review (1967 to date); chairman Contentious Business Law Society (1972-1975); Legal Aid Committee (1969-1972); Examining Board Incorporated Society of Valuers and Auctioneers (1981-1984); member Home Office Law Revision Committee (1971); chairman Council and trustee Imperial Society of Kts Bachelor (1981 to date) chairman Mario and Franco Restaurants Ltd (1968-1977); trustee W Ham Boys' Club (1979 to date) president (1981 to date); member Garrick Club.

Biography: lives Berkshire; born 25.07.1915; married to Leah with 2 children. Educated Burlington College; author of 'Law on the Remuneration of Auctioneers and Estate Agents'(1947); (ed) 'Bateman's Law of Auctions'(1954); author of: 'The Law of Auctioneers and Estate Agents Commission'(1957); 'Crime and Criminal Procedure'(1963); 'Guide to Law and Practice under the Criminal Justice Act'(1967); 'The Technique of Persuasion'(1970); (3rd edition 1984); 'Not without Prejudice'(1982); section 'Halsbury's Laws of England'; 'The Camden Town Murder'(1987); 'Murder at the Villa Madeira'(1988); 'Rasputin in Hollywood'(1990); contributor to legal and forensic scientific journals; press; legal discussions on radio and TV.

Leisure: painting; reading; writing; music; eating.

NATHAN Lord

consultant DENTON HALL BURGIN & WARRENS Five Chancery Lane, Clifford's Inn, London EC4A 1BU.

Career: admitted (1950); partner Herbert Oppenheimer Nathan & Vandyk; became senior partner (1978-1987); became consultant (1987-1988); became consultant Denton Hall Burgin & Warrens (1988).

Activities: associate member Bar

Association of City of New York and New York County Lawyers' Association; chairman House of Lords Select Committee on Murder and Life Imprisonment; member Royal Commission on Environmental Pollution (1979-1989); House of Lords Select Committee on European Communities (1983-1988 & 1990 to date); chairman Environment Sub-committee (1983-1987 and 1990 to date); chairman Ad-hoc Sub-committee on the European Company Statute (1989-1990); president UK Environmental Law Association (1987 to date); chairman Institute of Environmental Assessment (1990 to date); chairman National Council for Voluntary Organisations Working Party Report 'Effectiveness and the Voluntary Sector'reported (1990); vice-chairman Committee on Charity Law and Practice reported (1976); chairman Working Party on Energy and the Environment (reported 1974); chairman Royal Society of Arts (1975-1977) (vice-president 1977 to date); vice-chairman Cancer Research Campaign (1987 to date) (chairman Executive Committee 1970-1975) (treasurer 1979-1987); chairman Arbitration Panel The Securities Association; founder and chairman The America-European Community Association Trust; president Jewish Welfare Board (1967-1971); hon president Central British Fund for Jewish Relief and Rehabilitation (chairman 1970-1977); member of: Athenaeum; Cavalry & Guards.

Biography: lives Petworth; born 05.12.1922; married to Philippa with 3 children. Educated at Stowe School; New College Oxford (1946 MA); Sussex (1988 hon LLD); papers: 'Is Charity Redundant'(1975); 'Innovation: Secrecy and Protection'(1976); MacMillan Education Lecture on Energy and the Environment; Garner Lecture (UK Environmental Law Association) 'Fencing our Eden'.

NAYLOR Lynne

partner AVERY NAYLOR LANE & WILSON 35/36 Walter Road, Swansea, West Glamorgan SA1 5NW.

Career: articled John Morse & Co (1976-1978); admitted (1979); assistant solicitor (1979-1982); became partner (1982).

Activities: Regional Duty Solicitor Committee South Wales (1984); chairman/administrator Swansea Local Duty Solicitor Committee (1984); Law Society Standing Committee Criminal Law (1985); Crown Court Rule Committee (1986); legal advisor National Childrens

Homes South Glamorgan and Dyfed areas (1986 and 1987); legal advisor Disabled Drivers' Club, Swansea.

Biography: lives Swansea; born 25.06.1953; single. Educated at Bentley Lane Primary School, Leeds; Alterton High School for Girls, Leeds; University College of Swansea (1974 BSC); correspondence course College of Law (1974-1976).

Leisure: gardening.

NEATE Francis

partner SLAUGHTER AND MAY 35 Basinghall Street, London EC2V 5DB.

Career: articled Slaughter and May (1964-1966); admitted (1966); assistant solicitor (1966-1972); became partner (1972).

Activities: chairman Commercial Banking Committee of the section on business law of the International Bar Association; vice-president Berkshire CCC; trustee Richmond CC; president Falkland CC; member MCC.

Biography: lives London SW15; born 13.05.1940; married to Patricia with 4 children. Educated at St Wilfrid's School, Seaford (1947-1951); St Paul's School, London (1951-1958); Brasenose College Oxford (1962 BA); University of Chicago Law School (1963 JD).

Leisure: family; cricket.

NEEDHAM George

partner COOPER SONS HARTLEY & WILLIAMS 9 Terrace Road, Buxton, Derbyshire SK17 6DU.

Career: articled with father at TA Needham & Son (1967-1969); admitted (1969); assistant solicitor Norton Rose Botterell & Roche (1969-1971); became partner Towns Needham & Co (1971-1974); became partner Cooper Sons Hartley & Williams (1974).

Activities: member negligence panel SolicitorsComplaints Bureau; member Legal Aid Area Committee; Deputy Registrar of High Court and County Court.

Biography: lives Chinley nr Buxton; Oxford; London and Manchester; born 31.03.1945; married with 1 child. Educated at Manchester Grammar School (1956-1963); Worcester College Oxford (1963-1966); College of Law (1966-1967).

Leisure: reading (particulary medieval and slavonic history); theatre; walking.

NELSON Bernard

partner WHITE & CASE 66 Gresham Street, London EC2V 7LB.

Career: joined White & Case (1975); admitted New York (1976); associate New York (1975-1977 & 1980-1988); Paris (1977-1980); became partner (1984); London (1988 to date).

Activities: US representative on the steering committee of the Permanent Tax Commission of the Union Internationale des Avocats.

Biography: lives London SW3; born 09.05.1950; married to Jane with 3 children. Educated at Yale College (1972 BA); Harvard Law School (1975 JD).

Leisure: collecting antiquarian books and maps.

NELSON Richard

senior partner NELSON JOHNSON & HASTINGS Pennine House, 8 Stanford Street, Nottingham NG1 7BQ.

Career: articled J & K Bright Richards & Flewitt; admitted; assistant solicitor; assistant solicitor Freeth Cartwright & Sketchley; became partner (1980-1983); became senior partner Nelson Johnson & Hastings (1983).

Activities: member Criminal Business Committee Notts Law Society; vice-chairman The Nottinghamshire Hospice; committee member Old Nottinghamians Society; member Old Nottinghamians CC (former captain 1st XI).

Biography: lives Nottingham; born 14.06.1950; married to Elizabeth with 1 son and 1 daughter. Educated at Greenholme School; Nottingham High School; Bristol University (1972 LLB hons).

Leisure: sport; cricket; rugby; comedy; cinema; theatre.

NELSON-JONES John

business development partner FIELD FISHER WATERHOUSE 41 Vine Street, London EC3N 2AA.

Career: articled Gregory Rowcliffe & Co (1960-1963); admitted (1963); assistant solicitor Nicholas & Co (1964-1965); assistant solicitor Howard Kennedy & Co (1966-1967); became partner Peacock Fisher & Finch (now Field Fisher Waterhouse) (1968).

Activities: tax editor Law Society's Gazette (1972-1980); chairman Business Law Section Holborn Law Society (1985-1986); chairman Travel and Tourism Law Committee of International Bar Association (1987 to date); council member National Consumer Council (1987 to date) (chairman NCC's Legal Advisory Panel

1987 to date); member Board of Job Ownership Ltd; member Council of City Technology Colleges Trust; member Hurlingham Club.

Biography: lives London; born 26.07.1934; married to Helene with 2 children. Educated at Repton; Trinity College Oxford (1955-1958); joint author of: first three editions Nelson-Jones 'Practical Tax Saving' and of 'Package Holiday Law and Contracts'; principal author 'Employee Ownership - Legal and Tax Aspects'; contributor of chapters on Commercial Agency and Franchising.

Leisure: reading; classical music; tennis.

NELSON-JONES Rodney

partner in charge of medical litigation department FIELD FISHER WATERHOUSE 41 Vine Street, London EC3N 2AA.

Career: articled Prothero & Prothero (1973-1975); admitted (1975); assistant solicitor (1975-1977); assistant solicitor L Bingham & Co (1977-1978); became partner (1978); became partner Field Fisher & Martineau (now Field Fisher Waterhouse) (1983); equity partner (1985).

Activities: past chairman Spaid Legal Working Party; member of M1 Air Disaster Solicitors Steering Committee; member Campden Hill LTC.

Biography: lives London W9; born 11.02.1947; married to Kusum. Educated at Repton; Hertford College Oxford (1970 PPE); Herbert Ruse Prize in Law Society's exams; author of: 'Product Liability - The New Law under the Consumer Protection Act 1987' with Peter Stewart (1987); 'Medical Negligence Case Law' with Frank Burton (1990); 'Nelson-Jones and Nuttall's Tax and Interest Tables' with Graeme Nuttall (1988, 1989, 1990); contributor of articles to the Law Society's Gazette on personal injury interest limitation, provisional damages and fatal accident damages.

Leisure: cinema; tennis; travel.

NETTLESHIP Robert

partner MORGAN BRUCE PO Box 45, Princess House, Princess Way, Swansea SA1 5LW.

Career: articled Andrew Thompson & Partners; admitted (1959); assistant solicitor Beor Wilson & Lloyd (1959-1961); became partner Collins Woods & Vaughan Jones (1961-1967); founded own practice (1967); merged to form Geo L Thomas Netleship & Co (1969); merged with

Morgan Bruce & Hardwickes (1988); merged with Collins Woods & Vaughan Jones to form Morgan Bruce (1989).

Activities: member of: Cardiff and County Club; Bristol Channel Yacht Club; Pennard Golf Club (honorary); City of Swansea Swimming Club (vice-president).

Biography: lives Swansea; born 30.01.1936; married to Judith with 2 children. Educated at Stowe.

Leisure: swimming; music; singing in church choir; opera.

NEWELL David

head of government and legal affairs department THE NEWSPAPER SOCIETY Bloomsbury Square, 74-77 Great Russell Street, London WC1B 3DA.

Career: articled Lawford & Co (1976-1978); admitted (1978); lecturer in law Leicester University (1978-1986); became head of government and legal affairs department The Newspaper Society (1984).

Activities: secretary of Parliamentary and Legal Committee of Guild of British Newspaper Editors (1984 to date); member Law Society's Employment Law Committee; the Media Law Group; Law Society/Guild of Editors' Joint Committee; the Advertising Standards Authority's Code of Advertising Practice Committee; the Advertising Association's Public Action Group; Politicians Working Party and International Working Party; Fleet Street Lawyers' Society; member Campaign for Freedom of Information Council.

Biography: lives London; born 21.09.1951; married to Cora with 1 daughter, Rebecca. Educated at Shrewsbury School (1965-1970); Birmingham University (1973 LLB); College of Law (1973-1974); Southampton University (1975 M Phil); UK Press Gazette Special Award (1988); Campaign for Freedom of Information Award (1989); numerous books and articles.

Leisure: walking; swimming; windsurfing; sailing; theatre; cinema.

NEWMAN George

Queen's Counsel and head of chambers 1 Crown Office Row, Temple, London EC4Y 7HH.

Career: called to the Bar (1965); pupillage with Christopher French QC; QC (1981); Recorder (1985); Bencher Middle Temple (1989).

Biography: lives Mayfield; born 04.07.1941; married to Hilary with 2 sons and 1 daughter. Educated at Lewes County Grammar School; St Catharine's College Cambridge (1964); Squire Scholar; Blackstone Scholar; joint contributor to 4th ed Halsbury's Laws 'Agency'.

Leisure: mountains; sea; countryside.

NICHOLAS Paul

partner and head of insurance/professional indemnity department REYNOLDS PORTER CHAMBERLAIN Chichester House, 278/282 High Holborn, London WC1V 7HA.

Career: articled Reynolds Porter (1968-1970); admitted (1970); assistant solicitor (1970-1972); became partner (1972).

Activities: legal adviser to Headmasters' Conference and Incorporated Association of Preparatory Schools; governor Lockers Park School; member of: Ashridge Golf Club; Connaught Snooker Club.

Biography: lives Felden; born 24.04.1946; married to Elsa with 1 son and 1 daughter. Educated at Mill Hill School; Emmanuel College Cambridge (BA LLB).

Leisure: watching all sports except tennis.

NICHOLLS Patrick

senior partner DUNN & BAKER 212 Southernhay East, Exeter.

Activities: Parliamentary Under Secretary of State Department of Employment; Member of Parliament for Teignbridge; former vice-chairman Society of Conservative Lawyers; member of Employment Bill Standing Committee (1987 & 1988); member Video Recording Standing Committee (1984); member Police and Criminal Evidence Bill (1984); member Carlton Club.

Biography: lives Farringdon; born 14.11.1948; married with 3 children. Educated at St Peter's School, Harefield; Redrice College, Andover; College of Law Guildford; Exeter Technical College.

Leisure: riding; theatre; opera; historical research.

NICHOLLS Trevor

senior partner GREENLAND HOUCHEN 38 Prince of Wales Road, Norwich NR1 1HZ.

Career: National Service in the army; commissioned in the Royal Norfolk Regiment; seconded to 1st Battalion Sierra Leone Regiment, Royal West African Frontier Force (1953-1955); assistant superintendent of Police, Sierra Leone Police Force (1955-1961); law clerk Greenland Houchen (1961); admitted (1971); assistant solicitor (1971-1972); became partner (1972); became senior partner (1988).

Activities: member Norfolk Club.

Biography: lives South Norfolk; born 02.05.1935; married to Margaret with 5 children. Educated at Norwich Cathedral Choir School; Norwich School.

NICHOLSON Graham

managing partner FRESHFIELDS Whitefriars, 65 Fleet Street, London EC4Y 1HT.

Career: articled Freshfields; admitted (1974); assistant solicitor (1974-1980); partner (1980); New York office (1979-1980); Singapore office (1980-1983); managing partner company department (1986-1989); became managing partner (1990).

Biography: lives London W8 and Suffolk; born 22.02.1949; married to Pamela with 1 daughter. Educated at Bloxham School (1962-1967); Trinity Hall Cambridge (1971 MA).

Leisure: music; tennis; sailing.

NICHOLSON John Alasdair

partner in private client department BLYTH DUTTON 8 & 9 Lincoln's Inn Fields, London WC2A 3DW.

Career: articled Long & Gardiner (now Blyth Dutton) (1958-1963); admitted (1963); assistant solicitor (1963-1966); became partner (1966).

Activities: member Council of the Law Society (1985 to date) (member Professional Purposes Committee 1985-1987) (member Professional Development Committee 1986-1987) (member Adjudication Committee 1987-1988) (member Training Committee 1988 to date); member Holborn Law Society (1972 to date) (joint secretary 1973-1979) (president 1985-1986); member Lowtonian Society; member Court of Assistants of the Worshipful Company of Coachmakers & Coach Harness Makers of London (clerk to the Company 1978-1984); hon secretary Livery Companies Golfing Society; member of: Savile Club; MCC; Wig & Pen Club.

Biography: born 18.12.1938; 2 children. Educated at KCS Wimbledon; College of Law.

Leisure: cricket; fishing; DIY.

NICHOLSON Malcolm

partner SLAUGHTER AND MAY 35 Basinghall Street, London EC2V 5DB.

Career: admitted; became partner Slaughter and May.

Biography: lives Essex; born 04.03.1949; married with 4 children. Educated at Haileybury; Cambridge (BA LLB); Brussels (Lic en Droit Europeen); contributor to Bellamy and Child 'Common Market Law of Competition'.

NICHOLSON Robert

managing partner NICHOLSON CADGE & GILBERT 23 Alexandra Road, Lowestoft, Suffolk NR32 1PP.

Career: articled Taylor & Humbert (1970-1973); admitted (1973); assistant solicitor Nicholson Cadge & Gilbert (1973); became partner (1973).

Activities: director Adnams & Co PLC; member Royal Norfolk & Suffolk Yacht Club.

Biography: lives nr Lowestoft; born 04.03.1948; married to Stephanie with 3 children. Educated at King's College Choir School; Shrewsbury School; Birmingham University Law Faculty (1969 LLB); College of Law Guildford (1970).

Leisure: music; horse riding; sailing.

NOBLE John

senior partner BARTLETT GREGORY COLLINS & SNOW National Westminster Bank Chambers, 143 High Street, Bromley, Kent BR1 1JG.

Career: articled Ironside & Co (1949-1954); admitted (1954); assistant solicitor Patersons Snow & Co; assistant solicitor Lawrence Graham & Co; assistant solicitor Bartlett & Gregory; became partner.

Activities: costs certifyer; non-council member Property and Commercial Services Committee; Costs Certifying Committee; member National Protocol Working Party; sponsor Sevenoaks Christmas Fat Stock Show; member of: Kent Archaeological Society; RSPB.

Biography: lives nr Maidstone; born 01.12.1931; married to Cynthia with 2 sons. Educated at Rugby; joint editor of 4th edition of 'The Expense of Time'; sole editor of 'An Approach to Non-Contentious Costs'.

Leisure: 'rescue' archaeology; birdwatching; sheep farming; keeping geese for Christmas market; 18th-century architecture.

NODDER Edward

partner intellectual property and company commercial departments BRISTOWS COOKE & CARPMAEL 10 Lincoln's Inn Fields, London WC2A 3BP.

Career: articled Bristows Cooke & Carpmael (1978-1980); admitted (1980); assistant solicitor (1980-1985); became partner (1985).

Biography: lives East Sussex; born 29.06.1956; married to Rosalind. Educated at Lewes Grammar School; Christ's College Cambridge (1977 BA) (1980 MA); College of Law.

NORBURY Peter

partner ALEXANDER TATHAM & CO 30 St Ann Street, Manchester M2 3DB.

Career: articled Alexander Tatham & Co (1976); admitted; assistant solicitor; became partner (1984).

Biography: lives Ashton-under-Lyme; born 12.01.1953; married to Elizabeth with 1 son. Educated at Manchester Grammar School; Sheffield University (1975 LLB).

Leisure: all sports.

NORMAN Ronald

senior commercial partner MALKIN JANNERS PO Box No 243, Inigo House, 29 Bedford Street, London WC2E 9RT.

Career: articled Norton Rose (1968-1970); admitted (1970); assistant solicitor (1970-1975); assistant solicitor Travers Smith Braithwaite (1975-1978); head of commercial department Janners (1978-1988); head of commercial department Malkin Janners (1989).

Activities: member Cumberland Lawn Tennis Club.

Biography: lives London NW11; born 01.07.1945; married with 2 children. Educated at Highgate School; Gonville and Caius College Cambridge (MA LLB); Exhibitioner; magazine articles on general private company/commercial subjects.

Leisure: tennis; skiing.

NORRIS John

managing partner LUPTON FAWCETT Yorkshire House, Greek Street, Leeds LS1 5SX.

Career: admitted (1963).

Activities: president Leeds Law Society (1986); chairman North Rigton PC; member of: Leeds Club; Pannal GC (past captain); Harrogate Tennis Club; Taveners Club; Romany CC (past captain).

Biography: lives Harrogate; born 11.11.1938; married to Angela with 2 children. Educated at Leeds Grammar School; Pocklington School.

NORRIS William

partner ALLEN & OVERY 9 Cheapside, London EC2V 6AD.

Career: articled in Bedford and Weybridge (1954-1959); admitted (1959); lecturer Gibson & Weldon (now College of Law) (1959-1961); assistant solicitor Allen & Overy (1961-1964); became partner (1964).

Activities: chairman Revenue Law Committee of the Law Society; member Addington Society.

Biography: lives London; born 11.05.1937; married to Catherine with 3 children. Educated at Bedford School (1944-1954).

NORTH Peter

principal Jesus College and pro vice-chancellor UNIVERSITY OF OXFORD Oxford OX1 3DW.

Career: teaching associate Northwestern University School of Law, Chicago (1960-1961); assistant lecturer University College of Wales (1961-1963); lecturer Nottingham University (1963-1965); lecturer Worcester College Oxford (1965-1968); Fellow and Tutor in Law Keble College Oxford (1965-1976); University lecturer (CUF) Oxford (1966-1976); Fellow by Special Election Keble College Oxford (1976-1984); Law Commissioner for England and Wales (1976-1984); hon Fellow Keble College (1984); Associe de l'Institue de Droit International (1985); hon Bencher Inner Temple (1987); hon Fellow University College of North Wales (1988).

Activities: CBE (1989); Fellow of the British Academy (1990); chairman Faculty of Law University of Oxford (1971-1975); member Hebdomadal Council University of Oxford (1985 to date); member Council of Reading University (1986-1989); member Lord Chancellor's Advisory Committee on Legal Education (1973-1975); member Council of the Society of Public Teachers of Law (1971-1975); member Economic and Social Research Council Social Sciences and the Law Committee; Government and Law Committee (1982-1985); member Editorial Committee of the British Year Book of International Law (1983 to date); member Council of Management of British Institute of International and Comparative Law and chairman of the Private International Law Section of its Advisory

Board (1986 to date); chairman Conciliation Project Advisory Committee Lord Chancellor's Department (1985-1988); chairman Road Traffic Law Review (1985-1988); representative of the UK in negotiations within EEC on variety of Conventions and Community instruments (1977-1984); member various working parties advising UK Government on a range of mainly international legal matters (1978-1984); chairman management Committee Oxford CAB (1985-1988); member United Oxford & Cambridge Universities Club.

Biography: lives Oxford and Gloucestershire; born 30.08.1936; married to Stephanie with 1 daughter and 2 sons. Educated at Oakham School; Keble College Oxford (1959 BA) (1960 BCL) (1963 MA) (1976 DCL); editor Oxford Journal of Legal Studies' (1987 to date); author of: 'Occupier's Liability' (1971); 'The Modern Law of Animals' (1972); assistant editor: 'Chitty on Contracts' (26th edition 1989); 'Halsbury's Laws of England' (4th edition 1975); chapter on Torts in 'Annual Survey of Commonwealth Law'; author of 'Private International Law of Matrimonial Causes' (1977); editor 'Contract Conflicts' (1982); author 'Cases and Materials on Private International Law' with JHC Morris (1984); author 'Cheshire and North, Private International Law' (11th edition 1987); articles and notes in legal journals.

NORTHAM John

senior and managing partner JAQUES & LEWIS 2 South Square, Gray's Inn, London WC1R 5HR.

Career: articled Jaques & Lewis (1957-1960); admitted (1960); assistant solicitor (1960-1963); became partner (1963).

Activities: chairman Southgate Round Table (1969-1970); trustee Hadley Wood Association; captain Hadley Wood Golf Club (1988-1989).

Biography: lives Hadley Wood; born 22.07.1935; married to Jill with 4 children. Educated at Highgate School; Cambridge University (1957 BA) (1958 LLB); McMahon Prize (1958).

Leisure: golf.

NUTTALL Graeme

tax partner FIELD FISHER WATERHOUSE 41 Vine Street, London EC3N 2AA.

Career: articled Field Fisher & Martineau (1982-1984); admitted (1984); assistant solicitor (1984-1988); became partner

(1988); firm now Field Fisher Waterhouse.

Activities: associate member Institute of Taxation (1985).

Biography: lives London SE13; born 29.12.1959; married to Elizabeth with 1 child. Educated at Price's Grammar School, Fareham; Peterhouse Cambridge (1981 MA); College of Law Guildford (1981-1982); various articles and publications including 'Employee Ownership: Legal and Tax Aspects'(1987) with John Nelson-Jones; 'Nelson-Jones and Nuttall's Tax and Interest Tables'(annually) with Rodney Nelson-Jones; 'Sponsorship, Endorsement & Merchandising - A Practical Guide'(1990) with Richard Bagehot.

O

O'BRIEN Roger

senior partner LAWSON COPPOCK & HART 18 Tib Lane, Cross Street, Manchester M2 4JA.

Career: articled Lawson Coppock & Hart (1957-1962); admitted (1962); assistant solicitor (1962-1966); became partner (1966).

Activities: General Commissioner of Income Tax; member (former president) Manchester Incorporated Law Library Society; governor of Culcheth Hall School; member of: St James's Club, Manchester; Bowdon Hockey Club; Budworth Sailing Club.

Biography: lives Hale; born 03.07.1940; married to Barbara with 2 children. Educated at St Ambrose College, Hale Barns, Manchester University; College of Law.

Leisure: hockey; sailing.

O'BRIEN William

partner RUSSELL JONES & WALKER 324 Gray's Inn Road, London WC1.

Career: articled Robin Thompson & Partners; admitted (1979); assistant solicitor Hextall Erskine & Co (1979-1983); assistant solicitor WI Corlett (1983-1985); assistant solicitor Russell Jones & Walker (1985-1986); became partner (1986).

Activities: member Society of Labour Lawyers; member of: Scottish RAC; Copthorne Waterside Business Club.

Biography: lives London N5 and Manchester; born 15.07.1955; single. Educated at Berkhamsted School; Birmingham University (1976 LLB hons);

College of Law Lancaster Gate.

Leisure: theatre; opera; literature.

O'CALLAGHAN Vincent

partner DAVIES ARNOLD COOPER 6-8 Bouverie Street, London EC4Y 8DD.

Career: Zurich Insurance Company (1958); National Motor & Accident & Contingency Group; specialised in personal injury litigation on behalf of plaintiffs with WH Thompson (1965-1970); articled Davies Arnold Cooper; admitted (1975); became partner (1975).

Activities: member Joint Working Party (Law Society/Bar/Institute of Actuaries) on the actuarial assessment of damages in personal injury and fatal accident litigation; consulting editor to Personal & Medical Injuries Law Letter; directorships with Java Properties Limited and Martath Management Limited; member of the International Bar Association (section on business law); participated as panellist at IBA Conference in Strasbourg on 'Disaster Litigation Worldwide'(1989).

Biography: lives Purley; born 28.12.1940; married to Anne with 3 children. Educated at Christ the King College, Cork; College of Law Lancaster Gate (1971-1972).

Leisure: family; sailing; skiing.

O'HARE John

principal lecturer COLLEGE OF LAW Bishopthorpe Road, York YO2 1QA.

Career: called to the Bar Lincoln's Inn (1972); pupillage Kenneth Farrow; (1972-1973); taught Bar finals and Solicitorsfinals College of Law Chancery Lane (1973-1989); College of Law York (1989).

Biography: lives York; born 26.02.1949; divorced with 1 child. Educated at Bromley Boys' Grammar School; Leicester University (1971 LLB hons); College of Law Chancery Lane (1971-1972); Sir Thomas More Bursary; author of 'Civil Litigation'with Robert Hill.

Leisure: bridge; cycling; living in France.

O'MEARA Barry

deputy group solicitor IMPERIAL CHEMICAL INDUSTRIES PLC ICI Headquarters, 9 Millbank, London SW1P 3JF.

Career: articled Bailey Shaw & Gillett; admitted (1962); assistant solicitor Henry Pumphrey & son (1962-1965); legal department Imperial Chemical Industries Limited (1965).

Activities: president European Company Lawyers' Association (1987-1990); chairman Law Society Commerce & Industry Group (1977-1978).

Biography: lives Caterham; born 28.08.1939; married with 2 sons. Educated at Charterhouse School.

O'NEILL David

senior property partner HOOD VORES & ALLWOOD The Priory, Church Street, Dereham, Norfolk NR19 1DW.

Career: National Service (1948-1950); articled Joynson-Hicks & Co (1950-1956); admitted (1956); assistant solicitor (1956-1958); became salaried partner (1958); became partner (1960-1965); became partner EF Turner & Sons (1965-1968); became partner Hood Vores & Allwood (1970).

Activities: member Norfolk & Norwich Law Society Committee (1980 to date) (president 1988-1989); member of: Royal West Norfolk Golf Club; Brancaster Staithe Sailing Club.

Biography: lives Colkirk; born 29.05.1930; divorced with 2 daughters. Educated at Uppingham; inaugurated and in (1986) achieved nearly 100% acceptance by Society members of conveyancing guidelines which to all intents and purposes were the forerunner of the TransAction Protocol inaugurated by the Law Society in (1990).

Leisure: golf; shooting; sailing.

O'SULLIVAN Roderic

partner HOLMAN FENWICK & WILLAN Marlow House, Lloyds Avenue, London EC3N 3AL.

Career: admitted (1970).

Activities: member of: RAC; Hurlingham.

Biography: lives London SW3; born 30.05.1944; married to Hedderwick with children. Educated at Downside School.

Leisure: sailing; tennis; skiing.

ODY Jonathan Wilmot

partner NORTON ROSE Kempson House, PO Box 570, Camomile Street, London EC3A 7AN.

Career: articled Rommey Fraser & Ody (1960-1964); admitted (1965); assistant solicitor Pattinson & Brewer (1964-1967); became partner (1967-1969); assistant solicitor Freshfields (1969-1972); assistant solicitor Norton Rose (1972-1973); became partner (1973).

Activities: member of: MCC; le Cercle de la Fraternite, Claviers.

Biography: lives London SW3 and Claviers, Var, France; born 24.12.1941; married to Noelle with 4 children. Educated at The Elms School (1950-1955); Malvern College (1955-1959).

OERTON Richard

consultant BIRCHAM & CO 1 Dean Farrar Street, Westminster, London SW1H 0DY.

Career: articled family firm Barnstaple, Devon (1953); admitted (1959); assistant solicitor and salaried partner in Bournemouth area; textbook editor, Butterworths (1968); Law Commission (1972) (became senior staff member land law and landlord and tenant teams 1978); part-time private practice (1985); consultant Bircham & Co (1988).

Activities: member Howard League for Penal Reform, Institute for the Study and Treatment of Delinquency, Justice, Clarity.

Biography: lives London NW5; born 21.04.1936; married to Marion with 3 children. Educated at Sherborne School; Sols Finals (hons); Sir George Fowler Prizeman; editor of: Underhill on Trusts (12th edition 1970) and supplements; supplements to Williams on Wills, Williams on Title, Encyclopaedia of Forms and Precedents (1968-1972); author of: 'Who is the Criminal?'(1968); 'A Lament for the Law Commission'(1987); Wills Division of Butterworths' Wills Probate and Administration Service (1990); contributor to: SolicitorsJournal; Law Society's Gazette; New Law Journal; Conveyancer; Criminal Law Review; Law Notes; Capital Taxes; Trusts and Estates; British Journal of Medical Psychology; Howard Journal; Social Science Quarterly.

OFFER Michael

managing partner in charge of the company/commercial department and of practice development LAWRENCE JONES Sea Containers House, 20 Upper Ground, Blackfriars Bridge, London SE1 9LH.

Career: articled Thompson Quarrell & McGaw (1964); admitted; assistant solicitor Lawrence Jones & Co; became partner (1973).

Activities: member IBA; member Asia Pacific Lawyers' Association; member SolicitorsEuropean Group; Fellow Chartered Institute of Arbitrators; Liveryman City of London.

Biography: lives London N16; born

28.09.1942. Educated at Cathedral Choir School, Salisbury; St Paul's School, London; St Catharine's College Cambridge.

Leisure: walking; sailing; windsurfing.

OGDEN Sir Michael

Queen's Counsel 2 Crown Office Row, Temple, London EC4Y 7HJ.

Career: called to the Bar Lincoln's Inn (1950); QC (1968); Bencher Lincoln's Inn (1977).

Activities: Recorder (1971); Knighted (1989); FCI Arb.

Biography: lives London W8 and Newmarket; born 1926; married with 4 children. Educated at Downside; Jesus College Cambridge (MA).

OGLETHORPE Bill

senior partner PYE-SMITHS 4 New Street, Salisbury, Wilts SP1 2QJ.

Career: Sapper (1944-1947); articled to father (1947-1951); articled to cousin; became partner Clark Oglethorpe & Sons (1953-1964); became partner Pye-Smiths (1964).

Activities: Downton Parish Councillor; secretary Downton Moot Preservation Trust Ltd; company secretary Abbeyfield (Salisbury & Wilton) Society Ltd; chairman Brian Whitehead Sports Centre Association Downton; various other 'good works'.

Biography: lives Downton; born 04.09.1926; married with 3 children. Educated at Marlborough College; Manchester University; Trinity Hall Cambridge (BA LLB).

Leisure: gardening; dinghy sailing.

OGLEY James

finance partner OXLEY & COWARD 34 Moorgate Street, Rotherham, South Yorkshire S60 2HB.

Career: articled Oxley & Coward (1960-1965); admitted (1965); assistant solicitor; became partner.

Activities: area commissioner St John Ambulance Brigade Rotherham area (1981 to date); former secretary and vice-president-elect Rotherham Rotary Club; member South Yorkshire Archives Consultative Council.

Biography: lives Wickersley; born 25.05.1941; married to Susan with 2 children. Educated at Brocksford Hall, Doveridge; Uppingham School; Sheffield.

Leisure: squash; travel; farming.

OLDALE Keith

head of company commercial department ROWE & MAW 20 Black Friars Lane, London EC4V 6HD.

Career: articled Rowe & Maw; admitted (1962); assistant solicitor; became partner (1965).

Activities: former member British Film Fund Agency (until the Quango was wound up 1987); member of Amicable Society of St Clement Danes.

Biography: lives Eversley; born 29.11.1937; married with 6 children. Educated at Henry Fanshawe School; (1959 LLB hons).

Leisure: estate management.

OLIVER David

Queen's Counsel 13 Old Square, Lincoln's Inn, London WC2A 3UA.

Career: called to the Bar (1972); Standing Counsel to the Director-General of Fair Trading (1980-1986); QC (1986).

Biography: lives London SW13 and Norfolk; born 04.06.1949; married to Judith with 1 son and 2 sons by previous marriage. Educated at Westminster Under School (1957-1962); Westminster School (1963-1967); Trinity Hall Cambridge (1971 BA); Institut D'Etudes Europeenees, Brussels (1972-1973); (Licence Special En Droit Europeen).

Leisure: gardening; bird watching; rough shooting; tennis.

OLIVER Stephen

Queen's Counsel and head of chambers 4 Pump Court, Temple, London EC4Y 7AN.

Career: National Service Sub-Lieutenant Royal Navy (Submarines) (1957-1959); called to the Bar Middle Temple (1963); practiced at Bar in London and Manchester (1964 to date); Bencher Middle Temple (1988); Recorder (South-Eastern Circuit).

Activities: assistant Parliamentary Boundary Commissioner (1978 to date); member Parliamentary and Taxation Committee of Historic Houses Association; member English Heritage Tax Group; chairman Blackheath Concert Halls; member Groucho Club .

Biography: lives London SE3; born 14.11.1938; married to Dawn with 3 children. Educated at Rugby; Oriel College Oxford (1962 BA) (1965 MA).

Leisure: music; sailing.

O

O

OLSWANG Simon

senior partner SIMON OLSWANG & CO
1 Great Cumberland Place, London
W1H 7AL.

Career: accountancy articles Deloitte
Haskins & Sells (1965-1966); articled
Brecher & Co (1966-1968); admitted (1968);
assistant solicitor (1968-1971); became
partner (1971-1981); founded own practice
(1981).

Activities: admitted California Bar (1978);
guest speaker at: annual UCLA
Entertainment Law Symposium, Los
Angeles (1979 & 1987); the NSW Sydney
Film Symposium (1980); The Royal
Television Society Symposium (1986); The
Institute of International Business Law and
Practice of the International Chamber of
Commerce and the International Bar
Association Conference (1987); European
Co-productions in Film and Television
Symposium, Munich (1988); Marketing for
Lawyers' Conference (1989); member
Arbitration Panel American Film
Marketing Association; member British
Screen Advisory Council (1985); active
participation in the affairs of the New
North London Synagogue (founder and
past council member); member of: Royal
Motor Yacht Club; Parkstone Yacht Club;
Arts Club; BAFTA.

Biography: lives London N6 and Dorset;
born 13.12.1943; married to Susan with 3
children. Educated at Bootham School,
York (1957-1961); Durham University (1964
BA Econ).

Leisure: travel; skiing; sailing; reading
history.

ORCHARD John Charles Johnson

managing partner PINSENT & CO Post &
Mail House, 26 Colmore Circus,
Birmingham B4 6BH; also London and
Brussels.

Career: National Service Sub-Lt RNR
(1958-1960); articled Sydney Morse & Co
(1963-1967); assistant solicitor (1967-1968);
became partner Pinsent & Co (1970).

Activities: Director SolicitorsIndemnity
Mutual Insurance Association.

Biography: lives nr Stratford upon Avon;
born 09.03.1939; married to Cynthia with 2
children. Educated at Harrow; Emmanuel
College Cambridge (1963 MA) (1967 LLB).

Leisure: Chinese ceramics; English period
furniture; pre-Columbian Mochican and
early Cypriot pottery; fly fishing; shooting;
gardening; prawning.

ORCHARD Neville

consultant SPEECHLY BIRCHAM
Bouverie House, 154 Fleet Street, London
EC4A 2HX.

Career: articled Goodman Brown &
Warren; admitted (1956); assistant solicitor
Tackley Fall & Read; assistant solicitor
Edmund Hemming & Co; assistant
solicitor Herbert Oppenheim Nathan &
Vandyk; became partner Bircham & Co
(1963).

Activities: director Davies Laing & Dick
Ltd; director The Singapore Para Rubber
Co PLC; governor Wetherby, Pembridge
Hall and The Falcons Schools; member of
Cripplegate Ward Club (former master).

Biography: lives London EC2; born
10.05.1930; married to Tryphena with 2
children. Educated at Berkhamsted;
Peterhouse Cambridge (MA); Exhibitioner;
State Scholarship.

Leisure: Church committees; astronomy.

ORCHARD Steve

chief executive LEGAL AID BOARD
Newspaper House, 8-16 Great New Street,
London EC4 3BN.

Career: civil servant Lord Chancellor's
Department (28 years); administrator of the
London Civil Courts based in the RCJ
(1984-1988); became chief executive of the
Legal Aid Board (1989).

Biography: lives Bracknell; born 05.08.1944;
married to Pauline with 2 children.
Educated at Swanage Grammar School.

Leisure: walking; eating; drinking; cooking.

ORR Michael

senior partner MILLS & REEVE
3/7 Redwell Street, Norwich, Norfolk
NR2 4TJ.

Career: commissioned Suffolk Regiment
(1956-1959); articled Mills & Reeve (1963-
1965); admitted (1965); partner (1966-1987);
became senior partner Mills & Reeve
Francis (1987).

Activities: president Norfolk & Norwich
Incorporated Law Society; trustee Theatre
Royal Norwich; governor King Edward VI
School, Norwich; member of: Oxford &
Cambridge Golfing Society; Hunstanton
Golf Club.

Biography: lives Norwich; born 03.03.1938;
married to Clarke with 4 children.
Educated at Clifton Preparatory School
(1949-1952); Clifton College, Bristol (1952-
1956); Balliol College Oxford (1962 hons).

Leisure: skiing; theatre; reading; golfing;
walking.

OSBORNE Anthony

managing partner CLARKE WILLMOTT &
CLARKE 6 Hammet Street, Taunton,
Somerset TA1 1RG.

Career: assistant solicitor Clarke Willmott
& Clarke (1972-1974); became partner
(1974); became managing partner (1988).

Activities: member numerous local
committees.

Biography: lives South Somerset; born
20.10.1944; married to Anna with 3
children. Educated at Beaminster School,
Dorset; Bristol University (1966 LLB).

Leisure: country pursuits.

OSBORNE Jim

senior partner MACROBERTS
152 Bath Street, Glasgow G2 4TB.

Career: apprentice MacRoberts (1946-1949);
admitted (1949); National Service with
Army Legal Aid Service (1949-1951);
assistant solicitor (1951-1955); became
partner (1955).

Activities: member Dean's Council of the
Royal Faculty of Procurators in Glasgow;
member Royal Scottish Automobile Club.

Biography: lives Paisley; born 12.01.1930;
married to Margaret with 1 child. Educated
at Airdrie Academy; Glasgow University
(1949 BL).

Leisure: golf; bridge; walking.

OSBORNE Simon

solicitor to BRITISH RAILWAYS BOARD
Macmillan House, PO Box 1016,
Paddington Station, London W2 1YG.

Career: articled Goodman Derrick & Co
(1971-1973); admitted (1973); assistant
solicitor Calvert Smith & Sutcliffe (1973);
British Railways Board legal department
(1973-1981); head of Parliamentary and
commercial division (1981-1986); became
solicitor to the Board (1986).

Biography: lives London; born 26.01.1948;
married to Fiona with 2 daughters and 1
son. Educated at Aldenham School (1961-
1966); Kingston Polytechnic (1970 LLB);
College of Law Lancaster Gate (1970-1971).

OSTRIN Anthony

senior partner YAFFE JACKSON &
OSTRIN 81 Dale Street, Liverpool L2 2HZ.

Career: articled Goldrein & Co (1962-1965);
admitted (1965); assistant solicitor John A
Benn Twyford & Co (1965-1968); became
partner Yaffe Jackson & Ostrin (1968).

Activities: hon secretary Merseyside Drugs

Council; member Liverpool Law Society; member Management Committee of Toxteth Activities Group; former lay member Liverpool Family Practitioner Committee; lay member Alder Hey Hospital Ethical Committee; member local housing association; chairman student hostel; member of local tennis club.

Biography: lives Liverpool; born 31.08.1941; married to Beverly with 2 children. Educated at Liverpool College (1949-1959); Liverpool University (1962 LLB hons); article published in Law Society's Gazette on the Prevention of Terrorism Act and PACE (1988); article 'Attempting the Impossible' published in JP Magazine.

Leisure: photography; pottery; music.

OVERS John

commercial tax partner BERWIN LEIGHTON Adelaide House, London Bridge, London EC4R 9HA.

Career: admitted (1978); assistant solicitor (1978-1981); became partner Berwin Leighton (1981).

Biography: lives London; born 15.08.1953; married to Elana with 2 children. Educated at City of London School; St Peter's College Oxford (1975 BA) (1977 MA); occasional articles.

Leisure: tennis; photography; music.

OWEN Gerald

Queen's Counsel 3 Paper Buildings, Temple, London EC4Y 7EU.

Career: QC (1969); Recorder of the Crown Court (1979).

Activities: chairman Medical Appeal Tribunal (1984).

Biography: lives London; born 29.11.1922; married to Phyllis with 2 children. Educated at Kilburn Grammar School; St Catharine's College Cambridge (1943 MA); Diploma in Statistics (1945); London University (1946 LLB).

Leisure: music; opera.

OWEN Philip

Queen's Counsel 1 Brick Court, Temple, London EC4Y 9BY.

Career: Royal Welch Fusiliers (1949-1945); Major TARO; called to Bar Middle Temple (1949); Bencher (1969).

Activities: member General Council of the Bar (1971-1977); deputy chairman Quarter Sessions Montgomeryshire (1959-1971); Cheshire (1961-1971); Recorder Merthyr

Tydfil (1971); Recorder Crown Court (1972-1982); Leader Wales and Chester Circuit (1975-1977); Chairman Adv Bd constituted under Misuse of Drugs Act (1974 to date); legal assessor to General Medical Council (1970 to date); General Dental Council (1970 to date) RICS (1970 to date); JP Montgomeryshire (1959); JP Cheshire (1961); vice-president Montgomeryshire Conservative and Unionist Association; president Montgomeryshire Society (1974-1975); director Swansea City AFC Ltd (1976-1997); member of: Carlton; Pratt's; Cardiff and County; Welshpool and District Conservative; Bristol Channel Yacht (Mumbles).

Biography: lives Llanbrynmair; born 10.01.1920; married with 3 sons and 2 daughters. Educated at Hozzis Hill, Newbury; Winchester College; Christ Church Oxford (MA).

Leisure: amateur bassoonist; shooting; fishing; forestry; music; Association football.

PACKHAM Rosalind

partner and head of planning department SAUNDERS SOBELL LEIGH & DOBIN 20 Red Lion Street, London WC1R 4AE.

Career: called to the Bar (1982); planning lawyer Country Landowners' Association (1983-1987); head of planning department Stephenson Harwood (1987-1988); admitted (1989); assistant solicitor Saunders Sobell Leigh & Dobin (1989); became partner (1989).

Activities: member Private Bills Panel CBI (1983-1987); member Land Use Panel CBI (1985-1987).

Biography: lives Datchet; born 24.02.1953; married to Michael with 1 daughter. Educated at Slough High School for Girls; King's College London (LLB hons); College of Law; articles in Country Landowners' Journal and Country Life.

Leisure: reading; cooking.

PAGE Richard

training manager BAKER & McKENZIE Aldwych House, Aldwych, London WC2B 4JP.

Career: articled Alsop Stevens Batesons & Co; admitted; assistant solicitor Gillespie & Co (1972-1974); lecturer Nottingham Polytechnic (1974-1975); senior lecturer

(1975-1979); principal lecturer (1979-1984); senior assistant secretary and head of continuing education at the Law Society (1984-1988); became training and education manager Baker & McKenzie (1988) and editor Professional Lawyer (1990).

Activities: member Academic and Professional Development Committees Nottingham Polytechnic (1974-1984); member Education Committees and Advisory Groups at the Law Society (1984-1988); member Education and Training Sub-committee of the City of Westminster Law Society (1988 to date); hon secretary British Institute of Management Westminster branch (1985-1987) (member Executive Committee 1984 to date); Reader in the Church of England; admitted Southwell Minster (1983); licensed in the Diocese of Guildford (1987 to date); member Guildford Diocesan Board of Readers (1989 to date).

Biography: lives Woking; born 20.03.1948; divorced. Educated at The Judd Grammar School, Tonbridge; Leicester University (1969 LLB); City of Liverpool College of Commerce (1970); OU post-experience certificate on the EEC (1974); MBIM (1984); articles on legal education in Law Society's Gazette (1984-1989) and Legal Issues (1989).

Leisure: rural life in England, Wales and France; the National Parks of the USA.

PAINTER Nick

partner specialising in company acquisitions and disposals SIMPSON CURTIS 41 Park Square, Leeds LS1 2NS.

Career: articled Howes Percival (1981-1983); admitted (1983); assistant solicitor (1983-1985); assistant solicitor Simpson Curtis (1985); associate (1985-1988); became partner (1988).

Biography: lives Ilkley; born 03.02.1959; married to Jayne with 1 daughter. Educated at Gowerton Grammar School, Swansea (1970-1974); Haverfordwest Grammar School (1974-1977); Keble College Oxford (1980 MA); College of Law Chester (1980-1981).

Leisure: football; cricket; squash; cinema; theatre.

PALLEY Marc

partner BERWIN LEIGHTON Adelaide House, London Bridge, London EC4R 9HA.

Career: articled Allen & Overy (1976-1978); admitted (1978); assistant solicitor (1978-

P

1979 & 1982-1985); Dubai office (1979-1982); became partner Berwin Leighton (1985).

Biography: lives Kent; born 02.05.1954; married to Sabina with 3 sons. Educated at Clifton College; St John's College Oxford (1975 BA).

PALLISTER Tim

partner SLAUGHTER AND MAY 35 Basinghall Street, London EC2V 5DB.

Career: articled Mills & Reeve (1958-1963); admitted (1963); assistant solicitor Slaughter and May (1964-1971); became partner (1972); partner responsible for firm's Paris office (1973-1980).

Activities: member Law Society; member International Bar Association; member of: Royal Automobile Club; Norfolk Club; Sheringham Golf Club.

Biography: lives London SW3; born 02.07.1940; married to Christine with 3 children. Educated at Bloxham School.

Leisure: motoring; tennis; skiing; golf; country pursuits.

PALMER Malcolm

administrative partner BAKER & MCKENZIE Aldwych House, Aldwych, London WC2B 4JP.

Career: articled Linklaters & Paines (1957-1960); admitted (1960); assistant solicitor Rickerby & Mellersh (1960-1961); assistant solicitor Baker & McKenzie (1962-1963); consultant on English commercial and tax law to Baker & McKenzie, Chicago (1963-1965); became partner (1964); became senior partner Hong Kong office (1975-1981); returned London (1981).

Activities: member Baker & McKenzie London Management Committee; chairman International Professional Development Committee (1984-1985); member of: Reform Club; Hurlingham Club; RAC.

Biography: lives London; born 22.10.1933; married to Rachel with 2 sons and 1 daughter. Educated at Charterhouse; Queen's College Cambridge (MA); Law Society Finals (1960 hons); various publications on UK taxation of intellectual property income; securities for banks and the Hong Kong companies ordinance; lectured at Henley Administration College, Management Centre Europe and elsewhere on legal structure and implications of international joint ventures.

Leisure: bridge; bowls; buying and occasionally reading books.

PALMER Nigel

partner media and communications group SJ BERWIN & CO 236 Gray's Inn Road, London WC1X 8HB.

Career: articled Denton Hall & Burgin (1976-1979); admitted (1979); assistant solicitor (1979-1982); salaried partner (1983-1985); equity partner (1985-1988); joined SJ Berwin & Co as partner (1988).

Activities: speaks on merchandising and film financing at seminars; member of: United Oxford & Cambridge Club; Copinger Society.

Biography: lives London SE10; born 12.05.1950; single. Educated at Little Appley, Isle of Wight; St Edward's School, Oxford; Christ Church Oxford (1971 BA) (1982 MA); College of Law (1976 & 1978); sundry articles on merchandising and media matters; regular 'VERDICT' column for 'Screen International'.

Leisure: reading; music; opera; swimming; theatre; film; gardening.

PANNETT Alan

director of training ASHURST MORRIS CRISP Broadwalk House, 5 Appold Street, London EC2A 2HA.

Career: called to the Bar Gray's Inn (1979); lecturer in law Oxford Polytechnic (1979); senior lecturer (1986); head of the law unit (1987); became director of training Ashurst Morris Crisp (1988); Visiting Professor in professional development Nottingham Law School, Nottingham Polytechnic (1990).

Activities: Visiting Tutor Lady Margaret Hall and St Hugh's College Oxford; member Gray's Inn; member Friends of the Earth.

Biography: lives Middlesex; born 06.03.1957; 1 child. Educated at Hayes County Grammar School; Bristol University (1978 LLB); Inns of Court School of Law; author of: 'Recruitment and Training in the Solicitors Practice' (1989); 'Torts' (1989); 'A Level Law'; 'Principles of Hotel & Catering Law' (1989).

Leisure: classic and sports cars; swimming; overseas travel.

PANNICK David

Junior Counsel to the Crown 2 Hare Court, Temple, London EC4Y 7BH.

Career: called to the Bar (1979); Junior Counsel to the Crown (common law) (1988).

Biography: lives Hertfordshire; born 07.03.1956; married to Denise with 3 children. Educated at Bancroft's School, Woodford Green; Hertford College Oxford (1978 MA BCL); Fellow All Souls College Oxford (1978); author of: 'Judicial Review of the Death Penalty' (1982); 'Sex Discrimination Law' (1985); 'Judges' (1987).

PANNONE Rodger

senior partner PANNONE BLACKBURN 123 Deansgate, Manchester M3 2BU.

Career: articled Casson & Co; admitted (1969); assistant solicitor WH Thompson (1969-1971); became partner (1971-1973); became partner with Conn Goldbery (1973) which became Goldberg Blackburn & Howards and then Pannone Blackburn (1987); founded Pannone Napier (1985); founded Pannone De Backer (1988).

Activities: former member Supreme Court Rule Committee; member Supreme Court Procedure Committee; solicitor adviser to Lord Chancellor on civil justice producing the Civil Justice Review (1988); member Council of the Law Society (1979 to date); former chairman Contentious Business Committee; former member Law and Procedure Committee; member Adjudication Committee and amongst others the Wine Committee; member St James's Club; Northern Lawn Tennis Club.

Biography: lives Manchester and Rosgill; born 20.04.1943; married to Patricia with 3 children. Educated at St Brendan's College, Bristol; College of Law London; Law School, Manchester; many articles and broadcasts.

Leisure: fell walking; all holidays; sport; food and wine.

PAPATHOMAS Maro

in-house lawyer TRANSATLANTIC SEAWAYS LTD Irongate House, 22-30 Duke's Place, London EC3A 7EP.

Career: articled Wilde Sapte (1978-1980); admitted (1980); became in-house lawyer Transatlantic Seaways Ltd (1980).

Activities: nutrition consultant at the Hale Clinic, London; member of; Grosvenor House Health Club; Natural Medicines Society; British Society for Nutritional Medicine; Institute for Optimum Nutrition; Institute for Complementary Medicine; Rags; Mortons; Business Network; N.C.A. (Nutrition Consultants' Association)..

Biography: lives London NW3; born 09.10.1955; single. Educated at South Hampstead High School for Girls;

University College London (1977 LLB hons); College of Law (1978-1979); Diploma from Institute of Optimum Nutrition (1987).

Leisure: opera; travel; swimming; skiing; gym; yoga; reading.

PARK Andrew

Queen's Counsel Gray's Inn Chambers, Gray's Inn, London WC1R 5JA.

Career: Bigelow Teaching Fellow Law School University of Chicago (1960-1961); assistant lecturer LSE (1961-1962); lecturer (1964-1968); lecturer University of Lagos (1962-1964); called to the Bar Lincoln's Inn (1964); pupillage (1965-1966); revenue bar (1966 to date); QC (1978); Bencher Lincoln's Inn (1986); Recorder (1989).

Activities: chairman Taxation and Retirement Benefits Committee of the Bar Council (1978-1982); treasurer Senate of Inns of Court and the Bar (1982-1985); chairman Revenue Bar Association (1987 to date); member St George's Hill Lawn Tennis Club.

Biography: lives Thames Ditton; born 27.01.1939; married to Marny with 3 children. Educated at Leeds Grammar School (1947-1957); University College Oxford (1960 BA) (1964 MA); Winter Williams Law Scholar.

Leisure: squash; tennis; hill walking in the Yorkshire Dales.

PARK Bill

partner and head of litigation department LINKLATERS & PAINES Barrington House. 59-67 Gresham Street, London EC2V 7JA.

Career: articled Hart Jackson & Sons (1950-1955); admitted (1955); National Service Army Legal Aid (1955-1957); assistant solicitor Leslie C Powell (1958-1961); became partner Morrison & Masters (1961-1966); assistant solicitor Linklaters & Paines (1967-1971); became partner (1971).

Activities: past president London Solicitors Litigation Association; member of Council London International Arbitration Trust; member Council of Management British Institute of International and Comparative Law and Executive Committee; member of Board of London International Court of Arbitration; member of various other organisations associated with the law; associate member Chartered Institute of Arbitrators.

Biography: lives London W11 and High Lorton; born 28.05.1934; married to Valerie

with 1 son and 1 daughter. Educated at Belmont (Mill Hill Preparatory); St Bees; Samuel Herbert Easterbrook Prize (1952); author of: Oyez Practice Notes on Hire Purchase and Credit Sales (1957); Collection of Debts (1962); Discovery of Documents (1966); consulting editor of 'Style and Hollander Documentary Evidence' and 'International Commercial Litigation'; numerous articles and contributions to published papers.

Leisure: farming in W Cumberland; fox hunting (fell packs); collecting books on Cumbria; generally living in Cumbria.

PARK Keith

senior partner KEITH PARK Claughton House, 39 Barrow Street, St Helens, Merseyside WA10 1RX.

Career: articled Gair Roberts (1967-1969); admitted (1969); assistant solicitor Linaker & Linaker (1970-1972); founded own practice (1972); took over Taylor & Hickson (1985).

Activities: handling the litigation for haemophiliacs who are infected by the HIV virus or have contracted Aids and are suing or proposing to sue the Government and the Health Authorities for negligence; director Keith Park Homes Ltd.

Biography: lives Ormskirk; born 26.10.1946; divorced with 2 sons. Educated at Wintringham Grammer School, Grimsby (1957-1959); Holt High School, Liverpool (1959-1964); Liverpool University (1967 LLB hons).

Leisure: boating; fell walking; sports; photography.

PARK Michael

senior partner PAULL & WILLIAMSONS Investment House, 6 Union Row; Aberdeen AB9 8DQ.

Career: articled Paull & Williamsons (1959); admitted; assistant solicitor; partner; became senior partner (1986).

Activities: member Council Law Society of Scotland (1974-1985); vice-president Law Society of Scotland (1979-1980) president (1980-1981); CBE (1982); chairman Aberdeen Citizens Advice Bureau (1976-1988); member Criminal Injuries Compensation Board (1983 to date); holder of commission as temporary Sheriff; part-time lecturer in Constitutional Law at Aberdeen University; developed legal broadcasting (regarded by many as 'the voice/face of Scots Law'); did 120 or so live legal items of interest on Grampian

Television on Tuesday night news magazine programme; presented own 5 half-hour programmes 'Cause for Concern' on Grampian Television; also BBC Television and ITV/ITN appearances including 'Out of Court'; appears frequently on BBC Radio Scotland/Radio 4 interview programmes and phone-ins; for several years weekly 15 minute radio spot on local commercial radio (Northsound); broadcast nationwide in UK; Republic of Ireland; Hong Kong; Vienna; Berlin; broadcast on farming programmes on farming topics and BBC Radio Scotland 'Thought for the Day'.

Biography: lives Aberdeen; born 07.04.1938; married to Elizabeth with 2 sons. Educated at Aberdeen Grammar School; Aberdeen University (MA LLB).

Leisure: gardening; golf.

PARKER Anthony

senior partner STUCHBERYS & FRANCIS ALEXANDER & CO 1 Park Street, Maidenhead, Berks SL6 1SN.

Career: articled in City; assistant solicitor in West End (1 year); assistant solicitor Stuchberys & Francis Alexander & Co (1967-1970); became partner (1970).

Biography: lives Maidenhead; born 01.01.1941. Educated at St Paul's School; London University (LSE) (1959-1962).

PARKER William N

partner FRESHFIELDS Whitefriars, 65 Fleet Street, London EC4Y 1HS.

Career: admitted (1966); assistant solicitor Freshfields (1967-1972); became partner (1972).

Activities: member City of London Law Society - Company Law sub-committee.

Biography: lives London W2; born 23.07.1941; married to Vanessa with 2 children. Educated at Herbert Strutt School; Sheffield University (1962 LLB).

Leisure: opera; gardening.

PARR Martin Roger

partner WILLEY HARGRAVE Park Lane House, Westgate, Leeds LS1 2RD.

Career: articled Lupton & Fawcett; articled Willey Hargrave; admitted (1971); assistant solicitor (1971-1972); became partner (1972).

Biography: lives near Leeds; born 06.12.1946; married to Elizabeth with 2 children. Educated at Manchester University (1968 LLB hons); College of

P

P

Law Liverpool.

Leisure: cricket; history; gardening; whiskey!.

PARSLOE John

director MERCURY ASSET MANAGEMENT PLC 33 King William Street, London EC4R 9AS.

Career: overseas career officer British Council (1965-1969); articled Clifford Chance (1969-1971); admitted (1971); assistant solicitor (1971-1973); assistant solicitor Lovell White Durrant (1974-1978); Mercury Asset Management (1979).

Activities: member RAC Club.

Biography: lives Epsom; born 14.10.1939; married to Maggie with 3 children. Educated at Bradfield College; Queen's College Oxford (MA); Robert Innes Prize; Samuel Herbert Easterbrook Prize.

PARSLOW Robert

senior partner HYDE MAHON BRIDGES 52 Bedford Row, London WC1R 4UH.

Career: articled Hyde Mahon & Pascall (1952-1955); admitted (1955); assistant solicitor (1955-1958); became partner (1958); became senior partner (1983).

Activities: member Legal Aid Area No 13 Committee; member Law Society.

Biography: lives Oxted; born 19.06.1929; married to Shirley with 2 children. Educated at Harrow School; Peterhouse Cambridge (1952 MA); Solicitors Final Examinations (1955 hons).

Leisure: foreign travel.

PARSONS John

solicitor HUMPHREY & PARSONS Cambrian House, Machynlleth, Powys SY20 8AL and Cambrian Chambers, Cambrian Place, Aberystwyth, Dyfed SY23 1NY.

Activities: clerk to Commissioners of Taxes (Machynlleth division); part-time clerk Machynlleth Town Council; member Associated Law Societies of Wales; Mid-Wales Law Society; Aberystwyth Law Society; West Wales Law Society; stood as Liberal Candidate in the last three General Elections; member National Liberal Club.

Biography: lives Machynlleth; born 19.04.1930; 1 son. Educated at Corris Primary; Machynlleth Grammar School; Liverpool University (LLB hons); College of Law Guildford (hons).

Leisure: communal interest and sports.

PARSONS Robert

consultant LOOSEMORES Alliance House, 18-20 High Street, Cardiff CF1 2BZ.

Career: teacher St Julian's High School, Newport (1971); articled Loosemores; admitted (1976); became partner (1976).

Activities: founding partner Lawyers' Planning Services; director CARE for the Family; leader Glenwood Church Centre; frequent speaker at national and international law conferences.

Biography: lives Cardiff; born 10.10.1948; married to Dianne with 2 children. Educated at Howardian Grammar School, Cardiff; College of Law Guildford (1975-1976); contributor to various legal journals.

PASSMORE Jeremy

partner private client department THOMSON SNELL & PASSMORE 3 Lonsdale Gardens, Tunbridge Wells, Kent TN1 1NX.

Career: articled Frere Cholmeley; admitted (1977); assistant solicitor (1977-1979); assistant solicitor Thomson Snell & Passmore (1979-1981); became partner (1981).

Biography: lives Tunbridge Wells; born 30.03.1952; married with 3 children. Educated at Yardley Court Prep School, Tonbridge (1960-1965); Cranleigh School (1965-1969); Trinity College Cambridge (1973 BA) Open Exhibitioner; College of Law Lancaster Gate (1975).

Leisure: family; environmental matters; gardening; reading; theatre; various sports.

PATERSON Frances

claims manager WREN MANAGERS LTD New City Court, 20 St Thomas Street, London SE1 9RR.

Career: articled Kennedys (1971-1973); admitted (1973); assistant solicitor (1973-1978); became partner (1978-1987); became partner Rowe & Maw (1987-1989); became claims manager Architects Mutual, The Wren Insurance Association Ltd (1989).

Activities: treasurer and membership secretary Society of Construction Law (1985 to date); member Committee British Insurance Law Association (1986-1989); Visiting Fellow Centre of Construction Law King's College London; member United Oxford and Cambridge Universities Club.

Biography: lives London N1; born 24.11.1948; married to Ronald. Educated at Benenden School, Kent; King's College London (1970 LLB AKC); various articles

in Professional Liability Today; Construction Industry Law Letter; Architects' Liability.

Leisure: walking; trekking; travelling.

PATON Richard

partner ALSOP WILKINSON India Buildings, Liverpool L2 0NH.

Career: articled Slaughter and May (1970-1972); admitted (1972); assistant solicitor Slaughter and May (1972-1977); assistant solicitor Alsop Stevens Batesons & Co (1977); became partner (1979).

Activities: member Law Society Standing Committee on company law (1983 to date); lectures on: protection of minority shareholders; Financial Services Act 1986; taxation of deferred consideration; 1992 - company law aspects; member of the Liverpool Racquet Club.

Biography: lives Chester; born 11.02.1947; married with 3 children. Educated at Radley College (scholar); Clare College Cambridge (1971 MA); College of Law Guildford.

Leisure: tennis; gardening; photography; golf; reading; walking.

PATRICK Derek

senior partner LACEYS 5 Poole Road, Bournemouth.

Career: articled Lester & Russell (1947-1952); admitted (1953); National Service with 4th/7th Royal Dragoon Guards (1953-1955); (Gazetted subaltern 1954); assistant solicitor Laceys (1955-1958); became partner (1958).

Activities: Fife & Forfar Yeomanry/Scottish Horse (TA) (1954-1963) (retired as Captain); member Legal Aid Certifying Committee (9 years); member Hunt Committee; past member Committee of several yacht clubs; treasurer PCC; member of: Portman Hunt Club; numerous yacht clubs.

Biography: lives Winterborne, Zelston, Dorset; born 01.09.1929; married. Educated Canford School (1943-1947).

Leisure: hunting; sailing; imbibing vintage claret and port; opera; ballet.

PATTEN Alan

senior property partner HARBOTTLE & LEWIS Hanover House, 14 Hanover Square, London W1R 0BE.

Career: articled Harbottle & Lewis; admitted (1969); assistant solicitor (1969-1971); became partner (1971).

220

Activities: member of: Savile Club; Sherborne Golf Club; Royal Horticultural Society.

Biography: lives London SW18 and Sherborne; born 18.07.1943; married to Valerie with 2 children. Educated at Taunton School; Manchester University (1965 LLB).

Leisure: golf; walking; gardening; films; theatre.

PAUL Christopher

partner and head of commercial property department BURSTOWS 8 Ifield Road, Crawley, West Sussex RH11 7YY.

Career: articled Wilde Sapte; admitted (1980); assistant solicitor (1980-1982); assistant solicitor Burstows (1982-1984); became partner (1984).

Activities: committee member Crawley Chamber of Commerce.

Biography: lives Wineham; born 23.09.1955; married with 2 sons. Educated at Wallington Grammar School for Boys; Nottingham University (1977 LLB hons); College of Law Guildford.

Leisure: golf.

PEARLMAN Joseph

senior partner PEARLMAN GRAZIN & CO 5/6 Park Place, Leeds LS1 2RV.

Career: admitted; National Service Second Lt; assistant solicitor (6 months); founded own practice (1958).

Activities: hon solicitor to Ramblers' Association; secretary and president Leeds and West Riding Medico Legal Society; public relations officer Leeds Law Society; former president and former non-council member Adjudication Committee of Solicitors Complaints Bureau; member Yorkshire Dales National Park Committee appointed by Secretary of State for the Environment; former chairman Open Spaces Society; member Royal Commonwealth Society.

Biography: lives Leeds; born 26.04.1933; married with 2 children. Educated at Keighley Boys' Grammar School; London University (1956 LLB); various articles in the Journal of Environment & Planning Law; The Magistrate; Solicitors Journal, etc.

Leisure: regular rambler, drinker and eater; extensive world travel.

PEARN John

senior partner and head of agricultural department SLEE BLACKWELL 1 South Street, South Molton.

Career: articled Gilbert H Stephens & Sons (1972-1976); admitted (1974); assistant solicitor (1974-1976); became partner (1976); became senior partner (1982).

Activities: member Devon & Exeter Law Society Committee; member local Land Registry Users' Committee; chairman North Devon Lawyers' Group (1990-1991); farmer.

Biography: lives Bratton Fleming; born 18.04.1950; married to Sara with 2 daughters. Educated at Chafyn Grove School, Salisbury (1958-1963); Sherborne (1963-1968); UWIST, Cardiff (1971 LLB); College of Law Guildford (1971-1972).

Leisure: horse racing (owner and former amateur jockey); hunting; skiing; literature; travel.

PEARSON Graham

consultant ROTHERHAM & CO 8 & 9 The Quadrant, Coventry CV1 2EG.

Career: articled Rotherham & Co (1939-1942); war service in army (1942-1947); commissioned (1943); served with Fife and Forfar Yeomanry in NW Europe and Germany; resumed articles Rotherham & Co (1947-1948); admitted (1948); assistant solicitor (1948-1951); became partner (1951); became senior partner (1973-1989).

Activities: member Warwickshire Law Society (president 1988-1989); life member Coventry Godiva Harriers.

Biography: lives Lapworth; born 18.04.1923; married to Faith with 3 children from previous marriage. Educated at Coventry Preparatory School; Cheltenham College; Birmingham University (LLB); James of Hereford Scholar (Cheltenham College (1937).

Leisure: involved for many years in athletics both as a runner and administrator; represented the AAA and Midland Counties AAA on numerous occasions in track events; breeder of thoroughbred racehorses.

PECK David

senior partner BIRKBECK MONTAGU'S 7 St Bride Street, London EC4A 4AT.

Career: articled Birkbeck Julius Coburn & Broad (1963-1965); admitted (1965); assistant solicitor (1965-1967); partner (1967-1985); became senior partner Birkbeck Montagu's (1985).

Biography: lives London W2 and Brinton, Norfolk; born 03.05.1940; married to Still with 3 children. Educated at Wellingborough School; St Johns College

Cambridge (1962 BA) (1967 MA).

Leisure: golf.

PEDDIE Peter

partner FRESHFIELDS Whitefriars, 65 Fleet Street, London EC4Y 1HT.

Career: articled Freshfields (1954-1957); admitted (1957); assistant solicitor (1957-1960); became partner (1960).

Activities: CBE (1983); governor Canford School (1981 to date); special trustee Middlesex Hospital (1977 to date); member of Council Middlesex Hospital Medical School (1977-1988); member Law Society's Standing Committee on Company Law; member Parochial Church Council; member City of London Club.

Biography: lives London SW13 and Mattingley; born 20.03.1932; married to Charlotte with 4 children. Educated at Canford School; St John's College Cambridge (1954 BA); Law Society Finals (1957 hons).

Leisure: gardening.

PEDRO Melvin

partner company and commercial department MANCHES & CO Aldwych House, 71-91 Aldwych, London WC2B 4RP.

Career: articled Clifford Chance (1981-1983); admitted (1983); assistant solicitor (1983-1984); assistant solicitor Manches & Co (1984-1988); became partner (1988).

Biography: lives Buckhurst Hill; born 16.09.1957; married to Tracy. Educated at Central Foundation Boys' Grammar School; Durham University (1980 BA hons).

Leisure: football; squash; tennis; badminton; bridge.

PEGG David

senior partner GISBY HARRISON 126 Crossbrook Street, Cheshunt, Herts EN8 8JS.

Career: articled mid-Wales (1958-1961); admitted (1961); assistant solicitor CO Harrison (1961-1964); became partner (1964); became senior partner Smith and Harrison and Chalmers-Hunt & Gisby (1983); firm became Gisby Harrison (1989).

Activities: member and chairman former Legal Aid General Committee; committee chairman Legal Aid Area Committee; member Law Society and Solicitors Benevolent Society; member Herts Law Society (1961 to date) (committee member

P

1975-1978) (president 1985-1986); member Hertfordshire Family Practitioner Committee .

Biography: lives Nazeing and Welshpool; born 18.09.1937; married to Jean with 2 children. Educated at Welshpool Grammar School; King's College London (1958 LLB); Gibson & Weldon Guildford (1958-1961).

Leisure: various sporting interests.

PELTOLA Lauri

resident partner PROCOPE & HORNBORG OY 7th Floor, Burne House, 88/89 High Holborn, London WC1V 6LS.

Career: Ministry for Trade & Industry, Helsinki (1974-1976); Procope & Hornborg (1976-1980); called to the Finnish Bar (1978); partner (1980); became resident partner in London (1984); court practice (1977); SG Archibald, Paris (1980) .

Biography: lives London; born 24.05.1950; married to Kirsti with 2 children. Educated at Helsinki University Faculty of Law (1974 LLM).

PEMBRIDGE Eileen

founding partner FISHER MEREDITH 2 Binfield Road, London SW4 6TA.

Career: freelance interpreter/translator and scientific precis writer for various UN agencies and African and Islamic Development Banks (1967-1972 and intermittently until 1984); articled (1972-1974); founded Fisher Meredith (1975).

Activities: member Law Society Council for South London (1990 to date); co-opted member Council Courts & Legal Services Committee (1987-1990); member Legal Aid Practitioners' Group Committee (vice-chair 1985-1987) (chair 1987-1988).

Biography: lives London SE21; born 15.03.1944; married to Andrew with 1 daughter. Educated at Worcester Girls' Grammar School; Gloucester High School for Girls; University of Cambridge (degree in Natural Sciences); Bath University (post grad diploma in language studies); College of Law (Solicitors professional examination); various articles in legal press on legal aid and LCD treatment thereof.

Leisure: long distance walking and all things countrified; keep fit; squash; fencing; skating; tennis; BBC World Service; gardening; visiting small Caribbean islands; reading novels in French, Russian or Spanish; sailing (with old 'Mirror'); playing with small children.

PENDLEBURY Alan

senior litigation partner CLARKE WILLMOTT & CLARKE 6 Hammet Street, Taunton, Somerset TA1 1RG.

Career: articled Russell & Russell (1949-1954); admitted (1954); assistant solicitor Watterson Moore & Co (1957-1959); became partner (1960-1969); became partner Clarke Willmott & Clarke (1969).

Activities: chairman Dorset & Somerset Agricultural Wages Committee (1974); international exchange and charity involvement through Rotary International; member Taunton Rotary Club.

Biography: lives Taunton; born 31.08.1932; married to Irene with 2 children. Educated at Bolton School (1942-1949); Manchester University (1949-1950).

Leisure: armchair geography and travel; Anglican Church activities; campanology; bridge; wine; gardening; walking.

PENN Graham

partner and director of banking research CAMERON MARKBY HEWITT Sceptre Court, 40 Tower Hill, London EC3; partner in the banking department specialising in asset-based financing, banking regulations and international banking.

Career: Williams and Glyn's Bank (1975); lecturer in commercial law University College Cardiff (1983); lecturer in banking law Queen Mary College London (1984); assistant director Centre for Commercial Law, Queen Mary College (1984-1988); senior visiting lecturer University College London (1988 to date); assistant solicitor Cameron Markby (1988); became partner and director of banking research (1989); elected fellow of the Chartered Institute of Bankers (1990).

Activities: chief examiner (Practice and Law of International Banking) The Chartered Institute of Bankers (1983 to date); editor of The Journal of International Banking Law (1984 to date); senior visiting lecturer University College London; regularly lectures throughout UK and abroad on banking law and related topics.

Biography: lives Loughton; born 17.05.1956; married to Jane with 2 children. Educated at Hull University (1981 LLB); Chester College of Law (1982); author of 'Banking Supervision' (1988); co-author of: 'The Law Relating to Domestic Banking' (1987); 'Law and Practice of International Banking' (1987); 'Company Law' (1987); contributor to 'Gore-Browne on Companies' (1985 to date); writes monthly column for 'Banking World' (1983 to date); editor of The Journal

of International Banking Law (1984 to date); writes for various legal journals in banking and related fields.

Leisure: church; cricket; squash; swimming; reading; theatre.

PENNINGTON Robert

professor of commercial law UNIVERSITY OF BIRMINGHAM Faculty of Law, Birmingham B15 2TT.

Career: admitted (1951); senior lecturer and reader Law Society's School of Law (1951-1962); member Board of Management the College of Law (1962); senior lecturer in commercial law University of Birmingham (1962-1968); professor of commercial law (1968).

Activities: Government adviser and draftsman on company legislation, Trinidad (1967); Seychelles (1970); UK special legal adviser on company legislation to the Commission of the European Communities (1973-1979); member Law Society's Company Law Committee (1973-1984).

Biography: lives Claverdon; born 22.04.1927; married to Patricia with 1 daughter. Educated at Holly Lodge Grammar School, Warley; Birmingham University (1943-1946); author of 'Pennington's Company Law' (6th edition 1990); 'Companies in the European Communities' (3rd edition 1982); 'Directors' Personal Liability' (1987); 'Company Liquidations: The Substantive Law and the Procedure' (1987); 'The Law of Investment Marketing' (1989).

Leisure: industrial archaeology (particularly metalliferous mining); local history of south western Britain; walking.

PEPPITT John

Queen's Counsel 3 Gray's Inn Place, London WC1R 5EA.

Career: called to the Bar Gray's Inn (1958); QC (1976); Recorder of the Crown Court (1976); Bencher Gray's Inn (1982).

Activities: commissioner of Inland Revenue (1983); chairman Mental Health Review Tribunals (1984).

Biography: lives nr Maidstone; born 22.09.1931; married to Judith with 3 sons. Educated at St Paul's School (1945-1950); Jesus College Cambridge 1954 BA) Exhibitioner; Lord Justice Holker Senior Scholar (1958); Stuart Cunningham Macaskie Award Winner (1958).

Leisure: collecting watercolours; sheep-breeding and rearing; restoring antique furniture.

PERCIVAL Ian

Queen's Counsel 5 Paper Buildings, Temple, London EC4Y 7HB.

Career: Major The Buffs Alamein, Burma (1940-1946); called to the Bar Inner Temple (1948); QC (1963); Recorder Deal (1971); Recorder of the Crown Court (1971); Knight Bachelor (1979); Her Majesty's Solicitor General (1979-1983) .

Activities: MP for Southport (1959-1987); member Her Majesty's Most Honourable Privy Council; Chairman Conservative Parliamentary Legal Committee; Reader of the Inner Temple (1989); Treasurer (1990); member of Royal Economic Society; Liveryman and member of the Court of the Worshipful Company of Arbitrators; hon member of the Order of the COIF (USA); member of: Carlton; Beefsteak; Rye Golf Club; Royal Birkdale Golf Club; City Livery.

Biography: lives London and Kent; born 11.05.1921; married with 2 children. Educated at Latymer Upper School; St Catherine's College Cambridge (1947 BA hons); Entrance Scholar Inner Temple; Fellow Chartered Institute of Arbitrators; Fellow of the Institute of Taxation; some pamphlets.

Leisure: parachuting; windsurfing; tennis; golf; farmer.

PERCIVAL Michael

senior partner and head of private client division HOWES PERCIVAL Oxford House, Cliftonville, Northampton NN1 5PN.

Career: articled Chamberlain & Co (1961-1966); admitted (1966); assistant solicitor family firm Howes Percival (1966); became partner (1966); became senior partner (1984).

Activities: member Law Society; member SBA; Deputy High Court & County Court Registrar (1983-1988); clerk to Commissioners of Taxes for Northampton Districts 1 & 2 (1988 to date); council member Northamptonshire Law Society (1982 to date); chairman South Midlands branch of the Solicitors Family Law Association (1988-1989); president Northampton & District branch of Multiple Sclerosis Society; elected member Northampton District Health Authority (1987-1990); trustee Northamptonshire Natural History Society and Field Club; trustee St Christopher's Church of England Home for the Elderly, Northampton; member of: Northampton Football Club (rugby); Northamptonshire County Cricket Club; Dallington Lawn Tennis Club; Brancaster Staithe Sailing Club, Norfolk.

Biography: lives Northamptonshire; born 11.07.1943; married to Jean with 3 daughters. Educated at Berkhamsted School, Hertfordshire (1953-1961).

Leisure: walking; tennis; sailing; skiing.

PERELL Edward

resident managing partner DEBEVOISE & PLIMPTON 1 Creed Court, 5 Ludgate Hill, London EC4M 7AA.

Career: associate Debevoise & Plimpton, New York (1965-1972); admitted to New York Bar (1966); partner (1973 to date); became resident managing partner London (1989).

Activities: former chairman and director Federation of Protestant Welfare Agencies, New York; former president and director Graham-Windham Family Services, New York; member Yale Club of New York.

Biography: lives London SW3; born 30.03.1940; married to Nan with 2 children. Educated at Phillips Academy, Andover, Mass; Yale College (1962 BA): Yale Law School (1965 LLB); articles on cross-border mergers and acquisitions and US securities laws.

PERRETT Desmond

Queen's Counsel 2 Crown Office Row, Temple, London EC4.

Career: National Service with Royal Navy (1955-1957); called to the Bar Gray's Inn (1962); Midland & Oxford circuit (1963); Recorder of the Crown Court (1978); QC (1980); Bencher Gray's Inn (1989).

Activities: member Senate of the Inns of Court and the Bar (1983-1987); chairman Cricket Council Appeals Committee; member governing body Harris Hill School; trustee Highclere Maintenance Trust; member MCC.

Biography: lives Newbury; born 22.04.1937; married to Pauline with 2 children. Educated at Westminster School (1951-1955).

Leisure: shooting; fishing; cricket; local history and topography.

PERRY John David

managing partner SIMPSON CURTIS Dauntsey House, Frederick's Place, Old Jewry, London EC2R 8PS.

Career: articled Clifton Woodward & Smith (1964-1966); articled McKenna & Co (1966-1967); admitted (1967); equity partner McKenna & Co (1971-1975); became partner Knapp-Fishers (1975-1987); founded own practice (1987); became managing partner Simpson Curtis (1989).

Activities: UK representative CBS Inc (1972); director Ecuador Travel Ltd (1975); director and chairman Spiteri Ltd (1978); director and chairman Marriott Hotels and Catering (Holdings) Ltd (1979); European Counsel Marriott Corporation (1987 to date); chairman Marquis Hotels Ltd Partnership (1987); chairman Marriott Roissy Service SA (1985); director Arbiter Group PLC (1987); director Caterair UK Ltd (1989); member International Bar Association; member City of London Solicitors' Company; member Music Business Lawyers' Association; member of: Haydn-Mozart Society; Wigmore Lawn Tennis Club.

Biography: lives London SE21; born 10.09.1941; married to Kristian. Educated at King Edward VII School, Sheffield; Queen's College Oxford (1963 BA) (1964 BCL) (1967 MA); (1967 Solicitors Finals Hons).

Leisure: cricket; tennis; soccer; travel; archaeology; classical music; opera; current affairs.

PERRY Philippa

director of research and training BARLOW LYDE & GILBERT Beaufort House, 15 St Botolph Street, London EC3A 7NJ.

Career: articled Linklaters & Paines; admitted (1985); lecturer in information technology law at the Centre for Commercial Law Studies London University (1985-1987); specialist information technology law Slaughter and May (1987-1989); became director of research and training Barlow Lyde & Gilbert (1989).

Biography: lives London; born 29.04.1959; married to Kevin. Educated at Chelmsford County High School for Girls; Queen Mary College London (1980 LLB hons); Cambridge (1981 LLB); Harvard (1983 LLM).

Leisure: badminton; theatre; opera; entertaining.

PERYER Roger Norman

senior litigation partner D J FREEMAN & CO 43 Fetter Lane, London EC4A 1NA.

Career: admitted (1959); assistant solicitor Stiteman Neate & Topping (1959-1961); became partner (1961-1976); became partner DJ Freeman (1976).

P

Activities: member of the Chartered Institute of Arbitrators; Freeman of the City of London; Liveryman of the Worshipful Company of Solicitors; member of the Negligence Panel of the Solicitors Complaints Bureau; served as committee member for Holborn Law Society (1970s); member Law Society; member of: MCC; Leander Club; RAC; Temple Golf Club; Stewards Henley Royal Regatta.

Biography: lives London W14; born 27.02.1937; divorced with 2 children. Educated at King's College School, Wimbledon.

Leisure: golf; boating; shooting.

PESCOD Michael

partner SLAUGHTER AND MAY 35 Basinghall Street, London EC2V 5DB.

Career: articled Slaughter and May (1968-1970); admitted (1970); assistant solicitor (1970-1976); became partner (1977).

Activities: member of: MCC; RAC; Euston.

Biography: lives London W11 and Somerset; born 04.01.1946; married to Bettina with 1 child and 2 stepchildren. Educated at Royal Grammar School, Newcastle upon Tyne; University College Oxford (1967 BA); various articles principally about takeover bids.

Leisure: sport; literature; music.

PETERS Brian

senior partner HANCOCK AND LAWRENCE Old Mansion House, Quay Street, Truro, Cornwall TR1 2HD and Great Office, Cross Street, Helston, Cornwall TR13 8NF.

Career: National Service with Royal Air Force Police; articled Falmouth; admitted (1965); assistant solicitor Hancock and Lawrence (1965-1968); became partner (1968); became senior partner (1986).

Activities: President Cornwall Law Society (1989-1990); member of: Mylor Yacht Club; Helford River Sailing Club; Cadgwith Pilot Gig Club.

Biography: lives Helston; born 30.10.1938; married to Barbara with 4 children. Educated at Truro Cathedral School; College of Law Lancaster Gate.

Leisure: sailing; rowing; any activity connected with the sea; walking; reading; singing traditional Cornish songs.

PETTERSON David Charles

intellectual property consultant TAYLOR JOYNSON GARRETT 10 Maltravers Street, London WC2R 3BS.

Career: articled Woodham Smith; admitted (1961); assistant solicitor (1961-1965); partner (1965-1990); became consultant Taylor Joynson Garrett (1990).

Activities: member Licensing Executives' Society; Churchwarden; bible study leader.

Biography: born 28.01.1939; married to Jennifer with 1 son and 1 daughter. Educated at Chigwell School.

Leisure: steam railways (signalman; restoring signal equipment and coaches); HGV licence holder; motorcycles.

PFISTER Charles

senior partner ATKINS WILSON & BELL 3 Jenner Road, Guildford, Surrey GU1 3AQ.

Career: articled Atkins Walter & Locke; admitted (1973); assistant solicitor (1973-1975); became partner (1975); merged with Gerald Wilson & Bell (1976); became senior partner Atkins Wilson & Bell (1987).

Activities: president West Surrey Law Society (1989-1990); member of: The County Club; West Surrey Golf Club; The Post House Hotel Health and Fitness Club.

Biography: lives Godalming; born 29.01.1950; married to Karen. Educated at Perrott Hill, Somerset; Canford School, Dorset; College of Law.

Leisure: golf; cricket; squash.

PHILIPP Thomas

first American partner resident in London BAKER & MCKENZIE Aldwych House, Aldwych, London WC2B 4JP.

Career: admitted Wisconsin (1975); admitted Illinois (1976); assistant solicitor Baker & McKenzie, Chicago (1976-1983); became partner Baker & McKenzie, London (1983).

Biography: lives London NW3; born 18.05.1950; married to Barbara with 3 children. Educated at Marquette University High School, Milwaukee; Georgetown University, Washington DC (1972 BA); University of Wisconsin (1975 JD); articles in Acquisitions Monthly; author of: 'Multi-Country Acquisitions: The Practical Legal Aspects' with James Rider; 'International Mergers and Acquisitions' (1989).

PHILLIPS Alun

director of legal services ROYAL BOROUGH OF KENSINGTON & CHELSEA Town Hall, Hornton Street, London W8 7NX.

Career: articled Tatton Gaskell & Tatton (1972-1974); admitted (1975); assistant solicitor London Borough of Brent (1976-1980); assistant borough solicitor London Borough of Hammersmith & Fulham (1980-1989); borough solicitor Royal Borough of Kensington & Chelsea (1989-1990); Director of Legal Services (1990).

Activities: secretary to mini and junior sections of Saracens RFC.

Biography: lives London N22; born 10.09.1949; married with 1 son. Educated at Abermad Preparatory School, Aberystwyth; Dulwich College; King's College London (1971 LLB hons).

Leisure: skiing; squash; circuit training.

PHILLIPS Carey

consultant GF LODDER & SONS 50 Henley Street, Stratford on Avon; Warwickshire CV37 6QL.

Career: articled to father (1936-1937); (father died 1937 and practice purchased by GF Lodder & Sons); articled GF Lodder & Sons; War Service in Royal Armoured Corps (1940); OCTU Royal Military College, Sandhurst; commissioned Royal Tank Regiment (1941); served with 143rd Regiment Royal Armoured Corp; served with 400 Independent Scorpion Squadron (Flail Tanks) Egypt (1942); Far East (1942-1946); repatriated on Python with the rank of Major; admitted (1947); assistant solicitor GF Lodder & Sons (1947-1950); became partner (1950); became senior partner (1984); consultant (1990).

Activities: one-time secretary of Stratford on Avon Rotary Club; member of Union Club.

Biography: lives Stratford on Avon; born 25.10.1919; married to Sally with 5 children. Educated at Emscote Lawn Preparatory School; Malvern College.

PHILLIPS Eric

senior partner MORGAN BRUCE & HARDWICKES 3 Museum Place, Cardiff CF1 3TX.

Career: member of the Bar (1949-1959); assistant solicitor Hardwickes (1959-1961); became partner (1961-1987); became partner Morgan Bruce & Hardwickes (1987); senior partner (1989).

Activities: chairman Wales Region of Mental Health Review Tribunals; legal member Medical Appeal Tribunals for Wales; specialist in intellectual property law.

Biography: lives Cardiff; born 01.03.1924; married with 2 children. Educated at Howard Garden High School, Cardiff; St John's College Oxford.

Leisure: all forms of physical recreation in particular swimming, walking, training; opera listening and viewing .

PHILLIPS Jeremy

joint managing partner HOLT PHILLIPS 11-12 Queen Square, Bristol BS1 4NT.

Career: landscape gardener (1976); articled John Lloyd & Co (1977-1980); admitted (1980); assistant solicitor Cartwrights (1980-1982); became partner (1982); joint-founder Holt Phillips (1984).

Activities: member Welshback Squash and Health Club.

Biography: lives Hawkesbury Upton; born 20.01.1954; married to Mary with 1 daughter and 2 sons. Educated at Belmont Preparatory School, Mill Hill; Harrow School; Southampton University (1975 BA hons); occasional contributor to the press on matters concerning licensing law.

Leisure: family; battling with smallholding; many animals and overgrown garden.

PHILLIPS John F

Queen's Counsel and head of chambers 1 Verulam Buildings, Gray's Inn, London WC1; Arbitrator (Commercial, Medical, Agricultural).

Career: official Royal Courts of Justice (Court of Protection) (1933-1944); legal and Parliamentary secretary and assistant general secretary National Farmer's Union (1945-1956); secretary and chief executive Institute of Chartered Secretaries and Administrators (1957-1976).

Activities: CBE (1977); OBE (1957); O St J (1982); president (1977) and member of Council Institute of Chartered Secretaries and Administrators; president (1976) and member of Council Chartered Institute of Arbitrators; chairman and director Private Patients Plan (1958-1984) (president 1984 to date); chairman Associated Examining Board (1958 to date); chairman Southern Examining Group for GCSE (1986 to date); deputy chairman Eggs Authority (1970-1980); chairman Houghton Poultry Research Station (1978-1987); deputy chairman Business Education Council

(1976-1982); member Animal Health Trust; member of: Athenaeum; United Oxford & Cambridge Universities Club; City Livery.

Biography: lives London N2; born 09.06.1911; married to Olive with 3 children. Educated at Cardinal Vaughan School, Holland Park; London University LSE & Birkbeck (LLB hons); Trinity Hall Cambridge (LLB LLM); City University (DCL Hon); Fellow British Institute of Management (Companion); FRSA; author of: 'Court of Protection' Practice (6th & 7th eds 1939 & 1954); 'Agriculture Act 1947' (1948) 'Arbitration Law Practice & Precedents' (1988); several others.

Leisure: travel; theatre; charitable trusts.

PHILLIPS Robert

partner MCKENNA & CO Mitre House, 160 Aldersgate Street, London EC1A 4DD.

Career: admitted (1971); assistant solicitor (1971-1979); became partner (1979); senior resident partner Hong Kong (1983-1988); co- ordinator of McKenna & Co's international major projects unit (1988-date).

Activities: set up McKenna & Co's China Data Base and China News Letter; participated in and promoted courses for the greater use of private sector finance for public sector works including Build, Operate and Transfer, also known as Design, Build, Finance and Operate.

Biography: lives North East Surrey; born 15.05.1947; married to Eleanor with 3 children. Educated at St Mary's College, Southampton; College of Law Guildford.

Leisure: to be earnestly hoped for.

PHILPOTT Fred

barrister and joint head of chambers 9 Devereux Court, London WC2R 3JJ.

Career: Intelligence Corps with Regular Army (1963-1969); called to the Bar Gray's Inn (1974); pupillage with Michael Gettleson; co-founded Chambers at 9 Devereux Court (1986).

Biography: lives London SE15; born 10.11.1947; married to Elizabeth. Educated at John Lyons School; King's College London (1973 LLB); Inns of Court School of Law (1974); co-author of 'Sale of Goods Litigation'.

PHIPSON John

partner LINKLATERS & PAINES Barrington House, 59-67 Gresham Street, London EC2V 7JA.

Career: articled Linklaters & Paines (1959-1964); admitted (1964); assistant solicitor (1964-1970); became partner (1970).

Activities: vice-president Honourable Artillery Company; member HAC (TA) (1959-1975) (Major TD); member Court of Assistants (1972 to date); member Players' Theatre.

Biography: lives near Tunbridge Wells; born 29.11.1940; married to Harriet with 4 children. Educated at Rugby School; College of Law Lancaster Gate.

Leisure: family; keeping house from falling down; drinking?!.

PICKLES Tony

senior partner OXLEY & COWARD 34 Moorgate Street, Rotherham, South Yorkshire S60 2HB.

Career: articled Oxley & Coward (1944); military service (1944-1947); admitted; became partner (1952).

Activities: president Doncaster and District Law Society (1969); chairman Yorkshire Rent Assessment Committee (1982 to date); member Sheffield Philharmonic Chorus (hon sec 25 years); president Tickhill Cricket Club; member Rotherham Club.

Biography: lives Doncaster; born 23.09.1926; married to Judyth with 4 children. Educated at Rotherham Grammar School; Sedbergh School.

Leisure: rugby union supporter; pianist.

PIKE John

joint managing partner commercial property department BOOTH & CO Sovereign House, South Parade, Leeds LS1 1HQ.

Career: articled Booth & Co (1969-1971); admitted (1972); assistant solicitor (1972-1976); became partner (1976); partner in charge of practice development; member firm's Board of Management.

Activities: hon secretary West Riding branch of the Council for the Protection of Rural England; former chairman Boston Spa & Tadcaster Round Table; member Wetherby 41 Club.

Biography: lives Wetherby; born 04.10.1947; married to Rosemary with 3 children. Educated at QEGS, Wakefield; Keighley School; Jesus College Cambridge (1969 BA) (1972 MA); Open Exhibition at Jesus College.

Leisure: squash; walking; gardening; watching most sports.

P

PILSWORTH Ian L

manager Legal Services Department
LONDON ELECTRICITY PLC Templar
House, 81-87 High Holborn, London
WC1V 6NU.

Career: articled London Borough of Enfield
(1974-1977); admitted (1977); assistant
solicitor; senior assistant solicitor; chief
assistant solicitor (1977-1985); head of legal
section London Electricity Board (1985-
1989); became manager of Legal Services
Department (1989), which includes
insurance responsibility (from 1989).

Activities: chairman Edmonton
Conservative Association (1989-1990);
governor Latymer School, Edmonton;
District Health Authority member for
Haringey.

Biography: Newcastle upon Tyne
University (1973 LLB); College of Law
Chester (1974).

PINCOTT Andrew

managing partner ELBORNE MITCHELL
Three Quays, Tower Hill, London
EC3R 6DS.

Career: articled Arthur Palmer & Co;
admitted (1974); assistant solicitor (1974-
1976); assistant solicitor Elborne Mitchell
(1976); partner (1980); became managing
partner (1988).

Activities: chairman British Insurance Law
Association (1987 & 1988).

Biography: lives London N1; born
24.12.1949; single. Educated at Barry
Grammar School; Bristol University (1971
LLB hons); Faculte de Droit at Aix en
Provence (1975-1976); Institute of
International and Comparative Law
Scholarship (1975); articles on the law of
insurance and reinsurance; lectures in
these topics at City Polytechnic as part of
continuing education courses for solicitors.

Leisure: opera; stage design; French
literature and theatre; Japanese culture;
food and wine; gardening; sunshine.

PINSON Barry

Queen's Counsel and head of chambers
11 New Square, Lincoln's Inn, London
WC2A 3QB.

Career: military service (1944-1947); called
to the Bar Gray's Inn (1949); Bencher
(1981).

Activities: trustee Royal Air Force Museum
(1980 to date); member Arts Club.

Biography: lives London SW1; born
18.12.1925; married to Anne with 2

children. Educated at King Edward's High
School; Birmingham University (1945 LLB
hons); Fellow of the Institute of Taxation;
author of 'Revenue Law' (17 eds).

PIRRETT David

partner ROSS HARPER & MURPHY
4/6 Regent Way, Hamilton M13 7AJ.

Career: apprentice Headrick Inglis Glen &
Co (1969-1971); admitted (1971); Court
assistant Maclay Murray & Spens (1971-
1973); assistant solicitor RH & M (1973-
1974); became partner (1974).

Activities: reporter to Scottish Legal Aid
Board; secretary to Society of Solicitors of
Hamilton & District; member of:
Strathaven Golf Club; Strathaven Rugby
Club; Trades House of Glasgow; Cordiners
(former Deacon); Council member of Law
Society of Scotland.

Biography: lives Strathaven; born
25.08.1946; married with 2 children.
Educated at Uddingston Grammar School;
St Andrew's University (1969 LLB).

Leisure: sailing (Firth of Clyde, Western
Isles); golf; skiing; supporting Motherwell
Football Club.

PISTORIUS Brian

general counsel KPMG PEAT MARWICK
MCLINTOCK 1 Puddle Dock, Blackfriars,
London EC4V 3PD.

Career: articled Bell Dewar & Hall,
Johannesburg (1953-1955); admitted South
Africa (1956); legal department large
mining and finance house Johannesburg
(1955-1957); assistant solicitor Durban
(1957-1959); became partner Garlidre &
Bausfield (1960-1976); admitted England
(1979); became partner Barlow Lyde &
Gilbert (1979); chairman Executive
Committee (1985-1986); admitted Hong
Kong (1986); became senior partner (1988)
resigning 1990 to become general counsel
KPMG Peat Marwick McLintock.

Activities: Notary Public South Africa
(1959); member Law Society Council Natal
(1964-1976) (vice-president 1970-1972);
examiner in practice and procedure (1968-
1976); member Board of Faculty of Law
University of Natal (1968-1976); member
National Legal Aid Board (S Africa) (1969-
1972); chairman Valuation Appeals Board
Borough of Umhlanga Natal (1973);
member South African Law Society
Committee for Legal Education (1967-1972)
(chairman 1969-1972); member South
African Law Society Committee for Legal
Aid (1967-1972); Deputy Mayor Borough of
Kloof Natal (1970); member Board of

Control Attorneys Notaries &
Conveyancers Fidelity Fund (1970-1972);
member South African Law Society
Standing Committee on Continuing Legal
Education (1974-1976); member Committee
(Natal Section) Mountain Club of South
Africa (1958-1961); member Finance
Committee Natal Region Progressive Party
of South Africa (1962-1963); member Board
of Fulton School for the Deaf nominated by
Bishop of Natal (1971-1975); Captain 6th
SA Armd Division Signals Regt (1949-
1956).

Biography: lives Cranleigh; born 20.02.1931;
married to Meridythe with 3 children.
Educated at Durban High School; Jeppe
High School; Witwatersaand University
(1952 BA) (1955 LLB); College of Law
Guildford (1977).

Leisure: golf; travel; sailing; opera; ballet.

PITTS John

chairman LEGAL AID BOARD Newspaper
House, 8-16 Great New Street, London
EC4A 3BN.

Career: research officer Shirley Institute
(1948-1953); director Mond Division and
deputy chairman Agricultural Division ICI
PLC (1953-1978); chairman and chief
executive Tioxide Group PLC (1978-1987);
chairman Legal Aid Board (1988 to date).

Activities: president Chemical Industries
Association (1984-1986); vice-chairman
Shildon & Sedgefield Development
Agency (1982 to date); member Chemicals
Economic Development Committee (1981-
1987); member Council CBI (1984-1987);
member of Royal Automobile Club.

Biography: lives London NW1 and
Carthorpe; born 06.10.1925; widowed and
remarried. Educated at Trowbridge High
School; Bristol University (1948 physics).

Leisure: studying history of the marine
steam engine; gardening.

PLATT Eleanor

Queen's Counsel One Garden Court,
Temple, London EC4Y 9BJ.

Career: called to the Bar Gray's Inn (1960);
Recorder of the Crown Court (1982); QC
(1982).

Activities: treasurer Family Law Bar
Association (1990 to date) Matrimonial
Causes Rule Committee (1986); chairman
Law Parliamentary & General Purposes
Committee of the Board of Deputies of
British Jews (1988).

Biography: lives London SE21; born
06.05.1938; married with 2 children.

Educated at Hove County Grammar School; University College London (1959 LLB).

Leisure: the arts; travel; skiing.

PLUMTREE John

partner GEPP & SONS 58 New London Road, Chelmsford CM2 0PA.

Career: office boy Chelmsford (1948-1949); articled Brentwood (1949-1954); admitted (1954); assistant solicitor Grimsby (1954-1956); became partner Hilliard & Ward (1957-1975); became senior partner (1975-1989); became salaried partner Gepp & Sons (1989).

Activities: Governors past chairman St Cedd's School Chelmsford; hon legal adviser and area councillor National Operatic & Dramatic Association; president Chelmsford Amateur Operatic Society; member of: Colchester Club; Colchester Garrison Officers' Club.

Biography: lives Colchester; born 21.10.1928; married with 3 children. Educated at King Edward VI Grammar School, Chelmsford; College of Law London.

POLLARD Neil

senior partner DUTHIE HART & DUTHIE 517/19 Barking Road, Plaistow, London E13 8PS.

Career: articled (1953-1958); admitted (1958); personal assistant to the managing director of a limited company (2 years); assistant solicitor in Luton (2 years); assistant solicitor Duthie Hart & Duthie (1962); became partner.

Activities: president West Essex Law Society (1987-1988); member Committee of the London Criminal Courts Association (1982 to date); set up Duty Solicitor Schemes in all Magistrates' Courts in West Essex; member Law Society Advisory Committee on Duty Solicitors; member London Area 13 Duty Solicitor Committee; president London Criminal Courts Solicitors Association; member Area Legal Aid Committee; member Royal Corinthian Yacht Club.

Biography: lives Althorne nr Burnham; born 25.11.1935; single. Educated at Queen's College, Taunton; College of Law.

Leisure: sailing; opera; gardening.

PONSFORD Ian

consultant PENNINGTONS incorporating GAMLENS 37 Sun Street, London EC2M 2PY.

Career: RAF (1939); qualified as pilot and became flying instructor USA; operational flying on Spitfires (1943-1946); articled Holborn (1946); admitted (1949); assistant solicitor Gamlens (1951-1954); partner (1954); became consultant Penningtons (1990).

Activities: chairman Solicitors Wine Society (1974) (president 1985-1989); founder and chairman Vinifrance Ltd; member Royal Air Force Club.

Biography: lives Northamptonshire; born 20.03.1922; married to Cynthia with 2 children. Educated at Abbotsholme School; London University (1939-1940); Distinguished Flying Cross and Air Force Cross.

POOLE David

Queen's Counsel 1 Dean's Court, Crown Square, Manchester M3 and 1 Crown Office Row, Temple, London EC4.

Career: called to the Bar Middle Temple (1968); Recorder (1983); QC (1984).

Activities: Chairman Association of Lawyers for Defence of Unborn.

Biography: lives Manchester; born 08.06.1938; married to Pauline with 4 sons. Educated at Ampleforth; Jesus College Oxford (MA) Meyricke Exhibitioner; UMIST (Dip Tech Sc).

POPE Julian

partner and head of Construction Group DENTON HALL BURGIN & WARRENS Five Chancery Lane, Clifford's Inn, London EC4A 1BU.

Career: articled and assistant solicitor Lovell White & King (1975-1980); assistant solicitor Denton Hall Burgin & Warrens (1980-1982); became partner (1982); Hong Kong (1980-1988).

Biography: lives London; born 05.06.1952; married with 2 children. Educated at Haileybury (1965-1969); Kent University (BA hons); Law Society Professional Exams (1975).

POPPLE Chris

partner responsible for acquisition and disposal of development land including town & country planning and probate and trust RIGBEYS 42-44 Waterloo Street, Birmingham B2 5QN.

Career: articled Starkie & Gregory; admitted (1965); part-time lecturer Nottingham Polytechnic (1962-1966); assistant solicitor Chattertons (1966-1967);

partner (1967-1972); co-senior partner (1972-1977); assistant solicitor Rigbey Loose & Mills (1977); became partner (1977).

Activities: former chairman Woodhall Spa Round Table; past chairman Sutton Park 41 Club; chairman Sutton Coldfield Philharmonic Society; chairman local residents' association; Birmingham Diocese licenced to administer communion; former member Diocesan monitoring group in respect of Church Urban Fund; member of: the Birmingham Club; Moor Hall Golf Club.

Biography: lives Birmingham; born 25.06.1940; married to Jill with 3 children. Educated at Nottingham High School (1948-1959); Emmanuel College Cambridge (1962 BA) (1963 LLB) (1966 MA) Senior Exhibitioner; author of articles for Birmingham Post.

PORTEOUS Christopher

solicitor to the Commissioner of Police for the Metropolis New Scotland Yard, Broadway, London SW1H 0BG.

Career: articled to the clerk of Malling RDC (1954-1960); admitted (1960); LCC (1960-1962); legal assistant with New Scotland Yard (1962-1968); senior legal assistant (1968-1976); assistant solicitor (1976-1987); became solicitor to the Commissioner of Police for the Metropolis (1987).

Activities: Anglican reader Rochester Diocese (1958 to date); member Rochester Diocesan Pastoral Committee (1984-1989); chairman Metropolitan Police Civil Staff Welfare Committee.

Biography: lives South East London; born 08.11.1935; married to Brenda with 4 children. Educated at St Dunstan's Preparatory School; Dulwich College; College of Law; articles in Police Review and Policing.

Leisure: writing hymns and verse.

PORTER Jim

joint senior partner THOMPSON SMITH & PUXON 4 North Hill, Colchester, Essex CO3 3SP.

Career: articled Thompson Smith & Puxon (1948-1953); admitted (1953); National Service with Royal Engineers (1953-1955); assistant solicitor Surrey and London (1955-1957); assistant solicitor Thompson Smith & Puxon (1958-1959); became partner (1959).

Activities: clerk to the Commissioners of Income Tax Colchester Division (1970);

president Suffolk & North Essex Law Society (1982); trustee Winsleys Almshouses Colchester; member of: Colchester Rotary Club (president 1981); Colchester Golf Club.

Biography: lives Colchester; born 06.09.1930; married to Elizabeth with 2 sons and 1 daughter. Educated at Hill Crest Preparatory School; Charterhouse.

Leisure: golf; tennis.

PORTER John

senior partner LAWSON LEWIS & CO 11 Hyde Gardens, Eastbourne, East Sussex BN21 4PP.

Career: Royal Artillery (1943-1947) (captain); articled Leslie Bunker (1948-1951); admitted (1951); assistant solicitor (1951-1955); became partner Lawson Lewis & Co (1955) .

Activities: member Council of the Law Society of England and Wales (1974); chairman Legal Aid Committee England and Wales (1981-1983); part-time chairman Social Security Appeal Trib nals; member Remuneration and Practice Development Committee and Wills and Equity Committee of the Law Society; member of: Army and Navy Club; Royal Eastbourne Golf Club; Devonshire Club; The Eastbourne Club.

Biography: lives Eastbourne; born 10.07.1925; married to Mary with 2 children. Educated at Brighton College; Glasgow University; Travers Smith Scholarship (1951).

Leisure: snooker; golf; opera.

PORTER Neil

partner BURGES SALMON Narrow Quay House, Prince Street, Bristol BS1 4AH.

Career: articled Porter & Co; admitted (1960); assistant solicitor (1960-1964); qualified as teacher (1968); taught in Botswana (1968-1969); taught Bristol (1969-1971); senior research fellowship at Bristol University (1971-1974); lecturer in education Bristol Polytechnic (1974-1977); lecturer in law Bristol Polytechnic (1977-1978); assistant solicitor Burges Salmon (1978-1980); became partner (1980).

Biography: lives Bristol; born 31.01.1935; married to Christine with 3 children. Educated at Repton School (1948-1953); Wadham College Oxford (1964-1966); Bristol University (1966-1968) (PGCE); Senior Research Fellowship (1971-1974) (MEd SSRC).

Leisure: music; walking; photography; gardening.

PORTER Robin

partner property department WILDE SAPTE Queensbridge House, 60 Upper Thames Street, London EC4V 3BD.

Career: articled Titmuss Sainer & Webb; admitted (1971); assistant solicitor (1971-1974); assistant solicitor Wilde Sapte (1974-1975); became partner (1975); partner in charge New York office (1984-1987); liaison partner to the Japan Association (1987 to date).

Activities: member Practice Development Committee (1987-1988); member IBA section on business law; Freeman of the City of London; Freeman of the Worshipful Company of Musicians; member of: English Speaking Union; Cumberland Lawn Tennis Club.

Biography: lives London NW2 and Castle Acre; born 15.09.1945; 2 sons. Educated at Arnold House School, London; Highgate School; University of Leeds (LLB); College of Law Lancaster Gate.

Leisure: reading; theatre; films; listening to classical music and jazz; tennis; skiing; computers.

POTTER Charles

Queen's Counsel 4 Pump Court, Temple, London EC4Y 7AN.

Career: Army (RAC) (1942-1946); assistant lecturer in law LSE (1947-1949); called to the Bar Middle Temple (1948); pupillage Chancery (1949-1950); practice at Chancery Bar (1950-1964); practice Revenue Bar (1964-1988); QC (1970); Bencher Lincoln's Inn (1979).

Activities: arbitrator; chairman Revenue Bar Association (1978-1988); part-time special commissioner tax appeals (1986-1989); part-time VATT chairman (1986-1989); member Garrick.

Biography: lives London WC2 and Salcombe; born 24.05.1922; single. Educated at St Dunstan's College; London University (1947 LLB); co-author of 'Tax Planning with Precedents' (1954 and subsequent eds).

Leisure: sailing; farming; travel; theatre; walking; architecture.

POTTS Christopher

partner MIDDLETON POTTS 3 Cloth Street, Long Lane, London EC1A 7LD.

Career: articled City of London (1961-1964); admitted (1965); assistant solicitor (1965-1967); became partner (1967-1976); founded Middleton Potts with William

Middleton (1976).

Activities: member of: City of London Club; several sports clubs and societies.

Biography: lives Forest Row; born 01.07.1939; married to Nadine with 3 children. Educated at The King's School, Macclesfield; Sutton County Grammar School; London School of Economics and Political Science (1961 LLB hons).

Leisure: listening to music (particularly opera); reading; sporting activities (particularly golf and tennis).

POTTS John Edward Collins

senior partner SINTON & CO 32 Portland Terrace, Newcastle upon Tyne NE2 1SQ.

Career: articled Newcastle upon Tyne City Council (1960-1963); admitted (1963); assistant solicitor (1964); assistant solicitor Sinton & Co (1964-1965); became partner (1965).

Activities: chairman Rent Assessment Panel; joint hon secretary Literary & Philosophical Society, Newcastle upon Tyne.

Biography: lives Riding Mill; born 19.09.1935; married with 4 children. Educated at Durham School; St Catherine's College Oxford (1960 BA).

POULSEN Randi Bach

resident partner BERNING SCHLUTER HALD & ANDERSEN 16 Blackfriars Lane, London EC4V 6EB.

Career: lecturer on legal procedure and bankruptcy law at Copenhagen University (1982-1985); admitted (1989); became partner Berning Schluter Hald & Andersen.

Activities: lectures on business establishments abroad for various institutions including The Danish Law Society and The Federation of Danish Industries; member of: The Law Society; EEC Lawyers' Society; European Solicitors Group; Danish Law Society; Federation of Danish Industries.

Biography: lives London SW6; born 03.04.1957; married to Kurt with 1 child. Educated at London University (1986 LLM); Candidata Juris (1981); languages: English; Scandinavian; German; articles on the registration of ships, debt collection, arbitration, conveyance of real property, investments and establishments abroad.

POWELL David

group legal director MIDLAND BANK PLC Poultry, London EC2P 2BX.

Career: National Service as Flying Officer in RAF; admitted (1962); assistant solicitor (1964-1968); deputy legal adviser BLMC (1969-1973); director of legal services BL (1974-1983); became group legal director Midland Bank PLC (1984).

Activities: director of: BL International Ltd; BL International (Holdings) Ltd; BL Portugal; BL Pension Trustees Ltd (1980-1983); Midland California Holdings Ltd; Midland/Montague Investment Co; member Legal Committee of Society of Motor Manufacturers and Traders (1974-1983).

Biography: lives London W9; born 09.02.1936; divorced. Educated at Gowerton Grammar School; Christ's College Cambridge (BA LLB MA); Yale Law School (1963 LLM) Graduate Fellow; Harvard Business School (1982 SMP 18).

Leisure: reading; music; social bridge.

POWELL-SMITH Christopher

head of corporate department MCKENNA & CO Mitre House, 160 Aldersgate Street, London EC1A 4DD.

Career: articled Henry Sissmore & Co (1954-1959); admitted (1959); assistant solicitor McKenna & Co (1959); Royal Artillary (1959-1961); assistant solicitor McKenna & Co (1961-1964); became partner (1964); managing partner (1982-1986); head of corporate finance (1986-1987); head of corporate department (1987).

Activities: director of: Carlsberg Brewery Ltd; Chairman Black and Decker Group Inc; member of the Law Society; member International Bar Association; asst of the Court of the Honourable Artillary Company; member The City of London Solicitors' Company; member The London Concert Choir; committee member of The Union Jack Club; member of: City of London Club; Royal Mid-Surrey Golf Club; Thurlesdon Golf Club.

Biography: lives Kew and Devon; born 03.10.1936; married to Jennifer with 4 children. Educated at City of London School (1946-1953); Clement's Inn Prize; Travers Smith Scholarship; author of: 'Legal Aspects of International Cross Border Acquisitions' (1989).

PRATT John

partner NEEDHAM & JAMES Windsor House, Temple Row, Birmingham B2 5LF.

Career: articled Lovell White & King (1975-1977); admitted (1977); assistant solicitor (1977-1983); assistant solicitor Needham & James (1983-1984); became partner (1984).

Activities: chairman London Young Solicitors Group (1981-1982); chairman National Committee of Young Solicitors of England and Wales (1984-1985); member London Young Solicitors Committee; member National Committee of Young Solicitors (1980-1986); member Law Society's Law Reform Committee (1982-1984) International Relations Committee (1985-1986) Solicitors European Group Committee (1985-1987) Gazette Committee (1986-1987); member Law Society's Gazette's Advisory Committee (1987 to date); member Birmingham Young Solicitors Committee (1983-1986); member Council of the Birmingham Law Society (1986 to date); hon member Young Lawyers' Division of the American Bar Association.

Biography: born 26.04.1951; married to Barbara with 4 children. Educated at Dulwich College; Hertford College Oxford (1973 BA hons); Universite d'Aix-Marseille (1973-1974 Diploma in Comparative Law); author of 'Sold - but with no safety net attached' Times (1989); Needham & James Competition Law Manual (1989); Franchising, Law and Practice (1990).

Leisure: wine; food; theatre; politics; tennis.

PRESKETT Alan

partner in charge of the commercial department HART BROWN & CO 8 Guildford Road, Woking, Surrey GU22 7PX.

Career: articled Hart Brown & Co (1960-1965); admitted (1966); assistant solicitor (1966-1968): became partner (1968).

Activities: Commissioner for Oaths; former member West Surrey Law Society; member Management Committee Woking Citizens Advice Bureau; former director of a number of companies mainly in publishing; original director Home & Law Magazines Ltd (now part of the Maxwell Group).

Biography: lives Guildford; born 10.06.1942; married to Hilda with 2 sons. Educated at Woking County Grammar School for Boys; College of Law Lancaster Gate and Guildford; author of: 'Exchange Contracts Conveyancers' Handbook'.

PRESLAND Frank George

partner FRERE CHOLMELEY 28 Lincoln's Inn Fields, London WC2A 3HH.

Career: articled Prestons & Kenleys (1970-1972); admitted (1973); assistant solicitor Frere Cholmeley (1973-1976); became partner (1976); member executive committee (1981).

Activities: member Law Society Legal Aid Committee (1985 to date); member Little Ship Club.

Biography: lives Thames Ditton; born 27.02.1944; married to Julia with 2 children. Educated at Sunbury Grammar School; London University (1965 BSC); University College of Rhodesia & Nyasaland (1962); Fairbridge Rhodesian Scholarship; written various minor articles.

Leisure: cruising and occasional racing in own yacht.

PRESTIGE Colin

consultant LAWRENCE GRAHAM 190 Strand, London WC2R 1JN.

Career: articled Lawrence Graham (1950-1953); admitted (1954); assistant solicitor (1954-1959); partner (1959-1989); second senior partner (1987-1989); became consultant (1989).

Activities: chairman Law Society Young Solicitors Group (1960-1961); member Law Society Council (1967 to date) ('father' 1987 to date); chairman Non-Contentious Business Committee (1974-1977) (vice-chairman 1971-1974); vice-chairman Professional Purposes Committee (1980-1982 & 1983-1984); chairman Accounts Rules Sub-committee (1981-1984); chairman Library Sub-committee (1970-1985); member Investigation Committee of Solicitors Complaints Bureau (1987 to date); founder and committee member Holborn Law Society (1962 to date) (hon treasurer 1963-1971) (vice-president 1971-1973) (president 1973-1974); member Worshipful Company of Solicitors (1988 to date); member Land Registration Rules Committee (1970 to date); chairman Rent Assessment Appeals Committee Greater London (1965-1968); member Incorporated Council for Law Reporting (1984 to date); member Council Selden Society (1988 to date); member Committee of Management Solicitors Staff Pension Fund (1988 to date); member Committee Records Preservation Section of British Records Association (1988 to date); trustee D'Oyly Carte Opera Trust (1964 to date); trustee Friends of D'Oyly Carte (1981 to date); director Royal Theatrical Fund (1967-1979 and 1989 to date); member Garrick Club.

Biography: lives London; born 19.11.1926. Educated at Bradfield College (1940-1945); Oriel College Oxford (1950 BA) (1954 MA); FRSA (1967).

PRESTON Christopher

senior tax partner WATSON FARLEY & WILLIAMS Minories House, 2-5 Minories, London EC3N 1BJ.

Career: articled Lees Smith Matthew & Wheeler (1970-1975); admitted (1975); assistant solicitor Norton Rose Botterell & Roche (1975-1982); became tax partner Watson Farley & Williams (1982).

Activities: founder member and national secretary of VAT Practitioners' Group; member Revenue Law Committee of Law Society; chairman of Law Society's Sub-committee on VAT; Fellow of Institute of Taxation; member of: MCC; Oriental Club.

Biography: lives Woldingham; born 09.10.1950; married with 2 children. Educated at Sutton County Grammar School for Boys; author of 'VAT Guide and Casebook'; contributor to 'Tax Practitioner'; lectures on various tax matters.

Leisure: riding; bridge; pottering in the garden.

PRESTON Miles

partner in charge of matrimonial department RADCLIFFES & CO 5 Great College Street, Westminster, London SW1P 3SJ.

Career: articled Radcliffes & Co; admitted (1974); assistant solicitor (1974-1978); associate (1978-1980); became partner (1980).

Activities: served on Sir Gervase Sheldon's Family Law Liaison Committee (1982); founder member Solicitors Family Law Association (Committee 1982-1988 and chairman Working Party on Procedure 1982-1988); founder member International Academy of Matrimonial Lawyers (1986) (governor Main Academy 1986 to date); Parliamentarian main Academy (1989 to date); president-elect English Chapter (1986-1989); president (1989); president European Chapter (1989 to date); member Council of Osteopathic Educational Foundation; member Old Salopian Committee (Old Boys' Association for Shrewsbury School); member of: Turf Club; Leander Club.

Biography: lives London; born 12.04.1950; married to Jane with 2 children. Educated at Shrewsbury (1963-1968).

Leisure: travel; historic houses; rowing.

PRESTON Robin

partner and executive partner media and technology department THEODORE GODDARD 150 Aldersgate Street, London EC1A 4EJ.

Career: articled Simmons and Simmons (1967-1969); admitted (1969); assistant solicitor (1969-1972); became partner (1972-1976); assistant solicitor Theodore Goddard (1976-1977); partner (1977); member firm's management committee (1985); became executive partner media and technology department (1990).

Activities: member City of London Solicitors' Company Commercial Law sub-committee.

Biography: lives London SW15; born 30.09.1943; married to Pat with 1 daughter. Educated at Portora Royal School, Enniskillen; Sidney Sussex College Cambridge (1965 MA hons).

Leisure: photography; reading; travel (especially Italy).

PRICE Diane

consultant in intellectual property and competition law and training officer MARTINEAU JOHNSON and law lecturer BIRMINGHAM UNIVERSITY Faculty of Law, PO Box 363, Birmingham B15 2TT.

Career: articled Martineau Johnson (1984-1986); admitted (1986); assistant solicitor (1986-1987); became consultant and training officer (1988); part-time lecturer in law Birmingham University (1984-1987); became full-time lecturer in law (1987).

Activities: member Birmingham University Board of Continuing Education; member Competition Law Association.

Biography: lives Aldridge; born 31.10.1960; married to Andrew with 1 son Edward Andrew. Educated at Aldridge Grammar School (1972-1979); University College London (1982 LLB hons); College of Law Guildford (1983); Clare College Cambridge (1984 LLM hons); articles in: European Competition Law Review; Modern Law Review; Company Lawyer; Solicitors Journal; Law Society's Gazette; Law for Business.

Leisure: swimming; badminton.

PRICE Leolin

Queen's Counsel 10 Old Square, Lincoln's Inn, London WC2A 3SU.

Career: called to the Bar Middle Temple (1949) Lincoln's Inn (1959); QC (1968); QC Bahamas (1969); QC New South Wales (1987); Bencher Middle Temple (1970); treasurer Middle Temple (1990).

Activities: vice-chairman Society of Conservative Lawyers; governor Hospital for Sick Children Great Ormond Street; chairman Institute of Child Health; chairman Child Health Research Investment Trust PLC; chancellor Diocese of Swansea & Brecon; member Carlton Club.

Biography: lives London and LLanbedr nr Crickhowell; born 11.05.1924; married with 4 children. Educated at The Judd School, Tonbridge; Keble College Oxford (MA); treasurer Oxford Union Society (1948); president Oxford Conservative Society (1948).

PRICE Richard

mergers and acquisitions partner MCKENNA & CO Mitre House, 160 Aldersgate Street, London EC1A 4DD.

Career: articled McKenna & Co; admitted (1977); assistant solicitor; partner in charge Middle East operations (1984-88)..

Biography: lives London SW14; born 27.05.1953; married to Griffin with 2 children. Educated at Cowbridge Grammar School; Leeds (1974 LLB hons); articles in: Middle East Economic Digest; International Financial Law Review; Euromoney.

Leisure: golf; squash..

PRICE Richard

partner and head of intellectual property department TAYLOR JOYNSON GARRETT, 10 Maltravers Street, London WC2R 2BS.

Career: articled Joynson-Hicks & Co (1968-1970); admitted (1970); assistant solicitor and partner (1970-1975); became partner Courts & Co (1975-1977); became partner Woodham Smith (1977-90); re-joined Taylor Joynson Garrett (May 1990).

Activities: hon solicitor Surrey Bird Club; founding member and Secretary, Patent Solicitors Association; member Executive Committee Community Trademarks Office; member Standing Advisory Committee on Trademarks (DTI); appeared on BBC TV's 'The Money Programme' (1988); member of: Royal Automobile Club; Riverside Racquets Club; British Ornithologists' Union; British Ornithologists' Club; numerous natural history societies and trusts.

Biography: lives London W12; born 07.01.1946; married to Helen with 3 sons. Educated at Lynton Preparatory School, Epsom; Kingston Grammar School; Bristol University (1967 LLB); College of Law (1967-1968); articles in The Lawyer on Community Trademark Matters.

Leisure: natural history and conservation

(particularly birds); photographer of birds, butterflies and plants; hockey; cricket; tennis; golf; sailing.

PRICHARD Cameron

senior partner ANDREW & CO
St Swithin's Square, Lincoln LN2 1HB.

Career: articled Andrew & Co (1958-1961); admitted (1961); assistant solicitor (1961-1963); became partner (1963); became senior partner (1985).

Activities: member local Legal Aid Committee; panel solicitor Solicitors Complaints Bureau; chairman local charitable housing committee; member committee on housing for elderly; member committees dealing with the Arts locally; member Lincoln Golf Club.

Biography: lives Lincoln; born 09.09.1936; married to Patricia with 2 children. Educated at Kilmarnock Academy; Lincoln School; Manchester University (1958 LLB hons).

Leisure: the Arts; golf; gardening.

PRICHARD Mick

senior partner ROOKS RIDER 8 & 9 New Square, Lincoln's Inn, London WC2A 3QJ.

Career: articled Ward Bowie & Co (1949-1951); admitted (1951); assistant solicitor (1951-1953); assistant solicitor Jaques & Co (1953-1955); assistant solicitor Rooks & Co (now Rooks Rider) (1955); became senior partner .

Activities: member City Livery Club.

Biography: lives Eton; born 02.09.1925; married with 4 children. Educated at Wimbledon College; King's College London (1949 LLB); various Law Society Finals Prizes including Scott Scholarship & Clement Inn Prize.

Leisure: reading; walking; skiing.

PRIDEAUX Walter

joint senior partner WHITE & BOWKER 19 St Peter Street, Winchester, Hants SO23 8BV.

Career: articled Kennedy Ponsonby & Prideaux (1960-1963); admitted (1963); assistant solicitor (1963-1964); assistant solicitor White Brooks & Gilman (1964-1966); partner (1966-1983); senior partner (1983-1990); became joint senior partner White & Bowker (1990).

Activities: board member Law South; member Winchester City Council (1976-1990); governor Peter Symond's Sixth Form College and Perins Community School;

Liveryman Goldsmiths' Company; member Hampshire Green Jackets.

Biography: lives Arlesford; born 19.11.1937; married to Lenore with 3 children. Educated at St Aubyn's, Rottingdean; Eton; Trinity College Cambridge (1961 BA) (1971 MA).

PRIMOST Norman

barrister specialising in property law and head of chambers 1 Temple Gardens, Temple, London EC4Y 9BB.

Career: called to the Bar Middle Temple (1954); National Service in RASC censoring mail at military corrective establishment, Colchester (1954-1956); pupillage with Montague Waters QC (1956-1957); general common law practice with emphasis on landlord and tenant law; became head of Chambers (1986).

Activities: member of: Wig & Pen Club; King's Head Theatre Club.

Biography: lives Hampstead, London NW3 and Bournemouth; born 25.06.1933; married to Debbie with 1 daughter and 3 sons. Educated at The Hall School, London; St Paul's School, London; London School of Economics, (1953 LLB hons); Trinity Hall Cambridge; legal correspondent Stock Exchange Journal (1967-1969); editor Restrictive Practice Reports (1969-1971).

Leisure: theatre; chess; modern literature; classical music.

PRINSLEY Mark

partner ROWE & MAW
20 Black Friars Lane, London EC4V 6HD.

Career: articled McKenna & Co (1979-1981); admitted (1981); assistant solicitor McKenna & Co (1981-1984); assistant solicitor Rowe & Maw (1984-1987); became partner (1987).

Biography: lives London N10; born 27.05.1956; married to Judith. Educated at Guisborough Grammar School; Brasenose College Oxford (1978 BA hons).

Leisure: walking; gardening.

PRITCHARD John

proprietor LEGALEASE 3 Clifton Road, Maida Vale, London W9 1SZ.

Career: articled WH Thompson & Partners; admitted (1974); consultant Powell Magrath & Spencer (1977-1990).

Activities: member of: Holland Park Tennis Club; Bentley Driver's Club; Bosham Sailing Club.

Biography: lives London NW6 and Bosham, West Sussex; born 18.06.1949; married to Mary with 3 children. Educated at Penarth Grammar School, Glamorgan; Bristol University (LLB); author of various books and magazines including: 'Penguin Guide to The Law'; 'The Legal 500'; 'Law Firms in Europe'; editor of: The Practical Lawyer; Legal Business Magazine.

Leisure: being with non-lawyers.

PRITCHARD Kenneth

secretary LAW SOCIETY OF SCOTLAND 26 Drumsheugh Gardens, Edinburgh EH3 7YR.

Career: articled John Ross & Co (1954-1955); admitted (1955); assistant solicitor J & J Scrimgeour (1955 & 1957-1959); became partner (1959-1976).

Activities: hon visiting professor in law Strathclyde University; Sheriff Court Rules Council (1973-1976); member Dunpark Committee on reparation following conviction (1973-1976); member Council of the International Bar Association; member of the Court of the University of Dundee; member of: New Club; Hon Company of Edinburgh Golfers.

Biography: lives Edinburgh; born 14.11.1933; married to Gretta with 2 sons and 1 daughter. Educated at Dundee High School; Fettes College Edinburgh; St Andrew's University; articles in Journal of the Law Society of Scotland and international legal journals.

Leisure: golf.

PRITCHARD Michael

senior partner SHARPE PRITCHARD Queen Anne's Chambers, 3 Dean Farrar Street, Westminster, London SW1H 9JX.

Career: National Service commissioned in Royal Artillery (1953-1955); admitted (1963); became partner Sharpe Pritchard (1963).

Activities: admitted Roll A Parliamentary Agent (1965); member Society of Parliamentary Agents (1965 to date) (secretary 1971-1977) (president 1985-1987); admitted Reader (C of E) (1975); former member Rochester Diocesan Synod, Rochester Diocesan Board of Finance, Rochester Bishop's Council and former chairman Rochester Diocesan Stipends Committee.

Biography: lives Purley; born 03.04.1935; married with 3 children. Educated at Claremont School; Charterhouse; Balliol College Oxford 1955-1958 BA).

P

PROCTER Gerald

senior partner STAMP JACKSON & PROCTER 5 Parliament Street, Kingston upon Hull HU1 2AZ.

Career: articled; Travers Smith Scholar and Karuth Prizeman (1950-1955); admitted (1955); National Service pilot (1955-1957); assistant solicitor (1957-1960); became partner Stamp Jackson & Procter (1960).

Activities: local politics (1968-1981); president and chairman Kingston upon Hull Conservative Federation; president Hull Junior Chamber of Commerce and Shipping; president Hull Incorporated Law Society; legal adviser to British Junior Chambers of Commerce; chairman Hull Watch Committee and Development Committee; chairman Humberside County Council Planning and Transportation Committee; vice- chairman Humberside County Council; member Carlton Club.

Biography: lives Hedon nr Hull; born 28.05.1931; married to Pauline with 3 children. Educated at Holgate Grammar School, Barnsley; Hull Grammar School.

Leisure: flying; music; languages.

PRYER John

chief land registrar HM LAND REGISTRY 32 Lincoln's Inn Fields, London WC2A 3PH.

Career: executive officer Treasury Solicitor's Department (1948) called to the Bar Gray's Inn (1957); legal assistant HM Land Registry (1959-1965); assistant land registrar (1965-1976); district land registrar Durham (1976-1981); deputy chief land registrar (1981-1983); chief land registrar (1983).

Activities: CB (1986); associate member Royal Institution of Chartered Surveyors (1986); former member Council of Licensed Conveyancers.

Biography: lives Ware; born 05.09.1929; married to Moyra with 1 son and 1 daughter. Educated at Beckenham and Penge County Grammar School; Birkbeck College London (BA hons); author of official Land Registry publications; articles in journals; contributing editor to 'Ruoff and Roper on Registered Conveyancing' and 'Land Registration Handbook'.

Leisure: reading.

PSYLLIDES Milton

partner EVERSHED WELLS & HIND 10 Newhall Street, Birmingham B3 3LX.

Career: articled Evershed & Tomkinson (1976-1978); admitted (1978); assistant solicitor (1978-1981); became associate (1981); became partner (1984); firm merged with Wells & Hind (1989).

Activities: director of Shire PLC; chairman First Roman Property Trust PLC; chairman Roman Rentals 001 PLC to 055 PLC incl; member Birmingham Law Society Company and Commercial Law Committee.

Biography: lives Sutton Coldfield; born 30.10.1953; married to Lynne with 1 son and 1 daughter. Educated at Torriden Primary School; Brockley County Grammar School; Liverpool University (1975 LLB).

Leisure: keep fit; family life.

PUGH Michael James

senior litigation partner BARLOW LYDE & GILBERT Beaufort House, 15 St Botolph Street, London EC3A 7NJ.

Career: worked in London and abroad (1965-1967); articled GC Davies & Partners (1967-1972); admitted (1972); assistant solicitor Barlow Lyde & Gilbert (1972-1975); became partner (1975).

Activities: chairman Insurance Committee of the International Bar Association (1984-1988); vice-chairman Committee on International Tort and Insurance Law and Practice of the American Bar Association; chairman designate of the British Insurance Law Association; member of: Reform Club; Bentley Drivers' Club; Jaguar Drivers' Club; Historic Sports Car Club.

Biography: lives Wimbledon; born 23.04.1948; married to Shirley. Educated at All Hallows Preparatory School (1956-1962); Downside School (1962-1965); College of Law (1968 & 1970); author of a number of articles in legal, insurance and accountancy journals chiefly on the subject of professional liability.

Leisure: mountain walking; bird watching; music; wine; motor cars.

PUGH-THOMAS Anthony

partner litigation sector LOVELL WHITE DURRANT 21 Holborn Viaduct, London EC1A 2DY.

Career: articled Simmons & Simmons; admitted (1965); assistant solicitor Durrant Cooper & Hambling; subsequently Durrant Piesse and now Lovell White Durrant (1965-1967); became partner (1967).

Activities: president London Solicitors Litigation Association (1980 & 1981); member Law Society and co-opted member Civil Litigation Committee; Freeman of the City Solicitors' Company; committee member City of London Law Society; council member Justice; hon solicitor to the Georgian Group; nominated member of the Court of Appeal (civil division) Users' Committee; member International Bar Association and its Banking Law sub-committee; member of: Oriental Club; Travellers' Club.

Biography: lives London SW15; born 14.07.1939; married to Rosemary with 2 daughters. Educated at The Leas, Hoylake; Repton; Jesus College Cambridge (MA LLM); articles in Litigation; The Chief Executive; Law Society's Gazette; Solicitors Journal; City of London Solicitors' Company Newsletter; Journal of International Banking.

Leisure: collecting prints and pottery; growing unusual plants from seed.

PURCHAS Robin

Queen's Counsel 2 Harcourt Buildings, Temple, London EC4.

Career: called to the Bar Inner Temple (1968); practised in local government rating, administration and Parliamentary work (1969 to date); QC (1987); Recorder (1989).

Activities: member Attorney General's Panel (1982-1987); member of: The Queen's Club; Royal West Norfolk Club; Royal Worlington Club.

Biography: lives London and Sudbury; born 12.06.1946; married to Anne with 2 children. Educated at Summerfields, Oxford; Marlborough College; Trinity College Cambridge (MA) Senior Exhibitioner; Foster Bolton Prize (1968).

Leisure: opera; music; theatre; tennis; golf; shooting.

PURIE-HARWELL Kaushalya

barrister and head of chambers 1 Mitre Court, Temple, London EC4Y 7BS.

Career: principal SG High School for Girls, India (1946); deputy director of public instruction, State of Himachal Pradesh (1950); lecturer in English literature Wilson College, University of Bombay (1953); journalist, London; called to the Bar Inner Temple (1960); pupillage K Homer, Pump Court; head of Chambers 1 Mitre Court (1967).

Activities: lectured in law of accountancy, catering, motoring; law reporting for all England LR; counsellor at free legal advice centres; actively engaged in setting up educational and charitable trust to enable young persons in India to learn more of the world by travel and education; member of: University Women's Club; Wig & Pen Club; India International Centre, New Delhi.

Biography: lives Headley and Perthshie; born 1920s; married to John. Educated at Kinnaird College for Women, Lahore; Punjab University, Lahore; Government College, Ludhiana; Punjab University, New Delhi.

PURSER Gavin

senior partner LAWRENCE GRAHAM 190 Strand, London WC2R 1JN.

Career: commission in army; admitted (1963); assistant solicitor (1963-1967); partner Middleton Lewis & Co (1967-1977); partner Lawrence Graham (1977); became senior partner (1987); specialised in shipping law.

Activities: member Athenaeum.

Biography: lives Charlwood; born 31.05.1936; married to Mary-Ruth with 2 children. Educated at Cottesmore Preparatory School; Lancing College.

Leisure: tennis; golf; shooting; gardening.

PURTON Peter

a senior partner NORTON ROSE Kempson House, Camomile Street, London EC3A 7AN.

Career: commissioned 3rd Regiment Royal Horse Artillery serving in BAOR (1951-1953); commissioned 290th (City of London) Field Regiment RATA (1953-1960); admitted (1958).

Activities: legal member Royal Town Planning Institute (LMRTPI) (1968); legal adviser to: The Baltic Exchange; The National Heart & Chest Hospital; member council of the Law Society for the City of London Constituency (1969-1986); chairman of: Law Reform Committee (1972-1975); Planning and Development Law (1974-1984); Law Office Management and Technology (1981-1986); Legal Expenses Insurance (1983-1986) (with the Law Society of Scotland); member Scott Committee on Property Linked Unit Trusts; member Lord Chancellor's Law Reform Committee; member The Wine Standards Board of the Vintners Company; chairman Family Welfare Association (1982 to date).

Biography: lives Dunton; born 18.07.1933; married to Mary with 3 children. Educated at Aldwickbury School, Harpenden (1940-

1946); Aldenham School, Elstree (1946-1951); formerly joint general editor 'Organisation and Management of a Solicitor's Practice'; joint general editor Butterworth's Planning Law and Practice; numerous articles and lectures on environment, planning law & practice, management and technology.

PUXON Margaret

Queen's Counsel Francis Taylor Building, Temple, London EC4Y 7BY.

Career: gynaecologist and obstetrician (1946-1955); practising barrister since called to the Bar Inner Temple (1954); QC (1982); Recorder (until 1984).

Activities: Privy Council member Council of Royal Pharmaceutical Society; member Clinical Trials Ethical Committee of Royal College of General Practitioners.

Biography: widowed with 3 children. Educated at Birmingham University (1942 MBchB) (1946 MD); Fellow Royal College of Obstetricians and Gynaecologists; author of 'The Family and The Law'; numerous contributions on medico-legal subjects to gynaecological text books; various journals; proceedings of Royal Society of Medicine; etc.

PYSDEN Edward

partner ALEXANDER TATHAM 30 St Ann Street, Manchester M2 3DB.

Career: articled Alexander Tatham & Co (1970-1972); admitted (1972); assistant solicitor (1972-1974); became partner (1974).

Activities: non-executive director UMIST Ventures Ltd; member St James's Club.

Biography: lives Macclesfield; born 06.05.1948; married to Anna-Maria with 3 children. Educated at Dulwich College; King's School, Macclesfield; Manchester University (1969 LLB).

Leisure: squash; gardening; postcard collecting.

QUARRELL John

partner and head of pensions department NABARRO NATHANSON 50 Stratton Street, London W1X 5FL.

Career: clerical officer HM Land Registry Harrow (1966-1969); documents clerk Clerical Medical & General Life Assurance

Society (1969-1973); articled Nabarro Nathanson (1973-1976); admitted (1976); assistant solicitor (1976-1978); became partner (1978).

Activities: hon sec Association of Pension Lawyers (1984-1988) (committee member 1988 to date); member Education Committee of National Association of Pension Funds; member Council of Pensions Management Institute (1989); member Law Society.

Biography: lives Southborough; born 27.10.1948; married to Teresa with 2 daughters. Educated at St Gregory's Secondary School, Kenton; Polytechnic of Central London (evening classes) (1976 LLB); Fellow of the Pensions Management Institute (1987); author of 'The Law of Pension Fund Investment'; editor Trust Law & Practice; consulting editor Butterworths/NAPF Pensions Legislation Service; regular contributor to Pensions & Employee Benefits; occasional articles in other periodicals.

Leisure: actively involved in Roman Catholic parish; Scout Association; Guide Association (wife and daughters all active); gardening; wine; 60s rock music.

RABIN Michael

partner FINERS 179 Great Portland Street, London W1N 5FD.

Career: articled with small family practice and Thornton Lynne & Lawson; admitted (1959); assistant lecturer in law London School of Economics (1960-1961 hons); assistant solicitor Richards Butler (1961-1963); became partner Gershon Young & Co (1964).

Activities: assistant examiner Law Society Finals in commercial law (1965-1968); member Legal Aid Local and Area Committees (1975-1985); secretary International Lawyers' Group (1984-1987) (chairman 1987 to date); member of: MCC; Queen's Club; The Rugby Club.

Biography: lives London NW11; born 11.12.1934; married to Tamara with 2 sons. Educated at Raines Grammar School, London; London School of Economics (1956 LLB hons); Ford Foundation Fellowship to Tulane University of Louisiana, New Orleans, USA (1960 LLM).

Leisure: tennis; swimming; cycling; watching cricket, rugby and athletics; theatre; reading and other sedentary activities; foreign travel; foreign languages.

R

RADCLIFFE Neville

senior partner BROWNE JACOBSON
44 Castle Gate, Nottingham NG1 6EA.

Career: articled Southern Ritchie and
Southern; admitted (1957); assistant
solicitor Browne Jacobson (1957-1961);
became partner (1961); became senior
litigation partner .

Activities: area chairman No 10 East
Midlands Legal Aid Area Committee;
member Nottinghamshire Law Society
(president 1988-1989); member
Notinghamshire Law Society; member
Nottinghamshire Medico-Legal Society
(president 1988-1989); visiting lecturer in
law Nottingham University; member Law
Advisory Council Nottingham University
and Nottingham Polytechnic; member
Solicitors Assistance Scheme; member of
Nottingham and Notts United Services
Club; Nottingham Rugby Football Club.

Biography: lives Nottingham; born
21.08.1932; married to Mabel with 2
daughters. Educated at the Grammar
School, Colne; Manchester University (LLB
hons).

Leisure: fell walking; rugby football;
cricket; soccer; gardening; travel; musician;
attending concerts; meeting friends.

RAE Maggie

partner HODGE JONES & ALLEN
148-150 Camden High Street, London
NW1 0NG.

Career: called to the bar (1973); pupillage
in the Temple; barrister Tony Gifford's
Chambers; admitted (1977); assistant
solicitor Hodge Jones & Allen (1977-1978);
became partner (1978).

Activities: lectures Warwick University;
actively involved local level Labour party;
member Fabian Society's National
Executive; chair governors of special
school for delicate children in Tower
Hamlets.

Biography: lives London E9; born
20.09.1949; single. Educated at infant
schools in England, Scotland and West
Africa; Gt Yarmouth High School for Girls;
Warwick University (1971 LLB); author of:
'Women and the Law'; 'Children and the
Law'; FRG's first 'Guide to Care
Proceedings'; NCCL's 'First Rights'; a law
workbook for the Open University.

Leisure: climbing; walking; gardening.

RAE Scott Alexander

partner MORTON FRASER MILLIGAN
WS 15-19 York Place, Edinburgh EH1 3EL.

Career: admitted solicitor and Writer to the
Signet (1968); assistant solicitor (1968-
1970); became partner Morton Fraser &
Milligan WS (1970).

Activities: The Law Society of Scotland:
chairman Board of Examiners; examiner in
taxation; member Revenue Committee;
investor Protection Committee; Trust
Working Party; member of Council of
International Academy of Estate & Trust
Law; member VAT Tribunal (Scotland);
former tutor in taxation and former course
leader in post graduate diploma course at
Edinburgh University; contributor to a
number of LSS PQLE courses on tax, tax
planning, etc.

Biography: lives Peeblesshire; born
17.12.1944; married to Annabel with 3
children. Educated at Daniel Stewarts
College, Edinburgh; Edinburgh University
(1966 LLB hons); International Private Law
Medal (1965); Hastie Scholarship (1966).

Leisure: fishing; rural/quasi agricultural.

RAFIQUE Syed Tariq Daud

barrister 8 King's Bench Walk, Temple,
London EC4Y 7DU.

Career: called to the Bar Lincoln's Inn
(1961); Karachi High Court Bar (1962);
High Court Karachi Bench (1962-1971);
English Bar (1971 to date).

Activities: vice-chairman Race Relations
Committee of the Bar; chairman
Association of Muslim Lawyers; member
of: Questors Theatre, Ealing;
Commonwealth Society; Labour Party.

Biography: lives London W5; born
27.09.1937; married to Farida with 3
children from former marriage. Educated
at Karachi Grammar School; Westminster
City School; Christ's College Cambridge
(1959 BA Hons).

Leisure: swimming; community politics;
golf; reading; going to plays.

RAISMAN Jeremy

partner and head of company/commercial
department and member management
committee JAQUES & LEWIS 2 South
Square, Gray's Inn, London WC1R 5HR.

Career: articled Norton Rose (1953-1959);
admitted (1959); assistant solicitor Clifford-
Turner & Co (1959-1962); assistant solicitor
and partner Nabarro Nathanson (1962-
1967); became partner Jaques & Lewis
(1967).

Biography: lives Peaslake nr Guildford;
born 06.03.1935; married to Diana with 3
children. Educated in India (1935-1945);

Dragon School, Oxford (1945-1948); Rugby
School (1948-1953).

Leisure: beagling (former master of
hounds); hill walking; sailing; surfing; golf;
tennis; riding.

RAKISON Robert

joint senior partner RAKISONS
27 Chancery Lane, London WC2A 1NF.

Career: articled Tarlo Lyons & Aukin;
admitted (1974); assistant solicitor (1974-
1975); became junior partner (1975-1976);
assistant solicitor Travers Smith
Braithwaite & Co (1976-1979); founded
Rakisons with Tony Wollenberg (1979).

Activities: first secretary of IAG
International; chairman Richmond Football
Club (rugby); committee member London
Rowing Club; chairman St Mary's Barnes
Scout Group; member various local
committees for preservation of local
amenities and environment; member of:
Leander Club; Remenham Club;
Roehampton Club.

Biography: lives London SW13; born
19.09.1947; married to Scota with 4
children. Educated at Carmel College;
Kingston Polytechnic (1970 LLB hons).

Leisure: family; rowing; rugby; the Arts.

RAMAGE Roderick

partner KENT JONES AND DONE
Churchill House, 47 Regent Road, Hanley,
Stoke on Trent ST1 3RQ.

Career: articled Foysters (1963-1965);
admitted (1966); assistant solicitor (1966-
1967); assistant solicitor Taylor Hindle &
Rhodes (1967-1969); partner (1969-1972);
assistant solicitor Kent Jones and Done
(1972-1979); became partner (1979).

Activities: experimental work on computer
aided expert systems for preparation of
legal documents (1988 to date); member of:
CTC; Daimler & Lanchester Owners' Club;
Veteran Cycle Club; Border Bridleway
Association.

Biography: lives Congleton; born
08.10.1939; divorced with 2 children.
Educated at Monkton Combe School;
London School of Economics (1962 BSc
Econ); articles and precedents in New Law
Journal (1970-1972); editor Kelly's
Draftsman (1973 to date 13th 14th & 15th
eds); compiler of Ramage: Companies Acts
Table A (1982-1985 1st & 2nd eds); co-
author of Note on Belgian and English Law
on One Man Companies in Les Petites
Affiches (1984).

Leisure: reading; old cars and bicycles;
horse riding; DIY; cooking.

RANDALL John

director professional standards and development THE LAW SOCIETY Ipsley Court, Redditch B98 0TD.

Career: deputy president National Union of Students (1971-1973); president (1973-1975); assistant secretary Civil Service Union (1975-1977); assistant general secretary (1977-1981); deputy general secretary (1981-1987); director professional standards and development The Law Society (1987).

Activities: various appointments within the trade union movement and the Labour Party; member of: Orion Harriers; South London Harriers.

Biography: lives Midlands; born 23.11.1947. Educated at Wallington County Grammar School for Boys; York University (1971).

Leisure: running; music; wine.

RANDS Harvey

partner and head of litigation MEMERY CRYSTAL 31 Southampton Row, London WC1B 5HT.

Career: admitted (1976); assistant solicitor Rubinstein Callingham (1976-1977); assistant solicitor Stilgoes (1977-1978); became partner (1978-1980); became partner Memery Crystal (1980).

Activities: ACI Arb; member Brooks's Club.

Biography: lives London NW3; born 14.06.1951; married to Anne with 4 children. Educated at Pilgrim School, Bedford; The City University (1972 BSC); College of Law Lancaster Gate (1972-1973 & 1975).

Leisure: shooting; riding; gardening.

RANKMORE Charles

senior litigation partner KINGSFORD STACEY 14 Old Square, Lincoln's Inn, London WC2.

Career: articled Kingsford Dorman (1968); admitted (1970); assistant solicitor (1970); became partner (1970).

Biography: lives London N8; born 26.04.1946; married with 1 daughter. Educated at Liverpool College; King's College London (1967 LLB hons).

Leisure: tennis; music; travel.

RASKIN Susan

partner in charge of conveyancing, matrimonial and probate departments RUSSELL JONES & WALKER 15 Clare Street, Bristol.

Career: articled Chas D Mason (1962-1966); admitted (1967); assistant solicitor Ledbury Merry & Co (1966-1968); law lecturer and senior law lecturer Bristol Polytechnic (1974-1983); became partner Raskin & Raskin (1969-1988); lecturer Bath University (1975-1977); became partner Russell Jones & Walker (1988).

Activities: governor Bath High School (1983 to date); member ad hoc sub-committees Women's National Commission on Illegitimacy and Matrimonial Law Reform; listed in Debretts Directory of Distinguished People; developing expertise in French and Spanish law; member Association of University Women; member Bath Bach Choir; member Association of Women Solicitors; member Chantry Singers; member Cannons Sports Club.

Biography: lives Bath; born 28.03.1942; married to James with 3 children. Educated at Plymouth High School; Tiffin Girls School; College of Law Guildford.

Leisure: choral singing; playing piano; hill walking; swimming; dressmaking; learning foreign languages.

RAWLINS Christopher (Kit)

barrister Albion Chambers, Broad Street, Bristol BS17 6QA.

Career: regular army officer Gloucestershire Regiment serving in West Indies, Cyprus, Egypt and Kenya (1946-1956); called to the Bar (1957); advocate Supreme Court of Kenya and partner Geoffrey White & Co, Nakuru, Kenya (1957-1964); practising Albion Chambers (1964 to date); Assistant Recorder.

Activities: member Army & Navy Club.

Biography: lives nr Chipping Sodbury; born 21.04.1926; married with 1 son. Educated at Eton College; Aberdeen University.

Leisure: field sports (especially shooting and fishing).

RAWLINS David

partner FIELD FISHER WATERHOUSE 41 Vine Street, London EC3N 2AA.

Career: admitted; assistant solicitor Field Fisher Waterhouse; became partner.

Biography: lives London W11; born 04.01.1933; married to Jean with 1 child. Educated at St Edward's School, Oxford; College of Law London.

Leisure: hunting; fishing.

RAWSON-MACKENZIE Duncan

senior partner CRIPPS HARRIES HALL 84 Calverley Road, Tunbridge Wells, Kent TN1 2UP.

Career: articled Freer Bouskell and Halsey Lightly & Hemsley (1958-1961); admitted (1961); assistant solicitor Cripps Harries Hall (1961-1962); became partner (1962); became head of probate and trust department (1963); became senior partner (1986).

Activities: General Commissioner of Taxes.

Biography: lives Tunbridge Wells; born 25.10.1934; married to Pamela with 2 children. Educated at Cothill House (1943-1948); Eton College (1948-1953); Trinity College Cambridge (1958 BA) (1959 LLB).

Leisure: general sporting activities including golf and tennis; foreign travel; classical civilisation.

RAWSTORNE Martin

partner BATTEN AND CO Church House, Yeovil, Somerset BA20 1HB.

Career: taught English literature at St Thomas Anglican Secondary School, Kuching Sarawak, Malaysia (1962); articled Oswald Hickson Collier & Co (1963); assistant solicitor; assistant solicitor Batten and Co (1968-1972); became partner (1972); specialises in UK and continental European agricultural law.

Activities: founder member UK Agricultural Law Association affiliated to Comite European de Droit Rural; interest in International Drama Cooperation; governor and legal adviser to British American Drama Academy.

Biography: lives Ilminster, Somerset; born 24.03.1940; married to Mary with 3 children. Educated at Highfield School, Liphook; Eton College; Christ Church Oxford (MA).

Leisure: local politics; lawn tennis; sailboarding; photography; music; Chinese language, history and politics.

RAY Ralph

senior partner and tax trust partner WEDLAKE SAINT 14 John Street, London WC1N 2EB.

Career: admitted (1956); Theodore Goddard (1956-1962); became tax trust partner Wedlake Saint.

Activities: Council of Institute of Taxation (1973-1988); member Law Society Revenue sub-committee on capital taxes; member of Ravells.

R

235

Biography: lives London; born 20.10.1930; married to Dorothy with 5 children. Educated at St Paul's (FTII BSC Econ); lectures widely and writes on tax matters; author of: 'Practical Inheritance Tax Planning'; Accountants/Tax Digests 'Revenue Aspects of Partners Agreements'; 'Wills and Post Death Planning'; 'Settlements: A Practical and Tax Planning Approach'.

Leisure: painting; allotment; walking; travel.

RAYNER Stephen A

senior partner RAYNER DE WOLFE 31 Southampton Row, London WC1B 5HJ.

Career: articled Osmond Bard & Westbrook; admitted (1957); founded own practice (1957); took over Hudson & Co and Mark Lemon Hudson & Co (1968); merged with De Wolfe & Co (1983).

Activities: former visiting lecturer School of Business Studies Hatfield Polytechnic; past president (instigated formation) of international network of lawyers 'Interleges' (1989); member Law Society's International Committee (chairman sub-committee on relations with Central and Eastern Europe); past chairman Solicitors European Group; past chairman Holborn Law Society Education and Training Committee; member Holborn Law Society Committee; past chairman London Legal Education Committee (LLEC); represented Law Society on visits to Moscow, Leningrad, Berlin (GDR), Prague, Warsaw and Brussels (1989-1990); governor boarding school specialising in ballet training; chairman British Czechoslovak Law Association; lectures and articles on legal aspects of Central and Eastern Europe.

Biography: lives London NW3; born 12.07.1934; married to Hana with 2 children (one a solicitor). Educated at City of London School (1945-1951); University College London (1954 LLB); Law Society Finals (Honours) (1957); Maurice Nordon Prize (1957).

Leisure: music; bridge; spending weekends in New Forest cottage; golf; tennis; skiing; cricket.

RAZZALL Tim

partner and chief executive FRERE CHOLMELEY 28 Lincoln's Inn Fields, London WC2A 3HH.

Career: teaching associate North Western University, Chicago (1965-1966); articled Frere Cholmeley (1966-1969); admitted (1969); assistant solicitor (1969-1973);

became partner (1973).

Activities: chairman Policy & Resources Committee; deputy leader Richmond Council (1983 to date); treasurer Liberal Democrats; non-executive director: CALA PLC; WEA Records Ltd; ISS Holdings Ltd; member of: National Liberal Club; MCC.

Biography: lives London SW13; born 12.06.1943; married with 2 children. Educated at St Paul's School; Worcester College Oxford (1965 BA).

READ Dudley Poole

partner DIBB LUPTON BROOMHEAD and PRIOR 117 The Headrow, Leeds LS1 5JX.

Career: articled in Wakefield to Dixon Coles & Gill; admitted (1957); National Service, commissioned with King's Own Yorkshire Light Infantry (1957-1959); assistant solicitor Shrewsbury (1959-1960); assistant solicitor Dibb Lupton (1960-1961); partner (1961).

Biography: lives in Wakefield; born 30.05.1934; married with 2 children. Educated at Mill Hill School (1947-1952).

Leisure: mountaineering.

READ Martin

managing partner READ HIND STEWART 10 Park Place, Leeds, W Yorks LS1 2RU.

Career: admitted (1971); assistant solicitor (1971-1973); became partner Read Hind Stewart (1973); appointed Professor of Law Practice Management (1990).

Activities: president Bradford Law Society (1980); chairman and majority shareholder J Jolly (Poultry Packers) Ltd (1978-1984); director and shareholder Betterbake Products Ltd (1985); Professor of Law Practice Management, undertakes Management Consultancy for legal profession, and presents seminars on management effectiveness to law firms and non-legal organisations; member of: Alwoodley Golf Club; Chapel Allerton Tennis Club; South Caernarvonshire Yacht Club Ltd; International Food and Wine Society.

Biography: lives Collingham; born 21.08.1945; married to Jane with 2 children. Educated at Giggleswick School, Settle; College of Law Guildford.

Leisure: cricket; golf; tennis; watersports.

READ Martin

commercial partner SLAUGHTER AND MAY 35 Basinghall Street, London EC2V 5DB.

Career: articled Hammond Suddards (1959-1962); admitted (1962); assistant solicitor Slaughter and May (1963-1971); became partner (1971).

Activities: vice-chairman Law Society Standing Committee on Company Law; former chairman Company Law Sub-committee of City of London Law Society; member of: MCC; Royal St George's.

Biography: lives Chesham Bois and Bath; born 24.07.1938; married to Laurette with 2 daughters. Educated at Queen Elizabeth's Grammar School, Alford; Wadham College Oxford (1959 MA); articles on company law for various journals.

Leisure: golf; lawn tennis; reading; theatre; watching cricket.

READ Richard Thomas Andrew

senior partner ASSHETONS 99 Aldwych, London WC2B 4JF.

Career: articled in London (1956-1961); admitted (1961).

Biography: lives London; born 28.05.1939; 2 children. Educated at Bedford School; College of Law.

REED Denis

director of legal personnel STEPHENSON HARWOOD One St Paul's Churchyard, London EC4M 8SH.

Career: law costs draftsman and head of personnel and administration Clifford-Turner (now Clifford Chance) (1967-1982); partner The Room Twelve Partnership (1982-1987); became director of legal personnel Stephenson Harwood (1987).

Activities: non-executive director The David Andrews Partnership; member MCC.

Biography: lives Brentwood, Essex; born 18.05.1949. Educated at Aveley County High School, Essex.

Leisure: cricket; golf.

REES Allen

senior partner REES PAGE 17 Wellington Road, Bilston, West Midlands WV14 6AD.

Career: articled in Cardiff; admitted (1961); became partner in a litigation practice; conveyancing and litigation work for National Coal Board; head of legal department of an American Company; assistant solicitor Darbey-Scott-Rees (1965); became partner (1966).

Activities: chairman and member West Midland Rent Assessment Panel (1968 to date); chairman Social Security Tribunals (1980 to date); part-time chairman Industrial Tribunals (1982 to date); represents practice as head office solicitors of Birmingham Midshires Building Society; past member Bilston Round Table (chairman 1974); executive committee member Old Monmouthians' Club (1966-1977) (president 1977); member Bilston Rotary Club (1966 to date) (president 1984-1985); member Legal Aid Area Committee (1975 to date); Negligence Panel Representative for Wolverhampton Area of Law Society (1982 to date); member of: Wolverhampton Lawn Tennis and Squash Club; Old Monmouthians' Club.

Biography: lives Albrighton nr Wolverhampton; born 11.05.1936; married to Nerys with 2 daughters. Educated at Westbourne House Preparatory School (1941-1949); Monmouth School (1949-1955); University of Wales (1958 LLB); writes in the Solicitors' Notebook for the Solicitors Journal (1968 to date); occasionally reviews new law books for the Journal.

Leisure: squash; canoeing; shooting; skiing; gardening.

REES Andrew

partner and head of corporate services EVERSHED WELLS & HIND 10 Newhall Street, Birmingham B3 3LX.

Career: articled (1978-1980); admitted (1981); became partner Evershed Wells & Hind (1985).

Activities: various public and private company non-executive directorships.

Biography: lives Birmingham; born 20.07.1954; married to Monica with 4 sons. Educated at Culford School; Fitzwilliam College, Cambridge (1977 MA).

Leisure: shooting; travel; athletics.

REES Joan

partner WALTONS & MORSE Plantation House, 31-35 Fenchurch Street, London EC3M 3NN.

Career: articled Waltons & Morse; assistant solicitor (1959-1971); became partner (1971).

Activities: member United Universities Club.

Biography: lives London SW3; divorced with 3 children. Educated at High School for Girls, West Hartlepool; Lady Margaret Hall Oxford (hons).

Leisure: art history and looking at pictures in terms of social history and ideas; keeping up with the children; dogs; cats; talking to friends; travelling.

REES Philip

head of chambers 34 Park Place, Cardiff.

Career: called to the Bar (1965); Recorder (1983).

Activities: member Legal Aid Area Committee (No 5 South Wales); member of: Glamorgan Wanderers RFC; Cardiff and County Club.

Biography: lives Cardiff; born 01.12.1941; married to Catherine with 2 children. Educated at Monmouth School; Bristol University (1963 LLB).

Leisure: squash; watching rugby; walking; music.

REEVES Anthony

managing partner KENT JONES & DONE Churchill House. 47 Regent Road, Hanley, Stoke on Trent ST1 3RQ.

Career: admitted (1965); assistant solicitor; became managing partner Kent Jones & Done (1978).

Activities: non-executive director of: Steelite Int PLC; Bullers PLC (1984-1986); PMT Ltd (1987 to date); Stoke City FC (1984-1985); chairman The CAS Group PLC (1985 to date); senior trustee The Beth Johnson Foundation (1972 to date); member North Staffs Medical Institute Council (1979-1982); chairman Law Society Working Party on Coal Mining Subsidence (1985 to date).

Biography: lives North Staffordshire; born 05.03.1943; married with 3 children. Educated at Hanley High School; College of Law.

Leisure: active country sportsman; environmentalist; Friend of the Royal Opera House & Royal Ballet and of the Royal Academy.

REGAN Michael

partner in charge of office at Lloyd's ROWE & MAW Suite 894, Lloyd's, One Lime Street, London EC3M 7DQ.

Career: articled Rowe & Maw (1978-1980); admitted (1980); assistant solicitor (1980-1985); became partner (1985); became head Lloyd's branch (1988).

Activities: panel member for the monitoring of articles by the City of London Law Society (1989-1990); working member of Turnkey Heavy Plant sub-committee of Committee T of IBA (1987-1989); tutored at the centre for construction law and project management King's College London.

Biography: lives London W6; born

04.10.1955; married to Henrietta with 1 child. Educated at Westcliff High School for Boys; Pembroke College Oxford (1977 MA); College of Law Lancaster Gate (1977-1978); contributes to the Construction Law Journal, Estates Gazette and insurance publications; assisted in the writing of 'Management Contracting' by Rowe & Maw (1989).

Leisure: watching cricket; travel.

REID Andrew

senior partner REID MINTY AND CO 92 Seymour Place, London W1H 5DB.

Career: admitted (1979); founded Reid Minty and Co (1980).

Activities: member Law Society's Negligence Panel; member Marlborough Street Magistrates' Court Duty Solicitors Scheme Committee; former member West London Law Society Committee; licensed racehorse trainer; member of: Bucks; Oakley Hunt Club; Annabels.

Biography: lives London; born 02.03.1954; single. Educated at UCS Frognal; University College London; ACI Arb.

Leisure: field sports; classic cars.

REID Bill

partner HALL PRATT & PRITCHARD General Buildings, 9 Waterloo Road, Wolverhampton, West Midlands WV1 4DT.

Career: articled Hall Pratt & Pritchard (1956-1959); admitted (1959); National Service 2nd Lt Royal Artillery (1960-1962); assistant solicitor Hall Pratt & Pritchard (1962-1964); became partner (1964).

Activities: president Wolverhampton Law Society (1987-1988); member of TA (1962-1988) chief of staff 23 Artillery Brigade; Lt Colonel; TD; hon Colonel No 1 (Wolverhampton) Area Army Cadet Force; member Walsall Rugby Union Football Club; National Artillery Association; West Midlands TAVRA.

Biography: lives nr Shifnal; born 27.08.1935; married to Sylvia with 2 sons. Educated at Lead Hills School, Abington; Queen Mary's Grammar School, Walsall; St John's College Cambridge (1956 BA) (1959 MA).

Leisure: sport; hill walking .

REID Jim

senior partner BISHOP AND ROBERTSON CHALMERS 2 Blythswood Square, Glasgow G2 4AD.

Career: articled Bishop Milne Boyd & Co; admitted (1956); assistant solicitor (1956-

R

1958); partner (1958); senior partner Bishop & Co (1984); became senior partner Bishop and Robertson Chalmers (1986).

Activities: member Scottish Board of Alliance & Leicester Building Society; former president local bowling club; organist and choirmaster (1946-1963); member of: The Royal Scottish Automobile Club; Whitecraigs Bowling Club; Glasgow Indoor Bowling Club.

Biography: lives Newton Mearns; born 25.02.1932; married to Maimie with 3 daughters. Educated at Kilmarnock Academy; Glasgow University (1953 MA) (1956 LLB).

Leisure: bowling (flat green); church music; gardening.

REID Robert

Queen's Counsel and head of chambers 9 Old Square, Lincoln's Inn, London WC2A 3SR.

Career: called to the Bar Lincoln's Inn (1965); Bencher (1988); pupillage with Judge Peter Crawford QC and Mr Justice Harman; QC (1980); Recorder of the Crown Court (1985).

Activities: Deputy High Court Judge (Chancery Division) (1984 to date); joint treasurer of Barristers' Benevolent Association (1987 to date) (committee member 1984-1987); member Senate of Inns of Court and the Bar (1977-1980); advised at Mary Ward Legal Advice Centre (1966-1972); member of Bar Council (1990 to date); member of: MCC; Guildford Fencing Club; Leatherhead Cricket Club.

Biography: lives mid-Surrey; born 23.01.1943; married to Anne with 3 children. Educated at Marlborough; New College Oxford (1964 BA) (1968 MA); Buchanan Prize Lincoln's Inn; Mansfield Scholarship; author of books on 'The Rent Acts 1968 & 1974' published by Estates Gazette; specialist editor 'Megarry Rent Acts' (11th ed).

Leisure: cricket (NCA qualified coach); fencing; gardening.

REID William

partner HALL PRATT & PRITCHARD General Buildings, 9 Waterloo Road, Wolverhampton, West Midlands WV1 4DT.

Career: articled Hall Pratt & Pritchard (1956-1959); admitted (1959); National Service as 2nd Lt Royal Artillery (1960-1962); assistant solicitor Hall Pratt & Pritchard (1962-1964); became partner (1964).

Activities: president Wolverhampton Law Society (1987-1988); member Territorial Army (1962-1988); chief of staff 23 Artillery Brigade with rank Lt Colonel; awarded TD; hon colonel No 1 (Wolverhampton) Area Army Cadet Force; member National Artillery Association and West Midlands Tavra; member Walsall Rugby Union Football Club.

Biography: lives nr Shifnal; born 27.08.1935; married to Sylvia with 2 sons. Educated at Lead Hills School, Abington; Queen Mary's Grammar School, Walsall; St John's College Cambridge (1956 BA) (1959 MA).

Leisure: sports enthusiast; hill walking.

REITH David

commercial partner LINDSAYS WS 11 Atholl Crescent, Edinburgh EH3 8HE.

Career: articled Lindsays (1972-1974); admitted (1974); assistant solicitor Frere Cholmeley (1974-1975); assistant solicitor Lindsays WS (1975-1977); became partner (1977).

Activities: Notary Public; director Scottish Historic Buildings Trust (Ltd); director Solway Heritage Ltd; secretary Lothian Building Preservation Trust; hon solicitor Architectural Heritage Society of Scotland; member Scottish Lawyers' European Group; member International Bar Association; member European Lawyers' Association (UAE); member Law Society of Scotland; member the Cockburn Association; member New Club, Edinburgh.

Biography: lives Edinburgh; born 15.04.1951. Educated at Edinburgh Academy; Fettes College; Aberdeen University (1972 LLB).

Leisure: skiing; curling; wine; conservation of buildings.

RENWICK George

partner SLAUGHTER AND MAY 35 Basinghall Street, London EC2V 5DB.

Career: teaching Associate Northwestern University Chicago School of Law (1962-1963); admitted (1966); assistant solicitor (1966-1970); became partner Slaughter and May (1970); admitted in Hong Kong (1978).

Activities: member Law Society Revenue Law Committee (1975-1985); member Lawyers' Supper Group; member of: Addington Society; Athenaeum Club; MCC.

Biography: lives London; born 27.07.1938; married to Elizabeth with 1 child. Educated at Charterhouse; New College

Oxford (1962 BA) (1965 MA); author of 'The Aftermath of Furniss -v- Dawson' (1986).

REYNOLDS Peter

senior partner GORNA & CO Virginia House, Cheapside, Manchester M2 4NB.

Career: prosecutor Military Government Court, Bonn (1945-1946); admitted (1949); became senior partner Gorna & Co (1984).

Biography: lives Southport; born 15.01.1925; married with 4 children. Educated at William Hulme's Grammar School, Manchester; Manchester University (1948 LLB hons).

Leisure: jogging.

RHODES John

partner MACFARLANES 10 Norwich Street, London EC4A 1BD.

Career: articled Macfarlanes (1968-1970); admitted (1970); assistant trust and estates department White & Case, New York (1971-1972); assistant solicitor Macfarlanes (1972-1975); became partner (1975).

Activities: chairman Cambridge House Law Centre (1980-1987); member City of London Club.

Biography: lives London NW1 and Nr Saffron Walden; born 16.02.1945; married to Christine with 2 sons. Educated at King Edward VI School; Jesus College Cambridge (1964-1967); written various articles on tax and trust law.

Leisure: tennis; squash; skiing; woodlands.

RHODES Martyn

joint senior partner CATTERALLS PO Box 43, 15 King Street, Wakefield, West Yorkshire WF1 2SL.

Career: articled Catterall Pell & Moxon (1960-1965); admitted (1965); assistant solicitor (1965-1968); partner (1968); became joint senior partner Catteralls upon merger with Higgins Mason & Co (1990).

Activities: Associate of the Chartered Institute of Arbitrators; member of: Rotary Club of Wakefield; Wakefield Golf Club.

Biography: lives Huddersfield; born 28.06.1943; married to Janet with 2 children. Educated at Queen Elizabeth Grammar School; Leeds University (1960-1961).

Leisure: golf; walking; cycling; gardening; swimming.

RHODES Peter

senior partner TAYLOR HINDLE &
RHODES AND MARSH & CO Astley
House, 23 Quay Street, Manchester
M3 4AX.

Career: RAF (1945-1948); articled Samuel
Bishop & Sons (1948-1953); admitted
(1953); assistant solicitor (1953-1954);
assistant solicitor Wilfrid Taylor and
Hindle (1954-1959); became partner Taylor
Hindle & Rhodes (1959).

Activities: Bishop of Manchester's legal
assessor under Clergy Discipline Acts; hon
supernumerary assistant organist
Manchester Cathedral (1956-1986).

Biography: lives Manchester; born
26.11.1926; married to Mary with 3 sons.
Educated at Manchester Grammar School;
Manchester University (1951 LLB hons);
Solicitors Finals (1953 hons).

RICE Gordon

senior partner GILBERT STEPHENS
17 Southernhay East, Exeter EX1 1QE.

Career: articled in Coventry (1943);
Japanese translator and interpreter with
RAF (1943-1947); admitted (1951); assistant
solicitor (1951-1953); assistant solicitor
Gilbert H Stephens & Sons (1954); became
partner.

Activities: Deputy Registrar High Court &
County Court (1969 to date); chairman
National Insurance & Industrial Injuries
Local Appeal Tribunal (1971-1979); part-
time chairman Industrial Tribunals (1979 to
date); member Legal Aid Area Committee.

Biography: lives Exeter; born 22.12.1925;
married to Dallow with 5 children.
Educated at King Henry VIII Grammar
School, Coventry; Birmingham University
(1949 LLB); School of Oriental & African
Studies, London University (1944).

Leisure: church warden; family; woodland
interests.

RICHARDS Garry

partner MICHAEL FREEMAN & CO
1 Great Cumberland Place, London
W1H 7AL.

Career: articled Wegg-Prosser & Co (1970-
1972); admitted (1972); assistant solicitor
Tuck Mann & Geffen (1972-1974); senior
commercial solicitor EMI Limited (1975-
1979); became partner Michael Freeman &
Co (1980).

Biography: lives Chesham; born 21.03.1947;
married to Linda with 2 children. Educated
at Llandovery College; University College
of Wales (1969 LLB); College of Law

Guildford.

Leisure: theatre; cinema; reading; walking;
golf; swimming; spectator rugby, cricket,
horseracing and other sports.

RICHARDSON Jeremy

partner TAYLOR VINTERS
119 High Street, Newmarket, Suffolk
CB8 9AG.

Career: admitted (1970); clientele drawn
exclusively from bloodstock racing
industry.

Activities: secretary The Injured Jockeys'
Fund; solicitor to The National Trainers'
Federation; member Racing Welfare
Committee; lectures and writes articles on
equine law.

Biography: lives Newmarket; born
14.01.1944; married (1973) Valerie Bridget
de Stacpoole; 2 children, (1974) Jemma and
(1978) Patrick.

Leisure: cricket; sailing; horseracing; tennis;
squash; reading; television.

RICHARDSON Martin

director of education and training
BERWIN LEIGHTON Adelaide House,
London Bridge, London EC4R 9HA.

Career: lecturer in law Hitchin College
(1968-1970); lecturer; senior lecturer;
principal lecturer in law Liverpool
Polytechnic (1970-1989); became director of
education & training Berwin Leighton.

Activities: education consultant North
West Independents Printing and
Publishing Training Group (1976-1982); JP
Liverpool Bench (1983-1990); member
Athenaeum, Liverpool.

Biography: lives Cambridge; born
01.09.1944; married to Pauline with 2
children. Educated at Queen Elizabeth
Grammar School, Wakefield; Newcastle
University (1966 LLB) (1977 LLM);
Bradford University (1987 MBA).

Leisure: choral music; The Yorkshire Dales;
cricket; rugby.

RICHARDSON Michael N

partner and head of company and
commercial department LAWRENCE
GRAHAM 190 Strand, London WC2R 1JN.

Career: Coward Chance (1960-1962); Jaques
& Co (1963-1973); deputy chairman Henry
Ansbacher & Co Ltd (1970-1977);
Richardson & Oakley (1977-1985); became
partner Lawrence Graham (1985).

Activities: member of: IOD; Oriental Club;

MCC.

Biography: lives Berkshire; born 23.02.1935;
married to Moers with 4 children.
Educated at Dulwich College; College of
Law.

Leisure: all sports; gardening; music.

RICKFORD Jonathan

director of government relations BRITISH
TELECOMMUNICATIONS PLC British
Telecom Centre, 81 Newgate Street,
London EC1A 7AJ.

Career: teaching associate School of Law
University of California at Berkeley (1968-
1969); called to the Bar (1970); lecturer in
law London School of Economics (1969-
1972); legal assistant and senior legal
assistant Department of Trade and
Industry (1972-1976); Department of Prices
and Consumer Protection (1976); senior
legal assistant Law Officers' Department
(1976-1979); assistant secretary (legal)
(1979-1982); under secretary (legal)
Department of Industry (1982-1984);
admitted (1985); solicitor to Department of
Trade and Industry (1985-1987); solicitor
and chief legal adviser British
Telecommunications PLC (1987-1989);
became director of Government relations
(1989).

Activities: member Royal Dart Yacht Club.

Biography: lives London; born 07.12.1944;
married with 3 children. Educated at
Lambrook School, Bracknell; Sherborne
School; Magdalen College Oxford (BA
hons) (BCL); Gibbs Prizeman in Law
(1967).

Leisure: sailing; walking; refurbishing
antiques.

RICKLESS Elwood

managing partner WHITMAN &
RANSOM 11 Waterloo Place, London
SW1Y 4AU.

Career: associate counsel Allied Signal
Corp, New York City; counsel
Rinderknecht & Co, Zurich (1959-1963);
conseil juridique Paris (1963-1972); became
managing partner Whitman & Ransom
(1972).

Activities: lecturer International Taxation
Management Centre Europe (1970-1976);
member Board of Directors Citizens'
Utilities Corp, Stamford, USA; chairman
schools committee Harvard Club of
London; member RAC.

Biography: lives London SW1; married to
Regina with 2 children. Educated at
Harvard College Magna Cum Laude (1951
BA); (1958 MA LLB).

R

RIDDLE Howard

senior partner EDWARD FAIL
BRADSHAW & WATERSON
402 Commercial Road, Stepney, London
E1 0LG.

Career: Social Science Research Council of
Canada (1970-1975); articled Edward Fail
Bradshaw & Waterson (1976); admitted;
assistant solicitor; became senior partner
(1985).

Activities: member Thames Duty Solicitor
Committee; member Law Society Area
Committee.

Biography: lives Bethersden; born
13.08.1947; married to Hilary with 2
children. Educated at The Judd School,
Tonbridge; London School of Economics
and Political Science (1968 LLB hons).

Leisure: rugby; football.

RIDLEY Michael

partner entertainment department
DENTON HALL BURGIN & WARRENS
Five Chancery Lane, Clifford's Inn,
London EC4A 1BU.

Career: articled Lewis Lewis & Co;
admitted (1980); rights manager at The
National Theatre (1980-1981); senior
solicitor London Weekend Television
(1981-1989); solicitor Denton Hall Burgin &
Warrens (1989); became partner (1990).

Activities: trustee St Paul's Art Centre, Isle
of Dogs.

Biography: lives London E10; born
21.10.1955; single. Educated at Woodhouse
Grammar School, London; Durham
University (1977 BA).

RIGBY Rodney

consultant DALE & NEWBERY
1 Shepperton House, Green Lane,
Shepperton TW17 8DN.

Career: articled Wilkinson Howlett &
Moorhouse; Dale & Newbery (1964);
admitted (1965); assistant solicitor (1965-
1970); became partner (1970); became
senior partner (1985).

Activities: founder secretary Thames Valley
Cricket League; former chairman Slough
Hockey Club and Slough Cricket Club;
chairman Pizza Express London Hockey
League (1984 to date); member Ashford
Manor Golf Club.

Biography: lives Ascot; born 19.06.1939;
married to June with 2 children. Educated
at Mostyn House School; Wrekin College;
College of Law.

Leisure: golf.

RILEY Martin

senior partner MERCERS 50 New Street,
Henley on Thames, Oxon RG9 2BX.

Career: Lloyds Underwriters (1953-1958);
articled Marshall & Eldridge (1959-1963);
admitted (1963); Public Trustee (1963);
assistant solicitor Mercers (1963-1964);
became partner (1964); became senior
partner (1977).

Activities: chairman of the managers of
Turners Court (school for underprivileged
boys) Oxfordshire County Councillor
(1970-1981).

Biography: lives Henley on Thames; born
15.11.1931; married with 3 children.
Educated at Bradfield College; Queen's
College Cambridge; occasional articles in
Country Life and the Antique Collector.

RIMMER Stephen

senior partner STEPHEN RIMMER & CO
28 Hyde Gardens, Eastbourne .

Career: admitted (1975); founded own
practice (1981).

Activities: member Royal Golf Club.

Biography: lives Eastbourne; born
05.08.1952; married to Isabel with 2 sons.
Educated at Hastings Grammar School;
College of Law.

Leisure: golf; tennis; windsurfing.

RINK John

partner ALLEN & OVERY
9 Cheapside, London EC2V 6AD.

Career: articled Allen & Overy (1970-1972);
admitted (1972); assistant solicitor (1972-
1977); became partner (1977).

Activities: member City of London
Solicitors' Intellectual Property sub-
committee; governor King's College
School, Wimbledon; member of: Royal
Wimbledon GC; Royal West Norfolk GC.

Biography: lives Wimbledon; born
25.10.1946; married to Elizabeth with 2
children. Educated at Sedbergh School;
London (LLB).

Leisure: golf; skiing; fell walking; music;
opera; theatre.

RIPPON Lord of Hexham

Queen's Counsel 2 Paper Buildings,
Temple, London EC4Y 7ET.

Career: called to the Bar Middle Temple
(1948); Bencher (1976); Privy Counsellor
(1962); QC (1964).

Activities: MP for Norwich South (1955-
1964); MP for Hexham (1966-1987); Life

Peer (1987); Parliamentary Secretary
Ministry of Housing and Local
Government (1961-1962); Parliamentary
Secretary Ministry of Aviation (1959-1961);
Minister of Public Buildings & Works
(1962-1964) (Cabinet 1963-1964); Minister
of Technology (incorporating Ministries of
Industry, Aviation, Energy and Supply)
(1970); Chancellor of the Duchy of
Lancaster (1970-1972); responsible for
negotiating Britain's entry into the
European Community; Secretary of State
for the Environment (incorporating the
Ministries of Housing, Transport and
Public Building & Works) (1972-1974); chief
opposition spokesman on European
Affairs (1974) and on Foreign and
Commonwealth Affairs (1974-1975); leader
of Conservative Group in European
Parliament (1977-1979); Admiral of the
Manx Herring Fleet (1971-1974); chairman
British Section European League for
Economic Cooperation (1967-1970)
(president 1970-1983) (chairman 1983 to
date); chairman Conservative Party
Parliamentary Foreign and
Commonwealth Affairs Committee (1979-
1981); president Association of District
Councils (1986 to date); president Town
and Country Planning Association (1987 to
date); member of: Pratts; Whites; MCC.

Biography: lives London EC4 and
Broomfield; born 28.05.1924; married with
1 son and 3 daughters. Educated at King's
College, Taunton; Brasenose College
Oxford (1944 MA) Hon Fellow; Fellow
Institute of Arbitrators; Robert Garroway
Rice Pupillage Prize; Hon LLD London
University.

RITCHIE Shirley Anne

Queen's Counsel 4 Paper Buildings,
Temple, London EC4Y 7EX.

Career: called to the Bar South Africa
(1963); called to the Bar Inner Temple
(1966); QC (1979); Recorder (1981); Bencher
Inner Temple (1985).

Activities: member Senate of Inns of Court
and Bar (1978-1981); member Criminal
Injuries Compensation Board (1980 to
date); member Mental Health Review
Tribunal (1983 to date); member General
Council of the Bar (1987); chairman
Barristers' Benevolent Association (1989 to
date).

Biography: lives London E1 and Pennal;
born 10.12.1940; married to Robin Anwyl
with 2 sons. Educated at St Mary's
Diocesan School for Girls, Pretoria; Rhodes
University, Grahamstown (1960 BA) (1963
LLB); FRSA.

RIX Bernard

Queen's Counsel 3 Essex Court, London EC4Y 9AL.

Career: called to the Bar Inner Temple (1970); tenant 3 Essex Court (1971); QC (1981); Recorder (1990); Bencher, Inner Temple (1990).

Activities: member Senate of the Inns of Court and Bar (1981-1983); member Bar Council (1981-1983); associate of Milbank, Tweed, Hadley & McCloy, New York (1969-1970); director London Philharmonic Orchestra (1986 to date); chairman British Friends of Bar Ilan University (1987 to date) (member Board of Trustees 1988 to date).

Biography: lives London; born 08.12.1944; married to Karen with 3 children. Educated at St Paul's School, London (1957-1962); New College Oxford (1966 BA) (1968 BA); Harvard Law School (1969 LLM); Ella Stephens Scholar (1962); Kennedy Scholar (1968).

Leisure: music; opera; Italy; formerly fencing.

ROACH David

senior partner GREGSON OWLES & ROACH Park House, 3-5 Leigh Road, Leigh-on-Sea, Essex SS9 1JP and GREGSON ROACH 14 Billett Street, Taunton, Somerset.

Career: articled Mills and Reeve; admitted (1961); assistant solicitor Barrington & Sons (1961-1964); assistant solicitor Gregson & Golding (1964-1965); became partner (1965).

Activities: member of: Queen Hythe Ward Club; Royal Burnham Yacht Club; Law Society Yacht Club.

Biography: lives Burnham on Crouch; born 10.04.1939; married with 2 children. Educated at King Edward VII School, Norwich.

Leisure: sailing; 'playing at property'.

ROBERTS Brian

partner in charge employers' liability and public liability personal injury department CARTWRIGHT & LEWIS 100 Hagley Road, Edgbaston, Birmingham.

Career: articled Lenton Lester & Co; admitted (1963); assistant solicitor (1963-1966); assistant solicitor Cartwright & Lewis (1966-1968); became salaried partner (1968-1971); became equity partner (1971).

Activities: Deputy Registrar of the High and County Courts for the Midland &

Oxford Circuit (1983 to date); chairman of the Board of the Walsall Masonic Co Ltd.

Biography: lives Rowney Green nr Alvechurch; born 25.08.1937; married to Rosemary with 3 sons. Educated at Lichfield Grammar School; Borrowcop School, Lichfield; Wednesbury Technical College (1961 LLB).

Leisure: family; church; gardening.

ROBERTS David

partner VEALE WASBROUGH 17 Berkeley Square, Bristol BS8 1HD.

Career: National Service in Libya (1954-1956); commissioned RASC; articled Sibly Clough & Gibb (1957-1960); admitted (1960); assistant solicitor (1960-1963); became partner (1963-1974); became partner Veale Benson (1974); merged to become Veale Wasbrough (1988); Recorder of the Crown Court (1990).

Activities: council member Bristol Law Society (1973-1985) (president 1983-1984); member Law Society's Criminal Law Committee (1981-1989); Law Society's representative on Home Office Steering Committee on tape recording of police interviews with suspects; member Law Society's Committee producing National Duty Solicitor Scheme; founder member Bristol Branches of Justice (1962); Amnesty International (1962); NCCL (1969); formerly actively involved in organisations in Bristol committed to the elimination of racial discrimination and peaceful transition to a multi-cultural society; chairman Lord Mayor of Bristol's Committee for International Human Rights Year (1968); occasional lecturer to police on their role in a democratic society; sometime member committee providing accommodation for ex-offenders and of a parole board local review committee; governor Redland High School for Girls (1975 to date).

Biography: lives near Bristol; born 21.06.1931; married to Jane with 1 daughter. Educated at Coatham Grammar School, Redcar; Llandrindod Wells County Grammar School; London School of Economics (1954 LLB); occasional articles.

Leisure: enjoys company of wife and daughter, labrador dog and friends; walking for pleasure; travel; reading poetry, good writing and history; admiring good paintings; collecting old letters from people in interesting situations, often military conflict.

ROBERTS Hilary

head of chambers 49 Westgate Chambers, Commercial Street, Newport, Gwent.

Career: called to the Bar (1978); pupillage London and Cardiff; Newport Chambers (1982).

Activities: member United Services Mess, Cardiff.

Biography: lives Cardiff; born 30.09.1953; married to Shirley with 1 son. Educated at Whitchurch Grammar School, Cardiff; University College of Wales (LLB hons); College of Law.

Leisure: politics; rugby.

ROBERTS Jeremy

Queen's Counsel 2 Dr Johnson's Buildings, Temple, London EC4 7AP.

Career: called to the Bar (1965); Recorder (1981); QC (1982).

Biography: lives Brentford; born 26.04.1941; married to Sally. Educated at Winchester College; Brasenose College Oxford (1964).

Leisure: gardening; opera; theatre; exploring canals.

ROBERTS John

managing partner WINTER-TAYLORS Park House, London Road, High Wycombe, Buckinghamshire HP11 1BZ.

Career: articled Grylls & Paige; admitted (1957); assistant solicitor Winter-Taylors (1959-1961); became partner (1961); now managing partner.

Activities: HM Coroner for South Buckinghamshire; Recorder in Crown and County Courts; president of the Mental Health Review Tribunals; regional chairman for the Oxford and Wessex Health Regions for the Mental Health Review Tribunals (1981); past president Berks Bucks & Oxon Incorporated Law Society; member Law Society Negligence Panel; hon solicitor & trustee of local St John Ambulance Brigade (serving brother of the Venerable Order of St John of Jerusalem); hon solicitor for welfare officers and local Royal British Legion branches and clubs; hon solicitor to the Wycombe Judo Centre; hon solicitor to the High Wycombe Dog Rescue & Welfare Society; chairman Buckinghamshire Housing Association Limited; director Wycombe Wanderers Football Club Limited; past chairman and present governor Pipers Corner School; president High Wycombe and District Show Association; trustee Wycombe Almshouses; Liveryman and member of the Court of Assistants of the Feltmakers' Livery; Liveryman of the Coopers' Company; president Rotary Club of High Wycombe (1989-1990); past chairman and past president High Wycombe Round Table; past chairman 41 Club; past captain Whiteleaf Golf Club; president of High Wycombe Sports Club; director of the Solicitors Benevolent Association; member of: Wig & Pen Club; Oriental Club.

Biography: lives Speen; born 11.06.1935; married to Pat with 4 children. Educated at Mount House Preparatory School; Blundells School Law School (hons).

Leisure: golf; hill walking; reading.

ROBERTSON Alastair

company solicitor BICC PLC Devonshire House, Mayfair Place, London W1X 5FH.

Career: articled Herbert Smith & Co (1970-1972); admitted (1972); assistant solicitor (1972-1978); group legal adviser The General Electric Co PLC (1978-1988); became company solicitor BICC PLC (1988).

Activities: member CBI Competition Law Panel; former member Competition & Licensing Committee of the Trade Marks Federation; member Hampstead Cricket Club.

Biography: lives London SW6; born 17.06.1947; married to Vanessa with 2 sons. Educated at Winchester College; St Peter's College Oxford (1969 BA hons).

Leisure: cricket; fishing; opera.

ROBERTSON Ranald

partner and head of information technology group STEPHENSON HARWOOD One St Paul's Churchyard, London EC4M 8SH.

Career: admitted New Zealand (1973); EMI Music (1974-1980); admitted (1980); contracts manager CAP Group (1981-1982); legal services manager (1982-1987); assistant solicitor Stephenson Harwood (1987-1988); became partner (1988).

Activities: co-founder and board member Federation Against Software Theft (1974-1986) (chairman 1985-1986); founder chairman Legal Affairs Group of Computing Services Association (1982-1987); member British Computer Society Intellectual Property Committee; member Editorial Board of the Computer Law and Security Report; member editorial panel of Applied Computer and Communications Law; contributor to Encyclopaedia of Information Law.

Biography: lives London SW6; born 23.04.1948; married with 2 children. Educated at Pukekohe High School, New Zealand (1960-1966); Auckland University (1968-1971) (1972 LLB).

ROBINS John

consultant TROWERS & HAMLINS 6 New Square, Lincoln's Inn, London WC2A 3RP.

Career: RAF (1945-1948); articled Saw & Sons and JK Edmondson & Co (1950-1952); admitted (1953); assistant solicitor Trower Still & Keeling (now Trowers and Hamlins) (1953-1958); became partner (1958-1989); became consultant on retirement (1989).

Activities: Local Director, Guardian Royal Exchange Assurance; Chairman Examinations Board for the College of Estate Management's Certificate in Residential Estate Agency; former member Legal Aid Certifying and Area Committees; former panel chairman Legal Aid General Committee; former member Management Committees of the World of Property Housing Trust and Chislehurst and Mottingham and Sidcup Housing Associations; member Committee Hurst Johnian Club; member committee of North West Kent branch of Oxford Society.

Biography: lives Bromley; born 18.07.1926; married to Hazel with 2 children. Educated at Carn Rea Preparatory School; Hurstpierpoint College, Sussex (1940-1945); St John's College Oxford (1950 BA MA); article in the Solicitors Journal on compulsory land registration.

Leisure: holidaying abroad; studying 20th-century military history.

ROBINSON Brian

partner and head of company and commercial department HOLMAN FENWICK & WILLAN Marlow House, Lloyds Avenue, London EC3N 3AL.

Career: articled Finch Turner & Taylor (1960-1963); admitted (1964); assistant solicitor (1964); lecturer in company law & equity Victoria University of Wellington, New Zealand (1964-1966); assistant solicitor Holman Fenwick & Willan (1966-1968); became partner (1969).

Activities: member Malden Golf Club.

Biography: lives Kingston-upon-Thames; born 27.03.1940; married to Jennifer with 2 children. Educated at Heversham Grammar School (1951-1953); Burnley Grammar School (1953-1957); The London School of Economics & Political Science (1960 LLB hons) (1962 LLM); various articles in New Zealand law journals (1964-

1965).

Leisure: golf; theatre.

ROBINSON David Michael

head of shipping and aviation BERWIN LEIGHTON SOLICITORS Adelaide House, London Bridge, London EC4R 9HA.

Career: cadetship in the Merchant Navy with Overseas Tankships UK Ltd (now Texaco Oil Co) (1961-1966); navigation officer (1966); chief officer (1969-1972); Berwin Leighton (1973); became partner (1980).

Activities: member Baltic Exchange (1983) member of: Pump Club; South Benfleet Social Club.

Biography: lives South Benfleet; born 01.02.1945; married with 3 sons. Educated at Hull Nautical College (1966 & 1968); University of Wales Cardiff (1972 BSC hons) (1973 MSC); College of Law Lancaster Gate; author of 'The Seafarer and the Law' (1976).

Leisure: shipping; economic studies; horticultural pursuits.

ROBINSON Jeremy

senior partner and chairman practice development committee ANSTEY SARGENT & PROBERT 4, 5 & 6 Barnfield Crescent, Exeter, Devon EX1 1RF.

Career: articled Davidson Holloway & Smart; admitted; assistant solicitor Anstey & Thompson (1967-1971); became partner (1971); became senior partner (1983); merged with Sargent & Probert (1989).

Activities: vice-chairman Devon Community Housing Society; hon solicitor Devon County Agricultural Association; former chairman Devon Young Solicitors; member board of West of England school for children with little or no sight; member Executive Committee Devon & Exeter Spastics Society; former member Devon & Exeter Incorp Law Society Committee; member of: Burnham & Berrow Golf Club; East Devon Golf Club; Exeter & County Club.

Biography: lives Budleigh, Salterton; born 04.01.1941; married to Victoria with 2 children. Educated at Seafield School, Bexhill; Charterhouse; Christ's College Cambridge (1963 BA).

Leisure: golf; gardening.

ROBINSON Joel

founder JOEL Z ROBINSON Warnford Court, 20 Throgmorton Street, London EC2N 2AT.

Career: admitted New Zealand (1968); articled Titmuss Sainer & Webb (1972-1974); admitted (1974); articled Donovan Leisure Newton & Irvine, New York (1974-1976); admitted New York (1976); as multi-admitted practitioner established first firm permitted to practice as English solicitors/New York attorneys (1977); opened New Zealand office (1985).

Activities: assisted in development of procedure which solicitors - MAPs - are permitted to practice transnational law in more than one country under present restrictive rules; arranged for exhibition of British original of Treaty of Paris 1783 (an operative treaty) in New York and Washington (1983); member University Club, New York.

Biography: lives Park Slope, New York; born 22.06.1946; married to Goulston with 4 children. Educated at Auckland Grammar School; Auckland University (1969 LLB); author of article in Export Times (UK) (1990); various articles on transnational legal problems.

Leisure: music; swimming.

ROBINSON Vivian

Queen's Counsel Queen Elizabeth Building, Temple, London EC4Y 9BS.

Career: called to the Bar Inner Temple (1967); Recorder of the Crown Court (1986); QC (1986).

Activities: member of the Bar Council Professional Standards Committee; member Council of Legal Education; member MCC.

Biography: lives London; born 29.07.1944; married to Louise with 3 children. Educated at Queen Elizabeth Grammar School, Wakefield; The Leys School, Cambridge; Sidney Sussex College Cambridge (1966 BA).

Leisure: gardening; reading.

ROBSON David

Queen's Counsel and head of chambers New Court Chambers, Broad Chare, Newcastle upon Tyne 1.

Career: teacher of English at experimental multilateral unit Co Durham (1961-1963); called to the Bar Inner Temple (1965); head of Chambers (1980 to date); junior North Eastern Circuit (1970); Recorder North Eastern Circuit (1979); QC (1980); Bencher Inner Temple (1988).

Activities: president Herrington Burn YMCA (1987 to date); director amateur theatre productions; adviser to Royalty Studio Theatre and Royalty Theatre;

member Durham County Club.

Biography: lives Rothbury; born 01.03.1940; single. Educated at Robert Richardson Grammar School, Ryhope; Christ Church Oxford (1961 MA); Profumo Prize in Criminal Law (1964).

ROCHER Philip

partner in charge WILDE SAPTE 200 Park Avenue, New York, NY 10166, USA.

Career: articled Kenneth Brown Baker Baker (1979-1981); admitted (1981); assistant solicitor Wilde Sapte (1981-1985); partner (1985-1988); became partner in charge New York office (1988).

Activities: licensed foreign legal consultant in the State of New York; member American Bar Association International Law & Practice Section European Law Committee; member New York State Bar Association International Law & Practice Section Western European Law (1992) Committee; member American Arbitration Association Panel of Arbitrators.

Biography: lives Greenwich, Connecticut, USA; born 05.02.1956; married to Lesley with 2 children. Educated at Ashville College, Harrogate; Birmingham University (1978 LLM).

Leisure: golf; spectator of all sports.

ROCHEZ Nicholas

managing partner DAVIES ARNOLD COOPER 12 Bridewell Place, London EC4V 6AD.

Career: articled Davies Arnold Cooper (1978-1980); admitted (1980); assistant solicitor (1980-1984); partner (1984-1988); became managing partner (1988).

Biography: lives in Ham, Chichester; born 13.11.1954; married to Hazel with 3 children. Educated at Ardingley College, Sussex; Middlesex Polytechnic (1977 BA); City of London (1981 Business Law MA); various articles on insurance and reinsurance in Reactions and The Review.

Leisure: family; horse racing; sailing.

RODDICK Winston

Queen's Counsel 1 Harcourt Buildings, Temple, London EC4Y 9DA.

Career: master of laws University College London (1966); called to the Bar (1968); QC (1986); Recorder (1987); member Wales and Chester Circuit.

Activities: member Welsh Language Board (chairman Legislation Committee);

member of: Cardiff and County Club; National Liberal Club.

Biography: lives Cardiff; born 02.10.1940; married with 2 children. Educated at Caernarfon Grammar School; University College London (196 LLB) (1966 LLM).

Leisure: walking the countryside.

ROEBUCK Robin

senior partner NALDER & SON Farley House, Falmouth Road, Truro, Cornwall TR1 2AT.

Career: articled Ivens Thompson and Green (1957-1962); admitted (1962); assistant solicitor Nalder & Son (1962-1964); became partner (1964).

Activities: Notary Public (1982); member Child Care Panel; member Magistrates' Court Users Group; member Negligence Panel Solicitors Complaints Bureau; member Cornwall Panel of Guardians ad Litem & Reporting Officers' Committee; chairman and vice-chairman Service Committees of the Family Practitioner Committee; member No 4 (South Western) Area Legal Aid Committee; ; member of: Royal Cornwall Yacht Club; Flushing Sailing Club; St Mawes Sailing Club; Law Society Yacht Club.

Biography: lives near Falmouth; born 12.11.1938; married to Jenny with 2 children. Educated at Cheltenham Grammar School; Bristol University; author of 'A Licensing Guide' for licensing clients.

Leisure: in partnership with wife in a farm of 186 acres (a mixed farm of beef and cereals); breeds racehorses; yacht racing; other activities connected with the sea; cross country skiing; classic motor cars; shooting; food and wine.

ROGERS David

partner in charge common law section of DAVIES ARNOLD COOPER 12 Bridewell Place, London EC4V 6AD.

Career: legal executive with Gaster & Turner and WH Thomson; articled Holman Fenwick & Willan (1970-1975); admitted (1975); assistant solicitor (1975-1977); assistant solicitor Davies Arnold Cooper (1977-1979); became partner (1979).

Activities: lectures in relation to marine personal injury claims; industrial deafness claims with particular relevance to the marine industry; industrial disease and carcinogenic claims arising out of the operation of chemical carriers; crisis management and 'disaster' litigation.

Biography: lives Colchester; born 01.05.1947; married to Maureen with 3 children. Educated at Sloane Grammar School; College of Law Lancaster Gate.

Leisure: golf; chess; cricket.

ROGERS Dorcas

partner WALTONS & MORSE Plantation House, 31-35 Fenchurch Street, London EC3M 3NN.

Career: articled Trowers & Hamlins (1982-1984); admitted (1984); assistant solicitor (1984-1987); assistant solicitor Waltons & Morse (1987-1989); seconded to Ushijima & Associates, Tokyo (1988-1989); specialises in corporate services; ship finance; EC competition law.

Biography: lives London; born 17.01.1960. Educated at Brighton and Hove High School (1965-1978); University College London (1981 LLB hons); College of Law (1982).

Leisure: theatre; cinema; fine arts.

ROGERS William Scofield

partner and head of corporate department THEODORE GODDARD 150 Aldersgate Street, London EC1A 4EJ.

Career: articled Theodore Goddard (1958-1961); admitted (1961); assistant solicitor (1962-1965); became partner (1965).

Activities: non-executive director United Racecourses (Holdings) Ltd (Epsom, Kempton and Sandown Park); council member The National Horseracing Museum; member The Twelve Club.

Biography: lives Esher; born 23.01.1936; married to Hilary with 3 stepchildren. Educated at St Andrew's School, Pangbourne; Radley College, Abingdon; Worcester College Oxford (BA hons).

Leisure: horseracing; croquet; theatre.

ROLFE Malcolm

senior partner SMART & SPICER 35/7 Gildredge Road, Eastbourne, East Sussex BN21 4RX.

Career: articled Harris & Harris (1960-1965); admitted (1965); assistant solicitor Kennedy Ponsonby & Prideaux (1965-1968); assistant solicitor Argles & Court (1968-1973); assistant solicitor Smart & Spicer (1973-1974); became partner (1974).

Activities: solicitor Sorrel Drive; member Eastbourne Law Society (president 1988-1989); member of: Willingdon Golf Club; Eastbourne 41 Club; Meads Tennis Club.

Biography: lives Eastbourne; born 10.01.1942; married to Susan with 2 children. Educated at King's School, Rochester (1950-1960).

Leisure: golf; tennis; badminton; classical music.

ROMERO Eduardo

partner in charge EDUARDO ROMERO & ASSOCIATES Grosvenor Gardens House, 35-37 Grosvenor Gardens, London SW1W 0BS.

Career: admitted Argentina; admitted Spain.

Activities: founding chairman of The Lawyers' Club; founder of Club Argentino; founder International Lawyers' Forum; founder International Consultants' Group; founder European Seminars; member of: Canning Club; IBA; The Law Society (overseas member).

Biography: born 02.05.1946; married to Ann with 2 children. Educated at Sagrado Corazon; Tucuman University, Argentina; Central School of Planning & Statistics, Warsaw; Sorbonne, Paris; London School of Economics; various articles on Latin American law.

Leisure: tennis; gardening.

ROSE Aubrey

partner OSMOND GAUNT & ROSE Winston House, 349 Regent's Park Road, Finchley, London N3 1DH and Furnival House, 14-18 High Holborn, London WC1Y 6BX.

Career: articled (four and a half years); admitted (1951); founded own practice (1952); amalgamated with two firms (1971).

Activities: appeared on TV and radio about human rights and race relations legal battles; advised governments, Prime Ministers of overseas Commonwealth countries on commercial and diplomatic matters; active in Commonwealth matters; adviser to national bodies and religious groups; OBE (1986); member Race Relations Committee of the Law Society; deputy chairman British Caribbean Association; former chairman Jewish Defence and Group Relations Committee; member Board of Deputies of British Jews; Advocate at Scarman Tribunal; trustee of the Urban Trust; lectured at International Bar Association meetings on nationality law; Patron of New Assembly of Churches; award from Islamic body; member working group of Commonwealth Human Rights Initiative; Freeman of City of

London; member Institute of Journalists.

Biography: lives Barnet; born 01.11.1926; married to Sheila with 2 children. Educated at Central Foundation School; Chiswick County School; Preston Manor County School; Law Society's School of Law; written articles and books on legal subjects.

Leisure: gardening (show garden open to public and for events); sport; lecturing; Commonwealth affairs; writing and lecturing on environmental and communal affairs.

ROSE Keith

senior partner CC BELL & SON 48/50 Harpur Street, Bedford MK40 2QT.

Career: Army (1944-1947); articled (1947-1950) Field Roscoe & Co (1 year); admitted (1950); assistant solicitor (1950-1951); became partner (1951); sole practitioner (1952-1962); became senior partner (1962).

Activities: director EF Taylor & Co Ltd (1965) (chairman 1970 to date); chairman No 11 (eastern) Legal Aid Area (1988-1989); member regional panel Monitoring of Articled Clerks; member Bedford Club.

Biography: lives Biddenham; born 22.11.1925; married to Carol with 1 son. Educated at Bedford School.

Leisure: shooting.

ROSE Michael

senior partner CLARKE WILLMOTT & CLARKE 47 High Street, Wellington, Somerset TA21 8QX.

Career: Royal Navy; articled (1958-1961); admitted (1961); assistant solicitor in Salisbury; assistant solicitor Clarke Willmott & Clarke (1964-1967); became partner (1967).

Activities: assistant deputy coroner West Somerset (1966); deputy coroner (1968); coroner (1983).

Biography: lives Wellington; born 23.02.1933; married to Gillian with 3 children. Educated at Royal Naval Colleges, Dartmouth and Greenwich; College of Law Guildford.

Leisure: sailing; skiing; beagling.

ROSKILL Julian

partner and head of the employment group ROWE & MAW 20 Black Friars Lane, London EC4V 6HD.

Career: articled Allen & Overy; admitted with them (1974); became partner Rowe &

Maw (1988).

Activities: member and secretary City of London Solicitors' Company Employment Law sub-committee; member of the Employment Lawyers' Group and Industrial Law Society; lectures on employment law and practice.

Biography: lives London; born 22.07.1950; married with 2 children. Educated at Horris Hill; Winchester College.

Leisure: photography; theatre; listening to classical music/opera; tennis.

ROSS Denis J

consultant and member corporate finance department SJ BERWIN & CO 236 Gray's Inn Road, London WC1X 8HB.

Career: articled Hyman Isaacs Lewis & Mills (now Beachcroft Stanleys); admitted (1952); assistant solicitor Bartlett & Gluckstein (1952-1955); partner (1955); senior partner (1985); firm amalgamated with Crawley & De Reya to become Bartletts de Reya (1978); firm dissolved (1988); became consultant to SJ Berwin & Co (1988).

Activities: president City of Westminster Law Society (1986-1987); member Holborn Law Society; trustee of the Victorian Community Centre; member of the Council of the Family Holiday Association; member of: MCC; Royal Automobile Club.

Biography: lives London NW11; born 10.07.1923; married to Shifra with 4 children. Educated at Haberdashers' Aske's, Hampstead; University College London (1950 LLB); College of Law (1952 hons); commercial editor of and author of articles and reviews in the Law Society'sGazette.

Leisure: tennis; golf; skiing; watching cricket and rugby; reading; music.

ROSS Howard

tax partner CLIFFORD CHANCE Royex House, Aldermanbury Square, London EC2V 7LD.

Career: articled Slaughter and May; admitted (1970); assistant solicitor (1970-1974); legal department head office of Bank Leumi (1974-1976); assistant solicitor Slaughter and May (1976-1978); assistant solicitor Clifford Turner (now Clifford Chance) (1978-1981); became partner (1981).

Activities: member Law Society Oil Tax Committee; member ATI; member Reform Club.

Biography: lives Pinner; born 12.08.1945;

married to Jennifer with 3 children. Educated at Owens Grammar School; London School of Economics (1966 LLB first class hons); member Israel Bar; author of 'Mens Rea for Murder' Modern Law Review (1967); editor of international tax chapters in Clifford Chance 'Doing Business in House'; 'Transfer pricing - A new approach' for the Tax Journal (1989); Clifford Chance technical publication 'Structuring buy out and other investment funds'.

Leisure: jogging; magic.

ROSS Murray J

partner and head of property department WITHERS 20 Essex Street, London WC2R 3AL.

Career: company secretary and general manager legal affairs 3M United Kingdom PLC; became partner Withers.

Activities: member Law Society Land Law and Conveyancing Committee; member of: MCC; National Trust for Scotland.

Biography: lives Sunningdale; born 31.03.1947; married with 2 sons. Educated at Dulwich College; College of Law Lancaster Gate; author of 'Drafting and Negotiating Commercial Leases'; co-author 'Drafting and Negotiating Commercial Leases in Scotland'; advisory editor and contributor to Volume 22 Encyclopaedia of Forms & Precedents (5th edn): Landlord and Tenant; Blundell Memorial Lecture (1990).

ROTHWELL John Dominic

senior partner WALTONS & MORSE Plantation House, 31/35 Fenchurch Street, London EC3M 3NN.

Career: National Service 2nd Lt in 10th Royal Hussars (POW) (1955-1957); articled Neish Howell Haldane (later called Macfarlanes) (1960-1963); admitted (1964); assistant solicitor (1963-1965); assistant solicitor Allen & Overy (1965-1967); assistant solicitor Waltons Bright (1967-1968); became partner (1968); firm became Waltons & Morse (1975).

Activities: member British Property Federation; Lloyd's underwriter; member of: Cavalry & Guards Club; City University Club.

Biography: lives London SW19 and North Devon; born 11.04.1937; married to Anne with 2 daughters. Educated at Ampleforth College, York; Brasenose College Oxford (1960 BA now MA).

Leisure: forestry (timber grower in Devon).

ROWAN Robert

senior partner CARTER FABER 10 Arthur Street, London EC4R 9AY.

Career: claims officer Guardian Royal Exchange Assurance (1955-1963); admitted (1970); assistant solicitor (1970-1971); became partner Carter & Co (1971); firm merged to become Carter Faber (1986).

Activities: hon solicitor to the Cruising Association; Liveryman of the Worshipful Company of Carmen; member of: Lloyds; Royal Automobile Club; Royal Harwich Yacht Club; Law Society Yacht Club.

Biography: lives London SE1 and Writtle, Essex; born 29.11.1934; married with 2 children. Educated at Westcliff High School; College of Insurance; College of Law; Fellow of the Chartered Insurance Institute.

Leisure: sailing; shooting.

ROWE Colin

partner HALLIWELL LANDAU St James's Court, Brown Street, Manchester M2 2JF.

Career: articled in Liverpool; admitted (1978); assistant solicitor Foysters (1979-1981); partner (1981-1987); became partner Halliwell Landau (1987).

Activities: Notary Public; secretary Manchester Young Solicitors' Association (1982-1985) (chairman 1985-1986); member Young Solicitors Group National Committee (1983-1990) (national chairman 1988-1989); member Law Society Standards & Guidance Committee (1988-1990); member Law Society Land Law & Conveyancing Committee (1986-1988); member Manchester Law Society Conveyancing Committee (1988-1990); member of: Wig & Pen Club; Alderley Edge Cricket Club; Valley Lodge Country Club; Downhill Only Club.

Biography: lives Alderley Edge; born 30.07.1953; married to Anne with 2 children. Educated at Sunnymede Preparatory School, Southport; Merchant Taylors' School, Crosby; Liverpool Polytechnic.

Leisure: squash; tennis; skiing; riding; fell walking.

ROWE Paul

partner in charge of professional negligence WANSBROUGHS WILLEY HARGRAVE 8 Broad Quay, The Centre, Bristol BS99 7UD.

Career: articled Lawrence & Co and Gouldens (1970-1972); admitted (1972); assistant solicitor Wansbroughs (1972-

R

1975); became partner (1976).

Activities: member Hawks Club.

Biography: lives Bristol; born 12.05.1947; married to Cilla with 2 daughters. Educated at Salisbury Cathedral School; Sherborne School; Cambridge (1969 BA).

Leisure: cricket; rackets; golf; cellist; opera; walking with family; bird watching.

ROWLEY Jim

partner and member of the executive EVERSHED WELLS & HIND 10 Newhall Street, Birmingham B3 3LX.

Career: National Service commission with Royal Artillery; articled Evershed & Tomkinson (now Evershed Wells & Hind) (1958); assistant solicitor; became partner (1966).

Activities: former treasurer Birmingham Law Society.

Biography: lives Birmingham; born 25.03.1935; married to Janet with 2 daughters. Educated at King's School, Worcester; King's Scholar; Trinity Hall Cambridge (1958 MA); Open Exhibition to Trinity Hall; Dr Cooper's Law Studentship.

Leisure: early music.

ROYCE John

Queen's Counsel and head of chambers Guildhall Chambers, 23 Broad Street, Bristol BS1 2HS.

Career: qualified as solicitor (1969); called to the Bar Gray's Inn (1970); Recorder of the Crown Court (1986); QC (1987).

Activities: member of: Hawks Club; St Enodoc Golf Club.

Biography: lives Bristol; born 27.08.1944; married to Gillian with 3 children. Educated at The Leys School, Cambridge (1958-1963); Trinity Hall Cambridge (1966 BA) (Hockey Blue 1965 & 1966).

Leisure: golf; cricket; skiing (Austrian qualified ski instructor); collecting corkscrews.

ROZENBERG Joshua

legal correspondent BBC TV NEWS Television Centre, London W12 7RJ (081-576 1789).

Career: trainee journalist BBC (1975); admitted (1976); first legal correspondent BBC Radio News; presenter 'Law in Action' (1985); legal correspondent BBC Television News (1988).

Biography: lives London W12; born 30.05.1950; married with 2 children. Educated at Latymer Upper,

Hammersmith; Wadham College Oxford (1971 BA) (1976 MA); author of: 'Your Rights and The Law' with Nicola Watkins (1986); 'The Case for the Crown' (1987).

RUSHTON John

partner litigation department ROWE & MAW 20 Black Friars Lane, London EC4V 6HD.

Career: articled Freshfields (1973-1975); admitted (1975); assistant solicitor (1975-1980); assistant solicitor Rowe & Maw (1980-1981); became partner (1981).

Biography: lives Loughton; born 22.03.1950; married to Jennifer with 2 children. Educated at Uppingham School; Sidney Sussex College Cambridge (1972 BA); Liverpool Polytechnic (1972-1973); Associate Chartered Institute of Arbitrators and member Society of Construction Law.

RUSSELL David

senior partner BLAKE LAPTHORN 8 Landport Terrace, Portsmouth, Hampshire PO1 2QW.

Career: articled Blake Lapthorn and Kingsford Dorman (1953-1958); Easterbrook prize; admitted (1958); National Service Commission (1958-1960); became partner Blake Lapthorn (1961).

Activities: clerk to General Commissioners of Taxes Havant District and Portsmouth District (1974 to date); director Portsmouth Building Society (1974-1989) (chairman 1986-1989); governor Portsmouth Grammar School (1979 to date) (chairman 1988 to date); former president South East Hampshire Chamber of Commerce & Industry; member of: Royal Naval & Royal Albert Yacht Club; Avenue Squash Club; Havant Hockey Club.

Biography: lives Havant; born 02.07.1936; married to Irene with 4 children. Educated at Dulwich College.

Leisure: squash; skiing; caravanning; theatre; walking.

RUSSELL Dick

managing partner TITMUSS SAINER & WEBB 2 Serjeants' Inn, London EC4Y 1LT.

Career: articled Titmuss Sainer & Webb; admitted (1968); assistant solicitor; partner; head of corporate department (1985-1987); became managing partner (1987).

Biography: lives London SW7; born 16.10.1942; divorced with 1 son and 1 daughter. Educated at Nottingham High School; University College Oxford (BA

hons).

Leisure: walking; bird watching; cookery; opera; cricket.

RUTHERFORD Margaret

arbitrator, lecturer, writer, chairman Registered Homes Tribunal, president Mental Health Review Tribunal, Thurlow, Munstead Park Godalming, Surrey GU8 4AR.

Career: called to Bar Inner Temple (1966); Salzburg Seminar in American Studies (1970); lecturer in law Guildford College of Technology (1966 to date); arbitrator (1977 to date); adjudicator Westminster Small Claims Court (1979); senior lecturer at College of Law Guildford (1970 to date); appointed Chairman Registered Homes Tribunal (1987); President Mental Health Review Tribunal (1989).

Activities: Chartered Institute of Arbitrators (1971) (Fellowship 1973) elected to the Council (1985) member of Executive Committee; chairman Arbitration Committee; member Special Fellowship Applications Committee; Professional Conduct Committee; Convenor of ABTA Panel; lecturer on arbitration at Chartered Institute Residential courses, Young Solicitor and Law Society groups, RICS; tutor at courses; Freeman City of London (1981); Freeman of the Worshipful Company of Arbitrators (1981); member Court of Assistants; guest speaker at VI International Congress of Maritime Arbitrators, Monte Carlo (1983); presented Blundell Memorial Lecture on Documents Only Arbitrations (1984); member Law Society working party on arbitration; lectured to the Institute of Arbitrators, Hong Kong (1987 & 1989); lecturer on continuing professional education courses, in-house and otherwise; at College of Nursing, to Consumer bodies, etc; elected vice-president Chartered Institute of Arbitrators (1990); member University Women's Club.

Biography: homes near Guildford and in Provence; married to Michael with 1 son. Educated at Rosebery School for Girls; University of London (LLB hons); FCI Arb; Murray Buxton Prize (1981); writer on legal topics in Solicitors Journal; New Law Journal; Family Law; Law Society'sGazette; Arbitration Journal, etc; book critic on family law for legal journals; contributor to Ronald Bernstein's Handbook on Arbitration Practice; editorial board of Lawline.

Leisure: France and French food; opera; walking; work.

RUTHERFORD-WARREN Alastair

head of law section BARCLAYS BANK PLC 16/17 Old Bailey, London EC4M 7DN.

Career: admitted (1965); assistant solicitor Herbert Oppenheimer Nathan & Vandyk (1965-1968); legal officer Barclays Bank Trust Co (1968-1972); various managerial appointments (1972-1986); deputy head of law section (1986-1990); became head of law section (1990).

Biography: lives East Horsley; born 16.11.1941; married to Jennifer with 3 daughters. Educated at Bradfield College, Berks; The Administrative Staff College, Henley (1978); Oxford University Business School (1983).

Leisure: sailing; gardening; cooking; walking.

RUTMAN Laurence David

senior property partner ASHURST MORRIS CRISP Broadwalk House, 5 Appold Street, London EC2A 2HA.

Career: became partner Paisner & Co (1960-1974); became partner Ashurst Morris Crisp & Co (1974).

Biography: lives London SW3 and Edenbridge; born 08.10.1937; married to Sandra with 3 children. Educated at Hendon County School (1949-1956); University College London (1959 LLB); Yale (1959-1960 LLM).

Leisure: farming; opera; books.

RYAN Gerard

Queen's Counsel practising at Parliamentary Bar and Local Government and Planning Bar 2 Harcourt Buildings, Temple, London EC4Y 9DB.

Career: called to the Bar Middle Temple (1955); National Service commissioned in Royal Artillery (1955-1956); pupillage with HAP Fisher, 3 Hare Court (1957); common law Bar (1958-1965); Parliamentary and Local Government and Planning Bar (1965 to date); QC (1981); Recorder of the Crown Court (1984); Bencher of the Middle Temple (1988).

Activities: member Local Government and Planning Bar Association (1986 to date); chairman Examinations in Public into Structure Plans; chairman Tribunal of Inquiry into the gas explosion at Loscoe, Derbyshire (1987-1988); member United Oxford & Cambridge Universities Club.

Biography: lives London SW1 and West Sussex; born 16.12.1931; married to Sheila with 2 sons. Educated at Clayesmore School, Iwerne Minster; Brighton College; Pembroke College Cambridge (1953 BA MA); Harmsworth Law Scholar (1956); co-author of 'Outline of the Law on Common Land' (1966).

Leisure: gardening; natural history; conservation; walking.

RYAN Kevin

partner ALLEN & OVERY 9 Cheapside, London EC2V 6AD.

Career: assistant solicitor Tolhurst & Fisher (1965-1968); assistant solicitor Allen & Overy (1968-1971); became partner (1972).

Activities: member City of London Law Society's Land Law sub-committee (1986 to date).

Biography: lives Guildford; born 29.10.1942; married to Elizabeth with 1 daughter and 2 sons. Educated at Beaumont College, Old Windsor .

Leisure: horse riding; skiing; reading.

RYLANCE Paul

director of professional development SJ BERWIN & CO 236 Gray's Inn Road, London WC1X 8HB.

Career: called to the Bar (1980); lecturer Inns of Court School of Law (1982-1987); practice at the Bar (1981-1987); head of training Slaughter and May (1987-1990); became director of professional development SJ Berwin & Co (1990).

Activities: visiting fellow Centre for Commercial Law Studies Queen Mary and Westfield College London; visiting lecturer Brunel University; former visiting lecturer Surrey University and Kingston Polytechnic; founder and chairman Legal Education and Training Group (July 1988 to July 1990); member Law Society's Academic Consultative Committee (1989 to date); member Council for the Accreditation of Teacher Education (1990 to date); Editor 'Business Law Europe' (UK section).

Biography: lives Surbiton; born 10.12.1957; single. Educated at St Nicholas School, Shoreham; St Andrew's High School, Worthing; Kingston Polytechnic (1979 BA hons); Inns of Court School of Law (1979-1980); Lloyd Scott Memorial Prize (1980).

Leisure: jazz music; ancient history; oriental cookery.

SABBERTON David

partner and head of residential conveyancing/development department HEWITSON BECKE AND SHAW Shakespeare House, 42 Newmarket Road, Cambridge CB5 8EP.

Career: articled Wild Hewitson & Shaw; admitted (1968); assistant solicitor Tree Russell & Co (1969-1970); became partner Wild Hewitson & Shaw (1971); firm merged with Becke Phipps (1989).

Activities: member of: Hawks Club; Gogagog Golf Club.

Biography: lives Cambridge; born 17.10.1943; married to Sandy with 2 children. Educated at Stowe School; Trinity Hall Cambridge (1965 MA).

Leisure: golf; hockey; tennis; cricket.

SACHER Jonathan

partner PAISNER & CO Bouverie House, 154 Fleet Street, London EC4A 2DQ.

Career: admitted advocate of the Supreme Court of South Africa (1978); articled Paisner & Co (1978-1980); admitted (1981); assistant solicitor (1981-1984); became partner (1984); specialisation in insurance and reinsurance litigation.

Activities: chairman London Young Solicitors Group (1985-1986); member Young Solicitors Group (1984-1988); member AIJA; member British Insurance Law Association; member Law Society'sInternational Committee (1987-1988); member Law Society'sChina Working Party (1987-1988); trustee Maxwell Law Scholarship.

Biography: lives London; born 12.03.1955; married to Marla. Educated at Herzlia, Cape Town; University of Cape Town (1975 BA) (1978 LLB); article in Law Society'sGazette on Immigration and Nationality; articles in Reactions Magazine on Employee's Shares in Insurance Companies (1989); Reinsurance in the Middle East (1990).

SACKER Tony

partner and head of company commercial department KINGSLEY NAPLEY 107-115 Long Acre, London WC2E 9PT.

Career: articled Friedman Fredman (1958-1963); admitted (1963); assistant solicitor (1963-1964); became partner (1964-1966); became partner Egerton Sandler (1967-1976); became managing partner (1976-

S

1989); became partner Kingsley Napley (1989).

Activities: president City of Westminster Law Society's(1987-1988); member Law Commission Standing Conveyancing Committee; member committees of various charities.

Biography: lives London W1; born 02.03.1940; married to Frances with 2 children. Educated at Owen's School, London; article in Law Society'sGazette 'The Recruitment Crisis: Making the best of Human Resources' (1988).

Leisure: theatre; eating out; computers.

SALANDER Axel

resident partner DRES DABELSTEIN & PASSEHL International House, 1 St Katherine's Way, London E1 9UN.

Career: admitted (1986); Rechtsanwalt with Dres Dabelstein & Passehl, Hamburg (1986-1987); became partner and opened London office (1989); assistant lawyer Ingledew Brown Bennison & Garrett (1987-1989); co-founder Lauritzen & Salander, Hamburg (1987-1989).

Activities: spokesman for West German student athletics team (1982-1983); member of: German Association of International Maritime Law; Achilles Club; Haringey Athletics Club; LG-Wedel-Pinneberg, West Germany.

Biography: lives Brighton; born 06.09.1955; married to Fiona with 1 son. Educated at Otto Hahn Gymnasium, Geesthact; Highgate School (1970-1973); St John's College Oxford (1976 BA); Christian Albrechts Universitat, Kiel (1976-1983 First State Examination in Law); joint publication on subject of certain aspects of English arrest proceedings in German legal journal Transportrecht (1986).

Leisure: politics/economics; sailing; track and field athletics (West German national team 1975-1983) long jump and 400m hurdles); coaching.

SALISBURY Robert

senior partner GAMLIN KELLY & BEATTIE 31-33 Russell Road, Rhyl, Clwyd LL18 3DB.

Career: articled clerk to Flintshire County Council (1970-1974); admitted (1973); assistant solicitor (1973-1974); assistant solicitor Gamlin Kelly & Beattie (1974); became partner (1974).

Activities: membership secretary Chester and North Wales Law Society; member North Wales CBI.

Biography: lives Rhyl; born 18.02.1948; married to Irene with 4 children. Educated at Mold Alun Grammar School (1959-1966); Liverpool University (1969 LLB).

Leisure: family life.

SALT David

partner BIRD & BIRD 2 Gray's Inn Square, London WC1R 5AF.

Biography: lives London; born 09.10.1954; married to Julia with 2 children. Educated at Newcastle School; Keble College Oxford (MA).

Leisure: ornithology; sailing; tree planting; opera.

SALTER David

partner and head of family law department BOOTH & CO Sovereign House, South Parade, Leeds LS1 1HQ.

Career: articled Mills & Reeve (1970-1972); admitted (1972); assistant solicitor (1972-1974); assistant solicitor Barber Robinson (1974-1975); assistant solicitor Booth & Co (1975-1978); became partner (1978).

Activities: Deputy Registrar (North-Eastern Circuit); member Law Society's Child Care Panel; member Law Society's Family Law Committee; member Family Law Sub-committee of Supreme Court Procedure Committee; member Solicitors Family Law Association Main Committee; chairman Solicitors Family Law Association Procedure Working Party; member Board of Family Mediators' Association; member (immediate past chairman) West and North Yorkshire Solicitors Family Law Association; member Leeds Law Society Contentious Business Sub-committee; chairman Ripon/Leeds area of Royal School of Church Music; organist and choirmaster Knaresborough Parish Church.

Biography: lives Harrogate; born 27.08.1948; married to Anne with 3 children. Educated at Ecclesfield Grammar School; Pembroke College Cambridge (MA LLM); general editor Longman Litigation Practice; Humphreys' Matrimonial Causes (16th edition); Matrimonial Consent Orders and Agreements (1st edition); co-author 'Family Courts Emergency Remedies and Procedures'.

SALTER John Rotherham

a senior partner and chair of property and planning department and chair of environmental law group DENTON HALL BURGIN & WARRENS Five Chancery Lane, Clifford's Inn, London EC4A 1BU.

Career: Lt Royal Artillery (1951-1953); Law Society Honours (1959); became partner Denton Hall Burgin & Warrens (1961).

Activities: president Oxford University Law Society (1955); vice-chair IBA Committee (now Section) of Energy and Natural Resources Law (1976-1979); vice-chair IBA Committee on International Environmental Law (1979-1982); secretary-treasurer (1982-1984); vice-chair (1984-1986); chair (1986-1988) Section on Business Law of the International Bar Association; treasurer Anglo-American Real Property Institute (1985-1986); trustee Petroleum Law Education Trust (1980 to date); IBA Educational Trust (1983 to date); vice-chair American Bar Association's Committee on Comparative Government Law (1988 to date); council member Town & Country Planning Association (1985-1988); president the Silver Wine Label Circle (1986-1988); chair the Silver Society (1986-1987); consultant United Nations Industrial Development Organisation (1983-1984); Fellow of the British Institute of Management (1984 to date); Fellow Royal Society of Arts (1984 to date); Associate Chartered Institute of Arbitrators (1987 to date); Fellow Royal Geographical Society (1987 to date); Freeman City of London and City of Glasgow; member Oxford & Cambridge Club.

Biography: lives Sevenoaks; born 02.05.1932; married to Cynthia with 1 son and 2 daughters. Educated at Queen Elizabeth's School; Ashridge College; Lincoln College Oxford; King's College London; joint editor 'Planning Law for Industry' (1981); contributor 'United Kingdom Oil and Gas Law' (1984); Halsbury's Laws of England vol 51 part 8 'Environment and Consumers' (1986); contributor 'Law of the European Communities' (1986); 'UK Onshore Oil and Gas Law' (1986); contributor Vaughan's 'Law of the European Communities Service' (1990); contributor of numerous articles and publications published by International Bar Association.

Leisure: the arts; archaeology; sailing.

SAMSON John

partner NABARRO NATHANSON 50 Stratton Street, London W1X 5FL.

Career: admitted (1970); assistant solicitor Nabarro Nathanson (1970); became partner (1972).

Activities: General Editor - Property Law Bulletin (1984 to date); lectures on property law for Hawkesmere; Profex; Henry Stuart conferences and others; youth club leader; school governor; member Kollel Lev Aryeh Leib.

Biography: lives London; born 30.04.1946; married to Millie with 7 children. Educated at Christ's College, Finchley; King's College, London (LLB); contributor of articles on business leases; rent review & VAT to 'Rent Review and Lease Renewal' and 'The Valuer'.

SAMUELS Alec

14 Redhill, Bassett, Southampton SO1 7DB.

Career: barrister (1952); lecturer in law University of Southampton (1954-1984).

Activities: JP (1973 to date); member Medico-Legal Society; member British Academy Forensic Sciences; member Statute Law Society; member Open Spaces Society; member National Federation Consumer Groups; member Magistrates' Association; member Board Criminal Law Review; director of Research Justice; member United Oxford and Cambridge University Club.

Biography: lives Southampton; born 1930. Educated at Selhurst Grammar School, Croydon; Magdalene College Cambridge.

SAMUELS John EA

Queen's Counsel and head of chambers 22 Old Buildings, Lincoln's Inn, London WC2A 3UJ.

Career: called to the Bar Lincoln's Inn (1964); member South Eastern Circuit; QC (1981); Recorder (1985); Deputy High Court Judge (1981 to date); Bencher, Lincoln's Inn (1990).

Activities: chairman Joint Regulations Committee of Inns Council and Bar Council (1987-1990); member Senate of Inns of Court & The Bar (1983-1986); chairman Senate Working Party on Organisation and Administration of Barristers' Chambers; first chairman and organiser Bar Council/CLE training course for pupils and new tenants; member Council of Legal Education (1983-1990); member Professional Standards Committee (1987-1990); member Bar Representation Committee (Lincoln's Inn) (1982-1990); member Justice (chairman several working parties); member Bar Council Working Party on EC directive relating to recognition of higher education diplomas; former member TA; former member Richmond Twickenham & Roehampton Health Authority; former member Kingston and Richmond Family Practitioner Committee; trustee Richmond

Parish Lands Charity (1986 to date); member Athenaeum.

Biography: lives Richmond; born 15.08.1940; married to Maxine with 2 sons. Educated at Charterhouse; Perugia; Queen's College Cambridge (1963 BA) (1966 MA); Mansfield Scholar Lincoln's Inn (1963); contributor to Halsbury's Laws of England (4th ed); Editor 'Counsel's Guide to Chambers Administration' (Action Pack) 2nd ed (1988).

Leisure: restoration; conservation; serendipity.

SANDISON Francis

partner in the tax department FRESHFIELDS Whitefriars, 65 Fleet Street, London EC4Y 1HS.

Career: articled Freshfields; admitted (1974); founder member tax department (1975); 6 months as foreign associate Sullivan & Cromwell, New York (1977); became partner (1980).

Activities: member Revenue Law sub-committee City of London Law Society; member Steering Committee Institute for Fiscal Studies Capital Taxes Group; spoken at a number of conferences; member of the Addington Society.

Biography: lives Churt nr Farnham; born 25.05.1949; married to Milva with 1 son. Educated at Glasgow Academy; Charterhouse (Senior Scholar); Magdalen College Oxford (Demy) (1971 BCL); (1975 MA); author of 'Tolley's Profit Sharing' (1979); co-author of: 'Whiteman on Income Tax' (1988); 'Business Operations in the United Kingdom' (1988); contributor 'Simon's Taxes'; 'Tolley's Tax Planning' (until 1988); articles in professional press.

Leisure: keen salmon fisherman; good wine; photography; reading.

SANDS Charles

partner and head of the international finance and banking section HERBERT SMITH Watling House, 35 Cannon Street, London EC4M 5SD.

Career: articled Herbert Smith & Co (1959-1960 & 1964-1966); admitted (1966); assistant solicitor (1966-1972); became partner (1972).

Activities: member Banking Committee of the ICC; member of Royal Automobile Club.

Biography: lives London SE11; born 09.03.1938; divorced with 2 sons. Educated at Marlborough College; Lincoln

College Oxford (1963 BA).

Leisure: squash; tennis; golf; riding; walking; gardening.

SANDS Derek

partner KIRK JACKSON 97-101 Chorley Road, Swinton, Manchester M27 2AB.

Career: articled Addleshaw Sons & Latham (1961-1965); admitted (1965); assistant solicitor (1965-1966); assistant solicitor Cartwright & Backhouse (1966-1967); assistant solicitor Kirk Jackson (1967-1968); became partner (1968).

Activities: former membership secretary Manchester Young Solicitors Association (chairman 1973-1974); council member Manchester Law Society (1974 to date) (president 1985-1986); member Law Society Council (1986 to date) Legal Services Committee; Legal Aid Committee; International Committee; Training Committee; former member Child Care Appeal Panel; Family Law Committee chairman (from Sept 1990); former member Mental Health Review Tribunal Appeal Panel; chairman Entry Casework Committee B member Specialisation Litigation Case Work Committee; involved in drafting constitution of the Manchester Law Centre (member management committee; treasurer; chairman); former member Steering Committee of the Salford Law Centre; former member North Western Legal Services Committee; former nominee of the Manchester Law Society on the Manchester Marriage Guidance Council Executive Committee; member local Rotary Club (chairman of various committees and president 1984-1985).

Biography: lives Alderley Edge; born 26.01.1940; married with 3 children. Educated at Manchester Grammar School (1951-1958); Manchester University (1961 LLB hons); John Peacock Prize for Conveyancing (1962); GH Charlesworth Scholarship (1964-1965); George Hadfield Prize (1964-1965); John Peacock Prize (1964-1965); Broderip Prize for Conveyancing (1964); Stephen Heelis Gold Medal.

Leisure: tennis; travel; music; wining and dining.

SANTOW Kim

senior partner FREEHILL HOLLINGDALE & PAGE Birchin Court, 19/25 Birchin Lane, London EC3V 9DJ.

Career: part-time lecturer Sydney University; became partner Freehill Hollingdale & Page (1964); co-founder

S

London office (1990).

Activities: former member various Law Society committees; former trustee Sydney Opera House (1986-89); trustee Sydney Grammar School; trustee (former Chairman) of Malcolm Sargent Cancer Fund for Children in Australia; former director The Greater Union Organisation Pty Ltd and Amalgamated Holdings Ltd; member legal advisory committee to the Commonwealth Attorney General on companies and securities law; former member Corporate Crime Task Force set up by Attorney General for NSW; founder director Australian Commercial Disputes Centre; member of: Sydney University Boat Club (rowing Blue); Australian Clu, University and Schools Club.

Biography: lives London NW3 and Hunters Hill, Sydney; born 11.03.1941; married to Leonora with 3 sons. Educated at The Friends School, Tasmania; Sydney Grammar School; Sydney University (1960 BA) (1963 LLB) (1970 LLM Hons); various articles on company and securities law and trade practices in Australian Law Journals; paper on infrastructure financing for Australian Minerals & Petroleum Law Association.

Leisure: tennis; music; chess; sculling; reading; occasional writing.

SARGINSON David

senior partner SARGINSON & CO 11 Warwick Row, Coventry CV1 1EQ.

Career: admitted (1958); founded own practice (1961); took over Mealand Robinson & Co (1979).

Activities: former Deputy Coroner for the City of Coventry; Coroner (1984); director Sarginson Bros Ltd (1969) chairman 1984); former chairman West Midlands Rent Assessment Panel; West Midlands representative on the Council of the Coroners' Society; Warwickwickshire representative of Solicitors Benevolent Association; member of Institute of British Foundrymen; member of: Drapers' Club; Morton Morrell Tennis Court Club.

Biography: lives Coventry; born 09.05.1936; married to Pamela with 2 children. Educated at Wrekin College, Shropshire.

Leisure: real tennis; gardening; France.

SAUL Dorothy

senior solicitor BRITISH TECHNOLOGY GROUP 101 Newington Causeway, London SE1 6BU.

Career: articled Slaughter & May (1980-

1982); admitted (1982); assistant solicitor (1982-1983); assistant solicitor Taylor Garrett (1983-1985); assistant solicitor British Technology Group (1985-1987); became senior solicitor (1987).

Activities: chair NRDC branch of IPMS; director London Cycling Campaign (1986-1988); co-secretary of a fine wine company (1984-1986); member Council of Management of Ukela; member C & I Group Committee and Activities Sub-committee; member of: CTC; LCC; AWS; SWS.

Biography: lives South Nutfield, Surrey; born 05.05.1957; married to John Jolliffe, Actuary partner with R Watson & Song, Reigate. Educated at James Allen's Girls School; Southampton University (1979 LLB hons); College of Law Guildford (1980).

Leisure: flying light aircraft; long-distance cycling and cycle touring; wine tasting; good food and restaurants; skiing; theatre; opera; the arts; voluntary work and campaigning on environmental issues and for 'green groups'.

SAUL Pat

senior partner WALTER GRAY & CO 17 High Street, Ventnor, Isle of Wight PO38 1RZ.

Career: articled in Long Eaton (1947-1952); admitted (1953); assistant solicitor Isle of Wight (1953-1958); married and had family (1958-1965); assistant solicitor Walter Gray (1965-1972); became equity partner (1972); chairman of the firm (1986); became senior partner (1987).

Activities: former marriage guidance counsellor; former County Scout secretary; former governor of Sandown High School; formerly involved with PTAs as secretary; chairman IW branch Carers National Association; chairman District Scout Council; secretary Ventnor Town Trust; member of (former president) IW Club; UK Federation of Business and Professional Women (representative on Carers' National Association).

Biography: lives Ventnor; born 09.05.1931; married to Ian with 3 children. Educated at Loughborough High School; Nottingham University; Gibson & Weldon Guildford (1952).

Leisure: bird watching; gardening.

SAVAGE Robert

senior partner FARNFIELD & NICHOLLS The Square, Gillingham, Dorset SP8 4AX.

Career: articled in the City; admitted

(1966); assistant solicitor Lincoln's Inn Fields (1966-1967); assistant solicitor Theodore Goddard & Co (1967-1969); assistant solicitor Farnfield & Nicholls (1969-1970); became partner (1970); became senior partner (1986).

Activities: member Salisbury Health Authority; chairman The Managers of the Old Manor Hospital, Salisbury under the Mental Health Act 1983; former member Dorset Law Society Committee; member Yeovil County Court Liaison Committee; member Solicitors Family Law Association.

Biography: lives Shaftesbury; born 19.05.1941; married to Jane with 4 children. Educated at MerchantTaylor's School, Northwood; St Peter's College Oxford (1963 MA).

Leisure: squash; walking; food; wine; theatre; music.

SAX Richard Noel

managing partner and head of family law department RUBINSTEIN CALLINGHAM POLDEN & GALE 2 Raymond Buildings, Gray's Inn, London WC1R 5BZ.

Career: articled BA Woolf & Co and Rubinstein Nash & Co; admitted (1967); became equity partner Rubinstein Nash & Co (1968); amalgamated Rubinstein Callingham (1976); became managing partner Rubinstein Callingham Polden & Gale (1984).

Activities: founder member and committee member Solicitors Family Law Association (chairman 1987-1989); outside member Law Commission working party on family property and the matrimonial home (1972-1973); member SFLA Committee (1984 to date); member Board of Family Mediators' Association; member Advisory Board Institute of Family Therapy; lectured and spoke on family law on various occasions including National Young Solicitors Conference, Family Law Conferences, Bath University, Newcastle University, etc; various SFLA reports to the Law Commission, LCD, etc; various radio and TV appearances and press interviews (1979 to date); member Law Society's Family Law Committee (1989 to date); Deputy Registrar Divorce Registry London; member MCC.

Biography: lives Beckenham; born 26.12.1938; married to Margaret with 3 daughters. Educated at Tonbridge School; St John's College Oxford (1962 BA MA); Senior Scholar; articles on child maintenance in Family Law.

Leisure: family; gardening; archaeology

and history; visiting churches and art galleries; watching cricket; current affairs; theatre.

SAYER Richard

partner INCE & CO Knollys House, 11 Byward Street, London EC3R 5EN.

Career: articled Ince & Co (1962-1966); admitted (1966); assistant solicitor (1966-1970); became partner (1970).

Activities: hon secretary City of London Admiralty Solicitors Group (1972 to date); member Lloyds Form of Salvage Agreement Working Party (1985 to date); member Admiralty Court Committee (1987 to date); member International Bar Association; supporting member of the London Maritime Arbitrators' Association; subscribing member of the Association of Average Adjusters; member of the Baltic Exchange; governor Seaford College, Sussex; trustee United Response and associated charities for the handicapped; member MCC.

Biography: lives Roehampton; born 07.05.1943; married with 2 sons. Educated at Framlingham College, Suffolk; Tours University, France; College of Law Lancaster Gate (1965-1966); occasional papers and lectures on maritime law.

Leisure: golf; cricket; hockey; shooting.

SAYERS Maurice George

senior partner STILWELL & HARBY 110 Maison Dieu Road, Dover, Kent CT16 1RT.

Career: office boy Stilwell & Harby (1942-1944); junior clerk (1944-1946); admitted (1961); assistant solicitor (1961-1963); partner (1963-1971); became senior partner (1971); Army (1946-1949); Deputy Magistrates' Clerk Dover (1949-1961).

Activities: president Kent Law Society (1979-1980); president Dover Deal & Sandwich Law Society (1987-1989); president Dover Chamber of Commerce (1969-1970); chairman Alkham Valley Society; former chairman and president Dover Round Table; president Dover Rugby Club (former captain); former captain Dover Swimming Club; member Royal Cinque Ports Yacht Club.

Biography: lives Dover; born 04.09.1928; married to Pamela with 3 children. Educated at Dover Grammar School for Boys; College of Law Lancaster Gate.

Leisure: rugby; swimming; fly fishing; gardening; part-time farmer.

SAYERS Michael

senior corporate finance partner NORTON ROSE Kempson House, PO Box 570, Camomile Street, London EC3A 7AN.

Career: articled Neish Howell & Haldane (now Macfarlanes) (1959-1960); admitted (1960); assistant solicitor (1960-1962); assistant solicitor Norton Rose Botterell & Roche (now Norton Rose) (1962-1964); became partner (1965).

Activities: member City University Club.

Biography: lives London NW2 and Holwell, Oxfordshire; born 23.04.1934; married to Peta with 3 children. Educated at Winchester College; Magdalen College Oxford (1957 MA hons).

Leisure: walking; reading; travelling; seeing friends.

SCAMELL Ernest

barrister and head of chambers 5 New Square, Lincoln's Inn, London WC2A 3RJ.

Career: called to the Bar (1949); practice at Bar (1954 to date); head of Chambers (1971).

Activities: professor of English law London University (1966-1990); vice-provost University College London (1978-1984); member Holy Trinity Meccano Club.

Biography: lives Ashford; born 09.03.1928; married to Ragnhild with 4 children and 1 stepchild. Educated at Fray's College, Uxbridge; King's College London (1947 LLB hons) (1948 LLM); author of 'Precedents for the Conveyancer' (1956-1977); editor 'Lindley on Partnership' (12th & 13th eds); joint editor (14th & 15th eds).

Leisure: flying; model building and collecting.

SCANLAN Charles

partner SIMMONS & SIMMONS 14 Dominion Street, London EC2M 2RJ.

Career: articled Simmons & Simmons (1967-1970); admitted (1970); assistant solicitor (1970-1973); became partner (1973).

Activities: Freeman of the City Solicitors' Company.

Biography: lives London NW8; born 23.12.1944; married to Dorothy with 2 sons. Educated at St Benedict's School, Ealing; Balliol College Oxford (1966 BA hons); co-author of 'Know Your Rights'.

Leisure: history.

SCHEPS Adrian

partner and head of commercial department WALKER MARTINEAU 64 Queen Street, London EC4R 1AD.

Career: articled Herbert Oppenheimer and Nathan & Vandyk (1972-1974); admitted (1974); assistant solicitor Freshfields (1974-1975); legal adviser on company law reform and harmonisation of EEC law (1975-1979); legal adviser Allied-Lyons PLC (1979-1982); became partner Walker Martineau (1983).

Activities: member Honourable Society of Artificers.

Biography: lives Pinner; born 12.02.1946; married to Cheryl with 1 daughter. Educated at William Ellis School, Highgate (1959-1964); Merton College Oxford (1971 BA DPhil).

Leisure: bridge; opera; most spectator sports.

SCHMIDT Karsten

partner and head of German department BAKER & MCKENZIE Aldwych House, Aldwych, London WC2B 4JP.

Career: German Bar (1956); Illinois, USA Bar (1960); US Supreme Court Bar (1961) (first ever non-American); founder German office Baker & McKenzie, Frankfurt (1962 to date); senior partner; German Notary (1969); professor INSEAD, Fontainebleau (1974-1975); visiting professor Columbia University Parker School of Law (1978-1981); visiting professor John F Kennedy University, Buenos Aires (1981).

Activities: hon legal adviser HM Consul General Frankfurt (1973 to date); hon legal adviser British Chamber of Commerce in Germany (1974 to date); chairman The Jane Goodall Institute (UK) for Wildlife Research; chairman Scholarship Foundation of the British Chamber of Commerce in Germany; executive vice-president British Chamber of Commerce in Germany; vice-president Confederation of British Chambers of Commerce in Continental Europe (1985-1989); hon starter German Open Golf Championship; member various golf clubs in Germany and UK; member Bucks Club; appointed OBE (1983) for services to British interests.

Biography: lives Coombe Hill; born 13.10.1927; married with 3 children. Educated at Hamburg University (1952 LLB) (1957 Dr); Academy of International Law, The Hague (1950-1953); Indiana University (1959 JD); numerous articles in legal journals in particular on anti-trust, professional development and European integration; editor of 'Trade Partners'.

SCHOLES Rodney James

Queen's Counsel 25 Byrom Street, Manchester M3 4PF and 5 Essex Court, Temple, London EC4Y 9AH.

Career: called to the Bar Lincoln's Inn; member Northern circuit (1968 to date); Recorder of the Crown Court; QC.

Biography: born 26.09.1945.

SCIENCE Austen

development partner MINCOFF SCIENCE & GOLD Kensington House, 4/6 Osborne Road, Newcastle upon Tyne NE2 2AA.

Career: admitted (1961); assistant solicitor (1961-1962); became partner (1962).

Activities: vice-president British Amusement Catering Trade Association; former vice-chairman local Sports Aid Foundation; involved in local inter-faith and racial harmony activities; member of: Arcot Golf Club; Northumberland Lawn Tennis Club.

Biography: lives Newcastle upon Tyne; born 11.08.1938; married to Jennifer with 2 children. Educated at Clifton College; contributor to Encyclopaedia of Forms and Precedents on Clubs and revising Halsbury's Laws of England on Clubs.

Leisure: golf; tennis.

SCOBLE Peter

partner BOODLE HATFIELD 43 Brook Street, London W1Y 2BL.

Career: articled Joynson Hicks & Co; admitted (1962); assistant solicitor Boodle Hatfield & Co (1962-1964); became partner (1964).

Activities: member Council of The Law Society (1986 to date); member City of Westminster Law Society (past president); member SBA Justice; long standing involvement with training and monitoring of articled clerks; former member of London Legal Education Committee organising lectures on behalf of the Central London local Law Societies; governor Papplewick School; member of: MCC; Wig & Pen; Lowtonian Society.

Biography: lives Halstead, Kent; born 08.03.1938; widowed with 3 children. Educated at Papplewick Prep School, Ascot; Malvern College; College of Law Lancaster Gate.

Leisure: tennis; golf; philately; music (particularly opera); gardening.

SCOPES Richard

partner WILDE SAPTE Queensbridge House, 60 Upper Thames Street, London EC4V 3BD.

Career: articled Ashurst Morris Crisp & Co (1963-1969); admitted (1969); director Scopes & Sons Ltd (1970-1974); assistant solicitor Wilde Sapte (1976-1980); became partner (1980).

Activities: member Law Society; member City of London Solicitors' Company; member Queenhithe Ward Club.

Biography: lives Flamstead; born 06.06.1944; married with 1 daughter. Educated at University College School; College of Law Lancaster Gate (1969); Magdalene College Cambridge (1976 LLB).

Leisure: wine; antiques; painting; opera.

SCORER Tim

partner BARLOW LYDE & GILBERT Beaufort House, 15 St Botolph Street, London EC3A 7NJ.

Career: articled in East Grinstead and Crawley; admitted (1966); assistant solicitor Josselyn & Sons; partner (1967-1976); assistant secretary professional and public relations Law Society (1976-1978); assistant solicitor Barlow Lyde & Gilbert (1978-1981); became partner (1981).

Activities: Freeman of City of London; Liveryman and hon solicitor to Guild of Air Pilots & Air Navigators; international vice-president Lawyer-Pilots Bar Association of USA; hon solicitor to: Army Parachutes Association; European General Aviation Safety Foundation; Helicopter Club of GB; chairman Lawyers' Flying Association; member of: Royal Aero Club; Aircraft Owners' and Pilots' Association; Popular Flying Association; Flying Farmers' Association; Suffolk and North Essex Law Society.

Biography: lives Lavenham, Suffolk; born 25.06.1941; divorced with 3 children. Educated at New Beacon, Sevenoaks; Repton School; Sussex School of Law; College of Law; numerous articles, features and presentations on various aspects of aviation law and practice.

Leisure: flying (private pilot and aircraft owner); photography; classic cars; travel; music.

SCOTT Ian

partner ASHURST MORRIS CRISP Broadgate House, 7 Eldon Street, London EC2M 2HD.

Career: articled Sharpe Pritchard & Co (1965-1967); admitted (1967); assistant solicitor Ashurst Morris Crisp (1968-1972); became partner (1972).

Activities: member of: City of London Club; Roehampton Club.

Biography: lives London SW15; born 12.09.1942; married to Mary with 3 children. Educated at Sherborne School; London School of Economics (1964 LLB hons).

Leisure: hockey; tennis; sailing; theatre.

SCOTT Ian

senior partner BRISTOWS COOKE & CARPMAEL 10 Lincolns's Inn Fields, London WC2A 3BP.

Career: Army; admitted (1953); assistant solicitor Bristows Cooke & Carpmael (1953-1959); became partner (1959); became senior partner (1982).

Biography: lives Brighton; born 17.06.1927; married to Lesley-Jane with 1 child. Educated at West Downs, Winchester; Sherborne School.

Leisure: reading; sailing; walking.

SCOTT Kenneth

senior partner EATON SMITH & DOWNEY Britannia Buildings, St Peter's Street, Huddersfield, West Yorks HD1 1BB.

Career: articled Eric Watts Moses; National Service with Royal Navy; assistant solicitor Richard Reed (1954-1959); assistant solicitor Eaton Smith & Downey (1959-1963); became partner (1963).

Activities: member of: Huddersfield Golf Club; Royal St David's Golf Club; The Arts Club; The Senior Golfers' Society.

Biography: lives Huddersfield; born 26.01.1930; married to Ruth with 3 children. Educated at Durham School; King's College, Newcastle.

Leisure: golf.

SCOTT Peter

barrister practising commercial and common law Fountain Court, Temple, London EC4Y 9DH.

Career: called to Bar (1960); pupil AS Orr (1960); QC (1978).

Activities: various Bar Council Committees; chairman of the Bar (1987); Centre for Commercial Law Studies.

Biography: lives London W8; born 19.04.1935; divorced. Educated at Monroe High School, Rochester, USA; Balliol College Oxford (1959 MA hons); Harmsworth Scholar.

SCOTT Roger Martin

barrister and head of Chambers 5th Floor, St Paul's House, 23 Park Square, Leeds 1.

Career: called to the Bar (1968); pupillage with HA Richardson (1968); tenant 38 Park Square (1969); co-founder Chambers 23 Park Square (1982); head of Chambers (1985); Assistant Recorder (1985); Recorder of the Crown Court (1989).

Biography: lives Dacre nr Harrogate; born 08.09.1944; married to Diana with 3 children. Educated at Mill Hill School, London; St Andrew's University (1966 LLB).

Leisure: golf; theatre; walking in the Dales.

SCOTT Sue

senior solicitor WOOLWICH BUILDING SOCIETY Corporate Headquarters, Watling Street, Bexleyheath, Kent DA6 7RR.

Career: articled Blount Petre & Co (1979-1981); admitted (1981); assistant solicitor DM Landsman & Co (1981-1982); assistant solicitor Woolwich Equitable Building Society (1982-1986); became senior solicitor (1987).

Activities: treasurer and committee member South London Law Society (1982-1989); examiner in mortgage and land law for Chartered Building Societies Institute.

Biography: lives Chislehurst; born 29.04.1957; married to Patrick. Educated at Swanley Comprehensive School; King's College London (1978 LLB hons); City of London Polytechnic (1978-1979); distinction Law Society Part II; co-author of 'An Introduction to the Building Societies Act 1986'.

Leisure: cooking; gardening; handicrafts.

SCOTT-BAYFIELD Julie Ann

libel partner MISHCON DE REYA 125 High Holborn, London WC1V 6QP.

Career: admitted (1965); assistant solicitor (1965-1966); partner Oswald Hickson Collier & Co (1966-1981); partner Peter Carter-Ruck & Partners (1982-1988); partner Mishcon de Reya (1988 to date).

Activities: Freeman City of London Solicitors Company; member Law Society; member City of Westminster Law Society; member Media Society; lecturer in libel and copyright; member of: Reform Club; Royal Ocean Racing Club; Groucho Club; Roehampton Club.

Biography: lives London SW15; married with 2 children. Samuel Herbert

Easterbrook Prize (1962).

SCRAGG Peter

senior litigation partner GOODGER AUDEN 2/4 Lichfield Street, Burton on Trent DE14 3RB.

Career: trainee technical adviser International Computers and Tabulators Ltd (1960-1961); articled Thorpe & Thorpe (1961-1964); admitted (1965); assistant solicitor Goodger Lowe & Co (now Goodger Auden) (1965-1966); became partner (1966).

Activities: member Legal Aid Appeals Committee Area No 10; Notary Public (1989); member of: The Burton Club; Bretby Rotary Club.

Biography: lives Alrewas; born 05.04.1938; married to Diane with 3 children. Educated at North Mimms Boys' School; Hertingfordbury School; Hertford Grammar School; Ramsey Grammar School; University College London (1960 LLB).

Leisure: walking; travelling; (trekking in Ladakh in Himalayas, Northern India (1988); reading; gardening.

SCRIVENER Anthony

Queen's Counsel 8 New Square, Lincoln's Inn, London WC2A 3PQ.

Career: called to the Bar Gray's Inn (1958); QC (1975); Recorder (1975); Bencher Lincoln's Inn (1986).

Activities: member Bar Council (vice-chairman); chairman International Practice Committee.

Biography: lives Pinner; born 31.07.1935; married to Iren with 2 children. Educated at Kent College; University College London (1955-1958); Holt Scholar Gray's Inn.

Leisure: motor sport; tennis; chess; walking the dog; mountain climbing.

SCRUTTON David

partner KENNEDYS 104A High Street, Brentwood, Essex CM14 4AP.

Career: junior clerk Barlow Lyde & Gilbert (1961); articled (1971); admitted (1976); assistant solicitor (1976-1981); assistant solicitor Kennedys (1981); became partner (1982); opened specialist office (1988).

Activities: member of: Lawyers' Flying Association; Upminster Bach Society.

Biography: lives Upminster; born 01.03.1945; married to Nora with 2

children. Educated at State secondary modern.

Leisure: flying; walking; collecting antiques; objets d'arts; chorister.

SEABROOK Michael

partner corporate services department EVERSHED WELLS & HIND 10 Newhall Street, Birmingham B3 3LX.

Career: articled Lovell White & King (1974-1976); admitted (1976); assistant solicitor Clifford-Turner (1977-1979); assistant solicitor Needham & James (1980-1981); became partner (1981-1986); became equity partner Evershed & Tomkinson (1986); member firm's liaison committee whose work eventually led to establishment of Eversheds Group; involved in articled clerk recruitment on behalf of firm and Eversheds Group.

Activities: chairman Fourth Roman Property Trust PLC (BES company) and 54 separate PLCs Roman Rentals 56 PLC to Roman Rentals 109 PLC (BES link companies); director LCL Ltd and Leicester Circuits Ltd; former member committee of the West Midlands branch of Solicitors European Group; member of: Copt Heath Golf Club; Knowle & Dorridge Cricket Club; Warwickshire Imps Cricket Club; Warwickshire Pilgrims Cricket Club; Bacchanalians Golfing Society.

Biography: lives Dorridge; born 24.03.1952; married to Hilary with 2 children. Educated at King Edward's School, Birmingham; Exeter University (1973 LLB); article in Law Society's Gazette.

Leisure: family; club cricket; golf; watching sport (particularly rugby internationals); non-law reading.

SEABROOK Robert

Queen's Counsel and Leader of South Eastern Circuit 1 Crown Office Row, Temple, London EC4Y 7HH.

Career: called to the Bar Middle Temple (1964); pupillage with Anthony (now Lord Justice) McCowan (1964-1965); Recorder of the South Eastern Circuit Bar (1982-1984); QC (1983); Recorder of the Crown Court (1985); Leader of the South Eastern Circuit (1989).

Activities: member Bar Council (1989 to date); vice-chairman Bar Committee (1990); chairman South Eastern Circuit Fees & Legal Aid Committee (1987-1989); member Brighton Festival Committee (1976-1986); Liveryman of the Curriers Company (1972 to date).

Biography: lives London SE11 and Brighton; born 06.10.1941; married to Liv with 3 children. Educated at St George's College, Salisbury, Southern Rhodesia; University College London (LLB).

Leisure: travel; listening to music; wine.

SEARLE Geoffrey

managing partner and member of planning group, property department DENTON HALL BURGIN & WARRENS Five Chancery Lane, Clifford's Inn, London EC4A 1BU.

Career: articled in Central London (1963-1968); admitted (1968); assistant solicitor Brentwood District Council (1969-1971); assistant clerk of the Council (1971-1973); assistant solicitor Denton Hall & Burgin (1973-1977); became partner (1977); member Management Committee (1984-1986); admitted Hong Kong (1986); managing partner (1988).

Activities: member International Bar Association; founder member UK Environmental Law Association; associate member American Bar Association; member Asia Pacific Law Association; member Committee of Management British Chapter International Real Estate Federation.

Biography: lives near Brentwood and Westminster; born 21.06.1945; married to Nicole with 3 children. Educated at Bancroft's School, Woodford Green; College of Law; joint author of Volume 5 of'The British Tax Reporter on Capital Gains Tax and Development Land Tax' (1986).

Leisure: family; reading; swimming; listening to pop music; conversation with young adults.

SEGAL Nick

partner business reconstruction and insolvency group ALLEN & OVERY 9 Cheapside, London EC2V 6AD.

Career: articled Cameron Markby (1980-1982); admitted (1982); assistant solicitor (1982-1986); partner (1986-1989); became partner Allen & Overy (1989).

Activities: senior visiting Fellow Centre for Commercial Law Studies Queen Mary College London; member of International Bar Association; Association Europeene des Practiciens des Procedures Collectives; RAC Club; holder of Insolvency Practitioner's licence.

Biography: lives London SW6; born 20.10.1956; married to Genevieve.

Educated at Poole Grammar School; St Peter's College, Oxford (1979 MA hons); Carl Albert Prizewinner (1979); country correspondent ESC Journal of International Banking Law; contributor to: Gore-Browne on Companies (44th ed chapters 31-34 on administration orders, voluntary arrangements, receivers and liquidations); Totty & Jordan on Insolvency; Boyle & Bird's Company Law (2nd ed); series of articles on banking and insolvency law.

Leisure: golf; theatre; good literature; astronomy.

SEWELL Peter

partner and head corporate department FLADGATE FIELDER Heron Place, 3 George Street, London W1H 6AD.

Career: partner David Alterman & Sewell; merged to become Fladgate Fielder.

Biography: lives London; born 23.08.1933; separated with 1 son. .

SHANKLAND David

partner commercial property LOVELL WHITE DURRANT 21 Holborn Viaduct, London EC1A 2DY.

Career: articled Lovell White & King (1964-1967); admitted (1967); assistant solicitor (1967-1971); became partner (1971).

Activities: solicitor to the Honourable Society of Lincoln's Inn; member Committee U Business Law Section of the International Bar Association; member Law Society.

Biography: lives nr Haywards Heath; born 30.09.1939; married to Virginia with 3 children. Educated at Bramblette School, East Grinstead (1948-1953); Tonbridge School (1953-1958); Trinity College Cambridge (1963 BA); articles in IBA's Journal.

Leisure: fly fishing; tennis; skiing.

SHANNAN Robin

partner corporate law department McCLURE NAISMITH ANDERSON & GARDINER 292 St Vincent Street, Glasgow G2 5TQ.

Career: apprentice North of Scotland Hydro-Electric Board (1975-1977); admitted (1977); assistant solicitor McClures (1977-1980); became partner (1981); member management committee; assistant solicitor Clifford Turner (1980-1981) .

Activities: member Arbitration Panel of the American Film Marketing Association;

member Law Society of Scotland Working Party of Banking Law; member International Bar Association; member Scottish Council for Civil Liberties; member Amnesty International; member of: Western Baths, Glasgow; The Royal Faculty of Procurators in Glasgow.

Biography: lives Glasgow; born 26.01.1952; married to Pia with 1 daughter. Educated at Wishaw High School; Bo'ness Academy; Dundee University (1973 MA) (1975 LLB).

Leisure: family life; theatre; music; reading.

SHARP Peter

litigation partner WILDE SAPTE Queensbridge House, 60 Upper Thames Street, London EC4V 3BD.

Career: articled AJ Harry & Co (1978-1980); admitted (1982); assistant solicitor Wilde Sapte (1982-1984); became partner (1984).

Biography: lives London SW17; born 16.04.1956; married to Pippa with 2 children. Educated at Berkhamsted School; Oxford University (BA hons).

Leisure: family; motor racing; cycling.

SHARPLES Clive

partner and head of residential development department SAUNDERS SOBELL LEIGH & DOBIN 20 Red Lion Street, London WC1.

Career: admitted (1974); assistant solicitor (1974-1978); became partner Saunders Sobell Leigh and Dobin (1978).

Activities: member Conveyancing Committee of Housebuilders Federation.

Biography: lives Farnham and Bournemouth; born 01.09.1947; married to Billie with 3 children. Educated at Headlands Grammar School, Swindon; Fitzmaurice Grammar School, Bradford on Avon; Kingston Polytechnic (1972 LLB).

Leisure: riding; game shooting.

SHAW Andrew

equity partner BAILEYS SHAW & GILLETT 17 Queen Square, London WC1N 3RH.

Career: teacher evening school in Brent; teacher Davies Laing & Dick; lecture tour USA (1964-1965); articled Elliot & Macvie; admitted; assistant solicitor Wilkinson Kimbers & Stadden; assistant solicitor Simmons & Simmons; assistant solicitor Baileys Shaw & Gillett; became partner (1974).

Activities: lecturer on funding agreements

and institutional finance; expert on commercial leases; member International Bar Association; member of: The Executive Club International; Old Millhillians.

Biography: lives Edgware, Devon and Spain; born 05.11.1942; married to Diane with 1 daughter. Educated at Belmont School; Mill Hill School; London School of Economics (BSC); article in Sunday Times on local card charge searches.

Leisure: gardening; reading; walking.

SHAW Martin

practice development partner SIMPSON CURTIS 41 Park Square, Leeds LS1 2NS.

Career: articled Simpson Curtis (1966-1969); admitted (1969); assistant solicitor (1969-1971); became partner (1971); head corporate department (1980-1988); practice development partner (1984).

Activities: part-time lecturer in law Leeds Polytechnic (1969-1971); chairman Legal Resources Group (1988); chairman Minstergate PLC (1985-1989); chairman ABI Caravans Limited (1986-1988); chairman Minster Corporation PLC (1988-1989); director Leeds Business Venture (1982); member the Law Society; Leeds Law Society (1969); Solicitors European Group (1975); American Bar Association (corporation, banking and business law section and international law and practice section); International Bar Association (business law section); governor Richmond House School; governor Gateways School; member Leeds Chamber of Commerce and Industry; Yorkshire and Humberside Development Association; member Variety Club of Great Britain; member of: The Leeds Club; Alwoodley Golf Club; Chapel Allerton Lawn Tennis & Squash Club; Headingley Rotary Club.

Biography: lives Leeds; born 31.10.1944; married to Christine with 3 children. Educated at Leeds Grammar School; University College London.

SHAW Michael Bernard

partner and head of private client department MARTINEAU JOHNSON St Philip's House, St Philip's Place, Birmingham B3 2PP.

Career: National Service commission in the Royal Artillery; articled Burton Yeates & Hart; admitted (1957); assistant solicitor Johnson & Co (1957-1960); became partner (1960); became partner Martineau Johnson (1987) upon merger with Ryland Martineau.

Activities: Registrar of Birmingham C of E Diocese; member The Birmingham Club.

Biography: lives North Worcestershire; born 23.02.1931; married to Susan with 1 child. Educated at Charterhouse; College of Law Lancaster Gate.

Leisure: gardening; fell walking; painting; photography; archery.

SHAW Peter

senior partner HEWITSON BECKE & SHAW Shakespeare House, 42 Newmarket Road, Cambridge CB5 8EP.

Career: articled Parrot & Coales; admitted (1949); assistant solicitor Mallam Lewis & Norris (1949-1952); assistant solicitor Wild & Hewitson (1952-1955); became partner (1955).

Activities: former chairman Cambridge Round Table; former president Cambridge Rotary Club; former president Cambridge & District Law Society; chairman Directors of the Cambridge Water Company; chairman Cambridge branch of the RNLI.

Biography: lives near Cambridge; born 27.03.1925; married with 3 children. Educated at Aylesbury Grammar School.

Leisure: live theatre; opera; ballet; art.

SHAW Trevor

director, secretary and group legal advisor to ASSOCIATED BRITISH FOOD PLC Weston Centre, Bowater House, 68 Knightsbridge, London SW1X 7LR.

Career: articled MA Jacobs & Sons (1952-1957); admitted (1957); became partner A Kramer & Co (1957-1968); Associated British Food PLC (1968).

Activities: member Annabels.

Biography: lives London; born 28.09.1933; married to Paula with 2 children. Educated at Bedales School, Petersfield; London University (LLB hons).

Leisure: music; ballet; tennis; antiques.

SHAW Tony

barrister and head of chambers 4 Brick Court, Temple, London EC4Y 9AD.

Career: called to the Bar Middle Temple (1972); legal research unit, Bedford College, London (1972-1975); Divisional Court QBD (1974-1976); tenant 4 Brick Cout (1977).

Biography: lives London SW17; born 04.10.1948; married to Faugust with 2 children. Educated at King's School, Canterbury; Trinity College Oxford (BA) Major History Scholar; Astbury Scholar

Middle Temple; co-author 'Extradition' 4th ed Halsbury's Laws of England; 'Informal Applications for the Writ of Habeas Corpus'; 'Judicial Recommendations for Minimum Periods of Imprisonment for Murder'.

Leisure: reading; history; administering Chambers.

SHEARER Roy

senior partner LINDSAYS WS 11 Atholl Crescent, Edinburgh EH3 8HE.

Career: apprentice Edinburgh; admitted; assistant solicitor Lindsays (1969-1971); became partner (1971); became senior partner (1988).

Biography: lives Edinburgh; born 02.02.1943; married to Ann with 5 children. Educated at George Watsons College, Edinburgh; Edinburgh University (1963 MA) (1967 LLB).

Leisure: golf; tennis (former county player); squash; rugby (Watsonians briefly).

SHELDON Mark

senior partner LINKLATERS & PAINES Barrington House, 59-67 Gresham Street, London EC2V 7JA.

Career: National Service as Lt Royal Signals; articled Linklaters & Paines (1953-1956); admitted (1957); assistant solicitor (1957-1959); became partner (1959); opened branch office in New York (1972-1974); became senior partner (1988).

Activities: council member Law Society (1978 to date) deputy vice-president (1990-1991); (treasurer 1981-1986); member Court of City of London Solicitors' Company (1985 to date); master of the Company and President of the City of London Law Society (1987-1988); member Council of the Corporation of Lloyd's (1989-1990); member Financial Reporting Council (1990 to date); member of Courts and Legal Services Committee (1989); Training Committee (1987-1989); Examination Casework Committee (1987-1989); Training Review Casework Committee (1987-1989) and Revenue Law Committee (1976-1978 & 1989) of the Law Society; director Law Society Trustees Ltd (1981 to date); member The Justinians (1967 to date); member of: The Travellers' Club; The City of London Club.

Biography: lives London W8 and Oxfordshire; born 06.02.1931; married to Catherine with 1 son and 1 daughter. Educated at Stand Grammar School, nr Manchester; Wycliffe College,

S

Gloucestershire; Corpus Christi College Oxford (1953 BA hons MA); City of London Solicitors' Prize (1957).

Leisure: music; English watercolours; wine and food; swimming.

SHELFORD Bill

partner in the property department CAMERON MARKBY HEWITT Sceptre Court, 40 Tower Hill, London EC3N 4BB.

Career: articled Waltons Bright; admitted (1969); assistant solicitor (1969-1970); became partner (1970); elected senior partner (1990).

Activities: member of property department Cameron Markby Hewitt advising on all aspects of commercial real estate. Formerly member of the management group. Member of: City of London Club, Brook's.

Biography: lives Sussex; born 27.01.1943; married to Annette with 3 children. Educated at Eton College (1956-1961); Christ Church Oxford (1965 MA).

Leisure: tennis; skiing; attempting to look after smallholding.

SHEPPARD John

partner HOLMAN FENWICK & WILLAN Marlow House, Lloyds Avenue, London EC3N 3AL.

Career: articled Holman Fenwick & Willan (1955-1959); admitted (1959); assistant solicitor (1959-1963); became partner (1963).

Activities: member Oxford & Cambridge United Universities Club.

Biography: lives London W8 and Nantmor; born 15.11.1932; married to Alexandra with 4 children. Educated at Oundle (1946-1950); Exeter College Oxford (1955 BA) (1956 MA).

Leisure: golf; theatre; jogging.

SHER Jules

Queen's Counsel 3 New Square, Lincoln's Inn, London WC2A 3RS.

Career: articled in South Africa; admitted South Africa; called to the Bar England and Wales (1968); QC (1981); Recorder (1987); Master of the Bench of the Honourable Society of the Inner Temple (1988).

Activities: member of the Supreme Court Rule Committee; member of the Chancery Bar Association; member of the Commercial Bar Association.

Biography: lives London NW11; born 22.10.1941; married to Sandra with 3

children. Educated at Athlone High School; University of the Witwatersrand (1961 BCOMM) (1964 LLB); New College Oxford (1967 BCL).

Leisure: tennis; music.

SHERR Avrom

director of legal practice, Warwick University; professor of law, Liverpool University (April 1991); head of Centre for Research in Professional Law, Liverpool University (April 1991); director of training MACFARLANES 10 Norwich Street, London EC4A 1BD.

Career: articled Coward Chance; admitted; lecturer in law at Warwick University (1974); Warwick Legal Practice programme; became director of Legal Practice (1976); taught in USA (1970s); University of San Francisco (1982); visiting professor UCLA (1984-1985); became director of training Macfarlanes (1987).

Activities: consultant to the Law Society in relation to advocacy training in the light of the Green Papers and as consultant and trainer in practical legal skills generally; member Client Counselling Competition Committee (1983 to date); member Law Society Race Relations Committee (1986 to date); treasurer Legal Education and Training Group of In-house Training Directors (1988 to date); member Law Centres Federation Executive Committee (1979-1983); Minister to the Coventry Hebrew congregation; school governor.

Biography: lives Finchley Central and Coventry; born 28.03.1949; married to Lorraine with 3 sons. Educated at Carmel College; School Bursary Scholarship; London School of Economics (1971 LLB); author of:'Client Interviewing for Lawyers - An Analysis and Guide' (1987);'Freedom of Protest, Public Order and the Law' (1989); video film and manual'Client Relations' (1985); articles in Journal of Law and Society; International Journal of Law and Economics; Fiscal Studies No 3; Modern Law Review.

Leisure: driving slow cars; tennis; eating; childrens' homework; maintaining attempt not to take anything or anybody too seriously; DIY; photography.

SHERRARD Michael

Queen's Counsel and head of chambers 2 Crown Office Row, Temple, London EC4Y 7HJ.

Career: Recorder of the Crown Court; Master of the Bench Middle Temple; QC (1968).

Activities: member Winn Committee on Personal Injury Litigation; DOT inspector London Capital Group (Stonehouse); chairman Normansfield Hospital Inquiry; member Council and Executive Committee of Justice; member Working Party on Science and Society.

Biography: lives London W1; born 23.06.1928; married to Shirley with 2 sons. Educated at King's College London (LLB); numerous articles Law and Accountancy.

Leisure: Oriental art; opera; company of granddaughter.

SHILLITO Richard

partner OSWALD HICKSON COLLIER & CO Essex House, Essex Street, London WC2R 3AQ.

Career: trainee journalist with Yorkshire Weekly Newspaper Group Ltd (1970-1972); articled Oswald Hickson Collier & Co (1973-1976); admitted (1976); assistant solicitor (1976-1984); became partner (1984).

Biography: lives London SW19; born 13.03.1948; married to Sally with 3 daughters. Educated at Westminster School; Magdalen College Oxford (1970 PPE hons); articles in Marketing; Law Society's Gazette and occasional contributor to the Gazette of Law & Journalism, Australia.

Leisure: music; sailing.

SHINDLER Geoffrey

partner HALLIWELL LANDAU St James's Court, Brown Street, Manchester M2 2JF.

Career: articled March Pearson & Skelton; admitted; became partner (1971-1986); became partner Halliwell Landau (1986).

Activities: director various private companies in Manchester region; trustee private and charitable foundations; member Executive Committee North West Arts; former member Salford Family Practitioner Committee; former chairman Local Review Committee (parole) and member board of visitors HM Prison Manchester; member of: St James's Club; Lancashire County Cricket Club.

Biography: lives Manchester; born 21.10.1942; married with 3 children. Educated at Bury Grammar School (1954-1962); University of Cambridge (1962-1966); Open Scholar Gonville and Caius College; WM Tapp Scholar; (MA LLM); joint author of'Law of Trust' (1984); occasional lecturer in private taxation, trusts and the administration of estates.

Leisure: thespian (much in demand as director of contemporary plays and as an actor); active professional theatre and opera attender.

SHIPWRIGHT Adrian

tax partner SJ BERWIN & CO
236 Gray's Inn Road, London WC1X 8HB.

Career: Linklaters & Paines (1974-1977); official student and tutor Christ Church Oxford; lecturer in law Oxford University (1977-1982); partner Denton Hall Burgin & Warrens (1982-1987); became tax partner SJ Berwin & Co (1987).

Activities: visiting professor King's College London.

Biography: born 02.07.1950; married to Diana with 1 son and 1 daughter. Educated at King Edward VI School, Southampton; Christ Church Oxford (1972 BA) (1973 BCL) (1977 MA); editor and contributor to:'Strategic Tax Planning'; author:'UK Tax and Land Development';'UK Tax and Intellectual Property';'Volume 5 CCH British Tax Reporter'.

SHORT Michael

partner in charge of trade union and employment law department
ROWLEY ASHWORTH 247 The Broadway, London SW19 1SF.

Career: articled Lovell White & King (1977-1979); admitted (1979); assistant solicitor (1979-1980); assistant solicitor Lawford & Co (1980-1983); became partner (1983-1988); became partner Rowley Ashworth (1988).

Activities: member Industrial Law Society Executive Committee (1982-1989); advises number of large trade unions on legal matters.

Biography: lives Beckenham; born 02.05.1951; married to Anne with 2 sons. Educated at St Philip's Grammar School, Edgbaston; Sussex University (1973 BA hons); contributor to Industrial Law Journal; member Advisory Editorial board of Encyclopaedia of Labour Relations Law.

Leisure: sport; politics; discourse.

SHRAGO Ivor

partner commercial and industrial and Head of the Property Department
HAMLIN SLOWE PO Box 4SQ,
Roxburghe House, 273-287 Regent Street, London W1A 4SQ.

Career: articled H Davis & Co (1961-1966);

admitted (1966); assistant solicitor (1966-1968); partner (1968-1981); became senior partner (1981); merged with Hamlin Slowe (1987).

Activities: chairman British Anzani PLC (1978-1980); lectured in contract and property law; member of; Savile Club; East India Club; Lansdowne Club.

Biography: lives Teddington; born 13.12.1942; married with 1 daughter and 1 son. Educated at William Ellis School, London (1953-1961).

Leisure: hill walking; skiing; running; reading; theatre; cycling; concerts.

SHULMAN Jeremy

senior partner SHULMANS
21 York Place, Leeds LS1 2EX.

Career: articled Willey Hargrave (1973-1975); admitted (1975); assistant solicitor Fingret Paterson & Co (1975-1981); became partner (1976); founded own practice (1981); founded first legal insolvency practice in England and Wales Isadore Goldman Shulman (1989).

Activities: chairman Yorkshire Young Solicitors' Group (1979); chairman Professional and Public Relations Sub-committee of National Committee of Law Society's Young Solicitors' Group (1983-1986); chairman Independent Broadcasting Authority Local Radio Advisory Committee - Leeds/Wakefield (1981-1985); member Independent Broadcasting Authority General Advisory Committee (1985 to date); national chairman of the Law Society's Young Solicitors' Group (1987); member Law Society's Professional and Public Relations Committee (1983-1987); member Law Society's 1992 Working Party (1988 to date); member National Committee of Law Society's Young Solicitors' Group (1979-1989); set up Young Solicitors' Group network of media spokesmen; involved in a number of Young Solicitor Group publications/conferences; member of: Leeds Club; Wig & Pen Club; Moor Allerton Golf Club; Yorkshire County Cricket Club; Chapel Allerton Lawn Tennis and Squash Club.

Biography: lives Leeds; born 03.03.1952; married to Angie with 1 son. Educated at Richmond House School (1956-1960); Leeds Grammar School (1960-1969); Birmingham University (1972 LLB); College of Law Guildford (1972-1973) (Distinction Company Law); licensed insolvency practitioner.

Leisure: family; tennis; golf; watching

cricket and rugby; keen supporter Yorkshire County Cricket Club; music; the country.

SHURMAN Laurence

the Banking Ombudsman Citadel House, 5/11 Fetter Lane, London EC4A 1BR.

Career: articled John H Sinton & Co (1954-1957); admitted (1957); assistant solicitor Haswell Croft (1957-1958); assistant solicitor Hall Brydon (1958-1960); assistant solicitor Kaufman & Siegal (1960-1961); partner Shurman & Bindman (1961-1964); partner Shurman & Co (1964-1967); partner Kingsley Napley (1967-1975); managing partner (1975-1989).

Activities: legal member Mental Health Review Tribunal (1976 to date); president City of Westminster Law Society (1980-1981); member Council of Justice (1973 to date); member Leander.

Biography: lives London N6; born 25.11.1930; married to Mary with 3 children. Educated at Newcastle upon Tyne Grammar School; Magdalen College Oxford (MA); author of 'The Practical Skills of the Solicitor' (2nd ed 1985); contributor on Mental Health Review Tribunals in vol 26 Atkin's Encyclopaedia of Court Forms (2nd ed 1985).

Leisure: law reform; literature; fell walking; swimming; jogging.

SIBLEY Edward

senior litigation partner BERWIN LEIGHTON Adelaide House, London Bridge, London EC4R 9HA.

Career: articled Clifford Turner (1961-1964); admitted (1965); assistant solicitor Berwin & Co (1965); became partner (1968); founder partner Berwin Leighton merger (1970); admitted New York State Bar (1985); former managing partner Berwin Leighton.

Activities: member Litigation sub-committee City of London Solicitors' Company; member National Committee Union Internationale des Advocates; member American Bar Association; International Bar Association; the Law Society; New York State Bar; chairman Appeals Committee Youth Clubs UK; chairman Youth Committee Eastern Counties Rugby Union; governor Daiglen School; member of: Reform Club; Wig & Pen Club.

Biography: lives High Beach; born 21.07.1935; married to Sonia with 3 children. Educated at Rhymey Grammar

S

School; University of Wales (1961 LLB hons); College of Law Lancaster Gate (1964).

SILBER Stephen

Queen's Counsel 3 Gray's Inn Place, Gray's Inn, London WC1.

Career: called to the Bar (1968); QC (1987); Recorder of the Crown Court (1987).

Biography: lives London NW8 and Wiltshire; born 26.03.1944; married to Lucinda with 2 children. Educated at William Ellis School, London; University College London; Trinity College Cambridge; Heidelberg University; various articles.

Leisure: photography; walking; theatre; watching sport.

SILVERMAN Frances

principal lecturer COLLEGE OF LAW Braboeuf Manor, St Catherine's, Guildford, Surrey.

Career: articled in London; admitted (1973); College of Law (1973); became principal lecturer (1984).

Activities: voluntary work for CAB legal advice sessions .

Biography: lives near Billingshurst; born 03.09.1949; married with 2 sons. Educated at Alice Ottley School, Worcester; College of Law; author of: Silverman's Standard Conditions of Sale; Silverman's Searches and Enquiries; Handbook of Professional Conduct for Solicitors; contributor to Encyclopaedia of Forms and Precedents; Lawyers Remembrancer.

Leisure: passionate gardener and embroiderer (City and Guilds Embroidery Certificate; exhibits regularly as member of a group); tennis; pianist.

SIM Andrew

deputy solicitor and head of litigation division BRITISH RAILWAYS BOARD Macmillan House, PO Box 1016, Paddington Station, London W2.

Career: articled British Railways Board (1973-1975); admitted (1975); solicitor in commercial division (1975-1980); solicitor in litigation division (1980-1982); head of litigation division (1982 to date); became deputy solicitor (1986).

Biography: lives near Edenbridge; born 27.11.1948; married to Antonia with 3 children. Educated at Haileybury College, Hertford; City of London Polytechnic (1970 business law hons); College of Law Lancaster Gate (1971).

SIMANOWITZ Arnold

executive director ACTION FOR VICTIMS OF MEDICAL ACCIDENTS Bank Chambers, London Road, Forest Hill, London SE23 3TP.

Career: articled Levy Berman & Boerbaitz, Cape Town (1956-1961); admitted (1961); kibbutz worker (1961-1962); articled Sydney Hackman & Co (1962-1966); admitted (1966); admitted solicitor and barrister Zambia (1966); assistant solicitor Ellis & Co, Zambia (1966-1969); partner Armstrong & Co (1969-1975); partner Simanowitz & Brown (1975-1981); became director Action for Victims of Medical Accidents (1982).

Activities: chair Croydon Council for Community Relations (1974-1976); councillor London Borough of Croydon (1971-1974); chair Croydon North East Labour Party (1985-1989); consultant editor Personal & Medical Injuries Lawletter; editor The AVMA Medical & Legal Journal.

Biography: lives London SE19; born 12.12.1938; married with 2 children. Educated at Sea Point Boys' High School, Cape Town; University of Cape Town; written widely on medical accidents including: articles in: LAG Bulletin; The Lancet; Journal of the Medical Defence Union; contributor to 'Medical Negligence' - Powers and Harris (1990) and 'No Fault Compensation in Medicine' - Mann & Havard.

Leisure: travel; fell walking; rambling; politics; current affairs.

SIMEY George

senior partner FORD SIMEY DAW ROBERTS 8 Cathedral Close, Exeter, Devon EX1 1EZ.

Career: TA 4th Battalion The Devonshire Regiment and 1st Battalion The Wessex Regiment; retired Captain; admitted (1960); became partner Ford Simey Daw Roberts.

Activities: previous Under Sheriff Exeter; previous Under Sheriff Devon; former Chairman Devon and Cornwall CAB; former Chairman management committee Exeter CAB; former Chairman Governors of All Hallows School; member Exeter Housing Society Committee; former local Director Eagle Star Insurance Co Ltd; clerk to the General Commissioners in Exeter; clerk to the St Edmunds and St Mary Stepps Chrities; member of: Exeter Chamber of Commerce and Trade, Exeter CAB management committee, Riding for the Disabled Regional Committee; Trustee

for the Devonshire War (1914-1918) Memorial Scholarship Fund; member Exeter and Country Club; Hon Solicitor to the Devonshire & Dorset Regiment.

Biography: lives Exeter; born 23.04.1937; married with 4 children. Educated at All Hallows; Cranmore Hall; Downside (captain of shooting).

Leisure: gardening; tennis; stamps; listening to classical music; ballet; watching rugger; horses.

SIMKIN Graham

partner and head of corporate services and intellectual property group BOODLE HATFIELD 43 Brook Street, London W1Y 2BL.

Career: articled Boodle Hatfield (1974-1976); admitted (1976); assistant solicitor (1976-1978); became partner (1978); seconded to Paris as General Counsel to Terre Armee Internationale SA (1980-1984); founded intellectual property group (1985); head of corporate services (1988); member management committee (1988).

Activities: member RAC.

Biography: lives London; born 14.07.1952; married to Susan with 4 children. Educated at Handsworth Boys' Technical School; Leeds University (1973 LLB).

Leisure: theatre; wine appreciation.

SIMMONDS Jeremy Basil Canter

partner and head of banking and property finance department GLOVERS 115 Park Street, London W1Y 4DY.

Career: articled Radcliffes & Co (1964-1966); admitted (1967); assistant solicitor (1967-1969); partner (1969-1973); partner Glovers (previously Glover & Co) (1973 to date).

Activities: various public engagements including address to Royal Society of Arts (1974) speaking on the law of fish farming; member London Division Royal Naval Reserve (1963-1982); Reserve Decoration (1979); retired Lt Commander (1982); Liveryman of Fishmongers' Company (1980 to date); member Shellfish Association of Great Britain; chairman East Berkshire branch National Asthma Campaign; member Naval Club.

Biography: lives Cookham Dean, Berkshire; born 02.07.1941; married to Sally with 2 sons and twin daughters. Educated at Eagle House, Sandhurst; Trinity College, Glenalmond; Keble College, Oxford (1963 BA); two articles published in Solicitors' Journal (1990).

Leisure: walking; photography.

SIMMONS Michael

senior partner MALKIN JANNERS
PO Box 243, Inigo House, 29 Bedford
Street, Covent Garden, London WC2E 9RT.

Career: articled Whitehouse Gibson &
Alton (3 years); admitted (1958);
commission in Royal Air Force; became
salaried partner Malkin Cullis & Sumption.

Activities: admitted Hong Kong (1982);
member International Bar Association;
member American Bar Association; Fellow
of the British Institute of Management;
member Chartered Institute of Marketing;
member IBA; joint vice-chairman
Committee 10 of General Practice Section;
chairman Trustees of Divorce Conciliation
& Advisory Service; member Immigration
Committee of Justice; management
consultant to the professions in general
and lawyers in particular; member Law
Society; member RAC.

Biography: lives London N6 and
Roccatederighi, Italy; born 19.05.1933;
married with 4 children. Educated at St
Paul's School, London; Emmanuel College
Cambridge (1955 BA).

Leisure: journalism; listening to jazz;
watching association football; travel;
music; films.

SIMON Lyddon

partner RADCLIFFES & CO
10 Little College Street, Westminster,
London SW1P 3SJ.

Career: admitted attorney Transvaal, South
Africa (1959); admitted England (1963);
assistant solicitor (1963-1967); became
partner Radcliffes & Co (1967).

Activities: president Radcliffes Trustee
Company SA, Geneva; member Brooks's.

Biography: lives London; born 30.12.1934;
married with 2 children. Educated at King
Edward VII School; Witwatersand
University (1955 BA) (1958 LLB).

Leisure: sailing; squash; tennis.

SIMONS Bernard Michael

senior partner SIMONS MUIRHEAD &
BURTON Lading House, 10-14 Bedford
Street, London WC2E 9HE.

Career: taught at University of Virginia
Law School (1965-1966); articled Clinton
Davis & Co; admitted (1969); became
partner Sears Simons & Co; became
partner Clinton Davis Simons & Co;
became partner Simons Muirhead & Allan
(1972); firm became Simons Muirhead &
Burton (1987).

Activities: Assistant Recorder; member
Committee of the London Criminal Courts
Solicitors' Association (current chair Ethics
Committee); secretary Criminal Law
Committee of International Bar
Association; trustee of New Horizon Youth
Centre; many television appearances;
member Groucho Club.

Biography: lives London N5; born
23.03.1941; single. Educated at Wyggeston
Grammar School for Boys; Trinity Hall
Cambridge (1964 MA LLB) (Dr Cooper's
law studentship); wrote and presented a
series of six programmes about the law
'Cautionary Tales' on Channel Four
television; written articles in legal
periodicals both in this country and the
United States.

Leisure: opera; travel; gossip.

SIMONS Jonathan

senior partner HART FORTGANG
26 Market Place, London W1A 4BY.

Career: articled Landy Laufer (1966);
admitted (1971); assistant solicitor Hart
Fortgang (1971-1974); became partner
(1974); senior partner (1989).

Activities: member Legal Aid General
Committee (1976-1988); member Central
Middlesex Marriage Guidance Council
Management Committee (1974-1986);
member of: Law Society; Sandy Lodge Golf
Club; Northwood Squash Centre.

Biography: lives Hatch End; born
15.06.1947; married with 2 children.
Educated at Hasmonean Grammar School.

Leisure: sport.

SIMPSON Alasdair

senior partner MANCHES & CO
Aldwych House, 71/91 Aldwych, London
WC2B 4RP.

Career: articled Gregsons (1965-1967);
admitted (1967); assistant solicitor
Manches & Co (1967-1968); became partner
(1968); became senior partner (1981).

Activities: holds non-executive
directorships in substantial companies
within the shoe retailing and
manufacturing industries; wife and he
became first couple to be admitted at the
same admission ceremony (1967); legal
adviser to RAC Motor Sports Association,
The All England Showjumping Centre at
Hickstead and to a major French
corporation involved in the UK water
industry; member of: Royal Automobile
Club; Turf Club.

Biography: lives London NW3; born

10.03.1943; married to Jane with 3 children.
Educated at Queen Elizabeth Grammar
School, Carmarthen; London University
(LLB).

Leisure: charity and community work from
a low profile; tennis; thoroughbreds; claret;
Provence.

SIMPSON David

partner in charge of commercial
department TRUMP & PARTNERS
34 St Nicholas Street, Bristol BS1 1TS.

Career: articled Peter Wood (1961-1964);
admitted (1965); assistant solicitor in
Temple (1965-1967); assistant solicitor
Trump & Partners (1967-1970); became
partner (1970).

Activities: General Commissioner of Taxes
(1974 to date); chairman commissioners
(1986); President Bristol Law Society (1989-
1990); chairman No 4 Legal Aid Area
Committee; member Law Society Working
Group on Arbitration; member Institute of
Arbitrators (South West Committee);
member Council Bristol Law Society;
member British Institute of Management
(Bristol branch); company secretary of 40-
50 private companies inluding travel and
theatre ticket agencies; member Bristol &
Wessex Aero Club; governor various
schools in maintained and independent
sector; member Institute of Directors.

Biography: lives Burrington nr Bristol; born
31.01.1938; married with 4 children.
Educated at Queen's College; Christ's
College Cambridge (1961 BA) (1965 MA);
Exeter University (European Community
Law).

Leisure: flying light aircraft.

SIMPSON David

partner BOOTH & CO PO Box 8, Sovereign
House, South Parade, Leeds LS1 1HQ.

Career: partner Booth & Co.

Activities: member Alwoodley Golf
Course/Club.

Biography: lives Leeds; born 17.02.1941;
married. (1967 BA).

Leisure: golf.

SIMPSON Desmond

senior partner RC MOORHOUSE & CO
16 & 17 East Parade, Leeds LS1 2BR.

Career: articled Reginald Moorhouse (1948-
1951); admitted (1951); assistant solicitor
(1951-1955); became partner (1955).

Activities: licensed insolvency practitioner;

S

member Leeds Club.

Biography: lives Harrogate; born 11.05.1926; married to Patricia with 4 children. Educated at Wrekin College, Wellington.

SIMPSON Jane

partner and head of family law department MANCHES & CO Aldwych House, 71/91 Aldwych, London WC2.

Career: articled Manches & Co; admitted (1967); assistant solicitor (1967); became partner (1967-1968); counsellor with London Marriage Guidance Council (1972-1977); returned Manches & Co (1977).

Activities: co-founder Solicitors' Family Law Association; member Main Committee and chairman of the Education Committee.

Biography: lives London NW3; born 15.07.1942; married to Alasdair with 2 daughters and 1 son. Educated at Channing School, Highgate; University College London (1964 LLB).

Leisure: music; theatre; walking; horse racing.

SIMPSON John

Queen's Counsel 5 Paper Buildings; Temple, London EC4Y 7HB.

Career: called to the Bar Middle Temple (1937); pupillage with Mr John Bassett; Royal Artillery Military Intelligence and Control Commission for Germany (legal division) (1939-1945); successive legal appointments in Government service (1946-1972); retired as second legal adviser to the Foreign and Commonwealth Office; QC (1980).

Activities: led United Kingdom delegation at two sessions of the United Nations Sea Bed Committee (1971 & 1972); alternate president Arbitral Tribunals International Telecommunications Satellite Organisations (1974 & 1976); Freeman City of London (1976); member Dubai/Sharjah Boundary Court of Arbitration (1978-1981); chairman Appeals Board UNESCO (1980-1985).

Biography: lives London SW1; born 09.10.1912; married. Educated at George Watson's College, Edinburgh (1924-1930); Edinburgh University (1934 MA hons D Litt); CMG (1958); TD (1950); author of 'Germany and the North Atlantic Community: A Legal Survey' (with Sir Maurice Bathurst) (1956); 'International Arbitration: Law and Practice' (with Lady Michael Fox) (1959).

Leisure: literature; formerly hill walking.

SIMPSON John Rowton

senior partner HARVEY INGRAM STONE & SIMPSON 37 New Walk, Leicester LE1 6TX.

Career: articled Herbert Simpson Son & Bennett (1951-1954); admitted (1954); assistant solicitor (1954-1960); became partner (1960-1978); became senior partner Stone & Simpson (1978-1988); became senior partner Harvey Ingram Stone & Simpson (1988).

Activities: captain Leicestershire Golf Club (1972); president Rugby Football Union (1988-1989); Lt-Colonel Royal Engineers (1965) TD DL; chairman East Midlands Cadet Committee TAVR (1985-1989); member East India Club.

Biography: lives Leicester; born 19.09.1926; married to Roxane with 3 children. Educated at Rugby School (1940-1944); Magdalene College Cambridge (1951 MA LLM).

SIMPSON Keith

joint founding partner SIMPSON ROBERTSON & EDGINGTON 'Barringtons', Hockley Road, Rayleigh, Essex SS6 8EH.

Career: articled Mitchell Williams & Roland Thomas (1970-1972); admitted (1972); assistant solicitor (1972-1975); founded Simpson Robertson & Edgington (1975).

Activities: chairman Southend on Sea Young Solicitors' Group (1979-1981); Southend on Sea & District Law Society treasurer (1981-1988) (president 1988-1989) (joint secretary (1990 to date); member Essex County Cricket Club.

Biography: lives Leigh on Sea; born 18.02.1948; married to Denise. Educated at Royal Liberty School, Romford; Mid-Essex Technical College (1970 LLB hons); University of London (1969); Law Society (1970).

Leisure: fine dining; theatre; classical & contemporary concerts; foreign travel; bridge; most sports as spectator (particularly cricket).

SIMPSON Michael

partner and head of litigation department TODS MURRAY WS 66 Queen Street, Edinburgh EH2 4NE.

Career: apprentice Lindsays WS (1965-1967); admitted (1967); Writer to the Signet (1967); assistant solicitor J & RA Robertson WS (1967-1969); assistant solicitor Tods Murray WS (1969-1970); became partner

(1970).

Activities: member of: New Club; the Royal Scots Club.

Biography: lives Edinburgh; born 30.10.1941; married to Lesley with 3 children. Educated at Rugby School; Magdalen College Oxford (1963 BA); Edinburgh University (1965 LLB).

Leisure: reading; gardening; shooting; golf.

SINCLAIR Neil

senior partner BERWIN LEIGHTON Adelaide House, London Bridge, London EC4R 9HA.

Career: became senior partner Berwin Leighton (1970).

Activities: creator of the PINCs concept for property securitisation.

Biography: lives London; born 17.09.1937; married with 3 children. Educated at Caius College Cambridge; author of 'Warranties and Indemnities on Share Sales'; general editor and contributor to 'Practical Commercial Precedents'; contributor to 'Real Estate Finance'.

Leisure: mathematics; cycling.

SINCLAIR Sir Ian (McTaggart)

Queen's Counsel 2 Hare Court, Temple, London EC4Y 7BH.

Career: assistant legal adviser Diplomatic Service (1950-1957); called to the Bar Middle Temple (1952); legal adviser to the British Embassy, Bonn (1957-1960); legal adviser to UK delegation negotiating British entry into the EEC (1960-1963 & 1970-1972); legal adviser to UK Mission to UN and British Embassy, Washington (1964-1967); legal counsellor to the Foreign and Commonwealth Office (1966-1971); deputy legal adviser (1971-1973); second legal adviser (1973-1976); legal adviser (1976-1984); retired (1984); KCMG (1977); QC (1979); Bencher (1980); since retirement from FCO, has acted as Counsel for the UK government and foreign governments in several major international arbitrations, and has also advised on questions of public international law, private international law and comparative law.

Activities: deputy chairman of UK delegation to Vienna Conference on the Law of Treaties (1968-1969) (member Panel of Conciliators under Annex to the Convention (1981 to date); member International Law Commission (1981-1986); member Panel of Arbitrators of International Centre for Settlement of Investment Disputes (1988 to date);

member Bureau Steering Committee on Legal Cooperation in Europe (Council of Europe) (1979-1981); member panel of legal experts under INTELSAT Convention (1989 to date); chairman Public International Law Section of British Institute of International and Comparative Law; chairman International Committee of the International Law Association on 'Legal Aspects of Extraterritorial Jurisdiction'; member Executive Council, British Branch of International Law Association; hon member American Society of International Law (1987); associate member Institut de Droit International (1983) (member 1987); visiting professor McGeorge School of Law, Sacramento (1986); visiting professor in international law King's College, London (1989 to date); member Athenaeum.

Biography: lives London SW19 and Chithurst, West Sussex; born 14.01.1926; married to Barbara with 3 children. Educated at High School of Glasgow; Merchiston Castle School, Edinburgh (hon scholar); King's College Cambridge (1948 BA) (1949 LLB 1st class hons); author of: 'Vienna Convention on the Law of Trustees' (1973 & 1984); 'International Law Commission' (1987); contributor to 'Satow's Guide to Diplomatic Practice' (5th ed 1979); 'The Law of Sovereign Immunity: Recent Developments' (1980); numerous articles in British Year Book of International Law, the International and Comparative Law Quarterly and other legal journals.

Leisure: watching sea birds; golf; walking.

SINCLAIR HODGE Hamish (James)

senior commercial property partner DUNDAS & WILSON 25 Charlotte Square, Edinburgh EH2 4EZ.

Career: apprentice Dundas & Wilson (1964-1966); admitted (1966); assistant solicitor (1966-1968); became partner (1968).

Activities: member of: Bruntsfield Links Golfing Society; Blairgowrie Golf Club.

Biography: lives Edinburgh; born 30.11.1942; married with 2 children. Educated at Cambusdoon Prep School, Alloway; Fettes College, Edinburgh; Edinburgh University (1964 LLB).

Leisure: golf; curling.

SKELDING Barry

partner ROWE & MAW 20 Blackfriars Lane, London EC4V 6HD.

Career: articled Gamlens (1964-1969); admitted (1970); associate Gamlens (1970); group property solicitor EMI Ltd (1970-1980); assistant solicitor Rowe & Maw (1980-1981); became partner (1981).

Activities: member Royal Marlborough.

Biography: lives Radlett; born 02.01.1945; married to Margaret with 2 daughters. Educated at The Stationers' Company's School.

Leisure: competitive squash and tennis; music.

SKELTON Frank

a senior partner WYNNE BAXTER GODFREE 47 Gildredge Road, Eastbourne, East Sussex BN21 4RY.

Career: articled Town Clerk of Eastbourne County Borough Council (1961-1964); admitted (1964); assistant solicitor (1964-1965); assistant solicitor Wintle & Co (1965-1967); became partner (1967); became senior partner (1978); became senior partner Wynne Baxter Godfree upon merger with Wintle & Co (1988).

Activities: Cambridge Soccer Blue (1957-1959); captain Cambridge AFC (1959); president Downing College Amalgamation Club (1959-1960); president Eastbourne Law Society (1983-1984); member of: Hawks Club; Royal Eastbourne Golf Club.

Biography: lives Eastbourne; born 10.07.1936; married to Jane with 1 daughter and 1 son. Educated at North Manchester Grammar School; Downing College Cambridge (1960 BA) (1963 MA); Pilley Scholarship.

Leisure: golf; tennis; fell walking; old buses and trams; wine; sport.

SKELTON Jonathan

partner COZENS-HARDY & JEWSON Castle Chambers, Opie Street, Norwich, Norfolk NR1 3DP.

Career: articled Bond Pearce & Co (1971-1973); admitted (1973); assistant solicitor (1973-1975); assistant solicitor Cozens-Hardy & Jewson (1975-1976); became partner (1976).

Activities: former part-time lecturer Norwich City College on a legal executives' part one course; member Broadlands Rotary Club.

Biography: lives Norwich; born 09.01.1947; married to Anne with 4 children. Educated at Abbotsholme School; Exeter University (1968 LLB); Oxford (1970 BCL).

Leisure: walking; sailing; gardening; swimming.

SKINNARD Nicholas

partner BLIGHT BROAD & SKINNARD George Place, Callington, Cornwall.

Career: articled in Plymouth; admitted (1983); assistant solicitor Blight Board & Skinnard (1983-1987); became partner (1987).

Activities: member of: Vincent's Club; Royal Western Yacht Club.

Biography: lives South East Cornwall; born 22.11.1956; married to Paula with 1 son. Educated at Mount House School; Canford School; Oriel College Oxford (1981 BA hons) (1986 MA).

Leisure: rugby football; sailing.

SKINNER Jeremy

general corporate partner (previously tax partner) LINKLATERS & PAINES Barrington House, 59-67 Gresham Street, London EC2V 2JA.

Career: articled Linklaters (1962-1965); admitted (1965); assistant solicitor (1965-1967); became partner (1967).

Activities: governor Rugby School (1975 to date); member Law Society Tax Committee (1980-1984); founder and member Executive Committee Institute for Fiscal Studies; member of: Brooks's Club; HAC.

Biography: lives London W2 and North Hertfordshire; born 15.11.1936; married to Judy with 3 children. Educated at Rugby School; Clare College Cambridge (1960 BA).

Leisure: tennis; hunting.

SLADE David

partner STEPHENSON HARWOOD One St Paul's Churchyard, London EC4M 8SH.

Career: admitted (1966); assistant solicitor (1966-1969); became partner Constant & Constant (1969-1985); became partner Stephenson Harwood (1985).

Activities: member Baltic Exchange.

Biography: born 03.07.1941; married to Barbara with 3 children. Educated at St Peter's School; Emmanuel College Cambridge (1966 MA LLM).

Leisure: collecting paintings; antique furniture.

SLATER Richard

partner company/commercial department SLAUGHTER AND MAY 35 Basinghall Street, London EC2V 5DB.

Career: articled Slaughter and May (1970-1972); admitted (1972); assistant solicitor

S

(1972-1979); became partner (1979); Hong Kong office (1981-1986).

Biography: lives London NW8; born 18.08.1948; married to Julie with 3 children. Educated at University College School, Hampstead; Pembroke College Cambridge (1969 BA) (MA); article in Journal of Business Law and Transnational Law of International Business Transaction; fortnightly article in Trade Finance Asia (1985-1986).

Leisure: travel; photography; reading; theatre; opera; cinema; tennis; real tennis.

SLEATH Mike

partner in the property department SIMPSON CURTIS 41 Park Square, Leeds LS1 2NS.

Career: articled Simpson Curtis; admitted (1977); assistant solicitor ASDA Group PLC (1978-1981); assistant solicitor Simpson Curtis (1981); became partner (1981).

Activities: sports secretary Leeds Law Students' Society (1976-1977); chairman Yorkshire Young Solicitors' Group (1983); member National Committee of Young Solicitors' Group (1984-1988); member Planning & Environmental Law Committee of the Law Society (1987 to date); member Non-Contentious Business sub-committee of Leeds Law Society (1987 to date); hon legal adviser to the Thorp Arch Village Society; member of: Alwoodley Golf Club; Scarcroft Golf Club; Boston Spa Badminton Club.

Biography: lives Boston Spa; born 06.12.1952; married to Katie with 1 son and 1 daughter. Educated at Northampton Grammar School (1964-1971); Southampton University (1974); College of Law Chester.

Leisure: sport; golf; badminton; squash; cricket; family.

SLEIGHTHOLME John

barrister and head of chambers 38 Park Square, Leeds LS1 2PA.

Career: articled to the Town Clerk of Leeds; admitted (1968); West Riding County prosecuting solicitor (1968-1973); partner Carter Bentley & Gundhill (1973-1982); called to the Bar Gray's Inn (1982); head of Chambers (1986).

Activities: former solicitor agent to the DHSS and Selby District Council; various Legal Aid Committees; Freeman City of Glasgow; member of: Oakdale Golf Club; North Leeds Cricket Club; the Romany Cricket Club; Harrogate St Andrew's

Society.

Biography: lives Boston Spa; born 06.01.1942; married to Maureen. Educated at Leeds Grammar School; Leeds University (1965 LLB hons); College of Law Guildford (1968).

Leisure: most sports; playing cricket and golf; theatre; eating out; fine wines; foreign travel; novels with historical background; San Francisco; West coast of Scotland.

SLINGER Edward

senior partner RAMSBOTTOM & CO 25/29 Victoria Street, Blackburn BB1 6DN.

Career: articled Sharples Sons & Slinger (1958-1961); admitted (1961); assistant solicitor Ramsbottom & Co (1961-1964); became partner (1964).

Activities: president Old Accringtonians Association (1968); president Blackburn Incorporated Law Association (1986-1987); inaugural chairman Area 7B Regional Duty Solicitor Committee; Deputy Registrar (1981-1988); Assistant Recorder (1988 to date); hon solicitor Matthew Brown Lancashire Cricket League; member Blackburn Incorporated Law Association; local representative Solicitors' Benevolent Association; vice-chairman Discipline Committee of Test & County Cricket Board; governor St Leonard's C of E School, Samlesbury; governor Westholme School, Blackburn; official steward British Horse Society Pony Club Tetrathlon Competitions; member of: Lancashire CCC (trustee and vice- chairman; chairman Cricket Sub-committee); MCC; Commonwealth Lawyers' Association.

Biography: lives Samlesbury; born 02.02.1938; married to Rosalind with 4 children. Educated at Balliol College Oxford (1956 BA).

Leisure: completed Manchester Piccadilly Marathon (1984).

SLINGSBY Charles Anthony

senior commercial partner PAYNE HICKS BEACH 10 New Square, Lincoln's Inn, London WC2A 3QG.

Career: articled Macfarlanes; admitted (1969); assistant solicitor; became partner Payne Hicks Beach (1972).

Activities: past chairman London Young Solicitors; past chairman Solicitors' European Group; past president Young Lawyers' International Association; vice-president Association Europeene des Avocats; represents Law Society on Union International des Notaires Latins; secretary

Douglas Bader Foundation; member of: Garrick; Oriental Club; Hurlingham Club; RAC.

Biography: lives London W1; born 07.06.1943; married to Charlotta with 2 children. Educated at Rugby; Exhibitioner University College Oxford; Universite de Nancy; Post-qualifying Education Diploma in Insolvency Law and Administration, Institute of Chartered Secretaries (1988); Associate of Institute of Arbitrators (1985); articles in Law Society's Gazette and joint publication for use by Japanese businessmen investing in Europe.

Leisure: travel writing; photography; whitewater rafting; gardening.

SLY Christopher

partner and head of tax department JAQUES & LEWIS 2 South Square, Gray's Inn, London WC1R 5HR.

Career: articled Church Adams Tatham & Co (1972-1974); admitted (1974); assistant solicitor Jaques & Lewis (1974-1978); became partner (1978).

Biography: lives London N10; born 13.09.1949; married to Jill with 2 children. Educated at King's College School, Wimbledon; St John's College Cambridge (1971 BA hons) (MA); College of Law Lancaster Gate (1971-1972).

Leisure: theatre; cinema; family; travel; bridge.

SMALLWOOD Charles

litigation partner WATSON FARLEY & WILLIAMS Minories House, 2-5 Minories, London EC3N 1BJ.

Career: called to the Bar; articled Holman Fenwick & Willan; admitted (1979); assistant solicitor (1979-1983); Hong Kong office (1981-1983); became partner Watson Farley & williams (1983).

Activities: member RAC Club.

Biography: lives London SE10; born 11.02.1949; married to Tessa with 2 children. Educated at Wellington College, Crowthorne; Oxford (1971 LLB); occasional contributor to 'Credit and Finance Law'.

Leisure: sailing; skiing.

SMART Norman

consultant FIELD FISHER WATERHOUSE 41 Vine Street, London EC3N 2AA.

Career: Army 2nd Lt RA (1945-1948); articled (1951-1954); admitted (1954); assistant solicitor (1954-1959); became partner (1959).

Activities: patron of Gower Festival and Swansea Festival of Music and the Arts; member United Oxford and Cambridge University Club.

Biography: lives London W2 and Swansea; born 12.01.1927; married to Vera. Educated at Eton College; Edinburgh University; King's College Cambridge (MA LLB); minor scholar.

Leisure: contract bridge player; writer.

SMERDON Richard

senior lawyer of the corporate and commercial department OSBORNE CLARKE 6 Middle Street, London EC1A 7JA.

Career: articled Slaughter and May (1963-1966); admitted (1966); assistant solicitor Osborne Clarke (1968-1969); became partner (1969).

Activities: choral exhibitioner at Christ Church; president Oxford University Law Society (1962); lectured in law at the Western Reserve Law School, Cleveland, Ohio; member Small Business Committee and High Technology Sub-committee American Bar Association; member Schola Cantorum (a group attached to the Benslow Music Trust); member Help Tibet Trust; founder and past chairman The Coach House Small Business Centre; chairman St Andrew's Conservation Trust; chairman Bath International Festival Foundation; member choir of St Mary's Church, Barnes; recently returned from 3 months sabbatical in India where worked with missionaries of charity (Mother Teresa); hon life member Gloucestershire County Cricket Club.

Biography: lives London SW13 and Bristol; born 20.05.1942. Educated at West House Preparatory School, Birmingham; King Edward's Grammar School, Aston; Christ Church Oxford (1966 MA); joint editor Butterworths Company Law Service.

Leisure: singing; early music; opera; theatre; eating and entertaining; reading books on cricket.

SMITH Alan

secretary and solicitor to SMITHS INDUSTRIES PLC 765 Finchley Road, London NW11 8DS.

Career: brand assistant Procter & Gamble Ltd; articled Pennington & Son; admitted; assistant solicitor Smiths Industries (1966-1969); head of legal department (1969-1972); special director (1972-1977); deputy secretary (1977-1983); associate director

(1983-1986); became secretary (1986).

Biography: lives London; born 15.05.1938; married with 2 children. Educated at Cheltenham Grammar School; Pembroke College Oxford (1961 MA); College of Law (1962-1963).

Leisure: tennis; opera; ballet; theatre.

SMITH Charles

partner PENNINGTONS 9-19 London Road, Newbury, Berks RG13 1JL.

Career: articled Watsons & Morse; admitted (1966); set up consultancy department Jordan & Sons Ltd (1966); joined board as director of legal services (1976); private practice Hong Kong (1980); founded Court Business Services Ltd (1980); became partner Penningtons (1985).

Activities: lectured extensively to local law societies; groups of accountants; company secretaries and academic institutions; hon solicitor to local chamber of commerce; school governor; member Royal Commonwealth Club.

Biography: lives Newbury; born 24.05.1942; married to Judith with 3 children. Educated at Mercers School; Eltham College; London University (1964 LLB hons); written several articles published in the legal and accountancy technical press both in Hong Kong and UK; conceived, wrote and edits the encyclopaedia 'Company Procedures Manual'.

Leisure: hang-gliding.

SMITH David

contact partner commercial property department SHEPHERD & WEDDERBURN WS 16 Charlotte Square, Edinburgh EH2 4YS.

Career: admitted (1971); assistant solicitor (1971-1974); became partner Shepherd & Wedderburn (1974).

Activities: member of: The Honourable Company of Edinburgh Golfers; Bruntsfield Links Golfing Society.

Biography: lives Edinburgh; born 17.11.1947; married to Anne with 1 son and 1 daughter. Educated at Fettes College, Edinburgh; Edinburgh University (1969 LLB).

Leisure: hockey; golf; walking.

SMITH Janet

Queen's Counsel 5 Essex Court, Temple, London EC4 9AH.

Career: called to the Bar Lincoln's Inn

(1972); QC (1986); Recorder of Crown Court (1988).

Activities: member Criminal Injuries Compensation Board (1988).

Biography: lives Bolton; born 29.11.1940; married to Robin Mathieson with 3 children from first marriage. Educated at Bolton School.

SMITH Michael

senior partner TITMUSS SAINER & WEBB 2 Serjeants' Inn, London EC4Y 1LT.

Career: articled Titmuss Sainer & Webb (1963-1970); admitted (1970); assistant solicitor (1970-1972); became partner (1972).

Biography: lives near Guildford; born 30.05.1945; married to Wendy with 2 children. Educated at Cheltenham College Junior School; Cheltenham College; Sorbonne, Paris.

Leisure: opera; good food and wine; skiing.

SMITH Paul

partner CUFF ROBERTS NORTH KIRK 25 Castle Street, Liverpool L2 4TD.

Career: articled Cuff Roberts & Co (1975-1977); admitted (1977); assistant solicitor (1977-1980); became partner (1980).

Activities: member Liverpool Young Solicitors' Group (1980-1988) (chairman 1985); member National Committee Young Solicitors' Group (1981-1988 (secretary 1984-1988); member Law Society Land Law and Conveyancing Committee (1982-1984) and Professional Purposes Committee (1984-1986); member of: Oxton Cricket Club; Liverpool Racquet Club.

Biography: lives Birkenhead; born 05.04.1953; single. Educated at St Anselm's College, Birkenhead; University College London (1974 LLB).

Leisure: tennis; music; theatre; cinema; walking.

SMITH Peter

head of Programme Legal Services THAMES TELEVISION 306 Euston Road, London NW1 3BB.

Career: lecturer/senior lecturer in law University Hall (1973-1974) and Wolverhampton Polytechnic (1974-1982); called to the Bar Middle Temple (1980); legal adviser Midland News Association 'Express & Star' (1977-1982); became legal adviser Thames Television (1982-1987); 'News on Sunday' (1987) .

Biography: lives Wimbledon; born 21.07.1951; single. Educated at Lincoln School; Kingston Polytechnic (1973 LLB); Inns of Court School of Law (1979-1980); contributor to 'International Media Law'; various newspaper articles; TV programmes: 'Murder at the Farm' (1987); 'Waldheim' (1988).

Leisure: reading nineteenth and twentieth century novels; history; politics; soccer; cricket; running; Wolverhampton Wanderers FC.

SMITH Peter

senior partner SMITH LLEWELLYN PARTNERSHIP 18 Princess Way, Swansea SA1 3LW.

Career: articled Ivor Evans & Benjamin; admitted (1972); became partner (1972-1975); founded practice with HM Spring (1975).

Activities: hon secretary Aberavon Green Stars RFC, Port Talbot.

Biography: lives Neath; born 25.08.1948; married to Anita with 1 child. Educated at St Clare's Convent, Porthcawl; Dyffryn Grammar School, Port Talbot; College of Law Guildford (1972 hons); Assoc Law Society of Wales Prize Winner (1972).

Leisure: all sports; antique collecting.

SMITH Peter

chief executive NORTON ROSE M5 GROUP The Priory Queensway, Birmingham B4 6BS.

Career: lecturer in law Hull University (1971-1973); lecturer in law Nottingham University (1973-1984); senior lecturer (1984-1987); warden Cripps Hall (1978-1985); director of training M5 (1987-1988); managing director M5 Ltd (1988-1990); became Chief Executive Norton Rose M5 Group (1990).

Biography: lives Harborne; born 23.09.1950; married to Louise with 1 child. Educated at Manchester Grammar School; Nottingham University (1971 LLB); various texts on the English legal system in particular (with SH Bailey) 'The Modern English Legal System', welfare law and company and commercial law; articles and reviews in journals.

Leisure: association football; cricket.

SMITH Peter

partner BERRY & BERRY 1/5 Longley Road, Walkden, Worsley, Manchester M28 6AA.

Career: articled Hall Brydon & Co; admitted (1954); assistant solicitor (1954-1957); assistant solicitor Alan Ashcroft (1957-1959); became partner JW Francis & Co (1959); amalgamated with Berry & Berry (1961).

Activities: panellist on the Solicitors' Complaints Bureau; chairman Social Security Appeal Tribunals (1978 to date); president Bolton Law Society (1985); member local CAB management Committee; member Rotary Club of Walkden.

Biography: lives Bolton; born 31.03.1931; married to Sheila with 4 children. Educated at Ackworth School, Yorkshire; Manchester University (1951 hons).

Leisure: choral singing; Rotary activities; helping to run local Abbeyfield Society; walking; gardening.

SMITH Richard

partner and head of divorce and family department PARIS SMITH & RANDALL 9 College Place, Southampton.

Career: articled Bell Pope & Bridgwater; admitted (1970); assistant solicitor (1970-1972); assistant solicitor Paris Smith & Randall (1972-1973); became partner (1973).

Activities: former member Law Society Yacht Club Dinghy Team; member of: Southampton and District Solicitors' Golf Society; Stoneham Golf Club; Southampton Shipping Golfing Society; Trojans Club (former hon sec).

Biography: lives Southampton; born 30.07.1945; married to Jane with 2 children. Educated at Oakmount Prep School, Southampton; King Edward VI School, Southampton; Canford School, Wimborne (head of house; deputy head of school; 1st XV rugby; 1st XI hockey; captain sailing; captain fives; winner National Public Schools Sailing Championships); Southampton University (1967 LLB hons) (sailing colours); College of Law Guildford.

Leisure: tennis; golf; snow and water skiing; dinghy sailing; windsurfing.

SMITH Robin

managing partner DIBB LUPTON BROOMHEAD 6 Butts Court, Leeds LS1 5JX.

Career: articled Dibb Lutpon (1964-1966); admitted (1966); assistant solicitor (1966-1969); became partner (1969-1986); became managing partner (1986); became managing partner Dibb Lupton

Broomhead (1988).

Activities: chairman Solicitors' Financial and Property Services Limited (1988 to date); chairman the Law Society Professional and Public Relations Committee (1986-1987); chairman the Law Society Remuneration and Practice Development Committee (1987-1988); secretary Leeds Law Society (1980-1982); council member the Law Society (1982 to date); pioneered development of legal applications software for County Court debt collection with Simon Chalton (1970s); formed (with Simon Chalton) Law Data Systems Ltd (1977); member TA (The Light Infantry) for 22 years (recently retired with rank of Lt Colonel); trustee RC Diocese of Leeds; member of: Army and Navy Club; Leeds Club.

Biography: lives Leeds; born 15.02.1943; married to Jennifer with 1 son and 1 daughter. Educated at St Michael's College; Manchester University (1963 LLB); College of Law Guildford (1963-1964).

Leisure: golf; tennis.

SMITH Roger

senior partner PRICE & SON 33 Hill Lane, Haverfordwest, Dyfed SA61 1PS.

Career: articled Price & Son; admitted (1955); National Service commissioned in the Gunners (Royal Artillery) (1955-1957); assistant solicitor Price & Son (1958-1961); became partner (1961).

Activities: Undersheriff for the Town and County of Haverfordwest (retired); president of the West Wales Law Society (1976-1977); president Pembrokeshire Law Society (1984-1986); member Legal Aid Area Committee; Rotarian; member Cardiff & Country Club.

Biography: lives Haverfordwest; born 09.05.1932; married to Sadie with 1 son. Educated at Llandovery College; University College of Wales (1952 LLB hons).

Leisure: golf.

SMITH Roger

director LEGAL ACTION GROUP 242 Pentonville Road, London N1 9UN.

Career: articled Allen & Overy (1971-1973); admitted (1973); solicitor Camden Law Centre (1973-1975); director West Hampstead Law Centre (1975-1979); researcher NCCL/freelance advocate (1979-1980); solicitor Child Poverty Action Group (1980-1986); became director Legal Action Group (1986).

Activities: took Jackie Drake's invalid care allowance case to the European Court and won on unlawful discrimination against married women (1986).

Biography: lives London with partner and 2 children. Educated at Whitgift, Croydon; York University (BA); author of 'Children & The Courts' (1981); numerous articles largely in LAG's Legal Action.

Leisure: flute playing; walking; reading.

SMITH Tim

head of legal and business affairs AVL LABELS (VIRGIN RECORDS LTD) Kensal House, 553-578 Harrow Road, London W10 4RH.

Career: articled Balin & Co (1978-1982); admitted (1983); assistant solicitor (1982-1983); assistant solicitor Leonard Ross & Craig (1983-1985); assistant solicitor Clintons (1985-1987); partner (1987); became head of legal and business affairs AVL Virgin Records Ltd (1989).

Activities: heavily involved in local Baptist Church (lay preacher); member Albanian Society.

Biography: lives Croydon; born 05.04.1958; married. Educated at Reigate Grammar School; College of Law Chancery Lane and Guildford.

Leisure: playing football; cricket; music; theatre; restoring 1956 Vauxhall Wyvern; collecting 1930s memorabilia.

SMITH Timothy

senior partner LEE CROWDER 24 Harborne Road, Edgbaston, Birmingham B15 3AD.

Career: articled Sharpe Pritchard & Co (1950-1953); admitted (1953); assistant solicitor Richards Butler & Co (1953-1955); assistant solicitor Lee Crowder (1956).

Activities: director Airflow Streamlines plc; British Empire Medal; member Army & Navy Club.

Biography: lives Worcester; born 29.08.1926; married to Elizabeth with 3 children. Educated at West House Preparatory School; Rugby School; University College Oxford (MA).

Leisure: gardening; fishing.

SMITHSON Bobby

senior partner STANTON CROFT 46 Grainger Street, Newcastle upon Tyne NE1 5LB.

Career: taught classics, games, cricket,

rugger and rugby fives Durham School; articled Wilkinson Marshall Clayton & Gibson (1965-1967); admitted (1968); assistant solicitor Haswell Croft & Co (1968-1969); became partner (1969); firm amalgamated with Stanton Atkinson & Bird to become Stanton Croft & Co (1971); became senior partner (1988).

Activities: chairman Northumberland County Cricket Club (1984 to date); president Northumberland Schools' Cricket Association; president Northumberland Cricket Association; member of: Hawks Club; Northumberland Golf Club Ltd.

Biography: lives Gosforth; born 23.01.1930; married to Sheila with 1 daughter. Educated at Durham School (1943-1948); St John's College Cambridge (1953 BA hons) (1957 MA).

Leisure: golf; Shakespeare (reading and theatre); Times Crossword (non-competitive); classical music; opera; concerts; amateur piano playing; bridge.

SNAPE Royden

consultant to DAVID SNAPE Wyndham House, Wyndham Street, Bridgend, Mid Glamorgan CF31 1EP.

Career: Royal Regiment of Artillery (1940-1946); commissioned (1941); Major (1946); admitted (1949); founded own practice (1949).

Activities: deputy circuit Judge (1975-1979); Crown Court Recorder (1979); chairman Medical Appeal Tribunal (1985 to date); member of: Royal Porthcawl Golf Club; Cardiff Athletic Club; Glamorgan County Cricket Club.

Biography: lives Cowbridge; born 20.04.1922; married to Jo with 2 children. Educated at Bromsgrove.

Leisure: golf; rugby union football; cricket; swimming.

SNOWDON Bill

a commercial lawyer, partner in charge of marketing and practice development PHOENIX WALTERS 48 The Parade, Cardiff CF2 3AB.

Career: articled Adams & Black (1977-1979); admitted (1979); became partner Phoenix Walters (1982).

Activities: monthly radio broadcasts on general legal topics on local commercial radio station (3 years).

Biography: lives Cardiff; born 12.09.1954; married to Joan with 2 children. Educated at Radnor Road Primary School, Cardiff

(1959-1965); Cantonian High School, Cardiff (1965-1972); Queen Mary College, London (1973-1976); College of Law Lancaster Gate (1977).

Leisure: junior level and veteran rugby including various international tours; golf.

SOBELL Brian

senior partner SAUNDERS SOBELL LEIGH & DOBIN 20 Red Lion Street, London WC1R 4AE.

Career: articled to father (partner and one of the founders) at Saunders Sobell Leigh & Dobin (1954-1959); admitted (1959); assistant solicitor (1959-1960); became partner (1960); became senior partner (1974); became managing partner (1988).

Activities: vice-captain Hartsbourne Golf Club.

Biography: lives Radlett; born 31.08.1937; married to Angela with 4 children. Educated at St Paul's School; College of Law Lancaster Gate.

Leisure: golf.

SOLOMON David

partner and chief executive DJ FREEMAN & CO 1 Fetter Lane, London EC4A 1BR.

Career: admitted (1955); National Service with Royal Hampshire Regiment (1955-1957); assistant solicitor (1957-1961); became partner Nabarro Nathanson (1961-1968); private business activities (1968-1976); became partner DJ Freeman & Co (1976).

Activities: member Council Oriental Ceramic Society.

Biography: lives London N6; born 31.08.1930; married to Hazel with 3 children. Educated at Torquay Grammar School; author of numerous articles and lectures on: property development agreements; overseas investment in UK property; unitisation and securitisation of property.

Leisure: collecting early Chinese ceramics; architecture; modern art; music; Tai Chi.

SOUNDY Andrew J

partner ASHURST MORRIS CRISP Broadwalk House, 5 Appold Street, London EC2A 2HA.

Career: admitted (1966); assistant solicitor Ashurst Morris Crisp (1966-1969); became partner (1969).

Activities: member Cavalry & Guards Club.

S

Biography: lives Mattingley; born 29.03.1940; married to Jill with 1 son and 2 daughters. Educated at Boxgrove School, Guildford (1948-1953); Shrewsbury School, Salop (1953-1958); Trinity College Cambridge (1963 MA).

Leisure: pedigree cattle breeding; opera; tennis; good living.

SOUTHEY Verner George

senior company commercial partner CLYDE & CO 51 Eastcheap, London EC3M 1JP.

Career: admitted Rhodesia (1967); assistant attorney Rhodesia (1967-1970); became partner Calderwood Bryce Hendrie & Partners, Bulawayo (1970-1975); admitted England (1977); became partner Wedlake Bell (1978-1979); became partner Elborne Mitchell (1979-1986); became partner Clyde & Co (1986).

Biography: lives London; born 01.10.1942; married with 2 children. Educated at Aidan's College, Grahamstown; Cape Town University (BA); external student London University (LLB).

SOUTHWELL Richard

Queen's Counsel 1 Hare Court, Temple, London EC4.

Career: QC.

Activities: Deputy President Lloyds Appeal Tribunal; Chairman, Legal Services and Professional Standard Committees of Bar Council.

Biography: married to Belinda. Educated at Maidwell Hall, Winchester; Trinity College Cambridge; author of 'Quality of Justice' the Bar Council's 'Blue Book' response to the Lord Chancellor's Green Papers.

SPALDING Bruce

barrister New Court, Temple, London EC4Y 9BE.

Career: called to the Bar (1955).

Activities: part-time chairman Social Security Tribunals (1989 to date); member Bar Council and Law Society Joint Working Party on Intellectual Property (1977 to date); member Travellers' Club.

Biography: lives London; born 28.07.1930; divorced with 1 child. Educated at Clifton Hall School; Merchiston Castle School; St Andrew's University(1952 hons).

Leisure: reading; golf.

SPEKER Barry

senior partner SAMUEL PHILLIPS & CO 86 Pilgrim Street, Newcastle upon Tyne NE1 6SR.

Career: articled in Newcastle upon Tyne; admitted (1971); assistant solicitor Samuel Phillips & Co (1971-1973); became partner (1973); became senior partner (1987).

Activities: member and interviewer for Law Society's Child Care Panel; member Law Society's Mental Health Review Tribunal Panel; local Law Society contact person for Lawyers for Enterprise Scheme; chairman Professional Purposes Sub-committee of Newcastle Law Society; member Council Newcastle upon Tyne Incorporated Law Society; member Area No 8 Legal Aid General Committee; member BAAF Legal Group Committee; legal adviser Barnardo's North East; legal adviser to NSPCC, Newcastle upon Tyne; legal adviser to Newcastle Health Authority; member Committee of North East Medico-Legal Society; member of Committee of West Newcastle Victim Support Scheme; member Executive Committee North East Council on Addictions (NECA); treasurer Lifestyle; regular lecturer on child care law, mental health law and medical negligence and contributer to courses and seminars; convenor of North East Child Care Panel Support Group; member of the Advisory Group to the North of Tyne Panel of Guardians ad Litem; member Arcot Hall Golf Club.

Biography: lives Newcastle upon Tyne; born 28.06.1947; married with 2 children. Educated at Heaton Grammar School, Newcastle-upon- Tyne; London University (LLB hons); London University Prize winner (1967).

Leisure: golf; local debating society; amateur dramatics; football; The Times Crossword.

SPEKER David

partner and head of litigation department KINGSLEY NAPLEY 107/115 Long Acre, London WC2E 9PT.

Career: admitted (1969); assistant solicitor (1969-1974); became partner Kingsley Napley (1974).

Activities: vice-president City of Westminster Law Society; member golf club committee.

Biography: lives London; born 19.11.1943; married to Sheila with 1 son and 1 daughter. Educated at Heaton Grammar School, Newcastle upon Tyne; Durham

University (LLB); College of Law Guildford (1965-1966).

Leisure: golf; sport generally; theatre; food.

SPENCE Malcolm

town and country planning Queen's Counsel 8 New Square, Lincoln's Inn, London WC2A 3QP.

Career: pupillage with Nigel Bridge (now Lord Bridge of Harwich); Chambers of John Widgery QC (1959 to date); Recorder of the Crown Court; Bencher of Gray's Inn.

Activities: member of the Committee of Local Government and Planning Bar Association; member of Hawks Club.

Biography: lives Richmond; born 23.03.1934; married to Jane with 2 children. Educated at Summer Fields, Oxford; Stowe; Gonville and Caius College Cambridge (MA LLM); Gray's Inn James Mould Scholar; Holker Senior Exhibitioner; Lee Prizemen; author of 'Rating and Valuation Law Practice and Procedure'.

Leisure: trout fishing.

SPENCER Derek Harold

Queen's Counsel 5 King's Bench Walk, Temple, London EC4.

Career: 2nd Lt King's Own Royal Regiment; served in Nigeria (1954-1956); called to the Bar Gray's Inn (1961); Recorder of the Crown Court (1979); QC (1980).

Activities: Councillor London Borough of Camden (1978-1983) (deputy leader Conservative group 1979-1982); MP for Leicester South (1983-1987); PPS to Home Office Ministers (1986); PPS to Attorney General Rt Hon Sir Michael Havers QC MP (1986-1987); secretary Conservative Backbench Legal Committee (1985-1986); member Norfolk Club.

Biography: lives London SW1; born 31.03.1936; married to Caroline with 3 children from first marriage. Educated at Clitheroe Royal Grammar School; Keble College Oxford (1959 MA) (1960 BCL); Holt Scholar; Arden Scholar of Gray's Inn.

Leisure: reading; swimming; travelling.

SPENCER John Needham

clerk to the justices LAW COURTS Westwey Road, Weymouth, Dorset DT4 8BS.

Career: called to Bar Inner Temple (1963); deputy clerk Inner London Magistrates' Court (1964-1965); deputy chief clerk (1965-1973).

Activities: hon legal adviser Brentford and Chiswick CAB (1968-1973); training officer for Dorset Magistrates; secretary Dorset branch of the Magistrates' Association; secretary Weymouth & Portland advisory sub-committee on the appointment of Magistrates; member Lord Chancellor's Magistrates' Courts Rules Committee; member Magistrates' Association Road Traffic Committee.

Biography: lives Sherborne; born 07.06.1936; married to Brenda with 2 children. Educated at Stamford School; Cambridge (1958 BA) (1959 LLB) (1961 MA) (1985 LLM); joint editor Wilkinson's Road Traffic Offences (1979 to date); author 'Questions and Answers on Motoring Law'; series of articles on the Monmouth Rebellion and many articles on legal and historical topics in various legal journals including the Justice of the Peace, the Journal of Criminal Law and the Solicitors Law Journal.

Leisure: historical and literary dabbling; village pastimes.

SPENCER Shan

partner and head of litigation department WILLIAM PRIOR & COMPANY 4th Floor, Bernard House, Piccadilly Plaza, Manchester M1 4DD.

Career: articled Addleshaw Sons & Latham; admitted (1977); assistant solicitor William Prior & Co (1978-1980); became partner (1980).

Activities: licensed insolvency practitioner (1987); member Association of Women Solicitors.

Biography: lives Hale; born 05.01.1953; married to Andrew with 2 children. Educated at Altrincham County Grammar School for Girls; Sheffield University (1974 LLB).

Leisure: badminton; reading; theatre.

SPOKES John

Queen's Counsel 3 Pump Court, Temple, London EC4Y 7AJ.

Career: called to the Bar Gray's Inn (1955); Bencher (1985); Western circuit; head of Chambers (1982 to date); QC (1973); Recorder of the Crown Court (1972).

Activities: legal assessor to the General Medical Council (1982 to date); Chancellor of Winchester Diocese (1985 to date); chairman Data Protection Tribunal (1985 to date); member Bar Council (1961-1964); junior prosecuting Counsel to Inland Revenue on Western circuit (1972-1973);

chairman Statutory Inquiry under National Health Service Act - Sharon Campbell Inquiry (1988); council member Medico-Legal Society; member of: Leander; Vincent's; United Oxford & Cambridge University.

Biography: lives Winchester; born 06.02.1931; married to Jean with 2 children. Educated at Westminster School; Brasenose College Oxford (1951-1954 MA).

Leisure: walking; gardening; ornithology.

SPRAGUE Christopher William

partner and specialist in maritime and insurance litigation INCE & CO Knollys House, 11 Byward Street, London EC3R 5EN.

Career: articled Simmons & Simmons (1966-1969); admitted (1970); assistant solicitor Ince & Co (1970-1974); became partner (1975).

Activities: subscribing member Association of Average Adjudicators; supporting member London Maritime Arbitrators' Association; lecturer on maritime law topics; member Thames Regional Umpires' Commission; Liveryman Worshipful Company of Barbers; member Guildford Diocesan Bellringers' Guild; member of: United Oxford & Cambridge Club; London Rowing Club; Leander.

Biography: lives Shamley Green; born 19.08.1943; married to Clare with 4 daughters. Educated at St Edward's School, Oxford; Christ Church Oxford (1965 MA); College of Law; articles on transport law in Business Law and on disaster litigation in Bulletin of International Litigation Practitioners' Forum.

Leisure: reading history; rowing; bellringing.

STALLARD William

senior partner JOHN STALLARD & CO 3 Pierpoint Street, Worcester WR1 1TD.

Career: National Service with 1st Battalion The Worcestershire Regiment (1956-1958); articled Waltons (1961-1964); admitted (1965); became partner John Stallard & Co (1965).

Activities: president West Midlands Association of Law Societies (1988-1989); president The Worcester and Worcestershire Incorporated Law Society (1988-1989); hon secretary Cheluvelt Homes; Governor of The Royal Grammar School Worcester; governor Ellerslie School Malvern; member of: Union & County

Club Worcester (chairman); Hadley Bowling Club; The Clothiers Company, Worcester; Worcester Hockey Club; Worcestershire County Cricket Club.

Biography: lives Colwall; born 15.03.1938; married to June with 3 children. Educated at Bromsgrove School (1951-1956); St John's College Cambridge (1961 MA LLM).

Leisure: rugby; football; cricket; tennis; squash; athletics; hockey (former county player); history; music; theatre; arts; fine wines; travel.

STAMLER Sam

Queen's Counsel and head of chambers 1 Essex Court, Temple, London EC4Y 9AR.

Career: called to the Bar (1949); QC (1971); Bencher Middle Temple; Recorder (1974-1989).

Activities: member Athenaeum.

Biography: lives London; born 03.12.1925; married to Honor with 3 children. Educated at Berkhamsted; King's College Cambridge (MA LLB).

Leisure: walking; swimming; grandchildren.

STANBROOK Clive

senior partner STANBROOK AND HOOPER 42 Rue du Taciturne 42, 1040 Brussels, Belgium.

Career: called to the Bar (1972); pupillage 5 Pump Court (1972-1973); pupillage 5 Paper Buildings (1973); Brussels (1977); QC (1989).

Activities: president of the British Chamber of Commerce for Belgium and Luxembourg (1985-1987) (chairman Legislation and Taxation Committee 1983-1984); OBE (1988).

Biography: lives Brussels; born 10.04.1948; married to Julia with 4 children. Educated at the Dragon School, Oxford; Westminster School (1961-1966); Milton Academy, USA (1966-1967); University College London (1971 LLB hons); author of 'Extradition - the Law and Practice ' (1980); 'Dumping' (1980); co-author 'Dumping and Subsidies' (1983); co-editor 'International Trade Law and Practice'.

Leisure: tennis; sailing.

STANFIELD Brian

legal director UK trading operations GRAND METROPOLITAN PLC 11/12 Hanover Square, London W1A 1DP.

Career: articled Alastair Thomson (1955-

S

1958); admitted (1958); assistant solicitor Allbone George & Co and Taylor Wilcocks & Co (1958-1961); legal adviser (South); assistant legal adviser and senior assistant legal adviser Esso UK Ltd (1961-1970); group solicitor Watney Mann Ltd (now Grand Metropolitan PLC) (1970); became legal director UK trading operations.

Activities: member City of Westminster Law Society (president 1978-1979); Court assistant Worshipful Company of Makers of Playing Cards Master (1992-1993); Court City University; director Business in the Cities; member of: Savile Club; Lansdowne Club.

Biography: lives Epsom; born 12.07.1934; married to Janet with 2 children. Educated at Tottenham County School; London School of Economics; articles in Law Society's Gazette (1970s).

STANGER Elizabeth

partner and head of litigation department REES EDWARDS MADDOX King Edward House, New Street, Birmingham B2 4QW.

Career: articled Ryland Martineau & Company; admitted (1981); assistant solicitor (1981-1983); assistant solicitor Rees Edwards Maddox (1983); became head of litigation department (1984); became associate partner (1985); became equity partner (1986).

Activities: member Birmingham Young Solicitors' Group (1981-1988); member National Committee of Young Solicitors (1981-1987); non-council member Law Society Indemnity Committee (1986-1987); non-council member Law Society Standards and Guidance Committee (1987 to date).

Biography: lives Menith Wood; single. Educated at Eastbourne Girls' High School; Birmingham University (1985-1988 LLB).

Leisure: entertaining and socialising; theatre; opera; bridge; skiing; riding; reluctant gardener.

STANGER Kenneth

senior partner MCKINNELLS 188 High Street, Lincoln LN5 7BE.

Career: articled British Oxygen Co Ltd; admitted (1963); assistant solicitor (1963-1966); became partner McKinnells (1966); became senior partner (1979).

Biography: lives Lincoln; born 17.04.1934; married to Glynis with 3 children and 2 stepchildren. Educated at Barking Abbey School; external (LLB); Associate of Chartered Institute of Bankers

(distinction).

Leisure: walking; music; photography.

STANLEY Derek

barrister and head of chambers 3 Fountain Court, Steelhouse Lane, Birmingham B4 6DR.

Career: called to the Bar Gray's Inn (1968); Midland and Oxford Circuit; pupillage and tenancy 3 Fountain Court; Recorder (1988); head of Chambers (1989).

Activities: circuit representative on Bar Council (1986-1988) .

Biography: lives Birmingham; born 07.08.1947; married with 3 children. Educated at Solihull; Inns of Court School of Law (1965-1968).

Leisure: Church music; squash.

STANNARD Paul

partner and head of pensions department TRAVERS SMITH BRAITHWAITE 10 Snow Hill, London EC1A 2AL Tel: 071-248 9133.

Career: admitted (1982); assistant solicitor (1982-1987); became partner Rowe & Maw (1987); became partner Travers Smith Braithwaite (1989).

Activities: chairman Association of Pension Lawyers' Education & Seminars Committee.

Biography: Educated at Port Moresby High School, Papua New Guinea; Trinity College Cambridge (1979 BA) (MA); College of Law Chester (1980); Associate of the Pensions Management Institute (1987).

STAPLE George

senior litigation partner CLIFFORD CHANCE Blackfriars House, 19 New Bridge Street, London EC4V 6BY.

Career: articled Walker Charlesworth and Jefferson (1958-1962); associate Condon and Forsyth, New York (1963); admitted (1964).

Activities: DTI Inspector Consolidated Gold Fields plc (1986); Aldermanbury Trust plc (1988); Chairman of Tribunals, The Securities Association; member Commercial Court Committee (1977 to date); governor City of London Polytechnic (1982 to date); member Council of the Law Society (1986 to date) (treasurer since 1989); member of: Brooks's; City of London Club; MCC.

Biography: lives London SW11; born 13.09.1940; married to Olivia with 4

children. Educated at Haileybury; College of Law; Fellow Chartered Institute of Arbitrators.

Leisure: cricket; gardening; hill walking.

STAPLEY John

partner in charge commercial property department SAUNDERS SOBELL LEIGH & DOBIN 20 Red Lion Street, London WC1R 4AE.

Career: articled Saunders Sobell Leigh & Dobin; admitted (1964); assistant solicitor (1964-1965); became partner (1965).

Biography: lives Hertfordshire; born 31.01.1942; married with 3 children. Educated at Bancrofts School, Woodford; College of Law.

Leisure: family; sporting activities; theatre; films; reading; antiques.

STARLING Christopher

senior partner HOOD VORES & ALLWOOD The Priory, Church Street, Dereham, Norfolk NR19 1DW.

Career: articled Leslie Allwood; admitted (1958); National Service in the Intelligence Corps (1958-1959); assistant solicitor (1959-1961); became partner (1961); became senior partner (1978).

Activities: part-time Coroner Dereham District of Norfolk; clerk to General Commissioners of Income Tax; president Norfolk & Norwich Law Society (1976); vice-chairman Eastern Area Legal Aid Committee; chairman elect Norwich & Norfolk Solicitors' Amicable Society.

Biography: lives near Dereham; born 30.10.1935; married to Sally with 2 daughters. Educated at Lisvane School, Scarborough; King Edward VI School, Norwich; Felsted School.

Leisure: collecting etchings; visiting Venice and remote Greek islands.

STEDMAN Graham

company partner MISHCON DE REYA 125 High Holborn, London WC1V 6QP.

Career: admitted (1980); assistant solicitor Forsyte Kerman (1980-1982); assistant solicitor and equity partner Speechly Bircham (1982-1989); became partner Mischcon de Reya (1989).

Activities: governor Thornhill Primary School; member Federation against Software Theft; member of Bentham Club.

Biography: lives London N1; born 10.05.1956; married. Educated at

Gravesend School for Boys; University College London (1977 LLB); College of Law Lancaster Gate (1977-1978); co-author of 'Shareholders' agreements' and 'Computer Contracts'; author of various articles on company and computer law topics.

Leisure: football; running; skiing; cinema; travel.

STEEL David

Queen's Counsel 2 Essex Court, Temple, London EC4.

Career: called to the Bar (1966); QC (1981); associate member Hong Kong Bar; member Gibraltar Bar; Wreck Commissioner (1983); Assistant Recorder (1988).

Activities: Junior Counsel to Treasury (Admiralty) (1979-1981); (Common Law) (1979-1981); member Panel of Lloyd's Arbitrators (1982 to date); chairman Commercial Bar Association; Associate Coudert Bros, New York (1968); member of: Turf; Beefsteak; Leander.

Biography: lives London SW10 and Oxfordshire; born 07.05.1943; married to Charlotte with 2 children. Educated at Eton College; Keble College Oxford (MA); co-editor of: 'Kennedy on Salvage'; 'Temperely: Merchant Shipping Acts'; 'Commercial and Admiralty Court Forms'.

Leisure: shooting; fishing; reading.

STEEL Elizabeth

partner CUFF ROBERTS NORTH KIRK 25 Castle Street, Liverpool L2 4TD.

Career: articled Percy Hughes & Roberts (1955-1960); admitted (1960); assistant solicitor (1960-1967); assistant solicitor John A Behn Twyford & Co (1967-1968); became partner (1968-1980); became partner Cuff Roberts North Kirk (1980).

Activities: Recorder (1989); vice-president Liverpool Law Society (1988-1989); president (1989-1990); national vice-chairman Young Conservatives (1965-1967); member Cripps Committee (1967-1969); member Race Relations Board (1970-1978); chairman North West Advisory Council and member General Advisory Council of the BBC (1979-1982); member of board of directors Liverpool Playhouse (1968 to date) deputy and vice-chairman (1980-1988); chairman steering Committee Hillsborough Solicitors' Group (1989-1990); member Liverpool Law Society Committee; former chairman Legal Education Sub-committee; member of: University Women's Club; associate

member Athenaeum.

Biography: lives Liverpool; born 28.11.1936; married to Stuart Christie with 1 son and 1 daughter. Educated at Howells School, Denbigh; Liverpool University (1958 LLB).

Leisure: theatre (both watching professional and performing/directing amateur); music; needlework; cooking; reading; entertaining; being entertained.

STEEL James Cuthbert

senior partner POWELL EDDISON FREEMAN AND WILKS 14 Albert Street, Harrogate HG1 1JW.

Career: admitted (1939); served in destroyers North Sea, North and South Atlantic and Mediterranean with Royal Navy (1940); assistant solicitor Powell Eddison Freeman and Wilks (1949); became partner .

Activities: past Deputy District Registrar and Deputy County Court Registrar; past president Harrogate and District Law Society; past president Harrogate Rotary Club; held most lay offices in Harrogate Methodist Circuit.

Biography: lives Knaresborough; born 17.05.1917; married to Elizabeth with 3 children. Educated at West Leeds High School; Leeds University (1938 LLB).

Leisure: shooting; love of countryside.

STEEL Roger

head of litigation department and employment group FRERE CHOLMELEY 28 Lincoln's Inn Fields, London WC2A 3HH.

Career: articled Frere Cholmeley (1974-1976); admitted (1976); assistant solicitor (1976-1982); founded employment group (1976); became partner (1982); became head of department (1987).

Biography: lives Stoke D'Abernon nr Cobham; born 18.02.1952; married to Prue with 2 daughters. Educated at St Martin's C of E Primary School; Scarborough High School for Boys; University College London (1973 LLB hons); College of Law Lancaster Gate (1974); school captain; author of series of articles in Department of Employment 'Employment Gazette'; contributor to other publications on employment issues.

Leisure: gardening; swimming; travel.

STEINFELD Alan

Queen's Counsel 24 Old Buildings, Lincoln's Inn, London WC2A 3UJ.

Career: admitted to Lincoln's Inn (1966);

called to the Bar (1968); commenced practice in Chambers of George Newsom QC (1969); QC (1987).

Activities: member of: RAC; Cumberland Lawn Tennis Club.

Biography: lives London NW8; born 13.07.1946; married to Josephine with 2 children. Educated at City of London School; Downing College Cambridge (1967 BA hons) (1968 LLB); Arnold McNair Scholarship; Whewell Scholarship; Hardwicke Scholarship.

Leisure: tennis; sailing; skiing; windsurfing; theatre; opera; relaxing in Turkish baths.

STEPHENS Jeremy

partner LOVELL WHITE DURRANT 65 Holborn Viaduct, London EC1A 2DY.

Career: articled Lovell White & King (1960); admitted; assistant solicitor; became partner (1968).

Activities: member Cavalry & Guards Club.

Biography: born 26.07.1937; married with 4 children. Educated at Downside School; St John's College Cambridge (1960 BA hons).

Leisure: ocean sailing.

STEVENS Hugh

partner BRODIES 15 Atholl Crescent, Edinburgh EH3 8HA.

Career: examiner Capital Taxes Office (1971-1977); assistant solicitor Brodies WS (1977-1981); became partner (1981).

Activities: tutor at University (1981-1987); senior tutor and national course convener (1987 to date) in Wills Trusts and Executries.

Biography: lives Dunfermline; born 05.11.1949; married with 3 children. Educated at Edinburgh University.

STEVENS Stuart

barrister and head of chambers 3 King's Bench Walk, Temple, London EC4.

Career: called to the Bar Gray's Inn (1970); head of Chambers (1982).

Activities: member Race Relations Committee of the Senate of the Bar.

Biography: lives London WC1; born 30.04.1947; divorced with 2 sons and 1 daughter..

STEWART Barry

barrister and head of chambers 71A Borough Road, Middlesbrough, Cleveland.

Career: assistant governor HM Prison

S

Service (1965); called to the Bar Gray's Inn (1968); North Eastern Circuit; counsel and attorney at law Federal Courts USA; member New York Bar (1987).

Activities: member Cleveland Steering Committee on tape-recorded police interviews; member Labour Party; Methodist local preacher accredited (1964) Danby circuit.

Biography: lives Staithes; born 03.09.1943. Educated at Robert Richardson Grammar School, Ryhope; Nottingham University (1964 LLB hons); Fitzwilliam College Cambridge (1965 Dip Crim); (1986 JD) (ZUP).

Leisure: foreign travel.

STEWART Douglas

senior partner J & F ANDERSON WS 48 Castle Street, Edinburgh EH2 3LX.

Career: Royal Air Force; articled Strathern & Blair WS; admitted (1951); in charge of branch office of MacArthur Stewart & Orr (1951-1954); law secretary's office of the Scottish Provident Institution; became partner J & F Anderson WS (1961).

Activities: solicitor Crown Estate Commissioners; Notary Public; president Watsonian Club; examiner of intrants Society of Writers to the Signet; session clerk Braid Church Edinburgh; hon treasurer Friends of the National Museums of Scotland; hon secretary and treasurer The Stewart Society (1967-1987); council member Royal Celtic Society; former member Business Committee of the General Council of Edinburgh University; Fellow of the Society of Antiquaries of Scotland; member of New Club.

Biography: lives Edinburgh; born 22.05.1927; married to Catherine with 2 children. Educated at George Watson's College, Edinburgh; Edinburgh University (1949 MA) (1951 LLB).

Leisure: overseas travel; local Hellenic Society; reading in archaeology and astronomy; swimming; keen rugby spectator.

STEWART Gordon

partner ALLEN & OVERY 9 Cheapside, London EC2V 6AD.

Career: admitted (1980); became partner in business reconstruction and insolvency group Allen & Overy.

Activities: lectures widely on banking and insolvency matters; member of: The Royal Scottish Automobile Club; Barbican Health & Fitness Centre.

Biography: lives London SW6; born 16.05.1956; married to Fiona. Educated at Hutchesons Boys' Grammar School; University College Oxford (MA) (BA 1977); author of 'Administrative Receivers and Administrators' (1987); contributor to 'Insolvency' by Totty and Jordan.

Leisure: running; golf; chess; bridge; wine.

STEWART Heather

partner in charge of branch offices READ HIND STEWART 15 The Grove, Ilkley, West Yorkshire LS29 9LW.

Career: articled in Leeds (1965-1970); admitted (1970); assistant solicitor (1970-1974); partner Stewart & Co (1980-1985); partner with Simpson Wade (1985-1987); partner with Read Hind Stewart (1987 to date).

Biography: lives Ilkley; born 05.06.1947; married with 2 children. Educated at Morrison's Academy, Crieff.

STEWART James

Queen's Counsel 40 Park Cross Street, Leeds LS1 2QH and 3 Temple Gardens, London.

Career: called to the Bar Inner Temple (1966); Junior NE Circuit (1970); QC (1982); Recorder of the Crown Court (1982).

Activities: member of: Bradford Club; Leeds Taverners.

Biography: lives Bradford; born 02.05.1943; married to Helen with 2 children. Educated at Cheltenham College; Leeds University (1965 LLB hons).

Leisure: cricket; tennis; squash; golf.

STEWART Peter

partner FIELD FISHER WATERHOUSE 41 Vine Street, London EC3N 2AA.

Career: articled Field Fisher Martineau (now Field Fisher Waterhouse); admitted (1982); assistant solicitor (1982-1985); became partner (1985).

Activities: member Institute of Travel & Tourism; member International Forum of Travel and Tourism Advocates; member International Bar Association.

Biography: lives Goudhurst; born 03.02.1956; married. Educated at Campbell College, Belfast; Pembroke College Cambridge; co-author of: 'A Practical Guide to Package Holiday Law and Contracts'; 'Product Liability - the New Law under the Consumer Protection Act 1987'.

Leisure: golf; tennis; cinema; theatre.

STEWART Robin

Queen's Counsel and recorder of the Crown Court 2 Harcourt Buildings, Temple, London EC4Y 9DB.

Career: called to the Bar Middle Temple (1963); pupilled to P Colin Duncan QC; practised NE Circuit (1970 to date); prosecuting counsel to the Inland Revenue NE Circuit (1976-1978).

Activities: QC (1978); Recorder of the Crown Court (1978); Liveryman The Glaziers' Company; member Oriental Club.

Biography: lives London W4 and Yorkshire; born 05.08.1938; married with 3 children. Educated at Abberley Hall, Worcester; Winchester College; New College Oxford (1961 BA) (MA).

Leisure: music; Scottish family history; pictures; silver; gardens.

STOAKES Christopher

partner STEPHENSON HARWOOD One St Paul's Churchyard, London EC4M 8SH.

Career: articled Freshfields (1980-1983); admitted; assistant solicitor; editor Euromoney Publications PLC (1983-1988) (International Financial Law Review; founding editor Global Investor); became director of marketing Stephenson Harwood (1988); became partner (1990).

Biography: born 22.01.1958; married. Educated at Charterhouse; Worcester College Oxford (MA Jurisprudence).

STOCK Michael

senior partner GABB & CO 32 Monk Street, Abergavenny; Gwent NP7 5NW.

Career: articled Gabb Price & Fisher (now Gabb & Co) (1952-1957); admitted (1957); assistant solicitor (1957-1958); became partner (1958).

Activities: president Council of the Monmouthshire Incorporated Law Society (1985-1986); addressed seminars from time to time on taxation and agricultural matters; member of: MCC; Abergavenny Cricket & Hockey Club.

Biography: lives Eardisley; born 03.02.1935; married to Rebecca with 4 children and 3 stepchildren. Educated at Dean Close School, Cheltenham; Cardiff University.

Leisure: cricket; music (classical, opera, traditional jazz); plays piano; organist in parish church; horses and horse-racing; home and family.

STOCKWELL Tony

partner and head of banking and asset finance department STEPHENSON HARWOOD One St Paul's Churchyard, London EC4M 8SH.

Career: articled Stephenson Harwood (1972-1974); admitted (1974); assistant solicitor (1974-1978); became partner (1978).

Activities: member City of London Law Society Sub-committees on Banking Law and Insolvency law; occasional speaker at conferences on security and insolvency law; member Editorial Board of Journal of International Banking Law.

Biography: lives London; born 14.01.1949; married. Educated at The Grammar School, Enfield; Clare College Cambridge (1971 BA hons); legal editor Tolley's 'Employees' Rights in Receiverships and Liquidations'; articles in Journal of International Banking Law and International Financial Law Review.

STONE Andrew

partner corporate department and head of finance LEWIS SILKIN 1 Butler Place, Buckingham Gate, London SW1H 0PT.

Career: admitted (1977); became partner Lewis Silkin (1977).

Activities: board member and hon legal adviser to Crusaid; non-executive director Ian Greer & Associates (parliamentary lobbyists).

Biography: lives London; born 16.07.1953; single. Educated at Roundhay Grammar School, Leeds; Nottingham University (1974 LLB); College of Law.

Leisure: cinema; reading.

STONES Nic

senior partner WIGGIN AND CO The Quadrangle, Imperial Square, Cheltenham, Glos GL50 1YX.

Career: articled Rickerbys and Freshfields (1965-1970); admitted (1970); assistant solicitor (1970-1974); assistant solicitor Wiggin and Co (1974-1975); became partner (1975); became senior partner (1986).

Activities: former captain of the Law Society Golf Club (1986-1987); speaker at various conferences on international taxation and trusts; member of: MCC; Royal Jersey Golf Club.

Biography: lives Cheltenham and Morzine, France; born 19.10.1946; married with 3 children. Educated at Haileybury; College

of Law Guildford.

Leisure: tennis; golf; skiing; fine food and wines.

STOWE Grahame

senior partner GRAHAME STOWE BATESON & CO Portland House, 7 Portland Street, Leeds LS13 3DR.

Career: articled Leem Solicitors (1972-1974); admitted (1974); became partner (1974-1981); founded practice with Arthur J Bateson (1981).

Activities: president Mental Health Review Tribunal; chairman Supplementary Benefit Appeal Tribunal .

Biography: lives London and Leeds; born 22.05.1949; married to Marilyn with 1 son. Educated at Allerton Grange School, Leeds; Leeds University; Fellow Chartered Institute of Arbitrators.

Leisure: squash.

STRACHAN (Ian) John

senior partner PETERKINS Burgh House, 7-9 King Street, Aberdeen AB2 3AA.

Career: National Service (Sub-Lt RNVR); assistant solicitor Whyte & Connon (1956-1958); partner Davison & Garden (1958-1972); senior partner (1972-1989); became senior partner Peterkins (1989).

Activities: Notary Public; JP; Burgess of Guild; chairman Hunter Construction (Aberdeen) Ltd; director of: William Wilson Holdings Ltd; Osprey Communications plc; member of: Royal Northern Club; East India Club; Aberdeen Petroleum Club.

Biography: lives Aberdeen; born 09.08.1929; widowed with 1 son and 2 daughters. Educated at Fraserburgh Academy; Aberdeen University (1954 MA LLB).

Leisure: salmon fishing; shooting.

STRACHAN Dale

partner commercial property department BRODIES WS 15 Atholl Crescent, Edinburgh EH3 8HA.

Career: apprentice Archibald Campbell & Harley WS (1977-1979); admitted (1979); assistant solicitor Brodies WS (1979-1983); became partner (1983).

Activities: member International Bar Association; member Scottish Arts Club.

Biography: lives Edinburgh; born 12.10.1956; married to Ghillean with 1 child, Kyle. Educated at George Heriot's School, Edinburgh; Aberdeen University

(1977 LLB).

Leisure: fishing; skiing; paragliding.

STRACHAN Mark

barrister 1 Crown Office Row, Temple, London EC4.

Career: called to the Bar (1969); QC (1987); Recorder (1990).

Biography: lives London W8; born 25.09.1946. Educated at Orange Hill School, Edgware; St Catherine's College Oxford (1967 BA) (MA); (1968 BCL); Open Exhibitioner; Nancy University (1968-1969 Doctorat en Droit); Major Scholar Inner Temple; French Government Scholar; various legal articles in Modern Law Review; New Law Journal; Solicitors' Journal.

Leisure: France; antiques; food.

STRACHAN Russell

senior pension law partner LOVELL WHITE DURRANT 65 Holborn Viaduct, London EC1A 2DY.

Career: articled Lovell White & King (1967-1969); admitted (1970); assistant solicitor (1970-1975); became partner (1975).

Biography: lives London; born 30.03.1945. Educated at St Paul's; Wadham College Oxford (1966 BA).

STRATTON David

deputy senior partner HALLIWELL LANDAU St James's Court, Brown Street, Manchester M2 2JF.

Career: articled to the Town Clerk Warrington County Borough Council (1969-1971); admitted (1971); assistant and principal assistant solicitor (1971-1972); assistant group legal adviser Christian Salvesen Properties Ltd (1972-1975); group legal adviser (1975-1979); became partner Halliwell Landau (1979).

Activities: member St James's Club, London.

Biography: lives Hale; born 16.05.1947; married to Ruth with 6 children. Educated at Altrincham Grammar Shool for Boys; Colwyn Bay Grammar School; Leeds University (1968 LLB hons); Liverpool College of Commerce (Law Society Finals).

STREAT Ian

senior partner and head of litigation department WARNER GOODMAN AND STREAT 14/16 Portland Terrace, Southampton SO9 4ZQ.

S

Career: articled WH Heelis & Son and Gregory Rowcliffe & Co (1961-1964); admitted (1965); assistant solicitor Gregory Rowcliffe & Co (1965-1967); assistant solicitor Streat Daunt & Farmiloe (now Warner Goodman & Streat) (1967-1969); became partner (1969).

Activities: clerk to Southampton General Commissioners of Taxes; chairman Litigation sub-committee Hampshire Incorporated Law Society; member Taxation and Legal Committee of Southampton Chamber of Commerce; member British German Jurists' Association; member Solicitors' European Group; member Southampton Master Mariners' Club.

Biography: lives Winchester; born 16.02.1937; married to Jennifer with 3 children. Educated at Seascale Preparatory School, Cumbria; Kingswood School, Bath; Ecole des Roches, Normandy; Jesus College Cambridge (1961 BA) (1962 LLB) (1968 MA); Open Exhibition Jesus College (1955); Solicitors' Final Examination (1964 distinction).

Leisure: swimming; walking; reading; music; foreign languages; lay reader Church of England.

STREATHER Bruce

senior partner STREATHERS, 16 Clifford Street, London W1X 1RG.

Career: articled Frere Cholmeley (1969-1971); admitted (1971); assistant solicitor Swales (1971); became partner (1972-1977); became partner Streathers (1977).

Activities: member of: Royal and Ancient Golf Club of St Andrews; Sunningdale Golf Club; Little Aston Golf Club; Oxford and Cambridge Golf Society; Vincents.

Biography: lives London; born 03.06.1946; married to Geraldine with 3 daughters. Educated at Packwood Haugh Ruyton Towns XI (1954-1959); Malvern College (1959-1964); Oxford (1968 BA) (1976 MA).

Leisure: family; golf; theatre; skiing.

STREET Robert

partner CHAFFE STREET Brook House, 70 Spring Gardens, Manchester M2 2BQ.

Career: articled Coward Chance (1973-1975); admitted (1975); assistant solicitor (1975-1977); assistant solicitor Harold Chaffe & Co (1977-1978); became partner (1978); firm divided into Chafes and Chaffe Street (1983).

Activities: secretary local branch Kidney Research Association; member of: St

James's Club; Prestbury Golf Club.

Biography: lives Prestbury; born 25.05.1951; married to Janet with 1 son and 1 daughter. Educated at Stockport Grammar School; Liverpool University (1972 LLB); College of Law Guildford.

Leisure: golf; cricket; fell walking; watching sports (particularly cricket).

STRINGFELLOW Richard

head of financial services department EVERSHED WELLS & HIND 14 Fletcher Gate, Nottingham.

Career: articled Hunt Dickins & Willatt (1950-1955); admitted (1955); commissioned in the Admin Branch RAF (1955-1957); assistant solicitor Keogh & Co (1957-1958); assistant solicitor Wells & Hind (1958-1959); became partner (1959); became senior partner (1987-1989); firm amalgamated with Evershed & Tomkinson (1989).

Activities: member of: Notts Athletic Club; Nottingham Anglo-French Society.

Biography: lives Nottingham; born 17.06.1933; married to Beryl with 3 children. Educated at Queen Elizabeth's Grammar School, Mansfield; Nottingham University; examinations in French of the Institute of Linguists.

Leisure: long distance running; skiing; listening to music.

STROYAN Colin SR

senior partner BRODIES WS 15 Atholl Crescent, Edinburgh EH3 8HA.

Career: Black Watch (RHR) (1945-1948); apprentice Thomson Dickson & Shaw WS (1951-1954); admitted (1954); assistant solicitor (1954-1955); became partner John C Brodie & Sons (1955).

Activities: TD; WS; director: Royal Trust Bank; Iowa Loan Co; Swilken Golf Company and others; commanded TA Battalion 6/7th Black Watch (1964-1966); member of Lloyds; member of: Naval & Military; Honourable Company of Edinburgh Golfers; New Club.

Biography: lives Doune; born 24.03.1927; married to Caroline with 3 children. Educated at St Peter's Court, Broadstairs; Harrow; Edinburgh (1954 BL).

Leisure: landowner; shooting; fishing; stalking; gardening.

STUBBINGS Simon

partner THEODORE GODDARD 150 Aldersgate Street, London EC1A 4EJ.

Career: articled Theodore Goddard (1969-1972); admitted (1972); assistant solicitor (1972-1977); became partner (1977).

Activities: member City of London Law Society Revenue Law Sub-Committee; member of New Grampian Squash Club.

Biography: lives London N1; born 16.01.1945; married to Joan with 1 daughter and 1 son. Educated at Michaelhouse, Natal, South Africa (1959-1963); Trinity College Dublin (1968 BA); author of chapter on Director's Benefits in Tolley's Company Law.

Leisure: squash; home-brewing.

STUBBLEFIELD Rodney

senior partner PENNINGTONS incorporating GAMLENS 37 Sun Street, London EC2M 2PY.

Career: admitted (1961); assistant solicitor (1961-1962); became equity partner Gamlens (1962); became senior partner (1989); firm now Penningtons incorporating Gamlens.

Activities: member Solicitors' Assistance Scheme (1981 to date); junior vice-president Holborn Law Society (chairman Conveyancing Standing Committee (1982-1989) (member and officer of various committees over last 10 years); governor Sutton Valence School; member of: RAC; Wentworth Club.

Biography: lives Sunningdale; born 10.10.1937; married to Jenny with 1 son and 1 daughter. Educated at Durston House, Ealing; Sutton Valence School, Kent; University College London (1958 LLB); various papers on Property Law Reform for HLS.

Leisure: squash; tennis; bridge.

STUBBS Ian

a senior partner in the private client department MACLAY MURRAY & SPENS 151 St Vincent Street, Glasgow G2 5NJ.

Career: trainee chartered accountant Thomson McLintock & Co; qualified (1968); apprentice Maclay Murray & Spens (1968-1971); admitted (1971); assistant solicitor (1971-1973); became partner (1973).

Activities: member Law Society of Scotland Board of Examiners (1976-1986) (latterly chairman); senior tutor wills, trusts & executors Glasgow University (1980-1986); non-executive director First Northern Corporate Finance Ltd (1983-1988); council member Institute of Chartered Accountants of Scotland (1986 to date) member Finance & General Purposes Committee (1986 to date) (Taxation Committee 1986-1988); (Business Legislation Unit 1988 to date) (Professional Examination Board 1988 to date); speaks and lectures on topics including inheritance tax, partnership law and tax, agricultural and landed estate law and tax (including forestry), valuations of private limited company shares and wills, trusts and executries at both Law Society and Institute of Chartered Accountants of Scotland PQE courses/conferences; one of the original solicitors behind formation of SEAL Limited; member Scottish Royal Automobile Club.

Biography: lives Whitecraigs; born 14.11.1943; married to Joan with 3 children. Educated at Marr College, Troon; Glasgow University (1965 LLB); Institute of Chartered Accountants of Scotland (1968 CA).

Leisure: jogging to keep fit (has run several marathons and half marathons); gardening; hill walking; paintings (and collecting); bird watching; country interests.

STUBBS John

manager commercial law branch NATIONAL POWER PLC Sudbury House, 15 Newgate Street, London EC1A 7AU.

Career: articled Earle & Walker (1974-1976); admitted (1976); assistant solicitor Richards Butler & Co (1976-1980); legal assistant Central Electricity Generating Board (1980-1984); senior solicitor - commercial (1984-1988); became manager commercial law branch (1988); company secretary National Power (North) Limited.

Activities: visiting speaker Institute of Petroleum and Mineral Law, Dundee University; member Shoreham Port Authority; committee member Electricity Supply Industry Arbitration Association.

Biography: lives London N3 and Minehead; born 15.01.1951; married to Pauline with 3 children. Educated at Finchley Grammar School; Queen Mary College London (1972 LLB hons); College of Law (1974); City of London Polytechnic (1986 MA CNAA).

Leisure: walking; shooting; opera.

STURT Richard Harvey Brooke

senior partner MOWLL & MOWLL 34 & 36 Castle Street, Dover, Kent CT16 1PN.

Career: articled Mowll & Mowll; admitted (1966); assistant solicitor (1966-1967);

became partner (1967); became senior partner (1984).

Activities: solicitor to the Dover Harbour Board (1979 to date); Deputy Coroner for East Kent (1972-1979); HM Coroner for Kent (Canterbury and Dover District) (1979 to date) (conducted Herald of Free Enterprise inquest 1987); clerk to the governors of the King's School, Canterbury (1979 to date); legal adviser to the Independent Schools' Action Committee (1980-1982); president South Eastern Coroners' Society (1981-1982); director Dover & Folkestone BS (1978-1984); governor: Betteshanger School (1978-1980); Northbourne Park School (1980-1985); founder and chairman East Kent Holiday Music Trust; trustee of various charities; chairman of Gateway Broadcasting Ltd (1982-1984); chairman Invicta Sound PLC (1984 to date); contributed to discussions organised by Home Office into planning for civil emergencies (1988-1989); conducted numerous prosecutions for government departments for maritime offences committed in the English Channel and Southern North Sea; Fellow Royal Society of Arts; member of: Athenaeum; Flyfishers' Club.

Biography: lives Deal; born 14.11.1939; married to Ann with 4 children. Educated at Marlborough College (Open Scholarship 1953); Peterhouse Cambridge (1961 BA) (1965 MA); author of: 'Fishery Protection and Foreign Sea Fishing Boats' (1973); 'The Collision Regulations' (1976 & 1984); Halsbury's Laws of England 4th edition Fisheries (1976); Ports and Harbours (1981); European Communities (Fisheries) (1986); Vaughan on European Community Laws - Fisheries (1987); The Role of the Coroner with Special Reference to Major Disasters (1988).

STUTTER John

partner HARBOTTLE & LEWIS Hanover House, 14 Hanover Square, London W1R 0BE.

Career: corporal then sergeant Intelligence Corps Trieste Security Office (1949-1950); articled Devonshire & Co (1953-1956); admitted (1956); assistant solicitor Simmons & Simmons (1956-1959); assistant solicitor Harbottle & Lewis (1959-1960); became partner (1961).

Activities: member of: Oriental Club; Aldeburgh Yacht Club.

Biography: lives London SW17; born 20.04.1930; married to Jane with 5 children. Educated at Finchley Grammar School; Magdalene College Cambridge (1953 BA

now MA); (1954 LLB now LLM).

Leisure: cycling; sailing; skiing.

SUDDARDS Roger Whitley

consultant HAMMOND SUDDARDS Empire House, 10 Piccadilly, Bradford BD1 3LR.

Career: partner Last Suddards (1952-1988); became senior partner; became consultant Hammond Suddards (1988).

Activities: CBE (1987); Deputy Lt of County of West Yorkshire (1990); lecturer at the Leeds School of Town Planning; planning law consultant to the United Nations Development Programme and the governments of Mauritius and Saudi Arabia; member of the Law Society Planning Law Committee (1964-1981); hon member ISVA; hon member Yorkshire & Humberside area of RIBA; chairman working party on the future of Bradford churches (1978-1979); chairman of the Board (1969-1986); vice-chairman and then chairman Bradford Grammar School; chairman Bradford Disaster Appeal Fund (1985-1989); chairman Yorkshire Building Society; chairman of Council and pro-chancellor Bradford University; chairman Hammond Suddards Research Ltd; chairman Yorkshire Television Telethon Trust; member The Civic Trust; member West Yorkshire Residuary Body; member Law Society Bye-Laws Revision Committee; member Committee of the National Museum of Photography, Film and Television; member Editorial Board of the Journal of Planning and Environmental Law ; member of: The Bradford Club, Bradford; The Arts, London.

Biography: lives Bradford; born 05.06.1930; married to Elizabeth with 2 daughters. Educated at Bradford Grammar School; legal member The Royal Town Planning Institute; produced many articles on town planning law both in this country and in the Third World; "Town Planning Law of West Indies" (1974); "History of Bradford Law Society (1975); "Listed Buildings" (1982 & 1988); "A Lawyer's Peregrination" (1984 & 1987); "Bradford Disaster Appeal" (1986).

Leisure: theatre; music; reading; travel.

SUGGETT John

partner JAMES ELDRIDGE & SONS Avenue House, Avenue Road, Freshwater, Isle of Wight PO40 9UZ.

Career: articled Foskett Marr Gadsby & Head (1970-1972); admitted (1972); assistant solicitor (1972-1973); assistant

S

solicitor James Eldridge & Sons (1973-1975); became partner (1975).

Activities: past member Committee Isle of Wight Law Society (1976-1990) (president 1988-1989); member operating staff Isle of Wight Steam Railway (director 1989 and chairman 1990); qualified guard, signalman and operating manager.

Biography: lives Northwood; born 05.04.1947; married to Janet with 2 children. Educated at Penarth Grammar School; Queen Mary College London (1969 LLB).

SULLIVAN Jeremy

Queen's Counsel 4-5 Gray's Inn Square, London WC1R 5AY.

Career: called to the Bar Inner Temple (1968); QC (1982); Recorder (1989).

Activities: member Parliamentary Bar, Planning and Local Government Bar, Administrative Law Bar Association.

Biography: lives London and Wotton Underwood; born 17.09.1945; married to Ursula with 2 children. Educated at Framlingham College; King's College London (1967 LLB) (1968 LLM); LMRTPI (1976); articles in Journal of Planning Law.

Leisure: railways; canals; walking; gardening; reading history.

SULTOON Jeffrey

partner corporate finance department ASHURST MORRIS CRISP Broadwalk House, 5 Appold Street, London EC2A 2HA.

Career: articled Freshfields (1975-1978); admitted (1978); assistant solicitor (1978-1981); assistant solicitor Ashurst Morris Crisp (1981-1986); became partner (1986).

Biography: lives Cobham; born 08.10.1953; married to Vivien. Educated at Haberdashers' Aske's, Elstree; St Edmund Hall Oxford (1974 MA); College of Law (1974-1975); author of 'Tolley's Company Law - Dividends and Universal Checklist for any Transaction'.

SUMMERFIELD Peter William

partner specialising in international commercial litigation and transnational business NABARRO NATHANSON 50 Stratton Street, London W1M 5FL.

Career: National Service in Egypt and Malta (1952-1954); articled Herbert Oppenheimer Nathan & Vandyk (1957-1960); admitted (1960); assistant solicitor (1960-1965); partner (1965-1988); became

partner Nabarro Nathanson (1988).

Activities: visiting professor University of the Pacific, McGeorge School of Law (member Board of Visitors and Chairman International Board of Advisors); accredited lawyer in UK to Governments and Embassies of Switzerland and Austria; member of: The Law Society of England and Wales; The European Group of The Law Society; The International Bar Association; The American Bar Association; The British-German Jurists' Association; the Institute of Directors; Society of English and American Lawyers; American Chamber of Commerce (UK); The Anglo-Austrian Society; The Anglo-German Society; The Anglo-Swiss Society; The British-Swiss Chamber of Commerce; British Chamber of Commerce in Germany; German Chamber of Industry & Commerce in the UK; British Chamber of Commerce in Spain; The Japan Association; The Finnish-British Trade Guild; The Norwegian Chamber of Commerce; the Swedish Chamber of Commerce; David Lloyd Leisure Centres.

Biography: lives London N2; born 03.06.1933; married to Marianne with 5 children. Educated at The Hall School, Hampstead (1940-1945); William Ellis School, London (1945-1952); Pembroke College Oxford (1957 BA hons) (1960 MA hons) State Scholarship; president Sir William Blackstone Law Society; president Sir Thomas Browne Dramatic and Literary Society; member Oxford Union Debating Society; represented College at tennis and chess; co-editor 'Dispute Resolution for the International Commercial Lawyer' (1988).

Leisure: tennis; theatre; opera.

SUMPTER Robin

senior partner RAC SYMES & CO 110 High Street, Scunthorpe, S Humberside DN15 6HF.

Career: articled RAC Symes & Co (1949-1953); admitted (1953); National Service with Royal Artillery; 2nd Lt 1st Singapore Regiment RA; became partner RAC Symes & Co (1965).

Activities: chairman Social Security Appeals Tribunal (1969-1989); president Lincolnshire Law Society (1986-1987) (member Council 1972-1989).

Biography: lives nr Scunthorpe; born 06.04.1931; married to Aileen with 2 children. Educated at Brigg Grammar School.

Leisure: hockey (former player; now umpire; Lincolnshire County player 1957-

1964); cricket; golf.

SUMPTION Jonathan

Queen's Counsel 1 Brick Court, Temple, London EC4.

Career: called to the Bar (1975); QC (1986).

Biography: lives London SE10; born 09.12.1948; married to Teresa with 3 children. Educated at Eton College; Magdalen College Oxford (1970 hons).

Leisure: history; music.

SUNNUCKS James Horace George

barrister and head of chambers 5 New Square, Lincoln's Inn, London WC2A 3RS.

Career: called to the Bar Lincoln's Inn; pupillage Michael Albery QC; practised from Chancery Bar and Octagon House, Norwich; Bencher Lincoln's Inn (1980).

Activities: member Institute of Conveyancers (1974) (president 1988-1989); member Senate of the Inns of Court and Bar (1982-1985); member various Bench Committees, Lincoln's Inn; member Parole Review Committee Chelmsford Prison (1970-1982) (former chairman); assistant Parliamentary Boundary Commissioner of Wandsworth, Camden and Wiltshire (1975-1985); member of: United Oxford & Cambridge Universities Club; Norfolk Club; Garrick Club.

Biography: lives London WC2 and Colchester; born 20.09.1925; married with 4 sons. Educated at Wellesley House, Broadstairs; Wellington College; Trinity Hall Cambridge (MA); editor Williams and Mortimer on Executors; contributor to Halsbury's Laws of England 'Executors' and 'Lien'; various articles on legal topics; DL (1990).

Leisure: gardening; local history; sailing.

SUSSKIND Alan

managing partner ROSS HARPER & MURPHY 455 Paisley Road, Glasgow.

Career: articled William Armour & Son and with Procurator Fiscal Service, Dumbarton, Glasgow and Kilmarnock; assistant solicitor Ross Harper & Murphy; became partner; became managing partner.

Activities: Dean of Shawlands and District Faculty; member O & M and Legal Aid Committees of Law Society of Scotland.

Biography: lives Glasgow; born 04.09.1957; married to Angela with 2 children. Educated at Hutchesons Grammar School; Strathclyde University (1977 LLB); article in Law Society Journal on genetic fingerprinting (1989).

Leisure: competitive squash; running; reading science fiction.

SUTCLIFFE Ian

consultant MOUNSEYS 19 Castle Street, Carlisle, Cumbria CA3 8TW.

Career: senior partner Mounsey Bowman & Sutcliffe (1959-1986); senior partner Mounseys (1987-1989); became consultant (1989).

Activities: president Carlisle Law Society (1984); Registrar Carlisle Diocese (1959); legal secretary to Bishop of Carlisle (1989); clerk to Dean and Chapter Carlisle Cathedral (1989); Registrar to Archdeaconries (1959); member Border and County Club.

Biography: lives Carlisle; born 30.01.1931; married with 3 sons. Educated at Marlborough College (1944-1949); Emmanuel College Cambridge (1954 BA) (1955 LLB) (MA).

Leisure: hockey; golf; tennis; walking; shooting; theatre; music.

SUTTON Bill

partner BLACKHURST PARKER AND YATES 22 Edward Street, Blackpool Lancashire FY1 1DP.

Career: articled Beor Wilson and Lloyd and Chamberlain & Co (1948-1952); admitted (1952); commissioned RASC and RA (1952-1957); assistant solicitor Stringer and Stringer (1955-1956); assistant solicitor Blackhurst Parker and Co (1956-1958); became partner (1958) .

Activities: Notary Public; former president Blackpool and Fylde District Law Society; former member Law Society Non-Contentious Costs Committee; liquor licensing work throughout England; member of: Fylde Rugby Club; Royal Lytham St Anne's Golf Club; Lytham Yacht Club.

Biography: lives Lytham; born 13.12.1930; married to Jill with 1 son, 2 stepsons and 3 daughters. Educated at St Andrew's School, Pangbourne; Winchester College.

Leisure: watching rugby and cricket; music; bridge; snooker.

SUTTON Richard

partner DIBB LUPTON BROOMHEAD & PRIOR 117 The Headrow, Leeds LS1 5JX.

Career: articled Dibb Lupton & Co; admitted (1973); assistant solicitor Cleary Gottlieb Stein & Hamilton, New York

(1973-1974); became partner Dibb Lupton & Co (1976-1988); became partner Dibb Lupton Broomhead (1988).

Activities: member Patent Solicitors' Association; International Bar Association; associate member Institute of Patent Agents.

Biography: lives North Yorkshire; born 05.05.1947; married with 2 children. Educated Charterhouse School (1960-1964); Royal Agricultural College (1966).

Leisure: usual country activities.

SUTTON Robert

partner MACFARLANES 10 Norwich Street, London EC4A 1BD.

Career: articled Macfarlanes (1976-1978); admitted (1978); assistant solicitor (1978-1980); seconded to White & Case, New York (1980-1981); became partner (1983).

Activities: member City Club.

Biography: lives London; born 19.01.1954; married to Tiggy with 2 children. Educated at Winchester College; Magdalen College Oxford (1972-1975); articles on 'Timetable of a hostile bid'; 'The role of the lawyer in takeovers' and 'Acquiring a people business in Japan'.

Leisure: rackets; sports; poker.

SWIFT John

Queen's Counsel 4 Raymond Buildings, Gray's Inn, London WC1R 5BP.

Career: called to the Bar (1965); QC (1981).

Biography: lives South Oxfordshire; born 11.07.1940; married to Jane with 2 children. Educated at Birkenhead School; University College Oxford (1963 1st Class hons Jurisprudence); School of Advanced International Studies, John Hopkins University, Bologna (1964 Diploma with distinction); contributor to: 'Bellamy & Child Common Market Law of Competition'; 'Butterworth's Encyclopaedia of Forms and Precedents' and other publications on EEC and UK competition law.

Leisure: golf; coastal cliff path walking; gardening; travel.

SWIFT Philip

partner TAYLOR VINTERS Lushington House, 119 High Street, Newmarket, Suffolk CB8 9AG.

Career: articled Moore & Blatch (1960-1963); admitted (1964); assistant solicitor (1964-1967); assistant solicitor Taylors

(1967-1968); became partner (1968).

Biography: lives Weston Colville; born 23.05.1939; married to Perdita with 3 children. Educated at Stone House, Broadstairs; Radley College, Abingdon; King's College Cambridge (1960 MA); author of one chapter in Michael Simmons' book 'Successful mergers' (1989).

Leisure: golf; tennis; watersports; skiing; bridge; gardening; walking.

SWIFT Robert

partner LINKLATERS & PAINES Barrington House, 59-67 Gresham Street, London EC2V 7JA.

Career: articled small city firm; admitted (1967); solicitor patent and trademark department EMI Ltd (1967-1971); assistant solicitor Linklaters & Paines (1971-1974); secondment to White & Case, New York (1974-1975); became partner Linklaters & Paines (1976); head of Intellectual Property Department (1982).

Activities: member of Patent Solicitors' Association; member City of London Law Society Intellectual Property sub-committee (deputy chairman); member joint Bar-Law Society Working Party on Intellectual Property Law; member Computer Law Group; USTA; member of: Riverside Club; West Middlesex LTC.

Biography: lives London W5; born 13.08.1941; married to Hilary with 3 children. Educated at John Marshall High School, Los Angeles; London School of Economics (1963 LLB); author of various articles.

Leisure: music; walking; eating; a bit of gentle squash; travel.

SYKES Robert

senior partner POWELL & SYKES 136 Highgate, Kendal, Cumbria LA9 4HN.

Career: district officer Overseas Civil Service Tanganyika (1960-1962); articled Yarde & Loader (1963-1966) .

Activities: president Westmorland Law Society; trustee Francis C Scott Charitable Trust; board member Outward Bound Mountain School, Ullswater.

Biography: lives Kendal; born 30.12.1934; married with 4 children. Educated at Blundell's School, Tiverton; Christ Church Oxford (MA).

Leisure: mountain travel; pteridology.

S

SYKES Roger

partner WHITEHEAD MONCKTON 72 King Street, Maidstone ME14 1BL.

Career: articled in North London; assistant solicitor Whitehead Monckton (1977-1979); became partner (1979).

Activities: HM Coroner for Maidstone (1986 to date); member management committees of local mother and baby home and Maidstone Citizens Advice Bureau.

Biography: lives nr Maidstone; born 19.01.1949; married to Sabrina with 2 children. Educated at Sutton Valence School; London University (1971).

SYKES Sir John

partner in charge of probate and trust department TOWNSENDS 18 London Road, Newbury, Berks RG13 1AW and 42 Cricklade Street, Swindon, Wilts SN1 3HD.

Career: articled Gamlens (1965-1968); admitted (1968); assistant solicitor (1968-1969); assistant solicitor Townsends (1969-1971); became partner (1972).

Activities: president Swindon Chamber of Commerce (1981) (hon solicitor 1975 to date); governor Swindon College (1981-1989); governor Swindon Enterprise Trust (1982-1989); hon solicitor to Thamesdown Community Trust (1976 to date); trustee Roman Research Trust.

Biography: lives Marlborough; born 07.06.1942; married to Susan with 3 sons. Educated at Shrewsbury School; Worcester College Oxford (1963 MA hons) .

Leisure: local history (research and lecturing); Anglo-Indian history.

SYMONDS John

senior partner TG BAYNES & SONS 27 Upper Wickham Lane, Welling, Kent DA16 3AB.

Career: articled Good Good & Co (1947-1952); admitted (1952); National Service in Army (1952-1954); assistant solicitor (1954-1957); became partner TG Baynes & Sons (1957); became senior partner (1985).

Activities: non-executive director WPP Group PLC.

Biography: lives Sidcup; born 04.11.1929; married to Alwyn with 3 children. Educated at City of Bath Grammar School (1940-1945); Roan School, Greenwich (1945-1946); Department of Slavonic Studies Cambridge (Army Russian Course) (1952-1953).

Leisure: sailing; gardening; property development.

SYMONDS Malcolm

company secretary and legal adviser TOTAL OIL GREAT BRITAIN LTD Legal Department, 33 Cavendish Square, London W1M 0JE.

Career: articled Radcliffes & Co (1962-1967); admitted (1967); assistant solicitor (1967-1969); assistant solicitor Shapley Barnet Marsh & Co, Nairobi (1970-1972); assistant solicitor Total Oil (1972); senior solicitor; legal manager; became company secretary and legal adviser (1989).

Biography: lives Ashstead and Chichester; born 02.04.1944; married to Linda with 2 children. Educated at Alleyn's School, Dulwich (1955-1962); London University (1967 LLB).

Leisure: geology (particularly tertiary research); photography.

SYSON Michel James

commercial conveyancing partner KENNEDYS Longbow House, 14-20 Chiswell Street, London EC1Y 4TY.

Career: articled Kennedys; became partner (1966).

Activities: hon solicitor Ealing Chamber of Commerce & Industry; member of: Gerrards Cross Golf Club; Oxford & Cambridge Universities Club; Stewards' Club, Henley Royal Regatta.

Biography: lives Gerrards Cross; born 26.07.1933; married to Lavinia with 1 child. Educated at Lord Williams' Grammar School, Thame; Keble College Oxford (1958 MA).

Leisure: theatre; French literature; music; golf.

T

TABACHNIK Eldred

Queen's Counsel 11 King's Bench Walk, Temple, London EC4.

Career: advocate of Supreme Court of South Africa (1966); lecturer in law University College, London (1969-1972); called to the Bar (1970); QC (1982); Master of the Bench of the Inner Temple (1988).

Activities: member Reform Club.

Biography: lives London SW20; born 05.11.1943; married to Jennifer with 3 children. Educated at Cape Town University (1963 BA) (1965 LLB); London University (1969 LLM).

Leisure: reading; communal and charitable work.

TADIELLO Derek

construction law partner WILDE SAPTE Queensbridge House, Upper Thames Street, London EC4V 3BD.

Career: civil engineer London Borough of Camden (1972-1977); articled Kennedys; admitted; assistant solicitor Stephenson Harwood (1983-1986); became partner (1986-1987); head of small construction law unit Titmuss Sainer & Webb (1987-1989); became partner Wilde Sapte (1989).

Activities: member CIB-W87; member Public Relations Committee of British Academy of Experts; member Society of Construction Law; Freeman City of London Solicitors' Company.

Biography: lives Berkhamsted; born 13.04.1951; married to Alison with 1 son and 1 daughter. Educated at Ranelagh School; the City University, London (1972 BSC hons).

Leisure: eating; wine; travel; walking; the environment; theatre; swimming.

TAMLIN Keith

Senior Partner CUFF ROBERTS NORTH KIRK 25 Castle Street, Liverpool L2 4TD.

Career: articled WT Husband & Son; admitted (1954); assistant solicitor North Kirk & Co (1954-1960); became partner (1960); amalgamated with Cuff Roberts (1982).

Activities: president of the Liverpool Law Society (1983); president Liverpool Junior Chamber of Commerce; president Liverpool Round Table; Group 1 (Employer) UK member of Economic and Social Committee in Brussels; member Post Office Users' National Council; member Council of the Retail Consortium; member Council of the Advertising Association; director Mail Order Traders' Association; director several companies including Everton Football Club; member of the Council of the Confederation of British Industry; member The Athenaeum.

Biography: lives Liverpool; born 19.07.1928; married to Marian with 2 children. Educated at Ruthin School; LLB.

Leisure: swimming; golf; walking.

TANDY David

partner and head of private client department TITMUSS SAINER & WEBB 2 Serjeants' Inn, London EC4Y 1LT.

Career: estate duty office of Inland Revenue (1967-1973); articled Titmuss Sainer & Webb (1973-1975); admitted (1975); assistant solicitor (1975-1976);

became partner (1976).

Activities: member City of London Solicitors' Company Committee (1989).

Biography: lives Crawley; born 25.06.1944; married to Catherine with 2 children. Educated at Bexley Grammar School; University of London (1970 LLB external); City of London College (Diploma in Civil Law).

Leisure: shooting.

TAPSFIELD Richard

partner LINKLATERS & PAINES Barrington House, 59-67 Gresham Street, London EC2V 7JA.

Career: articled Linklaters & Paines (1974-1976); admitted (1976); assistant solicitor (1976-1978 & 1979-1982); became partner (1982).

Activities: member Society of Construction Law; associate member Chartered Institute of Arbitrators.

Biography: lives Tunbridge Wells; born 21.05.1951; married to Penelope with 2 children. Educated at Hulme Preparatory School for Boys; The Manchester Grammar School for Boys; Selwyn College Cambridge (1973 BA) (1975 MA).

Leisure: African wildlife; skiing; gardening; fatherhood.

TATTAM Soren

partner and head of company commercial department MARCH PEARSON & SKELTON 41 Spring Gardens, Manchester M2 2BB.

Career: articled March Pearson & Skelton; admitted (1978); assistant solicitor (1978-1983); became partner (1983).

Activities: Consul of Sweden in Manchester; secretary North Western Area National Association of Paper Merchants; governor Wilmslow Prep School Trust Ltd; member of: St James's Club; Licensing Executives Society; L'Association Europeenne D'Etudes Juridiques et Fiscales; Law Society Solicitors' European Group.

Biography: lives Alderley Edge; born 14.07.1953; married to Sherran with 1 child. Educated at Rodkille School, Copenhagen; Askims Skola, Gothenburg; Taby Hogskola, Stockholm; Bramhall County Grammar School; City of London Polytechnic (BA); author of United Kingdom chapter for 'Security on Movable Property and Receivables in Europe' (1988).

Leisure: reading; gardening; DIY; foreign travel.

TAYLOR Barton

equity partner and head of commercial litigation department RUSSELL JONES & WALKER Swinton House, 324 Gray's Inn Road, London WC1X 8DH.

Career: articled RD Edwards and Morgan, Swansea (1965-1970); admitted (1970); assistant solicitor Gregsons (1970-1972); salaried partner Alexander Rubens Weeil and Co (1972-1976); partner Russell Jones & Walker (1977).

Activities: member Jury List Committee.

Biography: lives Richmond; born 03.08.1944; married with 2 children. Educated at Hereford Cathedral School; College of Law Guildford.

Leisure: tennis; rugby union football.

TAYLOR Bill

Queen's Counsel 17 Old Buildings, Lincoln's Inn, London WC2A 3UP.

Career: Royal Artillery France, Belgium, N Africa, NW Europe (1939-1946); called to the Bar Inner Temple (1946); Lincoln's Inn (1953); Bencher Lincoln's Inn (1976); QC (1981) .

Activities: lecturer in construction of documents Council of Legal Education (1952-1970); Conveyancing Counsel of the Court (1974-1981); chairman VAT Tribunals (1988-1990); member General Council of the Bar (1971-1974); member Senate of the Inns of Court and the Bar (1974-1975); member Inter-professional Committee on Retirement Provision (1974 to date); member Land Registration Rule Committee (1976-1981); member Standing Committee on Conveyancing (1985-1987); member Incorporated Council of Law Reporting (1977 to date) (vice-chairman 1987 to date); vice-president Bar Musical Society.

Biography: lives London SW7; born 27.07.1917; married to Julia with 2 children. Educated at Peter Symond's School, Winchester; Christ's College Cambridge (1938 BA) (1942 MA); co-editor 'Deeds and other Documents' Halsbury's Laws of England (4th ed); articles in periodicals.

Leisure: sailing; shooting; music.

TAYLOR Cavan

deputy senior partner LOVELL WHITE DURRANT 65 Holborn Viaduct, London EC1A 2DY.

Career: articled Herbert Smith & Co (1958-1961); admitted (1961); legal department The Distillers Co Ltd (1962-1965); assistant solicitor Piesse & Sons (1965-1966); became partner (1966).

Activities: member International Bar Association; member UK Oil Lawyers' Group; chairman governing body of King's College School, Wimbledon (1973 to date); member of: Law Society; Justinians; City of London Solicitors' Company.

Biography: lives Cobham; born 23.02.1935; married to Helen with 2 daughters and 1 son. Educated at King's College School, Wimbledon (1942-1953); Emmanuel College Cambridge (1958 BA) (1959 LLM); occasional articles on commercial topics in legal journals.

Leisure: reading; gardening; sailing.

TAYLOR George

partner BRODIES WS 15 Atholl Crescent, Edinburgh EH3 8HA.

Career: partner Torrance Baird (1967-1989); became partner Brodies WS (1989).

Activities: secretary Scottish Association of Manufacturers' Agents (1970-1975); independant secretary Scottish Knitwear Trade Joint Industry Committee (1975-1980); director (Property and Franchising) Olivers (UK) Ltd (1980-1986); member of: RSAC; North Berwick Golf Club.

Biography: lives North Berwick; born 01.11.1942; married to Helen with 2 children. Educated at Paisley Grammar School; Glasgow University (1963 MA) (1965 LLB); Royal Faculty of Procurators Gold Medal; general articles on Scottish law for English trade journals.

Leisure: music; golf.

TAYLOR Neil

Queen's Counsel 2 King's Bench Walk, Temple, London EC4Y 7DE.

Career: called to the Bar (1949); head of Chambers 2 Dr Johnson's Buildings (1957-1987); QC (1975); Recorder (1983); Bencher of Inner Temple (1983).

Activities: Deputy High Court Judge from time to time; member of: Leander Rowing Club; Old Salopian Club.

Biography: lives Epping and County Antrim, Northern Ireland; born 20.02.1922; married with 3 children. Educated at Shrewsbury School (1936-1941); Oriel College Oxford (1946-1948) State Bursary in Science; (1948 MA hons).

Leisure: farming; forestry.

T

TAYLOR Paul

partner INGLEDEW BOTTERELL Milburn House, Dean Street, Newcastle upon Tyne NE1 1NP.

Career: articled Nottinghamshire County Council (1969-1971); admitted (1971); assistant solicitor (1971-1974); senior assistant solicitor Leicestershire County Council (1974-1977); group planning advisor Hoveringham Group Ltd (1977-1982); assistant solicitor Ingledew Botterell (1982-1983); became partner (1983).

Activities: member Law Society's Planning Law Committee.

Biography: lives Ponteland; born 19.08.1947; married to Barbara with 2 children. Educated at Exeter School (1958-1965); Nottingham Regional College of Technology (1968 LLB).

TAYLOR Raymond

partner BEVAN ASHFORD Gotham House, Tiverton, Devon EX16 6LT.

Career: articled Penny & Harward (1965-1968); admitted (1968); assistant solicitor (1968-1969); became partner (1969); became equity partner (1971); thereafter equity partner successor firms to Penny & Harward.

Activities: clerk to General Commissioners of Income Tax for Divisions of Taunton Tiverton and Axminster; vice-president Association of Clerks to Commissioners of Taxes for Great Britain; member Law Society's Revenue Law Committee.

Biography: lives Taunton; born 28.09.1942; single. Educated at King's College, Taunton (1955-1960); Oriel College Oxford (1963 BA MA); Solicitors' Finals (1967 hons).

Leisure: literary interests.

TAYLOR Richard

partner and head of commercial and litigation department MCKENNA & CO Mitre House, 160 Aldersgate Street, London EC1 4DD.

Career: articled McKenna & Co; admitted (1969); assistant solicitor (1969-1974); seconded to German lawyers for six months (1973); (shorter periods with Dutch and French lawyers); became partner (1974); established office in Brussels (1988).

Activities: speaks at conferences on European Community law; committee member of the Solicitors' European Group; invited by the London office of the Commission of the European Communities to be one of a small number of outside speakers to explain the policy of the Commission at conferences and seminars on the subject of the internal market; member Roehampton Club.

Biography: lives London SW13; born 06.02.1945; married to Jean with 1 daughter. Educated at St Benedict's School; Corpus Christi College Oxford (1966 MA); College of Law Lancaster Gate (1966-1967); written a number of articles on UK competition law and European Community law; edits firm's monthly bulletin on European Community law.

Leisure: tennis; cricket; opera; theatre; wine tasting; travel; reading travel books (particularly about Asia and Far East).

TAYLOR Sue

partner company and commercial department FRERE CHOLMELEY 28 Lincoln's Inn Fields, London WC2A 3HH.

Career: articled Frere Cholmeley; admitted assistant solicitor (1978); became partner (1985).

Biography: Educated at Beverley High School for Girls; Exeter University (LLB); St Anne's College Oxford (BCL).

TAYLOR Victor G

assistant secretary LONRHO PLC Cheapside House, 138 Cheapside, London EC2V 6BL.

Career: articled Baileys Shaw & Gillett (1951-1956); admitted (1957); National Service; commissioned in the Army in Kenya (1957-1959); Company Secretary's department The English Electric Co Ltd (1959-1963); John Holt & Co (Liverpool) Ltd, Lagos, Nigeria (1963-1975); general manager investment division, England (1975-1981); became Assistant Secretary Lonrho Plc (1981).

Activities: member The Queen's Club.

Biography: lives London W14; born 23.09.1934; married to Margaret with 2 daughters. Educated at Bancroft's School, Woodford Green; College of Law Lancaster Gate.

Leisure: tennis; piano playing; oil painting.

TAYLOR W Nicholas

partner and head of the planning and environment department BERWIN LEIGHTON, Adelaide House, London Bridge, London EC4R 9HA.

Career: articled chief executive Dorset County Council; admitted (1974); local government solicitor Dorset and Avon County Councils; assistant secretary Association of County Councils; joined Berwin Leighton (1984). Became a partner (1985). Member of the Board of Management.

Activities: former member CBI London Region Task Force on Inner Cities; former Regional Councillor London Region CBI; member Land Use panel of CBI; regular speaker at conferences on planning, urban regeneration and the environment.

Biography: lives Kew; born 09.03.1949; married to Jacqueline with 2 children. Educated at Fitzmaurice Grammar School; New College Oxford (1970 BA MA in School of Modern History); College of Law Lancaster Gate (1971 & 1973).

Leisure: walking; tennis; antiques and porcelain; music; theatre; opera.

TEMPLE Anthony

Queen's Counsel 4 Pump Court, London EC4.

Career: Crown Law Office, Western Australia (1968-1969); 4 Pump Court (1970); QC (1986); Recorder of the Crown Court (1989).

Biography: lives London; born 21.09.1945; married with 2 children. Educated at Haileybury and ISC; Worcester College Oxford (1967 MA).

Leisure: modern pentathlon; travel.

TEMPLE Euan

partner and head of company/commercial department HUNT DICKINS Leeds House, 14 Clumber Street, Nottingham NG1 3DS.

Career: articled Andrew & Co (1968-1970); admitted (1970); assistant solicitor (1970-1971); assistant solicitor Kingsford Dorman (1971-1973); became partner Ashton Hill & Co (1973-1980); became partner Temple Wallis (1980-1987); became partner Hunt Dickins (1987).

Activities: Notts Law Society secretary (1983-1985); regional secretary to East Midlands Association of local Law Societies (1985 to date); secretary Solicitors' European Group (East Midlands Branch) (1988 to date); playing member South Nottingham Hockey Club .

Biography: lives East Bridgford; born 07.01.1946; married to Patricia with 4 children. Educated at Fettes College (1959-1964); Pembroke College Cambridge (1967 MA).

Leisure: Western European history; political biography; fell-walking; hockey playing and coaching.

TENCH David

head of legal department CONSUMERS' ASSOCIATION 2 Marylebone Road, London NW1 4DX.

Career: admitted (1952); assistant solicitor (1952-1958); Inland Revenue (1958-1969); Consumers' Association (1969).

Activities: member Farrand Committee (1984); Parliamentary lobbyist; promoted (inter alia) Unfair Contracts Terms Act (1977) and House Buyers' Bill (1983).

Biography: lives Amersham; born 14.06.1929; married to Elizabeth; 3 children. Educated at Merchant Taylors' School, Northwood; author of: 'The Law for Consumers' (1962); 'The Law for Motorists' (1964); 'The Legal Side of Buying a House' (1965); 'Wills and Probate' (1966); 'Towards a Middle System of Law' (1982) .

TERZEON Paul

partner in charge of recruitment and training of articled clerks and solicitors KINGSLEY NAPLEY 107-115 Long Acre, London WC2 9PT.

Career: articled Hempsons (1975-1977); admitted (1978); assistant solicitor (1978-1979); assistant solicitor Bird & Bird (1979-1981); assistant solicitor Kingsley Napley (1981-1982); became salaried partner (1982); became partner (1986).

Activities: member Law Society and local Law Society; member British Academy of Forensic Sciences.

Biography: lives London and Hertfordshire; born 03.09.1951; married to Hilary with 2 children. Educated at St Michael's College, Hitchin; The Polytechnic, Regent Street (1973 BSC).

Leisure: leisurely country pursuits.

THEYER Nigel

commercial property partner BOND PEARCE 1 The Crescent, Plymouth, Devon PL1 3AE.

Career: articled Bond Pearce (1975-1977); admitted (1977); assistant solicitor (1977-1982); became partner (1982).

Activities: member Plymouth Law Society; member of: Hawks Club; Oxford & Cambridge Golf Society; Yelverton Golf Club; Saints Cricket Club.

Biography: lives Plymouth; born 22.02.1953; married with 2 daughters. Educated at Buxton College; Peterhouse Cambridge (1974 BA hons) (MA); contributor to Butterworths Encyclopaedia Forms and

Precedents Fifth Edition Volume 37.

Leisure: sport; collector of 'Spy' cricket cartoons and PG Wodehouse novels.

THOMAS (R) John (L)

Queen's Counsel Four Essex Court, Temple, London EC4Y 9AJ.

Career: called to the Bar Gray's Inn (1969); pupillage 4 Essex Court (1971); general commercial practice (1972 to date); QC (1984); member of the Bar and QC of the Eastern Caribbean Supreme Court, St Vincent and the Grenadires Circuit; Recorder, Wales & Chester Circuit (1987).

Biography: lives London NW3 and Brecknock; born 22.10.1947; married to Elizabeth Ann Buchanan with 1 son and 1 daughter. Educated at Rugby School; Trinity Hall Cambridge (1969 BA); University of Chicago Law School (1970 JD); Commonwealth Fellow; articles and papers on shipping, insurance and reinsurance law.

Leisure: gardens; walking; opera.

THOMAS Andrew

partner responsible for recruitment and training LEWIS SILKIN 1 Butler Place, Buckingham Gate, London SW1H 0PT.

Career: articled Lewis Silkin (1972-1974); admitted (1974); assistant solicitor (1974-1976); became partner (1976); managing partner (1988-1989).

Activities: member Executive Committee of the Legal Aid Practitioners' Group (1984 to date); member Law Society By-Laws Revision Committee (1987); member Law Society Entry and Training Committee (1987-1988); member Law Society Remuneration and Practice Development Committee (1988 to date); evening voluntary worker at West Stepney/Tower Hamlets Law Centre (1974-1984); member Management Committee of North Lewisham Law Centre (1983-1987).

Biography: lives London SE21; married to Eileen with 1 daughter. Educated at Portsmouth Grammar School; University of Wales Institute of Science and Technology Cardiff (1970 LLB); London School of Economics (1971 LLM); College of Law Lancaster Gate (1972 hons).

Leisure: singing with the London Chorale; long distance running; opera.

THOMAS David

managing partner LEEDS LLOYD WHITLEY Castle Chambers, Castle Street, Liverpool L2 9SH.

Career: articled FS Moore & Price (1967-1969); admitted (1969); assistant solicitor (1969-1971); became partner (1971); became senior partner (1982); FS Moore & Price amalgamated with GF Lees & Son to form Lees Moore & Price (1984); amalgamated with Edward Lloyd & Co and Whitley & Co to form Lees Lloyd Whitley (1988); managing partner Lees Lloyd Whitley (1988).

Activities: president Liverpool Law Society (1987-1988) (vice-president 1986-1987) joint secretary 1985-1986) (secretary (1981-1985); council member Law Society (1987 to date); chairman Specialisation Committee; member Standards & Guidance Committee; Standards & Guidance Casework Committee; Revenue Law Committee.

Biography: lives Scorton; born 07.11.1945; separated with 4 children. Educated at St Anselm's College, Birkenhead; Liverpool University (1966 LLB hons) .

Leisure: reading (particularly history and naval aviation); fell walking.

THOMAS James

partner and head of probate and trust department READ HIND STEWART Ivebridge House, 59 Market Street, Bradford BD1 1SL.

Career: articled Bird & Bird; admitted (1979); assistant solicitor; assistant solicitor Palmer Whieldon; assistant solicitor Henman Ballard & Co; assistant solicitor Read Hind Stewart; became partner (1987).

Biography: lives Leeds; born 07.07.1953; married to Susan with 2 children. Educated at St Edward's School, Oxford; Durham University (1975 hons).

Leisure: cricket; golf; running; theatre.

THOMAS Neville

Queen's Counsel and head of chambers 3 Gray's Inn Place, London WC1R 5EA.

Career: called to the Bar Inner Temple (1962); QC (1975); Master of the Bench Inner Temple; Recorder (1975-1981).

Activities: member Garrick.

Biography: lives London SW5 and Berriew; born 31.03.1936; married to Jennifer with 2 children. Educated at Ruthin School, North Wales, London University School of Slavonic Studies; Oxford Unversity (1960 BA) (1961 BCL).

Leisure: reading; gardening; fishing.

T

THOMAS Rodney

senior partner PICKERING & BUTTERS 19 Greengate Street, Stafford ST16 2LU.

Career: articled Pickering & Pickering (1960-1963); admitted (1963); assistant solicitor (1963-1964); became partner (1964); merged with Butters (1975).

Activities: former president Stafford & District Law Society; former adviser Stafford & District Marriage Guidance Council; former member of Stafford Round Table (former chairman and president); member of: Stafford 41 Club (former chairman); Stafford Rotary Club.

Biography: lives Stafford; born 22.04.1936; married with 3 sons. Educated at Old Hall School, Wellington; Shrewsbury School; St Catherine's College Cambridge (1960 BA) (1961 MA).

Leisure: gardening; skiing; walking; swimming.

THOMAS Roger

partner, member of board and head of company/commercial department PHILLIPS & BUCK Fitzalan House. Fitzalan Road, Cardiff CF2 1XZ.

Career: articled Phillips & Buck (1967-1969); admitted (1969); became partner (1969).

Activities: member of Court of National Museum of Wales (1983 to date) (member of Council 1985 to date); member Welsh Council of Confederation of British Industries (1987 to date); vice-chairman Council of Management of Techniquest (1989 to date); chairman Cardiff branch of British Institute of Management (1988-1990); Fellow of British Institute of Management; member of: Cardiff and County Club; Penarth Yacht Club; Teifi Boat Club.

Biography: lives Penarth; born 22.07.1945; married to Rhian. Educated at Penarth County School (1958-1960); Leighton Park School, Reading (1960-1963); Birmingham University (1966 LLB).

Leisure: sailboarding; hill walking; choral singing.

THOMPSON Anthony

Queen's Counsel 1 Essex Court, Temple, London EC4Y 9AR and 17 Avenue de Lamballe, 75016 Paris, France.

Career: called to the Bar Inner Temple (1957); 1 Essex Court (1968 to date); QC (1980); Recorder of the Crown Court (1983); Bencher Inner Temple (1986); admitted avocat Paris Bar (1988); admitted Singapore; Hong Kong; St Vincent.

Activities: chairman Bar European Group (1984-1986) (vice-chairman 1982-1984); co-chairman Commission on Banking Law of the Union Internationale des Avocat (1988 to date); Arbitrator International Chamber of Commerce, Paris; Associate Chartered Institute of Arbitrators.

Biography: lives London and Gloucestershire; born 04.07.1932; married to Francoise with 2 sons and 1 daughter. Educated at Latymer; University College Oxford (MA); La Sorbonne, Paris.

Leisure: lawn tennis; walking; theatre; cinema; food; wine.

THOMPSON Brian

partner BRIAN THOMPSON & PARTNERS 102 St George's Square, London SW1V 3QY.

Career: articled WH Thompson (father's firm) (1947-1951); admitted (1951); became partner (1951).

Activities: submitted some evidence to the Royal Commission on Civil Liability and Compensation for Personal Injury (chairman Lord Pearson).

Biography: lives London SW7; born 13.04.1926; single. Educated at Dartington Hall School; Imperial College London (1945 BSC).

THOMPSON Peter

solicitor to Departments of Health and Social Security A102 Richmond House, 79 Whitehall, London SW1A 2NS.

Career: called to the Bar Lincoln's Inn (1961); practised at common law Bar (1961-1973); Law Commission (1973-1978); Lord Chancellor's Department (1978-1983); DHSS Solicitors' Office (1983-1988); solicitor to DH and DSS (1989 to date).

Activities: general editorship of The County Court Practice (1989 to date) (assistant editor 1981-1989).

Biography: lives North London; born 30.07.1937; married with 2 daughters. Educated at Worksop College; Christ's College Cambridge (1960 BA) (LLB MA); author of: 'The Unfair Contract Terms Act 1977' (1978); 'The Recovery of Interest' (1985).

Leisure: writing (particularly plays).

THOMPSON Peter

partner and head of employment law services HOWES PERCIVAL Oxford House, Cliftonville, Northampton NN1 5PN.

Career: assistant solicitor Littlewoods Organisation PLC (1970-1974); company solicitor (1974-1979); personnel manager (1979-1982); private practice (1982-1987); became partner Howes Percival (1987); member strategic board.

Activities: part-time chairman Industrial Tribunal Manchester (1983-1989) (Nottingham 1989 to date); member of: Royal Birkdale Golf Club; The Northamptonshire Golf Club.

Biography: lives Northampton; born 18.01.1946; married to Elisabeth with 3 children. Educated at King George V School, Southport; Leeds University (1967 LLB hons); OU Diploma Industrial Relations; articles in Law Society's Gazette ; various newspaper and journal articles.

Leisure: golf; literature; music.

THOMPSON Robin

senior partner ROBIN THOMPSON & PARTNERS Bainbridge House. Bainbridge Street, London WC1A 1HT.

Career: Army for 4 years; obtained rank of Captain; articled father's firm; admitted (1950); became partner.

Activities: member the Winn Committee on personal injuries litigation and author of 'Minority Report'; past treasurer of the Society of Labour Lawyers.

Biography: lives London NW3; born 15.09.1924; son David Thompson partner in charge Nottingham office; 1 daughter. Educated at Dartington Hall School; Loughborough College; author of: 'Accidents at Work' (1963) (subsequently reprinted and revised) and 'Injuries at Work' (1990) with Brian Thompson and Partners).

Leisure: golfing; photography; messing about in boats; entertaining 13 year old daughter.

THOMPSON Roger

managing partner WARNER GOODMAN & STREAT Portland Chambers, 66 West Street, Fareham, Hants PO16 0JR.

Career: articled Goodman & Kent (1959-1962); admitted (1962); assistant solicitor (1962-1965); became partner (1965).

Activities: former chairman Havant Rugby Club; member Round Table; member Rotary Club; member several sporting clubs.

Biography: lives Hayling Island; born 15.10.1935; married to Christine with 4 children. Educated at Warwick School; King Edward VIII School, Sheffield.

Leisure: sport.

THOMSON John

senior partner STREATHERS
37 Bushey Green, Catford, London
SE6 4AX.

Career: articled Streather & Co; admitted;
assistant solicitor Baines & Baines; partner
(1984); became partner Streather & Co;
Streather & Thomson Streatham: and
Streather Thomson Hauser Clapham.

Activities: member Croham Hurst Golf
Club.

Biography: lives Banstead; born 02.07.1957;
married to Lesley with 3 children.
Educated at Trinity Academy, Edinburgh;
King's Norton Grammar School,
Birmingham; Emanuel Grammar School,
Swansea; Selhurst Grammar School,
Croydon; University College London (1979
LLB); College of Law Lancaster Gate (1979-
1980).

Leisure: golf.

THORNE Clive

partner and head of intellectual property
group DENTON HALL BURGIN &
WARRENS Five Chancery Lane, Clifford's
Inn, London EC4A 1BU.

Career: articled Clifford-Turner (1975-
1977); admitted (1977); assistant solicitor
(1977); assistant solicitor Beachcroft
Hyman Isaacs (1977-1980); associate (1980);
admitted Hong Kong (1984); associate
Baker & McKenzie, Hong Kong and
London (1980-1987); barrister and solicitor,
Victoria (1985).

Activities: member Anti-Counterfeiting
Group Law Reform Committee; member
United States Trademark Association;
member Society of Conservative Lawyers;
member United Oxford & Cambridge
University Club.

Biography: lives Woking; born 21.01.1952;
married (1) Catherine Sykes (diss 1982); (2)
Alison Healy. Educated Eastbourne
Grammar School; Trinity Hall Cambridge
(1974 BA hons) (1978 MA hons); Dr
Cooper's Law Studentship (1974-1975); co-
author of 'Intellectual Property - The New
Law'; author of numerous articles on
intellectual property matters.

Leisure: walking; flute playing; English
music; opera; politics.

THORNEYCROFT John

senior partner MANBY & STEWARD
Ninth Floor, Mander House,
Wolverhampton, W Midlands WV1 3NE.

Career: admitted (1966); assistant solicitor
Manby & Steward (1966-1968); became

partner (1968).

Activities: Registrar of Diocese of Lichfield;
legal secretary to Bishop of Lichfield;
member Wolverhampton Law Society
Council (1973-1976); member Shropshire
Law Society Council (1984-1987).

Biography: lives Shifnal; born 09.12.1939;
married with 4 children. Educated at
Wellington College, Berks; Pembroke
College Cambridge.

Leisure: squash; tennis; jogging; church
and charitable activities.

THORNEYCROFT Max

managing partner/corporate finance
partner GOULDENS 22 Tudor Street,
London EC4Y 0JJ.

Career: articled Macfarlanes; admitted
(1975); assistant solicitor Norton Rose
(1975-1981); assistant solicitor Gouldens
(1981-1983); became corporate finance
partner (1983); became managing partner
(1987).

Biography: lives London N1 and
Gloucestershire; born 02.09.1949; married
to Jenny with 2 children. Educated at
King's School, Macclesfield; Lincoln
College Oxford (1972 BA); author of UK
section on 'The Regulations Governing
Mergers and Acquisitions across the
European Community' produced by
International Financial Law Review (1989)
and 'Western European joint ventures and
alliances' published by Acquisitions
Monthly (1990).

Leisure: opera; riding; sailing; skiing.

THORNTON Robert

partner and senior member commercial
property department FORSYTE KERMAN
71 New Cavendish Street, London W1.

Career: articled Dodd Lampliffe &
Fenwick; admitted (1970); became equity
partner (1970-1979); became partner
Forsyte Kerman (1979).

Activities: member London Regional
Council CBI; chairman Kingdomwide
Limited and Kingdomwide Developments
Ltd; member Apex Trust Employers'
Advisory Group; member British Council
of Shopping Centres; member British
Property Federation; member International
Real Estate Federation; director London
Property Co PLC.

Biography: lives London W2; born
01.06.1947; divorced. Educated at Preston
Manor County Grammar School; College
of Law; contributor to quarterly newsletter
issued by Household Mortgage

Corporation PLC.

Leisure: property development in England
and France; tennis.

THORPE John

senior partner SHOOSMITHS &
HARRISON Compton House, Abington
Street, Northampton NN1 2LR.

Career: articled Phipps & Troup; admitted
(1963); assistant solicitor Boyes Turner &
Burrows; partner Shoosmiths & Harrison
(1964); managing partner (1987); became
senior partner (1989).

Activities: past president
Northamptonshire Law Society (1984); past
chairman Daventry Round Table; past
chairman ISAC Committee North
Oxfordshire; trustee (past president)
Daventry & District Sports Club; trustee
Nene Foundation; member of: 41 Club;
Staverton Park Golf Club; Northampton &
County Club; Trevose Golf & Country
Club.

Biography: lives Everdon; born 17.10.1939;
married to Susan with 3 children.
Educated at Oundle School.

Leisure: tennis; cricket; gardening; walking.

THRELFELL John

partner in charge of civil litigation
BRAY & BRAY 1, 3 & 5 Welford Road,
Leicester LE2 7AN.

Career: articled Leicester City Council;
admitted (1971); assistant solicitor Grimsby
Borough Council; assistant solicitor Bray &
Bray; became partner (1973).

Activities: president Leicestershire Law
Society (1989-1990).

Biography: lives Leicestershire; born
05.10.1946; married to Madeleine with 3
children. Educated at Bridlington School;
King's College London (1968 LLB).

Leisure: gardening; skiing; badminton.

THRING Jeremy

senior partner THRINGS AND LONG
Midland Bridge, Bath, Avon BA1 2HQ.

Career: commissioned 3rd King's Own
Hussars (1955-1957); North Somerset
Yeomanry (1957-1964); admitted (1962);
assistant solicitor (1962-1965); became
partner Thring Sheldon Rutherford (now
Thrings and Long) (1965).

Activities: member Bath Hospital
Management Committee (1967-1974);
chairman Community Health Council
(1974-1978); president Bath Law Society

T

(1984-1986); deputy Lt for Avon; director Coutts Bank (local); Notary Public; director Sun Alliance (local); member Bath District Health Authority (1982 to date); trustee of: Bath Institute for Rheumatic Diseases Trust; Bath Institute for Research into the Care of the Elderly;; National Eye Research Centre (Bristol); Bath Unit for Research into Paediatrics; Avon & Bristol Red Cross - special appeal fund; member Avon Game Conservancy (1979 to date); governor Bath High School; member Bath County Club.

Biography: lives Bradford on Avon; born 11.05.1936; married to Cynthia with 2 children. Educated at Winchester College.

Leisure: stalking; shooting; fishing; breeding Soay sheep.

THUM Max

senior litigation partner ASHURST MORRIS CRISP Broadwalk House, 5 Appold Street, London EC2A 2HA.

Career: commissioned pilot officer RAF (1955-1957); admitted (1955); assistant solicitor Lewis & Lewis and Gisborne (1955-1957); advocate and assistant solicitor Rodyk & Davidson, Singapore (1957-1960); Singapore Bar (1958); professional purposes department Law Society (1961); became partner Sharpe Pritchard & Co (1962-1966); became senior litigation partner Ashurst Morris Crisp (1967).

Activities: member International Bar Association; associate member American Bar Association; member RAC.

Biography: lives London SW7 and Hampshire; born 15.02.1933; married to Valerie; 3 children by previous marriage. Educated at Ecole Internationale de Geneve (1937-1939); Chigwell School (1940-1950); College of Law (1952-1955).

Leisure: photography; opera; swimming; tennis; cars.

THURMAN Roderick James

partner and head of corporate law department EDWARDS GELDARD 16 St Andrew's Crescent, Cardiff CF1 3RD.

Career: administrative officer University of Zambia law department (1970-1971); articled Macfarlanes (1971-1973); admitted (1973); studied in Germany (Heidelberg) (1973-1974); assistant solicitor Herbert Smith & Co (1974-1976); assistant solicitor Edwards Geldard (1976-1977); became partner (1977); became head of corporate department (1983).

Activities: member of: Royal Porthcawl Golf Club; Cardiff & County Club.

Biography: lives Usk; born 16.07.1948; married to Jacqueline with 4 children. Educated at Bridgend Boys' Grammar School (1959-1967); Birmingham University (1970 LLB hons).

Leisure: golf; skiing; walking; gardening; theatre; opera.

THURSTON SMITH Martin

corporate partner TODS MURRAY WS 66 Queen Street, Edinburgh EH2 4NE.

Career: apprenticeship Tods Murray WS (1974-1976); admitted (1977); assistant solicitor (1977-1978); became partner (1978).

Activities: member Law Society of Scotland pensions working party.

Biography: lives Edinburgh; born 20.11.1951; married to Diana with 1 son and 1 daughter. Educated at The Edinburgh Academy; Christ's College Cambridge (1973 BA) (1974 LLB); occasional articles for non-academic publications.

Leisure: hill-walking.

TIFFIN Jeremy

partner HILL DICKINSON DAVIS CAMPBELL Pearl Assurance House, Derby Square, Liverpool L2 9XL.

Career: articled Davis Campbell & Co; admitted (1975); assistant solicitor (1975-1979); became partner (1979); firm amalgamated (1989).

Activities: member Legal Aid Area Committee; member Merseyside Medico-Legal Society Committee; member of: Liverpool Racquets Club; The Northern Club (president); Blundellsands Tennis Club.

Biography: lives Blundellsands; born 16.11.1950; married to Gillian with 2 children. Educated at Merchant Taylors' School; Sheffield University (1972 LLB hons); Liverpool Law School (1973); co-author of 'The Examination of a Horse prior to Purchase' tape/slide programme sponsored by the College of Continuing Veterinary Education.

Leisure: tennis; squash; skiing; travel; music; wines.

TILLY Hugh

partner TILLY BAILEY & IRVINE York Chambers, York Road, Hartlepool TS26 9DP.

Career: admitted (1973).

Activities: Notary Public.

Biography: lives Hartlepool; born 01.01.1944; married to Val with 1 child. Educated at Repton; College of Law.

Leisure: trout fishing; racing pigeons.

TILLY John

senior and managing partner TILLY BAILEY & IRVINE York Chambers, York Road, Hartlepool TS26 9DP.

Career: articled to father; admitted (1971); assistant solicitor (1971-1972); became partner (1972-1984); became senior partner (1984); became managing partner (1989).

Activities: Notary Public (1970); president Hartlepool Law Society (1981-1982); member General Committee Hartlepool Law Society (1975 to date); member Conveyancing Committee Hartlepool Law Society (1989); director various property companies; director Hartlepool Statutory Water Co.

Biography: lives Hartlepool; born 22.04.1940; married to Veronica with 2 children. Educated at Repton Preparatory School; Repton School.

Leisure: farming.

TIMS Brian

managing/senior partner AMERY-PARKES 12A London Street, Basingstoke, Hants RG21 1BG.

Career: articled Amery-Parkes; admitted (1965); assistant solicitor (1965-1968); partner (1968); managing partner (1986); became joint senior partner (1989); former chairman firm's managing committee.

Activities: former hon secretary Basingstoke Area Committee of Hampshire Incorporated Law Society; chairman of the governors of local county primary school; vice-chairman local parish council; past captain golf club.

Biography: lives Newbury; born 03.08.1943; married to Christine with 2 children. Educated at Hampton Grammar School; LOMAT residential training at Sundridge Park Management Centre; Institute of Linguists Grade I Certificate in French.

TISDALL Miles

partner and head of litigation department LARCOMES 168 London Road, North End, Portsmouth, Hants PO2 9DN.

Career: admitted (1968); assistant solicitor (1968-1973); assistant solicitor Larcomes

T

(1973-1974); became partner (1974).

Activities: former member Law Society's Negligence Panel; former member Law Society Legal Aid Committee (Area No 3); solicitor to major Diocese; one of advisory solicitors to regional office of major clearing bank.

Biography: lives Emsworth; born 02.12.1941; married to Elizabeth with 3 children. Educated at Uppingham; College of Law.

Leisure: sailing; sailboarding; classical music.

TITHERIDGE Roger

Queen's Counsel and head of chambers 1 Paper Buildings, Temple, London EC4Y 7EP.

Career: called to the Bar Gray's Inn (1954); Western Circuit; Recorder (1972); QC (1973); Deputy High Court Judge (1984); master of the Bench Gray's Inn (1985); leader Western Circuit (1989) .

Activities: member Hampshire Club.

Biography: lives Kingston-upon-Thames; born 21.12.1928; married to Annabel with 2 children. Educated at Midhurst Grammar School; Merton College Oxford (1953 BA) (MA) Exhibitioner; Holker Senior Scholarship Gray's Inn (1953).

Leisure: tennis; sailing; gardening.

TOBIAS Paul

partner and head of probate department HART BROWN & CO West Bank, 4 Jenner Road, Guildford, Surrey GU1 3PW.

Career: articled Hart Brown & Co (1978-1980); admitted (1980); assistant solicitor (1980-1982); became salaried partner (1982); became equity partner (1984); head of probate department (1989).

Activities: member of: West Byfleet Squash Club; Chris Lane Tennis & Health Centre.

Biography: lives Woking; born 23.02.1955; married with 2 children. Educated at Farnborough Grammar School; Birmingham University (1977 LLB hons); College of Law Guildford (1977-1978); magazine and newspaper articles tax planning.

Leisure: tennis; squash.

TOBIAS Peter

compliance officer SCHRODER INVESTMENT MANAGEMENT LIMITED 36 Old Jewry, London EC2R 8BS.

Career: articled Hunters; admitted (1971);

became chief executive Executor and Trustee Co of Schroders.

Activities: assistant Director of Sim; school governor.

Biography: lives Woodford; born 09.04.1944; married with 3 children. Educated at William Ellis, London; Manchester University (1966 LLB hons).

TOLLETT Michael

partner EVERSHED WELLS & HIND 10 Newhall Street, Birmingham B3 3LX.

Career: articled Harold Roberts & Lea (1950-1954); admitted (1954); assistant solicitor Evershed & Tomkinson (1954 & 1956-1959); National Service as intelligence officer in the Royal Air Force (1954-1956) (pilot officer); became partner Evershed & Tomkinson (1959).

Biography: lives Solihull; born 11.05.1931; married to Ann with 2 children. Educated at King Edward The Sixth's Grammar School, Camp Hill, Birmingham (1942-1943); King Edward The Sixth's School, Birmingham (1943-1949); Birmingham University Open Scholar (1949) (1952 LLB hons).

TOMLINS John

senior partner EDWIN COE 11 Stone Buildings, Lincoln's Inn, London WC2A 3TH.

Career: articled Edwin Coe & Calder Woods (1960-1965); admitted (1965); assistant solicitor (1965-1969); junior partner (1969-1986); became senior partner (1986).

Activities: treasurer of The Friends of the Geffrye Museum (1980 to date); member Blackwater Sailing Club.

Biography: lives Maldon; born 05.10.1942; married to Anna with 3 children. Educated at Wallop School, Weybridge; Bradfield College, Berks; College of Law Lancaster Gate (1961); Guildford (1964-1965).

Leisure: sailing; local parish and parochial parish affairs.

TOMS Bate C

partner DOBSON SINISI & TOMS 64 London Wall, London EC2M 5TP.

Career: associate and then European Counsel at two large US firms (1977-1986); partner Pepper Hamilton & Scheetz (1986-1990); became founding partner Dobson Sinisi & Toms (1990).

Activities: editor of: Yale Law Journal

(1975-1977); Oil and Gas Law & Taxation Review (1982 to date); Journal of International Banking Law (1986 to date); member United Oxford & Cambridge Universities Club.

Biography: lives London SW7; born 22.09.1949; married to Jocelyne with 1 child. Educated at Woodberry Forest School (1967); Institute d'Etudes Politiques de Paris (1969-1970); Washington and Lee University (1971 BA); Magdalene College Cambridge (1973 Law Tripos); Yale Law School (1975 JD); Yale Graduate School (1977 MS); author of: 'Compensating Shareholders Frozen Out in Two-Step Mergers' in Columbia Law Review vol 78 (1978); 'The French Response to the Extraterritorial Application of United States Antitrust Laws' in The International Lawyer vol 15 (1981); 'Offshore Share Offerings' in Journal of International Banking Law vol 1 (1986).

Leisure: golf; sailing.

TOOMEY John

partner in property department ROWE & MAW 20 Black Friars Lane, London EC4V 6HD.

Career: articled Rowe & Maw (1969-1971); admitted (1971); assistant solicitor (1971-1973); became partner (1973); staff partner and member Executive Committee (1978-1986).

Activities: school governor; member Bentham Club.

Biography: lives Mayfield; born 18.07.1946; married to Dilys with 3 children. Educated at Bishop Challoner School; University College London (LLB).

Leisure: family; golf; turning 3 acres of farmland into garden; music; walking.

TOOTAL Christopher Peter

partner and head of intellectual property law section HERBERT SMITH Watling House, 35 Cannon Street, London EC4M 5SD.

Career: chartered patent agent (1962); articled Herbert Smith (1964); admitted; became partner (1968).

Activities: member Standing Advisory Committee on Intellectual Property; chairman Patent Solicitors' Association; chairman joint working party of the Bar and Law Society on intellectual property; member Royal Harwich Yacht Club.

Biography: lives Ardleigh; born 10.03.1936; married to Alison with 2 children. Educated at Repton; Queen's College

T

Oxford (1958 BA BSc).

Leisure: music; sailing; photography.

TOTTY Peter

partner ALLEN & OVERY 9 Cheapside, London EC2V 6AD.

Career: admitted (1964).

Activities: licenced insolvency practitioner; member Council of Insolvency Lawyers' Association; member Insolvency Practitioners' Association; member City of London Law Society Insolvency Law Sub-committee; member Joint Bar Council and Law Society Insolvency Law Committee; member International Bar Association Committee J (Insolvency); leads firm's business reconstruction and insolvency group.

Biography: lives London SE21 and New Forest; born 10.06.1938; married to Gillian with 2 children. Educated at Wirral Grammar School; Oxford (1961) (1964 MA); author numerous articles; co-author: 'Corporate Insolvency' with Michael Crystal QC; Longman's 'Insolvency' (3 vols) with Michael Jordan.

Leisure: sailing.

TOUBKIN Michael

legal adviser BANQUE NATIONALE DE PARIS PLC 8-13 King William Street, London EC4P 4HS.

Career: articled EF Turner & Sons; admitted (1969); assistant solicitor Sinclair Roche & Temperley (1969-1971); legal department Shell International Petroleum Co Ltd (1971-1973); shipping department William Brandts' Sons & Co Ltd (1973-1974); legal department Commonwealth Development Corporation (1974-1978); legal adviser Nordic Bank PLC (1978-1985); became legal adviser Banque Nationale de Paris PLC (1985).

Activities: member The Kandahar Ski Club.

Biography: lives Oxshott; born 15.03.1944; married to Phyllis with 2 children. Educated at Charterhouse; Ecole Lemania, Lausanne.

Leisure: reading.

TOULSON Roger

Queen's Counsel 2 Crown Office Row, Temple, London EC4Y 7HJ.

Career: called to the Bar Inner Temple (1969); QC (1986); Recorder .

Activities: member Old Millhillians.

Biography: lives Guildford; born

23.09.1946; married to Elizabeth with 4 children. Educated at Mill Hill School (1959-1964); Jesus College Cambridge (1964-1968); Scholar.

Leisure: skiing; tennis; gardening.

TOWERS Lennox

managing partner BOOTH & CO Sovereign House, South Parade, Leeds LS1 1HQ.

Career: articled Booth & Co; admitted (1971); assistant solicitor (1971-1974); became partner (1974).

Biography: lives Menston; born 24.09.1946; married to Jan with 3 children. Educated at Hutchesons' Boys' Grammar School, Glasgow; Leeds Grammar School; Exeter University (1968 LLB).

Leisure: walking; sailing; family pursuits.

TOWNEND James

Queen's Counsel and head of chambers 1 King's Bench Walk, Temple, London EC4Y 7DB.

Career: called to the Bar (1962); QC (1978); Recorder (1979); Master of the Bench Middle Temple (1987).

Activities: member Kingston and Esher DHA (1983-1986); member Bar Council (1984-1988); chairman Sussex Crown Court Liaison Committee (1980-1989); chairman Family Law Bar Association (1986-1988); member Bar Yacht Club.

Biography: lives Kingston-upon-Thames; born 21.02.1938; married to Airelle with 1 stepdaughter. Educated at Tonbridge School; Lincoln College Oxford (1963 MA hons).

Leisure: sailing; fishing; walking.

TOWNSEND Nick

managing partner EDGE & ELLISON Regent Court, Regent Street, Leicester LE1 7BR.

Career: articled Harding & Barnett and Gardiner & Millhouse (1963-1969); admitted (1970); ICFC (1970-1971); ran nightclub in Spain (1971); assistant solicitor Gardiner & Millhouse (1974-1976); became partner (1976-1978); founded Marron Townsend (1978-1980); founded own practice (1980); merged with Stauntons (1987); merged with Edge & Ellison (1989).

Activities: chairman Tamborough Properties PLC; member Leicester Squash Club.

Biography: lives Leicester; born 08.04.1946;

married to Lis with 1 daughter. Educated at Kimbolton.

Leisure: keen game shot; squash.

TRAVERS Iain

partner and head of regional office, Doncaster NABARRO NATHANSON 50 Stratton Street, London W1X 5FL.

Career: articled Nabarro Nathanson; admitted (1977); assistant solicitor (1977-1980); became partner (1980); set up property litigation department (1987).

Activities: seminars; lecturing.

Biography: lives London SW11 and Wiltshire; born 06.09.1952; married. Educated at Oratory School, Berkshire; City of London Polytechnic (1973 BA hons); book reviews; articles in Estates Times and Property Management.

Leisure: skiing; good food and wine; entertaining; country walks.

TREVES Vanni

senior partner MACFARLANES 10 Norwich Street, London EC4A 1BD.

Career: articled Macfarlanes; admitted (1965); secondment to White & Case (1968-1969); became partner Macfarlanes (1970); senior partner (1987).

Activities: chairman BBA Group PLC; non-executive director Saatchi & Saatchi Co plc (1987-1990); non-executive director Oceonics Group PLC; trustee J Paul Getty Jr Charitable Trust and 29th May 1961 Charitable Trust; governor Hall School; hon treasurer London Federation of Boys' Clubs; member of: Boodles; Bucks Club; City of London Club.

Biography: lives London N1 and Suffolk; born 03.11.1940; married to Angela with 3 children. Educated at St Paul's School; University College Oxford (1961 BA); University of Illinois (1962 LLM) (Fulbright Scholar).

Leisure: walking; eating; English watercolours.

TRITTON Clare

Queen's Counsel and head of European Law Chambers, Hamilton House, 1 Temple Avenue, London EC4.

Career: called to the Bar (1968); formerly practised private international and commercial and common law; now practising in European Community law; QC (1988).

Activities: Chairman Bar European Group

(1982-1984); UK rapporteur to FIDE (1988); member European Committee of British Invisible Exports Council; vice-chairman International Practice Committee of the Bar Council; set up the largest barristers' Chambers practising solely European Community law in the UK.

Biography: lives London SW11; born 18.08.1935; married to Andrew McLaren with 2 sons and 1 daughter. Educated at Convent of the Holy Child, Mayfield St Leonards; Birmingham University (1958 BA hons); Inner Temple Pupillage Award; European Community law courses at Exeter University and Polytechnic of Central London; various articles in legal periodicals on the Brussels Convention of Jurisdiction and Judgements; contribution to 'Towards a Community Air Transport Policy' (1989) and published widely articles on various aspects of European Community law.

Leisure: travelling; gardening; reading.

TROMANS Stephen Richard

partner and head of environmental law department SIMMONS & SIMMONS 14 Dominion Street, London EC2M 2RJ.

Career: articled Wild Hewitson & Shaw, Cambridge (1979-1981); admitted (1981); lecturer in law and Fellow of Selwyn College Cambridge (1981-1987); partner Wild Hewitson and Shaw (later Hewitson Becke & Shaw) (1988-1990).

Activities: book reviews editor Journal of Environmental Law; associate lecturer in law Department of Land Economy, Cambridge; specialist advisor to House of Lords Select Committee on the European Communities Sub-committee F (Environment); council member of UK Environmental Law Association; member Law Society's Standing Committee on Planning Law and Chairman of Environmental Law Sub-committee; Fellow of the Royal Society of Arts.

Biography: lives Impington, Cambridge; born 02.02.1957; married to Caroline with 3 children. Educated at Rowley Regis Grammar School; Selwyn College Cambridge (1987 BA hons); author of 'Commercial Leases' (1987); co-author of Sweet & Maxwell's 'Planning Law, Practice and Precedents' (1990); written various articles on property, planning and environmental law in academic and professional journals.

Leisure: family; music; tennis.

TROTT Philip

partner and head of immigration and employment law department THOMSON SNELL & PASSMORE 6th Floor Tower House, 8-14 Southampton Street, London WC2E 7HA.

Career: articled Dale Parkinson & Co (1977-1978); articled Lawford & Co (1978-1979); admitted (1979); assistant solicitor (1979-1982); partner (1982-1989); became partner Thomson Snell & Passmore (1989).

Activities: member Industrial Law Society (1978 to date); hon legal adviser to King's Cross CAB (1979 to date); adviser of art law (1983-1984); founder member Central London Legal Action Group (1984-1985); member Executive of Immigration Law Practitioners' Association (1984-1990); chairman Immigration Law Practitioners' Association (1986-1988); speaker and lecturer at conferences and seminars.

Biography: lives Teddington; born 05.06.1952; single. Educated Dauntsey's School, Devizes (1963-1964); Portsmouth Grammar School (1964-1971); Oxford Polytechnic (1971-1973 HNC); University College London (1976 LLB hons); College of Law (1976-1977); contributor to: Chartered Surveyor Weekly; American Immigration Journal; Immigration and Nationality Law & Practice; New Gazette of Hong Kong Law Society.

Leisure: sailing; swimming; squash; hill walking; flying; travelling.

TROTTER John

senior litigation partner BATES WELLS & BRAITHWAITE 61 Charterhouse Street, London EC1M 6HA.

Career: admitted (1973); assistant solicitor Bates Wells & Braithwaite (1973).

Activities: manager of the Parlex Group of European Lawyers; member Seaview Yacht Club.

Biography: lives Esher and Isle of Wight; born 16.11.1948; married with 2 children. Educated at King's School; Nottingham University (LLB hons); author of articles relating to child abuse enquiries.

Leisure: reading; water sports; skiing.

TROWER Anthony Gosselin

senior partner TROWERS & HAMLINS 6 New Square, Lincoln's Inn, London WC2.

Career: war service (7 years); articled Trower Still and Keeling (1946); became senior partner (1976) and then senior partner Trowers & Hamlins.

Activities: member of: Travellers' Club; Alpine Club; St James Club Manchester.

Biography: lives Stanstead Abbots; born 12.07.1921; married to Catherine John with 5 children. Educated at Durnford; Eton College.

Leisure: farming; shooting; country sports; climbing; hill walking; maintenance of the integrity of the Church of England.

TRUMP Bill

senior partner TRUMP & PARTNERS 34 Saint Nicholas Street, Bristol BS1 1TS.

Career: articled Trump & Partners (1957-1961); admitted (1961); became senior partner (1961).

Biography: lives Bristol; born 15.05.1939; married to Sally with 3 children. Educated at Dean Close, Cheltenham; Bristol University.

Leisure: farming 120 acres sheep, beef and arable; property investment and development; sailing.

TUCKEY Simon

Queen's Counsel 4 Pump Court, Temple, London EC4 7AN.

Career: called to the Bar (1964); general common law on Western Circuit; commercial practice London; QC (1981); Recorder of the Crown Court (1984); Bencher Lincoln's Inn (1989).

Activities: chairman Review Panel Financial Reporting Council (1990).

Biography: lives London NW1; born 17.10.1941; married to Jennifer with 3 children. Educated at Plumtree School, Zimbabwe.

Leisure: tennis; sailing.

TUDOR JOHN William

partner and head of banking department ALLEN & OVERY 9 Cheapside, London EC2V 6AD.

Career: articled Allen & Overy (1967-1969); admitted (1969); assistant solicitor (1969-1970); became partner (1972); banker Orion Bank Ltd (1970-1972).

Activities: member City of London Solicitors' Company Banking and Insolvency Committees (1980-1985); non-executive chairman Suttons Seeds Ltd; non-executive chairman Horticultural & Botanical Holdings Ltd; appeal steward British Boxing Board of Control; member The Justinians.

Biography: lives Hertfordshire; born

T

26.04.1944; married with 3 daughters. Educated at Cowbridge School, Glamorgan (1955-1963); Downing College Cambridge (1966 MA) (Associate Fellow); various articles on the law relating to Sovereign immunity.

Leisure: shooting; rugby; books; music.

TULLY David

managing partner ADDLESHAW SONS & LATHAM Dennis House, Marsden Street, Manchester M2 1JD.

Career: articled Addleshaw Sons & Latham (1959-1964); admitted (1964); assistant solicitor (1964-1969); became partner (1969); became managing partner (1989).

Activities: chairman National Young Solicitors (1977); president Manchester Law Society (1985); joint chairman joint committees Law Society/RICS on model forms of commercial leases; occasional lecturer on matters relating to commercial leases; member of: Wig and Pen; Racquets Club, Manchester; St James's Club, Manchester (chairman 1976).

Biography: lives Hale; born 13.03.1942; married to Susan with 3 children. Educated at prep school, Twyford; public school, Sherborne.

Leisure: shooting; fishing; golf.

TUNNICLIFFE John

senior partner FEW & KESTER Montagu House, Sussex Street, Cambridge CB1 1PB.

Career: RAF (1945-1948); articled at Rochdale (1952-1956); admitted (1956); assistant solicitor Few & Kester (1956-1960); became partner (1960); became senior partner (1983).

Activities: member Council of the Law Society (1969-1989); member Discipline Committee of the Architects' Registration Council; member Hawks.

Biography: lives Cambridge; born 24.05.1926; married to Sonia with 3 children. Educated at North Manchester School; Manchester Grammar School; Trinity College Cambridge (1949 BA) (1951 MA); Manchester University (1954 LLB); articles and contributions to various legal periodicals.

Leisure: golf administration; minor journalism; English and French grammar, syntax and vocabulary; New Testament Greek; history; archaeology; reading and writing verse; music (including playing New Orleans jazz); current affairs; stock exchange investment.

TURNBULL John

managing partner and head of company/commercial department BIRCHAM & CO 1 Dean Farrar Street, Westminster, London SW1H 0DY.

Career: articled Bircham & Co; admitted (1977); assistant solicitor (1977-1979); became partner (1979); became managing partner (1988).

Activities: company secretary of highly successful BES company Finotel PLC (1983 to date); member of: Institute of Directors; Sunningdale Golf Club.

Biography: lives London N10; born 16.10.1950; married with 1 child. Educated at Marlborough College; Balliol College Oxford (1973 MA); College of Law.

Leisure: golf; music; gastronomy; cricket; gardening; travel; skiing.

TURNER Amedee

Queen's Counsel 1 Essex Court, Temple, London EC4.

Career: called to the Bar (1954); patent attorney Kenyon & Kenyon, New York (1957-1960); London Patent Bar (1960 to date); QC (1976).

Activities: MEP (1979, 1984 & 1989); member Legal Affairs; Energy and Technology & Development Committees (various times); Chief Whip European Democratic Group (1989); Rapporteur in European Parliament; Trade Mark Regulations & Directive computer chip topographies Directive; computer software copyright Directive; etc; member Carlton Club.

Biography: lives London; born 26.03.1929; married to Deborah with 2 children. Educated at Temple Grove; Dauntseys; Christ Church Oxford; author of 'The Law of Trade Secrets' (1962 & 1968); 'The Law of the New European Patent' (1979).

TURNER David

senior partner LACE MAWER King's House, 42 King Street West, Manchester M3 2NU.

Career: admitted (1952); assistant solicitor (1952-1954); partner Francis & Turner Bolton & Walkden (1954-1957); became partner AW Mawer & Co (1957).

Biography: lives Poynton; born 04.06.1929; married to Doreen with 1 son. Educated at Ruthin School, Clwyd; Manchester University (1950 LLB).

TURNER Hamish

senior partner KITSONS 2 Vaughan Parade, Torquay TQ2 5EF.

Career: admitted (1957); assistant solicitor (1957-1962); became partner Kitsons (1962); National Service Commission in the Army and served in Cyprus and Jordan.

Activities: Deputy Coroner (17 years); HM Coroner Torbay & South Devon (1982); member of successful consortium applying for franchise for commercial radio in Exeter and South Devon and director and company secretary of Devonair Radio Ltd; PR for South Devon area of Devon & Exeter Law Society (10 years); former chairman of Young Members' Group of Devon Solicitors; founder chairman Douglas House, Cheshire Home at Brixham; national trustee of Leonard Cheshire Foundation (10 years); founder chairman (now president) of Torbay Victims of Crime Support Scheme; vice-chairman governors South Devon College of Arts and Technology.

Biography: lives Torquay; born 02.12.1932; single. Educated at All Hallows School Devon.

Leisure: gardening; former acting member of various operatic societies; golf.

TURNER John

senior partner STANLEY TEE & COMPANY 6 High Street, Bishop's Stortford, Herts CM23 2LU.

Career: National Service with Royal Air Force (1952-1954); commissioned in the RAFVR; admitted (1961); assistant solicitor (1961-1962); became partner Stanley Tee & Company (1962); became senior partner (1981).

Activities: Commissioner for Oaths; General Commissioner of Taxes; trustee Stort Enterprise Trust; governor Herts and Essex High School; governor St Mary's Roman Catholic School; former member Hertfordshire Law Society Committee; former member Harlow Group Hospitals Management Committee; member The Twelve Club.

Biography: lives Bishop's Stortford; born 26.09.1933; married to Mary with 3 children. Educated at Bishop's Stortford College; Christ's College Cambridge (1957 hons) (1961 MA); Exhibition (1955); Batchelor Scholarship (1957).

Leisure: golf; swimming; gardening; sailing; theatre; eating out.

TURNER Roger

senior partner STAFFURTH AND BRAY York Road Chambers, Bognor Regis, West Sussex PO21 1LT.

Career: admitted (1962); assistant solicitor Staffurth & Bray (1964-1966); became partner (1966); became senior partner (1984).

Activities: president Chichester & District Law Society (1988-1989); charter member Bognor Regis Lions Club (1966); member executive committee Bognor Chamber of Trade; president Bognor branch RNLI.

Biography: lives Bognor Regis; born 22.05.1940; married to Janet with 2 children. Educated at St John's College, Southsea.

TURNER Stephen

head of taxation department SIMPSON CURTIS 41 Park Square, Leeds LS1 2NS.

Career: National Service in Royal Armoured Corps - commissioned in Royal Tank Regiment (1957-1959); articled Simpson Curtis (1962-1965); admitted (1965); assistant solicitor (1966-1969); became partner (1969).

Activities: assistant secretary and secretary Leeds Law Society; ex-treasurer Yorkshire County Hockey Club; trustee Educational Charitable Trust; director Charitable Investment Holding Company; member of: Leeds Club; Lightcliffe Golf Club; Bradford Hockey Club (vice- president); Yorkshire County Hockey Association; Yorkshire County Cricket Club.

Biography: lives near Leeds; born 19.07.1938; married to Rita with 1 son and 1 daughter. Educated at Malsis Hall; The Leys; Christ's College Cambridge (1959-1962).

Leisure: golf; walking.

TWEEDIE David Allison Osborne

partner GREGORY ROWCLIFFE & MILNERS 1 Bedford Row, London WC1R 4BZ.

Career: articled Gregory Rowcliffe & Co (1965-1968); admitted (1968); assistant solicitor (1968-1969); became partner (1969).

Activities: former hon legal adviser Neighbourhood Advice Centre, Kentish Town; member Management Committee Hammersmith & Fulham Community Law Centre Ltd (1982-1985); member International Bar Association (publications officer for Committee O 1978-1979); member American Bar Association;

member Holborn Law Society; councillor London Borough of Hammersmith & Fulham (1982-1986); contested Glasgow (Springburn) parliamentary constituency, General Election (1983); member London Fire & Civil Defence Authority (1986); former school governor; trustee Pocklington Apprentices' Trust; member of: Brooks's; Hurlingham Club; Blackmoor Golf Club; Royal Society for Asian Affairs.

Biography: lives London SW6; born 15.09.1941; married with 2 children. Educated at Eton College; New College, Oxford (1963 BA hons) (1967 MA); College of Law, London & Guildford; author of various articles for the legal and professional press; the Law Society's Gazette; The Times, etc.

Leisure: golf; tennis; study of 18th-Century history.

TWEMLOW Tony

managing partner CUFF ROBERTS NORTH KIRK 25 Castle Street, Liverpool L2 4TD.

Career: articled Cuff Roberts & Co (1965-1968); admitted (1968); assistant solicitor (1968-1971); became partner (1971); firm merged with North Kirk & Co (1982) and with Banks Kendall (1987).

Activities: licensed insolvency practitioner; member National Committee of the Young Solicitors' Group of the Law Society (1971-1979) (secretary 1976-1978) (chairman 1978-1979); former member Land Law & Conveyancing and Non-Contentious Committees of the Law Society; non-Council member Remuneration and Practice Development Committee; member Remuneration Certifying Casework Committee; director Solicitors' Benevolent Association; chairman Liverpool Board of Legal Studies; member General Committee Liverpool Law Society; deputy vice-chairman of the Royal Liverpool Philharmonic Society; member Royal Liverpool Philharmonic Choir (1965 to date); member Lyceum Club.

Biography: lives West Kirby; born 02.12.1943; married to Margaret with 3 children. Educated at Calday Grange Grammar School; Cambridge University (1962 BA) (1965 MA).

Leisure: music; tennis.

TWIGG David

partner in criminal department RUSSELL JONES & WALKER New Oxford House, 16 Waterloo Street, Birmingham B2 5UG.

Career: articled in Manchester; prosecuting lawyer (latterly as senior Crown prosecutor) in the West Midlands (1978-1988); secretary and chairman Crown Prosecution section Association of First Division Civil Servants (1987-1988); Russell Jones & Walker (1988); became partner (1990).

Activities: former chairman Committee of the Law Society Prosecutors' Group.

Biography: lives Leamington Spa; born 26.06.1949; married to Anne. Educated at Manchester Grammar School; Manchester University (1972 LLB hons).

TWISS Charles

HQ director of legal services BRITISH GAS PLC Rivermill House, 152 Grosvenor Road, London SW1V 3JL.

Career: articled Dodds Ashcroft & Cook (1965-1967); admitted (1967); assistant solicitor Streat Daunt & Farmiloe (1968-1971); partner (1971-1977); local government assistant controller (legal) London Borough of Harrow (1977-1980); solicitor to the board Eastern Electricity (1980-1985); became HQ director of legal services British Gas PLC (1985).

Activities: member Royal Harwich Yacht Club.

Biography: lives Suffolk; born 10.04.1943; married to Sylvia with 2 children. Educated at Boteler Grammar School, Warrington; Hertford College Oxford (1964 BA) (1969 MA); contributor to 'Managing Legal Practice in Business' (1989).

Leisure: sailing; tennis; country pursuits.

TYLER John

partner and head of commercial division CRIPPS HARRIES HALL 84 Calverley Road, Tunbridge Wells, Kent TN1 2UP.

Career: short service commission admin branch RAF (final rank Flight Lt) (1952-1958); director and co secretary Atcost Group of Companies (1958-1969); articled Cripps Harries Hall (1970-1972); admitted (1973); assistant solicitor (1973-1974); became partner (1974).

Activities: hon auditor Law Society (1980-1981); director and chairman Jones Clifton Group of Companies (1974 to date); hon solicitor various local organisations; Liveryman Worshipful Company of Carmen; director Heatherlands Home for the Handicapped; chairman local committee of Nuffield Hospital.

Biography: lives Tunbridge Wells; born 21.11.1931; married to Patricia with 2 children. Educated at Magnus School, Newark (1942-1948); University of Nottingham (1952 BA).

Leisure: golf; skiing; swimming.

TYLER Richard

partner ATTERSOLLS
40 West Street, Reigate, Surrey RH2 9BT.

Career: admitted (1971); assistant solicitor (1971-1973); became partner (1973-1983); founded Richard Tyler & Company (1983); merged with Attersoll Smith (1985).

Activities: secretary South East Surrey Law Society; member Committee of Association of Surrey Law Societies (1988 & 1990); director National Conveyancing Network (1989-1990); chairman Homecharter Users Group; member AIM Charter Users' Association Management Team; associate member American Bar Association and Practice Management Division; second vice-president Reigate Rotary Club; chairman Salford's Community Aid Project; former borough and parish councillor; thespian and founder chairman Salford's Theatre Arts Group.

Biography: lives Reigate; born 21.09.1946; married to Gaynor with 3 children. Educated at Chislehurst and Sidcup Grammar School; Llandrindod Wells Grammar School; University College of Wales (1967 LLB); Southwark Pastoral Auxilliary.

Leisure: fly fishing; walking; digging holes.

TYRRELL Alan

Queen's Counsel and head of chambers Francis Taylor Building, Temple, London EC4Y 7BY.

Career: called to the Bar Gray's Inn (1956); Western circuit (1956); Recorder of Crown Court (1972); QC (1976); Bencher Gray's Inn (1986); partner Stanbrook and Hooper (1984-1989); head of Chambers (1986); The Lord Chancellor's Legal Visitor (1990 to date).

Activities: member European Parliament (London East) (1979-1984) (member delegation to US Congress on 10 occasions 1980-1984); chairman Bar European Group (1986-1988); chairman International Practice Committee (1988) (vice-chairman 1989 to date); member Bar Council (1988); chairman London Region National Federation of Self-Employed at Single Businesses (1977-1979); member of: Hampshire Club; Exeter and County Club.

Biography: lives London NW11; born 27.06.1933; married to Elaine with 2

children. Educated at Bridport Grammar School; London School of Economics (1954 LLB hons).

Leisure: breeding budgerigars; bridge.

U

UNGER Andy

senior lecturer in law SOUTH BANK POLYTECHNIC Department of Law & Government, 103 Borough Road, London SE1 0AA.

Career: PR & admin assistant Riverside Studios Theatre (1982-1983); articled G Houghton & Son (1985-1987); admitted (1987); assistant solicitor (1987-1989); part-time tutor Holborn Law Tutors (1986-1988); part-time lecturer Middlesex Polytechnic (1988-1989).

Activities: national chairman Trainee Solicitors' Group (1986-1987); external examiner CPQS (National Nursery Examination Board) Kilburn Polytechnic; member Law Society Standing Committee on Entry and Training (1987-1989); member Law Society Advocacy Training Sub-committee (1989-1990); member National Young Solicitor Committee; cash auditor international ELSA (European Law Students' Association); teaches introductory courses on English law to European students (East & West) through ELSA; convenor Central London Legal Action Group; member Law Society Central-East European Working Party.

Biography: lives London SW12; born 06.10.1959; single. Educated at Shephalbury Comprehensive School; King's College London (1982 LLB hons); College of Law Chancery Lane (1986).

Leisure: walking in England; pubs; parties; reading.

UNMACK Tim

senior partner BEAUMONT AND SON Lloyds Chambers, 1 Portsoken Street, London E1 8AW.

Career: articled Beaumont and Son (1961-1964); admitted (1965); assistant solicitor Linklaters & Paines (1965-1967); became partner Beaumont and Son (1968); became senior partner (1987).

Activities: former chairman Royal Philanthropic Society; member sub-committee of International Chamber of Commerce on formulation of INCOTERM - FOB AIR; member Committee on Air

Traffic Control Liability of International Law Association; member Air Law Group Committee of The Royal Aeronautical Society; member Royal Society of Asian Affairs; member United Oxford & Cambridge University Club.

Biography: lives Reigate; born 05.08.1937; married with 2 children. Educated at Radley College; Christ Church Oxford (MA).

Leisure: languages; sailing.

URQUHART Tim

partner OSBORNE CLARKE
30 Queen Charlotte Street, Bristol BS99 7QQ.

Career: articled Warren Murton & Co (1964-1968); admitted (1970); assistant solicitor (1970-1972); became partner (1972).

Activities: Registrar of Bristol Diocese (1972); member Bristol European Legal Activities Group; secretary The Anchor Society; Regent The Commanderie de Bordeaux Bristol Chapter; member Clifton Club.

Biography: lives Bristol; born 18.12.1944; married to Fern with 2 children. Educated at Braydlea-Avondale; Clifton College.

Leisure: charitable work; photography; wine; travel.

V

VALENTINE Richard

senior partner BARLOWS
55 Quarry Street, Guildford, Surrey GU1 3UE.

Career: articled Brig HG Smith; admitted (1954); assistant solicitor Collyer & Bristow (1954-1959); assistant solicitor Wells & Philpot (1959-1962); became partner (1962); firm amalgamated with Barlows (1974).

Activities: member County Club Guildford; Bramley Golf Club.

Biography: lives Cranleigh; born 10.08.1929; married to Margaret with 1 son. Educated at Brentwood.

VALLANCE Richard

partner and head of litigation department COMPTON CARR 6 Dyer's Buildings, Holborn, London EC1N 2JT.

Career: articled Cole & Cole (1965-1970); admitted (1970); travelled USA (9 months);

assistant solicitor Compton Carr (1971); became partner (1972).

Activities: boxed for Oxford (half blue).

Biography: lives Saffron Walden; born 26.01.1947; married to Robyn with 2 children. Educated at St Dunstan's Preparatory School, Burnham on Sea; King's School, Bruton; College of Law Lancaster Gate.

Leisure: tennis; squash; theatre; reading; gardening.

VALLINGS Robert

partner RADCLIFFES & CO 10 Little College Street, Westminster, London SW1P 3SJ.

Career: articled Radcliffes & Co (1963-1968); admitted (1968); assistant solicitor (1969); became partner (1970).

Activities: chairman of governors of boys' preparatory school; governor of girls' public school; Lt Cdr (retd) Royal Naval Reserve; member of: Naval & Military Club; Richmond FC.

Biography: lives London SW3; born 18.11.1943; married to Penny Lalonde with 1 son and 1 daughter. Educated at Rugby.

Leisure: sport particularly rugby football.

VAN GELDER John

litigation partner HARVEY INGRAM STONE & SIMPSON 20 New Walk, Leicester LE1 6TX.

Career: articled Hunt Dickins (1971-1974); admitted (1974); assistant solicitor Harvey Ingram (1974-1977); became partner (1977).

Activities: secretary of Leicestershire LTA junior training committee (promotion of junior tennis).

Biography: lives Quorn; born 23.03.1946; married to Barbara with 2 children. Educated at Nottingham High School (1957-1965); Exeter University (1968 hons); Freie Universitat, Berlin (1966); University of Alberta (1969 MA); 'Applications to the European Court of Justice' published in the Journal of the Law Society of Scotland (1978).

Leisure: skiing; tennis; opera; wine; photography.

VAN OPPEN Richard

consultant BEVAN ASHFORD Raleigh Hall, Fore Street, Topsham, Exeter, Devon EX3 1HU.

Career: articled Northampton; admitted (1962); assistant solicitor (1962-1965);

became partner Bevan Ashford (1965).

Activities: Notary Public (1970); HM Coroner for Exeter & East Devon (1985); leader Exeter City Council (1973-1979) (Mayor 1979-1980) (hon Alderman 1981 to date); vice-president Exeter Constituency Conservative Association; hon solicitor to Exeter Rowing Club; hon solicitor to Devon Trust for Nature Conservation; chairman Exeter Canal and Quay Trust and Market House Trust; member of the Council of the Coroners' Society for England & Wales.

Biography: lives Topsham; born 01.08.1937; married to Annette with 2 children and 3 stepchildren. Educated at Bedford School.

Leisure: politics; sailing.

VARLEY Philip

senior partner VARLEY HIBBS & CO Kirby House, Little Park Street, Coventry CV1 2JZ.

Career: articled to father (1938); served in Royal Warwickshire Regt World War II (1939-1946); (prisoner of war in Germany 1940-1945); completed articles with Callingham Griffith & Bate and Owen Bailey & Hulme (1946-1948); admitted (1948); assistant solicitor Varley Hibbs & Co (1949); became partner .

Activities: served in Territorial Army (until 1952); TD; president Warwickshire Law Society (1984-1985); chairman St John's Ambulance Association (Leamington Spa) (1963-1988); awarded the Order of a Serving Brother of St John; hon legal adviser and trustee for the Royal Fusiliers Regimental Association (Warwickshire area) (president Leamington Spa branch); member Army & Navy Club.

Biography: lives Barford nr Warwick; born 14.05.1920; married to Jill with 2 children. Educated at Downside School, nr Bath; Birmingham University (LLB hons) (presented 'in absentia' whilst prisoner of war (1943-1944).

Leisure: shooting.

VAUGHAN SALZ Anthony Michael

head of corporate finance group of company department FRESHFIELDS Whitefriars, 65 Fleet Street, London EC4Y 1HS.

Career: articled Kenneth Brown Baker Baker (1972-1974); admitted (1974); assistant solicitor (1974-1975); assistant solicitor Freshfields (1975-1977 & 1978-1980); assistant solicitor Davis Polk &

Wordwell, New York (1977-1978); became partner Freshfields (1980).

Activities: member Trevose Golf Club.

Biography: lives nr Winchester; born 30.06.1950; married to Sally with 1 son and 2 daughters. Educated at Summerfields School, Oxford; Radley College, nr Oxford; Exeter University (1971 LLB hons); College of Law Lancaster Gate (1972 hons); chapters in Tolley's Company Law (first edition) and Mergers and Acquisitions.

Leisure: spending time with family and at home; fighting the garden; fishing; golf; tennis; horses.

VEEDER Van Velhten

Queen's Counsel 4 Essex Court, Temple, London EC4Y 9AJ.

Career: called to the Bar Inner Temple (1971); QC (1986).

Activities: member DTI Departmental Advisory Committee on Arbitration Law member Arbitration Court of the London Court of International Arbitration (LCIA); member of: Aldeburgh Yacht Club; Orford Sailing Club; Little Ship Club.

Biography: lives London; born 14.12.1948. Educated at Neuilly, Paris; Clifton College, Bristol; Jesus College Cambridge; co-editor of 'Arbitration International'.

Leisure: travelling; reading; sailing.

VENABLES David

official solicitor to THE SUPREME COURT 81 Chancery Lane, London WC2A 1DD.

Career: articled Palmer Bull & Mant (1951-1956); admitted (1956); RAF (1957-1958); assistant solicitor Sherrard & Sons (1959-1960); legal assistant Official Solicitor's Office (1960-1977); assistant Official Solicitor (1977-1980); became Official Solicitor (1980).

Activities: secretary Lord Chancellor's Committee on the Age of Majority (1965-1967).

Biography: born 14.10.1932; married with 1 son and 1 daughter. Educated at Denstone (1945-1949); College of Law (1952-1956); author of 'A Guide to the Law affecting Mental Patients' (1975); contributor to Halsbury's Laws of England (4th ed).

Leisure: vintage cars; motoring history; military history.

V

V

VERDIN Peter

senior partner HEALDS Moot Hall Chambers, 8 Wallgate, Wigan WN1 1JE.

Career: admitted (1957); assistant solicitor Healds; became partner (1960).

Activities: member Council of Law Society representing Merseyside and South West Lancashire (1974); chairman Remuneration Committee (1980-1984); chairman Contingency Planning Working Party (1984-1986); former Chairman Rent Assessment Committee; president Wigan Law Society (1988-1989); president North Western Law Societies (1974); member Standards & Guidance Committee of the Law Society; part-time chairman Industrial Tribunals; member of: RAC; Lymm Golf Club.

Biography: lives Lymm, Cheshire; born 04.03.1934; married with 4 children. Educated at Ushaw College, Durham; Durham University (1954 LLB hons).

Leisure: golf.

VOGE Julian CA

partner, corporate department, BRODIES WS 15 Atholl Crescent, Edinburgh EH3 8HA.

Career: admitted (1982); assistant solicitor in Edinburgh and London; became partner Brodies WS (1987); Writer to the Signet; Notary Public.

Activities: part-time tutor in company law Edinburgh University; member Scottish Franchise Advisory Group; member International Jugglers' Association; member New Club.

Biography: lives Edinburgh; born 03.02.1958; single. Educated at Daniel Stewarts and Melville College, Edinburgh; Edinburgh University (1980 LLB hons).

VOGEL David

partner specialising in corporate finance TITMUSS SAINER & WEBB 2 Serjeants' Inn, London EC4Y 1LT.

Career: articled Titmuss Sainer & Webb; admitted (1972); assistant solicitor (1972-1975); became partner (1975).

Biography: lives Bushey; born 02.08.1948; married to Michele with 3 children. Educated at Haberdashers Askes, Elstree; University College London (1969 LLB); London University (1970 LLM).

VOKES David

managing partner PHILLIPS & BUCK Fitzalan House, Fitzalan Road, Cardiff CF2 1XZ.

Career: articled Jeremy & Jenkins (1970-1972); admitted (1972); assistant solicitor AL Jeremy & Co (1972-1975); assistant solicitor Phillips & Buck (1975); became partner (1975); became staff partner (1981-1988); became managing partner (1989); Eversheds' Board member (1989); chairman Eversheds' Human Resources Committee (1989).

Activities: solicitor to the Guild of Freemen of the City of Cardiff; member local Law Society; member South Wales Committee of South Wales Institute of Marketing; member of: Cardiff & County Club; Penarth Yacht Club; Cardiff Golf Club.

Biography: lives Cardiff; born 02.01.1947; married with 3 sons. Educated at Fitzalan High School; Exeter University (1969 LLB); College of Law (1969-1970).

Leisure: sailing; golf; skiing; running; walking.

VON BENZON Nicholas

partner responsible for litigation in firm's East Sussex offices and overall responsibility for matrimonial work CRIPPS HARRIES HALL Croham House, Croham Road, Crowborough, East Sussex TN6 2RL.

Career: articled in East Kent initially with father's practice Daniel & Edwards; admitted (1979); assistant solicitor in East Kent; solicitor Thomas Tilling PLC; solicitor London Insurance Brokers Ltd; assistant solicitor Cripps Harries Hall (1987); became partner.

Activities: formerly lectured extensively on professional negligence; helped to set up Law Society's compulsory continuing education course on office management; member Solicitors' Family Law Association; Anglican priest; governor local C of E primary school; member Bewl Valley Sailing Club.

Biography: lives Heathfield; born 28.02.1954; married to Mariana with 2 children. Educated at St Lawrence College, Ramsgate; Kent University (BA); College of Law; articles in Law Society's Gazette; edits newsletter which circulates nationally among ordained ministers who work in secular employment.

Leisure: church activities; dinghy sailing; horse riding; hill walking.

VOREMBERG Rhoderick

partner WILSONS Steynings House, Chapel Place, Fisherton Street, Salisbury, Wilts SP2 7RJ.

Career: short service limited commission Royal Horse Artillery (1973); articled Burges Salmon; admitted (1980); assistant solicitor (1980-1982); assistant solicitor Wilsons (1982-1985); became partner (1985).

Activities: member county Londoners' Association Wiltshire Committee and Taxation Sub-committeee; hon secretary English Eight Club; member Hawks Club.

Biography: lives Salisbury; born 19.11.1954; married to Susan with 3 children. Educated at Cumnor House School, Danehill (1963-1968); Rugby School (1968-1972); Magdalene College Cambridge (1978 BA hons); College of Law Guildford (1978-1979).

Leisure: match rifle shooting (represented England in Elcho Match 5 times); fly fishing; country sports; printing; typography; bibliography.

W

WADDELL Jeremy

partner and head of commercial department THOMSON SNELL & PASSMORE 3 Lonsdale Gardens, Tunbridge Wells, Kent TN1 1NX.

Career: articled Coward Chance & Co (1959-1962); admitted (1962); assistant solicitor (1962-1963); assistant solicitor Gouldens (1963-1966); associate Carson Ladson & Co, Nassau (1966-1973); assistant solicitor Thomson Snell & Passmore (1974-1976); became partner (1976).

Activities: treasurer Tunbridge Wells, Tonbridge & District Law Society; member Executive Committee of Rusthall Lodge Housing Association; member Tunbridge Wells Squash Club.

Biography: lives Langton Green; born 14.07.1936; married to Christine with 2 children. Educated at Diocesan College, Cape Town; Lincoln College Oxford (1957 BA); Cornell University USA (1957-1958) Telluride Exchange Scholar; Fulbright Travel Scholarship; London School of Economics (1974 LLM).

Leisure: tennis; squash; walking .

WADE Robert

partner and head commercial property department BOOTH & CO Sovereign House, South Parade, Leeds LS1 1HQ.

Career: articled Clifford Turner & Co (1966-1968); admitted (1968); assistant solicitor

(1968-1969); assistant solicitor Booth & Co (1969-1970); became partner (1970); chairman Management Board.

Activities: member Norton Rose M5 Group Board; president West Riding Opera; member Old Millhillians.

Biography: lives Leeds; born 22.05.1943; married to Elizabeth with 4 children. Educated at Mill Hill; Trinity College Cambridge (MA) (LLM).

Leisure: singing; tennis; formerly hockey.

WADE Sir William

consultant barrister Gonville and Caius College, Cambridge CB2 1TA; Gray's Inn Chambers, Gray's Inn, London WC1R 5JA; Tel: Cambridge (0223) 332400; Chambers 071 430 1522.

Career: HM Treasury (1940-1946); Fellow Trinity College and lecturer and reader Cambridge University (1946-1961); Professor of English law Oxford University and Fellow of St John's College Oxford (1961-1976); master Gonville and Caius College Cambridge (1976-1988); Professor of English law Cambridge University (1978-1982); hon Bencher Lincoln's Inn (1964); QC (1968).

Activities: FBA (1969) (vice-president 1981-1983); member Council on Tribunals (1958-1971); member Council Statute Law Society (1989); constitutional commissions and work in Uganda, Seychelles, Barbados, Hong Kong, Australia; lecturships in USA, Turkey, Scandinavia, India, Japan; member of: United Oxford & Cambridge Universities Club; Alpine Club.

Biography: lives Cambridge; born 16.01.1918; married to Marjorie with 2 children. Educated at Shrewsbury School; Gonville and Caius College Cambridge (1939 BA) (1959 LLD); Henry Fellow Harvard (1939); Commonwealth Visiting Fellow, Australia (1972); author of 'Real Property' (with Sir Robert Megarry) (5th ed 1984); 'Administrative Law' (6th ed 1988); 'Constitutional Fundamentals' (1980); 'Towards Administrative Justice' (1963); 'Legal Control of Government' (1972).

Leisure: gardening; music; mountaineering (formerly).

WAINWRIGHT Jill

partner in charge of private client department RAKISONS 27 Chancery Lane, London WC2.

Career: articled Davis Campbell & Co; admitted (1981); assistant solicitor and partner Robertson Thomas & Stevens (1981-1987); partner Reynolds Johnson &

Green (1987-1989); became partner Rakisons (1989).

Activities: PRO for BB & O Law Society; member Committee BB & O Young Solicitors' Group (former chairman); former member Chiltern District Council Housing Committee; member SFLA.

Biography: lives Chesham; born 1957; single. Educated at Southport High School; Sheffield University (1978 LLB); College of Law Chester; articles on the law in local paper and other publications.

Leisure: sailing; skiing; fitness training; writing.

WAITE Ian

senior partner STEPHENS & SCOWN 3 Cross Lane, St Austell, Cornwall PL25 4AX.

Career: articled Stephens & Scown (1953-1956); admitted (1956); assistant solicitor (1956-1959); became partner (1959); became senior partner (1967).

Activities: secretary China Clay Council; chairman of trustees St Austell China Clay Museum Ltd; governor Truro High School for Girls; council member Cornwall Independent Hospitals Trust Ltd, Truro; trustee First Air Ambulance Service Trust; member Oriental Club.

Biography: lives Truro; born 02.09.1930; married to Annabella with 2 daughters and 2 stepsons. Educated at Rugby School; Magdalene College Cambridge (1953 MA); Solicitors' Finals (1956 hons).

Leisure: golf; model railways; music; painting.

WAKEFIELD Carol

head of litigation department LLOYDS BANK PLC 78 Cannon Street, London EC4P 4LN.

Career: admitted (1981); assistant solicitor Durrant Piesse (1981-1987); became head commercial banking litigation department Lloyds Bank PLC (1987).

Activities: member Law Society's Solicitors' European Group and Commerce and Industry Group; founder member Conseil D'Administration AEDBF; member Wentworth Club.

Biography: lives Walton-on-Thames; born 25.07.1957; married with 1 child. Educated at Twickenham Grammar School for Girls; St Anne's College Oxford (1978 BA hons) (1985 MA).

Leisure: reading; walking; tennis; gardening.

WAKERLEY Richard

Queen's Counsel 4 Fountain Court, Steelhouse Lane, Birmingham B4 6DR.

Career: called to the Bar Gray's Inn (1965); QC (1982); Recorder (1982).

Activities: deputy leader Midland & Oxford Circuit (1989 to date).

Biography: lives Atherstone; born 07.06.1942; married to Marian with 2 sons and 2 daughters. Educated at De Aston School, Market Rasen; Emmanuel College Cambridge (1964 MA).

Leisure: bridge; gardening.

WALFORD Christopher

partner ALLEN & OVERY 9 Cheapside, London EC2V 6AD.

Career: articled Allen & Overy (1959-1962); admitted (1962); assistant solicitor (1962-1970); became partner (1970).

Activities: member of: MCC; City Livery Club.

Biography: lives London EC4 and Berkhamsted; born 15.10.1935; married to Anne with 2 sons. Educated at Charterhouse; Oriel College Oxford (1959 MA hons).

Leisure: music (listening); sport (spectator); bridge.

WALKER Andrew

managing partner LOVELL WHITE DURRANT 21 Holborn Viaduct, London EC1A 2DY.

Career: teaching associate North Western University School of Law, Chicago (1966-1967); articled Wilkinson Kimbers & Staddon (1968-1970); admitted (1970); assistant solicitor (1970-1971); assistant solicitor Lovell White & King (1971-1975); became partner (1975); admitted Hong Kong (1982); Hong Kong office (1982-1987).

Activities: member The Hong Kong Club.

Biography: born 06.05.1945; married to Hilary. Educated at Giggleswick School; Exeter College Oxford (1966 BA) (MA).

Leisure: opera; classical music; ornithology; squash; bridge.

WALKER Andrew

partner specialising in family law FOOT & BOWDEN 70/76 North Hill, Plymouth, Devon PL4 8HH.

Career: articled Plymouth (1962-1967); admitted (1967); assistant solicitor Weston-super-Mare (1968-1969); assistant solicitor Foot & Bowden (1969-1971); became

W

partner (1971).

Activities: member Solicitors' Family Law Association (1973); founder member and chairman Plymouth and District Family Conciliation Service; Deputy Registrar (1987); Deputy District Registrar; secretary Broadreach House, Drug and Alcohol Addiction Treatment Centre; treasurer Devon & Cornwall Solicitors' Family Law Association; member office cricket team; member of: St Mellion Golf and Country Club; Royal Western Yacht Club.

Biography: lives Cornwall; born 10.01.1944; married to Nicky with 2 children. Educated at Wellingborough School (1952-1962); College of Law London and Guildford (1964).

Leisure: sailing; walking; shooting; theatre.

WALKER Andrew

partner and head of corporate department and member management committee SIMPSON CURTIS 41 Park Square, Leeds LS1 2NS.

Career: articled Linklaters & Paines (1968); assistant solicitor Bury & Walkers; assistant solicitor Simpson Curtis (1973-1974); became partner (1974).

Activities: member Collingham branch of Elmet Conservative Association; lectured at public seminars on Stock Exchange flotations; privatisation of bus companies and employee share ownership schemes; member Law Society; Leeds Law Society; Solicitors' European Group; Licensing Executives' Society; the American Bar Association; International Bar Association; member of: Collingham & Linton Sports Association; Collingham & Linton Cricket Club (patron); Collingham Lawn Tennis Club; Linton Tennis Club.

Biography: lives Wetherby; born 09.01.1944; married to Jennifer with 1 daughter and 1 son. Educated at Moorlands Preparatory School, Leeds; Leeds Grammar School; Magdalene College Cambridge (hons) (MA); College of Law Guildford; articles in the Yorkshire Post on stock exchange flotations, The Financial Services Act (1986) and protection of the minority shareholder.

Leisure: theatre; local politics; conservation; country pursuits; horse riding; skiing; sailing.

WALKER Barry

partner ASHURST MORRIS CRISP Broadwalk House, 5 Appold Street, London EC2M 2HA.

Career: articled Gouldens (1957-1962);

admitted (1962); assistant solicitor Paisner & Co (1963-1967); became partner (1967-1974); became partner Ashurst Morris Crisp (1974).

Biography: lives London SW3 and Chalfont St Giles; born 30.08.1939; married to Hazel with 4 children. Educated at Milbourne Lodge; Cranleigh.

WALKER Brian

one of the senior partners and head of litigation and divorce LEE & PRIESTLEY, 41-43 Sunbridge Road, Bradford BD1 2AS.

Career: Lee & Priestley (1957); articled (1960s); admitted (1973); became partner (1973).

Activities: member Bradford Law Society General Council, County Court Committee and Professional Purposes Committee; member Law Society Area 9 Committee; member Huddersfield Town Gentlemen's Sporting Club.

Biography: lives Bradford; born 17.11.1941; married to Pamela with 2 children. Educated at Morley Grammar School; College of Law Guildford; Leeds Technical College.

Leisure: tennis; cricket (organises the firm's cricket matches against other professional firms); watching football (Huddersfield Town); keen gardener; keen walker.

WALKER Ian James

partner and joint head of personal injury litigation department RUSSELL JONES & WALKER Swinton House, 324 Gray's Inn Road, London WC1X 8DH.

Career: articled Russell Jones & Walker and Tuck & Mann & Geffen; admitted (1974); assistant solicitor (1974-1977); became partner Russell Jones & Walker (1977).

Activities: former member Committee of London Solicitors' Litigation Association; lead solicitor King's Cross disaster; member Wig & Pen Club.

Biography: lives Caterham; born 15.04.1950; married to Gillian with 3 children. Educated at Whitgift School, Croydon; College of Law Guildford; co-author of 'Tribunals - Practice and Procedure' (1985).

Leisure: golf; sailing; walking; music; family.

WALKER John

senior partner ALLAN JANES 21 Easton Street, High Wycombe, Bucks HP11 1NU.

Career: National Service as Russian linguist; articled Booth & Co (1961-1965);

admitted solicitor (1965); assistant solicitor Simpson Curtis & Co (1965-1967); assistant solicitor Allan Janes & Co (1967-1971); became partner (1971); became senior partner (1982).

Activities: member of: High Wycombe Squash Club; Farnham Common Music Club; Gerrards Cross Squash Club; Benslow Music Trust.

Biography: lives Gerrards Cross; born 11.06.1937; married to Penelope with 2 children. Educated at Queen Elizabeth's Grammar School; Pembroke College Oxford (1961 BA hons).

Leisure: squash; playing the piano; hill walking; cross country skiing.

WALKER John Adrian Harrison

senior partner HFT GOUGH & CO 38/42 New Lowther Street, Whitehaven, Cumbria CA28 7JU.

Career: National Service in Royal Corps of Signals (1948); Eaton Hall Officer Cadet Training Unit commissioned 2nd Lt REME (1949); articled Summer & Singleton (1951-1956); admitted (1956); gazetted 2nd Lt Westmorland and Cumberland Yeomanry (TA) (1957); became partner HFT Gough & Co (1958).

Activities: assistant Deputy Coroner for West Cumbria (1961); HM Coroner for West Cumbria (1979); former member and chairman Local Committee No 8 Legal Aid Area; member and former Commodore Harrington Sailing & Fishing Club.

Biography: lives Workington; born 07.06.1929; widowed with 2 children. Educated at Haileybury College, Hertford (1943-1948).

Leisure: gardening; sailing; visiting historic buildings.

WALKER Paul Christopher

partner LAWRENCE GRAHAM 190 Strand, London WC2R 1JN.

Career: administrative trainee Home Office (1972-1974); articled Allen & Overy (1974-1976); assistant solicitor (1976-1979); executive then manager corporate finance department Hill Samuel & Co (1979-1984); assistant director corporate finance department J Henry Schroder Wagg & Co (1985-1986); became partner Lawrence Graham (1986).

Biography: lives London W4; born 27.08.1950; married to Sandra with 2 daughters. Educated at Charterhouse; St John's College Oxford (1972 BA hons MA); author of: 'The City Institutions - A Guide to their Financial Services' (1984).

WALKER Raymond

Queen's Counsel and head of chambers 1 Harcourt Buildings, Temple, London EC4.

Career: called to the Bar Middle Temple (1966); QC (1988).

Activities: member of: Garrick; Royal West Norfolk Golf Club; Huntercombe Golf Club.

Biography: lives London SW3; born 26.08.1943; married to June with 1 son. Educated at Radley College; Trinity Hall Cambridge (BA).

Leisure: golf; tennis; skiing; sailing; opera.

WALKER Ronald

Queen's Counsel and head of chambers 12 King's Bench Walk, Temple, London EC4Y 7EL.

Career: called to the Bar (1962); senior lecturer College of Law (1963-1968); practice at Bar (1968 to date); QC (1983); Recorder (1986).

Biography: lives Barnes; born 24.06.1940; married to Caroline with 2 sons. Educated at Owens School, London; University College London (1961 LLB); author of 'Walker & Walker, The English Legal System' (1967 6th ed 1985); contributing editor to Bullen and Leake and Jacob's Precedents of Pleading (13th edition 1990).

WALKER Timothy

Queen's Counsel Fountain Court, Middle Temple, London EC4 9DH.

Career: assistant lecturer in law King's College London (1967-1968); called to the Bar Inner Temple (1968); QC (1985); Recorder of the Crown Court (1986).

Biography: lives London SW10; born 13.05.1946; married to Mary with 2 daughters. Educated at Harrow School; Entrance Scholar; Leaving Scholar; University College Oxford (1964-1967) (MA Jurisprudence 1st class hons); Plumptre Scholar (1965); Profumo Scholarship Inner Temple (1968); Eldon Law Scholar (1969).

WALKEY Justin

partner BIRD & BIRD 2 Gray's Inn Square, London WC1R 5AF.

Career: articled Lawrence Graham (1980-1984); admitted (1984); assistant solicitor Bird & Bird (1984-1987); became partner (1987).

Activities: member St Mellion, Cornwall.

Biography: lives London N21; born 30.10.1957; married to Stella with 2 children. Educated at Westbury House Prep School, Westmeon; Sherborne; Polytechnic of Central London (1979 BA hons); College of Law Lancaster Gate (1979-1980).

Leisure: sports; music; painting; sculpture.

WALKLEY Geoffrey

partner and head of intellectual property section NABARRO NATHANSON 50 Stratton Street, London W1X 5FL.

Career: articled Bartlett & Gluckstein (1966-1968); admitted (1968); assistant solicitor (1968-1971); salaried partner (1971-1975); equity partner (1975-1988); became partner Nabarro Nathanson (1988); editor firm's '1992' Newsletter.

Activities: hon secretary Maylandsea Bay Yacht Club.

Biography: lives Hornchurch; born 25.07.1944; married to Barbara with 2 children. Educated at East Ham Grammar School; King's College Durham University (1962-1965 LLB).

Leisure: sailing; skiing; handicrafts.

WALLACE Duncan

Queen's Counsel 1 Atkin Building, Gray's Inn, London WC1R 5BQ.

Career: Western Circuit and general practice Chambers of GRF Morris QC (1948-1951); specialist practice (construction law) Chambers of EV Rimmer QC (1951 to date); QC.

Activities: visiting professor King's College London; arbitrator; member Bar Sub-committeee on Exclusion Clauses Reform; member Sub-committee to Law Reform Commission on Defective Premises Act; member Editorial Board Construction Law Journal; member of: Lansdowne Club; Hurlingham Club.

Biography: lives London W11; born 21.04.1922; divorced. Educated at Loretto School, Musselburgh; Oriel College Oxford (1948 MA); editor 'Hudson On Building Contracts' (1959; 1965; 1970 & 1979); author of: 'Building and Civil Engineering Standard Forms' (1969); 'Further Building and Engineering Standard Forms' (1973); 'The International Civil Engineering Contract' (1974); 'The ICE Conditions of Contracts' (1978); 'Construction Contracts (Principles and Policies) (1986); many articles and papers in the LQR; Construction Law Journal; International Construction Law Review; etc.

Leisure: collecting paintings (Orientalist and modern British) and ceramics; shooting; conservation.

WALLER Philip

barrister and head of chambers 2 Gray's Inn Square, Gray's Inn, London WC1R 5AA.

Career: called to the Bar (1975); pupillage and worked for law firm in the USA (1975-1977); became head of Chambers (1988).

Activities: member Family Law Bar Association; member Criminal Bar Association; member South Eastern Circuit; member Ecclesiastical Law Society; closely involved in the life of St Albans Cathedral (member Cathedral Council).

Biography: lives St Albans; born 12.10.1952; married with 2 daughters. Educated at Whitgift School; Exeter University (1974 LLB hons).

Leisure: family; music (especially early music); theatre; wine; historic houses and gardens.

WALLIS Andrew

partner JAQUES & LEWIS 2 South Square, Gray's Inn, London WC1R 5HR. Telephone: 071-242 9755; Fax 071-405 4464; Telex 27938 and Suite No. 2, Seaton House, 17-19 Seaton Place, St Helier, Jersey JE2 3QL. Tel: 0534-37321; Fax: 0534-38163; Telex: 4192145 and 18 St George's Street, Douglas, Isle of Man. Tel: 0624-26557; Fax: 0624-72502; Telex: 628369.

Career: articled London Borough of Southwark (1967-1970); admitted (1970); suburban firms (1970-1972); assistant solicitor Jaques & Lewis (1972-1974); became partner (1974).

Activities: formerly hon legal adviser to CAB and charities.

Biography: lives London N1; born 05.12.1945. Educated at Emmanuel School; King's College London (1967 LLB).

Leisure: music; sailing; politics; theatre.

WALLIS Peter

clerk to ASHFORD, TENTERDEN, DOVER AND EAST KENT AND FOLKESTONE AND HYTHE JUSTICES The Law Courts, Castle Hill Avenue, Folkestone, Kent CT20 2DH.

Career: service commission as pilot RAF (1967-1972); articled clerk to Dartford and Bexley Justices (1972-1976); admitted (1976); clerk to Tonbridge & Malling Justices (1977-1988); became clerk to

W

Ashford, Tenterden, Dover and East Kent Justices (1988) and Folkestone and Hythe Justices (1990).

Activities: training officer Magistrates (Kent); council member and assistant hon secretary Justices' Clerks' Society (1983 to date); member Regional Duty Solicitor Committee (No 2 Area); member DVLC/Courts Liaison Group; member Management Committee Kent Family Conciliation Service; member Editorial Board Wilkinson's Road Traffic Law Bulletin.

Biography: lives Maidstone; born 31.03.1945; married to Ann with 2 children. Educated at Maidstone Grammar; Lincoln College Oxford (1967 BA) (1975 MA); general editor Wilkinson's Road Traffic Offences (1987 to date); author of: 'The Transport Act 1981' (1982); 'The Transport Acts 1981 and 1982' (1985); contributor to various journals.

Leisure: cricket; tennis.

WALLIS Tim

partner CRUTES 27 Portland Square, Carlisle CA1 1PE.

Career: articled Crutes (1976-1978); admitted (1978); assistant solicitor (1978-1981); became partner (1981).

Activities: former hon secretary Carlisle and District Law Society; member Law Society Civil Litigation Committee; member Round Table.

Biography: lives nr Pennine Way; born 06.04.1954; married to Ann. Educated at Carre's Grammar School; Newcastle upon Tyne Polytechnic (1975 BA hons).

Leisure: bassett hounds; skiing; windsurfing; Nottingham Forest FC; walking; sailing; driving.

WALMSLEY David

senior partner HAWKINS RUSSELL JONES Midland House, Wratten Road East, Hitchin SG5 2AL.

Career: articled McKenna & Co (1962-1966); admitted (1966); assistant solicitor Hawkins Russell Jones (1967-1969); became partner (1969).

Activities: former member Law Society Local Committee; member of: Blueharts Hockey Club; John O'Gaunt Golf Club.

Biography: lives Letchworth; born 25.05.1941; married to Andy with 2 children. Educated at Hitchin Boys' Grammar School; Eton College; Keble College Oxford (1962 BA).

Leisure: hockey; golf.

WALMSLEY Keith

area director LEGAL AID OFFICE City House, New Station Street, Leeds LS1 4JS.

Career: articled GA Pratt (1951-1955); admitted (1956); National Service RAF; assistant solicitor Cyril Morris & Co; assistant solicitor Law Society Manchester (1967); deputy local secretary Leeds (1969); assistant area secretary (1980) area secretary (later amended to area director) (1985).

Activities: member Leeds Local Law Society; former treasurer Accrington Golf Club; competition and handicap secretary Woodhall Hills Golf Club (former junior organiser and captain); secretary of the Association of Bradford Union Past Captains.

Biography: lives Pudsey; born 24.12.1932; married to Marian with 2 sons. Educated at Peel Park Council School, Accrington; Accrington Grammar School; Manchester University; College of Law Guildford.

Leisure: theatre; philately; golf.

WALROND Bill

senior partner PARTRIDGE & WILSON 88 Guildhall Street, Bury St Edmunds, Suffolk IP33 1PT.

Career: admitted (1958); National Service (1958-1960); assistant solicitor Partridge & Wilson (1960-early 1970s); became partner (early 1970s); became senior partner (1988).

Activities: Coroner for the district of West Suffolk; member Area Committee No 11 (Eastern) Legal Aid area; member of Law Society; Suffolk & North Essex local Law Society; member of: London Gliding Club.

Biography: lives nr Bury St Edmunds; born 23.12.1935; married to Sallie. Educated at St Ronan's Preparatory School and Repton Public School.

Leisure: glider pilot to 'Gold C' standard.

WALSH Jonathan

partner and head of private client department and family law department TAYLOR JOYNSON GARRETT 10 Maltravers Street, London WC2R 3BS.

Career: admitted (1969); assistant solicitor (1969-1973); became partner Joynson-Hicks (1973-1989); became head of private client department on merger with Taylor Garrett (1989).

Activities: former member Solicitors' Family Law Association Committee on Procedure; member of: Boodles; Queens.

Biography: lives London SW15; born 21.04.1944; married with 4 children.

Educated at Eton College; Sorbonne.

Leisure: real tennis; lawn tennis; shooting.

WALSH Paul

partner intellectual property department BRISTOWS COOKE & CARPMAEL 10 Lincoln's Inn Fields, London WC2A 3BP.

Career: articled Linklaters & Paines (1980-1983); admitted (1983); assistant solicitor Bristows Cooke & Carpmael (1983-1988); became partner (1988).

Activities: lectures on biotechnology licensing copyright law and technology transfer.

Biography: lives London N6 and Cambridgeshire; born 21.12.1956; married to Caroline. Educated at Salvatorian College (1969-1975); Oxford University (1979 BA).

Leisure: English and American literature; film; theatre.

WALTON Anthony

Queen's Counsel Francis Taylor Building, Temple, London EC4Y 7BY.

Career: called to the Bar Middle Temple (1950); QC (1970); Bencher Middle Temple (1978).

Activities: lecture to Malaysian Bar Association (1984); associate member Chartered Institute of Patent Agents; ICC arbitrator; Freeman City of London; Liveryman Worshipful Company of Gunmakers.

Biography: lives London SW2; born 04.05.1925; married to Jean with 1 son. Educated at Dulwich College Prep School; Dulwich College (Scholar); Hertford College Oxford (1950 MA BCL); Baring Scholarship; president Oxford Union (1945); contributor to: Halsbury on Arbitration; Russell on Arbitration; author of English section Langen's 'Internationale Lizenzvertrage'; co-author 'Digest of Patent Cases'; author 'Encyclopaedia British & European Patent Law'; contributor to Whitebook & Atkins CC Forms; Patents; Trade Marks; various articles.

Leisure: interested in education.

WALTON Miles

partner corporate tax department WILDE SAPTE Queensbridge House, 60 Upper Thames Street, London EC4V 3BD.

Career: articled Kenneth Brown Baker Baker (1978-1980); admitted (1980);

assistant solicitor Slaughter and May (1980-1983); assistant solicitor Wilde Sapte (1983-1984); became partner (1984).

Biography: lives London SW11; born 15.07.1955; married to Lorraine with 1 son and 1 daughter. Educated at Ratcliffe College, Leicester; Brasenose College Oxford (1977 MA); College of Law Chester (1978); ATII (1983); chapter on business tax anti-avoidance in ICAEW Tax Service.

Leisure: saxophone and clarinet in big band; wine tasting; yachting; scuba diving.

WALTON Paul

management partner HILL DICKINSON DAVIS CAMPBELL Pearl Assurance House, Derby Square, Liverpool L2 9XL.

Career: admitted (1969); assistant solicitor Davis Munro (1969-1971); became partner Davis Campbell & Co (1971-1989); became management partner Hill Dickinson Davis Campbell (1989).

Activities: created Knight of St Gregory by Pope (1987); member Monarchist League; member Liverpool Racquet Club.

Biography: lives Hoghton; born 18.05.1945; married with 3 children. Educated at King George V School, Southport; Exeter University (1966 LLB) Lloyd Parry Prize in Constitutional Law and Bracton Law Society Prize; College of Law (1966-1967).

Leisure: anti-abortion causes; philately; opera; history; antiques; herb collecting; flower growing; squash.

WANDER Charles

resources partner and partner in corporate department FLADGATE FIELDER Heron Place, 3 George Street, London W1H 6AD.

Career: articled Walters Vandercom & Hart (now Fladgate Fielder); admitted (1979); assistant solicitor; became partner (1982).

Activities: chairman Miles 33 User Group; member RAC.

Biography: lives Middlesex; born 22.01.1954; married to Karen with 2 children. Educated at Manchester Grammar School; Wolverhampton Polytechnic (1976 LLB hons).

Leisure: reading; fishing; computers; tennis; family; travel.

WARD Christopher

managing partner CLARKS Great Western House, Station Road, Reading RG1 1SX.

Career: articled in Maidenhead; admitted

(1965); assistant solicitor (1965-1971); became partner Clarks (1971).

Activities: member Berkshire County Council (1965-1981) (leader and chairman of finance and policy committee); Member of Parliament for Swindon (1969-1970); member of: Carlton Club; United & Cecil Club; Berkshire Athenaeum.

Biography: lives Maidenhead; born 26.12.1942.

WARD Helen

partner and head of matrimonial department PENNINGTONS Clement House, 99 Aldwych, London WC2B 4LJ.

Career: articled Ward Bowie ; admitted (1978); became partner (1978); firm amalgamated with Penningtons (1985); became head of matrimonial department (1985).

Activities: treasurer and member Main Committee of the Solicitors Family Law Association; Fellow of International Academy of Matrimonial Lawyers (European Chapter); lectures to legal profession at seminars and local Law Society meetings on various aspects of family law and practice.

Biography: lives London; born 28.05.1951; married to Alan with twin daughters; 2 stepdaughters and 1 stepson. Educated at King Alfred's School; Birmingham University (1973 LLB) .

Leisure: enjoying family.

WARD Ian

partner shipping insurance and international trade group LOVELL WHITE DURRANT 21 Holborn Viaduct, London EC1A 2DY.

Career: deck officer Merchant Navy and Royal Naval Reserve (1953-1964); called to the Bar Middle Temple (1962); barrister Admiralty Chambers (1965-1975); admitted (1976); became partner (1976).

Activities: Fellow Chartered Institute of Arbitrators.

Biography: lives Kew and Newport Dyfed; born 17.09.1936; married to Vivienne with 2 daughters and 1 son. Educated at Bembridge School; Thames Nautical Training College, HMS Worcester; Inns of Court School of Law.

Leisure: sailing; walking.

WARD John

partner BEALE & COMPANY Garrick House, 27-32 King Street, London WC2.

Career: admitted (1975); assistant solicitor Beale & Co (1975-1977); became partner (1977).

Activities: member Reform Club.

Biography: lives Esher; born 22.11.1950; married to Myril with 4 children. Educated at University College London; articles in The Structural Engineer.

Leisure: family.

WARD Tony

partner CLIFFORD CHANCE Blackfriars House, 19 New Bridge Street, London EC4V 6BY.

Career: articled Town Clerk's office Northampton County Borough Council (1969-1971); admitted (1971); assistant solicitor (1971-1974); senior assistant solicitor legal department Aylesbury Vale District Council (1974-1976); deputy borough solicitor Hammersmith & Fulham London Borough Council (1976-1978); assistant solicitor Coward Chance (1978-1985); became partner (1985-1987); became partner Clifford Chance (1987).

Activities: member Law Society (1980); Freedom of City of London (1980); member International Bar Association (1981); Liveryman The Worshipful Company of Solicitors (1983); chairman The Joint RICS Bar Council Law Society Planning Law Conference (1987-1988); member the joint RICS Bar Council Law Society Planning Law Conference Committee (1985 to date); member Law Society Planning Law Committee (1985 to date); Council member British/Polish Legal Association (1989 to date).

Biography: lives London EC2; born 23.06.1947; single. Educated at Northampton Trinity High School; Lanchester Polytechnic, Coventry (1968 LLB); College of Law Guildford (1969 hons); written numerous articles, papers and lectures to professional journals and organisations on town planning topics.

Leisure: tennis; squash.

WARE James Henry

marketing partner and head of music department DAVENPORT LYONS 1 Old Burlington Street, London W1X 1LA.

Career: articled Biddle & Co; became partner Saunders & Ware (1974-1977); head of legal and business affairs Virgin Group (1977-1980); MD CBS Song Ltd (1980-1984); VP CBS Inc and regional head CBS Songs Intl, Europe (1983-1985); became partner Davenport Lyons (1986).

Activities: director Music Royalties Monitoring Service (1985 to date); former council member Mechanical Rights Society; past chairman MRS Audit Committee; council member Brent Community Law Centre; council member Fantasy Factory Video (video charity); general interest in all aspects of copyright and particular interest in music and computer software; member Athenaeum.

Biography: lives London N1; born 29.10.1946; married to Vanessa with 4 children. Educated at Bryanston School; St John's College Oxford (BA hons); Solicitors' Finals (hons); occasional articles on the music business.

Leisure: hill walking; playing the oboe.

WARE Jeremy

joint senior partner TALLENTS GODFREY & CO 3 Middlegate, Newark, Notts NG24 1AQ.

Career: articled Hugh Tallents (1954-1957); admitted (1958); assistant solicitor Murray Hutchins & Co (1957-1960); became partner Tallents & Co (1960-1970); became joint senior partner Tallents Godfrey & Co (1988).

Activities: president Nottinghamshire Law Society (1986-1987); clerk to Commissioners of Taxes Newark Division; president Grantham Division Conservative Association; chairman Lincolnshire Conservative European Council.

Biography: lives Brant Broughton; born 29.10.1932; married to Jane with 3 children. Educated at Bramcote; Scarborough; Winchester; Lincoln College Oxford (1954 hons MA).

Leisure: shooting; fishing; gardening.

WARNER David

senior partner WARNER CRANSTON Pickfords Wharf, Clink Street, London SE1 9DG.

Career: admitted (1973); assistant solicitor Lovell White & King (1973-1978); worked in Brussels office (1975-1977); founded David Warner & Co (1979).

Activities: member of: City of London Solicitors' Company; Worshipful Company of the Makers of Playing Cards (member of the Court of Assistants); United Oxford & Cambridge Universities Club.

Biography: lives London NW8 and Oxfordshire; born 28.08.1947; single. Educated at Whitgift School; St Edmund Hall Oxford (1968 MA).

Leisure: bee-keeping.

WARNFORD-DAVIS Mandy

partner in company/commercial department ROWE & MAW 20 Black Friars Lane, London EC4V 6HD.

Career: articled Titmuss Sainer & Webb (1976-1979); admitted (1979); assistant solicitor (1979-1982); assistant solicitor Rowe & Maw (1982-1985); became partner (1985).

Biography: lives London SW7; born 19.06.1954; single. Educated at Heathfield School, Ascot; St Hugh's College, Oxford (1975 BA hons).

Leisure: opera; reading; travel; backgammon.

WARRINER Frank

consultant CRIPPS HARRIES HALL 84 Calverley Road, Tunbridge Wells, Kent TN1 2UP.

Career: articled RWG Braithwaite; admitted (1958); assistant solicitor (1958-1962); partner (1962-1965); founded practice with wife (1965-1988); became consultant Cripps Harries Hall (1988).

Activities: coroner for West Kent (1971 to date); former part-time chairman of industrial tribunals (1977-1983); part-time legal chairman Pension Appeals Tribunal (1986 to date); Tunbridge Wells Borough Councillor (1969-1972); director Solicitors' Benevolent Association; life governor Imperial Cancer Research Fund; conservator Epsom and Walton Downs (1963-1967); former treasurer Langton Green Parish Church; former vicar's warden St Mark's Church, Broadwater Down.

Biography: lives Tunbridge Wells; born 28.01.1930; married to Helen with 5 children. Educated at Clarks Modern School for Boys, Ilford; London (1955 External LLB); Solicitors' Finals (1958 hons); Open University (1986 BA).

Leisure: keen cyclist (cycle tour member Spain over Pyrenees 1988).

WATCHMAN Paul Q

associate, head of the planning and environmental law department BRODIES WS 15 Atholl Crescent, Edinburgh EH3 8HA.

Career: LLB (1975); apprentice Bird Semple & Crawford Herron (1975-1977); admitted (1977); research fellowship Glasgow University (1977-1979); lecturer in law Dundee University (1979-1988); senior lecturer in law (1988-1989); senior assistant Brodies WS (1989-1990).

Activities: chairman Social Security Appeal Tribunals (1984 to date); case editor and co-editor Scottish Planning Law & Practice (1981-1987); chairman Law Society of Scotland Law Reform Committee Social Security Law Working Group; convenor and contributor to Law Society of Scotland PQLE courses on landlord and tenant, administrative law and planning law; research on consultancy basis for Scottish Office Convention of Scottish Local Authorities, Scottish Consumer Council; organised post-qualifying education for Law Society of Scotland, legal groups and local authorities on planning housing and landlord and tenant law.

Biography: lives Wormit; born 17.11.1952; married to Janet with 1 child. co-editor 'Justice, Lord Denning and the Constitution' (1981); co-author of: 'Homelessness and the Law' (1983); 'Developments in Homelessness and the Law' (1986); 'Homelessness and the Law in Great Britain' (1989); 'Crime and Regulation' (1990); 'The Local Ombudsman' (1990); 'Stair Encyclopaedia of the Laws of Scotland'; contributions to collections of essays and legal and professional journals.

Leisure: golf; writing; music.

WATERSON Nigel

senior partner WATERSON HICKS 14/20 St Mary Axe, London EC3A 8BU.

Career: called to the Bar Gray's Inn (1973); articled Constant and Constant (1976); admitted; assistant solicitor (1976-1978); co-founder and senior partner Horrocks & Co (1978-1990); co-founder and senior partner Waterson Hicks (1990).

Activities: supporting member London Maritime Arbitrators' Association; regular attender American Maritime Law Association events; given various papers on maritime subjects; member of: Carlton Club; Marine Club; Guards Polo Club; Coningsby Club.

Biography: lives London SW6; born 12.10.1950; married. Educated at Leeds Grammar School; Queen's College Oxford (1971 MA).

Leisure: politics; music; reading; sailing; writing on the law; shooting.

WATKINS Bill

partner LOVELL WHITE DURRANT 73 Cheapside, London EC2V 6ER.

Career: commission Royal Artillery (1952-1954); articled Slaughter and May (1957-

1960); admitted (1960); assistant solicitor (1960-1969); assistant solicitor Durrant Cooper & Hambling (1969-1970); became partner (1970) .

Biography: lives Bramsholt; born 29.08.1933; married to Anne with 4 children. Educated at King's School, Canterbury; University College Oxford (1957 MA).

Leisure: walking; industrial archaeology.

WATKINS James

senior partner LINKLATERS & PAINES 14th Floor, Alexandra House, Chater Road, Hong Kong.

Career: articled Linklaters & Paines (1967-1969); admitted (1969); assistant solicitor (1969-1975); became partner (1975).

Activities: member of: Hong Kong Club; Shek-O Country Club, Hong Kong; Annabels; Hurlingham.

Biography: lives Hong Kong; born 26.09.1945; divorced with 2 daughters. Educated at Archbishop Holgate's School, York; Leeds University (1966 LLB); College of Law Guildford.

Leisure: tennis; golf; reading; music; theatre.

WATKINS Lindsay

senior partner EDWARD LEWIS & CO Waterloo House, Fitzalan Court, Newport Road, Cardiff CF2 EL1.

Career: National Service with RAF; articles in Cardiff; admitted (1957); assistant solicitor for short spells South Wales; assistant solicitor Edward Lewis & Co (1961-1964); became partner (1964); became senior partner (1978); founded firm's London office.

Biography: lives Penarth; born 30.11.1930; married to Meriel with 2 children. Educated at Hereford Cathedral School; St John's College Cambridge (1953 BA); (1958 MA); Cardiff University (1954); College of Law Guildford (1956).

Leisure: opera; theatre; travel; rugby.

WATKISS John

partner TURNER KENNETH BROWN 100 Fetter Lane, London EC4A 1DD.

Career: articled Ernest W Long & Co; admitted (1961); assistant solicitor Simmons & Simmons (1961-1968); assistant solicitor EF Turner & Sons (1968-1969); became partner (1969).

Activities: member of: City Livery Club;

Moor Park Golf Club; Glass-sellers Company.

Biography: lives Rickmansworth; born 14.09.1937; married to Susan with 3 children. Educated at Mill Hill.

Leisure: golf; gardening; music.

WATMORE Leslie

senior partner L WATMORE & CO Chancery House, 53/66 Chancery Lane, London WC2A 1QU.

Career: admitted (1957); assistant solicitor (1957-1959); became partner L Bingham & Co (1959-1976); founded own practice L Watmore & Co (1976).

Activities: chairman No 13 Legal Aid Area (1981-1984); member of: RAC; City Livery Club; Cordwainer Ward Club; West Kent Golf Club.

Biography: lives London; born 08.05.1929; married to Iris with 2 children. Educated at St Olave's Grammar School, Southwark; Keble College Oxford (1953 MA); articles on pneumoconiosis and limitation.

Leisure: golf; hill walking.

WATSON Andrew

partner and head of personal injury/medical negligence unit THOMSON SNELL & PASSMORE 3 Lonsdale Gardens, Tunbridge Wells, Kent TN1 1NX.

Career: articled Thomson Snell & Passmore (1973-1975); admitted (1975); assistant solicitor (1975-1981); became partner (1981).

Activities: member Legal Aid Area Committee (1986 to date); chairman Tunbridge Wells Runners; member local Headway Group.

Biography: lives Tunbridge Wells; born 29.03.1950; married to Lea. Educated at King's School, Worcester; St John's College Oxford (1971 hons); Open Scholar; Casberd Scholar; HWC Davis Prize Winner; Law Society Finals (hons).

Leisure: running; fell walking; reading; music; cooking.

WATSON Sir Andrew

head of No 4 Fountain Court chambers, Steelhouse Lane, Birmingham 4.

Career: National Service (1956-1958); Anglo American Corporation (1958-1964); called to Bar (1966); practised at 1 Harcourt Buildings (1966-1970); practised in Birmingham (1970-1989).

Activities: Recorder; stood in Sutton Coldfield in 2 elections; chairman Parish Council.

Biography: lives Stratford on Avon; born 30.12.1937; married to Christabel with 3 children. Educated at Eton College.

Leisure: politics; gardening; playing tennis; tasting wine; walking in mountain areas.

WATT James

partner HEMPSONS 33 Henrietta Street, London WC2E 9NH.

Career: National Service (1954-1956); articled GV Bull Wright & Bull (1957-1961); admitted (1962); assistant solicitor Kennedys (1962-1963); became partner (1963-1967); assistant solicitor Hempsons (1967-1968); became partner (1969).

Activities: trustee Iolanthe Trust; member NSPCC Professional Advisory Committee; occasional lecturing at conferences on medico-legal and ancillary topics; member Law Society.

Biography: lives London SW15; born 23.07.1935; married to Patricia with 5 children. Educated at Kingsmead School, Hoylake (1944-1949); Giggleswick School, Settle (1949-1954); College of Law Lancaster Gate; occasional articles in professional journals on medico-legal topics.

Leisure: music; gardening; reading.

WATT Nigel GM

partner LINDSAYS WS 11 Atholl Crescent, Edinburgh EH3 8HE.

Career: apprentice Hagart & Burn-Murdoch WS (1972-1974); admitted (1974); assistant solicitor (1974-1976); became partner (1977-1984); became partner Lindsays WS (1985).

Activities: member of: Rotary Club of Edinburgh; Gullane Golf Club; Bruntsfield Links GS; Royal Aberdeen Golf Club.

Biography: lives Gullane; born 17.11.1950; married to Joanne with 2 sons. Educated at Aberdeen Grammar School; Aberdeen University (1972 LLB).

Leisure: golf; hill walking.

WAY Patrick

tax partner GOULDENS 22 Tudor Street, London EC4Y 0JJ.

Career: Lawrence Graham (1977-1982); assistant solicitor Nabarro Nathanson (1982-1985); became tax partner (1985-1987); became tax partner Gouldens (1987).

W

Activities: Tax Committee member of the BES Association.

Biography: lives London SW19; born 06.02.1954; married to Judith with 3 sons. Educated at Solihull School (1965-1972); Leeds University (1975 BA); author of 'Death and Taxes'; 'Maximising Opportunities under the BES'; 'BES and Assured Tenancies'; 'Share Sales and Earnouts' (to be published 1991); contributor to 'Tolley's Tax Planning 1991'.

Leisure: gardening and tennis.

WEATHERILL Barry

senior partner WEDLAKE BELL 16 Bedford Street, Covent Garden, London WC2E 9HF.

Career: articled Wedlake Letts & Birds (1964-1966); admitted (1966); partner (1967); finance partner Wedlake Bell (1975-1981); senior partner (1984 to date).

Activities: director of: Brillo Manufacturing Co of GB Ltd (1975-1986); Trident Group Printers Ltd (1974-1979); Phoenix Securities Ltd (1984-1987); chairman First Mortgage Securities Treasury Holdings Ltd (1987-1989); director of First Mortgage Securities Ltd and All England Ground Ltd (1990); member of Committee of Management Wimbledon Championships (1981 to date); chairman The Prentice Cup Committee (1971-1988); secretary Council of International Clubs (1969 to date); council member Guide Dogs for the Blind Association; member of: All England Lawn Tennis Club; Berkshire Golf Club; The Jesters; Hawks Club.

Biography: lives Berkshire; born 17.07.1938; married with 3 children. Educated at Caldicott School; Felsted School; Clare College Cambridge (1962 BA hons).

Leisure: lawn tennis; golf; skiing; opera; theatre; gardening; constructive thought.

WEAVER Oliver

Queen's Counsel Erskine Chambers, 30 Lincoln's Inn Fields, London WC2A 3PF.

Career: called to the Bar Middle Temple (1965); tenant Erskine Chambers (1966); QC (1985).

Activities: panel of chairman Authorisation/Disciplinary Tribunal of the Securities Association (1988 to date); member General Council of the Bar (1982-1985); vice-chairman Law Reform Committee of the Bar (1987-1989); member Incorporated Council of Law Reporting (1986 to date).

Biography: lives Albany; born 27.03.1942;

married to Julia with 3 children. Educated at Friends' School, Saffron Walden (1952-1960); Trinity College Cambridge (1963 BA) (1964 LLB) (1966 MA) (1986 LLM) president Cambridge Union Society Michaelmas (1963); junior editor Gower's Modern Company Law 3rd ed (1969).

Leisure: fishing; racing; gun dogs; sheep.

WEBB Robert S

Queen's Counsel and head of chambers 1 Harcourt Buildings, Temple, London EC4Y 9DA.

Career: QC; head of Chambers; practising barrister.

Activities: Chairman Air Law Group of Royal Aeronautical Society; vice-chairman Air Law Committee of International Bar Association; member International Academy of Trial Lawyers (IATL), International Association of Defence Counsel; member of: Royal Wimbledon Golf Club; Royal Lytham St Anne's Golf Club; Prestbury Golf Club.

Biography: lives London N1; born 04.10.1948; married to Angela with 2 children. Educated at Wycliffe College, Gloucs; Exeter University (1971 LLB).

Leisure: fly fishing; golf.

WEBB William John

senior partner SHERWOOD WHEATLEY 48 High Street, Kingston upon Thames, Surrey KT1 1HW.

Career: articled Kingston upon Thames; admitted (1968); assistant solicitor (1968-1971); assistant solicitor Sherwood Cobbing & Williams (1971-1975); became partner (1975); merged to become Sherwood Wheatley (1987).

Activities: Deputy County Court Registrar (1984-1988); member of: Home Park Golf Club; Old Tiffinians Sports Association.

Biography: lives Thames Ditton; born 24.12.1941; married to Elisabeth with 4 children. Educated at Woking County Grammar School for Boys (1952-1960); Southampton University (1963 hons).

Leisure: all types sport (particularly rugby; cricket; golf); theatre.

WEBBER John

senior partner RUSSELL JONES & WALKER Swinton House, 324 Gray's Inn Road, London WC1X 8DH.

Career: articled Tuck & Mann and Russell Jones & Walker; admitted; assistant solicitor; became partner; became senior

partner (1978).

Activities: member Holborn Law Society Committee (1981); member Supreme Court Procedure Queen's Bench Sub-committee; member of: RAC; Riverside Club; Itchenor Sailing Club.

Biography: lives Twickenham; born 16.05.1946; married to Anna with 2 children. Educated at Royal Grammar School Guildford.

Leisure: sailing; skiing; squash.

WEBSTER Michael

senior partner ROWE & MAW 20 Black Friars Lane, London EC4V 6HD.

Career: articled Herbert Smith & Co; admitted (1967); assistant solicitor McKenna & Co (1968-1970); assistant solicitor Travers Smith Braithwaite (1970-1973); assistant solicitor Rowe & Maw (1973); became partner (1973).

Activities: served on Rowe & Maw's Managing Board on two occasions; chairman Aim Limited Solicitors' Charter Users' Group (1984-1986); member The Computer Law Group; lectured for Legal Studies and Services on directors' duties and responsibilities and joint venture agreements; member of The International Bar Association Committee R (Computers and Technology Law); member of: Honourable Artillery Company; Berkhamsted Lawn Tennis and Squash Rackets Club; Ashridge Golf Club.

Biography: married with 3 children. Educated at Berkhamsted School; Bristol University (LLB hons); author of 'Legal Aspects of Computer Contracts' - Computing Services Association Journal (1986); 'Taking and Granting Security over Software' - Computer Law and Practice (1988).

Leisure: wood-cutting; walking in remote places with binoculars; golf; tennis; cross-country cycling; theatre.

WEDDERBURN Lord of Charlton

barrister 15 Old Square, Lincoln's Inn, London WC2A 3UH and Cassel Professor of Commercial Law LONDON SCHOOL OF ECONOMICS Houghton Street, London WC2A 2AE.

Career: called to the Bar Middle Temple (1953); Queen's Counsel (1990); lecturer in law Cambridge University (1953-1964); Cassel professor of commercial law London University at London School of Economics and Political Science (1964 to date); visiting professor School of Law UCLA (1967); visiting professor Harvard

Law School (1969-1970); general editor Modern Law Review (1971-1988).

Activities: general editor Modern Law Review (1971-1988); chairman London and Provincial Theatre Councils (1973 to date); independent chairman Independent Review Committee (TUC) (1976 to date); member Bullock Committee on Industrial Democracy (1976-1977); life peer (1977); member Group of Experts on the European Company (ETUC/EEC) (1989 to date); president Institute of Employment Rights; hon president European Association of Company Registration Agents; member Executive Committee International Society of Labour Law.

Biography: lives London N6; born 13.04.1927; married to Frances with 4 children. Educated at Aske's Hatcham School, New Cross; Whitgift School, Croydon; Queen's College Cambridge (1949 MA LLB); Chancellor's Medal for English Law; Certificate of Honour Bar Examinations (1953); Fellow British Academy (1981); hon Dottore Giurisprudenza Pavia University (1987); assistant editor 'Clerk and Lindsell on Torts'; author of: 'The Worker and The Law' (1986 3rd ed); 'Diritto Del Lavoro In Europa' (1987) with B Veneziani and S Ghimpu; 'Cases and Materials on Labour Law' (1967); 'Industrial Conflict - A Comparative Legal Survey' (1972) with B Aaron; many other articles and contributions to books.

Leisure: Charlton Athletic FC.

WEEDON Lord Alexander of

chairman NATIONAL WESTMINSTER BANK PLC 41 Lothbury, London EC2P 2BP.

Career: called to the Bar Middle Temple (1961); QC (1973); Bencher of the Middle Temple (1979); QC New South Wales, Australia (1983); chairman National Westminster Bank PLC (1989).

Activities: chairman of the Bar of England and Wales (1985-1986); trustee National Gallery (1986 to date); chairman Panel on Takeovers and Mergers (1987-1989); Life Peer (1988); member Garrick.

Biography: lives London SW1 and Aylesbury; born 05.09.1936; married to Marie with 2 sons and 1 daughter. Educated at Brighton College; King's College Cambridge.

WEEKES David

senior partner GREENWOODS 30 Priestgate; Peterborough PE1 1JE.

Career: articled local firm (1956-1961); admitted (1961); assistant solicitor Greenwoods (1961-1962); became partner (1962).

Activities: Deputy Registrar; member Cambridge Legal Aid Area Committee; member of: Peterborough Town Sports Club; Flying Services Club.

Biography: lives Wansford nr Peterborough; born 29.03.1938; married to Stephanie with 3 children. Educated at Deacons School, Peterborough; College of Law Lancaster Gate.

Leisure: veterans' hockey and squash; gardening; family.

WEETCH Andrew

partner OXLEY & COWARD 34 Moorgate Street, Rotherham, South Yorkshire S60 2HB.

Career: design engineer British Steel (1972-1973); articled Oxley & Coward (1972-1979); admitted (1979); assistant solicitor (1979-1982); became partner (1982).

Activities: formerly on General Committee of Barnsley Law Society; member Lindrick Golf Club.

Biography: lives Rotherham; born 03.07.1951; married to Eleanor with 3 children. Educated at Birkdale Preparatory School (1956-1964); Shrewsbury School (1964-1968); Sheffield University (1968-1972).

Leisure: golf.

WEIL Simon

partner specialising in commercial property law and the law of charities BIRCHAM & CO 1 Dean Farrar Street, Westminster, London SW1H 0DY.

Career: articled Bircham & Co (1978-1980); admitted (1980); assistant solicitor (1980-1983); became partner (1983); in charge of catering (1983 to date) and marketing (1988 to date); member firm's Premises & General Purposes Committee (1984-1985); member Staff Committee (1985-1988); jointly responsible for recruitment of articled clerks (1985-1990).

Activities: member Oxford & Cambridge University Club.

Biography: lives London N5; born 21.03.1955; married to Glenda with 4 children. Educated at Scarsdale Villas (1958-1961); Bousfield (1961-1964); Chiswick & Bedford Park Prep (1964-1966); City of London School (1966-1972) Corporation Scholarship; Trinity College Cambridge (1977 BA); (1986 MA); College

of Law Lancaster Gate.

Leisure: history; opera and serious music generally; riding; tennis; singing; swimming; politics (especially Central Europe); drama; films; novels; cooking; lunching and dining in restaurants; struggling to be a practising Christian.

WEISMAN Malcolm

barrister and head of chambers 1 Gray's Inn Square, London WC1R 5AA.

Career: called to the Bar Middle Temple; Recorder of the Crown Court.

Activities: assistant commissioner of Parliamentary Boundaries (1976-1982); deputy circuit Judge (1978-1980); secretary-general Allied Air Forces Chiefs of Chaplains' Committee; member Courts of East Anglia, Warwick & Lancaster Universities; member Ministry of Defence Advisory Committee in Chaplaincy.

Biography: lives London; married to Rosalie with 2 children. Educated at Parmiter's School; Harrogate Grammar School; London School of Economics; St Catherine's College Oxford; Blackstone Pupillage Prize.

Leisure: reading; walking; music; doing nothing.

WELCH Sir John

partner WEDLAKE BELL 16 Bedford Street, Covent Garden, London WC2E 9HF.

Career: articled Freshfields (1957-1960); admitted (1960); became partner Bell Brodrick & Gray (1961-1971); became partner Wedlake Bell (1972).

Activities: director John Fairfax (UK) Ltd; Registrar Archdeaconry of London; member Court of Assistants of The Worshipful Company of Parish Clerks (Master 1967); member of Court of Assistants of The Worshipful Company of Haberdashers; formerly member of the Court of Common Council (City of London) (1975-1986); chairman of the Planning and Communications Committee (1981-1982); chairman London Homes for the Elderly (1981-1990); Commander Order of St John; member of: City Livery Club (president 1986-1987); MCC; Surrey County Cricket Club; The Hurlingham Club; Walbrook Ward Club (chairman 1977-1978).

Biography: lives London SW6; born 26.07.1933; married to Kerry with 3 children. Educated at Marlborough College; Hertford College Oxford (MA).

W

WELTON Brian

partner and head of commercial conveyancing FOOT & BOWDEN 70/76 North Hill, Plymouth PL4 8HH.

Career: articled Foot & Bowden (1971-1975); admitted (1975); assistant solicitor (1975-1976); became partner (1976).

Activities: member Plymouth Proprietary Library.

Biography: lives Plymouth; born 28.10.1938; married to Irene with 3 children. Educated at Plymouth Secondary School for Boys; Plymouth Polytechnic; College of Law Chester.

Leisure: photography; riding; music; literature.

WESTCOTT John

partner VEALE WASBROUGH 14 Orchard Street, Bristol BS1 5ER.

Career: National Service with 13th/18th R Hussars (1949); articled Wincanton (1950-1955); admitted (1955); assistant solicitor London and Salisbury (1955-1960); assistant solicitor Veale Benson (1961-1964); became partner (1964); managing partner Veale Wasbrough (1988).

Activities: president Bristol Law Society (1981); member Law Society Family Law Committee; member LCD Conciliation Committee; local articled clerks conciliation officer; trustee Bristol Family Conciliation Service; vice-president Avon Youth Association; chairman Southmead Youth Centre; chairman Kingswood Schools (former approved school); chairman Bristol Home Start; legal chairman (part-time) Pensions Appeal Tribunal; member of: Bristol Rugby Club; Somerset County Cricket Club; Wincanton Race Club.

Biography: lives Bristol and Baltonsborough; born 22.02.1930; married to Anne with 2 children. Educated at Taunton School; articles in Law Society's Gazette ; Family Law; Modern Law Review.

Leisure: village cricket; walking; dry stone wall building.

WESTMACOTT Philip

partner intellectual property department BRISTOWS COOKE & CARPMAEL 10 Lincoln's Inn Fields, London WC2A 3BP.

Career: trainee Tube Investments Ltd (1972-1975); articled Lovell White & King (1976-1978); admitted (1978); assistant solicitor Bristows Cooke & Carpmael (1978-1985); became partner (1985).

Biography: lives Wimbledon; born 15.04.1954; married to Susan with 3 children. Educated at Newcastle Preparatory School; Gilling Castle; Ampleforth College; Trinity College Cambridge (1975 BA); College of Law (1976).

Leisure: walking; skiing; sailing; cycling.

WESTON Adrian

deputy senior partner HARVEY INGRAM STONE & SIMPSON 20 New Walk, Leicester LE1 6TX.

Career: articled Harvey Clarke & Adams (1958-1961); admitted (1961); assistant solicitor Ingram & Co (1961-1963); became partner (1963); firm merged to become Harvey Ingram (1970); merged to become Harvey Ingram Stone & Simpson (1988).

Activities: director of: Everards Brewery Limited; Invicta Plastics Limited; Atkinson Design Associates Limited; Portland House School Trust Limited: Pal International Limited; governor Ratcliffe College; chairman the Hockey Association (1972-1978) (now vice-president); chairman Leicestershire Sports Advisory Council; member of: County Cricket Club (vice-president); British Sportsmen's Club; The Royal Air Force Club; Leicestershire Golf Club.

Biography: lives Leicester; born 07.06.1935; married to Bridget with 1 daughter and 1 son. Educated at Radcliffe College; Queen's College Oxford (1958 MA).

Leisure: golf; history; music.

WHALLEY Guy

partner FRESHFIELDS Grindall House, 25 Newgate Street, London EC1A 7LH.

Career: articled Freshfields (1956-1959); admitted (1959); assistant solicitor (1959-1964); became partner (1964); became recruitment and training partner (1977).

Activities: non-executive director Higgs and HIll PLC (1972 to date); governor Royal Academy of Music (1980 to date); governor Beechwood Park School (1974-1988); (chairman 1975-1985); co-opted member Oxford University Appointments Committee (1982 to date); member Education & Training Committee City of London Law Society; member of: MCC; Ashridge Golf Club.

Biography: lives London EC4 and Chipperfield; born 26.05.1933; married to Sarah with 1 son and 1 daughter. Educated at Rugby School (1946-1951); Gonville and Caius Cambridge (1956 BA); (1960 MA).

Leisure: music; gardening; golf; cricket; watercolour painting and drawing; hill walking.

WHALLEY Michael

resident partner MINTER ELLISON, Australian Solicitors, 20 Lincoln's Inn Fields, London WC2A 3ED.

Career: articled Ellis Peirs & Young Jackson; articled Freshfields (1976-1979); admitted England, Victoria, NSW and Australian Capital Territories; assistant solicitor Ellison Hewison & Whitehead (now Minter Ellison) (1979-1982); became partner (1982).

Activities: regular speaker on Australian legal issues to business conferences in UK and Europe; member of: Melbourne Cricket Club; Royal South Yarra Lawn Tennis Club; the Lawyer's Club; professional and business societies and associations.

Biography: lives London; born 03.09.1951; married to Karen Goldie-Morrison with 2 daughters. Educated at Geelong Grammar School, Victoria; Melbourne University (LLB hons BComm); contributes to number of legal journals including Butterworths Journal of International Banking and Financial Law; paper on impact on Australian business of the EEC 1992 program for Australian Studies Centre of London University.

Leisure: tennis; snow skiing; computer programming; flying; bringing up children.

WHARTON Mike

partner property department DJ FREEMAN & CO 1 Fetter Lane, London EC4A 1BR.

Career: articled Martin Nicholson Hortin & Nash; articled Raymond-Barker Nix & Co; articled Lawrence Graham; admitted (1968); assistant solicitor (1968-1972); assistant solicitor Staffurth & Bray (1972-1974); partner (1974-1977); assistant solicitor DJ Freeman & Co (1977-1979); became partner (1979).

Activities: member of: Institute of Advanced Motorists; Allard Owners Club; Wentworth Club.

Biography: lives Woking; born 06.03.1943; single. Educated at KCS Wimbledon; occasional articles for Estate Times.

Leisure: motoring; classic cars; golf; American vernacular music of the late 1950s.

WHEELDON John Michael

senior partner PALMER WHEELDON Daedalus House, Station Road, Cambridge CB1 2RE.

Career: articled David Brayshaw (1954-1958); admitted (1958); assistant solicitor Stanley Green (1961-1963); became partner (1963); firm became Palmer Wheeldon (1979).

Activities: part-time chairman Industrial Tribunals; president Cambridgeshire and District Law Society.

Biography: lives Cambridge; born 03.12.1935; married to Pamela with 3 children. Educated at High Storrs Grammar School, Sheffield; Sheffield University (1956 LLB hons); Solicitors' finals (1958 hons); Clement's Inn and Edmund Thomas Child Prizes.

Leisure: English literature; choral singing; sailing; walking.

WHEELHOUSE Alan

senior partner FREETH CARTWRIGHT Willoughby House, 20 Low Pavement, Nottingham NG1 7DL.

Career: articled Wells & Hind (1958-1961); admitted (1961); assistant solicitor Freeth Cartwright & Sketchley (1961-1963); became partner (1963); became senior partner Freeth Cartwright (1974).

Activities: president Nottinghamshire Law Society (1985-1986) (past council member); governor Nottingham High School; past president Old Nottinghamians Society; president Old Nottinghamians Cricket Club; president Notts Cricket Association; committee member Nottinghamshire County Cricket Club; district chairman XL Club; vice-president Nottinghamshire Football Club.

Biography: lives Nottingham; born 04.03.1934; married to Jennifer with 3 daughters. Educated at Nottingham High School; Emmanuel College Cambridge (1958 MA) (1959 LLB).

WHITBY Charles

Queen's Counsel 12 King's Bench Walk, Temple, London EC4Y 7EL.

Career: called to the Bar Middle Temple (1952); QC (1970); Recorder (1972); Bencher (1977).

Activities: member Criminal Injuries Compensation Board (1975 to date); member General Council of the Bar (1969-1971; 1972-1978); member of: United Oxford & Cambridge Universities Club; RAC (Steward); Garrick Club; Woking Golf Club.

Biography: lives London SW1; born 02.04.1926; married to Eileen. Educated at Hamilton House School, Ealing; St John's School, Leatherhead; Peterhouse Cambridge (1949 BA) (1951 MA) Scholar; contributed to: 'Master and Servant' Halsbury's Laws of England (3rd ed vol 25 1959); 'Master and Servant' Atkins Encyclopaedia of Court Forms (vol 25 1962).

Leisure: boating; fishing; cinema; theatre; golf; watching soccer.

WHITE Andrew

company commercial partner LOVELL WHITE DURRANT 21 Holborn Viaduct, London EC1A 2DY.

Career: admitted (1967); assistant solicitor (1967-1972); opened office for Lovell White & King and resident in Brussels (1972-1973); became partner (1973).

Activities: member RORC.

Biography: lives Henham; born 12.10.1942; married with 2 children. Educated at St Benedict's School, Ealing; Trinity Hall Cambridge.

Leisure: sailing; travel; good food and wine.

WHITE Andrew

partner ROWE & MAW 20 Black Friars Lane, London EC4V 6HD.

Career: articled Warren Murton & Co (1972-1974); admitted (1974); assistant solicitor (1974-1977); assistant solicitor Rowe & Maw (1977-1979); became partner (1979).

Activities: member Association of Pension Lawyers (1984 to date) (past chairman Legislative and Parliamentary Sub-committee).

Biography: lives London N4; born 01.01.1950; single. Educated at Manchester Grammar School; University College Oxford (1972 MA); Law Society Finals (hons); articles in various pensions magazines.

Leisure: reading history and related topics.

WHITE David

partner THOMSON SNELL & PASSMORE 3 Lonsdale Gardens, Tunbridge Wells, Kent TN1 1NX.

Career: articled Thomson Snell & Passmore (1968-1970); admitted (1970); assistant solicitor (1970-1973); became partner (1973).

Activities: chairman Hellingly Parish Council; Governor Claremont CPS, Tunbridge Wells.

Biography: lives Hellingly; born 03.02.1946; single. Educated at Judd School, Tonbridge; London University (1967 LLB hons); Convocation Trust Prize (1966); contributor to 'Magna Legal Precedents'.

Leisure: beef and poultry farmer; keen countryman.

WHITE John

senior partner BERRYMANS Salisbury House, London Wall, London EC2M 5QN.

Career: articled Berrymans (1946-1951); admitted (1951); became senior partner (1989).

Activities: member of: MCC; Hadley Wood GC; Royal Cromer GC.

Biography: lives Hadley Wood; born 1929; married to Myrle with 2 children. Educated at Minchenden; London University (1950 LLB).

WHITE John

senior banking partner CAMERON MARKBY HEWITT Sceptre Court, 40 Tower Hill, London EC3N 4BB.

Career: articled Cameron Kemm & Co (1957-1962); admitted (1963); assistant solicitor (1963-1964); became partner (1964); became partner Cameron Markby (1980); became partner Cameron Markby Hewitt (1989).

Activities: member International Bar Association; member West Herts Club.

Biography: lives Tylers Green; born 06.07.1938; married to Carolyn with 3 children. Educated at Wrekin College; member editorial board Journal of International Banking Law; contributed one chapter to 'Legal Issues of Cross Border Banking'.

Leisure: hockey fanatic; cricket enthusiast; student of port.

WHITE Patrick Bazley

partner BAZLEY WHITE & CO 8 Portman Street, Portman Square, London W1H 0BA.

Career: articled in London suburbs (1969-1971); admitted (1971); assistant solicitor Kenwright & Cox (1973-1974); partner (1974-1986); founder member of Bazley White & Co (1986).

Activities: Deputy Registrar (1986); assessor on reviews of taxation in High

W

Court; member Law Society Contentious Business Committee (1984-1987); Civil Litigation Committee (1987 to date); Practice & Procedure Sub-committee Solicitors' Family Law Association; Chancery member Supreme Court Procedure Main Committee (1984 to date); passive member Selden Society; member Wig & Pen Club.

Biography: lives Colchester; born 27.06.1947; married to Patricia with 2 sons and 1 daughter. Educated at St Ignatius College, London; London School of Economics (1968 LLB hons).

Leisure: family; gardening; DIY; swimming; tennis; physical exercise.

WHITE Stewart

partner and head of telecommunications group DENTON HALL BURGIN & WARRENS 5 Chancery Lane, Clifford's Inn, London EC4 1BU since (1988).

Career: articled Sly & Russell, Sydney (1973-1976); admitted NSW (1976); assistant solicitor Linklaters & Paines, London (1977-1978); admitted UK (1979); assistant and senior associate Allen Allen & Hemsley, Sydney (1979-1983); partner Blake Dawson Waldron, Sydney (1983-1988); became partner Denton Hall Burgin & Warrens (1988).

Activities: chairman International Bar Association Communications Law Sub-committee (vice-chairman Committee L Entertainment Copyright & Communications Law); chairman Media & Communications Law Committee of Lawasia; chairman Organising Committee of the Legal Symposium of the International Telecommunication Union ITU-COM (1989); member Organising Committee Legal Symposium of ITU's TELECOM (1991); member NSW Committee Cambridge Commonwealth Trust; member of: Royal Sydney Yacht Squadron; Bosham Sailing Club; Australian Club; Australian Jockey Club.

Biography: lives London SW6; born 23.07.1951; married to Elisabeth with 2 children. Educated at Newington College, Sydney; Sydney University (BA hons) (LLB); Downing College Cambridge (LLM International Law); number of journal articles.

Leisure: opera; swimming; bridge; walking; sailing; horse racing.

WHITEHEAD Fraser

partner RUSSELL JONES & WALKER 324 Gray's Inn Road, London WC1X 8DH.

Career: articled (1973-1975); admitted (1975); assistant solicitor (1975-1978); became partner Russell Jones & Walker (1978).

Activities: Chairman of Trustees Child Accident Prevention Trust; London internship supervisor School of Law University of San Diego; member Main Committee Holborn Law Society; member Executive Committee of Society of Labour Lawyers; member of Committee London Solicitors' Litigation Association; member Management Committee Mary Ward Legal Settlement; advisor to Islington Legal Advice Centre; member Labour Party and Islington South Constituency Management Committee; member American Trial Lawyers' Association; member Association of Personal Injury Lawyers; member Zanzibar Club.

Biography: lives London; born 14.12.1950; single with 1 daughter. Educated at Pocklington, Yorks; Sheffield University; College of Law.

Leisure: travelling.

WHITEHEAD John

senior partner BURROUGHS DAY ROBERT SMITH 14 Charlotte Street, Bristol BS1 5PT.

Career: articled Birkbeck Montagus; admitted (1957); admitted barrister and solicitor British Columbia Canada (1959); assistant solicitor Clay MacFarlane & Co British Columbia (1959-1960); assistant solicitor A Peter Steele-Perkins (1961-1963); assistant solicitor Burroughs Day & Blackmore (1963-1965); became partner (1965).

Activities: Commissioner for Oaths; Notary Public (British Columbia); member Area No 4 Legal Aid Committee; member Bristol South Rotary Club.

Biography: lives Bristol; born 16.05.1931; married to Rosemary with 2 children. Educated at Radley College; Sidney Sussex College Cambridge (1954 BA) (1957 MA); solicitors' finals (1957 hons).

Leisure: music; gardening; walking.

WHITEHOUSE Chris

member financial planning department BOODLE HATFIELD 43 Brook Street, London W1Y 2BL.

Career: called to the Bar Inner Temple (1972); lecturer; senior lecturer; principal lecturer and reader at College of Law (1972-1987); joined Boodle Hatfield (1987).

Biography: lives Richmond on Thames;

born 03.01.1948. Educated at Priory Grammar School; Wirral Grammar School; Oxford (1969 BA) (1970 BCL); Bar Finals (1970-1971); Duke of Edinburgh Scholar (1967); author of standard text book 'Revenue Law Principles and Practice' (8th edition 1990); joint author of 'McCutcheon on Inheritance Tax (3rd edition 1988 part of the British Tax Library) .

Leisure: theatre; music and opera; sports especially association football; tennis; squash; bridge.

WHITFIELD Alan

director commercial department BRITISH TELECOM The Solicitor's Office, 81 Newgate Street, London EC1A 7AJ.

Career: articled Linklaters & Paines (1977-1979); admitted (1979); assistant solicitor Brussels office (1979-1980); London (1980-1981); solicitor with British Telecom (1981-1989); became director commercial department (1989).

Biography: lives Harpenden; born 13.12.1954; married to Ann with 2 children. Educated at Cowley School, St Helens; Lincoln College Oxford (1976 BA); College of Law Chester (1976-1977).

Leisure: house; children; music; food.

WHITFIELD-JONES Clive

managing partner, head of property department and property finance team JEFFREY GREEN RUSSELL Apollo House, 56 New Bond Street, London W1Y 9DG.

Career: articled Chethams (1973-1975); admitted (1975); assistant solicitor Coward Chance (1975-1976); assistant solicitor Jeffrey Green Russell (1976-1978); became partner (1978); became head of property department (1980); became managing partner (1985); senior partner (from August 1991).

Activities: Royla Automobile Club and various equestrian associations.

Biography: lives London, Wimbledon; born 10.12.1949; married to Rosemary (also a solicitor) with 3 children. Educated at Denbigh Grammar School; Keele University (1972 BA hons 1st class); College of Law Lancaster Gate.

Leisure: travel; equestrian sports; shooting; motorcars; theatre; cinema; good restaurants.

WHYBROW Stephen

managing partner MCKENNA & CO Mitre House, 160 Aldersgate Street, London EC1A 4DD.

Career: articled McKenna & Co (1969-1971); admitted (1971); assistant solicitor (1971-1977); became partner (1977).

Activities: member Institute of Directors.

Biography: lives Boxted nr Colchester; born 13.03.1946; married to Annette with 1 son and 1 daughter. Educated at Bishops Stortford College; St John's College Cambridge; author of Longman's Commercial Precedents - Employment Section.

Leisure: family; gardening; cricket; walking.

WICKERSON Sir John

senior partner ORMEROD WILKINSON 10 High Street, Croydon, Surrey CR2 1DT.

Career: admitted (1960); assistant solicitor (1960-1962); became partner Ormerod Morris & Dumont (1962).

Activities: member Council Law Society (1969-1989); chairman Contentious Business Committee and Remuneration Committee; president Law Society (1986-1987); president London Criminal Courts Solicitors' Association (1981-1983); member Farrand Committee on Conveyancing; member Matrimonial Causes Rules Committee; solicitor to National Fund for Research into Crippling Diseases and other charities; director R Mansell Ltd.

Biography: lives Purley; born 22.09.1937; married to Shirley with 1 child. Educated at Christ's Hospital; London University (LLB); author of 'Motorist and The Law'.

Leisure: sport; reading; music.

WIGGIN Harry

partner BURGES SALMON Narrow Quay House, Prince Street, Bristol BS1 4AH; a member firm of the Norton Rose M5 group of legal practices.

Career: articled in London; admitted (1965); assistant solicitor (1965-1970); partner Freshfields (1970-1973); founded Wiggin and Co (1973-1986); became partner Burges Salmon (1986).

Activities: chairman Special Committee of Tax Law Consultative Bodies; member Law Society Revenue Law Committee; member British Branch Committee of International Fiscal Association; lectures on taxation topics; member of: Brooks's Club; Gresham Club.

Biography: lives Wye Valley; born 12.08.1939; married with 3 children. Educated at Eton College; Trinity College Cambridge (1961 MA); various articles.

Leisure: photography; field sports; gardening.

WIGHTMAN David

senior partner TURNER KENNETH BROWN 100 Fetter Lane, London EC4A 1DD.

Career: articled Kenneth Brown Baker Baker; admitted (1962).

Activities: member International Bar Association; member Society of Construction Law; member Law Society; member Society of English and American Lawyers; member Travellers' Club.

Biography: lives Horsham; born 03.04.1940; widowed with 2 children. Educated at King's College School, Wimbledon; joint editor in chief 'International Construction Law Review'.

Leisure: farming; tennis.

WIGHTMAN John

chairman MORTON FRASER & MILLIGAN WS 19 York Place, Edinburgh EH1 3EL.

Career: apprenticed to Macandrew Wright & Murray WS (1957-1960); joined family firm Morton Smart MacDonald & Milligan WS (now Morton Fraser Milligan WS) (1960); chairman (1988).

Activities: Commodore Royal Naval Reserve (1982-1985); church elder St George's West Church of Scotland; vice-convener committee on chaplains for the Forces; vice-chairman Territorial & Auxiliary & Volunteer Reserves Association (Lowland); member of: Royal Scots Club; Naval Club; RNVR.

Biography: lives Edinburgh and North Berwick; born 20.11.1933; married to Isla with 3 children. Educated at Daniel Stewart's College; St Andrew's University (1955 MA); Edinburgh University (1960 LLB); modified (RNR) Ship Command Royal Navy.

Leisure: ornithology; sailing.

WILKIN Ashley James

head of regional private client department FLADGATE FIELDER Walgate House, 25 Church Street, Basingstoke, Hampshire RG21 1QQ.

Career: articled in London; admitted (1975); assistant solicitor (1975-1976); head of probate department W Bradly Trimmer & Son (1976); partner (1977); partner in charge of the Alton office (1987) on merger with Walters Fladgate; on merger with

Fielder Le Riche (1988) became member of the Management Board and member of Fladgate Fielder's Business Plan Committee.

Activities: TA (decoration); served with Queen's Regiment; commanded South East District training team Aldershot; member Chamber of Commerce (former president); founder director East Hants Enterprise.

Biography: lives Dockenfield nr Farnham; born 09.01.1951; married to Susan. Educated at Portsmouth Grammar School; Birmingham University (1972 hons); College of Law.

WILKINSON Charles Edmund

senior partner BLYTH DUTTON 8 & 9 Lincoln's Inn Fields, London WC2A 3DW.

Career: articled Blyth Dutton (1965); admitted; assistant solicitor; assistant solicitor Clifford Turner (1969-1973); became partner Blyth Dutton (1974).

Activities: Freeman of City of London; Liveryman Coachmakers and Coach Harness Makers; member of: Hurlingham Club; Roehampton Club; Royal Ashdown Golf Club.

Biography: lives London; born 06.06.1943; married to Gillian Alexander with 2 children. Educated at Haileybury MSC; Clare College Cambridge (1965 MA); Law College (1965).

WILKINSON Jeremy Squire

consultant ADDLESHAW SONS & LATHAM Dennis House, Marsden Street, Manchester M2 1JD.

Career: articled March Pearson & Green (1959-1962); admitted (1962); assistant solicitor Addleshaw Sons & Latham (1962-1965); partner (1965-1990).

Activities: secretary Manchester Incorporated Law Library Society; solicitor to statutory railway company; chairman Board of Management Cheadle Royal Hospital; governor Cheadle Hulme School; chairman Talyllyn Railway Preservation Society; trustee Narrow Gauge Railway Museum Trust; member of: Welsh Mines Society; Northern Mines Research Society.

Biography: lives Wilmslow and Tywyn; born 04.06.1936; married to Alison with 2 children. Educated at Wilmslow Preparatory School; Terra Nova School; Rugby School; Cambridge (MA LLM).

W

WILKINSON Sam

senior partner DAVEY SON & JONES 10/12 Dollar Street, Cirencester, Glos GL7 2AL.

Career: articled in Swansea; admitted (1961); assistant solicitor Davey Son & Jones (1962-1965); became partner (1965); became senior partner (1981).

Activities: secretary North Cerney Cricket Club; member Cirencester Squash and Tennis Club; Cirencester 41 Club.

Biography: lives Cirencester; born 31.12.1935; married to Jane with 3 children. Educated at Dudley Grammar School; Tettenhall College, Wolverhampton; Swansea Grammar School; University College London (1958 LLB hons).

Leisure: cricket; squash; tennis; cycling; gardening.

WILLIAMS Alan Pete

partner DENTON HALL BURGIN & WARRENS Five Chancery Lane, Clifford's Inn, London EC4A 1BU.

Career: admitted (1969); assistant solicitor (1969-1972); became partner Denton Hall Burgin & Warrens (1972); established Hong Kong office (1976-1979).

Activities: Fellow of the RSA; member Publishers' Association Law Panel; Editorial Board member of International Media Law; member of: MCC; RAC; Groucho Club; Associate member of the Inner Magic Circle.

Biography: lives London; born 27.10.1944; married to Lyn with 1 daughter. Educated at Merchant Taylors' School; Exeter University (LLB hons); contributions to: Law Society's Gazette; International Media Law; 'Publishing Agreements'; co-author 'Intellectual Property - The New Law'.

Leisure: music; theatre; sport (particularly cricket); rebuilding Shakespeare's Globe on Bankside; walking; photography.

WILLIAMS Charles

partner specialising in shipping and trade litigation WILDE SAPTE Queensbridge House, 60 Upper Thames Street, London EC4V 3BD.

Career: articled Thomas Cooper & Stibbard (1977-1979); admitted (1979); assistant solicitor Lovell White & King (1979-1982); assistant solicitor Richards Butler (1982-1988); assistant solicitor Wilde Sapte (1988-1989); became partner (1989).

Activities: member RAC.

Biography: lives Carshalton; born

17.12.1953; married to Lesley with 2 sons. Educated at Shrewsbury School; Birmingham University (1975 LLB hons).

Leisure: family life.

WILLIAMS Chris

partner EDGE & ELLISON 148 Edmund Street, Birmingham, B3 2JR.

Career: articled in South Birmingham; admitted (1969); assistant solicitor (1969-1971); became partner Glaisyers (1971); partner Edge & Ellison (1990).

Activities: former vice-chairman Solihull Chamber of Trade; member Birmingham Chamber of Commerce; member of: Copt Heath Golf Club; Hampton Sports Club.

Biography: lives Knowle; born 20.01.1945; married to Jane with 2 children. Educated at Hallfield Preparatory School; Malvern College, Worcestershire; College of Law.

Leisure: golf; hockey; Francophile; serious music.

WILLIAMS Gareth

Queen's Counsel and head of chambers Farrar's Building, Temple, London EC4Y 7BD.

Career: called to the Bar (1965); QC (1978); Recorder of the Crown Court (1978).

Activities: Deputy High Court Judge; member Bar Council; former leader Wales & Chester Circuit; chairman Professional Conduct Committee; chairman Bar Committee.

Biography: born 05.02.1941. Educated at Mostyn CP School; Rhyl Grammar School; Queen's College Cambridge (MA LLB hons); University Prize Jurisprudence.

WILLIAMS Geoffrey C

partner WATSON FARLEY & WILLIAMS Minories House, 2-5 Minories, London EC3N 1BJ.

Career: admitted (1970); assistant solicitor (1970-1974); partner Norton Rose Botterell & Roche (1974-1982); founding partner Watson Farley & Williams (1982).

Biography: lives London W1; born 15.04.1944; married to Susan with 3 children. Educated at Dublin University (BA LLB); College of Law Guildford.

Leisure: cricket; theatre; opera; fishing.

WILLIAMS Graeme

Queen's Counsel and head of chambers 13 King's Bench Walk, Temple, London EC4 and King's Bench Chambers, Wheatsheaf Yard, Oxford.

Career: called to the Bar Inner Temple (1959); pupillage with D Lowe (1959); practice in London; Oxford and Midland and Oxford circuit; Recorder (1982); QC (1983).

Activities: member Legal Aid No 3 Area Committee.

Biography: lives London NW1; born 05.07.1935; married to Anna with 2 daughters. Educated at Tonbridge School (1948-1953); Brasenose College Oxford (1958 BA) (1968 MA).

Leisure: gardening; music; travel.

WILLIAMS Hugh

partner in charge of insurance services group JAQUES & LEWIS 2 South Square, Gray's Inn, London WC1R 5HR.

Career: articled Frere Cholmeley & Co; admitted (1976); assistant solicitor (1976-1977); partner Alexander Rubens (1977-1980); partner Russell Jones & Walker (1980-1988); founding partner Jaques & Lewis Insurance Group (1988).

Activities: chief coach Christ's College Boat Club, Cambridge; chairman of The Tideway Scullers' School; member assorted Old Boy and Dining Clubs.

Biography: lives London W4; born 24.10.1950; married to Gilly with 3 children. Educated at The Dean's School, Singapore; Maidenhead Grammar School; Christ's College Cambridge (1973 BA) (1976 MA); various articles on the subject of insurance law for newspapers, specialist magazines and other publications.

Leisure: rowing; sculling; long-distance running; formerly rugby union and karate.

WILLIAMS Huw

partner EDWARDS GELDARD 16 St Andrew's Crescent, Cardiff CF1 3RD.

Career: articled Morgan Bruce & Nicholas (1976-1978); admitted (1978); assistant solicitor Mid Glamorgan County Council (1978-1980); senior assistant solicitor (1980-1984); principal assistant solicitor (1984-1987); associate Edwards Geldard (1987-1988); became partner (1988).

Activities: secretary Cardiff and South East Wales branch of the Oxford Society; member United Oxford & Cambridge University Club.

Biography: lives Cardiff; born 04.01.1954; single. Educated at Llanelli Grammar School; Jesus College Oxford (1980 MA); College of Law Guildford.

Leisure: skiing; swimming; books; art history; architecture.

WILLIAMS James

partner BREEZE & WYLES
114 Fore Street, Hertford, Herts SG14 1AG.

Career: admitted (1966); assistant solicitor
(1966-1967); became partner (1967).

Activities: former member Round Table;
chairman Herts County Day (2 years);
chairman Perry Green & Green Tye Society.

Biography: lives Much Hadham; born
10.05.1941; married to Priscilla with 2
children. Educated at Tonbridge School;
Bristol University (LLB hons).

WILLIAMS John

senior partner LEIGH WILLIAMS
King's House, 32-40 Widmore Road,
Bromley, Kent BR1 1RY.

Career: admitted (1962); became partner
with father Bill Williams; amalgamated
with Gunson & Leigh to form Leigh
Williams (1986).

Activities: member Croydon & District
Law Society; member Overseas Committee
of the Magistrates' Association; past
president Bromley & District Law Society;
Justice of the Peace South East London
Commission (1966 to date); hon secretary
the Magistrates' Association SE London
branch; hon solicitor and council member
Commonwealth Magistrates' Association;
council member International Association
Juvenile and Family Courts Magistrates;
director Churchill Theatre Trust; member
Bromley Hockey Club; chorus member
Kentish Opera Group; chorister St Francis
of Assisi, West Wickham; founder
president Langley Park Rotary Club;
member Croydon Medico/Legal Society.

Biography: lives Croydon; born 13.11.1935;
married to Patricia with 4 children.
Educated at Beckenham and Penge
Grammar School; Downing College
Cambridge (1959 MA LLB).

WILLIAMS John

partner TURNER KENNETH BROWN
100 Fetter Lane, London EC4A 1DD.

Career: called to Bar (1961); worked for
Inland Revenue; articled Peacock &
Goddard; admitted (1966); became partner
(1966); senior resident partner in Hong
Kong office (1985-1988); member
Management Committee (1988 to date).

Activities: lectures and seminars on tax,
trusts and offshore vehicles; member of:
Brooks's; Burhill Golf Club; Royal Cinque
Ports Golf Club; St George's Hill Tennis
Club; The Royal Hong Kong Jockey Club;
The Foreign Correspondents' Club (Hong
Kong).

Biography: lives Walton on Thames; born
17.12.1936; married to Gillian with 2
children. Educated at St John's College,
Southsea; Inns of Court School of Law;
College of Law.

Leisure: golf; opera; theatre; tennis.

WILLIAMS June

director policy and legal LEGAL AID
BOARD Newspaper House, 8-16 Great
New Street, London EC4A 3BN.

Career: articled in Birmingham; admitted
(1955); assistant solicitor (1955-1956);
Dudley County Borough Council (1956-
1963); Deputy Town Clerk Oldbury (1963-
1967); Birmingham Legal Aid office (1967-
1975); Brighton Legal Aid office (1975-
1977); deputy director head office London
(1977-1989); Legal Aid Board (1989);
secretary to the Board and its committees
and directing the legal section and the
secretariat.

Activities: member International Board
Soroptimist International.

Biography: lives Brighton; born 04.06.1930;
widowed. Educated at Sutton Coldfield
High School for Girls; Edinburgh
University (1951 MA); Birmingham
University (1954 LLB).

Leisure: walking; theatre; opera; concerts;
reading.

WILLIAMS Melville

Queen's Counsel and head of chambers
15 Old Square, Lincoln's Inn, London
WC2A 3UH.

Career: called to the Bar Inner Temple
(1955); common law practice as junior
barrister (1955-1957); QC (1977); legal
assessor to the General Medical Council
and General Dental Council (1982); Crown
Court Recorder (1985); Bencher of Inner
Temple (1985).

Activities: member Independent Review
Body of the Coal Industry (1985); member
American Bar Association; member
Association of Trial Lawyers of America;
president Association of Personal Injury
Lawyers.

Biography: lives nr Dorking; born
20.06.1931; married to Jean with 4 children.
Educated at St Christopher's School,
Letchworth; St John's College Cambridge
(1954 History and Law); articles/papers;
'Arbitrators and Awards' (1959); 'Forum
Shipping and the Brussels Convention'
(1989).

Leisure: mountain walking (house in North
West Scotland); golf; travel.

WILLIAMS Paul

senior partner JACKLYN DAWSON &
MEYRICK WILLIAMS
Equity Chambers, John Frost Square,
Newport, Gwent NP9 1PW.

Career: articled Husband Tillyard & Rees
(1964-1970); admitted (1970); assistant
solicitor John W Davies & Co (1970-1972);
assistant solicitor Jacklyn Dawson &
Meyrick Williams (1972-1973); became
partner (1973) .

Activities: chairman Rent Assessment
Panel for Wales (1981 to date); lectures at
Newport Enterprise Agency; member
Newport Constitutional Club.

Biography: lives Llansoy nr Usk; born
26.04.1946; married to Sheila. Educated at
Cardiff High School for Boys; College of
Law Guildford; written articles for
Newport Enterprise Agency and local
Gwent Business Directory.

Leisure: walking; reading; bridge; medieval
history and architecture.

WILLIAMS Philip

consultant EVERSHED WELLS & HIND
10 Newhall Street, Birmingham B3 3LX.

Career: articled JM Day (1955-1958);
admitted (1958); assistant solicitor in
private practice and local government
(1958-1966); deputy town clerk Norwich
City Council (1966-1969); town clerk
Coventry City Council (1969-1973); county
secretary West Midlands County Council
(1973-1986).

Activities: member council of Law Society
(1979 to date); chairman local government
Legal Society (1977-1978); member various
Law Society Committees; chairman Law
Reform Committee; chairman Planning
Law Committee; chairman Employment
Law Committee.

Biography: lives Coventry; born 25.10.1932;
married to Margaret with 2 sons. Educated
at Wycliffe College; St John's College
Cambridge (1955 BA) (1958 MA);
McMahon Law Scholarship; various
articles on local government and Law
Society matters.

Leisure: golf; rugby football (spectator);
classical music; classical literature.

WILLIAMS Robin

head of commercial litigation practice, with
particular responsibility for the insurance
and reinsurance practice McKENNA & CO
908 Lloyd's, 1 Lime Street, London
EC3M 7DQ.

Career: articled McKenna & Co; admitted

W

(1973); assistant solicitor (1973-1979); became partner (1979); member of Board of firm; finance partner for commercial litigation department.

Activities: associate member Lloyd's; member ABA; member IBA; speaker at various seminars on insurance matters particularly environmental insurance; seminars: Product Liability Insurance Seminar (1988); Is Reinsurance Litigation Inevitable? (1988); Data Ownership & Security - The Legal View (1988); Environmental Insurance Coverage Issues (1989); Environmental Insurance Coverage Issues for IBC Seminar (1989); Environmental Law Seminar (1989); Standard Insurance Policies for Law & Business Forum 'Corporate Environmental Responsiblities' (1989); The Role of Insurance in Environmental Issues (1989); Insuring for Environmental Risk for Environment Council (1990); The Insurability of Environmental Risks for Law & Business Forum 'Environmental Law & The Corporation - The New Imperatives' (1990); Is Insurance the Answer? for Law & Business Forum 'Hazardous Waste Management & Liaiblity' (1990); Insurance Coverage Issues for IBC Financial Focus Ltd 'Pollution, Environmental Impairment & Waste' (1990); The Insurability of Environmental Risks for Law & Business Forum 'Environmental Law & Practice' (1990); member of: Old Hamptonians Association Football Club; Old Hamptonians Association Golf Society; Foxhills Country Club.

Biography: lives Guildford; born 06.02.1949; married with 2 children. Educated at Hampton School; University College Oxford (1970 MA); author of: Comment: 'The Changing Insurance Market' (1989); Reoccurring Questions for ReActions (1989); 'Towards A Greener Spain' for ReActions (1989); Environmental Impairment Liability Policies; Enviro Risk (1990); The Insurance of Environmental Risks - Time for a New Approach (1990); Environmental Risks: Who Pays the Bill? for Global Reinsurance (1990); Current International Issues for Environmental Claims Journal (1990).

Leisure: playing for Old Hamptonians veterans' football team; gardening; horse racing; sport; food and drink; theatre.

WILLIAMS Sarah

deputy banking ombudsman THE OFFICE OF THE BANKING OMBUDSMAN Citadel House, 5/11 Fetter Lane, London EC4A 1BR.

Career: articled Penningtons; admitted (1973); assistant solicitor Few & Kester; assistant solicitor Francis & Co; assistant solicitor Thames Water Authority; assistant solicitor Professional Purposes Department The Law Society; the office of the Banking Ombudsman (1986); became deputy banking ombudsman (1989).

Biography: lives London SW20; born 03.02.1948; married to Adrian. Educated at Malvern Girls' College; Leeds University (1969 LLB hons).

Leisure: theatre; concerts; tennis.

WILLIAMS Sir Max

consultant CLIFFORD CHANCE Blackfriars House, 19 New Bridge Street, London EC4V 6BY.

Career: admitted (1950); assistant solicitor family firm in Fishguard (1950-1958); became partner Clifford Turner (1958); became senior partner (1984-1987); became joint senior partner Clifford Chance (1987-1989); became senior partner (1989); retired (1990).

Activities: Knight (1983); member Royal Commission on Legal Services (1976-1979); president of the Law Society (1982-1983); lay member of Council of International Stock Exchange (1984 to date); director Royal Insurance Holdings PLC (1985 to date); master of the City of London Solicitors' Company (1986-1987); president of the City of London Law Society (1986-1987); chairman of the Review Board for Government Contracts (1986 to date); director of 3i PLC (1988 to date); former hon treasurer of Wildfowl Trust; member of: Garrick Club; Flyfishers' Club.

Biography: lives Harpenden; born 18.02.1926; married to Jenifer with 2 children. Educated at Nautical College, Pangbourne; Birmingham University (1983 LLD hons).

Leisure: fishing; golf.

WILLIAMS Spencer

partner property department ROWE & MAW 20 Black Friars Lane, London EC4V 6HD.

Career: articled Tackley Fall & Read (1966-1971); admitted (1971); assistant solicitor (1971-1973); assistant solicitor Freshfields (1973-1979); became partner Braby & Waller (1979-1989); became partner Rowe & Maw (1989).

Biography: lives Ealing; born 1946; married to Liz with 3 sons. Educated at Durston House, Ealing; Bloxham School.

Leisure: theatre; watercolour painting; gardening; swimming.

WILLIAMSON Jim

senior partner and chairman management committee personal communications and administration BRAY & BRAY 1 3 & 5 Welford Road, Leicester LE2 7AN.

Career: articled Freer Bouskell & Co (1959-1962); admitted (1962); assistant solicitor (1962-1964); assistant solicitor K I Maclean (1964-1965); assistant solicitor Bray & Bray (1965-1966); became partner (1966); became senior partner (1989).

Activities: treasurer St John's Church, Billesdon; member Commercial Committee of Leicester Tigers RFC; past president Old Wyggestonian Association; member of: Oadby Wyggestonian RFC (past president); Kibworth (Leics) Bowling Club.

Biography: lives Frisby by Gaulby; born 22.04.1938; married with 3 children. Educated at Wyggeston Grammar School (1949-1956); Nottingham University (1959 LLB); College of Law Guildford (1961-1962).

Leisure: rugby union; swimming; bowls.

WILLIAMSON Peter

managing partner TURNER KENNETH BROWN 100 Fetter Lane, London EC4A 1DD.

Career: articled Ward Bowie & Co; admitted (1972); assistant solicitor (1972-1974); became partner Kenneth Brown Baker Baker (1974); member Management Committee.

Activities: President Holborn Law Society (1989-1990); member of: MCC; Travellers' Club.

Biography: lives Chesham Bois; born 20.08.1947; married to Patricia with 2 children. Educated at Berkhamsted School.

Leisure: cricket; classical music; numismatics.

WILLIAMSON Raymond

partner MacROBERTS 152 Bath Street, Glasgow G2 4TB.

Career: articled MacRobert Son & Hutchison (now MacRoberts) (1966-1968); admitted (1968); assistant solicitor (1968-1972); became partner (1972).

Activities: Law Society of Scotland: member of council; convener Employment Law committee; convener Guarantee Fund; member Industrial Law Group; external examiner in various mercantile law subjects at Glasgow University; chairman Scottish National Orchestra; chairman The John Currie Singers; Governor The High School of Glasgow; member of: Royal Scottish Automobile Club; The Glasgow Art Club; The College Club Glasgow University.

Biography: lives Newton Mearns; born 24.12.1942; married to Brenda with 2 children. Educated at The High School of Glasgow; The Glasgow University (1966 MA LLB).

Leisure: music; fine art.

WILLIS Arthur

consultant to FLINT BISHOP & BARNETT Royal Oak House, Market Place, Derby DE1 2EA.

Career: articled in Huddersfield; admitted; assistant solicitor in Huddersfield, Bradford and Barnsley; assistant solicitor Flint Bishop and Barnett (1955-1956); partner (1956); senior partner (1976); became consultant (1990).

Activities: Deputy Registrar in the High Court and County Court; chairman National Insurance Tribunal (12 years); Assistant Deputy Coroner for South Derbyshire; chairman Disciplinary Committee of the Derbyshire Family Practitioners' Committee for Doctors and Dentists (12 years); advises football clubs on liquidation proceedings; member of: Farmers' Club; The Wig & Pen Club; Kedleston Park Golf Club.

Biography: lives Derby; born 30.05.1927; married with 2 children. Educated at Almondbury Grammar School, Huddersfield; monthly digest for the benefit of own office.

Leisure: enthusiastic gardener; keen golfer; enjoying countryside; reading books; dabbling in painting.

WILLIS David

partner and head of private client department FRERE CHOLMELEY 28 Lincoln's Inn Fields, London WC2A 3HH.

Career: called to the Bar; articled Frere Cholmeley (1973-1975); admitted (1975); assistant solicitor (1975-1978); became partner (1978).

Biography: Educated at Oxford University (1967 MA hons).

WILLMER John Franklin

Queen's Counsel 7 King's Bench Walk, Temple, London EC4Y 7DS.

Career: called to the Bar Inner Temple (1955); QC (1967); Bencher of Inner Temple (1975).

Activities: member Panel of Arbitrators appointed by Committee of Lloyd's for salvage arbitrations (1967 to date); Wreck Commissioner for England and Wales (1967-1979 & 1987 to date); General Commissioner of Income Tax for Inner Temple (1982 to date); member Admiralty Court Committee; Lay chairman North Camden Deanery Synod (1970-1976); Churchwarden St John-at-Hampstead (1976-1979); member London Diocesan Synod and Bishop's Council (1970-1979); member Edmonton Area Synod and Bishop's Council (1979 to date); member London Diocesan Board for Social Responsibility (1979 to date); member United Oxford & Cambridge University Club.

Biography: lives London NW6; born 30.05.1930; married to Nicola; divorced; married to Margaret with 4 children by first marriage. Educated at The Hall School, Hampstead; Abberley Hall; Winchester College; Corpus Christi College Oxford (1950-1953) (1957 MA); Council of Legal Education (1953-1954); joint winner Miles Clauson Memorial Prize (1953); captain College Boat Club (1952-1953).

Leisure: walking; visiting ancient buildings and archaeological sites; active in church synodical government.

WILLOUGHBY Jeremy

director and company secretary GARTMORE INVESTMENT MANAGEMENT LIMITED Gartmore House, 16-18 Monument Street, London EC3R 8QQ.

Career: research officer Bank of London & South America; articled Addleshaw Sons & Latham (1974-1977); admitted (1977); assistant solicitor Allen & Overy (1978-1981); solicitor Gartmore Investment Management Limited (1981-1989); became director (1989).

Activities: member of: MCC; Groucho's; City of London Club.

Biography: lives London N1; born 03.06.1948. Educated at Ashlyn's School, Berkhamsted; University College of Wales (1970 BSC); London School of Economics and Political Science (1971 MA); SSRC Studentship (1970-1971).

Leisure: opera; theatre; art; collecting prime ministerial memorabilia and Vanity Fair cricket prints.

WILLOUGHBY Peter

partner TURNER KENNETH BROWN 100 Fetter Lane, London EC4A 1DD and 1901 Worldwide House, 19 Des Voeux Road, Central, Hong Kong.

Career: admitted (1962); admitted Nigeria (1962); admitted Hong Kong (1973); professor of law and head of Department of Professional Legal Education, Faculty of Law, Hong Kong University (1973-1986); became partner Turner Kenneth Brown (1986).

Activities: chairman Joint Liaison Committee on Hong Kong Taxation; member Hong Kong Inland Revenue Board of Review; member Hong Kong Standing Committee on Company Law Reform; member Hong Kong Law Society's Disciplinary Panel; JP (Hong Kong); member Hong Kong Air Traffic Licensing Authority; member English Law Society's Revenue Law Committee; member English Law Society's VAT Sub-committee (1987 to date); member Hong Kong Law Reform Commission (1980-1987) (chairman Committee on Insurance Law Reform 1982-1986); chairman Hong Kong Law Society's Revenue Law Committee (1974-1987) (member Free Legal Advice Panel 1974-1987); member Hong Kong Securities Commission (1984-1989).

Biography: lives Guildford and Hong Kong; born 17.02.1937; married to Ruth with 2 children. Educated at Merchant Taylors' School, Sandy Lodge; London School of Economics (1958 LLB) (1960 LLM); author of 3 volume loose leaf encyclopaedia 'Hong Kong Revenue Law'; various books and articles .

WILLS Ted (Edward William)

Official Solicitor CHURCH COMMISSIONERS 1 Millbank, Westminster, London SW1P 3JZ.

Career: articled in The Temple (1957-1960); admitted (1960); Treasury Solicitor's office Legal Civil Service (finally as head of lands advisory section) (1961-1985); became Official Solicitor Church Commissioners (1985).

Activities: representative member on Government Land Transactions Committee; member Churches Main Committee and many ad hoc Committees.

Biography: lives London SW15; born 11.09.1932; married to Jocelyn with 1 son. Educated at Gosport County Grammar School; Bristol University (1954 LLB).

Leisure: art; history; photography.

W

WILSON (Alan) Martin

Queen's Counsel 6 King's Bench Walk, Temple, London EC4Y 7DR.

Career: schoolmaster (1961-1962); called to the Bar (1963); Chambers at 2 Fountain Court, Birmingham (1963-1982); pupillage with HJ Garrard; joined Oxford Circuit; Deputy Circuit Judge (1978); Recorder Midland and Oxford Circuit (1979); QC (1982); Chambers at 6 King's Bench Walk (1982 to date).

Activities: chairman Midland & Oxford Circuit Sub-committee on Criminal Justice Bill; member Midland & Oxford Circuit Liaison Committee with Crown Prosecution Services; occasional member Hong Kong Bar Association; member of: Bar Yacht Club; Sloane Club.

Biography: lives Peopleton; born 12.02.1940; married to Julia with 3 children. Educated at Kilburn Grammar School; Nottingham University.

Leisure: literature; sailing; shooting; travel.

WILSON Atholl

senior partner RAWORTHS Eton House, 89 Station Parade, Harrogate HG1 1HF.

Career: articled Booth & Co (1959-1963); admitted (1964); Queener & Courtney Attorneys Columbia USA (1964-1965); assistant solicitor Trollope & Winkworth (1965-1968); assistant solicitor Raworths (1968-1971); became partner (1971); became senior partner (1986).

Activities: president Harrogate and District Law Society (1985-1986); chairman Harrogate and District Association for Mental Health; Fellow Woodard Corporation; vice-chairman Council of Queen Ethelburgas School for Girls, Harrogate.

Biography: lives Harrogate; born 27.03.1941; married to Rosemary with 2 daughters. Educated at Bramcote Preparatory School, Scarborough; Uppingham School, Rutland.

WILSON Bruce

partner in charge of family law MILLS & REEVE Francis House, 3-7 Redwell Street, Norwich NR2 4TJ.

Career: articled Mills & Reeve (1964-1967); admitted (1967); assistant solicitor (1967-1970); became partner (1970).

Activities: member of: The Norfolk Club; Norfolk Broads Yacht Club.

Biography: lives Mulbarton; born 09.03.1942; married to Anita. Educated at

Norwich School; King's College London (1964 LLB).

Leisure: fast cars; travelling in France; wine; reading; gardening.

WILSON Colin

senior partner TURNERS 1 Poole Road, Bournemouth BH2 5QQ.

Career: articled EW Marshall Harvey & Dalton (1960-1965); admitted (1966); assistant solicitor (1966-1967); became partner Turners (1967).

Activities: member Law Society Committee for interviewing prospective articled clerks (1960s); various former posts as hon solicitor to local charitable and other organisations; former member Bournemouth & Wimborne Round Table; hon solicitor to St Thomas Garnett School Trust; company director of caravan and leisure company; member Royal Motor Yacht Club.

Biography: lives Wimborne; born 06.09.1941; married to Priscilla with 2 children. Educated at St Peter's School; College of Law.

Leisure: tennis; sailing; skiing.

WILSON David

senior partner STEVENS & BOLTON 5 Castle Street, Farnham, Surrey U9 7HT.

Career: management trainee BOAC (1960-1965); admitted (1965); assistant solicitor Stevens & Bolton (1967-1968); became partner (1968); became senior partner (1989).

Activities: Notary Public; chairman local choral society.

Biography: lives Farnham; born 28.07.1936; married with 3 children. Educated at Geelong Grammar School, Victoria, Australia; Stubbington House, Fareham; Winchester College; New College Oxford (1959 MA).

Leisure: choral singing; marathon running (5 completed London marathons); tennis; hill walking.

WILSON Gerard

senior partner JONES MAIDMENT WILSON 5 Byrom Street, Manchester M3 4PF.

Career: office boy Theo M Cohen (1963); legal executive; articled (1968-1973); assistant solicitor (1973-1978); became partner Jones Maidment Wilson (1978) .

Activities: member of: Bramhall Golf Club;

Northern Squash Club; Bramhall Lawn Tennis Club; Village Squash Club; Withington Golf Club.

Biography: lives Bramhall; born 22.10.1947; married to Evelyn with 2 children. Educated at Xaverian College .

Leisure: golf; gardening; music (piano and harmonica).

WILSON Michael

partner and head of litigation department STEPHENSON HARWOOD One St Paul's Churchyard, London EC4M 8SH.

Career: National Service commission Royal Artillery; admitted (1961); assistant solicitor (1961-1966); became partner Stephenson Harwood (1966).

Activities: member of: Gresham Club; PCC.

Biography: born 09.09.1934; married to Mary Rose with 3 children. Educated at Rugby; Oriel College Oxford (1958 MA Jurisprudence).

Leisure: family; racing; tennis; rugby; gardening.

WILSON Michael

partner and head of litigation department BERWIN LEIGHTON Adelaide House, London Bridge, London EC4R 9HA.

Career: articled Slaughter and May; admitted; assistant solicitor Berwin Leighton (1977-1979); became partner (1979).

Activities: member City of London Solicitors' Company; member Law Society; non-executive director Spreckley Villers Hunt & Co Ltd; Freeman of City of London; associate member Lloyd's of London; member Asia Pacific Lawyers' Association; member International Bar Association; member South Western Legal Foundation; member of: RAC.

Biography: lives Ashtead; born 06.12.1942; married to Maureen with 2 children.

Leisure: tennis; squash; swimming; travel; reading; music.

WILSON Nicholas

advisor and member of executive committee NATIONAL WESTMINSTER BANK PLC, 41 LOTHBURY, LONDON EC2P 2BP.

Career: articled Keeble Hawson Steele Carr & Co (1956-1961); admitted (1961); assistant solicitor Slaughter and May (1961 & 1963-1967); partner (1968-1990); joined National Westminster Bank plc (1990).

W

Activities: member DTI Advisory Committee on Company Law (1974-1978); member Bank of England City Capital Markets Committee (1974 to date); member The Stock Exchange New Issues Procedures Committee (1989-1990); member Bullock Committee (1975-1976); member of: The Justinians; The Bond Club of London.

Biography: lives Guildford; born 27.09.1935; married with 3 children and 4 stepchildren. Educated at Repton School; Sheffield University (1959 LLB); Harvard Law School (1962 LLM); University of California (Berkeley post graduate research); Harkness Fellowship; author of 'Freedom of Contracts' and 'Adhesion Contracts' (1964).

Leisure: gardening; music; poetry.

WILSON Nicholas AR

Queen's Counsel Queen Elizabeth Building, Temple, London EC4Y 9BS.

Career: called to the Bar (1967); QC (1987); Recorder of the Crown Court (1987).

Activities: family law.

Biography: lives London W2 and Broadway; born 09.05.1945; married to Margaret with 2 children. Educated at Bryanston; Worcester College Oxford (1966 jurisprudence 1st class hons); Eldon Scholarship (1967).

Leisure: music; antiques; racing.

WILSON Paul Ian

senior partner JOELSON WILSON & CO 70 New Cavendish Street, London W1M 8AT.

Career: articled WR Bennett & Co, Bloomsbury; assistant solicitor Lionel Leighton & Co (now Berwin Leighton) (1961-1965); assistant solicitor Joelson & Co (1965); became equity partner (1965); firm became Joelson Wilson & Co (1971); became senior partner (1982).

Biography: lives Harrow on the Hill; born 26.12.1935; married to Elaine with 3 children. Educated Kilburn Grammar School; Bristol University (1957 LLB hons).

Leisure: mountain walking and skiing in Switzerland; gardening; playing golf; travel; visiting Edinburgh where he has a flat; following careers of children through university and wife as author.

WILSON Peter

senior partner WILSON & BROWNE 41 Meadow Road, Kettering, Northants.

Career: admitted (1970).

Biography: lives Kettering; born 14.06.1943; married with 2 children. Educated at Cheltenham College; St Andrew's University (1966 LLB).

WILSON Richard

senior partner GORDONS 14 Piccadilly, Bradford BD1 3LX.

Career: articled Gordons (1958-1963); admitted (1963); assistant solicitor (1963-1964); became partner (1965); became senior partner (1982).

Activities: miscellaneous directorships of private companies; non-executive director and deputy chairman Central Motor Auctions PLC; Notary Public and one of the last Commissioners of Oaths; chairman of the Bradford Support Group of NSPCC; member of: The Bradford Club; Yorkshire County Cricket Club; Bradford 41 Club.

Biography: lives Bradford; born 17.04.1941; married to Paddy with 4 children. Educated at Bradford Grammar School; part-time Leeds University (1961 LLB).

Leisure: the arts; music; walking.

WILSON Robert William

HM Coroner for East Berkshire 'Oak Trees', West End, Waltham St Lawrence, Berks RG10 0NN.

Career: admitted (1951); appointed Coroner (1969); senior partner Colemans (1980-1989).

Activities: chairman Waltham St Lawrence Parish Council; member Lloyds Yacht Club.

Biography: lives Waltham St Lawrence; born 18.09.1926; married to Pamela with 2 children. Educated at Retford Grammar School; Intelligence Corps (1945-1948).

WILSON Roger

partner MALCOLM WILSON & COBBY Highworth, 3 Liverpool Terrace, Worthing; West Sussex BN11 1TA.

Career: articled Price Atkins & Price (1953-1958); admitted (1958); served as 2nd Lt Royal Tank Regiment (1958-1960); assistant solicitor Malcolm Wilson & Cobby (1960-1962); became partner (1962).

Activities: secretary Worthing Law Society (1987 to date) (president 1981-1982); member Royal Ocean Racing Club.

Biography: born 19.08.1935; married to Ingrid with 1 daughter and 2 stepsons. Educated at Solihull, Warwickshire.

Leisure: tennis; bridge; sailing.

WILSON Sir David

partner and head of tax department SIMMONS & SIMMONS 14 Dominion Street, London EC2M 2RJ.

Career: admitted Barrister (1954); practised at tax chambers (5 Paper Buildings) (1954-1961); joined Simmons & Simmons (1961); admitted (1962); became partner (1963).

Activities: member City of London Law Society; member Revenue Law sub-committee; member of: Arts Club; Royal Southern Yacht Club.

Biography: lives Oxshott; born 30.10.1928; married to Margareta with 3 children. Educated at Deerfield Academy, Mass, USA; Harrow School; Oriel College Oxford (1952 MA); Brisco Owen Scholar.

Leisure: shooting; sailing; golf.

WINSOR Thomas Philip

assistant solicitor in energy and natural resources group NORTON ROSE Kempson House, PO Box 570, Camomile Street, London EC3A 7AN.

Career: apprentice Thorntons & Dickies WS (1979-1981); admitted (1981); assistant solicitor (1981-1982); sole practitioner (1982-1983); assistant solicitor Dundas & Wilson CS (1983-1984); became assistant solicitor Norton Rose (1984).

Activities: member Society of Scottish Lawyers in London (president 1987-1989); member Dundee University Petroleum and Mineral Law Society (president 1987-1989); guest lecturer at the Centre for Petroleum and Mineral Law Studies, Dundee University (1985-1990); member UK Oil Lawyers' Group; member Law Society of Scotland; member The Law Society; member American Society of International Law; member International Bar Association (section on Energy and Natural Resources Law).

Biography: lives Brenchley; born 07.12.1957; married to Sonya. Educated at Grove Academy, Broughty Ferry; Edinburgh University (1979 LLB); Dundee University (1983 Diploma in Petroleum Law); co-author 'Oil and Gas Law: The Joint Operating Agreement' (1989).

Leisure: swimming; golf; Scottish legal history; politics; travel; antique books; reading.

WINSTANLEY Robert

joint senior partner WINSTANLEY-BURGESS 378 City Road, London EC1V 2QA.

Career: articled Dawson & Co (1971-1973);

W

admitted (1973); assistant solicitor (1973-1975); co-founded Winstanley-Burgess (1975).

Activities: Deputy County Court Registrar (1987 to date); council member Law Society representing Constituency No 4 (1985 to date); chairman Law Society's Mental Health sub-committee (1986-1990); vice-chairman Remuneration and Practice Development Committee of the Law Society; member Legal Aid Board's Duty Solicitor Sub-committee; member Law Society's Advocacy Training Committee; member United Oxford & Cambridge University Club.

Biography: lives London W4; born 04.11.1948; married to Josephine with 2 children. Educated at Glyn Grammar School, Epsom; St Catharine's College Cambridge (1973 MA); College of Law Lancaster Gate.

Leisure: cricket; motorcycling.

WINTLE Giles

secretary company law INSTITUTE OF CHARTERED ACCOUNTANTS IN ENGLAND AND WALES Chartered Accountants' Hall, Moorgate Place, London EC2P 2BJ.

Career: admitted (1958); assistant solicitor and partner (1958-1968); quotations department and secretary to the council The Stock Exchange (1968-1975); joined staff Institute of Chartered Accountants in England and Wales (1976).

Activities: Freeman of the City of London Solicitors' Company; member of the Court of the Armourers' & Brasiers' Company (Master 1989); member of: Law Society Yacht Club; Wandsworth Society.

Biography: lives London SW17; born 27.02.1935; married to Elizabeth with 3 children. Educated at Westminster School; College of Law.

Leisure: light engineering; sailing; gardening.

WINWARD Richard

partner and joint head construction law department WINWARD FEARON & CO 35 Bow Street, London WC2E 7AU.

Career: articled Slater Heelis & Co; admitted (1972); assistant solicitor McKenna & Co; assistant solicitor Masons; founding partner Winward Fearon & Co (1986).

Activities: member Appeal Committee of British Academy of Experts; lectured on construction law problems; member

Farmers' Club.

Biography: lives Whaddon; born 20.09.1947; married. Educated at Audensham Grammar School; Sheffield University (1969 LLB hons); author of: 'Applications for Summary Judgement in Construction Disputes' (1984); 'The Demise of Tortious Liability and the Resurrection of Contract Law' (1989); joint author of 'Collateral Warranties: A Practical Guide for the Construction Industry' (1990).

Leisure: field sports; motor racing.

WISEMAN Alan

partner and head of one of the firm's commercial conveyancing teams BRECHER & CO 78 Brook Street, London W1Y 2AD.

Career: Sub-Lt RNVR (1951-1953); articled Nicholson Graham & Jones (1957-1960); admitted (1960); assistant solicitor (1960-1963); assistant solicitor Brecher & Co (1963-1965); became partner (1965).

Biography: lives London N2; born 17.02.1934; married to Judy with 2 sons and 1 daughter. Educated at Stockport Grammar School (1945-1952); St Catharine's College Cambridge (1957 BA) (1958 MA); Civil Service Commissioners' Exam in Russian (1954).

Leisure: crosswords; cinema; reading; jogging; skiing.

WISEMAN Richard

legal adviser SHELL INTERNATIONAL PETROLEUM COMPANY LIMITED Shell Centre, London SE1 7NA.

Career: articled Mackrell & Co; admitted (1974); legal division Shell UK (1975-1980); legal division Shell International (1980-1984); Shell Australia (1984-1986); admitted Victoria, Australia (1985); returned to Shell International Petroleum Co Ltd (1986).

Biography: lives London N3; born 11.08.1951; married with 2 children. Educated at Emmanuel School, London; College of Law Lancaster Gate; articles on international sale of goods.

Leisure: painting; calligraphy; visual arts.

WITHERS Ian

partner EDGE & ELLISON Rutland House, 148 Edmund Street, Birmingham.

Career: articled Redfern & Co (1963); admitted (1970); assistant solicitor (1970-1973); partner O'Dowd & Silk (1973); senior partner (1983); firm amalgamated with Glaisyers; senior partner (1985-1990);

became partner Edge & Ellison (1990).

Activities: member of: Harborne Club (past president); Birmingham Club.

Biography: lives Birmingham; born 14.05.1946; married to Charlotte with 4 children. Educated at King Edward School for Boys; College of Law Lancaster Gate.

Leisure: gardening; socialising; eating out.

WOLF Piers

partner EVERSHED WELLS & HIND 10 Newhall Street, Birmingham B3 3LX.

Career: articled Skelton & Co (1961-1966); admitted (1966); assistant solicitor Freshfields (1967-1972); assistant solicitor Evershed & Tomkinson (now Evershed Wells & Hind) (1972); became partner (1973).

Activities: member Law Society's Company Law Committee (1989); member Warwickshire County Cricket Club.

Biography: lives Dorridge; born 26.01.1943; married to Jennifer with 2 children. Educated at Bedford school.

Leisure: reading; listening to music; gardening.

WOLSELEY BRACHER George Anthony

senior partner BRACHERS Somerfield House, 59 London Road, Maidstone, Kent ME16 8JH.

Career: articled to family firm (1955-1958); admitted (1958); partner (1958-1978); became senior partner (1978).

Activities: treasurer Kent Law Society (1962-1976); president Kent Law Society (1977); member of: The Oxford Union; The Ebury Court.

Biography: lives Maidstone; born 20.09.1932; married to Sarah with 3 children. Educated at Marlborough and Hertford College Oxford (1955 MA).

Leisure: classical music; opera; sailing; field sports (particularly wild fowling); travel; gardening.

WOLTON Harry

Queen's Counsel and head of chambers 5 Fountain Court, Steelhouse Lane, Birmingham B4 6DR.

Career: called to the Bar (1969); QC (1982); Recorder (1985).

Activities: trustee National Head Injuries Association; member Sette of Odd Volumes.

Biography: lives London; Warwickshire

and Herefordshire; born 01.01.1938; married to Julie with 3 children. Educated at Hallfield; King Edward's School, Birmingham; Birmingham University.

Leisure: farmer.

WOOD Bruce

partner MORTON FRASER MILLIGAN WS 19 York Place, Edinburgh EH1 3EL.

Career: admitted (1976); admitted Writer to the Signet (1979); apprentice solicitor Morton Fraser & Milligan (1974-1976); became partner (1977); became part-time lecturer in conveyancing Edinburgh University (1979).

Activities: World chairman of Interlaw the worldwide association of business law firms; convener of the teachers of conveyancing of the Scottish Universities for the Diploma in Legal Practice (1985-1988); member Law Society working party on security over moveable property (1987-1989); world chairman of Interlaw the worldwide association of business law firms; Notary Public (1979); member of: Mortonhall Golf Club; Edinburgh University Staff Club.

Biography: lives Glencorse; born 02.10.1951; married to Agnes with 3 children. Educated at Madras College, St Andrew's; Edinburgh University (1973 LLB); Scots Law Society Prize; Vans Dunlop Scholarship; Lord Cooper Memorial Prize; University of California (Berkeley) (1974 LLM); Sarah Lowenhaupt Scholarship; Fulbright travel grant; author of 'Location: Leasing & Hire of Moveables' (1988); 'Leasing of Moveables' (1982); 'Recent Authority on Missives' (1982); 'The Consumer Credit Act - Conveyancers in Distress' (1985); 'Die Floating Charge Als Kreditsicherheit im Schottishchen Recht' (1980) with Gunter Bottger.

Leisure: Scottish country dancing (and teaching it); golf; hill walking.

WOOD Ian

partner and head of intellectual property department HOPKINS & WOOD 2-3 Cursitor Street, London EC4A 1NE.

Career: research assistant physics department Durham University; articled Clifford-Turner (1975-1977); admitted (1977); assistant solicitor (1977-1979); assistant solicitor Bird & Bird (1979-1980); consultant Hopkins Fuller (1981-1982); co-founder Hopkins & Wood (1982).

Activities: associate Chartered Institute of Patent Agents; associate Institute of Trademark Agents; member Union of European Practitioners in Industrial Property.

Biography: lives East Molesey; born 31.03.1950; married to Jenny with 2 children. Educated at Hampton Grammar School; Durham University (1971 BSc hons: physics); (1973 MSc: nuclear physics).

Leisure: gardening; family.

WOOD Jonathan

partner KINGSFORD STACEY Lincoln House, High Street, Harpenden, Herts AL5 2SX.

Career: articled Marcy & Co (1963-1968); admitted (1968); firm merged with Kingsford Dorman; assistant solicitor (1968-1969); became partner Kingsford Dorman (1969); firm merged with Routh Stacey (1987).

Activities: member Rotary Club of Harpenden.

Biography: lives Harpenden; born 21.01.1944; married to Jackie with 3 daughters. Educated at Chigwell School, Essex (1953-1963); College of Law (1963-1968).

Leisure: classical music; tennis; chess; mountain/hill walking.

WOOD Philip

partner ALLEN & OVERY 9 Cheapside, London EC2V 6AD.

Career: admitted (1970); assistant solicitor Allen & Overy (1970-1973); became partner (1974); specialises banking; corporate finance; shipping; aircraft.

Activities: visiting Professor Queen Mary & Westfield College, University of London, visiting Fellow and external examiner Faculty of Law, King's College; member Banking Law sub-committee City of London Solicitors' Company.

Biography: lives Shere; born 20.08.1942; married with 4 children. Educated at St John's College Johannesburg; University of Cape Town (BA); Oxford (BA); Law Society Clement's Inn Prize; Sheffield Prize; Edmund Thomas Child Prize; author: 'Law and Practice of International Finance' (1980); 'Encyclopaedia of Banking Law' (1982); 'English & International Set-Off' (1989); 'Law of Subordinated Debt' (1990).

Leisure: piano; walking; landscaping; motor touring; architecture.

WOODBRIDGE Anthony

senior partner TURBERVILLE WOODBRIDGE 122 High Street, Uxbridge, Middx UB8 1JT.

Career: articled Speechly Mumford and Soames; became partner Woodbridge and Sons (1969-1983).

Activities: clerk to the Commissioners of Income Tax Uxbridge Division; company secretary Abbeyfield Uxbridge Society Ltd; chairman of Governors Fulmer County First School; member of Denham Golf Club.

Biography: lives Buckinghamshire; born 12.08.1942; married to Lynda with 1 son. Educated at Stowe School; Trinity Hall Cambridge (MA).

Leisure: walking; cycling; travel.

WOODCOCK Caroline

solicitor TRAFALGAR HOUSE DEVELOPMENTS HOLDINGS LTD 21 Tothill Street, London SW1H 9LN.

Career: articled Wimpey Group Services Ltd (1977-1979); admitted (1979); assistant solicitor (1979-1982); proof-reading in Germany (1982-1984); Kall-Kwik Printing (UK) Ltd (1984-1985); became solicitor commercial property division Trafalgar House Developments Holdings Ltd (1985).

Biography: lives Welwyn; born 01.12.1954; married to Ian with 1 daughter. Educated at Beverley High School for Girls; Stanwell Comprehensive School, Penarth; Eastbourne School of Domestic Economy (1973); Nottingham University (1976 LLB hons); College of Law Chester (1977).

Leisure: walking.

WOODESON Hugh

senior partner HUNTERS 9 New Square, Lincoln's Inn, London WC2A 3QN.

Career: articled Monier-Williams & Keeling; admitted (1969); assistant solicitor Hunters (1969-1971); became partner (1971-1986); became senior partner (1986).

Activities: member Solicitors' Family Law Association; member Roehampton Club.

Biography: lives London SW13; born 04.11.1943; married to Gill with 3 children. Educated at St Neot's Preparatory School; Bradfield College; King's College London (1965 LLB hons).

Leisure: tennis; golf; painting; ornithology; reading; jazz.

WOODHOUSE Charles

partner FARRER & CO 66 Lincoln's Inn Fields, London WC2A 3LH.

Career: admitted (1966); assistant solicitor (1966-1969); became partner Farrer & Co (1969).

W

Activities: director Peko Exploration (UK) Ltd; vice-chairman Solicitors' Staff Pension Fund; vice-chairman Land Settlement Association Limited; hon legal adviser Commonwealth Games Council for England; legal adviser Central Council of Physical Recreation; legal adviser Amateur Athletic Association, British Sports Association for the Disabled and several other sports representative and governing bodies and charities; president Guildford Cricket Club; committee member Surrey County Cricket Club; former chairman Surrey Championship; member of: United Oxford & Cambridge Club; MCC; Free Foresters; Worplesdon Golf Club; Marlborough Blues CC.

Biography: lives Guildford; born 06.06.1941; married to Margaret with 3 children. Educated at Marlborough College; McGill University; Peterhouse Cambridge; author of 'Sport and the Law : Some Current Issues' (1981); co-author of The Palmer Report 'Amateur Status and Participation in Sport' (CCPR) (1988).

Leisure: cricket; golf.

WOODROFFE Geoffrey

professor associate and director CENTRE FOR CONSUMER LAW Brunel University; managing director GW CONSULTANCY LTD; consultant BELLS POTTER & KEMPSON, SOLICITORS Farnham, Surrey.

Career: articled Cameron Kemm; admitted (1963); assistant solicitor; lecturer College of Law; board of management (1972); senior lecturer Brunel University (1976); founded Centre for Consumer Law (1982).

Activities: member SPTL Council; member National Consumer Council legal advisory panel; member National Federation of Consumer Groups Legislation Committee; member editorial board European Consumer Law Journal; joint editor, Journal of Consumer Policy; member Property and Commercial Services Committee Law Society; 'expert' consultant to Consumer Policy Service of EC Commission; well-known conference speaker to lawyers and businessmen.

Biography: born 21.12.1934; married with 3 children. Educated at Bec School; St John's College Cambridge (1959 BA hons) (MA); state scholarship; author of: 'Consumer Law and Practice' (1980 & 1985); 'Goods and Services - the New Law' (1982); 'A Buyer's Guide to the Supply of Goods and Services Act 1982' (1983); 'Consumer law in the EEC' (1984); Management of Engineering Projects (Legal Aspects

chapter) (1988); Model Business Contracts (Conditions of Sale and Purchase) (1988).

Leisure: walking; music (particularly 20th-Century); cycling; arts and crafts generally (collecting and viewing).

WOODROFFE Peter

senior partner WOODROFFES York House, Westminster Bridge Road, London SE1 7UT.

Career: Lt Royal Northumberland Fusiliers (1945-1948); articled to father KD Woodroffe (1949-1952); admitted (1953); assistant solicitor (1953-1956); became partner (1956); became senior partner (1963).

Activities: Conservative member of Westminster City Council (1962); secretary to the governors Mill Hill School (1981 to date); partner Crofts & Ingram and Wyatt & Co; underwriting member Lloyds; member of: Boodles; The Berkshire GC; Rye GC; Royal Cinque Ports GC; the firm Woodroffes has practised under that name since 1877 and PM Woodroffe is third generation of family to practise in partnership; Freeman of the City of London (1984); Honorary Citizen State of Texas USA (1967).

Biography: lives London SW3 and near Rye; born 02.08.1927; married to Amanda with 2 sons. Educated at Mill Hill; College of Law (1952).

Leisure: skiing; golf; tennis.

WOODROW John

partner NORTON ROSE Kempson House, Camomile Street, London EC3A 7AN.

Career: Ford Motor Co Ltd (1954-1956); articled Merton Jones Lewsey & Jefferies (1956-1959); admitted (1959); assistant solicitor Clifford Turner (1959-1961); assistant solicitor and partner Stones Porter (1961-1965); became partner Norton Rose (1965).

Activities: member Education and Training Committee City of London Solicitors' Company; recruitment and training of articled clerks and personnel; president Old Aldenhamian Society; governor Aldenham School; trustee various Aldenham charities; member of: MCC; City of London Club; Ashridge Golf Club; Southgate Hockey Club.

Biography: lives London W11 and Tring; born 12.04.1933; married to Daphne with 3 daughters. Educated at Hendon Preparatory School; Aldenham School, Elstree; University College London (1954 LLB).

Leisure: golf; tennis; collecting Tunbridge ware, antique maps and stamps; travelling.

WOOF Richard

senior partner DEBENHAM & CO 20 Hans Road, Knightsbridge, London SW3 1RT.

Career: articled Foot & Bowden, Plymouth (1957-1962); admitted (1963); assistant solicitor (1963-1964); assistant solicitor Debenham & Co (1964-1967); partner (1967); became senior partner (1974).

Activities: Lt in TA (1959-1964); commercial property editor Law Society's Gazette (1975 to date); director Caribeach (St Lucia) Ltd and Cove Hotels (Antigua) Ltd.

Biography: lives Hascombe; born 14.06.1940; married to Christine with 1 son and 1 daughter. Educated at St Michael's School, Otford; King's College, Taunton.

Leisure: painting; organ playing; quarter horse racing; carriage driving.

WOOLF Fiona

partner MCKENNA & CO Mitre House, 160 Aldersgate Street, London EC1A 4DD.

Career: assistant solicitor Coward Chance; assistant solicitor McKenna & Co (1978); became partner (1981); ran Bahrain office for 3 years.

Activities: Law Society Council member; member Law Society Company Law Committee; vice-chairman International Committee of the Law Society; member Bank of England City EEC Committee.

Biography: lives Epsom; born 11.05.1948; married. Educated at St Denis School; Keele University (BA); Strasbourg University (diploma in comparative law).

Leisure: singing; opera; fell walking.

WOOLF Geoffrey

partner and head of property department STEPHENSON HARWOOD One St Paul's Churchyard, London EC4M 8SH.

Career: articled Stephenson Harwood (1968-1970); admitted (1970); assistant solicitor (1970-1975); became partner (1975).

Biography: lives London NW11; born 13.10.1946; married to Josephine with 2 children. Educated at Harrow County Grammar School; King's College London (LLB hons).

Leisure: family life; opera; theatre.

WOOLLEY David

Queen's Counsel 2 Mitre Court Buildings, Temple, London EC4Y 7BX.

Career: called to the Bar (1962); pupillage with M Griffiths and D Trustam Eve; QC (1980); Crown Court Recorder.

Activities: inspector National Gallery Extension Inquiry (1984); member of: MCC; The Queen's Club; Oxford & Cambridge.

Biography: lives London SW1 and Marlborough; born 09.06.1939; married to Mandy. Educated at Winchester College; Trinity Hall Cambridge; visiting scholar Wolfson College Cambridge (1983-1986); articles in The Town Hall and The Property Owner.

Leisure: theatre; opera; riding; real tennis.

WORDSWORTH Bryan

senior partner EASTLEYS
The Manor Office, 12 Victoria Street, Paignton, Devon TQ4 5DW.

Career: articled Tuck & Mann (1949-1954); admitted (1954); National Service with executive branch of Royal Navy (Ordinary Seaman then Sub-Lt) (1954-1956); assistant solicitor Eastleys (1956-1958); became partner (1958) .

Activities: clerk to the General Commissioners of Income Tax for the two divisions of Torquay and Paignton; member of Financial Intermediaries' Managers' & Brokers' Regulatory Association (FIMBRA); president Devon & Exeter Incorporated Law Society (1974-1975) (hon treasurer 1975-1988); set up financial services department in the firm which became separate partnership of which he is senior partner (1974); outside lecturer for College of Law for continuing education course on financial services (1987 to date); consultant to solicitors on financial services; drafts software for solicitors' financial services .

Biography: lives Newton Abbot; born 16.02.1931; married to Marilyn with 4 children. Educated at Cranleigh School; King's College London (1953 LLB); legal/financial columnist for the Town & County Magazines publications of Devon Life; Cornish Life and Somerset & Avon Life (1986 to date); contributor to College of Law booklets on financial services; regular local radio broadcaster on legal and financial matters; chairman Paignton Round Table (1964); churchwarden; member of: Rotary Club of Paignton (president 1969), Royal Dart Yacht Club (past rear Commodore).

Leisure: sailing; skiing.

WORTHINGTON Allan

partner MCCLURE NAISMITH ANDERSON & GARDINER
49 Queen Street, Edinburgh EH2 3NH.

Career: articled Connell & Connell WS (1965-1967); admitted (1967); legal department National Coal Board (1967-1983); head of litigation (1983-1987); solicitor NCB (Scotland) (1987-1989); became partner McClure Naismith Anderson & Gardiner (1989).

Biography: lives Edinburgh; born 01.08.1944; married to Margaret with 2 children. Educated at Highfield Primary CE School; Wigan Grammar School; St Andrew's University (1965 LLB).

Leisure: rugby union; curio collecting; gardening.

WREN-HILTON Michael

senior partner WREN-HILTON APFEL
32 Orchard Road, St Anne's, Lytham St Anne's FY8 1PF.

Career: admitted (1953); became partner E Wren-Hilton & Son (1953); became senior partner Wren-Hilton Apfel (1985).

Activities: Deputy Circuit Judge Northern Circuit (1973-1978); president Fylde Medico/Legal Society; chairman Merseyside Legal Aid Area; member Blackpool & Fylde District Law Society (past president); past president Association of North West Law Societies; chairman Fylde Conservative Association; member of: Royal Lytham & St Anne's Golf Club; St Anne's Conservative Club.

Biography: lives Lytham St Anne's; born 03.01.1928; married to Jean with 4 children. Educated at Mount St Mary's; Lancaster Royal Grammar School; Manchester University (1948-1949).

Leisure: golf; gardening; St John Ambulance.

WRIGHT Antony

senior partner WRIGHT SON & PEPPER
9 Gray's Inn Square, London WC1R 5JF.

Career: articled Wright Son & Pepper (1956-1961); admitted (1961); Cabinet Sarrut (avocat) Paris (1961-1962); became partner Wright Son & Pepper (1963); became senior partner (1980).

Activities: secretary (later chairman) Holborn Law Society Conveyancing Section (1972-1980) (member Committee 1976-1980); member Solicitors' Assistance Scheme; member Solicitors' Negligence Panel; expert witness on conveyancing matters; chairman local residents' association; member various Conservative party committees; member Wycombe Conservative Association.

Biography: lives High Wycombe; born 22.11.1939; married to Vanessa with 2 daughters. Educated at Charterhouse; occasional articles in Law Society's Gazette and Holborn Law Society Report.

Leisure: gardening; snorkelling; skiing.

WRIGHT C John

partner and head of construction and technical department WARNER CRANSTON Pickfords Wharf, Clink Street, London SE1 9DG.

Career: articled Herbert Oppenheimer Nathan & Vandyk (1974-1976); admitted (1976); litigation assistant Coward Chance (1976-1979); assistant solicitor McKenna & Co (1979-1984); assistant solicitor Warner Cranston (1984); became partner (1984).

Activities: associate of the Chartered Institute of Arbitrators; member International Bar Association; member Society of English & American Lawyers; member Society of Construction Law; member American Society in London.

Biography: lives London SW14; born 02.05.1952; married to Jan with 2 sons. Educated at Hereford Cathedral School (1963-1969); St John's College Cambridge (1973 BA) (1977 MA); College of Law Lancaster Gate (1974); author of miscellaneous articles published in 'Atlantic' magazine (1987).

Leisure: horseracing; cricket; theatre; wines; restaurants.

WRIGHT David

senior partner MARSHALL & GALPIN
Vanbrugh House, 20/22 St Michael's Street, Oxford OX1 2EA.

Career: National Service with Royal Artillery (1950-1952); articled Kerwood & Co (1955-1958); admitted (1958); assistant solicitor (1958-1959); assistant solicitor Henry F Galpin & Co (1959-1963); partner (1963); amalgamated with Marshall & Eldridge (1974); became senior partner (1987).

Activities: Under Sheriff Oxfordshire (1988 to date); clerk to the City of Oxford Charities; member General Synod and lay reader of Church of England; member Clarendon Club, Oxford.

W

Biography: lives Oxford; born 21.03.1932; married with 4 children. Educated at Cheltenham College; St Edmund Hall Oxford (1955 BA MA).

WRIGHT Desmond

Queen's Counsel and head of chambers 1 Atkin Building, Gray's Inn, London WC1R 5BQ.

Career: QC (1974); Bencher Lincoln's Inn.

Biography: lives London; born 13.07.1923; married to Elizabeth with 2 children. Educated at Giggleswick; Worcester College Oxford; Cholmeley Scholarship Lincoln's Inn; author of 'Wright on Walls' (1953).

WRIGHT Michael

Queen's Counsel 2 Crown Office Row, Temple, London EC4Y 7HJ.

Career: called to the Bar Lincoln's Inn (1957); QC (1974); Recorder (1974); Bencher Lincoln's Inn (1983).

Activities: leader South Eastern Circuit (1981-1983); chairman of the Bar (1983-1984) (vice-chairman 1982-1983); chairman Professional Conduct Committee (1982-1983); chairman Fees & Legal Aid Committee (1978-1982); member Legal Aid Area Committee No 2 (1972-1982); member Supreme Court Rules Committee (1972-1974); vice-chairman Appeal Committee of the Institute of Chartered Accountants in England and Wales; legal assessor Royal College of Veterinary Surgeons.

Biography: lives London and Sussex; born 26.10.1932; married to Kathleen with 3 children. Educated at The King's School, Chester (1945-1951); Oriel College Oxford (1956 BA); (1978 MA); Tancred Student; King George V Pupillage Scholarship.

WRIGHT Richard

partner DIBB LUPTON BROOMHEAD & PRIOR Temple Bar House, 23-28 Fleet Street, London EC4Y 1AA.

Career: articled Simmons & Simmons; admitted (1964); assistant solicitor (1964-1968); became partner William Prior & Co (1968).

Activities: member Justice Committee on Bankruptcy; member Council of the Insolvency Lawyers' Association; lectured for College of Law and commercial organisations on insolvency.

Biography: lives Shipbourne; born 13.05.1941; married with 2 children. Educated at Bryanston School, Blandford

Forum; Cambridge University (1963 LLB MA).

Leisure: golf; tennis; classical music; opera.

WYLD David

litigation partner MACFARLANES 10 Norwich Street, London EC4A 1BD.

Career: barrister chambers of Geoffrey Rippon QC and George Dobry QC (1968-1971); articled and assistant solicitor Linklaters & Paines (1972-1979); became partner Macfarlanes (1980).

Activities: chairman City of London Law Society Litigation Committee; member of: Marylebone Cricket Club; Berkshire Golf Club.

Biography: lives London SW1 and Petersfield; born 11.03.1943; married to Caroline with 2 sons by first marriage and 2 daughters by second marriage. Educated at Hawtreys Preparatory School (1951-1956); Harrow (1956-1961); Christ Church Oxford (1964 hons); article on Letters of Request under the Hague Convention in IBA magazine (1987).

Leisure: golf; walking; gardening; tennis; shooting.

WYNNE Geoffrey

senior banking partner WATSON FARLEY & WILLIAMS Minories House, 2-5 Minories, London EC3N 1BJ.

Career: articled Slaughter and May; admitted (1975); assistant solicitor (1975-1979); Royal Bank of Canada (London) Ltd (1979-1981); executive director Orion Royal Bank Ltd (1981-1983); assistant general counsel of Royal Bank of Canada (1983-1985); became partner Watson Farley & Williams (1985).

Activities: course director Cadmans Educational Courses on financial services, banking and insolvency; speaker and/or chairman number of courses particularly run by IBC (legal studies and services).

Biography: joint editor of Credit Finance Law; member editorial boards of: Butterworth's Journal of International Banking; International Financial Law Review; International Banking and Financial Law Bulletin; contributor to Butterworth's Handbook of Corporate Finance.

Leisure: charitable work; theatre; keep fit; golf; classic cars.

WYNNE-WILLSON George

solicitor claims department LONDON INSURANCE BROKERS LIMITED Hilton House, 161-166 Fleet Street, London EC4A 2DY.

Career: articled Wilkinson Kimbers & Staddon (now Alsop Wilkinson) (1971-1973); admitted (1973); deputy local secretary Legal Aid Area 13 (London East) (1974); assistant area secretary (1977); area director (1983); Legal Aid Board area manager London (1989-1990) joined London Insurance Brokers Limited (1990) .

Biography: lives London SW6; born 20.02.1947; married to Caroline with 1 daughter. Educated at Wellington College, Crowthorne; Trinity College Dublin (1969 BA).

Leisure: reading; walking; visual arts.

Y

YABLON Anthony

partner JAQUES & LEWIS 2 South Square, Gray's Inn, London WC1R 5HR.

Career: articled Jaques & Lewis (1963-1965); admitted (1965); assistant solicitor (1965-1966); became partner (1966).

Activities: director of Kerr Herrmann & Stagg Ltd and Ian Hodgkins & Co Ltd; member Oxford & Cambridge University Club.

Biography: lives London NW8; born 16.04.1940; married to Rosemary with 2 children. Educated at Bradford Grammar School; Rugby School; Pembroke College Oxford (1962 MA).

Leisure: squash.

YATES David

international director professional development BAKER & MCKENZIE Aldwych House, Aldwych, London WC2B 4JP.

Career: assistant lecturer in law Hull University (1969-1972); lecturer in law Bristol University (1972-1974); lecturer in law Manchester University (1974-1976); senior lecturer in law (1976-1979); visiting professor of law (1979-1980); foundation professor of law Essex University (1979-1987); visiting professor of law (1987 to date).

Activities: various legal consultancies with variety of public and private bodies (1973-1987); visiting professor of law Universities of New South Wales and Sydney (1985);

foundation dean of law Essex University (1979-1984) (pro-vice-chancellor 1985-1987); principal of Dalton Hall Manchester University (1976-1980); member Advisory Committee of American Institute for Law Training; lecturer on landlord and tenant and commercial law and on legal training topics; General Editor of Professional Lawyer; member editorial boards of: Journal of Contract Law; Urban Law and Policy; Review of International Business Law; member United Oxford & Cambridge Club.

Biography: lives London SW19; born 05.05.1946. Educated at Bromley Grammar School (1957-1964); St Catharine's College Oxford (1967 BA) (1971 MA); College of Law Guildford (1968-1969); David Blank Scholar (1964-1967); Frank Alan Bullock Prize (1967); author of: 'Local Authority Housing' (sectional contribution to the Encyclopaedia of Social Welfare Law 1977); 'Exclusion Clauses in Contracts' (2nd ed) (1982); 'A Comparison of the Experimental Housing Allowance Program and Great Britain's Rent Allowance Programme' (with O Hetzel and J Trutko) (1978); 'Leases of Business Premises' (1979); 'Landlord and Tenant Law' (with AJ Hawkins) (2nd ed) (1986); 'Standard Business Contracts' (with AJ Hawkins) (1986); numerous notes and articles in various legal journals.

Leisure: squash; tennis; swimming; jogging; cooking; food; wine; theatre; music (especially opera).

YEAMAN Keith

Partner RICKERBY JESSOP Ellenborough House, Wellington Street, Cheltenham, Gloucestershire GL50 1YD.

Career: articled Sir Ian Yeaman (father) in Rickerby Mellersh & Co; admitted (1959); became partner (1960) .

Activities: formed (with His Honour Judge Sir Jonathan Clarke) the Gloucestershire & Wiltshire Young Solicitors' Group (1962); secretary to the Gloucestershire & Wiltshire Incorporated Law Society (1964-1983) (president 1980); chairman National Committee of the Young Solicitors' (1967); president Association of South Western Law Societies (1981); served on the Council of the Law Society (1983-1989) - member of the Society's Indemnity Insurance Committee; director Indemnity Fund Ltd; member Strategy Committee; member Training Committee; chairman of the Gazette Editorial Board; vice-chairman Wills & Equity Committee; past member TA (RGH) and Inns of Court Regiment;

member of several school governing councils; member of East India & Sports Club.

Biography: lives London SW7 and Forthampton; born 20.07.1931; married to Bulger with 2 daughters. Educated at Cheltenham College.

Leisure: most country pursuits.

YOUARD Richard

Investment Referee THE OFFICE OF THE INVESTMENT REFEREE 6 Frederick's Place, London EC2R 8BT.

Career: articled Slaughter and May (1956-1959); admitted (1959); assistant solicitor (1959-1968); partner (1968-1989).

Activities: inspector appointed by DTI (1987); member City of London Solicitors' Company Committee on Sovereign Immunity (1977-1978) (leading to State Immunity Act 1978); lecturer on legal topics (principally at the Centre for Commercial Law Studies, King's College, London, and the City University Business School); member Home Office Committee on London Taxicab and Car Hire Trade (1967); chairman National Federation of Consumer Groups (1968); clerk to the governors and governor Bradfield College (1968 to date).

Biography: lives London N1; born 27.01.1933; married with 3 children. Educated at Horris Hill School (1941-1946); Bradfield College (1946-1951); Magdalen College Oxford (1956 BA); City of London Solicitors' Company Prize (1959); honorary Senior Research Fellow King's College London (1988); contributor of the banking documents in Butterworths Encyclopaedia of Forms & Precedents (1986); contributor to various books and journals (principally on legal aspects of international finance including Sovereign Borrowers (1984); current issues of International Financial Law (1985); Butterworths Banking and Financial Law Review (1987); Journal of Business Law and Euromoney (regular column at one time) and International Financial Law Review.

Leisure: vegetable gardening; electronics (holder of amateur transmitting licence); bee-keeping; map collecting; jazz; playing trumpet/cornet; Welsh history.

YOUNG David

Queen's Counsel 6 Pump Court, Temple, London EC4Y 7AR.

Career: called to the Bar Lincoln's Inn (1966); QC (1980); Recorder SE circuit;

Bencher Lincoln's Inn.

Activities: chairman Plant and Seed Varieties Tribunal.

Biography: lives London SW1 and Dorset; born 30.09.1940; married to Anne with 2 children. Educated at Monkton Combe School; Oxford University (1964 MA); joint editor of 'Terrell on Patents' (12 & 13th eds); author of 'Young on Passing Off'.

Leisure: equestrian activities; skiing; walking.

YOUNG Graham

senior partner TOWNSENDS 42 Cricklade Street, Swindon, Wilts SN1 3HD.

Career: National Service with Royal Corps of Signals (1954-1956); commissioned and served in Germany (1955-1956); articled Herbert Smith; admitted; assistant solicitor; assistant solicitor Townsends; became partner; became senior partner (1985).

Activities: part-time chairman DHSS Appeal Tribunal and Rent Assessment Panel; president Gloucestershire and Wiltshire Incorporated Law Society (1986-1987); company secretary Prospect Foundation Limited; hon secretary Swindon and North Wilts branch NSPCC and member Central Executive Committee; regular weekly legal programme on WR (later GWR) (1984-1988) (BBC Wiltshire Sound 1989 to date); regular lecturer on the subject of wills and other aspects of law.

Biography: lives Fairford; born 20.12.1935; married to Pam with 3 children. Educated at Culford School, Bury St Edmunds; Trinity College Cambridge (1960 BA hons MA); (1960 LLB hons); letters in legal press; occasional articles for local Chamber of Commerce, etc.

Leisure: swimming; DIY.

YOUNG John

partner CAMERON MARKBY HEWITT Sceptre Court, 40 Tower Hill, London EC3N 4BB.

Career: articled Maxwell Batley & Co (1953-1957); admitted (1958); assistant secretary Law Society (1958-1964); became partner Markby Stewart & Wadesons (now Cameron Markby Hewitt) (1965).

Activities: national chairman Young Solicitors' Group (1965-1966); president Young Lawyers' International Association (1968-1969); member Council of the Law Society (1971 to date); chairman Society's International Relations Committee (1983-1987); leader of UK delegation to CCBE

Z

(Council of Bars and Law Societies of the European Community) (1984-1987); member of Council of International Bar Association (1983 to date); governor of the College of Law (1975 to date); Master of the City of London Solicitors' Company (1989-1990); chairman of Solicitors' Indemnity Fund Limited (1990).

Biography: lives Plaxtol; born 28.07.1934; married to Yvonne with 4 children. Educated at Cranbrook; Law Society's School of Law (1956 LLB); Law Society Finals (1957 hons); author of sundry articles for legal periodicals.

Leisure: music (particularly as choirmaster/organist of local church); gardening; family.

YOUNG John

partner and head of litigation department BIRKETT WESTHORP & LONG 20/32 Museum Street, Ipswich IP1 1HZ.

Career: National Service commissioned in Northamptonshire Regiment and seconded to King's African Rifles (1954-1956); articled Birketts (1956-1961); admitted (1962); assistant solicitor (1962-1965); became partner (1965); firm amalgamated to become Birkett Westhorp & Long (1989).

Activities: member Law Society Insolvency Casework Committee.

Biography: lives East Bergholt nr Colchester; born 22.10.1935; single. Educated at Bedford School; Solicitors' Finals (hons).

YOUNG Maureen

management partner and head of family law department DIBB & CLEGG 31 Regent Street, Barnsley, South Yorkshire S70 2HJ.

Career: operational research officer East Midlands Gas (1969-1973); articled Dibb & Clegg (1974-1977); assistant solicitor (1977-1980); became partner (1980); became management partner (1987).

Activities: committee member South Yorkshire branch of Solicitors' Family Law Association; founder member and hon treasurer Sheffield Women Lawyers; member Barnsley Law Society (president 1988-1989); former chairman Barnsley & District Family Conciliation Service Steering Committee; member Sunday Times Wine Club.

Biography: lives Chapeltown; born 13.07.1948; married to Stuart. Educated at Birkenhead High School; St Mary's College Durham University (1969 BSC).

Leisure: fell walking; gardening.

Z

ZERMAN Per

head London office REUMERT & PARTNERS One Knightrider Court, London EC4V 5JP.

Career: head of section, legal department of Danish Ministry of Foreign Affairs (1982); trainee advokat Trolle Damsbo & Lund-Andersen (1983-1985); admitted (1985); advokat (1985-1986 & 1988);stagiaire Linklaters & Paines (1987-1988); became resident partner London office Reumert & Partners (1989).

Activities: member working group under Danish Law Society on the Danish legal profession and the single market (1992); member Reform Club.

Biography: lives London SW8; born 08.09.1958; single. Educated at Maglegaardsskolen, Copenhagen; Gentofte Statsskole, Copenhagen; Copenhagen University (1982 candidatus juris); London School of Economics (1987 LLM); post-qualification courses in Denmark and England; articles in Danish law journals; author of Danish book on the regulation of foreign investments in The People's Republic of China (1988); co-author of the Danish chapter in 'European Corporate Finance Law' (Euromoney, 1990).

Leisure: history; travel; skiing.

ZETTER Howard Keith

senior litigation partner SAUNDERS SOBELL LEIGH & DOBIN 20 Red Lion Street, Holborn, London WC1R 4AE.

Career: articled Saunders Sobell Leigh & Dobin (1966-1971); admitted (1971); became partner (1971); became head of litigation department (1982).

Biography: lives Radlett; born 10.10.1946; married to Jennifer with 2 children. Educated at East Ham Grammar School for Boys; College of Law Lancaster Gate.

Leisure: horse riding; cycling; jogging; spectator soccer and rugby union; theatre; good food and wine.

ZIEGLER Oliver

senior partner MOORE & BLATCH 48 High Street, Lymington, Hants.

Career: articled Collyer Bristow & Co (1947-1950); admitted (1950); assistant solicitor (1950-1951); assistant solicitor Moore & Blatch (1951-1952); became partner (1953); became senior partner (1972).

Biography: lives Ringwood; born 09.12.1925; married to Margaret with 2 children. Educated at St Cyrman's, Eastbourne; Eton.

Leisure: trying to keep up with an over-large garden.

ZIMAN Lawrence

partner NABARRO NATHANSON 50 Stratton Street, London W1X 5FL.

Career: articled Herbert Oppenheimer Nathan & Vandyk (1960-1963); admitted (1963); assistant solicitor (1963-1965); became partner (1965); founding partner Berwin & Co (now Berwin Leighton) (1966); executive Industrial Reorganisation Corporation (1969-1970); founded Ziman & Co (1970); merged with Nabarro Nathanson (1977).

Activities: member Lansdowne Club.

Biography: lives Cobham; born 10.08.1938; married to Joyce with 2 children. Educated at City of London School; Trinity Hall Cambridge (1959 BA hons) (MA); University of Michigan Law School; general editor Butterworths Company Law Service.

ZIMMERMAN Jay

partner BINGHAM DANA & GOULD 39 Victoria Street, London SW1H 0EE.

Career: associate Debevoise & Plimpton, New York (1980-1982); associate Bingham Dana & Gould, Boston (1982-1986); became partner (1986); became resident partner London (1987).

Activities: member American Bar Association; International Bar Association; Boston Bar Association; member Harvard Club.

Biography: lives London SW3; born 15.03.1954; married to Laura with 2 children. Educated at Harvard College (1976 BA Magna Cum Laude); Harvard Law School (1980 JD Cum Laude).